1,000,000 Books
are available to read at

Forgotten Books

www.ForgottenBooks.com

Read online
Download PDF
Purchase in print

ISBN 978-0-282-92445-4
PIBN 10873519

This book is a reproduction of an important historical work. Forgotten Books uses state-of-the-art technology to digitally reconstruct the work, preserving the original format whilst repairing imperfections present in the aged copy. In rare cases, an imperfection in the original, such as a blemish or missing page, may be replicated in our edition. We do, however, repair the vast majority of imperfections successfully; any imperfections that remain are intentionally left to preserve the state of such historical works.

Forgotten Books is a registered trademark of FB &c Ltd.
Copyright © 2018 FB &c Ltd.
FB &c Ltd, Dalton House, 60 Windsor Avenue, London, SW19 2RR.
Company number 08720141. Registered in England and Wales.

For support please visit www.forgottenbooks.com

1 MONTH OF FREE READING

at

www.ForgottenBooks.com

By purchasing this book you are eligible for one month membership to ForgottenBooks.com, giving you unlimited access to our entire collection of over 1,000,000 titles via our web site and mobile apps.

To claim your free month visit:

www.forgottenbooks.com/free873519

* Offer is valid for 45 days from date of purchase. Terms and conditions apply.

English
Français
Deutsche
Italiano
Español
Português

www.forgottenbooks.com

Mythology Photography **Fiction**
Fishing Christianity **Art** Cooking
Essays Buddhism Freemasonry
Medicine **Biology** Music **Ancient Egypt** Evolution Carpentry Physics
Dance Geology **Mathematics** Fitness
Shakespeare **Folklore** Yoga Marketing
Confidence Immortality Biographies
Poetry **Psychology** Witchcraft
Electronics Chemistry History **Law**
Accounting **Philosophy** Anthropology
Alchemy Drama Quantum Mechanics
Atheism Sexual Health **Ancient History**
Entrepreneurship Languages Sport
Paleontology Needlework Islam
Metaphysics Investment Archaeology
Parenting Statistics Criminology
Motivational

A HISTORY OF
SAVANNAH
AND
SOUTH GEORGIA

BY
WILLIAM HARDEN

VOLUME II

ILLUSTRATED

27492

THE LEWIS PUBLISHING COMPANY
CHICAGO AND NEW YORK
1913

Ra_Bk

N. W. JONES.

History of Savannah and South Georgia

ANCESTORS OF WYMBERLEY JONES DE RENNE. The first of the Jones family to come out from England to America was Dr. Noble Jones, the great-great-grandfather of Wymberley Jones De Renne, at present living upon the old family estate, Wormsloe Plantation, near Savannah. Dr. Noble Jones was the father of Noble Wymberley Jones, the grandfather of Dr. George Jones, and the great-grandfather of George Wymberley Jones De Renne. Hereafter follow accounts in greater or less detail of the lives of each of these gentlemen, who have since their earliest connection with America been makers of her history, and prominent and successful in a high degree.

Dr. Noble Jones was bred to the profession of physic and lived at Lambeth, a village in the County of Surrey, situated on the south side of the river Thames, opposite Westminster, in which county his ancestors were born and resided. Being intimately acquainted with General Oglethorpe, he was induced by the general to accompany him on his first voyage to America in 1732. This friendship lasted all their lives. After General Oglethorpe returned to England to live, he sent Colonel Jones his portrait, with his Indian pupil standing by his side, reading. This portrait was lost when Savannah was captured by the English.

Dr. Noble Jones' family then consisted only of his wife and two children—a daughter and a son, Noble Wymberley Jones. It was his first intention to accompany the general without his family, but his wife objected to being left. Having promised the General to accompany him, he concluded to bring his family, not however, with an intention of remaining permanently, but after his arrival he was so pleased with the country that he decided to stay. Before leaving England, Doctor Jones, by deeds, to which the seal of the corporation of the Trustees of the Colony of Georgia was affixed, was appointed, November 7, 1732, conservator of the peace, and on the next day, November 8, 1732, he was appointed recorder in the place of Thomas Christie. How long he remained recorder is not certain, but he still held that office in 1735, and was succeeded by Thomas Christie. He was appointed surveyor by General Oglethorpe February 1, 1734, but did not give satisfaction and was discharged by the trustees and also suspended from the office of constable, which he had held for some time. To the last office he was soon re-appointed. That he was a good surveyor was testified to by Mr. Stephens in a letter to the trustees December 31, 1740. Other letters endorsed Mr. Stephens' opinion. He was also appointed by General Oglethorpe "Agent for the Indians," and for Tomo-chi-chi in particular.

533

During this time he was very active protecting the southern frontier. He writes to General Oglethorpe July 6, 1735: "I have been twice to the most southern parts of the province; the first time upon an alarm with about fifty men (all volunteers except ye scout boat), the particulars of which voyage (for fear of false account comes to your hands) I will send by next. The second time was with Captain Dunbar, who, I do not doubt, has informed you thereof before now."

The constables were responsible for the colonists attending to their military duties, and Jones and Fallowfield are mentioned as the two constables "in whom the civil and military power was lodged." Each of these two controlled three wards.

On the 10th of April, 1738, Mr. Stephens writes: "The two constables, Jones and Fallowfield (which was all we had), came early to town on the present occasion, conferring on the affair they came about, which was more immediately to look into the condition of the arms. It was resolved (for experiment's sake) to order the drum to beat immediately to arms, that thereby we might see how alert the people were and what number would get together on a sudden without previous notice. It was so done, and in less than an hour's time we saw eighty odd men in the center of the town with their proper arms, well appointed, and all able men, freeholders. Such as were absent were, almost every man, abroad busy planting."

When General Oglethorpe invaded Florida and laid siege to St. Augustine, some forty volunteers under Noble Jones joined the South Carolina regiment, in which he held a lieutenant's commission. On their return the company was disbanded in Savannah, according to the General's orders, and Noble Jones was sent to Charleston to collect the pay due them.

Soon after Noble Jones' arrival in the colony, he leased from the trustees the southern end of the Isle of Hope; later he received a grant from the trustees, which, in turn, was exchanged for a royal grant when the crown took charge of the colony. He named his place Wormsloe and built on it a watch house to protect Jones' Narrows. Later he built a large, tabby fort, the ruins of which are still well defined. This fort was successfully defended by his daughter Mary against a party of Indians during her father's absence. The other two-thirds of the Isle of Hope were owned by Messrs. Fallowfield and Parker. All three acted as magistrates at the same time "by Colonel Oglethorpe's orders until the trustees' further pleasure be known." Wormsloe is mentioned in the London Magazine of August, 1745; "We arrived in somewhat more than two days at the Narrows, where there is a kind of Manchicolas Fort for their defense, garrisoned from Wormsloe, where we soon arrived. It is the settlement of Mr. Jones, ten miles southeast of Savannah, and we could not help observing, as we passed, several pretty plantations. Wormsloe is one of the most agreeable spots I ever saw, and the improvements of that ingenious man are very extraordinary. He commands a company of marines who are quartered in huts near his place, which is a tolerable defensive place with small arms. From this house there is a vista of near three miles cut through the woods to Mr. Whitefield's orphan house, which has a very fine effect on the sight."

When the Spaniards invaded Georgia in 1742, Noble Jones who was in command of a company of scouts with General Oglethorpe's regiment on St. Simons, prepared to resist the Spanish army which had landed there. It was through his vigilance that General Oglethorpe was enabled to surprise and thoroughly defeat them at Bloody Marsh. Captain McCall gives the following account of this affair: "Capt. Noble Jones, with a detachment of regulars and Indians, being out on a scouting expedition, fell in with a small detachment of the enemy's advance, who were surprised and made prisoners. From these prisoners information was obtained that the whole Spanish army was advancing. This was immediately communicated by an Indian runner to the General, who detached Captain Dunbar with a company of grenadiers to join the Regulars and Indians, with orders to harass the enemy on their advance. These detachments, having formed a junction, observed at a distance the Spanish army on the march, and, taking a favorable position near a marsh, formed an ambuscade. The enemy fortunately halted within one hundred paces of this position, stacked their arms and made fires and were preparing their kettles for cooking when a horse observed some of the party in ambuscade, and, frightened at the uniform of the soldiers, began to snort and gave the alarm. The Spaniards ran to their arms, but were shot down in great numbers by Oglethorpe's detachment, who continued invisible to the enemy, and after repeated attempts to form, in which some of their prominent officers fell, they fled with the utmost precipitation, leaving their camp equipage on the field, and never halted until they got under cover of the guns of their battery and ships.''

The first official notice of the appointment of Noble Jones as a captain was on the 21st of March, 1842-43. Egmont's Journal has this reference: "Noble Jones, made a captain by Oglethorpe," but he fulfilled the duties of a captain, and was so called before that date. After his return from the Spanish campaign he seems to have devoted himself to his scout boat duties (captain of which he had been named by General Oglethorpe), and to the improvement of Wormsloe. He raised mulberry trees and silk worms, and the colony in a measure depended upon him for worm seed.

He and Captain Demetree cruised together with scout boats to intercept unlawful trading at Tybee. On December 22, 1739, "with boat well armed he captured a schooner in Ossybaw Sound and carried her around to Tybee.''

Meanwhile, he did not neglect his military duties in Savannah, and when in 1749 Mary Musgrave, now Mary Bosomworth, assumed the title of Independent Empress, and, putting herself at the head of a large body of warriors, set out for Savannah to demand from the president and council a formal acknowledgment of her assumed rights the militia was ready to receive her. President Stephens put the town into the best state of defense possible and received the Indians boldly. Jones' History of Georgia says: "The militia was ordered under arms, and as the Indians entered town Capt. Noble Jones at the head of a troop of horses stopped them and demanded to know whether their visit was of a friendly or hostile nature. Receiving no reply he commanded them to ground their arms, declaring that his instructions were not to suffer an armed Indian to set foot in the town, and that he was determined to enforce the order at every hazard. The Indians reluctantly submitted. Later, at their solicitations, their arms were returned to them, but strict orders were issued not to allow them any ammunition. When at last an amicable adjustment of existing difficulties had been effected, Mary, drunk with liquor, rushed into the Assembly and told the president that the Indians were her people and that he had no business with them. Mary had been arrested and locked up and had just been released. The president calmly threatened to confine her again. Turning to Malachte in a great rage, she repeated to him with some ill-natured comments what the president had said. Malatche thereupon sprung from his seat, laid hold of his arms, and calling upon the rest to follow his example, dared any man to touch his queen. In a moment the whole house was filled with tumult and uproar. Every Indian having a tomahawk in his hand, the president expected nothing but instant death. During this confusion, Capt. Noble Jones, who commanded the guard, with wonderful courage interposed and ordered the Indians immediately to surrender their arms. This they reluctantly did. Mary was conveyed to a private room, where a guard was placed over her, and all further communication with the Indians was denied her during her stay in Savannah."

About this time the expediency of subordinating Georgia to South Carolina was in certain high quarters seriously discussed and gave the trustees some concern. Before they could communicate with President Stephens, Captain Demetree landed at Causton's Bluff with boats, which, having brought the last of Oglethorpe's disbanded regiment to Charleston on their way to England, were returning to Frederica in his charge. He had a small detachment of ten or twelve men and said that he was on his way to Frederica to assume command at that point; that he took orders only from the governor of South Carolina, and that the trustees were cognizant of the fact. As he failed to report to the president and his assistants and disclose to them his orders or his intentions, they were at a loss to understand his extraordinary conduct and ordered Capt. Noble Jones to wait upon him and demand an explanation of and an apology for his discourtesy. Captain Demetree's reply to Captain Jones was that he was acting under the instructions from His Grace, the Duke of Bedford, and that he was to receive his orders from and report only to the governor of South Carolina. He reluctantly appeared before the council in answer to their summons. After Captain Demetree had made ample apology to the council, he was permitted to assume command of the military forces stationed at Frederica. The annexation of Georgia to South Carolina was to be accomplished at this time by stationing officers from three independent South Carolina companies in proper places in Georgia, "to preserve the possession of the province."

On July 13, 1750, the trustees recommended to the common council that Noble Jones be appointed an assistant in and for the province of Georgia, and the appointment under seal was sent to him July 16, 1750.

On April 18, 1751, the trustees recommended to the common council his appointment as Register of the Province, and his appointment followed on May 24, 1751.

About the middle of May of this year news came from Augusta that there was fear of an Indian invasion. "Accordingly the Magazine was examined, officers were appointed and ordered to muster and discipline the militia, a troop of horses was ordered to be raised composed of such inhabitants as were possessed of three hundred acres of land. Noble Jones was appointed Colonel, and his son, Noble Wymberley Jones, who had been a cadet in Oglethorpe's regiment, was appointed to command the Dragoons."

The alarm was exaggerated, but it served to bring out the militia, which consisted of 220 men, infantry and cavalry, and when they paraded (on the 16th of April, 1751, under the then Capt. Noble Jones) they "behaved well and made a pretty appearance." Noble Jones was appointed to "accompany Mr. Robinson in his inquiry into the state of the colony." According to Mr. Habersham, he was a stiff churchman and took a great deal of voluntary trouble in building the church, and in all church matters greatly aiding his friend, Rev. Mr. Zouberbuhler.

In the last year of the trustee's government of the colony, he was captain of the Marines and scout boat at Wormsloe, assistant to the president, register of the province, commissioner to treat with the Indians, member of the council to report on the state of the colony, and colonel of the regiment.

The trustees surrendered the colony to the British government on the 23d of June, 1752, and Benjamin Martin was appointed agent of the colony in England. Upon the death of President Parker, who had succeeded President Stephens (the first president of the colony appointed in April, 1741), Patrick Graham became president. His assistants were James Habersham, Noble Jones, Pickering Robinson and Francis Harris.

On the 6th of August, 1754, Capt. John Reynolds was appointed governor of the province and Noble Jones was confirmed as member of councils. On the 27th of November, 1754, Governor Reynolds, with the advice of the board, appointed Noble Jones and William Spencer, esquires, judges to hold the approaching court of oyer and terminer, and on December 12, 1754, Noble Jones and Jonathan Bryan were appointed as judges to hold the first general court in the province.

On March 29, 1757, "Noble Jones of His Majesty's Council, was appointed one of the new commissioners of the peace." This appointment was made before the Lords of Trade had heard from Governor Reynolds, who on Wednesday, December 15, 1756 "acquainted the board that he had thought proper to suspend Noble Jones, Esq., from all offices, for reasons which he would lay before the king." Governor Reynolds "removed Mr. Noble Jones from the board and bench to gratify Mr. Little, and it is positively affirmed, to promote the establishment of Bosomworth's titles to the Indian lands with a view to sharing the spoils." Governor Reynolds was summoned to England to answer for his conduct in Georgia. He embarked in a merchant vessel in February, 1757, resigning the government into the hands of Lieutenant Governor Henry Ellis, who became governor in chief on May 17, 1758. Noble Jones was re-instated by an order of the English council to Governor Ellis May 31, 1759, with his former precedence as councillor and also as senior justice of the general court.

Under Governor Ellis he was one of His Majesty's council, senior justice of the general court, colonel of the regiment and treasurer of the province, having been appointed to this last office by Governor Ellis on the 16th of February, 1760. "He had no salary, but a commission of five per cent, which on the last year's tax amounted to sixty-five pounds sterling, and may this year amount to eighty pounds." Governor Ellis resigned his office on account of ill-health and handed over the government to Lieutenant-Governor James Wright, who was appointed governor in chief on the 20th of March, 1761. In the following letter to the Lords of the board of trade, Governor Wright commends Noble Jones' services as chief justice of the colony after Mr. Simpson's death and before Mr. Anthony Stokes' arrival:

SAVANNAH, GA., Sept. 28, 1769.

"My Lords:—I take the liberty to acquaint your lordships that Noble Jones, Esq., senior judge of the courts here, has in every respect done and performed the office and duties of chief justice from 20th of October, 1768, when Mr. Simpson died, to the arrival of Mr. Stokes; and although Mr. Jones was not bred to the law, yet I believe that justice only was administered during that time and with integrity, and I have not heard any complaint made or fault found with his conduct. I therefore submit to your lordships whether it may not be reasonable that Mr. Jones shall receive the salary from the death of Mr. Simpson to the appointment of Mr. Stokes, and half of it from the appointment of Mr. Stokes to his arrival here. I have given Mr. Jones two certificates of his having done his duty here and have the honor to be, my Lords, Your Lordships' most obedient and obliging servant,

JAMES WRIGHT,

The Right Honorable Lords of Trade."

On the 10th of July, 1771, Governor Wright availed himself of a leave of absence, and three days afterward Mr. James Habersham took the usual oath of office and entered upon the discharge of the gubernatorial duties.

In a long letter to the Earl of Hillsborough, Governor Habersham relates that the assembly had against royal orders elected Noble Wymberley Jones, the son of Noble Jones, three times speaker in succession, and that they refused to leave this fact out of their minutes on the subsequent election of Archibald Bulloch, and that he had dissolved the assembly. Noble Wymberley Jones was as ardent a patriot as Noble Jones, his father, was a thorough Royalist. His opposition to the crown and his upholding of the cause of liberty seems to have embittered Mr. Habersham, who, not able to punish the son, brought his spleen to bear upon the father. He writes to the Earl of Hillsborough, April 30, 1772: "My Lord, it is very painful to me to say or even insinuate a disrespectful word of anyone, and every person who knows me will acknowledge that it is contrary to my disposition to dip my pen in gall; but I can not help considering Mr. Jones' conduct for some time past in opposing public business as very ungrateful and unworthy of a good man, as his family have reaped more advantages from government than any one I know in this province. He was several years first lieutenant and sergeant in a company of rangers paid by the crown, and in these capacities met with great indulgence. His father is the king's treasurer, and if I am not mistaken, reaps very considerable emoluments from it. But his accounts have never been clearly stated and examined by any assembly that I know of; and such an inquiry may not be agreeable. Governor Wright in his speech to the assembly in October, 1770, recommended our financial and public accounts to be examined entire but that assembly was dissolved in February following and no steps taken therein, and many people suspect that this very necessary examination operates with some to retard and impede progress. I sincerely meant to recommend this inquiry to the late assembly in the strongest terms, and as we now have no assembly I shall require the treasurer to lay before me in council a clear account of the produce of our funds, also the certificates that have been issued for different purposes, and of every account that may be necessary to post me with the state of the treasury, and after that is done I shall pursue such measures as seem necessary for the service of his majesty and the province, of which I shall inform your lordship."

That the treasurer's accounts were examined and approved of at times by the deputy auditor and the governor, is shown by a treasury account signed "Noble Jones, treasurer," February 26, 1767. Audited by Gray Elliott, Det. Aud. Gen., 6th February, and approved by James Wright 10th of February.

On further deliberation Mr. Habersham either found out that the accounts had been audited, or that an investigation was unnecessary, as there is no record of one having taken place—and as Noble Jones continued treasurer until the day of his death, which occurred three years afterward, it would seem reasonable to suppose that Mr. Habersham's fears were groundless. During Governor Wright's administration he took part in all important matters appertaining to Georgia,

and his fidelity and absolute devotion to the crown were unswerving.
In a card appearing in the Georgia Gazette, September 7, 1774, his name appears with James Habersham, Josiah Tattnall and ninety-three others, criticizing the meeting at Tondee's Tavern in Savannah, and protesting that the resolutions there should not be adopted as reflecting the sentiments of the people of Georgia. He performed his judicial duties up to the last. Upon the assembling of the general court on the 10th of October, 1775, one of the jurors summoned refused to be sworn. Others "behaved insolently," and the conduct of the business was practically obstructed. Mr. Noble Jones, one of the associate justices, was then "lying extremely ill." He died on the second of November following, at Wormsloe, and was buried near the fort on the place he loved so well. His remains were removed from Wormsloe to the colonial burying ground in Savannah, and later to Bonaventure cemetery near Savannah. His death was hastened by the dissensions among the Colonists; he could not sympathize with the idea of separation from or independence of the mother country, and he saw nothing but storms and trouble ahead for his beloved Georgia. During a long life, in which he held nearly every office in the province, if he was found fault with he never failed upon investigation of the charges against him to rise higher in the public esteem. Notwithstanding the zealous patriotism of Noble Wymberly Jones, he was a devoted son, and though then first elected a member of the continental congress, remained with his father at Wormsloe until the latter's death. On Noble Jones' tombstone at Bonaventure cemetery is inscribed the following:

NOBLE JONES, of Wormsloe, Esq.,

SENIOR JUDGE OF THE GENERAL COURT AND ACTING CHIEF JUSTICE OF THE PROVINCE OF GEORGIA.

FOR TWENTY-ONE YEARS MEMBER AND SOMETIMES PRESIDENT OF HIS MAJESTY'S COUNCIL.

COLONEL OF THE FIRST GEORGIA REGIMENT.

DIED NOVEMBER 2, 1775. AGED 73.

W. J. DE RENNE.

Noble Wymberley Jones, already mentioned in connection with some of the more important concerns of the Province of Georgia, was born near London, England, in 1723. Coming to Georgia at a tender age he secured an appointment as a cadet in Oglethorpe's regiment. Having studied medicine and received his degree, he was promoted to first lieutenant, and with the rank and pay of surgeon, was assigned to a company of rangers in the pay of the crown. After a few years passed in military service he resigned from the army and entered upon the practice of his profession in Savannah. He arose rapidly in the public esteem as a citizen and physician, winning golden opinions from the community. No idle spectator of passing events or indifferent to political preferment, he was in 1768 elected speaker of the Lower House of the Assembly of the Province of Georgia. By that body he was placed upon a committee to correspond with Dr. Benjamin Franklin—who had been appointed an agent "to represent, solicit and truthfully account the affairs of the colony of Georgia in Great Britain"—and gave such instructions as might appear necessary for the public welfare. Re-elected to this position in 1770, so pronounced and influential had become his views and conduct in opposition to the objectionable and oppressive acts of parliament, and in support of American ideals, that Governor Wright, exercising the power vested in him, refused to sanction this choice and ordered the house to select another speaker.

Incensed at this affront offered to one who had been aptly termed the Morning Star of Liberty in Georgia, and resenting what they deemed an unwarrantable interference with the power resting solely with them to nominate and judge of the qualifications of their own presiding officer, the members of the house passed resolutions complimentary to Dr. Jones and declared that the "sense and approbation this house entertains of his conduct can never be lessened by any slight cast upon him in opposition to the unanimous voice of the Commons House of the Assembly in particular and the Province in general." Criticising the action of the executive, they resolved "that this rejection by the governor of a speaker unanimously elected was a high breach of the privileges of the house and tended to subvert the most valued rights and liberties of the people and their representatives." This bold assertion the council was pleased to stigmatize as "a most indecent and insolent denial of his majesty's authority," and the governor, wielding the only punitive weapon at his command, dissolved the assembly on the 22d day of February, 1770.

Adhering to the preference shown on a former occasion, and resolving to rebuke the late interference on the part of the executive, at the first session of the eighth General Assembly of the Province, convened at Savannah on the 21st day of April, 1772, the Commons house perfected its organization by electing Dr. Jones as speaker. Officially informed of this action, the Hon. James Habersham, who, during the absence of Sir James Wright, was occupying the gubernatorial chair, responded: "I have his Majesty's commands to put a negative upon the speaker now elected by the Commons House, which I accordingly do; and desire that you will inform the house that I direct them to proceed to a new choice of speaker."

Despite this inhibition, and in direct opposition to the injunction of the executive, thrice did the house adhere to its selection; and it was only by dissolving the assembly that the governor was able to carry his point. It was upon this occasion that Governor Habersham wrote the letter of April 30, 1772, to the Earl of Hillsborough, commenting at length upon this matter, and which is quoted in the foregoing date upon the life of Col. Noble Jones.

The truth is, that while Gov. Habersham was loyally seeking to carry out the instructions of the king and to support the authority of Parliament, Dr. Jones "was in sympathy with those who considered taxation without representation as wholly unauthorized, and who were zealous in maintaining what they regarded as the reserved rights of the colonists, and the privileges of provincial legislatures." Both were true men but they viewed the situation from different standpoints. An honored servant of the crown, Mr. Habersham was confronted with peculiar duties and stringent oaths. Dr. Jones, on the contrary, was a representative elected by the people, was free to give expression to his own views and the sense of his constituents at an epoch when American liberty was being freely discussed and proclaimed. Of each it may be fairly said that he was pure in purpose, wise in counsel, and fearless in action, enjoying in a conspicuous degree the esteem and affection of the community. But their political paths henceforward diverged. The one clave to the crown and shared its fortunes, while the other cast his lot with the Revolutionists and became a favored leader of the patriot band.

With Archibald Bulloch, John Houstoun and John Walton, he issued the public call on July 20, 1774, which convened the citizens of Georgia at the Watch House in Savannah. The resolutions then adopted, and the measures there inaugurated, gathering potency and allegiance as they were discussed and comprehended, proved effective in unifying public sentiment in support of the plans suggested by the Liberty Party, and paved the way for sundering the ties which bound the Province to the British empire. Of the committees then raised to conduct the public affairs of the colony and to minister to the relief of the "suffering poor" of Boston, Noble Wymberley Jones was an active member. He was also elected with Archibald Bulloch and John Houstoun, a delegate to the Continental Congress, by a convention of patriots assembled at Savannah on the 8th of December, 1774, and again by the Provincial Congress of January, 1775. These three, concluding very properly that inasmuch as they had been nominated by the political convocation which in reality embraced only four of the twelve parishes then constituting the Province of Georgia, they could not be justly regarded as representatives of the entire colony, were yet persuaded that the will of those who commissioned them should be formally made known and the mind of Georgia be freely interpreted, and on the 6th of April, 1775, addressed the following communication to the president of the Continental Congress:

"Sir: The unworthy part which the Province of Georgia has acted in this great contest leaves room to expect little less than censure or even indignation of every virtuous man in America. Although on the one hand we feel the justice of such a consequence with respect to the Province in general, yet on the other hand, we claim an exemption from it in favor of some individuals who wished a better conduct. Permit us therefore in behalf of ourselves and many others of our fellow citizens warmly attached to the cause to lay before the respectable body over which you preside, a few facts, which we trust will not only acquit us of supineness, but also cause our conduct to be approved by all candid and dispassionate men.

"At the time the late congress did this Province the honor to transmit to it an extract from their proceedings, included in a friendly letter from the Honorable Mr. Middleton, the sense and disposition of the people in general seemed to fluctuate between liberty and convenience. In order to bring on a determination respecting the measures recommended, few well affected persons in Savannah, by public advertisement in the *Gazette*, requested a meeting of all the parishes and districts by delegates or representatives, in Provincial Congress. On the day appointed for this meeting, with concern they found that only five out of twelve parishes to which they had particularly written, had nominated and sent down delegates; and even some of these five had laid their representatives under injunctions as to the form of an association. Under these circumstances those who met saw themselves a good deal embarrassed. However, one expedient seemed still to present itself. The house of assembly was then sitting, and it was hoped there would be no doubt of a majority in favor of American freedom. The plan therefore was to go through what business they could in Provincial Congress, and then with a short address to present the same to the house of assembly, who it was hoped would by votes in a few minutes and before prerogative should interfere, make it the act of the whole Province.

"Accordingly the congress framed and agreed to such an association and did such other business as appeared practicable with the people, and had the whole just ready to be presented, when the governor, either treacherously informed, or shrewdly suspecting the step, put an end to the session. What then, could the congress do? On the one hand, truth forbid them to call their proceedings the voice of the Province, there being but five out of twelve of the parishes concerned; on the other, they lacked strength sufficient to enforce them on the principle of necessity. They found the inhabitants of Savannah not likely soon to give matters a favorable turn. The importers were mostly against any interruption and the consumers very much divided. There were some of the latter virtuously for the measures; others strenuously against them; but more that called themselves naturals than either. Thus situated, there appeared nothing before us but the alternative of either commencing a civil war among ourselves, or else of patiently waiting for the measures to be recommended by the general congress.

"Among a powerful people provided with men, money and conveniences, and by whose conduct others were to be regulated, the former would certainly be the result that would suggest itself to every man removed from the condition of a coward; but in a small community like Savannah (whose members are mostly in their first advance towards wealth and independence, destitute of even the necessities of life within themselves, and from whose junction of silence so little would be had or lost to the general cause), the latter presented itself as the most eligible plan, and was adopted by the people. Party disputes and animosities have occasionally prevailed and show that the spirit of freedom is not extinguished, but only resting for a time until an opportunity shall offer for calling it forth.

"The congress convened at Savannah did us the honor of choosing us delegates to meet your respectable body at Philadelphia on the 10th of next month. We were sensible of the honor and importance of the appointment and would gladly have rendered our country any service our poor abilities would permit of; but alas with what face could we have appeared for a Province whose inhabitants had refused to sacrifice the most trifling advantages to the public cause, and in whose behalf we did not think we could safely pledge ourselves for the execution of any measures whatever?

"We do not mean to insinuate that those who appointed us would prove apostate or desert their opinions, but that the tide of opposition was great; that all the strength and virtue of these our friends might not be sufficient for the purpose. We beg, sir, you will view our reasons for not attending in a liberal point of light. Be pleased to make the most favorable representation of them to the honorable, the members of congress. We believe we may take upon ourselves the satisfaction, notwithstanding all that has passed, that there are still men in Georgia who, when occasion shall require, will be ready to evince a steady allegiance and manly attachment to the liberties of America. For the consolation of these they find themselves in the neighborhood of a Province whose virtue and magnanimity must and will do lasting honor to the cause, and in whose fate they seem disposed freely to involve their own.

"We have the honor to be, sir, your most obedient and very humble servants,

NOBLE WYMBERLEY JONES,
ARCHIBALD BULLOCH,
JOHN HOUSTOUN.''

The news of the affairs at Concord and Lexington reached Savannah on the 10th of May and caused the wildest excitement. The thunders of the 19th of April aroused the Georgia Parishes from their lethargy and multiplied patriots within their borders. The magazines at the eastern extremity of Savannah,—built of brick and sunk some twelve feet under ground,—contained a considerable amount of ammunition. So substantial was thus structure that Governor Wright deemed it unnecessary to post a guard for its protection. The excited revolutionists all over the land cried aloud for powder. Impressed with the importance of securing the contents of this magazine, there quietly assembled Dr. Noble Wymberley Jones, Joseph Habersham, Edward Telfair, William Gibbons, Joseph Clay, John Milledge and some other gentlemen, at the residence of Dr. Jones, at a late hour on the night ,of the 11th of May, 1775, and proceeding to the magazine, broke it open and removed therefrom some six hundred pounds of powder. A portion of the rest was sent to Beaufort, South Carolina, for safe keeping, and the rest was concealed in the garrets and cellars of the houses of the captors. Although Governor Wright offered a reward of one hundred and fifty pounds sterling for the apprehension of the offenders, it failed to elicit any favor, although the actors in the affair are said to have been well known in the council. The tradition lives and is generally credited that some of the powder so obtained was forwarded to Cambridge and was actually expended by the patriots in the memorable battle of Bunker Hill.

On the 22d of June, 1775, in response to a call signed by Dr. N. W. Jones, Archibald Bulloch, John Houstoun and George Walton, many of the inhabitants of the town and district of Savannah assembled at the Liberty Pole in Savannah and elected a council of safety with instructions to maintain an active correspondence with the continental congress and with the councils of safety both in Georgia and other provinces, with a view to bringing about a union of Georgia with her sister colonies in the cause of freedom.

Of the provincial congress which assembled in Savannah on the 4th of July, 1775, Dr. Jones was a member accredited from the "town and district of Savannah." In this congress every parish was represented. Dr. Jones was of the committee then selected to frame a suitable address to the inhabitants of Georgia, advising them of the true nature of the disputes existing between Great Britain and her American colonies, and informing them of the deliberations and conclusions of the present congress. He was also chosen with John Habersham, Archibald Bulloch, Rev. Dr. Zubly and Dr. Lyman Hall to represent Georgia in the Continental Congress. Georgia was now in acknowledged sympathy with her sisters and took her place by regular representation in the national assembly. Of the Council of Safety which ordered the arrest of Governor Wright, Dr. Jones was a member.

Upon the capture of Savannah in December, 1778, Dr. Jones removed to Charleston, South Carolina. There, upon the fall of that city in 1780, he was taken prisoner by the British and sent in captivity to St. Augustine, Florida. Exchanged in July, 1781, he went to Philadelphia and there entered upon the practice of his profession. While a resident of that city he was elected to the Continental Congress by the General Assembly of Georgia.

Shortly after its evacuation by the king's forces in 1782, Dr. Jones returned to Savannah, repaired the desolations which war had wrought in his comfortable home, and resumed his professional labors. He was a member of the committee which received and saluted President Washington with an address of welcome upon the occasion of his visit to

Savannah in 1791. Dr. Jones presided over the constitutional convention which assembled at Louisville, Jefferson county, in May, 1795, and amended the constitution of Georgia. In 1804 he was president of the Georgia Medical Society. He died in Savannah, January 9, 1805, honored by the community as an accomplished gentleman, an influential citizen, a skillful physician and a sterling patriot.

Of his son, Dr. George Jones, no fitter expression as to his life and work might be made than is embodied in a set of resolutions adopted at a meeting of the bar of the federal and state courts, at the court house in Savannah, on November 14, 1838, on the day following his death. Here is given entire the resolutions adopted on that sad occasion : "Dr. George Jones, a distinguished citizen of Savannah, died November 13, 1838. His career of public service began in early youth. He endured, the last two years of the Revolutionary war, the hardships of a soldier, and manifested, in confinement on board an English prison ship, the fortitude and constancy of a youthful patriot. When the war was concluded, though still a very young man, he received strong proofs of public confidence by being placed in official relations to his fellow citizens, the duties of which required the ability, discretion and industry of matured manhood. He was subsequently one of Georgia's prominent legislators, and in the convention which framed our present constitution, was a leading member as a delegate from Chatham county. He was frequently afterward a member of the general assembly in both branches. Its history shows him to have been pure and disinterested, at all times inflexible in support of correct principles and in opposition to those schemes of personal aggrandizement which were unfortunately corruptly consummated by the alienation of the most valuable portion of the state's territory. The estimation in which his character and attainments were held induced the legislature, though he was not a lawyer, to elect him judge of the superior court for the eastern circuit. His demeanor as a judge was dignified, courteous and patient, and when he voluntarily retired from the appointment it was regretted by the bar, the officers of the court and the public. From the bench he was transferred to the senate of the United States. His services in that capacity being terminated, he was called by general consent to other stations of usefulness.

"It was truly said of him that he took office from a sense of obligation rather than from any desire for distinction. He was for many years one of the members of the superior court, and its record showed that he was a faithful administrator of its duties, vigilant in all that regarded the rights of the widow and orphan. He served efficiently as mayor of Savannah for two years, from September, 1812, to September, 1814.

"He was amiable, philanthropic, considerate, firm, forbearing, delicate in his intercourse with society. He had a modesty in speech and manner, at all times and to all persons, worthy of remembrance and imitation, and to these graces were added the belief and humility of a Christian."

In setting forth details concerning the life of George Wymberley-Jones De Renne, it has seemed expedient to make free quotation of excerpts from an address given by a prominent resident of Savannah on an occasion of considerable importance. Here follows portions of the address referred to; with occasional paraphrase:

"Although born in the city of Philadelphia on the 19th of July, 1827, Mr. George Wymberley-Jones DeRenne, was in every thought and emotion, a Georgian most loyal. In the paternal line he was the direct descendant of Col. Noble Jones,—the trusted lieutenant of Oglethorpe,—his great-grandson, to speak in exact terms, and the grandson of Noble Wymberley Jones. And among the patriot names shedding lustre upon the period when our people were engaged in the effort to rid themselves of kingly rule, none in Georgia was more conspicuous for purity of purpose, wisdom of counsel and fearlessness in action than was he. Speaker of the provincial legislature at a time when it was no light matter to incur the displeasure of a royal governor, arrested and confined because of his sympathy with the revolutionists, and upon the termination of the war, selected a representative from Georgia in the congress, as physician, legislator, patriot, citizen, he won the confidence and esteem of all.

"Thus does it appear that Mr. De Renne was the legitimate inheritor, in the fourth generation, of illustrious traditions and of memories personal and precious connected with the history and honor of Georgia. With him they were family legacies. He accepted them as such, and the allegiance which bound him to home and state was inseparable from the ties which united him to kindred and lineage. They were indissolubly interwoven, and whenever the name of Georgia was uttered, there came heart throbs of loyalty and pride most peculiar and pleasureable.

"The first eleven years of his life,—that tender period when impressions the most abiding are formed,—when loves are cemented which the vicissitudes of subsequent age cannot impair,—that morning of existence whose sunlight fades not from memory,—were passed at Wormsloe on the Isle of Hope, the abode of his ancestors. There in infancy were his loves of Georgia begotten. There was his knowledge of home and country localized. There were attachments born which remained ever part and parcel of his inner being.

"When not yet twelve years old, upon the death of his father, he accompanied his mother to Philadelphia. There he pursued his academic studies and was, in due course, admitted as a member of the collegiate department of the University of Pennsylvania. His proficiency in the acquisition of knowledge, and his intellectual capabilities attracted the notice and evoked the commendation of his teachers. It was natural that he should seek an education in that city and from that institution, for both were allied to him by ties of no ordinary significance. His maternal grandfather,—Justice Thomas Smith,—had been for many years a prominent lawyer and a distinguished judge in Philadelphia, and his maternal great-uncle, the Rev. William Smith, D.D., was the first provost of the institution now known as the University of Pennsylvania. He was a noted teacher, an accomplished writer and an eloquent divine. A native of Scotland and a graduate of the University of Aberdeen, shortly after his removal to America he identified himself with all that was progressive and of high repute in the City of Brotherly Love. After a long life spent in the rendering of important service to the literary, educational and religious interests of the country, he died in the city of his adoption on the 14th of May, 1803. His scholarly works and the institutions he founded are living monuments to his memory.

"In his maternal home, and upon the benches whence had gone forth many who had been instructed by his distinguished relative, Mr. De Renne found opportunity for earnest study. Graduating with honor, and selecting medicine as the profession best suited to his tastes, he became a private pupil of Dr. Samuel Jackson and entered the medical school of the University of Pennsylvania. This college was at that time probably the most noted in the United States, and the facilities there afforded for mastering the mysteries of the healing art were unsurpassed this side of the Atlantic. Mr. De Renne's graduating thesis was entitled 'Theory Concerning the Nature of Insanity.' It was, in 1847, privately printed, to the number of forty-eight copies, for special distribution. Striking in thought and composition is this production, indicating an amount of careful research, delicate analysis, and philosophical deduction quite uncommon in one who had barely attained unto his majority. It elicited the praise of his preceptors, who earnestly hoped that his talents and acquirements would be consecrated to the calling which sweeps in its high scope the whole range of physical and moral science. But with Mr. De Renne there was no intention of applying himself to the active pursuit of the profession to the privileges of which he had just been admitted as a doctor of medicine. His affections turned to his island home beneath the Georgia magnolias, and his thoughts were of a quiet, independent life, devoted to the exhibition of hospitality, the pursuit of literature, and the enjoyment of dignified repose.

"Shortly after graduation he repaired to Wormsloe and there fixed his residence. With all its wealth of magnificent live-oaks, palmettoes, pines, cedars and magnolias, with its quiet, gentle views, balmy airs, soft sunlight, swelling tide, inviting prospects and cherished traditions, this attractive spot had uninterruptedly continued to be the home of his ancestors from the date of its original cession from the crown to his great-grandfather, Capt. Noble Jones. Here were the remains of the tabby fortification which he had constructed for the protection of his plantation,—then an outpost of the town of Savannah,—and there, vine covered and overshadowed by oaks and cedars, they will endure for unnumbered years, constituting one of the most unique and interesting historical ruins on the Georgia coast. During his residence at this charming abode, which continued, with occasional absences, until the late war between the states, Mr. De Renne guarded his ancestral domain with the tender care and devotion of a loyal son, adding to the recollections of the past literary and cultivated associations in the present, which imparted new delights to the name of Wormsloe.

"His carefully selected library contained works of high repute, and of great rarity in certain departments. His reading was varied and accurate. Communing often with his favorite authors, he maintained an active acquaintance with the ever expanding domain of scientific and philosophical inquiry. His liberal education, enriched by study, travel and observation, enabled him to appreciate and cultivate those standards in literature and art which give birth to the accurate scholar and the capable critic.

"To familiarize himself with the history of Georgia and rescue her traditions from forgetfulness were ever his pleasure and pride. During his sojourn in London he obtained favored access to the records in the various public offices and to the treasures of the British Museum. Thence did he procure copies of all papers throwing light upon the early life of the colony. We have no hesitation in expressing the opinion that in a thorough acquaintance with the history of Savannah and that of Georgia, both as a colony and a state.—he was excelled by none.

"During his residence on the Isle of Hope the literary tastes of Mr. De Renne found expression in the following publications,—with one exception bearing the imprint of Wormsloe,—and executed in the highest style of the printer's art.

"In 1847 he reprinted the rare and valuable political tract by George Walton, William Few, and Richard Howley, entitled 'Observations upon the effects of certain late political suggestions, by the Delegates of Georgia.' Two years afterward appeared the caustic 'Observations on Dr. Stevens' History of Georgia.' In 1849 was issued the second of the Wormsloe quartos, entitled 'History of the Province of Georgia; with Maps of Original Surveys; by John Gerar William

DeBrahm, His Majesty's Surveyor General for the Southern District of North America.' This was a most valuable publication. DeBrahm's manuscript, from which the portion relating to Georgia was thus printed, exists in the library of Harvard University, at Cambridge, Massachusetts. Mr. De Renne did for Georgia what Mr. Weston has accomplished for South Carolina. The next year the third of the Wormsloe quartos presented the interesting 'Journal and Letters of Eliza Lucas,' the mother of Generals Charles Cotesworth and Thomas Pinckney.

"So charmed was Mr. De Renne with 'A Bachelor's Reverie' by Ik Marvel, that in 1850, by permission of and as a compliment to the author, he had a beautiful edition of twelve copies privately printed.

"In 1851 Mr. De Renne published, as his fourth Wormsloe quarto, the 'Diary of Col. Winthrop Sargent, Adjutant General of the United States Army during the Campaign of 1791.' Only such portion of the diary was printed as related to St. Clair's expedition. Of these quartos but a very limited edition was printed, and the copies were donated to famous libraries and placed in the hands of favored friends. Of the first quarto there are only twenty-one copies; of the second, forty-nine; of the third, nineteen; and of the fourth, forty-six. They are all remarkable specimens of typography and literary taste; and, in addition to the historical value they possess, are highly esteemed because of their rarity.

"Soon after the inception of the war Mr. De Renne transferred his residence from Wormsloe to the city of Savannah. The desolations consequent upon the failure of the Confederate cause pressed sorely upon the coast region of our state, sadly altering the conveniences of life, changing the whole theory of our patriarchial civilization, and begetting isolation and solitude where formerly existed inviting mansions,—the centres of sympathies and social life which in their essential characteristics can never be revived.

"His residence in Savannah,—the abode of the choicest hospitality, within whose walls dwelt comfort, refinement and elegance most attractive,—could never in his affections supplant the love he cherished for the old homestead on the Isle of Hope. During the winter and spring, one day in each week he dedicated to the sweet influences of Wormsloe, where secluded from the turmoil of busy life, he surrendered himself to the contemplation of scenes and the revivification of memories upon which time had placed its seal of consecration.

"Of the public spirit which characterized Mr. De Renne as a citizen of Savannah,—the public spirit of a high-toned, independent gentleman solicitious for the general welfare, yet courting neither personal advantage nor political preferment,—of the sterling qualities which he exhibited in the business affairs of life and in the administration of his ample fortune,—of the active and intelligent interest he manifested in everything promotive of the material and intellectual progress of the city,—of his many charities, unheralded at the times of their dispensation, I may not speak. They are fresh in the recollection of us all. Were he here he would tolerate no mention of them, and now that he is gone, as his friend, I will do no violence to his known wishes.

"I cannot refrain, however, from reminding you of two princely gifts which will identify his memory with Savannah so long as human structures endure. I refer to his munificent donation of a commodious and substantial building on West Broad street to be used as a public school for the education of the children of citizens of African descent, and to his presentation, to the Ladies' Memorial Association, of that admirable bronze statue of a Confederate soldier which surmounts the monument erected by fair hands in the military parade of Savannah in honor of our Confederate dead.

"A meeting of the Ladies' Memorial Association was held June 3d, 1879, at six o'clock, at the lecture room of the Independent Presbyterian church, when, after the transaction of the usual routine of business, the following communication from Mr. G. W. J. De Renne was submitted by the president and ordered to be read:

"SAVANNAH, MAY 21, 1879.
"To the President of the Ladies' Memorial Association, Savannah:

"'MADAM: In pursuance of the proposition made and accepted in April of last year, I now present to the Ladies' Memorial Association a bronze statue of a Confederate soldier.

"'It represents him as he was,—marked with the marks of service in features, form and raiment;—a man who chose to be rather than to seem, to bear hardship than to complain of it;—a man who met with unflinching firmness the fate decreed him, to suffer, to fight and to die in vain.

"'I offer the statue as a tribute to the "MEN" of the Confederate army. Without name or fame or hope of gain, they did the duty appointed them to do. Now, their last fight fought, their suffering over, —they lie in scattered graves throughout our wide Southern land, at rest at last, returned to the bosom of the loved Mother they valiantly strove to defend.

"'According to your faith, believe that they may receive their reward in the world to come:—they had none on earth.

"'With the expression of my profound respect for those women of the South who, true to the dead, have sought to save their memory from perishing, I am, madam,
Very respectfully, etc.,
G. W. J. DE RENNE.'

"The following resolutions were then offered and unanimously adopted by a rising vote:

"'Whereas our fellow citizen, G. W. J. De Renne, has presented to this association the bronze statue of a Confederate soldier now crowning the monument erected in the military parade of this city to the memory of the soldiers who perished for the cause they held more precious than life;

"'Therefore, Resolved, that we, as members of this association, individually and as a body, do hereby unanimously express our grateful appreciation of this noble gift; recognizing its great merit not only as a work of art, but as a signal ornament to our beloved city, and as a valued contribution to the public sentiment worthy of the munificent and solemn purpose of the donor.

"'Resolved, that we do hereby accept this tribute with profound gratitude, and, in the name of all who are true to these heroic dead, we reverently consecrate it to the memory of the Confederate army who 'went down in silence.'

"'Resolved, that two copies of these proceedings be signed by each of the officers of this association;—one copy to be presented to G. W. J. De Renne, Esq., and the other to the Georgia Historical Society, with the request that it may be placed for preservation in the archives of the society.

HENRIETTA COHEN, *President.*
S. C. WILLIAMSON, *Treasurer.*
S. C. MANN, *Secretary.*'

"Thus are the name, the generosity and the patriotism of G. W. J. De Renne indissolubly linked with the holiest monument erected within the confines of the monumental city:—a monument redolent of the

SAVANNAH AND SOUTH GEORGIA 549

prayers, the loves and the tears of mother, wife, sister, daughter;—a monument crystallizing in towering and symmetrical form the memories of the Confederate struggle for independence; a monument standing as a spotless, imperishable, just tribute to our Confederate dead.''

HON. CHARLES GORDON EDWARDS. In March, 1907, there took his place in the Congress of the United States, representing the First District of Georgia, a young statesman of the type upon which the south founds its hope—the Hon. Charles Gordon Edwards, of Savannah. So excellent was the record made by him in the Sixtieth Congress that he was returned at the next election. He is particularly well fitted by nature and training for the duties of his office and combines in himself the theoretical and practical, which produces the man who begets great ideas and knows how to make them realities. He has carried with him to the National Assembly well defined and unfaltering ideas of duty towards his constituents and is in refreshing contrast to the self-seeking politician who has proved the menace of modern society. In truth he has been very successful in keeping his political skirts free from corruption. As a lawyer he has already taken rank among the most able in the city.

Mr. Edwards is a native son of Georgia, his birth having occurred in Tattnall county, July 2, 1878. His parents are the Hon. Thomas J. and Annie (Conley) Edwards, who reside at Daisy, Tattnall county, the former being, indeed, a life-long resident of that section. He served with distinction as a Confederate soldier in the war between the states, enlisting as a member of the Fifth Georgia Cavalry, but early in the great conflict he became a courier on the staff of Gen. Bob Anderson, in which capacity he spent the greater part of his army service. He became one of the best known and most highly trusted couriers in the Confederate army, his services taking him from northern Virginia through the Carolinas and Virginia to Florida. His military career it would be impossible to exceed in interest, filled as it was with thrilling adventures and escapes from the enemy. The forbears of the subject on both sides of the family have for many years been identified with this part of the south. His paternal grandfather, Dr. William H. Edwards, was one of the pioneers of the county and assisted in laying the paths straight and clean for the coming of latter day civilization. His great-grandfather, Willis F. Edwards, was a soldier in the Continental line from North Carolina in the Revolutionary war, and at the conclusion of his services in the cause of independence, he settled in Georgia. The maternal grandfather, Rev. William Fletcher Conley, also a pioneer of Tattnall county, assisted in the suppression of the Indians. He was a son of William F. Conley, a Virginian and a soldier in the Revolutionary war. Thus it will be seen that the gentleman from Georgia is a thorough American, which in this day of foreign invasion is coming to be a notable distinction. He has inherited the patriotism of his ancestors and is very loyal to American institutions.

Mr. Edwards received an excellent education, attending the Gordon Institute at Barnesville, Georgia; the University of Florida; and the University of Georgia. He graduated in the law department of the latter in the class of 1898, receiving the degree of B. L. He immediately began the practice of law at Reidsville, the county seat of Tattnall county, where he remained until December, 1900, in which year he located permanently in the city of Savannah. Here he soon found the recognition to which his gifts entitled him. Upon first arriving he formed a partnership with Capt. R. J. Travis and later with A. L.

Alexander. The latter partnership existed until his election to Congress.

In the election of 1906, Mr. Edwards was elected to Congress, representing the First District of Georgia and throughout the city there was at that time and still persists a conviction that the right man had triumphed and that the interests of the people would be well represented. He took his seat in the National Assembly on March 4, 1907, as a member of the Sixtieth Congress. He was reelected in 1909 and on March 4, 1910, became a member of the Sixty-first Congress. At the time of his appearance in the Sixtieth Congress he was the youngest member of that body. Mr. Edwards has in every way justified the confidence of his constituents and has made a fine record for practical usefulness, all of which has made him justly beloved in Savannah and throughout the First District. He is a member of the important Rivers and Harbors Committee, one of the seven big committees of the House. He is also a member of the Committee on Elections, in which committee he is ranking Democrat, ranking next to the chairman. He is identified with the Committee on Alcohol Liquor Traffic and he has taken part in the enactment of much important legislation. At home, in state affairs, it was largely through his agitation, eloquent and logical, that the Georgia State Drainage Law was enacted, under which a vast acreage of rich land, particularly in the vicinity of Savannah and in southeast Georgia is being scientifically drained and reclaimed for agricultural purposes. As such land is now practically waste land the beneficence of this measure will readily be seen, and will conduce in material fashion to the prosperity of the section. It will result not only to adding greatly to the agricultural wealth of the state by coming under cultivation, but it will also have a tendency to decrease malaria and other diseases arising from low, swampy and flooded lands.

Besides his work as a statesman and in the law profession, Mr. Edwards in commercial life has substantial interests in naval stores, saw mills, farming and banking. He was formerly a member of the Oglethorpe Light Infantry in Savannah, in which he became a lieutenant. He is a member of Epworth Methodist Episcopal church, and a trustee of the Southern Methodist College at McRae, Georgia. He has many fraternal and social affiliations, being identified with Sigma Nu fraternity, the Knights of Pythias, the Odd Fellows, the Elks, the Oglethorpe Club, the Georgia Bar Association, the Savannah Bar Association, the Sons of Confederate Veterans, and he is also a Knight Templar Mason and a Shriner.

Mr. Edwards was happily married December 17, 1902, his chosen lady being Miss Ora Beach, of Waycross, Georgia, daughter of Hon. William W. and Margie (Hinson) Beach. They share their hospitable and attractive home with one son, Charles Beach Edwards.

HON. WILLIAM W. OSBORNE is a member of the firm of Osborne & Lawrence, general practitioners of law. The firm has been general counsel for the Savannah Electric Company, which has operated the street railway system since 1897. Mr. Osborne has been a member of the state legislature from Chatham county, session of 1892-93, and state senator in the session of 1894-95. While in the lower house he was chairman of the committee on immigration and in the upper, chairman of the committee on railroads.

Mr. Osborne was born at Graniteville, October 19, 1867. His parents were John H. H. and Mary Stoney (Wilson) Osborne. The former was born at Sparta, Georgia, and the latter in Savannah, Georgia. In his early childhood, Mr. Osborne removed with his parents to Savannah.

He was reared in this city. Here he received his public school education, graduating from the high school in 1882. For his higher education he became a student in Mercer University at Macon in 1882 and 1883. The following year he entered the University of Georgia at Athens, from which institution he was graduated in 1885. With the idea of adopting the law as his profession he entered the law office of Denmark & Adams and was admitted to the bar on December 7, 1886. For a time he practiced alone, but subsequently formed a partnership with the late Pope Barrow, a gentleman of many distinctions, who had been United States senator and who later became judge. This partnership continued from 1894 until 1902, and in the year last mentioned, Mr. Osborne formed a second partnership with Alexander L. Lawrence, which has continued to this day.

In 1906, Mr. Osborne organized the Exchange Bank of Savannah, and is president of the same. In 1910-1911, Mr. Osborne was elected to the office of president of the Georgia Bankers' Association. In addition to the foregoing honors, Mr. Osborne was elected and served as solicitor general for the eastern circuit, superior court, for three terms of four years each, his tenure of office extending over the period comprised within the dates January 1, 1896, and January 1, 1908.

Mr. Osborne was married in 1894 to Miss Louette Dale. They have two daughters: Kate Dale and Mary Stoney.

GEORGE J. MILLS. One of Savannah's leading citizens is George J. Mills, who has come to attain an admirable and influential position among the able financiers of the city. The success attained in his business enterprises has been greatly owing to his steady persistence, stern integrity and excellent judgment, qualities which cause him to take rank with the eminent men in this section of the state, besides winning for him the confidence and esteem of the public to a marked degree. Mr. Mills was born in this city on the 7th day of June, 1850, the son of Capt. J. G. and Hettie Mariah (Cope) Mills. Captain Mills was born at St. Marys, Camden county, Georgia. For a long number of years before the war he was a prominent figure in maritime affairs on the Atlantic ocean. Starting as a youth before the mast, he was promoted through his own merit and efficiency to higher positions and became the master of a sailing vessel. Later Captain Mills went into the ocean shipping business for himself; he established and for several years was the owner of the Mills line of sailing vessels, operating between Savannah and Liverpool, and in this business he accumulated a comfortable fortune, all the more creditable from the fact that he started in with nothing. The Mills line of sailing vessels had to go out of business on account of the war, and after the termination of sectional hostilities, Captain Mills became a member, with his brother, of the firm of T. R. & J. G. Mills, cotton merchants of Savannah; which business was continued until about 1874, when Captain Mills retired from active business life. He died on September 24, 1880.

Mr. Mills is bound to Savannah by all the most important associations of life. He was reared and educated in the city of his birth and has been in business here ever since he became of age. He found his first field of occupation in his father's cotton business, and afterward, with the elder gentleman went into the private banking business, in which he continued after the demise of Captain Mills. His unusually fine business qualifications have brought success to a number of enterprises. He is a capitalist, having large financial interests in various important commercial and industrial concerns and he is one of the financial bulwarks of Savannah. He is chairman of the Sinking Fund

Commission of Savannah. He was made a member of this commission in 1907, and has served upon it continuously since that time. He is a director of the Central of Georgia Railway; a director of the Merchants' National Bank; and a director, or stockholder in various other corporatons. He has also acted efficiently and with public spirit in various philanthropic movements in the city and is president of the Savannah Hospital Association and a director of the Savannah Port Society. He is chairman of the board of trustees of the Independent Presbyterian church. Regarded as a citizen, Mr. Mills belongs to that useful and helpful type of men, whose ambitions and desires are centered and directed in those channels through which flows the greatest and most permanent good to the greatest number. His sympathies are ever with his less fortunate brothers and with no one is the betterment of the "other half" a more vital issue.

Mr. Mills was married in Savannah, Miss Euphemia F. Postell, member of a prominent South Carolina family of that name, becoming his wife. Mrs. Mills is a sister of that well-known gentleman, Col. C. Postell, of Savannah. Their daughter, Sarah C., is the wife of Henry W. Hodge, a civil engineer and bridge builder of New York City.

HON. GEORGE W. TIEDEMAN. Savannah for three elections chose the same man for her chief executive. Such confidence is sufficient proof of the worth of the Hon. George W. Tiedeman, ex-mayor of Savannah. Before becoming identified with the civic affairs of the city, Mr. Tiedeman had won prominence as an able and energetic business man, and he has carried his methods of doing business into the direction of the city's affairs. His administration was productive of many public improvements, and was particularly diligent in measures for the protection of the public health and the proper sanitation of the city, and for its freedom from bribery and misuse of funds, such as most American cities of today have to endure. The movement for a "Greater Savannah" received the most enthusiastic support from the administration, and the great stride forward that Savannah has taken in recent years is due in no small part to the personal influence of Mr. Tiedeman. His whole administration not only thought for the present but made preparation for the future. In the optimistic mind of Mr. Tiedeman, there has never been the least doubt but that Savannah would have a prominent place among the greater American cities and in his plans for her welfare he looked far ahead and attempted to meet the demands of such a city as it now seems certain Savannah will become. In short, to quote the words of William Harden, the administration of Mr. Tiedeman "has been essentially a constructive administration."

Mr. Tiedeman was born on the 11th of September, 1861, in Charleston, South Carolina. Here he was reared and educated, imbibing with the lessons he learned at school, the fine ideals and courtesy of bearing for which the men of this old city are noted. Growing up during the years following the Civil war he of necessity saw the courage with which a defeated people took up their burdens and set out to bring order out of chaos. He was only a boy during the greatest period of suffering, but his impressionable mind was impressed by the love that the people of the South bore for their country, and by the way in which they set to work to repair the ravages of war. He determined at this time that when he grew to manhood he would do everything in his power to make his country as prosperous as she was before the war. He was educated in private schools and in Charleston College, and in 1887 he came to Savannah.

He went into the wholesale grocery business on his arrival in the city and since that time he has been successfully engaged in this line of business. In addition to his political activities he has been prominent in the world of finance and in society. He is president of the Georgia State Savings Association. He is a member of the Board of Trade and of the Chamber of Commerce. In the world of sport and of society he is much sought after, and is a member of the Oglethorpe Club, the Yacht Club, the Automobile Club and the Golf Club.

Mr. Tiedeman received considerable preparatory training for his present position through his service as an alderman, for he was brought to a clear realization of the great necessity for improvement in many branches of the public affairs through this close connection with them. He was elected mayor in January, 1907, for a term of two years, was re-elected in January, 1909, and again in January, 1911. Savannah has never passed through a more prosperous period. She has held her proud position of being the largest market in the world for naval stores; her business, both in exports and imports, has been greatly increased and indeed she has advanced to the rank of fifth city in the United States in amount and value of exports. Many new industries have found a location in the city, and trade in all branches has received an impetus. The city limits have been extended, and during the season of 1911-12, the record for handling and exporting cotton was broken.

It is not possible to mention all of the beneficial results of Mayor Tiedeman's administration, and only the more important and those which will have the most far reaching results can be mentioned. Among these is the part that the city has had in the improvement of that beautiful southern section which is now the site of some of the finest homes in the city. This tract of land is owned by the Chatham Land & Hotel Company and the Ardsley Park Land Corporation, and this land has been brought within the city limits on a lot basis, thus increasing the taxable values of the municipality, and aiding in the rapid development of the section. A large amount of street paving has been done, greater in extent than has been completed during any previous period of the same duration. Some of this paving had been agitated for years but things seemed to stand still until Mr. Tiedeman appeared on the scene. For a city as dependent as is Savannah upon her harbor, it had been allowed to fall into a shameful state of disrepair and one of the most necessary deeds of the administration was the repair of all the slips and public docks. The water system and the storm sewerage system were extended to meet the needs of the growing city, and the street lighting system was practically made over by the installation of a new type of more brilliant lights in every section of the city. Bonaventure cemetery was developed and put in its present beautiful condition, and Daffin Park was also improved and thrown open to the public. The fine statue of General Oglethorpe, upon which work had ceased to be done for lack of funds, was now completed, the necessary money being appropriated for the purpose from the public treasury. Several thousands of dollars were spent in the laying of concrete and stone sidewalks, and an ordinance that was of especial importance to people of all classes was passed. This was a milk ordinance, and the officers of the administration have been extremely careful that this law should be enforced.

The achievement which stands out above all the others, and which brought to Mr. Tiedeman the thanks of a devoted city was the successful culmination of the bond election on December 6, 1911, by which the city is given the authority to spend $600,000 for the extension and completion of the sewerage and drainage system. This is one of the most beneficent measures ever passed in Savannah, for situated as the city is, drainage is a question of supreme importance to the health of the people. The work is to be carried on under the direction of a drainage commission composed of a number of the leading citizens. Mr. Tiedeman had long ago seen the necessity of such a measure, but he had not been able to make the city feel the necessity of it. In the election in which this was the issue Mr. Tiedeman took personal charge of the campaign, and carried it to a successful termination. He did not spare either his time or energy in placing before the public the necessity of this measure, and he set forth the advantages of the ordinance in so clear and sincere a manner that it was passed by an overwhelming majority. He has received full credit for his work in the formulation of the ordinance when it was as yet on paper, and the people have appreciated to the full his careful and painstaking selection of men of ability for members of the commission, who might be trusted with the administration of so large a sum of money. Mr. Tiedeman is very anxious to have some form of civil service regulation for all civil service employees, thus abolishing the old cries of favoritism, and securing more skilled service. He has strongly recommended this in his messages to the city council, and he is also a sincere advocate of a commission form of government.

Mr. Tiedeman was married in 1890 to Miss Floride Shivers of Savannah. In addition to their beautiful summer home at the Isle of Hope, they have a handsome city residence, and wherever they may be, their friends are always sure of a welcome. They are the parents of two children, Miss Inez Tiedeman and Carsten Tiedeman. Savannah is fortunate in having had such a mayor, for in the wave of progress and the new life that has swept over the South in the last few years, a strong hand is needed at the helm of those cities that will eventually become the great southern centers of trade. Some southern cities have suffered under the rule of a demagogue, and some from one who was too weak to rule and lacked the power of initiative, therefore Savannah should be proud that the man who for six years was at the head of her affairs was strong, conscientious, eager to do what will benefit the people and the city, and possessed of the brain and the wisdom to plan and carry out the necessary measures.

ABRAHAM MINIS. In the South, where family ties still bind and names still count, the Minis family are reckoned of the blue blood of Georgia, their history dating from colonial times and the grandfather of Abraham Minis having been the first male white child born in Georgia. The family is a historic one and it has been prominent in the history of the city for many generations. Abram Minis, youngest son of Abraham Minis, does not shine merely in the reflected light of his forefathers, but he is a citizen of ability, a lawyer of high standing at the bar and a man of property.

Abraham Minis, the second son of Isaac and Dinah Minis, was born in Savannah in 1820, and, in early youth was sent North to a school in Westchester, Pennsylvania, which stood very high and was kept by a Frenchman, a Mr. Bolmar.

Here he remained until the age of sixteen when, owing to his father having encountered business reverses, he determined to become self-supporting, a resolution which he carried out absolutely.

Securing a position with Padleford & Fay, then one of the leading houses on the Bay, it was characteristic of the man that he never filled another clerkship and that the heads of the firm became his warmest, lifelong friends.

Entering for himself the commission business, associated with Mr.

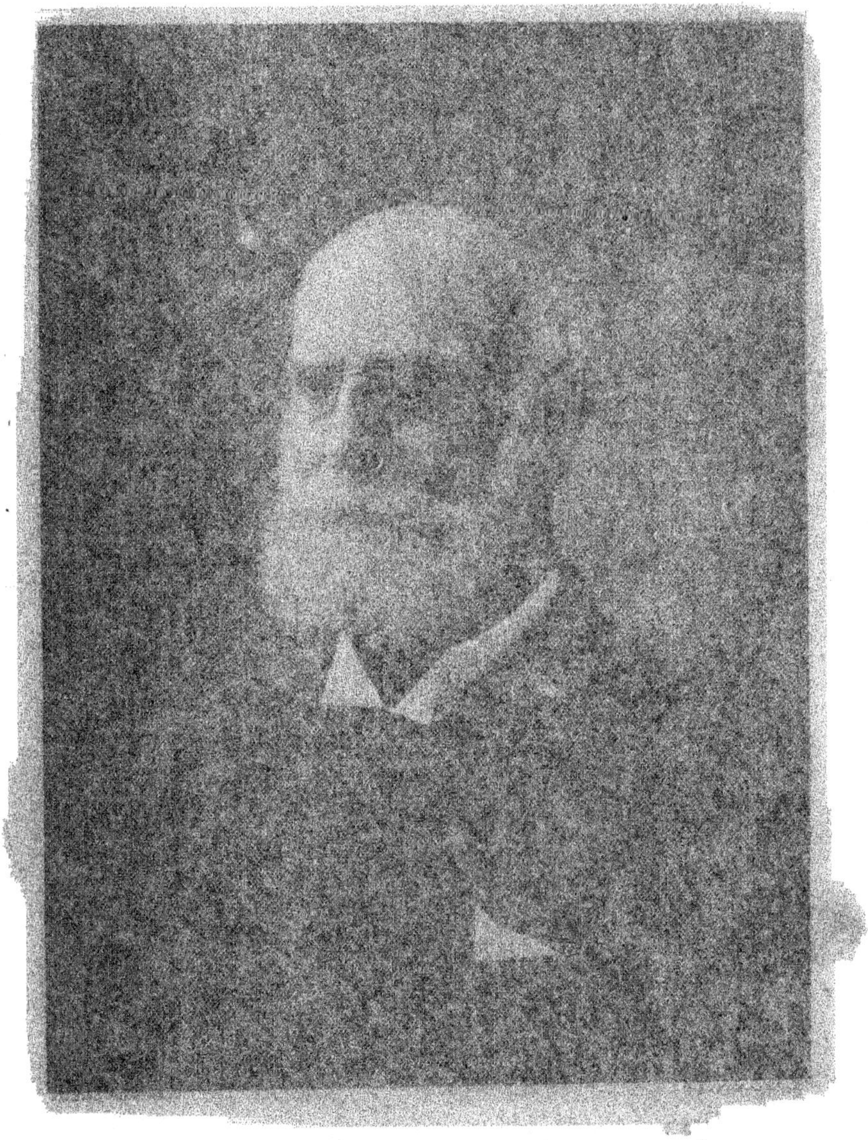

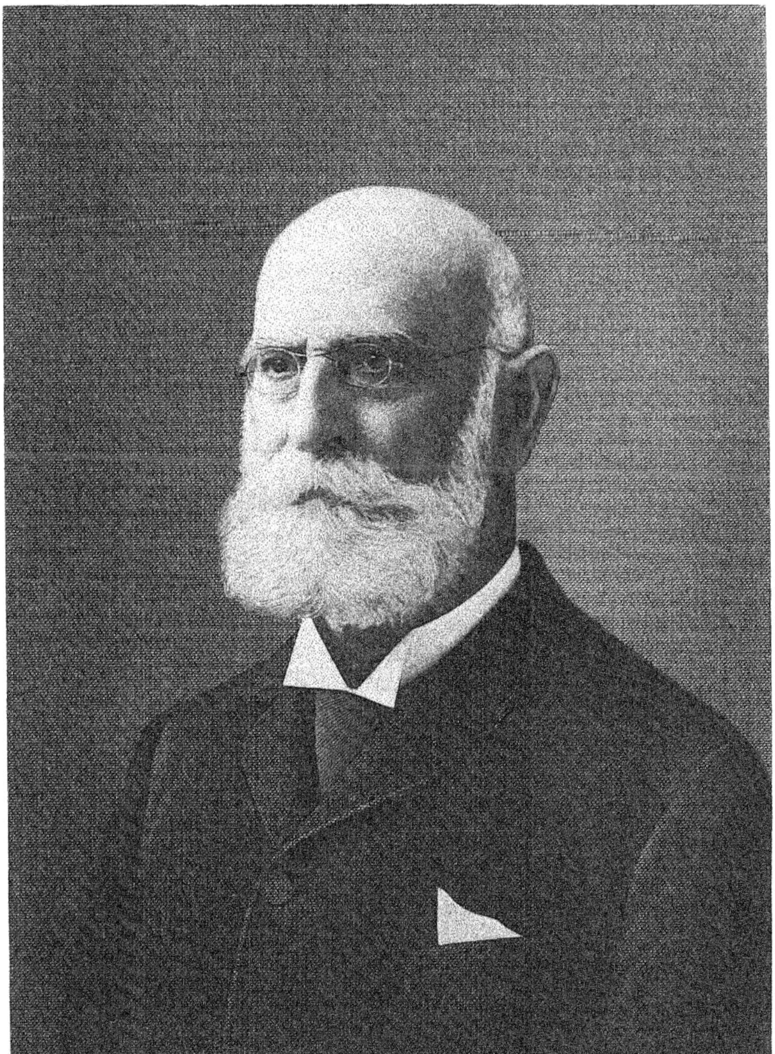

The Lewis Publishing Co

Eng'd by E. G. Williams & Bro. N.Y.

Abm: Minis

James H. Johnston, the firm being Minis & Johnston, he continued actively engaged in this pursuit until the day of his death, although, in consequence of years, the business changed to that of shipping.

Mr. Johnston retiring, Mr. Minis carried on the work alone until two of his sons were associated with him under the firm name of A. Minis & Sons.

One who knew him best wrote of him: "From his earliest years his course was one of duty well performed. Quiet and modest, yet firm and brave, he noted well his part as son, brother, husband, parent, neighbor and citizen. With no ambition but to be right, his amiable qualities made him beloved and respected by all who knew him, while all he did was based upon strictly moral and religious principle, unswerved by fear or favor."

All through the dark days of the yellow fever epidemic of 1876 he, with his eldest son, Mr. J. F. Minis, remained in Savannah doing all in his power, for those who needed assistance, in a quiet, unostentatious way of which the world knew nothing. His nature was one of the noblest simplicity, combined with the utmost moral strength and a deep sense of justice guided his every action.

The affection he inspired in the humble and lowly was attested when the longshoremen who had worked for him, as a spontaneous tribute, marched in a body to his funeral.

Many positions sought him. He rendered service as an alderman, acting as mayor, during the absence of that functionary, was a director of the Southern Bank and of the Central Railroad & Banking Company of Georgia.

For years he devoted much of his busy life to the presidency of the Union Society, and unbounded were his zeal and enthusiasm in behalf of this noble charity.

At the breaking out of the Civil war, physical disabilities rendering military service impossible, he entered the commissary department at Savannah, and, to help the cause, invested a large proportion of his means in Confederate bonds, although he had always been apprehensive of what proved to be the result of the desperate four years' struggle.

On the failure of the South, he was consequently left with the most limited resources.

Confronted with the disheartening task of beginning afresh his business career, he did so with the courage displayed by the best type of the men of the South, and the years brought their reward.

He died in New York City, November 6th, 1889, adding another honorable record to the family name, and was buried in Savannah.

Savannah is the native city of Abram Minis, his eyes having first opened to the light of day on May 16, 1859, within the pleasant borders of that city. His parents were Abraham and Lavinia (Florance) Minis. The latter's parents were Jacob L. and Hannah Florance. Mrs. Minis was born in New Orleans, Louisiana, May 26, 1826, and her marriage to Mr. Minis was celebrated in Philadelphia, October 22, 1851. Their union was blessed by the birth of six children, as follows: Jacob Florance Minis; Rosina Florance Minis, who died in infancy; Miss Maria Minis; Isaac Minis; Lavinia Florance Minis, the wife of Charles I. Henry, of New York City; and Abram Minis.

Isaac Minis, mentioned above, is now deceased, his death having occurred in New York City, June 8, 1893. His wife, to whom he was married in Savannah, March 9, 1886, was before her marriage, Miss Eugenia P. Myers of Savannah. She survives her husband and has two sons,—Isaac Minis and Carol E. Minis. Mr. and Mrs. Charles I. Henry have two daughters, namely: Harriet and Lavinia.

One of the subject's uncles, Philip Minis, married Miss Sarah A. Livingston, of New York, and their children are seven in number, and named as follows: Mrs. Alice Henrietta Poe, of Baltimore; Annie Livingston Spalding; Philip Henry; John Livingston; Mary Leila (Mrs. Poultney); and Augusta Medora. One of his aunts, Sarah Ann Minis, married Dr. Isaac Hays of Philadelphia, Pennsylvania, whose children were: Joseph Gratz; William DeWees; Harriet Minis; Theodore Minis; Frank Minis; Robert Griffith and Isaac Minis. Another aunt, Phillippa Minis, married Edward Johnson Etting, of Philadelphia, and their children were: Reuben; Charles Edward; Theodore Minis; Philippa Minis; and Harry Gratz.

The paternal father of the subject was Isaac Minis, who, although of the Savannah family, was born near Charleston, whence his parents and family fled from the British troops, which at that time were besieging the city of Savannah. They returned here after the close of the Revolution. On December 4, 1803, Isaac Minis married Miss Dinah Cohen, of Georgetown, who was born April 12, 1787, and died in Savannah, February 17, 1874. Her husband preceded her to the grave, his death occurring on November 17, 1856, in Philadelphia. He and his wife are buried in the family lot in Laurel Grove cemetery in Savannah. Isaac Minis served in the War of 1812 as a private in Capt. William Bulloch's company of artillery, first regiment of Georgia militia, commanded by General Johnston. Isaac Minis was the son of Philip and Judith (Pollock) Minis; Judith Pollock being a member of one of the first families that settled Newport, just as her husband belonged to a family that was numbered among the first settlers of the colony of Georgia. It is a somewhat interesting fact, in this connection, that Rhode Island and Georgia were the only ones of the colonies where Jews were not prohibited from settling.

Philip Minis, the great-grandfather of the subject of this review, as mentioned in a preceding paragraph, bore the distinction of having been the first male white child born in Georgia, his birth having occurred at Savannah, July 11, 1734, the year following the founding of the Georgia colony by Oglethorpe. In substantiation of this fact there are various authorities, among which is the following notice that appeared in the *Georgia Gazette* of the issue of Thursday, March 12, 1789, concerning the family of Philip Minis: "On Friday, March 6, 1789, departed this life, Mr. Philip Minis, merchant, age fifty-five years. He was the first male white child born in this state. His remains were buried in the Jews' burial ground on Sunday morning, attended by a large number of respectable citizens, who by their solemn attention evinced how sensibly they felt the loss the community has sustained in so valuable a man. He has left a disconsolate widow and five children, together with an aged and venerable mother and five sisters, to deplore their loss. He was an affectionate husband, a dutiful son, a tender father and a kind brother; in short, he was in every sense of the word, a truly honest man."

Philip Minis gave active aid and support to the colonists in their struggle with Great Britain, and on this account he was named in the Georgia Royal Disqualifying Act of 1780. When in 1779 the French auxiliaries besieged Savannah, Philip Minis acted as a guide, and was consulted as to the best place for landing. He also volunteered to act as a patriot guide thereafter. In 1780 the British passed their disqualifying act, whereby certain persons were disqualified from holding office, etc., because of their prominence in the "rebel cause," and the name of Philip Minis was one of the one hundred and fifty on the list of disqualified men.

The founder of the Minis family in Georgia was Philip Minis' father, Abraham Minis, who with his wife, Abigail Minis, and two daughters, Esther and Leah, also his brother, Simeon Minis, arrived in Savannah on a vessel from London, July 11, 1733, the year of Oglethorpe's founding of the colony of Georgia. There were thirteen Jewish families on this vessel; and the history of their organization for the journey in London and their trials and tribulation, as well as their successes, after their landing on Georgia soil in 1733, forms one of the interesting romances of the colonization of the new world. Abraham Minis, first American of the name, died in Savannah in 1757, and was buried in the first Jewish burial plot in the city. His widow, Abigail Minis, in 1760, received a grant of land from King George III. She lived to a great old age, her death occurring in Savannah, in October 11, 1794, aged ninety-three years and two months. The history of Mr. Minis' forbears is as interesting and gratifying as that of any other citizen of the old and historic city. Emerson has said: "Biography is the only true history." When Macaulay was shown the vast clustering vines in Hampton court, with trunk like a tree, he expressed a wish to behold the mother root in Spain from which the scion was cut. Similarly, the average person confesses to an eager desire to trace the ancestral forces that are united in every interesting character, mental and moral capital being treasures invested by forefathers, nature taking the grandsire's ability and putting it out at compound interest for the grandson.

Abram Minis, the present representative of the family, has in addition to his law practice, many other interests of broad scope and importance. He is a director of the following named enterprises: The Propeller Tow Boat Company; the Columbus Manufacturing Company; the Commercial Life Insurance & Casualty Company; the United Hydraulic Cotton Press Company; the Georgia Land & Securities Company, and the Georgia Cotton Mills. Although he bestows a profound attention on his affairs, business and professional, he is by no means a recluse, for he has many affiliations, and is one of Savannah's most prominent clubmen. He belongs to Landrum Lodge of Masons and of the Oglethorpe Club, the Yacht Club and the Golf Club. He is a member of the Sons of the Revolution and is also an honorary member of the Georgia Hussars, of which he was an active member for several years. He enlisted as a private in the Hussars in 1883, and was promoted through the various ranks to that of first lieutenant; it was while acting in such rank that he resigned. Following this he was made quartermaster of the First regiment of cavalry, National Guard of Georgia, with the rank of captain, and later was made adjutant with the rank of captain in the same organization. He is now on the retired roll of the Georgia state troops. In all public affairs in the city, which is dearest to him with the associations and traditions of centuries, Mr. Minis takes a keen and helpful interest and he stands as one of the aggressive and enterprising men who are aiding in the upbuilding of the city.

Mr. Minis has been twice married: His first wife was Miss Anna Maria Cohen, of Baltimore, Maryland, their union being solemnized October 8, 1890. She died May 24, 1891, in Savannah. The present Mrs. Minis was, previous to her marriage, Miss Mabel A. Henry, of New York City, where she married her husband on December 9, 1902. They have two children: Abram Minis, Jr., born November 6, 1903, and H. Philip Minis, born June 11, 1908.

THOMAS USHER PULASKI CHARLTON, the eldest son of Thomas and Lucy Charlton, was born near Camden, South Carolina, in 1780. His father came from Frederick, Maryland, and was a surgeon and lieutenant under Col. William Thompson in the Revolutionary forces of South Carolina; and later served in the legislature of that state. At the death of the father, the widow came to Savannah and settled there in 1790. Thomas Usher was called to the bar of the eastern judicial circuit in 1801, and in that year was elected a member of the Georgia legislature. In 1804 he became attorney-general, and in 1808 judge of the eastern circuit. Later he was elected mayor of Savannah and served in that office for six terms. He was head of the committee of safety in 1812, and performed devoted services during the epidemic of 1820. He again became judge, and died in 1835. He was of strong mentality and high courage, and had the judicial temperament. Many of his decisions appear in a volume of reports published by him. He partially completed a life of James Jackson, designed to cover the period of his military services. He was a close friend of that eminent man, who designated him as his literary executor. Having enjoyed the friendship of Jackson, he inherited from that great man some of his enemies, who, however, did not begin to give voice to their bitterness until years after Judge Charlton's death. He not only possessed decided literary ability but a high order of wit. He married, in 1803, Emily, daughter of Thomas Walter, of South Carolina, author of "Flora Caroliniana," the first considerable work on southern botany. Of this marriage were born his sons, Thomas Jackson Charlton and Robert Milledge Charlton. Charlton street was named for him.

ROBERT MILLEDGE CHARLTON, younger son of Thomas U. P. and Emily Charlton, was born in Savannah, Georgia, on January 19, 1807, and died there on January 18, 1854. He was called to the bar when very young, and served in the legislature at twenty-one. At twenty-three he was appointed district attorney by Andrew Jackson; and at twenty-eight was elected judge of the eastern judicial circuit. He was three times mayor of Savannah, and toward the end of his career became United States senator from Georgia. His practice at the bar was extensive and successful. Among the early Georgia reports is a volume published by him and containing his own decisions as well as those of the judges who held the bench in the eastern circuit subsequent to the publication of the reports of T. U. P. Charlton. He was a man of the finest sensibilities and highest ideals, loving his state and her people. He was at once firm and gentle; helpful and sympathetic. Devoted to the teachings of his own church, in his intercourse with his fellow man he knew no limitations of specific creeds or conditions, and became probably the most beloved citizen Savannah ever had. In 1829 he married Margaret, daughter of Peter Shick, whose ancestors had departed from Salsburg at the time of the Protestant exodus, settling in the colony of Georgia during the first years of its establishment. Judge Charlton was not only a learned lawyer and an orator, but a writer and poet. In his mind the wit of his father was tempered with a fine sense of humor, the evidences of which appear in his contributions to the Knickerbocker Magazine, the leading periodical of those times, in a series of sketches of life on the circuit. An edition of his poems, to which were added some of the productions of his brother, appeared in 1839, and another edition in 1842. Charlton county, Georgia, was named for him, and Charlton ward, Savannah.

WALTER GLASCO CHARLTON, youngest son of Robert M. and Margaret Charlton, was born in Savannah, Georgia, on June 5, 1851. He attended school in Savannah, and in Hancock county, Georgia, and Baltimore county, Maryland, under Richard Malcolm Johnston. In 1869 he matriculated at the University of Virginia, and came to the bar of the eastern circuit on January 22, 1873. In that year he became associated with Albert R. Lamar in the office of solicitor-general. In 1877 he was appointed reporter of the circuit; and in 1880 was elected solicitor-general. On February 11, 1908, he was appointed judge of the eastern judicial circuit and elected to that office during that year. In 1912, he was again elected. On February 11, 1874, he married Mary Walton, daughter of Richard Malcolm Johnston. He has filled several political positions, among them chairman of the Democratic party in Chatham for several years. His people have been Democrats literally from the day the party was formed. He is the author of several essays on epochs in Georgia history, and has delivered numerous speeches on occasions of historic celebrations. He has occasionally indulged in verse. His ancestors on both sides are identified with the history of Georgia and the United States. The Maryland Charltons held Mason and Dixon's line against Pennsylvania for many years. His great-grandfather Charlton volunteered in the Revolutionary forces in 1775, and his great-grandfather, John Shick, who afterward became a prosperous and prominent man, fought at the siege of Savannah, having his right arm shot off by a cannon ball from the British. Judge Charlton is at present president of the Georgia Society of the Cincinnati and of the Georgia Society of the Revolution.

HARRIS MACLEOD KING. Representing on both the paternal and maternal sides of the house families that have long been prominent in naval, military, civic and historical affairs of Georgia, Harris Macleod King has himself been actively associated with the development and promotion of the commercial interests of the state for upwards of thirty years, being now supervising inspector of naval stores for the state of Georgia, his home being in Savannah. A son of Col. Barrington S. King, he was born in Roswell, Cobb county, in 1860, a town which was named in honor of his great grandfather, Roswell King.

Roswell King was born in Sharon, Connecticut, May 3, 1765, being a son of Captain Timothy King, who was prominent on the Continental side in the naval service of the Revolutionary war, being commander of the brig "Defiance." Migrating to Georgia after the great struggle of the colonists for independence, Roswell King settled at Darien, in what is now McIntosh county. He subsequently married Catherine, a daughter of Josiah Barrington, who was born in Ireland, and emigrated to Georgia a few years after the arrival in this state of General Oglethorpe, who was his kinsman and friend. Old Fort Barrington on the Altamaha river, an outpost built long before the Revolution for defense against the Spaniards, was named for him.

Their son, Barrington King, Mr. King's grandfather, was born in Darien, Georgia, March 8th, 1798. About 1839, with a colony of several other families from the seacoast of Georgia, including the Bulloch's, Smith's, Lewis's, Dunwody's, Pratt's, and Goulding's, he immigrated to Cobb county, and located on the site which his father Roswell King had some years before purchased from the Indians, and founded the little village of Roswell, which, as previously stated, was named in honor of his father. His wife, whose maiden name was Catherine M. Nephew, was a daughter of James Nephew, who, during the Revolutionary war, served as lieutenant in Col. John Baker's regiment of the Liberty county, Georgia, militia.

Col. Barrington S. King was born while his mother was visiting the Bulloch family in Liberty county, the King home at that time having been in Darien, McIntosh county. Throughout almost the entire period of the war between the states, Colonel King served as a gallant soldier

Joseph McCarthy.

HON. JOSEPH MCCARTHY. It is safe to say that few men in the south are as well known in the labor world as Hon. Joseph McCarthy, the prominent Georgia legislator, fighter and friend of organized labor. An advanced student of philosophy, his mental power is for the most part directed toward the solution of problems affecting the whole of society. He is an inspiration to the class whose cause he champions, for he is of humble birth and has risen to his present high position through his own efforts. Besides being a member of the state legislature and a specialist in labor legislation, he is general foreman of the Central of Georgia Railroad shops and he is also the father of the county police bill of Chatham county. He is a particularly striking figure in Georgia affairs and a notable exponent of a great cause.

The Hon. Mr. McCarthy was born in Savannah in 1868, the son of Thomas and Eliza (Kehoe) McCarthy, both of whom were natives of Ireland. They followed the beckoning finger of opportunity from the shores of the New World and located in Savannah previous to the Civil war. Both are now deceased. The father's occupation was that of a blacksmith. Mr. McCarthy was reared in this city and received the greater part of his education in St. Patrick's parochial school. He learned the trade of machinist in the foundry and machine shops of the late J. W. Tynan, a prominent and well-known character of Savannah of former years. In 1890, the subject entered the employ of the Central of Georgia Railroad as a machinist in the Savannah shops and through his skill and efficiency was promoted to his present position. He is general foreman for the company in Savannah which includes both the locomotive and car departments, this being a position of importance and responsibility.

Mr. McCarthy has always been a strong union labor man and an ardent supporter of all measures of beneficence for the laboring classes. He is the leading exponent of union labor principles in the Georgia state legislature, in which he has served three terms: 1907-08; 1909-10, and 1911-12.

The record of Mr. McCarthy's achievements in the work to which he has devoted heart and hand can not be told more truly and concisely than in his own words, the account which follows having been published in the Savannah *Press*.

"When I was first elected to the legislature in 1907 and 1908, I met the father of the child labor bill, Hon. Madison Bell, of Fulton county, and before any committees were appointed he asked me to let him remain chairman of the labor committee, which I gladly consented to do on account of his experience and I was made vice-chairman of the labor committee of Georgia. We drafted the bureau of labor bill and introduced it in the house and when it came before the committee the Textile Manufacturers' Association appeared against it and finally defeated it in the committee room. In 1908 he modified the bill a little and introduced it again only to be defeated by the Textile Manufacturers' Association in the committee room. The Hon. Madison Bell, father of the child labor bill, declined to stand for reelection to the legislature in 1909-1910. I was reelected to the legislature and at that time Joe Brown was elected governor of Georgia. A committee of the working class appeared before Governor Brown and asked him to write the bureau of labor bill as a plank in his platform, which he did. I was then placed at the head of the labor committee of Georgia and in looking over the bill on which we had been defeated twice, I called on the Hon. J. Randolph Anderson who was the recognized leader of the Brown forces and he called a meeting in his room at the Piedmont Hotel. The gentlemen present were the Hon. J. Randolph Anderson, United States

Senator Terrell, Representative Evans, who was representing the working people of Bibb county, C. T. Ladson, attorney of the Georgia state federation of labor and myself. We discussed the bureau of labor bill and the committee left it to myself, Mr. Ladson and Mr. Evans to draw the present bill, which is now a law, and introduce it in the house. But it was again defeated in the committee room by the Textile Manufacturers' Association.

"The following year I introduced the bill again and, finally, after a hard fight, got it out of the committee room, only to be defeated on the floor of the house by those who were bitterly opposed to the bureau of labor. I was again elected to the legislature and Gov. Hoke Smith was reelected, after being defeated for one term. I made a trip to Atlanta and waiting on him, asked him to write the bureau of labor bill as a plank in his platform, which he did. When the Georgia legislature convened in 1910 I was again appointed chairman of the labor committee, with a new committee composed of members who had just been elected as representatives. This was composed of twenty-seven members of the house and all but a few were strangers to me. I seriously canvassed my committee to find if they were favorable to the people. I organized my committee and called a meeting. I was then notified by Hon. Henry Alexander, of Atlanta, an ex-member of the Georgia legislature and at one time on my committee, that he had been employed by the Atlanta Builders' Exchange, an association organized for the special purpose of defeating any labor legislation in the state. I notified Mr. Alexander of the date of the meeting and he appeared before the committee to fight the bill, but with all his power and the power of the Atlanta Builders' Association, he could not do a thing with the committee. The committee then recommended the favorable passage of the bill. The bill was so reported to the house, with recommendation that it do pass. It passed July 25, 1911, ayes, one hundred and eight, nays, thirty-five. The bill was immediately transmitted to the senate and there read the first time, July 31, and then referred to the senate committee on immigration and labor.

"The Textile Manufacturers' Association sent representatives before that committee and plead for it to be postponed for one week, so that they could have a hearing. I knew that this was the first move to try to defeat the bill. On the date set by the committee one hundred Textile Manufacturers' Association representatives appeared in a body. There was not a committee room large enough to hold these representatives, so the committee adjourned to the house. When the roll was called for the committee both sides answered ready. Mr. Anderson was allowed five minutes to speak for the bill. The gentleman in favor of the bill to follow Mr. Anderson was Mr. Ladson of Atlanta, and when he finished, Jerome Jones of Atlanta, who also favored the bill, spoke, which closed our side. Mr. Alexander, representing the Atlanta Builders' Exchange, was allowed to speak twenty-five minutes. He made one of the most telling speeches I have ever heard against the bill and this I saw, had terrible influence upon the senate committee. He told the senate committee that he voted against the bureau of labor bill while a member of the house, and that organized labor defeated him when he ran for reelection, one thousand to fifteen hundred votes. After he got through I knew that I could kill the influence and asked permission to speak five minutes in answer to Mr. Anderson's speech.

"I told the senate committee that I had been a member of the house when Mr. Anderson was a representative and that he was placed on my labor committee, was in favor of my bureau of labor bill and voted for it. I told the senate committee that what defeated him was the fact that the citizens of Atlanta were knocking at the legislature's door and demanding the passage of a local bill to elect their recorder by the vote of the people. Mr. Anderson took sides against the other three representatives and fought the bill viciously on the floor of the house, but was defeated and the bill was passed to elect the recorder by the vote of the people. There were members of the senate who could corroborate this and I completely destroyed the force of Mr. Alexander's speech. Senator Shingler of the tenth district, who fought the bill so vigorously, demanded of me if there were bureaus of labor in other states and I proved to him that thirty-five states had commissioners of labor.

"The committee went into executive session and I waited patiently until 7:30 o'clock, when they came out of executive session. Senator Morris, of the committee, told me that they could not agree and would have a meeting next morning. I then feared there was no hope for my bill and that they were playing for time to defeat its passage. The committee met again and did not agree and again Senator Morris came to me and asked if I would agree to an amendment to leave the office to be elected by the people. I told him it was one of the cardinal principles of the masses to elect to office by the vote of the people and that they could make no fight against it. The committee met and agreed and reported the bill to the senate with the recommendation that it do pass as amended. On the floor the next day, Senator Shingler, who fought every inch against the passage of the bill, asked that the bill be recommitted, but it was voted down and read the second time August 7, 1911. It was read the third time on August 15, 1911, and passed, ayes, twenty-three and nays, sixteen. I had finally seen the passage of my bureau of labor bill.''

Mr. McCarthy also gives the following enumeration of the achievements of organized labor.

"Organized labor has been a potent factor in the passage of the child labor law, the law in reference to headlights on engines, in reference to requirements of safety appliances, in providing regulation in reference to the convenience of female employes, and limiting the hours of employment. Organized labor was also an effective factor in the passage of the bill providing that administrators may recover in case of homicide and in rendering recovery possible even though the employe was to some extent negligent. Organized labor has also favored in legislative halls the protection of the indigent borrower from the excessive demands of the extortionate money lender. In the general sum total, the trend of influence of organized labor upon the Georgia legislature has been in favor of the amelioration of the burdens of the unfortunate and the exaltation of the individual into a higher and broader life. Organized labor has generally been favorable to education, and its representatives have encouraged the dissemination of knowledge everywhere. This is to be expected of any order whose purpose is to elevate mankind.

"I further state that when the whole state of Georgia was in a turmoil over the convict lease system, it was organized labor that wrote the clause to protect free labor and was one of the greatest factors in passing the bill which is now a law. I am eternally and forever opposed to child labor as a blight on civilization and I am tooth and nail for state-wide compulsory education and for furnishing free books to every child in Georgia. If wise heads and kind hearts continue to control the federation of labor so that the rights of both employer and employe will be recognized and the absolute necessity of aiding the welfare of both be accepted, the result will be beneficial to everybody. The best and noblest ideals of the individual of the organization are comprehended in the effort to uplift humanity and render it aid."

Mr. McCarthy was married in Savannah to Miss Minnie Baker, a native of Augusta, Georgia. Into their household have been born four children—Thomas, Minnie, Joseph, Jr., and Helen. The eldest son, Thomas, has charge of his father's interest in the grocery store of Greenfield & McCarthy on West Broad street. In May, 1912, Miss Minnie was married to Clarence L. Harris of Atlanta, son of C. L. Harris, a prominent insurance man of Atlanta. Mr. and Mrs. Harris reside at Atlanta.

ALBERT WYLLY. One of the most conspicuous figures in the recent history of Savannah is the well-known gentleman whose name introduces this review. An enumeration of the men of the state who have won honor and public recognition for themselves and at the same time have honored the community in which they live would be incomplete without reference to him as a political leader and director of opinion. Albert Wylly is active in the many-sided life of the city as property owner and county commissioner, and he is the scion of one of the oldest and most prominent families in all Chatham county. No name is more highly regarded and in many generations bearers of the name of Wylly have given valiant service to the country in times of both peace and war. The Wyllys are an exceptionally strong race of men, each generation having retained and transmitted the strength and virility of its predecessors. They have never deteriorated and down to the present time each generation of the Wyllys has been represented by strong, clean, high-minded citizens, upholding the traditional honor and high ideals of the family's progenitors. Without exception they have been highly educated and successful and prosperous in life. At the present time in Savannah the descendants of the three original Wylly brothers are among the most representative men of affairs in the city. Not only have they achieved personal success, but their devotion to the public good is not questioned and arises from a sincere interest in the welfare of their fellow men.

Albert Wylly was born in Savannah on the 25th day of October, 1859, the son of George W. and Sarah Anne (Revel) Wylly. George W. Wylly died at his home in Savannah in 1906 at the age of ninety years, his birth having occurred in this city in 1816. During the active period of his life he was one of the city's most prominent and successful business men and for a long number of years a leading figure in its affairs. He had held many positions of trust and responsibility at the hands of the public, among which was that of mayor pro tem of Savannah during the entire period of the war between the states, or until Sherman's army came into Savannah, upon which occasion he turned the city over to General Sherman. His eldest son, Col. William H. Wylly, commanded a regiment in the Confederate army. Another son, Dr. King Wylly, although a very young physician, acted in the capacity of surgeon for the Confederacy. Both of these sons have since died. Dr. King Wylly went to France at the breaking out of the Franco-Prussian war and became a surgeon in the French army. In testimonial of his services he was presented with the medal of the Legion of Honor, having distinguished himself in the siege of Paris. Two cousins of the subject's father—Capt. Robert Habersham Wylly and William C. Wylly, were also in the Confederate army and one of George W. Wylly's was a captain of the Jasper Irish Greens, going out from Savannah in the Mexican war.

George W. Wylly, father of the immediate subject of this brief review, was the son of William C. Wylly, who in turn was the son of Thomas Wylly and the latter was the son of William Wylly. Thomas Wylly was an officer in the American Revolution and thus the present generation are in direct line for membership in the Society of Cincinnati. William Wylly was a brother of Col. Richard Wylly and Campbell Wylly and it was these who founded the Wylly family in America. They were of an English family, but came from the North of Ireland early in the eighteenth century to the West Indies and went thence to Savannah not long after the founding of the city by Oglethorpe in 1733. Their descendants, as noted above, have resided here continuously ever since. Colonel Richard Wylly was a Continental officer in the Revolution. Mr. Wylly's paternal grandmother was Naomi (Dasher) Wylly, a daughter of Martin Dasher, who was the son of Thomas Dasher, all of Savannah and representative of another old family in the city. Thomas Dasher was an Englishman by birth, but followed the beckoning finger of opportunity from the shores of the new world. He located in Savannah and was given a grant of two thousand acres in its vicinity by the king of England. The subject's mother, whose demise occurred many years ago, was a member of the noted Chitty family of South Carolina, of French Huguenot descent.

Mr. Wylly and his brothers and sisters were all afforded the best of educational facilities both in America and Europe. He, himself, received his finishing education in Princeton University, where he was graduated in the class of 1879, a classmate and intimate companion of Woodrow Wilson, who graduated in the same class.

Mr. Wylly has always taken an active part in the affairs of the city and county and has large property and financial interests. He was elected a member of the board of county commissioners of Chatham county in 1903 and has since served in that capacity, with credit to himself and honor and profit to his constituents.

It is by no means difficult to understand Mr. Wylly's remarkable loyalty to the city with which his honored forebears have so long been identified and upon which his own interest and affection are centered. A glance at the careers of the present-day Wyllies is indeed edifying, for the usual student of biography confesses to an eager desire to trace the ancestral forces that are united in every son and daughter of unusual force and ability. No fine soul appears suddenly; the foothills slope upward, and mental and moral capital are treasures invested for us by our forefathers.

Mr. Wylly has three brothers and a sister, viz.: Fred C., Martin Dasher, George W. and Miss Naomi A. Wylly.

WILLIAM MURRAY DAVIDSON, property owner and real estate, dealer, is one of the prominent citizens of the city of Savannah, a power in the business world and of most distinguished stock. As his name indicates, he is of Scotch descent and is a fine representative of the people, who never conquered, though often beaten, finally gave kings to England, field marshals to France and Prussia and Russia, cardinals to Rome, the second greatest man to the Reformation and to America a body of citizens whose priceless value cannot be reckoned and who have made such an imprint upon our history that any of our citizens are proud to claim Scotch blood.

Mr. Davidson was born in Savannah on the 27th day of August, 1862, the son of Capt. W. M. and Sarah Anne (McIntire) Davidson. Captain Davidson was born in Dunfermline, Scotland, in the year 1821. He came to Savannah in 1840 and in 1844 established himself as a merchant in a location on Congress street between Jefferson and Barnard.

Before the war he had joined the Chatham Artillery of Savannah, of which he was second lieutenant when the war broke out. He gave up his business to go into the Confederate army and was in active service throughout the war. He was in command of the company of infantry that was the last to leave Savannah when General Sherman's army occupied the city, his command having had charge of the breastworks on the canal west of the city. After the war he resumed business, in which he continued for several years, and he served three terms as alderman of the city of Savannah. The demise of this highly respected and well remembered gentleman occurred in Savannah in 1894.

The paternal grandfather of Mr. Davidson was Capt. George Davidson of the British navy, who was captain of one of the quarter decks of the ship "Superb" under Nelson at the battle of Trafalgar. Following this battle he retired from the navy and became the owner of substantial property interests in Fifeshire. In his later years he came to America, but did not locate in Savannah. From that time he maintained his residence in New York and was buried in Greenwood cemetery. Mr. Davidson's grandaunt, on his father's side, was the wife of William Murray of Scotland, who was a distinguished jurist and held the position of lord advocate of Edinburgh. Lady Amelia Murray, his sister, was lady in waiting on the Duchess of Kent, mother of Queen Victoria. She made an extended visit to America during the period before the war in which slavery was the great issue of discussion. She traveled through the North and the South and visited for some time in Savannah. On her return to Scotland she wrote her views of the American situation, which, being published widespread and being contrary to the views expressed by Harriet Beecher Stowe in her work entitled "Uncle Tom's Cabin," was the cause of her dismissal from her position in the household of the Duchess of Kent; the official reason being her interference in American affairs. The Davidson family are prominently connected with the history of Dunfermline and the subject's father was the first child to be baptized in Dunfermline Abbey after the reinterring of the remains of King Robert Bruce in the abbey about 1822. The abbey and indeed the entire borough are rich in the most romantic Scottish history. In the latter many of the kings were born and in the former are interred many of the most celebrated characters in Caledonian annals. The mother of the immediate subject of this review was the daughter of Andrew McIntire, who came to Savannah from Donegal, Ireland, in 1820.

William Murray Davidson was educated in this city, taking his first draughts at the "Pierian Spring" as a pupil in the old Barnard street school, and subsequently becoming a pupil in Chatham Academy and studying under the private tutelage of Prof. C. C. Talliaferro. He also attended for three months Eastman business college at Poughkeepsie, New York. In 1879, at the age of eighteen years he took charge of his father's business and conducted the same about twenty years. For several years past Mr. Davidson has been engaged in real estate transactions and is the owner of valuable property interests in Savannah. He is a director of the Real Estate Bank and Trust Company and has other interests of broad scope and importance. He keeps in touch with all valuable public works and is a member of the Savannah public library board. He is president of the St. Andrews Society.

Mr. Davidson was married to Miss Jennie Wyly, who was born in Jacksonville, Alabama. They have one child, William Murray Davidson, and their household is the abode of culture and gracious hospitality. Mrs. Davidson is a direct descendant of John Sevier.

THOMAS PURSE. It is safe to say that no citizen of the commonwealth of Georgia is more widely and favorably known than Thomas Purse, secretary and superintendent of the Savannah board of trade, one of the most important and efficient bodies of its kind in the United States. Mr. Purse was elected to this highly important office in 1907, and he has since met its responsibilities with distinction. Since its organization in 1883 the Savannah board of trade has steadily developed into a powerful factor in the commercial life of the south and Mr. Purse has been influential in bringing about the accomplishment of its objects, which are: to maintain a commercial exchange; to promote uniformity in the customs and usages of merchants; to inculcate principles of justice and equity in trade; to facilitate the speedy adjustment of business disputes; to acquire and disseminate valuable commercial and economic information and generally to secure to its members the benefits of co-operation in the furtherance of their legitimate pursuits. Through one of its departments, naval stores alone, it is known throughout the world of trade and commerce; and its renown through its connection with the great lumber interests is almost equally widespread. The board's activities and usefulness, however, are not confined to these two industries; it is the keystone upon which rests all of the extensive commercial, industrial, mercantile and financial activities of Savannah. In aiding local concerns in the extension of Savannah's trade; in promoting substantial improvements of every kind in the city; in the building of new railroads; in opposing or favoring proposed state or national legislation, accordingly as it is objectionable or beneficent; in securing harbor and wharfage improvements; in locating new enterprises; in securing new territory for local concerns—in all of these and in many more ways the body has been of the greatest usefulness. In fact, it has done and is doing everything possible that it can do in a conservative way for the welfare and development of one of the most beautiful and progressive cities of the South.

Mr. Purse has become known as one of the expert board of trade officials in the country. With the foundation of expert knowledge as a statistician, which forms an important feature of the board's work, he is in addition a thoroughly live, resourceful and efficient official in carrying out the greatly varied activities of the board. He takes up the various matters affecting shipping interests, both ocean and rail, and is highly successful in adjusting such. He keeps in touch constantly with the many ramifications of the board of trade's interests, not only with local trade, but with the commerce of the world. His is a fascinating profession, and to meet its requirements he is peculiarly fitted.

Mr. Purse is a native son of Savannah and one of those who have elected to remain permanently within its borders. The date of his birth was March 19, 1874, and his parents were Capt. Daniel G. and Laura (Ashby) Purse, the former, now deceased, a native of Savannah, and the latter, who survives, a native of Fauquier county, Virginia.

Thomas Purse was educated in the public schools of Savannah and in the Georgia Military Institute, near Atlanta. For ten years he was employed in the accounting department of the Antwerp Naval Stores Company in Savannah. Following this he was connected as an expert accountant with the firm of Mustin & Marsh, public accountants, and in 1907, as previously mentioned, accepted his present position as superintendent and secretary of the Savannah board of trade.

Mr. Purse's wife, before marriage, was Miss Elizabeth Morrison, who was born in South Carolina. When she was a child her parents died and she was reared and educated by her grandfather, Hon. John Lawton, of Lawtonville, South Carolina, one of the leading citizens of that state. Mrs. Purse is now one of the well-known hostesses in exclusive social circles of the Forest city. Their union was celebrated on the 5th day of May, 1898, and they share their home with two children: Thomas, Jr., and Elizabeth Lawton.

Mr. Purse is a member of St. John's Episcopal church, and he is a Scottish Rite Mason. For some years previous to his marriage he was an active member of Company B, Savannah Volunteer Guards, and he is still interested in things military.

In 1908, Capt. Daniel G. Purse, father of the foregoing gentleman and one of Savannah's foremost citizens in any day or generation,

> "Gave his honors to the world again,
> His blessed part to Heaven; and slept in peace."

Captain Purse was one to whom public spirit and civic loyalty was far more than a mere rhetorical expression and it may truly be said that there was nothing of public import in the Forest city during his lifelong residence here in which he was not helpfully interested. It was, however, not merely in the capacity of a helper that he was valuable in the economic and civic history of his native city and state, for he was a man of great initiative, with a rare capacity for the handling of affairs of great scope and importance, and in the splendid ideas which he metamorphosed into realities he finished to himself a monument more enduring than bronze. When the nation went down into the valley of decision in the dark days of the '60s, firm in the conscientious conviction of the supreme right of the states to sever their connection with the national government, he enlisted in the Confederate service and served as officer during the war.

Captain Purse was born in this city November 14, 1839, the son of Thomas and Eliza Jane (Gugle) Purse, the former a native of Winchester, Virginia, and the latter of Savannah, Georgia. Thomas Purse came to this city in youth and played a prominent part in its affairs. In 1849-50 he represented his district in the state senate and in 1862 was mayor of Savannah; for many years before and after that period he was a member of the board of aldermen, and he filled many other civil and political positions of distinction and honor. He held the institutions of the South in ardent affection and it was a great trial to him that he could not enter the ranks of the Confederate army in Civil war times, but physical infirmities made this impossible. He passed to the great beyond at the age of seventy years, but there are many of the elder generation who still remember this man of fiery enthusiasm and loyal energy. He was one of the original projectors and promoters of the Central of Georgia Railroad. He was its first superintendent and he invented the first time-table ever employed in the operation of railroad trains, the equated principle which he formulated being now utilized on railroads throughout the world.

Capt. Daniel G. Purse received his early education in private schools in Savannah and Sandersville, Georgia, subsequently entering Emory College at Oxford, Georgia, which institution he left at the end of his junior year (in 1857), to take a commercial course in Pittsburgh, Pennsylvania, under Peter Duff, a celebrated accountant of that day. His first adventure as an active factor in the busy world was in a pedagogical capacity, taking charge of Monteith academy in Savannah, but retaining his preceptorship only for a twelvemonth. He then accepted a clerkship and shortly after bought out a paint and oil business, which he was successfully conducting at the outbreak of the war between the states. When hostilities began he was not able to leave with Company

A of the Oglethorpe Light Infantry, with which he had been previously connected. Later he took an active part in recruiting and organizing Company B, which was attached to the First Georgia Volunteer Infantry and of which he became third sergeant. He was serving as sergeant-major at Fort Pulaski when he was transferred to the ordinance department at Savannah and served most acceptably in this department from November, 1861, to November, 1864. Within this period he was tendered and declined a second lieutenancy in a camp of instruction in the northern part of the state and was offered the captaincy of a company in the field, but his services in the ordnance department were considered so valuable that it declined to release him at the time, with the understanding that he was to be commissioned and assigned to duty in the field as soon as he could be spared. In November, 1864, he was ordered to Augusta, Georgia, where he organized an engineer's supply station for the military department of Georgia, South Carolina and Florida, with a commission as military storekeeper of the corps of engineers and the pay and allowance of captain of infantry. He was always under the direct command of Gen. J. F. Gilmer, chief of engineers in the Confederate service. In 1862, while in the ordnance department, as the result of a severe illness, Captain Purse was rendered unfit for field service. He served in the engineer's corps until the close of the war, receiving a parole at Athens, Georgia, August 16, 1865, at the hands of Maj. M. A. Ewen, of the One hundred and sixty-sixth New York volunteers and provost marshal. He then returned to Savannah and in the beautiful old city lived out the remainder of his life.

He was long connected with the Central of Georgia Railway and for fourteen years successively was elected president of the Savannah board of trade, resigning in his fourteenth term on account of the pressure of private business interests. From 1881 to 1885 he served as president of the Savannah Bank & Trust Company. He was at the time of his death president of the Interstate Sugar-Cane Growers' Association, which accomplished a magnificent work in promoting the sugar industry in the South. He completed the circle of both the York and Scottish Rites of Masonry, taking the thirty-second degree in the latter. He was a leading member and communicant of St. John's church, Protestant Episcopal, in which he served as secretary, treasurer and vestryman, retiring as senior warden of the church, from parochial office, in 1895.

On December 20, 1865, Captain Purse was united in marriage to Miss Laura Ashby, daughter of Marshall and Lucy (Cooke) Ashby, of Fauquier county, Virginia. His married life was in all respects the fruition of his early hopes and the union was blessed by the birth of four children.

To enumerate the movements for civic and state progress and betterment with which Captain Purse was identified, would be almost to give a summary of the history of the progress of Savannah during the entire period of his active years, the impress of his enterprise, vigor and zeal being stamped upon every material undertaken that fostered the growth and prestige of the city of his birth. As alderman and chairman of the finance committee in 1877, after Savannah had been scourged and rendered almost bankrupt through the yellow fever epidemic of the preceding year, he succeeded in funding an oppressive bonded indebtedness upon terms much more favorable to the city than the most optimistic thought possible, maintaining, meanwhile, the respect and confidence of the city's creditors and his fellow citizens. When he advanced the idea that a railway should be constructed across nearly twenty miles of salt marsh to Tybee island, it was received with doubt and its author was pronounced a visionary; yet he built it, and the island is now the favorite summer resort of many Savannah and Georgia people. He was president of the road until it passed into the control of the Central of Georgia Railway, on terms most favorable to the original owners. The domestic water supply of Savannah was drawn from a muddy river and unsanitary surface wells. Captain Purse put down the first artesian well in Savannah and the second in the state, demonstrating the fact that unfailing crystal waters flow in subterranean channels to the sea, and as the result of his experimentation the towns, cities and islands of the south Atlantic coast have a pure water supply, drawn from depths ranging from two hundred to fifteen hundred feet. Savannah's entire water supply is now derived from artesian wells. Upon the very beach of Tybee island, where the salt waves wash its white sands, Captain Purse sunk artesian wells and fresh water was found for thirsty pleasure seekers. He was the leader in the project for the deepening of the channel in the river from Savannah to the sea. With unparalleled energy he instituted a campaign of education, enlisting the interest and support of congressmen in every state in the Union, at a time when there was a growing tendency to curtail river and harbor appropriations. By his pen and voice, by his visits to state governors and to commercial bodies in the principal cities of the West and South, and by attending meetings of state agricultural societies, he marshaled a corps of auxiliaries that made the way easy for the generous appropriations which resulted in the deepening of the channel of the Savannah river so that vessels drawing 32 feet can now enter and depart from the harbor, the result being that Savannah has stupendous shipping interests, ranking her as the first seaport of the south Atlantic coast.

During the five years the Savannah bureau of freight and transportation was in operation Captain Purse was its able and zealous commissioner, the organization doing a wonderful work for Savannah in the way of regulating freight rates and adjusting other matters touching the commercial welfare of the city. In purely local enterprises he was repeatedly chosen the leader; in securing the camp for Lee's army corps at Savannah in 1898; in bringing President McKinley and his cabinet to the city in 1899, and Admiral and Mrs. Dewey in 1900; in securing to Savannah its massive Georgia marble government building and in securing the site for the DeSoto hotel. He took great interest in legislation for the prevention of adulterated foods and contributed earnest and logical essays to the press of the country in advocacy of federal legislation in this direction. The pure syrup law of Georgia owes its passage largely to the public sentiment created by his public letters and his personal efforts throughout the state and at the national capital.

GEN. ALEXANDER ROBERT LAWTON. This celebrated lawyer, statesman and officer of the Civil war was born in St. Peter's Parish, Beaufort District, South Carolina, November 4, 1818, and died at Clifton Springs, New York, July 2, 1896. He was the son of Alexander James Lawton and Martha Mosse, natives of South Carolina and Georgia, respectively. The Lawton family was an old one in South Carolina, and General Lawton was the grandson of Joseph Lawton, a planter of Edisto Island, that state, who later removed to Beaufort District, South Carolina, where he passed the remainder of his life. He was a lieutenant in the Continental line in the war of the Revolution, and his patriotism and public spirit were transmitted in fullest measure to the subject.

At the age of sixteen years, young Alexander Robert entered West

Point Military Academy, and was graduated from that institution in 1839. He entered the United States army as second lieutenant in the First Artillery, but resigned his commission December 31, 1840, to enter the law school of Harvard University. After completing the law course there he settled in Savannah and in this city entered upon the career which was to prove so useful and distinguished. In 1855-56 he served as a member of the lower house of the legislature and in 1859-60 represented his constituency in the state senate, with an eye single to the interests of the people, accomplishing much in these years of public service.

When the Civil war opened he was colonel of the First Georgia Regiment of Infantry, composed of Savannah citizens, but on the day of the fall of Fort Sumter he was appointed brigadier general in the Confederate army, commanding the Georgia Military District, C. S. army. He served with distinction in the Army of Northern Virginia until severely wounded at the battle of Sharpsburg, Maryland. Upon his recovery, he was (in 1863) made quartermaster general of the Confederate army and held this position until the conclusion of the great conflict. The brigade of which he had command at the beginning of the war was assigned to Ewell's Division, Jackson Corps. General Lawton's military record was a gallant and unblemished one; he was a remarkably efficient officer, successful in inspiring his men with courage and greatly beloved by them.

At the close of the war, he accepted the new conditions with manly vigor and frankness, and gladly laying down the sword, betook himself to his law practice. He was again sent to represent Chatham county in the Georgia legislature, this time serving from 1870 to 1875. In 1877 he was a member of the Constitutional Convention; in 1876 was president of the State Electoral College; in 1880 and 1884 chairman of the state delegations to the national Democratic conventions. In April, 1887, he was appointed by President Cleveland to the post of minister to Austria, and his embassadorial duties he performed with distinction during that term. He was for many years general counsel and a director of the Central Railroad & Banking Company of Georgia, the responsibilities of which office is now successfully vested in his son, Col. A. R. Lawton. His identification with Georgia railway affairs did not end with this for he was also at one time president of the Augusta & Savannah Railroad. He was a curator of the Georgia Historical Society and served as alderman of the city of Savannah from 1853 to 1855. In all relations, he was a credit to his city and every cause with which he became aligned had reason to be proud of its representative. He was one of the most public-spirited of men, in his breast burning brightly the spirit of civic altruism and keen indeed was his recognition of individual obligation to the public weal.

In 1880, General Lawton became candidate for the United States senate in opposition to Gov. Joseph E. Brown. He entered the race entirely against his own will, without the slightest hope of success from the beginning, but as the generally accepted representative of those who desired to enter a strenuous protest against the placing of Governor Brown in the senate in succession to Gen. John B. Gordon. He was a great friend and admirer of General Gordon and one of the griefs and disappointments of his life was the happenings of the year 1880, to which he never referred with anger, nor with resentment, but always with deep sorrow. The tie between the two generals was strong indeed, and Lawton's Brigade, after the injury of its commander at Sharpsburg, became Gordon's Brigade.

General Lawton's marriage on November 5, 1845, proved in fullest degree the fruition of his early hopes. The young woman to become his wife was Sarah Hillhouse Alexander, daughter of Adam Leopold Alexander, of Washington, Georgia and of Sarah Hillhouse Gilbert, his wife. Mrs. Lawton was the second of the ten Alexander children, of whom the sixth was the late Gen. Edward Porter Alexander, chief of artillery, Longstreet's Corps, C. S. A., president of the Central Railroad & Banking Company of Georgia, etc.; the seventh member of the family was James Hillhouse Alexander, for many years a merchant in Augusta and for some time mayor of that city. The Alexanders were in truth an unusual family. The father was the same Adam Leopold Alexander, to whom is addressed the very beautiful dedication of Mr. Alexander H. Stephens' "Reviewers Reviewed," the same being the answer to the critics of his "War Between the States." The six daughters of Mr. Alexander were all remarkable women, and the very flower of the family was Mrs. Lawton, to whom was undoubtedly due a very large part of the successful career of her husband. She was a woman of the highest intellect and most extensive cultivation, with an unequaled will power and self control, truly,

"A noble woman, nobly planned,
To warn, to comfort and command."

Their domestic life was flawless; it was an ideal of Christian marriage; he a true and tender knight to his chosen lady; she the wise and charming counselor in all his undertakings.

General and Mrs. Lawton celebrated their golden wedding anniversary, November 5, 1895, surrounded by their children and grandchildren. The eldest daughter, Corinne Elliott, born September 21, 1846, died January 24, 1877. Louisa Frederika, born June 9, 1849, married in 1878 Leonard C. Mackall, of Baltimore, Maryland, and to their union three children were born, all of whom are living. Nora married in 1886 Henry C. Cunningham, of Savannah, Georgia, and they have one daughter living. Alexander Rudolf Lawton married April 27, 1882, Ella Beckwith, daughter of Rt. Rev. John W. Beckwith, Episcopal bishop of Georgia, and the two sons of this union both are living. Less than a year later General Lawton passed away and this beautiful companionship of half a century was terminated. Mrs. Lawton survived her husband but a year, dying in New York City, November 1, 1897.

The paternal grandfather of Mrs. Lawton, Adam Alexander, was a citizen of the old town of Sunbury, Liberty county, Georgia, and a surgeon-major in the Revolutionary war. Concerning her sisters the following data is herewith entered. The eldest, Louisa, married Maj.-Gen. J. F. Gilmer, chief of engineers, C. S. A.; Harriet married Wallace Cumming, cashier of the old Bank of the State of Georgia, and afterward a private banker in Savannah; Mary Clifford married George Gilmer Hull, prominent in railroad operations and construction in Georgia, before, during and after the war; Marion married the Rev. William Ellison Boggs, a distinguished Presbyterian minister and some time chancellor of the University of Georgia; and Alice married Col. Alexander C. Haskell of South Carolina, a distinguished Confederate soldier, who as chairman of the Democratic executive committee, was in charge of the celebrated South Carolina campaign of 1876, when Hampton was elected governor, and was afterward judge of the supreme court of South Carolina.

The following memorial of General Lawton, presented February 17, 1897, to the Supreme Court of Georgia by Judge Samuel B. Adams in behalf of the bar of Savannah, and ordered to be filed in the archives of the court and published, is an eloquent tribute to the subject both as a lawyer and as a man.

"Gentlemen of the Bar:

"Your committee appointed to submit a report touching upon the death of our late fellow member, Alexander R. Lawton, Esq., realizes fully their inability to do justice either to the subject or to your esteem for him, in a report as brief as this must be.

"Alexander Robert Lawton was born in St. Peter's Parish, Beaufort District, South Carolina, on the 4th day of November, 1818, and departed this life on the 1st day of July, 1896, having nearly completed his seventy-eighth year. He was the son of Alexander James Lawton and Martha Mosse. He was born upon the plantation purchased by his grandfather, Joseph Lawton, in March, 1776. His lineage was a proud one and he worthily bore his name.

"General Lawton became a member of this bar in 1843 and so contiuned until his death, although for some time before his decease he had retired from active practice. To the last, however, he was a member of our profession, took a lively interest in all that concerned it, and died the president of the Savannah Bar Association. His professional life in this city may, therefore, be said to have continued (the late war excepted) for more than fifty years. While he served his state and country in the legislature, in the field, as the quartermaster-general of the Confederacy, in the Constitutional Convention, and as a foreign minister, yet he was always a lawyer and cheerfully gave his full homage to the calling of his choice and affection, recognized always as a 'jealous mistress.'

"It is not in our province to speak of his career in public office, where fidelity to duty, singleness of purpose and intelligent appreciation of responsibility, characterized him; of his career as a soldier, signalized by calm, unflinching courage and devotion to the cause which he had espoused; but rather to call attention to those traits which distinguished him as a lawyer.

"The first and most important thought in connection with his career is that he illustrated, as so many others have done, that a man can be an eminently successful lawyer and yet a rigidly honest, candid and truthful man. General Lawton met with conspicuous success in his profession. He enjoyed more than a state reputation. He was in the front rank of the South's lawyers. For many years he did a large and lucrative practice, and, tested by any standard, he enjoyed the full measure of success. And yet the most cynical and uncharitable could never question the absolute rectitude and conduct of his speech. He was always and everywhere the high-minded, dignified, truth-loving gentleman, the soul of honor, despising every form of sham, dishonesty and deceit. No man, we assert, has ever lived in this community who enjoyed, or deserved, more fully than he did, the confidence of our people. No matter how sharp the difference in opinion and judgment, no one who knew him could ever question the honor or jurity of his purpose. With him 'duty' was always the 'sublimest word in the language;' and in every emergency he fully answered its most exacting demands. This was illustrated in his professional life. He was never unmindful of his duty to a client, to the court, or to his fellow lawyers.

"We have never had in Georgia any member of our profession who more carefully or consistently observed and enforced its ethics and its best traditions. He scorned the thought now unhappily finding expression in conduct, if not in spoken avowal, that the law was a mere money-making trade. With him it was always a profession, high and honorable, demanding for its proper pursuit, not only attainments of learning and mind, but also a high sense of honor and propriety, the best qualities of a gentleman.

"He practiced only in the courthouse; he argued his cases there only. He did not discuss them in the newspapers, or seek their applause. He never sought, directly or indirectly, newspaper advertisement of his professional achievements, or a newspaper reputation. At the same time he fully appreciated kind and pleasant allusions to him in the press, which were unsought and unsolicited, and came like other recognitions of his merit.

"General Lawton's mental characteristics were strong, clear common sense; the ability to grasp quickly, even intuitively, the salient points of a case, and to press them home with singular clearness and cogency. His speeches were short, pointed and pithy. He wasted no words, went at once to the heart of his subject, never floundered or wandered, and, when he was through, realized that he was, and sat down. Even in the most important cases, involving large amounts, he never made what may be termed a long speech. He simply could not discuss trifling or immaterial points, and confined his entire thought and effort to the salient and controlling features of his case. He used in his arguments very few law books. This does not mean that he did not consult a great many, if necessary, but that he selected the best and used only them. He loved to argue from reason and principle and was not a slave to mere precedent. He was not a case lawyer, but one well grounded in the fundamental maxims of the law, and he used most those books which dealt in these basic principles. In these days of digests and ready-made briefs, when the merest tyro, without any learning or perhaps the capacity to learn, can make a show of erudition by citing innumerable decisions without having read or understood any of them, this plan, so successfully pursued by General Lawton, is worthy of special mention.

"But, gentlemen of the bar, the necessary brevity of this report prevents us from saying much that we would like to say. We think of General Lawton today, not so much as the conspicuous citizen, or the eminent lawyer to whom came honors like that of the presidency of the American Bar Association, and a distinguished career; but rather as a member of our own, the Savannah bar, which is indebted to his stainless life in our midst for wholesome and ennobling lessons, for the honor his connection with us has done us, and for the rich legacy of his example. Let us gratefully cherish our proud recollections of him, and let us be stimulated by his career to a truer appreciation of the duties and dignity of our calling and of our obligation to its demands and responsibilities. Let us never disgrace it by conduct or word, and let us, as he did, 'magnify our office.'

"We submit the following resolutions:

"1. That this bar recognizes that in the death of General Lawton our profession has lost one of its real ornaments whose long and illustrious career has shed honor upon our profession and made it his grateful debtor.

"2. That a copy of this report and these resolutions be spread upon the minutes of our Superior Court, and another be sent by our secretary to the family of General Lawton.

"3. That the Superior and City courtrooms be draped in mourning for thirty days and that the judge of the Superior Court be requested to adjourn his court in honor of General Lawton's memory.

SAMUEL B. ADAMS,
POPE BARROW,
WILLIAM GARRARD,
WALTER G. CHARLTON,
P. W. MELDRIM,
Committee."

COL. ALEXANDER RUDOLF LAWTON. The history of the legal profession in the South presents a chronicle of importance and distinction and the state of Georgia has assuredly contributed its quota to the whole. In legal annals of the state a name of pre-eminence is that of Lawton, two generations of the family having been lawyers of honor and fame, who have done much to preserve the dignity of their calling and the honor which should be the pride of the profession. The city of Savannah has been the scene of their distinguished careers and the younger of these gentlemen, Col. Alexander Rudolf Lawton, is today one of Savannah's leading citizens. In addition to a large general practice, he is vice-president of the Central of Georgia Railway, and also one of its general counsel, and his remarkable grasp on corporation law is known beyond the boundaries of the state. He has been a marvel to the profession in many respects, seeming to leap into the arena fully armed and equipped for the fiercest fight and legal battle with most renowned barristers when a very young man. His reputation has been reinforced with the passing years and he is recognized as one of the masters of the craft throughout the state. The father of the foregoing, Gen. Alexander Robert Lawton, whose demise occurred July 2, 1896, was one of Georgia's greatest lawyers in any day or generation. He was also a splendid officer and a detailed account of his life and achievements will be given in the article succeeding.

Colonel Lawton is a native son of the Forest city, within whose delightful borders his birth occurred August 9, 1858. He received an unusually brilliant education and early in youth he came to the conclusion to follow in the paternal footsteps in the matter of a life work. When a lad eight years of age he was taken to Paris and in the French capital pursued his studies during the years 1866 and 1867. Thereupon returning to Savannah, he studied in public and private schools in this city and ultimately entered the University of Georgia, from which institution he was graduated in 1877, at the age of nineteen years, receiving the degree of Bachelor of Arts. During the ensuing summer, he was a student in the Eastman Business College, Poughkeepsie, New York, and in the fall entered upon his preparation for the law. He studied law in the law department of the University of Virginia in 1878 and 1879 and in the Harvard Law School in 1879 and 1880. In the year last mentioned he was admitted to the bar and entered upon the practice of the profession in Savannah. From the first his career has been of the most satisfactory character. He has been a member of the firm of Lawton & Cunningham, general counsel for the Central of Georgia Railway since 1887, succeeding General Lawton in this office on his retirement. His identification with the firm of Lawton & Cunningham, of which his father was at that time senior member, dates from the year 1882.

It is safe to say that probably in all the state there is no one more familiar with certain aspects of railway and maritime affairs than Colonel Lawton. He has been a director of the Central of Georgia Railway since 1896 and since 1904 has held the office of vice-president of the company. He is also a director of the Atlanta & West Point Railroad Company, the Western Railway of Alabama, the Ocean Steamship Company and the Savannah Trust Company. His position with the great railway mentioned gives an idea of his caliber, and so acceptably has he advised his clients in all dilemmas that he is regarded by them with admiration and gratitude.

Colonel Lawton is a member of the American Bar Association, the American Historical Association, the Southern Historical Society, the American Academy of Political and Social Science and the National

Geographic Society. He is president of the Georgia Historical Society, by virtue of which position he also is president of Savannah's notable institution, the Telfair Academy of Arts and Sciences, which is owned by and under the management of the Historical Society. He is a well-known clubman, his membership extending to some of the most notable organizations in the United States. Only partially to enumerate, these affiliations are with the Oglethorpe Club, of Savannah; the Capital City Club, of Atlanta; the University and City Midday clubs, of New York City; and the Metropolitan Club, of Washington, D. C.

Since youth, Colonel Lawton has been actively identified with things military in Savannah. In 1881, he enlisted as a private in the National Guard of Georgia and was promoted through the various ranks to that of colonel of the First Regiment of Infantry. During the Spanish-American war in 1898, he was colonel of the First Georgia Infantry, United States Volunteers.

Colonel Lawton was married in Atlanta, April 27, 1882, his chosen lady being Miss Ella Stanly Beckwith, daughter of the Rt. Rev. John W. and Ella (Brockenbrough) Beckwith, the former being bishop of the Protestant Episcopal church of Georgia. Colonel and Mrs. Lawton share their home with two sons, Alexander Robert, Jr., and John Beckwith. The family have an assured position in the most exclusive social circles in the city and their household is renowned for its culture and its gracious hospitality, exemplifying the highest social traditions of the South.

JOHN AVERY GERE CARSON. Prominent among the representative citizens of Savannah is John Avery Gere Carson, ex-president of the board of trade; president of the Carson Naval Stores Company; and prominent in commercial and financial affairs of the city. He has resided here for more than forty years and for a great portion of that time has figured conspicuously in the history of the city, to whose institutions he is very loyal and to whose welfare he is ever ready to contribute in any way within his power.

Mr. Carson, by the circumstance of birth, belongs to Baltimore, Maryland, his life record having begun in that city, February 19, 1856. He is the son of Carvill Hynson and Sarah Frances (Gere) Carson. As his name indicates his ancestry on both sides represents families of distinct prominence in the Colonial history of Maryland. His father was the son of David and Sarah Taylor (Hynson) Carson, the latter being the daughter of Charles and Sarah (Waltham) Carson. On the Hynson side the ancestry runs back through several generations to Thomas Hynson of England, who came to Maryland in 1650, settled at Kent in the then colony of Maryland, and became one of the commissioners in charge of the government of and holding of elections in Kent county. He also became a member of the Maryland assembly. On his mother's side Mr. Carson is descended from George Geer (as it was then spelled—now Gere), who with his brother, Thomas Gere, came from Hevitree, Devonshire, England, to America in 1621 and settled in the town of Enfield, Connecticut. Thus the family was founded on these shores only a few months after the arrival of the Pilgrim fathers. The mother of Mr. Carson was born in Baltimore, the daughter of John Avery Gere. This admirable lady is still living in Savannah, the possessor of universal respect and esteem. The father, who died on February 18, 1911, in Savannah, was born at Baltimore, November 14, 1830. A man of unblemished record, his memory will long remain green in the hearts of his numerous friends and admirers.

Mr. Carson received his education in the public schools of Baltimore

Yours Truly

J. W. J. Carson

and in the Normal College at Lycoming county, Pennsylvania. He came to Savannah with his parents in 1870 and has resided within the pleasant boundaries of the city ever since that time. On January 1, 1884, he became identified with Mr. J. P. Williams in the latter's business enterprises, and upon the organization of the J. P. Williams Company (naval stores) in 1897, Mr. Carson became vice-president of the concern. In January, 1910, he organized the Carson Naval Stores Company, which succeeded the J. P. Williams Company and of which he is president. The continual progress and present standing of the company is largely credited to the experience, executive ability, tireless energy, engineering skill and genius in the broad combination of applicable forces possessed by Mr. Carson.

This distinguished gentleman is ex-president of the Savannah Board of Trade, one of the strongest organizations of its kind in the South. He was for nine years, from 1900 to 1909, the president of the Merchants' National Bank of Savannah, and did much to add to the confidence felt in this important monetary institution. He was alderman of the city from 1889 to 1893. In 1893 he was elected by the largest vote received by any candidate, as a member of the first board of county commissioners of Chatham under the new law for such boards that went into effect at that time. He served in that capacity until 1897, with credit to himself and honor and profit to the people. He has always been interested in affairs military and was a lieutenant in the Chatham Artillery in 1895 and 1896. He has been deputy governor-general for Georgia of the Society of the Colonial Wars since its organization in 1896. Since starting in business as a young man his chief interests have been in grain, cotton and naval stores and he keeps in touch with Georgian resources and development.

Fraternally, Mr. Carson is a Mason and is entitled to the white-plumed helmet of the Knight Templar. He is a member of the Oglethorpe Club and a life member of the Savannah Volunteer Guards.

Mr. Carson was happily married January 29, 1879, his chosen lady being Miss Carrie Gordon Cubbedge, daughter of Stephen Jackson Maxwell and Caroline Rebecca (Tubbs) Cubbedge. They share their home, one of the most hospitable and delightful in Savannah, with four interesting children: John Avery Gere, Jr., Gordon Cubbedge, Edwin Williams, and Carvill Hynson.

J. FLORANCE MINIS, a retired citizen of Savannah, Georgia, belongs to one of the historic families of this state. The early record sets forth the fact that his great-grandfather, Philip Minis, was the first white male child born in Georgia.

J. Florance Minis was born November 12, 1852, son of Abraham and Lavinia (Florance) Minis. His father, a native of Savannah, was born November 4, 1820, and died November 5, 1889, his death occurring in New York City. For many years he was a prominent and successful merchant of Savannah. He had married in Philadelphia, Pennsylvania, October 22, 1851, Miss Lavinia Florance, a native of New Orleans, Louisiana, born May 26, 1826, daughter of Jacob L. and Hannah Florance, and their family consisted of six children: Jacob Florance Minis; Rosina Florance Minis, who died in infancy; Miss Maria Minis; Isaac Minis; Lavinia Florance Minis, wife of Charles I. Henry of New York City; and Abram Minis.

Isaac Minis died in New York City June 8, 1893. His wife, to whom he was married in Savannah March 9, 1886, was before her marriage Miss Eugenia Myers of Savannah; she survives her husband, and has two sons, viz.: Isaac M. and Carol Minis. Mr. and Mrs. Charles I. Henry have two daughters, namely: Harriet and Lavinia Henry. Philip

Minis, an uncle of the subject of this sketch, married Miss Sarah A. Livingston of New York, and their children are as follows: Mrs. Alice Henrietta Poe of Baltimore; Annie, Charles Spalding, Philip Henry, John Livingston, Mary Lela, and Augusta Medora Minis.

The paternal grandfather of J. F. Minis was Isaac Minis, and he, although of the Savannah family, was born in 1780, near Charleston, where his parents and family fled from the British troops, which at that time were besieging the city of Savannah. They returned to Savannah after the close of the Revolutionary war. Isaac Minis married Miss Dinah Cohen of Georgtown, South Carolina, December 4, 1803; she being the daughter of Solomon Cohen of that place. She was born in Georgetown, April 12, 1787, and died in Savannah, February 17, 1874. Isaac Minis, her husband, had died in Philadelphia, November 17, 1856; he and his wife were buried in the family lot in Laurel Grove cemetery in Savannah. Isaac Minis served in the War of 1812 as a private in Capt. William Bulloch's company of artillery, First Regiment of Georgia Militia, commanded by Colonel Johnston.

Isaac Minis was the son of Philip and Judith (Pollock) Minis; Judith Pollock being a member of one of the first families that settled Newport, just as her husband belonged to a family that was numbered among the first settlers of the colony of Georgia. An interesting fact, in this connection, is that Rhode Island and Georgia were the only two of the colonies where Jews were not prohibited from settling.

Going back to Philip Minis, the great-grandfather of the subject of this sketch, who bore the distinction of being the first male white child born in Georgia, it is found that this important event occurred at Savannah, July 11, 1734, the year following the founding of the Georgia colony by Oglethorpe. In substantiation of this fact, there are various authorities, among which is the following notice that appeared in the *Georgia Gazette* of the issue of Thursday, March 12, 1789, concerning the death of Philip Minis:

"On Friday, March 6, 1789, departed this life Mr. Philip Minis, merchant, age 55 years. He was the first white male child born in this state. His remains were buried in the Jews' burial ground on Sunday morning, attended by a large number of respectable citizens, who by their solemn attention evinced how sensibly they felt the loss the community has sustained in so valuable a man. He has left a disconsolate widow and five children, together with an aged and venerable mother, and five sisters to deplore their loss. He was an affectionate husband, a dutiful son, tender father and kind brother; in short, he was in every sense of the word a truly honest man."

Philip Minis gave active aid and support to the colonists in the struggle with Great Britain, and on this account he was named in the Georgia Royal Disqualifying Act of 1780.

The founder of the Minis family in Georgia was Philip Minis' father, Abram Minis, who, with his wife, Abigail Minis, and two daughters, Esther and Leah, also his brother, Simon Minis, arrived at Savannah on a vessel from London, July 11, 1733, the year after Oglethorpe's founding of the colony of Georgia. There were thirteen Jewish families on this vessel, and the history of their organization for the journey, in London, and their trials and tribulations, as well as successes, after landing on Georgia soil in 1733, forms one of the interesting romances of the colonization of the new world. Abram Minis died in Savannah in 1757 and was buried in the first Jewish burial plot in the city. His widow, Abigail Minis, in 1760 received a grant of land from King George III. She died in Savannah October 11, 1794, at the age of ninety-three years.

J. Florance Minis, the eldest of the children of Abraham and Lavinia

(Florance) Minis, was born November 12, 1852. In his early boyhood he attended Prof. W. S. Bogart's school at Savannah, and had as classmates Mr. H. H. Gilmer, Judge A. Pratt Adams, Judge Samuel B. Adams, the younger members of the Habersham family, the Owens boys and the Screven boys—all representatives of prominent families in Savannah. When he was fourteen years old he entered Washington College at Lexington, Virginia, of which Gen. Robert E. Lee was then president, and which, later, in his honor, was named Washington and Lee University. Of his own accord, Mr. Minis decided not to remain in college to graduate, but instead he returned to his home at Savannah, and on November 12, 1870, he entered his father's office as a clerk. He afterward became a member of the firm, the name of which was then changed to A. Minis & Son. In November, 1890, his father, Mr. Abraham Minis, died, and, Mr. Isaac Minis having previously become a member of the firm, the name was then changed to A. Minis' Sons. Upon the death of Mr. Isaac Minis in 1893, the business was continued by Mr. J. F. Minis under the firm name of J. F. Minis & Co. In 1905 Mr. Minis retired from active business, closed up the affairs of the old firm, and since then has devoted his attention to his private interests. He divides his time between his Savannah home, his country home "Rockwood" at Clarksville in Habersham county, and traveling in Europe.

While in active busines, Mr. Minis served one term as president of the Savannah Cotton Exchange. He is now a director of the Merchants National Bank, director of the Savannah Trust Company, director of the Southwestern Railroad Company, vice-president of the Savannah Brewing Company. In all the principal clubs of Savannah he has membership, and he is a member of the board of managers of the Georgia Historical Society and one of the curators of the Telfair Academy of Arts and Sciences. He was appointed by Gov. Joseph M. Brown as a member of the Oglethorpe Monument Commission, which had in charge the erection of the Oglethorpe Monument in Savannah, which was dedicated on November 23, 1910.

In 1890 Mr. Minis married Miss Louisa Porter Gilmer. Mrs. Minis is a daughter of Gen. Jeremy F. Gilmer, a distinguished engineer, a graduate of West Point, who, during the war between the states, was chief of engineers of the Confederate government. Her mother, Louisa P. (Alexander) Gilmer, was a daughter of A. L. Alexander of Washington, Wilkes county, Georgia.

GEORGE C. FREEMAN. As money, or any other medium of exchange, is the life-blood of business and commerce, it is evident that bankers, men who manage and control the circulating medium, stand related to the public as the physician who has his finger on the pulse of the patient and has the power of controlling his condition for better or worse. No member of the business community has a greater responsibility than the banker and any community or city is much to be congratulated which has at the head of its finances men of thorough training, stanch ability and moral dependability. No banker of the South is more closely typical of what is required in the financial manager and leader to inspire and retain business and commercial confidence than George C. Freeman, assistant to the president of the Citizens and Southern Bank, one of Georgia's most important monetary institutions. He has resided in Savannah since 1854, and has been identified with banking interests since 1873.

Mr. Freeman is one of the Forest city's venerable citizens, his birth having occurred in Bibb county, Georgia, August 16, 1833. He is the son of Azel R. and Delia (Shaw) Freeman. The father was born in

New Jersey in 1792. While still a youth he started out like the proverbial hero of romance to seek his fortunes, going with two companions to what was then known as the "West," crossing the 'Allegheny mountains and going down the Ohio river and finally locating in Lexington, Kentucky. When the War of 1812 came on Azel Freeman volunteered for service and joined the Kentucky Mounted Riflemen, with which organization he crossed the Ohio river and served with the same on the northern frontier. Upon the termination of hostilities, he returned to the Blue Grass state, but subsequently went thence to Nashville, Tennessee, which city remained his home for a number of years. In 1827 he removed from Nashville to Bibb county, Georgia, locating where the present city of Macon is situated, and in Bibb county he spent the years which remained to him before traveling on to the undiscovered country,

"From whose bourne no traveler returns."

The mother of the subject was a native of Massachusetts.

George C. Freeman was reared and educated in Bibb county. He came to Savannah in 1854, and ever since that time he has maintained his home in this city. His first employment in Savannah was in the office of Hudson, Fleming & Company, cotton factors, with whom he remained for six years. He then formed a partnership with A. H. Champion, under the firm name of Champion & Freeman, in the wholesale grocery business, their location being at the corner of Bay and Drayton streets. At the outbreak of the Civil war, in 1861, Mr. Freeman and Mr. Champion both joined the army of the Confederacy and their business, like that of many another Southern firm, became suspended on that account, to be resumed after the close of the war.

Mr. Freeman joined the Chatham Artillery in Savannah and was in service in Chatham county. In the second year of the war he was detached from his command and assigned to duty as assistant to the collector of the port of Savannah, under the Confederate government. The collector of the port was James R. Sneed and his chief deputy was Maj. Charles S. Hardee, who has for many years held the office of city treasurer of Savannah. A day or two prior to Sherman's entrance into Savannah, the collector of the port and his office force, taking their records, books, money and other possessions, went to Charleston, and of this historic party Mr. Freeman was a member. Within a few days they changed their headquarters from Charleston to Augusta; thence the Confederate authorities ordered them to Macon; from Macon to Milledgeville; and from the latter place they retreated to the plantation of Dr. T. A. Parsons, in Laurens county, whence they were ordered to Macon, where their effects were surrendered to the United States authorities and the party was paroled and returned to Savannah.

Upon the return of peace to the devastated country, the business of Champion & Freeman was successfully re-established and continued until 1877. Mr. Freeman, however, is best known for his long and honorable connection with banking business in Savannah. He entered upon his career in this field in 1873, when he was elected a director and vice-president of the Citizens' Mutual Loan Company, which began business in June of that year. He was one of the originators of that well-remembered financial institution and took an active part in the management of its affairs from the beginning. It was successful from the start and earned a good annual profit in dividends to its stockholders. In 1887 the Citizens' Bank was organized and by unanimous vote the Citizens' Mutual Loan Company was merged into that institution. The Citizens' Bank began with a capital stock of $200,000, and Mr. Freeman was the first cashier of the new bank. In 1890, the Citizens' Bank was reorganized and $300,000 was added to its capital, making its capital stock $500,000. Mr. Freeman remained as cashier after the reorganization, being the only one of the old officers retained after the reorganization.

In 1906 the Citizens' Bank was consolidated with the Southern Bank of the state of Georgia, with the name of the Citizens and Southern Bank, and of this substantial institution, as mentioned in a preceding paragraph, Mr. Freeman is an officer and assistant to the president; the increasing duties of the cashier's position being considered more than Mr. Freeman should discharge after his long years of service with the bank. The Citizens and Southern Bank is one of the largest and strongest banks in the South. It has a capital stock of $1,000,000, with a surplus and undivided profits running over a million dollars. It occupies the beautiful banking building constructed for its exclusive use, in the square surrounded by St. Julian, Bryan, Bull and Drayton streets, with entrances from both Bull and Drayton streets. Nothing could possibly be more advantageous than its situation. Besides his position of assistant to the president, Mr. Freeman is also secretary of the board of directors.

Mr. Freeman served five years as alderman of Savannah and was at one time chairman of the finance committee. He has been a member and officer of the Savannah Benevolent Association since 1866, and for ten years he was secretary, for nine years president, and for twenty-six years, treasurer, which latter position he now holds. He is a member of the Independent Presbyterian church and has been one of its board of trustees since 1878. He is the friend of good government and takes a public-spirited interest in all measures likely to advance the welfare of the beautiful old city to which he came over half a century ago.

Mr. Freeman laid one of the most important stones in the foundation of his success in 1862 by his marriage to Miss Sarah E. Davis, of Savannah, daughter of William H. Davis, one of the well-known early residents of the city and particularly well remembered for his prominent connection with the Republican Blues, one of Savannah's famous military organizations. Their union has been blessed by five children, two of whom now survive: Judge Davis, Freeman, lawyer, and judge of the city court of Savannah; and Miss Georgia Freeman, a member of the charming Freeman household, whose hospitality is thoroughly consistent with Southern traditions.

WILLIAM HAMPTON WADE. Of decided eminence in his profession is William Hampton Wade, of Savannah, whose abilities have brought him distinction at the bar and a large clientele. He is a native son of Savannah, his birth having occurred in this city on the 17th day of August, 1859. His parents were William and Margaret H. (Greene) Wade, both of whom are deceased. The father was a native of Bridgeport, Connecticut, and came to Savannah about the year 1850. He died early in the Civil war period, the subject being an infant at the time of his demise. At the time of the death of the elder gentleman he was one of the proprietors of a foundry in Savannah that was engaged in making cannon for the Confederate government. He was also the owner of a plantation in Chatham county, not far from Savannah, and his home there was known as "Hampton Place." The mother of the subject was the daughter of Herman and Harriet M. (Hart) Greene, and her birth occurred in Savannah in 1824. Herman Greene was the son of Zachariah Greene, who was a first cousin of Gen. Nathaniel Greene, the commander of Washington's forces in the Southern colonies during the Revolutionary war. Zachariah Greene was a very young man at the beginning of the Revolution, his years numbering about seventeen, but he joined the Continental army and was proffered a place on General Washington's staff.

William Hampton Wade was educated in the schools of Savannah and in the Virginia Military Institute at Lexington, from which he graduated in the class of 1880. Having come to the decision to adopt the law as his life work, he began his preparatory studies in Savannah under the late Judge Walter S. Chisholm, and was admitted to the bar in 1881. He has practiced law in Savannah since that time with the exception of a few years, when he was absent from the city. Of vigorous intellect, wide information and keen wit, his command of language is such as to make his speech apt and fitting at all times and careful in arranging and preparing his cases, he is never at a loss for forcible and appropriate argument to sustain his position. His reputation as one of the able lawyers of Savannah has been reinforced with the passing years. Besides his law practice he fills the office of county administrator and county guardian.

Mr. Wade was a member of the Savannah Volunteer Guards for about seven years and at the time of leaving the city in 1887 he had been appointed a lieutenant. He finds pleasure and profit in his fraternal relations, which extend to the Independent Order of Odd Fellows and the Knights of Pythias.

In the year 1906 Mr. Wade was married in this city to Miss Ada Hull, a native daughter of Savannah, her father being Fred M. Hull, the port warden of Savannah. They have one son, William Hampton Wade, Jr.

DAVID S. ATKINSON. In no profession is there a career more open to talent than is that of the law, and in no field of endeavor is there demanded a more careful preparation, a more thorough appreciation of the absolute ethics of life or of the underlying principles which form the basis of all human rights and privileges. Unflagging application and determination are the concomitants which insure personal success. Possessing the requisite qualities of the lawyer, is the young man whose name introduces this paragraph—Mr. David S. Atkinson.

Mr. Atkinson was born in Camden county, Georgia, November 1, 1884, the son of Dr. Dean Dunwody and Sarah Hardee (Scarlett) Atkinson, of Brunswick, Georgia.

Mr. Atkinson received the advantages of a thorough education, his public school training being supplemented by attendance in Gordon Institute at Barnesville, the University of Georgia at Athens, and the law department of Mercer University at Macon, from which last-named institution he was graduated with the class of 1907. He then entered upon the practice of law in Camden county and was, in 1909, appointed by Gov. J. M. Brown, judge of the city court of St. Marys, Georgia. In October, 1908, he established himself in the practice of law in Savannah.

Mr. Atkinson has become actively associated with the various affairs of Savannah. He was in 1913 appointed assistant city attorney of this city. He is a lieutenant in the First Regiment of Infantry, National Guard of Georgia, and a member of various clubs and societies. He is a past chancellor of the Knights of Pythias, a Mason, an Odd Fellow, an Elk, and Eagle, and is secretary and treasurer of the University Club of Savannah. Mr. Atkinson is unmarried.

COL. MICHAEL J. O'LEARY. Excelling in achievements and commanding success in several lines of endeavor, Col. Michael J. O'Leary, of Savannah, has won marked prestige as colonel of the First Regiment

M. J. O'Leary

of Infantry, National Guard of Georgia; has acquired prominence in commercial circles and engaged in the transfer of cotton; and as alderman was actively associated with the public interests of the city for one term.

Born in New York City in 1869, he was brought by his parents to Savannah when but a few months old, and is practically a Savannah product, having been brought up in this city, and here receiving his early education in Saint Patrick's school, and his commercial training in McCarthy's Business College. Since 1896, when he succeeded to the interests of Andrew McCormick, Colonel O'Leary has been actively and prosperously engaged in the cotton transfer business, which is the principal business of the kind in Savannah, in his operations enjoying the patronage of all the large cotton interests.

In 1888, responding to the lure of military life, Michael J. O'Leary enlisted as a private in the "Irish Jasper Greens," one of the companies of the First Regiment of Infantry, National Guard of Georgia. Subsequently receiving well-merited promotion, he was first made first lieutenant of his company, and later was commissioned major of his regiment. In 1908 he was again promoted, being made colonel of the First Regiment of Infantry, National Guard of Georgia, a position which he now holds. This regiment is famous in the military history of Georgia, its distinguished record being referred to at length in the historical portion of this work. At present the First Regiment is composed of twelve companies, including the Emmett Rifles, the German Volunteers, the Oglethorpe Light Infantry, the Savannah Cadets, the Irish Jasper Greens, the Republican Blues, and several out-of-town companies. Colonel O'Leary has rendered notably efficient service and given the highest of satisfaction as commander of his regiment, which is one of the military bulwarks of the state. For two seasons, in 1907 and 1908, the colonel was captain of the Georgia Rifle Team, representing the Georgia military organization in the rifle contests at Camp Perry, Ohio.

Elected alderman of the city in the fall of 1910, Colonel O'Leary took his seat in January, 1911, and is rendering excellent service in that capacity. He is one of the directors of the Savannah Fire Insurance Company. He is a director of the Chamber of Commerce; and of the Exchange Bank and a member of the Cotton Exchange; of the Savannah Automobile Club; the Hussars Club; the Guards Club; and fraternally is a member, and past state deputy, of the Knights of Columbus, and master of the fourth degree of the states of Florida, Georgia, North and South Carolinas.

Colonel O'Leary married, in Savannah, Josephine McCormick, and they have one daughter, Josephine O'Leary.

DR. RICHARD DENNIS ARNOLD, a physician and surgeon of considerable note, distinguished citizen and war mayor of Savannah, was born in that city on August 19, 1808. He passed away in the city of his birth in 1876, and he is mourned in the hearts of all who live to remember him today.

Dr. Arnold was the son of Capt. Joseph and Eliza (Dennis) Arnold; the former born in Rhode Island and the latter a native of Brunswick, New Jersey. No man was more generally or more favorably known in Savannah, few were more highly honored, and none have done more to promote the best interests of the city and to benefit the people individually and collectively than did Doctor Arnold. He died July 10, 1876, in the same house and in the same room in which he was born, the old family mansion still standing on the northwest corner of State and

Abercorn streets. He was a graduate of Princeton College, also of the Medical College of the University of Pennsylvania. 'In 1832 Doctor Arnold began the practice of his profession in Savannah, and success soon established him among the distinguished members of the medical profession. In 1839 he was elected to represent Chatham county in the state legislature, and the usefulness of his public service was such that many further political honors were bestowed upon him. In 1842 he was elected to the Georgia senate, and in 1843 he was elected mayor of Savannah, previously having served several terms as a member of the board of aldermen. He was again elected to the office of mayor in 1851, 1859 and 1863, and continued to hold that office until the close of the Civil war. General Sherman, upon his occupation of the city in December, 1864, convinced that Doctor Arnold was much better fitted to act as mayor than anyone that could be appointed from the army, retained Doctor Arnold in that position. He rendered service of great value to his people in those times in looking after the women and children and non-combatants.

Doctor Arnold was a prominent member of the American Medical Association, was elected first vice-president of that body in 1846, and was a member of the committee which drafted the association's code of ethics. In 1847 he was elected president of the Georgia Medical Society. His reputation as a physician was international, and he was especially well known as an expert in the treatment of fevers. In 1854, when the yellow fever epidemic swept over Savannah, Doctor Arnold rendered notably beneficent services, being unremitting in his attentions to the sick and suffering, and taking no heed of any danger to himself. His experience was wide and varied, and, a constant student, he wrote several masterful treatises on yellow and bilious fevers.

Doctor Arnold was a delegate to several national Democratic conventions, and was always enthusiastic in the cause of the party. He was deeply interested in the subject of education, and as a member of the board of education of Savannah, was able to do much for its advancement in his native city. He was one of the original members of the Georgia Historical Society.

Doctor Arnold was past master of Oglethorpe Lodge of the Independent Order of Odd Fellows and a member of Solomons Lodge, No. 1, Ancient Free and Accepted Masons. He was buried in Bonaventure cemetery and in respect to his memory a beautiful shaft was erected by the children of the public schools and the citizens of Savannah.

JOHN M. HOGAN. Among the prominent and valued citizens whom Savannah has been called upon to mourn within the past few years, none will be more generally missed than John M. Hogan, who, as cashier for many years of the Germania Bank, was closely identified with the financial interests of the city, while his connection with business, fraternal, military and educational associations brought him in contact with the membership of various city organizations. A native of Pennsylvania, he was born May 28, 1848, in Philadelphia, a son of Matthew and Anne (Higgins) Hogan, both of whom were born in Ireland, and died in Savannah.

As a young lad John M. Hogan came with his parents to Savannah, Georgia, where he acquired his early education, which was supplemented by a course of study in Spring Hill College, near Mobile, Alabama. Returning to Savannah from there, he entered the banking house of Wallace Cumming & Company, and subsequently remained with that firm and its successors, and with the Southern Bank of Georgia, until the organization of the Germania Bank, in 1889. Being then chosen cashier of that institution, Mr. Hogan retained the position continuously until his death, May 8, 1911, his long record of service in that capacity bespeaking in no uncertain tone his business ability, judgment and upright character. He was also secretary and treasurer of the Savannah Clearing House Association from its formation, in 1891, until his death. In a memorial issued by the clearing house association following his death, a beautiful and honest tribute was paid to his memory, as follows:

"Mr. Hogan's faithful and efficient services as an officer of this association were so appreciated by his associates that no other name was ever mentioned in connection with his office during his long incumbency of it. Mr. Hogan took an active interest in whatever tended to promote better banking methods. He was until his death a constant attendant upon the meetings of the American Bankers' Association, and he was for a time one of its vice-presidents. His sterling qualities, combined with his genial and courteous manner, won the friendship and affection of all his associates, and his death brings to each of us a profound sense of personal bereavement.

"As an expression of our sense of loss, it is

"Resolved, That in the death of John M. Hogan this association deplores the loss of a cherished friend and of a faithful officer, whose life and character exemplified the highest type of the upright business man and citizen."

The late Capt. Henry Blun, who was president of the Germania Bank, imposed great confidence in Mr. Hogan, and his long experience and irreproachable character made him a man of influence in financial circles.

Mr. John M. Hogan was a member of the Georgia Historical Society, and was vice-president of the Hibernian Society at the time of his death. He was a life member of the Savannah Volunteer Guards; a member of the Catholic Library Association; of the Savannah Yacht Club; the Oglethorpe Club; the Hussars Club; the Union Society; and the Chamber of Commerce. Fraternally he belonged to the Benevolent and Protective Order of Elks.

WILLIAM R. HEWLETT is an attorney of Savannah and since 1908 has been one of the United States commissioners for the United States court, Eastern district of Georgia. His reputation as one of the prominent lawyers of the state has been reinforced with passing years, during which he has appeared in connection with many of the important cases brought before the state and federal courts, with many noteworthy forensic victories to his credit. He is a strong advocate before judge or jury and not only marshals his causes with great ability, but also brings to bear the strength of a firm and upright character, so that he has gained and held the inviolable confidence and regard of his fellow practitioners and also of the general public.

Mr. Hewlett was born at Barnwell, Barnwell county, South Carolina, on the 20th day of September, 1869. He is the son of William Henry and Amelia H. (Fowke) Hewlett. The former, who has been deceased for several years, was a native South Carolinian, but came to Savannah to enlist in the Confederate army at the outbreak of the war, he joining the famous Georgia Huzzars of this city, of which he became lieutenant. He went with this organization to the Army of Northern Virginia; was wounded in one of the battles in that state; came home; and rejoined the army in South Carolina after he got well. He was the son of William H. and Elizabeth (Johnson) Hewlett.

The subject's mother, who is still living, comes from the well-known

Virginia family of that name. She is the daughter of Dr. Richard Chandler and his wife, whose maiden name was Harrietta (Allen) Fowke. Dr. Richard Chandler Fowke was the son of Dr. John Fowke, of Virginia, who served in the United States navy as a surgeon soon after the close of the Revolutionary war. Dr. John Fowke was descended from Roger Fowke of England, whose son, a colonel in the royal army, came to America about the time of the execution of Charles I and settled in the Old Dominion. Through marriage his descendants became connected with a number of the well-known families of Virginia, such as the Masons, Fitzhughs, Dinwiddies, Burdettes, Harrisons and Alexanders. The late Peter Daniel of the United States supreme court was of the Fowke connection.

Mr. Hewlett of this review received his general education in the schools of Barnwell and Charleston. He came to Savannah in 1886 and this city has since been his home. He studied law in Savannah and was admitted to the bar in 1898. He did not begin practice, however, until the year 1900, since which time he has been one of the active and successful practitioners at the Savannah bar and in the various federal and state courts. For a number of years he maintained a law partnership with Judge Walter W. Sheppard, which pleasant connection was dissolved in 1910 upon Judge Sheppard's appointment as judge of the Atlantic circuit of the superior court.

Mr. Hewlett is a prominent figure in several of the fraternal organizations. He is clerk and is practically at the head of the local lodge of Woodmen of the World; he is head officer of the fraternal Mystic Circle for the state of Georgia, and he is junior warden of the Royal Arcanum.

Mr. Hewlett was married June 2, 1893, to Miss Julia C. Erwin, a niece of Hon. Marion Erwin, United States district attorney for the Eastern district of Georgia, becoming his wife. Their union has been blessed with a daughter, Kathleen. The Hewlett homestead is a hospitable and charming abode and Mr. and Mrs. Hewlett hold high place in popular confidence and esteem.

WARING RUSSELL, JR. One of the most highly esteemed and popular citizens of Savannah, Waring Russell, Jr., has served continuously as clerk of the city court for upwards of fifteen years, administering the affairs of his office so ably and intelligently as to win the approbation of every member of the bar and of all others with whom he is brought into business contact. A native of Savannah, Georgia, his birth occurred December 2, 1854. He is of pioneer stock, his ancestors having come to this country with General Oglethorpe in 1733, being among the original settlers of Savannah, and subsequently identified with the history of the Revolutionary war.

His father, the late Judge Philip Moses Russell, was born December 17, 1815, in Savannah, a son of Isaac and Perla (Sheftall) Russell. At the age of eighteen years he began the study of law with his uncle, Hon. Mordecai Sheftall, at that time a leading member of the Savannah bar, but afterwards for many years judge of the court of common pleas and oyer and terminer of the city of Savannah, a position to which he was elected by the state legislature. Here it may be well to mention that the present city court of Savannah, with which some members of the Sheftall or Russell families have been officially connected for more than a century, was known before the Revolutionary war, and for some time after, as the mayor's court. In 1820 the name was changed to the "Court of Common Pleas and Oyer and Terminer," and in 1856 was again changed, becoming the "City Court of Savannah."

In 1835 Judge Philip M. Russell was appointed a director of the Savannah & Altamaha Canal Company, a position which he retained until receiving his appointment as deputy sheriff of Chatham county, and deputy United States marshal under Col. William I. Davis, positions in which, by urbanity of character and strict attention to and impartial discharge of his official duties, he made many personal and political friends. On June 15, 1843, Judge Russell was elected sheriff of the city of Savannah, and on April 9, 1844, was elected justice of the peace in the first district, defeating the Democratic and Whig opponents by a majority of twenty-five votes. While holding this office he was appointed inspector of customs by the collector, Gen. Edward Harden. Removing then to the second district, the judge was there elected justice of the peace in January, 1846, receiving a large vote. On January 1, 1850, he was elected clerk of the court of common pleas and oyer and terminer of the city of Savannah, and in January, 1853, he was elected city marshal of Savannah, an office which he filled acceptably for two years. In the year 1855 Judge Russell acted as clerk of the United States circuit and district courts, and in January, 1856, was elected clerk of the city court of Savannah, and held the position until the outbreak of the Civil war in 1861.

In 1853, Judge Russell was made a member of the "Republican Blues," a favorite volunteer company of the First Regiment of the Georgia Volunteers, in which he maintained his membership as long as he lived. When, by the occupancy of Fort Pulaski, the company entered into active service, Judge Russell was detailed to look after the comfort of the families of his fellow-members in service, and at the organization of the state forces, under Governor Brown's administration, was commissioned as captain and commissary of subsistence, and assigned to duty with Colonel Karkie's regiment, Gen. G. B. Harrison's brigade.

In September, 1863, the judge became a candidate for the legislature, and was elected the following month by a handsome majority of the votes cast, and two years later was re-elected by the highest vote in the county. At the expiration of his legislative term, Judge Russell, having become re-enfranchised under the reconstruction acts, resumed his position as clerk of the court of the city of Savannah, and continued in office several terms.

In 1876, Judge Russell was again the Democratic candidate for representative to the state legislature, receiving thirty-nine of the forty-two votes cast in the county convention, and was elected, leading his ticket by seventy-two votes. At the expiration of his term he had the honor of being re-elected to the legislature by a majority of two hundred votes over the highest candidate on the opposition ticket, and in 1886 was once more elected to the state legislature, leading his opponent at the polls by two hundred and ninety-eight votes.

Judge Russell served his people in various offices with conspicuous ability and untiring energy. He was clerk of the city court of Savannah for nearly thirty-five years, and was chief of the fire department for many terms. A stanch and unflinching Democrat in politics, he always received the highest vote cast for his ticket whenever he was the party's nominee for official positions. He represented his party in numerous conventions, and was chairman of the committee which notified Alexander H. Stephens of his nomination for governor. His death, December 11, 1902, at the ripe old age of eighty-eight years, removed from the community one of its best loved and most revered citizens.

Judge Russell married first, September 15, 1834, Elizabeth C. Ferre, of Philadelphia, Pennsylvania, who died October 10, 1886. He married second, in 1889, Eliza P. Aneker, of Philadelphia, also. He was the father of eleven children.

Waring Russell, Jr., the son of Judge Philip M. and Elizabeth (Ferre) Russell, was brought up and educated in Savannah, attending first the public schools, and later the private school taught by Prof. James F. Cann. On January 19, 1878, he was appointed deputy sheriff of the city court of Savannah by David Bailey, Esq., sheriff of said court. An extract from the minutes of the city court says that on July 20, 1880, the resignation of Waring Russell, Jr., as deputy sheriff was accepted with deep regret—David Bailey, sheriff, and approved with regret—William D. Harden, judge.

Mr. Russell resigned the office of deputy sheriff to accept the position of justice of the peace of the third Georgia district, to which he had been elected, after a heated contest, in March, 1880. Through continuous re-election he held the office until January, 1899, when he was elected clerk of the city court of Savannah, a position which his father had previously held for thirty-five years. On November 5, 1899, by legislative enactment, this office was made elective by the people, instead of by the mayor and alderman as formerly. At the ensuing election, in May, 1900, Mr. Russell was elected to this office by the people, being the only successful candidate for official honors on his ticket at that election. He has been continuously elected every two years since, and in every election has led his ticket. A thoroughly competent and efficient man in every respect, Mr. Russell has invariably had the unqualified endorsement and support of practically every member of the bar at each election. Universally popular in Savannah, he thoroughly understands political conditions, and being plain spoken, open and frank, with never a thought of resorting to political chicanery, it is said of Mr. Russell that he can have any public office which he desires.

Mr. Russell married, in Savannah, Miss Georgia A. Mendel, and they have three children, namely: Thomas Sheftall Russell; Mrs. Frances M. Harper; and Mrs. Georgia C. Smith. Thomas Sheftall Russell was educated in the public schools of Savannah, and was graduated from the high school and Chatham Academy. Subsequently studying law, he was admitted to the bar, but has never engaged in the practice of his profession. For several years past he has been chief deputy clerk of the city court, serving under his father, and giving universal satisfaction in the position.

DR. JAMES PROCTOR SCREVEN. (Prepared by Thomas F. Screven.) Dr. James Proctor Screven was born October 11, 1799, near Bluffton, in St. Peter's Parish, now Beaufort county, South Carolina, and died July 16, 1859 at the Hot Springs in Virginia, where he had gone in the hope of restoration to good health after an illness which began some time in the fall of 1858; this illness was probably attributable to his ardent and energetic attention to the Atlantic and Gulf Railroad (now a part of the Atlantic Coast Line Railroad) of which he was the faithful and first president.

Dr. Screven was the oldest son of Major John Screven, born January 18, 1777, in South Carolina, Major of the Second Battalion of Militia at Savannah, Georgia, and a planter in South Carolina and Georgia; he died November 20, 1830, at Savannah, his then place of residence and was there buried; his wife was Hannah (Proctor) Screven, born January 8, 1778, in South Carolina, and killed with her son John Screven, (born August 4, 1803) in the great storm of September 8, 1804, on Wilmington island, Georgia, by the fall of the family residence.

Hannah (Proctor) Screven was the second daughter of Richard Proctor, born 1734 in Charleston, South Carolina, and said to have been the first male baptized at St. Philip's church at Charleston; he died April 26, 1817, at the age of eighty-three years, in Savannah, Georgia, at the residence of his son-in-law, Major John Screven, and interred near Bluffton, South Carolina; and his wife, Mary Ann (Vinson) Proctor, born February, 1752, and died in 1822. She was a daughter of George and Martha Vinson of South Carolina.

Richard Proctor was a son of Stephen Proctor of Charleston, South Carolina, and Hannah (Simons) Proctor, his wife, widow of John Royer, and a daughter of Benjamin and Mary (DuPré) Simons of South Carolina, and of French Huguenot descent.

Dr. Screven's grandfather, Lieutenant John Screven, was born November 23, 1750, on James island, South Carolina; he died September 2, 1801, and was buried at Montpelier which is located on the southern shore of May river, or the River of May, and nearly opposite Bluffton, South Carolina; Lieutenant John Screven moved from South Carolina to the St. John's Parish, afterward known as Liberty county, Georgia, where his brother, James Screven, resided and became a planter there; he is recorded as becoming Lieutenant in Capt. James Screven's company of St. John's Rangers, by the Council of Safety of the State, and as engaged in the issue in 1776 of paper money for that state.

Dr. Screven's grandmother was Elizabeth (Pendarvis) Bryan, born May 23, 1755; died April 5, 1804; widow of Josiah Bryan (son of Jonathan Bryan) daughter of Joseph Pendarvis, whose pioneer ancestor was Joseph Pendarvis, died in 1694, and Mary Bedon, daughter of Col. Richard Bedon, and descended from George Bedon who came over from England with the Sayle colony in 1670. Josiah Bryan and Elizabeth Pendarvis were married August 14, 1770; he died 1774, leaving one son, Joseph, who was born August 18, 1773; by Elizabeth (Pendarvis) Bryan's first marriage she had one son. Her marriage to Lieut. John Screven occurred January 13, 1776, and they had thirteen children.

Dr. Screven's great-grandfather was James Screven of James island, South Carolina, born 1609, son of Samuel Screven, who was a son of the Rev. William Screven, born in Somerton, England, about 1629, an immigrant to Kittery, Maine, removed to South Carolina about 1696 with his family consisting of his wife, Bridget (Cutt) Screven and children, and Baptist congregation; founded the first Baptist church as its minister and died on the site of Georgetown, South Carolina, in 1713 and is there buried.

Dr. Screven's great-grandmother was Mary (Smith) Screven, born 1717, died 1758, a daughter of the second Landgrave Thomas Smith of South Carolina, son of Thomas Smith of Exeter, England, born 1643, first landgrave and governor of South and North Carolina, and Barbara Smith, his wife. Mary (Smith) Screven's mother, Mary, was a daughter of Col. Edward Hyrne, of Norfolk, England, and of North Carolina, and his wife, Elizabeth (Massingbird) Hyrne. (A bible record of the Girardeau family).

Dr. Screven completed his grammar school education at Willington, near Abbeville, South Carolina, under the tuition of Dr. Moses Waddell, then celebrated as a successful instructor of youth, and who became president of Franklin College, afterward the University of Georgia, at Athens, Georgia. He then entered the South Carolina College at Columbia, South Carolina, and graduated in 1817 with honor. Returning to Savannah he studied medicine under Dr. Wm. R. Waring, one of the leading physicians. Upon the completion of that course he entered the University of Pennsylvania, in Philadelphia, where he graduated April 6, 1820, obtaining a medical diploma, also one from the Medical Society of Philadelphia, dated at the time of his appointment to honorary membership in that society. This society appears to have been founded in the year 1779. Upon the completion of his course at the University, at his father's desire he obtained a French passport, dated May 27, 1820, and left for London, England, where he studied at Guy's and St. Thomas' hospitals, Sir Astley Cooper being one of the surgeons who gave him a certificate, dated April 13, 1821, of his diligent attendance upon the practice of surgery and medicine, in Guy's and St. Thomas hospitals for six months last past. Then he went to Paris, France, still in the active pursuit of his profesional studies, but also to learn their cognate branches. He was also a pupil of the celebrated Cuvier, as well as of others, the most distinguished of the French Medical school. Here he mastered the French language and probably the Italian. He numbered LaFayette as one of his friends.

The remainder of Dr. Screven's stay in Europe, which occupied over two years, was spent in travel in Switzerland and Italy. In the latter country, the late Hon. George Bancroft, the historian, was his companion. His son, John Screven, wrote: "I have long used a copy of Horace belonging to my father, evidently a *vade mecum* with him, as it was copiously marked with his references to objects of interest mentioned by the poet, and indicated not only his habitual closeness of observation but that he definitely associated those objects with the careful and well-directed maintenance of his classical studies. He made full and conscientious use of his European experiences, both in his profession and in the sciences, which later had their earlier accepted development in that period,—that is, in the first quarter of the nineteenth century. Without professing to apply himself to the sciences otherwise than as a man of advanced intelligence, he devoted much time to geology, mineralogy, conchology, chemistry and comparative anatomy," so when he and Dr. Joseph C. Habersham learned of the discovery of the remains of a strange animal on the shore of Skidaway island in Chatham county, his knowledge of anatomy convinced him that the remains were that of a megatherium, and to congratulate himself that he had been a pupil of Cuvier. He delivered his views on this interesting subject before the Georgia Medical Society, of which he became a member in 1823. Some of these remains were sent to the Smithsonian Institution at Washington, D. C., but were destroyed when the original buildings were burned. Portions of these remains were given to the Georgia Historical Society some time after his death. Another instance of the value of his observations in Europe was his letter to the council of Savannah in August, 1823, upon the subject of dry culture as observed in the south of Europe, which was referred to a committee and reported as "well calculated to set the question of the utility of dry culture at rest" and "after six years have passed away the operation of the dry culture system, imperfectly as that system has been enforced, it has given evidence the most conclusive of a favorable influence upon the health of Savannah." A newspaper of the time, September 16, 1823, stated: "No dispassionate man, after reading it can longer doubt. By the friends of Dr. Screven, this letter must be received as a most satisfactory evidence of the manner in which he has appropriated the time he passed in Europe—to his community and the country, this letter gives a high promise of future usefulness. We cannot close our remarks without expressing our approbation of the manly, dignified and chaste style of the writer."

Dr. Screven began the practice of medicine in Savannah in 1822-3. He and his brother-in-law, Dr. Wm. C. Daniell, formed a partnership and on April 23, 1823, they issued a public notice to the effect of their having procured the building occupied as a poor house and hospital, and would open May 1st next for the medical treatment of sick seamen and negroes.

Dr. Screven was elected January 8, 1824, by council "the first health officer under the new method."

Dr. Screven was alderman from April 13, 1826 to September 11, 1826; from then to September 10, 1827, and again from December 4, 1828.

Dr. Screven was married December 26, 1826 by the Rev. Abiel Carter, rector of Christ church at Savannah, to Miss Hannah Georgia Bryan, born August 31, 1907, daughter of Joseph Bryan and Delia (Forman) Bryan, (died December 16, 1825), daughter of Gen. Thomas Marsh Forman, of Rose Hill, Cecil county, Maryland.

Joseph Bryan and Delia Forman were married April 9, 1805, at the residence of Judge Ezekiel Forman Chambers, (a relative of General Forman) at Chestertown, Maryland. Joseph Bryan was born August 18, 1773, son of Josiah Bryan, and died September 5, 1812, at his own home, Non Chalanee, Wilmington island, and there interred. He was several times a member of the state legislature and once a member of the United States congress.

It is said that Joseph Bryan's popularity was greatly increased in the state by his successful fight, unarmed, with a bear, which he killed. At a house in the country, he desired at night a bath in a horse-water trough near the premises, which the bear also inclined to. A contest for the bath ensued, in which he succeeded by his great strength and courage. He resigned in 1806 from the United States congress before his term expired.

The distinguished John Randolph, of Roanoke, of Virginia, his dearest and most intimate friend, wrote of him in an obituary notice: "The character of Mr. Bryan was every way original. He was himself and no one else at second hand. Educated in Europe, which quarter of the globe he again visited for improvement by travel. He was every way free from taint of foreign manner. He lived and died a Georgian. Soon after his last return from Europe he was elected to congress from his native state. He took no part in the debates of the house, but his zeal against the Yazoo claims was not surpassed by even that of his friend, General James Jackson himself. In the spring of 1806, after serving three sessions in congress, Mr. Bryan resigned his seat, in consequence, it is believed, of his marriage the preceding year, with a beautiful and amiable lady of the eastern shore of Maryland, who, (with five children), survive him. Congressional life is incompatible with domestic enjoyments.

"His dissolution was uncommonly rapid; but his spirit retained its vigor to the last. He made light of his disease, and a few days before his death invited an old friend to dine with him next Christmas. All his fortitude could not save him. His complaint was of the liver, with dropsy.

"In person Mr. Bryan might have served as a model to the statuary. He possessed wonderful strength and activity of body, united to undaunted resolution; but he was not more terrible than generous as an enemy. The brave are always generous. As a friend, he was above all price. His mind was of the first order—stored with various but desultory reading; for he read solely for his own amusement. His integrity was unimpeached and unimpeachable; his honor unsullied. Quick in his resentments, but easily appeased when injured, and equally ready to acknowledge an error when wrong, provided the appeal was made to his sense of justice; for he knew not fear; he was brave even to rashness, and his generosity bordered on profusion. Strange, wonderful man! Some fatality must have taken him from the sphere for which nature designed him, and he has left his friends to regret that his talents, integrity, honor, unbounded and unexampled 'courage should be so early lost to them.''

Josiah Bryan, born August 22, 1746, in South Carolina, died 1774 at Brampton, Georgia, married August 14, 1770, Elizabeth Pendarvis, was a son of Jonathan Bryan and Mary (Williamson) Bryan, who were married October 13, 1737. Mary (Williamson) Bryan was a daughter of John Williamson, of South Carolina, and Mary (Bower) Williamson. Mary (Bower) Williamson was a daughter of William Bower and Martha (Hext) Bower. The latter was a daughter of Hugh Hext. William Bower and Hugh Hext came together from England to South Carolina. Their descendants were numerous and allied with prominent families of the province and state.

Jonathan Bryan, born 1708 in South Carolina and died 1788 at Brampton, his place of residence near Savannah in Georgia, was a son of the pioneer ancestor, Joseph Bryan and Janet (Cochran) Bryan, a daughter of Hugh Cochran of South Carolina. Mr. Bryan assisted Gen. James Oglethorpe in the selection of the site upon which Savannah stands; was useful in the construction of the country road leading to Darien and Frederica, and in 1740, as lieutenant of a company of "Gentleman Volunteers," attended General Oglethorpe's expedition to capture St. Augustine in Florida.

Mr. Bryan moved in December, 1752, with his family, to Savannah, permanently. With a high standing in South Carolina, he soon became more prominent in Georgia: One of the king's council; one of the judges of the court of oyer and terminer and the general court; treasurer of the province; captain of a company of horse militia; prominent in the councils of the malcontents with the actions of the British government in regard to taxation, who desired and finally succeeded in a separation of the province and state from the control of that government; resigned from the king's council, because of its threat to expel him, whereupon the Union Society bestowed upon him a silver vase, a gift expressive of the society's appreciation of his devotion to the cause of his fellow citizens; member of the Council of Safety and Executive Council, at one time acting as president of the state; in January, 1779, captured with his son, James, by the British at his "Union" plantation, twelve miles north and west of Savannah, but on the northern shore of the Savannah river, both taken to New York and held there in close and severe imprisonment for more than two years; when exchanged they returned to Georgia or South Carolina. Mr. Bryan's last effort for the colonists was his fighting with General Wayne in the latter's victory over the British and Indians near Savannah in the last year of the war.

His daughter, Mary, widow of John Morel, married in 1784 Richard Wylly, a distinguished officer of the Revolution and member of the Society of the Cincinnati; and another daughter, Hannah, married John Houstoun, lawyer by profession, son of Sir Patrick Houstoun, and member of the congress of the states, governor of Georgia, 1778, first mayor (1791) of Savannah, again governor of the state, judge, etc.

General Thomas Marsh Forman, born August 20, 1758, died 1845 and buried at his residence, Rose Hill, Cecil county, Maryland, was a son of Ezekiel Forman and Augustine or Augustina (Marsh) Forman, born 1744, daughter of Thomas Marsh and Mary (Thompson) Marsh, who was a granddaughter of John Thompson and Judith (Herrman) Thompson, and great-granddaughter of Augustin Herrman and Janetia Herrman, daughter of Casper and Judith Varleth.

Thomas Marsh Forman joined Smallwood's regiment in the Revolution as a cadet, shortly before the battle of Long Island, New York; the next winter was commissioned lieutenant in the 11th Pennsylvania regiment; then becoming captain in his uncle David Forman's continental regiment; and in 1779 succeeded James Monroe as staff officer to Maj. Gen. Lord Sterling. He served in the legislature in 1790, 1792, and 1800, and during the bombardment of Fort McHenry, War of 1812, commanded a brigade of militia. In his will, he bequeathed his estate to his grandson, Thomas Marsh Forman Bryan, son of Joseph Bryan and Delia (Forman) Bryan, provided he changed his name to Thomas Marsh Forman, which was done by the legislature of Maryland.

General Forman was descended from Robert Forman "who was driven from England by the persecutions of Archbishop Laud, and took refuge in Holland. His name and that of his wife, Johanna, are enrolled upon the church register at Vlissingen, Holland, the English name being Flushing. On Long Island, New York, he was one of the incorporators of Flushing in 1645, which was then governed by the Dutch, but the incorporators were Englishmen. The charter at Albany has Robert's name spelled "Firman," but in all documents signed by him it is spelled "Forman." He moved to Hempstead, Long Island, incorporated November, 1645. His name appears among the forty-three signers of a letter to Governor Stuyvesant agreeing to pay the "tenths" demanded by the governor, if it can be shown that they are legally obliged to do so. On December 9, 1658, Governor Stuyvesant chose to be magistrates Richard Gildersleeve and Robert Forman. On May 12, 1664, Robert Forman was one of the two magistrates at Oyster Bay, then under New England jurisdiction. His will, dated February 7, 1670 (record of Oyster Bay), mentions his sons, Moses, Aaron and Samuel. His wife was Johanna as shown by deed dated June 9, 1665. He died in 1671. Aaron Forman moved to Monmouth county, New Jersey, April 11, 1693. His son Samuel married in 1667 or 1668 Mary Wilbur, daughter of Samuel Wilbur and Hannah Porter.

Ezekiel Forman, father of Gen. T. M. Forman and son of Joseph and Elizabeth Lee Forman, married first Augustine, or Augustina, Marsh, daughter of Thomas Marsh and Mary (Thompson) Marsh; the latter a granddaughter of John Thompson and Judith (Herrman) Thompson; the latter a daughter of Augustin Herrman and Janitia his wife, daughter of Casper and Judith Varleth.

Ezekiel Forman was commissioned high sheriff of Kent County, Maryland, January 14, 1776; appointed paymaster to the eastern shore marching militia; member of the Council of Safety of Maryland and died at his wilderness plantation four or five miles from Natchez, Mississippi, having journeyed down the Ohio and Mississippi rivers to this plantation to cultivate tobacco. He wrote an interesting narrative of this journey, which has been printed, a copy being in the possession of the writer of this paper.

Augustine Herrman, colonist, first in New Amsterdam, now New York, and next Lord of Bohemia Manor in Maryland; he acquired this title and large tract of land through his making a valuable map of Maryland and Virginia at a cost to him of ten thousand dollars or two hundred pounds, which was an important acquisition to Maryland, and thereby the grant of the title of Lord and the Bohemia Manor. He was born at Prague, Bohemia, and died on his manor in 1686; his father and mother were Augustin Ephraim Herrman and Beatrice, daughter of Casper Redel of Prague, a patrician family. A copy of the above mentioned map is in the possession of the writer of these papers, and the original map has been in the map department of the British Museum these many years.

To return to Dr. Screven: A monument committee, composed of John Shellman, John Stevens, William B. Bulloch, J. V. Bevan, R. W. Habersham, A. Porter, James P. Screven, William Gaston, Alexander Telfair, A. B. Fanin and J. Bond Read, was formed to erect monuments to General Green and the Count Pulaski; and on November 30, 1826, the state authorized a committee, of which Dr. Screven was a member, to institute a lottery by which to obtain funds for these monuments.

In 1834 there was cholera in Savannah, and in December, the state appropriated $15,000 to be used in a Lazaretto to be located at Savannah, and Dr. Screven was one of a committee to select a site. This committee reported, February 5, 1835, in favor of the extreme western point of Tybee island, which was on Lazaretto creek.

About 1835, Dr. Screven retired from the practice of medicine and with his family resided at Non Chalanee, Wilmington island, for the purpose of actively prosecuting his planting interests there as well as in South Carolina and in Georgia on the Savannah river. This he followed successfully, thereby gathering large profits, and if he chose, the position of a man at ease in this world's goods. His energy and mental endowment allowed but little ease. However, about 1847-8, he and his family moved back to Savannah, and it is found that he was an alderman in the 61st, 62nd, 63d and 64th administrations of the city, and mayor in the 67th administration.

As alderman, during the calamitous yellow fever of 1854, he sent his family to Non Chalanee, Wilmington island, remaining himself unmindful of the dread fever. At one time, September 21, 1854, he as acting mayor, and Mr. Alderman Mallory, were the only ones of the mayor and aldermen, who were able to care for the interests of the city. Fortunately the fever did not attack him. His greatest misfortune was after the fever had almost ceased, when on November 7, 1854, his son, James, was drowned in the river north of Non Chalanee, while endeavoring to swim ashore to safety with a young lady who was visiting the family.

During the period from 1850 to and including 1857, the improvements to the city were the acquirement of the Springfield plantation, purchased by Dr. Screven and turned over to the city of Savannah at the purchase price; the establishment of Laurel Grove cemetery; introduction of gas; the building of water works; building of the Savannah, Albany and Gulf and Atlantic and Gulf railroads (now the Atlantic Coast Line Railroad), of which Dr. Screven was president; introduction of a public school system. For this, see Gamble-Mayor Myers report, 1799-1900. In 1855, Dr. Screven visited New York, England and France and Holland to observe the methods for the supply and purification of water, which might apply for use at Savannah. During his absence and without his knowledge, he was elected senator to the legislature by his fellow citizens. As mayor of the city his administration met with general approbation.

Dr. Cosmo P. Richardsone, the popular captain of the Savannah Volunteer Guards (organized 1802), having died early in 1852, Dr. Screven was soon after elected their captain, which met with hearty appreciation, for with his accustomed energy and intelligence, he thoroughly fitted himself by sincere devotion. And so he demonstrated his capacity as a military leader and the Guards flourished. One instance of his fondness for the corps was his gift of several lots of land in the southern section of the city. It should be mentioned that in 1835, he volunteered, probably with the Guards, to serve in Florida, against the Indians. He resigned his command about 1857, when his son, John, succeeded him.

Dr. Screven having died in Virginia in July, 1859, his remains were, there temporarily interred, and on the 9th of April, 1860, they were brought to his late residence at the southwest corner of Congress and Abercorn streets in Savannah. On that day the mayor and aldermen met and adopted the following resolutions, introduced by Mr. Alderman Abraham Minis: "Whereas, it has pleased Almighty Providence to remove from our midst one of our most cherished citizens—one who has served this community most zealously, faithfully and creditably—one who never took a place that he did not fill, and one than whom Savannah had never a more true and loving son, for whose prosperity life itself was not too great a sacrifice.

"Dr. James P. Screven was useful and honorable among men; discharging many public duties, and among them the mayoralty of our city, and no one in that capacity has ever labored more zealously and successfully for her weal; it is therefore meet that as his remains are borne from afar, whence he breathed his last, to mingle with the sands he loved so well, that this council shall endeavor to pay all respect to so much departed worth.

"Be it therefore resolved, That the Mayor and Aldermen, accompanied by the officers of the council, will, in their official capacity, as a body attend the funeral ceremonies of the honored deceased.

"Be it further resolved, That a copy of these proceedings be furnished to the family of the deceased, and be published in the gazettes of the city."

The funeral was held on April 10, 1860, and the remains placed in the Screven vault in Laurel Grove cemetery.

In the Savannah *Republican* was published: "The characteristics of Dr. Screven were not only an acute and comprehensive intellect, but an energy and perseverance of industry, which made him anywhere and everywhere a man of mark."

It was also written of him: "He was an extraordinary man, fitted by physical and intellectual equipment to lead in affairs requiring great energy, resolution, devotion and judgment. The public and private confidence, enlisted through these eminent qualities, entitled him to the distinctions he actually attained, and to them would have been added the highest honors of the state had his life been prolonged."

COL. JOHN SCREVEN. (Prepared by Thomas F. Screven.) In presenting a memorial of Col. John Screven, and of such as he, an eloquent tribute to the Confederate dead by a contemporary may be appropriately used: "Yes, strew their graves with roses, for we loved them and they loved us and gave their lives for us. Sprinkle them with lilies, for their motives were pure and their shields bright and stainless as their honor. Scatter them with forget-me-nots, for they dwell forever in our hearts, unforgotten. Cover them with immortelles, for their deeds are immortal, and while the rains descend to beautify their graves, while the sunshine gilds bright their memorial stones, while a southern emotion or impulse exists, we shall never cease to love and honor them;" and so with John Screven, for he occupied a sphere of love and reverence in the hearts and minds of his fellow men who mourned when he was removed from their sight and companionship.

Born in Savannah, Georgia, September 18, 1827, the oldest child of Dr. James Proctor Screven and Hannah Georgia (Bryan) Screven, he imbibed the teachings of tender parents and these sentiments, when developed, displayed him a man among men,—a mind well balanced, educated in scholarly knowledge and refinement, and equipped with energy and capacity to fill almost any position of honor and trust.

One of his courses of education was at a school near Philadelphia; the next being at Bolmar's (who had been a soldier, in the army of Napoleon the Great) at or near Princeton, New Jersey, where he was an apt and appreciative scholar; then at Franklin College, later the University of Georgia. At Franklin College, in the sophomore class, he contested for the prize medal offered to the best elocutionist. He and one other student were adjudged the best, and there being but one medal, another was furnished and presented to him. He did not graduate at this college, for when on a vacation at home, the faculty invited him not to return. Yet in after years, he was appointed one of the board of trustees for this university. Upon his retirement from college his studies were directed by a competent tutor. He then studied law with Judge William Law, one of the distinguished lawyers of Savannah. Finishing the course in law, he began the practice. At his father's solicitations he closed his office and undertook to manage his large planting interests. This he followed with unbounded energy, intelligence and success. He introduced rollers for crushing plowed land, rice plows and a rice sowing machine, which were valuable in the preparation of rice lands for cultivation and in the sowing of seed.

In the year 1847, Colonel Screven went to Europe, and meeting the Hon. George Bancroft in London, he was advised to begin his studies at Heidelberg. After a few months, his health not being good and a longing for home possessing him, he returned to Savannah to resume planting. In 1849 he married the beautiful and lovely in character Mary White Footman, a daughter of Dr. Richard and Mary Constance (Maxwell) Footman, a daughter of Benjamin and Mary (Habersham) Maxwell, a daughter of James and Hester (Wylly) Habersham, a sister of Col. Richard Wylly and daughter of Alexander Wylly. James Habersham was a son of Hon. James Habersham (a native of England, immigrant to the province of Georgia and who held many high and important offices in Georgia) and his wife Mary (Bolton) Habersham.

Colonel Screven's second marriage was to Mary Eleanor (Nesbit) Browne, widow of Col. Thomas Browne (colonel of Second Alabama Regiment of Cavalry, and killed at Murfreesboro), and daughter of Hugh O'Kiefe Nesbit of Macon, Georgia. She died in 1883. Colonel Screven had seven children by his first marriage and two by the second. Three children of the first marriage survived him, but two of these soon followed. One child of the second marriage survived him, and she died soon afterward, but there are descendants in the first, second and third generations.

Colonel Screven was elected, in 1858, captain of the Savannah Volunteer Guards. He was wonderfully successful in this command, the guards largely increasing in numbers and skill in the military exercises, and in popularity. They soon purchased a suitable building and lot for an armory on the corner of York and Bull streets. When General Sherman and his troops occupied Savannah, this building was burned. On January 3, 1861, Hon. Joseph E. Brown, governor of Georgia, as a precaution, ordered the seizure of Fort Pulaski at the mouth of the Savannah river. A detachment of the guards, under Captain Screven's command, the Oglethorpe Light Infantry, Capt. F. S. Bartow and the Chatham Artillery were sent to carry out the order and the fort was seized and occupied. The guards performed service at several periods during the months of January and February, 1861. Their next service under Captain Screven, clothed in Confederate gray (they were the first military companies to adopt the gray uniform) was in the Confederate states' service for sixty days, April and May, 1861, at a battery at Thunderbolt, Chatham county; the second term of service was for six months at Fort Screven and Battery Stiles on Green island, both under the command of Captain Screven. The third enlistment as the Savannah Volunteer Guards Battalion, in 1863, designated as the Eighteenth Georgia Battalion, of three companies, A, B and C, was on March 1, 1862, for three years, or the war. Captain Screven was elected major, but served only as acting such, not being commissioned by the state, but shortly after a commission was issued to him as major of artillery by the Confederate government. During this enlistment he was frequently absent from his command, having an additional duty imposed upon him by the authorities in supervising obstructions in the Savannah river by means of sunken cribs loaded with stone or brick; but he was permanently detached in December, 1862, from the command to take charge of the Atlantic & Gulf Railroad for the better transportation of government supplies and troops. Upon General Sherman's approach to Savannah in December, 1864, Colonel Screven, with the equipments of the Atlantic & Gulf Railroad, left the city for southwest Georgia, and, at Way's Station, in Bryan county, narrowly escaped capture by that general's troops, who were marching on Fort McAllister. Colonel Screven returned to Savannah in May, 1865. It was in 1864 that his services were required in Savannah in the work of raising troops. Succeeding with five companies, he was commissioned a lieutenant-colonel, and thence his title of colonel. The command of the Savannah Volunteer Guards fell to Capt. William S. Basinger of Company A, he being the senior officer. After the war, in 1872, he, Major Basinger, was elected major of the battalion of the Savannah Volunteer Guards and served for about ten years, after which he resigned, when the corps desired Colonel Screven to accept the command, but he declined the honor.

In 1859 Colonel Screven succeeded his father in the presidency of the Atlantic & Gulf Railroad. After the war between the Confederate states and the United States, he was retained in the presidency for many years, encountering serious difficulties in the management and maintenance of the road in consequence of the costs of its restoration of the roadbed and the poverty of the contiguous country, which indeed were largely attributable to the results of the war and course pursued by the victors. The company having gone into bankruptcy, he was retained as receiver. It was finally sold and was called the Savannah, Florida & Western Railway, now the Atlantic Coast Line.

Colonel Screven was elected the mayor of Savannah to serve during administrative periods from 1869 to 1873, but resigned before the expiration of the last period. In the election to that office in 1869, he represented the Democratic party of the city and was opposed by the Republican party. He received a majority of 2,010 votes over his opponent. Upon this result there was great rejoicing, evidenced by a grand parade of citizens bearing banners. Whilst mayor he was charged with mal-administration of the affairs of the Atlantic & Gulf Railroad, but at a meeting of the stockholders, he was re-elected president, and at a later public meeting of stockholders and citizens he was honorably exonerated from these charges. His administrative abilities and resolution were markedly judicious. An instance was while mayor of the city, during the regime of Aaron Alperio Bradley, the leader of the Republican negroes and carpet baggers, when anticipating the seizure by this class of the polls at an election to be soon held, he notified the volunteer companies of the city to be ready, sent to New York for a rapid fire gun, requested the aid of the authorities at Washington, D. C., and sending for one of the leaders of the white Republicans informed him that he would be the first one shot if any such action occurred. The white leader left Savannah that night and no disturbance occurred at the polls.

On March 11, 1873, Colonel Screven was persented with a handsome gift, upon which was inscribed: "Hon. John Screven, mayor of Savannah, 1869-1873. A token of esteem and affection from the Savannah Police Department, March 11, 1873."

Having been relieved of his railroad duties upon the sale of the Atlantic & Gulf Railroad, he was chosen an associate arbitrator of the Southern Railway & Steamship Association, and as such served with distinguished credit and approval.

He was the first president of the Sons of the Revolution, a member of the Jasper Monumental Association, president of the board of trustees of the Chatham Academy, member and third vice-president of the Confederate Veteran's Association, Camp 756, president of the Georgia Historical Society, trustee of the University of Georgia, member of the board of education, member of the legislature, 1859-60, judge of the inferior court of Chatham county from 1852, honorary member of the Savannah Volunteer Guards, commissioner on the construction of the state capitol at Atlanta, Georgia, member of the Savannah Benevolent Association, member of the Drainage Commission, 1877. In the yellow fever epidemic of 1876, "he rendered fearless, devoted and noble service." His oldest son, James Proctor Screven, died of this disease. Col. Screven was attacked, but recovered, having remained in the city to attend to his railroad duties.

Col. Screven's last public effort was in the fall of 1899, when an executive committee, of which he was chairman, made complete preparations for the reunion of the Georgia division of the United Confederate Veterans to be held in Savannah on November 22, 23, and 24, 1899. This was a notable event and was attended by numerous Veterans and Daughters of the Confederacy with their distinguished guests. On this occasion he delivered an address of welcome.

Col. Screven was an excellent presiding officer at meetings of clubs, associations, committees, and popular assemblies, for he understood parliamentary law and its application. In conversation, his charm of manner and his diction made him most entertaining. He was not given to story-telling. As an orator he had but few equals. As a writer he was lucid and cultivated. His mind was a storehouse of varied and valuable information acquired from youth to old age. In height he was about five feet ten and a half inches, slender in build, graceful in his movements, ever polite, easily approached, and kind and generous in all ways.

The following is copied from the report of the committee of the Georgia Historical Society on the death of Col. Screven, which occurred on January 9, 1900; the committeemen were members of the society: Col. George A. Mercer, Dr. R. J. Nunn, Judge Robert Falligant, B. A. Denmark, Esq., and J. R. Saussy, Esq.

"At the date of his decease he was president of the University Club of Savannah, president of the board of trustees of Chatham Academy, president of the Society of the Sons of the American Revolution and president of the Georgia Historical Society. It is to the dignified, able, and efficient discharge of the important functions of this last high office that your committee more particularly seek to pay merited tribute.

"Col. Screven was elected a member of our society on the 10th day of March, 1851. He was chosen a curator February 13, 1888. At the last date he was elected second vice-president and first vice-president on February 12, 1889. On June 16, 1898, upon the death of our then lamented president, the distinguished Henry R. Jackson, he was unanimously chosen president of the society, and filled the office up to the day of his death. For this position he was eminently fitted both by character and training. His conduct as man and officer was a model to all observers; his deportment was suave and winning; and his literary ability and culture, his love of art, his sympathy with every proper expression of beauty, were pronounced and abiding. One of the strongest qualifications he held for the position was his becoming attention to details. He fully appreciated the value of minutiæ and did not consider it the mark of a strong mind to neglect little things. While he accepted the rules which Shakespeare announced through the mouth of Lepidus that 'small to great matters must give way,' he did so with the frequent qualification of Enorbarbus, 'not if the small come first.' He knew that compacted grains of sand often make a surer foundation than mighty blocks of stone. In fine, he obeyed the injunction of the Apostle, and did all things, both great and small, at all times and in all places, decently and in order.

"Col. Screven was one of the last links left that bound us to a generation less materialized, less selfish and money loving, and in many respects possessing more high tones than our own. He belonged to that class of men who help to punctuate a cycle, and the bloom of whose life and character adorns a generation. He was always considerate and conciliating. His voice, like Cadelia's, was soft, gentle and low, and he was too refined a gentleman to be ever noisily demonstrative or otherwise. He was a very rare combination of the *fortiter in re* with the *suaviter in modo*. He always wore upon the iron hand the velvet glove. To the abounding virility of the strong man he united the gentle courtesy of the refined and delicate woman. The very atmosphere that he exhaled was redolent of his goodness and spread the pure contagion of his life and purpose. It was impossible to come within the sphere of his influence without feeling a sense of betterment, and realizing a consciousness of elevation. He was indeed a knight without fear and without reproach. What better can be said of him than that he was always a perfect southern gentleman, and at a period when to reach such an ideal was to be a little lower than the angels.

"Happy Historical Society to have numbered among its guides such noble characters, and to have been able to diffuse its divine purposes through the influences and example of such pure and lofty example! Be it therefore

"Resolved, 1st, That in the death of Col. John Screven the Georgia Historical Society has lost a most faithful and accomplished presiding officer, a wise counsellor, and a cherished and lamented friend.

"2d. That the city of Savannah has lost one of her most public spirited and useful citizens, who occupied a large place at every state of its progress, and in all its advancements, charities, and amenities was ever foremost.

"3d. That a certified copy of these proceedings be sent to the family of the deceased with the profoundest sympathy of the Society.

"4th. That they be spread upon the minutes of the Society upon pages specially set apart for that purpose.

"5th. That the chair of the late president be draped in mourning for a period of sixty days."

Hon. Robert Falligant, for the committee appointed by the board of managers to prepare suitable resolutions touching the death of President John Screven, made the following report which was ordered to be spread upon the minutes:

"Col. John Screven, Sons of the Revolution. A Minute.

"In common with many organizations of the city, civil and military, our Society mourns the loss of a distinguished son and a devoted president in the death of Col. John Screven. So broad and catholic was the spirit, so many and versatile were the gifts, so deep and profound the interest of Colonel Screven, that he touched the life of the city at every point, and while health and strength continued he never ceased to give himself and of the brilliant personality he possessed to the welfare of every institution that tended to broaden and enrich our communal life. And thus, as the municipality of Savannah mourns in his death the loss of one who filled with highest honor the office of chief executive; as the veterans of the past and the Volunteer Guards of the present stood together around his grave to testify to the fearless soldier in times of war and the wise counselor in times of peace; as state and city both remember with gratitude the illustrious statesman who reflected honor to the name of Georgia; so it seems good to us, his associates in the Society of the Sons of the Revolution, to enter this minute of respect and admiration upon the pages of our record. To us, in the more limited sphere of usefulness, as he was to others in the broader sphere of life's activities, Col. Screven was always the wise counselor, the helpful friend, the judicious manager of the patriotic interests of our Society. Himself the descendant of a long line of distinguished ancestry, he was particularly fitted to kindle and preserve a live interest in the deeds of the heroic men of the early days of our country. Possessing a fund of historic lore, well versed in the history of his native state, with a mind enriched by varied reading, it seemed to him—and through him to us—a duty to keep alive, by this Society the memory of the men whose wise statesmanship established, and whose blood cemented, the original Union of the States.

"A country gentleman of the old South! No better title can adorn his brow. Of all the crowns which eloquence, statesmanship, and chivalry have placed there, none did he wear with greater grace or with more perfect ease, for that title was his by heredity and his own developed culture. Standing before the young men of this generation they saw what type it was of grace and manhood—manly courage and womanly tenderness—that of the old South, at its very best, could produce for the inspiration of her sons and for the admiration of the world! As the shadows came out of the skies and fell upon his sleeping place, we seem to feel the historian's words of old: 'They buried him among the kings,' and with them came the poet's interpretation of them:

> " 'Yes, lay him down where sleep the royal dead,
> His steady hand no more the censer swings;
> Room for this man beside the bones of kings,
> For kingly was he, tho' uncrowned they said.
> Great hearted friend, thee, too, we counted bred
> For manhood, loftier than the tardy wings
> Of souls content with songs the caged bird sings
> Are wont to soar to. Thine it was to wed
> Far sundered thoughts in amity complete—
> With Christ's own freedom fettered minds to free;
> To thread the darkling patter where timid feet
> Faltered and slipped. Oh, it was not in thee
> To blanch at any peril! Then most meet
> That thou amidst the kings should buried be.'

"In sense of the loss this Society has sustained, in admiration of the character he bore,

"Resolved, that the secretary inscribe upon our minutes this testimonial to our late president, Col. John Screven; and to his family extend the profound sympathy of this Society in their bereavement—a loss to them too deep for words, and to us so great that our words do but feebly represent the sentiment of our hearts.

"R. FALLIGANT,
"CHARLES H. STRONG,
"POPE BARROW,
"Committee."

The following memorials and tributes are introduced to still further show how profoundly the death of Col. John Screven was felt by his friends and associates:

"Memorial and Tribute
to
Col. John Screven.
At Confederate Hall, February 6, 1900.

"The meeting was presided over by the newly elected president, Robert Falligant. Immediately after the meeting was called to order First Vice-President Louis G. Young moved to dispose of the reading of the minutes and the regular order of business.

"'At our last monthly meeting,' he said, 'there was one with us whom we loved to see here; his presence was a benediction, and we thought to have him with us many years, so we elected him to office, and we expected him to answer to the roll-call tonight, but our eyes were darkened; we could not see that his last was a farewell visit. Early in the morning of the ninth of last month the Great Captain called him and we can imagine his soldiery adsum as he joined the ranks of the hosts beyond the sky. John Screven, late lieutenant colonel in the provisional army of the Confederate states, is not here with us in the flesh tonight; they tell us he is dead, but as he lives in our hearts and is present in our thoughts, it is meet that we do homage to his memory.

"'I therefore move that the minutes of the last meeting and the regular business of this, be dispensed with, and that a committee of three be appointed by the chair to prepare a memorial and draft resolutions in commemoration of the death of our comrade and late third vice-president, Col. John Screven, the same to be presented and acted on at this meeting.'

"In seconding the motion Capt. M. P. Usina took occasion to introduce the response received by the executive committee of the reunion, of which he was a member with Colonel Screven, from the members of the family, of the deceased, replying to the action taken by the committee as follows:

"'The executive committee, Confederate Reunion: Gentlemen: The daughters and son of Col. John Screven thank you individually and collectively for your beautiful tribute to the memory of their father, and they beg that you will extend their thanks to the Confederate Veterans Association of Savannah for their presence at his funeral. He often spoke in the highest terms of the members of your committee, and he was exceedingly proud that he had the good fortune of being a member of your committee and of the association. It is most gratifying to them that he was held in such high esteem by yourselves and by the veterans, the memory of which they trust will ever be to them a pleasure and a joy.'

"Captain Usina also read a letter received by the members of Colonel Screven's family from Col. Thomas H. Carter, proctor and superintendent of grounds and buildings of the University of Virginia. Colonel Carter was a colonel of artillery in the Army of Northern Virginia. For a number of years he was associated with Colonel Screven as a member of the board of arbitration of the Southern Railway and Steamship Association. Colonel Carter wrote his letter to the family just after reading the announcement of Colonel Screven's death. In his letter he says: 'For sixteen years your father and myself stood together in the closest and most confidential bonds of friendship. His was the closest friendship formed by me since the days of my youth. In an acquaintance with a long line of men of the highest character, I never knew a nature more chivalrous, an honor more spotlessly bright, a sense of justice that more truly and bravely sought the right. As the needle with unerring instinct points to the pole, so his mind, by intuition, turned always to the truth. In arbitration, the most difficult, delicate and responsible, involving interests incalculable, he was ever true to the right, and as steady and brave as a veteran of a hundred fields. I esteem it one of the greatest privileges of my life to have known intimately a man so pure, noble and cultured, and can say in all sincerity that the earth that bears him dead bears not alive a truer gentleman.'

"Mr. Young's motion that the regular order of business be dispensed with and that the chair appoint a committee of three to prepare a suitable memorial to the late vice-president was unanimously adopted. The chair appointed Vice-President Young and Comrades Pope Barrow and J. R. Saussy. A short recess was taken while the committee prepared its report. When the meeting was again called to order the report was submitted by Vice-President Young as follows:

In Memoriam.
John Screven.
Born in Savannah, Georgia, Sept. 18, 1827.
Died in Savannah, Georgia,
January 9, 1900.

"His first American ancestor, the Rev. William Screven, emigrated from England in 1640, and located in Kittery, Maine, from which place, driven by persecution, he went to South Carolina, where he settled and founded the illustrious family from which sprung in due time the knightly comrade whose death we mourn.

"Colonel Screven was the eldest son of Dr. James Proctor Screven, and Hannah Georgia Bryan—his father an eminent physician and one of the leading men of the city and state; his mother a lineal descendant of Jonathan Bryan, one of the most prominent of the early settlers of the Colony of Georgia. Inheriting the intellectual and moral qualities which adorned generation after generation of his family, and which have made it conspicuous in public and private life, Colonel Screven, from youth to old age added lustre to the goodly name he bore. Studious and dutiful as a boy, he grew in knowledge, was educated with the best advantages, and, endowed with the nobility of soul which readily assimilated the refinement and virtues of a cultivated home, wherein dwelt all gentle, Christian virtue, he commenced life thoroughly equipped for the career of usefulness and honor which lay before him. Appreciating from the start the duty which he owed to God and his fellow men, he lived a faithful servant of both, and died as he had lived, in favor with God and man.

"Colonel Screven's was an active, useful life, surpassing in measure that of most men. Faithful and conscientious in the performance of his several callings, he was always ready to serve family, friend, city, country; and many and various were the places of honor and trust to which he was called. But the record of these is beyond the scope of this memorial. To the biographer must be left the details of a life replete with incident, and forming so important a part in the history of Savannah, that she must ever number him among the foremost and most illustrious of her sons. Ours the privilege as Confederate veterans to make mention of his services in the sacred cause for which we fought, the object of which is to sustain a principle,—the broad principle of constitutional liberty,—the right of self-government. Ours the part to recall his virtues,—to turn to them for consolation and example and to hold them up for the emulation of our youth.

"The simple account of Colonel Screven's record as a soldier, sanctioned by himself, runs thus: 'In 1858 he was elected captain of the Savannah Volunteer Guards, and his was one of the three companies designated to occupy Fort Pulaski, when it was seized by order of Governor Brown in the name of the state of Georgia, January 3, 1861. Although president of the Atlantic and Gulf Railway during this period, he was appointed Major of Artillery in the Confederate Provisional Army, and continued to serve with his command until December, 1862, when he was ordered by the commanding general to resume his railroad duties. In 1864, when Sherman commenced his movement towards the coast, Major Screven raised a local battalion of five companies to aid in the defense of Savannah, and was promoted to the rank of lieutenant colonel.' Thus was Colonel Screven active in war service, even before the Confederacy came into existence, and although but a short time in the field, always held commissions in the army, and left the field only at the call to more arduous and trying duties; if in a less conspicuous sphere, yet one in which he could serve his country to most advantage.

"The war ended, Colonel Screven took up the thread of life where it had been broken, and from that time to the close of an eventful and checkered career, so bore himself in public and private life that he has left to us the legacy of a spotless name. Upright in heart and mien, with nobility of soul stamped upon his face, he walked among us, the height of chaste thoughts so beaming from his countenance that men turned to look upon him and to gather inspiration to follow in his footsteps. No one could hold intercourse with him without feeling that: 'Here is a gentleman in whom I have an absolute trust.'

" 'He was a Christian, in faith, hope and charity;
An Israelite, indeed, in whom there is no guile.
A Knight in Chivalric,
Treuthe and honour, freedom and courtesie.'

"A gentleman! And 'what is it to be a gentleman? Is it to have lofty aims? to lead a pure life? to keep your honor virgin? to have the esteem of your fellow citizens and the love of your fireside? to bear good fortune meekly? to suffer evil with constancy? and through evil or good to maintain in truth always? Show me that happy man whose life exhibits these qualities, and him we salute as a gentleman.'

"Thus was he,
" 'And indeed he seems to me
Scarce other than my ideal knight,
Who reverenced his conscience and his king
Whose glory was redressing human wrong,
Who spake no slander, no, nor listened to it.
We have lost him, he is gone.

> We know him now; all narrow jealousies
> Are silent, and we see him as he moves,
> How modest, kindly, all-accomplished, wise;
> With what sublime repression of himself,
> And what limits and how tenderly;
> Not swaying to this faction or that;
> Not making his high place the lawless perch
> Of wing'd ambitions, nor a vantage ground
> For pleasure; but through all this track of years,
> Wearing the white flower of a blameless life.'

"Therefore, be it resolved, That in the death of John Screven, who was our third vice-president, our comrade, and one of the most devoted of our members to the sacred cause we represent, our association finds cause to mourn.

"That in contemplating his worth, his many virtues, and princely character, we find cause for gratitude and consolation in our grief.

"That in these times when our youth are misled by the teachings which measure success by the gain of money, we point them to an example of a life whose success lay in its wealth of honor, and truth and piety.

"That with a copy of these resolutions we extend to his family the heartfelt sympathy of the association."

In seconding the motion to accept the resolutions, Mr. Barrow said that he seemed to see again the slender, graceful form and gentle face which had been so familiar on the streets of Savannah. Mr. Barrow spoke from the long personal acquaintance and friendship with the deceased. He spoke especially of his grace and charm of manner, and said he never spoke a word or did an act that was unbecoming. His words and acts always seemed to suit the occasion. It was the nature of the man to act the gentleman. The sad feature of Colonel Screven's life, Mr. Barrow said, had been that his last days were not his best days. As he declined in years misfortunes had crowded upon him and he had been troubled with many cares. Mr. Barrow gave a tender and sympathetic account of his last visit to his deceased friend only two days before his death.

General McGlashan said that he had known Colonel Screven but a comparatively short time, but his strong individuality, his marked dignity of character and his purity of soul had drawn him strongly to him. He had been more strongly drawn to Colonel Screven, he said, during his association with him as a member of the joint executive committee, while the preparations for the recent reunion were in progress, the success of which had been largely due to the unceasing efforts, the wise judgment and the constant attention to details of the deceased. It was Colonel Screven who smoothed over all differences, preserved harmony and kept attention constantly centered upon their work. "Like his great prototype," said General McGlashan, "he was a man who drew all men to him. His heightened manner of looking at everything elevated us all. Colonel Screven was a man who typified in himself the highest type of a Georgia gentleman. In other words, he was a citizen of the first rank of the greatest nation on earth. In his death we have lost a warm, sincere, patriotic comrade, an officer who would have guided us wisely; a warm friend whose grasp was ever true; a Confederate whose heart was ever warm to the cause and whose effort since the struggle ended was ever to dignify the name of the Confederate soldier."

Mr. Saussy spoke of the galaxy of distinguished men who had

James P. Screven

been members of the association, but who had since become members of the great army beyond, among them the sturdy Lawton, the fiery Jackson and the brave McLaws. Among them all there was no man who filled so much the measure of a man as Colonel Screven. He was first of all a perfect gentleman, with an ease of manner which made it always a pleasure to be with him. Being possessed of unusual advantages in youth, he had made good use of these, becoming possessed of many accomplishments. He was thus fitted for the offices he had held, all of which he had discharged honorably and well. The reverses of later life had only served to bring out the strength and nobility of his character. His was a remarkably well-rounded character. Whatsoever things were true, honorable, just, pure and beautiful,—these were characteristics of him. Having lived a life worthy in all its parts that made man in the image of his Maker, he was able to gather the drapery of his couch about him and lie down to pleasant dreams.

Judge Falligant said that he could not allow the opportunity to pass without saying a word of tribute to the memory of one who was so highly esteemed by all. It had been peculiarly characteristic of the cause and the principle for which they had fought, he said, that the men who had stood up for this cause had been of the loftiest type of manhood. It was not necessary to run over the list of noble names embalmed in every southern heart. Of this type had been the man to whose memory they paid merited tribute. It is a type of civilization which is fast passing away and one never to be renewed in the history of the world. Judge Falligant closed with the idea that in the great moral world there is no death. While mortal frames perish, the moral truths which they have exemplified live on to exercise influence over the world of life.

The resolutions were then unanimously adopted and a copy ordered to be spread upon the minutes. Those members who did not make remarks gave their hearty endorsement to what had been said. It was a remarkable tribute to one who had so recently passed from their midst and to whom those present seemed to feel they were but rendering his just due.

CAPT. THOMAS F. SCREVEN. Distinguished not only as a splendid representative of the native-born citizens of Savannah, his birth having occurred in this city April 19, 1834, but for his honorable record as a brave and efficient soldier, and for the very efficient and creditable manner in which he is filling his present position as sheriff of Chatham county. He comes of honored pioneer stock, being a son of James Proctor and Hannah Georgia (Bryan) Screven, of whom an account may be found on another page of this volume.

Beginning his early studies at home, under the instruction of a private tutor in the family, Thomas F. Screven afterwards attended Miss Church's school and the Chatham Academy, in Savannah, and then entered Franklin College, now the University of Georgia, from which he was graduated with the class of 1852. For a short time thereafter he was engaged in mercantile pursuits in Savannah, but gave up his position in order to take up the study of medicine with Dr. R. D. Arnold. Finding that to his liking, he continued his studies at the old Savannah Medical College, where he was graduated in 1858. Subsequently his father sent him abroad, but after being in Europe but six months he was forced to return to Savannah on account of the ill health of his father. In caring for his father, Captain Screven subsequently traveled with him a good deal in those days, and never took up permanently the practice of medicine, although his professional knowledge was most usefully applied in treating the various ailments of the negroes belonging to the Screven family.

In 1852 Captain Screven had joined the Savannah Volunteer Guards, of which he was still a member when the dark clouds of war began to hover over the country. Following the secession of South Carolina from the Union, Governor Brown resolved to take possession of the forts and barracks on Georgia soil, a wise decision as subsequent events proved. Under his order to that effect, Colonel Lawton, of the First Volunteer Regiment, took fifty men of the Savannah Volunteer Guards (which were then commanded by Mr. Screven's brother, the late Col. James Screven, then captain), also taking a detachment from the Oglethorpe Light Infantry, and from the Chatham Artillery, and, on January 3, 1861, seized Fort Pulaski. Mr. Screven, who had assisted in the taking of the fort, was made second lieutenant junior of Company B, Savannah Volunteer Guards, on February 25, 1861. In March, 1862, he was commissioned first lieutenant of company A. S. V. G., and on May 10, 1863, was promoted to captain of said company, a position which he filled bravely and well until the end of the war, the Savannah Volunteer Guards having been organized as the Eighteenth Georgia Battalion, which served throughout the war with distinction.

Captain Screven's service was in Georgia, South Carolina, and Virginia. With his company he served for a time under fire of the terrible bombardment of Battery Wagner (Charleston Harbor). Going with his command to Virginia in May, 1864, he joined Lee's Army, and was stationed at Mattoax, on the Richmond & Danville Railroad. In October, 1864, the Captain went with the battalion to join the forces of the Richmond lines, and was there stationed at Chafin's farm. In April, 1865, Captain Screven returned to Georgia on a furlough, and on May 1, of that year, received his parol at Augusta.

For some time after the war, Captain Screven was engaged in agricultural pursuits on the Screven plantation, in Chatham county, but for many years past he has resided in Savannah, an honored and respected citizen. For a long while after the war the captain remained a member of the Savannah Volunteer Guards, serving as captain of Company B from 1872 until 1883. On retiring from the captaincy of the company, its members presented him with a beautiful silver set, and resolutions expressing their high regard for him, and their regret at his leaving them. On February 7, 1888, Captain Screven became a member of Camp No. 756, United Confederate Veterans. In 1906 the captain was elected sheriff of Chatham county, and has since filled the position with credit to himself and to the great acceptation of all concerned.

Captain Screven married first, in 1860, Miss Adelaide Van Dyke Moore, a daughter of Dr. R. D. and Elizabeth (Stockton) Moore, and granddaughter of Maj. Thomas Stockton, who served as major in the United States army, and at the time of his death was governor of Maryland. She passed to the life beyond in 1864. In 1866 the captain married for his second wife Miss Sallie Lloyd Buchanan, a daughter of Admiral Franklin and Ann Catherine (Lloyd) Buchanan, her father having been first a member of the United States Navy, and later of the Confederate States Navy.

CAPT. FRANCIS D. BLOODWORTH, vice-president of the National Bank of Savannah, and in many ways identified with the city's activities, is a native of the Empire State of the South.

It was in Spalding county, Georgia, October 16, 1842, that Francis D. Bloodworth was born, son of Solomon W. and Lucy (Thornton) Bloodworth, both natives of this state. He completed his education in

Marshall College, Griffin, Georgia, where he was a member of the Spalding Grays, one of the companies which were ordered to Virginia' by Governor Brown in April, 1861, upon the call of Governor Letcher of Virginia. They were sent to Norfolk to guard the stores abandoned by the enemy, and, with the other Georgia companies that went at the same time, were organized as the Second Independent Georgia Battalion, under the command of Colonel Hardeman, being the first troops from another state to arrive in Virginia. After a year's service in the vicinity of Norfolk, his battalion joined the army under General Lee, and participated in the Seven Days' battle around Richmond, and in the Manassas, Maryland and Fredericksburg campaigns. In the summer of 1863, Mr. Bloodworth, who had risen to the rank of first sergeant of his company, was detailed, owing to his physical condition, as clerk in a hospital in Atlanta, where he was on duty until January, 1864. Then he returned to his battalion in Gen. Ambrose R. Wright's brigade, Anderson's division, Gen. A. P. Hill's corps, Army of Northern Virginia, and fought through the Wilderness campaign. His health failed under this arduous service, and he was again disabled from active service until February, 1865, when he joined his command on the Petersburg lines. His last engagement was a fight between High Bridge and Farmville on the retreat to Appomattox, April 7, 1865, when he was slightly wounded, and captured. He was paroled at Burkesville, Virginia, shortly after General Lee's surrender, and returned to Griffin, Georgia.

Captain Bloodworth resided at Griffin until 1871, when he removed to Savannah and embarked in business as a commission merchant. And here he has since made his home, with the exception of two years, from 1893 to 1895, when he was engaged in manufacturing at Atlanta, and since 1895 he had held the important and responsible position of cashier and vice-president of the National Bank of Savannah, one of the strongest banking institutions of the state. This bank has a capital stock of $400,000, with surplus and undivided profits in excess of $600,000.

At the time of his leaving Savannah for Atlanta in 1893, Captain Bloodworth was vice-president of the Confederate Veterans' Association, a director of the Merchants National Bank, and a member of the sanitary board of the city of Savannah. And previous to that time he had served one term as president of the Cotton Exchange. Since then he served one term as president of the Georgia State Bankers' Association, and for several years, ending in 1911, he was president of the Savannah Clearing House Association. He is vice-president of the Savannah Port Society and a director of the Savannah Cotton Exchange. For a number of years he was an active member of the Georgia Hussars. Among other organizations of a social or business nature with which he is identified are the Oglethorpe Club, the Golf Club, the Yacht Club, the B. P. & T. Club and the Capital City Club of Atlanta.

Captain and Mrs. Bloodworth have two children: Lucy, wife of Mr. H. P. Inabnett of Tampa, Florida, and Effie, wife of Mr. F. M. Butler of Savannah. Mrs. Bloodworth, formerly Miss Sarah Allen, was born in Meriwether county, Georgia.

CAPT. FRANCIS P. MCINTIRE. This distinguished young citizen of Savannah is conspicuous in the affairs of this section of the state for three reasons. In the first place he is prominent in the military affairs of the state; in the second he is one of the standard-bearers of the Democratic party and holds the office of chairman of the executive committee of the same; in the third he is one of the ablest and most promising of Savannah lawyers, in his comparatively brief career having been connected with much important litigation and having earned the respect of bench and bar alike.

Captain McIntire was born in Savannah July 22, 1881, the son of James W. and Katherine (Foley) McIntire. The father, who is living in Savannah, is also a native of this city and a son of the late James McIntire, who when a small boy came from his native country, the north of Ireland, to Savannah, his arrival in this city being in antebellum days (some time in the early '50s). The wife of this immigrant ancestor was Frances (Noyes) McIntire. The family is really of Scotch origin. Captain McIntire's mother, who is deceased, was also born in Savannah and is the daughter of Owen Foley and Honoria Kirby, a native of Ireland, who came to Savannah about the year 1840. Thus the city is dear with many strong ties and associations to the immediate subject of these lines.

Captain McIntire received his first introduction to Minerva in the public schools of the city and was graduated from the high school in 1898. He subsequently matriculated in the Pennsylvania Military College, where he pursued a civil engineering course, and in 1901 received the degree of C. E. He attended the law department of the University of Georgia and in the class of 1903 received the degree of LL. B. He had in the meantime studied law in Savannah under Judge G. T. Cann, while that gentleman was judge of the court of chancery, and also under Judge Cann's brother, J. Ferris Cann. He was admitted to the bar in 1903, and since that time has been engaged successfully in the practice of his profession in this city.

For several years, Captain McIntire has been a prominent member of the Georgia Hussars, famous as the oldest military organization in the state, and for having taken a fighting part in all the wars from the Revolution to the Spanish-American, and whose membership has included many of the best-known citizens of Savannah during its long history. He enlisted in the Hussars as a private and through promotions became captain of the Georgia Hussars in 1905, which office he still holds.

Captain McIntire was married in Savannah in 1909, the young woman to become his wife and the mistress of his household being Miss Lucy H. Barrow, daughter of the late Judge Pope Barrow, a former governor of Georgia and United States senator. Mrs. McIntire's mother was Cornelia (Jackson) Barrow, daughter of the late Gen. Henry R. Jackson of Savannah. Their household, distinguished as one of the most charming in a city of attractive homes, is further made interesting by the presence of a son, James W. McIntire, Jr.

CAPT. DANIEL HOARD BALDWIN. Conspicuous among the enterprising and progressive men who during the middle of the nineteenth century were most intimately associated with the development and advancement of the mercantile prosperity of Chatham county, Georgia, was Capt. Daniel Hoard Baldwin, one of the foremost merchants of Savannah. A son of Tilley and Rebecca Hoard Baldwin, he was born, March 19, 1825, in Phillipston, Worcester county, Massachusetts. His mother dying when he was very young, his father married again, and to the influence of the lovely, sweet-faced Christian woman who became his step-mother he ever gave credit for all that was good in his character. His reverence and love for her remained unbroken and helpful until her death, which came as a great grief and loss to him after his marriage, and the birth of his first child.

Brought up in or near his birthplace, Daniel Hoard Baldwin worked as a lad for an uncle on a farm. A bright and cheery lad, full of life and spirits, his fondness for fun was rather a source of amazement to the stern and rugged New England farmer, who often called out, "There's that boy giggling again; what is he giggling at now?" The boy's strong and independent character, and his desire for greater advancement and advantages, lured him southward, and at the age of eighteen years he came to Savannah, Georgia, going into the home and office of another uncle, Mr. Loami Baldwin, head of the mercantile firm of L. Baldwin & Company. As a clerk he steadily and faithfully performed the duties then devolving upon him in that capacity, opening the office in the early morning, and clearing it up, work which is now done by unskilled labor. Industrious and persevering, he developed much business ability, making steady progress along the path of attainments until becoming a member of the firm, which, by the death of Loami Baldwin, was changed to the style of Brigham, Kelly & Company. The subsequent death of Mr. Kelly caused another change in the name of the firm, which became Brigham, Baldwin & Company, a firm which, it is said, did the largest shipping business in Savannah up to the Civil war.

During the war, Capt. Daniel H. Baldwin was in the commissary department, with which he was connected until 1865, when, in the spring of that year, he removed with his family to New York City. His former large business interests, and close touch with the people of Georgia, suggested to him the advisability of establishing a cotton commission business at a time when everything else was disorganized, and, availing himself of the opportunity, he organized the New York firm of D. H. Baldwin & Company.

The integrity and sterling honesty of Captain Baldwin was nuquestioned, as may be evidenced by the question of some business relation coming up to which he had "promised" his support. Someone being asked, "Has Baldwin signed the proposition?" the response from two prominent and wealthy business men was prompt and decisive—"No need for Baldwin to sign it if he said he would agree; do not doubt him, his word is as good as his bond."

About 1876 Captain Baldwin established, in Savannah, the firm of Baldwin & Company, cotton brokers. Prior to moving to New York his Savannah home was in the house now standing just east of Sullivan's grocery, on Congress street, between Bull and Whitaker, that having been his home from the time of his marriage up to the Civil war. The captain was a member of the Chamber of Commerce; of the United States Lloyds; and served several terms as a member of the board of managers of the Cotton Exchange.

His large-hearted generosity and kindly sympathy were known by all his associates, but to many of whom the world had no knowledge he stood as a strong, helpful adviser and friend, and by whom his memory will ever be cherished. In his domestic and family relations, Captain Baldwin was always a loving and ready helper, and, until the sudden death, by drowning, in 1880, of his youngest son and namesake, a blow from which he never recovered, his genial laugh and ready entrance into all gayety and fun were proverbial.

On September 19, 1855, Capt. Daniel H. Baldwin married Kate Philbrick, eldest daughter of Mr. Samuel Philbrick, a well-known and highly esteemed merchant of Savannah. Not long after the loss of his son, Captain Baldwin, on account of failing health, retired from active business. He died in New York from a stroke of apoplexy, June 10, 1887, leaving a widow and three children, namely: Mrs. Walter I. McCoy, of New Jersey; Mrs. A. L. Alexander, of Savannah; and George J. Baldwin, of Savannah.

George J. Baldwin was born August 18, 1856, in Savannah, in the family home on Congress street. He received superior educational advantages, in the spring of 1877 completing a four years' special course at the Massachusetts Institute of Technology, in Boston. He was subsequently superintendent of iron and gold mines in Alabama and Georgia from July, 1877, until October, 1879, when he became a member of the firm of Baldwin & Company, of Savannah, Georgia, dealers in fertilizers, cotton and naval stores factors. Later he organized the Baldwin Fertilizer Company, of Savannah, becoming its president and general manager. In 1894 Mr. Baldwin retired from active business, but resumed again in 1898, becoming interested in electric railway and lighting plants, and is now president of the Savannah Electric Company, and of numerous other industrial and heavily capitalized corporations, including the following: The Gainesville Midland Railway, a steam railroad running out of Gainesville; the Chestatee Pyrites Company, a Georgia mining corporation; and the Electric Railway and Lighting companies of Savannah, Georgia; Jacksonville, Florida, and Tampa, Key West, and Pensacola, Florida.

Mr. Baldwin is also a director in the Savannah Trust Company; the Columbus Electric Company of Columbus, Georgia; the National Bank of Savannah; and of the Augusta & Savannah Railroad Company. He is a member of the Savannah Cotton Exchange, and of the Savannah Chamber of Commerce.

In public, charitable and philanthropic movements Mr. Baldwin has long been active and influential. He is president of the Kate Baldwin Free Kindergarten, which was founded in 1900 by him and his mother, in whose honor it was named, and which has since been maintained by him free of any expense to the public. Mr. Baldwin is likewise president of the Associated Charities of Savannah; a trustee of the Georgia infirmary for colored people, and of the Chatham Academy. He is curator and vice-president of the Georgia Historical Society; and was the first chairman of the board of managers of the Savannah public library, and for many years was a member of that board, and of the park and tree commissioners of Savannah.

Among the many clubs and social organizations of which Mr. Baldwin is a prominent member mention may be made of the following ones in Savannah: The Oglethorpe, Cotillion, Golf and Automobile clubs, and the Savannah Volunteer Guards and Georgia Hussars. He is likewise a member of the Young Men's Christian Associations of both Savannah and Boston, Massachusetts. Among the New York clubs to which Mr. Baldwin belongs are the Southern Society, the Recess, the Automobile Club of America, and the Reform Club. He likewise belongs to the Muscogee Club, of Columbus, Georgia; the Capital City Club, of Atlanta, Georgia; the Lake Placid Club, of Lake Placid, New York; and the Highland Lake and Flat Rock Country clubs, of Flat Rock, North Carolina. Mr. Baldwin is also a member of the National Geographic Society; the Sierra Club, of San Francisco; the American Academy of Political and Social Science; the American Forestry Association; the National Society for the Promotion of Industrial Education, and of various other organizations.

Mr. Baldwin married, June 27, 1882, Lucy H. Hull, of Atlanta, Georgia, and they have two children, namely: George H., born in Savannah, April 23, 1883; and Dorothea C., born in this city, February 22, 1889.

Mr. Loami Baldwin, Mr. Baldwin's great uncle, established himself in business in Savannah prior to his marriage, which was solemnized in 1823, and since his coming here, nearly a hundred years ago, there has been a Baldwin continuously in business in Savannah.

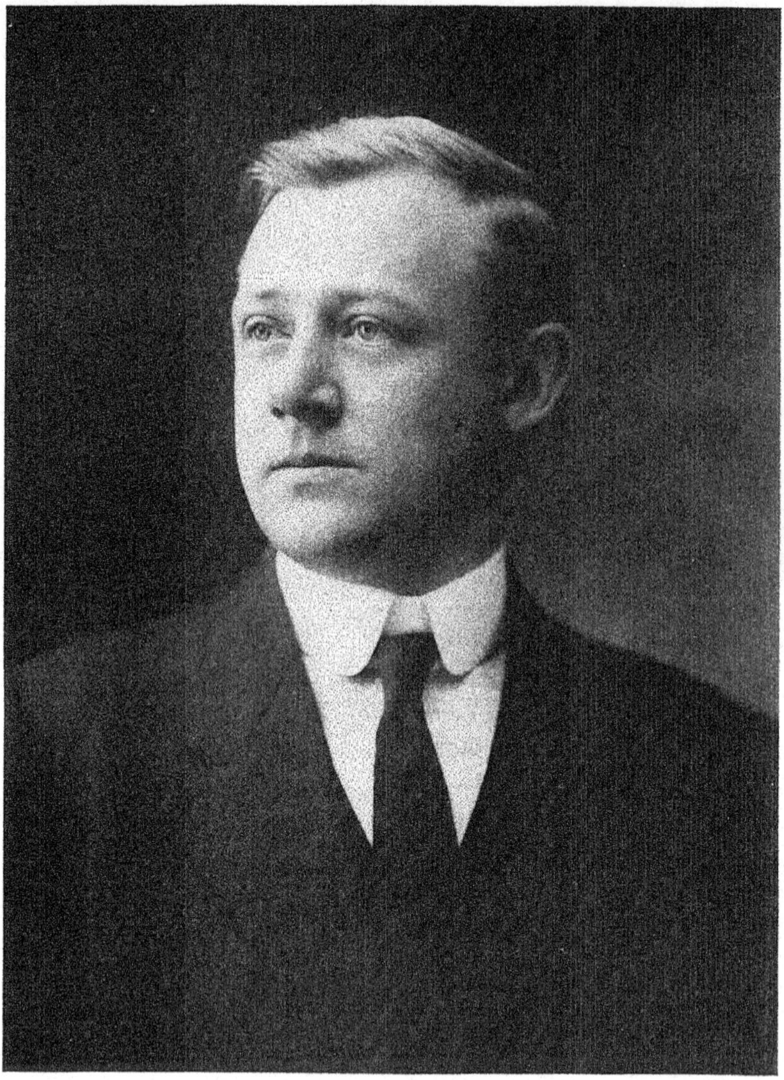

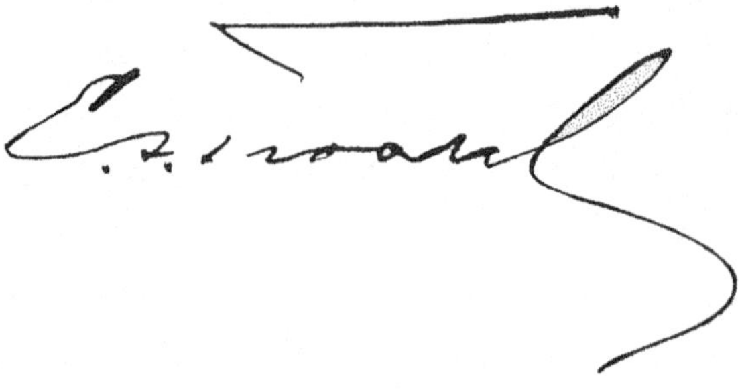

JOHN JACOB RAUERS. Intimately identified with many of the more, important industrial corporations of Savannah, John Jacob Rauers is recognized as a man of pronounced ability and keen business insight, and as a member of the firm of Williamson & Rauers, steamship and forwarding agents, is connected with one of the leading concerns of the kind on the south Atlantic coast. A son of the late Jacob Rauers, he was born in Savannah, in 1877, of German and Scotch ancestry.

A native of Bremen, Germany, Jacob Rauers immigrated to the United States as a young man, locating in Savannah in 1865. He was engaged in the cotton exporting trade for many years, but from 1881 until his death, in 1904, lived retired from business pursuits.

Jacob Rauers married, in Savannah, Joanna McDonald, who is still living. She was born in Scotland, and when a child came to this country to join her maternal uncle, James McHenry, who had previously established himself in business in Savannah, and was for many years one of the city's representative merchants, and a gentleman of the most exemplary character.

Bred and educated in Savannah, John Jacob Rauers began his business career at an early age. In May, 1901, he became junior member of the well-known firm of Williamson & Rauers, which as steamship and forwarding agents is conducting a large and substantial business. Besides this active connection, Mr. Rauers is associated with a number of the prominent corporations of Savannah, being one of the directors of the Savannah Trust Company; vice-president of the Savannah Hotel Company, owners of the De Soto Hotel; vice-president of the Southern Fertilizer & Chemical Company; a director of the Hydraulic Cotton Press Company; a director of the Hull Vehicle Manufacturing Company; and a director of the Savannah Brewing Company.

Since 1876 the Rauers family have been the owners of that historic spot, Saint Catherine's Island, off the coast of Georgia, where they maintain a summer home. Mr. Rauers has in his possession the various grants and deeds connected with the island since the first grant issued by George III. An interesting account of the island is given in connection with the historical portion of this work.

Mr. Rauers is a member of the Savannah Chamber of Commerce; of the Savannah Board of Trade; of the Cotton Exchange; and belongs to the Oglethorpe Club.

Mr. Rauers married, in Savannah, Marion Morrell Hammond, who was born in this city, a daughter of the late Capt. John L. Hammond, and into their home five children have made their advent, namely: Marion M., Jacob, Joanna McDonald, Katherine and Hammond.

EINAR STORM TROSDAL. No nation has contributed to the complex composition of our American social fabric an element of more sterling worth or one of greater value in fostering and supporting our national institutions than has Norway. In truth, the nation owes much to the Norwegian stock and has honored and been honored by many noble men and women of this extraction. Savannah has no more virile and progressive young citizen than Einar Storm Trosdal, vice-president and general manager of the South Atlantic Steamship Line, who was born at Christiana, Norway, in 1877.

Mr. Trosdal was reared and educated in Christiana, and in the excellent colleges of the capital city received the best of academic and business training. In the manner of so many of the fine flower of young European manhood, he answered the beckoning finger of Opportunity from the shores of the New World and severed old associations to come in quest of American resources and advantages. In 1898 he arrived in Savannah and became indentified with the firm of S. P. Shotter & Company, extensive operators in naval stores, the predecessors of the present American Naval Stores Company, which Mr. Shotter organized. Ever since that time Mr. Trosdal has been prominently connected with naval stores and shipping interests, and although his home and his business headquarters have remained in Savannah, his business has taken him on many journeys to various parts of the world. He is now vice-president and general manager of the South Atlantic Steamship Line, which carries on an extensive shipping business, especially in cotton and naval stores, to Europe and other ports, and he still retains his interest in the American Naval Stores Company, of which company he is a director.

Since establishing his home in Savannah, Mr. Trosdal has entered in a public-spirited way into the various activities of the city. He is interested in the success of good government and in his daily affairs manifests a generous regard for his fellows and as a large-hearted, whole-souled, companionable gentleman, actuated by principles of honesty and integrity, merits and commands the respect and good-will of all those with whom he comes into contact. He is a member of the Chamber of Commerce, the Cotton Exchange, the Oglethorpe Club and other organizations.

In the year 1904, Mr. Trosdal was married in this city to Miss Lucy Boyd, who was born in Savannah, the daughter of Dr. M. L. Boyd. They share their charming and well-directed home with two children, Einar Storm, Jr., and Beverly.

MICHAEL O'BYRNE. The law firm of which Michael A. O'Byrne is the senior member has had a long and favorable career in Savannah. It was originally composed of himself and the late P. J. O'Connor, with the firm name of O'Connor & O'Byrne. In 1896, Mr. Walter C. Hartridge was admitted to the firm, which then became O'Connor, O'Byrne & Hartridge. Mr. O'Connor, who had for many years been one of the prominent lawyers of Savannah, died in November, 1909, and on January 1, 1910, Mr. Anton P. Wright was admitted to the firm, the style of which was then changed to its present name—O'Byrne, Hartridge & Wright. It is one of the strongest law firms in Savannah and enjoys a large general practice, particularly in connection with real estate, corporation and commercial interests.

As a member of this firm, Mr. O'Byrne has gained reputation and practice with each succeeding year. Those who have entrusted important affairs to his management know how well and honorably he has guarded their interests. In all matters where the object is to safeguard the investment of capital, or where competent counsel is required in directing the organization and successful management of commercial and industrial enterprises in which weighty financial interests are involved, his services have been increasingly sought for. He has been especially successful in real estate and law and litigation affecting property interests, and his counsels are often required where such interests are involved.

In addition to his law practice, Mr. O'Byrne has many other interests that are of marked importance. He is the president of the Hibernia Bank, a successful financial institution of constantly growing prosperity, with capital, surplus and undivided profits in excess of $350,000. He has filled the position of president of this bank with such skill and prudence as to gain for it the highest confidence of the public. He is also the president and has charge of the finances of the John Flannery Company, the famous cotton house that was founded and for a long number of years controlled by the late Capt. John Flannery. He is first vice-president of the Commercial Life Insurance Company and a member of the executive committee of the board of directors of the Savannah Brewing Company.

For about twenty years Mr. O'Byrne was actively connected with the First Regiment Infantry, National Guard of Georgia, during most of the time being a member of the Irish Jasper Greens, one of the companies of that regiment. Mr. O'Byrne became sergeant of his company, and later was made quartermaster of the regiment. From this position he was later promoted to the rank of adjutant of the regiment.

Mr. O'Byrne has creditably filled several public positions of trust. For twenty years he has been a member of the Savannah board of education and has given much time to the duties and responsibilities of that office. He is commodore of the Savannah Yacht Club, also president of the Savannah Base Ball Association. In various other ways he is closely associated with the business and social affairs of the city. He is a member of the Savannah Automobile Club, the Oglethorpe Club, Golf Club and Music Club, and is president of the Atlanta Club.

Mr. O'Byrne has long been known for his quiet but powerful influence in local politics and in general civic affairs. In religious affiliation he is a Catholic and a member of the Cathedral parish in Savannah, and is chairman of its financial committee. Much credit is due to Mr. O'Byrne for his able assistance in the building of the beautiful cathedral of St. John the Baptist, one of the finest specimens of Gothic architecture in the United States. He was a member of the building committee, and was generous of his time and financial support during the erection of this noble edifice. He has similarly taken an active part in supporting various philanthropical and charitable organizations. He is a member of the Savannah Benevolent Association, member of the finance committee of the Associated Charities of Savannah, president of the Female Orphans Benevolent Society, vice-president of the St. Vincent de Paul Society, and is vice-president and trustee of St. Joseph's Male Orphanage, an institution of the diocese of Savannah, located at Washington, Wilkes county, Georgia. He has long been a prominent member of the Knights of Columbus.

Mr. O'Byrne was born in Savannah in 1861, attended the public schools of this city and received his finishing education at St. Vincent's University, near Pittsburg, Pennsylvania, the leading college of the Benedictine order in America. He was graduated from St. Vincent's with the class of 1881. He then studied law in Savannah in the office of Jackson, Lawton & Basinger, this firm being composed of Gen. H. R. Jackson, Gen. A. R. Lawton and Maj. W. S. Basinger, all of them distinguished lawyers and leaders at the Savannah bar. Mr. O'Byrne was admitted to practice in 1883. His law business, which forms the main part of all his activities, has been very profitable, and has made him one of the most substantial citizens of Savannah, a position in life that he has reached through his own efforts and ability.

Mr. O'Byrne has been twice married. His first wife was Miss Marie McDonough, a daughter of John J. McDonough, a prominent manufacturer and one time mayor of Savannah. She is survived by three children, namely: Eleanor, James Raymond, and Charles O'Byrne. Mr. O'Byrne's present wife, to whom he was married at her home in Bridgeport, Connecticut, was before her marriage, Miss Sara Lorene Wren, daughter of Peter W. Wren, a man of large affairs in Bridgeport and president of the Pequonnock National Bank of that city. Of this second union one child was born, Sara Wren O'Byrne.

CHARLES MAXWELL GIBBS. The gentleman, to a brief review of whose life and characteristics the reader's attention is herewith directed, is among the foremost business men of Savannah, and by his conservative methods has contributed in a material way to the industrial and commercial advancement of the city. He has in the course of an honorable career been successful in the business enterprises of which he is the head and is well deserving of mention in the biographical memoirs of Georgia. Charles Maxwell Gibbs belongs to fine old southern stock, and was born August 16, 1861, in the most crucial period of our national history, the guns of the Civil war echoing about his cradle. His parents were Leonard Young and Rosa Matilda (Williams) Gibbs. The former was born January 23, 1834, and died in Savannah, September 6, 1898. He served the South in the war between the states and in the defense of Fort McAllister was captured by Sherman's army, which was then entering Savannah, and was severely wounded in that engagement.

Mr. Gibbs' paternal ancestors were from Connecticut, and served in the War of the Revolution.

His mother was born in Savannah, March 5, 1840, and died in this city October 2, 1877. She was the daughter of Thomas F. and Mary Jane (Maxwell) Williams, the latter being a daughter of Col. William Maxwell, of Georgia, who was a member of the Provincial Congress of Georgia from 1775 to 1777.

Mr. Gibbs was graduated from the Savannah high school and spent three years in the Virginia Military Institute, from which he was graduated with the class of 1881. He early became engaged in his father's fertilizer business, with which as proprietor he is still identified.

He is affiliated with Ancient Landmark Lodge of Masons in Savannah and exemplifies in his own living the ideals of moral and social justice and brotherly love for which the ancient and august order stands.

Mr. Gibbs married in 1888 Miss Martha Louisa Rowland, a descendant of distinguished Georgia ancestry. She is a grand-daughter of Judge William B. Fleming, one of Georgia's noted jurists. They have one child, a daughter, Rosa Williams Gibbs.

CHARLES P. ROWLAND. Among the representative men of Savannah is Charles P. Rowland, property owner and engaged extensively in real estate business. The family was founded here in 1843 by the subject's father and in the ensuing sixty years the name has been one of the honored ones of the city and identified in praiseworthy fashion with business and municipal life, the attitude of the Rowlands, father and son, to the city, being public-spirited and altruistic.

Charles P. Rowland was born in Savannah on the 6th of June, 1877, the son of John C. and Mary (Gray) Rowland. The elder gentleman was born in Dutchess county, New York, May 20, 1827. He passed the days of his youth and his early manhood near Rochester, New York, and in 1843 came to Savannah to begin his business life. He embarked in a commercial career, becoming prominent as a cotton warehouseman and shipper. Notwithstanding his northern birth, he readily granted the justice of the southern contention for independence, and as early as January, 1861, enlisted in the Pulaski Guards, with which he served in garrison at Fort Pulaski. In August, 1861, he entered the regular Confederate service as first sergeant of the Washington volunteers, under Capt. John McMahon, which became a company of the First Regiment of Georgia, commanded by Col. Charles H. Olmstead. In the following winter he was promoted to second lieutenant. Lieutenant Rowland was part of the gallant garrison of Fort Pulaski during its bombardment by the Federal fleet and batteries, April 10 and 11, 1862, and which

Colonel Olmstead was compelled to surrender after all the guns that could be brought to bear on the enemy had been dismounted and the walls of the fort were breached. Following this event Lieutenant Rowland was taken as a prisoner of war by way of Hilton Head and Governor's Island to Johnson's Island, Ohio, where he was held until the latter part of the summer of 1862. Then being exchanged he returned to Savannah and rejoined his regiment and was promoted to first lieutenant. With this rank he served in Battery Wagner on Morris Island, South Carolina, during the great bombardment and assault in July, 1863, and in other operations around Charleston. In the spring of 1864 the regiment joined the Army of Tennessee and Lieutenant Rowland, in command of his company (Company K, First Georgia Regiment), participated in the battle of Kenesaw Mountain, the battles around Atlanta, Jonesboro, and other engagements of Mercer's Brigade with Hood's Corps in Tennessee. At the last he was a participant in the campaign in the Carolinas and surrendered with the army at Greensboro, North Carolina.

At the close of this worthy and honorable career as a Confederate soldier, John C. Rowland returned to his home in Savannah and re-engaged in business life of the city, in which he remained a potent factor up to the time of his death. He retired from the cotton business in 1880 and thereafter was engaged for the most part in real estate transactions, buying and selling his own property for investment, in which business he achieved substantial financial success, becoming one of the wealthy men of the city. He was one of the first directors and was vice-president of the Savannah Bank & Trust Company. He also served as alderman of the city of Savannah for one term. His death occurred on February 1, 1908. He held a place of highest esteem with the people of Savannah, for his usefulness as a citizen and business man and for his valiant service in the supreme struggle between the North and the South, as an upholder of the Confederacy. The subject's mother was born in Savannah and died in this city in 1906. She was the daughter of George S. Gray of this city. In addition to the immediate subject of this review, there was a son and a daughter, namely: Clifford G. and Helen C.

Charles P. Rowland was reared in Savannah and in the city of his birth has spent his entire life with the exception of the period of his higher education. He had his first introduction to Minerva in the public schools of the city and after finishing their curriculum, he entered Bingham Military Institute at Asheville, North Carolina, where he spent four years, and subsequently entered the Georgia Institute of Technology at Atlanta. In partnership with his cousin, John T. Rowland, he became established in the real estate and insurance business in Savannah in 1898 and after the retirement of the former, became associated with his brother, C. G. Rowland, and their business is one of the most extensive and prosperous in the city. Like his father, Mr. Rowland has been especially successful in the purchase and sale of local real estate for his own investment and he is acknowledged to be one of the best judges of property values in the city.

Mr. Rowland has always been interested in military affairs in Savannah, and for several years he was an active member of the Georgia Hussars, in which historic organization he rose to the rank of first lieutenant. He enlisted as a private in the Georgia Hussars on February 28, 1898, and receiving various promotions, received the rank above named on October 9, 1905, serving in that capacity until his retirement October 14, 1909. On May 14, 1910, he was appointed on Governor Brown's staff as aide-de-camp with the rank of lieutenant colonel. He is a member of the Sons of the Revolution; has taken the Scottish and York degrees in Masonry, and is also a Shriner.

Mr. Rowland was married on the 10th day of July, 1909, the lady to become his wife being Miss Minnie Coney Greenlee, of Asheville, North Carolina. They are prominent in exclusive social circles and maintain one of the attractive and hospitable households of the city.

CHARLES GRANDY BELL. Ranking high among Savannah's active, energetic and progressive citizens, Charles Grandy Bell, of the firm of Butler, Stevens & Company, now of Butler, Stevens & Bell, cotton factors and commission merchants, is widely known as a man of honor and integrity, and as one whose word and ability can always be relied upon in matters of business. A native of Florida, he was born, in 1858, in Madison county, near Greenville, coming from Virginian ancestry.

His father, Charles Grandy Bell, was born and reared in Virginia, being descended from the Norfolk family of that name. Locating in Florida in the forties, he was there a resident until his death, which occurred just prior to the outbreak of the Civil war, in which two of his uncles served, being soldiers in the Confederate army. He married Nancy Walker, who was born in Florida, where her parents settled on leaving South Carolina, their native state.

Brought up in Jefferson county, Florida, Charles Grandy Bell acquired his preliminary education in the schools of that county, after which he completed a course of study at Eastman's Business College, in Poughkeepsie, New York, being there graduated with the class of 1879. Following his graduation, he spent a year and a half in New York City, being employed in one of the largest dry goods establishments of that place, that of Lord & Taylor. Coming from there to Savannah, Georgia, in 1881, Mr. Bell has since made this city his home. In 1883 he became associated with the cotton industry of the South, in the year 1886 entering the employ of Butler & Stevens as bookkeeper and cashier. Displaying marked business acumen and judgment in that capacity, he was made a partner in the firm in 1891, whose members, Robert M. Butler, Henry D. Stevens, and Charles G. Bell, are of the highest standing in the commercial and financial world. This firm, which deals in cotton productions, is one of the largest and wealthiest firms of cotton factors and dealers in the South, its business being extensive and lucrative.

Prominently identified with many of the leading business organizations of the city, Mr. Bell is vice-president of the Savannah Bank and Trust Company, and is one of the oldest members of the Sinking Fund Commission of Savannah, of which he was for a number of years the secretary. For two terms, ending in 1910, he was president of the Savannah Cotton Exchange, to which he still belongs. He is a member of the board of trustees of the Independent Presbyterian church, and is president of the Young Men's Christian Association. Socially he is a member of the Oglethorpe Club.

Mr. Bell married, in Savannah, Miss Kate Maxey, who was born in Jacksonville, Florida, but came with her parents to Savannah in 1881. Four children have blessed the union of Mr. and Mrs. Bell, namely: Anna, Kate, Charles Grandy, third, and Suzanne.

MARCUS STEPHEN BAKER. One of the most conspicuous figures in the affairs of this section of the state is Marcus Stephen Baker, receiver of tax returns of Chatham county. He has held this responsible office since 1901 and is exceedingly popular and efficient. He was previously engaged in mercantile business and in general collecting and real estate.

Marcus S. Baker

Mr. Baker is a native Georgian, his birth having occurred at Hinesville, Liberty county, September 16, 1849. He is the son of Richard Fuller and Elizabeth G. (Dowsey) Baker. The father was born in Liberty county and died there in 1852, when Mr. Baker was an infant. Richard F. Baker was a son of Stephen Baker, also a life-long citizen of Liberty county. The former, at the age of eighteen, was orderly sergeant of Liberty Independent Troop, one of the oldest military organizations in Georgia. He was a planter by occupation. The Baker family, in truth, is one of the oldest in historic Liberty county, having been established there in 1752 by the subject's great-great-grandfather, Benjamin Baker, of Dorchester, South Carolina, who settled in Midway, Liberty county, in that year. The great-grandfather, John Baker, who died in 1792, was a member of the committee appointed by the convention at Savannah, Georgia, July 20, 1774, to prepare resolutions expressive of the sentiments and determination of the people of the province in regard to the Boston Port Bill. He was also a member of the provincial congress of Georgia from 1775 to 1777; he was a member of the Georgia council of safety in 1776; he was colonel commanding a regiment of militia of Liberty county from 1775 to 1783; he was wounded in the skirmish at Bulltown Swamp November 19, 1778; he defeated Captain Goldsmith at White House, Georgia, June 28, 1779, and participated in the capture of Augusta, Georgia, in May and June, 1781. He was lieutenant in the colonial wars. It will be seen that few citizens took a more active and useful part in the patriotic history of that stirring period.

The subject's mother, whose maiden name was Elizabeth G. Dowsey, removed to Savannah from Liberty county in 1854 and her demise occurred in this city in 1882. The children of this brave and admirable lady were reared in this city. One son, Richard F., is now a resident of the Forest city, and another, William E. Q. Baker, lives at Atlanta. Another brother, Robert Wilson Baker, was a Confederate soldier and was killed in the second day's fighting in the battle of Chickamauga. Another brother, M. M. Baker, served in the army of the Confederacy throughout the war and died December 23, 1909.

It has been seen that the early childhood of Mr. Baker was passed in Savannah. In 1859, when a lad of ten years, he returned to Liberty county to attend school under the tutelage of Prof. Moses Way at Taylor's creek, Professor Way being a well-known educator of that day. Afterward Mr. Baker studied under the direction of Prof. S. D. Bradwell, at Hinesville. That gentleman was also prominent in the educational world and had served as school commissioner of Georgia. In the first year of the war the subject went to Walthourville to attend school, and in 1863 he returned to his home in Savannah and finished his education in the public schools. The Baker family have for many generations been advocates of good education and have given their sons the best advantages possible, and it was only through the unsettled conditions of the war that Mr. Baker's education was terminated when it was. In 1866 he went to work as clerk in a wholesale grocery house in Savannah and later became outside salesman for a local hardware firm. Still later he engaged successfully in the general collecting and real estate business. In 1900 he was elected to the office of receiver of the tax returns of Chatham county, and assumed the duties of this office on January 1, 1901. He has been elected at each successive biennial election and is now (1913) serving on his seventh consecutive term in this office, which he has filled with remarkable efficiency and to the entire satisfaction of the public.

Mr. Baker holds the welfare of the city closely at heart and his influence and support are given to all beneficent measures. He is a member of Trinity Methodist church. He belongs to the Sons of the American Revolution, to which the patriotic services of his forbears make him eligible. Their even earlier patriotic activities entitle him to membership in the Society of the Colonial Wars. He stands high in Masonry, belonging to Landrum Lodge, No. 48, F. & A. M.; to Palestine Commandery, No. 7, Knights Templars; Alee Temple, A. A. O. N. M. S., of Savannah; Savannah Lodge, No. 183, B. P. O. Elks; Calanthe Lodge, No. 28, Knights of Pythias.

On the 5th day of January, 1874, Mr. Baker was married in Savannah, his chosen lady being Miss Fanny A. Krenson, a daughter of this city. Mrs. Baker's parents were Frederick and Sarah E. (Dean) Krenson, the latter descended from the Scotch family of MacDonalds, who were among the early settlers of McIntosh county, Georgia. To Mr. and Mrs. Baker have been born three children. Louise Elizabeth is the wife of Capt. Henry Blun, ex-postmaster of Savannah, and president of the Germania Bank; Laura Spencer is the wife of Irvin S. Cobb, formerly of Paducah, Kentucky, now of New York City, the famous feature writer and humorist for the New York *Sun*, New York *World*, *Saturday Evening Post* and various other publications; the third child, Marcus Stephen Baker, Jr., is postmaster at Savannah and one of the city's best known young citizens.

The Bakers are loyal Georgians and are prominent in a praiseworthy manner in the many-sided life of the city, enjoying general confidence and respect in a community of whose best traits they are typical.

RUFUS E. LESTER. Especially fortunate in the eminence and character of her citizens, it may be truly said that Savannah has no more honored name enrolled upon her list of representative citizens than that of the late Rufus E. Lester, who won distinction as a lawyer, and as a congressman, a brilliant and distinguished record. He was born in Burke county, Georgia, December 12, 1837, and died in Washington, District of Columbia, June 16, 1906.

Colonel Lester, as he was familiarly known, received his education principally in Mercer University, at Macon, Georgia, being there graduated in the twentieth year of his age. Subsequently studying law in Savannah, he was admitted to the bar in 1858, and in 1859 began the practice of his profession in that city, which continued to be his home as long as he lived.

Enlisting in the Confederate army in the spring of 1861, he remained in service throughout the war, going from Savannah to the front as an adjutant in the Twenty-fifth Georgia Regiment, which was first encamped in the vicinity of Savannah, near Tybee and Avondale. Going with his command from there to Mississippi, the colonel took part in the campaign of that state, afterwards meeting the enemy at the battle of Chickamauga, where he had two horses shot from under him, and was himself slightly wounded. Following this engagement, he was very ill for eighteen months, and remained in such poor health that he was assigned to the duty of inspector general under General Mackal, at Macon, Georgia, where he was stationed when the war closed. He had attained the rank of captain while in service, but after the war was always known as Colonel Lester. The colonel made a splendid record as a soldier, and in the book which he published Gen. N. B. Forrest commended Colonel Lester for extraordinary bravery and gallantry.

Resuming the practice of his profession in Savannah after the close of the conflict, Colonel Lester became active in public affairs, and in

1870 was elected to the state senate, representing the first senatorial district. Through successive re-elections, he continued a member of that body until 1879, during the last three years of that time serving as its president. From 1883 until 1888 he rendered excellent service as mayor of Savannah. In 1888 he had the honor of being elected to congress as a representative from the first congressional district of Georgia, which comprised ten counties, namely: Burke, Bulloch, Bryan, Chatham, Emanuel, Effingham, Liberty, McIntosh, Screven, and Tattnall. His services as congressman gave such general satisfaction that he was continuously re-elected every succeeding two years up to and including 1906, the year of his death.

Colonel Lester won a splendid record as congressman, and rendered services of great usefulness to his district in particular, and to the entire country in general. Honored by an appointment during his first year in congress upon the important rivers and harbors committee, he remained a member of that committee during his entire period of service, that comprising his most prominent and valued work. It was through the efforts of the colonel that Savannah received its continuous appropriation for harbor improvements, and this has proved the leading factor in the modern growth and development of the city. He also obtained the appropriation for the beautiful marble Federal building in which Savannah's postoffice is housed, and was likewise instrumental in having the Marine Hospital erected in Savannah, and in having the revenue cutter "Yamacraw" assigned for permanent duty in Savannah harbor.

Greatly beloved by his home people throughout his district, Colonel Lester was also held in the highest esteem and affection by the leading representatives of every section of the Union in the national congress. He was of large influence in that august body, and in the social and political affairs of Washington achieved, early in his career, a place of the highest rank. In the special proceedings in the house and senate on June 18, 1906, held in commemoration of Colonel Lester, memorial addresses were delivered by more than a score of the most prominent congressmen and senators, all eulogizing him in the most glowing terms. Within the limits of this sketch it would be difficult to condense those fine addresses, and, indeed, it mayhap will be more appropriate to here quote some excerpts from a tribute paid him by one of his own intimate friends and fellow citizens, Judge Samuel B. Adams, of Savannah, who said in part:

"Rufus E. Lester was admitted to the bar of Savannah when twenty-one years of age, and remained a member until his death. His professional career was interrupted by the war between the states, in which he was a Confederate soldier of gallantry and devotion from the beginning to the end of the struggle. He resumed his practice after the cessation of hostilities, and at once took a front rank at the bar which had more than its share of able and successful practitioners. Notwithstanding the fact he was often called into public service, he was always a lawyer, loving his profession and preferring its duties to those of office.

"I was a member of the bar with Colonel Lester for more than thirty years and had abundant opportunity of learning his power as a lawyer at our bar, and certainly no other lawyer lost fewer cases. He had a legal mind, one that saw quickly the strong points of his case, separated without delay the weak points, and pressed home those most worthy of consideration. Before a jury, if, under the charge, it was at liberty to find with him, he was almost invincible. He knew the men, knew how to talk with them, possessed their confidence, which he never abused, and, generally, secured their verdict. He was also strong before judges in purely legal arguments. When Mr. Lester urged a contention, judges knew he did it sincerely, and his ability and standing secured for its consideration an attentive and respectful hearing. I have often heard him make legal arguments of a high order of merit.

"He always practiced and illustrated the best ethics of an honorable profession, scorning always the arts and tricks of the shyster and pettifogger. While he struck hard blows in the courtroom and was a 'foeman worthy of any man's steel,' his blows were fair, never unworthy or unprofessional. His brethren of the bar trusted him absolutely without fear or misgivings, and rested securely upon any agreement that he would make, whether binding under the rules of the court or not. I knew him well, was honored with his friendship, and my deliberate conviction is that I never met a more honorable or trustworthy lawyer, or man, and a comparatively few who equaled him in his absolute sincerity, frankness and manliness.

"Mr. Lester was elected mayor of Savannah for three successive terms, and brought to the discharge of his duties the same efficiency and fidelity which distinguished him in all the relations of life. He was emphatically the mayor. His influence on his board was potential. This was due to his positive and virile character and the complete confidence reposed in his judgment and sincerity. He possessed to an extraordinary extent the elements of leadership, and these elements were manifest in the administration of the municipal government.

"An incident in his career as mayor illustrates the man and the officer. Some negroes were incarcerated charged with the murder for robbery of a family of white people living on the outskirts of the city. Feeling ran high. There was talk of lynching, and we were threatened with this unspeakable disgrace. A crowd gathered at the jail for the purpose of lynching. Mr. Lester was notified. He went to the jail immediately, personally took charge of the police present, mounted the steps, pointed out to the crowd the 'dead line' in front of the steps, and warned them that if a single member of the mob crossed that line he would order the police to shoot, and to shoot to kill. The crowd knew that he meant what he said, was utterly fearless, and would die before he would permit a lynching. The crowd quietly dispersing, it was not necessary to injure anyone, and Savannah's record remained unstained by that crime."

Perhaps Colonel Lester's most notable characteristic was his overflowing kindness and charity toward every human being, however poor or humble, with whom he came in contact. It was this trait that rounded out a beautiful character. He frequently did acts of thoughtful kindness, and did them so unobtrusively that they were never known to others, not even by his own family. It seemed perfectly natural for him to be a good and true man.

Colonel Lester married, in 1859, in Savannah, Miss Laura E. Hines, who was born in Burke county, which was likewise the birthplace of her father, James J. Hines, who was for many years a prominent business man of Savannah, where she was reared and educated. Mrs. Lester's mother, whose maiden name was Georgia Bird, was born in Liberty county, Georgia.

CHARLES C. LEBEY. Well and favorably known in connection with the cotton trade of Savannah, where he has charge of the local cotton of the Seaboard Air Line, Charles C. Lebey counts among his ancestors some of the more noteworthy families of the South. He was born in

Savannah, in 1868, this city having also been the birthplace of his father, David Christian Lebey, and of his grandfather, Christian David Lebey.

Andrew Lebey, the great-grandfather of Charles C. Lebey, was one of six brothers, natives of France, who came with Count d'Estaing's fleet from that country to assist the Continental army in its efforts to take Savannah from the British, whose forces had occupied the city almost from the beginning of the Revolution, the fleet making its appearance off the coast of Georgia in September, 1779. The Continentals, aided by Count d'Estaing's men, made an heroic and determined, but unsuccessful, assault on the British at Springfield Redoubt, on the western edge of Savannah. In the conflict that ensued, five of the Lebey brothers, Jerome, Louis, Philip, Augustine and John, were killed, while Andrew, the only surviving brother, was himself badly crippled. Remaining in this country after the war was over, Andrew Lebey settled on a farm in Ebenezer, Georgia, but afterwards returned to Savannah, where he spent the later years of his life. He married a widow, Mrs. Mary (Hines) Anderson.

Although born in Savannah, Christian David Lebey was educated in Connecticut, and subsequently established an extensive jewelry business in Savannah, where the greater part of his life was spent.

David Christian was a life-long resident of Savannah. He married Rosina I. Courtenay, who was likewise born in Savannah, being a daughter of Edward T. and Rosina (Bland) Courtenay, and a granddaughter on the maternal side of Richard Bland, who was of English lineage. On the paternal side she was a direct descendant of Carlisle Courtenay, the Earl of Devon, who was of French ancestry. The earl's sons removed to Ireland, and from that country John Courtenay, a member of that family, and the great-grandfather of Mr. Lebey, came to Savannah long before the Revolution, being accompanied on the voyage across the Atlantic by his brother, Charles, who settled at Charleston, South Carolina, and there became founder of the present prominent Courtenay family of that city. Edward T. Courtenay was for many years one of the leading cotton merchants of Savannah.

Charles C. Lebey was brought up and educated in Savannah, and now has charge of the local cotton of the Seaboard Air Line. For several years past Mr. Lebey has made his home at the suburban town of Pooler, in Chatham county, of which he is now serving his fourth term as mayor, having been re-elected to this position three successive times. Fraternally he is a member, and worshipful master, of Turner Lodge. No. 16, Ancient Free and Accepted Order of Masons, of Pooler; also a Scottish Rite and York Rite Mason and a member of the P. O. S. of A., the J. O. A. U., the K. of P. and the Redmen.

Mr. Lebey's wife, who prior to her marriage was Miss Mamie E. Amdreau, was born in Tampa, Florida.

WILLIAM VIRGINIUS DAVIS, vice-president and manager of the Savannah Trust Company, prominent banker, and well known for praetically all his life in Savannah, is one of the foremost figures in the business life of this city. He was born in Jacksonville, Florida, on June 14, 1871, and is the son of Thomas J. and Frances V. (Price) Davis. The father was born in Portsmouth, Virginia, and the mother in Wilmington, North Carolina. She died in 1896. For many years Thomas Davis was a grain merchant in Savannah, and he is still living in this city, but is retired from active business life.

Although born in Jacksonville, William V. Davis is practically a Savannahian, as his parents removed to the Georgia city when he was an infant, and he was reared and educated here, attending the public schools and Chatham Academy. In 1889, when he was eighteen years old, he went to Texas, locating at Palestine, where he became stenographer and secretary to Hon. Thomas M. Campbell, one of the prominent lawyers of that state, who was then the receiver and later the general manager of the International & Great Northern Railroad, and who was governor of Texas from 1906 to 1910. He was connected with Mr. Campbell's office for nearly four years and was then made ticket agent at Palestine for the I. & G. N. R. R., of which his uncle, D. J. Price, is general passenger agent. Mr. Davis remained in that position for one year, remaining at Palestine five years in all. In 1894 he returned to Savannah and since that time he has been continually associated with business interests headed by Capt. W. W. Mackall, a sketch of whose life appears elsewhere in this volume. Mr. Davis first entered Captain Mackall's law office as a clerical assistant, and studying law in the meantime, but has never practiced that profession. He became secretary of the various railroad and industrial corporations of which Mr. Mackall was the chief, prominent among which was the Georgia Construction Company, which built the Seaboard Air Line terminals in Hutchinson Island.

On October 1, 1902, the Savannah Trust Company, of which Mr. Mackall is president, began business, and Mr. Davis was made its secretary. He has been connected with this bank ever since that time. Upon the retirement of John Morris as treasurer of the company, Mr. Davis assumed the duties of that position in addition to the secretaryship. On January 22, 1907, Mr. Davis was elected to his present position of vice-president, and, as such, is the managing official of the company.

Few financial institutions in the South have been attended by such substantial growth and prosperity in so short a time as has the Savannah Trust Company. Under its charter it carries on both general banking and trust company business, besides a real estate department that is especially flourishing and successful. The capital stock is $500,000, with surplus and undivided profits of nearly $300,000. The management of the bank is conservative, efficient and economical, and it has returned most satisfactory dividends to its stockholders.

While living at Palestine, Mr. Davis was married to Miss Elizabeth Wyche Hunter. She died in that city. One daughter was born of this union,—Miss Wyche Hunter Davis, now at Orange, New Jersey, in Miss Beard's school. Subsequently Mr. Davis was married to Miss Winnifred Wright Bonney, of Norfolk, Virginia, and they have three children,—Thomas J.; William V., Jr.; and Frederick B.

Mr. Davis is a member of Westminster Presbyterian church, and is associated in a fraternal way with the Masonic order, being a member of Ancient Landmark Lodge, No. 231, A. F. & A. M., the Georgia Chapter of Royal Arch Masons, Palestine Commandery Knights Templar and is a Shriner. He is also a member of the Oglethorpe Club, the Yacht Club, the Guards Club and the Golf Club.

DAVID CRENSHAW BARROW, JR. The name borne by David Crenshaw Barrow, Jr., is a conspicuous one in the history of the state of Georgia. As educators, statesmen and members of the learned professions, several of the family have won distinction and high honors. He himself has not fallen behind the standard set him by his ancestors, and is one of the most prominent and successful members of the bar of Savannah. Gifted with a logical mind, he has had the best of training for his profession, and his success has been fully merited by his close application to his work and the careful preparation which he gives to each case.

David Crenshaw Barrow, Jr., is the son of Middleton Pope and Sarah Church (Craig) Barrow, both of whom are deceased. The Honorable Middleton Pope Barrow was born in Oglethorpe county, Georgia, on the 1st of August, 1839. He was educated at the University of Georgia, from which he received the degree of A. B. in 1859, and the degree of LL. B., in 1860. He was admitted to the bar in 1860, and began to practice law in Athens, Georgia. With the outbreak of the war, he enlisted in the Confederate army and served throughout the war between the states, as captain of artillery and as aid-de-camp, on the staff of Major General Howard Cobb. After the war he resumed the practice of his profession in Athens, and in 1877 was elected a member of the constitutional convention. During the session of 1880-81, he was a member of the Georgia legislature, and was elected to the United States senate from Georgia to fill a vacancy caused by the death of Hon. Benjamin Hill, and served from November 15, 1882, to the 3rd of March, 1883.

After the death of his first wife, Sarah Church (Craig) Barrow, Judge Barrow married Cornelia Augusta Jackson, daughter of the late Gen. Henry R. Jackson, of Savannah. There are five children living from his first marriage, namely, Middleton Pope Barrow, Elizabeth Church Barrow, James Barrow, David Crenshaw Barrow, and Dr. Craig Barrow. His second wife, who is now deceased, became the mother of six children, as follows: Florence Barclay, Davenport, Cornelia, Lucy Lumpkin, who is the wife of Francis P. McIntire; Patience Crenshaw Barrow and Sarah Pope Barrow. Only the last three named are living.

In 1893, Judge Barrow moved from Athens to Savannah, which city was his home during the remainder of his life. In 1900, he became judge of the superior court, of the eastern judicial circuit, and remained in this office until his death, which occurred on the 23rd of December, 1903. Judge Barrow was vice-president of the Georgia Historical Society, and held various honorary positions in other organizations. For many years he was one of the prominent figures in the political, business, and social life of the state of Georgia.

Dr. David Crenshaw Barrow II., a brother of Pope Barrow, a distinguished educator, has been for several years chancellor of the University of Georgia. The father of these two brothers was David Crenshaw Barrow I., a cotton planter of wealth and large affairs, who spent practically all of his life at his home in Athens and on his plantations in Oglethorpe county. He married Miss Lucy Pope, of Oglethorpe county, Georgia, the only child of Middleton Pope of that county, a direct descendant of the famous Nathaniel Pope of colonial Virginia. David Crenshaw Barrow I., who was born and lived in Baldwin county, after his marriage located in Oglethorpe county, but he owned plantations in both counties. He was the son of James Barrow, a native of Virginia, who entered the Continental army in North Carolina in 1776 and served in various capacities throughout the Revolutionary war. He was one of that brave little army, who under General Washington, watched through the long winter amid the cold and hardships of the camp at Valley Forge. He was sent under orders from General Lee to Savannah, and thereafter was in service in Georgia, South Carolina, North Carolina, Pennsylvania and New York, and was in the battles of Brandywine and Germantown. His last service in the war was in the North Carolina militia, and about 1800 he settled in Baldwin county, Georgia. His wife was Precious Patience Crenshaw, of Virginia.

Sarah Church (Craig) Barrow, the mother of David Crenshaw Barrow III., was the daughter of Col. Lewis Stevenson Craig, of Virginia, an officer of the United States army, who during the Mexican war, in which he was engaged, was promoted for gallantry from captain to lieutenant colonel. After the Mexican war he was placed in command of a department in California, and here he met his death at the hands of deserters. His wife was Elizabeth Church, the daughter of Alonzo Church, president of the University of Georgia, from 1829 to 1859.

David Crenshaw Barrow III., the subject of this sketch, was born on the Barrow plantation in Oglethorpe county, and grew to manhood in Athens, Georgia. He was graduated from the University of Georgia in 1894. After studying law for a time in the office of his father in Savannah he supplemented this preparation by a short course in the law department of the University of Virginia. He was admitted to the bar in Savannah in 1896 and commenced the practice of law in that year. From that time to the present his professional work has continued with uninterrupted success and he is now a lawyer of high standing at the Savannah bar.

For several years Mr. Barrow was an active member of the military organizations in Savannah. He enlisted for the Spanish-American war as a private in the Savannah Volunteer Guards, and served at Tampa, Florida, with the Second Georgia Regiment. Receiving honorable discharge from that organization, he accepted a second lieutenancy in what was known as Ray's Immunes, officially the Third United States Infantry. He went to Cuba with this regiment and served seven months in Santiago province, being adjutant of his regiment at the time of his resignation in January, 1899. Upon his return to Savannah he joined the Oglethorpe Light Infantry, one of the companies of the First Regiment of Infantry, National Guard of Georgia. He became captain of this company, from which rank he was promoted to major of the regiment. He was subsequently made lieutenant colonel and served in that capacity until he resigned from the regiment.

In 1906, Colonel Barrow was elected a member of the Georgia state legislature, as a representative from Chatham county, and served in the sessions of 1907 and 1908. In the session of 1907, he was one of those who fought the passage of the prohibition bill, and was one of the leaders of the famous filibuster against the passage of that bill. In the session of 1908 he was one of the active forces behind the legislation that abolished the convict lease system in the state of Georgia. He was assistant city attorney of Savannah for the year 1911-12. Fraternally, Mr. Barrow is a member of the Ancient Free and Accepted Masons, of the Benevolent Protective Order of Elks, and of the Knights of Pythias.

Mr. Barrow was married in Savannah, on the 10th of December, 1907, to Miss Emma Middleton Huger, a daughter of Joseph A. and Mary Elliott Huger. Mr. and Mrs. Barrow have two children, a son, Middleton Pope Barrow, and a daughter, Mary Elliott Barrow.

RAPHAEL THOMAS SEMMES, president of Semmes Hardware Company, one of the representative wholesale concerns of Savannah, was born at Canton, Madison county, Mississippi, on the 27th of July, 1857. His father, Dr. Alphonso Thomas Semmes, was born at Washington, Wilkes county, Georgia, on the 28th of April, 1830; and his mother, Mary Sabina (Semmes) Semmes, was born at Georgetown, now a part of the city of Washington, District of Columbia, on the 6th of December, 1832.

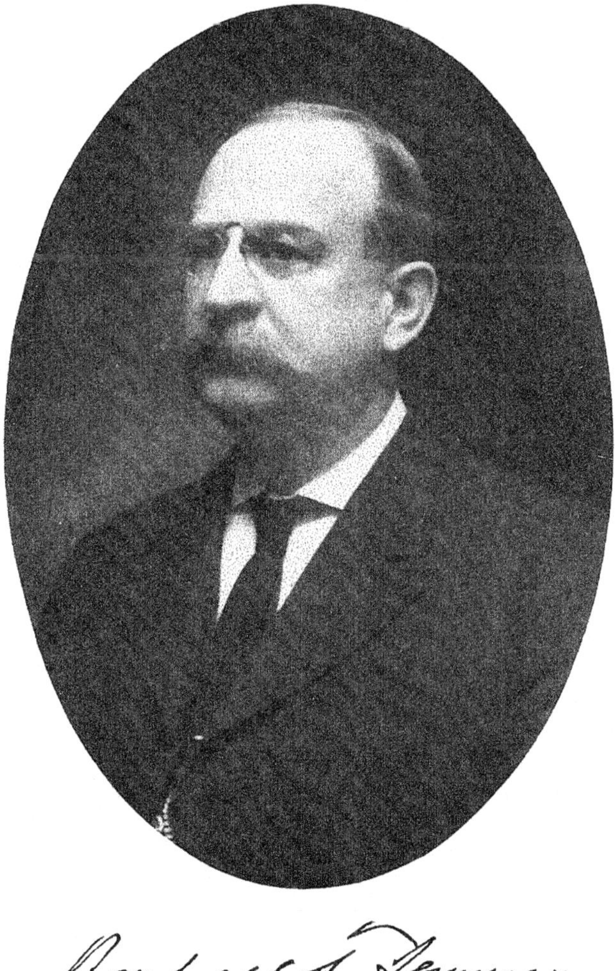

Dr. Semmes was a son of Thomas Semmes, Jr., and his first wife, Harriet Shepherd (Bealle) Semmes, the latter being a native of Columbia county,. Georgia, and a descendent of early settlers from Charles county, Maryland, whence her grandparents removed to Georgia. Thomas Semmes, Jr., was born in Wilkes county, Georgia, on the 19th of January, 1802, and was married on the 27th of January, 1829. He removed to Mississippi in 1852, and died at Canton, in May of 1862. He was the only child of Roger and Jane (Sanders) Semmes, who removed from Charles county, Maryland, to Wilkes county, Georgia. The former was born in Charles county, Maryland, in December, 1779, and removed to Wilkes county, Georgia, in 1800 or 1801, where he died in September, 1804. He was a son of Thomas Semmes, Sr., born 1753, who married a widow, Mrs. Mary Ann (Ratcliffe) Brawner, their marriage occurring in February, 1779, in Charles county, Maryland. In 1800, he removed to Wilkes county, Georgia, where he died on the 24th of June, 1824. He was a lieutenant in the Maryland line of troops in the war of the Revolution. (See Maryland archives.) He was a son of James Semmes II and Mary Simpson, his last wife, who was a daughter of Andrew and Elizabeth (Green) Simpson. Elizabeth Green Simpson was the daughter of Robert Green, and a granddaughter of Thomas Green, the first proprietary governor of the province of Maryland. James Semmes II was a son of James I and Mary (Goodrick) Semmes of Charles county, Maryland. James Semmes I was a son of Marmaduke Semmes of St. Mary's county, Maryland, and his mother, Fortune Semmes, was the widow of Bulmer Mitford (afterwards spelled Medford), who immigrated to Maryland in 1664. Her first husband died in 1666, and in July, 1668, she married Marmaduke Semmes, who in 1662 had been sworn in as doorkeeper of the upper house of the province of Maryland. (See Maryland archives.)

Mary Sabina Semmes, *nee* Semmes, mother of the subject of this sketch, was the seventh child of Raphael and Mary Matilda (Jenkins) Semmes of Georgetown, District of Columbia. The former was an uncle of Admiral Raphael Semmes of the Confederate navy, whom he adopted in childhood. Raphael Semmes, Sr., was born in Charles county, Maryland, on the 21st of August, 1786, and died on the 12th of October, 1846, at Georgetown, District of Columbia. He was a son of Joseph and Henrietta (Thompson) Semmes of Charles county, the former of whom served in the war of the Revolution (see Maryland archives), and the latter was a daughter of Richard Thompson of Charles county, the great-great-grandson of William Thompson, who settled in Maryland, in 1646. Joseph Semmes was born in 1754, in Charles county, and was a brother of Thomas Semmes, Sr., who became a resident of Georgia. They were sons of James Semmes II, and hence Joseph also was descended from Marmaduke Semmes I, and from Gov. Thomas Green, previously mentioned. Two other sons of James Semmes II, served in the Revolution, and both were killed in the battles of Long Island. One of these was Andrew Green Semmes, I, uncle of Andrew Green Semmes II, of Wilkes county, Georgia, who was the father of General Paul J. Semmes, a distinguished Confederate officer in the war between the states.

Mary Matilda (Jenkins) Semmes, the maternal grandmother of the subject of this review, was born on the 28th of December, 1800, in Charles county, Maryland, a daughter of Capt. Thomas Jenkins, of Revolutionary fame, and his wife, Mary (Neale) Corry, widow of Benjamin Leslie Corry, and daughter of Richard Neale, who was a great grandson of the famous Capt. James Neale, who was an early settler in Maryland and later was sent on an important mission to Spain in the interest of King Charles I of England, and who was still later one of those who stood on the scaffold with this unfortunate king when he was beheaded. He was a descendant of Hugh O'Neil, king of Ulster.

A notable member of the Semmes family, who once lived in Savannah, was Dr. Alexander Ignatius Semmes, a brother of Mary Sabina Semmes (mother of Raphael Thomas Semmes). Dr. Semmes was born in Georgetown, District of Columbia, was educated for the medical profession, both in America and in Europe, and practiced while living in Savannah. He married Miss Sallie Berrien, a daughter of the Hon. John McPherson Berrien of Savannah. She died without children, and after her death Dr. Semmes gave up the practice of medicine and became a Catholic priest and educator. He was professor of English literature in Pio Nono College, an institution for the education of priests, at Macon, Georgia. On account of ill health he later went to New Orleans to reside with his brother, Hon. Thomas J. Semmes, and died in that city. His reputation as a brilliant scholar is well known.

Andrew Green Simpson Semmes, a brother of Roger Semmes, the great-grandfather of Raphael Thomas Semmes, while never a resident of Savannah, had large business interests in the city. He was born in Charles County, Maryland, and came in 1800 to Wilkes county, Georgia, where he became in time, a wealthy man. He had large cotton and banking interests in Savannah, consequently was often in the city on short trips.

Dr. Alphonso T. Semmes, father of him to whom this sketch is dedicated, was an able physician, and during the war he served in the Confederacy for a time as a surgeon in the army, but for the greater portion of the time was in the hospital service. Thomas Semmes, Jr., of Georgia and later of Mississippi, grandfather of the subject of this sketch, crippled from paralysis and unable to fight for his country, equipped at his own expense a company, the Semmes Rifles. This company, raised in Canton, Mississippi, rendered valiant service in the ranks of the Confederacy.

Raphael Thomas Semmes secured his earlier educational training in the private schools in Canton, Mississippi, and supplemented this by the careful discipline and training of the Christian Brothers' College, in Memphis, Tennessee. Mr. Semmes had been in the Christian Brothers' College, barely a school year, not having reached the age of fifteen, when he left that institution in order to go to work; taking this step out of consideration for his father, who had suffered severe financial reverses through ill-advised investments in a cotton mill at Canton. In January, 1873, therefore, he became a clerk in a hardware store at Canton, and on the 9th of December, 1879, he located in Atlanta, Georgia, where he became a clerk in the hardware store of Tommey, Gregg & Beck. Two or three years later, when the firm was merged into a stock company, under the title of the Beck & Gregg Hardware Company, Mr. Semmes became a minority stockholder, and in 1891, when the concern increased its capital stock, he considerably increased his holdings. In January, 1896, he resigned his association with this company, having formed a business connection in Savannah, where he took up his residence in March of that year. In 1898, he individually established himself in the wholesale hardware business in Savannah, being the sole owner of the enterprise, but adopting the firm name of R. T. Semmes & Company. In 1901, he organized the Semmes Hardware Company, for the purpose of broadening and facilitating his business, and he has been president of the company since that time. This concern now takes rank among the leading enterprises of the kind in the southern states, and substantial growth and expansion of the same being due to the able and honorable methods and the energy and discrimination shown by

Mr. Semmes in its management. He is also a director of the Citizens and Southern Bank.

In politics, he is a staunch Democrat, and he and his wife are communicants of the Roman Catholic church, with which his ancestors have been always identified. He is a member of the Maryland Historical Society, the Virginia Historical Society, the Catholic Record Society of London, England, and of the Savannah Yacht Club. He is one of the founders of the "Society of The Ark and The Dove," whose membership is composed of descendants of those who with Lord Baltimore's original colony, sailed from England in 1633 in the Ark and the Dove and landed in Maryland, March 25, 1634. He was married on the 30th of April, 1891, to Miss Kate Flannery, daughter of Capt. John and Mary Ellen (Norton) Flannery, of Savannah, Georgia.

OLIN T. MCINTOSH. One of the most prominent and popular of the younger citizens of Savannah, Olin T. McIntosh, is a firm believer in the city and its prospects, and is never so happy as when working for its betterment, or saying a good word for it and its people. As president of the Southern States Naval Stores Company, he is intimately associated with the advancement of one of the important industries of this section of the state. A son of William Swinton and Ida S. (Talley) McIntosh, he was born, in 1881, in McIntosh county, Georgia, which was named in honor of one of his ancestors.

He is a lineal descendant in the sixth generation of John Mohr McIntosh, the immigrant ancestor, the line of descent being thus given: John Mohr,[1] William,[2] John,[3] John Nash,[4] William Swinton,[5] and Olin T.[6]

John Mohr[1] McIntosh, a native of Scotland, immigrated to this country in colonial days, settling in what is now McIntosh county, Georgia. Two of his sons, Gen. Lachlan McIntosh and Col. William McIntosh, served in the Revolutionary war, being officers in the Continental army. Col. William[2] McIntosh married Mary Mackay. Their son, John[3] McIntosh, who was a lieutenant colonel in the War of 1812, married Sarah Swinton. John Nash[4] McIntosh, major in United States army, who spent his entire life in McIntosh county, married Sallie Rokenbaugh. William Swinton[5] McIntosh, was a life-long resident of McIntosh county, his death occurring there in 1903.

Brought up and educated in McIntosh county, Olin T.[6] McIntosh has been connected with the naval stores industry since his early life, now being president of the Southern States Naval Stores Company, one of the prominent firms of naval stores factors in Savannah, the center of this immense industry. He has here been located in this business since 1896, and in the promotion of the business interests and prosperity of the city has been an active factor, in a public-spirited way being associated with the younger element that is doing great things for the growth and development of Savannah. For a number of years Mr. McIntosh was an active member of the Savannah Volunteer Guards, serving as lieutenant of Company A, of that famous organization. Fraternally, Mr. McIntosh is a member of the Ancient Free and Accepted Order of Masons the Benevolent and Protective Order of Elks, Sons of the Revolution and St. Andrew's Society.

Mr. McIntosh married Miss Janie Lawton, daughter of Asbury Lawton, of Lawtonville, who was born in South Carolina. Unto Mr. and Mrs. McIntosh two children have been born: Annie L., and Olin T., Jr.

BENJAMIN H. LEVY, leading merchant and public-spirited citizen, occupies the prominent place he does today in Savannah's business and social activities because years ago he came here and laid well the foundation for an honorable career; that the passing decades have witnessed dation for an honorable career; that the passing decades have witnessed his prosperity is due to his own keen insight into human nature and to his sterling qualities as an upright business man.

Benjamin H. Levy was born in Alsace-Loraine (then part of France), and came from his native land when a youth, to Savannah, Georgia. For a short time he clerked in the store of Julius Polinski, on Bryan street, before he made a business venture of his own. In 1871 he started out for himself, August 26th, opening a retail store at the corner of Bryan and Jefferson streets, where he remained until October, 1874. On that date he moved to the corner of Congress and Jefferson streets and here he soon built up a large country trade. In August, 1877, the business having increased, its quarters were extended to include an additional store room on Congress street, and he continued to do business at this location until 1885. In October of that year he removed to 161 Congress street, where he remained till October 1, 1895, when the present commodious quarters on West Broughton street, near Bull street, were occupied. In February, 1904, to accommodate increased business, another story was added to the building, making four stories. In 1891, a branch store was established at Brunswick, Georgia, which, like the parent establishment, has continued with undiminished success. The business was at first conducted by Mr. Levy, under his individual name. Later, his brother, Henry Levy, became a member of the firm, the name of which was then changed to B. H. Levy & Bro. On February 29, 1904, Arthur B. Levy, the son of B. H. Levy, and Sidney Levy, the son of Henry Levy, were admitted to the firm, and the name was changed to B. H. Levy Bro. & Company.

The Levy store handles both men's and women's clothing and furnishings, on a large scale, and is one of the most extensive establishments of its kind in Georgia. The store on Broughton street has a frontage of sixty feet, has four stories and basement, and is equipped and conducted in the most modern and up-to-date manner, one hundred and twenty-five people being employed. The "square-deal" spirit which pervades this establishment makes it popular alike with employe and patron.

Mr. Levy is active in both the business and the social life of Savannah. He is a director of the National Bank of Savannah, vice-president of the Georgia State Savings Association, director of the Savannah Fire Insurance Company. The board of curators of the Telfair Academy of Arts and Sciences includes him as one of its members, and he has fraternal identity with the Masonic order; he is a thirty-second degree Scottish Rite Mason and a Shriner.

Mr. Levy was married March 1, 1876, to Miss Rebecca Dryfus, of Savannah, and a native of Brockhaven, Mississippi. Besides the son above mentioned as being in business with his father, they have three other children: Stella, wife of Mr. Simon Gazan; Miss Lucile Levy and Miss Clarice Levy.

ROBERT TYLER WALLER. Of distinguished Virginia ancestry, Robert Tyler Waller, a well-known business man of Savannah, comes from a stock that has produced strong characters, particularly as soldiers, since early colonial days. A notable example of the soldierly element of the present generation of the family is Col. L. W. T. Waller, who successfully conducted operations against the insurgents in the Philippines, and later, when determined action was necessary, was sent to China. In the war between the states, every member of the Waller family in Virginia who was eligible to military duty joined the Confederate service.

A native of Virginia, Mr. Waller was born May 17, 1851, at Williamsburg, a son of William Waller, who was the third in direct line to bear that name.

Benjamin Waller, the great-great-grandfather of Mr. Waller, was a life-long resident of Virginia, and a man of great prominence and influence. He was born in 1716 and died in 1786. He was one of the leading members of the Virginia convention of 1775-1776, and during the Revolutionary war was judge of the admiralty court of that state. His son, Benjamin Carter Waller, was the next in line of descent, and his son, William Waller, second, married a daughter of Thomas and Mary, and granddaughter of Cyrus Griffin, who was the last president of the continental congress.

William Waller, third, spent his entire life in Virginia. He married Elizabeth Tyler, who also belonged to a noted Virginia family. Her father, John Tyler, a native of Williamsburg, Virginia, was active and prominent in public life, serving as a judge, a member of congress, United States senator, as vice-president, and as the tenth president of the United States. Her grandfather, the maternal great-grandfather of Mr. Waller, John Tyler, Sr., was born in Virginia in 1748. He, too, acquired distinction as a patriot and a statesman. He was a delegate to the Virginia convention of 1774; speaker of the House of Burgess; judge of the court of admiralty; as such deciding the first prize case after the War of the Revolution. He was called the "Patriot of the Revolution." He served as governor of Virginia, and was judge not only of the state district court, but of the United States district court.

Growing to manhood, Robert Tyler Waller completed his early studies in Lynchburg, at Norwood College, a famous institution of learning of the past generation. A resident of Savannah, Georgia, since 1871, he has been engaged, principally, in the cotton industry since that time. In 1905, Mr. Waller became a member of the firm of Derby & Waller, cotton warehouse men, and has since carried on an extensive and profitable business, their warehouse being one of the largest in the city. In September, 1912, Derby & Waller dissolved partnership, each party now being in business for himself.

Mr. Waller married, in Savannah, Miss Emily Greene Johnstone, who was born in Georgia, and likewise comes from a family of worth and distinction, being a great-granddaughter of Gen. Nathaniel Greene, the friend of George Washington, and commander of the troops of the Southern colonies during the Revolutionary war. Robert Tyler Waller, Jr., the only child of Mr. and Mrs. Waller, is treasurer of the Carson Naval Stores Company of Savannah.

CORNELIUS F. MOSES, manager for the Mutual Life Insurance Company, is the scion of one of the oldest families of South Carolina, whose history dates back to the period before the Revolutionary war. Mr. Moses was born in Augusta, Georgia, in 1865, where he was reared and educated. He was but twenty-one years of age when he first formed the connection with the Mutual Life Insurance Company of New York which has continued through all these years and as whose representative Mr. Moses is so widely known in the state of Georgia. His first work was as a local agent in Georgia, and through his energy and ability he was from time to time promoted to higher position. In 1898, he was appointed district agent at Savannah, and since that time he has made his headquarters in this city, here maintaining his residence. In 1905, the state was divided into two divisions, and Mr. Moses was appointed to his present position as general agent for the South Georgia territory, which embraces practically the southern half of the state. His first year's efforts in Savannah were rewarded by receiving the beautiful silver loving cup of his company, known as the "President's Cup," one of which was in that year presented to the agent in each state producing the largest amount of business. Mr. Moses' agency has never been a laggard one in the matter of productiveness, and it is recognized by the New York office as being the most productive agency of the company, in proportion to the population of the territory he represents. He is widely known as one of the most successful insurance men in the United States, and the record of his achievements in the insurance world is one of which he might well be proud. He was at one time president of the Savannah Life Underwriters' Association, at the present time he is vice-president of the Southern Managers Association of the Mutual Life Insurance Company, comprising all the southern managers of the company, and in the next year will be made president of the association. In a fraternal way, Mr. Moses is a member of Ancient Landmark Lodge No. 231, Ancient Free and Accepted Masons, and is a thirty-second degree Scottish Rite Mason, being affiliated with R. J. Nunn Consistory No. 1. He is a member of Alee Temple A. A. O. N. M. S., a member of the Oglethorpe Club, the Yacht Club, the Cotillion Club, and the Golf Club, being secretary of the last mentioned club, and an enthusiastic golfer.

In 1889, Mr. Moses was married at Washington to Miss Anna H. Sneed, a daughter of the late James Roddy Sneed, a prominent newspaper man, who was editor of the old Savannah *Republican* prior to and during the war.

THOMAS H. MACMILLAN. Noteworthy among the prominent business men and the active and enterprising citizens of Savannah, is Thomas H. MacMillan, one of the leading manufacturers of the city, a former member of the state legislature, and an ex-alderman. A native of North Carolina, he was born March 11, 1854, at Fayetteville, where he was brought up and educated.

Learning the trades of a machinist and coppersmith when young, Mr. MacMillan followed them in Fayetteville for several years. Locating in Savannah, Georgia, in December, 1878, he embarked in the manufacture of copper turpentine stills, a venture that proved so successful that he has continued it ever since, his plant being one of the substantial industries of the city. Associated in business with Mr. MacMillan is his brother, Ronald H. MacMillan, of Fayetteville, North Carolina, the firm name being MacMillan Brothers. The business of this firm has kept pace with the growth of the naval stores industry of the South, and in order to meet with greater facility the demands for their stills MacMillan Brothers maintain branch establishments at Jacksonville, Mobile and Pensacola.

The products of the MacMillan plants are notable throughout the turpentine regions for first-class material, honest, durable workmanship, and resultant satisfactory service to the user. In addition to the making of seamless stills, the MacMillan copper shops in Savannah, and the branch shops in Jacksonville, Mobile and Pensacola, manufacture other appliances used in the turpentine industry, doing general coppersmith work.

Mr. MacMillan has other interests of note, also. He established and for eight years was president, of the Savannah Blow Pipe and Exhaust Company, manufacturers of blow pipes systems. Withdrawing from that concern in 1911, he founded, in 1911, a new organization to carry on the same line of industry, it being the South Atlantic Blow Pipe and Sheet Metal Company, of which he is president, the headquarters of the company being in Savannah, with branch establishments at Jacksonville and Atlanta.

Thos. H. McMillan.

Mr. MacMillan is one of the directorate of the Citizens and Southern Bank; he is a member of the board of trade, of the chamber of commerce, and other business and social organizations. Fraternally he is a prominent member of the Ancient Free and Accepted Order of Masons, being a Knight Templar, a thirty-second degree Scottish Rite Mason, and a member of Alee Temple, Ancient Arabic Order of the Nobles of the Mystic Shrine.

For many years Mr. MacMillan has taken an active and public-spirited part in civic affairs. For two terms he served as alderman, and was chairman of the committee which had in hand the completion of the new water works system. He is a member of the Savannah park and tree commission, which is doing much towards improving and beautifying the city. During the administration of Governor Candler, Mr. MacMillan represented Chatham county in the state legislature, for two terms rendering appreciated service as a member of the finance and appropriation committees.

Mr. MacMillan married, in Savannah, Gertrude Bliss, who was born and educated in this city. Their union has been blessed by the birth of four children, namely: D. B. MacMillan, who has charge of the MacMillan interests in Pensacola; Thomas H. MacMillan, Jr., connected with the Savannah plant; Raymond H. MacMillan, representing South Atlantic Blow Pipe Company in Jacksonville; and Miss Alice MacMillan.

ROBERT P. LOVELL, of the firm of Edward Lovell Sons, hardware merchants of Savannah for many years, is one of the well-known business men of this city. He is the brother of Edward F. Lovell, who is his partner in the firm, and the son of Edward and Mary A. (Bates) Lovell.

Edward Lovell was born at Medway, Massachusetts, March 4, 1816. When he came to Savannah in 1835 the place was little more than a small seaport, but he remained in and of the city long enough to see it attain a growth and prominence which placed it among the foremost southern cities. Mr. Lovell's first business venture in Savannah as a young man of twenty-one was as proprietor of a gun store. He achieved success in the smaller venture, and was encouraged to reach out from time to time, until in 1857 he established the house of Lovell & Lattimore, his brother Nathaniel also entering the firm as a member. In 1868, Mr. Lovell retired from the firm of Lovell & Lattimore and in the fall of that year Edward F. Lovell entered into the partnership with William C. Crawford, which continued until the death of Mr. Crawford in 1884, when the firm was changed to Edward Lovell and Sons, the new members being Edward Lovell and Robert P. Lovell. The Lovell's have continued in the business established so many years ago by their father, and it has prospered in a manner highly pleasing to its members, and wholly consistent with the excellent management it has undergone in the passing years.

Mr. Lovell was for twenty-one years an active member of the Savannah Cadets, enlisting as a private, and he has occupied every rank in his company up to and including that of second lieutenant. He is a member of the Masonic fraternity, affiliating with Zerubbabel Lodge No. 15, the Georgia Chapter No. 3, R. A. M., and Palestine Commandery No. 7. He was for many years treasurer of the chapter and commandery.

In 1907, Mr. Lovell was elected mayor of the town of Tybee, on Tybee Island, and he has since served in that capacity. He has a summer home there, and has taken an active part in building up and maintaining Savannah's attractive coast resort.

In 1892, Mr. Lovell was married to Miss Katrina A. Schrim, who was born in this city. She is of German parentage, her father coming to this country from Germany in 1860. They have five children: Robert P., Jr.; William S.; Frank D.; Eleanor and Grace.

EDWARD LOVELL. Among those men who have contributed by their enterprise and public spirit to the permanent growth and prosperity of Savannah, Edward Lovell will always have a prominent place. Mr. Lovell was born at Medway, Massachusetts, on the 4th of March, 1816, and came to Savannah in 1835, then a little seaport having a limited commerce carried on by sloops and brigs, the river being too shallow to admit larger vessels. Mr. Lovell, as soon as he attained his majority, embarked in business for himself, his first venture being a gun store, and in addition to the sale of guns, he carried on a repair department. Three years of continued success in the primal undertaking warranted him in enlarging the business, and he then added a complete line of hardware and house-furnishing goods. Prosperity attended his every effort, and in 1848 he established the house known as Lovell & Lattimore, his brother Nathaniel coming into the firm as a member, as well as his friend, William Lattimore. The firm continued with this personnél until 1868. In that year his son, Edward F. Lovell, having reached his majority, Edward Lovell retired from the firm of Lovell & Lattimore, leaving the good will, the established stand of the business and the familiar firm name to his partners. Upon the death of Mr. Crawford in 1884, a new firm took its place, comprised of Edward Lovell and his two sons, Edward F. and Robert P. Lovell. The new firm soon came to be recognized as one of the largest hardware and iron houses in the state and has so continued, notwithstanding his death, which occurred on August 25, 1888.

Mr. Lovell, by his sagacity and experience laid the foundation broad and deep for an ever growing and successful business, and the impress of his wisdom and integrity is exemplified in the name of Edward Lovell Sons, under which the business still continues. Mr. Lovell was a man of great industry and application, but so methodical and exact was he in all his transactions that he was able to carry out every detail of business without hurry or confusion, accomplishing a vast amount of work without the apparent sacrifice of mental or physical activity. He was excessively loyal to his adopted city and had confidence in her ultimate success. He did not hoard his gains and after filling his coffers remove himself and his wealth to the place of his birth, there to enjoy in ease and comfort his well earned rest, but actively participated in every important enterprise that promised to advance the interest and prosperity of Savannah. He invested his income judiciously in permanent improvements, in real estate in and out of the city, and he became interested in financial and manufacturing ventures which have contributed largely to the growth and progress of Savannah. He was early interested in the Savannah & Ogeechee canal, which, in its day, floated millions of feet of lumber and timber to the city and before the construction of the Central railroad was an important highway of commerce to this point on the coast of Georgia. Mr. Lovell held the office of president of this company for many years. He was a director in the Atlantic & Gulf Railroad, president of the Savannah Brick Manufacturing Company, vice-president of the Oglethorpe Savings and Trust Company, while his name appeared as a stockholder and contributor to many of the corporations and associations formed for the promotion of manufacturing and commerce. Not only was Mr. Lovell loyal to his adopted home in contributing to its growth and material prosperity, but he was also true to it in time of war and pestilence. Although he was exempt from service by reason of his age, he served the Confederacy in superintending the construction of batteries and earthworks in the defense around Savannah. With the capacity and fitness for business so eminently displayed, Mr. Lovell possessed the estimable qualities of charity and benevolence, unostentatious but effective, dispensing relief to the needy and distressed with a lavish but discriminating hand. No worthy object ever appealed to him in vain.

Mr. Lovell was married on May 4, 1845, to Miss Mary A. Bates, of Cohasset, Massachusetts, who proved herself a devoted wife and constant companion. They became the parents of two sons, Edward F. and Robert P., who were associated with their father in business during the latter years of his life, and who now are carrying on the business founded by him. Both of them have been given more detailed mention in separate biographical sketches elsewhere in the pages of this work. The wife and mother did not long survive the death of her honored husband, her passing taking place on December 23, 1891. This worthy couple left a good name to their children, a heritage more lasting than wealth or earthly preferment. Mr. Lovell was social in his instincts and feelings, and while immersed in the cares of business and discharging many duties and trusts, both of a public and private nature, he found time to participate in the pleasant associations of Odd Fellowship as a member of Live Oak lodge, and he was for many years an honored member of that time-honored corps, the Chatham Artillery,—a military company which united the discipline of the soldier and the amenities of social engagement more successfully than any other of the volunteer militia of Georgia. Mr. Lovell was an honorary member of the Chatham Artillery at the time of his death. In connection with his military record, Mr. Lovell came of a family which has, since its establishment in America, given aid to the public cause. His father, Zachariah Lovell, son of Nathaniel, who was a Continental soldier in the Revolutionary war, and his great-grandfather, Hopestill Lovell, took part in the French and Indian war of 1745.

EDWARD F. LOVELL is a merchant of considerable prominence in Savannah, and is a member of the hardware firm established by Wm. C. Crawford and Edward F. Lovell. He was born in Savannah in 1847 and is the son of Edward and Mary A. (Bates) Lovell.

Edward Lovell was born at Medway, Massachusetts, March 4, 1816, and died in Savannah in 1888. He first came to this city in 1835. In the year 1848 he, in partnership with his brother, Nathaniel Lovell and William Lattimore, founded the firm of Lovell & Lattimore, hardware merchants. Edward Lovell was the senior member of the firm, and owner of one-half the business. The original place of business was on Bernard street, near Congress street, and the establishment was there maintained for a long period. In 1868 Edward Lovell sold his interest in the business to Nathaniel Lovell and William Lattimore, and he retired temporarily from the business, the two others mentioned continuing therein for many years thereafter. It was about the time that the elder Lovell disposed of his interests in the business that his son, Edward F. Lovell of this review, started in busines with W. C. Crawford, under the firm name of Crawford & Lovell, which was a hardware business, similar to that conducted by his father for so many years. In 1884 Mr. Crawford died, and at that time Edward Lovell, the father of Edward F. Lovell, came back into the hardware business. Robert P. Lovell, the brother of Edward F., also became a member of the firm at that time, and the firm was known as Edward Lovell & Sons. With the death of the father in 1888, the firm became Edward Lovell Sons, with Edward F. and Robert P. Lovell as the owners and members of the firm, and as such it has continued up to the present time. The elder Lovell was a man of the fine, sturdy type, possessing those qualities which made it possible for him to conduct his affairs along the lines of strictest integrity, and maintain business principles of the highest honor. He was far sighted and careful, and in the business world was known as a man of strength and wisdom. The business which he founded so many years ago still stands firm, a monument to the splendid business principles of the man who gave the best years of his life to its establishment and maintenance. In 1872 the Lovell store was removed from Congress street to Broughton street, and in 1906 was moved to its present position, 14-18 State street, West.

Both Edward F. Lovell and his father were Confederate soldiers in the Civil war. The elder Lovell was a member of Company A, Chatham Siege Artillery, in which he was very active, and he had charge of the work of placing the cannon for the defense of the city of Savannah. Edward F. Lovell joined Simmons' Battalion in the Georgia Reserves in 1864 on his seventeenth birthday. His service was mostly in the vicinity of Savannah till the occupation by Sherman's army, after which he was in the Carolinas till the close of the war.

Mr. Lovell is the oldest living director of the Citizens Southern Bank, Savannah's largest financial institution.

In 1870 Mr. Lovell was married in Savannah to Miss Emily Williams Dasher, a native of this city. They have three children: Edward F., Jr., Gilbert M., and Mary Laura, the wife of R. S. Cope.

THOMAS FREEMAN THOMSON. The gentleman to a brief review of whose life the reader's attention is herewith directed is one of Chatham county's most admirable public officials and business men and has by his enterprise and progressive methods contributed in a material way to the development of city and county. He has in the course of an honorable career been most successful in his various associations and is well deserving of mention in the biographical memoirs of this part of Georgia. Thomas Freeman Thomson, state and county tax collector, was born in Macon, Georgia, July 12, 1850, the son of Dr. Methven S. and Mary E. (Freeman) Thomson. He is of Scotch descent, the birth of his father having occurred at Perth, Scotland, January 7, 1815. The elder gentleman was reared and educated there and came to America at about the age of twenty-one years. He located in Macon, Georgia, about the year 1840 and resided there for over half a century, his demise occurring December 10, 1893. He had been all his life active in the practice of his profession and was widely known throughout middle Georgia. He was three times mayor of Macon, being the "war mayor" of the city and serving in such capacity throughout the period of the great conflict. Dr. Thomson is remembered by all as a man of the finest characteristics. The subject's mother, who died in January, 1887, was of an older family in Georgia. She was born on Staten Island, New York, October 24, 1824, the daughter of Azel Roe and Delia (Shaw) Freeman. Azel Roe Freeman was a soldier of the War of 1812, who removed to Macon with his family in 1827. Her brother, George C. Freeman, who is the father of Judge Davis Freeman, of the Savannah city court, removed from Macon to Savannah in 1854 and is still living in this city.

The youth of Mr. Thomson was passed in the troublous days preceding and during the Civil war. Mr. Thomson received as good an education as was possible under the circumstances. He received a good commercial training in Eastman's Business College at Poughkeepsie, New York, from which he was graduated in 1869.

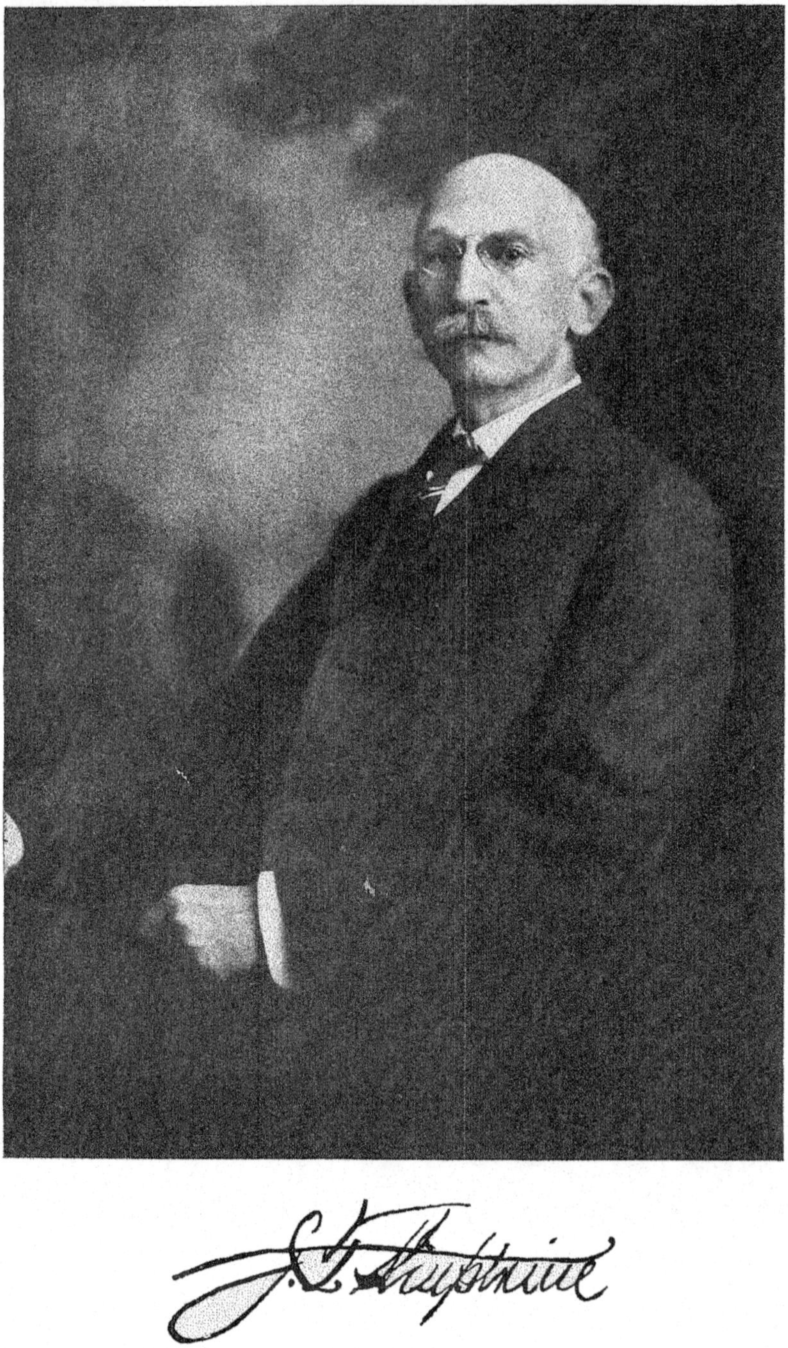

In January, 1870, Mr. Thomson came to Savannah, which has since been his home. His first position was in charge of the books of a wholesale and retail grocery house. From this position he went into the old Southern Bank, as bookkeeper; this bank, established in 1870, was the beginning of the present Citizens' & Southern Bank. Leaving the Southern Bank he became connected with the Merchants' National. Subsequently he became identified with the National Bank of Savannah, when it was established November 10, 1885, and for eleven years he was cashier of this bank. Altogether he was twenty-five years in the banking business in Savannah—six years with the Southern, eight years with the Merchants' and eleven years with the National Bank of Savannah.

For four years after retiring from the bank he was special agent for the New England Mutual Life Insurance Company. Then in 1901 he was elected to the office of state and county tax collector of Chatham county, which he has filled, by successive elections. ever since. He is a very popular official and his office has a wide reputation for efficiency.

Mr. Thomson is a Mason of statewide prominence, of both the York and Scottish Rites, a Knights Templar, and thirty-second degree Scottish Rite Mason, and in addition is a Shriner. He was for several years treasurer of the Scottish Rite bodies in Savannah. He was for ten years a member of military organizations in Savannah, first of the Savannah Cadets, and then with the Chatham Artillery. By election of the Savannah Cadets he is an honorary life member of that historic organization. He is also a life member of the Benevolent and Protective Order of Elks and no one is more beloved in fraternal circles. He and his wife are members of Wesley Monumental Methodist church.

Mr. Thomson was married in Savannah, Miss Margaret J. Meldrim, of this city, daughter of Ralph and Jane (Fawcett) Meldrim, becoming his wife. She is a sister of Gen. Peter W. Meldrim, one of the leading lawyers of Savannah. Mr. Thomson and his admirable wife are the parents of six children, all fine citizens and all sharing the high ideals of their parents. They are: Ralph M. Thomson, Rev. Thomas H. Thomson, Robert C. Thomson, Edward G. Thomson, Margaret M., wife of Mr. Earl Dasher, and Meldrim Thomson. There are seven grandchildren. Mr. and Mrs. Robert C. Thomson have three children: Thomas F., Jr., Robert P. and John L. Rev. Thomas H. Thomson and wife have two daughters, Eunice and Sarah; and Mr. and Mrs. E. L. Dasher have a son, Thomas Thomson Dasher. Mr. and Mrs. Meldrim Thomson, of Pittsburgh, Pennsylvania, have one son. Meldrim Thomson, Jr.

HERMAN C. SHUPTRINE. No name is more prominent in pharmaceutical affairs in Georgia than that of Shuptrine, the family, father and son, having been identified with this profession for a great many years. In addition to their prestige as good business men and exceptionally skilled druggists, the Shuptrines are public-spirited and of unswerving principles and none is more worthy of representation in a volume of this nature.

Herman C. Shuptrine, prominent Savannah druggist and president of the National Association of Retail Druggists, was born in this city, the son of the late James Thaddeus Shuptrine, and of his wife, whose maiden name was Sarah Newton. Of the former, whose much lamented demise occurred on August 15, 1911, more will be told in succeeding paragraphs. Herman C. was born in 1877, and here was reared and for the most part educated, his preliminary education being secured in the public schools of the city, after which he matriculated in Emory College, Georgia. Before he became of age, he entered his father's store and he has been connected with it ever since, becoming a skillful pharmacist and thoroughly skilled in merchandising methods. Since his father's death he has been president of the Shuptrine Company, which had been incorporated by his father. He is one of the prominent young business men of Savannah, aggressive and enterprising, of the type which is aiding in the upbuilding of the city. He is active in the many-sided life of the city and is a member of Ancient Landmark lodge of Masons and a former member of the Savannah Cadets.

In September, 1911, Mr. Shuptrine was elected president of the National Association of Retail Druggists, at the thirteenth annual convention of that body, held at Niagara Falls. He is probably the youngest druggist who has ever been at the head of the organization, of which over 17,000 druggists are members. This conspicuous honor came to him quite unsolicited, his election having been brought about through the influence of his wide circle of friends in the association, and it was a source of commendable gratification not only to himself, but to the druggists and citizens generally of his home city, Savannah. In 1907 he was elected a member of the Georgia board of pharmacy for a term of five years, and in 1912, re-elected to the same office, and is a member of the board of education of the city of Savannah. It is an eloquent commentary upon his ability and the respect and confidence in which he is held.

Mr. Shuptrine was married in Savannah on the 8th day of June, 1898, the young woman to become his wife and the mistress of his household being Miss Alice Elizabeth Vendeveer, who was born in this city. They share their attractive home with a son and a daughter, namely: James T. and Sarah.

James Thaddeus Shuptrine, father of the foregoing, was the second oldest druggist in Savannah and one of the Forest city's most highly esteemed citizens. He was a native Georgian, his life record having begun in Effingham county, on October 15, 1850. His parents were D. C. and Caroline (Newton) Shuptrine. He passed the early years of his life in his native county and received the education accorded to the usual youth of his day and generation. Immediately upon reaching manhood he became identified with the drug business and he continued in this field of endeavor until the time of his death. It is speaking with all due conservatism, to say that he was one of the most widely known druggists in all the length and breadth of the state.

He had spent the greater part of his life in this city, having taken up his residence here at the age of nineteen years. His first business venture was in the employ of the late J. M. Heidt, whose drug store was located on the corner of Whitaker and Congress streets. He remained with that gentleman for six years and following that connection took charge of the drug business of J. H. Polhill on Abercorn street. He remained with Mr. Polhill until 1876, and was in this association at the time of the yellow fever scourge which swept over Savannah in that year. It is characteristic that he remained at his post throughout that trying period.

Mr. Shuptrine went into business for himself in 1877, his store being located a few doors below the present location of the Shuptrine Company. He moved into his present commodious quarters on Congress street about fifteen years ago and in the year 1906 the business was incorporated. Mr. Shuptrine was particularly successful in his business ventures. Scrupulously conscientious in his dealings, kind and considerate in his private life, he won the admiration and respect of all with whom he came in contact. He was at one time president of the Georgia Pharmaceutical Association and for many years acted as its treasurer.

Mr. Shuptrine laid one of the most important stones in the foundation of his success by his marriage on February 17, 1876, to Miss Sarah, Newton. Their happy union was blessed by the birth of the following children: Mrs. Walter B. Stillwell, Mrs. F. E. Johnston, and Herman C. Shuptrine. He also had five grandchildren. He was essentially domestic in nature, finding his greatest pleasure about his own fireside. His home at 308 Bolton street, West, was known as one of the hospitable abodes of a city where hospitality has become a highly cultivated virtue.

Mr. Shuptrine was a member of Landrum Lodge of Masons and exemplified in his own life the ideals of moral and social justice and brotherly love for which the order stands. The Masonic body held the last ceremonial rites and consigned all that was mortal of him to the grave. He had for many years been a member of the First Baptist church and was a member of the board of deacons at the time of his passing to the Great Beyond. It has been said of him that he was recognized all over the state as a man of shrewd business sagacity, as well as an accomplished druggist. He was distinguished for unusual physical activity, and success was pretty sure to crown his undertakings. He was interested in all that pertained to the unity and advancement of his profession and retained his office of treasurer in the Georgia Pharmaceutical Association until the June before his death, when he was forced to retire on account of declining health. He was active in the local association of druggists up to a few years ago. The memory and influence of this gentleman will not soon be lost in the community which so profited by his good citizenship.

JOHN WARD MOTTE. In the field of production of naval stores, it is safe to say that no one man is more widely known than John Ward Motte, president of the Producers' Naval Stores Company and very prominent in the commercial affairs of Savannah. Mr. Motte is one of those native Southerners, who within recent years have manifested a remarkable capacity in the promotion and conduct of great commercial and industrial businesses amounting to genius and to them is due in great part the renewed prosperity of the South, which is going forward with leaps and bounds. This distinguished Savannah citizen was born at Cheraw, in Chesterfield county, South Carolina. His paternal ancestry is of French Huguenot origin, his forbears having located in Charleston, South Carolina, early in the history of that city and they and their descendants have resided there for many years. In 1889, Mr. Motte came to Savannah and this city has ever since been his home.

It was in the year above mentioned that Mr. Motte first became identified with the naval stores business and his main business interests have always been centered in the naval stores industry. He is the president of the Producers' Naval Stores Company, one of the most prominent and successful corporations engaged in this industry. This company is the successor to the John R. Young Company, which in turn was the successor to the Ellis-Young Company. Mr. Motte is also president of the Blue Creek Company, a large producing naval stores organization operating in Florida. He is financially interested in several other companies engaged in one way or another in the naval stores business. In addition to these he has many other interests of wide scope and importance. He is a director of the Savannah Bank & Trust Company, a history of which appears elsewhere in this work. It is this company which built the splendid fifteen-story office building at Bull and Bryan streets, perhaps the finest structure of its kind in the South, and a source of great pride to all Savannahians. The general offices of Mr. Motte's companies are in this building.

Mr. Motte is vice-president and director of the board of trade and for many years has been one of its most active and useful members. He has been either at the head of or a member of several important delegations from the board that have accomplished great results for Savannah. It is due to the public spirited efforts of such citizens as Mr. Motte that Savannah has become one of the wealthiest, most prosperous and most enterprising cities of the South. He is a man of splendid ability and the continual progress and present standing of those enterprises with which he is identified are largely to be credited to his experience, executive ability, engineering skill and genius in the broad combination and concentration of applicable forces.

The Chatham Nurseries (successors to the W. J. Stevenson Company), operating extensive green houses and a nursery in Savannah at Dale and Waters avenues, is fortunate in posessing Mr. Motte as president.

Mr. Motte was for several years an active member of the Savannah Volunteer Guards, and served with this command in the Spanish-American war. Upon his return to the city at the termination of the conflict he became an officer of the guards. Although eminently well fitted for the successful assumption of public trust, he has served in but one office, namely, county commissioner of Chatham county, to which he was elected in 1906 and re-elected in 1910.

He is a prominent club man, belonging to the Oglethorpe Club, the Savannah Yacht Club, the Masonic order, the Elks and other social and fraternal organizations.

JAMES FAIRLIE COOPER MYERS. It is distinctively within the province of this historical compilation to enter record concerning the captains of those staunch and important commercial and industrial concerns through which is being conserved the progress and prestige of Savannah. James Fairlie Cooper Myers is vice-president of the Germania Bank, also the American Naval Stores Company, of this city, a concern of national magnitude. He has been identified with the company in one capacity or another since 1881, when as a boy he secured a minor position with its principal predecessor, and no small degree of its rapid, steady growth and its present splendid scope and completeness may be partially traced to his executive ability, tireless energy, engineering skill and genius in the broad combination and concentration of applicable forces.

Mr. Myers was born in Atlanta, Georgia, on the 7th day of April, 1867. His parents were Francis Nimis Myers and Mary Fairlie (Cooper) Myers.

On his maternal side, Mr. Myers' ancestry presents an interesting and fascinating record. His mother, Mary Fairlie (Cooper) Myers, is the daughter of the late James Fairlie Cooper, who was a civil engineer of distinction and a resident of Alabama for a number of years. One of his most prominent achievements as an engineer was the building of the Western & Atlanta Railroad, which was financed by the state of Georgia, and of which he became manager after its completion. It was this which caused him to become a resident of Georgia.

Thomas Apthorpe Cooper, the eminent English actor, the stage tutor of the elder Booth and of Edwin Forrest, after his removal from London to New York, in 1830, married Miss Mary Fairlie, a young woman widely famed for her wit and beauty and for her artistic and intellectual qualities. She was the daughter of Maj. James Fairlie, who was aid-de-camp on the staff of General Washington in the Revolutionary war and who subsequently served as clerk of the supreme court of New York. Mary Fairlie was the granddaughter of Gov. Robert Yates of

New York (one of the colonial governors), and through this distinguished forbear the subject secured membership in the Society of Colonial Wars. The Fairlies were intimate friends of Washington Irving and Mary Fairlie was the original of the character Sophie Sparkle in "Salamagundi." One of the daughters of Thomas and Mary (Fairlie) Cooper, Priscilla Cooper, was likewise noted for her great charm of personality. She became an actress of note and her playing of the part of Virginia in her father's production of "Virginius," in which the latter played the title role, at the old Bowery theatre of New York, was a notable theatrical event of the early days. Priscilla Cooper gave up the stage upon her marriage to Robert Tyler, son of President Tyler. On account of the ill health of the wife of President Tyler, Priscilla Cooper Tyler became virtually the "Mistress of the White House" and her reign as such forms a delightful chapter in the social history of Washington.

Mr. Myers is one of Savannah's most distinguished members of the Sons of the American Revolution and his membership in the same comes from descent on his paternal side from Philip Minis, of whom he is the great-great-grandson. Philip Minis was born in Georgia in 1736 and it seems to be a pretty clearly established fact that he was the first white child born in the colony of Georgia, which was founded in 1733. On account of his activities in behalf of the Continental army during the Revolutionary war, he was named in the Georgia Royal Disqualifying Act of 1780. He passed to the great beyond in 1789.

Thus it will be seen that few have as inspiring a connection with the early years of American history and the spirit of the men who achieved American independence has come as a legacy to Mr. Myers, whose patriotism is manifest as a particularly fine type of citizenship. He is a genial gentleman, always courteous and considerate, of broad human sympathies and tolerance, and possessed of that sincere love of his fellow men without which there can never be the highest success. All measures likely to result in general benefit are sure of his support.

Mr. Myers was reared in Marietta, Georgia, where he attended school. In 1881, before he was fourteen years of age, he came to Savannah and soon after secured a position in the naval stores firm of S. P. Shotter & Company, with which business he has been connected ever since. It has since become the American Naval Stores Company, the organization of which was promoted by Mr. Shotter, and Mr. Myers holds the office of vice-president. The American Naval Stores Company is a very large and wealthy corporation, founded on Mr. Shotter's original company and embracing a number of other companies which have since been absorbed. Mr. Myers has made a splendid rise in the world of commerce. Besides the position above mentioned, he is president of the South Atlantic Steamship Company and of the National Transportation and Terminal Company. He is vice-president of the National Tank & Export Company and an officer of or financially interested in other commercial enterprises of importance. He has lived in Savannah continuously since 1881, with the exception of eight years, from 1886 to 1894, when he was a resident of New York City in charge of the offices of his company there. He is a director of the Germania Bank.

Mr. Myers was married in Savannah to Miss Lina Anderson, daughter of John W. Anderson. Their happy marriage has been blessed with a son and a daughter—John Anderson and Carolyn Cooper. To see Mr. Myers at his best socially it is necessary to meet him in his delightful home. There his easy dignity, generous hospitality and cordial ways mark him at once as a true gentleman.

ADAM COPE HARMON, for a number of years identified with the insurance business in Savannah and a resident of that city all his life, is a member of one of the oldest families known to the city. He was born here in 1850 and is the son of Abram and Anna Rosa (Cope) Harmon. The father was born near Lexington in lower South Carolina, and his father, the grandfather of Adam Cope Harmon of this review, was born in Germany. He came to America and located near Lexington, South Carolina, where he passed the remainder of his life. His son, Abram Harmon, came to Savannah in about 1830 and died in 1859. The mother of Adam Cope Harmon was Anna Rosa Cope. She was born in Savannah and there lived her entire life. She was the daughter of Adam Cope, one of the well known early citizens of Savannah, who was born in England and came to Savannah in the days of Oglethorpe. He furnished active aid and support to the Continental army during the War of the Revolution, after which he became prominent in the public affairs of the city. He was one of the marshals who officiated at the notable occasion of Lafayette's visit to Savannah in March, 1825, and was one of those to assist in the entertainment of the city's distinguished and honored guest.

Mr. Harmon is the youngest child of his parents. His oldest brother, Richard Fuller Harmon, now deceased, was in the cotton business in Savannah for many years and was a prosperous and prominent man. He was always active and prominent in public affairs, and Harmon street was named in his honor. He was a member of the city council, in which body he was chairman of the committee on streets and lanes. One other brother is living at Savannah—Abram W. Harmon.

The early education of Mr. Harmon was but a limited one, owing to the meagre school facilities that were available during and just following the war. He was a student in the private school of J. F. Cann for a short time, but the greater part of his education was self-acquired. Beginning life for himself he first went into the drug business, in which he was engaged for four years. He then became chief clerk in charge of the wharf for the line of steamships between Savannah and Washington and after some little time thus employed he went into the retail grocery business. He later engaged in the milling business, and conducted a rice and corn mill in Savannah. This latter venture proved to be most unprofitable, and upon getting clear of it he engaged in the brokerage business, and later in the rice trade. In about 1900 Mr. Harmon became established in the insurance business, in which he has since been successfully engaged. He is agent for the Continental Fire Insurance Company of New York, also general agent for the Pacific Mutual Life Insurance Company of San Francisco, each of which ranks among the highest of its class in the United States, and in the years which have elapsed since first identifying himself with the insurance busines, he has proven himself in every way fitted to handle the line in a successful manner, and the results of his labors have been profitable and pleasant.

Mr. Harmon is one of the directors of the Savannah Benevolent Association, and he is a member of the Masonic fraternity, being past master of Zerubbable lodge A. F. & A. M. and a Knights Templar.

In 1893 Mr. Harmon was united in marriage with Mrs. Isaquene (Lythgoe) Parrot, who was born in South Carolina of English parentage. Mr. Harmon has one son, Wayman Potter Harmon.

GORDON SAUSSY. The legal profession of Savannah, Georgia, includes among its members Gordon Saussy, who has been identified with the practice of law here for over fifteen years.

Norman

L. Norman

Mr. Saussy is a native of Savannah. He was born February 14, 1872, son of Robert and Gertrude L. (Keller) Saussy. His father, also a native of Savannah, born Dec. 24, 1840, now lives near this city, at Bonna Bella in Chatham county. For several years he was actively and prominently connected with the Central Railroad of Georgia and the Ocean Steamship Company. He was a member of the Georgia Hussars before the war, and upon the beginning of the conflict between the states he volunteered as a private, and served as such with efficiency and fidelity. In February, 1863, he was promoted to second lieutenant of Company A of the Hussars. October 27, 1864, he was seriously wounded at the battle of Wilson's Farm, near Boydtown plank road, below Burgess Mill, Virginia, and was incapacitated thereby till the close of the war. From 1866 to 1898, he made his home in New York City, where he was engaged in railroad and steamship service, and in the latter year he returned to his old home in Georgia. As above stated, he is now a resident of Bonna Bella, near Savannah.

Although born in Georgia, Gordon Saussy went to New York in early life and received his education there. He attended the College of the City of New York, and studied law in the law department of Cornell University, from which he was graduated in the class of 1896. That year he began the practice of his profession in Savannah, and here he has continued up to the present time.

NEWTON J. NORMAN. One of the most conspicuous figures in the recent history of this part of Georgia is the well-known gentleman whose name introduces this review. An enumeration of the men of this part of the state who have won honor and public recognition for themselves and at the same time have honored the community in which they live would be incomplete without reference to Newton J. Norman, a lawyer of admirable ability and solicitor general of the Atlantic circuit, comprising the five counties, viz.: Liberty, Bryan, McIntosh, Effingham and Tattnall.

Mr. Norman was born at Flemington, Liberty county, Georgia, September 12, 1855, the son of Capt. William S. and Susan Lorenna (Stacey) Norman. The father was born at Walthourville, Liberty county, Georgia, February 26, 1822, and died August 15, 1878. He was a lawyer by profession, a graduate of the State University at Athens, with T. R. Cobb, Charles C. Jones and others whose names are associated prominently with Georgia history, and afterwards studied law under Joseph Wilkins and Wm. B. Fleming. At the beginning of his law practice he removed from Walthourville to Hinesville, the county seat of Liberty county and situated about two miles from Flemington, and afterwards to Flemington. In addition to his professional interests he also became a large planter in Liberty county. At the beginning of the war he raised a company which was known as the Liberty Volunteers, becoming captain of the same and being stationed at Tybee island. After six months service his entire family were taken down with typhoid fever, which required his presence at home, and during which time his command joined the army of Northern Virginia. As soon as his family was sufficiently recovered for him to take up duties again for the Confederacy, he was appointed solicitor of revenue, under the Georgia Confederate government, for the counties of Liberty and Bryan, which position he held with efficiency until the close of the war. Upon the termination of the great conflict, he was elected judge of the county court of Liberty county, and after four years on the bench, he resumed the practice of law, in which he continued actively until his death. Captain Norman, in addition to his high repute as a lawyer and jurist, was also a writer of note, both of prose and poetry; his literary qualifications being of particularly high order. He was a member of and active participant of the affairs of old Midway church in Liberty county, the oldest and most historic church organization in Georgia. The subject's mother was likewise a native of Walthourville. She survived her husband for five years, her demise occurring on August 15, 1883. The family has long been established in this part of the South. Mr. Norman's paternal grandfather was William Norman, who was also a native of Liberty county, as was also the great grandfather, William Norman. The great-great-grandfather, also named William, was born in Dorchester, South Carolina and removed from that place to Midway, Georgia, March 22, 1771.

Newton J. Norman has passed his entire life in the state. He was reared and educated in Liberty county, one of the schools he attended being Bradwell Institute at Hinesville. He studied law under Judge John L. Harden and was admitted to the bar of Liberty county in 1894. Since that time he has maintained his residence and law practice at Flemington, but for several years has had a law office in Savannah, where he has his winter residence. He has occupied several public positions of importance and trust. In 1888, he was elected a member of the board of county commissioners of Liberty county. He resigned from that position to become a candidate for the state legislature, to which he was elected in 1890, serving one term. In the exciting race for United States senator, between Gen. John B. Gordon and Thomas M. Norwood, in that session of the legislature, it was Mr. Norman's vote, as will be recalled, that elected General Gordon to the senate.

Following this he was re-elected to membership on the board of county commissioners of Liberty county, but before his term expired he resigned as such and was elected in December, 1900 to fill an unexpired term as solicitor of the Liberty County court; at the end of this term he was elected to the position for a full term. In October, 1906, he was elected to his present position, solicitor general of the Atlantic circuit, and in 1910, he was re-elected to this position for another term of four years. He is one of the lawyers of whom Savannah is justly proud, his usefulness to the city and to the profession which he so greatly adorns being of the most definite sort. In addition to his duties as solicitor general, Mr. Norman has a general civil practice in courts other than his own.

Mr. Norman's wife before her marriage was Miss Minnie Box, who was born in Hampton county, South Carolina. They have three interesting children: Iola, Sarah Lorenna and Newton J. Norman, Jr.

Mr. Norman took a leading part in the reorganization of the old Midway church and in the re-establishment of regular religious services there after an interval of many years. At the meeting in which this reorganization took place he was elected president of the board of selectmen of the church and he has continued to take an active leading part in the affairs of that historic organization. Honored and respected by the people of both city and county, he enjoys a large measure of public esteem, not only for his professional achievements. but also for his worthy standing in the domain of private citizenship.

DANIEL REMSHART THOMAS. Mr. Thomas was born in Savannah August 27, 1843. He is a son of the late John T. Thomas, whose grandparents were among the French Huguenots who arrived in Charleston about the middle of the last century, while his maternal ancestors were Salzburgers and among the early settlers of the colony of Georgia.

As a child, a delicate constitution and imperfect sight interfered with Mr. Thomas' education. In 1862 he enlisted in the Confederate army with the Tattnall Guards, First Volunteer Regiment of Georgia. After a prolonged sickness he was, on the recommendation of the post surgeon and his commanding officer, detailed for duty at district headquarters and in the war tax office. His services in this position were mostly of a clerical nature and were performed with such exactness and efficiency as to win the highest commendation.

Soon after the close of the war Mr. Thomas began business as an insurance agent in Macon, where he remained until March, 1866. From Macon he returned to Savannah, and in July of the same year became associated with Capt. D. G. Purse (now deceased), in the commission, fertilizer and coal business, which, by the application of close and undivided attention, soon became large and profitable. In December, 1878, the firm of Purse & Thomas was dissolved, Mr. Thomas continuing in the coal trade.

In 1874, his sight having become so impaired and his suffering so great, Mr. Thomas sought the aid of an oculist and an optician, from which he obtained such relief and benefit as to greatly change his life and interest him in what was transpiring about him, especially with reference to public affairs in Savannah. In the compromise made by the city with the bondholders he took an active interest. In December, 1878, upon the organization of the Sinking Fund Commission, a new department of the municipal government of Savannah, Mr. Thomas was elected an original member of this commission and served as its secretary until January, 1883, when he resigned to accept the office of alderman, to which he was elected in that year. After serving six years in the council, he was in 1891 re-elected a member of and secretary of the Sinking Fund Commission, serving at that time six and a half years, after which he was again elected a member of the city council.

Mr. Thomas served the city with great usefulness as an alderman, under the administrations of Mayors Lester, Meldrim and Myers, for a period of thirteen and a half years. He was a member of the sanitary commission, making a thorough study of the city's system of sewerage and house drainage. He has long been known as one of the best posted authorities on these matters, and his advice, embodying the practical results of his knowledge thereof, has been considered of much value by each city administration. He was an active member and at various times chairman of several important committees of the council, including those on accounts, finance, streets and lanes, city lots and opening of streets. As chairman of the special committees on city extension and house drainage he took a very lively interest. In appreciation of his services to the city of Savannah Thomas park was named in his honor.

As treasurer of the committee for the relief of the sufferers by the Yamacraw fire, Mr. Thomas devoted a great deal of time to that beneficent work.

During the period that Mr. Thomas was a member of the council, no alderman was better acquainted with the affairs of the city than he. It is doubtful if the city ever had a public servant with such a thorough grasp of its varied affairs as had Mr. Thomas, nor one who so ably discharged his duties. The amount of money he has saved the city in various ways could hardly be estimated.

Fully a year before the expiration of Mayor Lester's last term, public sentiment apparently crystalized about Mr. Thomas as the best and most available successor. At a convention of the Democratic club held in Masonic hall January 4, 1889, Mr. Thomas was nominated for mayor, another candidate having been in the field for more than a month. The election came on in a few days and was a close one, Mr.

Thomas being defeated. The following strong endorsement of him is from an editorial in the *Morning News* appearing during that campaign: "Mr. Thomas is a man of fine business qualifications. He has proven himself to be one of the most competent and progressive councilmen the city has ever had. The greater part of the improvements that have been made during the last few years is the result of his earnest, consistent and conscientious efforts. He may not have pleased everybody, but he has done so much better than most of those who preceded him in his present position, that those who have been disposed to find fault have not found willing listeners. He is economical and careful."

Many of the large incorporated institutions of Savannah have received the benefit of the sound judgment and practical suggestions of Mr. Thomas. He has served as director of railroad companies, banks, investment companies and such enterprises as have contributed materially in building up the city. The Brush Electric Light & Power Company, which was succeeded by the Savannah Electric Company, and De Soto Hotel each received substantial support and liberal subscriptions from Mr. Thomas. In the former company he served as vice-president for many years. He was a director in the old Savannah & Western Railroad Company and in the Citizens' Bank, and is now a director in the Savannah Investment Company, and he is still a director of the Savannah Hotel Company, which built and owns and operates the De Soto Hotel. In 1910, after a service of thirty-one years in the various offices, including that of president, of the Union Society, Mr. Thomas retired, and is thus the only ex-president of that charity. By length of service, he is the senior ruling elder of the Independent Presbyterian church. Though no longer in public office, he is still keenly interested in all the important activities of the city, and, as in former years, his advice and counsels are sought in municipal affairs and in business matters.

Mr. Thomas was married in 1867 to Miss Jennie Manget of Marietta, Georgia, who still shares the fortunes of his life. They have two living children, Mrs. John A. Robeson and John Murchison Thomas. The latter has been a member of the firm of D. R. Thomas & Son since 1892. This firm, which was organized May 13, 1892, with father and son as senior and junior members, is one of the large and successful establishments of its kind in Savannah, carrying on an extensive coal trade. Mr. Thomas has taken the York rites in Masonry, being a member of Palestine commandery.

WILLIAM F. MCCAULEY. The banking interests of a community are so important to its prosperity, that to a large degree the outside world passes judgment according to the proved stability of its financial institutions and the personality of those who direct their policies. Among the old and substantial banks of Savannah, Georgia, the Savannah Bank & Trust Company occupies a foremost place, and as its able, alert, experienced and resourceful president, William F. McCauley is numbered with the leading financiers of the state.

William F. McCauley was born at Savannah, Georgia, and is a son of William J. and Susan (Timmons) McCauley. The father was of Irish ancestry but was born in South Carolina, and his death occurred during the boyhood of his son, William F. The mother still lives in her native city, Savannah. A fatherless boy has many drawbacks to contend with, especially when self-support is a necessity in early youth, but, on the other hand, this necessary effort is often a spur that arouses ambition and stirs up energy that results in a self-dependence that is the very foundation stone of business success. His education was secured in the Savannah schools. During his youth and early manhood he was connected with maritime affairs and was in the tug boat business, subsequently acquiring the proprietorship of a business of his own in this line in the harbor of his native city and continued until he became identified with the Chatham Bank as its cashier, which position he resigned in 1898. In 1900 he became cashier of the Savannah Bank & Trust Company, subsequently its vice-president and in 1906 assumed the presidency and the active management of this financial institution.

The Savannah Bank & Trust Company was founded in 1869, and enjoys the confidence of the entire financial field. Its original capital was $100,000, while at present, its capital, surplus and undivided profits amount to over $1,200,000. In January, 1912, the bank moved into its new building, situated at the corner of Bull and Bryan streets, Savannah. This handsome structure, fifteen stories high, fire-proof, and modern in every particular, was erected by the company which occupies the entire main floor, the whole of which is elegantly fitted for its accommodation and with every known convenience and safety appliance to ensure the rapid and satisfactory transaction of an immense banking business. To the completion of this handsome building Mr. McCauley has devoted much attention, having realized for some time that the old quarters were inadequate, and he is justly pleased to have so beautiful a home for the bank, the affairs of which he has so successfully guided for a number of years. While giving the larger part of his time to the bank, Mr. McCauley has not neglected his duties as a citizen and for a long period has been one of the dependable public men of Savannah, serving since 1906 as a member of the board of aldermen and in other positions where his public spirit and business sense have been particularly beneficial.

HUBERT O. YOUNG. The material growth and improvement of the city of Savannah, Georgia, have felt the influence of an active factor in the person of Hubert O. Young, contractor and builder, 518 West 40th street.

Mr. Young is a native of Oglethorpe, Macon county, Georgia, and was born in 1868, son of George T. and Muschogia (Draughton) Young, both deceased. George T. Young was born in Columbia, South Carolina, but when a boy came with his parents to Georgia, their settlement being in Macon county, where he was reared. His wife was a native of Georgia.

On his father's farm Hubert O. passed his boyhood and youth, with very meagre educational advantage. At the age of twenty-one years, he began to work at the carpenter's trade in Macon, with R. C. Wilder Sons. with whom he remained two years. Then he entered the car shops of the Central of Georgia Railway, at Macon, where he spent four years, and in that time thoroughly learned every detail of the car builder's trade. On leaving the car shops in June, 1891, he came to Savannah, which has since been his home. Here his initial work was as a journeyman on the Guckenheimer building on West Bay street, under John R. Eason, contractor. For ten years he worked as a journeyman, and during the ten years he also took a two years' course of mechanical and architectural drawing at the Y. M. C. A., Savannah, Georgia. Meanwhile he took a course in architectural and mechanical drawing, under the direction of the International Correspondence School of Scranton, Pennsylvania, and thus fitted himself for enlarging his efforts and going into business for himself. In 1903 he began business as a contractor and builder on his own account, without a dollar of capital, but with the ability to borrow money based upon a well-earned reputation for honesty and good workmanship.

His business has constantly grown until he has become a man of ample resources financially and with valuable property interests in Savannah. Unlike many contractors, he has never had financial reverses; on the contrary, his business each year has shown an increase in volume and in profit over the preceding year. He has erected some of the most important buildings in the city, prominent among which may be mentioned the cigar factory of the Lee Roy Myers Company, at the corner of Bryan and Abercorn streets, completed in the early part of 1912. This is one of the handsomest and most substantial cigar factories in the South, and was erected at a cost of $30,000. Another large contract that he carried out was the building of the complete plant of the Virginia-Carolina Chemical Company, one of the largest industrial plants in Savannah. He built the addition to the office building of the Central of Georgia Railway in Savannah. He constructed the substantial building on Drayton street owned and occupied by Henderson Bros., undertakers. At the time of the burning of the store of the Daniel Hogan Company on West Broughton street, Mr. Young was immediately engaged to rebuild it in the quickest possible time, which he accomplished by energetic work and the employment of extra forces of workmen and foremen. He also reconstructed the interior of the building formerly occupied by the Savannah Bank and Trust Company on Bay and Drayton streets. He built the fine residence of Mrs. John G. Butler at the corner of Montgomery and 36th streets, completed in the early part of 1912.

The uninterrupted success and progress of Mr. Young's business are attributable to his thorough knowledge of every phase of building construction and his promptness in carrying out his contracts; and to his integrity and square dealing in every transaction. This has earned for him high standing among the banks and business houses, who extend to him credit without question, whenever he desires it. In his work Mr. Young pays attention to the smallest detail, and in making his estimates for bidding on a contract he figures on the cost of all items separately and with accuracy, which enables him always to steer clear of possible loss. He has more than once been awarded contracts over bids that were less than his.

Since coming to Savannah, Mr. Young married Miss Lottie Eaton, who was born and reared in this city.

Fraternally, Mr. Young is a Mason and a Knight of Pythias, having membership in Clinton Lodge, No. 54, F. & A. M., and Myrtle Lodge, No. 6, K. of P.

HON. HENRY MCALPIN. A man particularly well fitted for important judicial position is the Hon. Henry McAlpin, judge of the court of ordinary, whose record for efficiency and judicial bearing has won the admiration of the entire Savannah bar. He was born in Savannah, the scion of families who have for several generations given splendid citizenship to the city and state and Georgia has no more loyal son than he. The year of his birth was 1860 and he is the son of James Wallace and Maria Sophia (Champion) McAlpin, both of whom were natives of Savannah and both of whom are deceased. The paternal grandfather, Henry McAlpin, was a native of Scotland who came to Savannah in 1805 and ever since that date the name McAlpin has been a prominent and honored one within its boundaries. On his mother's side, Mr. McAlpin is a great-grandson of Reuben Champion, who, at the age of fifteen enlisted in the Continental army and served until the close of the Revolutionary war, his demise occurring in 1832. He was the son of Dr. Reuben Champion, who was a surgeon in the Continental army and who died in 1777 while on duty at Fort Ticonderoga. Judge McAlpin's

R B Harris

maternal grandfather was Aaron Champion, who came to Savannah in 1812. Thus on both side of the house, the scene of a century's history has been laid in this city. The subject resides in the noted homestead, "The Hermitage," which is situated on the Savannah river, about two miles west of the city and which was built by his grandfather, Henry McAlpin. This stately old residence with its beautiful grounds and surroundings, is one of the show places of Savannah and one of the most celebrated in the South. It has been the scene of many notable gatherings, and in its time has entertained beneath its roof many of the socially and intellectually prominent. It has been the home of the McAlpins since the early '30s.

Judge McAlpin received the advantage of the best of educational facilities, first attending the schools of Savannah and then matriculating in Princeton University, New Jersey, from which famous institution he was graduated in the class of 1881. Following this he studied law in the law department of Columbia University, New York City, and also pursued his preparation for the profession of which he was to become an ornament in the law department of the University of Georgia at Athens, graduating from the latter institution with the degree of LL. B. in the class of 1883. In 1884 he began practice in Savannah and from the first has encountered success and has won an enviable reputation in the field in which have been his endeavors. In 1901 he was elected judge of the court of ordinary of Chatham, and this position he still holds, having been re-elected at each succeeding election, every four years. Under his administration Chatham county has won the reputation of possessing the best ordinary's office in the state of Georgia. This court has jurisdiction in all probate matters and litigation in connection with the settlement of estates. Judge McAlpin is especially well fitted for the adjudication of these important matters and his decisions have a remarkable record from the standpoint of non-reversal by the higher courts. His efficiency and ability as an ordinary are supplemented by a highly capable office force that keep everything systematically arranged, filed and indexed, in modern business method, making everything of easy convenience, not only to the office, but to the attorneys and others having matters to look up in connection with estates and litigation in connection therewith.

Judge McAlpin is a thirty-second degree, Scottish Rite Mason, and a Shriner. He is also prominent in Odd Fellowship, being Past Grand Master of Georgia. He also belongs to the Elks, the Knights of Pythias, and is president of the local lodge of Eagles. He is a member of the Oglethorpe Club, the Yacht Club and is an ex-captain of the Georgia Hussars. In addition to his official duties, he has other interests of wide scope and importance.

Judge McAlpin has one daughter, Mrs. Claudia Thomas (McAlpin) Whitney. She is the daughter of his first wife, whose maiden name was Claudia Thomas, who was a native of Athens, Georgia, and whose demise occurred in Savannah in May, 1908. His second wife, who, before her marriage, was Miss Isabelle Wilbur, was born in South Bethlehem, Pennsylvania.

RAYMOND VICTOR HARRIS, M. D. The life of the city physician and surgeon in these modern days is one of unceasing activity. Modern methods and the high speed with which civilization pursues its relentless way, make demands upon the time and energy of the physician greater, perhaps, than upon men in any other profession. The extent to which specialization is pushed, the deep study required to keep abreast of the discoveries of the age and the everlasting call of the suffering public, all combine to sap the vitality of the most rugged.

But as modern days are strenuous, so the modern man has something of power in his makeup which works best under pressure, Dr. Raymond Victor Harris, one of the distinguished young physicians of Savannah, is a modern instance of a man well equipped to handle the responsibilities of high medical positions. He is the son of one of the state's most noted physicians and comes of a fine, sturdy and capable race. The Harris's to which he belongs are a famous family in American history and it is notable for having kept up its vigor and high standing during all generations to the present. They are a stalwart race, usually not under six feet tall and though sometimes lacking in finished acquired scholarship, their natural intellectual gifts, added to inherited physical strength, have made them always leaders. They have been notably successful in politics and in the professions. They are of Celtic origin, and the branch from which Dr. Harris' family is descended was established in America by Henry Harris, who came from Wales in 1691 and obtained a grant of land at Mannikentown, Virginia. His immediate ancestor, his great grandfather, Nathan Harris, was born in Brunswick county, Virginia. His grandfather, Dr. Raymond Harris, established the family in Georgia.

Dr. Harris is a native Georgian, his birth having occurred at Darien, McIntosh county, October 6, 1880. He is the son of Dr. Raymond B. and Ophelia (Dasher) Harris. The mother is still living in Savannah, an admirable lady, secure in the respect of the community. The father died in this city May 15, 1910, but his value as a citizen and his high professional prestige will not soon be forgotten. Dr. Harris, the elder, was born at Palmero, Bryan county, Georgia, May 15, 1838. He studied medicine in the Savannah Medical College, from which institution he graduated in the class of 1859. When a few years later the long gathering Civil war cloud broke in all its fury, he became a surgeon in the Confederate army, his connection being with the Fifty-seventh Georgia Regiment of Infantry, and his service continued throughout the four years of strife. After the war he practiced medicine in Liberty county until 1876, in which year he located at Darien in McIntosh county, where he practiced until 1884, when he removed to Savannah. In October, 1880, he was elected to the Georgia state senate by a very small majority, the fight being a three-cornered one, and Dr. Harris having not one, but two opponents. He was alderman for two terms, from 1889 to 1895, under mayors Schwarz and McDonough; was a member of the board of sanitary commissioners, and fought the yellow fever epidemic of 1876. He was instrumental in building the crematory and also built the quarantine station while alderman, and seven years later sold to the government for $50,000 cash. As alderman, the doctor was chairman of the public health committee.

He owned and resided in a beautiful home, "Melrose," on LaRoche avenue, and the family were prominent in the social life of the city. He was a prominent member of the Georgia and the American Medical Associations and he continued actively in the work of his profession in Savannah until 1904, when he retired, his demise occurring some six years later, as recorded above.

Dr. Raymond B. Harris was a man of great ability and of striking individuality. He was of that type of man who, without effort, makes friends everywhere. In his size, physical make-up, mental qualities and in everything that goes to make a big, strong, broad-minded man of the widest sympathies, Dr. Harris was gifted by nature. Everywhere he inspired confidence, admiration and affection. During his life he was honored by many positions of trust; he served one year as chief surgeon of the United Confederate Veterans, by election at the annual reunion at New Orleans, and served in this position during the same year that Gen. Clement A. Evans was commander-in-chief. He had two brothers who, also were physicians,—Dr. Stephen Harris and Dr. Columbus Harris, the former dying from yellow fever contracted in the great epidemic in Savannah in 1859 and the latter's death occurring from the same cause in the epidemic of 1876.

Dr. Harris, in identifying himself with the profession to which he is an ornament, is but following in the footsteps of his forbears, and although his career has as yet been brief, he gives promise of sharing their distinction. He received his professional training in the University of Maryland, in Baltimore, and graduated with the class of 1903. He subsequently spent one year in the University of Maryland hospital and practiced for over a year in Baltimore. At his father's request he came back to Savannah in 1907, and began the practice of medicine in this city, having a general practice in medicine and surgery and holding the office of city physician. He is a member of all those organizations having as their object the advancement and unification of the profession, namely: The Chatham County, Georgia State and American Medical Associations, and he is the physician and surgeon for the Savannah base ball club of the South Atlantic League.

Dr. Harris was married on the 6th day of January, 1910, the young woman to become his wife being Miss Flora Middlebrooks, a daughter of Thomas E. Middlebrooks, of Oconee county, Georgia.

WILLIAM B. STILLWELL. A native son of Georgia, and a member of a distinguished Southern family, members of which have won eminence in the various walks of life, William B. Stillwell, son of Savannah, is a worthy representative of the best type of American citizenship, and during a long and honorable career has been identified with business enterprises of wide scope and importance, and has lent his influence to various movements in civic and social life. A brief outline of Mr. Stillwell's ancestry seems appropriate in a history of this nature. Nicholas Stillwell, the first of the name to land in America, brought to the aid of the infant colonies an iron will and mighty arm, and his descendants, settling North, South, East and West, have won enviable distinction in the pursuits of peace as well as in the art of war, many today occupying prominent positions in the army, in the national guard, and in the great enterprises and industries of the nation.

In direct line of descent from Nicholas Stillwell, his grandson, Maj. Thomas Stillwell, and great-grandson, John Stillwell, who won distinction during the Revolution, came Charles H. Stillwell, who, in addition to the spirit of his forefathers, was fortunate enough to inherit from his mother, a Huguenot of the South Carolina Colony, the spirit which animated the French martyrs. To him, although always beset by difficulties and adversity and twice made a cripple, the last time for life, the state of Georgia is indebted for nine sons and one daughter, who have worthily illustrated in their various vocations the indomitable energy, peerless courage and Christian faith which characterized their sire.

William Stillwell, one of the sons thus endowed, though starting without a dollar, amid confusion which follows in the wake of civil strife, has won both means and position even in a business which requires as much capital and individual effort for its successful prosecution as the lumber trade. He was born in Rome, Georgia, March 11, 1851, and his name is not quite half way down the official register of family births which must have overflowed the record pages in the old family Bible, for there were sixteen children. At the close of the war between the states, ten of these were living, nine boys and one girl, four boys older than William having seen service under the Confederate flag.

The family, which had during the war period "refugeed" pretty much all over the state, moved back to Rome at the close of hostilities, and William received his first experience in sawmill operations in an upright sawmill operated by his father, whom he assisted as yard man and general utility man. In February, 1866, he went into the employ of Millen & Wadley, at Savannah, Georgia, which firm afterward became Millen, Wadley & Company, by the admission of D. C. Bacon as junior partner. In 1876 Messrs. Bacon and Stillwell formed the firm of D. C. Bacon & Company, Mr. H. P. Smart being afterward admitted to this firm. The firm formed and operated a number of other companies, including the Vale Royal Manufacturing Company, the Atlanta Lumber Company, the Central Georgia Lumber Company, Screven County Lumber Company, and Amoskeag Lumber Company, Mr. Stillwell being for several years president of the last named company, as well as an officer in all of the others.

Mr. Stillwell was one of the organizers of the Savannah Board of Trade in 1883, and for two years was its vice-president, and later for two years its president; he was also a member of the Chamber of Commerce at its inception. He was one of the organizers and a member of the first board of directors of the Citizens' Bank, which, being merged with the Southern Bank in 1906, became the Citizens and Southern Bank. Mr. Stillwell was one of the promoters in the building of the South Bound Railroad and a director of the construction company which built it.

In 1887 the firm of D. C. Bacon & Company was dissolved and the firm of Stillwell, Millen & Company was established, with headquarters at Savannah; and L. R. Millen & Company of New York City, consisting of William B. Stillwell, Loring R. Millen and L. Johnson; R. H. and W. R. Bewick being admitted several years later. The firm owned and operated the Screven County Lumber Company, the Central Georgia Lumber Company and the Augusta Lumber Company, and also built and operated the Waycross Air Line Railroad and the Millen & Southern Railroad. In all of these companies Mr. Stillwell held official positions and was president of the Waycross Lumber Company.

In 1895 the lumber business of Stillwell, Millen & Company, L. R. Millen & Company, McDonough & Company, the James K. Clarke Lumber Company, Henry P. Talmadge and C. C. Southard, was consolidated into the Southern Pine Company of Georgia, and Mr. Stillwell became secretary and treasurer of the company, which position he has held continously since that time. Besides the prominent part taken by Mr. Stillwell in the city and state civic and business organizations, he suggested and was the main factor in the formation of the National Lumber Manufacturers Association, of which he is vice-president. By means of his position as a director in the National Rivers and Harbors Congress, and his connection for years and finally serving as the highest official of the National Hoo Hoo organization, Mr. Stillwell has a wide range of influential friends and acquaintances who have served him and the city in good stead when he has been called upon to represent Savannah and work for her interests. He took a prominent part in the securing of the government appropriation which gave deep water to Savannah—the city's greatest asset.

Mr. Stillwell has also been prominently connected with the military, fraternal and social organizations of the city; in fact in all the commendable activities and enterprises of Savannah he has given freely of his time and much unselfish personal service. He has always been actively at work for Savannah and South Georgia; he is really one man who seems to think of himself last of all. He is a member of the Baptist church and belongs to many social and fraternal orders, among which are the Elks, Masons and the higher degrees of the latter order, being a Knight Templar and a Shriner. He served for twenty years as a member of the historic Chatham artillery, and is now an honorary member of the corps, is also a life member of the Savannah Volunteer Guards and a pay member of the Savannah Cadets.

In 1875, Mr. Stillwell was united in marriage to Miss Mary Reily Royal, of the well known Carolina family of that name. They have three daughters, as follows: Edith, now Mrs. W. F. Train; Mamie R., now Mrs. James Tift Mann, and Laleah P.; and three sons: William H., Herbert L. and Walter B. Stillwell.

JAMES G. THOMAS, M. D. For many years one of the more prominent and able physicians of Savannah, the late James G. Thomas, M. D., acquired distinction not only for his superior professional knowledge and skill, but for his public-spirited, utilitarian and philanthropic benefactions. He was born June 24, 1835, in Bloomfield, Kentucky, and was there reared, acquiring a part of his early education in a monastery near that town. Beginning the study of medicine in Louisville, Kentucky, in the school of which the late Samuel D. Gross was the head, he later matriculated in the medical department of the University of the City of New York, being there graduated with the class of 1856.

Dr. Thomas began the practice of his profession at Bloomfield, Kentucky, his birthplace, but subsequently went to Mississippi, locating near Sardis, where he remained until the outbreak of the Civil war. Entering then the Confederate army as a surgeon, his duties in that capacity brought him to Savannah, Georgia, and here he continued in service until the occupation of the city by Sherman's army, when he left Savannah with the evacuating forces, and was thenceforward stationed in the Carolinas until the close of the conflict.

Returning to Savannah in 1865, Dr. Thomas resumed his labors as a physician and surgeon, attaining in due course of time the highest rank in his profession, and being rewarded by a very large general practice. An industrious worker and a deep student, the doctor kept pace with the latest discoveries in medical science, and had the distinction of being the very first physician in Georgia to make use of the thermometer in fever cases. He was especially active in promoting public hygiene, sanitation and drainage, and the health of the community. Vigilant and self-sacrificing in his services during the yellow fever epidemic of 1876, he contracted the disease himself just as the epidemic was nearing its close.

In 1875 and 1876 Dr. Thomas served through the sessions of the Georgia legislature, this apparent divergence from the line of his chosen vocation having been made by him in obedience to a sense of public duty, and in compliance with the earnest solicitations of eminent citizens, who desired to send to the legislature a public-spirited physician who would take the lead in procuring the enactment of laws relating to hygiene. He took an important part in the preparation and passage, in the session of 1875, of the "Act to create a state board of health for the protection of life and health, and to prevent the spread of disease in Georgia." A measure which the doctor there introduced for adopting a system of compiling and recording vital statistics was passed, but through lack of appropriation was never carried into effect.

On December 14, 1881, a Citizens' Sanitary Association, looking to the improvement of public health through the united efforts of private individuals, was organized in Savannah, and Dr. Thomas, who had strongly urged its creation, was elected its first president, and held the position until his death. He was one of the originators of the international medical congress, and was one of the two physicians appointed from the South to attend the conference held in Washington, District of Columbia, in 1884. It was while attending this conference in Washington, that the sudden death of Dr. Thomas occurred, December 6, 1884. The passing away of Dr. Thomas, just in the midst of a busy and useful life, was an event of universal regret and mourning in Savannah, his family and friends being deprived of a grand nature, while the city was bereft of a public benefactor.

Dr. Thomas married, in 1865, in Savannah, Margaret Owens, a daughter of George W. and Sarah (Wallace) Owens, both representatives of old and honored Savannah families. Her father, a native of Savannah, was a son of Owen Owens, who emigrated from Wales to Savannah soon after the close of the Revolutionary war. Her mother, Sarah Wallace, was a daughter of John and Mary (Anderson) Wallace, the said John Wallace, a native of Scotland, having served as British consul in Savannah years ago, while the Andersons have lived in the city since 1763.

Mrs. Thomas has two daughters, namely: Miss Mary B. Thomas and Miss Margaret G. Thomas.

Dr. Thomas was for some time a prominent member of the American Health Association, and of the National Board of Health. He was ever among the foremost in the establishment of philanthropical movements, being always willing to do the work of the humanitarian, and to turn aside even from the most congenial occupations of home life, and the routine of daily practice, to perform a worthy act of public duty, being not only a physician, but a patriot.

CHARLES H. DORSETT, engaged in the real estate and auction business and president of the Peoples' Savings & Loan Company, is a man whose life has been of unceasing activity and perseverance and the systematic and honorable methods which he has followed have won him the unbounded confidence of his fellow citizens in Savannah. In 1876 he became established in his present business, which he has ever since conducted. This is one of the oldest established institutions of its kind in Savannah. Among his other distinctions, Mr. Dorsett is a gallant ex-soldier, and he finds no small amount of pleasure and profit in renewing the old comradeship with those who carried arms with him in the troublous days of the '60s.

Mr. Dorsett is a native son of the city and one of those who have paid it the greatest compliment within their power by electing to remain permanently within its borders. He is the son of John and Sarah R. (Fletcher) Dorsett. His father was born in New York City and came to Savannah as early as 1839. He was a ship builder by occupation and had a large shipyard on the Savannah river. At the age of eleven months the subject had the misfortune to lose his father, but his mother survived her husband for many years, her summons to the Great Beyond occurring in 1893. Through his mother, Mr. Dorsett comes of an older Southern family; this admirable lady was born in Georgia and her parents were natives of South Carolina.

Young Charles was reared in Savannah and in its schools received his education. At the outbreak of the war between the states he was only in his teens, but his heart was with the cause of the South, and he believed in the supreme right of the states to sever their connection with the national government. As soon as possible he enlisted and during the latter part of the war was a member of Shellman's battalion, which was in service in Savannah and vicinity. For some years after the affair at Appomattox he was engaged in various occupations, but in 1876, as previously mentioned, he inaugurated his present real estate and auction business. Besides the agency business Mr. Dorsett is the owner of substantial property interests in Savannah and for more than twenty years he has been president of the Peoples' Savings & Loan Society, which makes loans on real estate and is well and favorably known to business men of the Forest city.

Mr. Dorsett is of sufficient social proclivity to find pleasure in his fraternal relations, and he enjoys membership in DeKalb lodge of Odd Fellows and of Landrum lodge of Masons. He was for one term a member of the board of county commissioners of Chatham county. He is intelligent and progressive and has the respect of the community in which he is so well known and in which his interests have always been centered.

Mr. Dorsett laid the foundations of a happy married life by his union in the year 1869, to Miss Josephine Frances Gross, of this city, where their nuptials were celebrated. They have one daughter, Mrs. J. E. D. Bacon, of Savannah.

MONGIN BAKER NICHOLS, auditor of traffic with the Central of Georgia Railway Company, at Savannah, Georgia, has been a resident of this city since his birth. In his association with business life he has been connected with but the one company with which he now is and he has filled numerous positions in the years that have intervened since he first took service with this company in 1892, beginning in the more humble capacity of stenographer and advancing constantly until he was promoted in 1907 to his present position.

Born in Savannah in 1874, Mongin Baker Nichols is the son of George Nicoll and Minnie (Mongin) Nichols. The father was born in Savannah and here lived all his life. He was identified with the printing and stationery business for a long period of years. He retired from active business in 1898, and died on April 13, 1905. Mr. Nichols was a member of the board of aldermen of Savannah on various occasions, serving several years in that capacity. Left an orphan at an early age, he made the best of every opportunity that presented itself at his door. He was the son of Abram Nichols, a native of New Jersey, and who in early life came to the southland and settled in Savannah. Abram Nichols was the first port warden of Savannah, was a member of the first board of fire commissioners, and was the commander of a mosquito fleet, fitted out in Savannah, and sent to Tybee island during the War of 1812 to protect Savannah from an invasion by the British fleet. He was the father of two sons and one daughter, George Nicoll Nichols, being the eldest son and the younger Edward Tattnall Nichols, who died in 1888, having achieved the rank of rear admiral of the United States navy.

The wife of George Nicoll Nichols and the mother of Mongin Baker Nichols of this review, was born in South Carolina, of Huguenot ancestry, and is still living in Savannah. Her family removed to Savannah in her early life and she was married to Mr. Nichols in 1872. Her mother was Eliza (Maner) Mongin, the daughter of Ruth (Stafford) Maner, who was the daughter of Col. William Stafford, the great-great-grandfather of the subject of this review. William Stafford was lieutenant colonel of a regiment of South Carolina troops in the War of the Revolution, in command at Black Swamp, near the Savannah river. The Mongin family, on the paternal side, is related in earlier generations to several famous characters, among them being Jonathan Edwards, an early president of Princeton University, and Phillipo Martin Angelo, an Italian refugee, who had been a soldier in the Vatican Guards. Mongin Baker Nichols is one of the five children of his parents. The others are: William N.; Fenwick T.; Oliver S.; E. McIntyre, and Minnie S. Nichols.

Mongin Baker Nichols was reared in Savannah and has lived in this city all his life. He was educated in private schools of the city, and in the old Savannah Academy conducted by Capt. John Taliaferro. After concluding his studies in the best private schools which the city afforded, young Nichols decided upon a business course for himself, and entered a business college, where he completed a thorough course in business training. His first position was in the capacity of stenographer in the office of the comptroller of the Central of Georgia Railway in 1892. In 1899 he was appointed station accountant, which position he occupied until 1907, in that year being promoted to his present position. He occupies the same position with the Ocean Steamship Company.

Mr. Nichols was for some years an active member of Company A, Savannah Volunteer Guards, enlisting as a private, and served as corporal, sergeant, and second lieutenant. He is a member of the Savannah Golf Club, Savannah Yacht Club, Business, Professional and Transportation Club, Guards Club, and of the Society of Colonial Wars, and is the historian of the Georgia Society of the Sons of the American Revolution. Since February, 1908, he has been secretary of the Southeastern Accounting Conference, which is composed of the accounting officers of common carriers in the territory south of the Ohio and Potomac rivers and east of the Mississippi river. His religious convictions have brought about his membership with the Baptist church.

JOHN HARDY PURVIS. The real estate and collection business of Savannah, Georgia, includes as one of its active, hustling factors the young man whose name introduces this review, John Hardy Purvis.

Mr. Purvis is of southern birth and parentage. He was born in Webster county, Georgia, in 1874, son of Edward B. and Welthea Evelyn (Watson) Purvis, both deceased. Edward B. Purvis, also a native of Webster county, was a Confederate soldier in the war between the states, and was in active service up to and including the battle of Gettysburg, where he was severely wounded, from which he never entirely recovered. His father, John Purvis, was an Englishman who, when a small boy, had come with his parents and several brothers to America, their settlement being in Virginia. Soon after he was grown, John Purvis came to Georgia and took up his residence in Webster county. Here he married Mrs. Mary Ann Askew. She had children by her first husband and also by Mr. Purvis, and altogether the Askews and the Purvises formed a large family, many of whom are still living in Webster county and in that section of southern Georgia. Welthea Evelyn (Watson) Purvis, the mother of John H., was born in North Carolina, and was a daughter of Hardy Watson of Raleigh, that state.

John Hardy Purvis passed the early years of his boyhood in his native county, attending school there and later in Savannah, to which city he came in 1885, and where he has since lived. About 1897 he engaged in the real-estate and collection business, which he has continued successfully up to the present time, his office being at 301 East Liberty street.

John Hardy Purnis.

Politically, Mr. Purvis is a Republican. He takes an active part in local and state politics; is thoroughly posted on the issues of the day, and in party councils exerts an influence that is felt for good.

On November 13, 1906 Mr. Purvis was married to Mrs. Honora O'Keefe, daughter of Mrs. Margaret Garrity, of Savannah, Georgia.

WILLIAM F. BRUNNER, M. D. Other men's services to the people and state can be measured by definite deeds, by dangers averted, by legislation secured, by institutions built, by commerce promoted. The work of a doctor is entirely estranged from these lines of enterprise, yet without his capable, health-giving assistance all other accomplishments would count for naught. Man's greatest prize on earth is physical health and vigor. Nothing deteriorates mental activity as quickly as prolonged sickness—hence the broad field for human helpfulness afforded in the medical profession. The successful doctor requires something more than mere technical training—he must be a man of broad human sympathy and genial kindliness, capable of inspiring hope and faith in the heart of his patient. Such a man is Dr. William F. Brunner, city health officer of Savanah, whose successful career has been due to the possession of innate talent and acquired ability along the line of one of the most important professions to which a man may devote his energies.

Dr. Brunner was born in Savannah in 1858, the son of C. W. and Frances (Haupt) Brunner, both of whom are now deceased. They were both natives of South Carolina, the father's birthplace having been Beaufort. He was a merchant by occupation and located in Savannah previous to the inception of the Civil war, subsequently taking an active part in the many-sided life of the municipality and enjoying general respect.

Dr. Brunner received an excellent education in private schools in this city and as a student in Locust Dale Academy, Madison county, Virginia. He studied medicine in the medical department of the University of Georgia, from which he was graduated with the class of 1877 and then spent the following year in post-graduate work in the medical department of the University of the City of New York. At that time (1878), yellow fever was epidemic in New Orleans, Memphis, Vicksburg, and other sections of the lower Mississippi valley and Dr. Brunner immediately after discontinuing his studies in New York went to the heart of the yellow fever district and offered his services to the Howard Association. He was immune, having had yellow fever in the Savannah epidemic of 1876. He began active work in Vicksburg, but a short time later went to the town of Lake, Mississippi, and took vigorous charge of the situation there, which was very serious, almost every person, including ministers, who was able to travel, having deserted the stricken town. He remained at Lake with a staff of nurses under his charge, doing all he could to alleviate the suffering, curing all cases possible and preventing the spread of the fever as far as possibly could be done with the means at hand and the panicky state of the populace. His work in this epidemic attracted the attention of the United States health officials, and Dr. Brunner was given a position on the Marine Hospital service of the United States, on the South Atlantic Coast, being engaged in the maritime quarantine service at that time for about four and a half years.

In April, 1888, Dr. Brunner was elected health officer of Savannah and after nine years in that position, resigned, and again entered the United States marine hospital, this time being assigned to duty at Havana, Cuba, where he had a staff of physicians and surgeons under his charge. He remained in that position until a short time before the occupation of Cuba by the United States, in 1898, being ordered out from Washington at that time. He then was assigned to duty in inspecting army camps at Tampa and other places in the South, and also at Montauk, Long Island. In September, 1898, he again joined his station at Havana and remained there until July 1, 1899, when he received an invitation from the city of Savannah to again become its health officer, which he accepted, entering his old duties again in that month, and has remained in that position ever since. His efficiency and success as an expert in preventative medicine and as a public health official are widely known and recognized; and his services are greatly appreciated by the citizens of Savannah. He is one of the most distinguished physicians, not only of Savannah, but of the entire South and his repute extends far and wide in the profession. He has never been a general practitioner, it will be seen, but has ever been engaged on special duty. The County, State and American Medical associations claim his membership.

Dr. Brunner, on December 14, 1883, was united in marriage to Miss Florence Richardson, of Savannah. They share their home of renowned hospitality with four children, namely: Florence Charlton, Albert Wylly, Frances L. and Ruth.

CAPT. WILLIAM H. ROBERTSON. As superintendent of the park and tree commission of Savannah, Capt. William H. Robertson has for many years been identified with one of the most useful and important departments of the municipality, and in that capacity has been largely instrumental in establishing and maintaining its title to the name of the "Forest City." Coming from thrifty Scotch ancestry, he was born in Savannah in 1881. His father, the late John G. Robertson, was a lifelong resident of Savannah, his death occurring here in 1907. He was connected during his active career with the Central of Georgia Railroad Company, of which he was paymaster. He married Annabelle Stephens Falligant, who survives him, and is still a resident of the city. She is a great-granddaughter of Louis Falligant, a native of France, who was the founder of the Falligant family of America, a record of which is given elsewhere in this work, in connection with the sketch of Raiford Falligant.

Reared and educated in Savannah, William H. Robertson attended the grammar schools, the Chatham Academy, and the private school of Lawrence & Morton. He subsequently made some preparation for the civil engineer's profession, and, although circumstances prevented his carrying out his desired plans, he did considerable construction work on jobs requiring engineering ability in Savannah and vicinity. Since 1898 Mr. Robertson has been connected with the park and tree commission of Savannah, at the present time being its superintendent. This department of the municipal government has in its charge the care and maintenance of all the parks, squares, cemeteries, and parked roadways of the city, and is the dominant factor in rendering it in truth a "city beautiful." As the city's main attraction to both visitors and residents lies in its parks, squares and beautiful trees o'ershading its broad streets and avenues, it will be seen that the park and tree commission department is of the utmost concern, requiring an expert knowledge of landscape gardening and forestry, as well as constant attention, and a genuine interest in this feature of the city's resources. In the successful carrying on of his work, Mr. Robertson employs about fifty men, keeping them all busy, and obtaining satisfactory results.

For a number of years Mr. Robertson has been prominently connected with the military life of Savannah. Enlisting December 4, 1899, in Company D, Savannah Volunteer Guards, which is officially known as the Coast Artillery Corps, he subsequently was promoted to. the rank of corporal, then sergeant, later becoming first sergeant, and on January 14, 1907, was commissioned captain of his company, a position which he has since held. Captain Robertson is a thoroughly efficient artilleryman, both from theoretical knowledge and actual practice, and as commanding officer is diligent in his post, and unflagging in his zealous efforts to maintain the high standard of his organization. An extended account of the corps appears in the general historical part of this work.

JOHN KIRK TRAIN, M.D., one of the prominent and successful members of the medical profession of Savannah, Georgia, is a son of one of Savannah's best known and most highly esteemed citizens, Prof. Hugh Fred Train, who for over forty years served as principal of the high school in this city. From a review of his life published a few years ago, we make the following excerpt:

Hugh Frederick Train is a native of the sturdy land of hills and heather, having been born in Murkirk, Ayrshire, Scotland, June 27, 1831. He was reared and educated in his native land, where he did efficient work as a university student and later completed a two years' course in a normal training school in the city of Glasgow. For five years thereafter he was a successful and popular teacher in the parish school of Perth. About this time alarming symptoms began to manifest themselves in the way of incipient disease of the lungs, and as his brother had died of tuberculosis Mr. Train was admonished by his medical adviser to seek a less rigorous climate, in order that his life might be prolonged and the disease possibly averted. Under the care of a friend and former schoolmate he was induced to come to America and settle in the South. In January, 1857, he took up his residence in Bluffton, Beaufort district, South Carolina, where he remained until the outbreak of the Civil war, being there engaged in teaching. In 1861, loyal to the cause of the Confederacy, he became a private in the Third Regiment of South Carolina state troops. His right arm being practically useless, as the result of an accident encountered when he was a boy, he was not able to take part in the tactical drill and manenvers, and consequently, after two months of irregular service, he was appointed by Col. Charles J. Colcock, commanding officer, to the position of commissary and acting quartermaster for the squadron, consisting of three companies, being first in camp at Bluffton and later at Camp Hartstein, and he was honorably discharged when the state troops were formally mustered into the Confederate service. After the close of the war Mr. Train found his home burned to the ground, his schoolroom plundered of everything movable and the whole country steeped in poverty. He remained in Bluffton one year, not earning enough to provide for ordinary necessities within the period, and then removed to Savannah, where, through the influence of Mr. Mallon, then superintendent of schools, he was appointed principal of the boys' grammar school. In the following year the board of education conferred upon him the appointment of principal of the Savannah high school, to succeed William H. Baker, who had been made superintendent, and this position he filled until his retirement in 1910. His long term of service is an unequivocal voucher for the successful work he performed and the high place he held in the esteem of both pupils and patrons. Here he now lives in quiet retirement, and he is perhaps more uniformly loved and respected in Savannah than any one of its most illustrious upbuilders, and his good work will continue to blossom and bear fruitage in this community as long as education is prized and knowledge is rewarded. In politics he is a staunch Democrat, and his religious faith is that of the Presbyterian church, both he and his wife having for many years been identified with the First Presbyterian church of Savannah. Mrs. Train was formerly Miss Elizabeth Frew, being a daughter of James and Mary Frew, of Savannah. They were married December 29, 1869, and of the six children given to them, only two are now living: William Frew Train, who is engaged in the insurance business in Savannah, and Dr. John Kirk Train, whose name introduces this sketch.

John Kirk Train was born and reared in Savannah. After his graduation from the high school he began the study of medicine, which he pursued in the medical department of the University of Virginia and in Bellevue Hospital Medical College, New York, graduating from the latter institution with the class of 1900. Following his graduation he spent three years as interne in Bellevue Hospital. He began the practice of his profession in Savannah in 1904, and from the time he opened his office has met with success. In addition to conducting a general practice, he is medical examiner for the Pacific Mutual Life Insurance Company, the Massachusetts Life and the Penn Mutual Life Insurance companies.

Doctor Train is a member of various medical societies, including the American Medical Association. He is ex-president of the District Medical Association of Georgia (comprised of the counties included in the first congressional district), and he is on the staff of the Savannah Hospital, St. Joseph's Hospital, the Telfair Hospital, and the Georgia Infirmary. For three years he was surgeon, with the rank of major, of the First Regiment of Georgia Infantry. Outside of Savannah he is a member of the Bellevue Hospital Alumni Society and of the Southern Society in New York City.

He is a member of Ancient Landmark Lodge, F. & A. M., a member of the Savannah Lodge of Elks, and is president of the St. Andrew's Society of Savannah.

Doctor Train has a wife and two children, Lilla and John Kirk, Jr. Mrs. Train, before her marriage Miss Lilla Comer, is a daughter of the late H. M. Comer, of Savannah, who was president of the Central Georgia Railway, and who was held in high regard as a leading and influential citizen.

HON. JOSEPH FRANCIS GRAY. On the roll of Savannah's conspicuous and progressive business men, none are eligible to a higher position than the Hon. Joseph Francis Gray, state railroad commissioner and executive officer of the Savannah Chamber of Commerce. Still to be numbered among the younger generation, he has for more than a decade been a brilliant figure on the stage of Savannah's railroad and commercial life. Mr. Gray is a native Georgian, his life record having begun in the city of Atlanta, on November 23, 1870. He is the son of Luke and Margaret (Carolan) Gray. His training for the responsibilities of life was acquired in St. Patrick's parochial school, of Augusta, and in St. Mary's College, at Belmont, North Carolina. His first adventures as an active factor in the world of affairs were in the capacity of stenographer for the late Patrick Walsh, editor of the Augusta *Chronicle* and at one time United States senator from Georgia. In January, 1887, he accepted a position as stenographer in the Augusta office of the Southern Express Company, with which he remained

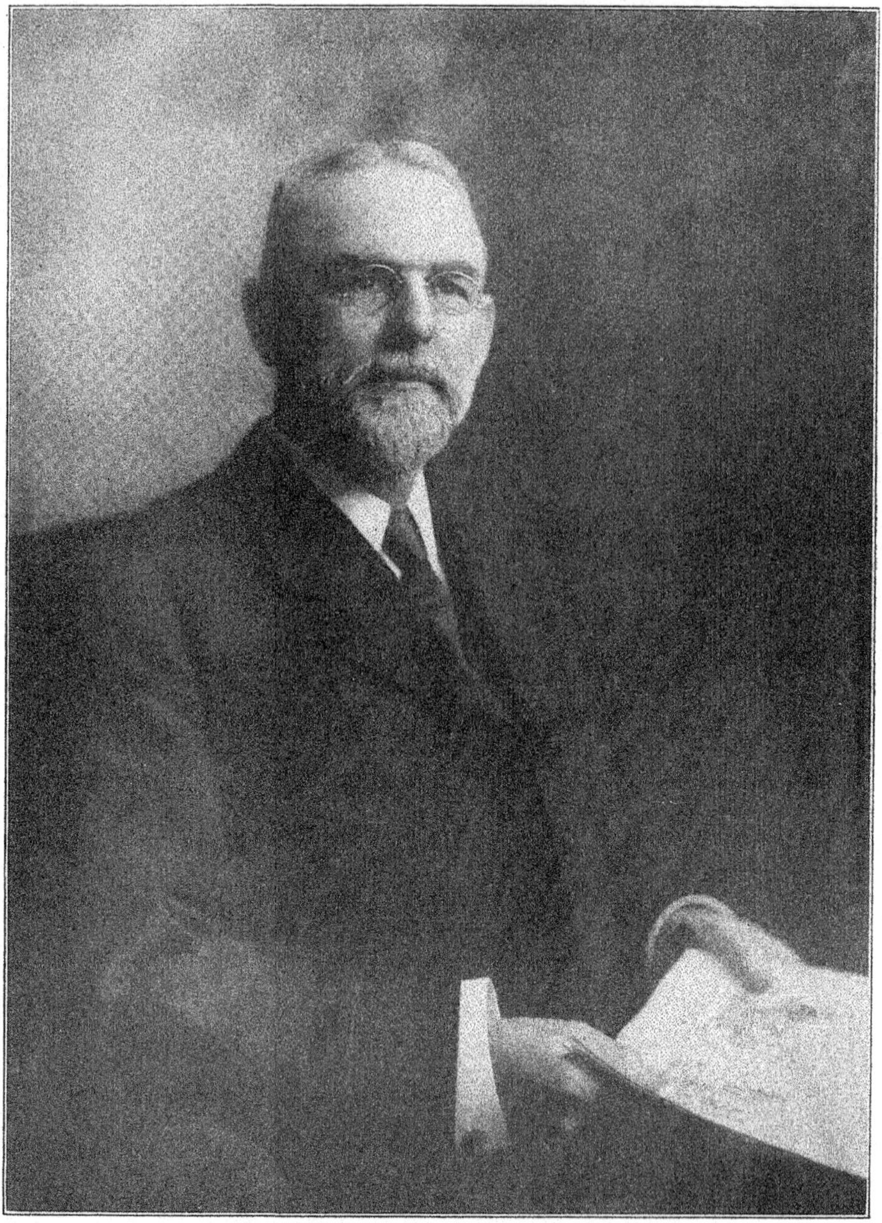

Wm. W. Williamson

identified until May, 1888. From the year last mentioned until 1890 he held a similar position in the office of the general freight and passenger agent of the Central of Georgia Railway in Savannah. From January, 1890, until October, 1893, he held the position of traveling freight agent for the Central of Georgia Railway. In his previous clerical positions he has assimilated a remarkable amount of information of a business character and was admirably fitted for the assumption of the duties of important positions. His advancement was steady. In October, 1893, he became superintendent and treasurer of the Millen & Southwestern Railroad with headquarters at Millen, Georgia. In February, 1900, he became superintendent of the Offerman & Western Railroad at Offerman, Georgia, and on July 15, 1902, became freight claim agent of the Central of Georgia Railway. In 1905 and 1906 he was auditor of traffic of the Central of Georgia Railway and in 1906 and 1908 was terminal agent in Savannah for the Central of Georgia and Southern railways.

In 1909, Mr. Gray severed his connection with railroad interests to become executive officer of the Savannah Chamber of Commerce, in which position he has entire managerial charge of this important organization. He is also its vice-president. The chamber of commerce under Mr. Gray's direction has become the most important factor in the modern growth and development of Savannah. It numbers among its membership a large number of Savannah's public-spirited citizens. Its quarters in October, 1911, were removed to the third floor of the new Savannah Bank & Trust building. In 1909, Mr. Gray also was made one of the state railroad commissioners of Georgia. Mr. Gray is a successful man. He has done things and has made an imprint upon many enterprises.

Mr. Gray was happily married on June 6, 1892, the young woman to become his wife being Miss Dora E. Gassman, daughter of Charles and Mary A (McLaughlin) Gassman. They have three interesting children: Joseph Francis, Jr., Mildred Lucile, and Charles Aloysius. Mr. and Mrs. Gray are communicants of the Catholic church and the former is affiliated with the Knights of Columbus.

MAJ. WILLIAM WAYNE WILLIAMSON is a scion of one of Georgia's oldest families. He was born in the city of Savannah, September 1, 1854, the son of John and Julia C. (Wayne) Williamson. His father, Judge Williamson, was born in Savannah, February 3, 1810. He was a merchant, cotton factor and rice planter for a long number of years and a citizen of well-deserved prominence. Although engaged for the greater part of his life strictly in commercial affairs, he was universally known as Judge Williamson for the reason that he was justice of the superior court of Chatham county before and during the war. He was also a member of and chairman of the Savannah city council at the time Sherman's army came into the city and during the entire period of the Civil war his most active efforts were given to the carrying out of measures of beneficence for his city and the cause of the Confederacy in general. He resigned from the city council to accept the position of city treasurer in 1866. In 1872 he was elected county treasurer, which position he held until his demise. He was a member of the first board of public education in Savannah, organized soon after the war, and at the time of his death was its treasurer and the only surviving member of the original board. At the time of his death he was the oldest living member of the Georgia Hussars. For a number of years he was warden and vestryman of Christ church; he was a member of the Union Society and of the Georgia Historical Society. After the war, having become too aged to enter active business life again, the mayor and aldermen honored him by electing him to the office of city treasurer, as before noted. He was re-elected to the office by the people, and served efficiently in such capacity for several years, his ability and public spirit being of the highest character. He died in 1885, while county treasurer, but although a quarter century has elapsed since he passed to the Great Beyond, his memory remains green with the older generation.

Major Williamson's grandfather, John Postell Williamson, was one of the wealthiest real estate owners and planters of Savannah in the first half of the last century. He was born in South Carolina, but made Savannah his home early in life. The Williamson family is of English origin, having been established in South Carolina, as early as 1690. John Postell Williamson's home in Savannah was the rendezvous for army officers following the Mexican war and the Indian wars in Florida— Sherman, Pope, Bragg, Ridgeley, Wade, Beckwith and Rankin being among the representatives of the government who received hospitality there. The old home of the Williamson family was at the northwest corner of Montgomery and State streets, which at that time was the fashionable residential section of the city. John Postell Williamson also owned Brampton and much other real property in and about the city. He operated a brick yard among other industries and is said to have built the old county court house.

The mother of the immediate subject of this review Julia C. Wayne, was born in Savannah in 1822 and died in 1892. She was the daughter of Gen. William C. Wayne and Ann (Gordon) Wayne and the granddaughter of Richard Wayne of England, who came to America in 1760. He married September 14, 1769, in South Carolina, Elizabeth Clifford, whose family were among the first settlers of that province and who were allied to the families of DeSaussure and Bacots. When the Revolutionary war broke out, Richard Wayne, who was designated by an act of the South Carolina legislature as a "leading merchant" of Charlestown, headed a petition to be armed on the side of the Crown, and in consequence his property was confiscated and he was banished from the colony. All of this, with the subsequent restoration of his property, is fully recorded in the reports of the Acts of the South Carolina Assembly. Richard Wayne, however, never returned to South Carolina to live. On being banished he came with his wife and children to Savannah about 1782 and became a successful planter. Gen. Anthony Wayne was one of the executors of his will.

Among the men of eminent ability of this family may be mentioned his son, Hon. James Moore Wayne, who was mayor of Savannah, judge of the superior court in this city, congressman from his district and finally associate justice of the United States supreme court. Another son was Gen. William Clifford Wayne, and one of his grandsons was Dr. Richard W. Wayne, who was at one time mayor of Savannah.

Major Williamson was reared in Savannah and received his education in the public schools, in Professor McLellan's private school and in Eastman's Business College of Poughkeepsie, New York. He began active business life in 1879 in the office of Wilder & Company, with which firm he remained as confidential clerk until the death of Mr. Wilder in 1900. Major Williamson then succeeded to the firm and taking Mr. J. J. Rauers as partner, established the present house of Williamson & Rauers, steamship and forwarding agents. This concern has a world-wide reputation as steamship agents. Major Williamson has unusual business and executive gifts of which the success of the firm is the logical outcome.

Major Williamson went through the public schools of Savannah, later took a course at Eastman's Commercial College at Poughkeepsie, New York, and then a mere youth, entered business with the firm of J. H. Gardner & Company, ship agents. He then went with the cotton firm of Andrew Low & Company (now out of existence), and after two years was sent by the firm, first to New Orleans and then to Galveston, Texas. He returned to Savannah in 1879, a young man of twenty-five, and was made confidential clerk of the firm of Wilder & Company. In the second year of service with that firm he was given power of attorney and put in charge of their freight business, in which position he remained until 1901. His entire service with that firm covered a period of twenty-two years. When Mr. Wilder died in 1901, Mr. Williamson associated himself with Mr. J. J. Rauers, under the style of Williamson & Rauers, and took over its business of Wilder & Company, which the firm of Williamson & Rauers have continued to successfully prosecute up to the present. This firm represents the North German Lloyd, the Hansa line (a German company) and other steamship companies. During all these years of steady-going business Mr. Williamson has been active in many directions and has been making character among his fellow-citizens. He has given an enormous amount of time to the public service and to the welfare of his native city, without any other compensation than that of the satisfaction which comes to the man who tries to serve his fellow-men. In 1895-96 he was president of the Cotton Exchange; and served again in that capacity in 1902-03. He is vice-president of the National Bank of Savannah; president of the Commercial Life Insurance Company, and for five years, from 1906 to 1910, inclusive, was president of the Chamber of Commerce. In the spring of 1907, while president of the Chamber of Commerce, Major Williamson, in company with Gov. Hoke Smith and G. Gunby Jordan, president of the Georgia Irrigation Association, visited Europe, and their efforts were successful in procuring the establishment of direct steamship communication with the Port of Savannah, so that the state received in 1907 the first cargo of selected immigrants arriving in Georgia since colonial days. Major Williamson's service to the state military covers a period of thirty-two years. In 1872 he joined the Savannah Volunteer Guards, organized in 1802. He joined as a private and held every office from private to captain. Finally in 1901, he advanced to the rank of major, which position he held until 1904, when he retired from active service. Certainly he had given a full measure of service. During his military service he was largely responsible for the establishment of Georgia's reputation in the rifle contests. Beginning in 1895, he was appointed by the Governor, captain of the state rifle team to represent the state at the annual rifle matches at Sea Girt, New Jersey. Major Williamson captained the team for five years. They came into competition with state teams from Massachusetts, New York, Pennsylvania, Connecticut, Maine, the District of Columbia, and other localities. From its first visit to Sea Girt the Georgia team steadily worked its way forward until 1897, when out of five team matches and twelve individual matches, the Georgia men won every one, except one individual match.

The things before mentioned have been merely a part of his immense activities in a public way. He has been, or is, a director in the Cotton Press Association, the Cotton Exchange, Tow Boat Company, Henderson-Hull Buggy Company, Young Men's Christian Association, a curator in the Georgia Historical Society, vestryman in St. John's Episcopal church, a commissioner of pilotage, a vice-president (for Georgia) of the National Rivers and Harbors Congress. As chairman of a committee composed of delegates from the Chamber of Commerce, Board of Trade, Cotton Exchange and Board of Aldermen, on several occasions, Major Williamson appeared before the Rivers and Harbors Committee of Congress, and secured for the city of Savannah large appropriations for the improvement of its harbor. The committee was in each case successful, and Savannah has in the last twenty-five years grown from a shallow-water port, with a depth of twelve feet, to a deep-sea port, which can accommodate vessels of twenty-seven foot draught. Major Williamson was also one of the active promoters of the automobile races of Savannah, which draw multiplied thousands of people to that city at their annual meets. In social life he is identified with the Oglethorpe Club, the Savannah Yacht Club, the Golf Club, the Savannah Volunteer Guards' Club, and the Cotillion Club, of which last named he has been chairman of the board since its organization. Politically, he is identified with the Democratic party, and in 1913 was elected alderman.

Major Williamson was married in 1904 to Miss Corinne Heyward, daughter of Robert and Mary Elizabeth (Stoney) Heyward. After the birth of two children, Mrs. Williamson passed away, leaving a surviving infant, William Wayne Williamson, Junior, and Major Williamson has since remained a widower. His preferred reading has been along historical lines, and it is a notable fact that every student of public men comes to be impressed with the fact that those men who are students of history show a larger measure of public spirit than those who are not interested in that direction. A knowledge of history seems to be one of the contributing factors in good citizenship; and when with this knowledge of history is combined a good ancestry, one can, in nearly every case, forecast what attitude the men possessing these qualifications will occupy upon public questions.

STEPHEN NATHAN HARRIS. The world instinctively and justly renders deference to the man whose success in life has been worthily achieved, who has obtained a competence by honorable methods, and whose high reputation is solely the result of pre-eminent merit in his chosen work. Among Savannah's young citizens and business men is Stephen Nathan Harris, president of the Harris Tire Company, manufacturers of automobile supplies, a concern which is a live factor in the city's prosperity. In this day when the automobile has taken so important a part in the world's affairs, Mr. Harris' business is one of remarkable possibilities and his thorough mastery of the business in all its details has constituted the basis of his steady advancement.

Stephen Nathan Harris is a native Georgian, his birth having occurred in Liberty county in 1877, the son of Stephen Raymond and Laura E. (McGillis) Harris. His father, who has lived in Savannah since 1886, was born in Liberty county, the ancestral home of this branch of the Harris family. S. R. Harris' father was Dr. Stephen Nathan Harris, who was born and died in Liberty county. The latter's father was Dr. Raymond Harris, a native of Virginia, who came to Georgia when a boy with his father and located in Liberty county. The subject's paternal grandmother, the widow of Dr. Stephen Nathan Harris, died January 15, 1913, in Savannah. The maiden name of the venerable and admirable lady was Emma A. Jones and her father was Capt. Joseph Jones of Liberty county. The latter was the son of Maj. John Jones, a South Carolinian, who served throughout the Revolutionary war, first as aide-de-camp to Colonel Elliott and later as aide-de-camp and major on the staff of General McIntosh. It was while acting in the latter capacity that he was killed in the siege of Savannah on October 9, 1779. The subject's grandmother is of Revolutionary descent on her mother's side also. Her mother, Elizabeth (Hart), Jones, was the daughter of Mary (Screven) Hart, who was the daughter of Gen. James Screven, of Georgia, a distinguished Revolutionary soldier, who was brigadier general of Georgia militia and was killed at the engagement at Midway Church, November 24, 1778. Capt. John Hart, the husband of Mary Screven Hart, mentioned above, was an officer of the Second South Carolina regiment in the Revolutionary war and was taken prisoner at Charleston, May 12, 1780. The scion of such ancestry, it is small wonder that the spirit of the men and women who achieved American independence burns in the breast of the young citizen whose name appears at the head of this paragraph. Although for only a few years an active member of the body politic, he has well performed his part therein, giving heart and hand to all measures which in his judgment promise well for the general welfare. His career has been such as to warrant the trust and confidence of the business world, for he has ever conducted all transactions on the strictest principles of honor and integrity.

Mr. Harris is almost a life-long resident of Savannah, having lived here since the age of six and having received the greater part of his education in this city. He is the president of the Harris Tire Company, one of the most flourishing business establishments in Savannah. This deals in general automobile supplies and its members are also branch managers of the Firestone Tire Company of Akron, Ohio. The Harris business was established in 1906.

Mr. Harris has from early boyhood been interested in affairs military and in 1896 enlisted as a private in the Savannah Volunteer Guards, joining Company B. With this company he went into service at the time of the Spanish-American war and had steady promotion, first becoming sergeant, then lieutenant and finally captain of Company B, which is his present rank. He is extremely popular with the boys, who find in him their gallant ideal of an officer.

Mr. Harris was married on April 24, 1901, to Miss Mary Coburn of this city. Mrs. Harris is a daughter of Moses Douville Coburn, who was a member of the society of Cincinnati.

SHELBY MYRICK has been engaged in the practice of the law in Savannah since 1897 and is recognized as one of the notable young lawyers of the city. His practice has grown as he has demonstrated his ability to handle with skill the intricate problems of jurisprudence and he possesses a distinctively representative clientage which has connected him with some of the most important litigation heard in the courts of this section. Also, for six years he held the office of city recorder.

Mr. Myrick was born at Forsyth, Monroe county, Georgia, on the 16th day of July, 1878, the son of Bascom and Mary Louise (Scudder) Myrick. His father was born in historic Liberty county in the town of Flemington and died in Americus, Georgia, August 8, 1895. He was one of the most prominent and successful newspaper men of the state and for several years previous to his decease he was the editor and publisher of the Americus *Times-Recorder*. The mother was born at Shelbyville, Tennessee, and is still living, making her home with the subject in Savannah.

The paternal grandfather of Shelby Myrick was Rev. Daniel J. Myrick, a widely known Methodist minister of the earlier years, who occupied some of the most prominent pulpits of the state in that denomination. He was born in Upson county, Georgia, and about the beginning of his ministerial career in Liberty county he was married to

Miss Mary Adeline Andrews, a member of one of the old families of that county. Rev. Myrick's mother, who was Elizabeth A. (Candler) Myrick, was the daughter of Col. William Candler, of Richmond county, Georgia, who was a member of a committee from that county appointed by virtue of an act of the Georgia legislature in September, 1777, "For the expulsion of internal enemies from this state." He was also colonel of a regiment known as "The Regiment of Refugees of Richmond county," which served in the War of the Revolution. Colonel Candler's regiment was at the field of Savannah and at the battles of Fish Dam Ford, Blackstock Farm and King's Mountain. Mr. Myrick, on his mother's side, is a great-great-great-grandson of Nathaniel Scudder, who was born in New Jersey in 1733 and was colonel of New Jersey Militia in the Revolutionary war. Colonel Scudder was killed in a skirmish at Shrewsbury, October 16, 1781.

Mr. Myrick received the greater part of his education in the University of Georgia and graduated from the academic department in the class of 1896. In the following year he graduated from the law department. He came from college to Savannah and began the practice of his profession in this city, which has continued with uninterrupted success, Mr. Myrick being on all sides recognized as one of the able attorneys of this bar. In 1901 he became city recorder of Savannah and held this office until 1907, with credit to himself and honor and profit to the people.

COL. GEORGE NOBLE JONES, a member of the Savannah bar and a representative citizen of Savannah, is descended from some of Georgia's famous historic characters. He was born in this city in 1874, son of George Fenwick and Anna Wylly (Habersham) Jones.

Both the Jones and the Habersham families were connected with the colony of Georgia from the time of its founding, taking a prominent part in its early history, the Revolutionary war, and events of importance in the state's subsequent history. Some of the most famous men and women in the history of Georgia were members of these two families, and a more extended mention of them will be found in the general history chapters of this work.

George Fenwick Jones, father of the subject of this sketch, was born in Savannah, and died in this city in 1876. By profession he was a lawyer. He was a son of George Noble and Mary (Savage-Nuttall) Jones, and this George Noble Jones' father was Noble Wimberly Jones, who in turn was the son of Dr. George Jones, United States Senator from Georgia. This brings the line of ancestry to Dr. George Jones' father, Dr. Noble Wimberly Jones, the great-great-grandfather of Col. George Noble Jones, who was born in England in 1732 and died in Savannah in 1805. He was an ardent supporter of the colonists' cause in the Revolutionary war; was speaker of the provincial legislature of Georgia in 1775; member of the Georgia Council of Safety in 1776; member of the Continental Congress from Georgia, in session at Philadelphia, first in 1775, and again in 1781-82. During the British occupation of Savannah he was imprisoned and sent to St. Augustine. His portrait hangs in Independence Hall in Philadelphia. It was in his infancy that he came to Savannah, being brought here by his parents. His father, Captain (later Colonel) Noble Jones was a member of Oglethorpe's party, landing here in the same ship with Oglethorpe in 1733 and being one of the original party that founded the colony of Georgia. Col. Noble Jones was a surveyor in his majesty's service in the new colony, and later became treasurer of the colony and a member of the council.

The mother of Col. George Noble Jones was a daughter of William Neyle and Josephine (Clay) Habersham. William Neyle Habersham's parents were Robert and Elizabeth M. (Neyle) Habersham, Elizabeth Neyle having come from a South Carolina family. Robert Habersham's father was Col. Joseph Habersham, who was an officer of the Contineutal line, Georgia troops, throughout the Revolutionary war, connected with the First Georgia Regiment, first as major and later as lieutenant colonel. Colonel Habersham was born in Savannah in 1751 and died in this city in 1815. Besides his military career, he was a prominent figure in national affairs after the Revolution, being postmaster general under both President Washington and President Adams. He was one of the charter members of the Society of the Cincinnati, when that society was organized in 1783.

The father of Col. Joseph Habersham was Gov. James Habersham, who came from England to Savannah about 1738, being the founder of the Habersham family in Georgia. He was governor of the colony during the absence of Governor Wright.

Another son of Gov. James Habersham was Maj. John Habersham, who was a prominent officer in the Revolutionary war, and was also an original member of the Society of the Cincinnati. He was the father of Dr. Joseph Clay Habersham, who was one of the early health officers of Savannah. Dr. Joseph Clay Habersham was the father of Josephine Clay Habersham, who married her third cousin, William Neyle Habersham, the maternal grandfather of Colonel Jones of this review. In this way the colonel is descended from both Joseph and John Habersham, brothers.

George Noble Jones was educated in the schools of Savannah and in the University of Virginia. His law course he pursued in the University of Georgia, where he graduated with the class of 1896, receiving the degree of LL. D. That same year he was admitted to the bar and began the practice of his profession in Savannah, and here he has since been engaged in the practice of law, with the exception of about one year's temporary absence, ending in the fall of 1911, in Florida, where he has extensive land interests.

For some years Mr. Jones was an active member of the Georgia Hussars, one of the most famous military organizations of the United States. It was founded in the early colonial days in Savannah, and Col. Noble Jones and Dr. Noble Wimberly Jones were both captains of the "First Troop of Horse," which was the name of the organization in those days. George Noble Jones was sergeant major of the First Regiment of Cavalry, of which the Hussars is a part. During the administration of Gov. Joseph M. Terrell, Mr. Jones was honored by being made lieutenant colonel and aide de camp on the governor's staff.

Colonel Jones was married in Savannah on April 6, 1904, to Miss Frances Meldrim, daughter of Gen. Peter W. and Frances P. (Casey) Meldrim. They have four children: Frances Meldrim, Anna Habersham, Noble Wimberly, and Caroline Wallace.

ROBERT VINCENT MARTIN, M. D. In no profession is there more constant progress than in that of medicine and surgery, thousands of the finest minds the world has produced making it their one aim and ambition to discover more effectual method for the alleviation of suffering, some more potent weapon for the conflict with disease, some clever device for repairing the damaged human mechanism. Ever and anon the world hears with mingled wonder and thanksgiving of a new conquest of disease and disaster which a few years ago would have been placed within the field of the impossible. To keep in touch with these discoveries means constant alertness, and while there may be in many quarters indolence in keeping pace with modern thought, the highest type of physician believes it no less than a crime not to be master of the latest means of science. To this type belongs Dr. Robert Vincent Martin, his constant thought and endeavor being devoted to the profession of which he is so admirable an exponent.

Dr. Martin was born in Barnwell county, South Carolina, in 1877, his parents being William E. and Sarah Harriet (Thompson) Martin. The father was born at "Mock Orange" plantation, the ancestral home of the Martins, in Barnwell county, South Carolina, and he and the subject's mother are now residents of Albany, Georgia. Since leaving the plantation early in life, the elder gentleman has been a railroad man.

Dr. Martin can trace his genealogy back to 1396, to Sir John Markham, judge of court of common pleas. The doctor's paternal grandfather was John Vincent Martin, of Barnwell county, who was a son of Judge William D. Martin, also of that county.

Judge Martin was a distinguished lawyer and jurist and a member of congress from South Carolina. He married the daughter of Dr. Peter Williamson of Edgefield, South Carolina, who was a surgeon of the Revolutionary war. Judge Martin was twice married, his second wife being the daughter of Chief Justice Dorsey of Maryland. The subject's mother, whose birthplace was in Charleston, South Carolina, is of English descent. Her family, as well as that of the Martins, are descended from ancestors whose names are promient in colonial and Revolutionary history. One of the first Martins in America was Capt. Abram Martin, a participant in the colonial wars and an early settler from England, of Westmoreland county, Virginia.

When Robert Vincent was a young boy, his parents left the old homestead in South Carolina and came to the Forest city, but did not reside here permanently, going from this city to Macon. In the latter city the subject received his preliminary education. He early decided to adopt the medical profession as his own and to gain the necessary preparation he matriculated in the Charleston Medical College of the state of South Carolina, from which he was graduated with the class of 1904. He went thence to New York City and entered the department of health, and during his connection therewith he was on duty particularly in that branch of the department devoted to contagious diseases. For his work in said department he was granted a diploma and his training thus received was of remarkably valuable character. Following this he served as interne in the New York City hospital, and from this entered the lying-in hospital as interne, receiving diplomas from both of these institutions. His work in these hospitals gave him a very wide range of experience for the beginning of his work as a regular practitioner.

Dr. Martin began his practice in Savannah in April, 1906, and has established a splendid name for himself as a physician and surgeon. He is a member of the staff of the Georgia Infirmary. With the county, state and American medical associations he has affiliation and he has served as second vice-president of the First Congressional District Medical Society. He is a member of the Landrum lodge of Masons and finds no small amount of pleasure in his relations with the ancient and august order. He has taken an active part in local military affairs; he joined the First Regiment of Infantry, National Guard of Georgia, becoming first lieutenant on March 28, 1907, and subsequently was promoted to his present rank, that of major of the medical department.

On January 8, 1913, Dr. Martin was united in marriage to Annie,

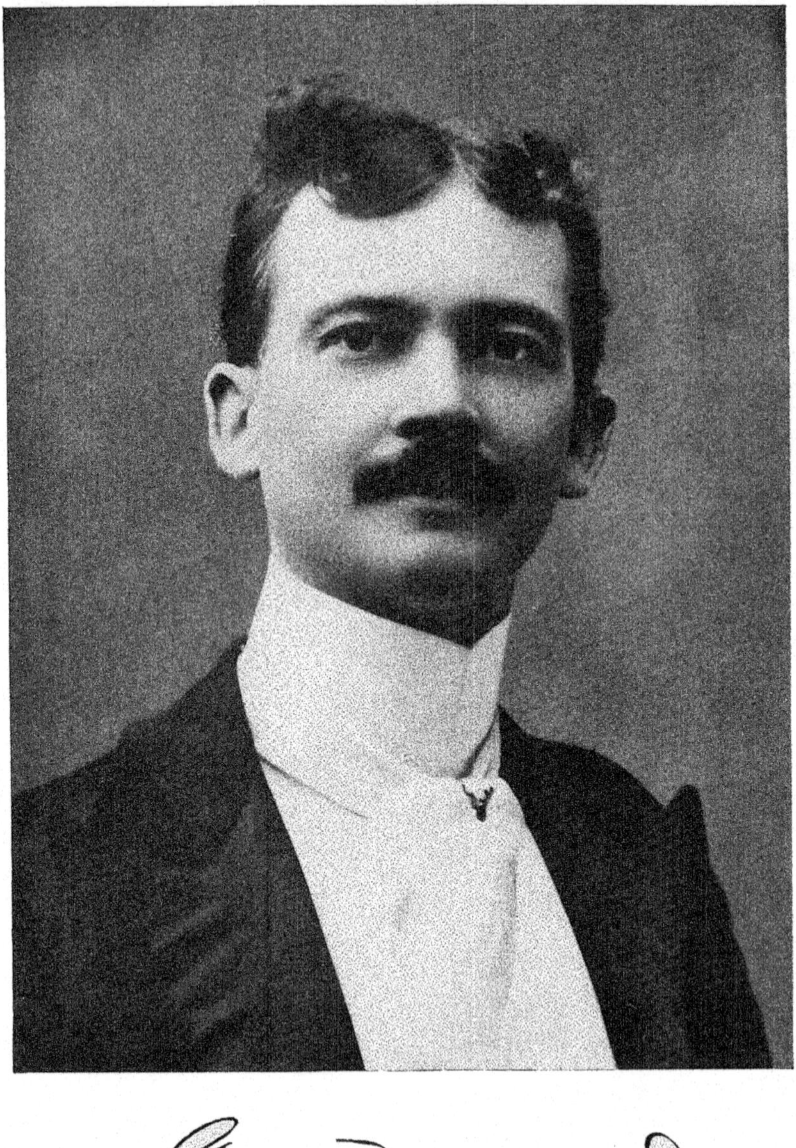

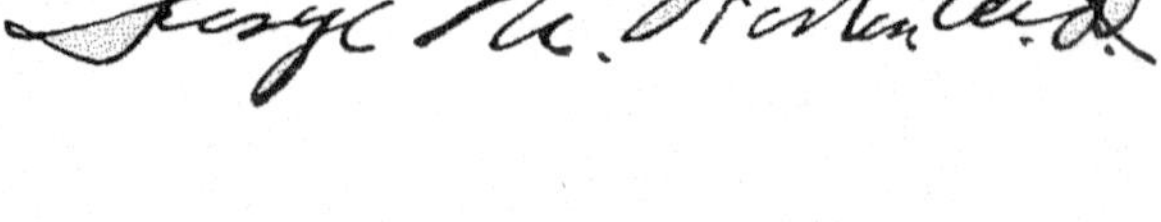

daughter of McDonald Dunwody and great-granddaughter of Gov. C. J. McDonald of Georgia.

DR. GEORGE MOSSE NORTON. One of the best known men in the medical profession in Savannah, is Dr. George Mosse Norton. His father and other members of his family were of the medical profession, and his ability in this line may be credited somewhat to inheritance. Born of one of the oldest southern families, he has lived up to the reputation for wit, and brilliancy and strength of character which had belonged to his ancestors for generations. Although one of the younger physicians in the city he has attained a success that an older practitioner might envy.

Dr. Norton was born in Savannah, Georgia, on the 29th of November, 1873, the son of Dr. Robert Godfrey Norton and Martha Jane (Edwards) Norton. He is descended from Jonathan Norton, a native of England, who early in life came to America and settled on the Island of St. Helena, off the coast of South Carolina. He was born in 1705 and died in 1774, his wife being Mary Ann Chaplin. One of his daughters, Dorothy Phoebe, became the wife of Dr. George Mosse. The latter was a notable character in the coast country of South Carolina and in Savannah. He was born, reared and educated for the medical profession in the University of Dublin, Ireland. Soon after his graduation he came as a physician to America and settled on the Island of St. Helena, where he subsequently became the owner of a large amount of landed property. In addition to this professional practice he was a large planter and a manufacturer of leather. He became in time a man of considerable wealth, and of prominence in this section of the country. Both the Nortons and the Mosses were originally members of the Protestant Episcopal church, but after coming to America they became devoted members of the Baptist church. Dr. George Mosse, at his own expense, built a house of worship on the Island of St. Helena. The advantages for education on the island were extremely meagre, so in order to better educate his younger children, in about 1799 or 1800, he removed with his family to Savannah. He had a large family and one of his daughters, Martha, became the wife of Col. Alexander Lawton. They were the parents of Gen. A. R. Lawton, now deceased, who was one of the most distinguished lawyers in Savannah, a brigadier general in the Confederate army, and for a long time the general attorney of the Central of Georgia Railroad. Members of the Norton family lived on the Island of St. Helena for over a hundred years and have been closely identified with the history of that island, as well as with the near-by towns of South Carolina; Beaufort, Bluffton, Robertville and Black Swamp, and with Savannah.

The great-great-grandfather of Dr. George Mosse Norton was William Norton, son of the original Jonathan Norton. William Norton married Mary Godfrey, and like, Dr. Mosse, removed in later life from the Island of St. Helena, to Savannah. One of his sons, the great-grandfather of the present Dr. Norton, was Robert Godfrey Norton, who was a soldier of the Continental line during the Revolutionary war. Robert Godfrey Norton married his cousin, Sarah Mosse, and most of his life was spent at Robertville, South Carolina. One of their sons was Dr. Alexander Norton, grandfather of Dr. George Mosse Norton. For a number of years Dr. Alexander Norton practiced medicine in the city and was the first official port physician of Savannah. He married Miss Julia Green, and after living for a number of years in Robertville, after the close of the Civil war, he again returned to Savannah and died here in 1869.

Dr. Robert Godfrey Norton was born in Robertville, South Carolina, on the 17th of March, 1841, and died in Savannah in 1900. He was a graduate of the College of Physicians and Surgeons of Baltimore, and also of the Charleston Medical College, and was one of the leading physicians in Savannah for many years. He was married in 1861 to Martha Jane Edwards, of Effingham county, Georgia, and they became the parents of the following children: Fannie Cone, who is now the wife of Gordan L. Groover, of Savannah; Robert G.; William Edwards; George Mosse, and Walter Abell. The latter is a physician and is practicing medicine in Savannah. Dr. William Edwards Norton, who was also a physician of Savannah, died in this city in March, 1911.

Dr. George Mosse Norton was reared in Savannah and was educated in the public schools of his home city and in the University of Georgia, at Athens. He studied medicine in the Southern Medical College at Atlanta, Georgia, from which he was graduated in the class of 1898. Two years later he went to New York City, where he took post-graduate work in the New York Post-Graduate Medical School. He then began his practice in Savannah and soon became one of the successful members of his profession in the city. He has continued to build up a large general practice, but of late years he has turned his attention more directly to surgery. He is a member of the Georgia and the American Medical Associations, and is a member of the staff of Park View Sanatarium. In his fraternal relations he is a member of the Masons and the Elks. For several years he was an active member of the Georgia Hussars, in which he was surgeon with the rank of lieutenant. He was awarded a medal for horsemanship by the Hussars in 1899.

The city of Savannah is noted for its historic old mansions, and the home of Dr. Norton is one of the most notable. It was originally built by Joseph Waldburg as a home for his family, and after his death it was occupied for many years by his son-in-law, Colonel Clinch, a native of South Carolina. The house is an example of that substantial style of architecture used by men of wealth in a former age, when timber was plentiful, and veneer was unknown. The walls of the house are more than two feet thick, and the brick of which it is built is all rosined as are the hardwood floors. The ceilings, walls, partitions and other inside wood work are all of the costliest and most durable materials. The interior furnishings, decorations and the wonderful chandeliers were all imported from Europe and most of these still remain to add to the artistic beauty of the house itself. A delightful garden on the Barnard street side of the house is in keeping with the rest, and on the west side is another garden which affords a charming playground for the children. The property has one hundred and twenty feet of frontage on Oglethorpe avenue, and from a financial standpoint is one of the most valuable in the city. The house is built with two stories and a basement, containing many rooms of the generous proportions that our ancestors enjoyed. It cost $55,000 and required three years and a half in building.

Doctor Norton was married in Savannah, October 6, 1902, to Miss Leila Exley, daughter of Marquis L. and Emma N. (Grovenstein) Exley. They have four children; Elizabeth Emma, Leila Lucile, Angela Willie, and George Mosse, Jr.

ALFRED KENT. The life of a good and just man and the record of his deeds are in themselves the purest biography, and in this connection something more than a simple announcement is due to the memory of one who was known to everyone in Savannah for his kindness and generosity to his fellow men, the late Alfred Kent. His talents as a business man made him a conspicuous figure in the commercial world of his native city, and he might have risen to a place of prominence in public life had his modesty not forbidden, but it is rather as a kindly, charitable philanthropist and true Southern gentleman that he is remembered by his fellow-townsmen, and he has left to his descendants the heritage of an honorable name and one on which there is not the slightest stain or blemish. Mr. Kent was born March 31, 1823, on West Broad street, opposite the head of St. Julian street, this part of the city having been the home of the Kent family since the early part of the nineteenth century. His parents were Ezra and Harriet (Vallotton) Kent, the latter having been the daughter of James Vallotton of South Carolina. Ezra Kent was born in Rhode Island in 1793 and came to Savannah about 1819. He was a wheelwright by trade and established in 1820 the business that was after his death continued by his son. After the custom of earlier days, the home and the shop were adjacent, and during all the years that the wheelwright and carriage business was carried on by the Kents, father and son, the work place adjoined the residence on West Broad street. This residence (No. 35 West Broad street), which until recently was occupied as a home by William Alfred Kent, the son of Alfred Kent, is one of the historic structures of Savannah. It is one hundred and fifty years old, one of the oldest houses in the city, and adjoining it on the south is the house in which President Monroe was entertained in May, 1819. It was moved in 1845 to its present location by Ezra Kent from the site where now stands Trinity Methodist church, on the west side of Telfair place, and still bears in its front the hole made by a cannon ball from Count d'Estaing's fleet during the siege of Savannah in 1779.

Alfred Kent, although never having received much school education, had finely developed natural talents which enabled him to carry on the various business affairs of life with great astuteness. He was a splendid judge of real estate and in early years made purchases of property at a very low price that later brought him a large profit. He was a born business man and money maker, and had he cared to, he no doubt could have become a man of very great wealth. He was not of an acquisitive nature, however, and his kind-heartedness and his leniency with those who owed him money kept him often from getting what was rightfully his. He never turned away anyone who was in need, neither would he ever sue a man for debt, and many times renters occupying houses belonging to him were allowed to become long overdue in their obligations. He was of that sturdy New England stock which was well grounded in the principle that better than honors and wealth is an irreproachable name. For many years he continued the carriage business which had been established by his father, but the latter years of his life were principally devoted to looking after his large and valuable real estate.

Mr. Kent enjoyed the distinction of being the oldest member of the Georgia Hussars, to which he had belonged since 1851, and of which in later years he was made an honorary member for life. As a citizen of Savannah he rendered valuable service to the Confederacy during the war between the states, and he was one of the committee of citizens whose duty it was to turn over the city to General Sherman upon the occasion of the occupation of the city in December, 1864. He took an active and influential part in public affairs, but never held but one office, that of tax assessor during the administration of Mayor Wheaton. He might have become more prominent in this respect if he had so desired, but he was a man of modest demeanor and never obtruded himself upon public attention. His counsels were often sought, however, where matters of importance in city affairs were under consideration, and his advice and suggestions were always appreciated. He was a lover of fine horses, and at all times had many in his stable, and he was an adept in handling fractious horses, always mastering them. He enjoyed most of all his home life, which was happy and congenial, and his keenest sorrow came with the loss of his wife, his life's partner of more than fifty years, whose death occurred in 1908, and who before her marriage was Sarah M. Ferrell, a native of South Carolina. In February, 1908, about one month after the death of his wife, Mr. Kent fell ill, and from this ailment he never recovered, his death occurring February 27, 1910. In the demise of this old and honored citizen the city of Savannah suffered a severe loss, and it will be long ere one to acceptably fill his place will be found.

William Alfred Kent, the only son of Alfred and Sarah M. (Ferrell) Kent, was born and spent all of his life in the city of Savannah. He was married in this city in 1876 to Miss Elizabeth J. Hood, daughter of Jason Paris and Sarah J. (Morrell) Hood, a descendant of the family of which General Hood was a member. Mr. Hood, who has been dead for several years, is well remembered by the older residents of Savannah. He was born in Wilkes county, Georgia, the son of Burwell Hood, a pioneer of the state, and was for several years a bookkeeper and accountant for Weed & Company and for the Central of Georgia Railroad. Mr. and Mrs. William A. Kent have had five children: Susie Vallotton, deceased, who was the wife of A. L. Stokes, of Charleston, South Carolina, and had one daughter—Susie Vallotton Kent Stokes; Alfred Duncan, who is married and has one daughter—Alfreda Mayla; William Hood, who is married and has two children—William Alfred, Jr., and Richard Hood; Miss Sadie; and Julia Holland, who married C. N. Wilson, of Bainbridge, Georgia, and has one son—William Carson.

JAMES THOMAS MCLAUGHLIN, D. D. S. One of the leading dental practitioners of Appling county, Georgia, and a man who has done much to advance the interests of his city and county, is James Thomas McLaughlin, D. D. S., of Baxley, who has acquired distinction in his chosen profession by close application, thorough mastery of the principles of the science and a delicacy and accuracy of mechanical skill so necessary in this important calling. Dr. McLaughlin was born February 7, 1882, in Wayne county, Georgia, on his father's farm, located near Odum, and is a son of J. A. and Rebecca (O'Quinn) McLaughlin, natives of Georgia, and now residents of Odum, where the father, a machinist by trade, has of recent years been engaged in the mercantile business. Dr. McLaughlin's maternal and paternal grandfathers served as soldiers in a Georgia regiment during the war between the states.

His great-grandfather was Scotch and French, was born in North Carolina and was named James McLaughlin. His grandfather was also named James.

James Thomas McLaughlin was five years of age when he was taken by his parents from the Wayne county farm to Brunswick, Georgia, where he commenced his education in the public schools. He was eleven years old when the family removed to Waycross, and after spending three years there and a like period in Statesborough, went to Fitzgerald, a locality in which the family remained two years. After finishing the graded course in the public schools, Dr. McLaughlin attended Blackshear high school, and on being graduated therefrom became a student in the Dental College, from which he was graduated in 1908 with high honors, being especially commended by his college preceptors for excellence in his work. Subsequently he took a course in the Southern College of Pharmacy, at Atlanta, and on leaving that institution began the practice of his profession at Bristol, but after one year there changed his field of operations to Baxley. Here he has established a most satisfactory professional business, his careful and skillful work having given him a high reputation. He has well appointed offices, the mechanical equipments of which are of modern design, while all work is executed with scrupulous fidelity and the utmost skill. The Doctor enjoys marked popularity and esteem in professional, fraternal and social circles, and is recognized as an able and progressive business man, energetic and public spirited. He belongs to the Blue Lodge of Masonry, the Knights of Pythias and the Woodmen of the World.

Dr. McLaughlin was married October 4, 1905, to Miss Jessamond Dae Carter, daughter of Dr. L. A. Carter, of Nashville, Georgia, and they have one child, James Treyvance, a bright lad of six years. Dr. and Mrs. McLaughlin are faithful members of the Missionary Baptist church, and are widely and favorably known in religious and social circles.

CHARLES ANDERSON DAVIS. A man who has ever been useful in his community, and an able assistant in promoting its agricultural prosperity, Charles Anderson Davis, of Hickory Head district, Brooks county, has nearly all of his life been a tiller of the soil, and in the independent occupation still finds his greatest pleasure. He was born on the farm which he now owns and occupies December 18, 1865, a son of Charles A. Davis.

Charles A. Davis, the father, was born, January 21, 1824, in Jones county, Georgia, but was brought up in Harris county, where his parents moved when he was a child, and where they spent their remaining years. He had a natural talent for music, with a clear, strong voice, and while a young man taught music, having classes in Lowndes county, and in various other counties in southwest Georgia. When ready to settle permanently in life, he bought a tract of land in Hickory Head district, in what is now Brooks county, and built a commodious and substantial log house, which has since been weather-boarded on the outside, and sealed inside. With the help of slaves he cleared a large part of the land, and carried on farming, being assisted by his slaves until they were freed. During the war between the states he served in the Georgia Reserves, going with his command to the defense of Atlanta. On the farm which he cleared from the forest, he resided until his death, October 8, 1884. He was a total abstainer from both liquor and tobacco.

The maiden name of the wife of Charles A. Davis was Henrietta McMullen. She was born in that part of Lowndes county now included in Brooks county, December 3, 1831, and died December 25, 1895. Her father, Hon. James McMullen, a native of Georgia, was taken by his parents to southwest Georgia when young, they having been among the earlier settlers of Thomas county. Some time after his marriage he removed from there to that part of Lowndes county now known as Brooks county, buying a tract of land in Hickory Head district. With the help of slaves he redeemed a farm from the wilderness, and there both he and his wife spent their last days. He was an active member of the Whig party, and represented his district one or more terms in the state legislature, and as that was before the days of railroads in this part of the country he journeyed to Milledgeville, then the capital of Georgia, on the back of a mule. To Charles 'A. and Henrietta Davis eight children were born, as follows: James R.; Fannie; Jefferson; Charles A., the subject of this brief biographical record; Henrietta; William J., who died at the age of twenty-seven years; and Maggie May.

Receiving his early educational advantages in the common schools, Charles Anderson Davis developed into manhood on the home farm, being trained to the habits of industry and thrift which laid the foundations of his subsequent success. At the age of twenty-one years he started in life for himself as an agriculturist, for four years having charge of his brother's farm, later superintending the management of Dr. McCall's and Judge Morton's estates. In 1898 Mr. Davis purchased the parental homestead, which he has since managed with most satisfactory results, as a general farmer and stock-raiser, being eminently successful. He has a very pleasant home, and in the yard in front of the house is a pecan tree that invariably attracts the attention of the passerby. The nut from which it sprang was planted by Mr. Davis' sister about fifty years ago, and the trunk is now fully twelve feet in circumference, the limbs being very long, and the shape symmetrical, the tree being, it is said, the largest tree of the kind in Georgia.

On October 18, 1899, Mr. Davis was united in marriage with Miss Clifford Anderson Arrington, a native of Brooks county, Georgia. Her father, Thomas Arrington, was born in Twiggs county, Georgia. Leaving home at the age of eighteen years, he became a pioneer settler of what is now Brooks county. Buying a tract of heavily timbered land, he felled the giant trees, uprooted the sod, and on the homestead which he hewed from the forest spent his remaining years, passing away in 1881, aged fifty-six years. Mr. Arrington was three times married, his first and second wives having been near relatives. He had four children by his first union, namely: William, Mattie, Louise, and Henry; but of his second marriage there were none. Mr. Arrington married for his third wife Fannie Denmark, who was born in Brooks county, Georgia, a daughter of Thomas and Amanda (Groover) Denmark. At his death he left her with six children to bring up and educate, namely: Annie D.; Briggs A.; Hattie; Clifford Anderson, now Mrs. Davis; Julia S.; and Thomas N. Mr. Arrington had assisted his older children, those by his first wife, to homes of their own 'ere his death, and therefore he left to his third wife and her children his entire plantation. Mrs. Arrington was a woman of much energy and ability, and she superintended the farm herself, making the rounds of the place on horseback, and proved herself such a good manager that she was enabled to give each of her children either a college or an academical education, fitting each for the vocation which he or she might choose. She died in June, 1900, having accomplished her life purpose. Mr. and Mrs. Davis have one child, Charles Anderson Davis, Jr., born June 11, 1909.

WILLIAM J. LEWIS. Postmaster at Dawson, Terrell county, since 1906, Mr. Lewis began his public career at the age of twenty-one as deputy sheriff in Columbia county, Florida. He has been a practical man all his life and was at work in a printing shop when eleven years old, and finally became head of a printing establishment of his own. Mr. Lewis belongs to an old family of the Carolinas and Georgia, which has furnished a number of soldiers, civil officials, and men of ability to the nation and community.

William J. Lewis was born January 10, 1874, and is a son of William Turner Lewis, who was born in Carroll county, Virginia, and a' grandson of Archibald Lewis, who was also born in that county of Virginia. It is believed that this branch of the Lewis family is directly descended from a General Hepsibah Lewis, who was a soldier of the Revolutionary war. Archibald Lewis, the grandfather, moved from Virginia into North Carolina and settled at Mt. Airy on the French Broad river, where he spent the remainder of his days.

William Turner Lewis, the father, was a youth when his father died and then came under the guidanceship of an older brother, Charles W. Lewis. This older brother went away to the war as a Confederate soldier on the beginning of hostilities. The younger boy wanted to enlist in the same regiment but his brother would not consent. He therefore ran away from home and when sixty miles from his home community enlisted in Captain Logan Whitlock's company with which he went into Virginia and participated in many of the historic campaigns and battles of the war. He was slightly wounded in the foot by a spent ball, but escaped capture. His service as a soldier continued until the close and he then returned home and with his brother engaged in the tobacco business for a while. Then with his brother he came into Georgia, and this migration was accomplished from beginning to end across country, with a team. William Turner Lewis located at Dawson where he was engaged in merchandising for a time and subsequently at farming near the town. He then returned to Dawson again, and once more became one of the local merchants. While in the war he had contracted inflammatory rheumatism and eventually was incapacitated for business, so that he was succeeded by his sons. He died greatly respected as a citizen and man on June 28, 1898. He had served as a deputy sheriff of Terrell county, and also as mayor of Dawson.

William Turner Lewis married Frances Cora Bell, who was born in Webster county, Georgia, daughter of Arthur and Eliza Bell. Her father was a well-to-do farmer in Webster county. Mrs. Lewis died in early life, and the father was again married, Mrs. Susan (Jones) Clarke, of Lee county, becoming his wife. The three children of the first marriage were Charles G., William J., and Archibald A., all of whom were carefully reared by their step-mother, who had two sons by her first marriage, named George E. Clarke and Albert S. Clarke.

While growing up to manhood in Dawson and Terrell county William J. Lewis attended the public schools, but most of his education was attained through practical experience and the inevitable education which goes with the printers' trade. When eleven years old he became printers' devil in the mechanical department of the *Dawson News,* and there learned the art preservative. When four years had passed and he had become an expert workman, he went to Murphy, North Carolina, where he was employed in typesetting for three years, and thence moved to Fort White, Florida, where he edited the *Fort White Herald.* Then at the age of twenty-one, Mr. Lewis was appointed deputy sheriff of Columbia county, Florida, and served two years in that office. Returning to Dawson in 1895, he took the position of foreman of the *News* office, and some time later bought the job printing department of the *News* and conducted a successful printing business until 1906. In that year he was appointed postmaster at Dawson, and has been continued in this office by reappointment to the present time.

Mr. Lewis on May 31, 1896, married Miss Selina Hay, a daughter of

Isaac and Mollie (Cannon) Hay, and a granddaughter of Martin Hay and Jeptha Cannon. Isaac Hay is one of the most successful farmers in South Georgia. Mr. and Mrs. Lewis have two children named Charles Arthur and Alice Maybell. The family worship in the Methodist church and Mr. Lewis is affiliated with Dawson Camp No. 74, of the Woodmen of the World, being consul commander.

JOHN A. FOSTER. Connected with the lumber interest of the south since boyhood and holding rank among the progressive men who have been instrumental in developing this industry in Georgia, John A. Foster is widely known among the business men of this state and more especially in the city of Savannah, where he is a member of the firm of Hilton & Dodge Lumber Company.

John A. Foster was born in Savannah, in 1853, a son of John A. and Ruth (Lachlison) Foster, natives respectively of Philadelphia, Pennsylvania and Preston, England, the mother being a sister of the mother of Joseph Hilton, whose sketch appears elsewhere in this work. A brother of Mr. Foster is Captain James L. Foster, an account of whose distinguished services as a soldier follows on a succeeding page.

John A. Foster was reared in his native city where he was brought up amid the excitement of war and in the hardships of reconstruction and resided there until 1869 when he went to Darien. Like his brother he has been connected with the Hilton & Foster Lumber interests, now known as the Hilton-Dodge Lumber Company, since 1869. At that time, when only sixteen years of age, he started at Darien as a board inspector, and in 1882 became a partner in the firm with which he has since been connected as a member. He had charge of the southern division of the Hilton-Dodge Lumber Company until 1907, in which year he came to Savannah. For several years he resided at Ceylon on the Santillo river, where the company had two mills and from that point moved to a home on St. Simon's Island, where his family resided until the removal to Savannah in 1907. Mr. Foster's long experience in the lumber industry has given him a vast and comprehensive knowledge of every detail of the business, and he is regarded as one of the best informed lumbermen in the state. He returned from Nicaragua, April 19, 1913, and is now negotiating with the government of Nicaragua for timber properties and a transcontinental railroad franchise, which looks very favorable. His business capacity is of a high order, but high as this ability has ranked in the special department of Georgia's industries to which his energies have been so long and so successfully devoted, it stands not higher than his personal character in the estimation of a large circle of acquaintances and of the people of that portion of the state where his large interests are centered.

Mr. Foster has been twice married, his first wife having been Miss Estella Floyd, who was the mother of four children, namely: Ruth, Katharine, Ida Hilton and Jule Floyd. Three years following the death of his first wife, Mr. Foster was married to Miss Augusta Russell, and they have five children, whose names are Georgia, Elizabeth Lachlison, Rosa Lee, Floyd and John.

CAPT. HENRY CUMMING CUNNINGHAM. A man of distinctive culture and forceful individuality, Capt. Henry Cumming Cunningham is an able and influential member of the Savannah bar, and a citizen of prominence. He was born April 5, 1842, in Savannah, a son of Dr. Alexander and Anna Frances (Mayhew) Cunningham, and in the city schools acquired his first knowledge of books.

In 1858 he entered South Carolina College, now the University of, South Carolina, and was there graduated with the class of 1861. Immediately after receiving his diploma, he entered the Confederate army as a private, and one year later, upon competitive examination, was appointed first lieutenant of artillery, and assigned to ordnance duty upon the staff of Gen. William B. Talliaferro, who was stationed in Savannah. Later Captain Cunningham was in service at Charleston, South Carolina, being with the army at the evacuation of that city. Subsequently, while holding a similar position upon the staff of Gen. Stephen Elliott, he participated in the battles at Averysboro and Bentonville, and in other engagements of the Carolina campaign, at the close of the conflict being paroled at Greensboro.

After the war Captain Cunningham returned to Savannah, and entered the service of the Central of Georgia Railway Company, first as a clerk, and later becoming treasurer of the company. Studying law in the meantime, the captain was admitted to the bar in 1872, and for four years was associated in the practice of his profession with Charles N. West. From 1876 until 1881, he maintained an individual practice, in the latter year forming a partnership with Gen. A. R. Lawton and A. R. Lawton, Jr., the firm of Lawton & Cunningham was established, and has been continued under this name ever since, a period of more than thirty years. Upon the withdrawal of General Lawton from the firm, Captain Cunningham became senior member of the firm, which is one of the leading law firms of Georgia. This firm is general counsel for the Central of Georgia Railway Company, and has an extensive and lucrative patronage.

From 1880 until 1887 Captain Cunningham was corporation attorney of Savannah, and he is now one of the members of the board of managers of the Georgia Historical Society. He is senior warden of the Christ church, Episcopal, and occupies an honored place among Savannah's most distinguished citizens.

Captain Cunningham married first, December 19, 1867, Miss Virginia Waldburg Wayne, a daughter of Dr. Richard Wayne, of Savannah. She died, leaving four children, of whom three are living, namely: Thomas Mayhew Cunningham; Mrs. Virginia C. Cleveland; and C. Wayne Cunningham. The captain was subsequently married to Miss Nora Lawton, a daughter of Gen. A. R. Lawton, and they have one daughter, Miss Sarah A. Cunningham.

WILLIAM BARRON CRAWFORD, M. D., Savannah, Georgia, is classed in the foremost rank of the younger members of his profession in this city, where he was born and reared.

Dr. Crawford dates his birth in 1876. Through his father, William C. Crawford, he traces the line of ancestry back to progenitors in Scotland; and through his mother, Mary (Barron) Crawford, he claims Irish blood.

The first of the Crawfords who came to this country from Scotland landed here as early as 1663 and made settlement in Appling county, Virginia, which was the home of the family for many generations. There were born his grandfather and great-grandfather Crawford, both named William, and both of whom, when the former was a small child, came to Georgia. In Muscogee county, near Columbus, Georgia, William C. Crawford, the doctor's father, was born, and from there, at the age of six years, was brought by his parents to Savannah, which city remained his home during the rest of his life, and where he died in 1883. He was a successful merchant, and for a number of years was a member of the hardware firm of Crawford & Lovell.

The doctor's mother died in Savannah in 1890. She was born in Philadelphia and in her childhood came to Savannah, where she grew up and married and where the rest of her life was passed. Her mother was a native of the city of Cork, Ireland, and a member of the O'Brien family which furnished a bishop to the Roman Catholic church.

After his graduation from the Savannah high school, William B. Crawford, having decided to enter the medical profession, went to New York to pursue his studies. There, in 1899, he graduated from the medical department of Columbia University, after which he spent two years as interne in Roosevelt Hospital. Returning to Savannah in 1901, he opened an office and began the practice of his profession among the people who had known him since childhood. Thoroughly fitted for his work, and with a deep interest in and love for it, his practice has been attended with success from its beginning, and today he occupies a position among the leading physicians of the city. He is consulting surgeon of St. Joseph's Hospital, and is identified with a number of medical organizations, including the American, the State and County Medical societies. He is a member of the Catholic church, and also has membership in the Hibernian Society, Knights of Columbus, and B. P. O. E.

Dr. Crawford's family consists of his wife and two children, Mary Barron and William. Mrs. Crawford, formerly Miss Rachel Miles Shellman, is a daughter of Maj. W. F. Shellman.

GRANTHAM I. TAGGART. In recalling the men who have contributed to the business prosperity of Savannah, Georgia, and whose names belong to the roll of men of distinction in military life, the late Col. Grantham I. Taggart claims prominent notice. His birth took place on October 17, 1828, at Northumberland, Pennsylvania, and his death occurred October 24, 1905, at Savannah, Georgia. His father was James Taggart and his grandfather was Capt. Joseph Israel Taggart who commnded a Delaware contingent in the Continental army in the Revolutionary war and was imprisoned on the British frigate, Roebuck.

In the schools of Northumberland, Pennsylvania, Grantham I. Taggart obtained his education and when he was sixteen years of age his practical father decided that his services could be profitably utilized in his grocery store. That the youth had other ambitions may be judged by the fact that he continued his studies at night in order to qualify himself for teaching school and in fact, taught two terms of school just across the Susquehanna river from his native place. Prior to this, however, he had had his first taste of military life, in 1845 enlisting as a volunteer for service in the Mexican war, and, although young, had been made second lieutenant of the Sixth Company, First Battalion, Third Regiment, Pennsylvania National Guard. Whether it was the times in which he lived that aroused his military spirit and later developed his powers, or, whether they were an inheritance from his Revolutionary grandfather, may not be determined, but it is certain that after the Third Regiment was sent back home on account of the cessation of the war, he continued in close touch with military matters and as a member of the state militia, studied tactics and the science of war.

In 1853 he left his native place and went to Philadelphia and there engaged as a clerk in several retail stores on Market street and later,

GRANTHAM I. TAGGART

in partnership with two other young men, embarked in the hat, cap and fur business in that city, and a satisfactory business was being done when the Civil war broke out. He joined the first volunteer company enlisted at Philadelphia and through the interest of Hon. Simon Cameron, then secretary of war, in President Lincoln's cabinet, who was a friend of his father, the young man was commissioned second lieutenant, and he continued in the Federal army until the close of hostilities between the North and South. A record is here presented of the battles in which he participated: 1861, Bull Run and Fredericksburg; 1862, Corinth, Island No. 10, New Madrid; 1863, Arkansas Post, Baker's Creek, Big Black River, Farmington, Grand Gulf, Jackson, Siege of Vicksburg, Port Gibson and Raymond; 1864, prior to accompanying General Sherman's forces on its march to the sea, Long Bridge, Roanoke Station, Reams Station, Siege of Petersburg, Spottsylvania Court House, Todd's Tavern, White Oak Swamp, Wilderness, Beaver Dam, Yellow Tavern, Meadow Bridge, Mechamp's Creek, Ashland and Hawk's Shop.

Colonel Taggart's connection with the history of Savannah began in the fall of 1864, when, as chief commissary of subsistence, under Gen. John A. McClernand, with the rank of captain, he entered Savannah and established headquarters for his department opposite the residence on Bull street, that was the headquarters of the commander, General Sherman. His services, however, were never strictly confined to the commissary department while chief in command, for he was such an efficient all-around soldier that he was needed in many departments. During the siege of Vicksburg he served under General Grant with the rank of lieutenant-colonel. At various times during the war, Colonel Taggart was detailed to conduct schools of instruction for officers in saber practice, being a skilled swordsman. He received many medals for conspicuous bravery in battle and efficiency on scouting expeditions, while, in the files of his letters and the documents preserved by his family, there are included many testimonials as to his ability as a soldier and officer as well as expressions of the highest personal regard, a number of these being from General Grant, having enjoyed the confidence and friendship of the great commander for many years.

Under date of August 23, 1864, Brig.-Gen. John H. Wilson wrote to Gov. Andrew G. Curtin, of Pennsylvania, as follows:

"Colonel Taggart is well qualified to command a regiment and has seen varied, active and honorable service in all parts of the country. I have known him from the beginning of the Vicksburg campaign, and have always found him at his post."

Under date of June 17, 1863, the following letter was written by Maj.-Gen. John A. McClernand, from the headquarters of the Thirteenth Army Corps, near Vicksburg:

"Permit me to recommend Lieutenant-Colonel Taggart, chief commissary of the Thirteenth Army Corps, for promotion in the line. He is an officer of remarkable activity, zeal and aptitude. I believe he would distinguish himself in command. He has afforded valuable services to me, not only in his own department, but in general service on several battlefields. He will fulfill every just expectation. I hope you will be pleased to give him a wider and more conspicuous field for the display of his talents." This letter was directed to President Lincoln.

In January, 1866, Colonel Taggart returned to Savannah, his previous experiences during war convincing him that here might be found an ideal home during peace. He established the coal business which has been continued by the family ever since, in his later years his two sons, Grantham I. and John P., under the firm name of Taggart & Company, assuming charge. This is one of the largest coal firms on the South Atlantic coast, being wholesale shippers. The firm are coaling contractors for steamships and they have English representatives in the firm of Hull, Blythe & Company, of London. With great foresight and judgment they are managing the coal situation precipitated by the recent conditions brought about by coal troubles in England, Wales and Germany. Colonel Taggart, late in 1866, embarked in a theatrical enterprise, in partnership with a brother of the late Fanny Davenport, taking over the management of the old Savannah theater and producing excellent plays presenting such noted people as Fanny Davenport and Joseph Jefferson. Although this venture was not a success it was not so much for want of business foresight as on account of the temper of the times and a lack of financial stability among people who formerly had been of independent fortune. It was some years later before complete confidence was restored and old-time conditions again prevailed. After his retirement from the theatrical business, Colonel Taggart devoted himself exclusively to his coal interests.

Colonel Taggart married Miss Martha Ethel Kirksey, who was born at Tallahassee, Florida, and died at Savannah, in 1903. Their two sons, as mentioned above, are prominent business men of this city and in addition to his coal connections, Grantham I. Taggart is also president of the Taggart-Delph Lumber Company of Savannah. While a resident of Pennsylvania, Colonel Taggart became identified with the Masonic fraternity and subsequently served as district deputy grand master of that state.

HARRY B. GRIMSHAW, superintendent of the Seaboard Air Line Railway, Savannah, Georgia, is prominent and popular alike in both business and social circles of this city. A brief review of his life gives the following facts:

Harry B. Grimshaw was born in Choctaw county, Alabama, in 1872. When he was a child, his parents removed to southern California, where he spent twelve years of his boyhood. Returning to Alabama, he began railroad service in 1890, at the age of eighteen, as a fireman, running out of Troy, on the old Alabama Midland Railway. He worked on that road till 1892, when he became an employe of the operating department of the old Savannah, Americus & Montgomery Railroad (now the Seaboard Air Line), and has remained with this system, under its different changes, ever since that time, with the exception of two years, when he was superintendent of the Savannah & Statesboro Railroad. Mr. Grimshaw has lived in Savannah since 1898.

On September 1, 1905, Mr. Grimshaw became superintendent of the Savannah division of the Seaboard Air Line, his jurisdiction then extending over the Savannah terminals and the lines west of Savannah extending to Montgomery, Alabama. On November 1, 1910, his jurisdiction as superintendent was expanded to include, in addition to the territory just mentioned, the main north and south line of the Seaboard extending from Columbia, South Carolina, to Jacksonville, Florida. This consolidated territory embraces 740 miles of railway, and is perhaps one of the largest divisions under one division superintendent. Mr. Grimshaw has rendered notably efficient and skillful services in railroad operation and is of high standing in railroad official circles.

While not a politician in any sense of the word, Mr. Grimshaw can be depended upon to support the best men and measures, and is recognized as an all-around representative citizen. In 1910 he was honored by being elected a member of the Savannah board of aldermen. Fraternally, he is an Elk and a Mason. He belongs to Ancient Landmark Lodge, No. 231, F. & A. M., and Richard Nunn Consistory, No. 1, in which he received the thirty-second degree, Scottish Rite; and he has membership in Savannah Lodge of Elks, No. 183.

ROBERT B. HUBERT, of Savannah, is a representative of one of the prominent families of southern Georgia.

He was born in Effingham county, Georgia, son of Hiram and Lela M. (Morton) Hubert, now residents of Quitman, Brooks county, this state. The Huberts are of French Huguenot descent, and the first of the family who came to America landed in the Old Dominion following the Edict of Nantes. From Virginia Hiram Hubert's father came to Georgia, about 1800, and made settlement in Warren county. The original home established by him in that county is still in possession of the Hubert family. Hiram Hubert, a native of Warren county, lived for several years in Effingham county, where he was a prosperous planter, and from whence he removed to Quitman, Brooks county, which, as above stated, is still his home. Mr. Hubert's mother, Lela M. (Morton) Hubert, was born at Halcyondale, Screven county, Georgia, where her father, who was a native of Massachusetts, had settled in the early days. Her father was of English descent and her mother, whose maiden name was Archer, was descended from one of the Salzburger colonists from Germany who settled in Effingham county in 1734. Mrs. Hubert's maternal grandmother was an Ennis, a member of a family who came direct from the north of Ireland to south Georgia previous to the year 1800. An uncle of the subject of this sketch, his mother's eldest brother, the late J. O. Morton, who died at Quitman, Georgia, in 1910, at the age of ninety-two years, was one of the oldest bankers in the United States and had been in the banking business at Quitman for a number of years.

Robert B. Hubert received his education in the public schools of Quitman and lived there with his parents until 1891, when he came to Savannah. This city has since been his home. In 1906, the Savannah Pure Milk Company, of which he was one of the organizers, was established, and he became its secretary and manager and continued with the company until it was dissolved, 1911. He is now in the dairy business for himself at 16 Estell avenue, where he has a large and modern plant.

Mr. Hubert is one of the prominent Masons of Savannah and Georgia. He is a member of Solomon's Lodge, No. 1, of Savannah, of which, in 1910, he served as worshipful master; also he is a Knight Templar Mason and a member of Alee Temple, A. A. O. N. M. S. of Savannah.

Mr. Hubert's wife, formerly Miss Josephine Boulineau Hodges, was born and reared in Savannah.

RAIFORD FALLIGANT. Among the more prominent members of the younger generation of the bar of Savannah is Raiford Falligant, who has attained a deservedly high place for ability and integrity in his profession. As indicated by his name he is of French stock and comes of a race distinguished for their patriotism and military enthusiasm, the Falligant history containing several pages unsurpassed in interest and romance. In days of peace, the stanch traits transmitted by his ancestors are revealed in the subject in a particularly good type of citizenship.

Savannah is the scene of the birth of Raiford Falligant, his life record having begun within the fair boundaries of the city on the 12th day of January, 1879. He is the son of Dr. Louis Alexander and Rosa

Oliver (Brown) Falligant. The father was born in Augusta in 1836 and died at his home in Savannah July 5, 1903. He was a physician and surgeon of unusual distinction and a veteran of the Civil war. He held the post of surgeon in the Confederate army; was stationed at Fort Pulaski just prior to its capture; and had charge of the medical department at the time Sherman's army came into Savannah. He had studied medicine in the medical department of Johns Hopkins University at Baltimore and his breadth of spirit led him in later years to perfect himself also in the homeopathic school and he combined the two schools in his practice. He was city health officer and an alderman of Savannah for a number of years. He achieved much well-merited fame as an expert on yellow fever, which came to him following his heroic services as a physician in Savannah during the yellow fever epidemic of 1876, at which time he was also a member of the sanitary board of the city. The federal authorities appointed him a member of the board of experts of the congressional yellow fever commission in 1878, in which capacity he went to New Orleans and gave his services to that city during the great epidemic of 1878. He was a member of the advisory council of the American Public Health Association; a member of the American Institute of Homeopathy and a member of the Homeopathic Yellow Fever Commission. He was one of the most public-spirited men in his profession and was connected with various other useful activities in connection. He wrote an exhaustive report of the yellow fever epidemic in Savannah in 1876, which was contributed to the medical press and afterward reprinted in pamphlet form. He was a member of the Society of Cincinnati, as was also his brother, Judge Robert Falligant.

Dr. Falligant had nine brothers and sisters; of these, the late Judge Robert Falligant was also a prominent citizen of Savannah, but in another profession—that of law. He was born in this city in 1839 and died here on January 3, 1902. He was a state senator for a number of years and later was judge of the superior court for the Savannah circuit. He was an able and accomplished jurist and did a large share in contribnting to the high professional prestige of the city which was the scene of his activities. During the war he was active in the Confederate army and was lieutenant in command of a field battery of Georgia troops. After the war he was captain for a number of years of the Oglethorpe Light Infantry.

Mr. Falligant's paternal grandfather was Louis Numa Falligant, who was the son of Louis Falligant, a Frenchman, and it is the record of the latter's life that gives to the Falligant family history a romantic tinge of the greatest interest. It was the latter who was a soldier under Napoleon on the Island of Martinique and founded the Falligant family on American soil. This Louis Falligant was born in the village of Paimboeuf, France; was well educated, trained for a soldier and became an ardent follower and admirer of Napoleon, whose army he joined. The Little Corporal sent him to the Island of Martinique in charge of the military stores on the island, a position of importance. There he met, wooed and married Miss Louise Benedict, a beautiful young American girl, who in early childhood had lost her parents, in Norfolk, Virginia, her home, and was taken by a neighboring family to Martinique. There she was placed in a convent conducted by French nuns, Josephine de la Pagerie, who later was to become the Empress Josephine, being a student in the convent at the same time, and the nun in charge of the school being an aunt of Josephine. Miss Benedict, thus accustomed to the French language from childhood, became very proficient in the tongue and when in later years she came to America with her husband, she had to acquire her native language.

About the year 1814, or shortly before the downfall of Napoleon, Louis Falligant and his wife left the Island of Martinique and went to Paris and later to Paimboeuf, the ancestral home of the Falligants. The downfall of Napoleon and the radical change of affairs in France led Falligant to long for other scenes and he decided to come to America, his wife's native country. With his wife and children he left France in the latter part of 1815 and first located in Philadelphia, becoming associated in business with Henry Dreeash. He soon removed from Philadelphia to Norfolk, Virginia, and in the fall of 1817 he came with his family to Savannah, where the Falligants have since resided, and where Louis Falligant resided until his death. His son, Louis Numa Falligant, was born on the Island of Martinique and was married in Augusta, Georgia, January 6, 1836, to Miss Eliza Robey Raiford, and these two were the parents of Dr. L. A. Falligant and Judge Robert Falligant, referred to in foregoing paragraphs.

Louise Benedict, through her ancestry, was a member of a prominent family in early colonial history. She was the granddaughter of Eli Benedict, descendant of an English family that came to America about the same time as the Puritans and with a number of other English families settled the town of Danbury, Virginia. Eli Benedict was a Royalist in the War of the Revolution and became a lieutenant in the English army, which he had joined at the age of eighteen. He died November 27, 1795, at the age of thirty-six. The subject's paternal grandmother, Eliza Robey (Raiford) Falligant, was born in North Carolina, daughter of Alexander Gray and Eliza (Battey) Raiford, and granddaughter of Robert Raiford, who was captain and brevet major in the Continental line in the American Revolution.

Mr. Falligant's mother, who is still living in Savannah, is the daughter of Marmaduke D. and Catherine Elizabeth (Salfner) Brown. Miss Salfner was the daughter of Matthew and Dorothy Salfner, who came with the Salzburger family from Germany to Savannah, about 1759, being among the earliest settlers of Chatham county. The present generation, as represented by the subject, still owns much valuable land in Chatham county that has been in the family since the first generation of Salfners, who received a grant of land at Vernonsburg (now White Bluff) from King George.

Mr. Falligant received his preliminary education in the public schools and subsequently matriculated in the University of Georgia, from the law department of which he was graduated in the class of 1899. Ever since that time he has been successfully engaged in the practice of his profession in this city and is one of Savannah's representative young citizens.

On the 21st day of April, 1908, Mr. Falligant became a recruit to the ranks of the benedicts, the young lady to become his wife being Miss Iola P. Baker, born in Macon, Georgia. They have a son, Raiford, Jr. They are prominent in the best social circles of the city, and Mr. Falligant is a member of the Society of Cincinnati.

JEFFERSON RANDOLPH ANDERSON was born in Savannah, Georgia, September 4, 1861, and has back of him an honorable and distinguished ancestry. He is the eldest of five children. In the paternal line he is descended from Capt. George Anderson, of England, who came to this country from Berwick on the Tweed, and was married in Trinity church, New York, on February 16, 1671, to Doborah Grant of that city, and settled in Savannah about the year 1763. Mr. Anderson's grandfather was Mr. George Wayne Anderson, who was a nephew of Justice James M. Wayne of the supreme court of the United States, and was for forty years prior to the Civil war the president of the old Planters Bank in Savannah, one of the greatest of the South's antebellum financial institutions. His father was Col. Edward Clifford Anderson, Jr., who, at the bloody cavalry battle at Trevillians Station, in Virginia, in 1864, succeeded to the colonelcy of the Seventh Georgia Cavalry in the army of the Confederacy; and who fell a victim at the post of duty in the yellow fever epidemic in Savannah in 1876.

In the maternal line, Mr. Anderson is a lineal descendant of Thomas Jefferson, third president of the United States and author of the Declaration of American Independence, his mother, Jane Margaret Randolph, of Albemarle county, Virginia, being a granddaughter of Col. Thomas Jefferson Randolph, of "Edgehill," in that county, and who himself was the eldest grandson of Mr. Jefferson.

Jefferson Randolph Anderson obtained his early education in various schools in Savannah, Georgia, and was graduated from the Chatham county high school in the class of 1877, and then entered the Hanover Academy of Hanover county, Virginia, of which Col. Hilary P. Jones was the principal. He remained a student there through two consecutive years, and in 1879 matriculated in the University of Virginia, spending there the scholastic years of 1879-80 and 1880-81, pursuing his studies in various branches in the academic department. He then went abroad and enjoyed superior educational advantages in the University of Gottingen in Germany, where for nearly two years he pursued the studies of history, literature and Roman, or civil, law under the celebrated jurist, Professor von Ehring. Returning to America in the summer of 1883, he again entered the University of Virginia, taking during the session of 1883-84 a part of the academic course and a part of the law course. He attended the summer law school of Prof. John B. Minor during the summer of 1884 and during the following session of 1884-85 took the remainder of the regular law course, being graduated in June, 1885, with the degree of Bachelor of Law.

While at the university, Mr. Anderson was a member of the Alpha Tau Omega fraternity, which he joined in 1879, and in 1883 he became a member of a student social organization known as the Eli Banana, composed of the leading students in the various Greek letter fraternities. He took active interest in all branches of student life, and in the spring of 1884 was the "bow oar" on the 'varsity crew. In June, 1884, he was elected by his fellow students to the position of "Final President" of the Jefferson Literary Society, which at that time was regarded, and perhaps still is regarded, as the highest honor which could be conferred by the students of the university upon a fellow student.

Mr. Anderson was admitted to the bar in Virginia and began practicing law in Savannah, Georgia, in November, 1885, in the office of his relative, the late Judge Walter S. Chisholm, one of the most distinguished lawyers in Georgia, who at that time was the general counsel for the Plant System of Railways, the Southern Express Company and many other large interests. In the summer of 1887 Mr. Anderson decided to branch out for himself, and as a preliminary step, took a course in practical business training in the Eastman Business College at Poughkeepsie, New York, and opened his law office in Savannah the following October. In May, 1890, he entered the law firm of Charlton & Mackall as junior partner, a partnership which the following year caused the firm style of Charlton, Mackall & Anderson to be adopted and which was retained until the retirement of the senior partner in June, 1900. This firm became in 1895 the general counsel for the Georgia & Alabama Railway and represented many large corporate, as well as private, interests. The firm of Mackall & Anderson then existed from July, 1900, until October,

1902, when it was dissolved and Mr. Anderson continued for some years alone in the practice. In February, 1908, he formed a co-partnership with Hon. George T. Cann, who resigned from the bench of the eastern judicial circuit of Georgia for that purpose, and this firm under the style of Anderson & Cann continued until January 1, 1911, when Hon. J. Ferris Cann became a member and the firm name was changed to Anderson, Cann & Cann. This firm is the division counsel for the portions in Georgia of the fourth and fifth divisions of the Seaboard Air Line Railway, and represents a large and influential clientele, their practice being general, although largely in the departments of corporation law and admiralty.

Mr. Anderson participates actively in the business life of his city and state. He is president of the Savannah & Statesboro Railway Company, whose management and affairs he personally directs. He is also president of the Georgia & Alabama Terminal Company, which owns the great export terminals used by the Seaboard Air Line Railway Company at Savannah; and he is a director in quite a number of business concerns, among others the Savannah Trust Company, the Atlantic Compress Company, the Savannah Electric Company, the Savannah Union Station Company, and the Chatham Real Estate & Improvement Company.

In the field of politics, Mr. Anderson is well and favorably known throughout the state. He represented his county in the legislature of 1905-06, and quickly earned a state-wide reputation for ability, earnestness and fairness as a legislator. He was re-elected for the session of 1909-10 and occupied the very important position of vice-chairman of the committee on rules, the speaker being exofficio the chairman. In politics, Mr. Anderson's chief interest seems to be in the direction of advocating conservatism in legislation and in matters relating to the education and improvement of the youth of his state. In the session of 1905, he was vice-chairman of the house committee, which created eight new counties in Georgia. He energetically supported the measure creating a juvenile reformatory and he was floor leader in the house for the movement which enacted the first child labor law in Georgia. In 1906 he actively assisted in the passage of the law which created the system of congressional agricultural schools in Georgia and he has been since its establishment the chairman of the board of trustees of the agricultural school for the first congressional district of Georgia. He was also chairman of the commission appointed by the state to erect in Savannah a monument to General Oglethorpe, the founder of the original colony of Georgia, the monument being erected in 1910. In the house of 1909 he introduced measures providing for the extension and improvement of the child labor law, for the appointment of a tax commission to revise and equalize the system and methods of state taxation, and for biennial instead of annual sessions of the legislature.

Mr. Anderson was re-elected for the succeeding term, session of 1910-11, and was influential in bringing about a great deal of helpful legislation. He was one of the authors of the bill creating the bureau of labor; he was the author of the bill reapportioning the state of Georgia into twelve congressional districts instead of eleven, providing for one additional congressman; he took an active part in the passage of the act increasing the borrowing power of the governor from $200,000 to $500,000, and also in that providing for the payment of corporation taxes in September instead of December. He was one of the authors of the general educational bill, which became a law. He was thus concerned in all the leading issues in the legislature and no member was prominent in a more effective or praiseworthy fashion. In the year 1912 Mr. Anderson was one of the eight delegates from the state at large to the national Democratic convention in Baltimore, and in October of that year he was elected to the senate of Georgia as senator from the first senatorial district for the term of two years.

Mr. Anderson during his earlier years took a strong interest in military matters. He was for several years an active member of the Georgia Hussars and later held a commission from the state as second lieutenant in the Savannah Volunteer Guards, two of the oldest and most historic military organizations in the South. He has also entered upon various congenial social relations, being a member of the Oglethorpe Club of Savannah, of which he is the vice-president; of the Capital City Club of Atlanta; the Savannah Golf Club; the Savannah Yacht Club; and the Georgia Historical Society. He is also a Royal Arch Mason, a member of the Knights of Pythias and of the Benevolent and Protective Order of Elks and of the Sons of the American Revolution. He is an Episcopalian and is one of the vestrymen of Christ church, Savannah.

Mr. Anderson was married November 27, 1895, to Anne Page Wilder, of Savannah, only child of Joseph J. and Georgia Page (King) Wilder. Mr. and Mrs. Anderson have had three children: Page Randolph Anderson, born August 27, 1899; Jefferson Randolph Anderson, born September 3, 1902, died November 29, 1903; and Joseph Wilder Anderson, born April 22, 1905. The family residence is in Savannah, with a summer home, "Oakton," at the foot of Kenesaw mountain, near Marietta, Georgia.

JULIAN SCHLEY. Conspicuous among the distinguished citizens who have given to Savannah its name as one of the most progressive and promising cities of the entire South is Julian Schley, known for many years as one of the leading insurance agents of the state. Belonging to a family that has been held in the highest esteem and honor throughout the state for many years, he has made Savannah his home since his boyhood days. A son of the late John Schley, he was born, August 7, 1852, at Richmond Hill, on the old Schley homestead, near Augusta, Georgia.

The Schley family was first represented on American soil by two brothers, John Jacob Schley and Thomas Schley, who, in 1745, emigrated from Germany to the United States, locating in the mountainous regions of Maryland, near Hagerstown and Frederick, where their families were born and reared, and where many of their descendants, people of prominence and worth, still reside. To those familiar with the history of our country, it is needless to say that various members of the Schley family have gained renown in different lines, and as physicians, jurists, and military and naval commanders have wrought much, not only for Maryland and Georgia, but for the United States. The late Admiral Winfield Scott Schley, of the United States navy, known as the "Hero of Santiago," and the late Judge William Schley, of Baltimore, famous for his decisions as a jurist in the Maryland courts, were both cousins of Julian Schley, of this brief biographical article.

Mr. Schley's grandfather, Judge John Schley, was a son of John Jacob Schley, Jr., who removed from Maryland to Georgia in the early part of the nineteenth century, locating in Jefferson county, at Louisville, which was then the capital of the state. Acquiring fame as one of the foremost lawyers of the state, Judge John Schley, presided over the bench of the middle circuit of Georgia from 1841 until 1845, during which time justice was the constant motive of his decisions. His brothers, Gov. William Schley and George Schley, were both men of prominence and influence.

Julian Schley

Hon. William Schley, who was governor of Georgia from 1835 to 1837, was a noted member of the Ancient Free and Accepted Order of Masons, his "history of Masonry" having been the first pretentious work of the kind written and published in this country. During his administration as governor, the charter of the Central Railroad of Georgia was granted. He and his brother, John Jacob Schley, Jr., were pioneers in the history of the railroads and cotton mills of the state, having the honor of erecting the second and third cotton mills established in Georgia.

George Schley, brother of Judge John Schley and Gov. William Schley, was for nearly half a century one of the foremost men of the city of Savannah, his death, on April 17, 1851, being a cause of general regret. The esteem in which he was held was voiced the following day in an editorial which appeared in the *Daily Georgian*, of Savannah, as follows:

We announce with sincere sorrow the death of George Schley, late postmaster of our city. His spirit departed from among us early on yesterday morning. The deceased gentleman had been a resident of Savannah for some forty-five years, having come from Louisville, this state, where his father resided, early in the present century, to embark in mercantile affairs. He became in time an officer connected with the Custom House, and afterwards a dry goods merchant. He was teller of the branch bank of the United States when it was first established here, in 1819.

Mr. Schley received from John Q. Adams the appointment of postmaster of Savannah, which position, under all changes of political power, he held to the hour of his death, enjoying the confidence of every administration. He had also the kind regard and respect of his immediate fellow citizens. He was for many years a commissioned officer of the Georgia Hussars, also a member of the city council; and during a long number of years was a director of the bank of the state of Georgia. He received from our county superior court the appointment of master in chancery, which post often required long and elaborate investigations of accounts. He was commissioner for half the states of the union to take acknowledgments and proofs of deeds. So accurate was his knowledge of the laws of insurance, especially of marine insurance, that contests arising under those laws were frequently referred to him for adjudication, in preference to litigation before the courts.

Mr. Schley was a gentleman in the highest meaning of the term; well educated, a man of literature—better read, perhaps, in the English classics than any other citizen among us; one whose library was his delight, and whose society was courted by men of intellectual refinement. No man who was ever honored by his friendship can forget his brilliant conversational powers. He was true to his friends and kind to his servants.

He was a brother of the late Judge John Schley, of Governor William Schley of Augusta, and of Philip T. Schley of Columbus. His family circle in Georgia and in the state of Maryland is large and of the first degree of respectabliity. Many a heart will be pained by the sad intelligence of his death. He was the intimate personal friend from earliest boyhood of the late Edward F. Tattnall, and was always the associate of William Gaston. The shipping in port was at half mast during the day.

Judge John Schley had a large family of children, consisting of seven sons and three daughters, as follows: John Schley, Jr., father of Julian Schley; George Schley; Dr. James Montfort Schley; Robert Schley; Judge William Schley; Philip Schley; Freeman Walker

Schley; Sara Schley; Anna Maria Schley; and Mary Ann Schley. Dr. James Montfort Schley and Judge William Schley, the third and fifth sons, are particularly well remembered by Savannahians, the former as a distinguished physician who practiced his profession in this city many years; the latter as a prominent lawyer and judge of the superior court of Savannah. The son Philip was also an able member of the bar and one of the leading lawyers of Columbus, who for many years was a resident of Savannah, living here prior to the war, and being owner of two brick houses on Whitaker street, immediately west of the residence of Gen. Peter Meldrim.

The eldest son of Judge John Schley, John Schley, father of Julian Schley, studied law when young, and subsequetly became one of the leading lights of the legal profession, as an attorney and jurist attaining note. Coming in 1854 from his home near Augusta to Savannah, he purchased the beautiful sea-island plantation known as "Beaulieu," which was located about twelve miles from the business portion of the city. In the second year of the Civil war he was forced to vacate his plantation, which was requisitioned by the Confederate government for the site of a fortification officially designated "Beaulieu Battery." He married Ellen McAlpin, who was born in Scotland, and came to Savannah with her father, Henry McAlpin, who built up the famous estate called "The Hermitage."

Spending his childhood days at "Beaulieu," Julian Schley came with his parents to Savannah in 1863, and since 1872 has been actively identified with the leading interests of this city. For the greater part of the time he has been connected with general insurance, and since 1888 has been general agent for the Penn Mutual Life Insurance Company. His relations with this company have been exceptionally pleasant and profitable, the business showing gratifying increase from year to year. One of the most esteemed and best-liked citizens of Savannah, Mr. Schley has been accorded many positions of honor in recognition of his progressive and liberal-minded character, and at the present time is a director of both the National Bank of Savannah, and of the Georgia State Savings Association.

Mr. Schley is also ex-president of the Savannah Life Underwriter's Association; ex-president of Saint Andrew's Society; a member of the Chamber of Commerce; and an ex-commodore of the Savannah Yacht Club, which he joined upwards of twenty years ago, and at the expiration of his term as commodore he became a life honorary member, and with which he has been officially connected most of the time since. He is a prominent member of the Democratic party, supporting its principles by voice and vote. Fraternally he is Knight Templar, Mason, and a charter member of Alee Temple, Ancient Arabic Order of the Nobles of the Mystic Shrine. Since his sixteenth year Mr. Schley has been a member of the Independent Presbyterian church of Savannah.

On December 31, 1878, Mr. Schley was united in marriage with Miss Eliza Ann Larcombe, of Savannah, and into their pleasant household four children have been born, namely: Julian Larcombe Schley, who at his graduation from the United States Military Academy at West Point, in 1903, stood seventh in a class of ninety-three members, and captain of engineers, and instructor, at West Point for four years and is now assistant to the engineer commission of the District of Columbia; Richard Larcombe Schley, a student at Princeton University, Princeton, New Jersey, is in partnership with his father, being a member of the firm of Julian Schley & Son, general insurance agents; Eliza Champion Schley; and Henry McAlpin Schley. Mr. Schley has a pleasant summer home on Vernon river, an arm of the sea, it being located on the site of his father's old estate, "Beaulieu."

JAMES M. DIXON. One of the leading business men and most loyal and progressive citizens of the historic old city of Savannah, which has been his home during his entire life thus far, is James M. Dixon, ex-chairman of the city council, and a man who is held in high esteem by business associates and the general public. He was born amidst the alarms and perils of the greatest Civil war known in history, having been ushered into the world April 10, 1864, at which time his mother was a refugee at Valdosta, Lowndes county, Georgia, during the occupation of her home city of Savannah by the Northern army. He is a son of William and Mary J. (Dent) Dixon, the father having been a valiant soldier of the Confederacy during the war.

Mr. Dixon has always been closely identified with the lumber interests of the South. He has for many years taken a strong interest in the affairs of the Savannah municipality and has served the public in a number of offices of trust. In 1896, Mayor Herman Myers appointed him chairman of the water commission, having in charge the public water works of the city, and he retained this position until the opposing political faction went into power, securing the abolishment of the commission by an act of the legislature. His services on the commission covered a period of three years. In January, 1899, the Citizens Club, with which Mr. Dixon was affiliated, was returned to power, and he, together with seven other candidates endorsed by the club, was elected alderman, serving as such for eight years. He became vice-chairman of the board in 1900, and in 1901, the same faction being returned to office without opposition, he was made chairman of the council. In 1903 he was again elected chairman of the city council, as was he also in 1905. The duties of the chairman were at times heavy and exacting, as he acted as mayor *pro tempore* in the absence of the mayor. He was a member of the building committee of the council which had charge of the construction of Savannah's city hall, one of the finest in the South, which was completed and dedicated in 1906. For two years from 1907 Mr. Dixon served as county commissioner of Chatham county. He gives stanch allegiance to the Democratic party. He is a life member of the Savannah Volunteer Guards, and was chairman of the board of stewards of the guards during the Spanish-American war. He is also a member of the Savannah Yacht Club, having served as commodore for several years, and a York and Scottish Rite Mason and a Shriner.

In 1899, Mr. Dixon was united in marriage to Miss Jessie Dale, of Savannah, and they are prominent in the social life of the city, having a beautiful home at the southeast corner of Abercorn and Hall streets. They have four children, namely: Helene, Meritt W., Jessie and James M., Jr.

GEORGE CUTHBERT HEYWARD, engaged in the cotton industry at Savannah, Georgia, is descended from Thomas Heyward, Jr., the South Carolina signer of the Declaration of Independence, and belongs to one of the most distinguished families of the South.

Mr. Heyward was born in South Carolina, December 24, 1846, son of Capt. George Cuthbert Heyward and wife, Elizabeth Martha (Guerard) Heyward, both natives of Beaufort county, South Carolina, her family, like his, being a prominent one. The Heywards for several generations had a residence in Beaufort county, also a residence in Charleston, and it was at the plantation home in Beaufort county, in 1822, that Mr. Heyward's father was born and reared. At the outbreak of Civil war between the states, he became captain of Company H, known as the Ashley Dragoons, a part of the Third South Carolina Cavalry, and as such served from the beginning to the close of the war, principally in the vicinity of Charleston and Savannah. His command fought Sherman's army both before it entered Savannah and afterward, while it was on the expedition through South Carolina. After the war he resumed operations on his plantation in Beaufort county, and died there on March 1, 1867. He was a citizen of sterling worth, and his soldier record was that of a brave, efficient Confederate officer.

Mr. Heyward's mother was the daughter of Dr. Jacob De Veaux and Alice (Screven) Guerard of Beaufort county, South Carolina; both of which, like the Heywards, were representatives of historic families in South Carolina. Shortly after her husband's death, Mrs. Heyward removed with her remaining family to Savannah, where she spent the rest of her life, and died in 1875.

Of the grandparents of the subject of this sketch, it is recorded that his paternal grandfather, Thomas Heyward, married Ann Eliza Cuthbert, daughter of Gen. John Alexander Cuthbert, of South Carolina, and granddaughter of Dr. James Cuthbert, of Castle Hill, Scotland, a member of a distinguished family there.

Mr. Heyward's great-grandfather was Judge Thomas Heyward, Jr., so called because his uncle was known as Thomas Heyward, Sr. Thomas Heyward, Jr., was one of the signers of the Declaration of Independence from South Carolina. In his youth he was sent to London to be educated, and while there he took up the profession of law. Returning to South Carolina just before the beginning of the Revolutionary war, he espoused the Continental cause, to the aid of which he devoted his time, his talents and his means. When the British took Charleston he was one of the seventy that were sent as prisoners to St. Augustine. Later, he was elected to the first Continental congress, which assembled in Philadelphia, and, as above indicated, subscribed his name to the most important American document. He served actively also with the continental troops, became a captain of artillery, crossed the Savannah river with his command during the siege of Savannah, and rendered efficient aid in the efforts to retake the city from the British. He was a friend of Washington, and upon the latter's visit to the South, after the war closed, he was a guest at White Hall, in Beaufort county at the home of Thomas Heyward, Jr. From White Hall, Washington was escorted by Thomas Heyward, Jr., to Purysburg, South Carolina, on the Savannah river, where the distinguished general was received by an escort from Savannah. Later in life, Thomas Heyward, Jr., became a judge of the circuit court in South Carolina. He died in April, 1809, at the age of sixty-three years. His grave is at "Old House" cemetery near Grahamville, South Carolina. The portrait of this distinguished man hangs in Independence Hall, Philadelphia.

Thomas Heyward, Jr., married Elizabeth Savage for his second wife, eldest daughter of Col. Thomas and Mary Elliott (Butler) Savage, and in this way the Heywards are connected with the well known Savage family. Through this marriage, also, is brought in a large circle of relatives, including the Elliott, De Renne, Noble, Jones, Clay and other families of note in South Carolina and Georgia colonial history.

Tracing back still further along the ancestral line, we find that Mr. Heyward's great-great-grandfather, Daniel Heyward, a wealthy planter, was a son of Capt. Thomas Heyward, of the British army, who for a time was stationed at Fort Johnson on James Island, and who, for his distinguished service in the army, particularly in fighting the Indians in America, was granted large tracts of land in St. Luke's parish, Beaufort district, South Carolina, in which was included the "Old House" tract, the family homestead. He also owned land on James Island; and in Charleston, from the corner of Meeting street to King street, on the south side, where the guard house once stood, was all the property of the Heyward family. Thus it is seen from the above brief outline that' the Heyward family from its early identity with America was one of wealth and influence.

Coming now to the direct subject of this review, George Cuthbert Heyward, following in the footsteps of his distinguished forefathers, he was ready when the call came to take up arms. He joined the Confederate army in the fall of 1863, and became a member of his father's command, Company H, Third South Carolina Cavalry. As recorded above, they were in service along the coast in South Carolina and Georgia, in the vicinity of Charleston and Savannah, were active in fighting in front of Sherman's army, and surrendered at Union Court House, South Carolina, in April, 1865.

Mr. Heyward has lived in Savannah since October, 1868, when he came to this city with his mother and other members of the family. Here he engaged in the cotton business, with which he has been actively connected ever since.

On June 22, 1875, Mr. Heyward was married to Miss Margaret E. Doar, daughter of Stephen D. Doar of St. James, Santee, South Carolina; and their children are as follows: George Cuthbert Heyward, Jr., Stephen Doar Heyward, Edward Lee Heyward, Arthur Smith Heyward, and Miss Elizabeth Heyward. The eldest son, named in honor of his father, is a lawyer in Savannah and is also engaged in the cotton business. He is a graduate of the law department of the University of Georgia at Athens, and is captain of Company A of the Savannah Volunteer Guards. November 8, 1911, he was married at Chestnut Hill, Philadelphia, Pennsylvania, to Miss Alice Stuart Hunter of that place, daughter of Mr. and Mrs. Allan Hunter. The second son, Stephen Doar, now a resident of Cleburne, Texas, married Miss Eleanor Blanche Allen of that place. The two other sons and the daughter are at home.

Mr. Heyward's eldest brother, the late J. Guerard Heyward, who died in Savannah in 1888, was a Confederate soldier in the war and was a prisoner on Johnson's Island, also at Moore's Island. He is survived by a widow, who before her marriage was Miss Pauline de Caradeue, and children, viz.: Mrs. Elise Howkins and Mrs. Arthur Overton and Miss Maud Heyward and Frank de C. and Walter Screven Heyward.

Another brother is Thomas Savage Heyward, who married Miss Mary Seabrook. They have two children, Clifford and Mary H.

Another of Mr. Heyward's brothers is T. Daniel Heyward who married Miss Selina Johnstone of North Santee, South Carolina, and they have five daughters: Selina, Isabelle, Elizabeth, Dorothy, Helen Hazel.

JUDGE JOHN E. SCHWARZ, judge of the police court of Savannah since 1907, and a prominent lawyer of the city, is one of the most popular citizens of his city, as well as one of the most influential. Born in Savannah and here reared, and taking his university training in the Georgia institution of learning, he is a distinctive Georgia product, and the results of his training and of his labors since entering upon the serious business of life have accrued to the general good of his native city and state.

Born in Savannah, Georgia, on August 31, 1878, Judge Schwarz is the son of Emil A. and Louise (Schoneck) Schwarz. The father was born in Bavaria, Germany, and with his parents immigrated to America in 1850, when the family located in New York City. In 1854 Emil Schwarz left his friends and family and came to the southland, settling in Savannah, where he lived until his death, which took place in 1894.

Mr. Schwarz became interested in the furniture and carpet business and conducted a representative business in this line at the corner of Bull and Broughton streets for a quarter of a century. At the inception of the Civil war he joined the Confederate army as a member of Company B, Savannah Volunteer Guards, and served throughout the war. His brother, the late Major Schwarz, who came to Savannah in 1858, also served the full duration of the war period, first as a member of the German Volunteers, and later as a member of Captain Phillips' company in the Thirty-second Georgia Infantry. Major Schwarz was for several years prominent in military circles of the state, becoming a major in the First Regiment of Infantry, retiring with the rank of lieutenant colonel, and afterwards serving four years on the staff of Governor Atkinson and the same period on the staff of Governor Chandler. The mother of Judge Schwarz, who was born in Alsace-Loraine, still lives in Savannah.

Judge Schwarz was reared and educated in Savannah, as a youth attending the private school of Capt. John Taliaferro, after which he entered the law department of the University of Georgia, finishing the prescribed course and receiving the degree of Bachelor of Laws from that institution in 1895, when he was but seventeen years of age, a most unusual accomplishment. He was considered too young to enter into actual practice of his profession at that time, and so turned his attention to his father's business, the death of the elder Schwarz having occurred some few months previous. In 1898 young Schwarz closed out the business which his father had so successfully conducted for the many past years, and in the following year he began the practice of law in the city of his birth. From its inception, his career has been one of worthy successes and accomplishments. He has founded an ever growing and lucrative practice, which he conducts aside from his duties as city recorder, to which office he was elected in 1907 by the city council of Savannah, his duties being those of judge of the police court. He was re-elected to the office in 1909 and again in 1911, succeeding himself in the office, which he has ever filled admirably. He is the only member of the old administration that holds over. The office having been changed from one elected by city council to one elected by popular vote, at the last election (1913) all the old administration was defeated with the exception of Judge Schwarz, who was unanimously elected.

Judge Schwarz was for seven years an active member of Company B, Savannah Volunteer Guards, enlisting as a private and receiving promotion to the rank of lieutenant of his company and sergeant major of his battalion. Resigning from the guards, he was elected captain of Company M of the First Regiment of Infantry, but after six months' service in that capacity he retired, his duties demanding too much time from his professional work. Judge Schwarz is a man of some prominence in fraternal circles, and is a member of the Elks of Savannah, with the pleasing distinction of having been elected for two successive terms to the office of exalted ruler of the lodge. He is president of the local lodge of Owls, and is a member of the Yacht Club, the Hussars' Club and the German Club.

Judge Schwarz was married to Miss Florence McDermott, of this city, and to them have been born a son and a daughter, John E., Jr., and Rosemary Schwarz.

HORACE A. CRANE. It is natural to look for the foremost citizens of a community among the recognized financiers, for a city's commercial importance and prosperity is largely indicated by the stability of its banks, and those who control these and direct their activities are, as a class, the safe, substantial, solid and dependable men. Among the prominent citizens of Savannah, Georgia, is Horace A. Crane, who is, vice-president of the Citizens and Southern Bank. He was born at St. Mary's, Georgia, in 1841, and is a son of Heman A. and Julia R. (Underwood) Crane.

Heman A. Crane, who, for many years was an esteemed and valued citizen of Savannah, was born in Litchfield county, Connecticut, from which section he came to Georgia in young manhood. He was a commission merchant and prior to 1843 engaged in this business at Darien, Georgia, which place, at that time, was an important shipping port. In the above year he removed to Savannah, in which city he made his home until his death, in 1879. In all that concerned the growth and development of this city he was deeply concerned and the general esteem in which he was held was expressed by resolutions adopted at the time of his decease, by one of the organizations to which he had belonged in life. This tribute we are permitted to copy:

"We are once more called upon to mourn the loss of one whose loss we share in common with a whole community. The sudden and unexpected demise of our late esteemed and beloved fellow member, Heman A. Crane, calls for no ordinary expression of feeling and opinion from the members of the Savannah Benevolent Association. Our deceased brother was one who gave character to our association, and during the dark days of 1876, while a fearful epidemic was raging in our midst, his self-sacrificing devotion in ministering to the wants of the sick, dying and distressed, was conspicuous and worthy of emulation. He was a sincere Christian, a noble friend, a charitable gentleman. While by his teachings he showed to others what they should do for the good of their fellow men, by his example he demonstrated to them how it might be done. He seemed to have adopted as the motto of his life, *Non sibi, sed aliis,* thereby illustrating his profession. He was truly a Christian man in every sense of the word. Be it therefore

"Resolved, that in the death of Heman A. Crane, our city has sustained the loss of one of its most useful and upright citizens, and the Savannah Benevolent Association one of its brightest ornaments; one whose daily life was an example worthy to be followed under any and all conditions."

Horace A. Crane was educated in his native city. Before he had yet established himself in business he became a soldier, in May, 1861, enlisting for service in the Civil war, in the Oglethorpe Light Infantry, Confederate army, which organization became Company B, Eighth Georgia Infantry, assigned to service in Virginia, his brother, William H., a member of the same company, being killed at the first battle of Manassas. On account of illness, Mr. Crane was given a furlough home after one year in the Virginia mountains, and later was commissioned a lieutenant in the First Georgia Battalion of Sharpshooters, whose commander afterward became Gen. Robert H. Anderson. This organization was ordered to Vicksburg, but, following the fall of that city, it was sent to North Georgia and from there to Tennessee and participated in the battle of Chickamauga. On the second day of this prolonged battle, Mr. Crane was severely wounded, this injury causing his being sent home to recuperate, and a year later, when but partially recovered, he was appointed adjutant of the garrison at Fort McAllister, having about 150 men. The fort was taken by storm by General Hazen, commanding a large force of Federal soldiers, December 13, 1864, and Mr. Crane was sent first to a military prison at Hilton Head, South Carolina, and six weeks later to Fort Delaware, where he remained a prisoner until the close of the war, when he was paroled and returned to Savannah.

Upon returning to Savannah after the war he became associated with his father in business and so continued until 1873, in that year becoming bookkeeper in the Southern Bank of the State of Georgia, of which, in 1877, he was made cashier. In 1881 he became vice-president of the institution and served continuously until 1906, when the Southern Bank was consolidated with the Citizens Bank, forming the present Citizens and Southern Bank, Mr. Crane retaining his official status in the new organization. The Citizens and Southern Bank has a capital of $1,000,000, a surplus of the same amount and undivided profits exceeding a quarter of a million dollars. For almost forty years Mr. Crane has been identified with this financial institution and his name has always added to its strength and his efforts to the extension of its prosperity.

Mr. Crane was married (first) to Miss Georgia Anderson, who died in 1880, survived by four children: William H., Horace A., Jr., Edward A., and Nina, who is the wife of John L. Hammond. Mr. Crane was married (second) to Miss Mary Cox, who was born in Georgia, and they have one son, H. Averill Crane. In all matters of great and general importance Mr. Crane's interest and assistance may be depended upon and more than once his keenness of business perception has proved of value in public matters.

ROBERT JESSE TRAVIS. Among the lawyers whose integrity and ability have given to the bar of Savannah its high reputation throughout the state is Robert Jesse Travis, of the firm of Travis & Travis, whose offices are located in suite 16-18 Provident building, Savannah, Georgia. Robert Jesse Travis was born January 13, 1877, in the town of Conyers, Georgia, the son of Dr. A. C. W. and Allie (Livingston) Travis. Dr. Travis was one of the best known physicians and surgeons in central Georgia, and was prominent as a surgeon in the Confederate service during the Civil war. He passed away in 1890, while his widow still makes her home in Covington, Georgia. Mrs. Travis is a woman of rare gifts and gracious refinement. Contributions from her pen have often found their way into print. She was born in Covington, Newton county, Georgia, June 17, 1845, the daughter of Robert Bass and Elizabeth (McLaughlin) Livingston. Robert B. Livingston is of distinguished ancestry, having been a grandson of William Livingston of colonial fame, and a direct descendant of Robert Livingston, who, in 1686, obtained a patent for the manor of Livingston, Columbia county, New York, and an account of whose life is to be found in Lossing's "Lives of the Signers of the Declaration of Independence."

The Rev. Jesse Travis, the grandfather of Robert Jesse, was a prominent Baptist minister and an associate of the Rev. Jesse Mercer, the founder of Mercer University of Macon, Georgia. Among the forebears of Mr. Travis, who were famous in Colonial and Revolutionary history, appear the names of Livingston, Bass, McLaughlin, Nicholson and Lewis, and including such well-known characters as the following: Amos Travis, an early settler in the state of Virginia; Richmond Terrell, the great-grandfather of Robert Jesse Travis, a native of Virginia, who served under Colonel Lynch's command in the southern campaign of the Revolution, and distinguished himself by valorous service in the battles of King's Mountain and Guilford Court House. John Nicholson, who served in the Revolution from Mecklenburg, North Carolina; Ebenezer Smith, a representative of Georgia in the war for independence; John Lewis, who settled in Hanover county, Virginia, and whose

Robt J. Travis.

nephew, Capt. Merriwether Lewis, became governor of the territory of Louisiana; and a member of the famous Lewis and Clark Expedition; and David Lewis, born in 1685, a son of John Lewis, a prominent figure in Albemarle county, Virginia, and related to Col. Barrett Travis, who lost his life in the Texas defense of 'the Alamo in April, 1836.

Robert Jesse Travis was graduated from Emory College, Oxford, Georgia, receiving the degree of Bachelor of Arts with the class of 1897, together with first honor and every scholarship medal in any department. In 1899 he was graduated from the University of Georgia, in the department of law, with the degree of Bachelor of Laws. He had at the same time been taking a post-graduate course in the literary department of the state institution. In the year 1897-98, he was principal of the high school at Madison, Georgia. In 1899, Mr. Travis entered upon the practice of his profession in Savannah, forming a partnership with Charles G. Edwards, under the firm name of Travis & Edwards, later entering into a partnership with his brother, John Livingston Travis, under the present firm style of Travis & Travis. The firm has an excellent professional business, and its members are popular and able, both as counselors and attorneys, at the Savannah bar. Both are members of the Savannah bar association.

In his political allegiance, Mr. Travis is a stanch Democrat, but although he is an enthusiastic worker in behalf of the candidates and measures of his party, he has himself never accepted public office. Fraternally, Mr. Travis is a member of the Ancient Free and Accepted Masons; is a past master of Landrum Lodge, Wise Master of Temple Chapter No. 1, Scottish Rite Masons, a Shriner, being Potentate of Alee Temple, Savannah, and a prominent figure at all state gatherings of the order. He is a member of the University Club, the Savannah Yacht Club, the Savannah Golf Club, and the Sons of the Revolution, and holds membership also in the Methodist Episcopal church South, belonging to the Wesleyan Monumental church of his home city.

Mr. Travis is known as one of the best rifle and revolver shots in the state, and until recently, when business caused him to give up rifle practice, he was a member of every Georgia team since 1902, holding the state and inter-state (southern) individual championship medals. He has been identified with the Georgia state troops since August 25, 1899, when he enlisted as a private in Company E, First Regiment of Infantry, and later in Company C, Savannah Volunteer Guards, known as the Coast Artillery Corps of Georgia. He has risen through the various ranks of promotion, and has served as corporal, first lieutenant and captain, and is still the captain of Company C. In 1903, he was appointed lieutenant-colonel and assistant judge-advocate in the Georgia state troops. He is also a member of the Savannah Volunteer Guards Club and the United Sons of Confederate Veterans. Captain Travis conducted the investigation which led to the finding of the exact location, on the west side of Savannah, of Spring Hill redoubt, where occurred one of the most sanguinary battles of the Revolution, in which the American and French forces, making an effort to retake the city of Savannah, which was occupied by the British, were repulsed after waging a battle in which they displayed great valor and bravery. On February 11, 1911, this spot was marked by a tablet commemorating the event, erected by the Georgia Society of the Sons of the Revolution, of which Captain Travis is vice-president. A notable gathering, consisting of prominent Georgians, United States government officials and a representative of the French government, were present at the dedication of the tablet, and Captain Travis had charge of the entire arrangement of the affair.

On November 27, 1902, was solemnized the marriage of Mr. Travis to Miss Rena Falligant, daughter of Louis A. and Rosa O. (Brown) Falligant, of Savannah. Captain and Mrs. Travis have three children: Robert Falligant, William Livingston and Margaret Elizabeth Travis.

THE LA ROCHE FAMILY HISTORY. In the year 1733 two brothers landed in America from the shores of England. Their names were John La Roche and Isaac La Roche. John La Roche was appointed by King James to assist in planning and laying off the present city of Savannah, and one of the sixteen tithings of the city according to the original plan was named in compliment to him by Gen. Oglethorpe La Roche Tithing. Some few years later on John La Roche returned to England and took up his abode in the royal family as privy counsellor to the king. Isaac La Roche decided to adopt America as his home and married Elizabeth Drummond, a lady of beauty and rare mental culture who had immigrated to America from Scotland a few years previous to her marriage. Elizabeth and her brother, Dr. Archibald Drummond, were the only surviving members of the Drummond family who had left their highland home for the New World.

Shortly after the marriage of Elizabeth her brother, Dr. Archibald Drummond, went to the West Indies and finally settled at or near Kingston, Jamaica, where he accumulated a large fortune. He never married and at his death bequeathed his large property by will to his sister, Elizabeth La Roche. The latter entrusted the recovery of this legacy to General Flournoy, of Augusta, Georgia, who from some cause failed to press the suit to a successful termination.

To Isaac La Roche and his wife, Elizabeth, were born one son, who was also named Isaac, and two daughters, Sarah and Elizabeth; after the birth of the third child their father died and their mother married again. Isaac on reaching the years of manhood married Eliza Oliver, who was the daughter of John Oliver of Augusta, Georgia. Her father was a graduate of Oxford College, England, and after coming over and settling in America he uniformed and equipped a military company at his own expense, to serve in defense of their country against the British. He was quite wealthy and while a resident of Augusta, Georgia, was a co-partner with General Fash in a large mercantile business in Charleston, South Carolina. From this late marriage were born the following children: Sarah E. La Roche, James A. La Roche, Oliver A. La Roche, Isaac D. La Roche, Adrian V. La Roche, Lawrence and John La Roche. Soon after the birth of John, the father died and their mother married Doctor Beaudry, to whom one child, a girl, was born. Isaac La Roche, the father of the children named above, three of whom are yet living, died about the year 1822. One of his sisters married a Mr. Votee, this one was Sarah; Elizabeth married a Mr. Craft.

James Oliver, grandfather of the children of Isaac La Roche and Elizabeth La Roche, *nee* Oliver, married Sarah McKay, who being left an orphan in early childhood, was reared by her uncle, Randolph Spalding, near St. Mary's, Georgia.

The brothers and sisters of Isaac La Roche were: Alice, deceased, was the wife of Edgar Williams; Ruth, deceased, was the wife of R. R. Richards; Amy, wife of Wm. E. Dunwody; Nellie, wife of Prof. Felix Lising; Ida, wife of L. L. Hunt; Isaac, mentioned below; Robert D.; Walter P.; Eva, wife of Gilbert W. Allen.

ISAAC DRAYTON LA ROCHE. The city of Savannah is fortunate in the possession of a representation of fine citizenship of French descent, this element being interesting, progressive and valuable. Of this is Isaac

Drayton La Roche, engaged in the real estate business in this city, who is descended from one of the founders of the colony of Georgia. He was born and reared in the Forest city in which for numerous generations his forbears have had their being, and is an able exponent of the strong initiative ability and progressive spirit that have caused the city to forge so rapidly forward.

Isaac Drayton La Roche was born within the pleasant boundaries of the city on the 3d day of March, 1859. The father of Mr. La Roche was born in Augusta, but was practically a life-long resident, coming here at an early age. In his own vocation Mr. La Roche is following in the paternal footsteps, the elder gentleman having been a successful real estate man, with substantial property interests in Savannah. and the Isle of Hope, where his home was located. He was also engaged in mercantile pursuits. He was the son of Isaac La Roche, who was for a long number of years one of the most prominent cotton factors of Georgia. The demise of Drummond La Roche occurred in 1895, but his memory remains green in the hearts of the citizens of Savannah. The La Roche family is prominently concerned in the events of the early history of Georgia and the subject's grandfather was one of the trustees of the colony.

Mr. La Roche, immediate subject of this review, received his education in the public schools of the city of Savannah and early came to the conclusion to enter the field of business. Some time before the attainment of his majority he became associated with his father in business, and succeeded that gentleman when he retired from active life. He is a successful dealer in real estate, being everywhere recognized as one of the city's experts in the placing of valuation, and he is also proficient as an auctioneer of real estate.

On the 5th day of November, 1884, Mr. La Roche laid the foundation of a happy household and congenial life companionship by his marriage to Miss Emma Ernst of this city, daughter of a descendant of one of the early German families. Their daughter, Georgia La Roche, thus shares the Teutonic and French elements, both of which have contributed in definite fashion to the early strength of Georgia. Miss Georgia graduated from the high school of Savannah at the age of fifteen years with first honors from a class of fifty-seven. Then to complete her education she attended the Mary Baldwin Institute at Staunton, Virginia. In 1912, she was married to Wm. A. Smith, of New Bedford, Massachusetts, but they now reside at San Francisco, California. He is associated with the San Francisco *Examiner*. The La Roche home is an attractive one and is known for its gracious hospitality.

CAPT. HENRY BLUN. America has been likened to a great meltingpot into which all the nations of the earth are cast in a constant tide of immigration, the result being the American citizen, virile, honest, progressive, with fine ideas of freedom and independence. It is generally acknowledged that one of the most desirable elements which enter into the great crucible is the German, the nation having everything to gain and nothing to lose from the assimilation of this brainy, honest and generally admirable stock, which has given to the world some of its greatest geniuses. To the Fatherland was Savannah indebted for one of her representative citizens, Capt. Henry Blun, president of Germania Bank and a Confederate veteran of the war between the states.

Captain Blun was born in the historic city of Worms, Germany, May 20, 1833. At the age of twenty, in 1853, he came to America, locating first in New York City, where he became a bookkeeper in a mercantile office. In December, 1854, he came to Savannah, which has ever since been his home, its charms and advantages appealing to him from the first. For some time before the war he was, associated with Thomas Walsh in the auction and commission business and in 1857 he formed a partnership with M. H. Meyer in the same line of business, in which he continued until about the time of the inception of the supreme struggle between the North and South.

Captain Blun volunteered for service in the Confederate army, early in 1861, and became a member of the German Volunteers, which organization was in service at Fort Pulaski at the mouth of the Savannah river and he was also with the forces on Tybee and Wilmington islands. Subsequently he became a member of the Savannah Artillery under Capt. George L. Cope, stationed at what was then known as Fort Jackson. In 1864, on account of ill-health, contracted from service on the coast, he was granted six months' furlough and on April 1, 1864, he left Savannah on the sloop "Maggie Blun," which he had bought and fitted up for blockade running, with a cargo of cotton, bound for Nassau, under agreement with the state of Georgia to dispose of the cargo to the best advantage. He successfully ran the blockade, disposed of the cargo at Nassau and turned over the proceeds to the agents of the state of Georgia at that place. He also delivered at Nassau, for mailing in the English mails, important dispatches and documents which had been entrusted to him by the Confederate government and addressed to Messrs. Mason and Slidell, the Confederate representatives in London, and which subsequently reached their destination safely. From Nassau, Captain Blun went on to Europe, visiting his home people in Germany, who were then living in the city of Mainz. He then proceeded to London and Liverpool, meeting in the latter city parties engaged in blockade running for the Confederacy and from Liverpool he embarked on the blockade running steamship "Banshee" for Wilmington, North Carolina. This steamship made a successful landing on the Carolina coast. Captain Blun had many interesting and dangerous adventures as a blockade runner, and the recountal of the same is a thrilling and picturesque tale. He was never lacking in bravery and was chosen for several perilous enterprises. His experiences as a blockade runner lasted six months, when, his furlough expiring, he returned to Savannah and took charge of a company of home guard, Company C of Colonel Pritchard's battalion. In command of his company he was on guard duty in Savannah until the occupation of the city by Sherman's army. He was then granted a parole which continued until the termination of the war.

After the war Captain Blun resumed business in association with Mr. Meyer and remained with him until 1870, when he became associated with George W. Wylly and R. M. Demere in the private banking business under the firm name of G. W. Wylly & Company. This firm was dissolved in 1873 and was succeeded by the banking firm of Blun & Demere, which continued in business until 1878. Captain Blun then withdrew and established a private banking business, which was succeeded in 1890 by the present Germania Bank, of which he was the president from its founding in that year. Captain Blun was the organizer and founder of the bank, an institution of which he was justly proud. Starting in with a capital stock of $50,000, it is now increased to $300,000. It is a highly prosperous financial institution and to be numbered among the monetary institutions which emphasize and exert marked influence in conserving the financial stability and commercial prestige of Georgia. Captain Blun was known as one of the ablest and most discriminating financiers of Savannah. The Germania building, the home of this bank, is a handsome eight-story structure, the first of

Savannah's tall office buildings. From the day of the organization of the bank it has been given the careful and strict conduct of Captain Blun. He was interested in all public matters, was essentially public-spirited, and for many years was a member of the Savannah board of public education. He was a member of several local clubs and was an adherent of the Catholic faith, as is also his family.

Captain Blun was happily married in Savannah on April 1, 1861, his chosen lady being Miss Catherine Savage, daughter of Michael and Catherine (Stafford) Savage. Their union has been blessed by the birth of several children, five of whom survive and are admirable members of society and expressive of the fine stock from which they spring. They are as follows: Augusta, wife of Dr. Matthew F. Dunn, of Savannah; Mary, wife of H. Clay Miner, of New York; Capt. Henry Blun, Jr.; Katherine E. Blun, wife of E. Clinton Jansen, of Denver, Colorado; and Walter Savage Blun. Capt. Henry Blun, Jr., is ex-postmaster of Savannah and a partner in the Neal-Blun Company, dealers in hardware and building supplies. He is also president of the Germania Bank. He is a graduate of Lehigh University and is prominent in social and business affairs of Savannah. Capt. Henry Blun died February 2, 1912.

CAPT. WILLIAM GRAFTON AUSTIN. The substantial and loyal citizens of Savannah have no finer representative than Capt. William Grafton Austin, who rendered the city most valuable and efficient service as chief of police for six years, the result of which made it remarkably free from crime and disorder, and the police force under his leadership reached a high point of efficiency. A son of Charles William and Georgia (Grafton) Austin, he was born in 1868 in Grimes county, Texas, being a member of the same branch of the Austin family from which Stephen F. Austin, the founder of the Austin colony of Texas, was descended, the immigrant ancestor of the family having been John Austin, who came from Kent, England, to America in the early part of the seventeenth century, and died in Greenwich, Connecticut, in 1657. He is the ninth generation removed from the founder of the Austin family of the United States, and seven generations removed from David Austin, who was the great grandfather of Stephen F. Austin, of Texas fame, this David having been the grandson of the immigrant, the lineage being thus traced: David Austin I., David Austin II., David Austin III., who during the Revolution was wounded in the defense of New Haven, Connecticut, against the British, and was afterwards collector of customs at New Haven, and was the founder, and first president, of the New Haven Bank; John P. Austin, born in New Haven, Connecticut, in 1774, was graduated from Yale College and died at Brazoria, Texas, in 1834, while visiting a son; Andrew Yates Austin, born in New Haven, Connecticut, in 1803, died in Willoughby, Ohio, in 1882; Charles William Austin; and William Grafton Austin.

Capt. Charles William Austin was born at Norwich, Connecticut, in 1833, and died in Savannah, Georgia, in 1889. Migrating to Texas in early manhood, he subsequently had a notable career, particularly in connection with the Confederate navy during the war between the states. His chief fame lies in the fact that he, in association with Capt. John A. Stevenson, was one of the designers and constructors of the Confederate ram "Manassas," the vessel which revolutionized naval warfare, displacing wood hulls for those of steel, that vessel having preceded the "Merrimac" and "Monitor." Following its completion the "Manassas" was placed in command of Capt. Charles William Austin, who while sailing her passed through some of the most dangerous and thrilling escapades of the war. His first encounter with the enemy after assuming command of the "Manassas" was at New Orleans, at the mouth of the Mississippi, where in a tilt with four of the Federal sloops-of-war Captain Austin came off victorious, but with his clothing nearly burned off him from the enemy's fire. He succeeded, however, in ramming and sinking the "Richmond," one of the enemy's fleet, in that engagement. In a later engagement the "Manassas," having her engine broken, had to run on a sand bank to save her crew, and was there abandoned.

Prior to the Civil war, Captain Austin had been captain of a steamer of the Harris-Morgan line, plying between New Orleans and Mobile. After the disaster to the "Manassas" he continued in active service in the Confederate navy until the close of the conflict, leading a life that was filled with most dangerous exploits in blockade running, and having narrow escapes from the enemy on both sea and land. Three times he was imprisoned, and each time made his escape, his most thrilling escapade having been when, in the closing days of the war, he successfully ran the Federal blockade in Galveston harbor, an event that is remembered by all of the old residents of that city as one of the most notable in the course of the war.

In 1875, Captain Austin came with his family from Texas to Savannah, Georgia, where he engaged in his old business, that of stevedoring, remaining a resident of the city until his death, in 1889, as mentioned above. He married Georgia Grafton, who is descended from the Harlan family of Kentucky, her mother having been a first cousin of the late Justice John Marshall Harlan, of the United States supreme court, and who also counts among her ancestors Nathaniel and John Harlan, founders of the city of Rochester, New York. After the captain's death she and her daughter, Miss Susie T. Austin, and her son, Andrew Y. Austin, returned to Texas, and are now living at Houston, that state.

One of Capt. Charles W. Austin's brothers, John P. Austin, belonged to Morgan's band of raiders, serving in the Confederate army, and was on land what the captain was on sea, an intrepid, fearless fighter, the entire Austin family having been then, as now, noted for coolness and bravery in face of danger.

Completing his education after coming to Savannah, William Grafton Austin attended the Barnard School, the Massie School, and the Chatham Academy. In 1887, he enlisted as a private in the United States army, in which he served five years, becoming first sergeant of Troop E, Seventh Cavalry, Custer's old regiment, being stationed at Fort Riley, Kansas. As sergeant of his troop, he took a prominent part in the suppression of the Sioux uprising in South Dakota, in December, 1890, and upon the earnest recommendation of his superior officers was awarded by the United States department a medal of honor for gallant conduct and conspicuous bravery in close-range fire at the battle of Wounded Knee, on December 29, 1890.

After leaving the regular army Capt. William G. Austin returned to Savannah, and was here for a number of years successfully engaged in the cotton business. In January, 1907, at the nrgeut solicitation of friends, he retired from his mercantile operations to take the position of chief of police of Savannah, an office which he filled with honor to himself, and to the great advantage of the city. Although a strict disciplinarian, it is recognized that through his severe training and experience the force of which he was at the head became one of the best and most efficient in the state, while he himself was an ideal head for a metropolitan police department.

In 1894, Capt. W. G. Austin joined the Savannah Volunteer Guards

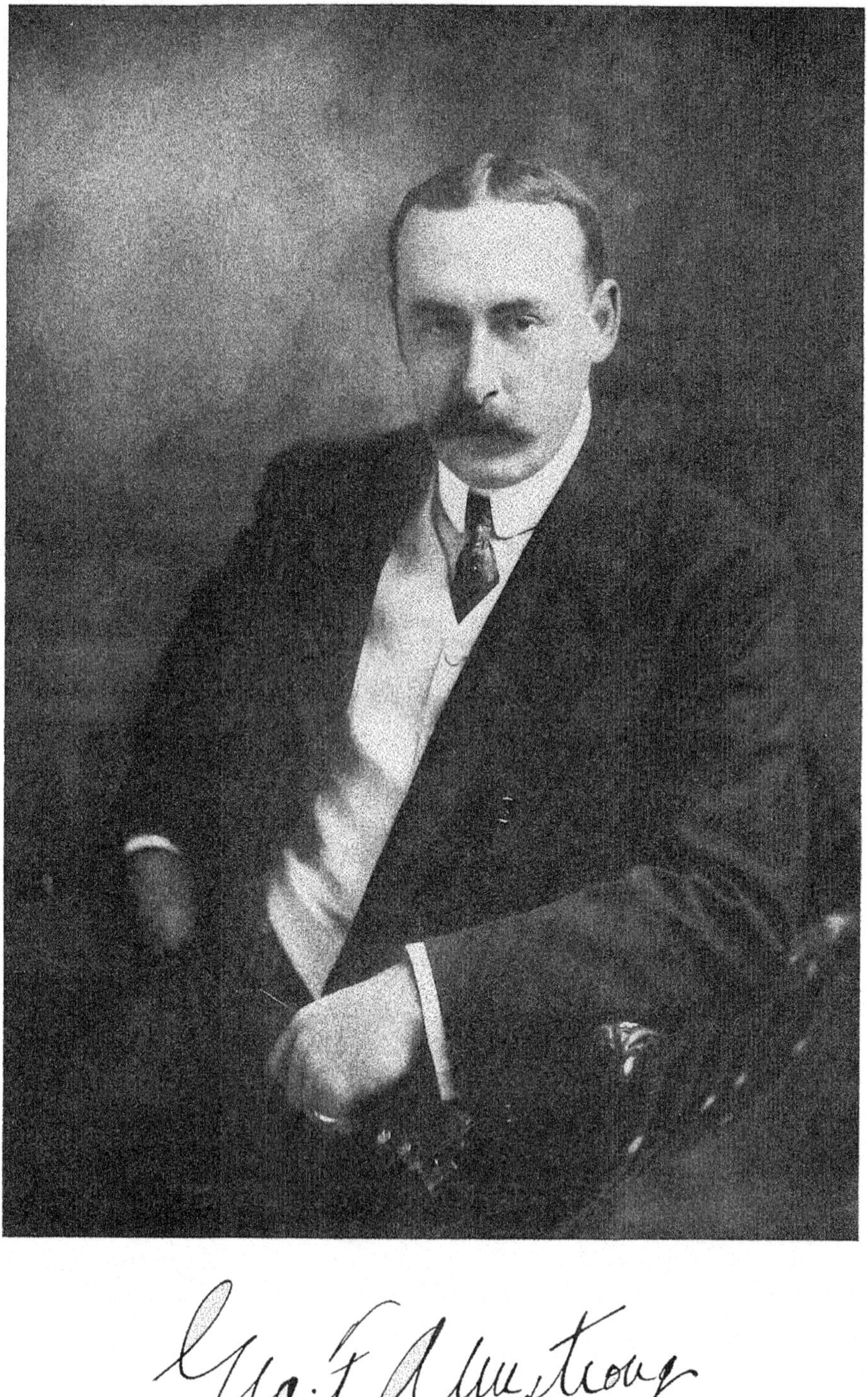

as a private, and having through various promotions become captain of Company A, commanded that company in the Spanish-American war; his company being a part of the Second Georgia Regiment of Volunteers. For a number of years the captain was a member of the Georgia Rifle Team, and is noted as an expert rifle shot. He retired from the captaincy of the company before he became chief of police.

Captain Austin organized, and is president of, the Savannah Motor Car Company, representing in Savannah the Cadillac automobile.

GEORGE F. ARMSTRONG. Savannah boasts an unusually large number of native born citizens, the fact finding explanation in the light of the splendid advantages, and the unusual attractions presented by the beautiful and historic old city, other sections not possessing charms sufficient to draw the Savannahian to them. Among the loyal native sons, a citizen of that type in which the city may well take pride—is George F. Armstrong, ship broker and prominent in maritime affairs. He was born at Guyton, Georgia, but he came to Savannah when two years old. His birth occurred on the 25th day of September, 1868, the son of Benjamin R. and Elizabeth (Ferguson) Armstrong. He is the scion of one of the eastern families which have found representation in the south, his father having been a native of Rhode Island. He came to Savannah, however, in young manhood, many years previous to the outbreak of the Civil war and the part he played in the many-sided life of the city was that of a contractor and builder. He was city assessor of Savannah for several years and was a prominent character in the public life of the city and in the fostering of its beneficial institutions and its upbuilding. He died in 1901, but his memory will long remain green in the community which he loved and which recognized his worth. The subject's mother was a southerner, Charleston, South Carolina, being her birthplace.

Mr. Armstrong was reared and educated in the city and since entering upon his business career he has been prominently identified with shipping and allied interests. He is a member of the co-partnership, which forms the firm of Strachan & Company, ship brokers, founded by Capt. George P. Walker and the late Capt. F. G. Strachan. This firm has for many years maintained extensive shipping interests centered at the port of Savannah, and is widely known for its prominent connection with maritime affairs. Its standing among shippers and ship owners is of the highest. In addition to the foregoing, Mr. Armstrong has other interests of broad scope and importance, among other things, being president of the Mutual Mining Company, extensive miners and shippers of Florida phosphate. He is a member of the board of pilotage commissioners of Savannah; he is a director of the Hibernia Bank and of the Commercial Life Insurance and Casualty Company. He is a member of the Savannah cotton exchange and board of trade and of the chamber of commerce. In the legitimate channels of business he has won the success which always crowns well-directed labor, sound judgment and untiring perseverance, and at the same time he has concerned himself with the affairs of the community in an admirably public-spirited fashion. He is also a great baseball enthusiast, and been president of the Baseball Club for several years and has been a large annual contributor to it.

Mr. Armstrong was for several years actively connected with the famous Chatham Artillery of Savannah, which he joined as a private in 1887 and of which he is now an honorary member. He is a veteran of the Spanish-American war, having been with the Chatham artillery at the time of that conflict, the organization being mustered into service as Battery B of Georgia, of which Mr. Armstrong was lieutenant.

Mrs. Armstrong before her marriage was Miss Lucy Camp, a member of the family of that name which comes from Suffolk, Virginia. Her marriage to the subject was celebrated in Ocala, Florida, on the 4th day of January, 1905, and the union has been blessed by the birth of a daughter, Miss Lucy Camp Armstrong. They hold a position of respect and prominence in the city and maintain a household of renowned hospitality.

GEORGE FRANCIS TENNILLÉ. As third vice-president of the Southern Cotton Oil Company, George Francis Tennille holds a position of great importance and responsibility, having immediate control of its Savannah works and offices, the plant in this city being the most extensive one of the company's system. A son of the late Capt. William Alexander Tennille, he was born, March 6, 1873, in New York City, and was there reared and educated, completing his early education at Columbia University, where he was graduated in chemistry in 1894.

His great-grandfather, Lieut. Francis Tennille, was the son of a French Huguenot, who emigrated from France after the Edict of Nantes, settling in Virginia. He was born in Virginia, in Prince William county, and came from there to Georgia in colonial days, locating in Washington county as a pioneer. During the Revolutionary war he enlisted for service in the Georgia Brigade of the Continental army, being mustered in as lieutenant of the second battalion, afterwards being promoted first to the rank of captain, later being commissioned lieutenant colonel. He had the distinction of being one of the charter members of the Society of the Cincinnati in Georgia. He married Mary Bacon Dixon, a daughter of Robert and Ann (Bacon) Dixon, and granddaughter of Gen. Nathaniel Bacon, of Virginia, who was a lineal descendant of the famous English family of that name.

Mr. Tennille's paternal grandfather, Col. Francis Tillman Tennille, was born near Sandersville, Washington county, Georgia, in 1799, and spent his entire life in his native state, dying in 1877.

Capt. William Alexander Tennille's birth occurred in Washington county, Georgia, in 1840. He was reared at Fort Gaines, Georgia, his father having large plantation interests in that vicinity, and was graduated from the University of Georgia with the class of 1860. Entering the Confederate army at the breaking out of the Civil war, he served until the close of the conflict in Company D, Ninth Georgia Infantry, at the close holding the rank of captain on the staff of Gen. "Tige" Anderson. Serving almost the entire time in Lee's Army of Northern Virginia, he proved himself a brave and efficient soldier, his military record, especially in the battle of Gettysburg, being spoken of in the highest terms by all who are familiar with it. Removing after the war to New York City, the captain was there a resident until his death, in 1905. He married Clara Tuttle, a daughter of George Hudson and Mary (Dawkin) Tuttle, and she is still living. She is a direct descendant of William Tuttle, who came from England to America in 1635, settling first in Boston, and later removing to New Haven, Connecticut. His descendants have furnished many distinguished names in American history.

Beginning his service with the Southern Cotton Oil Company in 1897, George Francis Tennille at first followed his profession of a chemist in the Savannah plant. Proving himself efficient in many dircetions, he was advanced to higher positions from time to time, being promoted first to the position of superintendent, then manager, later becoming district manager, and, in 1911, being made third vice-president of the company. This being an executive position with the concern makes it more or less of general jurisdiction. Mr. Tennille, however, has under his immediate charge the Savannah works and offices of the company, these comprising one of the main centers of the great corporation, which owns and operates over ninety cotton oil mills scattered throughout the South. The plant in Savannah covers more than twenty acres, it being one of the largest belonging to the Southern Cotton Oil Company, which ranks among the largest industrial organizations in the United States. It includes a large crude oil mill, a refinery, soap works, and plants for the manufacture of lard and paint. The headquarters of the freight department and of the company's chemical department are also located in Savannah, and are under Mr. Tennille's charge.

Mr. Tennille belongs to several patriotic, business and social organizations. He is a member of the Georgia Society of the Cincinnati; of the New York Society of the Sons of the Revolution; of the University Club of New York; the Society of Chemical Industry; the American Chemical Society; the Oglethorpe Club; the Yacht Club; the Golf Club; the Cotillion Club, and many others.

In Savannah, in 1903, Mr. Tennille was united in marriage with Miss Jessie Chisholm, a daughter of William W. Chisholm, and they have one child, Dorothy Tennille. Mrs. Tennille is descended from some of the oldest and most distinguished families of the South. Her grandfather, Murdock Chisholm, married Georgia A. Barnard, who belonged to that branch of the well-known Barnard family that is perpetuated by having had named one of the thoroughfares of Savannah, Barnard street. Mrs. Tennille's great-grandfather, Maj. John Barnard, was a member of the provincial congress assembled in Savannah, July 4, 1775, and assisted in raising the first liberty pole in the city. During the Revolutionary war he commanded a company which attacked the crew of a British frigate which had been landed on Wilmington island, and captured them all. He was finally himself taken prisoner by the British, but was later exchanged, and participated in the siege of Savannah, serving until the close of the struggle. Major Barnard was a son of Col. John Barnard of the British army, who, about 1743, came to Savannah in command of a regiment called the "Rangers," and settled on Wilmington island. He held his commission in the British army until his death.

William W. Chisholm married Jessie M. Fowke, a daughter of Dr. Richard Chandler Fowke, and granddaughter of Dr. John Sidneyham Fowke, who was a surgeon in the United States navy in the early part of the nineteenth century. The founder of the American family of Fowke was Col. Gerard Fowke, an officer of the British army, who settled in Virginia prior to 1657, and became an extensive landholder in both Virginia and Maryland. His son, Col. Gerard Fowke, Jr., and his grandson, Capt. Chandler Fowke, held military and civil positions in Maryland and Virginia. Among other prominent characters in the ancestral line of Mrs. Tennille were Capt. Adam Thoroughgood, who emigrated from England to Virginia in 1621; Thomas Harrison, of Fauquier county, Virginia; and Isaac Mazyck, who was born in Saint Martin's, France, immigrated to South Carolina about 1740, and became a prominent citizen of Charleston.

GEN. PETER WILTBERGER MELDRIM. One of the distinguished members of the bar of Georgia, Gen. Peter Wiltberger Meldrim, was born in Savannah, December 4, 1848, the son of Ralph and Jane (Fawcett) Meldrim. His earlier education was acquired in Chatham Academy and under private tutors, and he was graduated with honors from the academic department of the University of Georgia in 1868, being the anniversary orator of the Phi Kappa Society. He graduated from the law department of the University of Georgia in 1869, and during the following winter began the practice of his profession in Savannah. He went steadily and rapidly to the front, winning a large and lucrative clientele, and two days before the state election of 1881 was nominated for state senator and was elected, serving in that office for two terms. A writer, in summing up Mr. Meldrim's legislative service, said: "It was active, brilliant and of a high order. He was ever ready to give his vote and his voice to those measures or to those statutes which seemed to him to be essential to individual and public welfare. In all his acts he reflected the liberality and intelligence of his constituents, and for this was beloved and admired by all who witnessed his course. As chairman of the committee on military affairs, he was indefatigable in his labors in behalf of perfect organization, equipment and discipline of the volunteer troops of the state. His speeches on this subject before the committee and in the senate, were models of eloquence and logic. Then, when the bill to make tuition forever free at the State University was put upon its passage and the measure was violently opposed, he came to its rescue fearlessly and grandly, aiding materially in bringing about the happy result of its triumphant passage. His constituents and the people of Georgia have reason to be proud of his talents and character."

For several years General Meldrim was associated with Col. William Garrard in the practice of law, but for some years past the former has maintained his office and practice individually. He is an eminently successful lawyer, and in many of the decisions of Georgia, where General Meldrim's cases are involved, there are distinct compliments from the supreme bench. During a long period he was connected actively with the military establishment of the state. Although a youth, he reported for duty to Capt. William S. Chisholm at the time of Sherman's advance on the city in December, 1864, and was made corporal in the home guards organized by Captain Chisholm, serving in the trenches on the right of the line near the river and doing guard duty in the city. In later years he enlisted originally as a private in the historic Georgia Hussars, and was promoted to second lieutenant in January, 1889. Subsequently he became adjutant of the First Squadron of Georgia Cavalry, of which later he was promoted to major. From this rank he was advanced to lieutenant-colonel of the regiment, and was made colonel in February, 1900. He became brevet brigadier-general of the Georgia state troops in July, 1906, and brigadier-general commanding the Georgia state troops on September 24, 1907.

In 1891 General Meldrim was elected alderman, and in January, 1897, he was elected mayor of Savannah, and gave the city an efficient and creditable administration, during which much municipal improvement was carried out, particularly in street paving. In addition the jail was added to the police barracks and some new buildings were erected for the fire department. He has been president of the Hibernian Society since 1875; is ex-president of the alumni society of the University of Georgia and of the State Bar Association, and has for many years been a member of the board of trustees for the university. General Meldrim first suggested the erection of the monument to Sergeant Jasper, in Madison Square, Savannah, and then co-operated in the efforts which brought about the building of this memorial. In the American Bar Association he is chairman of the committee on jurisprudence and law reform, and he is one of the commissioners on uniformity of laws for the state of Georgia.

General Meldrim has achieved wide fame for his eloquence as a speaker; a reputation that had its beginning in his college days. Besides possessing the most pleasing oratorical graces, his addresses indicate deep scholarship and a wide range of reading and assimilation. Some of them are models of thought, form and diction. He has delivered notable speeches before the American Bar Association, as well as the Georgia and other state bar associations; also a large number of literary, historical and miscellaneous addresses. Upon the occasions of the presence of distinguished personages in the city, or in the formalities of extending invitation to such to be Savannah's guests, General Meldrim usually is chosen as the speaker to voice the city's welcome.

General Meldrim belongs to the Masonic and other orders. He is a member of the Oglethorpe Club, Capital City Club of Atlanta, Hussars Club, Yacht Club and the University clubs of Atlanta and Savannah, of the latter of which he is president. He was married June 30, 1881, to Miss Frances P. Casey, daughter of Dr. Henry R. and Caroline (Harris) Casey, of Columbia county, Georgia, and a grand-niece of Maj. John McPherson Berrien, who was one of Savannah's distinguished citizens of former years. General and Mrs. Meldrim have four children, namely: Caroline Louise, Frances Casey, who married Col. G. Noble Jones, Sophia d'A, and Jane. The Meldrim residence in Savannah is one of the most beautiful and stately homes in the South. It is possessed of historic interest from the fact that it was the headquarters of General Sherman upon the occupation of the city by the Federal army in December, 1864.

JAMES M. BARNARD figures in the business life of Savannah in three distinct capacities, namely: as ship broker, as president of the United Hydraulic Cotton Press Company and as president of the Savannah Hotel Company. A young New Englander, scarcely attained to his majority, his military connection at the time of the Civil war brought him to the seat of the conflict and his glimpse of the South falling upon the fertile imagination of youth, served so to enthrall him, that at the close of the war he severed the old associations and located in the city whose beauty is only equaled by its wealth of romantic history. He has resided here since 1865 and as one of the leading spirits in commercial and industrial life, has materially assisted in the growth and development of Savannah. He is known far and wide as a man of remarkable executive capacity, of fine initiative, with the power to make realities out of big ideas, and accustomed to "hitching his wagon to a star." Not only has he been successful in material ways, but his career has been such as to warrant the trust and confidence of the business world, for he has conducted all transactions according to the strictest principles of honor. His devotion to the public good is not questioned and arises from a sincere interest in the welfare of his fellow men.

Mr. Barnard was born in Boston, Massachusetts, on the 4th day of May, 1841. He is the son of Rev. Charles F. Barnard and he was reared and educated in the "hub of the universe." At the outbreak of the Civil war he enlisted in the Twenty-fourth Massachusetts Regiment, and participated in various important operations in the South. One of these of nearby interest, was the famous assault on Battery Wagner, in Charleston harbor, this being one of the bloodiest conflicts, numbers considered, in the history of the war. His service was three years in duration.

As mentioned previously, Mr. Barnard came to Savannah in the year 1865 and here he has ever since maintained his residence. During his half century's connection in this city, Mr. Barnard has been engaged with important interests in maritime affairs. Soon after beginning business here, the firm of Richardson & Barnard was formed, his partner being

Edward C. Richardson, now of Boston. Later C. S. Connerat became a member of the firm, but without change in its name. This firm were part owners and agents in Savannah of the old Boston Line, operating the two steamships, "Gate City" and "City of Columbus," between Savannah and Boston. This prosperous ocean passenger and freight business they conducted for several years and finally sold to the present Ocean Steamship Company. The old firm of Richardson & Barnard, not long after the war, built the Tybee telegraph line and they were the first to bring the telephone to Savannah; they built the telephone line between Tybee island and Savannah, which later they sold to the Bell Telephone Company. The telegraph and telephone lines were constructed originally for their own business. It will from this be seen that Mr. Barnard is an innovator in very definite fashion and he has ever kept well abreast of progress.

In 1890, the old firm of Richardson & Barnard was dissolved, and since that time Mr. Barnard has continued in the same line of enterprise under the name of Barnard & Company. He is also president of the United Hydraulic Cotton Press Company and of the Savannah Hotel Company, which owns and operates the DeSoto Hotel in Savannah, Mr. Barnard having been one of the originators of this admirable hostelry in 1890. This magnificent tourist and commercial hotel has been a most potent factor in the modern growth and development of Savannah, attracting annually great numbers of people to the Forest city to enjoy the climate and attractions, who would not have come but for the elegant comforts and conveniences of the DeSoto Hotel. The chambers are unusually large and peculiarly adapted to the climate, having the advantage of being all outside rooms. The water is supplied from an artesian well of great purity, seven hundred feet deep and situated on the grounds. The hotel is very spacious and covers an entire block. The open air cafe, in use from May to October, during the winter months is converted into a sunny sheltered piazza, one hundred and fifty feet long and thirty feet wide.

Mr. Barnard has been a member of the pilotage commission of Savannah for over twenty years and is chairman of the commission. He has a wide circle of friends, the boundaries of the state by no means limiting his acquaintance and popularity.

His wife, who is deceased and to whom he was married in 1866, was Miss Harriet L. Otis, who was born in Roxbury, Massachusetts. There are five children of the union: Theodore Otis Barnard, deceased; Mrs. Grace B. Brewster, William L. Barnard, and James H. Barnard, these three of Boston, and Mrs. Elsie B. Chisholm, wife of Frank M. Chisholm of Savannah.

FLEMING DAVIES TINSLEY. Among the foremost citizens of Savannah is Fleming Davies Tinsley, whose relation to the business community is concerned with the products peculiar to this section of the South, Mr. Tinsley being an exporter of cotton and phosphate rock. It is safe to say that he has no peer in his knowledge of these particular fields, and as one concerned in a line of industry which has important bearing upon the progress and stable prosperity of the community, he occupies a conspicuous position in business circles. He belongs to representative families of the South, on the maternal side coming of Revolutionary stock, this family—the Davies—having been prominent in this section previous to the struggle for independence.

Mr. Tinsley was born at the summer residence of his parents at Milledgeville, Georgia. Their home, however, was in Savannah, and as the greater part of his life has been passed within the boundaries of the beautiful and historic city, whose traditions are very dear to him, he maintains that he is a native Savannahian, and no one will gainsay this. He is the son of William B. and Sarah Grantland (Davies) Tinsley. The father was born in Hanover county, Virginia, and came to Savannah during the early '40s. For several years before the war and during the first of the supreme struggle between the North and South, he was the cashier of the old Savannah Bank, which occupied the building at No. 15 Bay street, East. Prior to the war between the states he held the office of state treasurer for several terms. This was previous to becoming cashier of the aforementioned bank. The demise of this gentleman occurred when the subject was a child, during the war, but he is still well and affectionately remembered by the older residents of Savannah. Mr. Tinsley had four older brothers in the Confederate service during the Civil war. His mother was the daughter of Judge William Davies, of Savannah, one of the distinguished lawyers of his day, and judge of the United States circuit court for the district of Georgia, and of the superior court for the eastern judicial circuit. Judge Davies was the son of Edward and Rebecca (Lloyd) Davies, the latter the daughter of Benjamin Lloyd of South Carolina, who was a lieutenant of artillery in South Carolina troops in 1779 and 1780. Mr. Tinsley's great-grandfather, Edward Davies, of Savannah, served as a member of the provincial congress of Georgia in July, 1775, and for that reason he was named in the celebrated "disqualifying act," passed by the royal council of Georgia.

Mr. Tinsley received his early schooling in the public schools of the city; afterwards he had private tutelage in Macon, to which city the family had temporarily removed. Upon growing to manhood, he entered business life, for which his tastes and abilities fitted him, his first association being in the office of Seymour, Tinsley & Company of Macon, wholesale grocers, the junior member of the firm being his brother, A. R. Tinsley. He remained in this business in Macon for some years and then went to Alabama, where he engaged in the fertilizing business. In 1899, he left Alabama and returned to his old home, Savannah, the memory of whose charms and advantages had ever remained vividly with him. Mr. Tinsley has encountered the best of fortunes here. He is the senior member of the firm, Tinsley & Hull, exporters of cotton and phosphate rock. This is a prominent firm widely and favorably known in the world of trade concerned with these two great industries.

Mr. Tinsley married Miss Martha Rodman Ruan, daughter of John G. and Amanda (Clark) Ruan. They are prominent in the social and benevolent activities of the community. Mr. Tinsley is a vestryman of Christ church. He is a member of the Cotton Exchange and the Chamber of Commerce, and a member of the Oglethorpe Club and of the Savannah Yacht Club. Besides his exporting business he has several additional interests of wide scope and importance, among other things being a member of the board of directors of the Merchants' National Bank of Savannah.

ANDREW JACKSON MOYE. A position of leadership in a community is not easily acquired except by hard work, careful management and enduring integrity. When his fellow citizens in Randolph county speak of Mr. Moye as the wealthiest or one of the wealthiest men of the county they also imply in this assertion that he has acquired this position of both affluence and influence by the most honorable means, and that his long life has been one of utmost honor in all its varied relations.

Past eighty years of age, Mr. Moye is one of the oldest residents of Randolph county, and represents a family which gave pioneer service in clearing the woods, and making farms and planting the early crops and founding of civilized institutions in this section of Georgia. Andrew Jackson Moye was born on a plantation about ten miles east of Barnwell Courthouse in South Carolina, December 12, 1832. His father was the Hon. Allen Moye, who was born on the same plantation in 1798. The grandfather was Matthew Moye who was born in North Carolina, whence he removed to South Carolina, purchasing land bordering upon Falttatcher creek, ten miles east of Barnwell Courthouse. The grandfather was a man of much ability and considerable property, and with the aid of his slaves cleared out a farm and made it his home until his death.

Allen Moye, the father, acquired a good education in his native district and was still a very young man when he was called into public affairs. He was elected a representative in the state legislature, a few weeks before he was twenty-one years of age. In 1834 he sold his estate in South Carolina and came into Georgia, settling in Randolph county. On that journey he was accompanied by his wife and six children, and they came through the woods and over the rough roads and trails with teams and wagons, bringing all their household goods and a large supply of agricultural implements, the slaves following along on foot. A tract of land three miles northwest of Cuthbert was the site chosen for his location. At that time the population in this district was very sparse and the Indians were still here and laid claim to the region as their hunting grounds. He was in Georgia in time to participate in the last great Indian war of 1836, when the southwestern Indians were finally defeated and compelled to remove to the West. In 1841, Allen Moye became a candidate for the state senate. During the campaign he attended a rally and barbecue at which he caught cold and his death occurred before the election. Allen Moye married Sarah J. Rice, daughter of Charles Rice, who so far as known was a lifelong resident of South Carolina in the Barnwell district. Mrs. Moye died in 1862 at the age of sixty years. Her ten children were named William, John, George, Andrew J., Mary, Benjamin, Wyatt, Allen, and Sarah.

Andrew Jackson Moye since he was two years of age has spent nearly all his life in Randolph county, and there is probably no other resident whose actions cover so much of the development of this section from its primitive conditions to the present time. As a boy he attended one of the neighborhood schools, that school being taught in a log building on the home farm. Subsequently the old frame courthouse at Cuthbert was removed in order to make room for a new brick structure, and the old building was then put to use as a school house, and as a boy he remembers that building as one of the institutions in Randolph county. Early in his youth he went to Georgetown, and became clerk in a general store. With the earnings of that occupation during two years he was enabled to advance his education, and attended the Brownwood Institute at Lagrange, and remained there as a student until the death of his brother George. Then at the solicitation of his mother he returned home to take charge of the farm. The following year he went to Eufaula, Alabama, where he was engaged in clerking for a time, after which he returned to the farm for a few months, and then moved into Cuthbert, where he was clerk in the store of Mr. Jesse E. Key until the latter's death. Then in 1859 he bought a plantation adjoining the old homestead and devoted all his time and attention to agricultural activities until after the war.

In 1864 Mr. Moye enlisted in Company B, of the Tenth Georgia

Infantry, and was engaged with this regiment in the defense of Atlanta. After the fall of that city he was in the battle at Griswolds Station, and while the army was on the march to Altamaha he was detailed as assistant quartermaster, being sent back to Macon where he remained until the close of the war. He was then paroled, and returned home to the farm, where he continued to live and manage the property until 1875. In that year he moved into Cuthbert and has since had his home in the county seat. His father soon after moving to Randolph county, bought a block of land west of and facing the public square in Cuthbert, and on a portion of this land Mr. A. J. Moye erected a building which he has since used for an office. For many years he has made a business of loaning money, and also employs his time in looking after his various investments, and other affairs.

In November, 1859, he married Laura J. West, who was born in Stewart county, a daughter of William and Laura Elizabeth (Pettit) West. Mr. and Mrs. Moye have five children: Andrew Clinton, Robert Leiden, Andrew Pettit, Loraine Mickle and Claude T. The son, Andrew Clinton, is a planter and has a mill and gin in Randolph county. He married Dixie Harris, and their two children are named Hubert Melton and Clinton. Robert L. is a practicing attorney and former mayor of Cuthbert, and by his marriage to Florence Powell has three children named Annie Laurie, Powell, and Eloise. Andrew P. is a merchant and planter, and married Lilla Tumlin, and their five children are Lewis, Guydon, Marie, Martha and Claude. Loraine M. married Elizabeth Walrath, and their two children are Laura Estelle and Andrew J. The parents of Mr. Moye were Baptists, and his wife is a member of that faith and has reared her children in the creed and practice of this religion.

HON. ALEXANDER A. LAWRENCE. One of the adopted sons of Savannah, Georgia, is Hon. Alexander A. Lawrence, member of the state legislature and an able lawyer of the city. He is qualified by his professional experience and success, his integrity and his qualities of mind and heart for the position to which his political and personal friends have called him.

Mr. Lawrence was born at Marietta, Georgia, on April 5, 1869, and comes of a Southern family, his father, Robert DeTreveille Lawrence having been born at Beaufort, South Carolina, and his mother, whose maiden name was Annie E. Atkinson, in Camden county, Georgia. They reside at the present time at Marietta, where the father has lived since 1842, having gone there as a child with his father in that year. The elder gentleman is a civil engineer by profession and he is a Confederate veteran of the Civil war, in which he served in the signal corps, in the southern army.

Mr. Lawrence, whose name heads this review, received his preliminary education in the common schools of this birthplace, Marietta, and subsequently entered the University of Georgia at Athens, from which institution he was graduated with the class of 1890. He had in the meantime come to the conclusion to adopt the law as his profession and made preparatory study for the profession at Brunswick, being admitted to the bar in 1891. He first hung out his shingle, as common parlance has it, at St. Mary's in Camden county, and remained there two or three years, from the first giving evidence of an unusually good legal mind. In 1894 he moved to Savannah and became established in the practice of law in this city, which has ever since been his home. In 1900 he formed a law partnership with W. W. Osborne, under the firm name of Osborne & Lawrence, and the same has developed into one of the prominent and successful law firms in the city. This concern, in addition to a large general practice, is the legal representative of the Savannah Electric Railway Company, which operates the electric street railway system in Savannah.

Mr. Lawrence is one who gives his support to the men and measures of the Democratic party. In 1904, in manifestation of the general high regard in which he is held, he was elected a member of the Georgia state legislature for the regular term of two years. Recommended by his past record in such capacity, he was again elected to the office in 1908 and once more succeeded himself in 1910. His legislative district embraces Chatham county. He has proved a most useful member of the state assembly, his work therein being to a considerable extent in the nature of opposing needless and harmful legislation, rather than in the introduction of new bills. In the session ending in 1911 he was chairman of the committee on constitutional amendments, and has been a member of both the general judiciary and the special judiciary committees.

Mr. Lawrence was formerly a member of the Savannah Volunteer Guards, and as such enlisted as a private for service in the Spanish-American war, his company being a part of the Second Georgia Regiment. Later he was transferred to the Third Georgia Regiment, in which he was made lieutenant of Company K.

Mr. Lawrence finds pleasure in fraternal association with his fellow men and is prominent in a number of organizations of such character, among which are the Masonic order, the Knights of Pythias, the Eagles, and the Benevolent Protective Order of Elks.

In 1900 Mr. Lawrence married Miss Isabel Ashby Paine, who was born in Charleston, South Carolina, and they have four interesting children, namely: Harriet, Alexander A., Jr., Ann and Virginia.

COL. SIGO MYERS. The name of Myers has figured with gratifying prominence in the life of Savannah for more than half a century as bankers, manufacturers, merchants and citizens of the highest type. The Myers brothers have ever been known as men who did things and their imprint is upon many splendid enterprises. In 1852 the little Bavarian family located within the fair boundaries of the South and in the ensuing years they have proved the possessors of all those characteristics which make the typical German so admirable an acquisition to our nation, and the support of our institutions. Sturdy integrity, indomitable perseverance, high intelligence and much business sagacity have been represented in them, and no more honored subjects could be represented in a work of this character.

Col. Sigo Myers, president of the National Bank of Savannah, succeeded to this position upon the death of his brother, the late Herman Myers, who from its founding until his decease on March 24, 1909, held that position. Herman Myers, who was the elder brother, was born in Bavaria, Germany, in 1847, the son of Sigmund and Fanny Myers, who in 1852, joined the numerous Teutonic company in quest of American independence and opportunity, and with their family crossed the Atlantic and shortly after arriving on our shores, located at Warm Springs, Bath county, Virginia, where their children were reared. There young Herman received his public school education, and, the family being in modest circumstances, he learned, like the usual German lad, a trade, his being that of a tanner. His father died in 1861 and the family removed to Lynchburg. In 1867, Herman Myers came to Savannah, which city remained his home until his death, his active and busy life attaining for him a position of relative distinction in the community with which his interests were allied. After coming here he became engaged in the cigar and tobacco business, and subsequently became a large handler and exporter of wool, under the firm name of H. Myers & Brother. He continued his interest in the cigar business, however, and in association with his brother, Sigo Myers, became an extensive manufacturer of cigars. He acquired the controlling interest in El Modelo Cigar Manufacturing Company, of which he was president and which maintained a large cigar factory at Tampa, Florida. He organized the Cuban American Cigar Manufacturing Company, into which El Modelo Company was merged and which maintained an office and factory at Havana, as well as in Tampa. This became one of the largest cigar manufacturing industries of the country. A few years before his death he disposed of his interests in the cigar manufacturing business and thereafter centered most of his activities in the banking business in Savannah.

He was the principal organizer and from its founding until the time of his decease was the president of the National Bank of Savannah, which began business in 1885. He promoted the erection of the National Bank building, the home of his bank, a splendid office building of handsome design, ten stories in height, standing at the corner of Bull and Broughton streets, the heart of the business section and one of the show places of the city. The capital stock of the bank is $250,000, while its surplus and undivided profits amount to nearly double that sum. It is one of the strongest financial institutions in the South and numbers among its board of directors a list of citizens whose business reputation and financial resources rank among the highest in Savannah. The bank has always been well managed to the extent that it gives the best of satisfaction in profits to its stockholders combined with the best of accommodations to its customers.

Herman Myers was one of the organizers and for years was president of the Savannah Grocery Company, wholesale. He was also the president of the Oglethorpe Savings & Trust Company, an auxiliary of the National Bank, organized to handle its large savings department. He was one of the organizers and promoters of the construction of the Southbound Railway Company, of which he was the vice-president until the time of its disposal to the Seaboard Air Line Railway Company. He was also largely interested in the old Savannah & Tybee Railroad and the Tybee Hotel Company. In addition to his Savannah interests he was a member of the syndicate which purchased the Macon Street Railway & Lighting System, and was president of the reorganized company.

In 1885, Herman Myers was elected a member of the board of aldermen of Savannah. He was continuously a member of the city council for ten years, serving on the finance committee during the entire period. For five years he was a member of the sanitary board. These duties equipped him well for the position of mayor, to which he was called by election of the people in 1895. He served out the term of two years, and then, after an interval of two years, he was again in 1899 elected mayor. He was re-elected in 1901, 1903, and 1905, the last three terms quite without opposition. His administration during those years was marked by the greatest permanent public improvements in the history of Savannah, including street paving, enlargement of the water works plant, street openings, and, the greatest achievement of them all, the building of the present city hall, one of the finest municipal buildings in the South. In Masonry he had taken the Scottish Rite degree. His life was in every way an honor to himself and to his home city, Savannah.

Although he has given "his honors to the world again, his blessed part to heaven," his benignant influence will not soon be lost in the city which was so much the better for his having lived in it.

Col. Sigo Myers, brother of the foregoing, was born in Bavaria in 1850, and was about two years old when his parents came to America. His boyhood history was nearly identical with that of his brother in rearing and education. Like Herman Myers he is entirely a self-made man, rising to his present position of wealth and influence in the financial world from the ranks. The Myers boys lost their father in early childhood, and, without any inheritance or financial assistance of any kind, found it necessary to begin earning their livelihood at an early age.

Sigo Myers came to Savannah in 1868, one year after his brother. For several years he was actively associated with his brother in the cigar manufacturing business and became president of El Modelo and the Cuban American Cigar Manufacturing Company, mentioned in a preceding paragraph. These interests took him away from Savannah for some years, during which he resided in Florida. As a capitalist he took a prominent part in the building up of Jacksonville, in which city, as well as in Tampa, he still holds large and important property interests. Previous to his brother's death he was vice-president of the National Bank of Savannah and upon his brother's death he became president of the institution, and through his wise, skillful and experienced management the bank has continued to flourish as it has from the beginning. He also succeeded his brother as president of the Oglethorpe Savings & Trust Company. In addition to those in Savannah and Jacksonville, he also has important financial interests in Macon and Columbus, Georgia. He is vice-president of the Muscogee Real Estate & Improvement Company of Columbus and is vice-president of the Macon Railway & Light Company. He is a director of the Glen Springs Company, Spartanburg, South Carolina, also a director of the Gainesville & Midland Railway. Mr. Myers has taken a very active part in the founding of the Jewish Educational Alliance, a non-sectarian institution, and to which he donated the building. He stands high in Masonry, being a thirty-second degree Scottish Rite Mason and a Shriner, and is president of the Masonic Temple Association. Under his administration, and the present trustees, ground for the temple was broken.

Colonel Myers has always taken an active interest in the famous military organizations of Savannah; he is one of the board of directors of the Savannah Volunteer Guards; he was a member of the Georgia Hussars for several years. Upon the election of Joe M. Brown as governor in 1909 he was appointed lieutenant colonel upon the governor's staff and served as such until the expiration of Governor Brown's term in June, 1911.

Colonel Myers takes an active interest not only in local affairs, but in matters generally of national and world-wide interest. He is known particularly as an ardent sympathizer with and prominent advocate of world-wide peace. On this subject he made a notable address on July 4, 1911, before the annual convention of the Witham Bankers' Association, at Warm Springs, Georgia, and a month or two later, while sojourning at Carlsbad, in Bavaria, he wrote a public letter on the subject of world-wide peace which received prominent space in the Paris edition of the New York *Herald*. Colonel Myers has an intimate knowledge, not only of national, but also of world politics, and, speaking not only as a citizen, but as a representative of the great banking interests which always are called upon to finance wars, his views on this important subject, and his enthusiastic advocacy of disarmament and of world-wide peace, receive the most respectful attention.

In July, 1911, he married Mrs. Nellie Simmonds, of New York.

EDWARD J. THOMAS of Savannah is one of the representative civil engineers of Georgia, and is county surveyor of Chatham county. He was born in Savannah on March 25, 1840, and is a son of Maj. John A. and Malvina H. (Huguenin) Thomas; the former was born in McIntosh county, Georgia, and the latter in Charleston, South Carolina. Maj. John A. Thomas was a planter by vocation, established in McIntosh county, and his death occurred there in 1858. He was a son of Jonathan and Mary Jane (Baker) Thomas. His wife, Malvina, was a daughter of John and Eliza (Vallard) Huguenin, both of whom were of French Huguenot stock. Mrs. Thomas survived her husband for many years, her death occurring in 1895.

Edward J. Thomas secured a good education in the academic sense, as well as in the line of his profession. He was graduated in the University of Georgia as a member of the class of 1860, receiving the degree of Bachelor of Arts. In early manhood he taught school for two months, but his vocation during practically his entire career has been that of civil engineering. For many years he was the civil engineer for the Savannah Street Railway Company, and for eight years he rendered most efficient services as county engineer for Chatham county.

The loyalty of Mr. Thomas to the cause of the Confederacy was manifested in a most unequivocal way during the war between the states. He served two years in the ranks, but on account of physical disability was appointed quartermaster sergeant in the Fifth Georgia Cavalry, with Wheeler's command in General Johnston's army, and surrendered at Greensboro. Many and thrilling were the experiences of Mr. Thomas during his military service, and at a meeting in February, 1912, of the Confederate Veterans' Association in Savannah, Mr. Thomas related some war-time reminiscences for the delectation of the assembly which were particularly well received. He had been asked to read a paper on the evacuation of Savannah, but upon reflection, he said he had come to the conclusion that as he had no business being in Savannah at the time of its evacuation, it might be more appropriate to change his topic to deal with interesting experiences of camp life, dealing particularly with those of the western cavalry just prior to the surrender of Atlanta. He said that after the big fight at Murfreesboro when his command was returning to Savannah the order was passed that every man without a mount could get a thirty days' furlough. The Confederate troopers owned their own horses, so Mr. Thomas gave his horse, saddle and bridle to his comrade, and thus being without a mount, took advantage of the furlough and spent thirty days at home, which explained how he came to be in Savannah at the time of its evacuation. Among other interesting things, he related how he recruited a horse in the bushwhacking country by the peculiar method of going out in the early morning before daybreak and rifling the nearest stable of its best mount for his use, and told how he saved his neck, likewise retained possession of a stolen horse, by the exercise of a bit of quick wit and strategy. These and many another experience, rich in movement and excitement, told by Mr. Thomas in his peculiarly interesting manner, proved a delightful offering in the program of the evening.

Mr. Thomas is a member of the United Confederate Veterans and of the University Club of Georgia. He is a Democrat in his political faith. He and his wife are members of St. John's Episcopal church. Mr. Thomas is now actively engaged in his profession and is at the head of the plans and specification committee of the drainage commission to devise and construct storm and domestic sewers for the entire city, as outlined in the $600,000 issue of bonds (1912).

On April 2, 1862, Mr. Thomas was married to Miss Alice G. Walthour, daughter of George and Mary (Russell) Walthour of Walthourville, Liberty county, Georgia. Seven children were born to them, namely: Abbott; Walthour; Julia, wife of C. H. Gibbes; Alice, married R. C. Gordon; Edward J., Jr.; Huguenin, and Dr. Marion R. Of these, Walthour died in youth, Mrs. Gibbes died in 1900, and Abbott died in 1912.

THOMAS RALPH MOYE, M. D., has been engaged in the practice of his profession in Abbeville for about fourteen years. He is a native of Georgia, born in Washington county on November 7, 1873, the son of Robert J. and Laura (Graybill) Moye, both natives of Washington county. The father is deceased, but the mother still lives. Robert Moye was a planter and merchant, and was prominent in the public life of his county, representing Washington county in the house of representatives in 1884-85, and in the senate in 1898-99. He was a highly esteemed citizen of his community, and his death was a distinct loss to the communal life.

Thomas R. Moye was educated in Washington and Johnson counties, with regard to fundamentals, and when he was sixteen years of age he entered the University of Georgia, from which institution he was graduated in 1894, after which he completed a course of study in the Physicians and Surgeons College in Atlanta, being graduated therefrom in 1899. Between the two college courses, however, the young man taught school in Butts and Franklin counties, as a means of furthering his progress in an educational way. Immediately following the completion of his studies Dr. Moye located in Abbeville where he has contiuued ever since, and he has been successful in building up a fine practice in this community. He has attained a high degree of prominence in a public way, and has been a member of the city council for a number of terms, and in 1909 was mayor of the city.

On Deecmber 20, 1899, Dr. Moye was united in marriage with Miss Rilla Leedy, daughter of J. D. and Annie E. Leedy, natives of Indiana. Mrs. Moye received her education in the schools of Bourbon, Indiana. Dr. and Mrs. Moye have one daughter—Annie Belle, born December 15, 1900. The family are members of the Methodist Episcopal church, and Dr. Moye is a member of the Knights of Pythias and the Independent Order of Odd Fellows.

Dr. Moye is one of a family of eleven children, of which number seven are now living. R. T. is a farmer in Washington county; Dr. L. G. is conducting a practice at Adrian, Georgia; E. L. is located at Augusta; B. H. is an attorney in Wrightville; Mattie is the wife of W. B. Daniels, a traveling salesman, and Lula is the wife of C. C. Battle, of Sorrento, Florida, Dr. T. R. Moye, making the seventh of the number.

CAPT. WALTER C. HARTRIDGE, solicitor general of the eastern circuit, superior court, and a member of one of the strongest law firms of Savannah—O'Byrne, Hartridge & Wright—is a native of the city in which he lives. He was born in 1870, a son of distinguished parents, Hon. Julian and Mary M. (Charlton) Hartridge.

Julian Hartridge was born in Savannah, Georgia, September 9, 1829, and died in Washington, District of Columbia, January 8, 1879. At the age of nineteen, he graduated with honors in the class of 1848 at Brown University, Providence, Rhode Island, and he studied law in the Harvard Law School, from which he received the degree of LL. B. in 1850. Returning to his home in Savannah, he entered the law office of Judge Robert M. Charlton and began the practice of his profession. Soon there-

Thomas R. Morge M.D.

after he was elected by the legislature to the position of solicitor-general of the eastern judicial circuit, in which office he proved his abilities as a lawyer of the first class. In 1859 he was elected to the general assembly of Georgia, and in 1860 was sent as a delegate to the national Democratic convention. At the breaking out of the war between the North and the South in 1861, he entered the service of the Confederate army, as second lieutenant of the Chatham Artillery of Savannah, and served in that capacity until 1862, when he was elected a member of the Confederate state congress. He served with distinction in this capacity until the close of the war and the consequent breaking up of the Confederacy. Then he returned to Savannah and resumed the practice of law, in partnership with Judge Walter S. Chisholm. In 1874 he was elected a member of the forty-fourth congress from the first district of Georgia. In that year also he presided over, as chairman, the first Democratic convention which gave to Georgia its first governor elected by her own people, following the reconstruction period. This convention made him also the chairman of the state Democratic executive committee. In 1876 he was an elector on the Tilden and Hendricks ticket, and in the same year he was elected to the United States congress. He had served out this term and was preparing to return to his home in Savannah, where it was his ambition to resume the practice of his profession and devote his time exclusively to it, when death overtook him, his demise occurring, as above stated, at Washington, on January 8, 1879.

Among the people of his native city and state Julian Hartridge was universally accorded a place of the highest distinction. He was handsome in person, accomplished in intellect, polished in manner; withal he was kind, gentle, considerate and generous, and he had a keen sense of honor. Endowed by nature with an intellect adapted to the discernment of truth, and embellished by literary attainments of the most liberal description—this, together with an honorable ambition and a persevering industry, rarely equipped him for the practice of law. As an orator his language was unusually chaste and elegant, as well as easy and fluent; his delivery, correct and impressive; his logic, clear and concise; his voice, musical and magnetic. As a legislator he was pre-emiuently conservative and just, and although a Democrat of the strictest sort, he did not hesitate to disregard the demands of mere party exigency whenever there was a conflict between them. His broad views of life and his sterling traits of character made him a man admired by the people among whom he lived—admired and looked up to and loved.

The wife of Julian Hartridge was before her marriage Miss Mary M. Charlton, eldest daughter of Judge Robert M. Charlton.

Walter C. Hartridge was reared in Savannah and received his education in the public schools and in Chatham Academy. He studied law in the office of Charlton & Mackall, was admitted to the bar in 1890 and began the practice of his profession, and he practiced alone for six years. In 1898 he became identified with the firm of O'Connor & O'Byrne, and the name was changed to O'Connor, O'Byrne & Hartridge. This firm style continued until January 1, 1910, when Mr. O'Connor's name was dropped, he having died in November, 1909; Anton P. Wright was then admitted to the company and the name became O'Byrne, Hartridge & Wright, which today represents one of the strongest legal firms in Savannah.

From time to time Captain Hartridge has been honored with important position. He was city recorder (police judge) of Savannah for four years, from 1897 to 1901. In November, 1908, he was elected solicitor general (prosecuting attorney) of the superior court, eastern judicial circuit, for a term of four years, and took charge of this office on

January 1, 1909. Here he has proved his efficiency; his service has received the high approbation of the people.

Before the Spanish-American war, Mr. Hartridge was an active member of the Savannah Volunteer Guards, Company D. This company enlisted for service in that war, in which it became Company B of the Second Georgia Regiment of Volunteers, of which company he was second lieutenant. Subsequent to the war he was made captain of Company D of the guards, which rank he held for about two years, until he tendered his resignation.

Captain Hartridge has been twice married. His first wife, who was Miss Bessie D. Hartridge, was a cousin. She died, leaving him with one son, Julian Hartridge. The present Mrs. Hartridge was before her marriage Miss Catharine McIntire, and is a daughter of James W. and Catharine (Foley) McIntire of Savannah.

CHARLES CLARKE MILLAR. Sometimes by executive order the wheels of a great railroad system are checked for a few moments to signalize the passing of a famous official, such is our appreciation of that which is spectacular and unusual. But when the stipulated time has expired work is resumed and those who did not know the man quickly forget the incident. It is the man whose passing can claim the thoughts of his fellow workmen and arouse their sorrow and regret who receives the truest tribute in this busy day and age, and such a man is invariably one who has worked with and worked for his associates, who has understood and appreciated them, rather than one far distant who by the chance of fortune or fate has attained to a directive capacity.

Of the latter class, the well-beloved leader and loyal co-worker, was the late Charles Clarke Millar, of Savannah, for forty years master car builder for the Central of Georgia Railroad. His long connection with the system as its master car builder was in itself a silent tribute to his ability and character, and there is another silent testimonial to his worth standing beside his grave in the beautiful cemetery at Savannah. It is a monument of chaste but striking design, and bears upon one face the following inscription:

CHARLES C. MILLAR

Died May 5, 1880   Age 64 years.

> Erected by the employes of the Central Railroad Car Department, with which he was connected as master car builder for forty years, in grateful remembrance of his many virtues.

This brief, but beautiful tribute from the grateful hearts of men who were for years intimately associated with Mr. Millar in their daily life, and who knew better than any others what a splendid type of character he possessed, indicates how fondly he was held in the affections of his friends and fellow workers.

Charles Clarke Millar was born at St. Mary's, Camden county, Georgia, March 19, 1816, and died at Savannah, Georgia, on May 5, 1880. He was a son of Jacob and Lydia (Pierce) Millar. Jacob Millar was born in Boston, Massachusetts, September 15, 1777, and settled at St. Mary's, Georgia, in 1809. He removed to Savannah with his family about 1837 and died in that city on August 29, 1854. His wife, Lydia Pierce, was descended from a long line of prominent New England ancestry, one of her forbears being Capt. Michael Pierce, who was distinguished for his service in King Philip's war. Jacob Millar himself was of English ancestry, the members of his family being early settlers in New England and members of the Plymouth colony, and thus of old Puritan stock.

In 1837, the year that he came of age, Charles Clarke Millar came to Savannah, which city continued his home as long as he lived. He entered the railroad service with the Central of Georgia, and in 1840 was appointed master car builder. He remained in that position continuously as long as he lived, covering a period of forty years, with the exception of the time that he was doing railroad duty for the Confedcracy during the war between the states. These duties, however, were mainly in connection with the Confederate government's use of the Central of Georgia, so that his service with that company was practically continuous. He espoused immediately and unequivocally the cause of the Confederacy when the war broke out, and his sympathies remained strongly with the latter.

As previously noted, his services were eagerly accepted and he was detailed on railroad duty, where his practical knowledge and efficiency made his service a particularly valuable one. During the two scourges of yellow fever in 1854 and in 1876, he remained in the city, attending to his business duties and preserving the routine of affairs, and in addition, aiding the sick and suffering in every possible way. He was a member of the Masons and the Odd Fellows, but took the keenest interest in the latter organization, particularly in its field of charity and practical usefulness. No more faithful member of the order ever was known in the vicinity, and he esteemed it a privilege to encounter a call to aid a sick or needy brother or his family.

His kindness to the distressed or suffering was by means limited to his fraternal affiliations, however, but his bounty was ample and free. He was kind and considerate to his men, and they reciprocated. He possessed a taste for good literature and was an insatiable reader. His well-stocked library was one of his most valued possessions and one that he delighted in, and many of his leisure hours were spent there, communing with the best authors. He was ever ready to lend a good book to any of his hundreds of employes, believing that the inspiration of a good book was one of the best resources of man.

In 1845 Mr. Millar married Miss Mary Letitia Yonge, who was born in Liverpool, England, but at the time of her marriage was a resident of Darien, Georgia. Of their children only one daughter survives the parents. She is Mrs. Carrie Millar Everitt, and she has five children: Edward Millar Everitt, Athol Everitt, Thomas B. Everitt, Horace P. Everitt, and Carrie, the wife of Louis Boyle.

Mr. Millar's brother, Horace P. Millar, was born in St. Mary's in 1826, and died in Savannah in 1867. He, like his brother, was a railroad man, but was not so well known in Savannah, having lived there for only two years prior to his death. He, too, left to his wife and children the heritage of a good name and an honorable record, and one could not ask for more.

JOSEPH HILTON. Standing in the front rank among the more prominent and more successful representatives of the lumber interests of Georgia is Joseph Hilton, of Savannah, president of the Hilton-Dodge Lumber Company, which has become a dominant force in the industrial and commercial life of the South. Starting in life for himself without capital, and without the assistance of influential friends, or the advantages that wealth can bring, he has steadily worked his way upward from the ranks, through his own ability and efforts building up this splendid business, which stands as a monument to his years of persistent and systematic application to his work.

Born in England, October 19, 1842, Mr. Hilton, in 1853, came to America with his parents, Thomas and Jane (Lachison) Hilton, who located in Darien, Georgia. At the outbreak of the Civil war he enlisted in the McIntosh Guards, of which he was made captain, and which, as Company B, Twenty-sixth Georgia Infantry, became a part of Stonewall Jackson's corps in the Army of Northern Virginia. Serving during almost the entire period of the conflict in Virginia, he received several promotions, at the time of the surrender, at Appomattox, being adjutant general of Gordon's old division, then under command of Gen. Clement Evans.

After the close of the war, in 1865, Mr. Hilton and his brother, Thomas Hilton, Jr., embarked in the lumber business with their father, in Darien, Georgia, under the firm name of Thomas Hilton & Sons, continuing the sawmill business established by the senior member of the firm before the war. Thomas Hilton, Sr., subsequently retiring from active pursuits, James L. Foster succeeded to his interests, and the firm name was changed to Hilton & Foster. Later this enterprising firm acquired the sawmill business of both Joseph P. Gilson and R. Lachlison & Son, and continued business under the name of the Hilton Timber & Lumber Company, operating four mills. In 1889 the business was again enlarged by being merged with the interests of Norman W. Dodge, which consisted of two mills on Saint Simon's island, the firm name then becoming the Hilton & Dodge Lumber Company, a name which it retained even after, in 1900, Mr. Dodge disposed of his interests, and retired from business.

In 1901 this corporation purchased the mill of the Vale Royal Manufacturing Company, in Savannah, and in 1906 acquired the Mill Haven lumber mill in Screven county, and in addition to those two plants the company also owned and operated a large three-band mill at Belfast; a mill at Darien; one near Brunswick; and another on the Satilla river.

In the autumn of 1911 the Hilton-Dodge Lumber Company, of which Mr. Hilton is president, was reorganized and reincorporated with a capital stock of seven and one-half million dollars. Under the previous organization this company had control of the following named plants: the Hilton-Dodge Lumber Company of Darien; the Mill Haven Lumber Company of Screven county; the Vale Royal Manufacturing Company of Savannah; the Savannah Mercantile Company; and the Southern Export Company of Savannah. The new corporation, with its greatly enhanced capitalization, was organized for the special purpose of bringing all of the business of these subsidiary companies under one head, and to build and operate additional plants, thus enlarging the scope and value of its business. The new charter of the corporation enables it to handle timber lands on a gigantic scale; to acquire and handle agricultural land and town property, and improve the same; to engage in the naval stores industry in all of its branches; to carry on agricultural and live stock business, and other enterprises that are naturally auxiliary to a great lumber industry. In 1913 they added a fleet of barges to their equipment at a cost of half a million dollars.

Mr. Hilton married Miss Ida Naylor, who belongs to a prominent and influential family of Savannah, and they have four children, a son, Thomas Hilton, a member of the Hilton-Dodge Lumber Company, and three daughters, namely: Ida, wife of J. Barton Seymour; Ruth, wife of Edmond B. Walker, and Miss Lucy G. Hilton.

CHARLES E. ADAMS, general manager of the Vidalia Ice & Coal Company, Vidalia, Georgia, is a native of this state. He is a son of

James Phillip Adams and wife, Ella (Thornley) Adams, and was born on his father's farm in Stewart county, one of a family of six children. In the common schools of his native county he received his early education, and at the age of thirteen years he went to Columbus, where he finished his schooling. His first business enterprise was at Charles, where for about twelve years he was engaged in merchandising. He came from there to Vidalia in 1909, and that year he and Mr. J. C. May, the furniture dealer of this place, organized the Vidalia Ice & Coal Company, of which Mr. Adams has since been general manager. Their ice plant has a capacity of ten to twelve tons per day, and the demand for ice product is such that it is the intention of the company to increase the capacity the coming year, Vidalia being a vantage point for this business, since a large quantity of ice is required for the refrigerator cars used in handling the fruit shipments to the north. Contrasting with the hard city water, the supply of their plant is soft and is especially adapted for boiler use and is in demand by the railroads. The company has a six-year water contract with the different railway lines of the city. Another feature of the business is the handling of coal, lime, cement and other building materials.

August 9, 1911, Mr. Adams took to himself a wife, wedding Miss Kate Brown, daughter of Mrs. Alice Brown, a native of North Carolina. Mr. and Mrs. Adams are members of the Baptist church, and, fraternally, Mr. Adams is identified with the Knights of Pythias. Both his father and grandfather served in the Confederate army during the late war, and fought bravely for their loved Southland.

WILLIAM ROBERT GOOGE, M. D., has been established in Abbeville for the past twenty-two years, and is by long odds the leading member of his profession in this locality. He was born in Berrien county, Georgia, on January 8, 1867, and is the son of Dr. Jas. A. and Annie (Smith) Googe. The father was a prominent surgeon and physician in his day, who was graduated from Oglethorpe Medical College in 1853. He served throughout the Civil war as a surgeon, and died in 1882.

As a boy Dr. Googe attended the common schools of his town and county, and graduated from the Johnsonville high school, after which he attended the Atlanta Medical College, graduating therefrom with the class of 1890, followed by a post-graduate course in 1902 at Tulane, New Orleans, Louisiana. He immediately located in Abbeville, which has been the scene of his professional labors throughout the long intervening years, and where he is known as one of the ablest men in his profession today. Dr. George is the official surgeon of the Sea Board Air Line and is county physician of Wilcox county. He is a member of the county board of education, and in that capacity has given efficient and valued service to the city and county. He is a member of the Tri-county Medical Association, which embraces Crisp, Dooly and Wilcox counties, and is prominent and active in the welfare and activities of that society.

On Christmas day, in 1892, was solemnized the marriage of Dr. Googe and Fannie Lott, the daughter of Jesse and Mary Lott, of Broxton, Coffee county. Mr. Lott is a merchant and planter of that place, and one of the prominent men of his community. The family is one of extraordinary prominence in southern Georgia. Mrs. Googe received her education in the schools of Coffee county, and finished at the Andrew Female College. Seven children were born to Dr. and Mrs. Googe, all of whom are living. Annie, aged eighteen, is a student at the state normal at Athens; Crisp, sixteen years old, is a student at home, as are also Jessie, aged fourteen, Pitman, twelve years old and Alton aged nine, while Mary, six years old, and Will, a babe of one year, complete the family.

Dr. and Mrs. Googe are members of the Methodist Episcopal church, and the doctor is a member of the Knights of Pythias, and also a Mason, and he is past master and past high priest.

ARTHUR PERRY JONES. Widely known as manager of the Vidalia Commission Company, which is carrying on a large wholesale and retail business, dealing in grain, provisions, lime, cement, seeds and building material, Arthur Perry Jones is a true type of the energetic and enterprising men who are so materially advancing the mercantile interests of Vidalia, and of Toombs county. A native of South Carolina, his birth occurred at Salkehatchie, Colleton county, May 26, 1878.

His father, Asbury Morgan Jones, was born and reared in Colleton county, South Carolina, and died in Pavo, Georgia, in 1908. He was a veteran of the Civil war, in which he rendered good service. He subsequently carried on a thriving business as a planter and a merchant for many years, in Colleton county, South Carolina, in his operations acquiring considerable property. The maiden name of his wife was Emeline Dassy Mood, of Charleston, South Carolina.

Receiving his early education in the town of his birth, Arthur Perry Jones completed his studies at the Stanley Business College, in Thomasville, Georgia. The ensuing year and a half he was employed as a telegraph operator, first with the F. C. & P. Railroad Company, now a branch of the Seaboard, and later with the Georgia Northern Railway Company, at Moultrie, Georgia. Going then to Tifton, Georgia, Mr. Jones was associated with the Western Union Telegraph Company for four and one-half years. Returning then to Tifton, he was manager of the Postal Company there for two years, after which he conducted a retail grocery in that city for two and one-half years. Disposing then of his store, Mr. Jones was for six months manager of the Postal Company at Thomasville, Georgia, after which he was agent for a year and a half, at Ashburn, for the Gulf Line Railroad Company. Coming from there to Vidalia, Mr. Jones became identified with the Vidalia Commission Company, which was incorporated January 1, 1911, as a stock company, and of which C. L. Herring is now president, and Mr. Jones is the efficient treasurer and general manager. This company was capitalized at $6,000, with the privilege of increasing it to $25,000, when occasion demanded, and is carrying on a rapidly growing business that even now amounts to $35,000 each year. The store occupies a floor space of three thousand, six hundred feet, and is well stocked with all goods handled by commission brokers, including groceries, grain, hay, flour, lard, hams, lime, cement, building materials, roofing, typewriting machines, showcases, and like productions, the business being extensive and lucrative.

On October 16, 1901, Mr. Jones was united in marriage with Allie Mae Harman, who was born, March 25, 1882, in Boston, Georgia, but was brought up and educated in Dixie, Brooks county, where she lived until her marriage. Her father, James Jackson Harman, was born in Ringgold, Georgia, April 17, 1855, and at the age of nine years, during the Civil war, accompanied his parents to Boston, whither they fled as refugees. On October 15, 1878, Mr. Harman married Sophronia Grovenstein, who was born, March 23, 1857, in Effingham county, Georgia, being a granddaughter of William Grovenstein, who was a lineal descendant of that branch of the Salsberger family that settled near Savannah, Georgia, in early colonial days.

Six children have been born of the union of Mr. and Mrs. Jones, namely: Agnes Lucile died at the age of twelve months; Asbury Harman, born in 1904; Emily Mae lived but one short year; Martha Perry, born in 1908; Alfred Joseph, born in 1910; and Margaret Louise, born in 1911. Fraternally Mr. Jones is a member of the Knights of Pythias. Religiously he, his wife, and his son Harman, are members of the Methodist church.

ALEXANDER S. MCQUEEN. Energetic, enterprising and progressive, A. S. McQueen has acquired prominence in business and political circles, being connected with the Citizens Bank of Vidalia, and is now in 1912, running, without opposition, as candidate for justice of the peace in the fifty-first district. A son of the late Philip A. McQueen, he was born, October 4, 1889, in that part of Montgomery county, Georgia, that is now included within the boundaries of Toombs county. He is of pioneer stock, his paternal grandparents, Angus and Harriet (McMillin) McQueen, having migrated from North Carolina to Georgia, settling in this state as planters, the grandfather subsequently serving in the Confederate army during the Civil war.

Philip A. McQueen was for many years one of the leading citizens of Toombs county. He served as county school commissioner for five years, in that position doing much to advance the educational standards. In June, 1908, in company with A. F. Sawyer, R. D. McQueen established The *Toombs County Local*, and on January 1, 1909, Mr. Philip A. McQueen bought Mr. Sawyer's interest in the paper, of which he was subsequently editor and general manager until his death, in July, 1911.

Philip A. McQueen married Minnie R. McLeod, whose father was born in Toombs county, about four miles from Vidalia, where his ancestors settled on coming from North Carolina to Georgia. Her father served as a soldier in the Civil war, being a member of General Wheeler's cavalry. Eight children were born of their union, all of whom are living, the five sons being as follows: H. M., assistant cashier of the First National Bank of Lyons, Georgia; R. D.; A. S., whose name we have placed at the head of this sketch; George D.; and Archibald A.

R. D. McQueen was born on the home farm, in Toombs county, July 8, 1887, and as a boy and youth received excellent educational advantages. Since the death of his father he has had the entire control of the *Toombs County Local*, a weekly publication issued Thursday of each week, and is managing it ably and successfully. He is a young man of considerable prominence in the community, and an active member of the Independent Order of Odd Fellows.

A. S. McQueen is a man of fine scholarly attainments, as a pupil in the Vidalia high school having won the state and first congressional distriet medals for the best essays, while at the Vidalia Collegiate Institute he was graduated with honors, being valedictorian of his class. He has since studied law and is now justice of the peace. He is a member of the Ancient Free and Accepted Masons, being now secretary of the local lodge, and belongs to the Oriental Order of Pilgrim Knights. Religiously he is a member of the Presbyterian church of Vidalia.

GEN. WILLIAM H. BOURNE. One of the important industrial enterprises that contribute materially to the commercial prestige of the city of Savannah is the Bourne Lumber Company, of which the gentleman whose name inaugurates this paragraph is president. He has for many years been one of the aggressive and enterprising business men who have aided in the up-building of the city and is especially well entitled to consideration in this volume. He comes of a prominent southern family, both sides of which produced Revolutionary soldiers and splendid citizens in times of peace and he is himself a veteran of the Civil war. He has for a long number of years been engaged in lumber manufacturing and in various phases of the lumber business.

General Bourne was born in Hanover county, Virginia, November 23, 1844, the son of John H. and Mary A. (McLeod) Bourne. His father was born at Hanover Court House, Hanover county, Virginia, and came with his family to Georgia in the year 1855. After living a short time in Chatham county he located permanently in Effingham county, where he established a sawmill, and engaged in lumber manufacturing and as a planter. He was a successful man of affairs, but died in comparatively early life, passing away in 1870, at the age of fifty-four. He was the son of Claiborne Bourne, who in turn was the son of Reuben Bourne, both of Hanover county, Virginia, the latter a soldier in the Continental line in the Revolutionary war.

The subject's mother, born in Richmond, Virginia, was the daughter of George W. McLeod, who was the son of Daniel McLeod, a native of Edinburgh, Scotland, who came to America from "the land o' cakes" and settled in Alexandria, Virginia. The maternal grandmother of the subject was Eliza M. (Tinsley) McLeod, daughter of Col. Jack Tinsley, of Virginia, who was a soldier in the Revolution. Mrs. John H. Bourne was born in 1822 and died in 1881.

The fact that William H. Bourne was a very young man at the outbreak of the Civil war did not prevent his immediate enlistment and it was his portion to see some of the hardest service of the great conflict. In 1861, quite at the beginning of hostilities, he enlisted at Savannah for service in the Confederate army, becoming a member of Company H, First Volunteer Regiment of Georgia. Company H was the second company of the Oglethorpe Light Infantry, one of Savannah's famous and historic military companies. In this service he was first engaged at Fort Pulaski, going there in October, 1861, and with the rest of his company he was captured there on May 11, 1862, and taken to Governor's island, New York. From there they were transferred to Fort Delaware, where in August, 1862, the company was exchanged. Upon the reorganization of his company in Savannah, Mr. Bourne continued with it and spent the summer of 1863 on Morris island, participating in the battle of Battery Wagner. In November, 1863, they returned to Savannah for winter quarters and in the latter part of April, 1864, they joined Mercer's Brigade in north Georgia. They participated in the battle of Lost Mountain, where General Bourne was wounded, and also in the battles of Kennesaw, Peach Tree Creek, Atlanta, Jonesboro and Lovejoy Station. Mercer's Brigade then went with the army that made the expedition into Tennessee, but on account of other duties, the forces with which Mr. Bourne's company were engaged did not engage in the actual fighting at the battle of Franklin. They went on to Nashville, but were not engaged in the battle of Nashville, having been sent to Murphysboro under General Forest. Subsequently they returned to Georgia, and then into the Carolinas, engaging in the battle of Bentonville, and surrendering with Johnston's army at Greensboro, North Carolina, when in the summer of 1865 the war ended. General Bourne enlisted with Company H, as stated above, as a private and remained with the same throughout the war, having been promoted to third sergeant of the company. General Bourne served as commander of the South Georgia Brigade, Georgia Division, United Confederate Veterans.

Following the general occupation of his father, General Bourne has practically all his life been associated in one way or another with the lumber industry in south Georgia, either as a manufacturer or as a dealer and he has also engaged extensively in the handling of timber lands. He located in Savannah after the war and has ever since resided here, witnessing a phenomenal half century of growth and development and at the same time contributing to it. He is the president of the Bourne Lumber Company, incorporated, whose manufacturing plant is located in Liberty county on the Seaboard Air Line Railway, their general offices being in Savannah, at 301-302 National Bank building. The company are manufacturers and wholesale dealers in long and short leaf yellow pine. It also owns the Bourne Brick Manufacturing Company, the plant of which is in Chatham county.

General Bourne was married in Savannah in the year 1869, to Miss Julia Backley, whose demise occurred in 1906. This admirable lady bore her husband five children, all sons, as follows: Walter L., who is secretary and treasurer of the Bourne Lumber Company; Lescoe J., vice-president of the same; Vernon C., engaged in the wholesale produce business at Brunswick, Georgia; Oran Tinsley, of the firm of O. T. Bourne & Company (lumber manufacturers); and Frank R., who is mill superintendent for O. T. Bourne & Company. The name of Bourne is well and favorably known throughout Chatham county, father and sons having proved themselves men of exceptionally fine citizenship. General Bourne is a member of the session of Westminster Presbyterian church.

CAPT. ROBERT G. TUNNO, captain and adjutant in the Savannah Volunteer Guards, has been connected with that organization since 1891. Enlisting as a private in Company B, of that battalion, he served in that capacity until 1894, since which time his rise in rank has been gradual, but continuous. He is now captain and adjutant of the entire battalion, which consists of four companies,—A, B, C, and D. He has served with entire satisfaction not only to the battalion, but to the state and federal military authorities as well. He has been connected with the naval stores industry almost continuously since leaving school.

Born in Savannah, in 1870, Captain Tunno is a lifelong resident of this city. He is the son of Capt. Matthew R. and Isabel C. (King) Tunno, both of whom are residents of Savannah. The father was born in Charleston, South Carolina, and upon the breaking out of the war between the states he entered the Confederate service as a member of the Charleston Light Dragoons, as a private. He later left this organization and joined the army of the West, becoming post ordnance officer at Columbus, Kentucky, holding this position until the evacuation of Columbus in September, 1861. He then became a staff officer with the rank of captain, on the staff of General Polk. In August, 1863, he was detailed to serve in the ordnance department at Columbus, Mississippi, continuing in that service until August, 1864. He then resigned, and again joined the Charleston Light Dragoons at Hixford, Virginia, remaining in active service with them until the close of the war, at which time he was with his command at Hillsboro, North Carolina. In 1866 Captain Tunno and his brother, Maj. William M. Tunno, who had also served with distinction as an officer in the Confederate army, came to Savannah and engaged in the banking and cotton business. In late years Captain Tunno, the elder, has been retired from active business life. The mother of Capt. Robert G. Tunno is a member of a well-known old Georgia family, and is a native of Savannah. Members of her family gave service to the cause of the Confederacy, among them being William C. King, first lieutenant of Company A of the Savannah

Volunteer Guards Battalion. He was killed at the battle of Sailors Creek, Virginia, in the latter part of the war. Another of her relatives, Colonel Bayard, was at one time the commander of the battalion. The Kings are also related to the Barrington family, which is descended from Col. Josiah Barrington of the English army who came to Georgia with General Oglethorpe at the time of the settlement of the colony.

Captain Tunno was reared in Savannah and received his schooling in private and public schools of the city and in Porter Academy, Charleston. He has led a life of military activity since his early manhood, enlisting on February 9, 1891, as a private in Company B, of the Savannah Guards Battalion (Coast Artillery Corps). February 1, 1900, he was promoted to first lieutenant of his company, acting as such until March 13, 1904, at which time he was elected captain of Company B. He served as such until April 28, 1906, when on account of business, he resigned from the captaincy. He at once re-enlisted in Company B as a private, and was sergeant and first sergeant of Company B from April 30, 1906, to October 5, 1909, when he was elected to his present position,—that of captain and adjutant of the entire battalion of four companies. His record throughout has been one of admirable efficiency, creditable to himself and to a family already distinguished for deeds of valor in a military way.

COL. CORNELIUS ALEX WEDDINGTON. That success is often the result of youthful enthusiasm and the uncompromising honesty that later in life are often battered down in the hard battles men have to fight to even hold a footing in the business world, is shown in the life of Cornelius Alex Weddington of Dublin, Georgia. Dependent on his own efforts for his education, he learned his hard lessons early in life, and entered upon his professional life as a lawyer with a knowledge of the world that does not come to many men until many years of experience have passed. His success as a lawyer, and his recognized ability as a public official have been only a just reward of hard and earnest work.

Colonel Weddington was born in Douglas county, Georgia, on the 11th of November, 1874. He is the son of Charles William Weddington and of Virginia L. Weddington, both of whom were born in Douglas county. His father was born in 1843, and his mother in 1853.

The early education of Colonel Weddington was obtained in the country school of Douglasville, Georgia, and after he had gained as much learning as the school master of the time was able to impart he became in turn a school master and until 1894 taught in the country schools of his native state. By dint of rigorous saving he was enabled to enter the University of Athens, at Athens, Georgia, at this time. He was graduated from this institution in 1898, and for a year read law with Dorsey Brewster and Howell of Atlanta. He was admitted to the bar in 1899.

Shortly after his admission to the bar, on the 5th of January 1900, he came to Dublin, Georgia, and began his practice of the law. His ability was speedily recognized and in 1903 he was elected city attorney, which office he held for a term of two years. In 1911 he was made city clerk, his term to expire in July, 1913. His rapid advance in his profession may be accounted for by the fact that he is possessed naturally of a keen logical mind and a capacity for hard work, but his speedy elevation to office is due to the fact that he has the highest regard for his profession and is one of that group of lawyers who are endeavoring to lift the stigma of corruption and dishonesty from the bar.

On the 18th of December, 1901, Colonel Weddington was married

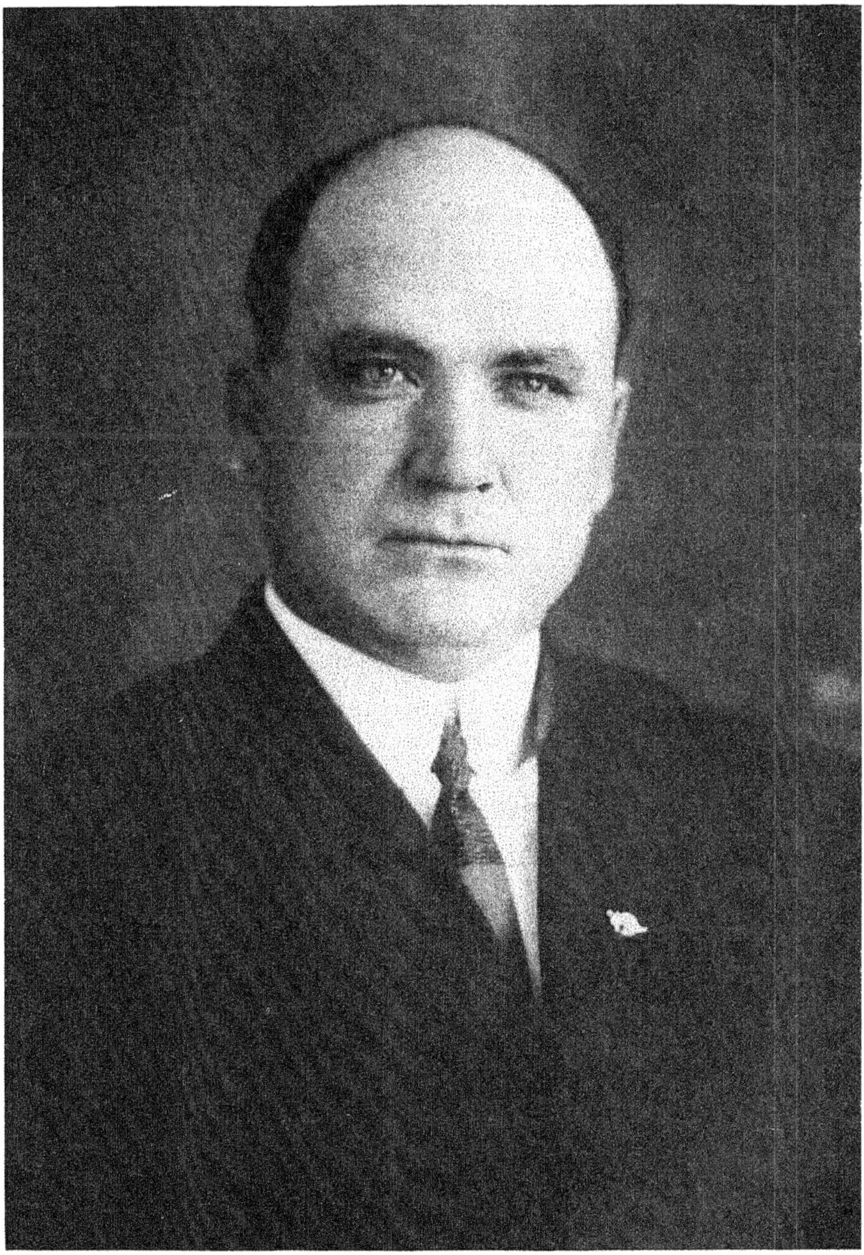

to Georgia Smith. His wife is the daughter of J. D. Smith, a man well known throughout the state for his activity in state affairs. Three' children have been born to them. Virginia was born on the 27th of October, 1902, Gladys on September 15, 1907, and the youngest, a son, C. A. Jr., on the 15th of December, 1900. All of the children were born in Dublin. Mrs. Weddington received her education in the schools of Dublin and finished at the seminary at La Grange, Georgia.

Colonel Weddington is very prominent in the various fraternal organizations of which he is a member. He is a Mason, being a member of Olivet Commandery of Knights Templars, No. 27, and is a Noble of the Mystic Shrine, belonging to Al Sihah Temple of Macon, Georgia. In the Knights of Pythias Colonel Weddington holds the office of Past Chancellor, in the Independent Order of Odd Fellows he is a Past Grand and also Past Exalted Ruler of Dublin lodge 1163 of the Benevolent and Protective Order of Elks. These various offices are the strongest evidence of Colonel Weddington's fine qualities as a man among men.

NICHOLAS PETER CORISH, a native born resident of Savannah and clerk of the city council since 1907, is the son of Richard and Ellen (Stafford) Corish, both natives of County Wexford, Ireland, born there in the year 1829, who came to the United States in their early years.

With the breaking out of the war between the states, Richard Corish promptly enlisted at Savannah in the Irish Jasper Greens, and for the first few months of the war was stationed at Fort Pulaski, near Savannah. The Irish Jasper Greens were a part of the First Volunteer Regiment of Georgia and were a notable company of brave and efficient soldiers. Later in the course of the war Mr. Corish was captured and confined as a prisoner of war at Fort Leavenworth, Kansas, where he underwent severe hardships and almost suffered starvation, his sole food for a long time consisting of nothing more than raw Irish potatoes. As a result of the intense suffering caused by the unhealthful conditions of the prison and the continued starvation rations, Mr. Corish was stricken with paralysis within a few years after the close of the war. Following the return of peace he had been successfully engaged in the tailoring business in Savannah, but his illness caused the discontinuance of the family income, and for a time the condition of the family was most serious. Mr. Corish died January 3, 1903, after a long and lingering illness, during which time his patient and courageous wife succeeded in rearing their children to years of usefulness and maintained the home comfortably and happily. She died January 24, 1910, after a long and useful life.

The son, Nicholas Peter, who was born in the year 1869, was educated in the primary schools of Savannah. His first position as a wage earner was as a messenger for the Western Union Telegraph Company in Savannah, and after a few years, when he had gained in knowledge and wisdom, he became identified with the real estate business and was thus occupied for a number of years. In January, 1907, Mr. Corish was elected to the office of clerk of the city council, coming into the office with the administration of George W. Tiedeman, mayor. He was re-elected in January, 1909, and again succeeded himself in the office in January, 1911. Mr. Corish carried on the duties of his office with conspicuous efficiency and his management of this important department of the municipal government has met with the endorsement of all classes, as was loudly attested by his third consecutive election to the office.

Mr. Corish enlisted as a private in his father's old company, the Irish Jasper Greens, and after serving for some time as a private was promoted from the ranks to the position of quarter-master-sergeant of the First Regiment of Infantry, National Guard of Georgia, under Colonel Mercer. He is a member of the Catholic church and is affiliated with the local lodge of the Knights of Columbus, of which he was financial secretary for a number of years. In the fall of 1911 Mr. Corish was elected president of the South Atlantic League of base ball clubs, composed of six teams, including Savannah.

Mr. Corish married Miss Mary Ellen Reynolds, daughter of Judge Samuel Reynolds on January 21, 1896, who was born and reared in Savannah, and they are the parents of six children: Eleanor Lucile; Mary Josepha; Julian Francis; Nicholas Peter, Jr.; Gertrude Reynolds and John Herbert, Julian Francis and Nicholas Peter, Jr., are twins.

ROBERT H. KNOX. Among the many progressive men who are making the city of Savannah, Georgia, a modern and up-to-date business center Robert H. Knox holds a prominent place. He belongs to that latest type of business men which believes a man should interest himself in affairs other than those pertaining to his own business in order to broaden his outlook and fit him for whatever responsibilities it may fall to his lot to shoulder. Therefore Mr. Knox has always taken a keen interest in politics, and before coming to Savannah was mayor of Darien, Georgia. His ability as a business man is unquestioned for he has attained his present high position by slow degrees, achieving success not through the fortunes of environment and good luck but by hard and conscientious work.

He is a prominent figure in the social world; is a member of the Oglethorpe Club of Savannah, the Savannah Yacht Club, and St. Andrews Society.

For a number of years Mr. Knox was prominently connected with the military organizations of the state. He was captain of the McIntosh Light Dragoons, which afterward became Troop "G," one of the companies of the First Regiment of Cavalry. Resigning this captaincy he became a member of the staff of Gov. W. Y. Atkinson, and was also on the staff of Gov. A. D. Candler. He is now on the retired list, holding the rank of lieutenant-colonel.

Fraternally Mr. Knox confines his interests to that oldest of orders, the Ancient, Free and Accepted Masons, being an affiliated past master of Solomon's Lodge, No. 1, the oldest Masonic lodge in the state.

Robert H. Knox was born in Savannah in 1862 while his mother was living temporarily in this city. His parents were Walter and Ellen (Hilton) Knox. His father was born in Charles county, Maryland, where his family had lived for several generations. His mother was born in England and came with her parents to Georgia in 1852. In 1817 his father came to Georgia and located in Wilkes county. Subsequent to this move the family lived for a time in Houston and Talbot counties in Georgia.

Robert H. Knox lived in the central part of Georgia until he was fourteen years of age when his parents moved to the southern part of the state and settled in Darien, McIntosh county.

On April 21, 1892, he married Miss Eloise M. Bennett, who was born in Walterboro, South Carolina. They have five children, namely: Eloise Bennett, Valencia Fraysse, Ellen Hilton, Robert Hilton and Janet Elizabeth.

Mr. Knox became connected with the lumber business of Hilton and Foster at the age of fifteen, and since that time has been associated more or less prominently with the lumber industries of the state. The

Geo. B. Davis

Hilton sawmill business was originally started at Darien before the war, having been founded by Mr. Knox's grandfather, Thomas Hilton, who took into partnership his two sons, Thomas and Joseph Hilton, under the firm name of Thomas Hilton & Sons.

After the war when Thomas Hilton, Sr., retired from the business James L. Foster entered the firm which then became known as Hilton & Foster. Subsequently the business of this firm and that of Hilton, Foster & Gilson, and also that of R. Lachlison & Son, were merged into the Hilton Timber and Lumber Company. The new company then owned and operated four lumber mills.

In 1889 the lumber business of Norman W. Dodge, who owned two mills on St. Simon's island, was consolidated with the Hilton interests, and the corporation then became known as Hilton & Dodge Lumber Company. At the same time a mill owned by Hilton & Foster on the Satilla river was taken in. Later the Altamaha mills near Brunswick were bought.

In 1901 the Hilton & Dodge Lumber Company purchased the mill of the Vale Royal Manufacturing Company in Savannah, and in 1906 came into control of the Mill Haven Company. In addition to these two mills the company at that time owned and operated four other plants, namely: a large band mill at Belfast, Georgia; a mill at Darien; one near Brunswick, and another on the Satilla river. The general headquarters of the company have been in Savannah since 1905, at which time Mr. Knox moved to Savannah.

In the fall of 1911 all of the interests of the company were consolidated with the Paschall and Gresham interests under the name of The Hilton-Dodge Lumber Company with a capital stock of $7,500,000. A large amount of capital was added for the purpose of enlarging the business and for carrying on more extensively such subsidiary enterprises as the handling of timber lands, agricultural lands, general merchandise, machinery and live stock.

The Hilton-Dodge Lumber Company, of which Robert H. Knox became president, is one of the largest lumber concerns in the South. It has seven large sawmills in Georgia and South Carolina and branch offices in New York City, Boston, Philadelphia, Portland, Maine, and Richmond, Virginia. It has agencies in Atlanta and New Haven, Connecticut. Also in Liverpool, Hamburg, Rotterdam, Antwerp, and Spain, covering eastern Europe, to which it does a large export business. It is now engaged in building a transportation line consisting of a powerful sea-going towboat and eight sea-going barges of large capacity. The tug is one of the largest on the Atlantic coast.

In addition to his connection with the Hilton-Dodge Lumber Company, Mr. Knox is president of the Savannah Timber Company, and is one of the directors of the Savannah Bank and Trust Company. He is also president of the Pulaski Realty Company, owning the Pulaski House property, and is largely interested in other real esate in Savannah.

GEORGE B. DAVIS. Let the man who is discouraged or feels that things are going hard with him and that luck is against him listen to the story of courage and steadfast determination as revealed in the life of George B. Davis, at present one of the ablest attorneys in Dublin, Georgia, and county solicitor. The same determination to succeed which showed itself in so marked a degree in his efforts to obtain an education, has been one of the characteristic elements in his success in the legal profession. Gifted with the power of clear and logical reasoning, and spendthrift as to the time and energy which he expends in working up a case to his satisfaction, his success has not been a surprise to those who know him best. He has been in practice in Dublin for only eight years and this is scarcely long enough to judge a man, but according to all who know him and particularly according to his brother lawyers, he is a man from whom great things are to be expected, not only in his own profession but in the political field.

George B. Davis was born in Montgomery county, Georgia, on the 19th day of March, 1881, his parents being Isham J. and Delilah Davis. His father was born in 1841 in Montgomery county and his mother was a native of Laurens county, Georgia. His father was a veteran of the Civil war, having served in Company F of the Forty-eighth Georgia Regiment throughout the whole of the war. He was not a wealthy man and was unable to give his son much of an education, partly on account of his poverty and party because of the scarcity of good schools in this section during the years when the lad was growing up. However, George Davis had made up his mind that he would become a lawyer, and when his mind has once been made up to a thing nothing less than a stick of dynamite would turn him from his purpose. Undaunted, therefore, by the discouragement he met from his family, he determined to consult a man whom he considered an authority, and coming to Savannah, Georgia, unfolded his plan to Donald Clark, only to be laughed at for his pains. Mr. Clark told him he could do nothing without an education and that the best thing for him to do was to go back to the woods and spend the rest of his life cutting trees and boxing them for turpentine. Indignant at the way his confidence had been received he turned away, saying nothing but making up his mind then and there that he would succeed in spite of everything. He therefore stopped on his way home and purchased a Blackstone and returned to the farm, apparently carrying out Mr. Clark's advice, for he set to work cutting trees the next day. At night after his work was done, however, he spent many a weary hour poring over his law books and by 1903, when he was twenty-two years of age, he had saved up enough money to enter Mercer University, at Macon, Georgia. That he had prepared himself very thoroughly and that he was a really brilliant student, is shown by the fact that he was graduated from this institution in a year. He was admitted to the bar on the 9th of June, 1904, and commenced practice on the 1st of September, 1904, locating at Dublin, Georgia, where he opened an office. His sole capital for this venture was a dollar and a half in cash and one shirt and two collars. He did not starve before he had his first client but he was not far from it. After the struggle of the first few months his ability began to be commented upon and he was presently on the high road to success, he being employed in and conducting some of the most important cases, criminal and civil, in that section of the state. He practiced until 1910, when he determined to enter the political field, and as a candidate for county solicitor conducted a personal campaign such as had not been seen in years, so energetic and earnest was the young politician. He won the coveted honor and is serving at present, his term expiring in 1914.

Mr. Davis is keenly interested in fraternal orders, believing that they are enabled to accomplish a great deal of good. He is a member of the Masonic order, belonging to the blue lodge and to the Eastern Star. He is also a member of the Knights of Pythias and of the Woodmen of the World. He is also a member of the Baptist church. When we consider that Mr. Davis is of Welsh and Scotch-Irish descent, we can easier understand some of the strong points of his character, for the Scotch-Irish who settled in the "up-country" of the South Atlantic states, were the very bone and sinew of the country. Much of his personal popularity is due to his open-hearted generosity, for every one is "kin" to him and he clings to the old southern ideals of hospitality. He is of the same family as the Calhouns and the Wests, who came to this country with Oglethorpe and located in the Carolinas in the early days. They have played an important part in the history of the section from colonial days down to the present.

In 1905, on the 29th of November, Mr. Davis was married to Anna Lizzie Bynum, a daughter of John L. Bynum, a prominent citizen of Columbia county, Georgia, well known there in business, as well as in other lines of endeavor. Mrs. Davis is a graduate of La Grange Female College at La Grange, Georgia. One daughter and one son have been born to Mr. and Mrs. Davis, Elizabeth and George Bynum by name, and their births occurred in Dublin in 1906 and 1912, respectively.

G. L. JOHNSON, general manager of the A. O. Johnson & Company, general mercantile establishment, Vidalia, Georgia, ranks with the representative citizens of the town.

Mr. Johnson is a native of Georgia. He was born on a farm in Manuel county, September 18, 1876, son of Emanual and Hattie (Oglesby) Johnson, and one of a family of nine children, all living except one. His father still maintains his home at the old farm in Emanuel county. Here G. L. Johnson passed the first twenty years of his life. When he left home to make his own way in the world, he found employment at Millian, Georgia, in the general merchandise store of T. Z. Daniels, where he filled a clerkship for eighteen months. The next eighteen months he was employed in the same capacity by V. L. Bourke, of that place, and then, having clerked for three years, he decided to engage in business on his own account, which he did at Butts, Georgia, and he was in business there five years. His next move was to Vidalia. Here he took charge of the A. O. Johnson & Company general merchandise store, which was organized in 1907, and which has since conducted a prosperous business.

Mr. Johnson has been twice married. By his first wife, who was Miss Roxie Gay, and whom he married March 8, 1900, he has one child, George Walton. This wife having died, he married Miss Marie Hall, a daughter of L. Hall, a native of this state. The only child by this wife died in infancy.

Both Mr. and Mrs. Johnson are members of the Baptist church. He has lodge membership in both the I. O. O. F. and the K. of P.

FOY O. POWELL, who is associated with John L. Sneed in the real estate and insurance business at Vidalia, Georgia, is one of the prominent and popular young men in both the social and business circles of the town, where he has resided since December 1, 1909.

Mr. Powell is a native of Alabama. He was born at Eufaula, January 4, 1883, son of F. R. and Carrie May (Dudley) Powell, the former a native of North Carolina and the latter of South Carolina. At Eufaula, Alabama, and at Clayton, Alabama, he received his education, being a graduate of the Clayton schools, with the class of 1903. Following his graduation he was for four years in the employ of his uncle, a furniture dealer at Eufaula. The next three years he was in the fire insurance business, for himself, and then he came from Eufaula to Vidalia and associated himself with Mr. Sneed, his present partner, with whom he is successfully engaged in the real estate, loan and insurance business.

Mr. Powell is a Knight of Pythias and a Methodist, and, like his partner, he is as yet unmarried.

JOHN L. SNEED. Vidalia, Georgia, includes among its enterprising, progressive element, a real estate and insurance firm whose members, John L. Sneed and Foy O. Powell, rank high as leading, up-to-date young men, prominent and active in business affairs and popular in the social circles of the town.

While Mr. Powell, as already stated in a personal mention of him on another page of this work, is a native of Georgia, Mr. Sneed hails from Virginia. It was at Charlottesville, Virginia, in 1879, that John L. Sneed was born, one of a family of ten children, all still living, of J. L. and Josephine A. (Moore) Sneed, both natives of the "Old Dominion." He received his education in the Virginia Military Institute and at the George Washington University, Washington, D. C., of which latter institution he is a graduate with the class of 1898, and he is a member of the Kappa Alpha fraternity. After his graduation he was employed in the engineering department of the Chesapeake & Ohio Railroad, and by the government as sanitary engineer, later, also, as engineer on the Norfolk-Southern, the Carolina, Clinchfield & Ohio, and the Georgia & Florida railroads. Deciding to settle down and establish himself in business, he took up his residence at Vidalia in the early part of 1910, and has since been identified with the interests of this place. With Mr. Powell he engaged in a general real estate, loan, and fire insurance business, placing loans for eastern capitalists and dealing in real estate both here and elsewhere, at this writing handling Florida lands. Also he is interested in the Vidalia Furniture Company, of which J. C. May is manager.

As showing his popularity, the second year of his residence in Vidalia, Mr. Sneed was elected to represent the First ward in the city council for a term of two years. Also he is a director in the Bonded Cotton Warehouse.

In Masonry Mr. Sneed has advanced to the higher degrees, including those of the Mystic Shrine, and his religious faith is that of the Episcopal church. He is unmarried.

ROBERT YOUNG BECKHAM, business manager of the Courier-Herald Publishing Co., has been identified with the printing business all his life. He began at the bottom of the ladder and has made steady progress in practical printing, until he is now filling a position of some importance in the business in this city. The *Laurens County Herald* was the recognized official organ of legal business for Laurens county and was so appointed on April 1, 1910, which, according to law, was the earliest possible date the company might assume that position after its organization.

Mr. Beckham was born July 30, 1880, in Zebulon, Pike county, Georgia, and is the son of R. Y. Beckham, Sr., and Laura Jordan. The father was a native son of Pike county and the mother was reared in Monroe county. The senior Beckham was clerk of the superior court of Pike county for twelve years, although his regular vocation is that of a farmer. The son, Robert Y. Jr., was reared on the home farm and educated in the Pike county common schools, after which he pursued a course of study at Jeff Davis Institute at Zebulon. In that place he entered a print shop and gave himself over to the careful study of the business, from the minor details up to the highest post in a newspaper office. He learned the multifarious intricacies of job printing as well as the successful conduct of a newspaper, and his thorough training made it possible for him to assume the complete charge of the establishment with which he is now connected. After learning the trade in Zebulon Mr. Beckham went to Atlanta where he was employed by the

R. Y. Beckham

Mutual Printing Company; he then came to Dublin and for two years was with the Mason & Patillo Company and together with them organized the Dublin Printing Company, which at that time published the Dublin *Times*, a semi-weekly paper, which was sold to A. P. Hilton in October, 1907. Mr. Beckham was thereafter associated for one year with the *Courier-Dispatch* as advertising manager, after which he purchased the Cordele *Dispatch*. He conducted that paper for a period of eight months, then disposed of it to E. T. Pound, his partner in the business, and went to Sandersville, where he purchased the Sandersville *Herald*. After a brief period of three or four months, he then purchased the Tennille *Tribune*, which he combined with the *Herald*. Later the *Herald-Tribune* and the Sandersville *Progress* were combined, and in that combination Mr. Beckham still retains an interest. It was on July 6, 1910, that Mr. Beckham became connected with the Dublin Printing Company. The *Laurens County Herald* was one of the popular and progressive papers of the county with a bona fide circulation of about 2,500 copies. They did an extensive job printing business, having a plant fully equipped with all that goes to make up a modern and complete job-printing establishment, and which enabled them to make a strong bid for the business of the district in their particular line.

About March 15, 1913, the Dublin Printing Company and the *Courier-Dispatch* consolidated their interests under the corporation name of the *Courier-Herald*, for the purpose of issuing a daily newspaper, known as the *Courier-Herald*, this being the only newspaper published in Laurens county. Mr. Beckham is now business manager of the Courier-Herald Publishing Company, which, besides publishing a daily and weekly newspaper, also operates one of the largest printing plants in this entire section of the state, the company being capitalized at $30,000.

Mr. Beckham was married on January 2, 1909, to Miss D'Nena Bridger, the daughter of Dr. Bridger, a well-known practicing physician of Perry, Houston county, Georgia. Two children have been born to Mr. and Mrs. Beckham: Robert Young, Jr., born September 17, 1909, and Willa Dixie, born May 27, 1911.

The family are members of the Methodist Episcopal church and Mr. Beckham is a member of the board of stewards of that church.

JAMES RUSK GRANT. An eminently useful and highly esteemed citizen of Hazlehurst, Jeff Davis county, James Rusk Grant is an able representative of the legal fraternity, as a lawyer meeting with pronounced success. A native of Georgia, he was born, March 30, 1876, in Clarkesville, Habersham county, a son of W. D. and Samantha J. (Holland) Grant, natives of South Carolina, and now residents of Clarkesville, Georgia. His father served throughout the Civil war as a private in the Twenty-fourth Georgia regiment, taking part in many engagements.

Receiving his preliminary education in Clarkesville, James Rusk Grant subsequently continued his studies one term at Clemson College, South Carolina. Beginning then to read law in his native town with Hon. J. C. Edwards, he applied himself diligently to his studies, making such progress that in March, 1898, he was admitted to the bar by Judge J. J. Kimsey, passing a good examination. After practicing his profession a short time in Clarkesville, Mr. Grant opened a law office at Clayton, Georgia, where he remained ten years, building up an excellent practice. In January, 1909, Mr. Grant located at Hazlehurst, and is here meeting with equally as good fortune, his legal skill and ability being recognized, and that it is appreciated is shown by his large and lucrative clientele. He has a large general practice, and has served as solicitor in both the county court and the city court. During the Spanish-American war, Mr. Grant served as a soldier in Company G, Second Georgia Volunteer Infantry. Active and public-spirited, he takes great interest in the affairs of town, county and state, and is ever willing to support all enterprises and projects for the benefit of the public.

Mr. Grant married, February 10, 1901, Mary T. Reynolds, a daughter of John A. Reynolds, editor of the Clayton *Tribune*. Her mother, whose maiden name was Jane Jackson, is a daughter of Rev. Jasper C. Jackson, a noted mountain missionary Baptist preacher, who served in the Confederate army during the Civil war. Four children have blessed the union of Mr. and Mrs. Grant, namely: Ellen, Willie J., Jesse, and James Rusk, Jr., a bright little fellow, born in 1910.

PETER S. HAGAN. Noteworthy among the valued and esteemed residents of Lyons is Peter S. Hagan, a man of intelligence and ability, now serving as clerk of the superior court. A native of Bulloch county, Georgia, he was born near Statesboro, July 6, 1863.

His father, M. F. Hagan married Elizabeth Sheffield, a daughter of Simeon and Keziah (Cone) Sheffield, who came from North Carolina to Georgia, locating in Bulloch county. Ten children were born of their union, as follows: W. L., engaged in agricultural pursuits in Bulloch county; J. F., a planter; J. S., a planter; Mary, who died, aged about sixty years, was the wife of the late T. J. Knight, of Bulloch county; Laura, died, aged about eighteen years; Margaret, who married first W. B. Williams, and after his death became the wife of H. F. Simmons, a dentist, in Brooklet, Bulloch county; Ella, wife of J. C. Ludlam, of Bulloch county; Lucia V., wife of A. J. Proctor, a planter in Stilson, Bulloch county; Effie, wife of M. R. Smith, also a planter in Bulloch county; and Peter S.

Living on the home farm until attaining his majority, Peter S. Hagan obtained his education in the public schools, in the meantime acquiring a practical knowledge of agriculture. On leaving home, he followed his trade of a carpenter for five years, being employed in Bulloch and Tattnall counties. Locating then in Montgomery, now Toombs county, he was for five years bookkeeper for Holmes & Ludlam, turpentine producers, and during the ensuing twelve years was engaged in mercantile pursuits at Vidalia, Georgia. Mr. Hagan was afterwards salesman for three years in the mercantile establishment of T. G. Poe. In August, 1910, he was elected to his present position as clerk of the superior court, an office which he filled so satisfactorily that he was urged to become a candidate for a second term.

Mr. Hagan married, in 1893, Mary P. Holmes, a daughter of B. P. and Laura (Ludlam) Holmes, natives of Horry county, South Carolina. Mrs. Hagan died in September, 1904, leaving four children, namely: Lottie, born in 1896; Annie Laura, born in 1898; Lila, born in 1900; and Lucille, born in 1904. Fraternally Mr. Hagan is a member of Vidalia Lodge, No. 330, Ancient Free and Accepted Masons, of Vidalia, which he joined in 1893, and of which he was for five years the secretary; and of the Independent Order of Odd Fellows. He attends the Baptist church, and is a liberal contributor towards its support.

COL. THOMAS J. PARRISH. An able and influential member of the bar, Col. Thomas J. Parrish has won prestige as a lawyer, his broad and comprehensive knowledge of law and of precedents bringing him well merited success. A native son of Georgia, he was born on a farm in Emanuel county, near Summit, and was there a resident until twenty-two years old.

Receiving his elementary education in the public schools of Emanuel county, Thomas J. Parrish continued his studies at the Agricultural College of the University of Georgia, in Dahlonega. He afterwards taught school two years, during which time he read law. Going then to Swainsboro, Emanuel county, he entered the office of F. H. Saffold, with whom he studied law until admitted to the bar, under state examination, in March, 1899. Mr. Parrish at once began the practice of his profession in Swainsboro, remaining there until 1905. In that year, at the organization of Toombs county, Mr. Parrish located at Lyons, the county seat, and has here built up an extensive and highly remunerative practice, being one of the leading lawyers of the city, and attorney for the Seaboard Air Line Railroad Company. He is active and prominent in public matters, and for two years served as mayor of Lyons, giving to the city a clean administration. Fraternally he is a member of Toombs Lodge, No. 195, Knights of Pythias, and a past councillor. He is an official member of the Methodist church, which he is serving as steward.

Mr. Parrish married Miss Berta Barnes, of Dawson, Georgia. She passed to the higher life, in December, 1907, leaving one child, Thomas J. Parrish, Jr.

Mr. Parrish's father, James M. Parrish, was born in Bulloch county, Georgia, while his wife, whose maiden name was Sarah Dixon, was born in Warren county, Georgia, where during the Civil war her father enlisted for service in the Confederate army.

MORGAN H. CLEVELAND. A public-spirited and esteemed resident of Hazlehurst, Morgan H. Cleveland has for many years been actively associated with the development of the industrial and agricultural interests of Jeff Davis county, and he rendered excellent service as city clerk at Hazlehurst for five months filling an unexpired term. A son of James Monroe Cleveland, he was born, May 22, 1856, on a farm in Stewart county, Georgia, near Lumpkin, coming from patriotic ancestry, his paternal grandfather, Benjamin Cleveland, having served in the Revolutionary war under Gen. Moses Cleveland, being major of his company.

James Monroe Cleveland was born in Franklin county, Georgia, where he grew to manhood. In his earlier life he participated in several engagements with the Indians, and in 1838 assisted in removing them from Georgia to a place beyond the Mississippi known as Indian Territory. He subsequently served in the Civil war, being commissioned as sergeant in a Georgia regiment of troops. He married Catherine Wright, a native of South Carolina, and they became the parents of several stalwart sons, as follows: Benjamin, Cromwell, Thomas, William, John, Ulisas, Joseph, Frank and the subject. Besides there were two daughters, Sultina and Eldora.

Brought up on the home farm, Morgan H. Cleveland was an ambitious student in his boyhood days, and after leaving the common schools of his native district he attended the State Normal school, in Athens, Georgia. Entering then upon a professional career, he taught school for eight years, being employed not only in Stewart county, but in Brown and Pulaski counties, as an educator being successful and popular. He has since been an active factor in advancing the agricultural prosperity of Jeff Davis county, owning and supervising an estate, which in its appointments and improvements compares favorably with any in the neighborhood.

Fraternally Mr. Cleveland is a member of the Ancient Free and Accepted Order of Masons; and religiously he and the family belong to the Missionary Baptist church. In 1899, Mr. Cleveland married Mrs. Rahabtuten, of Emanuel county.

JOHN GOLDWIRE MCCALL, LL. D. A man of broad culture and high mental attainments, John Goldwire McCall, LL. D., of Quitman, is a fine representative of the legal fraternity of Brooks county, and a credit to the profession which he has followed so many years, and with such distinguished success. A son of Francis S. McCall, he was born, January 18, 1836, in Screven county, Georgia. He is of Scotch ancestry, his great grandfather on the paternal side having emigrated from Scotland to America in early colonial days, settling, it is probable in the South, though very little is known of his subsequent history.

Rev. William McCall, father of Francis S. McCall, was a preacher in the Missionary Baptist church, and was also a planter of note, carrying on his agricultural labor with the help of slaves. He lived to a ripe old age, spending the later days of his long and useful life in Screven county. His wife, whose maiden name was Mary Pierce, survived him a few years. They reared eight children, as follows: George, Moses, Charles, Joshua, John, James, Francis S., and Laura.

A few years after his marriage, Francis S. McCall removed from Screven county, the place of his birth, to Telfair county, where he took up land, and was for a few years engaged in agricultural labors. Selling his plantation in 1845, he removed to Lowndes county, and there purchased a tract of land that is now included within the boundaries of Brooks county, it being situated nine miles south of the present site of Quitman. The family journeyed from one county to the other by private conveyances, the household goods having been transported in carts drawn by oxen or horses. At that time all of southern Georgia was but sparsely populated, while deer, bear, wild turkeys, and other game was plentiful, furnishing the new-comers with an ample supply of food. Clearing a space, he erected a house from timber which was first hewed ten inches square, and then split with a whip saw, that was operated by two of his slaves, one standing on top of the timber and the other below. Railroads, and telegraph and telephone lines were then unknown, and Tallahassee, seventy-five miles away, and Saint Marks, eighty-five miles distant, were the nearest markets and depots for supplies. The cotton and other surplus productions of the land had to be taken by team to one of these points, the teamster on his return trip bringing back a load of household supplies. All the sugar used was made at home, and in the smithy which stood upon the plantation a slave made all the plows, wagons and agricultural implements needed for use in carrying on the place, in the meantime tanning all the leather used for harnesses and shoes. The shoes, however, for the entire family, and for the slaves as well, were made by the typical cobbler of those early days. an Irishman who made the rounds of the new settlement each year. On the farm which he cleared and improved. Francis. S. McCall spent the remainder of his life, passing away in 1876, at the age of sixty-six years.

Francis S. McCall married Ann Dobson. She was born in Beaufort, South Carolina, where her father, an extensive and wealthy planter, was a lifelong resident. She died in 1901, aged eighty-five years. Thirteen children were born into their household, as follows: John Goldwire, James H., Rebecca, Jane, Wilson C., Mary, Elvira, Clementine, Joshua R., Richard M., Thomas B., Harry J., and Adda.

John Goldwire McCall received good educational advantages, in 18—, being graduated from the Union University, in Murfreesboro, Tennessee. A few months later he was made professor of Greek and Hebrew

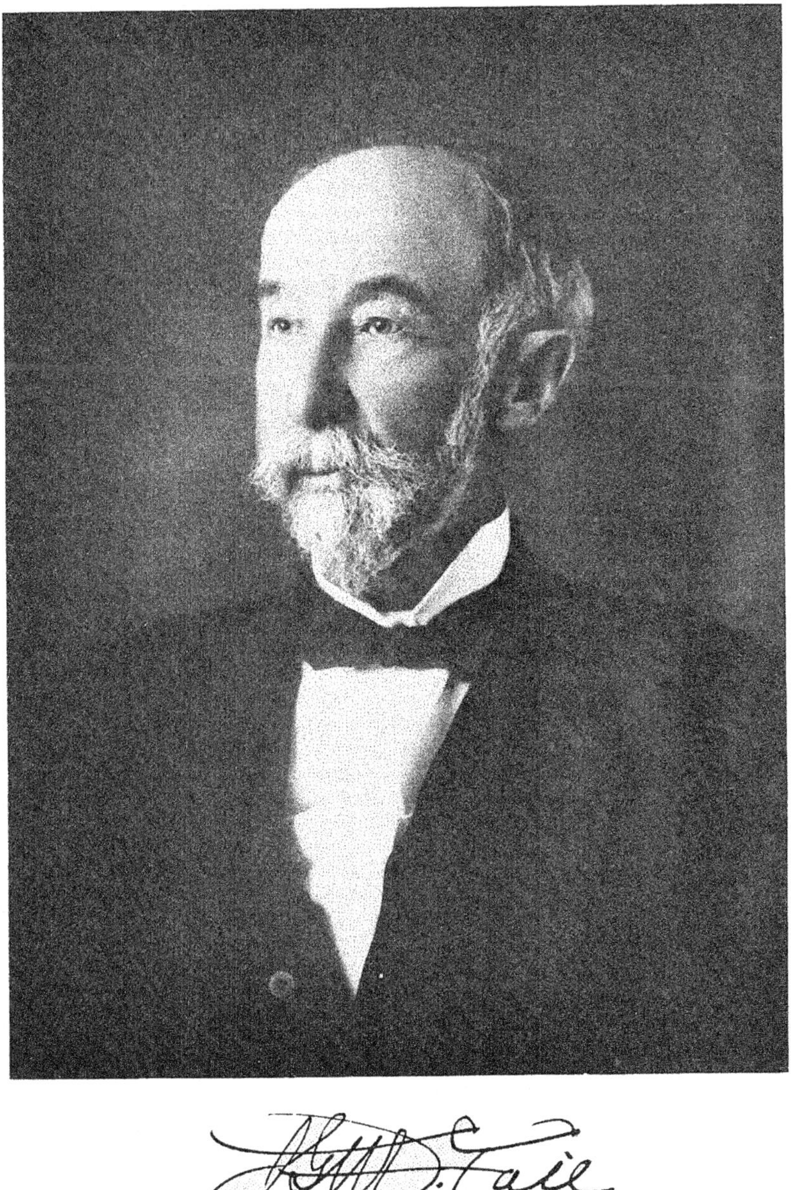

in that same institution, and was successfully filling that chair when war between the states was declared. Immediately offering his services to the Confederacy, Mr. McCall was commissioned first lieutenant of Company K,. Fiftieth Georgia Volunteer Infantry, and with his regiment joined the Army of the Potomac in Virginia, having command of his company until he was wounded. Immediately after the engagement at Sharpsburg, he was given charge of a section of artillery and of three companies of infantry that were guarding a bridge across Antietam creek, and while on duty he was severely wounded by a minnie ball passing through his face. He was immediately taken to the hospital for treatment, and during his convalescence he was elected ordinary of Brooks county, Georgia.

Being disabled for further service in the army, Mr. McCall returned to his native state to accept the position to which he had been chosen, and for four years filled the office acceptably to all concerned. While thus employed he studied law, and having been admitted to the bar located in Quitman as a lawyer, and has been in active practice here since, with the exception of four years when he was judge of the city court. Mr. McCall has been influential in public affairs, the people having great confidence in his ability, judgment and discretion. He has served as judge of probate for Brooks county, and as mayor of Quitman, administering the affairs of each office wisely and well. He is president of the board of trustees of Mercer University, which in 1894, conferred upon him the degree of LL. D.

Dr. McCall married, in 1867, Rosa Elizabeth Bobo, who was born in Glenville, Alabama, a daughter of Dr. Virgil and Sarah Hanson (Black) Bobo. She is a sister of Hon. Edward J. Black, and an aunt of Hon. George R. Black, members of congress. Dr. and Mrs. McCall are the parents of five children, namely: Rosa Lee, Rachel Black, Nonnie Bobo, John F. and Edna Florida.

Rosa Lee married John O. Lewis and has five children, Rosa Hunt, Minnie Cleborn, John O., Frank McCall and Virgil Bobo. Rachel Black, wife of Charles F. Cater, has one child, John McCall Cater. Nonnie B. is living with her parents. Edna F., wife of Albert L. Tidwell, has two children, Rose Elizabeth and Edna McCall. Dr. and Mrs. McCall and their family are members of the Missionary Baptist church. In politics the judge is a stanch adherent of the Democratic party.

JOHN AZARIAH MEWBORN. It is always pleasant and profitable to contemplate the career of a man who has made a success of life and won the honor and respect of his fellow citizens. Such is the record of the well-known gentleman whose name heads this sketch, than whom a more whole-souled or popular man it would be difficult to find within the limits of the county which is his home. John Azariah Mewborn is not a man who has exclusively confined his life to one line of endeavor. He was in educational work for twenty years, and after finishing his term as a director of the "young idea" he engaged for a short time in the mercantile business. He then first engaged in his present work, insurance, and has been successful as a representative of important companies in the line of life and fire insurance, casualty and loans.

Mr. Mewborn is a native Georgian. His birth having occurred in Gwinnett county, on a farm in the vicinity of Laurenville, the date of his nativity being July 15, 1859. The reverberations of the guns of the Civil war echoed about his cradle and many of his relatives participated in the great conflict between the states, his father losing his life on the field of battle, whence he had bravely gone forth in defense of the cause in which he believed. The subject remained upon the paternal homestead until about the age of twenty-four years. He drank of the "Pierian Spring" in the common schools of his district and then entered Gainesville College, from which institution he was graduated in 1888 with the well-earned degree of bachelor of arts. Thereafter he engaged in school teaching, in the state, and as previously mentioned, his pedagogical work extended over a period of a score of years and was of the most enlightened and satisfactory character. He continued in the mercantile business only for two years and then became representative at Rochelle, whither he had removed in the year 1908, for the Pennsylvania Mutual Life Insurance Company and proving exceedingly successful in this field, he added the general agency for fire insurance, casualty and loans, the latter addition being in the same year. He also handles real estate, and has located several families from other states.

Mr. Mewborn is the son of Archibald Marion and Cynthia I. (Noel) Mewborn, the former a native of Elbert county, Georgia, and the mother of Gwinnett. His maternal forebears were natives of Virginia and of Irish origin and the father's ancestry was English. The father enlisted at the time of the Civil war, was a member of the forty-second Georgia Infantry under Capt. L. P. Thomas and died in the service. His uncle, George Noel, also gave up his life for the cause of the Confederacy, but his brother, James, served throughout the dark days of the struggle and is still living at the present time, a veteran and respected citizen. Five paternal uncles, Jeff, James, John V., William M. and Martin C. were among the flower of young southern manhood who testified by enlisting to their conviction in the supreme right of the states to sever their connection with the national government, and all served in Georgia regiments. Martin was severely wounded while in the service.

Mr. Mewborn was happily married on January 24, 1895, his chosen lady being Clara Loveless, daughter of John G. and Sallie (Shockley) Loveless, the latter's father having originated the famous "Shockley apple." Their union has been blessed by the birth of one son, Fay Ellery, born January 8, 1903, and now ten years of age.

Fraternally Mr. Mewborn is a member of the Odd Fellows, and while at school was a member of the Ben Hill debating society. He attends the Methodist church. He is a man of fine character and takes a helpful and public-spirited interest in the affairs of town, church, county and state, exerting a very definite influence toward their advancement.

JUDGE DAVID BASCOM NICHOLSON is one of the most prominent members of his profession in this section of the state and having served since 1906 as judge of the city court. He has earned the reputation of being one of the most learned and impartial of jurists. He has an excellent legal equipment and has also brought to bear the strength of a fine and upright character, so that he has gained and held the inviolable confidence and regard of his fellow practitioners and of the general public. While a resident of his native state, North Carolina, he was sent to represent the interests of his county in the state legislature and in that body was recognized as one of its most intelligent and public-spirited members.

Judge Nicholson was born September 19, 1853, near Magnolia, Duplin county, North Carolina. He was reared to the age of fifteen years amid the rural surroundings of the father's farm. He received his early education in the public schools and also in private schools and subsequently entered Trinity College, now at Durham, from which institution he was graduated with the class of 1875, receiving the degree of bachelor of arts. He took post-graduate study and ultimately acquired the degree of master of arts. His first adventures as a wage-earner were in the capacity of a school teacher and during his pedagogical endeavors he also read law in spare minutes, pursuing this professional preparation under the direction of Col. W. A. Allen, a distinguished lawyer of Goldsboro, North Carolina. In 1880, the subject was admitted to the bar of the supreme court of North Carolina, and to inaugurate his practice, he removed to Kenansville, the judicial center of Duplin county, and there remained for two years. He represented Duplin county in the state assembly, as mentioned previously, and was instrumental in bringing about considerable helpful and wise legislation. Following that he removed to Clinton, Sampson county, North Carolina, where he practiced for ten years, and in 1893 he came to Abbeville, Georgia, where he resided two years, and then moved to Rochelle, where he has won recognition of the highest character. In that year he was appointed solicitor of the county court of Wilcox county, and he remained in that office until the establishment of the city court in 1896, when he was appointed by Governor Terrell judge of the city court, and subsequently, in 1908, he was elected to the same office for a term of four years, being at the present time the incumbent. Wilcox county looks upon this gentleman as an acquisition of great value and no matter with what responsibility entrusted he has never been found wanting.

Judge Nicholson is a son of Rev. David B. Nicholson, a distinguished member of the North Carolina conference of the Methodist Episcopal church South, and of his wife, Zilpha (Pearsall) Nicholson, both of these admirable people being natives of North Carolina.

He was happily married in 1876, his chosen lady being Miss Katie Powell, daughter of the late Col. Luke A. and Mary A. (Vann) Powell. Mrs. Nicholson's father was colonel of a regiment of North Carolina troops in the Civil war, and the record of that gentleman is gallant indeed. The children of Judge and Mrs. Nicholson are: Luke Powell, a locomotive engineer on the Atlantic Coast Line; Edwin Forrest, an electrical engineer of Americus, Georgia; David B., Jr., a Baptist minister of Macon, Georgia; and James Marvin, a student at Locust Grove Institute. Justin L. died March 5, 1909, and Mary died April 3, 1911.

Judge Nicholson is affiliated with the Knights of Pythias and the Odd Fellows and at college was a member of Chi Phi fraternity. He is a member of the Methodist Episcopal church, South, and his wife of the Missionary Baptist church at Rochelle. They maintain a household redolent of that warm and wholly charming hospitality for which the South is so justly famed.

WALTER G. BROWN, prominent banker and merchant of Rochelle, has been a resident of this city since 1898, and has been actively identified with the foremost business interests of the city in the years that have passed since his settling here. He was born in Dooley county, near Vienna, on June 1, 1862, and is the son of Judge Ira Brown and his wife, Henriette (Lasseter) Brown. The father was judge of the Dooley county court as long as forty years ago, and was one of the leading men of his community during his lifetime. He later occupied the same position in Wilcox county. There were seven children in the Brown family, of which Walter G. was one. Of his four sisters, but two are living today, Emma and Lucy, both married to prosperous farmers of Wilcox county.

Walter G. Brown received his early education in Dooley county.

In about 1882 he became interested in the merchandise business and established a store near Abbeville, where he continued for four years. He then located at Seville, remaining there in business for nine years, coming from there to Rochelle. Mr. Brown has prospered in his mercantile ventures, and he owns the building where his present business is conducted, a two story brick with a floor space of eighty-five by fifty feet, and boasting the only elevator in Wilcox county. In addition to his flourishing merchandise business, Mr. Brown is owner of the Brown Bank Company of Rochelle. This institution was organized as the Citizens Bank in 1908, under the laws of the state. In 1909, when the City Bank had been in operation one year, Mr. Brown bought it out, since which time it has been conducted as a private institution, and it is operated on a sound and conservative basis which has won and retained to it a high standing and the confidence and patronage of the best citizenship of Rochelle.

Mr. Brown was postmaster at Seville, under Grover Cleveland's last administration, a position which he most ably handled, and he has in other positions of a public nature exhibited the same characteristic efficiency and trustworthiness which marked his career as postmaster, and in the private business which he conducts.

On March 14, 1890, Mr. Brown was united in marriage with Miss Sallie Elizabeth Hardaman, daughter of J. D. Hardaman of Seville, but formerly from northern Georgia. Five children were born of their union, of which number four are living. Birdie died at the age of two years. Walter E., aged sixteen, is a student at the North Georgia Military School, in Dahlonega, Georgia. Annie Wilmer, seven years old; Mildred, aged five, and William, now two years of age, are the remaining members of the family.

Mr. Brown is a member of the Masonic fraternity, blue lodge degree, and is one of the most highly esteemed men in Rochelle.

JAMES ALEXANDER BUSSELL, M. D., has been engaged in the practice of medicine since 1893, and since 1896 he has been located at Rochelle, where he has become well and favorably known to the medical fraternity and where he has built up a practice in every way consistent with his splendid ability and his high character.

Born in Dooly county, Georgia, in 1873, Dr. Bussell is the son of W. A. and Edith Young (Raffield) Bussell, both of that county. The father was a veteran of the Civil war. Dr. Bussell is one of eight children, all of whom are living. They are: Lula, the wife of S. J. Barrett of Abba, Georgia; Mariette, married to W. J. C. Brown, also a farmer of Abba; Minnie, married to Medelton Grayham, a farmer of Isaac, Georgia; I. J., a farmer located in Abba; B. R., a doctor of Rochelle; Charles, a farmer living at Abba; James Alexander of this review, and William, a machinist of Abba.

At the age of four weeks James A. Bussell accompanied his parents to Irwin county, where his boyhood was spent, and it was there he received his preliminary educational training, finishing in the Rochelle high school. His medical training he received at the Atlanta Medical College, graduating therefrom with the class of 1893, beginning the active practice of his profession in the same year at Sibbie, Georgia, where he continued for three years. After he had located at Rochelle, Dr. Bussell completed a course in phamaceutics, and for three years or more conducted a drug store in this place, but the remainder of the time has confined his entire attention to his general medical practice.

In October, 1893, Dr. Bussell was married to Miss Ids Coffee, daughter of Mr. and Mrs. H. Coffee. Four children were born to Dr. and

J Henry Mitchell

Mrs. Bussell—Harry, Eva Mae, Sallie and James. The wife and mother died in September, 1902, and on January 20, 1904, Dr. Bussell married Mae Coffee, a sister of his first wife. They became the parents of two children—Ethel, born in May, 1907, and Earnest, born in 1905. Mrs. Bussell passed away on September 15, 1910, and Dr. Bussell contracted a third marriage in September of the following year, when Elizabeth Annie Coffee, a sister of his first and second wives, was united to him.

Dr. Bussell is a member of the Independent Order of Odd Fellows and the F. & A. M., and his wife is a member of the Methodist church, while he is a Baptist.

HENRY MITCHELL. For many years identified with the development and promotion of the lumber interests of Georgia, Henry Mitchell is now living retired from active pursuits in Waycross, enjoying to the utmost the well-merited reward of his long-continued and unremitting toil. Coming on both sides of the house from a long and honored line of pure Scotch ancestry, he was born, November 11, 1841, in the parish of Abernethy, Perthshire, Scotland, a son of William Mitchell.

His Grandfather Mitchell, a tiller of the soil, for many years operated the farm known at "Bartlett field," which was located about six miles north of Perth. He and his wife were both life-long residents of Scotland. They reared five children, one daughter and four sons. The daughter, Helen, married a Mr. White, and spent her entire life in her native country. All of the sons left Scotland, one of them, Henry, settling in London, England; Robert located permanently in Ireland; George came to America, settling in Wellington county, Ontario, Canada; and William also immigrated to America.

Born in the parish of Dron, Stirlingshire, Scotland, William Mitchell learned the trade of a tailor when young, and followed it for a number of years in Abernethy, Perthshire. Immigrating to America in 1848, he opened a merchant tailoring establishment in Guelph, province of Ontario, Canada, where he spent his remaining years, passing away at the advanced age of seventy-nine years. He married Jane Kinghorn, who was born in Perthshire, Scotland, of Scotch ancestry, and was there reared and married. Her brother, Joseph Kinghorn, was an expert steamboat engineer, and when the Turks bought steamships in Scotland he went to Turkey on board one of the vessels, and was for several years in the employ of the sultan, teaching the Turks how to operate the ships. Another of her brothers, Henry Kinghorn, immigrated to the United States, and served as foreman of the shipyard in New York when the steamers Atlantic, Pacific, Adriatic and Baltic were under process of construction. He continued a resident of New York until his death, and many of his descendants are still living there. Mrs. William Mitchell survived her husband about a year, dying at the age of seventy-nine years. Seven children were born of their union, as follows: William, deceased; Jane, wife of Richard Waldron, of Guelph, Ontario; Henry, the subject of the sketch; David, deceased; Robert, who was for many years a merchant in Guelph, and is now the postmaster; John, a carriage top manufacturer in Guelph; Helen, wife of Myron W. Burr, of Guelph, a furniture manufacturer, now retired.

In 1849 Henry Mitchell came with his mother, brothers and sisters to America, joining his father, who had emigrated from Scotland the previous year, in Canada, the ocean voyage in a sailing vessel having covered a period of six weeks. Landing in New York, the family went by way of the Hudson river and the Erie canal to Rochester, New York, thence by way of the Genesee river and Lake Ontario to Hamilton, Canada, where, there being no railroads, they took teams to convey them to Guelph. Continuing his education, which he had begun in Scotland, Henry Mitchell attended the schools of Guelph regularly until seventeen years old, in the meantime earning a little ready money by clerking during his leisure time in a store. Anxious then to secure congenial and remunerative employment, he bade good-bye to home and friends, and journeyed to New York City, where he expected to find his uncle, Henry Kinghorn. The uncle, however, had died. Concluding therefore to go farther south, Mr. Mitchell went to Charleston, South Carolina, where he hoped to have an opportunity to develop his mechanical ability by learning the machinist's trade. Finding no favorable opening in that city, he sought other employment, applying for work to Mr. James M. Rahb, who was the master mechanic and superintendent in the building of the Charleston & Savannah Railroad, of which a few miles only had then been completed. He began work as a common laborer, but after two days was given clerical work, later becoming first a fireman, and then a railroad engineer.

On the breaking out of the Civil war Mr. Mitchell was made sergeant of an independent company, and sworn into service, as an expert mechanic being placed on detached duty. He continued as an engineer, and in that capacity formed the acquaintance of General Lee, and was detailed to run his special train, having charge of the engine that drew the general's train while he had charge of the Georgia-Florida district. As previously stated, Mr. Mitchell's great ambition had always been to learn the machinist's trade, and while with General Lee left the train without permission to work in the railroad shops, which were under the supervision of his former employer, Mr. S. S. Haines, who was elected superintendent to take the place of the former superintendent. The commanding officer hearing of this, ordered Mr. Mitchell to headquarters. Mr. Haines accompanied him, pleaded his case most eloquently, telling the officers that as a good mechanic Mr. Mitchell was worth more to the Confederacy in the shops than at the front, putting his side of the case so effectively that Mr. Mitchell was allowed to remain in the shops, where he became familiar with all kinds of work.

A few days before the surrender of Fort Sumter, Mr. Mitchell was called there to adjust the sights of the cannon, and was afterwards one of the volunteers that undertook to blow up the Ironsides, and at the close helped to sink the Confederate boats that they might not be of service to the Federals. The close of the war left Mr. Mitchell penniless, but he and a companion, having found a boat adrift, established a ferry across the Ashley river, and for a few days carried on a profitable business, most of their patrons being Union soldiers. Entering then the employ of the United States government, under Bob Hunter, he was for a short time engaged in the construction of bridges, and the raising of sunken vessels.

Receiving financial aid then from his home people, Mr. Mitchell returned to Canada, and there served an apprenticeship of three years in the machine shops of F. G. Becket & Company. Returning then to the South, Mr. Mitchell was for a year employed as an engineer on the Fernandina & Cedar Keys Railroad. At the solicitation of Mr. S. S. Haines, he then went to Savannah, Georgia, and from that time until 1877 was an engineer on the Atlanta & Gulf Railroad. Resigning that position, he entered the employ of his father-in-law, for six months having charge of his saw mill in Screven, Georgia. The following two years he operated a saw mill at Ocean Pond, Florida, and subsequently became a partner in the firm of Dale, Dixon & Company, which was operating a planing mill in Savannah, and a saw mill in

Liberty county, Georgia. The latter plant Mr. Mitchell operated until it burned, six years later. Captain Dale died about that time, and Mr. Dixon and Mr. Mitchell purchased his interests in the business, and under the firm name of Dixon, Mitchell & Company operated a planing mill in Savannah, and a saw mill in Alexandria, Georgia, for several years. The partnership being dissolved in 1903, and the business disposed of, Mr. Mitchell located in Waycross, and was here profitably engaged in the lumber business until 1911, when he sold out, and has since lived retired from business cares, making his home with his son, Joseph D. Mitchell.

Fraternally Mr. Mitchell is a member of Waycross Lodge, No. 305, Ancient Free and Accepted Order of Masons; Waycross Chapter, No. 9, Royal Arch Masons; Damascus Commandery, No. 18, Knights Templar; and also belongs to Golden Rule Lodge of Savannah, Independent Order of Odd Fellows.

Mr. Mitchell married, in 1877, Kate Dale, who was born and educated in Savannah, a daughter of Capt. Joseph J. and Delia (White) Dale, the former of whom was a native of England, while the latter was born in the United States. Mrs. Mitchell died in 1883, in early womanhood, leaving two children, one of whom lived but eighteen months. The other child, Joseph Dale Mitchell, born in Wayne county, Georgia, but raised and educated in Savannah, was for many years associated in business with his father. He married Minnie Jones, and they have five children, namely: Katie Dale, Minnie, Joseph Dale, Jr., Nellie Burr, and William Bruce. He, too, stands high in the Ancient Free and Accepted Order of Masons, being eminent commander of Damascus Commandery, No. 18, Knights Templar.

J. MARK WILCOX. Talented, energetic, and well versed in legal lore, J. Mark Wilcox, of Hazlehurst, is rapidly winning for himself an honored position in the legal circles of Jeff Davis county, and deserves great credit for the position which he has won, not only as an attorney, but as a popular and esteemed citizen. He was born May 21, 1890, at Willacoochee, Coffee county, Georgia, of substantial Scotch-Irish ancestry.

His father, Jefferson Wilcox, M. D., is one of the best known and most prosperous physicians of Coffee county, and a man of prominence and influence. Very active in public affairs, he represented his district in the state legislature in 1892, 1894, and 1896, and 1898 served as state senator. During the Spanish-American war he raised a company of immunes, which was organized as Company B, Third United States Volunteer Infantry, and with them saw service in Cuba. He married Marion Henson, who was likewise a native of Coffee county, Georgia, and they are the parents of two children, namely: Ira E., of Savannah, Georgia, in the employ of the Southern Bell Telephone Company; and J. Mark, the subject of this brief biographical record.

After completing the course of study in the Willacoochee high school J. Mark Wilcox attended Emory College, in Oxford, Georgia, for two years. Going then to Macon, Georgia, he was graduated from the law department of Mercer University with the class of 1910. Immediately locating in Hazlehurst, Mr. Wilcox has met with most encouraging success in his professional practice, and as one of the younger generation of lawyers has a brilliant prospect for a prosperous future in his career. On November 9, 1911, he was appointed prosecuting attorney for Jeff Davis county, and is filling the position with characteristic ability. He is also a director of the Farmers State Bank of Hazlehurst, and its attorney.

SEABORN WALTER JOHNSON, M. D. Long familiar with the rudiments of medicine and surgery, Seaborn Walter Johnson, M. D., of Hazlehurst, has continually added to his knowledge by close study and earnest application, and through sheer merit has gained a fine reputation for professional skill and ability. He was born, February 7, 1859, in Appling county, Georgia, which was likewise the birthplace of his father, Matthew Johnson, and the county in which his Grandfather Johnson settled on coming to Georgia, in Bulloch county. The great-grandfather of Dr. Johnson was Mathew Johnson, a soldier in the Revolutionary army under General Washington, and his father, John Johnson, was born in Scotland in 1707, and came to America about 1730, with the Stewart clan, who were exiled from their native land and came to the colony of North Carolina.

Reared to agricultural pursuits, Mathew Johnson has been quite successful as a tiller of the soil, finding in farming both pleasure and profit. He married Elizabeth Cobb, who was born in North Carolina, a member of a family prominent in the Revolutionary war. She came with her parents to Georgia when about twelve years of age, settling in Jefferson county. She died on the home farm in Appling county. Five children were born of their marriage, as follows: Lewis W., a farmer in Appling county, died in 1886; Daniel W., postmaster at Nicholls, Coffee county; Seaborn Walter, the special subject of this brief sketch; Mary, wife of Jesse T. Sellars, a farmer in Jeff Davis county; and Marjorie, wife of W. P. Myers, of Baxley, Georgia.

Growing to man's estate beneath the parental roof-tree, Seaborn Walter Johnson successfully learned the three R's in the common schools, the body of instruction at that day, later attending Vanderbilt University in Nashville, Tennessee, for a year, studying in both the literary and medical departments. A man of his mental caliber naturally turns to a professional life, and his choice led him to continue the study of medicine. Going therefore to Atlanta, Georgia, he entered the College of Physicians and Surgeons, and was there graduated with the class of 1887, receiving the degree of M. D. Immediately locating in Graham, Appling county, Dr. Johnson remained there seven years, gaining wisdom and experience of value. He was afterwards settled for a number of years in Baxley, and in Douglas, in each place meeting with good success, his natural skill winning for him the confidence of the people, and gaining him a large patronage. In 1911 he took a post-graduate course in New York City, at the Bellevue hospital.

While living in Appling county, Dr. Johnson took much interest in local and state affairs, in 1890 and 1891 representing Appling county in the state legislature. While a member of that body, the doctor introduced and fathered the "Jim Crow" bill, which was passed during the same session, the bill providing for separate accommodations for white and black traffic on the railroads of the state, and being opposed by every Georgia railroad. Fraternally the doctor belongs to the Ancient Free and Accepted Order of Masons, being a member of Hazlehurst lodge, and to R. A. M. Chapter, No. 95. Both he and his wife are members of the Methodist church.

On November 27, 1890, Dr. Johnson was united in marriage with Miss Mamie K. Anthony, a daughter of Rev. J. D. and Josephine (Alexander) Anthony, and sister of Rev. Bascom Anthony, of the South Georgia Methodist denomination. Her father was dubbed the "Bishop of the Wire Grass," and at the time of the marriage of his daughter Josephine was living in Spring Hill, Montgomery county, Georgia. Dr. and Mrs. Johnson have four children, namely: Ruby Claire, born in 1894; Hallie R., born in 1896; Opal Anthony, born in 1900; and Grace, born in 1904.

ANSEL A. PARRISH. Among the active and prosperous business men of Valdosta is Ansel A. Parrish, born in that part of Lowndes county that is now Berrien county, Georgia, and a representative of one of the prominent pioneer families of this section. The family originated here with Henry Parrish, the grandfather of Ansel A., who took a leading part in the public affairs of his community and at one time was a member of the Georgia state legislature. Ansel A. Parrish was one of the many brave and loyal youth who, yet in their teens, so gallantly went to the defense of their beloved Southland in 1861-65, and he is one of the few remaining actors in that great struggle.

Henry Parrish, who was of North Carolinian stock, was reared and married in Bulloch county, Georgia, and removed from thence into southern Georgia in a very early day, locating in that part of Irwin county which later was transferred to Lowndes county and still later became Berrien county. He bought land about six miles east of the present site of Cecil and entered actively and prominently into the public life of this section. He died in middle life. His wife, who was a Miss Nancy Williams before her marriage, bore him twelve children and survived him fifty years, passing away at a remarkably advanced age. Ezekiel W. Parrish, born February 16, 1818, in Bulloch county, Georgia, son of Henry and father of Ansel A., was very young when his parents removed to southern Georgia and after his father's death he remained with his mother until his marriage, when he bought land one mile from where is now located the town of Cecil and there engaged in farming and stock-raising. In 1864 he sold his farm and received its value in Confederate money, which he still held when the war closed, but fortunately he had retained about seventeen hundred acres east of Hahira in Lowndes county. He settled on the latter estate, erected the necessary buildings and made it his home until his death on September 1, 1887. Martha C. (Wootten) Parrish, his wife, born in Taliaferro county, Georgia, had preceded him in death, her demise having occurred in June, 1871. She was a daughter of Redden Wootten and wife, the latter of whom was a Miss Bird before her marriage. Ezekiel W. and Martha C. (Wootten) Parrish were the parents of twelve children, namely: Nancy E., Redden B., Susan, Ansel A., James H., Joel W., Matthew R. A., Mary A. A., Ezekiel W. J., Martha M., John E. W. and Absolom B.

Ansel A. Parrish, born February 20, 1846, the fourth in this family, was reared amid pioneer scenes, for in his youth there were no railroads in this section of Georgia and his father went to Albany, Georgia, sixty miles away, to market his cotton. All cooking was done before the open fire and his mother would card, spin and weave the wool into homespun cloth which her deft fingers would then convert into garments for her family. Mr. Parrish received such educational advantages as the public schools of his day afforded, and when old enough took up duties on the farm. In May, 1864, he enlisted in Company B of the First Florida Special Battalion for service in the Confederate army and was assigned to the commissary department, where he continued until the close of the war. Returning to his Georgia home, he took up farming and also taught school to earn money, the money with which to advance his education. He was a student in the Valdosta Institute when occurred the death of Professor Varnedoe, then president of the institution. For sometime after concluding his studies there he clerked and then engaged in the mercantile business independently, continuing thus for seven years. He then took up the sale of sewing machines and when bicycles came into use he engaged in their sale and repair. One of the first in his city to see the future of the automobile, he opened a garage for the repair, storage and sale of automobiles and has continued in that line of business to the present time.

On July 16, 1874, Mr. Parrish was united in marriage to Mary Emma Peeples, a native of Berrien county, Georgia, and a daughter of Judge Richard A. and Sarah (Camp) Peeples, more specific mention of whom will be found in the sketch of C. B. Peeples appearing on other pages of this volume. Seven children have blessed the union of Mr. and Mrs. Parrish, namely: Carrie May, Maggie Alline, Charles E., Irene A., Ansel A., Richard E. and Edwin Willard. Carrie May is now Mrs. Francis H. Ramsey, of Valdosta, Georgia, and has one son, Francis H.; Maggie A., now Mrs. Albert N. Swain, resides in Richland, Georgia, and has three children, Albert N., Ansel Parrish and Emeliza; Charles E., married Julia Collier and has two children, Collier E. and Margaret; Irene married Dr. A. L. Smith, of Empire, Georgia and they have three children, Mary E., Dorothy and Samuel A.; and Ansel A., married Nona Hester and has a daughter, Caroline.

Mr. and Mrs. Parrish are members of the Tabernacle Baptist church at Valdosta and both are ardent advocates of temperance.

ROBERT BUTLER MYDDELTON. When it is stated that this esteemed citizen of Valdosta has served as clerk of the superior court in Lowndes county, Georgia, continuously since 1908 and that he succeeded his father, Robert Thomas Myddelton, the incumbent of that office for thirty-one consecutive years, further attestation as to the family's worth and standing will be unnecessary. Three generations of the Myddeltons have been native to Georgia soil and have sprung from their common ancestor, William Myddelton, who was born in England and came to America in colonial times, settling in South Carolina. William Myddelton was married in South Carolina to Margaret Thompson and removed from that state to McIntosh county, Georgia, where both spent the remainder of their lives as farmer people. Their son Augustus Myddelton, born in McIntosh county, Georgia, was reared in his native county to agricultural pursuits and after his father's death assumed charge of the home farm, which he conducted by slave labor. Later he removed from McIntosh county to Chatham county and bought a tract of land at Bethesda, ten miles from Savannah, where remained his home for about fifteen years. Removing from there to Bryan county, he bought a plantation of 720 acres on the Midway river, where he resided until March, 1863, when the war activities of the time having made his home in this section unpleasant and unsafe, he took his family to Valdosta, Lowndes county. He bought a home in the village and a farm a few miles out and continued his residence in Valdosta until his death in May, 1864, at the age of sixty. Mary Percival (Todd) Myddelton, his wife, was born in McIntosh county, Georgia, and was a daughter of John and Margery (Percival) Todd. She survived her husband many years and passed away at the advanced age of ninety. To this union were born the following children: John, Eugenia, Margaret, James, Ezra, Harriett, Samuel, Sara and Robert T.

Robert Thomas Myddelton, the youngest of this family and the father of our subject, was born near Savannah, Chatham county, Georgia, January 27, 1845, and was educated at Flemington, Liberty county. He was but a youth when the Civil war broke out, but fired with the zeal and loyalty which characterized the sons of the South, he enlisted in his seventeenth year in Capt. S. D. Bradwell's company of the Twenty-fifth Georgia Volunteer Infantry. After he had served about one year he was discharged on account of disability, but in 1864 he again enlisted, this time in the Twentieth Battalion of Georgia Cavalry

Carey M. Sweat.

and went with the command to Virginia, where it was transferred to the Jeff Davis legion (Mississippi troops) and served in Young's brigade of Wade Hampton's command. Young Myddelton was in active service until the close of the war, when he was paroled and returned to the home of his parents in Valdosta. For a time he clerked in a store there and then later engaged in the mercantile business independently, continuing it until compelled to give it up on account of ill health. Removing to a farm, he continued on it until 1878, when he began his duties as clerk of the superior court of Lowndes county, to which office he had been elected in the fall of 1877. By successive reelections he has continued in that office thirty-one years and then he resigned. Certainly no more eloquent testimony could be given of the confidence and esteem he has commanded from his fellow citizens. He has also served as a member of the city council several terms and also as mayor of Valdosta. In November, 1868, was solemnized his marriage to Euphemia Smith, who was born in Lowndes county to Duncan and Margaret (Dasher) Smith. They have reared eight children, as follows: Smith, Mary, Robert B., Effie, William, Ralph, Paul and Archibald. Both Mr. and Mrs. Myddelton are members of the Baptist church, and he affiliates fraternally with Valdosta Lodge No. 184, Free and Accepted Masons.

Robert Butler Myddelton was born in Valdosta, Georgia, March 6, 1873, was educated in the public schools of that city and when a mere boy took up responsible duties as a clerk in a store. At the age of sixteen he entered the employ of A. S. Pendleton, wholesale and retail groceries, with whom he remained four years. The following nine years were spent as a bookkeeper in the First National Bank of Valdosta, and then he was appointed deputy clerk of the superior court of Lowndes county and clerk of the city court of Valdosta. In the fall of 1908 he was elected clerk of the superior court to succeed his father, who had resigned, and by reelection he has been continued in that office to the present time, also in the office of clerk of the city court.

The marriage of Mr. Myddelton took place in November, 1898, and united him to Miss Maude Hodges, a native of Bulloch county, Georgia, and a daughter of Eli W. and Louise (Keller) Hodges. They have two children, Robert Hodges and Margaret Louise. Mr. Myddelton is a member of Valdosta Lodge No. 184, Free and Accepted Masons, Valdosta Chapter of Royal Arch Masons, Malta Commandery of Knights Templars, and of Alee Temple, A. A. O. N. M. S.

CAREY M. SWEAT. Possessing rare business ability and foresight, Carey M. Sweat occupies a position of prominence and influence among the substantial and influential residents of Waycross, being identified with various enterprises of magnitude and importance. A son of the late Capt. James A. Sweat, he was born, December 9, 1861, in Ware county, Georgia, on a farm lying five miles south of Waresboro.

Born and bred in South Carolina, Capt. James A. Sweat migrated in early life to Georgia, locating in what is now Pierce county. The southern part of the state was then but sparsely settled, being largely in its primitive wildness, with plenty of deer, turkeys and other wild game common to this region. The Indians here had their happy hunting grounds, and ofttimes caused the newcomers fear and trouble through murderous attacks, thieving and otherwise molesting them. The whites built log forts, to which the women and children repaired for safety when the redskins started out on a death-dealing mission, while the men organized companies for protection against the savages, James A. Sweat becoming a captain of one of those little brave bands of pioneer settlers. About 1853 Captain Sweat removed to Ware county, Georgia, and having purchased a tract of wild land five miles south of Waresboro erected first a log house, and later replaced the original structure with a substantial frame house. With the assistance of slaves, he cleared and improved a homestead, and later, as his means increased, bought large tracts of land in Ware and adjacent counties, becoming an extensive and prosperous landholder. He continued his agricultural operations until his death, at which time he was sixty-one years, one month, and fifteen days old.

Captain Sweat was three times married. He married first Elizabeth Newburn. She died in 1853, leaving eleven children, namely: Thomas, Martin, Bryant, Farley, Elias, Ancil, Charlotte, Cassie, Maria, Tabitha and Mary. He married for his second wife Mary Newburn, a sister of his first wife. For his third wife Captain Sweat married a widow, Mrs. Serena (Miller) Clough, who by her union with her first husband, Mr. Clough, had four children, Jonathan J. Clough, deceased; Mary, still living; Emma, and Lilla, deceased. She was born in Ware county, Georgia, a daughter of Martin and Nancy (Brewton) Miller, and granddaughter of William Miller, a pioneer of Bulloch county, Georgia, and a soldier in the Revolutionary war. By this union two children were born, namely: Carey M. Sweat, the subject of this sketch, and Frank L. Sweat.

Although young when his father died, Carey M. Sweat assumed the care of the home farm to a large extent. He attended the public schools as regularly as possible, acquiring a good knowledge of the common branches of study, while under his mother's guidance he was well trained to habits of industry and thrift. Succeeding eventually to the ownership of the parental homestead, he carried on general farming successfully until twenty-seven years old, when he made an entire change of occupation and residence. Removing to Waycross, Mr. Sweat's first introduction into the business world was as a manufacturer of turpentine, an industry in which he first embarked while living on the farm. His industrial and financial interests expanded rapidly, fortune smiling on his every effort, and he is now associated with many enterprises of note.

One of the organizers of the Waycross Exchange Bank, Mr. Sweat served as its president from its formation until 1910, and is now one of its directors. He was one of the six men who erected the Hotel La Grande block; is a stockholder in the Consolidated Naval Stores Company; a director in the Citizens Bank of Douglas, Georgia; a stockholder in the Southern Naval Stores Company; a stockholder, and vice-president, of the Texas Turpentine Company; a stockholder in the State Life Insurance Company; and a stockholder and the vice-president of the Newillard Naval Stores Company of Texas.

Politically Mr. Sweat is a stanch Democrat, but has been too much absorbed in his personal affairs to engage in politics, although he has served as a member of the city council. Fraternally he belongs to Waycross Lodge, No. 305, Ancient Free and Accepted Order of Masons; religiously both he and his wife are consistent members of the Methodist Episcopal church.

Mr. Sweat has been twice married. On April 27, 1887, he was united in marriage with Miss Mollie McDonald, who was born in Ware county, Georgia, a daughter of William A. and Mary Ann (Deen) McDonald. She died December 7, 1892, leaving two children, James Lester and Vera E. Mr. Sweat married second, May 14, 1901, Susan E. McDonald, a daughter of Col. William A. and Rebecca (Thompson) McDonald. Of this union six children have been born, namely: Thelma

Lucille, Lillian Marie, Carey McDonald, Ralph Franklin, Juniatta Rebecca, and Norman Ancil.

JAMES EVERETT GORNTO, now a resident of Valdosta, is a son of a soldier of the Confederacy and a grandson of one of the earliest settlers in this section of the state, and by these distinctions and by his own career as a worthy and progressive citizen he is entitled to mention among the representative men of southern Georgia. His nativity occurred June 24, 1854, in that part of Lowndes county that is now included in Brooks county, Georgia, and he is a son of James Gornto, who was born in Laurens county of the Empire state of the South. The grandfather, Nathan Gornto, was a stock-raiser in Laurens county, but as the country became more thickly settled and grazing facilities fewer he pushed on to the frontier and located in what is now Brooks county but then was included in Lowndes county. He purchased land there and grazed his herds on large tracts that were vacant, for at that time all of southern Georgia was sparsely settled. There were no railroads and no markets for produce nearer than the gulf ports, and the few farmers here at that time took their surplus crops to St. Marks or Newport, Florida with teams. As the land began to be taken up by settlers and farmed, he sold his land to a Mr. Spain and took his herds of cattle into Madison county, Florida, where he purchased land and where he continued to reside until his death when about ninety years of age. His wife was Esther Burnett before her marriage and she too lived to be full of years. The most of their descendants are located in Florida. Their son James, the father of James Everett, was but a boy when the family settled in Brooks county and was reared amid pioneer scenes. He began his independent career by working out on a farm and soon became an overseer, continuing thus employed several years. Later he bought land west of Quitman, Georgia, but after operating it several years he sold it and purchased another farm south of Quitman on which he resided thenceforward until his death at the age of eighty. In 1864 he joined the Georgia Reserves and went to the defense of Atlanta, serving with that command until the close of the war. He wedded Miss Mahala Dean, a daughter of John and Jane Dean, and she reached the age of seventy-eight years. They were the parents of seven children, namely: Jane, James E., Lavinia, Annie, Daniel, Sally and Elijah.

James Everett Gornto, the second of this family in order of birth, was the eldest son and as he grew up under the home roof his experiences were those which naturally come to a boy commendably assisting his parents in developing a productive farm, and while they were not notably different from those of many others, each had its value in developing self-reliance and the habits of industry and thrift. His earlier years of independent activity were spent as a farmer, and though he has not been following that vocation personally in recent years he has never ceased to be interested in agricultural pursuits and has an estate a short distance from Valdosta which he operates by the help of tenants. Upon leaving the farm he took up his residence in Quitman, where he clerked for a time and where he served as marshal three years; then in 1897 he removed to Valdosta, where he has since resided. Mr. Gornto has been thrice married. On January 1, 1874, he was united to Miss Fannie Groover, a daughter of Henry Groover, who at her death in 1879 left two daughters, Lavinia and Fanny. His second marriage occurred in 1882 when he wedded Miss Fanny Lightfoot, daughter of Dr. T. J. Lightfoot. At her death in February, 1889, there were left three children, Katie, Beulah and

Samuel. In November, 1889, Mr. Gornto took as his third wife Miss Ella Roberts, a daughter of Ashley G. Roberts, and to their union have been born three children, Lorenzo, Flora and James Everett, Jr. Mr. Gornto is a Democrat in politics and cast his first vote for Samuel J. Tilden for president. Fraternally he is affiliated with the Valdosta Lodge of Free and Accepted Masons and with the chapter of Royal Arch Masons in the same city and belongs to Alee Temple, A. A. O. N. M. S. He is also a member of the Benevolent and Protective Order of Elks.

REMER YOUNG LANE. The president of the Merchants Bank of Valdosta is one of the oldest residents of Lowndes county, and for more than half a century has been closely identified with its agricultural and business development. A pioneer himself, Mr. Lane also represents a family of Georgia pioneers, and its members have been worthily connected with civic affairs and business enterprise in America from before the Revolutionary war down to the present.

Remer Young Lane was born in that part of Emanuel now known as Jenkins county, Georgia, on November 18, 1826. His grandfather, Abraham Lane, a native of Duplin county, North Carolina, was one of seven brothers each of whom gave soldier's service to the cause of independence during the Revolutionary war. Soon after the close of that struggle he came into Georgia, locating in what is now Jenkins county, and took a pioneer's part as a settler and upbuilder of that region. Practically all of Georgia was then a wilderness, the land not yet surveyed, and many years passed before all the Indian titles were quieted. In this sparsely settled region he acquired several thousand acres, and spent the rest of his years in the management and cultivation of his broad acres. He died in 1826, aged eighty-one years. His wife, whose maiden name was Martha Wood, passed away some years before him.

John Lane, son of Abraham and father of the Valdosta banker, was born also in the present Jenkins county on April 1, 1795, and was reared amid pioneer scenes. Following in the footsteps of his father, he became a planter and with slave labor conducted a large estate. His death occurred at the early age of forty years. He married Mary Heath, who was born and reared in the same neighborhood with him. Her father, a native of Charlotte, North Carolina, was Louis Heath, who married a Miss Vickers. John Lane and wife had five children, and after the father's death the mother directed the home plantation and kept the children together until they had homes of their own. She lived to the age of about seventy years.

Remer Young Lane was in his ninth year when his father died, and he lived at the old home until he was twenty-one, being educated in the schools of the neighborhood. On leaving home he established a store at "No. 8" on the line of the Georgia Central in Burke county, and continued there for seven or eight years. The date of his settlement in Lowndes county was 1855, fifty-eight years ago. At that time the county comprised a large territory in southern Georgia, and the county seat was Troupville. Near Clyatville he bought a large tract of new land, and with the aid of slaves developed and farmed it for a number of years. Agriculture was his regular vocation until 1875, in which year he located in Valdosta. In association with Hon. A. T. McIntyre of Thomasville he engaged in banking, a business with which his name has been substantially identified ever since, and he is one of the oldest bankers of south Georgia. In 1889 he organized the Merchants Bank of Valdosta, and has been president of this institution ever since. Mr. Lane is one of the largest land owners of Lowndes county, his holdings comprising over four thousand acres, and through its management and his other business enterprises he has been for years one of the largest producers of actual wealth in this section of the state.

On September 13, 1855, Mr. Lane married Miss Henrietta Brinson. She too is a descendant of Georgia pioneers. Her parents were Mills M. and Sarah (Hines) Brinson, natives of Screven and Burke' counties respectively. Mr. and Mrs. Lane have reared seven children, namely: Mary, Walter Thompson, Mills B., John, Augustus H., Edward W. and Ben. Mary is the wife of E. P. S. Denmark, and her five children are Remer Z., Elisha P., Augustus H., Irwin and Mary Estelle. Walter T., a resident of Valdosta, married Katherine Gairard, who died, leaving three children, Katrina, Almerine and Walter T. J.; Mills B., who is president of the Citizens and Southern Bank at Savannah, married Mary Homer, and their children are Mary, Remer Y. and Mills B.; John, who is a planter in Lowndes county, married Emma Tillman, now deceased, and their children are Mills B. and Isaiah T.; Augustus H., the fifth child, is deceased; Edward W., who is president of the Atlantic National Bank of Jacksonville, Florida, married Anna Tollivar, and has two children, James T. and Edward Wood. Ben, the youngest of the family, is engaged in business at Douglas in Coffee county. One of Mr. Lane's granddaughters, Katrina Lane, married William Ashley, and their child, Mary Katrina, represents the fourth living generation.

BENJAMIN P. JONES, the president of the Valdosta Bank and Trust Company has had a long career in business, has won prosperity and influence much above that of the average man, and yet began with little or nothing and for a number of years had a hard struggle with the obstacles of business life. Mr. Jones is one of the prominent citizens of south Georgia, and has been identified with Valdosta from the time it was a small village.

Mr. Benjamin P. Jones was born June 25, 1837, in that part of Camden now Charlton county, Georgia. His grandfather was James Jones, thought to have been a native of Georgia, who was a Camden county planter, having a number of slaves, and died there at the age of seventy-five, his remains now reposing in the Buffalo churchyard. He married a Miss Davis, who was upwards of eighty when she died, and they reared a large family of children. They were Primitive Baptists in religion.

Burrell Jones, father of the Valdosta banker, was born in Wayne county, Georgia, April 29, 1803. About the time of his marriage he bought land near Folkston, living there a few years, and about 1840 returned to Wayne county and located on a farm near the present site of Lulaton, where he made his home until his death in 1877. He married Mary Margaret (known as Peggy) Mizell, who was born in Bulloch county, August 9, 1809. Her father, Jesse Mizell, of English stock and a native of North Carolina, was a soldier of the Revolution under Jasper at Savannah and with Marion during that leader's valorous excursions against the British. He was with the command when it crossed the Peedee river, first lay blankets on the bridge to deaden the sound of the horses' hoofs, and in this way surprised the enemy. Some years after the Revolution Jesse Mizell came to Georgia, living two years in Camden county, and then moved into the interior, settling near the present site of Folkston in Charlton county, where he bought land and was engaged in farming and stock raising until his death at the age of abouty sixty. He married a Miss Stallings, a native of North Carolina and of Dutch ancestry. Mary M. Mizell, the mother of Mr. Jones, spent her early life on the Georgia frontier, and for the lack of educational advantages she compensated by her great natural ability and force of character. Her husband was for many years an invalid, and the care of the children devolved entirely upon her. She reared them to habits of industry and honor, and they paid her all filial reverence. Her death occurred in 1885. Her nine children were named as follows: Harley, Joseph, Benjamin P., Margaret, James B., Nancy C., Harriet, Jasper N. and Newton J. Harley and Joseph were Confederate soldiers and died during their service for the southern cause.

Though in his youth he had little opportunity to obtain an education, Benjamin P. Jones managed to obtain an education largely through his own efforts at self-improvement and an ingrained habit of close observation. When he was seventeen he became a teacher, and while he did good service while in this occupation it may be remembered that qualifications for teaching were not very high at that period. Anyone could teach who could find others who knew less than himself, and there was no formality of examination. Intellectual curiosity was a passion with him from an early age, and the time most children give to play with their comrades he devoted to association in company with his elders, thus learning by listening. When he was twelve years old he once attended a court session, listening attentively to the evidence and the charge to the jury. At recess the judge asked why he was so absorbed in the proceedings. The boy replied that it was because he wanted to learn, and then asked the judge why he charged the jury as he did. That was equity, responded the judge, and after explaining the meaning of that word told the boy that if he ever had occasion to make out papers to make them out in accordance with equity and justice and he would sanction them if brought before his court. Chopping cotton at twenty-five cents a day and board was the means by which Mr. Jones earned his first money. A little later he became clerk in a general store at Lulaton, and after a time engaged in business for himself at Stockton, Georgia. Hardly had his trade started when a panic paralyzed all business, and he found himself in debt fifteen hundred dollars, which took him some time to pay off.

Early in 1861 Mr. Jones enlisted in Company D of the Twenty-sixth Georgia Infantry, and was with that command in the coast defense until the regiment was ordered to Virginia, when he secured a substitute. Confederate money was then plentiful but away below par, and he bought a farm for three thousand dollars, at war-time prices, going in debt for the greater part of this amount. He was busily engaged in farming until 1864, when he enlisted with the Georgia Reserves, being commissioned first lieutenant and being in actual command of his company. The Reserves went to the defense of Atlanta, but from Griffin his company was sent back to recruit and apprehend deserters, and he was on detached duty until the close of the war. After making three crops on his farm he sold the land for four hundred dollars, and with that money and what he had realized from his crops engaged in the mercantile business at Milltown in Berrien county. Nine days after opening his store an epidemic of smallpox broke out, he was quarantined fifty-two days, and at the end of that time offered to sell his entire stock for three hundred dollars but could not find a buyer. Owing to this circumstance he went on with his business, at the same time buying cotton and dealing in live stock, and in four years had so reversed the current of his previous fortunes that he had cleared up fourteen thousand dollars. Then selling out at Milltown he went to southern Florida, where he opened two stores and established a grist and saw mill, and was engaged in business there until 1874, when ill health compelled him to make a change. He sacrificed eight thousand dollars by the move, and then came to Valdosta, which was then a village. Here he bought an established general store and a home for three thousand dollars, and was prosperously identified with the mercantile enterprise of this city for twenty years. In 1894 Mr. Jones organized the Valdosta Guano Company, and in 1906 the Valdosta Bank & Trust Company, of which he has since been president, with his son C. L. as cashier.

On June 25, 1862, Mr. Jones married Miss Elizabeth Knight, who was born in Clinch county, October 18, 1843, representing an old family of southern Georgia. Her grandfather, Rev. William Knight, was a pioneer preacher in this part of the state. He married a Miss Cone. Jonathan Knight, the father of Mrs. Jones, was born in that part of Lowndes now Berrien county, and spent his life as a farmer in Clinch and Berrien counties. Mr. and Mrs. Jones reared thirteen children, named as follows: Jonathan H., Charles Lee, Frances M. McKenzie; Lillie Roberts, Samuel W., Elizabeth Fry, Benjamin U., Jimmie Staten Green, Eulah Norris, Pearl Mashburn, Lloyd E., Lotta and Audrey Terry.

Mr. Jones has been identified with the Masonic order since he was twenty-seven years old. He is a member of the Economic League of Boston, Massachusetts, a society for the betterment of mankind. He has been one of the influential men in political life for many years. His first presidential vote was cast for John C. Breckenridge in 1860. He was opposed to secession, in a speech in which he said that if the sixteen southern states would all go out in a body, taking the constitution in one hand and the flag in the other, he would favor the movement with his vote, but not otherwise. In subsequent years he has served as delegate to many county and state conventions, was a delegate to the national conventions that nominated General Hancock and Grover Cleveland, and was also one of the sound-money Democratic delegates of 1896 who nominated Palmer and Buckner. Since 1898 he has not been allied with any party, and as a free lance has supported the individual who best represents his ideas of government.

CHARLES B. PEEPLES. When a lad of six years Mr. Peeples came to Valdosta with his parents, and saw Valdosta grow from a mere hamlet to one of the flourishing cities of south Georgia and he took a very important part in its business and civic enterprise during these years.

Charles B. Peeples was born at Milltown, on September 2, 1854. He represents one of the old families of this part of the state. His grandfather, Henry Peeples, a descendant of pure Scotch stock, was a native of South Carolina, which was his home until 1835. With his own wagons and teams he then brought his family and household goods from his old home near Anderson to Jackson county, Georgia, later bought land in Hall county, where he was both a farmer and merchant. In 1848 he came to Lowndes county, settling on Flat creek about two and a half miles from where Allapaha now stands, and there established a store, the locality hence taking the name of "Peeple's Store." He continued in active business until his death at the age of sixty years. He married a Miss Smith, and the names of their eight children were Jackson, Thompson, Cincinnatus, John, Anson, Edwin, Richard and Josephine.

Judge Richard A. Peeples, father of Charles B., was born in South Carolina in 1829, and during his lifetime became one of the prominent men of south Georgia. His early years were spent in Hall county, where he made the best of his school opportunities and became a well educated man. During his youth he began helping his father in the store and continued with him until the latter's death. After his marriage he located at Milltown and was engaged in saw-milling for a time. Upon the organization of Berrien county in 1856 he was elected clerk of the superior court, removing his residence to Nashville, which was then but a mere hamlet, far from railroads. That was his home until 1860, at which date he moved to the new town of Valdosta, buying land in that town that adjoined the county's land. While clerk of court in Berrien county he had studied law, and on being admitted to the bar opened an office as one of the first lawyers resident in Valdosta. During the war between the states he commanded a company of Georgia Reserves, being stationed at Savannah until the capture of that city, and then in Columbia, South Carolina. After the fall of the latter city he was sent home sick, and was unable to rejoin his command before the close of the war. He was engaged in active practice at Valdosta until his death, which occurred in 1892. For twelve years he filled the office of city judge, and was one of the influential Democrats and public-spirited citizens of this part of the state. He was twice married. His first wife, whose maiden name was Sarah J. K. Camp and who was the mother of Charles B., was a native of Jackson county, and her death occurred at the age of thirty-two. Her father, Berryman Camp, was born in Jackson county in 1800, followed farming there many years, and later settled near Cedartown in Polk county, where he died. He married a Miss Lyle. The second wife of Judge Peeples was Sarah Virginia Dent, who is still living. By the first marriage there were four children—Henry C., Charles B., Mary Emma and Sally. The five children of the second marriage were Walter, Etta, Alexander, Fannie and Cincinnatus.

Charles B. Peeples during his youthful years in Valdosta attended the public schools, and when sixteen years old began learning the trade of brick layer, which he followed two years. For five years he sold sewing machines, then conducted a mercantile business until 1880, at which time he became a clerk for the Atlantic Coast Railroad Company, continuing five years. From 1887 Mr. Peeples conducted a successful business in the sale of builders' materials at Valdosta, and was one of the oldest merchants of the city.

On March 11, 1880 he was married to Lilla C. Keller. Mrs. Peeples, whose ancestry on both sides included some of the first settlers of Georgia, was born in Effingham county and was a daughter of Thomas M. and Margaret (Weisenbaker) Keller. Mr. Peebles was and his wife is a member of the Missionary Baptist church. As a Democrat he served several terms in the city council, was mayor for one term, and for ten years was chairman of the board of county commissioners. Fraternally he was a member of Phoenix Lodge, I. O. O. F. Mr. Peeples died October 6, 1912, and was buried in the Valdosta cemetery. Their adopted daughter is Mrs. T. B. Converse of Valdosta.

RANDOLPH AVERA. One of the first men to engage in mercantile business at Quitman was Randolph Avera, who died at his home in Quitman, December 22, 1912. Mr. Avera was born in Washington county, Georgia, on May 21, 1826. His father, David Avera, was born in the same county, February 2, 1800, where he was reared and married, and in 1828 moved to Crawford county, where he bought a planta-

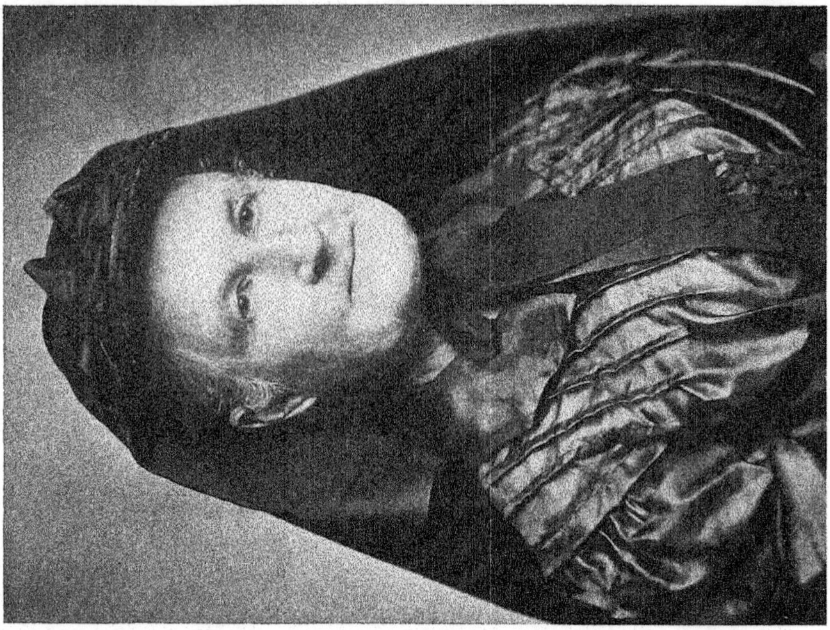

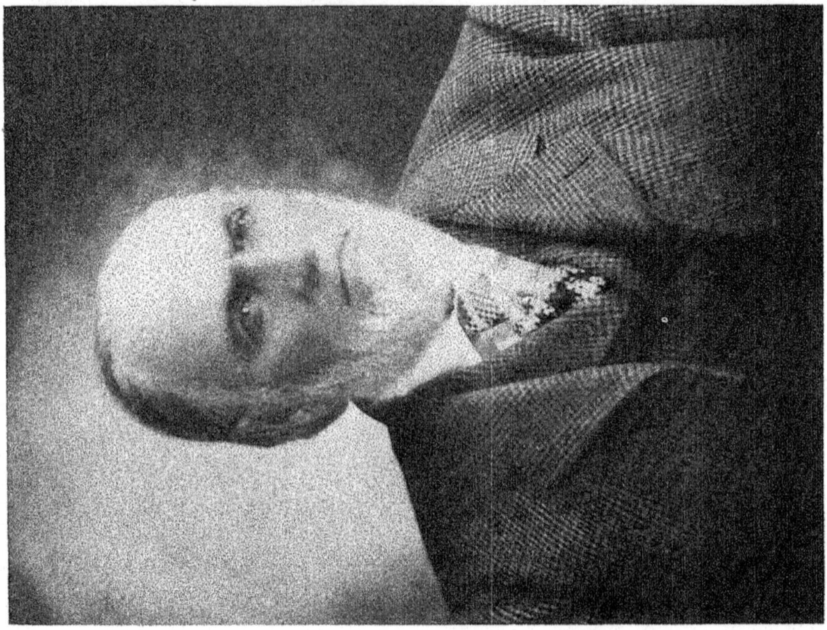

RESIDENCE OF MRS. RANDOLPH AVERA BUILT IN 1859

tion and operated it with his slaves for upwards of twenty years. He was also a member of the legislature. He then moved to the adjoining county of Houston, where he spent the rest of his days and died at the age of seventy-six in 1876. He married Elizabeth Hood. She was born in Washington county, and was a daughter of William Hood, a planter and lifelong resident of that county. David Avera and wife reared twelve children.

Randolph Avera spent his youth on the home farm and at the age of twenty-one began his independent career even with the world. He took up the carpenter's trade, and having served his apprenticeship followed it in various places until 1859. In that year he located at the new town of Quitman and with a brother established a store. He built the first brick store and set out the first shade trees—French mulberry. The town as yet had no railroad communication, and it was necessary to haul all goods in wagons from Dupont, forty miles away. When the war broke out Mr. Avera tendered his service to the Confederate government as a mechanic, and up to the close of the war was employed in the car-shops at Thomasville. After the war he was identified chiefly with the management of his home estate near Quitman, and lived retired up to the time of his death.

July 21, 1861, Mr. Avera married Mrs. Mary (Young) McElbeen, who represents one of the old and prominent families of south Georgia. She was born in Thomas county, September 29, 1830, and is a granddaughter of William and Mary (Henderson) Young. William Young in 1775, when the colonies were preparing to revolt from British rule, was a member of the council of safety at Savannah and on July 4th of that year represented the town and district of Savannah in the first assembling of the provincial congress. He was afterwards a planter of Screven county, where he spent his last days. Michael Young, son of this patriot and father of Mrs. Avera, was born in Screven county, January 16, 1797, later settled in Bulloch county, and in 1828 came and made settlement in the new county of Thomas. With wagons and other private conveyances he and his family and slaves arrived in what was then an almost unbroken wilderness, and the household camped in the forest while he and his helpers cut trees and made a log-cabin home. His location was three miles west of Thomasville. The Indians were still lingering in these hunting grounds, and all this part of the state was largely as nature had made it, so that Michael Young and his family were among those who bore the brunt of pioneer work and helped to prepare this region for the uses of subsequent generations. Michael Young had participated in one Indian war before coming here, and was engaged in another during the thirties. He cleared large tracts of land and resided in this vicinity until his death, which occurred August 24, 1856. He also was a member of the legislature and as there were no railroads here then he had to make the journey on horseback. The maiden name of his wife was Sarah Everett, who was a native of Bulloch county, and her death occurred on April 14, 1876. Her parents were Joshua and Jane (Carter) Everett, who, so far as known, were lifelong residents of Bulloch county. Michael Young and wife reared nine children, namely: James Everett, America, Remer, William Joshua, Mary Jane, Thomas Jones, John Carter, Sarah Lavinia, and Michael Henderson. The son John C. died while in school at LaGrange.

Mary J. Young was first married, in 1850, to William Henry McElbeen, who was born in Decatur county, Georgia, was reared on a farm, and on beginning his independent career bought land in his native county, where he and his wife lived until his death at the age of thirty-five. After the death of her husband Mrs. McElbeen with her three children returned to her parents in Thomas county. In 1857 coming to what is now Brooks county, where a brother had previously settled, she bought a tract of land to which the Quitman city limits have since been extended. At that time there was not a house on the present site of Quitman and the whole neighborhood was a pine forest. With the aid of her slaves she began improving her land, and her home for more than half a century has been on the estate which she thus undertook to develop. Log houses were the first homes both for her family and her slaves, but these have long since given way to comfortable frame dwellings. Her own home is a commodious colonial residence, situated well back from the street and in the midst of fruit and shade trees and is one of the most attractive homes in this vicinity.

The three children by her first marriage were Sarah America, William Henry and Susan Tallulah McElbeen. William Henry, born in 1853, died unmarried in 1881. Sarah America, born in 1851, married Dr. D. L. Ricks, and at her death on December 16, 1901, left eight children, namely: Mary Tallulah, William L., Eunice, Ethel, Cora Lee, Leila, Josie and Hugh. Susan Tallulah, who was born May 29, 1855, and died in 1895, married Joel K. Hodges, and left four children—Mary Effie, Clara Mec, Lula Mc. and Joel K.

Mr. and Mrs. Avera have reared four children—Clara Lavinia, James Walter, John Randolph and Charles Young. James W. married Maggie McMullen, and their three children are Mary Mec, Walter and James West. John R. married Beulah Whittington, and they are the parents of seven children, named Kathleen, Mary Jane, Virginia, John Randolph, Beulah, Benjamin W. and Dougald McDonald. Charles Y. first married Florrie McMullen, who died leaving two children, Maggie Daisy and Charles Young; and for his second wife he married Bertice Smith, and has one son, Henry Randolph, and a daughter, Ruth.

Mrs. Avera has five great-grandchildren. Her granddaughter, Mary Effie Hodges, married Joseph Austin Walker and has three children, Mary Bealer, Emma and Susan Tallulah. Her grandson, William L. Hicks, married Estelle Benedict and has a son Charles. Three other of her granddaughters are married—Cora Hicks, who married Mathew Fleming, Mary Mec Avera, who married Walter T. Horne, and Kathleen Avera married Paul C. Smith. To be the head of such a family is a proud distinction. Mrs. Avera is a member of the Methodist church, as are all the children except one, who is a Baptist.

ERASMUS DOUGLAS WHITE. The town of Dublin, Georgia, has since the year 1896 known the operations of Erasmus Douglas White along varied lines of enterprise and activity. As a member of the firm of White & White, which carries on one of the principal business concerns in the city, he is prominent and popular, while he is not less a leading figure in the administration of the affairs of the city. He has served as a member of the council, as mayor *pro tem.* and has been in charge of the municipal water and lights departments, and in all those lines of activity he has shown himself an ideal citizen and an excellent man of business.

Erasmus Douglas White was born in Screven county, near what is now called Middleground Postoffice, on November 24, 1865, and he is the son of Erasmus Downing and Mary Elizabeth (Southwell) White, both of whom were born in Screven county. The father was born in 1836 and died in 1908, while the mother still lives and makes her home in Sylvania, Georgia. They became the parents of ten children, of which number two are deceased. The father was a farmer, and passed his life in that vocation, and he was also a veteran of the civil war, having served in the Confederate army.

The early education of Erasmus D. White was secured in the country schools of Screven county, and he alternated his school attendance with work on the home farm. With the close of his school period he gave himself to the continued work of farming and therein was ocenpied until he reached the age of thirty years, and it was about then that he first came to Dublin. His first association with the business interests in the city was in the capacity of a grocer, and after some little time he closed out his grocery interests and accepted a position as superintendent of the light and water plants of the city. He also served as clerk of the city council, and a period of seven years was passed in these connections. For four years he was buyer for the Four Seasons Department Store, and in 1909 he purchased the business of which he had been manager for some time, and with O. D. White, is now engaged in conducting that business. Mr. White is also interested in agricultural activities and owns some of the best farm land in the vicinity.

Mr. White has given valued service to the city in many capacities. As a member of the city council in 1907 and 1908 he had a voice in one of the most successful administrations that the city has known, and during that time served as mayor *pro tem*. He has served as chairman of the street commissioners and of the light and water committees, and in 1910 was elected to the state legislature from his district. During that time he was a member of the committee on appropriations, the judiciary committee, the education committee, and the banking committee. Mr. White is distinctly in favor of compulsory education, and his opinions and influence bear no little weight in all circles of thinking people in Dublin.

On April 11, 1888, Mr. White was married to Miss Sarah J. McGee, a daughter of William H. and Rebecca McGee of Screven county. To them eight children have been born, named as follows: Eugene D., Rufus Lester, Tessie Sibley Lamar, Christopher Gadson, Cathleen, Brigham McGee, and William Herschel.

Mr. and Mrs. White are members of the Methodist church, and bear an active and worthy part in the activities of that body. They are among the more prominent of the citizenship of Dublin, and in this city enjoy the friendship of a large circle of people, where they occupy a leading part in the best social activities of the community.

Hon. ALBERT M. DEAL. To have lived honorably and well, to have employed to advantage the talents with which he was endowed and to have served his fellow men with distinction in various capacities has been the record of Hon. Albert M. Deal, of Statesboro, Bulloch county, Georgia. Although still on the sunny side of the half-century mark he has fufilled all the duties of citizenship, has helped to frame the laws for his constituents and assists in their administration. His abilities have won him substantial recognition and in his district he is today considered a type of the honorable, dignified Southern gentleman.

Statesboro was not the place of nativity of Mr. Deal, although he has spent the greater portion of his life there. He was born in 1868 in the nearby community of Stilson, also in Bulloch county. His parents were John and Susan (McElveen) Deal, the former a native of Bulloch county and now deceased. He was the son of James Deal, who was born in eastern Tennessee and who came as a boy with his father, Simon Deal, to Burke county, Georgia.

The Deals are one of the old families of this county. The great-

great-grandfather of the subject of this sketch was John Deal, one of three brothers who came to America not long before the Revolutionary war and took possession of a little island in Chesapeake bay, a part of Virginia. They located on this detached bit of the commonwealth and it is still known as Deal's island. John Deal subsequently went to North Carolina and thence to eastern Tennessee.

Albert M. Deal was reared on the Deal place near Stilson and attended the local schools. He then took a two years' course in the academic department of Washington and Lee University at Lexington, Virginia, graduating in the schools of history and political science. He also studied law in that department of the same university, graduating in the class of 1896. This was the last class taught by John Randolph Tucker, who died the following year.

In 1896 Mr. Deal began the practice of his profession in Statesboro, the county seat of Bulloch county, and has been so engaged since that time. The bar of Statesboro is notable for its high standing in the matter of ability and for maintaining the best ethics of the profession, and among these gentlemen Mr. Deal achieved and has ever maintained a position of the highest standing.

His knowledge of law, coupled with no little ability as a public speaker and a wide acquaintance among the people naturally drew his attention toward public affairs. He was solicitor for the county court of Bulloch county and later was chosen as county commissioner, serving several years. For five years, beginning with 1900, he was a member of the state legislature, representing Bulloch county. In the general assembly much of his duties was concerned with the judiciary committee, of which he was a member. He was one of the first to see the advantage of utilizing the labor of prisoners in making good roads. He had passed a special act by which Bulloch county was enabled to follow this plan, in advance of the general legislation on that subject which was later enacted.

Although his profession is that of the law, Mr. Deal's largest interests are those of agriculture. Reared on the farm, he has never given up his interest in or direct connection with the farming industry. Incorporated under the name of John Deal Company, he and other members of his family own over five thousand acres of agricultural land near Stilson, on which they carry on extensive farming, operating principally in cotton.

In addition to this Mr. Deal's home place, a mile and a half south of Statesboro, is a fine farm of 154 acres. His residence here is an extensive and commodious structure of modern type, fitted up with every convenience. It is regarded as one of the most attractive country seats in Bulloch county. Nearby, on the east, are the buildings and lands of the first congressional district agricultural school, credit for the successful establishment of which at Statesboro was largely due to Mr. Deal's enterprise and public spirit. He headed the list with a subscription of $1,000 toward a fund for the purchase of three hundred acres of land to be given in order to assure the location of the school in this community. This fund grew to something over $100,000, contributed by citizens of Statesboro and of Bulloch county.

Mr. Deal holds membership in the Presbyterian church and in his social relations belongs to the Masonic fraternity and K. of P. He was married in Stilson to Miss Azalia Mae Strickland, a native of Bulloch county, and they have five children—Roscoff, Stothard, William J. S., Ruby Ann and Ewell Morgan.

COL. J. MONROE BUSSELL. The young gentleman whose name stands at the head of this brief review is one of the promising members of his profession and at the present time holds the office of city attorney of Rochelle. In no profession is there a career more open to talent than is that of the law, and in no field of endeavor is there demanded a more careful preparation, a more thorough appreciation of the absolute ethics of life or of the underlying principles which form the basis of all human rights and privileges. Unflagging application and determination fully to utilize the means at hand are the concomitants which insure personal success and prestige in this great profession, which stands as the stern conservator of justice; and it is one into which none should enter without a recognition of the obstacles to be encountered and overcome and the battles to be won, for success does not perch on the banner of every person who enters the competitive fray, but comes only as the legitimate result of capacity. Possessing the requisite qualities of the able lawyer, Mr. Bussell doubtless has a successful career ahead of him.

He is a native son of the state, his birth having occurred on March 13, 1885, near Fitzgerald, Irwin county, Georgia, on a farm. His parents were J. M. Bussell and Mrs. Frances C. Bussell whose maiden name was Hill. Amid the scenes of his birth Colonel Bussell passed the roseate days of early youth, there remaining until sixteen-years of age. He received his early education in the public schools and subsequently entered the school at Norman Park, where he studied for a time. He drank deeper of the "Pierian Spring" in the Georgia Normal College and the business institute at Douglas, Georgia, and then entered Mercer University where he prepared for the profession, to which he hoped to devote his life. He entered in 1907 and was graduated in 1911 with the well-earned degree of LL. B. While in college he was associated with no fraternity institution. Shortly after he located at Fitzgerald, where he remained but five months and then came to his present location at Rochelle, where he is engaged in general practice and where in the month of March he was elected to the office of city attorney, and re-elected in January, 1913.

Colonel Bussell is one of a large family of children. His brother, J. A. Bussell, has for forty years been a farmer near Fitzgerald; a sister, Mahalie E., is the wife of Charles F. Dement; Isabella is the wife of J. Walter Ballenger; Amie E. is the wife of J. M. Fountain; and Pollie M. married Y. S. Gibbs, all of the aforementioned gentlemen being farmers in the vicinity of Fitzgerald.

Colonel Bussell is a member of the Missionary Baptist church, South. He is popular in the community; well informed, cordial and engaging.

JOHN CALVIN MAY. A young man of excellent ability and sound judgment, John Calvin May is identified with one of the leading mercantile enterprises of Toombs county, as part owner, and the manager, of the Vidalia Furniture Company, of Vidalia, carrying on an extensive and highly remunerative business. A son of John May, he was born September 18, 1880, in Russell county, Alabama, near the state line, and not far from Columbus, Georgia.

John May was born in Sumter county, Georgia, October 5, 1844, and was there reared to agricultural pursuits. In 1876 he moved to Alabama, and is still a resident of that state. During the Civil war he enlisted in Company F, Sixth Georgia Volunteer Infantry, which became a part of Colquitt's Brigade, and with his command participated in many engagements of importance. On September 30, 1864, at Fort Harrison, Virginia, he received wounds of such serious nature that he was unfitted for further duty in the army. He was twice married. He married first, October 23, 1868, Georgia Powell, who passed to the life beyond December 22, 1870. He married second, Fannie Powell, and they are the parents of six children, as follows: Lilla, wife of E. W. McLendon, a prominent planter of Omaha, Georgia; John Calvin, the special subject of this brief sketch; Georgia died at the age of ten years; Charles W. died at the age of twenty years, having received injuries that proved fatal while playing football at the Auburn, Alabama, Polytechnic Institute; Marie, a successful teacher in Russell county, Alabama; and Louise, who married Thomas Kirbo, of Omaha, Georgia, where they live, he being an extensive farmer and merchant. These children all received excellent educational advantages, with the exception of John Calvin, who began to hustle for himself when young, instead of continuing his studies.

Leaving the home plantation when eighteen years of age, John Calvin May began life for himself as a clerk in a general store, and subsequently located at Omaha, Stewart county, where he bought out Lee Kirbo, and was engaged in mercantile business for eight years. Coming from there to Vidalia in 1910, Mr. May, in partnership with Charles E. Adams and John L. Sneed, organized the Vidalia Furniture Company, the only exclusive furniture house in this part of Toombs county, and has since been manager of the large business built up by this wide-awake firm. This company occupies a floor space of six thousand, four hundred feet, which is devoted entirely to the display of its stock, which is valued at $5,000.00, and includes house furnishings of every description, from the kitchen to the parlor and the bed-rooms.

Mr. May was postmaster at McLenden, Georgia, for two years, where he had a branch store, and was there at the same time, from 1903 until 1905, agent for the Seaboard Air Line Railroad Company. He belongs to the Vidalia Chamber of Commerce, an organization of energetic and progressive business men, and is vice president of the Vidalia Ice & Coal Company, in which he is the heaviest stockholder. Fraternally he is a member, and master, of Vidalia Lodge, No. 330, Ancient Free and Accepted Order of Masons, which consists of one hundred members, and in which he has passed all the chairs; a member of the Oriental Order of Pilgrim Knights; and is a member, and master of finance, of the Knights of Pythias.

Mr. May married first, February 5, 1902, Maggie W. Lee, a daughter of Mrs. Sallie J. Lee, of Concord, Pike county, Georgia. Of the five children born of their union, three died in infancy; John C. May, Jr., and Louis R. survive. Mr. May married second, June 29, 1908, Martha E. Powell, a young lady of sixteeen years, a daughter of Henry M. Powell, of Omaha, Georgia. Two children have been born to Mr. and Mrs. May, namely: Louis Ouida, who lived but one short year; and Marjorie Deane.

SILAS MORTON YOUNG. A life of industry and usefulness was that of Silas Morton Young, who for many years was a successful farmer resident of Brooks county and is now deceased. He represented some of the oldest and most prominent families of Georgia.

He was born in Lowndes county on April 3, 1850. The Young family has been identified with Georgia since before the Revolution. William Young, great-grandfather of Silas M., was appointed to the council of safety in Savannah on June 22, 1775, and three weeks later represented the town and district of Savannah in the meeting of the provincial congress. He was later a planter in Screven county. He

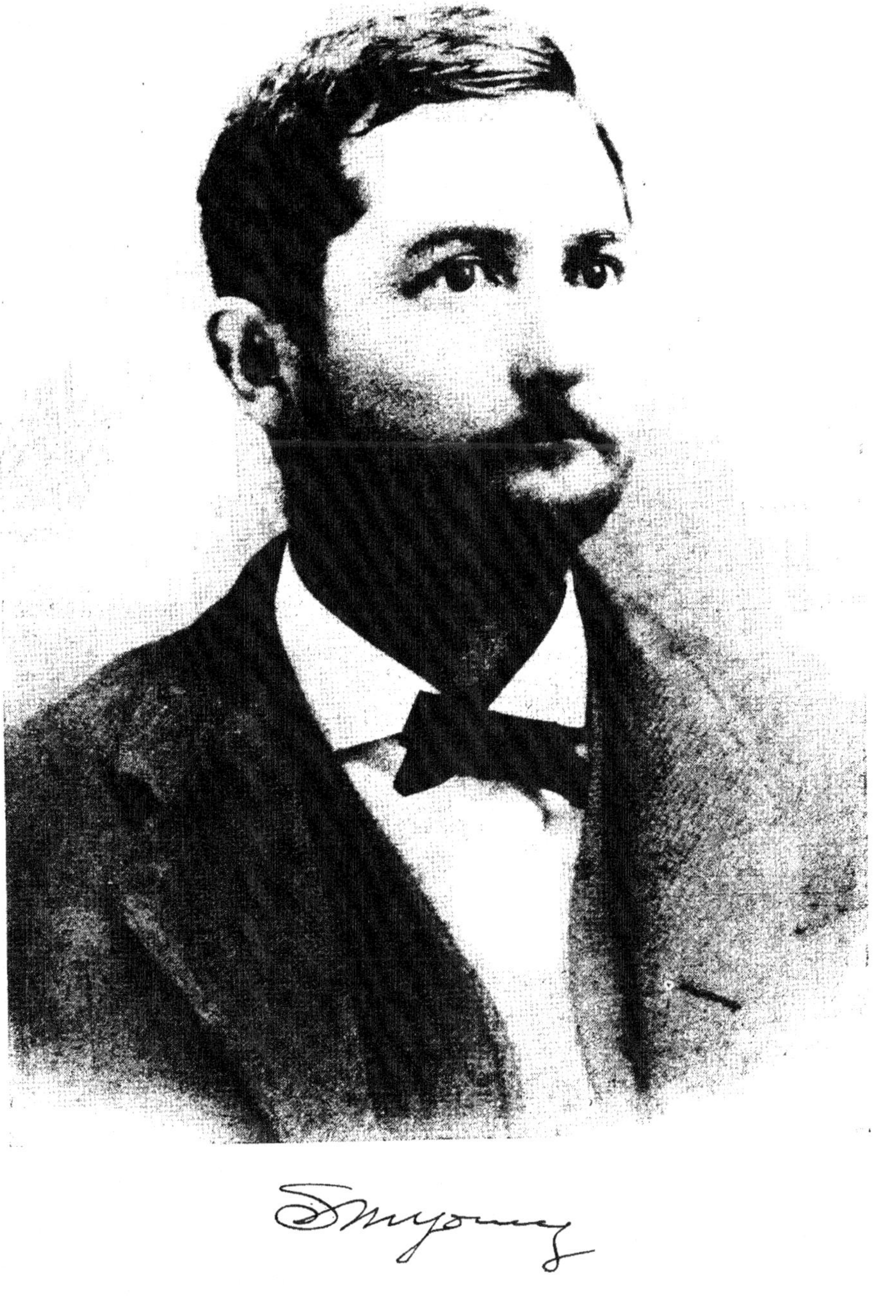

married Mary Henderson, and both he and his wife were buried on a hill overlooking the valley of the Ogeechee river in Screven county.

James Young, the grandfather, whose birthplace was probably in Screven county, during his young manhood moved to Bulloch county, where he bought land and was engaged in farming with a number of slaves. He afterwards bought the Jones homestead adjoining his first purchase, and there he and his wife spent their last days. He married Lavinia Jones, through whom another old Georgia family is properly introduced into this record. Her grandfather, Francis Jones, a native of Wales, who came to America in colonial times, lived for awhile in Virginia, and then became a pioneer settler of Burke county, Georgia. The deed to his land, given by the King of England and bearing the date of 1765, is now in possession of the descendant who owns the old homestead at Herndon, Burke county. Late in life Francis Jones, having given this original homestead to a son, moved to Screven county, where he bought a considerable tract of land. He finally went on a visit to Virginia, where he died and was buried. He was twice married, the first time in Wales to Mary Robins, and second to Elizabeth Huckabee. Three children were born of the first wife, and seven of the second, and one of the latter was James Jones, the father of Lavinia, who married James Young. James Jones was born in Burke county in 1764 and on September 27, 1791, married Elizabeth Mills. They settled in Bulloch county, where he bought land and was engaged in farming until his death, after which his widow sold the estate and with some of her children came to Lowndes county. James Young and wife reared ten children. The only one now living is Sarah A., the widow of James Oliver Morton (see sketch elsewhere).

Mathew Young, the son of James and father of Silas M., was a native of Bulloch county, where he was reared and married, and afterward came into southwest Georgia as one of the early settlers of Lowndes county. This was then a wilderness region, where wild game and Indians still abounded, and long before the railroads brought their attendant improvements and modern conditions. The cooking in the home was done at the fireplace, and the housewives carded, spun and wove the cloth with which all the family were dressed. Buying land in the southwest part of Lowndes county, Mathew Young improved a farm and lived upon it until his death. The maiden name of his wife was Emily Morton, who was born in Screven county, a daughter of Silas and Sabina (Archer) Morton and a sister of the late James Oliver Morton of Quitman (see sketch). She was a lineal descendant of the George Morton, an Englishman who joined the little colony at Leyden, Holland, and thence in the year 1622 crossed the Atlantic and settled among the other Pilgrims at Plymouth, Massachusetts. Through this Morton branch some members of the Young family can directly trace their ancestry to the oldest settlers of New England. Mr. and Mrs. Mathew Young reared seven children, named as follows: Michael, who settled in Nankin district of Brooks county; William, a soldier of the Civil war, who gave his life to the Southern cause on the field of battle; James, who served four years in the Confederate army and afterwards settled in Coryell county, Texas; Arminta, who married Isaiah Tillman of Lowndes county; Mathew, who settled in Hunt county; and Silas Morton, a brief sketch of whose career is now to be given.

After spending his youth on the family homestead he bought some land in the eastern part of Brooks county, where he resided until 1878, when he sold his place. He then bought a tract of a thousand acres six miles north of Quitman and engaged in farming and stock raising on an extensive and successful scale. He gradually added to his land holdings until at the time of his death they comprised upwards of twenty-five hundred acres, and he was one of the largest land owners of Brooks county. He had most of this land well improved and cultivated. A commodious residence, built in colonial style with broad verandas and as comfortable inside as it was attractive without, situated in a grove of fruit and native trees, was the home in which he spent the happiest years of his life, and where he died. The late Mr. Young was a director of the First National Bank of Quitman, was a Democrat in politics, and served his community several years as member of the school board. Fraternally he was affiliated with Shalto Lodge, F. & A. M.

Silas M. Young married, on October 17, 1871, Miss Ivy Johnson, who was born in what is now Brooks county and is still a resident on the homestead in the Morven district of this county. Her great-grandfather was Jonathan Johnson, who was a soldier of the Revolution and also fought in the Indian wars, and spent his last days in Tattnall county, Georgia. Her grandfather was Benjamin Johnson, Sr., who married Patsy Lane, and both were lifelong residents of Tattnall county. Benjamin Johnson, Jr., Mrs. Young's father, became one of the pioneer settlers of Brooks county, living there until his death in 1860, at the early age of twenty-seven. He married Mary Simmons, a native of Lowndes county. Her father, Ivy Simmons, a native of North Carolina, became a pioneer settler of Montgomery county, Georgia, where he resided for a time, and then came to Lowndes county and later to the east side of Brooks county, where he spent the rest of his life. He married Piety Joyce, who was a daughter of Henry Joyce, an early settler in South Georgia. Mary (Simmons) Johnson survived her husband more than half a century, her death occurring when she was eighty-seven years old. She reared two children, Mrs. Young and her brother, Benjamin, who now lives on the old Johnson homestead.

Mr. and Mrs. Young were the parents of the following children: Arminta Creech; Lane; Briggs: Morton; Rachel; Lavinia; James, who died at the age of twenty-one; and Annie, who died aged eighteen.

ATYS PERLETTE HILTON. In praising the founders of great enterprises, and lauding their farsightedness and their initiative, we often pass lightly over the work of a no less important class of men, that is those who take up the work which the pioneers have begun and carry it on successfully. They, too, must be men of force and executive ability. Such a man is Atys Perlette Hilton, cashier of the Commercial Bank of Dublin, Georgia. As yet only in his prime he has accomplished much, and is regarded as one of the strong men of his home city.

Atys Perlette Hilton was born in Sylvania, Georgia, on July 9, 1869. His father was James L. Hilton, of Taylor county, this state, and his mother, before her marriage, was Mary Lanier, a native of Screven county, Georgia. Mr. Hilton is the possessor of a good education, having received his preparatory education in the public schools of Sylvania, and completing his work at Emory College, one of the best colleges in the state of Georgia. After his graduation, which took place in 1895, and in which he was given the degree of A. B., Mr. Hilton taught school for a year and a half in his old home, Sylvania. He then came to Dublin and purchased the *Dublin Dispatch*. Here he gained his practical knowledge of journalism, a knowledge that afterwards aided him in making a success of his newspaper enterprises.

For a number of years Mr. Hilton worked for this newspaper, also for the consolidated *Dublin Courier-Dispatch,* and in 1907 he purchased the *Dublin Times.* In 1910 Mr. Hilton was appointed clerk of the city council, and he served in this position until 1911. With the organization of the Commercial Bank in 1911, in which Mr. Hilton took a very active part, he was elected cashier, and has held this office until the present time.

On March 14, 1899, Mr. Hilton was married to Luella Gilbert, of Albany, Georgia. She was the daughter of John and Lula Gilbert. Her father is now dead, but her mother is alive and makes her home with Mr. and Mrs. Hilton. In the fraternal world Mr. Hilton is a member of the Knights of Pythias.

CAPT. GEORGE ARCHIBALD JACKSON. Probably none of the colonial Georgia families through the different generations have given more worthy and efficient members to the varied professional, business and civic life of the state than the Jackson family, a prominent representative of which is Captain Jackson of Adel, Berrien county.

Of Scotch-Irish parentage, Benjamin Jackson, the founder of the family in Georgia, was a native of Virginia, whence he moved to North Carolina, settling in the Peedee river district, fought the British armies during the Revolution, and soon after that war came to Georgia and was one of the pioneers of Hancock county, while one of his brothers settled in Greene county. Benjamin was the great-grandfather of Captain Jackson.

John Jackson, grandfather, was born in Hancock county, Georgia, afterwards bought land in Screven county, employing a number of slaves in its cultivation, and resided there until his death, both he and his wife being buried in Sparta. On coming to Screven county soon after his marriage he bought land near the Ogeechee river, but from there moved to Hudson's Ferry, which continued his home until his death at the age of eighty-seven. John Jackson was a soldier of the War of 1812, so that the Jackson family has been represented in practically all of the great wars of the nation. The maiden name of his wife was Sarah Whitfield, and she was born in Putnam county, and her brother William lived in that county and another brother in Jackson county. Sarah (Whitfield) Jackson attained to a ripe old age, and she reared ten children, whose names were Thomas, John, William, George L., Andrew, Robert, Loreta, Sarah, Martha and one whose name is not now recalled.

Of this family, George Lewis Jackson was the father of Captain Jackson. He was born in Screven county on the 11th of February, 1811. During his youth he was converted and joined the Newington Missionary Baptist church, which he served as clerk for seven years, was licensed to preach in 1846 and the following year ordained at Newington. He was missionary for three years in the counties of Screven, Burke, Effingham and Chatham, and later spent many years of devoted service as pastor at different churches in these same counties, baptizing upwards of a thousand persons. He continued in the active work of his church until two weeks before his death, which occurred in his ninety-first year. His remains now rest in the Little Buckhead churchyard near Millen in Jenkins county.

Rev. George L. Jackson married Elizabeth Zetrower on April 18, 1836. She was born in Effingham county, a daughter of Solomon Zetrower, whose ancestors had come to Georgia with the Sulzbergers and settled at Ebenezer. She died in June, 1859, and left four children, namely: George A., Ann Lavinia, Solomon Z. and Julia E. Solomon Z. died unmarried; Ann L. married Dr. Thomas J. Ward of Burke county; and Julia E. married Dr. Edward Perkins, of Burke county.

George Archibald Jackson was born in Screven county, Georgia, May 21, 1839. During his youth he attended the public schools of Sylvania and also the high school. In November, 1860, he and 'some other associates formed a military company known as the Ogeechee Rifles. The Confederate records show that George A. Jackson was successively third, second and first lieutenant, with Andrew J. Williams as captain of the Rifles. Later the organization became Company D, then Company B, and finally Company K of the Twenty-fifth Georgia Infantry, C. S. A. The company was mustered into the Confederate service at Savannah on August 8, 1861. The Federal records show that George A. Jackson, captain of this company, was paroled in Augusta the 22d of May, 1865. From August, 1861, until the spring of 1863 Captain Jackson, with his command, was engaged in coast defense in Georgia, South and North Carolina, after which he joined the western army in Mississippi. With the fall of Vicksburg he went into Tennessee, participating at the battle of Chickamauga, and then fought Sherman's army all the way to Atlanta. When that city surrendered, he was ordered into Hood's command, with which he participated in the battles of Jonesboro, Franklin, Murfreesboro and Nashville. Captain Jackson was next sent into Mississippi and after a short time to South Carolina, being with the southern forces that interrupted Sherman's march at Branchville early in February, 1865, and also fought at Rays and Binache's bridges and at Orangeburg. At the last named place he was severely wounded and taken to the hospital at Columbia, being among those made prisoners when that city fell, and he was an eye witness of the burning of Columbia. In that city he remained in confinement until the end of the struggle a few weeks later, when his father sent a horse and cart to convey him back home. During his long and arduous service he was five times wounded, but not seriously until at Orangeburg.

As soon as he was able to get about on crutches, Captain Jackson commenced teaching school in Burke county and continued teaching four years. In the meantime he had married and bought a farm in Burke county, and there he lived and was engaged in the quiet pursuits of the soil for nearly twenty years. In 1884 he moved to Morgan county, and a year later to Walton county, where he bought a farm and resided until 1893. He was a resident of Irwin county about seven years, in 1900 came to Adel, living in town four years, and then bought a farm in Brooks county, on which he resided until 1909, since which date his residence has again been in Adel.

Captain Jackson has been well prospered in life and has a fine family. He was married on the 17th of January, 1866, to Lavinia Jamieson Zealy. Their marriage was the result of a rather romantic meeting, as will be mentioned. She was born at Orangeburg, South Carolina, October 8, 1843. Her grandfather, James Zealy, of English ancestry, was a native of Beaufort, South Carolina, as was also her father, Joseph T. Zealy. The maiden name of her grandmother was Rebecca Parsonage. Joseph T. Zealy, the father, learned the trade of carpenter, and was a carpenter and contractor of Orangeburg for a number of years. Later he acquired the then new art of photography, and had a gallery in Columbia and was in active business there until the city was captured and burned by the Federals on February 15, 1865. His home and gallery were both destroyed by the flames, but as soon as the bricks were cold he began cleaning them, and with this old material erected a building which he named the Phoenix. Financially he was at the very bottom, and with a capital of five dollars which he borrowed he engaged in mercantile business on a very modest scale. In a few years he was again fairly prosperous and finally sold out his business and lived retired.

His death occurred at the home of Captain and Mrs. Jackson in Walton county. The maiden name of his wife was Sarah Badger, who was born in Charleston, a daughter of James and Mary (Bell) Badger, both natives and lifelong residents of Charleston. Mrs. Zealey died in Charleston while on a visit to that city. She reared four children, Lavinia J., Anna, Richard and Mary G. Richard Zealey was a Confederate soldier, being a member of what was first known as the Richland Rifles, and later as Company A of the Fifteenth South Carolina Infantry. He was wounded in the battle of the Wilderness in June, 1864, and he died at home a month later as a result of these wounds. He had gone into the war when fifteen years old. His sister Lavinia, as a member of the Ladies Relief Corps, was one of the devoted southern women who carried the cheer of their presence and practical aid into the hospitals of the sick and wounded, and it was during these visits to the Columbia hospital that she met Captain Jackson, who soon after the war became her husband.

Mr. and Mrs. Jackson reared seven children: S. Annabel, Lizzie T., George L., Caroline W., Joseph Zealy, Henry Lee, Robert F., and a daughter Mamie who died at the age of seventeen months. S. Annabel married Jesse L. Watkins and has five children, Archie Jackson, William Mason, Jesse Bernard, Thomas S. and Winnie Bell. Lizzie T. married James Cooper, and their children are John Zealey, Lucille and Keith L. George married Miss Nannie Bracken and has one son, George Archibald. Caroline became the wife of Eugene M. Horn, and their children are Mattie C., Fannie E., E. M. and Lorell. Joseph L. married Evelyn Cunningham and has two children, Charles E. and Evelyn. Henry L., who married Alice Kent, has two children, Henry Lee and Flora A. Robert F. married Lela Wilkerson, and their children are Ouida and Robert Lee. The grandson, Archie J. Watkins, married Anna Miller, and their children, Archie Jackson, Jr., and Annabel, are the great-grandchildren of Captain and Mrs. Jackson. The captain and his wife are members of the Baptist church.

JOSEPH ZEALY JACKSON. Two of the sons of Capt. G. A. Jackson took up the profession of law and are now among the leading attorneys of Berrien county, the firm being J. Z. and H. L. Jackson at Adel.

The senior partner, Joseph Zealy Jackson, was born on the 27th of September, 1877, during the residence of his parents on a farm in Burke county. From his father and mother, who were both educated and cultured people, he received his first lessons and studied under their direction until he was about twelve years old, when he first attended the neighborhood school. He was also a student in the high school at Arabi in Dooly county, and later in a special school taught by Mrs. M. E. Fields at Sycamore, this state.

As the beginning of his practical career he learned the printing trade, and for about three years was employed in the offices of different newspapers. From that he turned his attention to law and entered Mercer University, where he was graduated in the law department in the class of 1900. For twelve years he has been actively engaged in his profession at Adel, and has gained recognition as an able lawyer, well versed in both the law and its practice. He has served five years as city attorney for Adel. In 1901 he prepared the code of ordinances for the town and revised it in 1912. In politics he is a democrat.

Mr. Jackson has fraternal affiliations with Adel Lodge No. 310, F. & A. M., Daisy Chapter No. 82, R. A. M., Malta Commandery No. 16, K. T., and is also a member of Adel Lodge No. 178 of the Knights of Pythias. He and his wife are members of the Methodist church. As mentioned in the sketch of his father, Mr. Jackson was married to Miss Evelyn Cunningham, and their children are Charles E., and Evelyn.

HENRY LEE JACKSON, son of Capt..George A. Jackson and junior partner in the law firm of J. Z. and H. L. Jackson at Adel, was born on the home farm in Burke county in 1879.

Reared on a farm, his father and mother being his first teachers, he continued his education in the public schools. He remained at home until twenty-one years of age, when he went to Macon and there learned the trade of carpentering, which he followed six years. He then took up the study of law and entered the law department of Mercer University, where he was graduated in 1908. In that year he formed the partnership with his brother, and their combined ability has brought them a large and successful practice. Mr. Henry L. Jackson affiliates with Adel Lodge No. 310, F. & A. M., and he and his wife are members of the Baptist church. He married Miss Alice Kent, and they are the parents of two children, Henry Lee and Flora A.

REV. DAVID JESSE MILLER. Coming from pioneer and Revolutionary stock, Rev. David Jesse Miller is distinguished not only for the honored ancestry from which he is descended, but for his own good life and works, having been intimately associated with the development and advancement of the agricultural and industrial prosperity of Ware county, and being now a member of the board of county commissioners, and an esteemed resident of Waycross. A son of Capt. David J. Miller, he was born, November 11, 1847, near Waresboro, Georgia. His great-grandfather, William Miller, presumably a native of South Carolina, served as a soldier in the Revolutionary war, and afterwards settled in Georgia, becoming a pioneer of Bulloch county, where he spent his closing years of life.

Henry Miller, Mr. Miller's grandfather, spent his early life in Bulloch county, Georgia. Subsequently locating, in pioneer times in Ware county, he bought land near Waresboro, and on the farm which he cleared and improved resided until his death, at the advanced age of eighty-three years, his body being then laid to rest in Kettle Creek cemetery, beside that of his wife. He reared four sons, William, Stephen, Henry, and David J., and two daughters, Nancy and Susan.

Capt. David J. Miller was born on the home farm in Bulloch county, Georgia, being there reared amid pioneer scenes, for in the days of his youth Ware county was a frontier region, over which the Indians roamed at will, frequently proving very troublesome to the white settlers. Joining the militia when young, he was made captain of a company, which he led against the savages. There were then two forts in this vicinity, one being located at Waresboro, and the other on the present site of Waycross, and whenever the Indians were on the war path the women and children took refuge in these forts, while the men pursued and fought the redskins. During all of his earlier life there were no railroads in the state, and he used to market his cotton and surplus farm products in Centerville and Saint Marys, fifty miles away, journeying there and back with teams, on his return trip being loaded with whatever merchandise was needed for family use, and for which he had invested the proceeds received from his cotton and other farm productions. He was quite successful as an agriculturist, and resided on his homestead until his death, at the age of seventy-two years. He married Loanza Dyer, who was born in Tattnall county, Georgia, and died in Bulloch county, when sixty-seven years old. The union of Captain and Mrs. Miller was blessed

David J. Miller

by the birth of twelve children, as follows: William, Henry, Thomas, James, David J., Stephen F., Nancy, Mary, Caroline, Susan, Serena, and Anna.

Leaving home at the age of twenty-one years, David Jesse Miller purchased land in Ware county, near Waycross, and for a few years successfully carried on general farming. While thus occupied he became interested in the turpentine industry, which was one of great importance and value, and, having removed to Waycross, was engaged in the manufacture of turpentine for ten years. Of late, however, Mr. Miller has devoted his time and energies to his official duties, since 1908 having rendered efficient service as county commissioner, and to his ministerial work, in which he has been actively engaged for upwards of thirty years. Mr. Miller united with the Methodist Episcopal church as a youth, and in 1879 was licensed as a local preacher, and has since preached in various places in Ware and near-by counties, being an effective and popular speaker.

Rev. Mr. Miller married, in 1869, Serena C. Sweat, who was born, in October, 1847, on a farm near Waycross, being a daughter of James and Mary (Blackburn) Sweat. Mrs. Miller passed to the life beyond in February, 1910, leaving five children, namely: Mollie, who married J. L. Stephens, and has eight children; Cora, wife of A. J. Williams, has seven children; Lovina married J. P. Lide, and they are the parents of five children; Della, wife of W. W. Webster, has four children; and James T., the only son, married Minnie Davidson, and they have eight children.

GEORGE PERRY LEGGETT. The ex-mayor of Adel in Berrien county is one of the progressive and enterprising young citizens of south Georgia, and by his ability and industry has acquired influence and leadership in his community. Mr. Leggett is a fine type of the young men who now and in subsequent years must share the increasing responsibilities for the development and welfare of their state.

George Perry Leggett was born at Naylor in Lowndes county on the 31st of July, 1879. His father, George W. Leggett, a native Georgian, was reared on a farm and was a young man at the time of the Civil war. Enlisting in one of the Georgia regiments, he went to Virginia and saw a long and arduous service in General Longstreet's corps, doing a soldier's duty until the close of hostilities. Afterwards locating at Naylor, he was engaged in farming there until 1890, then bought a farm in Taylor county, Florida, but three years later became one of the first citizens of the newly established town of Adel, where he engaged in the mercantile business a number of years. At the present writing he is farming near Milltown in Berrien county. The maiden name of his wife was Mattie Perry, who was born at Troupville, the one-time county seat of Lowndes county. Her father, William R. Perry, who was a pioneer settler in Lowndes county, afterward moved to Belleville, Florida, where he spent the rest of his days. Mattie (Perry) Leggett died in 1896. She was the mother of two sons, the younger, John Lewis, dying at the age of eighteen.

George P. Leggett received his education in the public schools of Naylor, in Florida and at Adel, during the residence of the family at these different places. As a boy he also assisted his father in the management of the store, and at the age of nineteen began his independent career in the railroad service, with which he has been identified ever since. His first experience was in the station at Adel, and a year later he was appointed station agent for the Georgia & Alabama at Rhine, where he remained a year. He then secured a transfer to the Adel station on the Georgia Southern & Florida line, and faithfully performed his duties there for seven years. At the end of that period Mr. Leggett took an excursion into other lines of business, and for three and a half years conducted a lumber yard at Adel. He then returned to railroad service as joint agent at Adel for the Georgia & Florida and the South Georgia & West Coast railways. This office has been under his management to the present time.

Mr. Leggett served two terms as mayor of Adel, and previously served as member of the town council. In politics he is a Democrat. He affiliates with the lodges of the Knights of Pythias and the order of Odd Fellows at Adel, and is one of the popular men of this community. He was married in 1900 to Miss Eva Rebecca Dopson, who was born at McRae in Telfair county, a daughter of Robert and Rebecca Dopson. Mr. and Mrs. Leggett are the parents of one son, named Julian.

LUCIUS M. STANFILL. From a farm hand at wages of three dollars a month to one of the most prosperous and enterprising merchants and bankers of Lowndes county, is a brief statement of the business career of Lucius M. Stanfill, of Hahira. To his own industry and integrity he has added an implicit trust in Providence and devoted service of his Lord, and he believes that his prosperity has come as a reward of his faith and works.

A native of Brooks county, where he was born on the 4th of January, 1864, he was the youngest child of Jesse John and Rebecca Miley (Tyson) Stanfill. It is thought that his father was born in one of the Carolinas. He was a carpenter by trade, following that occupation in Brooks county for some years. He was a soldier of the South in the war between the states, and his death occurred not long after he had returned from the front. The mother was a native of Thomas county, belonging to a pioneer family of that section. Her children were Joseph T., Mattie S. and Lucius M., and after the father's death she courageously managed to keep her family together until they became independent. Her death occurred at the age of fifty-two.

Lucius M. was a child when his father died, and as soon as old enough began earning his own living and contributing to the support of his mother. His first work was as a boy on a farm, getting $3 at the end of each month of labor. After several years spent in this way, he cropped land on the shares, and thus gradually got ahead a little. When eighteen years old he was converted and has ever since been a devout member of the Missionary Baptist church. Believing that all blessings come from the Lord, after his marriage he resolved to give a tenth of his profits to the Master's work. His wife did the same, taking a tenth of the proceeds from her poultry, dairy and garden. This plan had hardly been put into effect when prosperity came upon them and has been increasing ever since.

For seven years he operated the Richard Scraggs farm in Brooks county, and then came to Lowndes county, where he continued farming until 1895. In that year he became a cotton buyer for A. P. Brantley & Company, and also agent for the products of the Valdosta Guano Company. In 1901 he organized the Farmers Supply Company, of which he is half owner and superintendent, A. J. Strickland of Valdosta being president of the company. This company has at Hahira a large store for an extensive stock of general merchandise—furniture, stoves, etc., and also a fire-proof warehouse for a stock of wagons, carriages and farm implements. Besides this enterprise, Mr. Stanfill in 1911 erected in Hahira a two-story building, forty by eighty feet, with pressed-brick front, which is one of the finest business blocks in south

Georgia, and there established a large business under his own name and proprietorship. His stock comprises pianos, sewing machines, etc., and in a warehouse he handles such farm implements as are not carried by the Farmers Supply Company. Through these two concerns the customers of town and a large surrounding territory are supplied with nearly everything used at the home and farm.

At the organization of the Bank of Hahira in 1905, Mr. Stanfill became one of the directors, and since 1911 has held the office of president. He is owner of large tracts of land about Hahira as well as town property, and his influence in business and in citizenship extends to many directions. He is a director of the Georgia, Alabama & Western Railway, and is president of the Hahira Bell Telephone Company. During his boyhood he had little opportunity to gain an education, and during his own prosperous career has done all he could to extend the facilities of schools to the children of his generation. He has served as a member of the town school board and council, and is one of the trustees of the Oak Lawn Academy in Milltown. In national politics he is a Democrat, and is one of the zealous workers for the cause of prohibition. He has served as elector at large on the last two Prohibition presidential tickets.

Mr. Stanfill was married in 1885 to Miss Martha Belote, who was born in Lowndes county, a daughter of William and Martha (Barfield) Belote. They are the parents of three children, Minnie Lee, Mary Avey and Stephen. The daughter Minnie is the wife of B. L. Wilkinson, and they have a daughter named Mary Grace.

For more than a quarter of a century Mr. and Mrs. Stanfill have lived lives of trust in divine beneficence. The quality of his belief is well illustrated in the lesson he draws from the following incident. A number of years ago, while working among his bees and after hiving two swarms, he gave an orphan boy the choice of either swarm. Later in the same season, from the swarm which he kept, he took first $6 worth and later $2.80 worth of honey. From his other hives he got only a little honey from some and none at all from others. In this respect men are like bees, says Mr. Stanfill, that some will gather much, others little, and some nothing at all. In his own case he is assured that Providence has bestowed upon him the many rewards of a prosperous career.

EDWARD JOSEPH SMITH, M. D. The senior member of the medical profession at Hahira, Dr. Smith is both a successful and skillful physician and also a progressive citizen and busines man of this community.

Edward Joseph Smith is a native of Leesburg, South Carolina, where he was born October 20, 1872. The family were originally of Virginia, but the grandfather Smith was probably born in Edgecomb county, South Carolina, and spent most of his life there as a planter, operating his lands with slave labor. Grant S. Smith, father of the doctor, was born in Edgecomb county, and being a young man at the time of the war between the states he enlisted in a South Carolina regiment of cavalry, under the command of General, later Senator, Butler. His regiment was part of the Army of Northern Virginia, and he experienced a long and varied service in this principal seat of the war, including the Gettysburg campaign and the battles and movements about Richmond and Petersburg. He was never captured nor wounded, though several horses were shot from under him. When the war was over he came to Georgia and established a store and stock yard at Augusta, where he was successfully engaged in business until 1875. Failing health then caused him to sell out, and he spent his last days at Leesburg, South

Carolina, where he died in 1879. He married Elizabeth Crout, and she is still living, her home being in Augusta. She is a native of South Carolina, and her father, Uriah Crout, also born in that state and of German parentage, was a planter in the vicinity of Leesville until after the war, when he was engaged in mercantile business at Leesville, and lived to the ripe age of eighty-nine years. The three children of Grant S. Smith and wife are: Inez, the widow of W. D. Van Pelt, a former attorney at Augusta; Edward Joseph; and Harry L., who is in the service of the C. & W. C. Railroad Company at Augusta.

Dr. Smith spent his youth in Augusta, where he attended the public schools and Horton Institute. Early in life he made choice of medicine for his career, and in preparation he entered the medical department of the State University, where he was graduated M. D. in April, 1899. For the first two years he was engaged in practice at Augusta, and located at Hahira in 1901. He has a large practice and is a member of the county and state medical societies. The doctor is also secretary and treasurer of the Georgia, Alabama & Western Railroad Company. In politics he is a Democrat, and has been a member of the town council two years. His fraternal associations are with Pine Camp No. 265, W. O. W.

June 1, 1898, Dr. Smith married Miss Nellie Regina Mahoney, who was born in Augusta, a daughter of John J. and Mary Mahoney. Dr. Smith and wife are parents of three children: Virgil C., John Raymond and Dorothy.

JOHN A. HODGES. A native and lifelong resident of Lowndes county, the owner of many broad and fertile acres near Hahira, John A. Hodges has succeeded in life through ability and well timed industry, and has long been a prosperous and influential citizen of his community. He was born in Lowndes county on the 11th of February, 1849, and represents one of the old and prominent families of south Georgia.

His grandfather Nathan Hodges was, so far as known, a native Georgian, and about 1828 moved from Tattnall county to Lowndes county, settling some five miles south of the present site of Hahira. Lowndes county then comprised a much greater territory than at present, with Franklinville the county seat, which was subsequently transferred to Troupville. Nearly all the land was under state ownership, and directly from the commonwealth Grandfather Hodges bought a lot of four hundred and ninety acres, nearly all timber. His family were sheltered under tents while he was erecting the first log-cabin home. For many miles around no mills had yet been built. He had brought with him a steel mill, operated by hand, for grinding grain, and this became such an institution that the neighbors brought their packs of corn long distances to be ground into meal. The date of the Hodges settlement was also several years previous to the final expulsion of the Florida Indians, and it was a not infrequent occurrence that marauding bands crossed the border and disturbed the south Georgians. A log fort stood on the grandfather's place during these years, and it several times sheltered the inhabitants of this vicinity while hostile redskins were near. On this old homestead the grandfather and his wife spent their last years. They reared eight children, three sons and five daughters, namely: John, Daniel, Aleck, Elsie, Eliza, Caroline, Maria and Polly.

Of this family John was the father of John A. Hodges. He was born in Tattnall county, being nineteen years old when his parents came to Lowndes county. He was one of the militia or minutemen of the settlement during the period of Indian strife, and also participated in the final struggles that broke the power of the red men. These occurred in 1836, in which year there were three Indian battles, including the well-known conflict at Brush Creek, when the Indians made their last stand. On attaining his majority John Hodges bought a lot of land consisting of four hundred and ninety acres, and gave what was then considered a very good price for it, $50, a sum which would hardly buy one acre now. Not a railroad had yet come into this region. Marketing was difficult, and for several years the cotton from his and other plantations was hauled by team and wagon to Newport, Florida. He established on his farm one of the old cotton gins operated by mule power, its capacity during a long day's run being half a bale. He improved and developed a considerable quantity of land in this vicinity, and continued his residence there until his death in 1875 at the age of sixty-six years. The maiden name of his wife was Julia Ann Boyd, and she was a daughter of Banar and Sarah Boyd, also early settlers of Lowndes county. Her death occurred in 1872. Her twelve children were named as follows: Hardy, Polly Ann, Sarah J., Thomas B., Susan, George, John A., Julia, Laura, Charlotte, Henry B. and Samuel H.

The pioneer scenes which have been above referred to had not yet vanished from this section of Georgia during the childhood and youth of John A. Hodges, and his memory goes back to the time when deer, wild turkey and other wild game were plentiful among the sparse settlements. His mother did all her cooking at a fireplace, no stoves having yet been introduced, and she carded, wove and spun the wool or cotton or flax with which she dressed all the family in homespun. In such a household John A. acquired early habits of industry. His assistance when a boy was given to the farm labor, and when the weather did not permit outdoor labor he helped his mother at the wheel or loom. He is one of few men living who were once skilled in the old-fashioned art of spinning and weaving. Mechanical skill was one of nature's gifts to him, and though he never learned a trade for a regular vocation he had a practical craft for various lines of handiwork, and during his youth earned all his spending money through this skill, never calling on his father to supply him a cent. At the age of fourteen he made a substantial but plain saddle, which he sold for $10. Buying some brass tacks, he ornamented his next saddle, and secured $15 for it. He also made shoes.

When he was twenty-one he began his career as an independent farmer by working a tract of his father's land for half the crop. Four years later he bought two hundred and fifty acres at $2 an acre, paying two hundred in cash and obligating himself for the balance with twenty per cent interest. It took him six years to clear himself of the interest and principal. At his father's death he inherited land worth $300 and also bought the share of a sister. He later bought a tract of six hundred acres a mile north of Hahira, going in debt $2,400 with interest at fifteen per cent. It is on this latter land that he has spent most of his career as a general farmer. He has long been known as a practical farmer, one who could produce profits from his land, and besides his own prosperity his example has been valuable to the general welfare of this agricultural region. In 1912 Mr. Hodges moved to an attractive modern home which he had built on land adjoining the town of Hahira. His land holdings embrace upwards of fourteen hundred acres in the vicinity of Hahira, and for this material evidence of prosperity he owes all to his own efforts and good management.

At the age of thirty-two Mr. Hodges married Miss Susan L. Lawson. She is a native of Lowndes county, and a daughter of John and Mary A. (Sineth) Lawson. On the paternal side she is descended from Ashley Lawson (see sketch of Irvine and L. F. Lawson). Her mother was a daughter of William and Mary Sineth. The following children compose the family of Mr. and Mrs. Hodges: Lewis, Corine, Perry (deceased), Slater, Edward, Irene, Louell, Robert T. and Bevins. Lewis married Sally Marshall and has two children, Anna Lee and John Lewis. Corine is the widow of James Hall.

JAMES B. BAGLEY, M. D. Noteworthy for his keen intelligence, professional knowledge and skill, James A. Bagley, M. D., is meeting with excellent success as a physician, since locating at Waycross having acquired an excellent patronage. A native of Georgia, he was born, January 16, 1866, in Ware county, which was likewise the birthplace of his father, Berrien Bagley.

His paternal grandfather, Ransom Bagley, was a Virginian born and bred. As a young man he removed to North Carolina, being accompanied by two of his brothers, one of whom settled in Raleigh, that state, while the other brother located in Alabama. He, himself, came to Georgia, and having purchased land in Ware county carried on general farming with the help of slaves for a number of years, but subsequently removed to Florida, where he spent the remainder of his life.

Born in Ware county in 1815, Berrien Bagley was reared to agricultural pursuits, and when ready to begin life for himself bought land lying within three miles of the parental estate, and continued life as a farmer. There were no railways in the state when he was young, and he was forced to haul the surplus productions of his farm with teams to Savannah, a distance of one hundred miles, but ere his death there was a railroad within six miles of his home. Honest, industrious, and a good manager, he was very successful in his calling, acquiring a competency. On the farm which he improved he spent his last days, passing away in January, 1908, at the venerable age of eighty-three years. He married Eliza Thompson, a daughter of Rev. Henry Thompson, for many years a Methodist Episcopal preacher in Ware county. She passed to the higher life, aged eighty years. Of the twelve children born into their home, ten grew to years of maturity, namely: Mary J., Rachel, Julia, John W., Amanda, James B., Roan H., Thomas Berrien, Francis, and Ella.

Brought up on the home farm, James B. Bagley attended school as opportunity offered, in the meantime becoming intimately acquainted with farm work of all kinds. When he was eighteen years old his father gave him one hundred acres of land, and he began his career as an independent farmer. Having been trained to habits of industry and thrift, and well drilled in the art and science of agriculture, he succeeded from the start, and continued a tiller of the soil until 1892. Desirous then of gratifying a long cherished ambition, Mr. Bagley began the study of medicine in the Atlanta Medical School, from which he was graduated with the class of 1894. Immediately beginning the practice of his profession at Millwood, Ware county, Dr. Bagley continued there fifteen years, meeting with unquestioned success. Locating at Waycross in 1909, he has here built up a large and remunerative patronage, the people roundabout having great confidence in his skill and ability.

Dr. Bagley married, when a youth of eighteen summers, Miss Lucinda Meeks, who was born in the northern part of Clinch county, Georgia, eight miles from Pearson, a daughter of Mr. and Mrs. William Meeks. Four children have been born to the Doctor and Mrs. Bagley, namely: William Francis, now, in 1913, studying medicine; James Wesley; Daniel English; and Loney. The Doctor and his two

J. B. Bagley, M.D.

older sons are engaged in agricultural pursuits, conducting a stock and poultry farm near Beach. The Doctor and his wife are consistent members of the Primitive Baptist church, and their two older sons are affiliated by membership with the Methodist Episcopal church.

OLIN STEWART MCCOY. Numbered among the substantial and well-to-do residents of Cordele is Olin Stewart McCoy, who, as proprietor of McCoy's Steam Laundry, is conducting a lively and prosperous business. He was born, February 27, 1869, in Houston county, Georgia, which was also the birthplace of his parents, Meredith and Mary Emma (Blount) McCoy, neither of whom is now living. His father, who served as a member of a company of Georgia Cavalry in the Civil war, was for many years a merchant and farmer in Houston county, but spent his last days in Macon, whither he settled after selling his farm. He reared eight children, all of whom are living.

Completing his studies in the common schools of his native county, Olin Stewart McCoy accompanied the family to Macon, Georgia, when about nineteen years old, and there began life for himself in a mercantile establishment. In March, 1896, when the town of Fitzgerald was organized, in Ben Hill county, he located in the place, and was there a resident for five years. Coming to Cordele in 1901, Mr. McCoy was engaged in the bottling business until March, 1904, when he purchased his present steam laundry plant, which had been here established in 1902. Under his efficient management, the laundry is being conducted most successfully, employing about fifteen people, and being well patronized. The laundry is now housed in a building thirty-six feet by eighty feet, and is fully equipped with modern machinery of all the kinds required in an establishment of this kind. The business is rapidly increasing in size and value, and in order to meet its demands Mr. McCoy is now considering the erection of a brick building much larger than the present plant.

Mr. McCoy married Mae Terry, a daughter of James J. and Ida (Parker) Terry, natives respectively of Canada and Michigan. Mr. and Mrs. McCoy have two children, namely: Mary Lois, born in 1903; and Olin Terry, born in 1907. Mrs. McCoy is a member of the Baptist church, and is bringing up her children in the same religious faith.

IVY MILTON POWELL. A man of keen foresight and unquestioned business ability and judgment, Ivy Milton Powell occupies a conspicuous position among the enterprising and influential citizens of Cordele, as owner of the Cordele Electric Light & Power Company, and of Powell's Garage, being actively associated with two of the leading industrial enterprises of this part of Crisp county. A native of North Carolina, he was born, September 16, 1866, in Clinton, Sampson county, being a son of Milton and Elizabeth Powell, lifelong residents of North Carolina. He is one of a family of eight children, six sons and two daughters, as follows: J. W., who died in North Carolina; G. H., a miller in North Carolina; I. W., engaged in farming in his native state; O. J., engaged in mercantile business in North Carolina; Rev. L. J., a Baptist minister, now located in Grafton, West Virginia; Ivy Milton; Neely, wife of E. Williamson, a North Carolina farmer; and Livingston, who died, aged about thirteen years.

Growing to manhood in his native state, Ivy Milton Powell determined as a young man to try the hazard of new fortunes, and in his quest came to Georgia. About 1889 he took up his residence in Cordele, and has since acquired distinction along various lines of enterprise. In 1897, when the service of the Cordele Electric Light & Power Company was very unsatisfactory, Mr. Powell purchased the plant from the city, and has since so thoroughly improved and equipped it that it has now reached a high state of efficiency. For the past five years Mr. Powell has been actively engaged in the automobile business, for a year occupying his present location, his garage being a fully equipped building, sixty-two feet by one hundred twelve and one-half feet, with a cement floor. In this line he has built up a substantial business, handling both the Olds and the Overland machines, automobiles of the highest type of construction, and eminently satisfactory to all buyers. Mr. Powell is also an extensive landholder, owning a farm of one thousand, eight hundred and thirty-six acres adjoining the city.

Mr. Powell married, in 1890, Beulah Johnson, a daughter of William Johnson, of Worth county, Georgia, and they are the parents of three children, namely: Edwin, born in 1895; Ivy, born in 1900; and Louise, born in 1905. Mr. and Mrs. Powell are both Baptists in religion.

JOSEPH JACKSON COOPER, one of the best-known merchants of Vienna, Georgia, is successfully carrying on the business established and conducted by him in 1897. Born in Dooly county on January 16, 1869, he is the son of John C. and Mary (Moring) Cooper. The father was born and reared in Baldwin county, Georgia, while the mother is a native of Dooly county. John C. Cooper served the South during the Civil war, fighting with the Baldwin Blues, Fourth Georgia Regiment, and was captured just before the close of the war. He was a prisoner of war at Governor's island, New York, and participated in many of the hottest engagements of the struggle. After the close of the war he returned to his farm in Dooly county and there passed the remainder of his life. Mr. and Mrs. Cooper were the parents of four children: Lizzie, married to J. W. Bozemore, a farmer in Dooly county; J. B., also a farmer in Dooly county; Annie, the wife of J. B. Foreham, and the subject, Joseph Jackson.

The early life of Joseph Jackson Cooper was passed as a helper on the farm of his father and an attendant of the schools of the community wherein he was reared. He also attended the high school in Snow Springs. When he was twenty-two years of age he entered the service of the F. H. Bland Company, dealers in dry-goods, and after some time went from that firm to Pine Hurst, Georgia, with the firm of the Fullington-Barfield Company. He advanced rapidly with that firm and the last three years of his connection with them was as secretary and treasurer of the concern. In January, 1897, the young man decided to launch out into business on his own responsibility, and he accordingly located in Vienna, opening up an establishment as dealer in dry-goods, house furnishings, etc. He is the sole owner of the business, and in the years that have elapsed since its establishment, it has grown apace, expanding and reaching out into hitherto untapped channels of trade. The store occupies a two-story brick building at the corner of Union and Third streets, the property being owned by Mr. Cooper, who is also the owner of a handsome residence erected since his location in Vienna. Mr. Cooper has been able to give some of his time to civic matters, despite his necessarily busy life, and has served as a member of the city council, of the board of health, and is now a member of the school board. His presence on anything of a like nature is proof of honest effort being expended in the interests of the community, and Mr. Cooper has proved himself a citizen of a high order in the years of his residence in Vienna.

On October 2, 1896, Mr. Cooper was united in marriage with Miss Ella Lytle, the daughter of Thomas T. Lytle and M. T. (Smith) Lytle.

Sincerely yours,
Jas. M. Griggs

One child has been born to them, Lillian, now eight years of age. All members of the family are affiliated with the Methodist Episcopal church of Vienna.

DE WITT BUTLER THOMPSON has been a resident of Vienna for about twenty-one years, having come to this city in 1890. He is a native of the state of Georgia, born in Houston county on September 4, 1861, and is the son of Steven L. and Margaret Elizabeth Thompson, both of Houston county.

Mr. Thompson was educated in the common schools of his county and remained under the care and guardianship of his parents until he was sixteen, at which early age he took service with the Macon & Brunswick Railroad as water boy. He continued in railroad work in various capacities and eventually became a section foreman. After fifteen years in the employ of the Macon & Brunswick road he severed his connection with the company, and established the merchandise business which he is now conducting. He has prospered as a merchant, and has been the author of splendid accomplishments in industrial lines. To Mr. Thompson is ascribed the credit for the building of the first cotton gin in Vienna, and he was the first man to introduce the cylinder bail idea in this section of the country. He is the owner of a large quantity of real estate and owns the store building where he carries on his merchandise business. It is a fine up-to-date store, eighty by eighty-eight feet in size, and is well equipped and thoroughly modern. In addition he conducts a large warehouse where they handle cotton, hay, feed and other produce. He also owns his beautiful home in Vienna.

Mr. Thompson is a man who has taken his full share of the civic responsibilities of the community, and has served as alderman on the city board for two terms. He is always ready and willing to assume a generous part of the burdens of the communal life, and has ever acquitted himself as a most exemplary citizen in the long years of his identification with the business life of Vienna. The Thompson family has ever shared in the responsibilities of worthy citizens, and the father of Mr. Thompson, as well as two of his brothers, served their state in the years of strife between the North and the South.

Mr. Thompson was married on August 5, 1886, to Miss Margaret Daugherty, of Isle of Wight county, Georgia. She died on September 12, 1888, and on March 20, 1889, Mr. Thompson was united in marriage with Miss Jessie Crumpton of Florida. Six children have been born to them: Maggie, aged twenty-one years; Steven Milton, aged twenty; Mary, sixteen years of age; Sadie, aged thirteen years; Annie Lou, eleven years old, and D. B., Jr., aged five years.

Mrs. Thompson is a member of the Methodist Episcopal church, and is identified with the various organizations of that church.

HON. JAMES MATHEWS GRIGGS. A man of superior judgment and rare discrimination, thoroughly progressive and public-spirited, Hon. James Mathews Griggs, late of Dawson, attained distinction not only for his loyal citizenship and unquestioned legal ability, but for the services he rendered his fellow-men as a public servant. Summoned from the scene of his earthly endeavors while yet in the midst of life's most useful and honorable activities, his death having occurred January 5, 1910, his name will be held in loving remembrance and lasting honor in the annals of Terrell county. A native of Georgia, he was born, March 29, 1861, in La Grange, Troup county, of Welsh ancestry, being fifth in direct line of descent from the immigrant ancestor, his lineage being thus traced: William,[1] John,[2] Wesley,[3] Augustus Franklin[4] and James Mathews.[5]

William[1] Griggs was born and reared in Wales. In early manhood he came to America, accompanied by a brother who settled in New England, while he located in Virginia. During the Revolution he fought with the Colonists in their struggle for freedom, after which he settled permanently near Norfolk, Virginia, where he spent his remaining years.

John[2] Griggs was born and educated in Virginia, but when ready to begin life for himself migrated to Georgia, locating in Hancock county, which was his home for many years. He died, however, in Harris county, and his body was there buried on his son's plantation. The maiden name of his wife was Rebecca Pritchett. Wesley[3] Griggs engaged in agricultural pursuits, and with the help of slaves cleared and improved a valuable plantation in Putnam county, near Eatonton. He married Nancy Elizabeth Brown, a daughter of Jeremiah and Annie (Beasley) Brown, life-long residents of Clark county, Georgia.

Augustus Franklin[4] Griggs was born on the old home plantation in Putnam county, and was there brought up. He finished his education at Mercer University. Soon after the breaking out of the war between the states, he enlisted in Company E, Forty-first Georgia Volunteer Infantry, under command of Capt. Charles A. McDaniel. At Murfreesboro he joined Capt. C. B. Ferrell's Artillery Company, in which he served faithfully until the close of the conflict. He subsequently embarked in mercantile pursuits, first at La Grange, and later in Atlanta, Georgia, where he continued in business until his death, in 1870. He married Elizabeth Rebecca Mathews, who was born in Stewart county, Georgia, of distinguished ancestry, having been a descendant in the fifth generation from Isaac Mathews, who was a grandson of Sir Thomas Mathews, of Mathews county, Virginia, and a lineal descendant of Sir David Mathews, of Llandaff, Wales.

Isaac[3] Mathews, third in descent from Sir Thomas Mathews, the immigrant, married his cousin, Mary Mathews, who, like himself, was a Virginian by birth. Mary Mathews was the fifth in line of descent from one Samuel Mathews, the line being thus traced: Samuel,[1] Samuel,[2] John,[3] Samuel,[4] and Mary.[5]. Samuel[1] Mathews was born in England, a son of Tobias Mathews. When young he was sent by King James the First to Virginia, and by him appointed commander of the British army, later being made governor of the colony of Virginia. This Governor Samuel[1] Mathews married a daughter of Sir Thomas Hinton of Virginia. Their son, Samuel[2] Mathews, represented Warwick county, in the years 1652 and 1655, in the Virginia assembly. He was active in military and public affairs, having served as lieutenant colonel in the King's army, and as a member of the King's council. John[3] Mathews, the next in line of descent, was born in Virginia, and became a citizen of prominence. He married Elizabeth, the only daughter, and the heiress, of Michael Taverner, of York county, Virgina, and subsequently occupied the old Mathews homestead, "Denbeigh," near Blunt Point, Virginia. Samuel[4] Mathews, father of Mary Mathews, married a Miss Braxton, and their daughter Mary, as mentioned above, became the wife of Isaac[3] Mathews, and their son Moses was the great-grandfather of Elizabeth Rebecca Mathews.

Moses[4] Mathews learned the trade of a gun maker in Virginia, his native state, and when ready to establish himself in business removed to Winfield, South Carolina, where, during the Revolutionary war he made guns for General Sumter. His wife, whose maiden name was Sarah Findley, was born and bred in Virginia.

Their son, Rev. James [5] Mathews, went from Virginia to South Carolina, and did service as a soldier in the Revolutionary war. Soon after the close of the conflict he settled in Lincoln county, Georgia, where he bought a plantation, and in addition to his agricultural labors served as pastor of a Baptist church in Burke county, a brief account of his pastorate being given in Campbell's History of the Georgia Baptists. The maiden name of his wife was Rebecca Carlton. She was born, reared and educated in old Virginia. Her father, Robert Carlton, who, with his brother, Thomas Carlton, emigrated from England to America, settling in King and Queen county, Virginia, where he married a Miss Wafford. He fought with the colonists in their struggle for independence, and later, in 1785, migrated with his family to Georgia, becoming a pioneer settler of Wilkes county, where he spent his remaining days.

Rev. James [6] Mathews entered the ministry when a young man, and for a time preached in Wilkes county. Moving from there to Stewart county, he bought a plantation in the vicinity of Lumpkin, and for many years carried on farming with the help of slaves. He held pastorates in Lumpkin and Benevolence, and served as one of the first moderators of the Bethel Association. He died when but fifty years old, on his home plantation. He married Kiturah Pope, a descendant in the sixth generation from Lieutenant Colonel Nathaniel Pope, who was styled "A Gentleman of England," the line of descent being as follows: Lieutenant Colonel Nathaniel [1] Pope, Nathaniel [2] Pope, Nathaniel [3] Pope, John [4] Pope, John Henry [5] Pope, Capt. John [6] Pope, and Kiturah [7] Pope.

Lieut. Col. Nathaniel [1] Pope sailed from Bristol, England, for America in 1634, and located in Maryland, where he became a leader in affairs of state, in 1637 and 1638 serving as a member of the Maryland house of burgesses. Prior to 1650 he was granted by King Charles the First ten hundred and fifty acres of land in Westmoreland county, Virginia, and immediately assumed its possession, naming his new home place Pope's Creek. In 1652 he was appointed lieutenant colonel of militia, and had among his officers, as major, his son-in-law, John Washington, great-grandfather of George Washington. Nathaniel [2] Pope married Mary Sissons. Their son, Nathaniel [3] Pope, through whom the line of descent was continued, married Jane Brooks Brown, and continued a resident of Virginia until his death. Their son John [4] married his cousin, Elizabeth Pope. John Henry [5] Pope, a native of Virginia, married Mary Burwell. He was an ensign in the Revolutionary army, serving in North Carolina. After the war he came to Georgia, settling in Wilkes county, where he remained a resident until his death, in 1804. Of his five sons, one died ere the family left North Carolina, and the others settled in Georgia.

Capt. John [6] Pope commanded a company of North Carolina troops in the Revolutionary war, and after locating in Georgia had command of a body of soldiers in Wilkes county. He married Elizabeth Smith, and both spent their last years in Wilkes county. Kiturah [7] Pope, who became the wife of Rev. James [6] Mathews, survived him, and married for her second husband Henry Long. She died, at the age of seventy-six years, in Senoia, Georgia.

Elizabeth Rebecca [7] Mathews, mother of Hon. James Mathews Griggs, married first at a very early age Ephraim Smith Vernal. After his death she became the wife of Augustus Franklin [4] Griggs, whom she survived, passing away in Dawson, Georgia, June 21, 1910, having then lived a widow for forty years. She reared four children, as follows: Ella Vernal; James Mathews, the special subject of this sketch; Charles Brown, and Augustus Pope.

Hon. James Mathews [5] Griggs acquired his elementary education in the public schools of Senoia. After the death of his father he made his home for a time with Dr. Albert Mathews, in Elberton, where he continued his studies in the public schools. Subsequently completing the course of study in the Peabody Normal School, at Nashville, Tennessee, Mr. Griggs went from there to Palatka, Florida, where for two years he was principal of schools. Desirous of entering the legal profession, he then began the study of law in Canton, Georgia, with Hon. George Brown, and was admitted to the bar in 1884. Locating immediately in Jackson, Georgia, Mr. Griggs was for awhile there associated with Judge Marcus Beck. Going then to Berrien county, he embarked in journalistic work, editing a paper in Alapha.

Taking up his residence in Dawson in 1885, Mr. Griggs soon built up an extensive and lucrative law patronage, and likewise became prominent and influential in public affairs. From 1888 until 1893 he was solicitor general of the Pataula Circuit Court, and from 1893 until 1896 was judge of the Superior Court, Pataula Circuit. In 1896 Mr. Griggs was elected to represent the Third Congressional District of Georgia in the United States Congress, and gave such eminent satisfaction in that high position that he was continued as a representative to Congress by re-election until his death, in 1910. He served on many important committees, including that of Committee on Ways and Means. Mr. Griggs was not known as a temperance man or a church worker, but he won recognition as an able lawyer and legislator, and was popular with the masses.

On July 14, 1886, Mr. Griggs was united in marriage with Miss Theodosia Stewart, who was born in Randolph county, Georgia, a daughter of Hon. Daniel Randall Stewart, and granddaughter of John Stewart, who was for more than four score years a resident of Georgia. Mrs. Griggs's great-grandfather, Daniel Randall Stewart, was born and bred in Scotland, and there married Margaret Smith. Shortly after that important event, he came with his bride to America, crossing the ocean in 1800, and locating first in Buncombe county, North Carolina. Coming from there to Georgia in 1816, he purchased a tract of land bordering on Tobesofkee creek, in Bibb county. At that time all of South Georgia was in its primeval wildness, Indians claiming the country roundabout as their happy hunting grounds, while the forests were inhabted by deer, turkeys, and wild animals of many kinds. He subsequently moved to Marion county, where he resided until his death, at the advanced age of four score and four years.

John Stewart was quite young when brought by his parents to Georgia. When ready to establish a home of his own, he bought land in Randolph county, and was there engaged in general farming until his death, at the venerable age of eighty-nine years. His wife, whose maiden name was Catherine Giles, died when but forty-three years old. She was a daughter of John and Mary (Tarver) Giles, the former of whom was born in Jones county, Georgia, and the latter in Hancock county, of Virginian ancestry.

Honorable Daniel Randall Stewart, father of Mrs. Griggs, was born in Marion county, Georgia, and there obtained his early education in the rural schools. When seventeen years old he enlisted for service in the war between the states, joining the first body of state troops, and with his command going to the coast. Afterwards becoming a member of Company G, Fifty-fifth Georgia Volunteer Infantry, he served until the close of the conflict. Two of his older brothers served throughout the entire war, and a younger brother was an active participant during the latter part of the conflict. After the war, he was for a time employed as a clerk in the store of Captain Ben Smith, at Cuthbert, and later bought a farm lying twelve miles south of Cuthbert, and there spent the remainder of his active life engaged in agricultural pursuits. Active and alert, and possessing sound judgment and good executive ability, he was successful from the beginning of his career, by means of thrift and excellent management accumulating a fortune. On retiring from active business, he moved to Dawson, where his death occurred at the age of three score and ten years. Mr. Stewart became prominent in public affairs, for upwards of twenty years serving as jury commissioner, while for two terms he was representative to the State Legislature, and for one term was state senator.

The maiden name of the wife of Honorable Daniel Randall Stewart was Nancy Olivia Pope. She was born in Washington county, Georgia, a daughter of Reverend Wiley Mobley Pope, and is now living in Dawson with Mrs. Griggs, her only child. Her paternal grandfather, Jonathan Pope, was born and bred in Virginia, from there going as a young man to Sampson county, North Carolina, where he resided several years. In 1814 he migrated to Georgia, settling in Laurens county, where he bought a tract of wild land, and began the pioneer task of clearing and improving a farm. He was making very good progress in his work when, three years later, in 1817, he passed to the life beyond.

Jonathan Pope married Elizabeth Cooper, who was born in Duplin county, North Carolina, a daughter of Reverend Fleet Cooper, Jr. Her grandfather, Fleet Cooper, Sr., who married Emily Anders, a life-long resident of North Carolina, was one of the signers of the North Carolina Oath of Allegiance and Abjuration passed by the Assembly at Newbern, November 15, 1777. He was exempt from taxes in Duplin county, where, as far as is known, he spent his entire life. His son, Reverend Fleet Cooper, Jr., was a prominent preacher in North Carolina, holding pastorates in various Baptist churches, and both he and his father received large grants of land in Duplin county. The maiden name of his wife was Sarah Scott.

Reverend Wiley Mobley Pope was born in Sampson county, North Carolina. Studying for the ministry, he became a Baptist preacher, and after coming to Georgia held pastorates in both Laurens and Washington counties. After the death of his wife he moved to Randolph county, and for several years filled the pulpit of the Rehobeth Baptist Church, near Shellman. He married Martha Williams Bryan, whose father, Jason Bryan, migrated from North Carolina, his native state, to Georgia, and spent his last days in Washington county, where he was a successful agriculturist. Jason Bryan married Penelope Gainer, whose father, William Gainer, married, near Petersburg, Virginia, Martha Williams, and settled in Washington county, Georgia, where, in 1790, land was granted him by the Government. Ten children, nine daughters and one son blessed their union, a descendant of one of the daughters, having married Honorable Daniel Randall Stewart, as before mentioned.

Mr. and Mrs. Griggs were the parents of three children, namely: Ella Vernal, Daniel Stewart, and Augusta Pope. Ella Vernal Griggs, who married Edgar Whitfield Hollingsworth, died at the age of twenty-two years, leaving one child, Theodosia Hollingsworth. Augusta Griggs married Thomas B. Raines.

LUCIUS LAMAR WOODWARD, attorney-at-law of Vienna, Georgia, has been active in the practice of his profession in the town of his birth since he was admitted to the bar in 1897. He was born there on May 5, 1879, and is the son of Judge John Hartwell and Nancy B. (McCormack) Woodward, natives of South Carolina and Georgia, respectively.

Judge Woodward, for such he came to be in later life, was born in Sumpters district, South Carolina (now Sumpter county) on January 16, 1831. He is the son of Stephen and Jane (Barnett) Woodward, natives of South Carolina, and when he was about one year old accompanied his parents to Missouri county, Alabama, where they remained until he was about six years of age, when they moved to Georgia. The family located seven miles south of Macon, Bibb county, Georgia, where they made their home until 1863, at which time they settled in Dooly county, in which district Judge Woodward has since made his home. As a young man, he read law at the suggestion of Capt. Robert A. Smith, and took advantage of the generosity of Captain Smith by making use of his office and books, prosecuting his studies principally in the evenings. He was admitted to the bar in January, 1873, but deferred the initiation of active practice for some little time, owing to a prejudice peculiar to the South which held that a gentleman might not engage in the practice of law or kindred professions and continue to hold rank as a gentleman. It is worthy of mention that the natural good sense of Judge Woodward came to his rescue after a time, and he settled down to the practice of the profession for which he had so laboriously prepared himself. He attained a degree of prominence in the politics of his state, and served in the state legislature in 1871-72, and in 1880 was a member of the senate. He was judge of the county court of Dooly county for two terms, and in all these offices he acquitted himself as a gentleman and a scholar might be expected. During the Civil war Judge Woodward was not inactive. In February, 1862, he, with W. B. Busbee, organized the Whittle Guards, Company D, Tenth Georgia Battalion, and were immediately mustered into the service. He was offered the captaincy of the company, but declined and was unanimously elected first lieutenant. His health failed to such an extent that in August of that year he was compelled to resign. In July of 1863 his wife died, and Mr. Woodward again joined the army at Macon, where he was elected second lieutenant. He served two months and was again compelled to resign owing to the impaired condition of his health. Judge Woodward was thrice married. His first wife was Carrie Sheats, daughter of Benjamin S. Sheats of Clarke county. She passed away on July 6, 1863, leaving one child, Stephen B., born October 21, 1862, who lived to reach the age of twenty years, when he died on November 27, 1882. The second marriage of Judge Woodward occurred on July 18, 1865, when he married Miss Mamie McCormack of Hawkinsville, Georgia. Nine children were born of this union. They were: John M., a merchant of Hawkinsville, Georgia; William Thomas, who died at the age of eighteen months; James Madison, a farmer near Vienna; David M., expert accountant of Tampa, Florida; Charles Cannon, editor of the *Daily Tampa Times* of Tampa, Florida; Mary Jane, the wife of Charles H. Turton of Vienna; Lucius Lamar, practicing law in Vienna; Carrie Sheats, the wife of Charles Gurr of Vienna; Emma B., who shares her father's home. The second wife of Judge Woodward died on December 17, 1895, and in the following year he contracted a third marriage, when Emma Peacock, the daughter of John Peacock of Houston county, became his wife. She passed away on August 26, 1901.

Lucius Lamar Woodward was educated in the high school of Vienna after which he read law in the offices of his father, Judge Woodward, and Senator Crum. He was admitted to the bar on September 17, 1897, and took up the practice of law in Vienna almost immediately. He has gained a goodly clientele in the years of his labors and is highly regarded among the legal fraternity and among all those who have had occasion to look to him for legal aid or advice. His standing in the community is of a high order, and his circle of friends is unlimited, his long acquaintance in and about Vienna having won to him hosts of life-long friends. Mr. Woodward is a member of the Masonic fraternity, his affiliation being with the Shriners of Savannah, and he is a Baptist in his religious faith, while his wife is of the Methodist persuasion.

Mr. Woodward was married on October 21, 1909, to Miss Louie Fenn, the daughter of H. R. and Elizabeth (Collier) Fenn, natives of Dooly county. Two children have been born to them: Elizabeth Barmelia, and an infant son, Lamar Fenn.

COL. WILLIAM HERSCHELL DORRIS. In no profession is there a career more open to talent than is that of the law and in no field of endeavor is there demanded a more careful preparation, a more thorough appreciation of the absolute ethics of life or of the underlying principles which form the basis of all human rights and privileges. Col. William Herschell Dorris is a lawyer of the highest ideals and also a most public-spirited citizen, this fact having become happily evident in his administration as mayor of Cordele, his election to the mayoralty having occurred in 1910. He is a native son of the state, his life record having begun on a farm in the vicinity of Douglasville, Douglas county, August 9, 1871. He remained upon the parental homestead until the age of twenty-one years, gaining his elementary education in the public schools and under paternal instruction gaining a practical experience in the many sided science of agriculture. He entered Douglasville College about the age mentioned and was graduated from that institution of learning in 1892 with the degree of Bachelor of Arts. While in college he was a member of the Greek letter fraternity, Phi Cappi.

Having determined to adopt the profession of law as his life work, young Dorris began his study of Blackstone in the office of A. L. Bartlett, of Brownsville, Georgia, and was admitted to the bar in the year 1896, under examination by the committee appointed by the court. He engaged at once in general practice and his gifts and attainments have received signal recognition. He located at Cordele in the year 1896 and has ever since retained his residence here. He has been extremely loyal to its interest and it was due to his efforts that the fine Carnegie library, which is one of its most useful institutions, was secured for the city. He was a member of the first board of trustees appointed to supervise the affairs of the library. He served his city as alderman for two terms and in 1910 was elected mayor, of which office he is the present incumbent.

Colonel Dorris is the son of William C. and Matilda (Lowe) Dorris, both living and both natives of Georgia, the father's birthplace having been Carroll county, and the mother's Cobb county. His grandfather, Rev. John Dorris, was a distinguished member of the conference of the Methodist Episcopal church, South.

William C. Dorris served in the Civil war as first lieutenant of Company I, of the Fifty-sixth Georgia Infantry. He was in the thickest of the fight, serving at the siege of Vicksburg, at Missionary Ridge, at Baker's Creek, etc., and being captured at Vicksburg. The other members of the subject's family are James A., Marvin Homer, Mrs. Ola Stone, Mrs. L. C. Satterfield, Mrs. E. H. Huffines, and Miss Emma Dorris.

The colonel is a Mason of high standing, belonging to the blue lodge the chapter, the commandery at Cordele, and having "traveled east" with the Shriners at Savannah. He is a member of the Methodist Episcopal church at Cordele and is helpfully interested in all the good measures promulgated by the church. He is president of the Chamber of

Commerce and has for several years been identified in praiseworthy fashion with all public affairs looking toward the welfare and progress of city, county and state.

LEONARD MARCELLUS SUMNER. It is the privilege of the young men and young women who grow up in this country to select whatever occupation they desire and they may reserve the right to change such occupation whenever they please. In this way the occupation best fitted to them, or the one which they wish to pursue, is open to them at any time. It is not always that a young person is able to tell what pursuit he is best qualified to follow, so that as time passes and his own wants and abilities are developed, he may change his occupation and strike his proper sphere before it is too late. Then for the first time life is to him an earnest quantity. So the subject of this brief review has found it. Leonard Marcellus Sumner, now chief of police of Cordele, Georgia, and an admirable officer and citizen, was engaged in a number of occupations prior to his becoming a public official. He was born April 14, 1875, at Sumner, Worth county, Georgia, or rather on a farm in the vicinity of that place, and there he resided until reaching the age of twenty years. He received his first introduction to Minerva in the public schools and subsequently graduated from the higher department of the Sumner school.

In 1895, when about twenty years of age, Mr. Sumner was united in marriage to Miss Cora Balkcon, daughter of Alex and Josephine (Warren) Balkcon, the father an agriculturist of this section and a veteran of the Civil war, throughout the entire course of which he served. Their union has been blessed by the birth of the following interesting children: Leonna, aged fifteen; Janie, aged thirteen; Cora May, aged seven; and Irene, aged six. They are students in the Cordele graded school.

Upon first beginning his career, Mr. Sumner entered a mercantile and grocery establishment at Sumner and under McKinley's first administration, he was appointed postmaster and proved an efficient and faithful servant of Uncle Sam. Following his tenure of this office, he removed with his family to Cordele, where he accepted a position as clerk in the J. S. Pates dry-goods store, which he retained for six months. He then engaged with Carter & Darrough, dealers in musical instruments, and remained with this concern for one year and then became traveling salesman for the Cable Piano Company, an association which he did not terminate for a twelvemonth. It was ensuing upon this that Mr. Sumner became a member of the Cordele police force and he acted in the capacity of patrolman for four years, from 1905 to 1909, and in the latter year was made chief of police, which important office he has held to the satisfaction of the citizens for the space of four years.

Mr. Sumner is a popular and prominent Mason, belonging to the blue lodge, in which he is active, and also to the Independent Order of Odd Fellows and the Woodmen of the World, in the latter not taking an active part. He and his admirable wife are members of the Methodist Episcopal church.

The subject of this brief sketch is a son of Joseph M. and Jane (Young) Sumner, estimable citizens, both of whom survive at the present time. His grandfather and grandmother, also native Georgians, were Joseph and Mahala (Smith) Sumner, and the family is an old and prominent one in this county. Mr. Sumner is a member of a large family of brothers and sisters, as follows: Thomas J.; John M.; Robert O.; Henry L.; and Mrs. J. M. Williams; Mrs. M. C. Lemons; Mrs. A. E.

Bass; Mrs. Hattie Sykes; and Mrs. C. J. Williams, all this number being natives and residents of southern Georgia.

JAMES GORDON JONES. Exceptionally well fitted for the legal profession, not only by his natural gifts and ability, but through his high mental attainments, untiring industry, keen perceptive faculties, Col. James Gordon Jones has won an assured position among the foremost lawyers of Crisp county as a member of the firm of Crum & Jones, of Cordele, having a large and lucrative practice. A son of James F. Jones, he was born near Mountisville, Troup county, Georgia, September 20, 1870.

James F. Jones served in the Civil war as major of a company of Georgia infantry. A lifelong planter, he is now living in Hogansville, Troup county, an honored and respected citizen of seventy-three years. He married Araminta Seay, a native of Meriwether county, Georgia, and they have five children living as follows: William M., born in 1866, has for the past twenty years been engaged in farming in Texas and California; James Gordon, the special subject of this brief biographical record; and E. A., who has been engaged in the practice of law at LaGrange, Troup county, for four years; Mrs. J. W. Darden and Mrs. C. J. Daniel, who reside at Hogansville, Troup county; Mrs. F. P. Ayers, Hugh M. and Julia, who are deceased.

James Gordon completed his education in the high schools of Hogansville and after spending four years in California returned to Georgia and completed his study of law and was admitted to the bar at LaGrange on May 8, 1895, and has been admitted to practice in all the courts, having been admitted to practice in the supreme court of the United States, April 6, 1908. Mr. Jones located at Cordele, Georgia, July, 1896, where he has since been associated with D. A. R. Crum under the firm name of Crum & Jones, making a specialty of corporation law. This enterprising firm is division counsel for the Atlanta, Birmingham & Atlantic Railroad Company, and district counsel for the Georgia Southwestern & Gulf Railroad Company, and for the Southern Bell Telephone & Telegraph Company.

On April 7, 1897, Mr. Jones was united in marriage with Annie Lou Paul of Eastman, Dodge county, Georgia, a daughter of W. E. and Fannie (Childs) Paul. Four children have been born of the union of Mr. and Mrs. Jones, namely: Vannie, born June 12, 1899; Gordon, born April 7, 1903; Susie Pearl, born August 7, 1905; Edwin L., born January 7, 1907. Vannie died October 28, 1902, aged 3 years, 3 months.

LEON POWELL WIMBERLY, for sixteen years past the postmaster of Abbeville, is a native of the state of Georgia, born in Bibb county, city of Macon, on March 6, 1858. He is the son of Louis D. and Juliet Amanda (Powell) Wimberly, both natives of Bibb county. Louis Wimberly served in the Civil war in Cavalry regiment. He died at the age of thirty-five, when his son Leon Powell, was but twelve years old. The mother still lives, nearly eighty years of age, and makes her home in Hawkinsville, Pulaski county, Georgia.

Such schooling as Leon Wimberly secured was in the public schools of Macon, previous to his sixteenth birthday. When he reached that age he went to work on a farm, remaining there for two years and receiving as wages five dollars a month. He was employed on the farm of Dr. Virgil Walker in Wilcox county. When he concluded his two years of farm life, Mr. Wimberly engaged in the saw mill business, being occupied for five years driving a mule team. In 1890 he had saved some money from his previous years' labors, and he became a partner in the firm for whom he had been driving mules for five years, and the firm became known as the McLeod, Denard & Wimberly Company, dealers in general merchandise. Soon after that Mr. Wimberly bought the entire business, selling a half interest to C. A. Horne, and continuing with the trade until 1894, when they were burned out. Nothing daunted by his misfortunes, Mr. Wimberly again entered business alone, and after two years he sold out to one Mr. Fitzgerald and accepted a traveling position with L. Cohen & Company of Macon, dealers in whiskey, cigars and tobacco. He later became connected with Altmeyer & Flatau, dealers in the same commodities, with whom he continued for some time. Later he was appointed postmaster at Abbeville, which position he has retained since that time. He has also been engaged in merchandising from time to time, and has some farming interests as well, which he cares for in addition to his official business.

Mr. Wimberly was a member of the city council of Hawkinsville while he was identified with that place, and has discharged the duties of a loyal citizen in the most praiseworthy manner while he has been in Abbeville. He is prominent in fraternal circles of the city, holding membership in the Knights of Pythias, in which order he was past chancellor and representative to the grand lodge of Georgia for two terms. He is a Royal Arch Mason.

In 1891 Mr. Wimberly married Miss Ida R. Wilcox, daughter of T. D. and Roxie A. (Read) Wilcox of Irwin county. Six children were born to Mr. and Mrs. Wimberly, all of whom are deceased but one son, Leon, aged eighteen. Thomas died when about twelve years old; Justine P. died at the age of fifteen, while a student at Gordon Institute at Barnesville. Gerald was burned to death when three years of age. Two died in infancy. The wife and mother passed away on August 26, 1904. On February 14, 1906, Mr. Wimberly married Miss Carol M. Moorer of Savannah. Three children have been born to them, Juliet aged six years, Sarah, four years of age and Carol three years old.

COL. WADE HAMPTON LASSETER. When a man is a descendant of a family that has lived in the same section of the country for more than a generation, he naturally feels an affection for the very soil of that country that others could not feel. He consequently has a deeper rooted loyalty to the affairs of his community, and a firm determination to do his best towards furthering its interests. Such a man is Col. Wade Hampton Lasseter. He is as yet comparatively young in the practice of his profession, and one can not say what the future holds for him, but from what he has already accomplished, it is safe to say that greater successes await him, and that in whatever field his work may call him, he will ever be loyal to what he considers the best interests of his section and his people. As a lawyer, who has been in active practice for a little over seven years, he has proved to be worthy of the admiration that is accorded to him generally. He is a keen thinker, a clever speaker, and is honest and straight-forward in his methods. Is it any wonder that he is fast winning the trust of a large circle of men, and that he has recently been elected to the office of judge of the city court?

Col. Wade Hampton Lasseter was born on a farm near Hawkinsville, in Pulaski county, Georgia, the date of his birth being July 16, 1875. He was the son of Isaac S. and Martha (Ham) Lasseter. His father was a native of Twiggs county, and his mother was born in Dooly county, both counties of Georgia. His grandfather on his father's side was a native of North Carolina, who had emigrated to Georgia while still a young man. His maternal grandfather was a native Georgian. The father of Wade Hampton Lasseter was a private in the Eighteenth Georgia Infantry during the Civil war, and served through the long struggle between the states. Both he and his wife are living, and though they are past their prime they are still vigorous, and deeply interested in the affairs of the day. It is a matter of no small pride to them to see the way in which their son has won success for himself. Colonel Lasseter has several brothers, including Ed S., who is a resident of Cordele; S. L.; and H. S., who is a planter in Dooly county.

Colonel Lasseter only spent six months of his life on the farm where he was born, for his parents soon moved to Dooly county. There his father bought a farm near Vienna, and here the boy grew to manhood. He was naturally a leader among his young friends and was known for his ability along argumentative lines. He seemed to have that gift which seems peculiarly the property of the Southern man, that of oratory. There is no more popular course offered in Southern colleges today than that in public speaking, and witness how difficult it is to persuade students in Northern universities to take such a course. It was evident from an early day that he was destined for the court room. He remained on the farm until he was twenty-two years of age and then he was sent to Emory College, at Oxford, Georgia. His preliminary education had been received in the country schools, and since his preparation was not very good he had to work unusually hard while in college. This did not prevent him, however, from becoming very popular with his fellows, and he entered heartily into the activities of his student life. He was graduated from Emory in 1901, and thence went to Mercer University, at Mercer, Georgia. He spent three years here, completing his work in 1904. With a regretful sigh that his student days were over, he now settled down to practice in Vienna. He soon became known as a lawyer who knew his business and in a comparatively short time he had a flourishing practice. He was elected in June of 1911 to the position which he now holds, that of judge of the city court. Having so fine an education himself, and believing that it is the duty of every well educated man to enlist in the cause of education, he has been a prominent member of the county board of education since 1907. He has done everything in his power to bring the schools of the county into as good condition as possible, but the task is a difficult one, for the people in the South are just waking up to the crying need for educational facilities all over the country.

Colonel Lasseter is active in fraternal circles, having had many opportunities to observe the practical working of the theoretical principles of the various orders. He is a Mason, being a Royal Arch Mason. He belongs to the Knights of Pythias and to the Independent Order of Odd Fellows, and is also a member of the Benevolent Protective Order of Elks. Both he and his wife are regular attendants at the Methodist church in Vienna.

Colonel Lasseter was married on November 1, 1903, to Miss Eva Penney. They have two children. Their son Bill is seven years old, and the baby of two is named Mollie.

COL. JAMES OGLETHORPE VARNEDOE. Few Georgians have had careers of more varied activity than the present postmaster of Valdosta, Colonel Varnedoe. A veteran of two wars, a teacher, merchant and public official, he has long been one of the prominent citizens of southern Georgia and represents one of the oldest families of the state.

He was born at the Varnedoe summer home in McIntosh county of this state on June 24, 1842. His grandfather, Nathaniel Varnedoe, a native of South Carolina, on coming to Georgia settled in Liberty county, where he began his career as a planter and acquired large landed interests and many slaves. He was a cultured, prosperous Southern planter. Many of his summers were spent at Saratoga Springs, New York, at that time the most fashionable resort in America. Aside from this recreation afforded him by reason of his considerable wealth, he lived quietly most of his time in Liberty county and died there, aged about sixty-four. The maiden name of his first wife, the grandmother of the colonel, was Jones, and she was a sister of Moses and Samuel Jones. She passed away at middle age, leaving four sons and five daughters named as follows: Samuel McWhir, Nathaniel I., Leander L., Rufus A., Sarah, Louisa, Matilda, Claudia, and Anna. By his second marriage the grandfather had one daughter, Mary Ellen, and one son, who died aged eight or nine years, and whose name was Stockton.

Prof. Samuel McWhir Varnedoe, the first of the sons named above and the father of Colonel Varnedoe, was born on the Liberty county plantation in 1818, and was graduated with second honors from the state university, then known as Franklin College. He became one of the successful and inspiring teachers of his native state and also took an active interest in the politics of the time. In 1855 he was candidate of the American party for congress from the district that then embraced the greater part of south Georgia, being defeated by Mr. Seward of Thomasville. For some years prior to the war he was prosperously engaged in farming, having two plantations in Liberty county. With the overturn of the labor facilities by the war, he gave up the full operation of his lands and came to Valdosta, where he founded the Valdosta Institute, which, under his management until his death in 1870, was one of the fine and influential schools of Georgia, in which many men of the present generation received their training for honorable careers. Professor Varnedoe married Miss Caroline Fraser Law, who was born in Liberty county, a daughter of Samuel Law. She died at the age of seventy-six, the mother of five children, namely: Matilda Law, James Oglethorpe, Charles Carroll, Sarah Louise and Samuel LaMartine.

The education of James Oglethorpe Varnedoe was completed by graduation from the Oglethorpe University, and almost immediately he was ushered into the strenuous activities of war. Enlisting in 1861 in the Liberty county troop, attached to the Fifth Georgia Cavalry under Col. George R. Anderson, he was for a time in the coast defense, and later was sent to the western army under the command of Gen. Joe Wheeler, one of the conspicuous southern cavalrymen. In the campaign against Sherman's invasion he participated in some of its most notable battles. A short time before the close of hostilities he came home to get a fresh horse, and had gone as far as South Carolina on his way to rejoin his command when the news of Lee's surrender was received. At Macon he was paroled by the federal Gen. James Wilson.

After four years of military life he resumed civil pursuits in the capacity of a teacher, in charge of a school in Decatur county six months, after which he returned to Liberty county and farmed two years, taught a year in Brooks county, and assisted his father at the institute a year. He then became agent for the Southern Express Company and was located at Valdosta, resigning that work to become clerk and book-keeper for W. H. Briggs, a prominent Valdosta merchant, with whom he remained ten years. At the end of that time he himself became proprietor of a general store in Valdosta. In 1890 he organized the Valdosta Mercantile Company as a wholesale dry goods house, one of the successful mercantile firms of south Georgia.

In 1890 he became actively identified with the Georgia militia as captain of the Valdosta Videttes, and was promoted through the grades of captain, major, lieutenant colonel, to colonel. With the rank of major at the time of the breaking out of the Spanish-American war in 1898, he was appointed chief of the commissary department in the volunteer army. It is an interesting coincidence that on his entering the service he reported to Gen. J. H. Wilson, the federal leader to whom more than thirty years before he had surrendered at the close of the Civil war. He was assigned to General Wilson's staff, with which he served in Porto Rico until the troops were withdrawn from that island, and was then transferred to the staff of General Bates in Cuba. In 1899, at the close of his service, Colonel Varnedoe returned to Valdosta and resumed his regular business until President Roosevelt appointed him to the postmastership. He was reappointed by President Taft, and has given a very efficient administration of this local federal office.

Colonel Varnedoe was married in 1864 to Miss Harriet Louise Busby, a native of Liberty county. Her death occurred in 1897. The present Mrs. Varnedoe was Miss Anna Elizabeth Rogers, a native of Macon and daughter of William and Della Rogers. Mrs. Varnedoe is one of the talented Georgia women, known for her artistic accomplishments throughout the state. After her graduation from the Wesleyan Female College at Macon she studied art in Boston and later in France, some of her work having received the recognition most desired by artists, reception in the Paris Salon. She is the author of the painting of Gen. John B. Gordon, executed for the state of Georgia. Colonel Varnedoe by his first marriage has three children—Sarah Louise, David Comfort and Hallie Lois. Sarah is the wife of Judge John Cranford, and has four children—James Varnedoe, Hallie, Ora Lee and Sarah. David C. married Wenona Jones, and they are the parents of two children—Wyenelle and Virginia. Colonel Varnedoe is a member and ruling elder in the Presbyterian church.

WILLIAM BRECKINRIDGE CONOLEY. Twenty years ago Mr. Conoley was getting $25 a month as a "woods superintendent" in the turpentine industry of Georgia. His name is now associated as an official or stockholder in half a dozen or more of the important business and industrial enterprises of south Georgia. He had the ability and industry required by the modern world of affairs, and has been rewarded with prosperity and influence. Mr. Conoley is one of the prominent citizens of Valdosta, where he has resided since 1903.

William Breckinridge Conoley was born in Robeson county, North Carolina, on February 17, 1866. His family and its connections were prominent in that state from an early period. The great-grandfather Conoley, a native of Ireland, crossed the Atlantic and settled in Robeson county, North Carolina, buying land in the south part of the county, where he farmed until his death, and was buried on the homestead. A slab of light wood, inscribed with his name and date of death, marks his last resting place. Two brothers came with him to America, and they settled in New York.

William Conoley, son of this pioneer and grandfather of the Valdosta business man, was born in Robeson county early in the last century, and remained a lifelong resident and farmer of that vicinity, his death occurring at the age of about fifty years. He married Annie Patterson, a native of the same county and of pure Scotch ancestry, being a descendant of the Campbells of Scotland. She survived her husband, attaining the good old age of about eighty. Her six children were named John Alexander Patterson, James, Scott, Sidney, Ann and Sarah.

John Alexander Patterson. Conoley, the father, had an interesting career. Born in Robeson county, North Carolina, January 26, 1834, he was reared on a farm and at the time of his marriage bought a tract of unimproved land and built a log house with a clay floor and a dirt and stick chimney with large fireplace—this being the home in which he began wedded life and in which some of his children were born. His career as farmer was interrupted by the war, in which he made a fine record as soldier and officer. July 22, 1861, he enlisted in Company D of the Second North Carolina Cavalry, which was attached to Gen. J. E. B. Stuart's famous cavalry corps in the Army of Northern Virginia. His own service included many of the most important battles and campaigns of the war—Gettysburg, Fredericksburg, the Wilderness and many of the encounters and struggles about Richmond and Petersburg, being at the latter place when the mine was exploded. At one time he was knocked senseless by the concussion of a shell, and his comrades, thinking him dead, threw him into a pit, where he lay face upward in a pool of water until regaining consciousness, and then returned to his company. He was also once captured, but was soon exchanged. Enlisting as a private he was promoted by merit and faithful service through the different grades to major. At the end of the war he resumed farming for three years, was then in the turpentine industry four years, after which he returned to the quiet pursuits of the farm, and continued so until his death on October 25, 1904.

Major Conoley married Sarah Curry, who still resides on the old homestead in North Carolina. She was born in Robeson county, July 22, 1836. Her grandfather was Edward Curry, a native of Scotland, who afterwards immigrated to America and bought land near Lumber Bridge in Robeson county, where he spent the rest of his days, his body now resting in the Lumber Bridge churchyard. In Scotland he had been a distiller of brandy, and Robert Burns, as a revenue officer, had once raided his premises and cut his still in two pieces. He had it repaired and brought it to America with him. After his death his son, the father of Mrs. Conoley, had the still stored in a corn crib. He was often importuned to sell it, but always refused. About 1840 someone entered the crib, took the still and left ten dollars in payment. For many years nothing was known of its whereabouts, until 1905, when it was captured in a raid by U. S. revenue officers in Cumberland county and taken to Raleigh. Its peculiar construction attracted attention, descriptions were published in the press, and it was conclusively identified as the same which had been brought over by Edward Curry about a century before. Malcomb Curry, father of Mrs. Conoley, was a native and lifelong resident of Robeson county, where he died at the age of seventy-eight. He was a blacksmith and farmer, and had a shop on his farm. He married Catherine McNinch, of Scotch anecstry and a native of Robeson county. Sarah (Curry) Conoley is one of the venerable women who during early life were trained in the home industries which have long since passed out of fashion. She cooked by a fireplace, carded, spun and wove cotton and wool, and dressed her family in homespun clothes. She reared six children, whose names were: Catherine Ann Virginia, Charles Hamilton, Louvinia Robeson, John Lee, William Breckinridge and Alice Vitz Ellen. Industrious habits were part of the home training for all, and while the boys did the work of the farm the daughters were learning the same household arts of spinning and other things which their mother had employed. Mr. Conoley has two sisters, Jeanette and Catherine.

In this way the early years of William B. Conoley were spent upon the old homestead in North Carolina. At the age of sixteen he first left home, spending four months in Georgia, and two years later again came to this state to remain some eight months. Finally in 1890 he began his permanent residence in Georgia, beginning work for his brother, John L., as a "woods superintendent" in the turpentine industry. In this way he acquired a thorough knowledge of turpentine production, and in 1894 engaged in the business for himself in Colquitt county. Mr. Conoley was actively identified with this important line of Georgia manufacture until 1905, and from his success in this has transferred his interests and activities to various other important enterprises. In 1903 he moved to Valdosta, where he built his present attractive home. At the present time Mr. Conoley is owner of extensive farm lands in Lowndes and Colquitt counties, Georgia, and in Fernando and Pasco counties, Florida; is vice-president of the Valdosta & Moultrie Railroad Company; vice-president of the Valdosta Power & Light Company; a director in the Valdosta Bank & Trust Company; is stockholder in the Jacksonville Development Company and the Southern Drug & Manufacturing Company of Jacksonville, Florida, and a stockholder in the Valdosta Times Publishing Company; in the Citizens Bank of Moultrie and of the Valdosta Realty Company.

Mr. Conoley was married on December 20, 1893, to Miss Clara Alline Spivey, who was born in Lowndes county, a daughter of J. Benton and Adella Spivey. Clara A., William B., Jr., and Clyde Elizabeth are the names of the children born to Mr. and Mrs. Conoley. The first, Clara A., was born January 26, 1895, and died July 29, 1899. Mr. Conoley and his daughter are members of the Presbyterian church, while his wife belongs to the Missionary Baptist. Mr. Conoley is an active Mason, having membership in St. Johns Lodge, F. & A. M., Valdosta Chapter, R. A. M., Malta Commandery, No. 16, K. T., and the Alee Temple of the Mystic Shrine.

JOHN A. NEESE. One finds occupying the position of judge of the city court of Eastman, Georgia, a man who is worthy of the trust implied when he was appointed to this position. John A. Neese is a man who has scarcely reached his prime, yet has proved to be not only a clever lawyer but a broad minded citizen. Gifted with a natural eloquence, and with a logical and clear method of expression, his success is not to be wondered at. He is especially interested in educational affairs, believing that the South is more greatly in need of good schools than of anything at present. He is a native of the state of Georgia, and has grown up within her boundaries, and no man is more loyal to her interests or more interested in her future than is John A. Neese.

The maternal grandfather of Judge Neese, John A. Brown, was a veteran of the civil war, having participated in all of the campaigns, from Chattanooga to Dalton. The war proved fatal to him, for he died at home from sickness contracted during his years as a soldier. The father of Judge Neese was John Wesley Neese, a Methodist minister belonging to the North Georgia conference. He was born in 1840, and died on December 9, 1884. His wife was Sarah Elizabeth Brown, who was born in 1850, a native of Hart county, Georgia, and is still living.

Judge Neese was born on June 24, 1866, in Hart county, Georgia. He received his education in the district schools of North Georgia, his education being somewhat fragmentary, because of the frequent moves necessitated by the demands of his father's profession. He early in life determined to become a lawyer, and soon after leaving school, began to read law with J. F. L. Bond, of Danielsville, Georgia. He was admitted to the bar in 1894, at Danielsville, the county seat of Madison county. He opened his first office at Carnesville, Georgia, where he soon had a flourishing practice. He determined, after having practiced long enough to have added the lessons which experience teaches to those learned from his law books, that he was ready to attempt a larger field, and so in 1906 moved to Eastman. In 1910, on December 25th, he was appointed by Governor Brown as judge of the city court of Eastman, and has filled this rather difficult position to the satisfaction of both lawyers and citizens not of the profession.

Judge Neese was married on December 25, 1888, to Ella Tucker, a daughter of C. C. Tucker, of Hart county, Georgia, who was a prominent farmer in that section. Judge and Mrs. Neese are the parents of three children. The eldest of these, Wesley Lovick, was born on February 14, 1900, and is now employed by the government in the post-office department of Milledgeville, Georgia. Blanche, who was born on February 14, 1901, is living at home. Two of the children died in infancy, and the youngest, Donald, was born on February 14, 1902. The father of Mrs. Neese was a soldier in the Civil war.

From 1895 to 1902 Judge Neese was county school commissioner of Franklin county. He resigned from this post, but was immediately elected a member of the board of education of Franklin county, which post he resigned when he came to Eastman to live. In January, 1912, he was elected member of the city board of education for a four year term. Throughout these years of public service he won a reputation for progressive action which he has never lost. He is a member of the Masonic order, and belongs to the blue lodge. Both he and his wife are earnest members and workers in the Methodist Episcopal church.

JUDGE JAMES BISHOP, SR. The life of Judge James Bishop, Sr., has been intimately connected with the growth and development of Eastman, Georgia, and the surrounding country. Having lived all of his life in this section, he has taken an active interest in its prosperity and has had a hand in some of the most beneficial enterprises in the county. He is one of the men who is helping the South to win back the prosperity which was hers before the war swept away everything. People say, "It is Northern capital that is bringing wealth to the South." It is often true, and the South is grateful, but she is returning them fourfold the money which they are spending in her mines and cotton fields and mills; and it is to such men as James Bishop that the South turns her loving eyes, knowing that when he invests money he does it, thinking of the good it will bring to the country, and not purely of the money it will put in his pocket. He belongs to that class of men who favors inviting and welcoming capital and intelligence to his city, and to the county expert tillers of the ground, on whom the multiplied millions of earth are dependent for their bread and meat. He is in full sympathy and accord with every movement that tends to encourage and foster agricultural advancement, which he considers the most important avocation under the sun, and the only safe and sure vocation that keeps the nation alive and prosperous. Mr. Bishop believes firmly in the principles of brotherhood as set forth in the creed of the Masonic Order. He is a charter member of the Eastman lodge, and is a Royal Arch Mason, having been initiated, passed and raised to the sublime degree of a Master Mason in Mount Hope lodge, No. 9, F. & A. M., Hawkinsville, Georgia, in the twenty-second year of his age, and a few years afterward he became a member of Constantine Chapter No. 3, Macon,

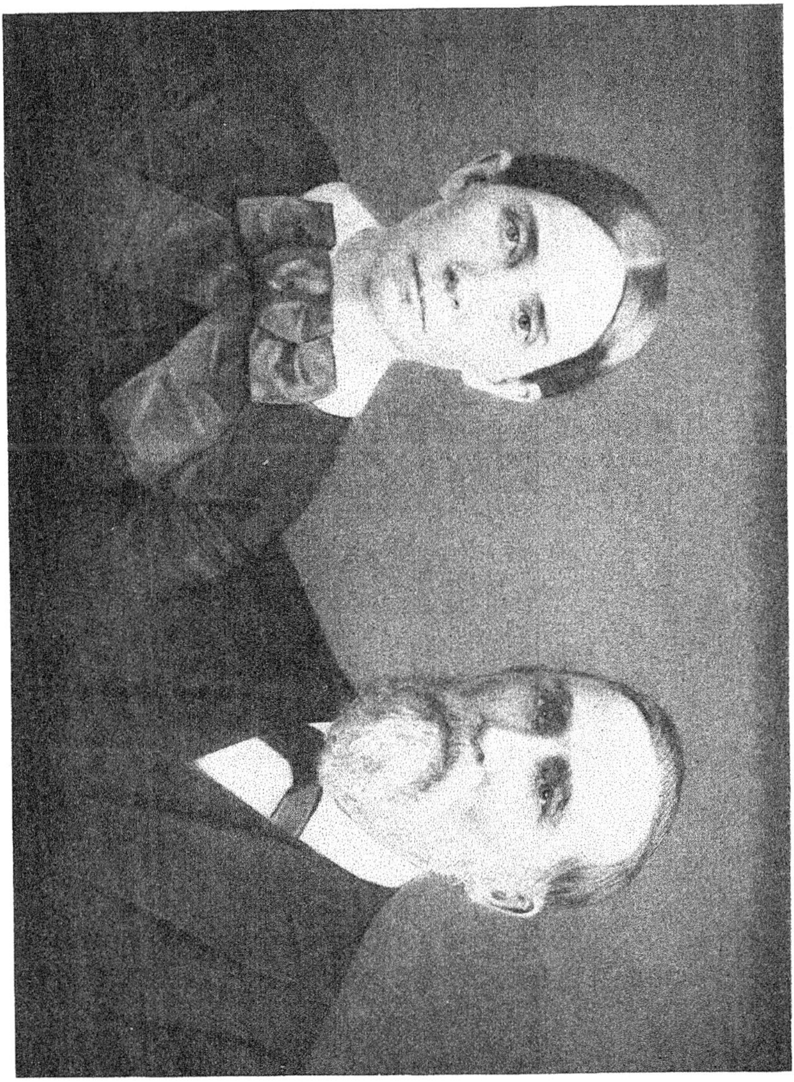

Georgia. He is perhaps among the oldest living members of that fraternity in the state, his Masonic years numbering sixty-two. His political creed in his early days was that of an Old Line Whig of the Clay and Webster type, both of whom he regarded as supreme models of American statesmanship and patriotism. After the war he identified himself with southern Democracy and has never since been known to vote any other than a straight Democratic ticket. During the war he belonged to the State Troops and was stationed for quite a while at Camp Rescue, Macon, Ga., on provost duty, and faithfully performing every other military duty required of him without a murmur. Before the war Judge Bishop was postmaster at Bishop's Store and after the war at Inglewood; and during the war he was appointed postmaster at Johnston Postoffice established by the Confederate government and named by President Davis in honor of his bosom friend, the lamented General Albert Sidney Johnston, who was killed at the Battle of Shiloh. All of these offices were located at the same place, on the very spot of his birthplace. He married Mary E. Guyton, daughter of Major Moses Guyton, an extensive planter of Laurens county, Georgia, but a native of South Carolina. Her mother before marriage was Mary Love, a native Georgian, a sister of Judge Peter E. Love, who was a member of congress from the second congressional district of Georgia when the state seceded from the Union. Mrs. Bishop was a lady of pronounced culture and refinement, with a finished education, which was primarily received from scholarly private teachers in her father's family, and afterwards at Charlestown Female Seminary, Massachusetts, and at LaGrange, Georgia. She was the instrument of organizing the first missionary society in Eastman, The Woman's Foreign Missionary Society of the Methodist Episcopal church, South Georgia Conference, and was instrumental in organizing many others in different counties, being vice president for the district. She also organized a society known as "The Dorcas Society," which afterwards merged into "The Woman's Home Mission Society." She died December 18, 1888, at their Inglewood home, where she was temporarily residing, but was buried in Woodlawn cemetery at Eastman. Mr. and Mrs. Bishop had born to them eight children, three sons and five daughters. The boys are all dead, the girls are all living. Saxon, the oldest, died at the age of twenty; Guyton, the youngest, at the age of one; James, Jr., the second child and son, at the age of fifty. He was happily married to Miss Minnie Douglas, of Talbotton, Ga., who is still living. He was a lawyer of marked ability. After graduating with a speaker's place at old Franklin College, now known as the University of Georgia, he read law under Colonel Clifford Anderson, former attorney-general, and was admitted to the bar in his young manhood, and was soon recognized and classed as one among the best lawyers in his judicial circuit. His first legal battle was by appointment of the court in the defense of the Eastman rioters. This unpleasant duty he reluctantly, though faithfully and fearlessly performed, under the most trying circumstances to his personal feelings. This trial resulted in the hanging of five negroes from the same scaffold, four men and one woman, a life sentence for nine, and a large number of acquittals. In addition to his general practice in the courts he was the leading attorney in this territory for the Southern Railway Company, and legal adviser and trusted representative of The William E. Dodge Land & Lumber Company, the largest concern of its kind in the state. Both of these positions he held without an effort from the time of his appointment to the day of his death, under the firm name of DeLacy and Bishop. He was mayor of Eastman for two years, giving the city the most satisfactory and brilliant administration it ever had. He was also judge of the city court of Eastman under Governor Chandler's administration. He died February 20, 1908, deeply mourned by a large circle of friends and acquaintances. Every order and organization of the city paid loving tribute to his memory, covering his casket with rare and costly flowers. In his death the city, county and state lost a useful citizen. He was held in high esteem by every one who knew him for his unblemished character and many virtues. He was emphatically a good man in its most extensive signification. Of Judge Bishop's five daughters, three are widows and two are unmarried. Mary, who now lives in Jacksonville, Florida, was married to G. F. Harrison, a native Georgian and farmer. He died May 9, 1907. Carolyn resides in Waynesville, N. C. Her husband was R. L. Bush, a North Carolinian and turpentine operator. He died April 11, 1898. Estelle, whose home is Orlando, Florida, was the wife of E. W. Bullock, a native of North Carolina and a naval stores dealer. He died December 1, 1910. Helen and Emma, the unmarried daughters, live with their father in Eastman. Each of Judge Bishop's widowed daughters have one or more grown sons, all brilliant young men, filling honorable and remunerative positions. He has twelve living grandchildren and four great grandchildren. The father of Judge James Bishop, Sr., was Simeon Bishop, a native of New Jersey. He came South when a young man to superintend a large lumber business near Darien, Georgia, but later made his home in the southern part of Pulaski county, where he conducted a large and lucrative mercantile business. He was a man of exceptional business capacity, much loved by his numeous customers, many of whom almost idolized him for his upright dealings and unbounded generosity. He died October 15, 1836, in the fortieth year of his age. Judge Bishop's mother before marriage was Nancy J. Daniel, whose parents moved from South Carolina to Georgia when she was quite young. She was a strong-minded woman of great force of character and determination. She died March 16, 1874, at the age of seventy-three. Judge James Bishop, Sr., the subject of this sketch, was born in Pulaski county, December 1, 1829. He was left fatherless when only seven years old. His mother gave him a liberal education in some of the best village schools of the state, but for the best part of his moral and mental training he feels deeply indebted to the Rev. Adam T. Holmes, a noted school teacher and distinguished Baptist minister and graduate of Yale College, under whose immediate supervision and tutorship he remained for four successive years. He read law under Judge A. H. Hansel, and though prepared for admission to the bar, decided to abandon the law and settle down on the old plantation where he was born, preferring the ease and independence of farm life to that of a profession. Here he remained until the close of the Civil war, when in common with all Southern slave holders his entire inheritance was almost completely wiped out, leaving him only a large body of land, a few horses and mules, with nothing to feed them on, and no one to look after them but himself. Soon after the surrender that part of Pulaski where his home is situated was cut off to help form the new county of Dodge, with Eastman as the county site. Judge Bishop, foreseeing the future possibilities of the new town, moved there while yet in its infancy and has lived to see it grow, as if by magic, from a mere hamlet to its present dimensions, with every element of industry, enterprise and intelligence that constitute a perfect and model city with undiminished lustre still in waiting. Judge Bishop was the second mayor of the town, succeeding General Ira R. Foster, the first incumbent, under whose administration as clerk of council, he formulated the original ordinances of the city, most of which are still in force. Within the last half century Judge Bishop has filled many places of honor and trust, among which may be mentioned that of merchant, Sunday school superintendent, jury commissioner, county school commissioner for twelve consecutive years, editor, express and railroad agent, newspaper correspondent, bank president and other positions of less responsibility, but equally important. He was also appointed by the governor of the state judge of the county court with limited criminal and civil jurisdiction. In every instance he gave perfect and entire satisfaction to all concerned, voluntarily resigning them one by one as best suited his convenience and pleasure. Judge Bishop has now retired from all business activities and will spend his remaining days in Eastman, the city of his cherished pride, where he has a choice home, plentifully stocked with fruits and flowers, with his dutiful and devoted daughter, Helen, at the head of the household, giving her life in adding comforts to her father's declining years.

PEYTON L. WADE is one of the men of note in the state of Georgia today. As a lawyer he has made a brilliant record, early becoming known not only as a man of splendid attainments in his profession but as a man who was worthy in every way to uphold the standard of honor and integrity that the family of which he is a member had always been noted for. A man was heard to remark the other day that one must go south in order to find the natural lawyer. If this is true, then Mr. Wade is a fair example, for he would seem to have been gifted by nature with those gifts of eloquence, logical reasoning and the power of persuasion that are of so great value to the successful lawyer. Adding to natural ability a tendency for hard work and a lasting enthusiasm, he has won from fate a fair measure of prosperity and is now in his prime, reaping the reward of years of hard work and close application.

Peyton L. Wade was born in Screven county, Georgia, on January 9, 1865, the son of Robert M. Wade and Frederica (Washburn) Wade. Screven county was the birthplace of the father as well as of the son, and the birth date of the former was March 4, 1840. The Wade family is an old and well-known family in Savannah and the vicinity, and Robert Wade added luster to the name. He was educated at the Georgia Military Institute, at Marietta, Georgia, being graduated from this institution in 1860. He then took up his medical studies in Savannah but they speedily came to an end, for the Civil war broke out and the young would-be physician turned soldier to defend his beloved Southland. He enlisted in the First Georgia Regulars, and was first lieutenant of the company. Afterwards he served on the staff of Gen. Frank W. Capers as aide, in the Georgia militia. After the Georgia militia were disbanded, he served in the Twenty-second Georgia Battery Artillery as hospital steward, in charge of a field hospital. After the evacuation of Savannah, was in the quartermaster's department for a time. He served in Virginia in the active campaigns there at the beginning, and later, as stated, in connection with militia and hospital department in the field. The story of the nobility and bravery of the surgeons and doctors during the Civil war has never been told, and probably never will be, for their heroism was like the work of the electricians in a play, carried on behind the scenes, and so easier forgotten than the spectacle being presented on the stage. In how many hearts today lingers the memory of such men as Dr. Wade, who helped to render bearable the terrible conditions that existed in the hospital camps. Lieutenant Wade was at the battle of Bentonville, and surrendered with Jos. E. Johnson. When there was no longer any need of his services and the war was a closed incident, he attended the medical department of the University of Maryland at Baltimore, from which he was graduated in 1872. He then moved to Athens, Georgia, and entered the practice of medicine, which he continued up to a short time before his death, which occurred in December, 1904.

The following notice in an Athens paper was a deserved tribute and expressed the feeling of the people among whom he lived for a quarter of a century:

"Dr. R. M. Wade is dead, and with his passing out there is removed one of the noblest, truest men that ever lived in Athens. We have known him for many years, and have observed his walk among us. He had a heart pure as gold and big enough to take in all the suffering and sorrow around him, and alleviate all the distress and suffering that came under his notice. Unostentatious, tender and true, he was an ornament to his profession and to society. He had been a sufferer for some years with Bright's disease and succumbed to the ravages of this fell destroyer on Wednesday at 6 o'clock. He and his good wife have raised a noble family of sons and daughters, who are ornaments to society. Their loss is great, because of the extreme tender affection each held for the other. He was a stanch member of the Methodist church, and that institution will miss him much. Our deepest sympathies go out to the bereaved in their great loss."

The wife of Dr. Wade was also a member of a very prominent family in this region, her father being Joseph Washburn, who was president of the old Savannah Bank for many years prior to the war of 1861, one of the best known financial institutions in the state at that time.

The schools of Georgia being very poor during the years that Peyton Wade was growing up, he was educated largely by private tutors, but the objection that is usually urged against this type of education, that is of the lack of inspiration through contact with other children, was needless in his case, for he was one of a large family, and soon learned the lessons of self-reliance and generosity. He was the eldest; next in order is Eugene W., who was born in 1868 and is now living in Galveston, Texas; Edward I., born in 1870, is a resident of San Francisco, California; Rosalie lives in Athens, Georgia, and she was born in 1873; Robert M., Jr., who was born in 1876, also lives in Athens; Macon, Georgia, is the home of Fred H., who was born in 1878; and the youngest, Georgia, is in Athens; her birth occurred in 1885. After his elementary education was practically complete, Peyton L. Wade attended the high school in Atlanta, Georgia, for a year, and then entered the State University of Georgia, from which he was graduated in 1886 with distinction, fifth in his class of forty-seven. He spent the next two years in reading law with his uncle, Ulysses P. Wade, at Sylvania, Georgia, and was admitted to the bar there in 1888, and returned to Athens, where after practicing his profession for a year, he came to Dublin, Georgia, where he has since remained.

He has never cared to take an active part in politics, as do so many men of the legal profession, for he feels that politics have often been the ruination of a good lawyer. Mr. Wade was married on April 13, 1895, to Gussie K. Black, a daughter of George R. Black, who was congressman from the Savannah district. Mrs. Wade's grandfather was Edward J. Black, in his day a distinguished lawyer, who also served in congress for several terms from the same district represented afterwards by his son, Geo. R. Black. Mr. and Mrs. Wade have one child, Frederica, who was born in Dublin, in 1901.

ROGER DYER FLYNT. The year 1902 saw Roger Dyer Flynt graduated from the law department of his alma mater, and the same year saw his establishment in practice in the city of Dublin, Georgia, where he associated himself in a partnership with L. R. Milton, under the firm name of Flynt & Milton.

Born on August 2, 1881, at Union Point, Greene county, Georgia, Roger Dyer Flynt is the son of William T. and Lilla (Moore) Flynt. The father was born on October 5, 1850, and the mother on May 26, 1856; she died the day before Easter Sunday, 1912. William T. Flynt is still living and enjoying life in the freedom from care in his declining years. They were natives of Taliaferro and Greene counties, respectively, and the father, who was a farmer during many years of his life, is now postmaster at Sharon, Georgia. He is a man of prominence in his section of the state, and served two terms in the state senate in the years 1890-91 and 1896-97. His service was for the nineteenth senatorial district, comprising the counties of Taliaferro, Warren and Greene. He now resides in Taliaferro county, which has always been his home, and where their son, the subject of this review, lived until he was twenty years of age.

Roger D. Flynt attended the country schools of his home community as a boy, later was entered at the Stephens high school at Crawfordville, Georgia, the same having been named for Alexander H. Stephens, and his old home being still used for the home of the teachers. In Mercer University, at Macon, Georgia, he studied law, and was duly graduated in 1902. Almost immediately thereafter he came to Dublin and formed a partnership with Mr. Milton, as previously stated, but their association continued only a short time. The next combination of which he was a member was that of Williams, Flynt & Blackshier. In 1905 Mr. Flynt withdrew from the firm and went to Crawfordville, where he edited the *Advocate,* Democratic, for a year, during 1906. His next entry into the law was at Dallas, Georgia, in partnership with a Mr. Whitworth. In that city he also did considerable newspaper work, finding himself with a peculiar talent for the work and his services always in demand, his connection with newspaper business in Dallas being on the *New Era.* In 1908 he returned to Dublin, here forming an association with M. H. Blackshier, which endured for a year, and he then joined forces with Judge Adams, and later became the partner of G. H. Williams, with whom he is now connected.

Mr. Flynt is a director of the Carnegie library of Dublin, as well as secretary and treasurer of the library. He is a member of the Baptist church. On October 10, 1912, he married Miss Nellie Louise Johnston, daughter of John G. Johnston, a business man of Dexter, Georgia. She is a graduate of the state normal school of Athens, Georgia.

Mr. Flynt is one of the seven children of his parents, all of whom are living. Fitzhugh C., the eldest, is a civil engineer of Nashville, Tennessee; Albert H. is principal of the school of Carlton, Georgia; Roger D. was the third born; Max S. lives in Atlanta, Georgia; Roy A. is assistant civil engineer of the L. & N. R. R. at Pensacola, Florida; Mabel and Donald are at home with the parents, and are students in the public schools. Mr. Flynt's maternal grandfather, Dr. W. A. Moore, was a physician who practiced a number of years at Union Point, Greene county, Georgia, and at Milledgeville, Georgia.

SOLOMAN HERRMAN. The city of Eastman is proud of her mayor, and she has a good right to be, for he is one of the most progressive men in this section of the state and has contributed largely to the success of the city and the surrounding country. His success has been due entirely to his own efforts, for with the exception of a good education he started out in life with little to help him in getting a start.

His business ability, especially along financial lines, is undoubted and his position as president of one of the most reliable and prosperous banks in Eastman is a proof of this fact. No measure conducive to the welfare of the people of Eastman is carried out without the aid or the leadership of Mr. Herrman, and the people of Eastman showed their appreciation of his services as well as their confidence in his sincere efforts to aid in the development of the city, and the cause of good government, by electing him mayor.

Soloman Herrman was born on August 20, 1859, in Dublin, Georgia. His parents, both natives of Germany, were Henry and Henrietta (Goodman) Herrman. The father emigrated from Bavaria, which was also the mother's native province, in 1849. He located in New York, where he married his wife, and where they resided for a short time. They came to Georgia about 1852, and located in Dublin, where Mr. Herrman went into the mercantile business. Soloman Herrman is the eldest of a family of four, the others being Dr. J. D. Herrman, Albert Herrman, who is in the insurance business in Eastman, and Mrs. S. Harris. Henry Herrman died in 1875, aged fifty-three, and his wife reached the age of sixty-six, dying in 1893.

Soloman Herrman received his earlier education in the schools at Dublin, Georgia, and his later education in the public schools of New York City. His parents moved back to this metropolis for the sake of giving their children a better education than they could secure in Georgia, and when they had completed their studies, the parents moved back to Georgia. Soloman Herrman entered the business world as a merchant, the scene of his first efforts being Eastman, though it was quite a different Eastman from the city today. He first came here in 1872, when the immense cotton trade which now amounts to about eighteen thousand bales per year, was only about two hundred. There was not a brick building in the place, where now there are between eighty and one hundred. Mr. Herrman has therefore grown up with the town, and with each step forward that she has made he has risen also.

The biggest feat which Mr. Herrman has accomplished in recent years is the organization of the Merchants and Farmers Bank. This bank was founded in 1905, and Mr. Herrman was one of the leading promoters who stood ready to support the enterprise should it show signs of failing. However, nothing like that happened, and the bank was a success from the very beginning. Mr. Herrman was elected vice-president, and held this position until the bank was organized in 1910 into the First National Bank, when he became president. This bank is one of the leading financial institutions in this part of the state. The capital stock is $100,000, and the corporation owns the building in which the bank is located, it having been built especially for the purpose.

Mr. Herrman was elected mayor in 1912 to succeed his brother, Doctor Herrman, who had served as the chief executive of the city for the two preceding terms. Soloman Herrman is also president of the Dodge Fertilizer Works, and is the principal owner in this enterprise. He is also deeply interested in agriculture and owns a plantation that supports about one hundred and fifty souls. About twelve hundred acres of this land is under cultivation, being planted largely in cotton. He handles about thirty plows, and raises on an average of three hundred bales of cotton yearly. His deep interest in educational matters is shown by his membership on the board of education for the city. He has been an active member of the board for sixteen years, and the present state of the city schools is due in no small measure to his efforts.

Mr. Herrman was married on December 7, 1892, to Sophie Bashinski of Tennille, Washington county, Georgia. She is the daughter of Sam Bashinski, a merchant of that place. Mr. and Mrs. Herrman have four children. Joseph was born on February 19, 1895; Thelma's birthday was July 15, 1898; September 3, 1900, saw the birth of Julian, and Jennie Claire was born on August 20, 1905.

Mr. Herrman is a Royal Arch Mason, a charter member of the chapter at Eastman, and a member of the blue lodge, also in Eastman. In his religious beliefs he is a Hebrew.

JOHN BENJAMIN CLARK, M. D., is one of the best known physicians in the central part of Georgia, and a man whose efficiency and lofty purpose entitle him to stand high among the names in the medical profession. Thoroughly grounded in the elements of medicine at several eastern schools of high standing he has since increased his knowledge by the experience gained from his large general practice. Although he has been an extremely busy man he has yet found time for civic and social interests and is a prominent and popular man in his locality.

Born in Dodge county, Georgia, March 29, 1869, his parents were Harlow and Cassie Annie (Miller) Clark. Dodge county, or Montgomery county, as it was called at that time, was also the birthplace of his father, who first saw the light on February 26, 1845. Mr. Clark, Sr., who is still living, ran away from home when he was fourteen years of age to enter the army, enlisting under Col. Alfred H. Colquist in Wheeler's Brigade. Many times during the war he proved himself a hero, and even after the surrender was in a battle below Atlanta. Dr. Clark's mother was born near Mt. Vernon, Montgomery county, September 19, 1846. The subject of this sketch was one of five children, four of whom, Symanthy T., Mary F. and Cassie G. are still living. His one brother, Bartlett Hamilton, died in March, 1905, just five days before he was to have been graduated from the law school of the University of Virginia.

Dr. Clark received his primary education in the public schools of Dodge county, and from them was sent to Dahlonega Agriculture College, where he took both the preparatory and college courses. He received his A. B. degree with the class of 1891. Most of his medical work was taken at the College of Physicians and Surgeons, Baltimore, Maryland; he supplemented the teaching he received there, however, by attending at the same time the lectures at Johns Hopkins University. After receiving his M. D. he at once started practice in Eastman, where his merits as a physician and his personal integrity soon attracted to him a substantial clientele. Dr. Clark has found opportunity among the many demands on his time for a participation in social affairs, and is a Royal Arch Mason and a Shriner K. T., holding membership in the Macon lodge. He is also a substantial landowner, owning the title deed to fourteen hundred acres of land, of which eleven hundred are under cultivation, and bearing sufficiently to support as tenants seventy-two people.

His wife, Annie M. Clark, is the daughter of Robert Harwell of Mechlinburg, Virginia, and is a graduate of St. Mary's Female Seminary of Maryland. They have had three children, Frederick Harlow, born in 1895; Alma May, born in 1898, and Mary Campbell, born in 1907. Frederick is at present a student at College Park, Atlanta.

JOSEPH DANIEL WILSON. An active and prosperous merchant, a whole-souled and pleasant gentleman, and a progressive citizen, Joseph Daniel Wilson of Quitman has contributed his full share in promoting the best interests of this section of Brooks county. A son of Jeremiah Wilson, Jr., he was born November 12, 1862, on the parental homestead in Brooks county, Georgia, four miles from Quitman.

His grandfather, Jeremiah Wilson, Sr., was born in Ireland. He lived for a while in Effingham county, Georgia, from there coming to the southern part of the state, and locating in that part of Lowndes county that is now included within the limits of Brooks county. The country roundabout was then heavily timbered, with only here and there an open place in which stood the cabin of the pioneer. Game of all kinds filled the forests, and the Indians, which still claimed this land as their happy hunting ground, made frequent raids upon the whites, ofttimes massacring many of the newcomers. The grandfather was a member of a company formed for defense against the hostile savages, and for services which he rendered in various Indian warfares was granted two lots of land. The tracts which he selected for his own were in that part of Lowndes county now included in Brooks county, one lying six miles north of Quitman, and the other four miles to the northwest. He located on the latter tract, the removal from Walton county being made with teams, the only mode of transportation in those early days, before railroads were dreamed of. Clearing a space, he erected a log house, splitting puncheon for the floors, and riving shakes for the roofs. He was a well educated man, and did much of the surveying of public lands. In 1858 he surveyed and platted the town of Quitman. A successful agriculturist, he carried on general farming with the help of slaves, continuing to reside on his farm until his death at the age of seventy-two years. His wife, whose maiden name was Betty Lucas, survived him a brief time.

The only son in a family of seven children, Jeremiah Wilson, Jr., was five years old when he came with his parents to Brooks county. Succeeding to the occupation in which he was reared, and inheriting the parental homestead, he carried on general farming throughout his active career, being assisted by slaves until they were freed. He was quite prosperous in his undertakings, and operated his land until his death, in 1891.

Jeremiah Wilson, Jr., married Delilah Robinson, who was born in Wayne county, Georgia, in 1829, a daughter of James Robinson. Her grandfather, Frederick Robinson, was born either in England, or in North Carolina, of English parents. He fought bravely for independence in the Revolutionary war, assisting the colonists in their heroic struggle. About 1818 he migrated to Georgia, becoming one of the early settlers of Wayne county. Purchasing land on the west side of the Altamaha river, he began the improvement of a farm, and was there a resident until his death. He married Jane Thomas, who was born in North Carolina, and died in Wayne county, Georgia.

One of a family of six children, James Robinson was born in Robinson county, North Carolina, and came with the family to Georgia as a youth. When ready to establish a household of his own, he bought land at Fort Barrington, Wayne county, and began life as a tiller of the soil. Moving with his wife and their three children to Lowndes county in 1834, he purchased land situated but two miles from Throopville, then the county seat, making the removal with teams of his own, they being not carriages, but carts drawn by oxen or horses. In 1836 he disposed of that farm, moving to the west part of the county, in the part now included in Brooks county. Purchasing a tract of land lying one mile west of Okapilco creek, Mr. Robinson erected a log house, and began the pioneer task of redeeming a farm from the forest.

People of this part of the Union then lived in a very primitive manner, there being neither railways in the state, and no convenient markets near. All cooking was done at the fireplace, there being no stoves, and all materials for clothing was carded, spun and woven at home, every housewife being proficient as a weaver and spinner, and also as a dressmaker and tailor.

The maiden name of the wife of James Robinson was Sarah Gibson. She was born in Wayne county, Georgia, where her father, Jack Gibson, was an early settler, and the owner of a large rice plantation which he operated with slave labor. Mrs. Delilah (Robinson) Wilson survived her husband but a short time, dying May 20, 1892. Thirteen children blessed their union, as follows: Sally; Betty; Jeremiah, the third; James, Frank; Alice; Henry; Janie; Joseph D., the subject of this sketch; Mary; Robert E. L.; Lillie; and Thomas Jackson.

Educated in the public schools of Brooks county, Joseph D. Wilson remained on the home farm until 1885, assisting in its labors. The soil having no particular attractions for him, he then began his mercantile career in Quitman, for three years being employed as a clerk. Embarking in business for himself as a haberdasher in 1888, Mr. Wilson has since built up an extensive and remunerative trade in Quitman and the surrounding country, being liberally patronized by the people, who have the utmost confidence in him.

In his political affiliation Mr. Wilson is a Democrat, and active in party ranks. He has filled various offices of trust and responsibility, for a dozen or more years having been a member of the city council, and in 1908 having been elected mayor of Quitman. Fraternally he belongs to Shalto Lodge, Free and Accepted Masons, and to the Royal Arcanum.

Mr. Wilson married in Baltimore, Maryland, in 1902, Daisy M. Justus, a daughter of Edwin Justus. Mr. and Mrs. Wilson are consistent members of the Methodist Episcopal church.

WELCOME HOPE THOMAS. Prominent among the active and progressive agriculturists of Brooks county is Welcome Hope Thomas, who owns and occupies one of the most attractive and desirable farming estates in the Grooverville district. A native of Florida, he was born, March 5, 1872, at Clear Harbor Water, of Virginian ancestry, his grandfather, Robinson Thomas, having been a life-long resident of Virginia.

Henry Robinson Thomas, Mr. Thomas's father, was born, reared and married in Brunswick county, Virginia. His health becoming impaired, he was ordered South, and spent ten years in Florida, during which time he lived in ten different places. Coming to Georgia in 1874, he settled in Quitman, Brooks county, where he was engaged in business as a merchant until his death, in 1880, while yet in the prime of life. His wife, whose maiden name was Matilda Catherine Simmons, was born in Mecklenburg, Virginia, a daughter of John and Jane Simmons, who spent their entire lives in the Old Dominion. She now makes her home in Brooks county, living with her son Welcome Hope Thomas. To her and her husband seven children were born, namely: Sally W., Minnie T., Florida V., Maggie M., Welcome Hope, John R., and Florence C.

Having completed his studies in the public schools of Quitman, Welcome Hope Thomas was there for four years clerk in a general store. Giving up that position, he settled in the Grooverville district, on the farm which he now owns and occupies, and for twelve years successfully carried on general farming. Returning then to Quitman, Mr. Thomas embarked in mercantile pursuits, and there continued in business until 1908. In that year he again assumed possession of his own farm, and in its management has met with most gratifying results. He has now one thousand and fifty acres of land, on which he has made improvements of value, his buildings being commodious and convenient, and pleasantly located. Here he carries on farming and stock raising in a profitable manner, never being satisfied with less than the best possible results.

Mr. Thomas married, in 1893, Lorena Groover, a daughter of Clinton D. and Alice (Joiner) Groover, and grand-daughter of James and Elizabeth (Denmark) Groover. Mr. and Mrs. Thomas are the parents of seven children, namely: Herman R., Allie C., Ernest G., Brantly D., Welcome Hope, Jr., Clinton D., and Lorena. Mr. and Mrs. Thomas are members of the Methodist Episcopal church. Politically Mr. Thomas is a Democrat, and fraternally he belongs to the Royal Arcanum, and to the Knights of Pythias.

WILLIAM MARSHALL. One of the colonial Georgia families is represented by William Marshall, of Hahira, Lowndes county, and the name has also been closely identified with the development and civic progress of south Georgia for a great many years.

Mr. Marshall was born in Lowndes county, January 13, 1848, and was a son of Matthew and grandson of Henry Marshall. Henry Marshall, a native of Georgia and descended from colonial settlers, moved from the northern part of the state to Irwin county, purchasing land and settling in a district now included in Berrien county. South Georgia was then a wilderness, most of the land in state ownership, deer, bear and wolves roamed everywhere through the woods, many of the Georgia Indians had not yet left and the Florida tribes were still occupying their aboriginal homes. Hunting parties of Indians often caused alarm, and more than once hostile raids were made from across the Florida line. A log fort protected every settlement, and there the women and children took refuge while the men stood guard or went in pursuit of the red foes. In this vicinity and amid such conditions the grandfather farmed and raised stock during his active career, and after the death of his wife spent the last years of a long life in the home of his son Matthew. His death occurred at the age of ninety-six. His first wife, the grandmother of William Marshall, was named Sarah McMullen, who was of Scotch ancestry. She died young, leaving four children. There were also several children by the grandfather's second marriage.

Matthew Marshall, who was born in this state and was reared in Irwin county, later came to Lowndes county and bought timbered land south of the present town of Hahira, where for many years he was engaged in general farming and stock raising. Railroads did not penetrate this vicinity for many years after his settlement, and he hauled his cotton and other products away to market at the nearest Florida ports. He was one of the successful men of his time, acquired large landed possessions and much stock, and gave each of his children a good start in life. Though past military age during the war, in 1864 he enlisted in the reserves and went to the defense of Atlanta, serving until the end of the war, escaping either wounds or capture. He then resumed farming and continued it until his death at the age of sixty-seven.

Matthew Marshall married Huldah Bradford. A native of Irwin county, she was a daughter of William and Elizabeth (Griffin) Bradford. Her father afterwards came to Lowndes county, settling seven miles south of Hahira, where he was engaged in farming until the death of his wife, after which he lived at the home of his daughter, Mrs. Marshall. Huldah (Bradford) Marshall died at the age of sixty-seven. She reared ten children, whose names were William, Henry, John, Mary, Frank, George, Matthew, Sarah F., Edward and Huldah.

Though only his early boyhood was passed before the war, William Marshall remembers when his old home vicinity had not yet emerged from its pioneer conditions. Cook stoves had not been introduced when he was a boy, and the housewives still carded and spun and wove, and his clothing as that of other members of the family was all homespun. His early traning gave him habits of industry, and he has never lacked that prosperity which is the reward of progressive effort and ability. On becoming of age he was given a tract of land which his grandfather had formerly owned and on which his uncle had built a frame house. There he was engaged in farming until 1893, at which time he sold out and bought an orange grove in Sumter county, Florida. He lived there until the grove was frozen, and was then engaged in truck farming in Dade county, Florida, until 1906, and after a year's residence in Perry, that state, he returned to Lowndes county and bought a farm near Hahira. In 1911 he retired from active pursuits, and has since resided in Hahira.

Though his energies have been devoted to practical business he has not failed to discharge the duties of good citizenship. In Lowndes and in Dade county, he has given sixteen years of service in the office of justice of the peace. In politics he is a Democrat. His father was a charter member of his Masonic lodge, and Mr. Marshall is likewise a charter member of Hahira Lodge No. 346, F. & A. M., and also became a charter member of the lodge organized at Lauderdale, Florida.

Mr. Marshall was married in 1870 to Miss Elizabeth Powell, who was born in Telfair county, this state, a daughter of Alexander and Elizabeth Powell. Mr. Marshall and wife became the parents of two sons, Alexander Hitch and John W. The first married Sally Allen. John W. married Jane A. Bellamy, and has one son named Brandt. Mrs. Marshall died March 6, 1913.

WILLIS H. KING AND JOHN H. KING. Well-known and highly respected citizens, as well as prominent and progressive agriculturists of the Grooverville district, Willis H. King and John H. King are of pioneer stock, being sons of the late James King, who spent the major part of his life in this part of Georgia, and grandsons of Willis King, one of the very early settlers of that part of Lowndes county that was set off as Brooks county.

Willis King was born, reared, and married in Edgefield district, South Carolina. In 1830 he came with his family to what is now Hickory Head district, Brooks county, Georgia, crossing the intervening country with teams, and bringing all of his worldly possessions. Southwestern Georgia seemed then one vast forest, the clearing of the few settlers being few and far between. Wild animals and game of all kinds roamed at will, while the Indians proved at times so troublesome and treacherous that it was necessary to build a fort as a place of refuge for the women and children when danger was nigh, while all of the men of the locality banded together to resist the attacks of the savages. The people of those days lived in a primitive manner, subsisting on the products of their land, game from the forest, or fish from the streams. There were then no railroads or near-by markets, all trading being done at the gulf ports in Florida. The land at that time was nearly all owned by the state, and for sale at prices low enough to attract much immigration. Acquiring large tracts of timbered land, Willis King cleared a good farm, and here spent the remainder of his life. His wife, whose maiden name was Nancy Williams, was born in Edgefield district, South Carolina, and 'died in Brooks county, Georgia, at the age of eighty years, outliving him. She reared nine children, as follows: Fanny, Mary, Barbara, Mahala, Elizabeth, David, James, Wilson, and Willis A.

Born in 1823, James King was a lad of seven years when he came with his parents to Lowndes county, Georgia. As soon as old enough to wield an axe or a hoe, he began to assist his father in the clearing and improving of a homestead. On attaining his majority, he bought of his father land in the Grooverville district, of what is now Brooks county, erected a small log cabin, splitting puncheon to cover one half of the earth floor, and for a while there kept bachelor's hall. When ready to marry, he built a two-story, double log house, and continued the arduous task of clearing and improving a farm. For several years he had to team all of his surplus produce to either Tallahassee or Newport, Florida, the round trip consuming much valuable time. Successful in his undertakings, he bought land at different times, becoming owner of two thousand acres in one body, besides owning outlying tracts. He was held in high respect as a man and a citizen, and his death, which occurred November 16, 1876, was a loss to the community. He married Catherine Brown, who was born in what is now Brooks county, Georgia, a daughter of Hezekiah and Eliza (Dixon) Brown, natives of Alabama. She passed to the higher life in 1881, having survived him nearly five years. She reared three children, namely: Willis H., John H., and Nancy. Nancy, now living at Saint James, Louisiana, is the widow of Thomas Carter, who at his death left her with four children, namely: Thomas Carter, of Ocala, Florida; Julia; Katherine Mae, and Mack. During the Civil war James King was detailed to care for the families of absent soldiers, but was not called out until sent to the defense of Atlanta.

Willis H. King was born in the Grooverville district, Brooks county, October 6, 1852, and as a boy and youth received a practical education in the common branches of study. He resided on the old homestead with his parents as long as they lived, and at the death of the mother, in 1881, succeeded to its ownership. He now owns six hundred and fifty acres of land, located in lots sixty-six, sixty-seven, seventy-two and twenty-six, and as a general farmer and stock-raiser is carrying on a successful and profitable business. He has never married, but after living by himself for many years is now a welcome member of his brother's household.

John H. King was born on the parental homestead, December 5, 1854, and like his brother was educated in the district schools, and taught to work on the home farm. At the time of his marriage he settled on his present farm of five hundred and forty acres, his land being located in lots number sixty-six, sixty-seven, seventy-two, and seventy-three. Here he is carrying on general farming with satisfactory pecuniary results, making a specialty of raising cattle and hogs.

Mr. J. H. King married, in 1876, Bethiah Elizabeth Williams, who was born in Fayette county, Georgia, a daughter of Joseph and Sarah (Rodgers) Williams. Her grandparents, John and Melinda (Welburn) Williams, were born in Virginia, of Welsh parents. Coming to Georgia, they located first in Henry county, but subsequently removed to Spaulding county, where the grandmother died, the death of the grandfather occurring later in Brooks county. Joseph Williams, Mrs. King's father, enlisted, in 1863, in the Confederate army, and served as a soldier until the close of the war. A few years later he removed to Texas, settling in Ellis county, where the death of his wife occurred. He afterwards came back to Georgia to visit, and while here was taken ill and died. His wife, whose maiden name was Sarah Rodgers, was born in Fayette county, Georgia, where her parents, Abner and Bethiah (Smith) Rodgers, settled on removing from Warren county, their birthplace. Bethiah Smith belonged to a family prominent in the history of Georgia, her mother before marriage having been a Miss Alexander, of Virginia.

Mr. and Mrs. King are the parents of ten children, namely: James, Willie, John, Joseph, May, Raymond, Turner, Ralph, Katherine, and Jessie. Mr. and Mrs. King are trustworthy members of the Missionary Baptist church, and have reared their children in the same religious faith.

PHILIP T. MCKINNON. Reared to the free and independent occupation of an agriculturist, Philip T. McKinnon has found his early training and experience of much value to him in his chosen work, which he is carrying on with unquestioned success, his farm, pleasantly located in the Grooverville district, being largely under cultivation, with improvements of a good, practical, and substantial character. He was born, October 19, 1851, in Thomas county, Georgia, a son of Angus B. McKinnon.

His grandfather, Peter McKinnon, a Scotchman by birth, was but an infant when left motherless, and very soon after he was brought to America by his father, who settled in North Carolina, where he again married, and reared a family. Brought up in his new home, Peter McKinnon began his active career as a North Carolina farmer, operating his land with slave labor. Late in life he migrated to South Georgia, bringing with him his family, live stock, and slaves, and locating in Thomas county, where he spent the remainder of his days.

One of a family of seven children, three sons and four daughters, Angus B. McKinnon was born in Rockingham county, North Carolina, where he acquired a good education for his times. Adopting a profession, he taught school as a young man in southwest Georgia for a few terms, and was so impressed with the future possibilities of this section of the country that he went back to his old home and induced his father and the family to return with him to this state. He bought land in Thomas county, which was then on the frontier, wild beasts and game of kinds abounding in the dense forests, which the Indians still claimed as their hunting grounds. Energetic and enterprising, he bought several different tracts of land in Thomas county, each of which, after he had partly improved it, and had erected a fair set of buildings, he sold at an advance. At the outbreak of the war between the states, he was too old for military duty, but during the last year of the conflict he joined the Georgia Reserves, a corps made up of boys and old men, and went to the relief of Atlanta. For a number of years after coming to Georgia to live, he taught school a part of each year, devoting the remainder of time to the care of his land. Disposing of his Thomas county land in 1866, he moved to Brooks county, where his death occurred when but sixty-five years of age.

Angus B. McKinnon was twice married. He married first Nancy McMullen, who died in early life, leaving him with two children, William and Patrick, both of whom served in the Confederate army, Patrick losing his life while in service. He married for his second wife Lucina Deakle, who was born in Emanuel county, Georgia, a daughter of Thomas and Wealthy (Cannon) Deakle, pioneers of Thomas county, where they settled when she was a child of four years. At her death she left several children, namely: Thomas P., Wealthy Ann, Duncan B., Philip T., Leon, Daniel J., and Henry Clay.

As a boy and youth Philip T. McKinnon attended the district schools, and on the family homestead acquired an excellent knowledge of the art of farming. Taking unto himself a wife, he left home, and bought land in Dixie district, and for four years was busily employed in improving his property. Selling out then, he bought another tract in the same district, where he lived another four years. Coming then to the Grooverville district, Mr. McKinnon purchased the farm which he now owns and occupies, and has since devoted his time and attention to general farming and stock-raising, pleasant and profitable branches of agriculture. His farm contains two hundred and eighty-six acres of land, on which he has made improvements of note, including a comfortable and conveniently arranged set of buildings, which are well located on high ground.

Mr. McKinnon married, October 6, 1875, Julia D. Beasley, who was born in Thomas county, Georgia, a daughter of James and Sarah A. (Ramsey) Beasley, and sister of David A. Beasley, in whose sketch, which appears elsewhere in this volume, further parental and ancestral history may be found. Into the home of Mr. and Mrs. McKinnon five children have made their advent, namely: James A., Ellis L., Sally E., Annie L., and Ida May. James married Rosa Groover, and they have three children, Esther, Ruth, and Ander. Ellis L. married Lois Rountree. Sally, wife of Felix Jarrett, has two children, Farris L. and Edna. Annie is the wife of Frank Groover. Politically Mr. McKinnon is an adherent of the Democratic party, and religiously both he and his wife belong to the Missionary Baptist Church.

ZADOC WASHINGTON HOWELL. In recording the names and careers of those families which have been most prominently identified with the material prosperity and social and civic affairs of south Georgia, considerable space must be given to the Howells and their connections, for they were almost at the forefront of the era of development in this part of the state, and the individual representatives of the family have never failed to give good accounts of themselves in all the responsibilities of life. One of the best known of them is Zadoc W. Howell, who for many years has been one of the large land proprietors and influential citizens of the Boston district in Thomas county.

He was born in the Glasgow district of Thomas county, September 8, 1849, that date itself being an early one in this history of this vicinity. This branch of the Howell family originally resided in North Carolina, the grandparents, so far as can be ascertained, having been lifelong residents at Snow Hills in that state. Barney Howell, the father of Mr. Z. W. Howell, with three brothers, Caswell, Payton and Turner, came to Georgia some time in the early forties and all settled in Thomas county. This migration was made in the fashion of the time, and several weeks were required for the wagons containing the goods of the party to be hauled along the long road into Southern Georgia. Thomasville was then a hamlet with only one store, and all the surrounding region little better than an unbroken wilderness, with wild game in abundance and Indians still numerous and protesting against their removal from these hunting grounds. For a time after his arrival here Barney Howell, who was then a young man, was mail carrier between this neighborhood and Monticello, Florida, making the horseback journey with great regularity and going via Troupville, which was then the county seat of Lowndes county. He later bought a tract of land, heavily timbered, in what is now the Glasgow district of Thomas county, and erected the log house in which he and his bride commenced housekeeping and in which their son Zadoc W. was born. During this period and for a long time afterward the absence of railroads compelled the planters to take their produce to distant markets, and the father hauled his to Tallahassee. On the return trip he brought back such supplies as could not be produced at home and such as were then considered among the prime necessities of import—salt, coffee and sugar. There was but little traffic at the time in dry goods, since the women of the household carded, spun and wove the cotton and wool into the cloth with which all were then dressed. After a residence for some years on the Glasgow tract the father sold and then bought in the Boston district, where he lived until his death at the age of about seventy.

Barney Howell married Smitty Ann Mooring, who was also born near Wilmington, North Carolina, her father, Henry Mooring, and wife, having spent all their lives in North Carolina. Mrs. Barney Howell survived her husband by a few years. She reared six children, named as follows: Virginia Caroline, Zadoc W., Rebecca Ann, Lizzie, Mary and Robert.

Zadoc W. Howell spent his early years on his father's farm and there acquired the training and experience which served him well when he began his own independent career. After his marriage, which occurred when he was nineteen, he settled on a place of one hundred acres which his father-in-law had bestowed upon the young couple, and this was the nucleus of the large farm which he still owns and occupies. As a farmer he was successful from the start, and from time to time has added to his estate until it comprised sixteen hundred acres, one of the best farm properties in the county. In addition to his regular pursuits he has for the past twenty-five years conducted a farm commissary. He has identified himself with the Farmers Alliance and the Grange, and he and his family are members of the Missionary Baptist church.

In 1868 Mr. Howell laid the foundation of his own home and his prosperous career by his marriage to Miss Minerva Cone, who was born on the 3d of April, 1848, in Thomas county, with which vicinity her family have been identified from the time of earliest settlement. Her grandparents, Joseph and Mary Cone, settled in Camden county, Georgia, towards the close of the eighteenth century, and from there came to Thomas county, where they spent the rest of their lives. James Cone, father of Mrs. Howell, was born in Camden county in 1800 and was a young man when he located in Thomas county. He bought land near Barwich, where he lived some years, and then bought an estate in lot 273 of the Boston district. He was a resident of Thomas county until his death at the good old age of eighty-seven. He married Rachel Lovett, who was born in Twiggs county in 1815. Her parents, James and Katie Lovett, came to that part of Irwin county, now Thomas county, in 1825, locating near the present site of Barwich, where they improved a farm and spent the rest of their days. Rachel (Lovett) Cone died in her ninetieth year. She reared nine children, whose names were Rachel, James, Francis Marion, Melissa, Minerva (Mrs. Howell), Mary V., Margian A., Walton and Warren.

Of the two children of Mr. and Mrs. Howell, James, the only son, died at the age of twenty-three. Their daughter, Emma Magnolia, is the wife of Augustus C. Milligan, who was a son of Edward A. and Lorena (Jones) Milligan (see sketch of Edward C. Milligan). The grandchildren of Mr. and Mrs. Howell by the marriage of their daughter are named James A., Troy Alabama, Myrtle Magnolia, Charlie Mae and Ocie Calloway Milligan.

DAVID A. BEASLEY. A native-born citizen of Brooks county, and one of the foremost agriculturists of Grooverville district, David A. Beasley, whose birth occurred June 8, 1858, has spent the larger part of his life in this county, and since attaining manhood has been conspicuously identified with its farming interests, being an extensive landholder and a skillful and successful tiller of the soil.

His grandfather, Thomas Beasley, was twice married, the maiden name of his second wife, Mr. Beasley's grandmother, having been Polly Brinson. Nothing whatever is known as to the birthplace of him, or of his wives, but they all spent their last years in Bulloch county. Five of his children by his second marriage, James, the father of David A., Moses, Annie, Rebecca, and Hannah, migrated from Bulloch county to South Georgia, coming in their own conveyance, which was a horse and cart, bringing their household goods and provisions with them and camping by the way. They located in that part of Thomas county now included within the boundaries of Brooks county, being among the earliest settlers of that place. South Georgia was then one vast wilderness, with here and there an opening in which the log cabin of the brave pioneer might be seen, and the land roundabout was for sale at a very low price. Wild game of all kinds was plentiful, and fish abounded in the streams, the skilful hunter and angler being thus enabled to furnish his table with plenty of fish, flesh and fowl.

James Beasley, the father of David A., was born in Bulloch county, Georgia, January 14, 1804. Coming with his brother and sisters to Brooks county, he bought a timbered tract on Piscola creek, and erected the customary log house of the pioneer. There were no railroads here for many years after he became a resident of the county, and when he began raising produce to sell he had to team it to either Tallahassee or Newport, Florida, being usually accompanied on such trips by some of his neighbors, many of whom, perhaps, lived a dozen miles away, these farmers taking along provisions and camping on the way, traveling together both as a matter of safety and of pleasure. In the meantime the women were equally as busy with pioneer tasks as the men, spending their leisure minutes in carding, spinning, weaving, and making the garments worn by the entire family, and doing all of their cooking by the open fireplace. In those days there was but little money in circulation, and they needed but little, their wants being but few. After clearing a part of his land, James Beasley sold out, and for five years resided in Thomas county. Returning then to Brooks county, he was here a resident until his death in the eighty-first year of his age.

James Beasley married Sarah A. Ramsey, who was born in North Carolina, a daughter of William Ramsey, and granddaughter of Matthew Ramsey, who emigrated from England to America in colonial times and fought in the Revolutionary war. William Ramsey was three times married. He married for his second wife Nancy Strahan, a sister of his first wife, and she was the mother of his daughter, Sarah A. Ramsey. Mrs. Sarah A. Ramsey survived her husband, passing away at the age of eighty-two years. Fifteen children blessed their union, namely: William T.; Marzell, deceased; Eli, deceased; James, deceased; Elizabeth, deceased; Eliza; Rebecca, deceased; Adam; Frank; Laura; Lovina; Thomas; Leonora; Julia; and David A. Four of the sons, William T., Eli, James and Adam served in the Confederate army, James being killed in battle, and Eli dying while in service.

David A. Beasley was reared and educated in Brooks county, and the days of his childhood and youth were not days of idleness. He began when young to assist on the farm, and has since continued in his early occupation, his long and varied experience in this industry making him an authority on agricultural matters. Mr. Beasley is now the owner of one thousand acres of land in the Grooverville district, where he is carrying on a remunerative business in general farming, including the raising of cattle and hogs.

Mr. Beasley has never married, but he is fortunate in having three of his sisters, Laura, Lovina, and Leonora, to preside over his household. He and his sisters are all members of the Missionary Baptist church, while their parents were both members of the Primitive Baptist church.

THOMAS BEASLEY. A well-known and highly respected citizen of Grooverville district, and one of its industrious and prosperous farmers, Thomas Beasley is a worthy representative of an honored pioneer, who dauntlessly pushed his way into an uncultivated country, coming to Brooks county as a young man, and leaving behind him a record for steadiness of purpose and persistent industry of which his descendants may well be proud. He was born September 6, 1852, in Brooks county, being the twelfth child in succession of birth of the fifteen children born of the union of James and Sarah A. (Ramsey) Beasley. An extended account of his parents may be found elsewhere in this volume in connection with the sketch of David A. Beasley, Mr. Beasley's brother.

Growing to manhood on the homestead, Thomas Beasley attended the district schools whenever opportunity offered, and until twenty-six years of age remained with his parents, the latter part of the time managing the home farm. Starting life for himself, he bought 135 acres of land, which are now included in his present farm. Sixty-five acres had been previously cleared, but no other improvements had been made. He has since erected a good set of buildings, and has invested his surplus cash in other lands, having now 380 acres of land, all in the Grooverville district. Here Mr. Beasley is successfully engaged in agricultural pursuits, in addition to carrying on general farming, making a specialty of raising cattle and hogs, a profitable industry.

Mr. Beasley married, in 1878 Alice Wilson. She was born in Brooks county, Georgia, a daughter of Jeremiah and Delilah (Robinson) Wilson, of whom a brief history may be found on another page of this work, in connection with the sketch of Joseph D. Wilson. Three children have been born to Mr. and Mrs. Beasley, namely: Alba, Thomas Hugh, and Carrie P. Alba married Joe F. Williams, and they have three children living, Paul, Will, and Ray. They lost Joseph W. and Olin W. Mr. and Mrs. Beasley are members of the Msisionary Baptist church.

REDDING GROOVER RAMSEY. A prosperous and progressive farmer of Grooverville district, Brooks county, Redding Groover Ramsey comes on both sides of the house of substantial pioneer stock, and is a native, and to the "manner born," his birth having occurred on the farm where he now resides, March 6, 1865, he being the youngest child of the late Owen Ramsey.

His grandfather, William Ramsey, was born, reared, and married in North Carolina. Migrating with his family to south Georgia in 1829, he brought his family and all of his worldly possessions with him, making the trip with ox teams, and being six weeks on the way, a part of his course being marked by blazed trees. Locating in the southern section of Thomas county, he bought a tract of heavily timbered land, erected a log cabin, and began to clear a farm from the forest, which was then inhabited by wild beasts and dusky savages. Industrious and ambitious, he subsequently bought other land in that vicinity, and was there a resident until his death, at the age of four score years.

He was twice married, by his first wife having one daughter, Sally Ramsey. He married for his second wife Dorcas Bevin, a native of North Carolina, and to them ten children were born, as follows: William H., Dorcas B., Richard, Ezekiel, Eliza, Elizabeth, Thomas, Owen, Julia and Henry.

But seven years old -when brought by his parents to Georgia, Owen Ramsey grew to manhood on the parental homestead, and in tender years began to assist his father in his pioneer work of eliminating a farm from the wilderness. Marrying at the age of twenty-three years, he built a small log cabin on land which his father had given him, and in that humble abode he and his bride began housekeeping, she performing her full share of labor, including the carding, spinning and weaving of fine linens and homespun goods. There being no railroads in those days, he used to team all of his extra produce to the gulf ports of Florida. After clearing a part of the land, he sold, and bought again in the same neighborhood. Coming to Brooks county in 1861, he came on to the farm on which his son Redding Groover is now living. It was then in its virgin wildness, but, nothing daunted, he built a small frame house in the woods, and began the improvement of a farm. A part of this farm was given to them by Mrs. Ramsey's father. His work, however, was laid aside when war between the states was declared, he enlisting in the Confederate army for service, and continuing with his regiment until his death, which occurred in Milledgeville, Georgia, in the fall of 1864.

The maiden name of the wife of Owen Ramsey was Martha Groover. She was a daughter of James and Elizabeth (Denmark) Groover, and a sister of Dr. James I. Groover, in whose sketch, which may be found on another page of this volume further history of her family may be found. She is still living, and can look back with pride and pleasure upon the work which she has accomplished. Left a widow with ten children, the oldest a boy of sixteen summers, she assumed the management of the home farm, continuing the improvements already begun, and wisely reared and educated her children, keeping them together until able to care for themselves, each one being now well established in life. There were seven boys and three girls in her family, as follows: James W., Thomas C., Columbus, Eliza J., Lizzie, Clayton H., Washington W., Owen L., Mattie J., and Redding G.

As soon as old enough Redding Groover Ramsey, who has always lived with his mother, began to superintend the work of the farm, and has greatly improved both the land and the buildings, which now bear comparison with any in the neighborhood.

Mr. Ramsey married, June 30, 1909, Maggie Harrell, who was born in Brooks county, Georgia, a daughter of Samuel and Laura (Albritton) Harrell, of whom a brief account is given elsewhere in this work, in connection with the sketch of M. J. Harrell. Mr. Ramsey is a member of the Methodist Episcopal church South, while his wife is a Baptist. Mr. Ramsey's mother is a member of the Missionary Baptist church, but his father was prominently identified with the Methodist Episcopal church, South, and for many years served as superintendent of its Sunday school.

ANSEL B. CONE, who for many years has been identified with the useful and honorable activities of Thomas county, and who is now living retired in Boston after a successful career as farmer and business man, was born in the Boston district of Thomas county on the 25th of May, 1846. The Cone family and its connections have been prominently identified with this portion of Georgia since pioneer times.

His grandfather, Joseph Cone, after many years' residence in Bulloch county, became one of the early settlers of Thomas county, locating, on Ancilla creek in what is now the Boston district, where he bought timbered land and improved a farm. There he resided until his death, and his great-granddaughter and her children now occupy the homestead. Joseph Cone married a Miss Stewart, whose parents came to America from their native Scotland, but after a residence of a few years on this side the Atlantic returned to Scotland, leaving some of their children here. The five children of Joseph Cone and wife were: James, John, Joseph, Matilda and Susan.

John Cone, father of Ansel B., was born in Bulloch county the 19th of April, 1806, and soon after his marriage there came to Thomas county. Here his father gave him land on Ancilla creek, on which he first erected a log cabin and later a substantial hewed-log house, in which his son Ansel and other children were born. For many years after the settlement of the Cone family, this part of Georgia had few improvements. Thomasville was a hamlet, with a log courthouse. Before the railroad era John Cone hauled his produce to St. Marks in Florida, this market journey requiring several days, and afterwards Tallahassee became the nearer market. He owned a number of slaves and was one of the prosperous men of this county. His death occurred on July 23, 1869. He married Civility Walker, who was born April 7, 1809, a daughter of Isham and Civility Walker, who were born respectively on April 7, 1769, and September 24, 1777, and who spent their last years in Bulloch county. Civility (Walker) Cone died on November 12, 1889, and her twelve children were named as follows: Isham W., William A., Elizabeth S., Joseph J., James F., Aaron P., Annie C., John D., Ansel B., Margaret S., Henry F. and King S. Six of these sons served in the Confederate army, James giving his life to the southern cause, and few southern families were better represented in the war by practical service than the Cones.

At the age of eighteen, in 1864, Ansel B. Cone likewise offered his services to the southern government. He enlisted in Company F of the Fifty-seventh Georgia, known as the "Dixie Boys," and was with the regiment in all the battles from Dalton to Atlanta, afterwards went with Hood's army in Tennessee, and at the close of the war surrendered at Greensboro, North Carolina. Following his return home he attended school for a while. After his father's death he assumed the management of the home farm until he was ready to embark upon his independent career. He then bought one hundred and eighty-four acres at ten dollars an acre, this tract adjoining the old homestead. His agricultural enterprise prospered from the start, and to his original place he added until his farm comprised five hundred acres. He gave his active supervision to this estate until 1887, but in December of that year established a warehouse in Boston, where he has since had his residence. After being in business fourteen years he retired, his attention having since been directed in a general way to his farm and to the management of his town real estate.

Mr. Cone is affiliated with Horeb Lodge No. 281, F. & A. M.; with J. M. Rushin Chapter, R. A. M., and for the past seventeen years has been commander of the Boston camp of the Woodmen of the World.

December 28, 1869, Mr. Cone married Miss Laura P. Johns. She was born in Bradford county, Florida, a daughter of Archibald Johns, who was an early settler of Bradford county, and had formerly been a resident of Bulloch county, this state. Mrs. Cone died on the 21st of November, 1870, leaving an infant daughter, Laura. Mr. Cone's second marriage occurred in February, 1872, when Mary J. Barrow, daughter of Joshua N. and Emeline (Ramsey) Barrow, became his wife. Mr. and Mrs. Cone are members of the Missionary Baptist church. Mr. Cone's only child, Laura, is now deceased. She married John J. Paramore and reared two children, named Dubel Ansel and Geneva Amanda. The grandson, Dubel A. Paramore, married Maude Norton, and they are the parents of two daughters, Laura Louise and an infant. Geneva Amanda married Mims Groover, and they have one daughter, Pearl E. Thus Mr. Cone is the great-grandfather of three.

THOMAS J. HIGHT. Among Thomas county citizens few have been more popularly known than Thomas J. Hight, who for a number of years rendered the county efficient service in the office of sheriff and has been a resident of the county for many years, now living retired at Boston.

Mr. Hight was born on a farm in Barbour county, Alabama, August 29, 1852. His father, Felix Franklin Hight, was born in Talbot county, Georgia, in 1817. The grandfather was Howell Hight, a native of Scotland, where the name was spelled McHight. At an early age Howell Hight, being left an orphan, made his way to America with a family named Cole, who settled in Georgia, and after his arrival here he simplified his name to its present form. He was reared to habits of industry, and after growing to manhood commenced a successful career as farmer in Talbot county, this state, where he acquired a large farm, having a number of slaves to operate it, and where he resided until his death. He reared a large family of children.

Felix Franklin Hight, the father, when a young man moved to Alabama, where he was an overseer on the plantation of Reuben E. Brown in Tallapoosa county. Later he bought land in Barbour county and conducted it with the aid of slave labor. In 1862 he joined the cavalry forces under General Joe Wheeler, and under that gallant leader participated in many of the hard-fought battles of the war. At its close he resumed farming and the raising of cattle, horses and hogs. He sold his farm in Barbour county in 1868 and bought a farm near Troy, in Pike county, where he lived until 1874, in which year he sold out and moved to Texas, where he bought a large tract of land and was engaged in farming and stock raising until his death in 1887. He was three times married. His first wife was Jane Padget, who died leaving two children, Robert Howell and Martha J. He married, second, Delilah Stuart, who was born in Barbour county, a daughter of Thomas and Jane (Lee) Stuart, and she died in 1862, leaving eight children, namely: Thomas J., Lorana Jane, Elizabeth, Josephine, John Alexander, Louise, Felix Franklin and Nathaniel W. His third wife was Elizabeth Stuart, a twin sister of his second wife. At her death in 1885 she left one daughter, named Roberta May. Robert Howell, the oldest son, enlisted at the first call for troops in Alabama in the First Alabama Regiment, and after serving the term of twelve months and being discharged, immediately re-enlisted in Company I of the Third Alabama Infantry. The regiment was in the Army of the Tennessee, under Generals Bragg, Johnston and Hood, in the battles of the Atlanta campaign, was with Hood about Nashville, and finally went to North Carolina. After the surrender at Greensboro he returned home.

Thomas J. Hight was reared and educated in his native state and remained on the farm until the age of twenty, when he became clerk in a store in Coffee county, Alabama, continuing at that one year. Then for two years he was employed at sawmilling in that state, and after a year spent in farming in Pike county came to Georgia and was a farmer in Boston district seven years. His next experience was as baggage master on what is now the Coast Line Railway, his run being from Waycross to Chattahoochee, Florida. Ill health compelled him to give up this occupation after a year, and he located at Boston. For fourteen years he served as the town marshal, after which for two years he was in railroad construction work. Mr. Hight was then chosen by the voters of Thomas county to the important office of sheriff, and he discharged the functions of that position eight years. Since leaving office he has lived retired in Boston.

At the age of twenty Mr. Hight was married to Mrs. Laura (Rembert) Dekel. She was a daughter of Caleb Rembert, Jr., and granddaughter of Caleb Rembert, Sr., the latter having been an extensive planter with an estate about twenty-five miles from Charleston, South Carolina. Mrs. Hight's first husband was Mathew Dekel. Mr. and Mrs. Hight have reared four children, Beulah, Sarah Elizabeth, Margaret L. and Thomas W. Beulah, who married Sterling Kingsley, died leaving two children, George Thomas and Georgie Louise, who now live with their grandparents, Mr. and Mrs. Hight. Sarah Elizabeth married J. B. Daniel, and has five children, named Emmett W., Annie L., Sarah, Hight and Emily. Margaret L. is the wife of R. Jones and has two children, William W. and Margaret C. Thomas W. married Minnie Jones and they are the parents of one son, Thomas W., Jr. Mr. Hight and wife are members of the Methodist church, South; he is a Democrat in politics and is affiliated with the Woodmen of the World.

EDWARD COKE MILLIGAN. None of the residents of the Boston district in Thomas county are better known or more closely associated with the varied activities of this vicinity than Mr. Edward Coke Milligan, merchant and farmer of Boston.

Mr. Milligan, who represents the sturdy Scotch-Irish stock was born in Dale county, Alabama, September 10, 1858. His grandparents were natives of the North of Ireland, and thence brought their children to America, first settling in North Carolina and after several years removing to Alabama, where they settled in Pike county, bought land and engaged in farming, and spent the rest of their days there. The grandfather was very proficient in the use of tools and did all his own building.

Edward Alexander Milligan, the father of the Boston merchant, was one of a large family of children, was born in the North of Ireland and was still young when the family crossed the Atlantic. Reared in Alabama at a time when free schools had not yet come into existence, he nevertheless made use of every opportunity and acquired a proficiency which enabled him when still in his 'teens to teach school. He thus earned the money with which to advance his education and preparation for a higher career. He took up the study of law, was admitted to the bar, and gained considerable success in the law at Newton, in Dale county, Alabama. He also bought a farm and combined legal practice with the pursuits of agriculture, operating his land with the aid of slave labor. In 1862 enlisting in an Alabama regiment, he served with his command in many of the important battles of the war. After the close of hostilities he returned home and resumed practice and farming. In 1877, having sold his Alabama interests, he came to Thomas county, Georgia, and in order to give his sons the benefit of farm life and training bought land in the Boston district. Here he was engaged in the active direction of his farm for ten years, and then removed to Moultrie, where he bought town property and farm lands in the vicinity, and as a resident of Moultrie continued farming and stock raising until his death, which occurred at the age of eighty-one years. The late Mr. Milligan married Lorena Jane Jones, who was a native of Oglethorpe county. Her father, Moses Jones, it is thought was also born in Oglethorpe county, where he spent many years as a farmer, and he afterward moved to Dale county, Alabama, where he continued the same occupation. He was a natural mechanic and built his own houses and farm wagons. He married a Miss Matthews, and she died in Oglethorpe county, and he spent his last years in Dale county. Mrs. Lorena Milligan, the mother, died at the age of sixty-five, and her children were named as follows: Edward Coke, Augustus Charles, John Calhoun, Mattie D., William Moses and Allie Cumy.

Edward C. Milligan was reared and educated in his native state of Alabama, but since the age of nineteen has been a resident of Thomas county. Three years later he began his independent career as a clerk in a general store at Boston, where during the next eighteen months he laid the foundation of a solid business experience. He then engaged in the livery business, and also bought land and practically throughout his career in business has been identified more or less actively with the cultivation of the soil. After about ten years in the livery business, he bought an interest in a cotton warehouse in association with Mr. A. B. Cone and six years later became sole proprietor of the establishment. In 1907, with a partner, he engaged in merchandising, and since 1910 has owned and conducted the business alone. For several years he also handled a large trade in fertilizers. Mr. Milligan is now owner of over four hundred acres in the Boston district, devoted to general farming, is proprietor of the cotton warehouse, and conducts a store with a stock that supplies nearly every want on the farm and home.

As one of the prosperous and influential business men of his community, Mr. Milligan has also performed public-spirited service for his home town. He is now a member of the council, and has served as mayor and also as president of the board of education. He affiliates with Horeb Lodge No. 281, A. F. & M., with the Odd Fellows, and with Columbia Camp of the Woodmen of the World. He and his wife are members of the Missionary Baptist church.

October 25, 1885, Mr. Milligan married Miss Florida Adora Taylor, who was born in Jefferson county, Florida, a daughter of Dr. Wesley and Jane (McCoy) Taylor. Mr. and Mrs. Milligan have reared five children, namely: Ernest Coke, J. Alexander, Jane Orina, Allie May and Wesley Alexander. Ernest C. married Hester Parker and has one son named Edward Carlyle.

EZEKIEL RAMSEY WHALEY. The prosperity and enterprise of the south Georgia agriculturist are well represented in Mr. E. R. Whaley, who for many years has directed the production of extensive lands in the Boston district of Thomas county, and is one of the well known and progressive citizens of that county.

Ezekiel Ramsey Whaley was born in the Boston district of Thomas county on the 19th of June, 1862, and represents pioneer families in this section of the state. His grandfather was named Ezekiel Whaley, who when a young man came from his native England to America, his brother being his companion on the voyage, and after arriving in this country joined the Revolutionary army as a fifer in General Washington's command, with which he served throughout the war. Later he became a settler in Lenoir county, North Carolina, where he bought land bordering on the Neuse river. He married a Miss Jarman, and both spent their last years in Lenoir county. They were the parents of three sons and several daughters. One of the sons, John, came to Georgia and lived in Hawkinsville, but as his only son died unmarried he left no descendants. Another son, Evans, settled in Florida and reared a large family.

Jarman Howell Whaley, the father of Ezekial R., was born in Lenoir county, August 10, 1809, was reared and educated there, and at the age of twenty-one came to Georgia and spent two years with his brother John in the central part of the state. He then moved to Thomas county, where he was one of the early settlers. Previously he had acquired the trade of clock maker, and was also possessed of considerable musical talent. So for some years after his location in Thomas county he gave his service to the community in repairing clocks and in teaching music, being the pioneer music teacher in this part of the state. After his marriage he lived two years at Grooverville, and then bought land in the Boston district. A log cabin was his first home, and with the aid of his slaves he cleared land for one of the early farms in that district. With subsequent prosperity he built a log house containing nine rooms, ceiled inside, making a very comfortable residence. For many years after his settlement here the country was without railroads, Newport and Tallahassee, Florida, were the nearest markets, and he hauled his products to those points. He remained a resident on his farm home until his death on the 30th of August, 1878. In 1864 he had joined the Georgia Reserves and participated with them in the defense of Atlanta.

Jarman H. Whaley married Eliza Ramsey, who was a native of Bladen county, North Carolina. Her grandfather was Mathew Ramsey, a native of England, who came to America in colonial times and served in the Revolution. William Ramsey, her father, was born, reared and married in North Carolina, and in 1829 came to Georgia, using teams and wagons to carry all his movable property and family and slaves, and driving his stock. He was one of the first settlers in what is now the Boston district of Thomas county. The land which he purchased was heavily timbered and he built a log house and cleared a farm from the midst of the wilderness. He was a devout Methodist, the first of that faith to settle in this vicinity, and he put up a commodious log building which was used as a church until one was erected in Grooverville. His death occurred on his homestead at the age of eighty-four. He married Dorcas Bivens, who survived him, and they reared a large family of children, one of whom was Eliza Ramsey, who became the wife of Jarman H. Whaley. The latter couple were the parents of eight children, namely: Julia, Laura, Ida, Ezekiel R., William, Anice, Olive and Birdie. Julia now makes her home with her brother Ezekiel and her sister Birdie. Ida married R. C. McMurray, and after her death her sister Laura became the wife of Mr. McMurray. William is deceased. Anice, also deceased, married P. P. Joiner. Olive is the wife of Dr. J. E. Watkins, a sketch of whom is found elsewhere in this work. Birdie is the wife of I. S. Futch.

Ezekiel R. Whaley received his early education in the common schools of the home neighborhood. When he was sixteen his father died, and that event threw the management of the entire home farm upon his shoulders, a responsibility he discharged with faithful effort, and with his mother helped to keep the family together until all became independent. He has been a successful and enterprising farmer from the beginning, and finally bought out the interests of the other heirs in the old homestead, which he continued to occupy until 1909. In that year, in order to give his children the advantages of the town schools, he moved to Boston, where he had built a fine large residence, with wide verandas and all the modern improvements. Mr. Whaley owns about nine hundred acres of the good farming land about Boston, and is still engaged in farming and stock raising on an extensive scale.

April 27, 1892, he married Miss Minnie Clauzelle Williams. Mrs. Whaley is a native of Eufaula, Alabama. Her grandfather, Zachariah Williams, spent all his life in the vicinity of Augusta, Georgia, and her father, Gazarway Williams, was born there, but when a young man went to Alabama and became one of the early settlers at Eufaula. With the aid of his slaves he conducted a large farm there and lived there until his death. His first wife was a Miss Abercrombie, who died leaving several children, and he afterwards married a Miss Lucy Belle Puryear, who was the mother of four children, namely: Minnie C. (Mrs. Whaley); Waller C.; Gazarway Davis; and Fay Belle.

The children of Mr. and Mrs. Whaley are Eldred Williams, Clauzelle, Rebecca, Julia, Mary Louise, Minnie Lee and Waller. Mr. Whaley and wife are members of the Methodist church South, at Boston, and he has served the church as steward and also as teacher in the Sunday-school. In politics he has taken an active interest in the Democratic party and in public affairs. He was elected county commissioner in 1894, serving until 1899, and was again elected to this office in 1909. Fraternally, he affiliates with Horeb Lodge No. 281, F. & A. M., and with J. M. Rusbin Chapter No. 23, R. A. M.

JASON M. RAMSEY. Born on the farm which he now owns and occupies, in the Grooverville district, Brooks county, on February 26, 1858, Jason M. Ramsey has long been an important factor in developing and promoting the agricultural prosperity of his community, and is held in high esteem by his neighbors and friends. His father, Richard Ramsey, was born in Bladen county, North Carolina, and his grandfather, William Harvey Ramsey, was born and bred in the same county.

While yet in the prime of a vigorous manhood William Harvey Ramsey left his native state, and, accompanied by his family, came to South Georgia in search of a more advantageous location, the overland journey made with ox teams consuming several weeks. Settling as a pioneer in Thomas county, he bought a tract of wild land, and with the help of the slaves which he brought with him cleared a farm from the wilderness, and was there employed in tilling the soil during his remaining days. He was a man of deep religious convictions, and the first Methodist to settle in what is now Thomas county. The first Methodist Episcopal church of that part of Georgia was the log cabin which he built, and in it the Methodists for miles around convened until the erection, several years later, of a church of that denomination in Grooverville. He was twice married, by his first wife having one daughter, Sally Ramsey. He married second, Dorcas Bivin, and to them ten children were born, as follows: William H., Dorcas B., Richard, Elizabeth, Ezekiel, Eliza, Thomas, Owen, Julia, and Henry. All of the sons served in the Confederate army.

Born March 6, 1822, Richard Ramsey was a small boy when brought by his parents from North Carolina to Georgia, where he grew to manhood, spending his earlier life on the home farm. For a few years after his marriage he was engaged in farming in the Boston district, of what is now Thomas county. Selling that property he removed to what is now Brooks county, buying a farm on the Boston and Grooverville road, and continued his chosen pursuit. Joining the Georgia Reserve Corps in 1864, he went to the defense of Atlanta, and served until the close of the war. Very successful in his agricultural work, he acquired a large tract of land, erected good buildings, and remained on his well-managed farm until his death, October 30, 1904. He married, January 23, 1846, Melvira Moye, who was born January 23, 1829, in Screven county, Georgia, a daughter of Furney Moye. Her father, whose birth occurred in 1785, was one of the pioneer farmers of Screven county, from there coming with his family to what is now Brooks county, and spending his remaining days in the Grooverville district. -Thirteen children were born to Richard Ramsey and his wife, as follows: Ella, Henry, Mary P., Gardner V., Jason M., Richard R., Annetta, Valeria P., Novella, Anna D., Homer H., Thomas L., and Evelina G. By his first wife, whose name was Narcissa Hurd, he had one son, William H. Ramsey.

Educated in the rural schools of his native district, Jason M. Ramsey became thoroughly versed in the theory and practice of agriculture when young, and later took charge of the home farm, and as his parents advanced in years looked carefully after their welfare. Subsequently purchasing the interests of the remaining heirs in the parental homestead, he succeeded to its ownership, and has since carried on general farming and stock raising most successfully, in his operations using modern methods.

In 1906, Mr. Ramsey married Hattie Louise Watkins, a daughter of Clark and Sally (Miller) Watkins, and granddaughter of Dr. Baker Ewing Watkins, of whom a brief account may be found on another page of this work, in connection with the sketch of Dr. J. E. Watkins. Coming to Georgia with his father in pioneer days, Clark Watkins lived in Colquitt county several years, but in 1886 bought land in the Boston district, Thomas county, and was there employed as a tiller of the soil until his death in 1890. Mr. and Mrs. Ramsey are people of much refinement, upright in principles, and are consistent and active members of the Methodist Episcopal church.

JOHN EWING WATKINS, M. D. For twenty years an active physician in southern Georgia, having a large practice and influential position as a citizen at Boston, in Thomas county, Dr. Watkins is the third doctor in as many successive generations of his family. For nearly a century the profession of medicine has been followed from father to son, and along with professional success have come honors in citizenship.

Dr. John E. Watkins was born in Colquitt county, Georgia, December 11, 1867. The family at a very early generation, probably about the time of the Revolutionary war or soon after, emigrated from the eastern colonies into the then west beyond the Blue Ridge mountains. From the best information obtainable, Joel Watkins, the great-grandfather of the doctor, was born in Tennessee, and from that state became an early settler in Whitley county, Kentucky. He married Martha Baker, a native of Virginia and a daughter of General Baker, who held a commission as an officer in the continental forces during the Revolution.

Hon. Baker Ewing Watkins, M. D., the grandfather, was born in Whitley county, Kentucky, in 1800, was reared and educated in his native state, and during his active career combined the professions of physician and a minister of the gospel for the Methodist church. In 1847, having sold his interests in Kentucky, he moved to Alabama, buying land in Coosa county and living there until 1859, when he sold out and came to Georgia. It was in this way that the family, planted in the west during one generation, was returned to the Atlantic slope during another. After two years in Webster county the grandfather bought a plantation in Terrell county, again selling this in two years, and finally bought an improved farm in Colquitt county, where he lived in the quiet pursuits of the country and in the practice of medicine until his death in 1877. He always took an interest in public affairs, and in 1825 served as a member of the Kentucky legislature. He married Sally

Berry, who was born in Kentucky and died in middle life, leaving thirteen children, whose names were: Willis, Emily, Adaliza, Crittenden, Elizabeth, Jackson, Virginia, Clark, Gideon, Harrison Lee, Sally, Harriet and Ruth.

The father of Dr. John E. was Harrison Lee Watkins, who was born in Whitley county, Kentucky, September 30, 1840, and was in his nineteenth year when the family came to Georgia. About that time he turned his attention to the study of medicine, but his course of preparation was interrupted by the outbreak of the war, at which time he entered the service of the Confederacy as hospital steward and remained until the end. He was in Atlanta during the siege, but at the fall of the city made his escape to Columbus. Though not yet a graduate in medicine, after the war he began practice in Colquitt county, and in 1869 settled at Tallokas, in Brooks county. He soon afterward entered the Southern Medical College at Savannah, where he was graduated M. D. with the class of 1873. Continuing his practice at Tallokas until 1881, he then returned to Colquitt county, and in 1887 removed to Thomas county, which remained his home until his death on August 22, 1906.

Dr. Harrison L. Watkins married Frances Miller. She was born in Sumter county, Georgia, a daughter of William H. and Amanda (Birdsong) Miller, her father being a native of Talbot county, this state. Her grandfather, William Miller, was a native of Ireland but of Scotch ancestry, and on coming to America became a pioneer settler in Talbot county, where he spent the remainder of his days. He married a Miss Simmons, who long survived him, dying at the extreme age of ninety-eight. William H. Miller removed from Talbot county to Sumter county, where he bought land and was engaged in farming and merchandising until his death, which occurred in middle life. Amanda Birdsong, his wife, was a daughter of James and Sally (McCoy) Birdsong, the latter a native of Upson county. James Birdsong was for many years a farmer in Talbot county, but removed from there to Alabama, where he spent the last years of his life. Mrs. Harrison L. Watkins (the mother) is now residing on the home farm in Thomas county with her son William Lee and family. The late Harrison L. Watkins was an influential Democrat, and represented his county in the state legislature during 1884-85.

During his boyhood John E. Watkins attended school in Brooks county, and at Boston, and then began his studies for his profession under the direction of his father and also under Dr. J. T. Culpepper. He afterward entered Atlanta Medical College, where he was graduated and received his degree of M. D. in 1891. After a brief practice in Climax, Decatur county, he came to Brooks county, practicing at Tallokas and Dixie until 1906, since which date he has attended to a growing business in Boston and vicinity.

Dr. Watkins was married in 1892 to Miss Olive Whaley, who was born in Thomas county, a daughter of Jarman Howell Whaley. The doctor and wife are the parents of the following children: Howell Lee, Frances, Elliott, Elizabeth, Merriam, Gaulden McIntosh and Olive. Dr. Watkins and wife are members of the Methodist church South, and he is a Democrat in politics, and a member of Horeb Lodge No. 281, F. & A. M., Boston.

JOSEPH WAY MOODY, D. D. S. The Moody family and its connections have been identified with south and southwest Georgia for upwards of a century, and have furnished a number of men notable for useful and honorable careers and public-spirited citizenship. As one of the younger representatives of the name, Joseph Way Moody has gained success in his profession at Boston in Thomas county, where he was born on the 10th of May, 1878.

His grandfather, S. S. Moody, was for nearly twenty years sheriff of Liberty county, and removed from that county to Savannah, where he was a cotton broker, and where he died during an epidemic of yellow fever. He married a member of the well known Georgia family of Bacons. Her first husband was named Way, and she was the mother of three children by that marriage, namely: Joseph Way, a graduate in medicine from the Jefferson Medical College of Philadelphia, who afterwards pursued his studies abroad in Paris, and who for many years was one of the foremost physicians of southeast Georgia, practicing in Chatham and Liberty counties; Moses Way, who devoted himself to the field of scholarship, became a teacher and later a minister of the Methodist church; and Cornelia Way, who married a Mr. Byrd and was a resident of Thomasville.

Dr. Moody's father was the late Prof. Axson Quarterman Moody who was born at Hinesville, Liberty county, May 4, 1840, and who died at his homestead near Boston in Thomas county, April, 1912. His only brother was William Benjamin Moody, who went away to the war when a boy and lost his life in one of the battles at Atlanta. The late Professor Moody, after fitting for college under the instruction of his half-brother, Rev. Moses Way, entered the junior class of Chapel Hill College of North Carolina and was graduated with first honors. In 1858, about the time Brooks county was organized, he settled at Grooverville, and was engaged in teaching until the war. He did a soldier's duty throughout that great struggle, and at its close located in Thomasville, where he became connected with the Fletcher Institute. Some years later removing to Boston, he began his long service as principal of the Boston Academy. During the quarter of a century in which he was the active head of that institution he taught and gave the inspiration of his character to hundreds of youth who have since filled worthy positions in life. While teaching he bought the interests of the heirs in the Daniels homestead near Boston, and that was his home until his death.

Professor Moody married Julia Catherine Daniels, who was born on the Daniels homestead a mile from Boston, and was a daughter of John and Elizabeth (Taylor) Daniels. Her grandfather, John Daniels, Sr., was one of the first settlers of southwest Georgia, locating there not long after the Florida purchase, when the south Georgia frontier first began to be settled. He settled in that part of Irwin county that is now Thomas county. Nearly all the land in this vicinity was still in state ownership, and could be bought for a price that little more than covered the cost of execution of the papers. He secured large tracts, which he did much to develop. He was also prominent in public life, representing his county in the legislature several times. As a legislator he journeyed to and from Milledgeville, then the capital, on horseback, and on one of his return trips brought along two young elm trees, which he gave to a neighbor. They were planted and are still standing, the only ones in this section, and interesting relics to the descendants of this pioneer legislator. He remained a resident of Thomas county until his death. John Daniels, Jr., father of Dr. Moody's mother, was reared in Thomas county and at the breaking out of the Civil war enlisted and died during his service for the southern cause. His widow afterwards married C. H. Hicks, who is deceased, and she is now living with her children. Professor Moody and wife reared three children, named William Benjamin, Joseph W. and Ethel May. The daughter is now the wife of A. E. Massey, who is superintendent of government contract work in New Orleans. Benjamin W., a graduate of the Atlanta Medical

College and the Atlanta School of Pharmacy, now represents the Parke-Davis Drug Company as city salesman in New Orleans. Professor Moody was twice married, his first wife having been Fanny B. Groover, who died leaving two children. The son L. G., practiced dentistry at Monticello, Florida, until his death, and the daughter, Fanny Byrd, is the wife of Samuel D. Groover.

The late Professor Moody was one of the prominent Masons of this vicinity. He became a member of the Grooverville lodge in 1867, this lodge having since been moved to Dixie and now known as Dixie lodge. When Horeb lodge was organized at Boston, he was one of its charter members. He was also a member of Thomasville chapter of Royal Arch Masons, was a charter member of J. M. Rushin Commandery of the Knights Templar, and at the time of his death had been for many years chairman of the committee on foreign correspondence.

Dr. Joseph W. Moody received his early education in the Boston public schools, and after graduation from the high school entered Atlanta Dental College, where he graduated with the class of 1903. Since that time he has been actively engaged in practice at his home town of Boston and has a large patronage. He has also been licensed to practice in Florida.

He was married February 22, 1905, to Miss Ann Elizabeth Groover, a daughter of Wiley and Virginia Groover, of Brooks county. One daughter, Virginia Groover Moody, has been born to their marriage. The doctor and wife are members of the Missionary Baptist church.

JOHN G. BURNEY. One of the progressive and successful merchants of the town of Boston, in Thomas county, Mr. Burney represents an old and respected family in this section of the state. He has been identified with this vicinity since he was born, and got his start and won an independent position in business through his ability and industry.

John G. Burney was born on a farm four miles north of Boston, on May 7, 1872. He is descended from the Scotch-Irish stock that so largely settled and gave character to the Carolinas and Georgia. James Burney, his great-granfather, was born in North Carolina, and from that state brought his family into southeast Georgia and become a pioneer of Glynn county. After a residence there for some years he moved to Florida, not long after the cession of that state by Spain, and served there during the seven years of Indian wars. He spent his last days in Duval county of that state. The maiden name of his wife was Elizabeth Freeman.

William Burney, the grandfather, was born and reared and married in Brunswick county, North Carolina, and after coming to Georgia bought land on Buffalo creek in Glynn county, where he was engaged in general farming and resided until his death at the age of seventy-one. His first wife died soon after coming to Georgia, and he then married Mrs. Rachel (Hunter) Johnson, who was born in Washington county, Georgia, and was a widow of John Johnson. She had three children by her first marriage and eight by the second.

The father of the Boston merchant was William J. Burney, who was born in Glynn county, January 11, 1832, spent his early life there, and after his marriage at the age of twenty-one engaged in farming. In 1861 he volunteered his services to the Confederate government, and was with the Fourth Georgia Cavalry in the coast defense until 1862. In the latter part of that year he put in a substitute, and after returning home removed his family, slaves and stock to Thomas county, where he bought four hundred and seventy acres in lot 331 of the Boston district. In 1864, when Sherman invaded the state, he again enlisted, this time in the Eleventh Georgia Infantry, and was at the defense of Atlanta and with the regiment in other service until the close of hostilities. Upon being paroled he returned to the farm, and has been a resident there ever since, being at this writing past eighty years of age and one of the venerable citizens of Thomas county. William J. Burney was married in 1856 to Miss Rachel Foreman, who was a native of South Carolina and daughter of Glover and Melinda Foreman. Mrs. Burney died in 1884, leaving nine children, named Frances, Ella, Lula, Claudia, William W., John G., Henry L., Alice and Margaret. In 1885 the father married for his second wife Mrs. Margaret (Anders) Anderson. She was a native of North Carolina, daughter of Owen and Mary Anders and the widow of Dr. Richard Anderson. Mr. Burney and his first wife were members of the Methodist church.

John G. Burney spent his early life on the home farm in Thomas county, getting a practical education in the common schools, and lived at home until he was twenty-four. He began his mercantile career as clerk in the hardware store of F. C. Ivey, at Boston, and by his steady application to business and ability had acquired an interest in the business by 1900, and in 1907 bought out the entire establishment. He carries a large and well selected stock of hardware, cutlery, stoves, harness, farm implements, paints, etc., and supplies a large trade throughout the vicinity about Boston. His is one of the largest stores in the Boston trading district, and he also has a commodious warehouse.

October 30, 1907, Mr. Burney married Miss Minnie Elizabeth Ingram. Mrs. Burney was born at Danville in the blue grass region of Kentucky, and her parents were D. N. and Emily Ingram. One son, John Glover, Jr., was born to Mr. and Mrs. Burney on December 10, 1910, and a daughter, Emily Ingram, born July 9, 1912. Mr. Burney and wife are members of the Boston Presbyterian church, and he is affiliated with the Horeb Lodge No. 281, F. & A. M.

JOSEPH STEBBINS NORTON. For a period of nearly forty years Mr. Norton was continuously identified with the business enterprise of Boston, in Thomas county, and while acquiring ample material prosperity has also rendered much useful service to his community as a citizen. He represented old and prominent families in Georgia and South Carolina, and many of his forefathers and relatives were men of mark in the profession and in business and civic affairs.

Joseph Stebbins Norton was born at Robertsville in the Beaufort district of South Carolina on the 31st of August, 1851. The founder of this branch of the Norton family in America was the Rev. Jonathan Norton, great-grandfather of the Boston business man. A native of England, he came to America during colonial times, settling at Hilton Head Island, South Carolina. He was a minister of the Baptist church and was pastor of the church at St. Helena Island and elsewhere in South Carolina.

Robert Godfrey Norton, the grandfather, was born at Bluffton in the Beaufort district, and became a prosperous planter in that vicinity. He also was honored with places of trust in the community, serving as sheriff and ordinary of the district for several years, and during his early life gave service to the united colonies as a revolutionary soldier. He was a lifelong resident of the Beaufort district. The maiden name of his wife was Sarah Morse. Her father, Dr. George Morse, who was throughout his life a resident of Beaufort district, was both a practicing physician and a minister of the Baptist church. Robert G. Norton and wife were blessed with long years and they celebrated the golden anniversary of their wedding day.

Alexander R. Norton, the father, was born on a plantation on the May river in Beaufort district, September 2, 1812. After his early training in the common schools he was graduated from the Charleston Medical College and later from the Savannah Medical College. His entire professional career was spent in Robertsville, South Carolina, where he gave arduous and unselfish service to a large circle of patients throughout many years. His death occurred at the age of seventy-five. (War record) Dr. Norton married Julia Elizabeth Greene, who was born in Screven county, Georgia, in 1817. Her father, John Greene, was also an active member of the medical profession, was a native Georgian, and in addition to his practice conducted a large plantation. It is also noteworthy that he was a pioneer in transportation business on the Savannah river, owning the first "pole boat" that plied between Savannah and up-river ports. Both Dr. Greene and wife are buried in the Buck churchyard on Brier creek, Screven county, near their old plantation home. Julia (Greene) Norton, the mother, died in her sixty-fourth year, and her seven children were named as follows: William B., John G., Robert G. Jr., Alexander C., Mary Eugenia, Susan Tallulah and Joseph S.

Joseph S. Norton, reared in one of the cultured homes of the south, received a good education, attending school in his native state and in Savannah, where the family lived during two years of the war. He began his business career with his brother at Stockton in Clinch county, and from there came to Boston in 1874. At that time Boston was a mere hamlet, and he was one of the first men of commercial enterprise to locate here, and was an important factor in the subsequent development of the town. He opened a store with a stock of general merchandise, and kept building and broadening his trade constantly for nearly forty years. He was at the head of the Norton Mercantile Company. For some time also he was engaged in sawmilling, and conducted one of the good farms in this vicinity.

Mr. Norton was married December 3d, 1874, to Miss Ella May Grovenstein. She was born in Effingham county, this state, a daughter of Benjamin and Emma (Metzger) Grovenstein. Both her parents were natives of Georgia, and their ancestry goes back to the original German stock that along with the Scotch-Irish and English composed the first Georgia colony, the Grovensteins and Metzgers having come in with the Salzbergers. Mr. and Mrs. Norton became the parents of ten children, named as follows: Binney A., Frederick S., Emma Augusta, Edward Judson, Bessie May, Hugh Grovenstein, Katie Eugenia, Josie Maude, Ruby Tallulah and Martha Louise.

Mr. Norton was a member of the Missionary Baptist church, as is his wife, he having served as clerk of the board. Fraternally he affiliated with Horeb Lodge No. 281, F. & A. M., and J. M. Rushin Chapter, R. A. M. In politics he was a Democrat, and for a time served as mayor of his home town of Boston. He died July 9, 1912.

JOHN W. DUKES. Only a few of the Georgian families of today can trace their ancestry in an authoritative line back to the original colony planted in this state over a century and a half ago. One representative of that period of beginnings in Georgia history is Mr. John W. Dukes, of the Boston district in Thomas county, who is only three generations removed from the founding of Georgia. His great-grandfather came to America with General Oglethorpe, and the Dukes family were among the very first settlers in Liberty and Tattnall counties.

John W. Dukes, who has spent a long and prosperous career in south Georgia, was born in what is now the Boston district of Thomas county, May 9, 1839. The date and place of his birth also indicate that the Dukes family, previously identified with the original colony of Oglethorpe, was in a subsequent generation likewise connected with the pioneer development and first settlement of southwest Georgia. His father, Edward C. Dukes, was born in Liberty county, January, 1810, and after reaching manhood brought his family to Thomas county. This migration was accomplished with horses and wagons and with slaves and many cattle. Only a few years before had the Floridas been transferred to the United States, and the entire southwest frontier of Georgia was a wilderness. Most of the land was owned by the state and sold as low as ten dollars per lot of four hundred and ninety acres. The father bought two lots numbered 330 and 331, built a log cabin in the forest, and then with his slaves set to work to clear up a farm. After a few years' residence there he gave one of his lots to a preacher friend, and moved to what is now the Dry Lake district of Brooks county. He bought a large tract of land, erected a commodious frame residence, and lived there until his death on July 17, 1855.

Edward C. Dukes married Nanny Hodges, who was born in Tattnall county, February 6, 1813, a daughter of William Hodges. She survived her husband and was married a second time, to John Hancock. Her death occurred in 1872. The twelve children of Edward A. and Nanny (Hodges) Dukes were: Martha A., Elizabeth J., Caroline, John W., George R., Elias C., Julia A., Edward T., Henry C., Millard F., Florence C. and William B. Of these, John W., George R., Elias C. and Edward T., were all soldiers for the Confederacy.

John W. Dukes was a child when the family moved to Brooks county, and was reared and lived at home until the war. In 1861 he enlisted in Company C of the Sixth Georgia Infantry, and was attached to Gordon's corps in the army of North Virginia. During the following three years he did a soldier's duty in many of the great battles of the war, including Gettysburg. In 1864, in the terrific struggles at the Wilderness, he was taken prisoner, was placed in the federal prison at Elmira, New York, and was not released until the end of the war. He was then carried as far as Point Lookout in Maryland, and from there made the best of his way home, walking most of the distance to southern Georgia.

In the meantime his mother had removed from the home farm, which he now took charge of and managed for three years. Then at the settlement of the estate, he bought the homestead and continued farming it for ten years, when he sold. He next bought a tract of timbered land on Mule creek in the Tallokas district of Brooks county, and after clearing up part of it traded for a farm and water-power site with a grist and saw mill on the Ochlochnee river in Thomas county. This place was exchanged two years later for his present homestead, situated close to the place on which he was born, and consisting of five hundred and twenty acres in lots 360 and 361.

In 1860, Mr. Dukes married Miss Wealthy E. Peacock, of an old and prominent family in this part of Georgia. She was born in Brooks county, a daughter of Dr. Howell and Mary (Mitchell) Peacock. Dr. Howell Peacock, who was a son of Robert and Wealthy (Howell) Peacock, was for many years a practicing physician, and spent his last years in Thomas county. His wife, whose maiden name was Mary Raines Mitchell, was a daughter of Col. Thomas Mitchell, a native of Virginia, who commanded a troop of cavalry during the Revolutionary war (see sketch of Hon. R. G. Mitchell elsewhere in this work). After a wedded companionship lasting nearly a half century, Mrs. Dukes passed away in 1909. She reared two children, Mattie and Edward. The latter has always lived at home and has been associated with his father in farming. The daughter Mattie is the wife of A. J. McKinnon, and has six children, Frank L., Clara May, Wealthy E., Lucy A., George R. and Howell E. Mr. Dukes, as was his wife, is a member of the Baptist church, but their children are all members of the Methodist church.

GEORGE W. HOWARD. Some of the earliest settlers of Thomas county and vicinity are represented by Mr. George W. Howard, who is himself somewhat of an old settler, having been born in what is now the Metcalf district of Thomas county on the 27th of August, 1846. At that time population was sparse and practically none of the modern improvements had appeared in the great forest-covered district of southwest Georgia.

This branch of the Howard family on coming from England had first settled in Maryland, but Mr. Howard's father, William Howard, was a native of Virginia. At the age of twenty-one he had left home and entered the employ of Dr. Epps, for whom he made an overland trip to Florida, taking along his employer's slaves. For several years he remained in Florida as an overseer of large plantations, and then came into southwest Georgia and bought two hundred and fifty acres of land in the present Metcalf district. Only a small clearing had been made in the midst of the forest which covered his purchase, and he erected a set of log buildings for shelter to his household and then set to work to clear the land for a farm. In those days and indeed for a number of years he marketed his crops in Tallahassee, all transportation being over the country roads and with wagons and teams. As a tiller of the soil he became very prosperous, acquired seven hundred and fifty acres of land and had a number of slaves to make the crops. His death occurred at the age of seventy-one, being caused by an accident at the cotton press.

William Howard married Miss Meeky Ferrell, whose family were likewise early settlers in this part of Georgia. She was born in North Carolina. Her father, Hutchins Ferrell, also a native of that state, brought his family and household in wagons and other conveyances to south Georgia, locating in Metcalf district of Thomas county. There he bought land and with the aid of his slaves cleared up another farm from the wilderness, thus adding to the productive area which has made modern conditions possible. Hutchins Ferrell spent the remainder of his life in this vicinity. He married Elizabeth Morgan, who survived his death many years. Mrs. William Howard, who died at the age of seventy-nine, was the mother of nine children, whose names follow: Elizabeth, George W., Anna, Jennie, Virginia, Amanda, John F., Thomas J. and Mary Lee. The father of this family was an old-line Democrat, and both he and wife were devout Methodists and brought up their children in the same faith.

During his boyhood spent on the home farm George W. Howard attended the common schools, and lived at home and assisted in the work of the farm until he was seventeen years old. In November, 1863, he offered his services to the Confederate government and became a soldier in Company D of the Second Florida Cavalry, serving with that regiment until the close of the war, when he returned home. After the death of his father he managed the home estate for several years, and finally bought a part of it from the other heirs, and made his home there until 1897. He then lived with his brother John until the latter's death, at which time he located on his present farm two miles west of Boston. His nephews are associated with him in the ownership of this place. Mr. Howard is a member of the Methodist church, and in politics follows the example of his father.

JOHN DAVID BOZEMAN. A well known and prosperous agriculturist of Brooks county, John David Bozeman has for nearly forty years been successfully engaged in his independent and useful occupation, his estate being situated three miles north of Quitman, on the Tallokas road, and being considered one of the most attractive in the vicinity. He was born October 26, 1836, in Jefferson county, Florida, a son of David Bozeman.

His paternal grandfather, Luke Bozeman, was born, it is supposed, in Maryland, where the name was formerly spelled Boseman, a form still retained by some members of the family. Migrating southward, he settled in Twiggs county, Georgia, as a pioneer. Georgia was then a frontier state, Indians being far more numerous than whites. Purchasing a tract of wild land, he reclaimed a homestead from the forest, and there spent the remainder of his years. He married Sarah Mann, who was also a native of Maryland, and to them five sons and three daughters were born as follows: Elizabeth, Dorothy, David, James, Luke, William and Eldred.

Born and reared in Twiggs county, Georgia, his birth occurring February 16, 1794, David Bozeman grew to manhood on the home farm, for many years assisting in its management. About 1830, accompanied by his brother-in-law, Solomon Mathews, and by Thomas Mathews, and their families, he removed to Florida. They made the trip with ox teams, taking along their household goods and stock, cooking and camping by the wayside, each night some of the men standing guard against the raids of Indians. They all located in Jefferson county, being among the earliest settlers of that place. For many years thereafter there were no railways in either Georgia or Florida, the people living in a very primitive style, with few conveniences of any kind. Their first act almost was to build a stockade or fort of logs, to which the women and children could flee when the dusky savages started on a raid. Taking part in the Indian war of 1836, David Bozeman served as first lieutenant of his company.

Soon after locating in Jefferson county, David Bozeman purchased from the government one hundred and sixty acres of land, and on it built of round logs the house which the family occupied a few years, when a substantial frame house was erected in its place. The nearest markets and trading points were Tallahassee and Port Leon, thirty-five miles distant, and all surplus productions of the land were hauled there by ox teams. He, in common with all of the pioneers, labored hard, in addition to tilling the land tanning the skins and making the shoes for the family, for several years using coon skins, while his wife did her cooking by the fireplace, and in addition to her other domestic duties used to card, spin and weave the material from which she fashioned all the garments worn by the family. On the farm which he cleared and improved, he lived until his death, February 16, 1848.

David Bozeman was twice married. He married first Sarah Mann, who lost her life by accident, having been burned to death. He married second, Catherine Barr, who was born in Florida, where her parents were among the first English speaking settlers. She died at the age of thirty-five years, while two of her brothers also lived to a very advanced age, Thomas Barr attaining the age of ninety-six years, and Rodger Barr living to the age of eighty-seven years. By his first marriage David Bozeman reared six children, as follows: Elisha Ward; Caroline and Mary Ann, twins; Luke; Elizabeth Mann; and Celia. By his second marriage he became the father of two children, John David and Sarah Ann.

When John David Bozeman was six years of age his parents located in the southern part of Jefferson county, about six miles from Monticello. In those days the wild beasts of the forest had not fled before the advancing steps of civilization, but, with the red skins, habited the vast wilderness. He was twelve years old when his father died, and from that time until nineteen years of age he lived with his oldest brother, Elisha Ward Bozeman. Beginning the battle of life then on his own account, he secured a position in a livery stable, receiving in addition to his board twenty dollars a month wages, the stable being located in Thomasville. At that time Brooks county had not been formed, the country roundabout being very thinly settled, and Troupville was then the county seat of Lowndes county. From 1854 until 1856 Mr. Bozeman drove a hack from Thomasville to Monticello, Troupville, and other points. In 1856 he began to learn the cabinet maker's trade, serving an apprenticeship of six months. Desirous then of learning the carpenter's trade, he entered the employ of John Wind, of the firm of Bowen Brothers & Wind, and worked on the Thomas county court house.

In April, 1859, when Quitman was platted, Mr. Bozeman settled in the new town as its first carpenter, and built for himself a log house in the southern part of the place. Early in 1862 he enlisted from Thomas county, in the company known as the "Seventeenth Patriot's," which was attached to the Twenty-ninth Georgia Volunteer Infantry, and became a part of the western army. He fought under General Bragg, Johnston, and Hood. After the battle of Nashville, the regiment was sent to Virginia, thence to North Carolina, where, on April 26, 1865, at Greensboro, it surrendered.

Returning to his home in Quitman, Mr. Bozeman was here engaged in carpentering until 1873, when he assumed possession of the land which he had previously purchased, it being located on the Tallokas road, three miles north of Quitman. By dint of hard work and good management he has here cleared and improved a valuable farm, having been very successful in his agricultural operations. His improvements are of an excellent character, including the erection of a good set of farm buildings, his house being most pleasantly situated in a grove composed of various kinds of forest trees, and being set well back from the street.

In July 1, 1858, Mr. Bozeman was united in marriage with Sarah Blanche Lewis, who was born in what is now Brooks county, Georgia, October 27, 1840. Her father, Irvin J. Lewis, was born in Bulloch county, Georgia, where his parents were early settlers. Left an orphan at an early age, he was reared by his uncle, Abner Groover, a pioneer of that part of Thomas county now included in Brooks county, it then having been an extreme frontier county. He was brought up on a farm, and on attaining manhood purchased land lying seven miles northwest of Quitman, and on the farm which he cleared he spent the remainder of his life. Mr. Lewis married Susan Thigpin, who was born in Wilkes county, Georgia, a daughter of Rev. Meles Thigpin, a preacher in the Primitive Baptist church. On coming from North Carolina, his native state, to Georgia, Mr. Thigpin lived first in Wilkes county, later becoming one of the original settlers of what is now Brooks county. Securing four hundred and ten acres of land, ten miles north of the present site of Quitman, he cleared a large plantation, and was there engaged in agricultural pursuits until his death. The maiden name of his wife was Sarah Whaley. Irvin J. and Susan (Thigpin) Lewis reared six children, as follows: Mary; Sarah Blanche, now Mrs. Bozeman; Caroline; Janie; Valeria; and Wiley Miles.

Mr. and Mrs. Bozeman have reared eight children, namely: Irvin Elisha (the first child born in Quitman); Alice P.; John D.; Willie L.;

Christopher L.; Susan; James C.; and Lewis I. Irvin E. married Martha Young, and they have three children, Evelyn, Francis, and Janie C, Willie married Houston A. Young, and they are the parents of four children, Lucretia, Tinly, Flavious, and Everett. Christopher married Lillie Oliff. Susan, wife of Frank M. Mathews, has four children, Joel, John B., Alice and Frank M. Janie, who married W. C. Parker, died leaving one daughter, Mary Blanche. John David, Jr., who became a lieutenant in the local militia, died in Jacksonville, Florida, aged twenty-seven years.

Politically Mr. Bozeman has always been a Democrat. He cast his first vote for governor in favor of Ben Hill, and gave his first presidential vote to John C. Breckinridge. Both he and Mrs. Bozeman are members of the Methodist Episcopal church, South.

Mr. Bozeman and Mr. Clinton Groover are the only living settlers now among the pioneers of this county.

WILLIAM NELSON CRANE. A man of good business capacity, intelligent and enterprising, William Nelson Crane holds high rank among the extensive and prosperous agriculturists of Brooks county, his well appointed estate being situated about six miles from Quitman, on the Tallokas road. A native of Brooks county, he was born October 26, 1859, on the farm of his father, Ephriam Thayer Crane. He comes of Revolutionary stock, and is the descendant of a New England family of prominence and worth, being a lineal descendant of the immigrant ancestor, Henry Crane, the lineage being thus traced: Henry[1] Crane, Ebenezer[2] Crane, Abijah[3] Crane, Abijah Barry[4] Crane, Ephraim Thayer[5] Crane, and William Nelson[6] Crane.

Henry[1] Crane was born in England in 1621, and died in Massachusetts in 1709. He was twice married, the maiden name of his second wife, from whom William Nelson Crane is descended, having been Elizabeth Kinstry. Their son, Ebenezer[2] Crane, born in East Milton, Massachusetts, August 10, 1665, married Mary Tolman, a native of Dorchester, Massachusetts. Abijah[3] Crane, born in Milton, Massachusetts, November 2, 1841, was a member of the party that, on December 16, 1773, threw the tea overboard in Boston Harbor, and was a brother of Col. John Crane, of Revolutionary fame. He married first Sarah Field, of Braintree, Massachusetts, and married second Sarah Beverly. Abijah Barry[4] Crane, a life-long resident of Massachusetts, was born August 24, 1777, in Boston, and died in 1854, in Medfield. The maiden name of his wife was Rachel Hatch Curtis.

Ephraim Thayer[5] Crane was born in Boston, Massachusetts, in 1816. Brought up and educated in his native city, he remained in Boston until about eighteen years of age, when, following the southward course of migration, he came to Georgia, locating in Savannah, where he found employment in the gun factory owned by Ned Lovell. A few years later he settled in what is now Brooks county, and having purchased a tract of land lying ten miles north of the present site of Quitman engaged not only in farming, but in the manufacture of fire-arms. He built up a substantial business, and continued his residence on the farm which he improved until his death, at the advanced age of eighty-two years. He married Mary Wilson, who was born in Brooks county, Georgia, a daughter of Jeremiah and Betty (Lucas) Wilson, of whom a more extended record may be found on another page of this work, in connection with the sketch of Joseph D. Wilson. She survived him, passing away at the age of four score and four years. Four children were born of their marriage, as follows: Abijah Barry Crane, who lost his life in the Confederate service; Julia E.; Isabelle; and William Nelson.

William Nelson[6] Crane was reared in Brooks county, educated in the rural schools, and early in life chose the free and independent occupation of his ancestors. Inheriting one hundred and fifty acres of the parental estate, located in the western part of the county, he was there prosperously employed in tilling the soil until 1897. Selling out in that year, Mr. Crane purchased his present fine property, which consists of four hundred acres of rich and fertile land, situated six miles north of Quitman, on the Tallokas road. Continuing his agricultural labors, he has met with most satisfactory results as a general farmer, each year reaping abundant harvests.

Mr. Crane married, in 1880, Annie M. Folsom, a daughter of Thomas and Victoria (Williams) Folsom. She was born in Brooks county, and here spent her entire life, her death occurring on the home farm in 1909. To them the following children were born: Eugene Thomas, who died at the age of eighteen years; Lucy; Ettie; Myrtie; Annie May; and William Bennett. Lucy, wife of A. J. Moran died in 1912, leaving three children, Gladys, Glenn, and Mary Lee. Ettie married Bluford Smith, and they have one child, Bluford Smith, Jr. Mr. Crane belongs to the Primitive Baptist church, of which Mrs. Crane was also an active and valued member.

ALPHA C. BERRY. Prominent among the enterprising, self-reliant, and progressive men who are so ably conducting the agricultural interests of Brooks county is Alpha C. Berry, a successful farmer living about five miles from Quitman, on the Tallokas road. A son of Rev. Joseph Festus Berry, he was born June 6, 1869, in Marshalltown, Iowa.

His grandfather Berry, was born in Stanton, Virginia, where his father located on coming to this country. An energetic, enterprising young man, he decided to begin life for himself in a newer part of the country, and, foreseeing in a measure the great development awaiting the then far West, he migrated to Illinois, settling in Washington county. Possessing excellent business ability and judgment, he became an extensive dealer in real estate, buying and selling several farms, always at a profit. He lived to the venerable age of ninety years.

The birth of Joseph Festus Berry occurred in Washington county, Illinois, in 1840. Brought up on a farm he acquired his preliminary education in the district schools, this being supplemented with a course of study at Bethany College, in Bethany, West Virginia. After his graduation from that institution he taught in the public schools of Illinois for a time. Ordained, at the age of thirty years, a minister in the Christian church, he preached for a short time in New York state, and subsequently taught school and held pastorates in Iowa, Nebraska, and Kansas. Coming to Georgia in the spring of 1886, Rev. Mr. Berry began his ministerial labors in Lowndes county, where he organized several Christian churches, including the one at Pine Grove, and also organized the Christian church at Quitman. Going to Missouri in 1907 he resided first in the Ozark region, moving from there to Dexter, Missouri, he was there a resident until his death in 1910. His wife, whose maiden name was Maria Parmley, was born in Warren, Ohio, and died in 1910, surviving him but one month. Seven children were born of their union, as follows: Alpha C., the subject of this sketch; Elpie Grace, of Little Rock, Arkansas; Dollie May lived but ten years; Scott, now an instructor at the University of Michigan, in Ann Arbor, and a man of brilliant mental attainments, earned as a student an international scholarship, which entitled him to a year's schooling in Germany and five hundred dollars in cash; Leslie Lee, a graduate of the Missouri Agricultural College, in Columbia, Missouri, is now one of the leading agriculturists and horticulturists of Dexter, Missouri; Milton, engaged in the grocery business at Denver, Colorado; and Bessie, residing at Little Rock, Arkansas.

After his graduation from the Valdosta Academy, in Valdosta, Georgia, Alpha C. Berry turned his attention to agriculture, for which he had a natural taste and aptitude. He first purchased, in Brooks county, two hundred and fifty acres of land lying two miles from Quitman, on the Morven road. Seven years later he sold at an advantage, and bought an estate of five hundred acres situated two miles northeast of Quitman. Ninety acres of the tract was under cultivation, and he improved one hundred more, and lived there seven years. Selling then, Mr. Berry purchased what was known as the Tom Folsom place, it being on the Tallokas road, five miles from Quitman, and here he has since been actively engaged in general farming and stock raising. His large and valuable estate contains nine hundred acres of land, two hundred and seventy-five of which he has under culture, while one hundred and fifty acres are covered with a magnificent growth of oak, hickory, pine, gum, poplar and ash timber, the remainder being covered with young pines. In the development and improvement of his land, Mr. Berry finds both pleasure and profit, his labors being well rewarded.

On January 3, 1894, Mr. Berry was united in marriage with Lillie Wilson, a daughter of Jeremiah and Delilah (Robinson) Wilson, of whom a more extended account may be found elsewhere in this volume, in connection with the sketch of Joseph D. Wilson. Mr. and Mrs. Berry are the parents of two children, namely: Julia and Delilah.

Religiously both Mr. and Mrs. Berry are consistent members of the Christian church. Mr. Berry is a member of the Hickory Head Club, an association of farmers organized in 1899.

ALBERT C. SWEAT. One of the ablest newspaper editors and managers in south Georgia is the present proprietor of the Nashville *Herald.* Mr. Sweat has been identified with the newspaper business nearly all his life, learning the art of sticking type when he was a boy, and through his own efforts and ability rising from the case to the chair of editor and owner.

He was born in Pierce county, this state, on the 7th of March, 1871. His only sister, Sally, the wife of J. A. Wade of Douglas, Georgia.

Owing to circumstances, Albert C. began earning his own way when a boy fifteen years of age, and his subsequent prosperity and influential position have been the result of his own endeavors. He first learned telegraphy, but was too young to be accepted as an operator, and for this reason he turned from what might have been a life vocation to employment in the office of the Blackshear *Georgian,* a weekly paper. There he learned the use of the composing stick, and in 1889, at the age of eighteen, became foreman for the Douglas *Breeze,* the first newspaper ever issued in Douglas. In a short time he became manager and editor of this paper and conducted it for six years. He also edited the Jesup *Sentinel* one year for Capt. Ben Miliken. Mr. Sweat then went to Texas and in 1899, with two associates, established a daily paper, the *Morning Sun,* at Denison. After a year he sold his interest in that publication, and, returning to Georgia, was engaged in publishing the Sparks *Enterprise* in Berrien county until December, 1903. At that date he removed his plant to Nashville and established the *Herald,* of which he is the sole owner, and which he has made successful as a business enterprise and influential among a large circle of readers. In 1912, Mr. Sweat erected at Nashville what is known as the Herald building, the first three-story structure in town. The two upper floors are used as an opera house, and the first floor is the home of the *Herald* and its job printing establishment. This handsome brick building, occupying ground thirty-three by ninety feet, is a credit to the enterprise of its builder and to the growing importance of Nashville as a center of population and commerce.

In Berrien county and elsewhere Mr. Sweat has always been an active and useful citizen. He is chairman of the board of county commissioners, is the present city clerk of Nashville, and has served in the city council and on the school board. He is also chairman of the Democratic executive committee of Berrien county. Fraternally he affiliates with Nashville Lodge No. 243, F. & A. M., the lodges of Woodmen of the World, Odd Fellows and Knights of Pythias, at Nashville, and the Tifton lodge of Elks.

In April, 1891, he married Miss Annie Glover. Mrs. Sweat is a native of Polk county, this state. They are the parents of four children, named Hoke, Glyds, Kate and Clifford. Mr. and Mrs. Sweat are members of the Methodist church at Nashville.

JUDGE JAMES B. HICKS. The career of James B. Hicks, attorney, judge, legislator, business man and all around good citizen, is one that one may contemplate with all pleasure and nothing of opposing sentiment. A straightforward statement of the facts of his progress from the rural districts which represented his home to his present high place in the social economic fabric of the county of which he is a resident cannot fail to prove of interest, and the record of his life thus far is here set forth, devoid of all attempt at embellishment or adornment of whatever variety.

James B. Hicks was born in Wrightsville, Georgia, on February 28, 1870, and he is a son of Dr. Henry and Nancy (Wright) Hicks. The father, long a practicing physician in his district, was born on the 15th of September, 1832, and died on June 24, 1900. The birth of the mother occurred on September 23, 1841, and she survived her husband some five years, passing away on April 27, 1905. Both were natives of Johnson county. The father served as a surgeon during the Civil war with the Confederate army, with Johnson's Grays, and four of his brothers also served in that regiment.

When James B. Hicks was five years old his parents moved to Laurens county, and there they lived on a farm for ten years. The boy attended the district schools during that time, and when he was fifteen the family moved to Milledgeville, Georgia, in order that the children might have greater educational advantages, school facilities in their former home district being of a limited nature. He attended school at Milledgeville in the Middle Georgia Military and Agricultural College for two years, and thereafter attended Mercer University at Macon, Georgia. He was graduated from the university in 1892 with his bachelor's degree, and came almost immediately to Dublin, where he took service with his brother, who was a member of the drug firm of the H. Hicks & Company, in the capacity of collector. After a year at this work he went to Atlanta, Georgia, where he read law under Hines, Shubrick & Felder for a year, and in 1893 he was admitted to the bar. He returned to Dublin at that time and began the practice of law, a profession in which he has experienced an unusually fair degree of success. He has taken a prominent place in the public eye, and his service as mayor of Dublin for two terms, 1899 and 1900, was one of the greatest values to the city. In 1902, Mr. Hicks was elected to the state legislature as a representative from his county, and something of the standing he enjoys in the county may be gleaned from the facts that of five candidates in the race for the legislative offices, with two to be elected, of two thousand, six hundred votes polled, Mr. Hicks received every vote in the county with the exception of about three hundred. He served through the years of 1902, 1903 and 1904, in the Georgia legislature, and was one of the several men who voted to change the legislative session from fall to summer.

After his nomination to the legislative office in 1902 Mr. Hicks was siezed with an attack of nervous indigestion, which clung persistently to him all through his legislative career, and so impaired his general health that when he left the legislature he repaired to his farm in the county and there continued for some time. He kept up a part of his law practice, however, during that time, spending a part of his time on the farm until 1911. On November 10th of that year he was appointed by Governor Hoke Smith as judge of the city court of Dublin to fill out the unexpired term of Judge K. J. Hawkins, who had been promoted to the bench of the superior courts of the Dublin circuit. In 1912, Mr. Hicks was a candidate for the judgeship for a full term, and made an excellent run for the nomination, being nominated by a majority of three hundred and forty-seven votes over the highest opponent. He was elected to the office and is now giving service in his capacity as judge.

Judge Hicks is a prominent Mason, with a membership in the blue lodge and the Royal Arch Masons. He is also a member of the Knights of Pythias and the Benevolent and Protective Order of Elks. He still retains membership in the Kappa Sigma, his college fraternity, and is a member of the Christian church. Among many other interests of Judge Hicks, he has continued to retain his identity with the agricultural activities of the county and is the owner of something like seventeen hundred acres of fine land.

Judge Hicks was one of the six children of his parents, all of whom are living with the exception of B. G. Hicks, who died at the early age of nineteen years, at Milledgeville, Georgia. The others are: Mrs. Leslie Kennedy, of Dublin; Mrs. Mabel A. Warthen, of Bartow, Georgia; Talmadge M., a practicing attorney of Dublin; and R. P., who is engaged in farming in the vicinity of Wrightsville, Georgia. The father raised a family by an earlier marriage and those children are Frances, Elizabeth and John W., both deceased; and Thomas B., of Dublin, Georgia.

The especially brilliant career of Judge Hicks thus far has been one that has brought honor to the family name, and established it even more firmly in the annals of his county, where the house of Hicks has long been known for many splendid qualities of heart and mind.

JUDGE ROBERT G. MITCHELL. A man of the true and noble character for which the sons of the Southland are noted, Robert Goodwin Mitchell has played his part bravely and well in all the activities of his life. He has served his state in times of war, suffering severe wounds in the service of the cause of the Confederacy, and has served it no less efficiently in times of peace, as a legislator, and also as an industrious private citizen and a Christian gentleman. A native of the community in which he has passed the greater part of his long and honored life. Judge Mitchell was born on a plantation in Thomas county, Georgia, July 15, 1843. His father, the Hon. Richard Mitchell, was born near Petersburg, Virginia, in 1797, the son of Col. Thomas Mitchell.

Col. Thomas Mitchell was a native of the Old Dominion state, and commanded a troop of cavalry in the War of the Revolution. After the colonies had been freed from the yoke of tyranny, Colonel Mitchell moved from Virginia, and settled in Montgomery county, Georgia, where he resided for some years. He finally left his home in that locality, however, and became one of the pioneer settlers of southern Georgia, establishing himself in Thomas county, on a tract of wooded land about nine miles southwest of Thomasville. There he built a log house, one of the early type, with a puncheon floor. He was the owner of a number of slaves, and set them to work to clear his land, and put it under cultivation. Colonel Mitchell is said to have been the first to grow sugar cane for market. He made what was called "sugar mush" of the cane, and hauled it in this form to the port of St. Marks, about sixty-five miles distant, for shipment to New York. This proved a profitable venture, and he continued to grow cane on his plantation until his death. He was buried on the plantation where he had lived, in the family burying ground, where his wife also sleeps.

The father of the subject of this history was a mere boy when his parents moved to Georgia. Having received a good education as a foundation for success, he started out as a young man in the mercantile business at old Hartford, Pulaski county, Georgia. After a time, however, he gave up this enterprise, and moved to Thomas county, where he bought land near his father's estate, and engaged in the pursuit of agriculture. He remained on this land where he had a number of slaves at work for him, until his death, which occurred on the twelfth of February, 1856. A member of the old Whigs, Richard Mitchell always took an active interest in public affairs. His devotion to his party and to the best interests of his community were rewarded in the 30's, by his election to the state legislature, a representative from Pulaski county.

Richard Mitchell was united in marriage to Sophronia Dickey, who was born near Sumpter, South Carolina, in the year 1808, and died many years after her husband, on the 17th of May, 1893, at the advanced age of eighty-five years. Sophronia Dickey Mitchell was the mother of nine children. One of these, a daughter, and the second child, died in infancy, but the rest lived to the age of maturity. Their names are as follows: Henry, Frances Nelson, Richard Raines, William Dickey, Sarah Ann, Robert Goodwin, Harriet E., and Amy Susan.

After some preliminary work in the neighborhood schools, Robert Goodwin Mitchell attended Fletcher Institute, at Thomasville, and later he was a student in the preparatory department of Mercer University for one term. When but eighteen years old, he volunteered for the Confederate service at Thomasville, and was mustered in Savannah in July, 1861, as color bearer, in Company E of the Twenty-ninth Regiment. Soon after this he was appointed sergeant and at the re-organization in 1862, was made second lieutenant of his company.

The Twenty-ninth was held on the coast, serving about Atlanta, and between that city and Charleston, until May, 1863, when it was sent to Mississippi as part of the command of Gen. W. H. T. Walker, for the re-enforcement of Gen. Joseph E. Johnston. There Lieutenant Mitchell participated in the fighting about Jackson, and the march toward Vicksburg, and when Gen. C. C. Wilson, of the Twenty-first Regiment, was put in command of the brigade, including the Twenty-ninth, he was appointed to his staff as aide-de-camp. In this capacity he participated in the gallant and important service of Walker's division at the battle of Chickamauga, and during one siege of Chattanooga, and the battle of Missionary Ridge.

General Wilson dying about this time at Ringgold, Gen. C. H. Stevens assumed the command of the brigade with his own staff, and Lieutenant Mitchell returned to his regiment, and was at once appointed adjutant, in which capacity he performed his duty brilliantly throughout the Dalton and Atlanta campaigns. He was in battle about Dalton, at Resaca, Cassville, New Hope Church, Kenesaw Mountain, Peachtree

Creek, and was in the battle at Atlanta in which General Walker was killed, on July 22, 1864, and after serving in the entrenchments under fire following this last-named engagement, was severely wounded on the line southwest of the city, August 9, 1864. His wound entirely incapacitated him for duty during the remainder of the war, and after remaining under treatment at Macon for some time, he returned home. He was forced, however, to use crutches for six months after peace had been declared.

The Twenty-ninth Regiment was commanded by Judge Mitchell's brother, Col. William Dickey Mitchell, who was severely wounded at Chickamauga. Having recovered from this wound, Colonel Mitchell joined Hood's command, and went on the Tennessee campaign, taking part in the battles of Murfreesboro, Franklin, and Nashville. He was captured in the battle of Nashville, and taken to Johnson's Island, Lake Erie, where he was detained as a prisoner of war until the contest was ended. Upon his return home he engaged in the practice of law at Thomasville, in which place he made his home, living in the honor and esteem of the entire community, and receiving many honors, among them the offices of county judge, in which capacity he was serving at the time of his death, which occurred in 1892.

It was while Robert G. Mitchell was disabled from the wound he received in the war that he began the study of law, a profession in which he was destined to attain many honors. After his admission to the bar, he formed a partnership with his brother William. In 1873 he was appointed solicitor general of the southern circuit of Georgia, a position which he held for about twelve years. At the end of this time he resigned, and in 1884 was elected to the state senate, serving in the session of 1884-5. In the year 1890, he was again chosen to receive the honor of the state senatorship, and represented his district in the legislature of that year, serving in that session and that of the following year as president of the senate. Upon the consummation of his term as senator, Judge Mitchell resumed the practice of his profession, and held no public office until 1903, when he was elected judge of the superior court of the southern circuit of Georgia, to succeed Judge Hansell. He resigned from this office in 1910, having been one of the best judges the state of Georgia has ever known.

Since his retirement from the judgeship, Judge Mitchell has been engaged in the peaceful pursuit of agriculture. He has a farm of about two thousand acres, situated from six to eight miles south of Thomasville. He resides in Thomasville on the outskirts of the city, in the home he has occupied since 1865. His house is a commodious frame structure, built in colonial style, with large pillars supporting the porch. It is situated about one hundred feet back from the street, in a lawn well-shaded by large oak and magnolia trees, and with an avenue of stately pecan trees leading to the door.

On the 21st of January, 1864, Robert G. Mitchell was married to Amaretta Fondren, who was born in Dublin, Laurens county, Georgia, the daughter of John G. and Nancy Thompson Fondren, both natives of Laurens county. For many years Mr. Fondren was in the mercantile business in Dublin, afterward coming to Thomas county, where he bought a large tract of land, on which he employed as many as two hundred slaves. He spent the last days of his life in Thomasville, where he died before the war. Judge and Mrs. Mitchell have been blessed with nine children, who have reached maturity, and two others, Rufus L. and Harriet E., who died in childhood, aged fourteen and five years respectively. The children who have survived are as follows: Minnie Lee, Frances, Annette, Robert Goodwin, John Fondren, Emmett, Carl,

Julian Raines, and Richard. Of these, Minnie Lee married Dr. W. W. Bruce, of Thomasville, and has one child, Helen; Annette is the wife of Theodosius Winn, a resident of Thomasville, and has three children, Davies, Nettie, and Sarah; Robert G., who is now an attorney of Blackshear, Georgia, is married to Mary O. Acosta, and has eight children, Blanche Acosta, Catherine, Robert Goodwin, Emily, Eustace, Mary Lillian, Nettie Fondren, and John Gorden; John F., married Anne Montgomery; Emmett married Augusta Bowen Lathrop, and has three children, Lathrop, Emmett, and Fondren. Carl is cashier of a bank at Lyons, Georgia, and Julian R. is a resident of Kansas City, Missouri. The judge's daughters received their education in the Thomasville schools, graduating from the Young Female College.

John F. took a law course at Athens, Georgia, and served three terms in the Georgia legislature and lacked but two votes of being elected speaker.

Mrs. Mitchell and the judge are both members of the Missionary Baptist church, and have reared their sons and daughters in the same faith. Besides his many interests in public and private life, Judge Mitchell has found time to affiliate with the Masonic fraternity, belonging to the Thomasville lodge of that organization. He is also a member of the W. D. Mitchell Camp of Confederate Veterans.

The following, which appeared in a paper in the locality in which Judge Mitchell makes his home, is a true testimonial of the esteem and honor in which he is so deservedly held:

"Throughout all his career, civil and military, he has been loyal to his country, his party, and generous and public spirited. * * * He did heroic service in redeeming Georgia from the second invasion, known as the 'reconstruction,' and he is one of the old guard, never departing from the faith, always holding to the time-honored principles of his party, warning against strange doctrines and new departures."

HON. ARCHIBALD THOMPSON MACINTYRE. Among the notable Georgia families none has been more conspicuous in public and professional life nor borne the responsibilities of citizenship with greater dignity and social service than have the MacIntyres during three generations of their residence in this state.

The family was identified with colonial and revolutionary times as well as the activities of the later national period. Daniel MacIntyre, the founder of the American branch, was a native of Scotland and a North Carolina settler. During the Revolution he served as a patriot soldier from January, 1777, to August, 1780. So far as known, he spent all his latter years in North Carolina.

Archibald MacIntyre, son of this Scotch immigrant and Revolutionary soldier, was born in North Carolina in 1776 and probably early in the following century came into Georgia, settling first in Twiggs county, and then becoming a pioneer of southwest Georgia, in Irwin county. He bought land in that part of the county now known as the Grooverville district of Brooks county. Archibald MacIntyre was a scholarly man, and by profession a civil engineer, and in the latter capacity made a number of surveys in this section of the state. With the aid of his slaves he cleared a farm, on which he resided until his death in 1830. Hannah Lawson, who became the wife of Archibald MacIntyre, also represented a prominent name in colonial history. Hugh Lawson, her great-grandfather, came to America and lived for a time in the Pennsylvania colony, and from there to Lunenburg, Virginia, in 1743, and was judge of the county court there in 1746. He later moved to Rowan county, North Carolina, where the records show that he bought land from Earl Granville in 1759. His death occurred in 1772. Roger Lawson, a Revolutionary soldier and the grandfather of, Hannah, married Hannah Thompson, whose father was a minister of the Presbyterian church. Their son, Col. John Lawson, the father of Hannah, was a commissioned officer during the Revolutionary war. He married Alice Moore. Hannah (Lawson) MacIntyre survived her husband and died in 1842. Roger Lawson and his son Col. John Lawson, both received grants of land for their services in the Revolutionary war.

Archibald Thompson MacIntyre, Sr., son of the above Archibald, was born in Twiggs county, Georgia, October 27, 1822, and in 1843 was admitted to the bar and opened an office at Thomasville. In a few years distinction and success came to him both in his profession and in public affairs. In 1847-48 he was a member of the state legislature. During the war he was a member of Gov. Joseph E. Brown's staff and for a time commanded a regiment of state troops. He was also a useful member of the state constitutional convention after the war. From 1876 until his death he served as one of the trustees of the state university, and for several years as trustee of the state insane asylum. During the forty-seventh congress he represented his district in the house, and honored his state by the quality of his service. The members of that congress, it will be remembered, voted themselves an increase of salary. His vote was cast against the measure, and after it had passed he turned the excess of his salary over the previous amount into the state treasury of Georgia. For thirty years he was a ruling elder of the Presbyterian church, and his life was lived in conformity with high ideals and religious convictions. His death occurred on the 2d of January, 1900.

The maiden name of his wife was America Young. She was born in Bulloch county, Georgia, a daughter of Michael and Sarah (Everett) Young. Her paternal grandparents were William and Mary (Henderson) Young, and her grandparents on the maternal side were Joshua and Jane (Carter) Everett—all of whom were, so far as known, life-long residents of Bulloch county. The Young family was prominent in Georgia from colonial times. William Young was member of a committee of safety appointed in Savannah on the 22d of June, 1775, and on the 4th of July, 1775, represented the town and district of Savannah in the session of the provincial congress of that date. America (Young) MacIntyre, whose death occurred in 1910, reared six children, namely: Hugh James, Archibald T., Jr. (see below), Mary America, Michael Young, William Remer and Daniel Irwin.

Archibald Thompson MacIntyre, Jr., was born on a plantation in Thomas county, June 6, 1852, and died in his home at Thomasville, July 11, 1897. In his comparatively brief span of life he added distinction to the name he bore, and was one of the leaders among his contemporaries of the Georgia bar and public life. At the age of seventeen, in 1869, a graduate of the state university, he then began the study of law and was admitted to the bar when nineteen. For a time he was associated with his brother Hugh and later with his father, and in his practice was early recognized as a lawyer of high attainments and successful ability. Though very young at the time, he took an active part in the reconstruction period, and was a bold and daring advocate of home rule. He was later prominent in Democratic politics, and chairman of the executive committee. He was an elector when Grover Cleveland was elected for the first time. In 1889 he was elected to the state legislature, and there as in every other position of responsibility discharged his duties with conscientious ability. Ill health finally compelled him to retire from law practice, and ended in his death, July 11, 1897, at the age of forty-five.

He was married on the 11th of December, 1880, to Miss Margaret Fraser Livingston, daughter of Hon. Thomas J. and Margaret S. (Wyche) Livingston, the history of this well known Georgia family being given in following paragraphs. Mrs. MacIntyre lives in one of the beautiful homes of Thomasville. Her four children are Hugh James, Archibald Thompson, Remer Young and William Fraser. Hugh is a successful attorney and the present mayor of the city of Thomasville. Archibald T. was cashier for a time of the First National Bank, of Thomasville. He died at the age of twenty-seven. Remer Young, is an electrician, and William F. is still pursuing his studies.

CAPT. THOMAS JOHN LIVINGSTON. A South Carolinian who for many years was prominent in the public life of the state of Georgia, the late Capt. T. J. Livingston was born at Abbeville, South Carolina, on the 25th of February, 1828, and was a son of Thomas and Margaret (Fraser) Livingston.

The first of the name to come to America was Robert Livingston, who settled in New York and lived there the rest of his life. He married Alida Schuyler. He was known as first lord of Livingston Manor. From him the line of descent is through the following: His youngest son Gilbert who married Cornelia Beekman was born in 1690 and died in 1746; was registrar of the colonial court of chancery, 1720; county clerk of Ulster county, 1722; member of the assembly for the manor, 1728-1737, and lieutenant colonel of the provincial militia. Cornelius, son of Gilbert, married a Taliaferro, and both died in Virginia. Their son Thomas was twice married, his wives being sisters, Mary and Nancy Childs, of Virginia. He was a private in Company Eight of Virginia, under Capt. Thomas Tebbs, April, 1777, as shown by record of Revolutionary war by W. T. R. Saffell, page 275. Thomas, a son of Thomas, married Margaret Fraser, of Abbeville, South Carolina and they were the parents of the late Captain Livingston. Leaving South Carolina, they became pioneers of Madison county, Florida. For a number of years after their settlement the Indians were so troublesome that each community had its fort or block-house, to which the inhabitants fled on the first alarm. Thomas Livingston, the father, was a lawyer by profession, but spent most of his years as a planter, having a large number of slaves. He and his wife spent their last years on the plantation home near Madison.

Thomas John Livingston, their son, was eight years old when the family moved to Florida, in which state he was reared and educated. He began his career as a farmer and was engaged in that occupation when the war between the states began. Raising a company for the Confederacy, he was made captain, and as a comrade wrote after his death, he performed his duty faithfully and with ability in every position he was placed. At the close of the war he entertained for a few days at his home Gen. J. C. Breckinridge, who was then trying to elude capture by his federal pursuers. Captain Livingston and Captain Tucker took this noted Confederate leader in a boat down the Suwanee river to the coast, whence he embarked for Cuba.

After the war Captain Livingston engaged in merchandising at Quitman, Georgia, for a time, and then retired to his farm in the Grooverville district of Brooks county. During succeeding years he took a high stand as an influential and able leader in civic affairs. He was chosen state senator and represented the counties of Brooks, Thomas and Colquitt. During his youth he united with the Methodist church, and for a quarter of a century was superintendent of his local Sunday-school. He was faithful in his religion, making it a practical guide in his everyday life, was a just and upright man, and a splendid type of the old southern gentleman. His death occurred at his homestead in Brooks county on the 15th of February, 1903.

Captain Livingston was twice married. Margaret S. Wyche, who' became his first wife, was born at Madison, Florida, daughter of John Scott and Hannah Lawson (MacIntyre) Wyche. Her ancestry is interesting. Henry Wyche, founder of the family in America, was born in England and came to the colonies about 1679, settling in Surry county, Virginia, and is mentioned as one of the foot soldiers of Surry county, Virginia. His son George (II) lived in Surry county, and George's son Peter (III) lived in Brunswick county, Virginia. George (IV), son of Peter, married a Miss Scott and became a pioneer settler in Richmond county, Georgia. Batte (V), the next in line, married a Miss Jarrett. John S. (VI), son of Batte, married Hannah Lawson L. MacIntyre. The latter was a daughter of Archibald and Hannah (Lawson) MacIntyre, and a lineal descendant of Daniel MacIntyre, founder of that name in America (see MacIntyre sketch). Captain Livingston's first wife died at the age of thirty-five, and he later married Ellen Groover. The children of Captain and Margaret (Wyche) Livingston were: Margaret Fraser, who became the wife of the late Archibald T. MacIntyre, of Thomasville (see preceding sketch); Lula Lawson, who married William H. Mitchell and lives in Thomasville; Irvene Camillas, who married, first, T. J. Howard, and, second, T. L. Shofner, and lives in Dade City, Florida; Thomas John, who married Mary McCall and lives in Fitzgerald. The children of Captain Livingston's second marriage are: Donald Madison; Emily Josephine, wife of McCall Quarterman, of Lane Park, Florida; LeRoy Rushin; and Helen Lucile, wife of R. W. Adams, of Boston, Georgia.

ROBERT EDWARD LEE BOWER. A prominent farmer and merchant of Dixie, Brooks county, Robert Edward Lee Bower takes an intelligent interest in everything tending to promote the welfare and progress of town and county, being a public-spirited and useful member of his community. A son of George McIntosh Troup Bower, he was born July 14, 1862, in Newton county, Georgia, of honored New England ancestry, being a direct descendant in the fourth generation of the noted sculptor, John Bower, and his wife, Honora Bower, *nee* Jacobs.

Ebenezer Bower, Mr. Bower's grandfather, was born, bred and educated in Providence, Rhode Island. Foreseeing the future development of the South, he came as a young man to Georgia, and lived for a while in Savannah, where he met and married an heiress, Miss Margaret McConkey. Removing with his bride to Jones county, Georgia, he became an extensive and prosperous planter and merchant, in the management of his land having plenty of help, owning as many as two hundred and fifty slaves. About 1830 he moved with his family to Florida, becoming a pioneer of Marianna, and there erecting the first brick house built in that locality. He operated large tracts of land, and leased many slaves to vessel owners doing shipping business between Apalachicola and Mobile. When he came South there were no railroads in Georgia, the country being largely in its pristine wildness, game of all kinds roaming at will through the forests, in which Indians still lived, and at times made raids upon the new settlers. All farm produce had to be teamed to either the Atlantic or gulf ports, the round trip having been long, tedious, and sometimes dangerous if the savages were on the war path. Both Ebenezer Bower and his wife spent their last years on their large estate in western Florida. They reared six children, five sons and one daughter.

George McIntosh Troup Bower was born in 1825, in Jones county,

Georgia, and as a lad of five years accompanied his parents to Florida. The facilities for obtaining an education in that state being then very limited, he was sent North, and in the public schools of Providence, Rhode Island, acquired his early book knowledge, which was subsequently supplemented by a course of study at Emory College, in Oxford, Georgia. When ready to establish himself in business, he settled in Newton county, Georgia, and was there an honored and esteemed resident until his death, in 1897. He became prominent in public affairs, holding many offices of trust and responsibility, including those of county judge and county sheriff. He was a great reader, and a constant student, remarkably well informed on all topics, and was very frequently called upon as an adviser and counsellor. During his life he saw wonderful changes in the face of the country roundabout, witnessing with just pride and gratification the growth of Georgia from a wilderness to a rich and prosperous state, in which are large and populous cities, and magnificent agricultural regions, while railroads traverse the country in every direction.

The maiden name of the wife of George McIntosh Troup Bower was Eliza Turner. She was born in Henry county, Georgia, and was brought up and educated in her native state. Her father, Rev. Allen W. Turner, a native of South Carolina, was educated for the ministry, and became a pioneer preacher of the Methodist Episcopal church in Georgia. He held pastorates in different places in Georgia, and as there were then no railways, nor even good carriage roads, he used to make his long trips on horseback, and did most of his preaching in log houses. He was offered the position of bishop of his church, but declined the honor, saying that he could do more real good as a pastor. He spent his last days in Palmetto, Georgia, and his wife, whose maiden name was Mary Dousing, died in 1878. Mr. and Mrs. George McIntosh Troup Bower reared the following named children: Augustus Rudolphus, Eugenia, Mary Fletcher, Chalmers Hendrick, Allen Ebenezer, Robert Edward, Stonewall Jackson, Annie, George, and Bennie Simms.

Obtaining his academical education at the seminary in Covington, Georgia, Edwin Robert Bower completed the course of study at Oxford, Georgia, at Emory College. Going then to Coweta county, he spent three years as clerk in a fancy grocery store, and the following two years was employed as a truck farmer in Lake county, Florida. Lured to Orange county, Florida, Mr. Bower embarked in mercantile pursuits in Orlando, where he conducted a grocery for a time, carrying a large stock of fancy goods. Returning to Georgia, he was for a year engaged in business as a merchant at Quitman, Brooks county, and was afterwards employed in farming in the Dixie district until 1901, when he resumed his former occupation in Dixie, where he is conducting an extensive and remunerative business as a general merchant, carrying a large stock of goods. Mr. Bower has been very fortunate in his agricultural operations. He is the owner of various farms, aggregating in all five hundred acres, the farms which are located in the Dixie, Dry Lake, and Grooverville districts, being operated by tenants.

Mr. Bowers married, in 1889, Catherine Puckett, who was born in Cumming, Forsyth county, where her father, Rev. Miles Puckett, who preached during his life in various places in Georgia, was then located. Neither he nor his wife, whose maiden name was Carrie Scott, are now living. Mr. and Mrs. Bower have six children, namely: Kittie Lee, Marie, R. E., Sybelle, Emory Scott, and Jack. Mr. Bower is a Democrat in politics, but has ever been too much engrossed with his private affairs to indulge in office holding, although he has for five years served as chairman of the Dixie school board. Both he and Mrs. Bower are consistent members of the Methodist Episcopal church.

CAPT. CHARLES THOMPSON STUART. Few men even in an extended lifetime of more than eighty years have careers of such varied activities and in so many parts of the world as Captain Stuart, of Thomasville, now retired after forty years in the hotel business in southern Georgia. For many years he followed the sea in the old wooden merchant marine, was a Southern soldier during the war between the states, and then during a period of forty years extended his genial hospitality as a landlord in Valdosta and in Thomasville.

Charles Thompson Stuart was born in Annapolis, Maryland, May 11, 1828. His grandfather emigrated from Scotland and founded this branch of the family in Maryland, where he spent the remainder of his life. The captain's father was Charles Stuart, a native of eastern Maryland. During his youth he received excellent educational advantages, and then entered a long career in public service. For a number of years he was connected with the state treasurer's department of Maryland, and under the administration of Gen. W. H. Harrison was given an appointment in the treasury department at Washington, where he continued until some time during the Civil war. After the war he moved his residence from Washington to New York City, where he died at the age of seventy-seven. The maiden name of his wife was Alicia A. Thompson, who was born in Annapolis, daughter of Henry Thompson, a capitalist of that city. She lived to the age of eighty-seven years, and she reared seven children, namely: John Nelson, Charles Thompson, Julia Ellen, William B., Mary A., Henry W. and Wilson W. Of the sons, John, Charles, William and Wilson wore the grey in the Confederate armies, and all but Charles met death in their devotion to the Southern cause.

Captain Stuart at the age of thirteen entered St. John's College in Maryland, but after two years had to relinquish his studies on account of ill health, and from that time forward until his retirement a few years since was engaged in an active and often arduous practical career. For three years he was apprentice in a mercantile house of Baltimore, and then took two voyages to Cuba and the West Indies. These were the start of his long seafaring adventures. In 1847 he sailed on a merchant vessel around Cape Horn to China and returned via Cape Hope, after sixteen months spent on all the seas and in many of the ports of the world. For twelve years he was identified with the merchant marine service, and came to know the world of that time as few other men did.

His retirement from the sea in 1861 was followed almost immediately by his enlistment in Company H of the Twenty-sixth Regiment in Gordon's famous brigade, and for several years he was with that command in its campaigns and numerous battles in Virginia. He was several times wounded, and at the battle of Monocacy, Maryland, toward the end of the war, a bullet passed through his left lung and thus dangerously wounded was captured on the field and kept a prisoner until the spring of 1865. Being then paroled he returned home, but was unable to resume service before the final surrender.

At the close of the war Captain Stuart came to southern Georgia, where nearly fifty years of his life has been spent. In December, 1865, he opened a hotel at Valdosta and conducted it as a popular hostelry for twenty years. He then moved to Thomasville and built the Stuart House, and continued as active proprietor of this well known hotel for twenty years and six weeks. Much to the regret of the large patronage he then sold and retired from active pursuits. His home is located on the same lot with the hotel, and here he is pleasantly spending a well-earned leisure.

Captain Stuart was married in the city of Baltimore, January, 1852, to Miss Ida Charlotte Marmelstein. She was born in Berlin, Germany, whence she came to America with her parents when two years of age. Her death occurred in 1910. The captain and Mrs. Stuart were the parents of six children, namely: Ida, Lillie, Lula, Ardie, Jessie and Ella. Ida is the wife of N. Lilienberg, and has one daughter named Agnes. Lillie is at home with her father. Lula married John McWilliams. Ardie married Etta Shackelford, and they have two daughters, Marie and Ida Virginia. Jessie is the wife of John T. West, and their two sons are Stuart and Thomas. Ella married C. M. Smith, and they are the parents of one son, Charles.

ROBERT J. HERRING, the prominent farmer and horticulturist of Thomas county, is one of the men who, by study and the use of scientific methods in agriculture, are showing the people of the locality the possibilities of south Georgia. Although he has spent the greater part of his life in the Thomasville district, Mr. Herring is a native of Sampson county, North Carolina, in which place he was born on the 16th of January, 1860. His father, John Herring, was born in the same county, and his father, Owen Herring, was a farmer and merchant of the locality for many years. Owen Herring's store was at a point on the Black river known as Herringville. When he had reached an advanced age, he sold out to his son John, and lived in retirement for the rest of his life.

Not only his father's business fell into John S. Herring's hands, but his father's office as well. John Herring served as postmaster at Herringville under both Federal and Confederate jurisdiction, and was actively engaged in business there until the time of his death, which occurred in February, 1865, a few weeks before Lee's surrender.

At his death, Mr. Herring left a widow and four small children. His wife, whose maiden name was Sarah Ellen Spearman, was born in Sampson county, North Carolina, the daughter of John Spearman, and is now the wife of Oliver C. Cleveland, a prominent resident of Thomas county, Georgia, then Mrs. Cleveland, then Mrs. Herring, remained in North Carolina for ten years, and then moved to Thomas county, Georgia, where she has ever since resided. Her children were named Robert J., Thomas E., William F., and Jefferson S. Of these, William F. died at the age of three years, and Thomas E. passed away in 1881.

Robert J. Herring was reared in the vicinity of his birth, attending the common schools of Sampson county. He was fifteen years of age when he migrated to Georgia with his mother, and after arriving at his new home, he continued to make his home with her until his marriage, which took place when he was twenty-five years of age. At this time, he settled on a tract of timbered land south of Thomasville, which his mother had given him, and there he commenced his career as an independent farmer. He had been well trained to habits of industry and thrift, and he soon had his farm cleared and in successful operation. He remained on his original property until 1895, in which year he sold out, and moved to the farm on which he now resides. This is in lot No. 103, Oak Hill district, Thomas county, and he had purchased it three years before he sold the land his mother had given him.

Since coming to his present farm Mr. Herring has been engaged in diversified farming, stock raising, and horticulture. He keeps in touch with the latest methods and ideas in agriculture by wide reading, and has been very successful in raising a large variety of fruits and farm products. It is such progressive men as he who are going to make the South a land of plenty.

In 1885, Mr. Herring was united in the bonds of matrimony with

Fannie Arnold. She was a native daughter of Thomas county, her father, John P. Arnold, having come to Georgia from Germany in his youth. Mr. and Mrs. Herring have been blessed with four children, Frances Ann, a school teacher; John Oliver, a clerk in Thomasville; Frank, with the Southern Express Company, at Thomasville office; Josephine. Mrs. Herring died January 16, 1909. The family are members of the Missionary Baptist church, and are valued workers in that congregation.

JAMES C. ADAMS. A man of good business judgment and tact, James C. Adams, of Boston, Georgia, has been actively associated with the advancement of the agricultural and mercantile interests of Thomas county, and is widely known as head of the prosperous firm of James C. Adams & Sons, druggists. A native of Brooks county, he was born December 21, 1850, in the Tallokas district, a son of Lasa Adams, and a grandson of Dennis Adams, a pioneer settler of Brooks county.

Migrating in pioneer days from North Carolina to Florida, Dennis Adams located near the present site of Wakena, Gadsden county, becoming one of the original settlers of that locality. His brother-in-law, a Mr. Carr, located on a tract of land two miles away. Indians were then very troublesome in that locality, and one night when Mr. Carr and his wife were away from home raided his place, and brutally massacred their two children. A slave made his escape to the Adams farm, and told Mr. Adams the tale, and Mr. Adams sent to Thomasville, Georgia, for aid. The following night the red skins paid a visit to the Adams cabin. The family were well prepared, and after several of the Indians had been killed the remainder retreated. Thinking it best to leave that region, Mr. Dennis Adams came to Georgia, locating in the Tallokas district, Brooks county, where he bought two lots of land, on which he resided until his death, three years later. By his two wives he had ten children, as follows: Joshua, Lasa, Dennis, Caswell, Cason, Sally, Rachel, Irene, Louisa, and Jane. His second wife, whose maiden name was Sally Williams, survived him about twenty years. She was a woman of much force of character, and in addition to keeping her family together, educated them, and trained them to habits of industry and thrift, enabling each one to gain success in after years.

Lasa Adams was young when the family came from Florida to Georgia to escape the malignant attacks of the Indians, although many red skins were then living in this vicinity, the dense forests being their happy hunting ground. The few daring white people of the county built a strong log fort to which the women and children were sent when ever trouble with the savages was brewing, and he immediately joined the company formed for protection against their raids, and took part, in 1836, in the battle of Brushy creek, when the Indians made their last stand in Georgia. When ready to begin the struggle of life on his own account, Lasa Adams bought land in what is now the Tallokas district, Brooks county, and engaged in farming. There being no railways in the state all transportation was by teams, and after his land became productive he used to take his cotton to Newport, Florida, going in company with several of his neighbors, some of whom perhaps lived miles away from him, each man taking provisions with him, and camping and cooking by the wayside.

In 1852, Lasa Adams sold his Brooks county land, moved to Florida, locating in Madison county, where he purchased a squatter's claim to a tract of government land situated about sixteen miles northeast of Monticello, and about the same distance northwest of Madison. A few acres had been cleared, and a log cabin had been erected. He continued the improvements, and there carried on general farming for some time. In 1864 he enlisted in the Florida Reserves, and continued in the Confederate service until the close of the war, when he again assumed charge of his farm. Selling out in 1870, he was for four years a resident of Jefferson county, Florida. Coming from there to Thomas county, Georgia, he bought land three miles south of Boston, and was there employed in tilling the soil for many years. Shortly before his death, which occurred in 1894, he returned to Brooks county, Georgia, and there spent his last days, passing away at the venerable age of eighty-three years.

The maiden name of the wife of Lasa Adams was Orpha Lee Holloway. She was born in Brooks county, Georgia, a daughter of William Holloway, one of the very first settlers of what is now Brooks county, he having been born and bred in Bulloch county. She died leaving four children, namely: Rhoda, who married William Hulet, of Brooks county; Jane, wife of J. M. Yates, of Brooks county; James C.; and Cason F., of whom a brief account may be found on another page of this volume.

Reared and educated in Florida, James C. Adams began life for himself on a farm in the Boston district, Thomas county, Georgia, his father giving him one hundred acres of land, forty of which had been improved, and on which a fair set of frame buildings had been erected. Industrious and enterprising, he succeeded in his undertakings, and as his means increased he invested in other tracts, and is now owner of five hundred and forty acres of good land in the Boston district. From his farm, which is devoted to general farming and stock growing, Mr. Adams receives a good annual income. In 1898, Mr. Adams removed to Boston in order that his sons might have better educational advantages, and here from 1900 until 1904 he carried on a thriving trade as a general merchant. Embarking in the latter year in the drug business in Boston, he has continued as druggist ever since, his sons being now associated with him, the firm name being James C. Adams & Sons.

In 1875, Mr. Adams was united in marriage with Mary Holman, who was born in Jefferson county, Florida, a daughter of Adam and Elizabeth (Smith) Holman.

Two children of the union of Mr. and Mrs. Adams are living, namely: Reddin W., who married Lillie Livingston; and De Roy. They lost by death four, who passed away in childhood. Mr. and Mrs. Adams are members of the Primitive Baptist church, to which Mr. Adams' parents also belonged.

JOHN CLEMENTS. One of the citizens of southwest Georgia who began their careers in log-cabin homes, labored with courage and industry to develop a wilderness of forest into a broad landscape of farms, and have subsequently reaped the rewards of such diligence in ample material prosperity, is Mr. John Clements, formerly of Irwin county, now a resident in Thomas county.

Mr. Clements was born in Irwin county, April 7, 1853, and represents a family which has been known with respect on this side of the Atlantic since colonial times. Joseph Clements, his great-grandfather, according to the best information, was a native of Virginia, whence he moved into South Carolina during colonial times, and spent the rest of his days there. He gave distinction to the family name by having served as a soldier in the continental armies during the Revolution.

Cornelius Clements, the grandfather, was born in the Darlington district of South Carolina, was reared to farm life, bought land in his native vicinity, but late in life moved to Georgia, being a resident of

Irwin county at the time of his death. He married Polly Register, who was a lifelong resident of South Carolina. She reared five sons and five daughters, the sons being named Elias, Jesse, Thomas, Richard and John.

Elias Clements, the father, was born and reared in Darlington district, South Carolina. His subsequent settlement in Georgia was due to a somewhat romantic circumstance rather than to any fixed purpose. When about twenty years old, in company with his father, he made a horseback journey to Alabama to visit an uncle. On their return they visited relatives in Laurens county, Georgia, where Elias concluded to tarry awhile before going back to South Carolina. He rented some land, made a crop, and in the meantime met his fate in one of the fair young women of that locality. His marriage took place shortly afterward, and the result was he never returned to his native state. He continued to make his home in Laurens county until 1852, in which year he moved to Irwin county, buying a farm two miles south of Irwinsville. This part of Georgia was still without railroads, and for some years after his settlement, Hawkinsville, fifty miles away, was the most convenient market and depot of supplies. After several years he sold his first place and bought an improved farm five miles north of Irwinsville, where he resided until his death, at the advanced age of eighty-seven. The young lady in Laurens county whose heart he had won was Elinzabeth (so she spelled her name) Turner, a native of that county. Her father was Ephraim Turner, a native of South Carolina and an early settler in Laurens county, where he spent the last years of his life; and her mother's maiden name was Sally Clements, who survived her husband and died in Irwin county. Mrs. Elias Clements died in 1882 at the age of sixty-two. Her six children were Mary, Cornelius, Ruth, John, Loupiney and Rachel.

The boyhood of John Clements was passed on a farm in Irwin county during the war-time era of the sixties. He made the best of limited opportunities to obtain an education, and became sufficiently advanced to teach one term of school in his home county. While living with his parents he bought a tract of timbered land near the old home, and his father later gave him another small acreage adjoining. On that he built a double "pen" house of round logs, and in that humble home he and his bride began their wedded career. After some years his family removed from this home to Ocilla in order that the children might have school advantages, while he remained to direct the operations of his farm. Mr. Clements prospered from year to year, and bought land until he was the owner of about two thousand acres. He built a commodious frame house to succeed the primitive dwelling of logs, and after a few years the family returned to occupy this home. The improvements on his farm compared favorably with any in Irwin county, and he was raised among the most progressive farmers of that county. In 1910, having sold his Irwin county property, Mr. Clements moved to Thomas county, where he bought his present fine farm of five hundred and sixty-five acres on the Summer Hill road four miles northwest of Boston. This homestead is well improved and has excellent buildings. In addition, he is interested in farming lands south of Boston and in Grady county, and owns some town real estate in Boston.

On the 25th of November, 1877, Mr. Clements married Miss Narcissa M. Pate. Mrs. Clements is a native of Wilcox county, this state, and a daughter of James and Jane (Moore) Pate. It is thought her father was born in Pulaski and her mother in Gwinett county, and they spent their last years in Wilcox county. The nine children in the Pate family were Bennett, John, Mary, Nancy, Sarah, Elizabeth, Narcissa, James H.

and Samuel. Mr. and Mrs. Clements have reared eight children, as follows: Jane, Loupiney, Annie, Emily, James E., Bessie, Mattie and Willie. Jane married Henry Lee Yarbrough, and her three children are Louise, Alma and Elmer. Loupiney died at the age of nineteen. Annie married James D. Gibbs and they are the parents of two sons, Clifford and James. Emily married George F. Moore and has two children, Lucile and Cecil. Bessie married Mr. G. B. Sweatt, of Irwin county. Willie married Anna L. Meadows of Thomas county. The other children are unmarried.

Mr. Clements and wife are active members of the Methodist church, and he was trustee and steward of his church in Irwin county. Fraternally he affiliates with Horeb Lodge No. 281, A. F. & A. M. He was secretary for both the local and county Farmers Union in Irwin county, and is still a member of the organization. In politics he has always adhered to Democratic principles. During his residence in Irwin county he served as a member of the local school board and also as county school commissioner. He held the office of postmaster at his home village of Tapley from the time it was established until discontinued through the operations of the rural free delivery.

JAMES I. GROOVER, M. D. Spending the best part of his life in the practice of medicine, James I. Groover, M. D., was for forty-five years one of the leading physicians of the Grooversville district, where he won an extended reputation for skill and ability, and built up a large and lucrative patronage. A son of James Groover, he was born November 18, 1835, in that part of Thomas county now included within the limits of Brooks county. His grandfather, John Groover, was of Dutch ancestry, and as far as known, was born in Bulloch county, Georgia, which was his home for many years, although his last days were spent in Brooks county.

Born September 6, 1798, in Bulloch county, Georgia, James Groover was there reared and married. Subsequently, accompanied by his wife and three children, he came to what is now Brooks county, making the entire journey in a cart drawn by one horse, and bringing with him in the one cart all of his earthly possessions. At the time of his arrival there were but two families in the vicinity, those of Willis King and Henry Melton. The county was in its original wildness, bear, deer, wolves, and game of all kinds sharing the forests with the Indians, who frequently so terrorized the few white settlers that they banded together for protection against their raids. There were no railroads for years after he came to this region, and he, in common with his neighbors, used to haul all of his produce to either Tallahassee or Newport, Florida. The land was for sale in lots of four hundred and eighty acres each, the prices ranging from $5.00 to $50.00 each. He purchased several lots, including lot number 509, on which he built a log house for his first residence. He subsequently whip-sawed lumber to erect a frame house in lot number 505, in what is now the Grooverville district, and continued his agricultural labors, with the assistance of his slaves clearing large tracts of land. In common with his neighbors he lived in a primitive manner, having very little farm machinery, while his wife, whose household conveniences were very limited, used to do all of her cooking by the open fireplace, and in addition to her other duties carded, spun, and wove all of the material from which she fashioned the garments worn by her family. He was a man of influence, his death, which occurred August 11, 1874, removing from his community one of its most valued citizens. He was active in religious work, and both he and his wives were members of the Missionary Baptist church.

James Groover was twice married. He married first, Elizabeth Denmark, who was born October 27, 1803, in Bulloch county, Georgia, and died in 1848, aged forty-five years. He married second, Mrs. Sarah Ann (Hagan) Groover, widow of Malachi Groover. His first wife bore him children as follows: Eliza, Redding J., Wiley W., Charles A., Thomas A., Clayton, Martha, Allen W., James I., Sally Ann, John Burton, Mary Jane, Daniel W., Henry C., Francis M., and Clinton D. By his second marriage he had one son, Fuller.

Laying a solid foundation in the pioneer schools of his native district for a good education, James I. Groover subsequently continued his studies in Thomasville two years, during his long vacations assisting his father in the work of the farm, when old enough going occasionally to either Tallahassee or Newport, Florida, with loads of farm produce, being several days in making the round trip. His natural inclinations turning him toward a professional career, he afterwards spent three years at the University of North Carolina, and at the age of twenty-five years was graduated from the Medical department of the New York University with the degree of M. D. Immediately locating in the Grooverville district, Brooks county, Doctor Groover had a long and eminently useful career as a physician, during the forty-five years that he continued in active practice gained to a marked degree the confidence of the community, and built up an extremely lucrative patronage. When ready to retire from his profession, the doctor announced his intention in church, arising in his seat and telling his friends that they would confer a favor upon him by never calling upon him again for professional services. At the outbreak of the Civil war Doctor Groover enlisted in the Brooks County Volunteers, which became a part of the Twenty-sixth Georgia Volunteer Infantry, and continued with his regiment in all of its marches, campaigns and battles, and after the surrender resumed his practice in Grooverville.

Doctor Groover has been twice married. He married first, in 1860, in New York City, Emily S. Johnson, a native of Connecticut. She died in 1885. The doctor married second, in 1887, Mittie Groover, who was born in Grooverville district, a daughter of Joseph Groover. By his first marriage Doctor Groover had one son, Clarence I. Groover, now publisher of the *Enquirer and Sun*, at Columbus, Georgia. He married Mary Davis, and they have two children, Emily and Herbert. The doctor is a member of the Episcopal church, to which his first wife also belonged.

WILLIAM HENRY WILSON. One of the active representatives of an old and well known family of South Georgia, William Henry Wilson, is a son of Jeremiah Wilson, Jr., and grandson of Jeremiah Wilson, Sr., the latter having made his name and work impressive among the old settlers of this part of the state as the man who made many of the first surveys in Thomas and Lowndes counties, especially in that part of Lowndes now included in Brooks county. The history of the various members of the Wilson family will be found elsewhere in this work under the name of Joseph D. Wilson.

William H. Wilson was born on the old home farm in this vicinity, July 10, 1859, and was reared and educated in Brooks county and lived at the parental home until his marriage. He began his independent career as a farmer on a small place bordering Mule creek in the Dry Lake district, but six years later bought the farm which he still owns and occupies, located four miles southeast of Boston in the Boston district of Thomas county. Here he owns 250 acres, with improvements, and for a number of years has carried on a prosperous business of general farming and stock raising.

Mr. Wilson was married at the age of twenty-four to Miss Hattie Julia Stanaland, a member of an old and well known family, the history of which will be found elsewhere in the sketch of J. O. Stanaland. Mr. Wilson and wife are the parents of six children, named as follows: James Stanaland, Nellie M., Henry Grady, Martha (died aged fifteen years), Joseph J., and Robert Lee. James S. married Katie Owen, and they have two children, Janette and Jewel. Mr. and Mrs. Wilson are members of the Primitive Baptist church.

DANIEL A. GROOVER. Closely identified with the agricultural interests of Brooks county, Daniel A. Groover is meeting with highly gratifying results in his pleasant and independent occupation, his estate, which is located in the Grooverville district, having substantial improvements, and being amply supplied with the necessary implements and appliances for carrying on his work. A grandson of John Groover, Sr., an early pioneer of South Georgia, he was born March 22, 1841, in Thomas county.

His great-grandfather, John Groover, was born either in Germany or America, of German parents. At the time of the Revolutionary war he was living near Cowpens, South Carolina, within sight of the field which later became the scene of a great battle. Joining the colonists in their struggle for independence, he was murdered by the Tories when home on a furlough.

John Groover, Sr., was born very near the line separating North Carolina from South Carolina. Migrating to Georgia in early life, he resided for many years in Bulloch county, from there coming to Thomas county, where his son, John Groover, Jr., father of Daniel A., had previously located. His brother, Solomon Groover, came with him to this section of the state, and they became the progenitors of the many families of Groovers now living in Brooks and Thomas counties. Locating in what is now the Grooverville district, Brooks county, John Groover, Sr., remained in that district until his death. He married and reared three sons and four daughters, as follows: John, James, Abner, Elizabeth, Hannah, Mary, and Barbara.

John Groover, Jr., was born in 1793, in Bulloch county, Georgia, and was there brought up and married. Subsequently, accompanied by his wife and their three children, and his brother James and family, he came with his own teams across the country to Brooks county, bringing with him his household goods and provisions, cooking and camping by the way. Locating in what is now Grooverville district, he purchased a tract of timber that was still in its virgin wildness, and in the space which he cleared erected the humble log cabin in which his son, Daniel A., first drew the breath of life. The land was in its primitive condition, its dense growth of timber being inhabited by the wily red man and the wild beasts of the forests, both at times proving troublesome, so much so that the settlers of that vicinity were forced to build a log fort to which the women and children could flee for protection when the Indians started on a rampage. There were but five families living near what is now Grooverville, and more than once these families, the women and children, sought refuge in the fort. After clearing quite a portion of his land, he sold out and purchased in lot 417, in the northwest part of Grooverville precinct, and was there employed in tilling the soil until his death, in 1859. He married Mary Redding, who was born in Bulloch county, Georgia, and lived to the advanced age of four score and four years. Eight children were born to them, as follows: John M., Elizabeth, Mary A., James H., Charles W., Sarah H., Albert J., and Daniel A.

Growing to manhood on the parental homestead, Daniel A. Groover has witnessed the growth of Brooks county from a vast wilderness to a rich agricultural region, dotted here and there with populous towns and villages, through which railroads now pass. In the days of his boyhood the forests were filled with wild beasts of all kinds, and game was abundant. Tallahassee and Newport, in Florida, were then the most convenient markets to which his father could haul the farm produce, the round trip to those places consuming at least five days. There having been no free educational institutions, he was forced to walk a distance of four miles whenever he attended school, which was very irregularly. Reared to habits of industry and economy, Mr. Groover remained with his parents until the outbreak of the war between the states, when he enlisted in the "Piscola Volunteers," which became Company G, of the Twenty-sixth Georgia Volunteer Infantry, known far and wide as the "Fighting Regiment." His regiment was assigned to Jackson Corps, Army of North Virginia, and he continued with it, taking an active part in all of its engagements until the battle of Gettysburg. Mr. Groover, who was then ill with typhoid pneumonia, was captured by the enemy and held as a prisoner-of-war at Forts Delaware and Point Lookout, for eight months. On being paroled he returned to Virginia, arriving at Appomattox just in season for the surrender. With several of his comrades he then started for home, walking across the states of Virginia, North Carolina and South Carolina, and on to Augusta, Georgia, from there going by rail to Albany, via Atlanta, and thence on foot to his old home.

On his arrival, Mr. Groover found that his father's estate had been settled and the farm sold subject to his mother's dower, Confederate money having been received in payment and thus lost. In 1865 he raised a crop on the old homestead, which he purchased the following year, and on which he has since resided. Mr. Groover now owns 264 acres in Brooks county, and seventy acres in Thomas county, and a large part of it is under cultivation and most intelligently managed. In 1907 Mr. Groover's home was burned and he erected the one that he and his family now occupy, it being situated in the Quitman and Boston road.

On October 6, 1861, Mr. Groover was united in marriage with Martha A. Groover, who was born in Brooks county, Georgia, a daughter of Joshua S. and Rebecca (Beasley) Groover, and granddaughter of Solomon Groover. Mrs. Groover passed to the higher life December 31, 1909, leaving a heaven-made vacant place in the home. Eight children were born of their union, namely: Mally A., Ophelia L., Mary Rebecca, Samuel Dickson, Janie E., John T., Julia R., and Mattie Lee, who died at the age of thirteen years. Mally A. married Annie Jarrett, and they have four sons, Wallace A., Daniel A., Felix, and Herman. Janie E., who married W. A. Simms, died March 2, 1906, leaving three children, Minor A., Sam Groover, and Martha A. Ophelia became the second wife of W. A. Simms. Mary Rebecca, wife of Hammond H. Groover, has one child, Eula K. Groover. Samuel Dickson married Fanny Moody, and at his death, which occurred in 1902, he left her with two children, James Russian and Samuel Daniel. John T. married Birdie Scruggs, and they have two children, Martha A. and Julia R. Julia is the wife of Jack Stringer.

ANSEL ALDERMAN. The Alderman family has become very well known in the southwestern part of Georgia, both on account of the industry and excellent character of the present generation, but also on account of the prominent part played by the early representatives of the name in the settling and opening up of the region where their descendants make their homes. The first American representatives of the family was David Alderman, who came to this side of the ocean from England in the latter part of the eighteenth century. His son, Timothy, and his grandson, James, the father of the subject of this sketch, were pioneers in Southwestern Georgia, and suffered the hardships of primitive existence in the very section which is now blessed with the advantages of civilization.

Ansel Alderman was born on a farm in the Tallokas district of Brooks county, on the fifth of April, 1867, one of the ten children of James and Jane Roberts Alderman. He passed his early years on the farm of his father, receiving his early education in the rural schools of his community. He was married when only seventeen years of age to Willie Murphy, and the parents of the young bride and groom fitted them out for their start in life, one family supplying them with land and the other with stock. By industry and thrift, indoors and out, the youthful couple soon managed to make a success of their small farm, and in time were able to add to the original tract until they possessed 650 acres, all in the Pavo district of Thomas county. Mr. Alderman continued to farm this land until the year 1902, when he moved to Pavo, where he has lived ever since, letting out his farm to tenants.

Willie Murphy Alderman, the wife who shared so many of the happy and prosperous years of his life, was the daughter of William Murphy, a native of one of the Carolinas, who was an early settler of Colquott county, Georgia, in which locality Mrs. Anselman was born. After a useful, though brief, career as a wife and mother, Mrs. Willie Alderman died in the year 1901, leaving seven children. These were: Jessie, who is now the wife of Mont Eller, and whose children are Clyde and Louis; James, Mattie, Romulus, Corbett, Tommy and Sabie. Ansel Alderman was married the second time to Lilla Pittman, who was born in Thomas county, Georgia, the daughter of Jack and Josephine (Hart) Pittman. Three children have resulted from this marriage, Aline, Willie Lee, and Lilla May.

Mr. Alderman lives quietly, seeking no public honor, but he is nevertheless a valued citizen of Pavo and lends his influence toward the good. Mr. and Mrs. Alderman are members of the Missionary Baptist church, and lend their support to the works of that congregation.

EZEKIEL ALDERMAN, the well known citizen and former hotel man of Pavo, was born in Thomas county, Georgia, August 13, 1850, a descendant of a family that had played its part in America since early colonial times. Mr. Alderman's great-grandfather, David Alderman, was a representative of a good old English family who settled in the United States while they were yet under the rule of Great Britain. He first made his home in New Jersey, but after living there for some time, he moved to North Carolina. There he spent a great many years, but late in life, his wife having died and his children being pretty well grown, he migrated to Bullock county, Georgia, with his family, and resided in that place until his death, which occurred at a good old age.

The grandfather of the subject of this sketch, Timothy Alderman, was born in North Carolina in the year 1801, and was a young man when he moved to Georgia with his father. After his marriage, which was solemnized in Bullock county, he changed his place of residence to Berrien county. While living in the latter place he explored the southwestern section of Georgia, and considering that that section of the state offered superior advantages for the settler, in the year 1835, he located at a place now included in Brooks county. At the time of his settlement in his new home, Southwestern Georgia was a wilderness. All kinds of game roved its tangled forests, and the red men still claimed it as their hunting ground. Nothing daunted by the obvious difficulties presented by life in this wild place, Timothy Alderman commenced at once to clear and put under cultivation the tract of timbered land he had brought in what is now the Tallokas district. By the time he had his farm in working condition, settlers were thronging the locality. Timothy Alderman sold out to one of these men and bought a farm south of Quitman. He resided there two years, but at the end of that time returned to the Tallokas district where he purchased a new farm and several hundred head of cattle, and engaged in stock raising. He died on this farm at the ripe old age of eighty-one years, leaving his wife, with whom he had shared fifty-five years of happy married life, to survive him. She passed away at the age of ninety-two years, after a long and useful life as wife and mother. Her maiden name was Sally Williams and she, like her husband, was born in the state of North Carolina. She reared seven daughters and four sons, namely: Nancy, Polly, Jinsey, Susan, Betty, Martha, and Jane, and James, Ezekiel, Henry and Timothy.

James Alderman was born in Bullock county, Georgia, in 1823. He was brought to the southwestern part of Georgia by his father when a mere lad and was reared amid the rigors and inspiring scenes of pioneer days. When he started out in life for himself, he purchased a tract of land about one mile west of Pavo, and there built himself a log house and engaged in farming. There were no railroads in those days and the nearest market he had for his produce was Tallahassee, which was a long and arduous journey from his farm. He hauled his commodities there by team, however, the journey consuming several days. After living on his original farm for several years, James Alderman sold it and purchased some land west of Thomasville. He only lived here two years, and at the end of that time he settled in what is now Brooks county, having bought a fine farm in the western part of the Tallahas district.

In the year 1864, when the memorable struggle between the states began, James Alderman enlisted in the Georgia state militia, and went to the defense of Atlanta. He served without interruption until the close of the war and then resumed farming on his last-purchased farm. In 1867 he sold his farm and rented land for a year, during which time he was looking around for an advantageous location. With the idea of finding a good place to settle in mind, he explored Florida, but that state did not come up to his expectations, so he returned to the Tallahas district and bought a farm from William Yates. In the year 1870 he sold his farm to Captain Wells and bought another large farm in the same district. Two years later he disposed of this land also and bought a small farm, upon which he lived for three years. At the end of that time he purchased a farm in the Pavo district. He stocked this farm with cattle and remained there engaged in stock raising until his death, which occurred when he had reached the ripe age of sixty-nine years.

The wife of James Alderman and the mother of the subject of this sketch, was Jane Roberts Alderman. She was born in what is now the Tallokas district of Brooks county, the daughter of Elias and Nancy Nevils Roberts. Mrs. Jane Alderman died at the age of sixty-five years, having reared ten children, Eliza, Elias, Timothy, Sally, Nicie, Ezekiel, James, Mary, Charles and Ansel.

The subject of this history was raised and educated in Brooks county and commenced his career as an independent farmer on rented land in the same locality. After renting for two years, he bought a tract of land in the Tallokas district from his father, and shortly afterward his father gave him one hundred acres adjoining his farm. He proved very successful in the pursuit of agriculture and added to his original farm until it included 525 acres, besides about one thousand acres of outlying land. In 1901 he removed to Pavo, in order to give his children the advantages of town schools. In Pavo he bought the hotel which he operated so successfully for several years and of which he is still the owner. Although he had the newer interests of town life to distract him, Mr. Alderman did not grow neglectful of his agricultural duties. He rented his farm property out to tenants and still keeps it under his supervision. In the town where he has made his home, Mr. Alderman enjoys the reputation of being not only a man of property, but a well-liked and prominent citizen. He is a valued member of the McDonald Lodge No. 172, of the Ancient, Free and Accepted Masons.

The marriage of Ezekiel Alderman to Mrs. Susan Elizabeth (Robertson) Beatty, took place when he was twenty-five years of age. She was the widow of Jackson Beatty and was born in Webster county, Georgia, the daughter of William and Matilda Hale Robertson. Mr. and Mrs. Alderman were blessed with eight children, Laura, Hugh, Frank, Charles, Deney, John, Hezekiah, and Sally Jane. Mrs. Alderman also had one son, Iverson J. Beatty, by her first marriage. Of these children, Laura is now the wife of D. M. Adams and has five children of her own, William E., Stanley, Ruth, Beulah, and Huson. Frank is married to May Simms and is the father of two children, Chester and Minnie Lee. Hugh Alderman married Nannie White from near Atlanta.

HEZEKIAH ROBERTS. A veteran of the war between the states and the first mayor of the town of Pavo, where he now resides, Hezekiah Roberts and his family have been identified with the substantial development of South Georgia since the beginning of settlement and progress in this region.

Mr. Roberts was born in that part of Lowndes county that is now the Tallokas district of Brooks county, on the 25th of December, 1840. His grandfather was Thomas Roberts, a Scotchman, who was born either in England or Scotland, and who on coming to America settled in Screven county, Georgia, where he spent the remainder of his days. He married a Miss Ponder, who died in Screven county and they were the parents of one son, Elias, and two daughters, Elizabeth and Patience.

Elias Roberts, after spending his youth in Screven county and a few years' residence in Chatham county, brought his family into the sparsely populated region of Southwest Georgia. He and his household made the removal in private conveyances and brought all their movable property, with slaves and live stock, locating in the west part of Lowndes county. Most of the land in this region was still owned by the state, though some of it had been purchased by non-resident speculators. Elias Roberts, having bought land bordering Mule creek, first built a house of round logs to shelter his family. Then his slaves laboriously whip-sawed boards from the native timber and with a skilled house-joiner and carpenter to direct the operations, a commodious two-story dwelling was erected. The boards were two and a half inches thick, were dove-tailed together at the ends, and were fastened to the studding with wooden dowel-pins in lieu of nails. When finished, and for some years afterward, this was the most pretentious residence in all this countryside. A few years after Mr. Roberts settled there, he was approached one day by a speculator, who owned several lots in this region, and who offered his land for sale at fifteen dollars per lot (a lot containing

490 acres). Mr. Roberts bought and paid the price asked for one lot, which was covered with fine oak timber, but told the speculator he thought the rest of his land was valueless for farming purposes. Elias Roberts remained a resident at the place of his first settlement until his death, at the age of sixty-three years. Before coming into this part of Georgia, he had served under General Jackson in the Florida Indian wars, and after coming here was a member of a company organized for protection against the Indians over the border, the company being several times called out to drive the red men back to their reservations. During such troublous times the Roberts homestead above described became the place of refuge for the women and children of the settlement, so that it served both as a residence and a fort. Elias Roberts had been a participant in the battle of Brushy Creek in 1836, when the Indians made their last great stand in defense of their hunting grounds.

Elias Roberts married Nancy Nevils, whose birthplace was at Statesboro, Bulloch county, Georgia. Her father, Jacob Nevils, was one of the very earliest settlers of Bulloch county, where he bought land and improved a farm, a part of which is now included in the town of Statesboro. There he resided until his death at the age of ninety-eight. His wife, whose Christian name was Nicey, attained to an even greater age, living one year beyond a century. They reared a large family of children, and Mrs. Elias Roberts likewise attained advanced age, being eighty-two at the time of her demise. Her nine children were John, Mary, Jane, Elias, James, Jacob, Nicey, Hezekiah and L. E.

As one of the youngest of this family, Mr. Hezekiah Roberts was about twelve years old when his father died, and as the older brothers had gone from home he became his mother's chief assistant in the management of the farm and slaves. He continued in this way until the breaking out of the war in 1861, at which time he enlisted in Company C of the Seventh Georgia Battalion, later being transferred to the Sixty-first Georgia Infantry. His first service was at Brunswick and Savannah, and he then went into the army of north Virginia under Stonewall Jackson, and his regiment saw almost constant movement of campaigning and fighting until September, 1864, when it was captured. He and his comrades were then confined at Point Lookout, Maryland, until 1865, when they were paroled. The war closed before he was exchanged, so he came home and resumed the work of the farm. He succeeded to the ownership of the old homestead which his father had carved out of the wilderness, and was there successfully engaged in general farming and stock raising until 1897. Since that year his home has been in Pavo, of which town, at its incorporation, he served as the first mayor.

Mr. Roberts was first married at the age of twenty-seven to Deney Morgan, who was born in Echols county, Georgia, a daughter of Elihu Morgan. She died in 1876. For his second wife Mr. Roberts married Moselle Peacock, a daughter of Delamar and Mary A. (McKinnon) Peacock, of Thomas county. The history of this well known family in Southwest Georgia is told in the sketch of Duncan D. Peacock, elsewhere in this work. By his first union Mr. Roberts has three children, John L., J. Sidney and Emma, and the four children of the second marriage are Mamie, Frank, Wessie and Jack H. John L., who is a physician at Pavo, married Eveline Gray and has one son, John L., Jr. J. Sidney married Annie Stevens and has four children: Thelma, Joseph Sidney, Ellis and Clara. Emma is the wife of Dr. J. W. L. Brannen, and their two children are Leone and Mamie Evelyn. Frank married Pearl Hutchins and has one daughter, Catherine. Wessie is the wife of H. C. Ford and they have one child, Hugh C., Jr. Mr. Roberts and wife are members of the Pavo Methodist church and he is a Democrat in politics.

ASBURY B. FINCH. Now a retired resident of Thomas county, Mr. A. B. Finch has had a long and active career and has well earned his material prosperity and the esteem of his family and fellow citizens.

He was born in Nash county, North Carolina, on the 2d of July, 1836. His family had been identified with North Carolina from colonial times. His grandfather, Allen Finch, was born in Nash county and so far as known both he and his wife spent all their lives in that vicinity. He owned and operated a farm located about forty miles from Raleigh, which was his nearest market and depot for supplies. In those days farmers bought but little at the stores, since all the household dressed in homespun, and most of the provisions were confined to what could be produced in the home locality. Berry Finch, the father of A. B. Finch, was also a native of Nash county and throughout most of his active career was employed as an overseer on large plantations. He died in Nash county at the age of seventy-five years. He married Nancy Carpenter, who died at the age of about seventy and they reared three sons and five daughters.

When A. B. Finch was eighteen years old he began learning the trade of cooper and this skill in handicraft gave him a steady vocation for many years of his active life. The war interrupted his work at this trade and he enlisted in Company D of the Fifth North Carolina Infantry. With this regiment he saw much arduous service in Virginia, serving under Generals Lee and Stonewall Jackson. At the battle of Williamsburg he was wounded in the left arm by a minie ball, and was in the hospital sixty days. He then continued with his regiment through its campaigns and marches until September, 1864, when he was captured and was kept a prisoner at Point Lookout, Maryland, until the close of the war. Returning home he resumed his trade, and with the exception of two years in South Carolina lived in Nash county until 1882. That was the date of his settlement in Thomas county, Georgia, which has been his home for the past thirty years. Here he bought a tract of timbered land in the Boston district and pursued his regular trade while superintending the clearing away of the forest. He is now owner of one of the most eligible farmsteads in this district, consisting of 264 acres, with 140 in cultivation, and with several sets of farm buildings. His homestead is located three and a half miles from the town of Boston, and there he and his wife live like the patriarchs of old, surrounded by their children and enjoying the fruits of a well spent life.

Mr. Finch was married at the age of twenty-five to Miss Rhoda Williams. They have nine children, whose names are Polly Ann, William H., Archie, John A., James, Rosetta, Nancy Jane, Joseph H. and Stella. All but the last named were born in North Carolina. Mr. and Mrs. Finch are earnest members of the Methodist church.

MARCUS H. ATKINSON. A native son of Georgia and representing one of the old families, Marcus H. Atkinson began business at Meigs when that town was a hamlet and for twenty years has been one of the principal business men and most influential citizens of that locality. He was one of the men who wore the grey during the war, and though the wound and hard service of that period impaired his physical powers, he has led a wonderfully active and enterprising career.

Mr. Atkinson was born on a plantation in Richmond county, Georgia, about twenty miles west of Augusta, on the 25th of January, 1841. His grandfather, Dickson Atkinson, a native of North Carolina, belonged to a family of seven brothers, one of whom settled in South Carolina and five of them in North Georgia. The grandfather was a young man when he settled in Richmond county, the lands there not yet having been surveyed. He bought eight hundred acres of state land, most of it heavily timbered, built a hewed log house and labored until he had made a productive plantation out of the former wilderness, where' he spent the rest of his life. He married a Miss Shepard, whose parents were among the pioneers of Richmond county, and she survived her husband by a number of years. She reared six children.

On this plantation in Richmond county were born two generations, the father, whose name was Zachariah Atkinson, and later, as already stated, Marcus H. Atkinson, the son of Zachariah. The latter was reared in his native county and having received four hundred of acres of land from his father, spent all his life in general farming and died on the plantation where he was born, at the age of sixty-five years. The maiden name of his wife was Ann Dye, a native of Burke county, Georgia. Her father, Avery Dye, a native of North Carolina, and a pioneer of Burke county, improved a plantation on Brier creek, where he spent the last of his days. He married a Miss Owens, who survived him some years, and they reared eight children. Mrs. Ann (Dye) Atkinson died in 1863, aged about fifty-five. She was the mother of six children, named as follows: Avery Dickson, William Shepard, Marcus H., Elizabeth Laura Ann, Robert Toombs, and George Crawford. The last-named was too young, but all the other four sons served with the Confederate army.

Marcus H. Atkinson, whose forefathers were thus closely identified with the early development of Georgia, was reared and educated in his native county, and at the age of twenty-one, instead of taking up the practical duties of civil life, engaged in the great war then in progress between the states. Enlisting in 1862, he became a member of Company D of the Twelfth Georgia Battalion of Light Artillery. Sent to Tennessee he was with the western army for a time, was then in Savannah and at Charleston during the siege, and early in 1864 joined Gordon's brigade in Virginia. At the battle of Monocacy Junction he was wounded in the left leg, was captured on the field and for three months remained a prisoner of war at Baltimore. Being exchanged at Savannah and disabled for further service, he returned home and was honorably discharged.

The war having soon closed, he engaged in farming for three years in Jefferson county, and in 1870 moved to Southwest Georgia, with which region his career has been identified ever since. Buying land in Brooks county, he was engaged in farming there until 1891, in which year he sold out and permanently located at Meigs in Thomas county. At that time Meigs was only a hamlet with two stores and a box-car served for the railway station. A cotton gin was his first enterprise in the village and he also bought land in the vicinity and engaged in farming. Later he also went into merchandising and established a saw-mill. The Atkinson Mercantile Company has for a number of years been one of the largest trading centers in this vicinity. He has also done considerable business in the buying and selling of timber lands and improved farms. His own farm, which he still operates, is located in the corporate limits of Meigs.

In 1866 Mr. Atkinson was married to Miss Eliza Arrington, who was born in Jefferson county, this state, a daughter of Leven Arrington. To their marriage one daughter was born, Ida, now the wife of Mr. Mack Simpson, and they now reside in Meigs. Mr. and Mrs. Simpson are the parents of seven children, namely: Zoah, Medford, Asa, Ela, Myers, Mercy and Margaret. Mr. Atkinson and wife are both members of the Methodist church.

HON. JAMES HORSLEY WHITCHARD. An honored and highly esteemed resident of Dawson, Terrell county, Hon. James H. Whitchard holds a position of note among the more useful members of the community, as a teacher having been an important factor in advancing the educational interests of Southwestern Georgia, while as the owner of a farm he has contributed towards the development of the agricultural prosperity of Terrell county. A son of John Whitchard, he was born August 29, 1853, at Garden Valley, Macon county, Georgia, of early colonial ancestry. The Whitchard family, according to tradition, is descended from one of three brothers that came to America at an early period of its settlement, and here spent their remaining years. But one of the brothers married, and from him are descended all of the Americans bearing the name of Witchard, Whitchard, Whichers, Whitcers, or Whittier.

John Whitchard was born in Crawford county, Georgia. Left an orphan in boyhood, he was brought up by his maternal grandfather, John Williams, being reared to agricultural pursuits. As a young man he purchased land in Crawford county, Georgia, and for a time operated it with slave labor. He subsequently removed to Macon county, where he continued as a farmer until after the breaking out of the war between the states, when he offered his services to the Confederacy. Enlisting, in 1862, as a private in the Tenth Georgia Battalion, he went with his company to Virginia, where he joined the Army of North Virginia. He was subsequently promoted to the rank of quartermaster of his battalion and continued with his command until the close of the conflict, taking an active part in the many battles in which the Army of North Virginia participated, being at Appomattox at the surrender. Returning to Macon county, he resumed business at Garden Valley, remaining there until 1877. Selling out in that year, he came with his family to Terrell county, and having purchased land lying three miles southwest of Dawson carried on farming until late in life, when he removed to Dawson, where he lived retired from active pursuits until his death, in the eighty-third year of his age.

The maiden name of the wife of John Whitchard was Nancy Jane Horsley. She was born in Upson county, Georgia, and died in Dawson, Georgia, in the eighty-second year of her age. Her father, James Horsley, who married Betsey Bullard, was born in South Carolina, of English lineage. Coming to Georgia in early manhood, he located first in Upson county, where he married, and for a time was engaged in farming. He was subsequently similarly employed for a number of years in Macon county, from there coming to Terrell county, where he and his wife spent the remainder of their lives, making their home with their children, Mr. Horsley living to celebrate the ninety-second anniversary of his birth, while Mrs. Horsley passed away at the age of four score and four years. Nine children were born to Mr. and Mrs. John Whitchard, namely: Antoinette, Loula, Mattie, William S., James Horsley, John Williams, Samuel M., Thomas O., and Lizzie.

Growing to manhood in Macon county, James Horsley Whitchard received a practical education in the public schools, and under his father's instructions was well trained in the different branches of agriculture. In 1878 Mr. Whitchard purchased, in Terrell county, land situated three and one-half miles from Dawson, and for a time was there prosperously engaged in farming. Retiring then from agricultural labors, be rented his land, and for eighteen years was actively engaged in educational work, teaching school in Terrell, Randolph and Webster counties, as an educator being successful and popular. In 1894 Mr. Whitchard was elected county school commissioner for Terrell county, and filled the responsible position ably and efficiently for six years, when he was elected as a representative to the state legislature. Although a resident of Dawson, Mr. Whitchard superintends the operation of his farm, in its management meeting with satisfactory results.

On December 10, 1884, Mr. Whitchard was united in marriage with Miss Leila Ada Jolly, who was born in Macon county, Georgia, a daughter of John Robert and Cynthia (McMickell) Jolly, natives of Macon and Marion counties, respectively.

In his political affiliations Mr. Whitchard is a Democrat and active in party ranks. Fraternally he is a member of P. T. Schley Lodge, No. 229, and of Lawrence Chapter, Royal Arch Masons. Both Mr. and Mrs. Whitchard are consistent members of the Missionary Baptist church.

WILLIAM CALLAWAY KENDRICK, M. D., who is also entitled to the term "Honorable," having served a number of terms in the state legislature, is a prominent physician and surgeon of Dawson, where his professional knowledge and skill have met with ample recognition. A son of James Cornelius Kendrick, he was born Hay 17, 1831, on a farm lying seven miles south of Morgan, in Morgan county, Georgia.

His grandfather, James Burwell Kendrick, was born and reared in Virginia and there married Mary Dowd, who was born in Ireland and at the age of ten years crossed the ocean with her parents, who settled in Virginia. About 1805, accompanied by his wife and children, he migrated to Georgia, locating in Morgan county. Buying a tract of land that was still in its primeval wildness, he began, with the help of slaves, to clear and improve a farm and was there a resident until his death.

One of a large family of children, James Cornelius Kendrick was born in Virginia, but while very young was brought by his parents to Morgan county, Georgia. Left fatherless when a lad of ten years, he subsequently made his home with an uncle until sixteen years old, when he joined the militia, and for two years served under General Jackson in the Indian wars. In his youthful days he was converted, and for many years he was a preacher in the Missionary Baptist church. He was also an agriculturist, being engaged in farming in Morgan county until 1836, when he purchased land in Meriwether county, and operated it successfully with slave labor for some time. Selling his holdings in that locality in 1850, he purchased a plantation in Sumter county, eleven miles west of Sumter, and continued in his free and independent occupation. At that time, and for a number of years afterwards, there were no railways in Southern Georgia, and the planters had to team their cotton to Macon, which was the nearest market and depot for supplies, bringing back with them all needed articles for the household, the round trip consuming a long week. After the close of the war he removed to Webster county, from there coming, in 1881, to Dawson to live with his son, Dr. William C. Kendrick, and died at the doctor's home at the venerable age of eighty-four years. His wife, whose maiden name was Mary Butler, was born in Green county, Georgia, a daughter of John Butler, and died in 1877, at the age of seventy-three years.

Mr. and Mrs. James Cornelius Kendrick reared eleven children, as follows: Butler; Burwell and John, twins; James B.; Catherine; William Callaway; Meredith; Benjamin J.; Melissa; Marian; and Isaac W. Five of the sons served in the Confederate army. William Callaway serving as surgeon, with the rank of captain; Burwell, Benjamin and Meredith each raised a company, of which he was commissioned captain. Benjamin was killed, in 1862, at the battle of Big Creek Gap, Tennessee, and Meredith was killed at the engagement near Marietta, Georgia, June 4, 1864. Isaac, who at the breaking out of the war was a youth in his teens, served as a private in the army. Burwell, the second son of the parental household, settled in Texas and at his death, which occurred at a ripe old age, left ninety-five descendants,

William Callaway Kendrick spent his youthful days on the home farm and was reared amid pioneer scenes. When he was a boy the women slaves used to card, spin and weave, and all the family, as well as the slaves, dressed in homespun. He obtained his rudimentary education in the rural schools of his neighborhood. Having decided to enter upon a professional career, he began the study of medicine with Dr. W. J. Reese, of Sumter county, and was graduated from the Metropolitan Medical College, in New York City, in the class of 1855. The following year Doctor Kendrick was engaged in the practice of medicine in Lee county, Georgia, and the next two years was similarly employed in Talbotton. Going from there to Arkansas, the doctor was located at Fort Smith until 1861, when he returned to Georgia, and enlisted as a private in the Twelfth Georgia Volunteer Infantry, in the company commanded by Captain Miles A. Hawkins. Going with his regiment to Virginia, he was soon promoted to surgeon, and with his command joined the Army of the Tennessee, with which he was connected until the close of the conflict.

Returning then to Georgia, Doctor Kendrick settled in Webster county, where he was actively engaged in the practice of his profession until 1881. Locating in Dawson in that year, the doctor has here continued his labors as a physician and surgeon with characteristic success for more than thirty years, with the exception of the time he has been obliged to devote to his official duties.

Doctor Kendrick cast his first presidential vote, in 1852, for the Whig candidate, Winfield Scott. In 1876 he was elected as a representative to the state legislature from Webster county, and after his re-election to the same position, in 1878, voted for Ben Hill for United States senator. In 1888 the doctor was elected to represent Terrell county in the state legislature and was honored with a re-election in 1892, and again in 1896, and in the latter year he cast his vote in favor of Sam Jones as United States senator. Since early manhood Doctor Kendrick has been an active member of the Ancient Free and Accepted Order of Masons. He is a past master of Furlow lodge, Sumter county, and is a member and past master of P. T. Schley Lodge, No. 229; a member of Lawrence chapter, Royal Arch Masons; and has served as a member of the finance committee of the grand lodge of Masons.

Doctor Kendrick has been twice married. He married first, in 1855, Nancy Kendrick, who was born in Talbot county, Georgia, a daughter of Burke Kendrick. She passed to the higher life in 1876. Their only child, Herschell V. Kendrick, died at the age of twenty-one years. The doctor married second, in 1877, Emma Corinne Foster, who was born in Lee county, Georgia. The doctor and Mrs. Kendrick have five children, namely: James B.; Juniata, wife of Dr. T. M. Meriwether; Mary B.; May Belle, wife of R. D. Smith; and Lessie Estelle, wife of Will C. Page.

ANDREW J. HILL. A man of excellent business qualifications, intelligence, and much enterprise, Andrew J. Hill is widely and favorably known in Terrell county as a successful agriculturist, and as a prominent warehouse man of Dawson, his home city. A son of Isaac Hill, he was born November 7, 1870, on a Stewart county farm, coming from pioneer ancestry. His grandfather, Green Hill, migrated from his native state. North Carolina, to Georgia in the very early part of the nineteenth century, becoming one of the first settlers of Houston county. Purchasing a tract of timbered land, he hewed, with the assistance of slaves, a farm from the dense wilderness, and there spent the remainder of his life.

Isaac Hill was born on the parental homestead, in Houston county, in 1814, and was early initiated into the mysteries of successful farming, as carried on in early days. A few years after his marriage, he moved to Monroe county, but not at all satisfied with his prospects in that section, returned with his family to Houston county, and there resided until 1851. Locating then in Stewart county, he bought a tract of standing timber, fourteen miles west of Lumpkin, and erected thereon the customary log house of the pioneer. The country roundabout was but sparsely settled, and deer, turkeys, and wild game of all kinds were plentiful, and formed to some extent the subsistence of the few inhabitants of that locality. For a number of years after his arrival in that county there were no railways, Georgetown, Georgia, and Eufaula, Alabama, being the nearest trading points. Persevering and industrious, he cleared quite a large tract of land, erected a good set of farm buildings, and was there engaged in tilling the soil until his death, March 17, 1897, at the age of eighty-three years. When a young man he took an active part in the Indian wars of that period and later served as one of the three judges of the inferior court of Stewart county.

Isaac Hill was three times married. He married first, Emily Stewart, who was born in Houston county, Georgia, a daughter of Thomas Stewart, a pioneer farmer of that county. She died in 1860. Eight children were born of their union, as follows: Isaac Thomas; Robert Green; William Russell; James Johnson; Nannie Mittie; John Calhoun, of whom a brief sketch may be found elsewhere in this volume; Benjamin L.; and Henry Clay. Mr. Isaac Hill married for his second wife Mrs. Ellen (Moffitt) Williams, She lived but a comparatively few years after their marriage, passing away in 1875. Of that union four children were born, namely: Mollie; Emma Eulala; Andrew J., the special subject of this brief personal review; and Walter L. Mr. Hill married for his third wife Mrs. Fanny (Ligeon) Boland, whose death occurred in 1900.

Acquiring a practical education in the district schools, Andrew J. Hill remained on the home farm until twenty-one years old, and while assisting in its management gained a practical knowledge of farming. Beginning the struggle for life for himself soon after becoming of age, he rented land in Terrell county, and met with such satisfactory results in his labors that he was ere very long enabled to buy a tract of land situated one and one-half miles from Dawson. Fortune smiled upon his every effort, and since making his first purchase Mr. Hill has invested in other tracts, and is now the owner of 650 acres of choice Terrell county land. In 1898 Mr. Hill embarked in the warehouse business in Dawson, and has since managed that successfully in addition to supervising his farms.

In 1897 Mr. Hill was united in marriage with Clemmie Bryant Harris, who was born in Terrell county, a daughter of Edward J. and Martha (Bryant) Harris. Her maternal grandfather, Lovett Bryant, was an extensive farmer of Stewart county, and served as one of the judges of the inferior court of that county and as county school commissioner. He lived to be upwards of ninety years of age and retained his mental faculties to a remarkable degree, being bright and active till the close of his life. Mr. and Mrs. Hill are both consistent members of the Methodist Episcopal church, South.

Ever interested in public affairs, Mr. Hill has served as a member of the city council, and as mayor of Dawson, filling the chair ably and acceptably. Fraternally he belongs to Dawson camp, Woodmen of the World, which was organized in 1897, being one of its charter members. He is fond of the chase and keeps a fine pack of hounds. He is a noted sportsman and as a crack shot has taken part in several target shooting tournaments.

JOHN CALHOUN HILL. Having accomplished a satisfactory work as a general farmer, acquiring a competency to live upon, John Calhoun Hill is now living retired from active business cares, near Dawson, enjoying to the utmost the well-merited reward of his many years of unremitting toil. He was born, in 1851, in Stewart county, Georgia, a son of Isaac and Emily (Stewart) Hill, of whom further notice may be found on another page of this volume, in connection with the sketch of Mr. Hill's brother, Andrew J. Hill.

John C. Hill was reared to a strong, self-reliant manhood on the parental farm, obtaining his education in the rural schools of his neighborhood. He became familiar with the various branches of agriculture while assisting his father on the homestead, and naturally adopted farming as his occupation. Mr. Hill did not become a landholder until after his marriage, his first piece of property having been a tract of land in Stewart county, on which he lived and labored industriously until 1879. Selling out in that year, he bought a farm in Quitman county, and was there a resident for nine years. Disposing of that property, Mr. Hill came to Terrell county, and having bought land four miles west of Dawson, was there actively and successfully engaged in general farming until 1912, in the meantime increasing the acreage of his farm by purchase. He now occupies a farm lying near his original estate and is living retired from active work.

Mr. Hill married, in 1873, Sarah Frances Bismuke, a daughter of William H. and Maria (Green) Bismuke, pioneer settlers of Stewart county, where both spent the closing years of their long and useful lives, Mrs. Bismuke attaining the venerable age of four score and ten years. Mr. and Mrs. Hill are the parents of eight children, namely: William Isaac, Miles Green, Addie Virginia, Alma, Pearl, John Carter, Emily May, and Fanny Ethel.

JOHN CULLEN HOLLINGSWORTH. An able representative of the prosperous business men of Dawson, John Cullen Hollingsworth, a hardware merchant, holds an acknowledged position of prominence among the progressive and public-spirited men of the city and county as a citizen faithfully performing duties imposed upon him in official capacities. He was born and reared in Barbour county, Alabama, of old Virginia ancestry, being a son of James Hollis Hollingsworth.

His paternal grandparents migrated from their native state, Virginia, to Georgia early in the nineteenth century, and for six years lived in the vicinity of Americus, Sumter county, making the removal with teams. White settlers were then few and far between, and the dense forests were apparently filled with all kinds of wild animals and game. Not pleased with their prospects in Georgia, they removed with their family to Alabama, becoming pioneer settlers of Barbour county, where they established a permanent home.

Born in Virginia, in 1832, James Hollis Hollingsworth was but three years old when his parents made the overland journey to Georgia, and but nine years of age when they migrated to Barbour county, Alabama, where he began as soon as strong enough to assist in clearing a homestead. At the breaking out of the war between the states, he enlisted in an Alabama regiment, and with the Confederate forces went to Virginia. He subsequently fought bravely in many of the noted battles of the war, including the battles at Fredericksburg and Gettysburg, and the different ones around Richmond and Petersburg, continuing in active service throughout the conflict, returning home after the final surrender. His father having died while he was an infant, the care of his mother and sister fell upon him at an early age. He rented a mule and a piece of land, and though he had a late start that year, he was blessed with a good crop, which he disposed of at a high price. After renting a few years, he bought a plantation in the northwest section of Barbour county, near Mount Andrew, on the plantation standing the log cabin in which his son, John Cullen, was born. The little cabin, with a few other rude log buildings, and a few cleared acres, constituted all of the improvements upon the place. He possessed good judgment and excellent executive ability, and with thrift and industry, both indoors and out, he and his family prospered, and in due course of time were installed in a substantial frame house. He also erected good barns and sheds for the shelter of his stock and machinery, and put up tenement houses. There he lived contented and happy until his death,

The maiden name of the wife of James Hollis Hollingsworth was Amanda Currington. She was a native of South Carolina. Surviving her husband, she now makes her home with her children, of whom she has five, all sons, as follows: George, John Cullen, James, Robert, and Edgar.

Receiving a good common school education in his youth, John Cullen Hollingsworth, at the age of seventeen, began life for himself as a teacher, and for four years taught school. Changing his occupation, he was clerk in a general store at Clayton, Barbour county, Alabama, until December, 1896. In January, 1897, Mr. Hollingsworth embarked in the mercantile business in Dawson, Georgia, with H. A. Petty, under the firm name of Petty and Hollingsworth, opening the first hardware store in the place, and for eight years carrying on a thriving business under that name. In 1905 the Hollingsworth Hardware Company was formed, with Mr. Hollingsworth as president of the corporation. Another store was purchased, the stock of the two establishments was consolidated, and this enterprising company now carries on an extensive and lucrative business, dealing in shelf hardware of every description, cutlery, kitchen furnishing goods, and farm implements, the firm aiming to anticipate as far as possible the wants and needs of their numerous patrons.

Mr. Hollingsworth married, August 10, 1905, Lillie Christie, who was born in Dawson, Georgia, a daughter of Samuel R. and Ella (Stevens) Christie. Three children have blessed the union of Mr. and Mrs. Hollingsworth, namely: Virginia, Ella May, and John Christie. Religiously Mr. Hollingsworth is an active member of the Baptist church, and superintendent of its Sunday school, and Mrs. Hollingsworth belongs to the Methodist Episcopal church. Fraternally Mr. Hollingsworth is a member of P. T. Schley Lodge, No. 229, Free and Accepted Masons, and of Lawrence chapter, Royal Arch Masons. He is now serving the city as a member of its common council, and is chairman of the board of county commissioners.

OWEN THOMAS KENYON, M. D. Engaged in the practice of a profession which is one of the most exacting of all the lines of occupation to which a man may devote his time and energies, Owen Thomas Kenyon, M. D., of Dawson, holds a position of note among the leading physicians and surgeons of Terrell county. A son of Dr. Solomon H. Kenyon, he was born, May 7, 1866, in Stewart county, Georgia, on a farm situated seven miles west of Lumpkin, coming from excellent New England ancestry. The immigrant ancestor of that branch of the Kenyon family from which Doctor Kenyon sprung was one John Kenyon, who was born in England in 1657, came to America as a young man, and settled in Hopkinton, Rhode Island, where he married Elizabeth Remington.

George Kenyon, the next in line of descent, was born in Hopkinton, Rhode Island, February 4, 1733, and there spent his entire life. He married Martha Hoxie, whose birth occurred in the same place, May 2, 1735. Their son, Solomon Kenyon, grandfather of the doctor, was born in Hopkinton, Rhode Island, and there resided until his death, September 1, 1857, during his active career having been prosperously engaged in agricultural pursuits. Both he and his wife, whose maiden name was Eunice Sheffield, were birthright Quakers and reared their children in that faith.

Solomon H. Kenyon was born in Hopkinton, Rhode Island, May 19, 1793, and there acquired the rudiments of his education. A natural mechanic, he learned the trade of a carriage maker, and subsequently earned enough money as a carriage manufacturer to pay his way through the state university at Burlington, Vermont, graduating first from the literary department, and later from its medical department. After taking a post graduate course in Boston, he was for three years engaged in the practice of medicine in Providence, Rhode Island. In 1829 Dr. Solomon H. Kenyon started for Florida, making the journey in a sailing vessel and being on the water six months, the voyage having been long and rough. A very few years later he came to Georgia, settling in Irwin county, where he became engaged in the practice of his profession and with a Mr. Bowen improved a water power on House creek, near Ocilla. South Georgia then had comparatively few inhabitants, neither the Indians or the wild beasts of the forest having yet fled before the advancing steps of civilization. A few years later he moved to Talbot county, where he practiced medicine until 1852, when he bought land in Stewart county, seven miles west of Lumpkin, and turned his attention to farming, retiring from his professional labors. He was a great reader and student, and when, after he had passed the allotted three score and ten years of man's life, a new grammar was introduced into the county schools, he attended school once again, and memorized the work. He died at the advanced age of four score and four years.

The maiden name of the wife of Dr. Solomon H. Kenyon was Luticia Pierce. She was born, August 18, 1820, a daughter of Allen and Sarah (Mulkey) Pierce, and died in 1895, at the age of seventy-five years. Her paternal grandfather, John Pierce, was a native of Ireland and a pioneer of Burke county, Georgia, of which her Great-grandfather Mulkey was also an early settler. Of the union of Dr. S. H. and Mrs. Kenyon, ten children were born, as follows: John, Solomon, Allen, Mina, George, Sally, Amos Hoxie, Martha, Eunice, and Owen Thomas. The four older sons served in the Confederate army, John and Solomon losing their lives while in the service.

Laying a substantial foundation for his future education in the public schools of Lumpkin, Owen Thomas Kenyon was graduated when young from its high school. Having inherited in no small measure the mechanical talent of his father, he earned enough money while yet a student to pay his college expenses, and in 1886 was graduated from the medical department of Tulane University, with the degree of M. D. Commencing the practice of his chosen profession in Webster county, Doctor Kenyon remained there until 1900, when he removed to Dawson, where he has since continued, having built up an extensive and highly remunerative practice, and has won an enviable reputation as a physician and surgeon. An attentive reader and close observer, the doctor has kept pace with all of the important advances made in medical and surgical science, and has taken a post graduate course at Tulane University, a course of six weeks in the Rhode Island state hospital, a special course at the Atlanta Medical College, and a course in the New York City Polyclinic.

Doctor Kenyon married, February 14, 1889, Mary Almira Kimbrough, who was born at Weston, Webster county, Georgia, a daughter of C. A. Kimbrough. Her paternal grandfather, Stephen P. Kimbrough, was born in Greene county, Georgia, but when a young man removed to Webster county, where he bought a large tract of land, which he operated with slave labor, owning a large number of slaves. He subsequently settled in Stewart county, where his death occurred when he was eighty-three years old. He married Agnes Peak, who lived to the age of eighty-nine years. C. A. Kimbrough enlisted in the Confederate army in 1864 and with his command went to Florida. At the close of the war he located in Webster county, where he still resides. He married Matilda Paschal, who was born in Putnam county, Georgia, where her father was an extensive farmer and a slave owner, who married Mary Ingram, a life-long resident of Putnam county.

Dr. and Mrs. Kenyon have two sons, namely: Stephen P. Kenyon, who was graduated from Mercer University in 1912 and now fills the chair of science in the Gainesville high school; and John C. Kenyon, a student. The doctor and Mrs. Kenyon are members of the Baptist church. Fraternally the doctor belongs to P. T. Schley Lodge, No. 229, Free and Accepted Masons.

GEORGE L. DUREN. Representing a family whose members have been identified by residence and citizenship with Georgia for more than a century, George L. Duren is one of the enterprising merchants of Meigs in Thomas county. Beginning when the present flourishing little city was a village, he has built up a large business, and has performed his share of the development which has been so notable in Southwest Georgia during the last quarter century.

This branch of the Duren family is of Scotch-Irish ancestry, and the great-grandfather of Mr. Duren came from the north of Ireland, the seat of the Scotch-Irish, and settled in Augusta, Georgia, where he spent the remainder of his days and followed his trade of blacksmith. He reared two sons, Thomas and George, but the former left Augusta and disappeared from the knowledge of the family. Mechanical skill has been almost a family asset of the Durens. The grandfather, George, was a skilled worker in wood and iron, and in his generation manufactured looms, spinning wheels, churns, carts and wagons. And his son, the father of the Meigs merchants, inherited the same genius but did not follow it as a regular gainful occupation, though he built the first wagon he ever owned.

George Duren, the grandfather, was born in Augusta and when a young man drove stages from Augusta to interior points, and later moved to Gwinett county, where he bought land and engaged in farming and resided until his death. He was known as a man of sterling character and was thoroughly honest in all his dealings. The maiden name of his wife was Sneed, and they reared ten sons and one daughter. All of the sons who were living at the time served in the Confederate army, and few families of the south were better represented at the front than the Durens.

W. N. Duren, the father, was born in Gwinett county on the 27th of September, 1824, was reared in his native county, and after attaining manhood bought a farm in the same county and also became proprietor of a grist mill on Yellow river. Being a miller, he was exempt from military service until the last call during the war, and was given what was really a greater responsibility, that of caring for the families of those who had gone to the front and supplying them with flour and meal for their daily bread. But in 1864, when Georgia became one of the principal centers of armed invasion, he joined the state militia and went to the defense of Atlanta. In 1865, having sold his possessions in Gwinett county, he came to Southwest Georgia, and bought land in the eastern part of Thomas county, where he spent the remainder of his years. He married Miss Elizabeth Flowers, a native of Gwinett county and daughter of James and Minerva (Chandler) Flowers. Both her parents were natives of Scotland and on coming to America first settled in North Carolina and later in Gwinett county, where they spent the rest of their lives, the mother being upward of seventy-six years at the time of her death. A few years after the Duren family moved to Thomas county the mother was left a widow with ten children to her care. She succeeded in keeping them all together until they were grown and had homes of their own. She spent her last days with a daughter in Thomasville, her death occurring at the age of seventy-six. The names of her ten children were: Mary J., Charlotte A., Reno M., William A., Emery G., Thomas C., Pinckney F., George L., Ella M. and Buna V.

Throughout practically all of his life George L. Duren has been a resident of Thomas county, and since childhood has witnessed the changes made by half a century in this part of the state. He was born in Thomas county, September 27, 1866, and when a boy attended the school in the neighborhood of his home. Up to the age of nineteen he assisted in the work of the farm, and then with a capital of three hundred dollars, given him by his mother, he opened a small store in Thomasville. That was the start of his long and successful career as a merchant. He was in business at Thomasville one year, then two years at Stone Mountain and five years at Cairo, after which he located in Meigs and as a merchant and public-spirited citizen has ever since been closely identified with this community. On coming here there were several frame but only one brick building in the village, and his own enterprise had a small frame structure for its first home. In 1905 he erected a commodious brick store, in which he carries a stock of general merchandise including almost everything in daily use in the house and on the farm. In 1913 he erected a large brick store in addition, in which he will carry a large stock of hardware, machinery, buggies and all kinds of feed stuffs.

Mr. Duren has been twice married. He was married in Gwinett county to Miss A. L. Williams, a native of that county and daughter of Pittman and Sally (Rowe) Williams. Mrs. Duren died at Cairo in 1895. By the second marriage, which was celebrated near Meigs, Miss Rosetta Vick became his wife. She was born in Colquitt county, this state, a daughter of James and Martha J. (Carlton) Vick. One daughter, Ola Belle, was born of the first marriage and the two children of the present union are Schley and Ella Vernon.

Mr. and Mrs. Duren are active members of the Missionary Baptist church. He is a prominent Mason, being master of Meigs lodge, F. & A. M., No. 459; Pelham chapter, R. A. M., and the Crusader Commandery K. T., No. 17, Bainbridge, Georgia. He is also a member of the Independent Order of Odd Fellows, the Knights of Pythias and the Woodmen of the World. Mr. Duren has always been one of the influential Democrats in his locality, has been a member of the district executive committee, and in Meigs has done his share of public service as member of the town council.

JAMES N. ISLER, M. D. Both as a physician and an enterprising business man, Dr. Isler has taken a prominent part in the improvement and development of the town of Meigs and its environs during the last fifteen years. It is due to the work and influence of such citizens that Southwest Georgia owes its rapid material progress of recent years.

James N. Isler has spent most of his life in this section of the state. Born on a farm in Calhoun county on the 21st of July, 1874, he was a son of Becton Isler, who was born in the same county in 1844. The grandfather, John Isler, was a native, it is thought, of Wilkinson county, this state, and a descendant of Swiss ancestors. The name is found in different states of the Union, sometimes being spelled Izler. The grandfather moved from Wilkinson county to Baker county during the early forties and settled in that part now included in Calhoun county. He bought land and devoted the rest of his career to the clearing and tilling of the soil. For many years after his settlement no railroads had penetrated into Southwest Georgia, and the farmers had to market their products at the river or gulf ports many miles away. It was a pioneer epoch in this region, when deer, turkeys and all kinds of game were plentiful. Calhoun county was the home of the grandfather until his death. He married a Miss Bailey.

Becton Isler (the father), though not sixteen years old when the war broke out, enlisted in a Georgia regiment, was for a time assigned to duty in guarding the magazines at Macon, and then took the field with his regiment and served until the end of the war. He then bought land in his native county and has ever since been identified with the agricultural interests of that locality. He was thrice married, and the maiden name of his first wife and the mother of the doctor, was Elizabeth Smith. Of her four children, one died in infancy and the others are named Judge Becton, James Nathaniel and Naomi Elizabeth. From the third marriage there are four children living: Guery Beaton, Louie, Jesse M. S. and Elsie.

Doctor Isler was reared and educated in his native county of Calhoun, attending the common schools and then the high school at Leary. His determination to study medicine was adopted at an early age and he began his reading when seventeen with Dr. W. R. Terry at Leary. In the fall of 1894 he entered the Southern Medical College at Atlanta, where he was graduated M. D. with the class of 1897. He chose for his residence and place of practice the city of Meigs, which had then had several years of slow growth. After two years he was induced to remove to Pearson in Coffee county, where he remained three years, and then returned to Meigs, which has been his home ever since. He enjoys a large practice, and is one of the most popular and successful physicians in Thomas county. Dr. Isler was married at Pearson in 1902 to Miss Lena, daughter of Louis and Phoebe (Simmons) Holtzendorff.

His part in the advancement of modern improvements and in civic and social affairs is not less important than his work in his profession. Realizing the need of the modern facilities of telephone service, a few years ago he established the Meigs Telephone Company, of which he is now sole owner. The service was at first confined to a small area about Meigs, but has been since extended to Mitchell and Grady counties, and in 1912 his system was established at Ochlochnee. In 1905 the doctor started a drug store in Meigs, and has since conducted one of the well appointed stores of the county. He is a stockholder in the Bank of Meigs.

Doctor Isler is a charter member, past master and was first junior warden of the Meigs Masonic Lodge, No. 459, F. & A. M., and is affiliated also with Pelham Chapter, R. A. M., and Crusader Commandery, K. T., at Bainbridge. His other fraternal associations include membership with the John B. Gordon Lodge, No. 163, K. of P., at Pelham, of which he is a charter member; member and past grand of Meigs Lodge, No. 241, I. O. O. F., and is one of the charter members; and past council, commander and camp physician of Meigs Camp, No. 157, W. O. W., and also one of the organizers. As a Democrat he has never taken any part in practical politics, but has done his duty as a voter and good citizen.

ANDREW JONES BOND, who belongs to one of the old families of Southwest Georgia, is a well known and prosperous citizen of Meigs. He is a native of Stewart county, having been born on a farm there the 1st of May, 1864.

His grandfather, Thomas Bond, a farmer by occupation, who so far as known was a life-long resident of Elbert county, reared seven sons and two daughters. John Rafe Bond, the father of Andrew J., was the seventh son, and was born at Elberton, Elbert county, in 1833. When a very young man he came to South Georgia, buying land in Stewart county, and was there successfully engaged in farming and stock raising until his death, which occurred in 1899. The maiden name of his wife was Martha Frances Broach, and she was a daughter of Thomas and Elizabeth Broach. She is still living, at a good old age, on the home farm in Stewart county, her son, John Willis, being manager of the estate. Her five children are Josephine, Andrew Jones, Eliza Cornelia, John Willis and Dora.

Andrew J. Bond was reared and educated in his native county, and has always been an industrious worker and good business manager. At the age of twenty-three he moved out to Texas, where he bought a tract of land in Hunt county and developed it as a farm, selling it at the end of three years. After six years' residence in Texas he returned to Georgia and for a time lived on the home place in Stewart county. In 1899 he bought land in Mitchell county six miles from Pelham, selling this in 1902, and during the following six years was a resident of the town of Pelham. After a sojourn of about six months in Florida he selected as his next place of residence the town of Meigs, where he is now owner of seventy-five acres within the corporate limits, and he also has a farm of 125 acres in Grady county. Most of his land is operated by tenants. He has been very successful in business, has developed a good deal of country property, and is a man of much enterprise. In 1905 he became a civil service employe of the government, and is still in charge of a rural mail route from Meigs.

Mr. Bond was first married in July, 1904, to Miss Eula Hand, whose father, Amos F. Hand, is a well known resident of Meigs. Mrs. Bond died in June, 1905. In 1907 he was united in marriage with Miss Vera May Young, daughter of William J. Young, of Meigs. The two children of Mr. Bond and wife are named Edgar E. and Velma Eilene.

JOE MCHANCOCK. Up to the time of his election to the office of ordinary of Turner county, Joe McHancock had devoted himself with all diligence to the farming industry, wherein he had experienced a very fair degree of success. His election to the office of ordinary came with the organization of the county in 1906 and continued for a term of four years, and as the incumbent of that office he verified to the utmost the expectations of his constituents, and proved himself a capable and wise official. Mr. McHancock has not relinquished his farming activities, but owns and operates a small and productive place, though his residence has been maintained in Ashburg since 1906.

Born on the 11th of September, 1859, in Pulaski county, Joe McHancock became a resident of Wilcox county in 1863. This county later was subdivided and Turner county was formed as a result, as was also Ben Hill county, in 1907, by act of legislature. The parents of Joe Mc- Hancock were Joseph J. and Sarah (Watson) Hancock. The father was born in 1818 and died in 1879. He was a farmer and divided his time between that work and the vocation of a Baptist minister, of the denomination known as Hard Shell. He was a pioneer preacher of his time, and was a resident of this community during the war. His wife was a daughter of Frederick Watson, one of the old settlers living in the vicinity of Houston county, near Perry, Georgia.

The early days of Joe McHancock were passed on his father's farm on the Allapha river, in Wilcox county, and there he early learned the business of farming under the insistent instruction of his parent. As a consequence, he turned his attention to that business when he reached years of manhood, and up to the time when he was elected ordinary of Turner county, had continued to devote himself to that industry. Mr. McHancock has been identified with the county in an official capacity since it was organized in 1905 and was chief clerk of the first ordinary of Turner county up to 1908, elected to that office with a majority of three to one. Since 1906 Mr. McHancock has maintained a residence in Ashburg, but he still conducts his farm in the vicinity of the city.

On February 22, 1870, Mr. McHancock was married to Mary W. McCall, and to them eight children were born. Mrs. McHancock died on June 11, 1905. The children are named as follows, in the order of their birth: John, of Lake Kerr, Florida, is assistant postmaster at that place and bookkeeper of a large lumber company; Dave is engaged in the livery business in Rebecca, Turner county, Georgia; Charles is a farmer of Rebecca; Samuel, also in the livery business; Essie, living at Atlanta, Georgia; Joe, Jr., Estelle and Domer are all students and living at home. In 1909 Mr. McHancock married Miss Nettie Barronton, the daughter of Mrs. J. W. Barronton, of Lafayette county, Georgia.

Mr. McHancock is a member of the Independent Order of Odd Fellows and the Rebekahs, and is also identified with the Masonic fraternity, Sycamore Lodge, No. 210, with membership in the Chapter, R. A. M. He and his wife are members of the Baptist church. Mr. McHancock is the youngest member in a family of eleven children. His brothers and sisters are named as follows: Martha, Elizabeth, Amanda, J. G. B., E. L., Catherine, Jane, John, Ellen and W. J. The latter is clerk of the supreme court of Wilcox county. J. G. B. McHancock was sheriff two terms in Irwin county, in 1876 and 1878, and E. L. McHancock was county treasurer of Irwin county two terms, in 1882 and 1884. All the family is yet living except Amanda, E. L. and Martha, and the children, grandchildren and great-grandchildren number over 420. The family is an old and well known one in this section of the state and many of the name have given valued service to the county and state in various capacities.

JOSEPH WESLEY CAMERON, clerk of the superior court of Telfair county, is a native of Georgia, born in the same county in which he now lives. His birth occurred on March 14, 1852, and he is the son of A. J. and Margaret Cameron, the father a native of Telfair and the mother of Tattnall county. The father was a gunsmith by trade and was foreman of the Georgia state army during the war, and for twenty-four years thereafter he was messenger of the Georgia senate, a position which he was filling when his death occurred, in 1888. The Cameron family is one which has been prominent in Georgia for a number of generations, and representatives of the family have ben identified with the fortunes of Telfair county since its organization in 1807. Duncan Cameron, the grandfather of Joseph Wesley Cameron, of this review, represented this county in the legislature five terms. He was a native of North Carolina, and the family is one of Scottish extraction. He also represented the county in the senate three terms and in the house two terms. The father, A. J. Cameron, was a member of both constitutional conventions after the close of the war. He was born in 1826 and died in 1888, as mentioned previously. The mother, who was born in 1825, died in 1898.

Mr. Cameron was the only child of his parents. He was educated primarily in the schools of McRae. On reaching years of maturity, he engaged first in the merchandise and timber business in this section, and he continued in that line of enterprise with more or less success until in 1890, when he was elected assistant doorkeeper in the house of representatives for a term of four years. In 1894 he was elected assistant doorkeeper in the senate for a five years' term, and on January 1, 1899, he took charge of the office of clerk of the superior court of Telfair county, his election to that position coming in the latter part of 1898. Mr. Cameron is still the incumbent of that office, a fact which is eloquent of ability and fitness for such a position.

Mr. Cameron is a member of the blue lodge of the Masonic fraternity, and with his family, is a member of the Methodist Episcopal church.

On May 11, 1876, Mr. Cameron was united in marriage with Mollie J. Paschal, daughter of William Paschal of McDuffie county, Georgia. William Paschal was a veteran of the Civil war, having served in the Georgia army. Twelve children were born to Mr. and Mrs. Cameron, of which number nine are yet living. Their names are here given in the order of their birth: Minnie Lee, the wife of W. H. Turner of Telfair county, is deceased; Annie Laurie, who married C. A. Graham, a contractor of McRae, is also deceased, her death occurring in 1898: Alice Jane, is the wife of W. W. Simmons, an architect and contractor of McRae; Maggie Mae is the wife of M. A. Birch, a farmer of Dodge county; William J. is a pharmacist of Montgomery county; Josie L. is a teacher in Glenwood; M. A. and Lillie Endell, living at home; Earl Duncan, Max Lamer and Joseph Terrill are still attending school in McRae.

ROBERT LEE GROOVER. One of the many enterprising men extensively engaged in farming in Brooks county, Robert Lee Groover has brought to his chosen calling superior knowledge, excellent judgment, and fine business methods, and his labors are crowned with success. A native of this county, he was born October 27, 1862, in Hickory Head district, not far from the birthplace of his father, Allen W. Groover.

His grandfather, James Groover, was born, reared and married in Bulloch county, Georgia. From there he came to Southwestern Georgia, making his way thither with teams, bringing with him all of his worldly possessions, including his household goods, his stock and his slaves. He located in that part of Irwin county that was later made into Lowndes county, and has since become a part of Brooks county. Buying a tract of timber, he erected a rude log house in the wilderness, and later sawed boards to seal the house and floors. For many years thereafter there were no railroads in this section of the country, all of the cotton produced being hauled to the gulf ports, fifty miles away, it taking a week to make the round trip. Indians were then numerous, and deer, bear and wild game of all kinds inhabited the deep woods. Clearing quite a tract of land, he was busily employed in cultivating the soil until his death, at a good old age. To him and his first wife, whose maiden name' was Elizabeth Denmark, twelve sons and four daughters were born, and by his second wife, one son was born.

Born in Hickory Head district, Brooks county, September 4, 1832, Allen W. Groover was brought up in what is now Brooks county. Inheriting a tract of land, he engaged in agricultural pursuits as a young man, continuing thus employed until the fall of 1862. Enlisting then in the Georgia Volunteer Infantry, he served with the Confederate forces until the close of the war. Returning home, he resumed farming on an extensive scale, becoming owner of about two thousand acres of land in Brooks county, where he continued a resident until his death, September 4, 1907. He married Martha McMullen, who was born in Brooks county, Georgia, a daughter of James McMullen. She died in 1892, leaving six children, as follows: Feliz R., Frank C., Robert Lee, Hattie, Eliza L., and W. Blewett.

An excellent scholar as a boy, Robert Lee Groover acquired a practical business education in the common schools, and until twenty-five years of age remained beneath the parental roof, being in the employ of his father. He then purchased land in the Nankin district and was there successfully engaged in tilling the soil until 1903. He then bought the place on which he is now living, it being the R. I. Denmark homestead property of seven hundred acres, and still retains the eleven hundred acres in the Nankin district.

In 1890 Mr. Groover married Peggie Wyche, who was born in Madison county, Florida, a daughter of James L. and Mary (Rossiter) Wyche. Five children have been born of their union, namely: Robert Lawrence, Allen W., Vann, Rossiter, and Frank Clayton. Religiously Mr. Groover is affiliated with the Missionary Baptist church, and Mrs. Groover is a member of the Presbyterian church. Politically a Democrat, Mr. Groover served for fourten years as county commissioner. He belongs to the Hickory Head Farmers' club, of which he has been president. He is a man of much ability and is now vice-president of the Bank of Quitman.

ALBERT JACKSON HODGES, a successful merchant and farmer at Morven, Georgia, was born in Brooks county of this state on September 9, 1867. His father, Joseph J. Hodges, was born in Bullock county, Georgia, in 1836, and his grandfather, James C. Hodges, was a native of the same county, where he was born of ancestors that were of English descent and were numbered among the early settlers of that county. James C. Hodges removed to southern Georgia in 1838 and located in that part of Lowndes county that is now included in Brooks county. At that time the greater part of southwestern Georgia was a wilderness, deer, bear, turkeys and many other kinds of game were still plentiful, and the Indians yet contested this as their hunting ground. He purchased a tract of timbered land five miles north of the present site of Quitman and began to hew a farm from the wilderness. There were no railroads in this section for many years afterward. He went to Newport, Florida, to market his products and on the return would bring back supplies for the house and farm, it requiring several days to make the trip. After clearing quite a tract of land there he sold his holdings and purchased land in Brooks county in the locality known as Okapilco, where he spent the remainder of his life and passed away during the war between the states. His wife, who was Miss Sarah Newton before her marriage, survived him many years and died at the advanced age of ninety-three. They were the parents of six children, namely: J. Lafayette, Robert L., Joseph J., Margaret, Mary and Maggie. All of the sons served in the Confederate army. Joseph J. Hodges, the father of Albert J., was reared on the farm. After he had attained his majority he went to Florida, where he clerked for an elder brother until the breaking out of the Civil war, when he enlisted in a regiment of Florida cavalry in which he served until the close of the war. He then returned to Brooks county, Georgia, the fortunate possessor of $200, which was his entire capital. With more valuable assets, however, in the way of energy, ambition and undaunted courage, he began anew his campaign for success. Purchasing the interests of the other heirs in the homestead of his father, he began farming in a small way and prospered from the start. As his means accumulated he invested in land until his holdings comprised about three thousand acres, besides outlying tracts, and he was also a stockholder in the banks at Pavo and Quitman, Georgia. He continued to reside on his estate until his death on July 25, 1910. The maiden name of his wife was Rachel Caroline Delk. She was born in Brooks county, Georgia, a daughter of John and Jane (Hodge) Delk, and still resides at the old homestead. Joseph J. and Rachel C. (Delk) Hodges became the parents of eight children, viz.: Albert J., Wesley, Sally, Charles W., James C., Eugene E., Judge R. and Mary. Wesley died at the age of seventeen and Charles passed to the life beyond when thirty years of age. Both parents were consistent members of the Methodist Episcopal church and the father was an ardent advocate of prohibition.

Albert Jackson Hodges, the eldest of his family and the immediate subject of this review, received his education in the common schools of Brooks county. Reared to habits of industry, he began in early youth to assist in the duties of the home farm and gained thereby a knowledge and a training that have been the foundation of his subsequent successful business career. He remained with his parents until twenty-three years of age and then purchased land near the old home, where he followed farming ten years. At the end of that period he removed to Morven to engage in the mercantile business and so continued there, carrying a large stock of general merchandise, including everything in daily use in the home and on the farm, until January 1, 1913, when the store and all the goods were burned. Since then he has been farming, his place of 350 acres adjoining the corporation of Morven, and is a stockholder in the Citizens banks at Quitman and at Morven. Mr. Hodges is also a member of the legislature and has been mayor of Morven two years.

At the age of twenty-three he was united in marriage to Mamie Griffin, who also is a native of Brooks county and is a daughter of Simeon and Emma Griffin. Mr. and Mrs. Hodges are both members of the Methodist Episcopal church. They have seven children: Euler F., Joseph J., Maude, Edwin D., Marion, Claude W. and Laura.

ASHLEY LAWSON. A life-long resident of Georgia, Ashley Lawson gained distinction not only for the active part he took in the development of the agricultural interests of the southern part of the state, but as a splendid representative of those brave men of old, who out of the dense forests of what is now Brooks county established for themselves permanent homes. A son of John Lawson, he was born in 1810, in Lawrence county, coming, probably, of Scotch ancestry. Lawson is a common and an honored name in all parts of the Union, many members of the family tracing their lineage back to one Roger Lawson, who resided in New York state during the Revolution, and was murdered by the Tories, he having reared eleven stalwart sons, who, as they grew to manhood, separated, settling in different localities in the north, south, east and west.

Born and brought up in North Carolina, John Lawson came when young to Georgia, traveling thither in his own conveyance. He located first in Laurens county, later coming south, and settling in that part of Irwin county which was subsequently converted into Lowndes county, and now forms a part of Brooks county. Purchasing land in the part now included in the Barney district, he began the improvement of a homestead. The wild and heavily wooded country roundabout was habited by wild animals of many kinds, and Indians were still numerous and troublesome. He began the pioneer labor of clearing the land, and raised his first crop on soil that had previously been used for the same purpose by the redskins. There being no railways in this vicinity for years after he came to Georgia, all surplus productions of the land had to be hauled to either Saint Marks, Georgia, or to Newport, on the Tallahassee, the general custom of marketing the goods being for a few of the neighbors to combine, and start with a number of teams loaded with produce, taking along with them provisions and cooking utensils, and camp by the way, on the return trip bringing home the household supplies needed. Having improved quite a tract of land, John Lawson occupied it several years, but later in life removed to Colquitt county, where he spent his declining days, passing away at the age of eighty-seven years. His wife, whose maiden name was Rachael Green, was born in North Carolina, and died, at a good old age, in Colquitt county. They reared four children, as follows: Eliza, Ashley, Greene, and Daniel.

The oldest son of the parental household, Ashley Lawson, began in his youthful days to assist in the arduous labor of redeeming a farm from the forest, sharing both the pleasures and hardships of frontier life. Little do the people of this day and generation realize what they owe to those brave spirits of old, who first uprooted the trees, ploughed the sod, and made a broad track for the advance of civilization. As a young man, Ashley Lawson joined a company organized for protection against the redskins, and was an active participant of the wars of 1836, when the Indians made their last stand in this part of Georgia. He was past military age when the war between the states broke out, but in 1864 he was called to the front, and, with the old and the young valiantly opposed the advance of the Federal army into Southwest Georgia.

Soon after attaining his majority, Ashley Lawson purchased land in Lowndes county, and on the farm which he reclaimed from its virgin wildness spent the remainder of his four score and four years of earthly life. During his active career he saw Lowndes county grow from a wilderness into a quite well developed farming country, with a railway passing through his own estate. He married Cynthia Folsom, who was born in Burke county, Georgia, a daughter of Lawrence A. Folsom, and granddaughter of William Folsom, who was born in England, and who, as far as is known, was the only member of his family to come to America. He settled in Virginia, and having purchased land lying on the Potomac river there spent his remaining years.

Born on the Virginia plantation, Lawrence Armstrong Folsom spent his early life with his parents. Lured southward as a young man, he lived for a time in Burke county, Georgia. In 1815, accompanied by three other enterprising and adventurous young men, James Rountree, Drew Vickers and Alfred Belote, he came to that part of Irwin county now included within the boundaries of Lowndes county, blazing his way through the wilderness on horseback. After exploring a considerable portion of South Georgia the quartet invested in government land, Mr. Folsom buying a tract about a mile from Little river; Messrs. Rountree and Vickers located near by; and Mr. Belote purchased land that included the present site of the village of Mineola. Going back to Burke county for their families, these gentlemen returned to Brooks county with their wives and children, making the overland trip in carts drawn either by horses or mules, following Indian trails a part of the way, at other times making their own path through the trackless woods. Whenever they came to a stream too deep to ford, they swam their stock across, and built rafts on which to take their carts and household goods across. Those four families were pioneers in very truth, being the first permanent white settlers of Lowndes county, more especially of its northern portion. There were no mills in that section of the country for several years thereafter, all the grain being ground in mills operated by hand. They kept sheep and raised cotton, and the women used to card, spin and weave the homespun material from which she fashioned all the garments worn by the family. The wild game found in the forests furnished the early settlers with a large part of their subsistence, while acorns, beech nuts and walnuts were so plentiful that the only need of feeding hogs was to keep them from growing wild, an occasional meal serving for that purpose. Very little ready money was then in cirenlation in the south, and in the newer settlements few store goods were used, salt, sugar and coffee being the principal articles brought in.

In the development of the community in which he located, Lawrence A. Folsom took an active part, and on the homestead which he built up spent the remainder of his life, passing away at an advanced age. His wife, whose maiden name was Rachel Vickers, was born in Virginia, and died on the home farm, in Lowndes county. They were the parents of nine children, as follows: William; John; Maston; Randall; James; Elijah; Cynthia, who became the wife of Ashley Lawson; Rachael, and Betsy.

Mrs. Ashley Lawson attained the age of seventy-two years, having reared a large family of children, namely: William, John, Hardy, James, Hugh, Greene, Nancy, Lawrence, Ivey, Martha, Irvin, Susie and Jane. Six of the sons, William, John, James, Hugh, Greene and Lawrence served during the war between the states in the Confederate army. Hugh and Greene died while in service, and Lawrence was severely wounded in battle.

LAWRENCE F. LAWSON. A prominent and prosperous agriculturist of Brooks county, and the proprietor of one of the most attractive estates in the Morven district, Lawrence F. Lawson is distinguished not only as a successful farmer, but as a veteran of the Confederate army, and as the descendant of an honored pioneer of southern Georgia. He was born January 29, 1849, in Lowndes county, Georgia, a son of Ashley and Cynthia (Folsom) Lawson, of whom an extended account is given elsewhere in this volume.

Growing to manhood on the homestead, Lawrence F. Lawson gleaned his early education in the rural schools, and under the wise instruction of his father acquired a proficient knowledge of farming. At the outbreak of the war between the states, he enlisted in Company H, Twenty-sixth Regiment of Georgia Volunteer Infantry, and at Staunton, Virginia, joined Stonewall Jackson's army. With his regiment he participated in many engagements of importance, at the second battle at Manassas being severely wounded. He lay upon the field between the two armies for several hours, seeing many of his comrades shot down, General Lawton having been standing by his side when he was wounded.

while Lieutenant Colonel Griffin fell dead at Mr. Lawson's feet. Of the twenty-eight men of his company that went upon the battlefield, four, only, escaped unhurt, the others being either killed or wounded.

After the battle was over, Mr. Lawson was taken to the field hospital for treatment, and for twelve months was unable to rejoin his command. Being then transferred to Liberty, Virginia, he remained there in duty until the close of the conflict. Returning home, he assisted his father, in the summer of 1865, in harvesting his crops, and then began life for himself as an independent farmer. Buying land in the Hahira district, Lowndes county, he lived there two years, and then sold and purchased two hundred and twenty-five acres in the Morven district, Brooks county. Mr. Lawson cleared one hundred acres of that tract, meeting with such encouraging success in his operations that he bought other tracts in that vicinity, obtaining title to upwards of two thousand acres. In 1881 he bought his present property, which borders on Lawson's pond, in the Morven district, it being one of the most beautiful and desirable locations in South Georgia. Near his house, which stands on high land, is a magnificent grove of oak, pine, and other trees native to this section, and within one hundred yards of his residence is a well of pure, cool, and sparkling water, none better to be anywhere found.

Mr. Lawson has been four times married. He married first Josephine Scruggs, who was born in Brooks county, a daughter of Richard and Mary (Goldwire) Scruggs. She died in early womanhood, leaving two children, Edwin and Luther. Mr. Lawson married second Mary Jones, who was born in Talbot county, Georgia, a daughter of Fennel and Susan (Brown) Jones. At her death she left one child, William. For his third wife Mr. Lawson married Laura Scruggs, a sister of his first wife, and to them six childern were born, Roberta, John Pleasant, James Bennett, Armsted, Richard Garland, and Mamie. After her death Mr. Lawson married Fannie King, who was born in Berrien county, Georgia, a daughter of James and Celia (Myers) King. Mr. and Mrs. Lawson are the parents of five children, namely: Yeatman, Sned, Hugh, Celia, and Rachael. Mr. and Mrs. Lawson are members of the Missionary Baptist church, to which his first and third wives also belonged, while his second wife was a member of the Methodist Episcopal church, South.

IRVIN LAWSON. As an active, enterprising, and industrious farmer, Irvin Lawson materially assists in maintaining the reputation of Brooks county as a superior agricultural region, having a well-appointed and productive farm in the Morven district. A member of the well-known and much respected Lawson family, and a descendant of the first settler of Southwest Georgia, he was born August 6, 1854, in Lowndes county, a son of Ashley and Cynthia (Folsom) Lawson, of whom a sketch may be found on another page of this work, and a grandson of John Lawson, the pioneer.

Acquiring his education in the public schools, Irvin Lawson was trained to habits of industry and thrift on the home farm, and remained with his parents as long as they lived, caring tenderly for them in their later years. His father gave him one-half of the old homestead property, and he, having purchased the remaining half from the other heirs, lived there until 1888. Selling out in that year, Mr. Lawson bought his present farm in lot number 225, Morven district, and has now three hundred acres of good land, on which he has improvements of a substantial character, including a comfortable set of farm buildings.

Mr. Lawson married, at the age of thirty-seven years, Lillie Scruggs, who was born in Brooks county, Georgia, a daughter of Richard and

Margaret (Horne) Scruggs, both natives of Georgia, her father having been born in the vicinity of Savannah, and her mother in Burke county. Mr. and Mrs. Lawson have four children, namely: Richard Ashley, Roy, Ernest, and Maggie.

An intelligent reader, taking a genuine interest in everything pertaining to his native state, Mr. Lawson is very familiar with the early history of Georgia, having acquired a large part of his historical knowledge first hand from his parents and grandparents, and through the reading of current literature keeps himself well informed on all the leading questions of the day.

ANGUS MORRISON. Devoting his time and energies to the development and advancement of the agricultural interests of Brooks county, Angus Morrison has for several years been actively and successfully engaged in general farming in the Morven district, where his property is finely located. He is distinguished as a native-born citizen, his birth having occurred in that district, February 9, 1864. He is a son of the late Angus Morrison, Sr., and a grandson of John Morrison, a pioneer of Georgia.

Born and educated in Scotland, John Morrison came to America when a young man, and after spending a brief time in North Carolina dauntlessly pushed his way to Montgomery county, Georgia, which was then but thinly populated. Buying a tract of wild land, he engaged in farming and stock-raising, remaining on the homestead, which he cleared and improved, until his death, while yet in the prime of a vigorous manhood. He married Catherine McCrimmon, who was also a native of Scotland. She was a woman of much ability and courage, and on being left a widow with a family to care for she immediately assumed the management of the home farm, on which she reared her children, giving to each a good education. She continued her residence on the farm, which is now owned by her great-grandson, until her death.

Angus Morrison, Sr., born in Montgomery county, Georgia, June 13, 1819, was but two years old when left fatherless. Receiving an excellent education, he embarked upon a professional career at the age of fourteen years, teaching first in Montgomery county, and later in Lowndes county, where he had charge of schools in various places. In 1857 he bought a tract of land in lot number 362, in what is now Morven district, Brooks county, and erected the house in which his widow now resides. Engaged both in teaching and farming, he was a resident of the district until his death, October 28, 1873.

On February 7, 1857, Angus Morrison, Sr., married Louisa Pike, who was born in that part of Lowndes county now included in Brooks county, March 22, 1834. Her father, Hon. John Joseph Pike, was born in Saint Augustine, Florida. His father being murdered by the Indians, he was taken, with the other children to the home of his grandfather, in Charleston, South Carolina. When large enough to care for himself he returned to Florida, where he took an active part in various Indian wars. Coming from there to Georgia, John Joseph Pike was one of the early settlers of that part now called Brooks county. Purchasing land north of Morven, he built a log house in the forest and began to clear a farm. There were no railways in this vicinity for many years thereafter the most convenient markets being either at Savannah or in the gulf ports, the round trip taking from one to two weeks. Deer, bear, panthers, wolves, wild turkeys, and game of all kinds were plentiful, and every man went armed as a protection against the hostile Indians. Mr. Pike had slaves and with their assistance cleared a large portion of the land, and until his death continued to reside on his farm, which is now owned by his great-grandson.

Hon. John Joseph Pike married Nancy Hall, who was born in Montgomery county, a daughter of Sion Hall. Her grandfather, Enoch Hall, came from North Carolina to Georgia, settling first in Montgomery county, but later removing to Appling county. His wife, whose maiden name was Jennie Jackson, was born and reared in North Carolina. Their son, Sion Hall, accompanied them to Georgia, and when ready to settle in life bought land in that part of Irwin county that was later made into Lowndes county, and is now a part of Brooks county. Purchasing large tracts of land he operated it with slave labor, and was also engaged in milling, having a grist mill and a sawmill on Little river, and a sawmill on Mill creek. Sion Hall, who lived to be nearly a hundred years old, continued a resident on the home farm until his death, and many of the descendants of him and his wife, whose maiden name was Mary Morrison, are still living in Brooks county. Hon. Joseph Pike was prominent in public affairs, serving as an officer in the state militia, and representing his district in the state legislature. Both he and his wife were influential members of the Primitive Baptist church.

Brought up and educated in Brooks county, Angus Morrison began life for himself as a railway employee, being first employed in the shops of the F. C. & P. Railroad Company, and later being an engineer on the same road, which is now called the Seaboard Air Line. After fifteen years' experience in that work, Mr. Morrison returned to Brooks county, and having purchased the estate which he now owns and occupies has since been prosperously engaged in farming and stock-raising. His farm, containing three hundred acres of rich land, is located at the Four Corners, five miles west of the village of Morven, and is one of the more desirable farms of that vicinity.

Mr. Morrison married, February 14, 1892, Anna Morrison Alderman, who was born in Marion county, Florida, a daughter of Hiram Alderman. Her grandfather, Samuel M. Alderman, was born and reared in North Carolina. He married Sarah Chestnut, and on coming to Georgia settled in Bulloch county, where he cleared and improved a homestead, on which they both resided during the remainder of their lives, her death occurring at the age of eighty-seven years. One of a large family of children, Hiram Alderman was reared in Bulloch county, Georgia, but as a young man went to Marion county, Florida, bought land, and in the log cabin which he built in the midst of the forest kept bachelor's hall two years. Returning then to Bulloch county, he married Emeline Jones, a daughter of Basil and Deborah (Bowen) Jones, who moved from North Carolina to Bulloch county, Georgia, in pioneer days. Returning with his bride to Florida he installed her as mistress of his cabin. Fifteen years later he disposed of that property, and purchased a farm in Bradford county, Florida, where both he and his wife spent their remaining days. They were the parents of nine children, as follows: Harmon; Deborah; Alice; Jane; Anna Morrison, wife of Angus Morrison; Laura; John; Basil; and Susan. Mr. and Mrs. Morrison have one child, Emma Lou Morrison, a student at the Norman Park Institute. Both Mr. and Mrs. Morrison are members of the Missionary Baptist church.

Mr. Morrison's mother is still living, a bright and active woman of seventy-eight years, with her mental faculties unimpaired. In her younger days she used to card, spin and weave, and for many years did all of her cooking by the fireplace. She is one of the few now living who have watched with pride the growth of Brooks county from a wilderness to a country in which are flourishing towns and cities, and rich agricultural regions. In the days of her girlhood the wild beasts of the forest had not yet fled before the advancing steps of civilization, but, with the dusky savage, inhabited the vast wilderness. Railroads, telegraph and telephone lines were then unknown, and the primitive cart, the only wheeled vehicle known by the early pioneers, has given way to the expensive carriages and automobiles now seen everywhere, not only in the streets of the cities and villages, but on the rural highways.

LLEWELLYN ROBINSON DIXON. A long and prosperous career was that of Mr. Dixon. Born in Georgia seventy-seven years ago, he had been identified with the southwestern part of the state since pioneer times when there were no railroads. He is a veteran of the Civil war, and for many years has successfully managed a large estate in Brooks county, his residence being in the village of Morven.

Llewellyn Robinson Dixon was born on a farm in Sumter county, August 26, 1836. His grandfather was a pioneer of Washington county, and there, it is thought, Pleasant Dixon, the father, was born and reared to manhood. From Washington he moved to Houston county, and after a few years to Sumter county and then to Pulaski county. Pleasant Dixon was a plantation overseer and managed a number of large estates in Georgia. He was overseer on Major McCormick's plantation until about 1846, when he settled in Dooly county and bought a farm of his own. In 1854, coming to that portion of Lowndes county now included in Brooks and buying land in the Morven district, he there devoted himself to the quiet pursuits of the farm until his death at the age of seventy-two. The maiden name of his wife was Fanny Lycett, and she was born in Washington county and her death occurred at the age of about eighty-six. She reared five children, Caroline, Moses, William, Lewellyn R. and Jimmie.

Mr. Dixon was a youth of eighteen when the family settled in Lowndes county (now Brooks), and at that time Troupville was the county seat. There was yet no railroad transportation for the products of this region, and the nearest markets were Tallahassee or Newport, Florida. His father often hauled his crops to one of these ports, and it required four or five days to make the round trip. Mr. Dixon lived at home most of the time until his marriage, when he settled on land inherited by his wife. When his brothers went into the war he returned to the home farm to care for his parents. But when practically all the youth of the South was needed to sustain that giant struggle he also left home in August, 1862, enlisted in Company A of the Second Florida Battalion. His command was soon sent to northern Virginia and placed in A. P. Hill's corps. He was engaged in many of the greatest battles of the war and served until the end. At the surrender at Appomattox he was a near observer of Generals Grant and Lee in their meeting, and was thus one of the actual witnesses of that culminating event in the war between the states. On being paroled he marched with his command to the James river, took boat to Fortress Monroe, was there transferred to a steamer which carried him to Savannah, and from there walked to Jessup and thence came by railroad the rest of the way to Lowndes county.

After nearly three years' absence in the army he resumed farming on the old homestead for five or six years, and then bought land about a mile northwest of Morven. Possessed of energy and good judgment, as the years went by he added to the sum of his material prosperity and has long since acquired a position of comfort and moderate affluence. He owned upwards of twelve hundred acres, and some years ago retired from the personal supervision of his property and lived retired in the village of Morven.

Mr. Dixon was married at the age of twenty-three to Miss Mary Beasley. She was born in Lowndes county, a daughter of Isaiah and

Polly (Campbell) Beasley, pioneer settlers of that county. Mrs. Dixon died at the age of twenty-five and left three children: Pleasant, Frankie and May, and he then married her sister, Catherine, his faithful companion for many years. Her death occurred in 1909. Mr. Dixon then married Mrs. Julia (Devane) Alderman. She was born in Brooks county, a daughter of John and Martha (Hicks) Devane, and her paternal grandparents were Benjamin and Mary (Rogers) Devane, and her maternal grandparents, Benjamin and Mosley (Brice) Hicks. Mrs. Dixon's first husband was Timothy Alderman, a Confederate soldier and until his death a farmer of Brooks county. Mr. Dixon's daughter Frankie married Moses Dixon, and their children are Pleasant, Llewellyn, William, Katie Lou and Temperance. Mary married Isom Walker and has one daughter, Mollie, who is the wife of Herbert Purvis, and their son Herbert is a great-grandchild of Mr. Dixon. By his second wife Mr. Dixon had seven children, namely: Jimmie, Emma, Annie, Alice, Mattie, Braxton and Estelle. Jimmie married Katie Briggs and has seven daughters, named Rachel, Inez, Jimmie, Julian, Estelle, Annie Lou and Reba. Emma is the wife of John Wiggins. Annie became the wife of John Moody, and their five children are Catherine, Braxton, Ina, R. F. and Frankie. Alice married George Edwards and has two children, Sally and Thelma. Mattie is the wife of William Council, and their three children are Emma Lee, Ralph C. and Alma. Braxton died at the age of twenty-one years. Estelle, who married John Hammett, died leaving an infant daughter, Estelle, who now lives with her uncle, John Wiggins. Mr. Dixon died December 20, 1912, and was buried at Mount Zion camp ground near Morven.

JAMES MADISON SCARBOROUGH. An active factor in the development of the agricultural resources of Brooks county, James Madison Scarborough has been industriously engaged in his useful vocation in the Morven district many years, by means of his ability and practical experience having become familiar with this branch of industry. A son of James Scarborough, he was born June 14, 1856, in Emanuel county. He is of pioneer stock, his grandparents having come from North Carolina to Georgia at an early day. They settled first in Bulloch county, from there moving to Emanuel county, where they spent their closing years.

Born and reared in Bulloch county, James Scarborough seized every opportunity to acquire an education, and being a diligent student acquired sufficient knowledge while young to begin life for himself as a teacher. He was also a natural mechanic, especially skilled as a wood worker, and in his leisure hours used to make chairs, spinning wheels, and other needed household articles. Industrious and thrifty, he accumulated some money, and made frequent investments in land, becoming owner of large tracts, which he devoted to farming and stock-raising. Disposing of all his Georgia property soon after the close of the Civil war, he bought land in Columbia county, Florida, where he lived and labored for nine years. Coming back to Georgia he purchased a farm in Colquitt county, seven miles from Moultrie, and continued his agricultural work a few years. Selling out then, he bought another piece of land in the same county, and on the farm which he improved resided until his death, at the age of seventy-four years. He married Elizabeth Lanier, who was born in Emanuel county, Georgia. She died at the age of forty-eight years, leaving a large family of children, as follows: Susan, Allen, Mary, Elizabeth, Miles, Nancy, James Madison, and Missouri and Mazelle, twins.

Acquiring a good common school education in Georgia and Florida,

James Madison Scarborough began when quite young to assist his father in the work incidental to life on a farm, remaining with his parents until twenty years of age. Accepting then a position as superintendent of a large plantation in Brooks county, he retained it for five years, managing it in a most satisfactory manner, the land yielding abundant harvests under his care. Mr. Scarborough then purchased his present farm of two hundred or more acres, it being finely located in lot number 329, Morven district, and as a farmer he has since met with characteristic success.

Mr. Scarborough married, in November, 1881, Catherine Morrison, who was born in Morven district, a daughter of Angus and Louisa (Pike) Morrison, of whom a brief sketch is given elsewhere in this volume. Two children have been born of their marriage, namely: Clara, living with her parents; and Lubie, wife of Frank Devane. Mr. Scarborough is not a politician in any sense implied by the term, but for twenty years he has served as justice of the peace. Fraternally he belongs to Morven lodge, F. & A. M. . Mr. and Mrs. Scarborough are both valued members of the Methodist Episcopal church.

KENDRICK J. HAWKINS. The appointment of a lawyer to the bench always calls forth a storm of comment and often occasions warm discussions and criticism, but in the case of Kendrick J. Hawkins, who is now judge of the superior court of the Dublin circuit, composed of the counties of Johnson, Twiggs and Laurens, Georgia, the approval was practically universal, and with the exception of his few enemies which fall to the lot of any strong man, everyone agreed that no one could have been selected who would fill the place to the greater satisfaction of the people. The faith which was thus reposed in him has been amply fulfilled, for his decisions have been made by a mind free from prejudice, and with a background of a wide and deep knowledge of the law and its puzzling technicalities, he has been able to make his court an example of real justice, and was re-elected in the primary of August, 1912, carrying every county in his circuit over strong opposition and a bitter fight.

Kendrick J. Hawkins is a native of the state of Georgia, having been born in Washington county, on the 6th of January, 1871. His father was William A. Hawkins and his mother was Mary (Mayo) Hawkins. His father was also a native of Washington county, where he was born on the 6th of November, 1836. His mother was born in Dougherty county, in 1851. Judge Hawkins' father was a veteran of the Civil war, having served throughout the long four years, and who came out of the conflict bearing the marks of the wound which he received at Chickamauga. When Kendrick Hawkins was but a lad his parents moved to Hancock county, Georgia, and here he attended school until he was fourteen years of age. His family not being so very rich in this world's goods, he was then forced to stop school and learn the printer's trade. He went to Warrenton and here he became master of this trade, later moving to Gibson, Georgia. At the age of seventeen he went into the newspaper business, and attained considerable success in this field, having many of the qualities necessary to the composition of a good newspaper man. He continued in this line of work until he was twenty-four, at which time he took up the study of law under the tutelage of Judge B. F. Walker, of the Toombs circuit court. His newspaper experience stood him in good stead in this study and after two years of close application he was admitted to the bar, in 1896.

He began to practice immediately after his admission in Gibson, Georgia, removing to Dublin, Georgia, in 1902. Here he proceeded to build up both a lucrative practice and a good reputation as a lawyer.

His arguments were always forceful, and his treatment of his cases was so clear and simple that he was seldom involved in useless technicalities. He was recognized as an unusually brilliant and clever attorney, and his appointment as judge of the city court in December, 1908, occasioned little, if any, surprise. A further triumph was in store for him, the more to be remembered as it was the last act of Governor Hoke Smith. This was his appointment by the governor on the 1st of January, 1912, as judge of the superior court of the Dublin circuit, which circuit was created by the legislature of 1911.

Some people attribute Judge Hawkins' success to their belief that talent of a certain order may run in a family. They point to the late Judge W. A. Hawkins, of the supreme court of Georgia, who lived at Americus, Georgia, before his death and was a relation of Judge Kendrick J. Hawkins, and say that the ability along legal lines is an inheritance of the Hawkins family. This is no doubt true to some extent, but the success of the judge is largely due to his own hard work and to the painstaking care which he exercised in all the work which he did.

Judge Hawkins was married on the 26th of February, 1900, to Mary Leola McNair, the daughter of L. F. McNair, of Jefferson county. No children have been born to the judge and his wife.

The subject of fraternal relationship has always been regarded with much interest by Judge Hawkins, and he is a member of various fraternal organizations, in which he takes an active part. He is a member of the Knights of Pythias, of the Benevolent Protective Order of Elks, of the Royal Arcanum, and of the Woodmen of the World.

LITTLE & PHILLIPS. The firm of Little & Phillips, contractors, have been located in Cordele, Georgia, since 1906, but they have been associated together since 1900. The firm, which is well and favorably known in and about this section of the state, was, during the early years of its existence, located at Fitzgerald, where they carried on a general contracting business, and where they built not only houses and business structures, but a fine reputation for competence, fair dealing and genuine business integrity. This reputation they have continued to deserve in the years of their association in Cordele, and nowhere may be found a firm more worthy of the fair reputation which this concern has won to itself. In Quitman and Fitzgerald the finest and best buildings of both a public and private nature have come into existence under the master supervision of this firm. Schools, churches, business blocks, residences, alike, have been reared to bear witness to the ability of these men in their constructive capacity, and the same is true of their years of activity in Cordele. Many neighboring towns, such as Americus and McRae, have called upon them when important building propositions were being planned, and scarce a town in south Georgia but offers material evidence of their prowess in their chosen field of labor.

Of the private life and origin of these men a few words will not be out of place in this brief review.

William Harmon Little, of the firm of Little & Phillips, was born in Schley county, Georgia, on October 16, 1870. He is the son of Joseph H. and Martha Francis (Harman) Little, natives of Meriweather county, Georgia. The father has followed farming all his life and lives now in Valdosta, Georgia. Their son, William H., was educated in the public schools of Schley and Terral counties, to the latter of which places the family moved when William was eleven years old. The father was a member of Company A., Twenty-seventh Georgia, Colquitt Brigade, during the Civil war. As a young man, William H. Little engaged in contracting, first as an employe until he had learned the trade, and later on his own responsibility. By constant study and diligent application to the subject, he has mastered every difficulty, and has reached the high place in the building world which he now occupies. Mr. Little is a Pythian knight and a member of the Masonic fraternity. He is a Baptist in his religious belief, while his wife is of the Methodist denomination.

Mr. Little was united in marriage with Miss Sallie Jones, the daughter of Thomas Anderson Jones, of Brooks county, Georgia. Four children have been born to them. They are: Miriam Nadine, aged ten years; Wilma, aged six; Fannie Joe, now three years of age, and an infant of three months, William H., Jr.

Wendle Councile Phillips, the partner of William H. Little, was born March 22, 1867, in Robinson county, North Carolina. He is the son of E. R. and Rose Ann (Mercer) Phillips, both of whom were of Irish descent. They came to North Carolina when young, settling in Robinson county, and there married. The father was a country school teacher and preacher of the Baptist church. During the Civil war he served in the army as a first lieutenant in a regiment of the army of the Confederacy. He still lives in North Carolina, where he and his wife reared a family of thirteen children, but six of whom are now living. They are J. R., Nettie, Mary Jane, Lula, Wendle C. and E. R., Jr. All are residents of North Carolina with the exception of Wendle C. Phillips. Such education as he received came to him through the avenues of the public schools of his home town, and at an early age he became responsible for his own progress in the world. He eventually entered the building and contracting field, first as a workman, but later as a contractor, and the present partnership between Mr. Phillips and his partner, Mr. Little, is a matter of thirteen years duration. Their association has ever been of the most agreeable nature, their natures blending to the extent that constant association in a business way only makes each the more valuable to the other.

Mr. Phillips married Miss Tommy Smith, the daughter of Thomas Smith, of Americus, Georgia. One child has been born of this union: Wendle Councile, Jr., born October 16, 1911.

CHARLES PAINE HANSELL. For nearly half a century a member of the Georgia bar and prominent in the civic life of Thomasville, Charles P. Hansell has himself been a successful lawyer and represents a name and family which have been notable in the law and public affairs of Georgia for fully a century. Mr. Hansell was born at Milledgeville on the 14th of September, 1844. A brief outline of his family antecedents is as follows:

South Carolina was the home of the Hansells previous to their removal to Georgia, and the great-grandparents were, so far as can be ascertained, lifelong residents of the Greenville district in that colony. The grandfather of Charles P. Hansell was William Young Hansell, a native of the Greenville district. When he was a child he lost his father, and at the age of twelve came to Georgia to make his home with his uncle, William Young. Making the best of his opportunities he acquired a common school education and then studied law in Milledgeville, and after admission to the bar engaged in practice there. He was one of the eminent attorneys of his time, and his name appears in the Georgia supreme court reports. His active practice continued until 1860, and he then lived retired until his death in 1867. The maiden name of his wife was Susan Byne Harris, representing another prominent family of this state. She was born on a plantation about two miles from Milledgeville, and her father, Augustin Harris, a native of Burke county, was directly descended from one of four brothers who came to America during early colonial times and settled in Virginia. Augustin Harris was a Baldwin county planter, having numerous slaves and being one of the prosperous men of his section. Susan (Harris) Hansell survived her husband until 1874, and she reared two sons, Andrew J. and Augustin H., and five daughters.

Augustin Harris Hansell, father of Charles P., was born at Milledgeville, August 17, 1817, and being reared in one of the prosperous homes of Georgia, was given excellent advantages. Prof. Carlisle Beaman was one of his tutors in general subjects, and he studied law under R. K. Hines and Iverson L. Harris. After admission to the bar he began practice at Milledgeville, and for a time served as private secretary for Governor Gilmer. In 1847 he was elected solicitor general, and two years later judge of the southern circuit, then embracing the greater part of south Georgia. Railroads had not yet penetrated to this region, and he journeyed from court to court in his private carriage. He resigned as judge in 1853 but was again elected to the same office in 1859. For some years, until 1850, he was a resident of Hawkinsville, then in Scottsboro two years, and in 1852 came to Thomasville, being one of the most prominent among the early settlers of this locality. During the war he served on the relief committee, and in 1864 spent three months distributing supplies to the soldiers around Atlanta and Marietta. In 1868 he left the bench, resuming private practice for four years, but in 1872 was again appointed judge of the southern circuit and continued in this office until 1903. For more than forty years he honored the bench with his character and ability, and his is one of the foremost names in the Georgia judiciary during the last half of the nineteenth century. On retiring from the bench he lived retired until his death in 1907.

Judge Hansell married Miss Mary Ann Baillie Paine, who was born in Milledgeville. Her father was Charles J. Paine, a native of Petersburg, Virginia, and a physician. As a young man he came to Georgia and was engaged in practice at Milledgeville until his death in 1857. Dr. Paine married Ann Baillie Davies, the daughter of William Davies, a native of Savannah, and granddaughter of Edward Davies, a native of Wales, who was one of the early settlers of Georgia. William Davies also conferred honor upon the legal profession of Georgia, and served as judge of the superior court and was mayor of the city of Savannah during the War of 1812. William Davies married Mary Ann Baillie, the maiden name of whose mother was Ann McIntosh, a daughter of John Mohr McIntosh, the immigrant ancestor of the noted McIntosh family. Judge Hansell's wife died in 1906, and her five children were as follows: Susan V., Charles Paine, Mary H., Frances B., and Sally H.

As a descendant of these conspicuous citizens and families of Georgians, Charles P. Hansell has himself borne a not inconspicuous part as a man and citizen. His early education was obtained in the common schools and in Fletcher Institute, and later in the Georgia Military Institute at Marietta. He was a young man of about eighteen when the Civil war came on, and on the 15th of May, 1862, he enlisted in Company B of the Twentieth Georgia Battalion of Cavalry. After two years engaged in the coast defense of Georgia and South Carolina, his command joined Lee's army in northern Virginia and served with Young's Brigade in Wade Hampton's division. He saw arduous service in the campaigns, marches and battles until the close of the war, and was paroled at Greensboro and returned home. In 1865 he was admitted to the bar, and has been continuously engaged in the practice of his profession from that time to the present, having won many honors in this long career. He has served as judge of both the county and city courts, and for two terms was mayor of the city of Thomasville. In politics he is a Democrat, and he and his family are members of the Presbyterian church.

Mr. Hansell was married in 1869 to Miss Margaret Charlton, who died October 5, 1889. She was born in Savannah, a daughter of Robert and Margaret Charlton (see sketch of Walter G. Charlton elsewhere in this work). Mr. Hansell's present wife is Mary (Glover) Hansell, who was born in Marietta, a daughter of John H. and Sarah E. (Brumby) Glover. Mr. Hansell has two daughters, Mary H., by his first wife, and Sarah G., by the second marriage.

COL. WILLIAM A. MCDONALD, deceased, was one of the gallant sons of the South that served in its defense as a soldier of the Confederacy in the great struggle of 1861-65, and during his lifetime was one of Georgia's prominent and worthy citizens, for many years a resident of Ware county.

Born in Bulloch county, Georgia, in 1817, he was a son of Dr. Randall McDonald, whose nativity had occurred on the Isle of Skye, Scotland. Donald McDonald, the father of Dr. McDonald, also was a native of Scotland, but in 1805 brought his family to America and became an early settler in Bulloch county, Georgia. There he purchased a tract of land and began its improvement, but a few years later was bitten by a rattlesnake and died from the effects. He left a widow and two children, a son and a daughter. The son Randall finally became an overseer. Through the large acquaintance he formed in this manner with wealthy planters he gained access to books and by self-instruction acquired a good general education and a practicing knowledge of medicine and surgery. Later he bought land in Ware county and became a successful planter, operating with slave labor. In those days there were no railroads in Georgia and the country was sparsely settled. Centreville was the principal market and depot for supplies. Indians were numerous and ofttimes troublesome, so that each settlement had a fort to which the women and children could repair for safety. Dr. McDonald continued a resident of his plantation until his death at the age of sixty-eight years. His wife was a Miss Catherine Miller before her marriage, a native of Bulloch county, Georgia, and a daughter of Henry Miller. Her grandfather was William Miller, one of the first settlers in Georgia, and her great-grandfather was D. J. Miller. She survived her husband several years and both are buried in the Kettle Creek cemetery in Ware county.

Col. William A. McDonald was largely reared in his native county but was still a boy when he accompanied his parents to Ware county. After he had begun his independent career he purchased large tracts of land there which he operated with slave labor. Upon the breaking out of the war between the states he entered the Confederate service and was commissioned captain of Company H of the Twenty-sixth Regiment of Georgia Volunteers, which was organized with C. W. Styles as colonel, and W. A. Lane as lieutenant colonel. This regiment was for a time on the Georgia coast under Lawton, accompanied that officer to Richmond, Virginia, in time to share in the seven days' battles, thenceforward serving in the army of northern Virginia until Appomattox, where, in the division commanded by Gen. Clement A. Evans and the corps of John B. Gordon, it shared in the last charge of that illustrious army. During this long and honorable service E. N. Atkinson succeeded Colonel Styles in the command of the regiment and William A. McDonald was a brave and able successor of Lieutenant Colonel Lane. Colonel McDonald remained in the service until the close of the war. His slaves were faithful and cultivated his land until his return from the conflict. His estate three miles from Waresboro, Ware county, remained his home until his death in his eightieth year. He was thrice married. His first wife was Tabitha Sweat, a native of Ware county and a daughter of Capt. James A. and Elizabeth (Newburn) Sweat, and to their union were born ten children. His second marriage was to Mary Ann Deen, who bore him seven children. The maiden name of his third wife was Rebecca Thompson and five children were reared from this marriage. Colonel McDonald left to his descendants the record of a brave soldier, a loyal son of the South and a citizen of worth, integrity and high respect.

Colonel McDonald served his district several terms in the state senate, and he was also a representative of his county in the legislature of his state. He was a member of the state senate at the time of his death, and served in all about forty years in the senate and in the house.

ALFRED JACKSON POWELL. An industrious and prosperous tiller of the soil, Alfred Jackson Powell, living in the Dixie district, owns and occupies a well-managed farm, on which he has a substantial set of farm buildings, located just outside the corporate limits of the town of Dixie, these with their surroundings having an air of neatness and prosperity that never fails to attract the attention of the passing traveler. He was born September 23, 1856, in Arkansas, where his father, Dr. Alfred Jackson Powell, was then engaged in the practice of his profession.

Dr. Powell was born in North Georgia, his parents having been farmers, who spent the later years of their lives in Wilkes county, Georgia. After his graduation from the Jefferson Medical College, in Philadelphia, Dr. Powell took a special course of study in the Baltimore hospitals, acquiring knowledge and experience of great value to him in his work. Returning then to his native state, he practiced medicine for awhile in Worth county, and then located in Arkansas, about twenty-five miles from Little Rock. Soon after the outbreak of the Civil war, the doctor came back to Georgia, settling his family in Dougherty county, and enlisted in the Confederate service as hospital surgeon, a position which be filled acceptably until the war was ended. Going then to Chihuahua, Mexico, Dr. Powell learned the language of the natives, and there continued his residence as a physician and surgeon until his death.

The maiden name of the wife of Dr. Powell was Georgiana Elizabeth Jordan. She was born in Bibb county, Georgia, a daughter of Joshua and Elizabeth (Hays) Jordan, being of Scotch-Irish descent. Removing from Bibb county to Worth county, Georgia, Joshua Jordan bought land on the Flint river, twenty-two miles from Albany, and was there extensively engaged in agricultural pursuits, operating his large plantation with slave labor, both he and his wife spending their last days there. For some time after the close of the war Dr. Powell's wife resided on her farm in Dougherty county, Georgia, but her later years were spent in Moultrie, Colquitt county, where her death occurred when she was about seventy-five years of age. She reared five children, as follows: Mary, Cynthia, Elizabeth, Alfred Jackson, and Florence, all of whom, with the exception of Elizabeth, are now living.

Acquiring his early education in the rural schools, Alfred Jackson Powell began when young to perform his full share of the manual labor incidental to life on a farm, becoming familiar with the theory and practice of agriculture. When twenty-two years of age he began work as a woodsman, and for twelve years was engaged in the turpentine business. Investing then his money in land, Mr. Powell bought sixty-five acres in the Dixie district of Brooks county, the improvements on the place consisting of a cleared and improved plot of a little more than twenty acres, on which stood a small board house. Beginning farming on a modest scale, Mr. Powell met with very encouraging success from the first. From time to time he has purchased other tracts lying near by, and now has a fine farm of three hundred and twenty-five acres, which he devotes to mixed husbandry, his land being under a good state of tillage, and yielding profitable harvests each season.

Mr. Powell married Alice McKinnon, who was born in Brooks county, Georgia, a daughter of William G. and Mary Jane (Groover) McKinnon, and a granddaughter of James Groover, one of the first settlers of Brooks county. Two children have been born of the union of Mr. and Mrs. Powell, Wallace and Mary E. Both Mr. Powell and his wife are identified by membership with the Missionary Baptist church.

REV. WILLIAM R. TALLEY. A fine representative of the professional and agricultural circles of Brooks county, Rev. William R. Talley, of Dixie, has gained distinction not only for the honorable ancestry from which he traces his descent, but for his industry, ability and integrity of purpose. He was born at Mount Zion, Hancock county, Georgia, February 16, 1844, a son of Rev. John Wesley Talley.

His grandfather, Caleb Talley, a native of Hanover county, Virginia, was a descendant of one of three brothers who came to America in colonial days, one of whom located in North Carolina, on the Roanoke river, one settling in Hanover county, Virginia, while the other took up his residence on the Susquehanna river, in Pennsylvania. Leaving Virginia in 1797, Caleb Talley traveled across the country by private conveyance to Georgia. He bought land in Lincoln county, but as it proved impossible to raise tobacco there at an advantage he moved to Greene county, leased manual labor school lands, and there raised tobacco on an extensive scale. Packing his tobacco when harvested into hogsheads through which he had drawn an axle, he attached shafts, and drew his entire crop to Augusta, seventy-five miles distant, where he received top prices for his loads. While yet a young man he served as a soldier in the Revolutionary war. He married Elizabeth Stuart, who was born in Virginia, of Scotch-Irish ancestry. She passed away at the age of seventy-five years, while his death occurred when he was but fifty-five years old. They were both members of the Methodist Episcopal church at Walker, Greene county, it being one of the oldest churches of that denomination in the state. They reared one daughter and five sons, the sons being named William, Nicholas, Alexander, Caleb, Elkanah, Nathan, and John Wesley. Caleb and Elkanah became farmers, and the other five became preachers in the Methodist Episcopal church.

On December 6, 1800, the birth of Rev. John Wesley Talley occurred in Greene county, Georgia, where he was reared. There having been in that early day no free educational institutions, he had but little opportunity to attend school, but through his own efforts he secured a fair education, and began life for himself as a merchant in Washington, Georgia. A man of deep religious convictions, he entered the ministry in 1827, and in 1828 joined the South Carolina Conference, which embraced the western part of North Carolina, and all of South Carolina, Florida, and Alabama. His first two appointments were in North Carolina, and his third was at Pensacola, Florida. There were then neither railways nor public roads of any account in this section of the country, and he made his rounds on horseback, following Indian trails, mostly, and preaching, generally, in log houses. In 1835 he was assigned to Macon, Georgia. A man of advanced ideas, broad-minded and liberal in his views, fully appreciating the value of a good education for girls as well as boys, he was one of the leaders in the movement of offering the girls the same facilities for acquiring knowledge that was as a matter of course afforded the boys. During his pastorate in Macon he agitated' the subject, and, supported by Elijah Sinclair, proposed the establishment of a female college in that city, and the two leaders in the movement worked to such good purpose that the Wesleyan College, for which they selected the site, was established in Macon. It was at first called the Georgia Female College, but was later changed to the Wesleyan Female College, a name which it still bears. During the Civil war he served as chaplain of the First Georgia Hospital, in Richmond, Virginia.

Being superannuated in 1871, Rev. Mr. Talley spent a few years with his son William, but in 1878 removed to Corsicana, Texas, where he resided until his death in 1885. He married Rosetta Ralston, who was born in Savannah, Georgia, a daughter of John Ralston, who came from Ireland with two of his brothers just after the close of the Revolutionary war. She died at the home of her daughter in Corsicana, Texas, at the advanced age of eighty-five years. They reared four children, namely: Elizabeth Stuart; John Shellman, a soldier in the Confederate army, died from the effect of wounds received at the second battle of Manassas; William R., the subject of this brief biographical record; and Sally C.

Completing his early education at Emory College, in Oxford, Georgia, Rev. William R. Talley began his professional career, at the age of twenty-two years, as a teacher in the Hancock county schools. Licensed as a local preacher in 1876, he preached in different places in Georgia, in addition to teaching and preaching turned his attention to farming. In December, 1880, Mr. Talley purchased his present farm in Dixie, where he has since resided. His one hundred and forty acres of land are under a high state of cultivation, and he has a substantial set of buildings, his house being most pleasantly located on a knoll overlooking Dixie valley. As a farmer and stock raiser he is meeting with well merited success, and as a man and a citizen he is held in high regard throughout the community.

Mr. Talley married, in 1872, Carrie Harvey, who was born in Marion county, Georgia, a daughter of Benjamin and Mary Harvey. Seven children have blessed their marriage, namely: Lizzie, John S., Eunice S., Ben H., Charles R., Sally Lee, and Elmer. Lizzie, wife of L. L. Stevenson, has two children, William and Shellman. Eunice, wife of W. L. Watkins, has three children, William Talley, Ruth, and Harrison. Ben married Mattie Stuart, and they have two children, Ben Harvey and Martha. Charles married Luella Hurt.

JOHN OBED STANALAND. A skilful and practical agriculturist, systematic and thorough in his methods, John Obed Stanaland is meeting with notable success in his pleasant and profitable calling, his farm, which is located in the Dixie district, having excellent improvements, the buildings being conveniently arranged, while his machinery is of the latest approved manufacture. He was born April 1, 1868, in Thomas county, Georgia, a son of Daniel B. Stanaland, and grandson of John Obed Stanaland, the first.

The pioneer ancestor of the Stanaland family in Georgia was Buz Stanaland, Mr. Stanaland's great-grandfather, who was born, it is thought, in South Carolina. Migrating to Georgia in early life, Buz Stanaland lived for awhile in Bulloch county. Later he came to southwest Georgia, making the removal with teams of his own, bringing his cattle and household goods with him, and settling on the old county road, ten miles north of Thomasville. Purchasing a tract of timbered land, he erected a log cabin in the wilderness, and began in reality to hew a homestead from the forest. He was the first to raise stock in this section of the state, and found the industry quite profitable. Successful in his work, he cleared a large part of his land, and in due course of time built a good hewed log house, sealing it inside and out, and there resided until his death, in the seventy-fifth year of his age. His wife, whose maiden name was Dolly Hollingsworth, survived him, being upwards of eighty years old at the time of her death. They, with one son and one daughter, lie buried in the family lot, on the old homestead. They were typical southerners in their generous hospitality, their latch string being always out. They reared five children: John Obed, Prissy, Zebulon, Thomas, and Amy.

John Obed Stanaland, the first, was born during the residence of his parents in Bulloch county, and with them came to the southwestern part of the state. He was early drilled in the branches of agriculture, and began farming for himself by renting a piece of land lying one mile from Thomasville, on the old Coffee road. Thomasville had then but one dwelling, a log house owned by James Kirksey, who was the only merchant in that vicinity, his store being also in a log building. While living on that land, he dug for Mr. Kirksey, the first well dug in Thomasville. After renting for a year, he bought land in Jefferson county, Florida, where he tilled the soil several years. Returning, however, to Georgia, he located in Thomas county, about a mile from the town of Boston, and in the log cabin which he erected lived a few years. He not only tilled the land, but he kept the family larder well supplied with the fruits of the chase, deer, bear, and wild game of all kinds being plentiful, and made all the shoes worn by his family, tanning all the leather used himself. His wife, who was a true helpmeet, used to card, spin and weave, and make all the clothing worn by her household. There being no railroads in those early days he used to market all of his surplus produce either in Tallahassee or in Newport, Florida, with teams, the round trip to the first mentioned place taking, if the roads were very good, three days, while a trip to Newport and back, under the same conditions, required a full week. He continued a resident of that farm until his death, at the advanced age of seventy-eight years. John O. Stanaland, the first, married Susan Melton, who was born in Bulloch county, where her father spent his entire life. The maiden name of the mother of Susan Melton was Davis. She survived Mr. Melton, and after his death came from Bulloch county to Thomas county, locating in the south part, where she bought a farm which she operated with slave labor, living upon it until her death, when over one hundred years of age. Both Mr. and Mrs. Melton were of New England ancestry. Of the union of John O. and Susan Stanaland, seven children were born and reared, as follows: James Alfred, John H., Benjamin, Daniel B., Jephtha C., Simeon, and Julia. All of these sons took an active part in the war between the states, Benjamin dying while in the service.

Daniel B. Stanaland was born in Thomas county, Georgia, near Boston, October 15, 1839, and there grew to man's estate. In 1861 he enlisted in the company known as the Dixie Boys, which was attached to the Fifty-seventh Georgia Regiment of Volunteer Infantry, which became a part of the Western army. With his command he participated in many important battles, and when Vicksburg surrendered was captured by the enemy. Exchanged about three weeks later he rejoined his regiment, and with it took part in various campaigns, continuing with his command until the close of the war. He served under Generals Joseph E. Johnston and J. B. Hood, toward the close of the conflict, being sent with his regiment to Virginia, marching through Georgia and the Carolinas to Virginia, and then fell back to Greensboro, North Carolina, where he surrendered. After returning home, he farmed for a number of years in Thomas county, and then came to Brooks county, to the home of his son, John Obed Stanaland. He married Elizabeth Mountain, who was born near Tallahassee, Florida, in 1845, a daughter of Jonathan and Martha (Lively) Mountain, natives, respectively, of Georgia and South Carolina. Three children were born of their marriage, namely: John Obed; William Henry, who died in the eighteenth year of his age; and Walter. The mother was a member of the Methodist Episcopal church, and in her daily life exemplified its teachings.

Educated in the district schools, and early initiated into the mysteries of farming, John Obed Stanaland remained a member of the parental household until twenty-two years old. Entering then the employ of the S. F. & W. Railroad Company, now the Atlantic Coast Line, he was for fourteen years identified with its roadway department. Lured back to the soil, Mr. Stanaland next purchased a tract of land in the Dixie district, near the Pidcock station, and has since been here actively and prosperously engaged in general farming and stock-raising, his success placing him among the wide-awake and progressive farmers of his neighborhood.

Mr. Stanaland married, November, 1891, Jimmie Alderman, who was born in Brooks county, Georgia, a daughter of Elias Alderman. She is of pioneer stock, being a granddaughter of James and Jane (Roberts) Stanaland, of whom a brief account is given on another page of this volume, in connection with the sketch of Ezekiel Alderman.

Elias Alderman was born in Thomas county, Georgia, in 1846, and was there reared to agricultural pursuits. Grown to manhood, he bought land near Pavo, lived there a number of years. Disposing of that property, he purchased a tract of land in lot No. 467, Tallokas district, Brooks county, and on the farm which he improved spent the remainder of his life, passing away in 1899. He married, in 1870, America Beaty, who was born in Brooks county, Georgia, a daughter of William Beaty, Jr., and granddaughter of William and Mary (Drew) Beaty. Born and brought up in Washington county, Georgia, William Beaty, Jr., came as a young man to Brooks county, locating near Harmony church, where he bought a tract of timber land. Clearing a space in the forest, he first erected a double log house, and then began the pioneer labor of redeeming a farm from the wilderness. There being no railways in the state at that time, he was forced to take all of his farm produce to Tallahassee for marketing purposes, making the round trip with a four-mule team, and being several days on the road. Clearing and improving a large farm, he was there a resident until his death, at the age of seventy-nine years. The maiden name of the wife of William Beaty, Jr., was Elizabeth Self, who was born in Telfair county, Georgia, where her parents, Thomas and Mary (Moore) Self, were early pioneers. Six children were born of their union, as follows: William; James; Berrien; America, who became the wife of Elias Alderman; Jackson; and Elizabeth. Mr. and Mrs. Elias Alderman reared eight children, namely: William; Jimmie, wife of Mr. Stanaland; Anna; Wessie; Shelby; Ona; Birdie; and Rupert.

Mr. and Mrs. Stanaland are the parents of four children, Ollie. Mat Hazel, Tinnie Lee, and Elias Alderman. Both Mr. and Mrs. Stanaland are faithful members of the Methodist Episcopal church.

JAMES M. PATTERSON. For nearly a score of years a resident of Brooks county, James M. Patterson has during that time been associated with the development and advancement of its agricultural resources.

his farming property being located in Dixie district. A son of the late John W. Patterson, he was born in 1853, in Muscogee county, Georgia.

His grandfather, John Patterson, was born, it is supposed, in North Carolina, and was of Scotch-Irish parentage. Soon after assuming the duties and responsibilities of a married man he migrated to Georgia, becoming an early settler of Burke county. In 1835 he moved to Muscogee county, Georgia, and having bought a tract of land near Boxspring was there engaged as a tiller of the soil during the remainder of his life. He married Sarah Wright, who was likewise of Scotch-Irish ancestry, and of their union seven children were born, as follows: Robert, Daniel, John W., Ruth, Margaret, Cornelia, and Catherine. True to the religious faith in which they were so strictly reared, both of the parents were communicants of the Presbyterian church.

John W. Patterson first opened his eyes to the light of this world in 1825, his birth occurring in Burke county, Georgia. When he was ten years old he accompanied the family to Muscogee county, which was his home for many years. In 1856 he came with his own family, and with that of his father-in-law, James McMurray, to Thomas county. Buying a tract of unimproved land lying three miles east of Boston, he erected a double log house in the timber, and immediately began the pioneer labor of clearing and improving a homestead. Five years later his work was interrupted by the breaking out of the war between the states. Hastening to the support of the Confederacy, he enlisted, in 1861, in the organization known as the Dixie Boys, a company which was attached to the Fifty-seventh Georgia Volunteer Infantry. Serving under Generals Johnston and Hood, he was with his regiment in all of its battles, including its many engagements on Georgia's soil against Sherman's forces, and in the battles at Franklin and Nashville, Tennessee. After the latter fiercely fought battle, his regiment was ordered to Virginia to join Lee's army, and had got as far as North Carolina when Lee surrendered. The Fifty-seventh Regiment then surrendered, and Mr. Patterson, with his comrades, returned to Georgia. Resuming his former occupation, he continued the improvements already initiated on his farm until 1870, when he sold out, although he continued a resident of Thomas county many years thereafter. In 1893 he moved to Brooks county, where, three years later, in 1896, his death occurred.

The maiden name of the wife of John W. Patterson was Cornelia McMurray. She was born in Muscogee county, Georgia, and was there brought up and married. Her father, James McMurray, was born in North Carolina, of Scotch-Irish parents. As a young man he came to Georgia, living first in Burke county, then in Muscogee county, from there coming, in 1856, as mentioned in the preceding paragraph, to Thomas county, buying land three miles east of Boston, and there living until his death, at the age of four score years. Mrs. Cornelia Patterson died at the early age of thirty-eight years, leaving five sons and two daughters, all of whom are now living, as follows: Harriet, James M., Robert C., Theodora M., Lila, John B., and Ernest E. She was a faithful and valued member of the Presbyterian church, to which her husband also belonged, and in which he served for several years as an elder.

But three years old when his parents settled in Brooks county, James M. Patterson here acquired a practical common school education. Early initiated into the secrets of good farming, he proved a faithful worker and remained with his parents until attaining his majority. He subsequently tried clerking for awhile, but on his marriage again turned his attention to farming, being located near Boston, Thomas county, until 1893. Since that time Mr. Patterson has been a resident of Brooks county, and has been busily employed in cultivating and improving his farming property.

In 1883 Mr. Patterson was united in marriage with Georgia Watkins, a native of Whitley county, Kentucky. Her father, Clark Watkins, came from Kentucky to Georgia in 1870, settling first in Colquitt county, from there coming, in 1884, to Thomas county, where he spent the remainder of his life. He was of honored ancestry, his mother, whose maiden name was Buchanan, having been a kinswoman of President James Buchanan. Mr. and Mrs. Patterson have nine children, namely: Edith I.; Cornelia, Eunice, Ruby, Deborah, Robert C., Frank, Edwin, and Georgia. Both Mr. and Mrs. Patterson are worthy members of the Presbyterian church and have reared their children in the same religious faith. Mr. Patterson is active in denominational work and for twenty years has served as an elder in the church. He is a Democrat in politics, and for a number of years has been secretary and treasurer of the West Side Farmers' Club.

CAPT. THOMAS NEAL GANDY. Occupying an honored position among the substantial business men of Brooks county, Capt. T. N. Gandy for a quarter of a century was actively identified with the advancement of the mercantile interests of Dixie as one of its leading general merchants. A son of Book A. Gandy, he was born December 30, 1836, in Thomas county, Georgia, of pioneer stock. According to tradition, the immigrant ancestor of the Gandy family came from England to America in colonial times, settling in South Carolina. He was twice married, his first wife bearing him twelve daughters, while his second wife became the mother of twelve sons, from whom the Gandys of the present generation are descended.

Brinkley Gandy, the captain's grandfather, was born and reared in South Carolina. In 1803, accompanied by his family, he came to Georgia, locating as a pioneer in what is now Montgomery county, where he bought land, and subsequently engaged in farming until his death. His wife, whose maiden name was Leah Nasworthy, was born in South Carolina, of English ancestry.

Born in Darlington district, South Carolina, in September, 1801, Book A. Gandy was but two years old when his parents brought him to Georgia. Growing to manhood in Montgomery county, he remained on the home farm until 1825, when he became one of the earlier settlers of Thomas county. Buying a tract of land five miles east of Thomasville, he began the pioneer labor of hewing a farm from the forest. Four of his brothers came with him to Thomasville, and each subsequently married, and raised large families. After clearing quite a portion of his land, he sold, and bought another tract twelve miles east of Thomasville, and was there a resident until his death, in the seventy-fifth year of his age. He married Elizabeth Browning, who was born in Montgomery county, Georgia. Her father, Daniel Browning, a native of North Carolina, settled in Montgomery county, Georgia, in 1803. In 1827 he removed to Thomas county, and having purchased land four miles east of Thomasville was there engaged in tilling the soil a number of seasons. Retiring then from active pursuits, he spent the remainder of his long life of four score years with his children. He married Honor Grace, who was born, it is thought, in Tattnall county, Georgia. Seven sons and three daughters were born into their household, all of whom were living at the breaking out of the Civil war, at its close the mother, one daughter and four sons had joined the silent majority on the other side. Of the marriage of Book A. and Elizabeth (Browning) Gandy, ten children were born, as follows: Thomas N., Henry, Book, Brinkley and Maria, twins, Fatima, Albert, Taylor, Mary and William. Five of the sons served in the Confederate army during the war between the states, four of whom, Henry, Book, Brinkley and Albert, lost their lives in the service.

Brought up in Thomas county, T. N. Gandy acquired his early education in the public schools, and was well trained in the different branches of agriculture as a youth. About 1859 his father gave him a farm, and two years later, at the outbreak of the Civil war, he enlisted in the company known as the Thomas County Volunteers. He was mustered in as first sergeant of his company, and six months later was promoted to the rank of lieutenant. The company was attached to the Twenty-ninth Georgia Volunteer Infantry, which was first sent to the Atlantic coast, and later to northern Georgia to oppose Sherman's forces. In the summer of 1864 Mr. Gandy was commissioned captain of a company of Georgia Reserves, which was assigned to the Twelfth Georgia Volunteer Infantry, and of that company he had command until the close of the conflict.

Returning then to Georgia, Captain Gandy resumed work on the farm which his father had given him. He subsequently sold out, purchased eleven hundred acres of land in the same county, and for eight years successfully managed his large plantation. Selling that property, Captain Gandy was for a few years engaged in the livery business at Thomasville. In 1887 he opened a general store in Dixie, and here, by his systematic business methods, his strict attention to all of its details, and his thoroughly upright dealings, he met with most gratifying results, winning for himself an honorable record as a merchant. He sold out his place of business in August, 1912.

Captain Gandy married, January 26, 1859, Miss Maggie Kemp, daughter of Peter and Alley Kemp, of Thomas county. Both the captain and Mrs. Gandy are members of the Methodist Episcopal church, South. Politically the captain was formerly a Whig, but is now an earnest supporter of the principles enunciated by the Democratic party. Although not an aspirant for public office, he has served as justice of the peace the past nine years.

FRANK M. AUSTIN. Heredity and environment, says Dr. Newell Dwight Hillis of Brooklyn, are but half truths and the part they play in determining a man's career are as nothing compared with the influence he can himself exert if he so prepares himself that he is ready when opportunity knocks at his door, and this statement of the noted divine is well borne out in the life history of Frank M. Austin, one of the foremost farmers of Brooks county. He was born in Dougherty county, Georgia, March 26, 1854, being the youngest child in a family of sixteen boys and girls born to John and Catherine Austin.

Mr. Austin was but seven years old when the war between the states occurred, and during the ensuing four years chaos reigned supreme. His opportunities for advancement in any direction were of the most meager, hard work, only, being in store for him. He had learned to read when quite young, and though he scarce saw the inside of a schoolhouse, he acquired a practical business education, and by extensive and intelligent reading has added to his store of knowledge until now but few are better informed in regard to the topics of the day than Mr. Austin. Inheriting a rugged constitution and an inclination for work, he entered the employ of the A. & G. Railroad Company, and for a number of years was connected with its roadway department. Resigning that position in 1882, Mr. Austin located in Dixie, Brooks county, where he was engaged in mercantile pursuits for seventeen years. Buying land in 1900, Mr. Austin embarked in farming, an occupation with which he has since been prominently identified, in addition to the care of his farm running a farm commissary. Mr. Austin owns 446 acres of rich and productive land, which he operates by tenants, cotton, corn, melons, and pindars being his principal crops, and bringing him a good annual income.

Mr. Austin married, at the age of twenty-four years, Mary Daniel. She was born in Thomas county, Georgia, a daughter of Aaron and Martha (Ivey) Daniel, and is of pioneer stock, her grandparents on both sides having been among the earlier settlers of southwest Georgia. Of the eleven children born to the marriage of Mr. and Mrs. Austin, three have passed to the life beyond and eight are now living, namely: Guy Leslie, Regina Frank, Frederick Lyle, Roy Coleman, Olah Matell, Mary Nadine, Elra Marion, and Annie Leone. Guy Leslie, a well-known physician of Berlin, Colquitt county, married Opal Elizabeth Smith, and they have one son, Philip Leslie. Regina Frank is successfully engaged in teaching. Frederick L. is in the employ of the Railroad Terminal Company at New Orleans. Roy, living in Brunswick, Georgia, is an employee of the Southern Railroad Company. The other four children are still in school. Mr. and Mrs. Austin are both identified by membership with the Methodist Episcopal church, South. Fraternally Mr. Austin is a member of Dixie Lodge, No. 242, Free and Accepted Masons. He cast his first presidential vote in 1876, for Samuel J. Tilden, and has since been a stanch supporter of the principles of the Democratic party. He has never been an office seeker, but has served as tax collector in Brooks county.

GEORGE W. AUSTIN. For many years prominently identified with the advancement of the mercantile and agricultural prosperity of Dixie district, Brooks county, George W. Austin is numbered among the representative men of Brooks county, and is well deserving of special mention in this biographical work. A native of Georgia, he was born in Laurens county, the date of his birth being June 7, 1849.

His father, John Austin, was a native of Georgia, and grew to manhood in Hancock county. Marrying at an early age, he lived for a time in Laurens county, going from there to Florida, where he was employed for a number of years as an overseer on large plantations. On his return to Georgia he located in Brooks county, where he spent the remainder of his long life, dying at the age of eighty-six years, at the home of his son, George W. Austin. His wife, whose maiden name was Catherine Bray, was born in North Carolina. and died in Brooks county, Georgia, at the age of four score and four years. Of their sixteen children, thirteen grew to years of maturity, as follows: William M., W. B., Joseph, Elizabeth, J. T., Mary, R. F., Lucinda, Newton J., Rachel, Crosby, George W., and Frank M.

Although there were no free schools in his vicinity when he was a boy, George W. Austin improved every opportunity for acquiring useful knowledge, securing largely through his own efforts a practical business education. At the age of nineteen years, having previously formed an intimate acquaintance with the numerous branches of agriculture on the home farm, he began life as a wage-earner, and for five years was in the employ of the A. & G. Railroad Company, now the Atlantic Coast Line, as section master in the roadway department. He was then made station agent at Dixie, Georgia, a position which he resigned at the end of five years. In the meantime Mr. Austin, who was a man of energy and enterprise, had embarked in the mercantile business in Dixie, starting with a fine stock of general merchandise. Accumulating considerable money as a merchant, he wisely invested it in land, buying at first one hundred acres, and in addition to conducting his store successfully was also engaged in agricultural pursuits. In 1909 Mr. Austin transferred his mercantile interests to his son, Hugh B., and is now devoting his time and energies to the management of his farm and of his private affairs. He has added to his landed possessions at different times, and now has title to about 650 acres of land, three hundred of which are under a high state of cultivation, producing good annual crops.

On February 15, 1877, Mr. Austin was united in marriage with Julia J. Benton, who was born in Dixie district, Brooks county, Georgia, a daughter of Shout Judson Benton. Mrs. Austin's grandfather, Joseph Benton, was born in North Carolina, where his father, Hugh Benton, settled on coming from France to this country. Brought up on a farm, he became an expert in the art of raising rice, and for many years was an overseer on rice plantations. He married Hannah Blocker, a native of North Carolina. Shout Judson Benton was born January 10, 1832, in Colleton county, South Carolina, and as a young man learned the carpenter's trade. Beginning work for himself in Brooks county, Georgia, he followed his trade in this section of the state many years, in the meantime buying and selling several different pieces of realty. He is now living retired in Dixie. Mr. Benton married Manira Maulden, who was born September 30, 1835, in what is now Brooks county, Georgia, where her parents, Holmes and Dicey (Millin) Maulden, were pioneer settlers. They reared a large family of children, as follows: Hugh, Elizabeth; Julia J., wife of Mr. Austin; Henry O.; Fanny; Viola; James; Jesse; Claudia; and Thaddeus, who lived but seven years, he having been the second son in succession of birth.

Eight children have been born of the marriage of Mr. and Mrs. Austin, namely: George R., Hugh B., Julia Ethel, Manira E., Mary Elizabeth, Winnie Davis, Harry Murray, and Alla Tutela. George R., who studied law, and was admitted to the bar, is now a bookkeeper for the Standard Supply and Fuel Company of Savannah; he married Stella Gibson, and they have three children: Catherine, Robert and Margaret. Hugh B. Austin, also a lawyer by profession, is one of the leading merchants of Dixie, where he is also engaged in the cross tie business; he married Josie Stewart, and they are the parents of five children: Christine, Manira, Stewart, George W., Jr., and Virgil. Julia Ethel died at the age of twenty-four years. Mary Elizabeth, wife of Ned B. Jones, has one son, Austin Jones. Mr. and Mrs. Austin are both trustworthy members of the Methodist Episcopal church, South, and fraternally Mr. Austin belongs to Dixie Lodge, No. 242, Free and Accepted Masons.

GROVER CLEVELAND EDMONDSON. A rising young attorney of Quitman, Grover Cleveland Edmondson has started in life with brilliant prospects for a successful career, and, continuing his present course, is sure to make for himself an enviable reputation, not only in legal circles, but in the business and social affairs of the community. A son of Simpson D. Edmondson, he was born in Tallokas district, Brooks county, Georgia, September 10, 1891, on the homestead cleared and improved by his grandfather, Rev. John Edmondson.

His great-grandfather, Isaac Edmondson, was a native of either England or Scotland. Immigrating to America in early manhood, he served as a soldier in the Revolutionary army, and at the close of the war settled in Bulloch county, Georgia. His health subsequently failing, he went to Savannah to consult a physician, and died in that city. His widow, Nancy Edmondson, survived him several years, and spent her last days in what is now Brooks county, Georgia, passing away in 1842. She was the mother of six children, as follows: Susan, Elizabeth, Sally, James, John and David.

Rev. John Edmondson was a lad in his teens when he came with his widowed mother and her family to Brooks county. All of southwestern Georgia was then a wilderness, inhabited by wild beasts of all kinds, and by the Indians, who at times were very troublesome. His educational advantages were exceedingly limited, although he attended school four months, earning the money to pay his tuition by splitting rails. He was an intelligent reader, however, and acquired a good knowledge of men and things. Beginning life even with the world, he invested his first money in land, buying a timbered tract, and for several years thereafter he and his faithful helpmeet occupied the humble log house which he erected, his little cabin having neither windows nor floors. In common with her few neighbors the wife used to card, spin and weave the homespun material with which the family was clothed, while he kept the family larder well supplied with wild game from the forests. He was quite successful, clearing and improving a farm with the help of slaves, and was there a resident until his death, in 1865.

The maiden name of the wife of Rev. John Edmondson was Martha Strickland. She was born November 13, 1814, in Tattnall county, Georgia, and at the age of fourteen years, on November 27, 1828, she was married. Her father, Archibald Strickland, came from one of the Carolinas to Georgia, and after living for awhile in Tattnall county removed to what is now Brooks county, becoming one of its earlier settlers. Buying land in the Tallokas district, he redeemed a farm from the wilderness, and here spent the remainder of his life, dying at a good old age. Mrs. Martha Edmondson survived her husband a number of years. Both she and her husband were active members of the Primitive Baptist church, he being one of its local preachers. They reared a family of ten children, as follows: Mary, Nancy, James, Martha, Louisiana, John A., Orpha V., Simpson D., Sally Ann, and William W.

Born in what is now Brooks county, Georgia, June 23, 1842, Simpson D. Edmondson was educated in the district schools, and as a youth was well trained in the various branches of agriculture. In 1861 he enlisted in Company C, Sixty-first Georgia Volunteer Infantry, which was assigned to the Army of North Virginia, and did gallant service under "Stonewall" Jackson. Taking part in all of the campaigns and battles in which his regiment was engaged, he was five times wounded at the battle of Antietam, four of the injuries being slight, and the last one, when he was hit by a minnie ball in the knee, being very serious. For eight months he was forced to use crutches, and was afterwards detailed to the commissary department, with which he was connected until the close of the war. He was present at the siege of Atlanta, and was one of the last to leave that city. Returning home at the cessation of hostilities, he resumed farming on the parental homestead, on which he is still living, having succeeded to its ownership.

On February 26, 1866, Mr. Simpson D. Edmondson married Mary A. Wade, who was born July 16, 1848, in Dooly county, Georgia, a daughter of Elijah Wade. Mr. Wade removed from Dooly county to Brooks county, and having bought land in the Tallokas district for many years engaged in both agricultural and mercantile pursuits, having a well stocked store on his farm, on which he resided until his death, at the age of seventy-five years. He married first Elizabth Reddick, who died at a comparatively early age, leaving three children, as follows: Mary A., wife of Simpson D. Edmondson; Fanny, and Lucy. Mr. Wade married for his second wife Mrs. Mary Peacock, who bore him four children, namely: Philip, Mitchell, Bury, and Wesley W. Mr. and Mrs. Simpson D. Edmondson are the parents of nine children, as follows: James W., Mattie, Fannie, Lucy, Jennie, May, Pearl, H. Turner, and

Grover C. They are valued and consistent members of the Methodist Episcopal church, and have reared their family in the same religious faith.

Gleaning his first knowledge of books in the rural schools, Grover Cleveland Edmondson afterwards continued his studies in the public schools of Quitman, and for a while read law in the office of his brother, James W. Edmondson. Subsequently entering the law department of Mercer University, he was there graduated with the class of 1908 and 1909. Being then admitted to the bar, Mr. Edmondson has since practiced law in Quitman and during the intervening three years has established one of the best practices in this section. A close student of criminal and constitutional law, Mr. Edmondson makes a specialty of criminal practice.

Keeping well informed on all topics of the day, governmental questions and political economics, he bids fair to become a state leader in political matters. He is a loyal Democrat and cast his first presidential vote for Oscar W. Underwood, and was appointed as a delegate to the Atlanta convention, which named the distinguished son of Alabama as Georgia's choice for the presidency.

In 1912 Mr. Edmondson announced his candidacy for representative from Brooks county in the general assembly, and after one of the most bitter local campaigns known to the county he received more votes than his five opponents combined.

During the campaign he was bitterly assailed by the legal organ of the county, opposed by every member of the bar, excepting Judge J. D. Wade and Hon. S. S. Bennet; every court house official, whom he designated as "Court House Ringsters," yet his support from the country was so overwhelmingly strong that nothing could defeat him.

On July 4th he addressed a gathering of over two thousand people at Quitman, and Hon. Joe Hill Hall, then a candidate for governor, being present, declared the speech to be the best stump speech he had ever heard.

Recognizing the necessity for a new constitution for the state, he started the agitation, which has met with tremendous encouragement from the leading newspapers and politicians of the state, and proposes to introduce at the next meeting of the legislature a bill calling a constitutional convention.

As a lawyer, politician and orator the merited success of this young man places him in that small circle of men in whom we find the mature thought of middle life combined with the energy of youth.

He is a devoted reader of the best literature, and in his library at Quitman the best works of the noted authors are found. Mr. Edmondson owns the largest private library in South Georgia, numbering over six thousand volumes of all kinds of books. His law library is the best equipped in the section.

Hon. Clark Howell, editor of the Atlanta *Constitution*, has termed Grover C. Edmondson as the "comer" in Georgia politics.

JAMES W. STRICKLAND. Eminently deserving of representation in this biographical work is James W. Strickland, who for the past ten years has served as clerk of the city council in Waycross, Ware county, performing the obligations of his office with ability. He was born June 7, 1847, on a farm near Blackshear, in that part of Ware county now included within the limits of Pierce county, Georgia, his father, Capt. Allen C. Strickland, having been born in the same locality.

James Strickland, Mr. Strickland's grandfather, came from North Carolina, his native state, to Georgia, at an early day, settling in what is now Pierce county. He first purchased 490 acres of land, which are now included within the limits of the city of Blackshear, the land being then in its primitive wildness. He bought other lands in that vicinity, and engaged in farming on an extensive scale, being assisted in his operations by slave labor, and there resided until his death. His wife, whose maiden name was Nellie Smith, survived him, passing away on the old homestead, near Blackshear. They reared a large family, and their descendants are now living in different parts of Georgia and Florida.

Soon after attaining manhood, Allen C. Strickland bought land in what is now Pierce county, and having acquired other land through inheritance, was employed in tilling the soil until after the breaking out of the Civil war, when he was commissioned captain of Company G, Fourth Georgia Cavalry, and went to the front with his command. Being taken ill, he returned to his home and there died in, 1862, while yet in the prime of life. Captain Strickland married Cassie Sweat, who was born in Ware county, Georgia, a daughter of Capt. James A. and Elizabeth (Newburn) Sweat, of whom a more extended account may be found on another page of this volume, in connection with the sketch of Carey M. Sweat. She survived him many years, and married for her second husband William Davis. By her first marriage she reared six children, and by her union with Mr. Davis became the mother of three children.

Brought up on the parental homestead, James W. Strickland attended school whenever opportunity offered, in the meantime becoming familiarly acquainted with farm work. In June, 1864, inspired by patriotic motives, he enlisted in the company formerly commanded by his father, Company G, Fourth Georgia Cavalry. Joining his command at Screven, Georgia, he served with his regiment in all of its engagements until the close of the conflict. Returning home then, Mr. Strickland farmed for a few months, and then attended school. In 1868 he embarked in the mercantile business at Blackshear, where he remained until 1890. Coming then to Waycross, Mr. Strickland was for twelve years proprietor and manager of a hotel, being very successful and popular as a host. In 1902 he was elected clerk of the city council, and continued in the office until 1913, discharging the duties devolving upon him in that capacity promptly and efficiently. He is a loyal Democrat in politics, and, with his family, belongs to the Methodist Episcopal church.

In 1870 Mr. Strickland married Annie E. Hendry, who was born in Savannah, Georgia, on the paternal side being a descendant of the pioneer family of that name that settled in Liberty county, Georgia, at an early day, and on the paternal side belonging to the Lee family of Virginia. Her father, Capt. E. D. Hendry, a native of Liberty county, Georgia, was commissioned a captain in the Confederate army, and after serving in the field for a year or two became a government official. Prior to his enlistment he had been engaged in mercantile pursuits in Blackshear, Georgia, and after its close he was engaged in business in Savannah for about four years. Returning to Pierce county in 1869, he remained in Blackshear until 1890, when he removed to Waycross, where he spent his remaining days, passing away at the venerable age of eighty-seven years. The maiden name of Captain Hendry's wife was Caroline Staley. She was born in Savannah, Georgia, her mother having been an Atkinson from North Carolina. Mr. and Mrs. Strickland have one daughter, Carrie E. Strickland.

JOHN LOTT WALKER, M. D. One of the best known members of the medical fraternity of Ware county, John Lott Walker, M. D., is devoted to his practice, and well deserves the reputation he enjoys of being one of the most skillful and faithful physicians of Waycross. A son of Elisha Walker, he was born on a farm in Washington county, the home farm having been located ten miles south of Tennille, and twelve miles west of Wrightsville. He comes of early colonial stock, the immigrant ancestor of the branch of the Walker family from which he is descended having come to America prior to the Revolution, locating very near the northern boundary line of North Carolina.

Lott Walker, the doctor's grandfather, was born in Laurens county, Georgia, in 1801, his father, also named Elisha Walker, having settled there on removing from North Carolina. During the earlier part of his active career, Lott Walker resided in Henry county, Georgia, from there removing to Johnson county, where his wife owned a tract of land that had come to her through inheritance. He purchased land adjoining hers and, with slave help, carried on general farming until his death, in 1880, at the age of seventy-nine years. He married Polly Walters, who was born in that part of Laurens county now included in Johnson county, being a daughter of Richard Walters, a farmer, who came from Virginia to Georgia. Eight children were born to Mr. and Mrs. Lott Walker, three of them being sons, Elisha, William and Moses, and five being daughters, as follows: Gatsy, Ann, Melissa, Mary and Eliza.

Born in Henry county, Georgia, in 1832, Elisha Walker settled in Washington county, Georgia, soon after his marriage, being there employed for a time in general farming. Subsequently buying land in Johnson county, he farmed with the help of slaves until the war between the states, and afterwards there continued his labors until 1906. Removing then to Wrightsville, he has since lived there retired from active pursuits, enjoying the fruits of his earlier years of toil. His wife, whose maiden name was Martha Webb, was born in what is now Johnson county, Georgia, in 1831, a daughter of Rev. John and Charlotte (Covington) Webb, and granddaughter of Rev. Covington, her father and maternal grandfather having both been ministers in the Methodist Episcopal denomination. Eight children were born of their union, namely: John Lott, Ann, Minta, Tabitha, Dolly, Nora, William, and Joseph.

Receiving his early education under private tutors, John Lott Walker first attended medical lectures in Louisville, Kentucky, at the Kentucky School of Medicine, and in 1879 was graduated from the Atlanta Medical College with the degree of M. D. The following seven years Doctor Walker was engaged in the practice of his profession at Wrightsville, Johnson county. In 1886 he removed to Waycross, where he has been in continual practice since, being one of the longest-established and most successful physicians in this part of the county. During the quarter of a century or more that the doctor has lived in Waycross, he has seen the city grow from a village of one thousand souls to a wide-awake, prosperous community of fourteen times as many inhabitants, while the surrounding country, which was but sparsely settled when he came here, has increased its population in a corresponding ratio.

Doctor Walker has invested largely in city property, wisely buying in the business section, where, on Jane street, he owns a commodious building. He has served three years as a member of the state board of medical examiners, and is now a member of the Waycross board of education and is a member of the state board of health. Fraternally the doctor belongs to Blackshear lodge. Ancient Free and Accepted Order of Masons; to Waycross Lodge, No. 27, Knights of Pythias; and to Waycross Lodge, No. 99, Independent Order of Odd Fellows.

Doctor Walker married, in 1883, Miss Laura Singleton, who was born and educated in Milledgeville, Georgia, being a daughter of Samuel and

Ann (Christian) Singleton, who reared four sons and four daughters, as follows: Samuel, Stewart, Charles, Robert, Bettie, Ellen, Martha, and Laura. Her father was in the employ of the state, and was also engaged for several years in the mercantile business at Eatonton, where his last days were spent. The doctor and Mrs. Walker have four children, namely: John S., Robert C., Annie Laurie, and Samuel E. The doctor and his wife are both members of the Methodist Episcopal church, and Mrs. Walker is a member of the Daughters of the American Revolution.

JAMES H. LATIMER, M. D. A well-known and successful physician of Ware county, and one of the foremost citizens of Waycross, James H. Latimer, M. D., has built up a large and lucrative practice in this section of the state and has here fully established himself in the esteem and confidence of his fellow men. A son of Dr. James Latimer, he was born September 9, 1869, in Coffee county, Georgia, of early colonial stock. His grandfather, Fleming Latimer, who, so far as known, was a life-long resident of South Carolina, was a lineal descendant of Lord Latimer, who fled from his native land to this country to escape religious persecution, settling in Manhattan Island, New York.

Dr. James H. Latimer's birth occurred June 10, 1829, in South Carolina. Receiving excellent educational advantages in his youthful days, he early determined to enter upon a professional career, and while yet a young man was graduated from the medical department of the state university, at Augusta, with the degree of M. D. After practicing medicine for a short time in Decatur county, Georgia, Dr. James Latimer subsequently spent a very few years in Appling and Coffee counties, and then removed with his family to Jeff Davis county, in 1872, locating at Hazlehurst, where he gained a fine reputation as a skillful and able physician, remaining there until his death, in 1907. The maiden name of his wife was Aleph B. Girtman. She was born in Coffee county, Georgia, in 1848, and is now living in Hazlehurst. Her father, Benjamin F. Girtman, owned a large plantation in the northern part of Georgia, and carried on farming with slave labor until his accidental death when less than forty years of age. The maiden name of his wife was Mary Simmons. Eleven children blessed the union of Dr. James Latimer and his wife, as follows: James H., the special subject of this brief biographical review; Ann Eliza and Mary Louisa, twins; Clem F.; Martha E.; Charles Albert; Aleph Letitia; Edgar F.; Ida Kate; Sarah, and Jennie.

Acquiring his rudimentary education in the public schools of Hazlehurst, James H. Latimer began the study of medicine with his father, and subsequently attended the Atlanta Medical College, on March 2, 1892, being graduated from that institution. Immediately beginning his professional career in Hazlehurst, Doctor Latimer continued there six years. Coming then, in 1898, to Waycross, which was then a comparatively small city, with a population of four thousand people only, he has remained here ever since, being a successful and popular physician. Keeping pace with the growth of the city, the doctor has been an important factor in advancing its material interests, in the meantime bending all of his energy towards making a success of his profession. He belongs to both the Ware County Medical Society and to the Georgia State Medical Society.

Fraternally the doctor is a member of Waycross Lodge, No. 305, Ancient Free and Accepted Order of Masons; Waycross Chapter, No. 9, Royal Arch Masons; Damascus Commandery, No. 18, Knights Templar; and of Alee Temple, Ancient Arabic Order of the Nobles of the Mystic Shrine.

Doctor Latimer married, November 24, 1892, Tallulah Estelle Brinson, who was born in Pierce county, Georgia, a daughter of David W. and Mary K. Brinson, natives of this state. The doctor' and Mrs. Latimer are the parents of four children, namely: Tallulah Elizabeth, Eva Grace, Marion, and Mary B. Both are members of the Baptist church.

DANIEL MARCUS BRADLEY, M. D. Actively engaged in one of the more important professions to which men devote their time and energies, Daniel Marcus Bradley, M. D., of Waycross, is numbered among the rising young physicians of Ware county, his skill in the diagnosis and treatment of diseases having gained for him the confidence of the people, and an extensive patronage. He was born November 7, 1884, in Liberty county, Georgia, which was likewise the birthplace of his father, Daniel Milton Bradley, Sr.

The doctor's great-grandfather was Ely Bradley. His grandfather, John S. Bradley, came with his parents from South Carolina, his native state, to Georgia when a child, locating in Liberty county. The country round about was then in its virgin wildness, Indians being numerous, and often troublesome, and deer, bear and wild turkey were plentiful, the pioneers of that day living largely on wild game. There were neither railroads nor convenient markets near, the surplus products of the farm being hauled many miles with teams. The pioneer women as well as the men had to make good use of every minute of their time, carding, spinning and weaving the homespun cloth, which they fashioned into garments for the family, and the yarn from which they knit the stockings, in the meantime doing all the cooking by the open fire. John S. Bradley succeeded to the occupation of his father, and becoming a landholder was engaged in farming in Liberty county until his death. The maiden name of his good wife was Jane Daniel.

Born in Liberty county, Georgia, January 24, 1850, Daniel Milton Bradley, Sr., there as a young man began his active career as a merchant, dealing in general merchandise for several seasons. Moving to Tattnall county, Georgia, in 1889, he has since been there successfully engaged in mercantile business, being one of the longest-established merchants of Hagan, and a citizen of prominence. He married Janie Brewton, who was born February 28, 1859, in Bulloch county, Georgia, a daughter of Simon and Matilda (Tippins) Brewton, natives respectively of Bulloch county, Georgia, and of Tattnall county. Seven children were born of their marriage, as follows: Rosamond N., John D., Bessie F., Daniel Marcus, Janie C., Willie D., and Waldo.

Being fitted for college in McRae, Georgia, Daniel Marcus Bradley, Jr., entered the medical departmnet of the University of Georgia, at Augusta, and was there graduated with the class of 1907. The following year Doctor Bradley was engaged in the practice of his profession at Guyton, Georgia, where he gained not only a fair share of practice, but experience of value. Coming from there to Waycross in 1908, he is here making rapid strides in his professional career, his wisdom and skill in dealing with difficult cases having placed him among the physicians of repute in this locality. He takes an intelligent interest in municipal affairs, and since 1910 has served as city health officer.

Fraternally the doctor is a member of Waycross Lodge, No. 305, Ancient Free and Accepted Order of Masons; of Waycross Chapter, No. 9, Royal Arch Masons; of Damascus Commandery, No. 18, Knights Templar; and of Alee Temple, Ancient Arabic Order of the Nobles of the Mystric Shrine.

On August 17, 1910, Doctor Bradley was united in marriage with Mary Gertrude, daughter of Chauncey G. and Mary Wallace (Moore)

Costin, of Pender county, North Carolina. She was adopted by Mr. and Mrs. Major L. Moore at the age of two years. They were formerly of Pender county, North Carolina, but now Waycross, Georgia. The doctor and Mrs. Bradley have one child, Daniel Marcus Bradley, third.

ARTHUR MERRILL KNIGHT. A man of pronounced business ability and acumen, Arthur Merrill Knight holds an assured position among the useful and highly esteemed citizens of Waycross, and has been a potent power in aiding the city's growth and improvement. A son of the late Albion W. Knight, he was born at White Sulphur Springs, Florida.

He comes of substantial New England ancestry, his paternal grandfather, Major Peter Merrill Knight, having been a life-long resident of Maine. He was a ship builder and planter, and was quite prominent in military circles, serving as major in a company of militia, a position to which he was appointed by King George. He married Sally Buxton, a native of Maine, and they reared two sons and two daughters, as follows: Albion W., father of the subject of this sketch; George A., a traveling salesman, who located in Florida, and whose son, Albion W. Knight, second, is now Bishop of the diocese of Georgia; Amanda M.; and Eliza J.

Albion W. Knight was born and reared in Maine, and was educated at Bowdoin College, in Brunswick, Maine, being graduated from both the literary and medical departments of that institution. Coming south after receiving his degree of M. D., Doctor Knight was actively and successfully engaged in the practice of medicine at White Sulphur Springs, Florida, until 1870, when he removed with his family to Jacksonville, Florida, where he continued the practice of his profession until his death, in 1889. Doctor Knight married Caroline Demere, who was born on Saint Simons Island, Georgia, a daughter of Raymond Demere, who was the third in direct line of descent to bear that name. The Demere family originated in France, the immigrant ancestor having been a Huguenot, who fled from his native country to America, settling in South Carolina, thence moving to Saint Simons Island, Georgia, which subsequently became the home of four generations of his descendants. The Demeres were extensive planters, very prosperous in their operations, at one time owning 360 slaves. Seven children blessed the marriage of doctor and Mrs. Knight, namely: Ann, Augustus Demere, Annie Elizabeth, Louis Buxton, Raymond Denery, Arthur Merrill, and Fraser Sinclair.

Completing his early studies at Saint John's church school, in Jacksonville, Florida, Arthur Merrill Knight began life as a wage-earner at the age of sixteen years, for two years clerking in a tobacco store, and for three years in a grocery. He was afterwards employed in the railroad service at Jacksonville until 1887, when he located in Waycross, Georgia, where he continued in the same line of work for thirteen years. Severing his connection with the railroad company in 1900, Mr. Knight engaged in banking. Close confinement and strict attention to business, however, did not agree with him, and on account of ill health he was forced to abandon active pursuits and go to the mountains to recuperate. Returning to Waycross after resting a few months, Mr. Knight embarked in the real estate and insurance business, with which he has since been identified, in his transactions being exceedingly prosperous.

Mr. Knight is likewise connected with various other enterprises of importance. He is secretary and treasurer of the Waycross Investment Company; secretary of the Waycross Reality and Improvement

Company; has been president of the board of education and also of the Waycross board of trade; is president of the board of trustees of the owners of the Young Men's Christian Association property; one of the directors of the Young Men's Christian Association, and senior warden of the Episcopal church.

Having cast his first presidential vote for General Hancock, Mr. Knight has since been a stanch adherent of the Democratic party. In the days when Waycross had but twenty-five hundred inhabitants, Mr. Knight was elected mayor of the city, and, through successive re-elections, held the position fifteen years. During that time the city schools were organized; streets were paved; and water and sewer systems were inaugurated; while the growth of the city was especially notable, during his administration the population being increased to nineteen thousand people. Fraternally Mr. Knight is a member of Waycross Lodge, No. 369, Benevolent and Protective Order of Elks. Religiously he and his family are members of the Grace Episcopal church.

In 1884 Mr. Knight married Susan Fatio, who was born in Jacksonville, Florida, a daughter of the late Col. Daniel Fatio, who commanded a Florida regiment in the war between the states. Mr. and Mrs. Knight are the parents of three children, namely: Jaquelin, who was graduated from the literary department of the University of Georgia, and from the Atlanta College of Physicians and Surgeons and was engaged in the practice of medicine at Waycross up to the time of his death, November 18, 1912; Arthur M., who was educated at the University of Georgia, is now in business with his father; and Gerald, attending the Waycross schools. The older son is a member of the Ancient Free and Accepted Order of Masons, as was also the deceased son.

GUSTAVUS P. FOLKS, M. D. Prominent among the best known and most highly esteemed residents of Waycross, Ware county, is Gustavus P. Folks, M. D., a retired physician, now carrying on a substantial business as an agriculturist, horticulturist and real-estate dealer. A native of Ware county, he was born in Waresboro, a son of Hon. William B. and Mary J. (Miller) Folks, and a brother of Hon. Frank C. Folks, M. D., in whose sketch, which appears elsewhere in this volume, further parental and ancestral history may be found.

Having laid a good foundation for his future education in the public schools of Lowndes county, and at Waycross, Gustavus P. Folks naturally turned his attention to the study of medicine, acquiring his first knowledge of that science under the tutorship of his father. Subsequently going to Louisville, Kentucky, he was there graduated from Louisville Medical College with the class of 1889. Locating at Dupont, Clinch county, Doctor Folks remained there ten months, meeting with encouraging success in his profession. Returning to Waycross, he was here actively employed as a physician for twelve years. Having in the meantime become specially interested in matters pertaining to the productions of the soil, the doctor retired from his professional labors and turned his attention to farming and the growing of fruit, in that industry planting the first peach orchard in Ware county. In addition to his agricultural and horticultural labors, he deals extensively in real estate, principally in timber lands, having now a well-established and profitable business. In 1910, Doctor Folks erected his present fine home on College Hill, a new residential part of Waycross, and there takes pleasure in welcoming his many friends and acquaintances.

Politically Doctor Folks invariably supports the principles of the Democratic party by voice and vote. Fraternally he is a member of Wakefield Lodge, No. 27, Knights of Pythias; of Waycross Lodge, No.

99, Independent Order of Odd Fellows; and of Waycross Lodge, No. 369, Benevolent and Protective Order of Elks. He also belongs to the Hoo Hoos, an organization composed of dealers in lumber and timber lands. Both he and his wife are members of the Methodist Episcopal church.

Doctor Folks married, in 1889, Belle C. Knox, who was born in Wayne county, Georgia, which was likewise the birthplace of her father, Capt. James Knox. Her paternal grandfather, Reddick Knox, was born in Pitt county, North Carolina, where his parents, who were of Welsh and Scotch ancestry, settled on coming to America. Brought up in his native state, he migrated to Georgia in pioneer days, he and his family making the removal with teams. At the end of two years of frontier life, he and his family went back to their old home, but later returned to Georgia, settling in Wayne county. Buying a tract of wild land, he improved a farm and there spent the remainder of his life. He married Ruhanna Taylor, who was born in North Carolina, and died on the home farm, in Wayne county, Georgia.

Born in 1830, Capt. James Knox grew to manhood beneath the parental roof-tree, and upon the breaking out of the war between the states offered his services to the Confederacy. Being commissioned captain of Company G, Twenty-sixth Georgia Volunteer Infantry, he went with his regiment to Virginia, and as a part of the Army of the Potomac was at the front in many engagements of importance. Being paroled at the close of the war, the captain turned his face homeward, and walked, barefooted, the greater part of the distance. Resuming his former occupation, he was for a while successfully engaged in farming, but later embarked in mercantile pursuits at Lulaton, Wayne county. In 1879 the captain came to Waycross, which was then a quiet village of about five hundred souls, and, having opened a general store, was here a resident until his death, in 1899.

Captain Knox married Mary Jane Jones, who was born in what is now Pierce county, near Big Creek, not far from the birthplace of her father, James Jones. Her paternal grandfather, the great-grandfather of Mrs. Folks, was born in North Carolina, of Welsh ancestry, and came to what is now Pierce county, Georgia, in pioneer times, when the Indians made such frequent raids upon the newcomers that it was necessary to have in each county one or more large log forts to which the settlers might flee for safety when the redskins became too troublesome. Securing title to extensive tracts of land, he carried on farming with slave labor until his death. James Jones, the father of Captain Knox's wife, became owner of a large plantation near the east end of the Okefinokee swamp, and was there profitably engaged in farming and stockraising the remainder of his life, passing away in 1850, being murdered by a slave belonging to one of his neighbors. The maiden name of his first wife, Mrs. Folk's grandmother, was Sarah Mizell. She spent her brief life in Georgia, dying in early womanhood. The wife of Captain Knox survived him several years, her death occurring in 1907, at the advanced age of seventy-five. She reared eight children, as follows: Sarah, who married Rev. John Strickland; Kate, deceased, was the wife of J. L. Courson; Mary died at the age of twenty-five years; Dora, wife of Andrew J. Miller; Belle C., wife of Dr. Gustavus P. Folks; William L.; Edward W., and James J. Dr. and Mrs. Folks have one child, Dorothy Mildred Folks.

HON. FRANK CLINGMAN FOLKS, M. D. A prominent and successful physician of Waycross, Hon. Frank Clingman Folks, M. D., has not only gained marked prestige in his profession, but is known as a progressive and public-spirited citizen, and as a man of the highest principles of honor and integrity. A native of Jefferson county, Georgia, he was born on a farm that is now included within the corporate limits of the city of Wadley, his father, Hon. William Bardon Folks, M. D., having been born, in 1830, in the same place, while his grandfather, Amos Folks, was a native of North Carolina.

His paternal great-grandparents were of English birth, or of English ancestry. After living for many years in North Carolina, they migrated to Georgia, making the removal with private conveyances, bringing with them their household goods, stock, and slaves. Buying land in Jefferson county, he improved a homestead, and there both he and his faithful helpmeet spent their remaining days.

A young boy when his parents moved to Georgia, Amos Folks assisted his father to some extent in the pioneer labor of improving the farm, and during his active career was a successful planter. He died while yet in manhood's prime, in Jefferson county. His wife, whose maiden name was Celia Lofly, was a life-long resident of that county. Three sons and one daughter were born of their marriage, as follows: Green, the oldest son, enlisted during the Civil war in the Confederate army, and died while in service, in Virginia; Solomon died in early manhood; William Bardon, father of Frank C. Folks, M. D., and Catherine, who married Dr. Seaborn Bell, of Emanuel county.

Acquiring his literary education in the schools of his native county, Dr. William Bardon Folks began the study of medicine under Dr. William Hauser, of Jefferson county, and was graduated from the Savannah Medical College with the class of 1855. Practicing but a short time in Jefferson and Washington counties, he located, in 1856, in Waresboro, then the county seat of Ware county. At that early day neither railroad, telephone or telegraph lines spanned the country; Ware county, and all of the nearby counties, being then in their pristine wildness. As the population grew, his practice increased, his visits, which extended many miles in either direction, were made on horseback, oftentimes the trails which he followed having been those made by the Indians. At the outbreak of the Civil war, he offered his services to the Confederacy, and being made surgeon of the Twenty-sixth Georgia Volunteer Infantry, he went with his regiment to Virginia, joining the Army of the Potomac. He continued with his regiment until the close of the conflict, when he resumed his practice in Waresboro. He subsequently settled in Yankee Town, afterward in Tibianville, where, in addition to his practice he engaged in mercantile business. Removing from there to Whigham, Decatur county, he was station agent on the Atlantic and Gulf railroad for two years, and during the next two years practiced medicine at Valdosta, Georgia, after which he lived for a while in Savannah.

When Waycross was first started, Dr. W. B. Folks was the first physician to locate in the new town, and built the fourth house erected within its limits. Here he was actively and prosperously engaged in the practice of his profession until about two years prior to his death, which occurred in 1886. Energetic and public-spirited, he became exceedingly influential in public affairs, and served two terms as mayor of the city, and represented the fifth district, which included Ware, Clinch and Coffee counties, in the State Senate, to which he was elected in 1878.

Dr. William B. Folks married Mary Jefferson Miller, who was born, in 1830, in Jefferson county, Georgia, whose parents were life-long residents of Jefferson county. Her grandfather, Thomas McWatty, immigrated from Scotland to America, settling in Jefferson county, Georgia, in pioneer days. She survived her husband many years, passing away in 1906. Five children blessed their union, as follows: Rosa, who died at the age of eighteen years; Frank Clingman, the special subject of this brief sketch; Chauncey M.; Gustavus P.; and William B., Jr. The father was a stanch Democrat in politics, and both he and his wife were members of the Methodist Episcopal church.

After completing the course of study in the public schools of Ware county, Frank Clingman Folks read medicine first with his father, and later with Dr. William Duncan, of Savannah. Then matriculating at the Savannah Medical College, he was there graduated with the class of 1876, receiving the degree of M. D. Immediately entering upon private practice of his profession, Dr. Folks was for four years located at Homerville, Clinch county, where he made rapid progress along the pathway of success. In 1880 he returned to Waycross, where he has since continued in his field of labor, having won a noteworthy position in the front rank of the medical fraternity of Ware county.

The doctor has taken quite an active part in public affairs, in addition to having served two terms as mayor of Waycross has represented the fifth district in the state senate, to which he was elected in the fall of 1888, just ten years after the election of his father to the same position from the same district. Fraternally he is a member of the Ancient Free and Accepted Order of Masons, and to the Independent Order of Odd Fellows. Religiously both the doctor and Mrs. Folks are valued members of the Methodist Episcopal church, South.

In 1877 Dr. Folks was united in marriage with Emma A. Morgan, who was born in Clinch county, Georgia, a daughter of Jonathan L. and Susan (Hargreaves) Morgan, who were born in Georgia, Mr. Morgan having been of Welsh lineage, and Mrs. Morgan of English ancestry. Eight children have been born to Doctor and Mrs. Folks, namely: Ada, who died in infancy; Rosa; Mabel; Frankie; Willie; Fleming; Robert, and Louise. Rosa married first George Bell, who died in early life, leaving one child, Sarah Bell; she married for her second husband P. K. Groff, of Akron, Ohio, and they have one son, Philip Folks Groff. Mabel, who married Charles Newton, has two children, Frances and Charles. Frankie, who became the wife of Walter P. Rivers, died March 1, 1912. Willie Folks, the doctor's oldest son, is a graduate of the Atlanta College of Physicians and Surgeons, and is now engaged in the practice of medicine at Waycross. Fleming was graduated from the Atlanta School of Pharmacy. Robert and Louise are both pupils in the Waycross high school.

EDWARD JEROME BERRY. Eminently capable, courteous, painstaking and accommodating, Edward Jerome Berry, of Waycross, clerk of the superior court, is administering the affairs of his office so wisely and conscientiously, and with such complete thoroughness as to win the approval of all concerned. A son of Francis C. Berry, he was born in Lexington, South Carolina, December 16, 1869, of English lineage, his great-grandfather Berry, a native of England, having immigrated to this country in colonial days, settling in South Carolina.

Alexander Berry, Mr. Berry's grandfather, was reared and educated in South Carolina, the larger part of his life having been spent in Charleston, where for many years he was employed as an accountant. His wife was a native, and a life-long resident, of that state.

The only son of his parents, Francis C. Berry was born, in 1829, in Charleston, South Carolina. Scholarly in his tastes and attainments, he embarked in a professional career when young, and after teaching school in various places in his native state, came, in 1882, to Georgia, and here continued his profession, teaching first in Appling county, and later in Ware county, where he spent the later years of his life, passing away in 1904. His wife, whose maiden name was Sarah Higgs, was born in Beaufort, South Carolina, being one of a large family of children born to Jacob and Sarah (Smith) Higgs, of whom but two are now living. She died in 1902, leaving three children, as follows: William Alexander, Francis M. and Edward Jerome.

Acquiring an excellent education in the schools of Ware county, Georgia, Edward Jerome Berry taught school from the age of eighteen years until twenty-three years old. He was afterwards employed for a time as a bookkeeper, and subsequently served for eighteen months as school commissioner. In 1901 Mr. Berry was elected clerk of the superior court, and has been confirmed in the office by successive re-elections ever since, performing the duties devolving upon him in that capacity to the absolute satisfaction of all with whom he is officially brought in contact.

Mr. Berry married, December 11, 1894, Miss Nellie Mizelle Cason, who was born in Ware county, Georgia, a daughter of J. Alfred and Nancy (Migell) Cason, natives respectively of Ware county, Georgia, and of Charlton county, they having been the parents of thirteen children, six sons and seven daughters. Mr. and Mrs. Berry have two children, namely: Ruby Irene and Edward James.

Fraternally Mr. Berry is a member of Wakefield Lodge, No. 27, Knights of Pythias; of Waycross Lodge, No. 99, Independent Order of Odd Fellows; of Waycross Lodge, No. 305, Ancient Free and Accepted Order of Masons; of Waycross Chapter, No. 9, Royal Arch Masons; of Damascus Commandery, No. 18, Knight Templars; and of Allah Temple, Ancient Arabic Order of the Nobles of the Mystic Shrine. Mrs. Berry is a member of the Ladies of the Modern Maccabees. Both Mr. and Mrs. Berry belong to the Methodist Episcopal Church.

THOMAS JEFFERSON DARLING. Prominent among the leading lumber manufacturers and dealers of Ware county is Thomas Jefferson Darling, of Waycross, who was for many years identified with the upbuilding and growth of this section of the state, and has contributed his full share towards advancing its material interests, as proprietor of the Darling Construction Company being associated with one of its most valuable industrial enterprises. A son of Dr. Thomas Jackson Darling, he was born, June 25, 1868, in Blackshear, Pierce county, Georgia, of New England lineage.

His grandfather, Joseph Darling, was born in 1784, either in Rhode Island, or in Georgia, of Rhode Island ancestry. For many years a resident of Richmond county, Georgia, he owned a large plantation on the Washington road, eight miles from Augusta, where both he and his wife spent their last years, at the close of life being buried side by side on the old home plantation, his death occurring October 4, 1844. He married Mary Manning Dunevan, who was born March 5, 1783, and died April 14, 1847, having survived him two and one-half years.

Born in Richmond county, Georgia, in 1828, Thomas Jackson Darling laid a solid foundation for his future education in the days of his youth, and was subsequently graduated from the Augusta, Georgia, Medical College with the degree of M. D. Beginning the practice of medicine in Blackshear, Pierce county, Dr. Darling continued there until the breaking out of the war between the states, when he offered his services to the Confederacy, and as a surgeon in the army continued in active service until the close of the conflict. Resuming then his practice in Blackshear, he remained there until his death, June 14, 1873, being one of the foremost physicians and surgeons of that part of the county.

The maiden name of the wife of Dr. Darling was Bashabee Elizabeth Godbee. She was born in Alabama, July 29, 1829, a daughter of Samuel Isaac Ivy Godbee, and grand-daughter of Samuel Godbee, who married

Elizabeth Moore, a daughter of Abner Moore. Samuel Isaac Ivy Godbee, who removed from Alabama to Georgia in 1830, and spent the remainder of his years in Richmond county, married Elizabeth Mobley, a daughter of James Alexander and Sarah (Wimberly) Mobley. The Moores, Mobleys and Wimberlys were among the early and prominent settlers of Richmond county. Dr. Darling's wife outlived him many long years, passing away October 9, 1903, leaving eight children, as follows: Rena, Mina, Dora, Will, Emma, A. C., Thomas Jefferson, and Edward Lee.

Receiving his preliminary mental training in the public schools of Blackshear, Thomas Jefferson Darling afterwards continued his studies at the Johnsonville High School. Apprenticing himself to a firm of builders at the age of seventeen years, in Orlando, Florida, he remained with his employers three years, and was afterwards foreman of a carpentering gang for four years, in Blackshear, Georgia, and in Waycross. Embarking then in business on his own account in Waycross, Mr. Darling built up a patronage that extended throughout southern Georgia, and into Florida, as a contractor and builder, filling many large contracts. In Jacksonville, Florida, Mr. Darling erected the magnificent Dyal Upchurch office building, and in Waycross has had the supervision of the building of many of its most substantial and handsome business blocks. He erected the Young Men's Christian Association Building, the Bunn Bell College Building, and many others of note. He has built three court houses, numerous school houses, and hundreds of dwellings in South Georgia, creations of his brains and hands being in evidence in many places. Retiring from the building industry in 1908, Mr. Darling has since been prosperously employed in the lumber business, having an extensive yard in Waycross, and a finely equipped planing mill.

On August 8th, 1895, Mr. Darling married Laura Le Count, who was born in Kekoshkee, Wisconsin, May 25, 1868, a daughter of Charles Le Count, and grand-daughter of John Hendrix Le Count. Her great-grandfather, John Le Count, was born at New Rochelle, New York, of French Huguenot ancestry, and served, so it is supposed, as a soldier in the Revolutionary war. John Hendrix Le Count, a native of New Rochelle, New York, served in the War of 1812, and Mrs. Darling now has in her possession his papers giving him an honorable discharge from the service. He subsequently removed to Wisconsin, locating at Hartford, where he spent his remaining years. He married Esther Smith, who was born in Dutchess county, New York, a daughter of Stephen and Deborah (Bashford) Smith, both of whom were life-long residents of Dutchess county, his birth occurring in 1770, and his death in 1845, while she was born in 1783 and died in 1851.

As a young man Charles Le Count migrated to Wisconsin, and until 1869 was there engaged in the hardware business. In that year he settled in Nebraska, in York, which was then a frontier town, seventy miles from a railroad. Opening a hardware store there, he built up a good business, and became prominent in public affairs, serving as treasurer of York county, as treasurer of the city of York, and as treasurer of the County Agricultural Society, and of seven other organizations of minor importance. On account of impaired health, Mr. Le Count sold out his Nebraska interests in 1885, and purchased an orange grove at Anthony, Marion county, Florida, where he lived until 1906. Coming then to Georgia, he resided in Waycross until his death, in February, 1907.

Mr. Le Count married Jane Amanda Littlefield, who was born, August 20, 1824, in Readsboro, Vermont, a daughter of Elisha Alvin Littlefield. Her grandfather, Asa Littlefield, who was born May 6, 1762, and died June 19, 1845, married, March 24, 1782, Lois Stark, whose birth occurred May 15, 1755, and who died April 25, 1740. In 1820 Elisha

Alvin Littlefield married Lydia Maria Parsons, a daughter of Joseph and Rachel (Battles) Parsons, who removed from Canada to Vermont, and they subsequently left New England, going to Kekoshkee, Wisconsin, where both spent their remaining years. Mr. and Mrs. Charles Le Count were people of sterling worth and integrity, highly esteemed in the business and social circles of Kekoshkee, and were valued members of the Universalist church. They reared four children, namely: Adelaide, John, Charles, and Laura, now Mrs. Darling. Mr. and Mrs. Darling are the parents of four children, namely: Thomas Jackson Darling, Charles Le Count Darling, Dorothea Darling, and Sunshine Darling. Politically Mr. Darling supports the principles of the Democratic party in state and town elections, and in national affairs is a Prohibitionist. Religiously both Mr. and Mrs. Darling are members of the Methodist Episcopal church.

PRATT ADAMS WILLIAMS, a recent acquisition to the town of Vidalia, Georgia, was born October 5, 1878, at Ellabell, Bryan county, this State, one of the family of twelve children of Judge P. W. and Mrs. Sarah Frances (Duggar) Williams, both natives of that county, and now residents of Lyons, Toombs county, Georgia. The other members of the family, including six sons and five daughters, are as follows: Pembroke C., Robert T., James J., Garland, Osgood, Teddy, Mrs. W. I. Graybill, Mrs. J. D. Bradley, Mrs. Charles Garbutt, and Miss Duluth and Miss Letha. Two of Mr. Williams' brothers, Pembroke C. and James J., are attorneys, the former a resident of Silver City, Idaho; the latter associated in practice with his father at Lyons.

Pratt A. Williams received his primary education in the common schools. Afterward he attended Bryan Institute and Hogan Academy, where he fitted himself for college. He is a graduate of Emory College, with the class of 1898, and of the law department of the University of Georgia at Athens. On the completion of his law course, he opened an office at Pembroke, Georgia, where he practiced his profession for a period of ten years, having large experience with criminal cases and practicing in all the courts. Four years he served as solicitor general of the Atlantic circuit.

On coming to Vidalia in August, 1911, he associated himself with Judge C. C. Curry in the practice of law, and soon afterward put on foot the organization of the Vidalia Loan & Trust Company, of Vidalia, of which he is president, and which will be in operation early in the summer of 1912, with a capital stock of $50,000.00.

In 1912 he entered the race for congress from the Twelfth District, opposing Hon. Dudley M. Hughs, M. C., and waged a heated campaign, but withdrew from the race before the election, because of a death in his family.

In 1901, Mr. Williams and Miss Annabelle Mathews were united in marriage. Mrs. Williams is noted for her musical attainments, and is a member of one of the distinguished families of the State. She is a daughter of Captain and Mrs. L. A. Mathews, of Dublin, Laurens county, and a grand-daughter of General Blackshears of both Indian and Civil war fame. Mr. Williams' grandfather, James T. Williams, also served in the Civil war, and as a soldier in the Confederate army proved himself loyal to the southern cause.

Fraternally, Mr. Williams is identified with the Junior Order of American Mechanics, and the Sigma Nu, the latter having membership in both the Emory and the University of Georgia chapters. He and his interesting family are a valued addition to the town of Vidalia.

WILLIAM NEYLE COLQUITT. Among the popular and talented young citizens of Savannah is William Neyle Colquitt, secretary to ex-Mayor Tiedman of the city and former lawyer and journalist. He comes of distinguished southern ancestry and has succeeded admirably in living up to the traditions of his antecedents. Mr. Colquitt is one of Savannah's native sons, his birth having occurred within the boundaries of the beautiful city, March 8, 1878. He is the son of Walter Wellborn and Lilla (Habersham) Colquitt. He received his preliminary education in the public schools of Savannah and then matriculated in the University of Georgia, being graduated from that institution in 1898 with the degree of LL.B. He hung out his maiden shingle in Atlanta, but dabbled in journalism, and finding it most congenial work, gave more and more of his attention to the affairs of the Fourth Estate. He came back to Savannah, and soon thereafter was proffered and accepted the city editorship of the Savannah *Press*. In 1907 he became secretary to the mayor of Savannah, and continued in that capacity until January, 1913.

Mr. Colquitt has always been active in the military life of his native city, although he declined an appointment to Annapolis, proffered to him on account of his having saved the life of the son of Hillary A. Herbert, formerly secretary of the navy. He was successively a member of the infantry, cavalry, artillery naval reserves and the governor's staff, and he is now secretary of the Savannah Volunteer Guards.

Mr. Colquitt has decided literary ability, having a forceful and interesting style. He has been the author of numerous magazine articles, mainly historical in their nature. He was formerly secretary of the board of managers of the Savannah public library, and he is still a member of the board, being chairman of the finance committee. He is a member of Sigma Alpha Epsilon fraternity and is secretary and treasurer of the Savannah Alumni Association. He was the author of the movement to erect a monument to Generals Screven and Stewart in Midway Cemetery, for which Congress has made available $10,000, and he is now secretary of the monument commission. In recognition of his services in this matter he was elected an honorary member of the Midway Society, the first in the history of the society, which has existed for more than a century.

Mr. Colquitt is everything that is patriotic and public-spirited. Being naturally enthusiastic, they are passionate emotions with him, and he has the gift of making fine realities out of his visions. He is a very popular citizen, his honorable life and commendable characteristics, combined with charming manners, having won him hosts of friends.

In 1905, Miss Dolores Boisfeuillet, daughter of Adrian S. Boisfeuillet, of Macon, became the wife of Mr. Colquitt, and their abode is now the center of gracious hospitality of the most charming southern type.

Walter Wellborn Colquitt, father of the foregoing, was born at Macon, Georgia, where he was reared and educated. About the time he became of age he located in Savannah, and was married in this city. He has been prominently connected with commercial affairs all his life, and at present his main interests are in the phosphate industry in Florida. During the first Cleveland administration he was chief of the revenue service of the United States, with headquarters at Washington. He is a half-brother of the late Alfred Holt Colquitt, who died in Washington City, March 26, 1894. Alfred Holt Colquitt was born in Walton county, Georgia, April 20, 1824; he graduated in the College of New Jersey in 1844, and in that year returned to Georgia and began the practice of the law. He served in the Mexican war and was elected to Congress in 1852 as a Democrat. In the war between the states he was a captain in the Army of the Confederacy. In 1876, this veteran of two wars was elected governor of Georgia and served one term. He was elected United States senator in 1882 and re-elected in 1888, his death occurring shortly after the close of his second term.

Governor Colquitt was the son of Walter T. Colquitt, one of the most distinguished lawyers of Georgia of the earlier days. He was born in Halifax county, Virginia, December 27, 1799, and died at Macon, Georgia, May 7, 1855. He was educated at Princeton College and admitted to the bar in 1820. About that time he came to Georgia, and in 1826 became a district judge, holding the first court ever held in Columbus, Georgia. He was a highly successful lawyer, and especially in criminal practice he was without a peer in the state. He was a member of the Georgia state senate from 1834 to 1837; a member of congress from Georgia from 1829 to 1843, and United States senator from 1843 to 1849.

The subject's mother, Lilla Neyle (Habersham) Colquitt, who passed away in Savannah in 1805, was a member of one of Georgia's distinguished families. She was the daughter of William Neyle Habersham, who was the grandson of Joseph Habersham, the first postmaster general of the United States, previous to which he had been acting governor of the colony of Georgia. Three of the Georgia Habershams were soldiers in the Revolutionary war.

JOSEPH THOMAS RAGAN. Widely and favorably known in the commercial circles of Terrell county, Joseph Thomas Ragan, of Dawson, holds a noteworthy position among the leading business men of his community, being officially connected with some of its more substantial and important industrial organizations. He was born, March 3, 1858, on a farm in Terrell county, a son of the late Dr. Spann Ragan.

His paternal grandfather, Joseph Ragan, was, it is thought, a lifelong resident of North Carolina, where he died while in manhood's prime. His wife, whose maiden name was Elizabeth Spann, married for her second husband Reddick Bryan, and came with him and her family to Georgia in pioneer days, making the removal with teams. After living for a time in Houston county, the family removed, in the forties, to Louisiana, and there both Mr. and Mrs. Reddick Bryan spent their remaining days, her death occurring at the age of eighty-five years. By her first marriage she reared two children, Spann Ragan and John Ragan. By her union with Mr. Reddick Bryan she reared six children, as follows: Joseph, Tillman, Terrell, Dolly, Amanda, and Georgia.

Spann Ragan was born in Greene county, North Carolina, and was a lad in his 'teens when he came with his mother and step-father to Georgia. He subsequently accompanied the family to Louisiana, where he began life for himself as a school teacher. Taking up the study of medicine while thus employed, he afterwards attended lectures in New Orleans, and still later was graduated from the Georgia Medical College, in Augusta, with the degree of M. D. Dr. Ragan then began the practice of his chosen profession in what was then Lee county, but is now Terrell county, settling ten miles east of the present site of Dawson. Being a physician, he was exempt from military duty during the Civil war, but in its last year he entered the Confederate service. He afterwards resumed the practice of his profession, in which he was actively engaged until his death, in 1874, at the comparatively early age of fifty-six years.

The maiden name of the wife of Dr. Spann Ragan was Julia Lou Speight. She was born in Greene county, North Carolina, which was likewise the birthplace of her father, Rev. Thomas Speight. In early life, Rev. Thomas Speight, who was a preacher in the Methodist Episcopal Church, came with his family to Georgia, locating in what is now Terrell county, in the eastern part. He bought land bordering on Kinchafoonee creek, and with slave labor improved a farm, on which he spent the remainder of his days. He married Julia Lou Pope, also a native of North Carolina, and they reared seven children, as follows: Thomas L.; John S.; Cicero C.; Skidmore; Mary; Eliza; and Julia Lou, who became the wife of Dr. Spann Ragan. The oldest son, Thomas L., became a preacher in the Methodist Episcopal church, and the others became successful agriculturists. Mrs. Spann Ragan survived her husband, passing away in 1884, aged fifty-five years. She reared five children, namely: Joseph Thomas, the special subject of this brief sketch; Elizabeth Lou, who has been postmaster at Bronwood the past eighteen years; Charles C., deceased; Mollie P., wife of C. N. Bryan, and Terrell B., who died in early manhood.

As a boy Joseph Thomas Ragan received ample opportunities for obtaining a practical common school education, and on the home farm was well trained in agricultural arts. When he was sixteen years of age his father died, and the care of the farm and the family devolved largely upon him. Equal to the task thus imposed, he continued the management of the parental acres until 1885, when he embarked in mercantile business in Bronwood. Meeting with well-deserved success in his undertakings, Mr. Ragan soon engaged in the warehouse business, continuing his residence in Bronwood until 1900. In that year he removed to Dawson, and when, a year later, the Southern Cotton Oil Company was formed, he became associated with that organization in an official capacity, and for the past ten years has been sole manager of its affairs. Mr. Ragan is also president of the Dawson Square Bale Gin and Mill Company, which is doing a flourishing business.

Mr. Ragan married on the 20th of September, 1889, in Bronwood, Georgia, Miss Mattie M. Moore, a daughter of Dr. Charles Reuben Moore, of pioneer ancestry, her great-grandfather, Richard Moore, who, it is said, was a native of North Carolina, having been one of the very early settlers of Burke county, Georgia. Mrs. Ragan's paternal grandfather, Henry Turner Moore, moved from Burke county, to Houston county, where he spent the later years of his life. He was twice married, by his first union rearing four children: Nancy, Seaborn, Dora, and Charles Reuben. By his second marriage he was the father of two children, Benjamin and Rebecca.

Charles Reuben Moore was born in Burke county, Georgia, and acquired his preliminary education in the district schools. His tastes and inclinations leading him to choose a professional career, he entered the Atlanta Medical College to pursue his studies, and after his graduation from that institution practiced first in Jefferson county, from there going to Starksville, Lee county, where he remained a short time. He subsequently removed to Weston, Webster county, from there going to Dawson, where he was successfully engaged in the practice of medicine for eight years. Returning then to Weston, he remained there in active practice as a physician and surgeon until his death, in 1882. He was highly esteemed, not only in his profession, but as a man and a citizen. He was prominent in public affairs, filling various local offices, and representing Webster county in both branches of the state legislature.

Dr. Charles R. Moore married Amelia Wynn Sharpe, who was born in Tattnall county, Georgia, and died in Webster county, aged fifty-two years. Her father, John Sharpe, was a Virginian by birth, and in his young manhood was captain of a steamboat, commanding, it is supposed, a vessel engaged in coastwise trade. On settling in Georgia he purchased land in Tattnall county, improved it with the assistance of slaves, and there carried on farming until his death. His wife, whose maiden name was Rebecca Lassater, was born in Burke county, Georgia, and died in Tattnall county. Mrs. Charles R. Moore, Mrs. Ragan's mother, died August 16, 1884. She reared nine children, as follows: Eudora, Fannie, Ora, Susie, Lula, Gertrude, Charles, Mattie, and Clarence. By a former marriage, Dr. Moore had three children, Emma, Jimmie, and Georgia. The doctor was a member of the Ancient Free and Accepted Order of Masons, and both he and his wife belonged to the Methodist Episcopal church.

Six children have been born of the union of Mr. and Mrs. Ragan, namely: Joseph Thomas, Jr.; Charles Ellis; Clarence Spann; Terrell Moore; Mattie E., who died in infancy, and Dorothy. Of the four sons, Joseph T., Jr., is in Atlanta with the Southern Cotton Oil Company. He is a noted musician, and is and has been for the past three years organist and musical director of the North Avenue Presbyterian church. Charles Ellis is connected with the Southern Cotton Oil Co. as traveling auditor. Clarence Spann is with G. W. Dozier & Co., dry goods merchants. Terrell Moore, the youngest son, is associated with his father in business at Dawson. The youngest is a daughter, Dorothy, now six years. The four sons, like their forefathers, are members of the Methodist Episcopal church. Both Mr. and Mrs. Ragan, true to the religious faith in which they were reared, are members of the Methodist Episcopal church, Mr. Ragan being assistant superintendent of the Sunday school in the church at Dawson for eight years. Mrs. Ragan is a valued member of the Methodist Episcopal Missionary Society. Mr. Ragan belongs to P. T. Schley Lodge, No. 229, Ancient Free and Accepted Order of Masons, Dawson, Georgia; to Forest City Lodge, Savannah, Knights of Pythias, and to the Independent Order of Odd Fellows.

LEE C. HOYL. A prominent citizen and well-known lawyer of Dawson, where he has an extensive practice, Lee C. Hoyl has won for himself an honorable name in the legal fraternity of Terrell county, his professional skill and ability being widely recognized. A native of Georgia, he was born in Dawson, where his father, the late Levi Clarke Hoyl, was for several years engaged in the practice of law.

Mr. Hoyl's grandfather, Rev. Thomas Latimore Hoyl, a native of Tennessee, was a preacher in the Methodist Episcopal church in that state until late in life, when, his wife having passed to the life beyond, he came to Dawson, Georgia, and spent the last years of his life with his son Levi. He reared seven children, as follows: John, Thomas, James B., Levi Clarke, Mahlon P., Andrew J., and Susan, who married E. H. Scovelle. Three of the sons, Thomas, Levi Clarke, and Mahlon P., served in the Confederate army during the Civil war, Thomas losing his life while in the army.

Born and bred in East Tennessee, Levi Clarke Hoyl acquired his education at Hiwassee College, and after his admission to the bar began the practice of law in Athens, Tennessee. Coming to Georgia in 1860, he opened an office in Americus, and continued his professional labors. Returning to Tennessee after the breaking out of the war between the states, he enlisted, at Cleveland, in Company E, Sixty-third Tennessee Volunteer Infantry, under command of Capt. Thomas Brown and Col. J. H. Rogers. Soon after entering the army, he was captured, and taken to Johnson's Island, in Lake Erie, where he was confined as a prisoner six months, when he was exchanged, and returned home. He had previously contracted rheumatism, at the time of his exchange having been helpless, and he never fully recovered his health. At the close of the war he again came to Georgia, and having purchased a tract of land six miles west of Dawson, embarked in farming. His health improving, he moved with his family to Dawson, and, in partnership with Major C. B. Wooten, was there actively engaged in the practice of his chosen profession until his death, September 1, 1898.

On August 8, 1867, Levi Clarke Hoyl married Mary Elizabeth Ozier, who was born in Harris county, Georgia, April 17, 1842, a daughter of Rev. Jacob Ozier. Her paternal grandfather, Jacob Ozier, Sr., was born in North Carolina, of French Huguenot ancestry, and died at the home of his son, in Randolph county, Georgia, when well advanced in years. Rev. Jacob Ozier, a native of North Carolina, studied for the ministry, and in earlier life was a Methodist Episcopal preacher in various places in South Carolina. About 1840 he came to Georgia, and having joined the Georgia Conference, held pastorates in different parts of the state. His health failing, he purchased a farm lying three miles south of Cuthbert, and there resided until his death, at the age of seventy-three years. He was twice married, his first wife having been a Miss Winn, who died in early womanhood. He married, second, Elizabeth Kaiger, who was born in South Carolina, and was educated in the city of Charleston. Her father, Major David Kaiger, was born, it is thought, in South Carolina. Coming to Georgia in early life, he bought land lying thirteen miles northeast of Dawson, and with slave labor improved a large farm, on which he spent the remainder of his years. Both he and his wife, whose maiden name was Barbara Crapps, lived long and useful lives, and at their deaths were buried on the home plantation. Mrs. Elizabeth (Kaiger) Ozier, Mr. Hoyl's maternal grandmother, died at the age of fifty-eight years. She reared eight children, as follows: Mary Elizabeth, widow of Levi Clarke Hoyl; Martha Matilda; Fredonia Pierce; Anna Capers; Florella Bascom; De Laura Zeuline; Hilliard, and David Henry. Mrs. Mary Elizabeth (Ozier) Hoyl was educated at the Andrew Female Seminary, in Cuthbert, and prior to her marriage taught school three years. She now resides in Dawson, and is the mother of five children, namely: Lee C., the special subject of this brief sketch; Thomas C.; James B.; Walter H., and Mary Lou. She is a faithful member of the Methodist Episcopal church, to which her husband also belonged, and has reared her children in the same religious faith.

Lee C. Hoyl received his early education in the South Georgia Male and Female College, in Dawson, later attending the University of Georgia. Subsequently studying law with his father, he was admitted to the bar by the late Judge J. M. Griggs, on December 3, 1894, and immediately became associated with his father in the practice of his profession. In 1898 Mr. Hoyl enlisted in Company G, Third Regiment, United States Volunteer Infantry, for service in the Spanish-American war. Being commissioned lieutenant of his company, Mr. Hoyl went with his command to Cuba. On the death of his father he resigned from the army, returned home, and has continued in active practice of his profession in Dawson ever since, at the present writing, in March, 1913, being city attorney.

Mr. Hoyl married, January 17, 1906, Elizabeth Peddy, a daughter of John W. Peddy, of Dawson. Mrs. Hoyl's paternal grandfather, Thomas B. Peddy, was born in Georgia in 1815, a son of Bradford Peddy, a farmer in Muscogee county. Removing to Alabama when a young man, he purchased land in Macon county, and was there prosperously engaged in tilling the soil for many years, residing on the home place until his death, in 1886. He served as a brave soldier in the Indian wars, but was too old for military service when the war between the states occurred. He married Nancy Holly, a native of Stewart county, Georgia.

John W. Peddy was born, October 19, 1851, in Alabama, in that part of Macon county now included within the limits of Lee county, and was reared on the home farm, and educated in the rural schools. Beginning life for himself at the age of twenty-one years, he was clerk in a mercantile establishment for two years, and the following season conducted a general store on his own account in Bulloch county. Locating then in Lee county, Georgia, he was there engaged in business two years. The ensuing ten years Mr. Peddy was a resident of Sumter county, Florida, during which time he was assistant postmaster and express agent. Coming from there to Dawson in 1890, he clerked in a store for three years, but has since been successfully engaged in the mercantile brokerage business. While living in Alabama and in Florida Mr. Peddy served as justice of the peace, and has held the same office in Dawson for eighteen years.

John W. Peddy has been twice married. He married first, in 1875, Mary Lizzie Harris, a daughter of Edmond Jackson and Martha Ann (Bryan) Harris; and a sister of Mrs. T. J. Hart, in whose husband's sketch, which appears elsewhere in this work, further parental history may be found. Mrs. Mary Lizzie (Harris) Peddy died February 22, 1893. Mr. Peddy subsequently married for his second wife Anna Maria McFarland. Of the eight children born of his first marriage, five grew to years of maturity, as follows: Susie Evelyn; Cecil Harris; Daniel Calloway; Bessie, now Mrs. Hoyl, and Annie Theo.

Mr. and Mrs. Hoyl have one son, Levi Clarke Hoyl. Fraternally Mr. Hoyl is a member of P. T. Schley Lodge, No. 229, Ancient Free and Accepted Order of Masons; of Lawrence Chapter, No. 96, Royal Arch Masons; of the Woodmen of the World; of the Royal Arcanum; and Sigma Nu Fraternity, Mu Chapter, University of Georgia.

CAPT. WILLIAM COUNT DILLON. Especially worthy of note in this volume among the many capable and intelligent men who have been actively associated with the agricultural interests of Terrell county is Capt. William Count Dillon, late of Dawson, who brought to his independent calling good business methods and excellent judgment, and whose labors were crowned with success. He was a native of Georgia, his birth having occurred in Augusta, November 5, 1836.

A small boy when his father died, he was brought up by an aunt, and began when young to be self-supporting. He was naturally a studious lad, but as he had little opportunity to attend school he obtained his education, principally, evenings, by the light of a candle. Industrious and thrifty, he saved his earnings, and when he had accumulated a sufficient sum to warrant him in becoming a landholder he purchased a farm in Baker county, Georgia, where he was soon busily and profitably engaged in raising cotton and corn. As his means increased, Mr. Dillon bought other land, and carried on farming on an extensive scale.

Renting his Baker county lands in 1879, Mr. Baker located in Terrell county, purchased a farm lying two miles east of Dawson, and was there a resident until his death, February 15, 1896.

While living in Augusta Mr. Dillon served as chief of police, in that capacity performing his duties faithfully and fearlessly, to a noticeable extent clearing the city of desperadoes. While thus employed the captain was shot, and carried the bullet in his body as long as he lived. Public-spirited and liberal, his influence and assistance were ever sought in behalf of undertakings for the public good and for the advancement of the best interests of his community. Although Captain Dillon acquired a large property, he did not obtain his wealth by penury, but by his business tact and ability, as is shown in his farming operations and in his wise investments.

Captain Dillon married Mrs. Mary Virginia (Elliott) Wilkinson, who was born January 6, 1845, in Baker county, where her father, James Elliott, was a farmer. By her union with her first husband, Dr. W. W. Wilkinson, Mrs. Dillon had one son, Walton Wilkinson, who died unmarried. Three children blessed the union of Captain and Mrs. Dillon, namely: George Crawford Dillon, who is an invalid; William Count Dillon, Jr., who died unmarried; and Susan Wright, who married Walter Aloisius Mercer, of Dawson, and has two sons, William D. Mercer and Walter A. Mercer.

Mrs. Mercer received her education first by private tutors in Dawson, then in Union Female College, under Mrs. James; then in Lake View University, at Birmingham, Alabama; then back to Eufaula, under Mrs. Simmons; then to Wesley Female College, at Macon.

Mrs. Mercer and her husband are both members of the Methodist Episcopal church, to which Mrs. Dillon, who died June 6, 1881, also belonged.

BYNUM H. HOOD. Resolute and earnest in purpose, energetic and progressive, Bynum H. Hood, late of Dawson, was for many years actively associated with the industrial and business prosperity of Terrell county, his death being a loss not only to his immediate family and friends, but to the entire community. He was born, November 11, 1836, in Meriwether county, Georgia, and was there reared to agricultural pursuits.

Joseph Hood, his father, was for many years engaged in agricultural pursuits in Meriwether county, Georgia. Coming from there to Terrell county, he purchased land lying one and one-half miles northeast of Dawson, and was there employed as a tiller of the soil during the remainder of his life.

An ambitious student, Bynum H. Hood received excellent educational advantages, completing his early studies in Forsyth, in Professor Morgan H. Looney's school. Public-spirited and patriotic, he enlisted, in April, 1862, in Company I, Forrest Cavalry, which became a part of Forrest's command, and was with his regiment in its many campaigns and battles. On July 23, 1863, he took part in the raid on Murfreesboro, when several Confederate prisoners there confined in jail were released, Congressman Richardson, who was under sentence of death as a spy, having been of the number. Mr. Hood also participated in the Battle of Perryville, Kentucky, and in the engagement at Chickamauga. In 1863, on account of physical disability, Mr. Hood was released from service by General Foster, but he continued with the army, and later was placed, by General Hood, on detached duty to obtain supplies for the army, a position which he filled until the final surrender, in May, 1865.

Returning to Georgia, Mr. Hood taught school in Meriwether county until January, 1866, when he accepted a position as teacher in the schools of Dawson. Obliged on account of ill health to resign his position in 1867, Mr. Hood did not remain idle, but with characteristic pluck and courage became successfully engaged in various enterprises, including the warehouse and lumber business. For many years there was but one railroad in Dawson, and Mr. Hood, perceiving the urgent need of better transportation facilities, conceived the plan of establishing a railway extending from Columbus to Albany. The project at the time seemed a big undertaking, but he, nothing daunted, began working at it with his customary vigor and zeal, interesting capitalists and influential business men, and through his untiring efforts the road was completed in 1889. Mr. Hood continued his residence in Dawson until his death, in 1905. Fraternally Mr. Hood was a member of P. T. Schley Lodge, No. 229, Ancient Free and Accepted Order of Masons, and he also belonged to Tom Brantley Camp, No. 404, Confederate Veterans.

On November 11, 1866, Mr. Hood was united in marriage with Miss Amanda A. Lasseter, a native of Sumter county, Georgia. Mrs. Hood's father, David Lasseter, was born, it is supposed, in Jasper county, Georgia. He was a pioneer of Sumter county, where he bought a tract of wild land near the present site of Plains, and with slave labor improved the homestead on which he spent his remaining days. Mr. Lasseter married Elizabeth Asbury Speer, who belonged to a prominent family of Georgia, of which she was a life-long resident. She passed to the higher life November 4, 1861, leaving eleven children, as follows: John H., Martha G., William F., James A., Simeon N., Jeremiah C., Henry M., Margaret J., Mary E., Amanda A., and Sarah C. All of the sons, with the exception of the elder one, served in the Confederate army. Henry lost his life in the service, having died the same date of his mother, but the others served throughout the entire war.

Mrs. Hood acquired her preliminary education in Dawson, attending first the school taught by Professor Tom Brantley, and afterwards was a pupil in Professor McNulty's school. Completing her early studies at the Americus Female College, she came to Dawson at the age of twelve years to open a private school. Her brother, Simeon F. Lasseter, M. D., was there engaged in the practice of medicine, and she started her school in his office, which was located on Stonewall street, adjoining the present site of the Presbyterian church. Very successful as a teacher, she continued in her chosen occupation several years, her school being well attended and very popular. Mrs. Hood is well educated, having been a reader of good literature, and a student all of her life. She is an interesting conversationalist, fluent in language, and a forceful writer whenever occasion requires it.

Mrs. Hood's parents were Methodists, but she departed from the faith in which she was reared, and before her marriage united with the Baptist church, of which Mr. Hood was also a member. In 1901 Mrs. Hood invited the daughters of veterans of the Confederate army to meet at her house, and there the assembled group of ladies organized the Mary Brantley Chapter, United Daughters of the Confederacy. Mrs. Hood was elected president of the chapter, and was continued in office, by re-election, until 1911. Mr. and Mrs. Hood had no children of their own, but they assisted many young people to acquire an education, and since the death of her husband Mrs. Hood has continued the good work, in many ways assisting those less fortunate than herself.

FRANCIS M. WHITTLE. Conspicuous among the foremost citizens of Savannah is Francis M. Whittle, who as division manager of the Virginia-Carolina Chemical Company is identified with one of its more important industries, at the same time being an active member of the public-spirited group of young men that are fostering the progressive movement for the greater development of the city. A son of the late Rev. Francis M. Whittle, he was born at Berryville, Clarke county, Virginia, on the paternal side tracing his ancestry back to John Rolfe and Pocahontas, the Indian princess, from whom were also descended the Randolph, Bolling, and other noted Virginian families.

Two of Mr. Whittle's uncles, the late Lewis M. Whittle, of Macon, and Col. Powhatan Whittle, settled in Georgia prior to the Civil war, both being lawyers. Colonel Whittle enlisted as a soldier in that conflict, and while serving as colonel of a Georgia regiment lost an arm at the battle of Gettysburg. A civil engineer in his earlier life, Lewis M. Whittle became a cripple as the result of an accident which befell him while he was assisting in the building of the railroad between Atlanta and Chattanooga. Going then to Macon, Georgia, he took up the study of law, was admitted to the bar, and became one of the most distinguished lawyers of the state. He was also prominent in public affairs, serving as member of the Georgia state senate under the Confederate regime.

Born in Mecklenburg county, Virginia, Rev. Francis M. Whittle, D. D., came from a family that for many generations had been prominent in the history of the Old Dominion. Admitted to the priesthood of the Episcopal church in Virginia, he was made rector of an Episcopal church in Louisville, Kentucky, prior to the Civil war. Soon after the outbreak of that conflict, on account of his unqualified adherence to the Confederate cause, he was taken prisoner by the Federal authorities and confined in prison for some time. Elected bishop of Virginia in 1868, he subsequently served in that capacity until his death, in 1905. He married Emily Carey Fairfax, who passed to the higher life. She was born in Virginia, a descendant of George Fairfax, a nephew of Lord Thomas Fairfax, one of the landed proprietors of Virginia, George Fairfax having married a Miss Carey, who was sister to the wife of Lawrence Washington.

Francis M. Whittle was educated, principally, in Richmond College, Virginia, and was early trained to business pursuits. Since 1897 he has been connected with Virginia-Carolina Chemical Company, during the first five years being located in Atlanta, Georgia. In 1902 he came to Savannah as division manager for the company, which is among the world's largest manufacturers of fertilizers, and whose Savannah plant is one of the city's greatest industries.

Progressive and enterprising, Mr. Whittle has ever evinced a warm interest in local progress and improvements, heartily endorsing all enterprises conducive to the welfare of the community. He is a member, and one of the directors, of the chamber of commerce; a member of the cotton exchange; of the yacht club; and of the automobile club. He is an Episcopalian and a vestryman of Saint John's church.

Mr. Whittle married Louise T. Hansell, of Roswell, Georgia, and into their home four children have been born, namely: Lucy, Mary A., Lulu T., and Emily Fairfax.

JOHN GOLASPY STANLEY. A man of marked enterprise and ability, John Golaspy Stanley is numbered among the substantial and prosperous agriculturists of Brooks county, and is also actively associated with various important enterprises in Quitman. A native of Georgia, he was born December 9, 1855, in Houston county, which was likewise the birthplace of his father, William Haddock Stanley.

Leary Stanley, his grandfather, was born in Goldsboro, North Carolina, November 24, 1802. As a boy he had no opportunity to attend school, but having mastered the alphabet he learned to read, and being a diligent student acquired a medical education without attending any educational institution. Coming to Georgia in early manhood, he bought timber land near Perry, Houston county, and on the farm which he reclaimed from its pristine wildness lived a number of years. Removing in 1857 with his family to Lowndes county, he purchased a tract of wild land lying four miles north of the present site of Quitman, in what is now included within the boundaries of Brooks county, and in addition to clearing and improving a farm was actively engaged in professional work, practicing medicine throughout Brooks and adjoining counties. He was very successful both as an agriculturist and a physician, and on the farm which he improved resided until his death, November 6, 1865, while yet in the prime of life. He married Charity West, who was born September 17, 1798, and died at the home of her oldest son,

William H. Stanley, April 26, 1878. Eight children were born to them, as follows: William H., John, James B., Sarah, Mattie, Susan, Ann, and Mary. All of the sons served in the Confederate army during the war between the states. John, who was then teaching in Texas, enlisted in a Texas regiment and was never again heard from. James B., a practicing lawyer, enlisted as a soldier, went to Virginia with his regiment, which was assigned to the Army of the Potomac, and bravely met his death on the field of battle.

Born on the home farm in Houston county, Georgia, November 24, 1831, William Haddock Stanley received a common school education, and soon after attaining his majority bought land in Houston county and was there employed in tilling the soil until 1856. Coming then to what is now Brooks county, he purchased a tract of timber situated eight miles south of the site of Quitman, a very few acres of his land having been previously cleared, and in the opening a set of buildings had been erected. All of southwest Georgia was then a wilderness, with comparatively few public highways and no railroads, Tallahassee and Newport, in Florida, being the nearest markets and depots for supplies. With the help of slaves he began the improvement of his land, continuing his agricultural labors until the outbreak of the Civil war, when he offered his services to the Confederacy.

Returning home at the close of the conflict, he continued the improvements previously begun on his homestead. The commodious frame house which he then erected was burned soon after its construction, and he then put up a less pretentious structure, in which he resided until his death, January 2, 1894. He married Mary J. (Baskin) Haddock, who was born in Houston county, Georgia, a daughter of William Baskin, and widow of William Haddock. She survived him, passing away February 26, 1896, leaving four children, namely: John Golaspy, Millard L., George W., and Mattie A. By her first marriage there were two sons, Franklin L. and James W.

After leaving the public schools John Golaspy Stanley entered the University of Georgia, in Athens, and was there graduated with the class of 1879. Not caring to adopt a profession, he embarked in the peaceful pursuit of farming. His father being in poor health, he returned home and for ten years superintended the work on the parental homestead. Buying then six hundred acres of land south two miles from the old home, he spent five years in adding to its improvements, living there until 1895. In that year Mr. Stanley bought the interests of the remaining heirs in the old homestead, which he has since managed with unquestionable success. He has now one thousand acres of valuable land, a good set of farm buildings, the improvements which he has made upon the place being of a substantial character.

Possessing excellent business tact and judgment, Mr. Stanley is identified with various organizations of importance. He is a director and vice-president of the First National Bank of Quitman, and one of the directors of the Alliance Warehouse Company. He is now president of the Hickory Head Agricultural Club, an old and influential society; a life member of the State Agricultural Society and a member of its executive committee; and is a trustee of the Eleventh District Agricultural School. He also belongs to the jury commission. He has always been a stanch supporter of the principles of the Democratic party and for ten years a member of the county board of education.

In 1891 Mr. Stanley married Frances Alberta Kinnebrew, who was born in Floyd county, Georgia, near Rome, a daughter of Newton Kinnebrew. Mrs. Stanley's grandfather Kinnebrew, who was of Scotch-Irish ancestry, was engaged in farming in Elbert county, Georgia, in his early life. He subsequently spent a few years in Chambers county, Alabama, but returned to Georgia, and spent his last days in Oglethorpe, county. Born and reared on a farm in Elbert county, Newton Kinnebrew succeeded to the occupation which he became familiar with in boyhood. He was a natural mechanic, and though he never learned a trade he could make anything in the line of furniture, wagons, or fashion any of the wood-work connected with farm machinery, being a skillful workman. He farmed for himself first in Oglethorpe county, Georgia, later in Chambers county, Alabama, finally settling on an estate in Floyd county, Georgia, where he resided until his death. The maiden name of the wife of Newton Kinnebrew was Mary E. Pinson. She was born in Oglethorpe county, a daughter of Thomas and Nancy (Patman) Pinson. Nine children blessed their marriage, as follows: Henry T.; Nannie S.; Sarah J.; Martha A.; J. Edwin; Olivia; Albin; Petty Alberta, now Mrs. Stanley, and J. Shannon.

Mr. and Mrs. Stanley are the parents of four children, namely: William K.; Baskin and Pinson, twins; and Nannie Belle, who lived but eighteen months.

DR. CHARLES HYATT RICHARDSON, practicing physician in Montezuma, and well known to the medical profession as well as the laity in this county, has been a resident of this region all his life. He followed in the footsteps of a worthy father, and in his capacity has carried on the good work that he laid down in 1886. Doctor Richardson has taken a notably important place in the communal life of Montezuma, and has given service in more than his medical capacity. As mayor of the city for three years and as alderman for seven years, much good has accrued to his community as a result of his whole-souled and honest services in those offices, and he occupied a sure place in the esteem and confidence of the people of his town and the surrounding region.

Born on March 3, 1859, Charles Hyatt Richardson is the son of Dr. Charles Hyatt Richardson and his wife, Margaret (Bettles) Richardson. Doctor Richardson was born in 1829 in Sumter county, South Carolina, and came from that place in 1855, locating at Fort Valley, Georgia, later engaged in practice in Byron. He died in 1886, after many years of faithful service in his medical capacity, and his name and fame is being carried on in the activities of his son, the subject of this review. The mother was born in Sumter county, South Carolina, also, and is still living at the age of eighty-six and makes her home in Byron, Georgia.

Doctor Richardson received his early education in the common schools of Byron and was later graduated from Mercer University with an A. B. degree, in 1878. He later entered the College of Physicians and Surgeons at Baltimore, Maryland, and was graduated in 1883, taking a post-graduate course in 1900 at the New York Post Graduate College. Following his graduation from Baltimore, he established himself in practice in Montezuma, where he has since carried on an active practice, and where he has gained reputation as a medical man of splendid ability.

His public service has been of a most praiseworthy nature, and it was during his administration as mayor, in which office he served three years, that Doctor Richardson brought about the establishment of the Carnegie library fund. Doctor Richardson was made chairman of the building committee and handled the fund thus donated. The building was erected at a cost of $10,000 and the library has about $5,000 worth of books. While he was alderman in 1889 the steel bridge spanning the Flint river was built by the city at a cost of $10,000, and the same has been a big source of growth to the city in that it has made possible easy access to the city from towns on the other side of the river, as a result of which trade has been on the continuous increase since that time. He was mayor of Montezuma while the A. & 'B. R. R. was in course of construction through the town, and upon its completion a banquet was held at Atlanta, at which Doctor Richardson, as mayor of Montezuma, was one of the principal speakers.

Doctor Richardson has always been held in high esteem by his brother physicians throughout the state, which is evidenced by the fact that he was elected vice-president of the State Medical Association in 1911. In 1912 he was elected president of the Third District Medical Association. This association will convene at Fort Valley, Georgia, on the third Wednesday in June under his presidency.

Recognizing his ability in pulmonary diseases, he was appointed by the president of its session in Augusta, Georgia, in 1912 (while he himself did not attend the meeting), as chairman of the committee on tuberculosis to write a series of articles on the great white plague.

In 1909 Doctor Richardson was appointed by Governor Smith as a member of the board of trustees of the state tuberculosis sanitarium to be established. At the first meeting of this board Doctor Richardson was appointed one of the five members of the executive committee whose duties were to select a location, build the sanitarium, and start it in operation. The terms of office of this board expired in January, 1913, and Doctor Richardson and three others were the only ones of the old board reappointed by Governor Brown, with twenty new members. Again Doctor Richardson was appointed one of the five members on the executive committee to control this sanitarium.

In 1889 the Central of Georgia Railroad decided to employ railroad surgeons on its road. Doctor Richardson was one of the first to be appointed as local surgeon for Montezuma and he has the honor of retaining this position to this day, twenty-four years of continuous service. Only two or three still hold the office now that were originally appointed.

In the spring of 1912, the political year in Georgia, it became Macon county's time to name the senator from the thirteenth district. The progressive element of the Democratic party in that county prevailed upon Doctor Richardson to enter the race. His opponent had represented the county twice in the house and was a gentleman of large and influential family connections. Doctor Richardson was elected in this race, carrying five precincts out of the seven precincts in the county. He will enter the Georgia senate as a progressive Democrat of the Woodrow Wilson type.

In addition to his many other interests, Doctor Richardson is deeply concerned in farming and on his eight hundred acres under cultivation, twenty plows are pressed into service in the preparatory seasons. He has twelve hundred acres in all, and his agricultural operations furnish employment to twenty families. He is a director in the First National Bank, owns a prosperous drug store in Montezuma, as well as other business property, and is a stockholder in a well known fertilizer company of the city.

In 1879 Doctor Richardson married Alice Cullen, the daughter of Dr. A. C. Cullen, of Sandersville, Georgia, a practicing physician of that place. Three children have been born to them: Dr. Charles Hyatt Richardson, III, a practicing physician of Macon, Georgia; Carrie, the wife of George W. Chastain, of Montezuma; and Augusta Cullen, who will graduate from Emory College in June, 1913. Doctor Richardson has one brother, C. C. Richardson, an attorney of Byron, who served as a member of the state legislature from his county for three terms, and a sister, who married Dr. C. Warren of Byron, Georgia, and who died in 1891.

DAVID WILLIAM PITTMAN. A man of mark and of recognized worth as a citizen, David W. Pittman, of Waycross, sheriff of Ware county, enjoys the confidence and esteem of his fellows to a high degree, and is filling the position to which he has been chosen with credit to himself and to the satisfaction of all. A native of Georgia, he was born December 10, 1872, in Ware county, which was likewise the birthplace of his father, Rev. Travis Pittman.

His paternal grandfather, Linsey Pittman, was born in Robinson county, North Carolina, and there "did his growing." Attaining his majority, he boldly struck out for himself, coming to Georgia and settling in Ware county, which was then a frontier region. Indians still inhabited the woods, far outnumbering the whites, and frequently terrorized the new settlers. He first purchased a tract of wild land on Kettle creek, and later bought land including the present site of the Congregational church. After improving a part of his land, he moved to the southern part of the county, and on the farm which he there bought and improved spent the remainder of his long life, passing away at the age of four score and four years.

Born in Ware county, Georgia, Travis Pittman assisted his father in the pioneer labor of redeeming a farm from the wilderness, and well remembered through his life many of the thrilling incidents of those early days. As a boy he heard the report of the guns when the Wilds family was massacred, and saw the soldiers rushing madly by in their pursuit of the fleeing savages. that having been one of the worst crimes committed by the redskins within his memory. On reaching man's estate, he bought land near the old homestead, and by dint of heroic labor cleared and improved a farm from its original wildness. In his early days, there being no railroads in this section of the country, he was forced to team all of his surplus farm productions to Centerville, and on the Saint Mary's river, forty miles away, that being the nearest market and depot of supplies. Selling his farm in 1886, he explored Florida, looking for a more promising location. After a thorough search in the more fertile parts of that state, he became convinced that Georgia had much greater advantages and resources, and came back to his native county. Purchasing land near Waresboro, he subsequently resided there until his death, in 1906.

Converted in his youth, Travis Pittman joined the Methodist Episcopal church, and having been licensed preached for some years in Ware and adjoining counties. He subsequently united with the Congregational Methodist church, which later became the Congregational church, and continued a preacher in that denomination, being for many years an earnest and zealous worker in the Master's vineyard.

Rev. Travis Pittman married Kate Mills, who was born in Milledgeville, formerly the capital of Georgia, being a daughter of Mr. and Mrs. George Mills. She is now living on the home farm, near Waresboro, where she is enjoying all the comforts of modern life. To her and her husband seventeen children were born.

An ambitious scholar when young, David W. Pittman attended the public schools of Ware county, in his thirst for knowledge oftentimes walking a distance of six miles to attend school. Assisting his father on the farm, he received an excellent training in habits of industry and economy, and when ready to begin life on his own account bought land in the vicinity of Waresboro, and was for several years actively engaged in agricultural pursuits. Removing to Waycross. he opened a grocery, which he managed for two years, and was afterwards similarly employed at Fort Meade, Florida, for a year. Returning then to his farm, which he still owns, Mr. Pittman continued general farming for some time, being quite successful as a tiller of the soil. In 1910 he was elected sheriff of Ware county and has since been a resident of Waycross.

Mr. Pittman cast his first presidential vote for William J. Bryan, and has always been a staneh adherent of the Democratic party. Fraternally he is a member of the Ancient Free and Accepted Order of Masons; of the Knights of the Modern Maccabees; and of the Woodmen of the World. Religiously both he and his wife are valued and active members of the Missionary Baptist church.

At the age of twenty-five years Mr. Pittman was united in marriage with Ida Rigdon, who was born in Waresboro, Georgia, a daughter of John and Sally (McQuaide) Rigdon, and into their home two children have been born, namely: Geneta and Bradford.

JOHN MADISON COX. A man of energy and brains, honest, efficient and progressive, John Madison Cox has been a dominant factor in the development and promotion of the mercantile prosperity of Waycross, as one of its leading merchants having the distinction of being the second to establish a wholesale grocery business in this section of Ware county. A son of James Madison Cox, he was born on February 27, 1868, in Woodville, Greene county, Georgia. His great-grandfather, Captain Stemridge Cox, a Virginian, born of Scotch-Irish ancestors, served as an officer in the Revolutionary war, having command of a company.

The grandfather of Mr. Cox, who was J. S. Cox, a life-long resident of Virginia, was not old enough to bear arms during the Revolution, but he entered the employ of the government, being engaged in the manufacture of guns in a government factory.

James Madison Cox was born and brought up in Mecklenburg county, Virginia. As a young man, seized by the Wanderlust, he migrated to Georgia, locating in Greene county, where he engaged in farming, and also in mercantile pursuits, opening a store at Woodsville. Although past military age at the breaking out of the war between the states, he enlisted during the second year of the struggle, went with his command to Virginia, where he took an active part in many battles of note. Returning to Woodville, at the close of the war, he resumed his occupation of farming and store-keeping, continuing both until well advanced in years, when he gave up all connection with business and thenceforward lived retired until his death, which came at the venerable age of ninety-two years. He married Sarah Ann Newson, who was born on a farm at Union Point, Greene county, Georgia, where her parents spent their last years. Four sons and three daughters were born of their marriage.

Obtaining his elementary knowledge in the common schools of Woodville, John Madison Cox completed his early studies at the Penfield high school, in Greene county. Industrious and self-reliant, he determined to become self-supporting, and with that object in view went to Brunswick, Glynn county, where he secured a position as traveling salesman for a wholesale house with which he was subsequently connected for eight years. Coming from there to Waycross, Mr. Cox was engaged in the brokerage business until 1901, when, realizing that this city was fast becoming a distribution point for a very large section of both Georgia and Florida, he established himself in business as a wholesale grocer, and the large trade which he now commands in that line shows conclusively that he made no mistake in the enterprise.

As a man and a citizen Mr. Cox possesses the highest regard of all who know him. An active worker in the Democratic ranks, he exerts much influence in local affairs, and for two years served ably and acceptably as mayor of Waycross. Fraternally he is a member of Waycross Lodge, No. 369, Benevolent Protective Order of Elks, and of the Knights of Pythias. He was for two years president of the Waycross board of trade.

Mr. Cox married on December 29, 1897, Miss Willella Lockhart, who was born in Opelika, Alabama, a daughter of Jesse Hamilton Lockhart. Her paternal grandfather, Richard Purycar Lockhart, was born in Virginia of colonial and revolutionary stock. Migrating to Alabama while a young man, he settled in Chambers county, becoming owner of a large plantation, which he managed successfully until his death. He married Sarah Hamilton Harris, a daughter of Judge Edmund Harris, a prominent lawyer of Lagrange, Georgia, and a granddaughter of Absolom Harris, whose father, Lieut. Benjamin Harris, was an officer in the Revolutionary war. The Harris family came from Greensville county, Virginia, to Georgia, settling in Hancock county, seven miles from Sparta. Judge Harris married Mary Rollins, who was a graduate of a Baptist college in Lagrange, and a woman of much culture and refinement.

The only child of his parents, Jesse Hamilton Lockhart, the father of Mrs. Cox, was educated in Lagrange, Georgia, and during his active career was identified with the railway service of the state, for a number of years serving as superintendent of the Louisville & Nashville Railroad. He is now living retired from active business. He married Ella Hurt, who was born in Hurtsboro, Alabama, and was educated in Georgia, having been graduated from the Wesleyan University, at Macon. She died at the early age of thirty-two years, her death occurring in Birmingham, Alabama, and her body being laid to rest in the cemetery at Auburn, Alabama. Her father, William Chappel Hurt, was born in Alabama, a son of Henry Hurt, who spent his entire life in Hurtsboro, where his ancestors settled on coming from Virginia to the South. William Chappel Hurt was a prominent and wealthy planter of Auburn, Alabama, and an active worker in the Methodist church, being especially interested in Sunday school work. He married Jane McTyeire, a sister of Holland Nimmons McTyeire, who was for many years the senior bishop of the Methodist Episcopal church, South, and from the time of the establishment of Vanderbilt University at Nashville, Tennessee, was one of its board of trustees, and lived on the university campus. Three children were born of the union of Jesse Hamilton and Ella (Hurt) Lockhart, namely: Willella, now Mrs. Cox; Jessie, the wife of G. W. Smith, of Brewton, Alabama; and Edith, the wife of Cecil Valentine Staton, of Waycross, Georgia. Mr. and Mrs. Cox are the parents of five children, as follows: John M., Jr.; Virginia Hurt, who died at the age of two years; Sarah McTyeire; William, and Elizabeth.

The wife and mother, who is one of the refined and cultured women of Waycross, received her education in the schools of Birmingham, and finished at Dr. Price's Female College at Nashville, Tennessee. Mr. and Mrs. Cox maintain a very pleasant home in which they entertain their friends with true southern hospitality, extending to them a most gracious and cordial welcome.

SIMON WOOD HITCH. An active and well-known member of the legal profession, Simon Wood Hitch has for many years been successfully engaged in the practice of law in Waycross, Ware county, where he has gained a large patronage. A son of the late Sylvanus Hitch, he was born in Clinton, Jones county, Georgia, coming on the paternal side of New England ancestry.

Born in New Bedford, Massachusetts, Sylvanus Hitch was left an orphan in childhood and was brought up in the home of his grandparents. Learning the tailor's trade in the old Bay state, he subsequently worked as a journeyman, and while yet a young man came south in search of a favorable opening. He located in Jones county, Georgia, at Clinton, which was then, although without railroad facilities of any kind, a place of considerable commercial importance, being a large cotton market. Opening a merchant tailor's establishment, he carried on business there until 1855, when he migrated to South Georgia, and purchasing a tract of land bordering on the Saint Mary's river, in Charlton county, he was employed in tilling the soil in that vicinity for ten years. Moving then to Clinch county, Georgia, he there lived retired from active business until his death, which occurred in 1880, he being seventy-two years of age at that time.

Sylvanus Hitch married Ann A. Nichols, who died in 1898, in Loudon county, Georgia, leaving seven children, as follows: Sylvanus; Simon Wood; Margaret Ann; Charles; Radford and Nannie. Her father, Simon Wood Nichols, was born in South Carolina. Coming from there to Georgia in early manhood, he was for several years a general merchant in Savannah, from there moving to Clinton, Jones county, Georgia. Instead of continuing in mercantile pursuits, he invested largely in real estate, buying extensive tracts of land in Appling, Ware and Clinch counties. Subsequently settling in Dupont, Clinch county, Mr. Nichols carried on farming for a while, but afterwards resumed mercantile business, in which he continued until his death, which came when he had attained a good old age. Mr. Nichols married Margaret Waver, who was born on one of the West India islands, of French parents, and she was a sister of John J. Waver. During one of the insurrections in the West Indies, she was carried by her parents to Savannah, Georgia, where she was brought up and educated. She survived her husband a few years.

Making good use of his time and advantages, Simon Wood Hitch attended Professor Landrum's school in Oglethorpe county, and afterward taught school in Clinch county for a few months. Desirous of entering upon a professional career, he subsequently studied law with his uncle, Congressman J. C. Nichols, and after his admission to the bar at the age of eighteen, located first in Clinch county. He later opened an office in Blackshear, Pierce county, where he practiced law for ten years. In 1887 he settled in Waycross, and in the practice of his chosen profession has here achieved well-merited success, his legal patronage being an extensive and remunerative one.

Mr. Hitch married, in Macon, Georgia, at the Wesleyan Female College, Miss Fannie Alice Myers, who was born in Augusta, Georgia. Her father, Dr. Edward Myers, was born in Orange county, New York, and was a son of Selim and Mary (Howell) Myers. Becoming a preacher in the Methodist Episcopal church, he was for a while a member of the Florida conference, later being associated with the Georgia and South Carolina conferences, and preaching in different parts of those states. For a time he was one of the professors of the Wesleyan Female Seminary, in Macon, later serving as president of that institution, an office of which he was the incumbent at the time of his daughter's marriage to the subject. Giving up that position, Doctor Myers became pastor of the Trinity Episcopal church in Savannah, Georgia. When, in 1876, yellow fever became epidemic in Savannah, he was at Cape May, attending a joint meeting of the Methodist Episcopal and the Methodist Episcopal church, South, looking to a national union. Returning to the stricken city to care for his flock, he was himself, taken ill with the disease, and lived but a short time, having given up his own life in an attempt to save others. He married Mary Mackie, who was born of Scotch ancestry, in Augusta, Georgia, where her father was for many years a banker. Mr. and Mrs. Hitch have four children, namely: Mary, the widow of Elbert P. Peabody, who has four children, Elbert P., Francis, Walton and Mary E.; Frank, who lived but twenty-one years; James, a missionary of the Methodist Episcopal church, South, to Korea; he married Reubee Lillie and has two children, Simon Herbert and Frances Elizabeth; Edward Sylvanus is the fourth child of Mr. and Mrs. Hitch. The wife and mother departed this life on November 6, 1912, after having reared to honorable manhood and womanhood her four children. In the foreign missionary work of the Methodist Episcopal church, South, she was most active, holding at the time of her death the position of conference secretary of the foreign department of the South Georgia Conference Missionary Society. She inherited her father's fine business ability and a deep religious experience made her a notable character as a wife, a mother and as a leader in all church work.

An active and influential member of the Democratic party, Mr. Hitch has served in various official positions. He was appointed by Governor Bulloch a member of the election board at the time of the three-days' election. Just following his admission to the bar he was appointed as solicitor general of the Brunswick judicial district, and served in that capacity for ten consecutive years. He has rendered appreciated service as a member of the Waycross board of education, having been a member when the present system of graded schools was adopted, and when the present fine school building was erected.

HON. JOHN MAY HOPKINS. Elected a member of the Georgia state legislature, in his twenty-second year, and thoroughly equipped for the profession of law, a business life, with its healthy problems and perplexities, has seemed to more closely appeal to him and in this field he has met with what must be gratifying success. He was born in Thomasville, Georgia, April 20, 1875, and is a son of Octavius and May Kell (Holmes) Hopkins.

The history of the Hopkins family is interesting and its earlier representatives were men of military prowess. Gen. Francis Hopkins, the great-grandfather of John May Hopkins, was a son of Rear Admiral Hopkins, of the British navy. General Hopkins commanded a regiment in the War of 1812, and to his marriage with a Miss Sears a family was born, one being named Thomas Spaulding.

Thomas Spaulding Hopkins was educated as a physician at the Charleston Medical College and during the Mexican war he served as assistant surgeon of a Georgia regiment of infantry, which was stationed at Fort Brock. After the close of the war he practiced medicine in Glynn and Wayne counties, Georgia, but when the war between the states became a fact he put aside his professional ambitions and raised a company which was known as the Wayne Rangers, of which he was commissioned captain and served as such until 1864, when he was appointed to the position of surgeon at Andersonville, Georgia. There he continued until the close of the war, when he removed to Thomasville, Georgia, where he continued the active practice of medicine and surgery for many years, his death occurring in his eighty-sixth year. He was twice married, first to Juliet Defoe, who, at death, left three children: Louise, Francis W. and Cecelia B. The second marriage of Doctor Hopkins was to Elizabeth Gignilliat, who was born at Oak Grove, near Brunswick, Georgia, and was a daughter of John May Gignilliat (who belonged to one of the old settled families of the state, and whose great-great-grandfather, Jean Francois de Gignilliat, and great-great-grandmother, Suzanne Le Sururier (Huguenot), were married in Charleston, South Carolina, in 1696). She died at the age of sixty-five years, and was the mother of the following children: Thomas W.; Octavius; James G.; Mary E.; John M., and Juliet.

Octavius Hopkins, second son of Doctor Hopkins and father of John May Hopkins, was reared and educated in Thomasville and at the age of twenty-one years embarked in the lumber business in which he continued his active interest at Darien, Georgia, until 1911, when he removed his field of operations to Wilmington, North Carolina, where he now operates a handle factory on an extensive scale. He married May Kell Holmes, who is a daughter of James and Susan (Clapp) Holmes. The father of Mrs. Hopkins, Dr. James Holmes, was a physician of McIntosh county, Georgia, born in Liberty county, Georgia, and of the Holmes family of Massachusetts. Her mother, who was born at Boston, Massachusetts, was a daughter of Derastus Clapp, and his wife Susannah (Bowditch) Clapp. Susannah Bowditch was descendant in the sixth generation of John Alden and Priscilla Mullins. Derastus Clapp was a lineal descendant in the seventh generation, from Roger Clapp, who came to America in 1630. He was born in New Hampshire and in early manhood went to Boston, Massachusetts. He was captain of a militia company and a member of the Ancient and Honorable Artillery. Thomas Clapp, who was president of Yale College for twenty-seven years, beginning 1739, was descendant of Roger Clapp's brother, Thomas. Five children were born to Octavius Hopkins and wife: John May; James Holmes; Thomas Spaulding; Lucile Clark, and Octavius, Jr.

John May Hopkins was educated at Thomasville in a branch school affiliated with the Georgia State University, and after completing his course in that institution, engaged in the study of law and subsequently was admitted to the bar. Although thus qualified, Mr. Hopkins practiced but a short time, having become interested in another direction. He was in charge of a survey party that explored the Okefenokee swamp and made surveys and estimated the amount, condition and quality of timber. After completing this survey he went to northern Michigan to gain a practical knowledge of the lumber business, entering the employ of Charles Hebard & Sons, lumber company, at their plant in Baraga county, Michigan, and remained there until 1908, when he returned to Georgia to establish the plant of The Hebard Cypress Company, at Hebardville, two miles from Waycross, in Ware county, and here installed one of the most complete plants of the kind in the whole country. This is a stupendous enterprise, 750 men being constantly employed, and the mills having a capacity of 125,000 feet of lumber per day of ten hours. Of this plant Mr. Hopkins is the general superintendent, and additionally he is general superintendent of the Waycross & Southern Railroad.

Mr. Hopkins was married first in February, 1913, to Miss Lily Schmidt Payne, who was born at Darien, Georgia, a daughter of W. H. Payne, and died in November, 1909. In June, 1911, Mr. Hopkins was married second to Miss Emily Walker, who was born at Fort Smith, Arkansas, and is a daughter of Alexander Walker, who was a resident of New Orleans, Louisiana. Mr. Hopkins had two children born to his first marriage: John May, Jr., and Lily Payne. Mr. and Mrs. Hopkins are members of Grace Episcopal church at Waycross. Through birth, rearing, education and association, Mr. Hopkins is a Democrat in his political attitude and that he should have been chosen as a state representative so early in his political career indicates a large measure of public confidence. He is identified fraternally with Damascus Commandery, No. 18, Waycross, Georgia.

HON. JAMES J. SLADE. Prominent and noteworthy among the talented, cultured and enterprising men who are, or have been in times past, identified with the educational, agricultural and business advancement of western Georgia, is Hon. James J. Slade, of Columbus, Muscogee county, who for many years was widely known as a popular and successful teacher. A son of Thomas B. Slade, a noted educator, he was born April 28, 1831, in Jones county, Georgia, coming from patriotic stock, his paternal great-grandfather, who was a life-long resident of North Carolina, having served as a soldier in the Revolutionary war.

Jeremiah Slade, his grandfather, was born on a farm in Martin county, North Carolina, and was there brought up and educated. Becoming a tiller of the soil from choice, though an attorney by profession, he succeeded to the ownership of the old home plantation, which was located six miles north of Williamston, and bordered on the Roanoke river, the locality being known as Marshpoint. There he spent his entire life, carrying on farming with slave help. His wife, whose maiden name was Janet Bog, was likewise a life-long resident of North Carolina. Of their union seven children were born and reared, as follows: Alfred, who became prominent in public affairs, was appointed United States consul to Buenos Ayres, and there died while in office; Jeremiah, although an expert swimmer, was drowned in the Roanoke river in early manhood; William succeeded to the ownership of the home plantation, and there spent his entire life; Thomas B., Mr. Slade's father; James, the youngest son, a physician, was appointed a surgeon in the United States army during the Mexican war, and died in Mexico during the war; Mary, the oldest daughter, married Dr. Pleasant Henderson; and Elizabeth, who became the wife of Mason L. Wiggins, of Halifax, North Carolina.

The birth of Thomas B. Slade occurred in Martin county, North Carolina, on the same plantation as did that of his father. Fitted for college at a preparatory school in Chapel Hill, North Carolina, he was subsequently graduated from the University of North Carolina, and was admitted to the bar. Locating soon after in Clinton, Jones county, Georgia, he began the practice of his profession. At the earnest solicitation of friends, however, he retired from the law and opened a school for girls in Clinton, where he met with great success as a teacher. He afterwards accepted the chair of philosophy in the Macon Female College, now the Wesleyan Female College, at Macon, and held the position until Bishop Pierce severed his connection with that institution. He then resigned his position, and for two years taught in a female college in Penfield, Georgia. Coming then to Columbus, Muscogee county, he established a female school, which he conducted successfully until the outbreak of the war between the states. Locating on his farm in Alabama after the close of the conflict, he remained there a few years and then returned to Columbus, and here continued his residence until his death, at the venerable age of eighty-two years.

The maiden name of the wife of Thomas B. Slade was Ann Jacqueline Blount. She was born in Washington, North Carolina, a daughter of James Blount, who migrated from his native state to Georgia and settled permanently in Blountsville, Clinton county. She survived her husband, attaining the advanced age of eighty-six years. She reared a family of eleven children, as follows: Janet E.; Mary; Anna; James J.; Emma; Thomas; Martha; Stella; Helen; John, and Fanny.

An ambitious student when young, James J. Slade prepared for college under his father's tuition, and in 1848 entered the University of North Carolina, from which he was graduated in 1852, with an excellent record not only for scholarship, but for promptness, having, like his father, never missed a roll call while there. Fitted for a professional career, Mr. Slade then taught school in Columbus for four years, and having in the meantime been admitted to the bar subsequently there practiced law for three years. Going then to Louisiana, he bought a plantation near Delhi, and managed it for a time with the assistance of slaves. At the breaking out of the Civil war he raised a company, of which he was elected captain, and took the entire company to camp and offered it to Governor Moore, who said that he could not accept the company, as already there were more men enlisted than were needed, and added that the war would soon be over. The company therefore returned to Delhi and disbanded. Soon after, Mr. Slade went back to his old home in Columbus, Georgia, and enlisted in Company A, Tenth Georgia Volunteer Infantry, and went with his command to Virginia. With the army of North Virginia he took part in the invasion of Maryland and in the battle of Antietam. Being taken ill after the last engagement, he was granted a furlough. On recovering his strength he was placed on detached duty, working between the western and eastern armies. Wool was then very much needed to make clothes for the soldiers and there was an ample supply in Texas. Quantities of it were started north in wagons, which were invariably captured by the Federals before it was taken across the Mississippi. Mr. Slade devised a means by which it might have been safely and surely transported to its point of destination, but the war terminated before his plan was put into execution. He was in Shreveport, Louisiana, when the war closed, and went immediately with his negroes to his plantation.

Deciding a short time later to return to Georgia, this being in 1866, he resumed his first occupation, that of a teacher, opening an independent school, which became an immediate success, and which he conducted until 1888, it being one of the leading institutions of the kind in this section of the state. He then embarked in the insurance business, in which he was also quite successful.

In 1878 Mr. Slade purchased from the General Benning's estate the Seaborn Jones homestead, which he has since owned and occupied. Located at Saint Elmo, two and one-half miles from the court house, it is a typical southern plantation home. The house, a commodious frame structure, sits well back from the street, and is surrounded by large shade trees.

Mr. Slade has been twice married. He married first Annie Graham, who was born in northern Georgia, a daughter of John Graham. She passed to the life beyond and her only child died in infancy. Mr. Slade married second Miss Leila B. Bonner, who was born in Columbus, Georgia, a daughter of Seymour K. and Marion (Huguenin) Bonner. Ten children have blessed the union of Mr. and Mrs. Slade, namely: William B.; Mary Janet; Thomas B.; Nora H.; Louisa; Marion; Charles; Effie May; Florence, and Seymour. William B. married Mary Brown, and they have four children, Roberta, Rhodes, Mary and Leila. Thomas, who married Miss Thirza Kirven, has two sons, Kirven and Thomas. Nora, wife of R. H. Scriven, six children, Leila, James, Nora, Maude, Thomas, and Marion. Louisa, wife of Dr. Theophilus West, has two sons, Slade and Marion. Charles married Miss Constance Thill and they have three children, Blount, Suzanne and William. Effie May, wife of

J. Lawrence Dozier, has four children, Anna, Lawrence, Florence and Seymour. Seymour Slade, the youngest son of the family, died in early, manhood.

Always taking a keen interest in anything pertaining to the public welfare, Mr. Slade has served as a member of the city council, and has twice had the distinction of being elected to the mayor's chair. He is a member of the Order of Cincinnati. Both Mr. and Mrs. Slade are members of the Missionary Baptist church, to which his parents also belonged, and in which his father was a licensed preacher.

ALEXANDER SHAW PENDLETON. One of the prominent commercial men of southern Georgia is Alexander Shaw Pendleton, a wholesale grocer at Valdosta, in whose veins is mingled the blood of several of of the South's leading families and whose lineal connections reveal the names of many able men, some of high position in government, others leaders in military affairs, and a number who have become eminent in professional life, especially in the field of literature. The Pendletons were originally an old and honored family of Norwich, Lancashire, England. The American branch originated with Philip Pendleton, who was born in England in 1650 and came to America in 1674. After six years here, or in 1682, he returned to England but later turned once more toward the New World and took up his residence in King and Queen county, Virginia. He married a Miss Isabella Hart, or Hurt, and died in 1721. Henry [2] Pendleton was a son of Philip [1] Pendleton, the emigrant, and the father of James [3] Pendleton. Henry [2] Pendleton was born in 1683 in Caroline county, Virginia, and died there in 1721, the same year his father died. Henry [2] Pendleton married, 1701, Mary Taylor, daughter of James [1] Taylor and Mary Gregory, his wife, ancestors of President Zachary Taylor. Their son, James Pendleton, was the great-great-grandfather of Alexander Shaw Pendleton, whose name introduces this review. James Pendleton, born in Virginia and a life-long resident of that commonwealth, served as high sheriff of Culpeper county in 1738. He married Elizabeth Clayton and their son, Capt. Philip Pendleton, born in Caroline county, Virginia, in 1732, was the next lineal ancestor of our subject. He commanded a company in the Revolutionary war and a valued heirloom in this family is the old Bible in which is preserved a record of his services as a patriot. He and his wife, Martha Aubrey, both life-long residents of Virginia, were the parents of Coleman Pendleton, the grandfather of our subject. Coleman Pendleton, born in Culpeper county, Virginia, August 4, 1780, migrated to Georgia and became an early settler in Putnam county, where he resided many years. Late in life he removed to Alabama and spent his last years in Tallapoosa county of that state, passing away there on May 31, 1862. He was married June 6, 1808, to Martha Gilbert, a daughter of Captain Benjamin and Hannah (Butler) Gilbert. They were married in 1779 in Bedford county, Virginia. Captain Gilbert entered the Revolution as a private in the command of Col. Charles Harrison, who served under General Washington, and in 1778 he was promoted to a captaincy. He was severely wounded at the battle of Monmouth, New Jersey, where his ankle was shattered by a musket ball, and as evidence of his valorous services during that great struggle for liberty he bore to his grave scars of wounds inflicted by British sabres. Coleman and Martha (Gilbert) Pendleton reared three sons and two daughters. The sons were William, who died in young manhood; Edmund, a well-known writer in his younger days, who successively became a successful physician, a professor of agriculture in the State University of Georgia, and finally late in life a wealthy manufacturer at Atlanta, Georgia; and Philip Coleman, the father of our subject.

Philip Coleman Pendleton was born in 1812 in Eatonton, Putnam county, Georgia, and for many years was prominently connected with the press of Georgia. Associated for a time with C. R. Hanleiter in the publication of the *Southern Post* at Macon, he severed his connection with that paper in 1836 to serve in the war against the Seminole Indians in Florida. About 1840, with Rev. George F. Pierre, afterward a bishop in the Methodist Episcopal church, he began the publication of the *Southern Ladies' Book* in Macon, but later changed the name of the periodical to that of *The Magnolia* and published it first in Savannah, Georgia, and then later in Charleston, South Carolina. Upon ceasing the publication of *The Magnolia*, which was the first magazine ever published south of Richmond, Virginia, he took up the practice of law in Sandersville, Georgia, and also published the *Central Georgian* until 1857, when he removed to Ware county and there bought a large tract of wire grass land which included the present site of Waycross, Georgia. He named his estate "Tebeau," after his wife's family name, and here he gave himself up wholly to agricultural pursuits for a few years. In the great issue between the South and the North he did not favor secession, but when war had actually begun he responded to the call of the Southland, enlisted for its service and was made captain of his company. When the Fiftieth Georgia Regiment was organized he was elected a major and served in that capacity through several of the Virginia campaigns. In 1863 he was obliged to resign on account of ill health. Disposing of his estate in Ware county, he then removed to Lowndes county, where he purchased a farm ten miles south of Valdosta. In 1867 he began the publication of the *Southern Georgia Times*, which he continued until his death in 1869 as a result of injuries received when thrown from a carriage. While living in Savannah he married Miss Catherine Tebeau, daughter of Frederick E. Tebeau, and a descendant of James Tebeau, one of the first settlers in Savannah. John, the son of James Tebeau, just mentioned, married Catharine Treutlen, daughter of Frederick Treutlen. The Tebeaus were French and the Treutlens were English. Frederick Treutlen was a native of Holland, but for political reasons fled that country with his wife and two sons, John Adam and Frederick, locating in London, England, where they resided a few years and where the wife and mother died. From there the father and his two sons embarked for America, but France and England being at war at that time, their vessel was captured by the French and all on board were taken to France and put in prison. There the father died. The sons were released after several months and returned to England, whence they once more turned toward the New World. Landing on St. Simons island, off the central coast of Georgia, they made their way from there to Savannah, where they arrived about two years after Governor Oglethorpe first settled there. The son John Adam finally settled in Effingham county and was governor of Georgia from May, 1777, to January, 1778. Frederick Treutlen, the other son, married Margaret Schadd, daughter of Col. Solomon Schadd, who settled on Wilmington island at the mouth of the Savannah river, in a very early day. His estate is still in the possession of descendants of his and the house which he built there in 1748 is said to be the oldest building yet remaining in Georgia. Frederick and Margaret (Schadd) Treutlen were the parents of Catherine, the wife of John Tebeau, who was a son of James, the early settler in Savannah, and father of Frederick E. Tebeau, the maternal grandfather of our subject. To Philip Coleman and Catherine (Tebeau) Pendleton were born the following children: William F.; James A.; Philip C.; Chas. R. Pendleton; Emline T.; Mary Z.; Louis B., and Nathaniel D., of whom James and Philip are deceased. William F. Pendleton, the eldest son, a captain of the Fiftieth Georgia Regiment during the Civil war, served three years and participated in nine of the hard fought battles of that conflict as well as in a number of minor engagements. He is now a bishop in the Swedenborgian church. Charles Rittenhouse Pendleton, who is well known throughout Georgia as the editor of the Macon *Telegraph,* ranks among the best journalists of our country and is well known for his independent views on political issues and for his fearless advocacy of them. Louis Beauregard Pendleton is a well known author and some of his novels and juveniles have been translated into four different languages. Nathaniel D. Pendleton is a minister in the Swedenborgian church.

Alexander Shaw Pendleton was born at Sandersville, Washington county, Georgia, March 17, 1855. He was educated at Valdosta Institute, Valdosta, Georgia, and after his father's death assisted his elder brother in the office of the Valdosta *Times* for a while. In 1873, then a youth of eighteen, he began his independent business career by opening a small grocery store at Valdosta, small because his means were very limited. His business steadily prospered and increased until 1897, when it had reached those proportions justifying a more effective business arrangement and one that would permit the business to branch out along more extensive lines. For this purpose there was organized The H. S. Pendleton Company, a wholesale grocery company, of which Mr. Pendleton has been president from the time of its organization to the present. He is a man of business ability and has not only achieved a gratifying personal success but has built up one of the most prosperous business enterprises of his city. Aside from his commercial interests he is interested in real estate and both agriculture and horticulture. At his city home he has a tract of five acres that is devoted to the raising of vegetables and fruits and he also owns a farm of one hundred acres located but a short distance from Valdosta.

In November, 1881, Mr. Pendleton was united in marriage to Susan Parramore, who was born in Thomasville, Georgia, a daughter of Noah Parramore and a granddaughter of John and Nancy (Brinson) Parramore. Noah Parramore was for some time an extensive farmer in Thomas county, Georgia, but after the war removed to a farm he purchased in Lowndes county, where he continued to reside until his death. His wife was Susan Dasher, a daughter of Christian and Elizabeth (Waldtheur) Dasher. Mr. and Mrs. Pendleton have six children living, namely: Philip Coleman; Elizabeth P.; Gertrude A.; Albert O.; Frederick W. and Alexis R. Francis, the sixth child in order of birth, died at the age of twenty. Their oldest son, Philip C., married Susan Hickey Corner and has two children, Catherine and Elizabeth; and Gertrude, their second daughter, is now the wife of Charles I. Harrell. Mr. Pendleton is a member of the Swedenborgian church and Mrs. Pendleton is affiliated with the Church of Christ.

THOMAS JEROME HART. Conspicuous among the active and enterprising men who settled in Dawson while it was yet a small village, and who became an important factor in developing and advancing its manufacturing and mercantile prosperity, was the late Thomas Jerome Hart, whose death on January 25, 1904, removed from the city one of its most respected and esteemed business men. Mr. Hart was born in Tuscumbia, Alabama, December 1, 1827, coming from honored New England stock.

His father, Thomas Jerome Hart, Sr., was born in Connecticut, of early English ancestry. When a young man he migrated to Alabama, settling in Tuscumbia, where he was engaged in manufacturing until his death, a few years later. He married Susan Allen, who was of Virginian ancestry. She was quite young when left a widow, with three small children, Thomas Jerome, the subject of this sketch; William; and Robert. Robert died unmarried. William, who died in early life, left a family, and his descendants are now living in Alabama.

Brought up and educated in Alabama, Thomas Jerome Hart served an apprenticeship at the carriage-maker's trade, making excellent use of his native mechanical ability. Subsequently locating in Dawson, Georgia, he established a carriage factory in the village, and subsequently erected the first brick building in the place. Making a specialty of manufacturing buggies, the products of his factory found a ready sale, and he became known far and wide as the manufacturer of the "Hart Buggy," which was recognized as the very best in the market. Successful from the start, Mr. Hart continued in active business in Dawson until called from the scene of his earthly labors to the life beyond.

Mr. Hart was twice married. He married first, soon after coming to Dawson, Sally Lassater, a native of Sumter county, Georgia. Her father, David Lassater, presumably a native of Jasper county, moved from there to Sumter county in pioneer days, and having purchased land near Plains carried on farming with slave help. Mr. Lassater married Elizabeth Asbury Speer, who died November 4, 1861, leaving eleven children, as follows: John H.; Martha G.; William F.; James A.; Amanda A., wife of Bynum H. Hood, of whom a brief personal record may be found on another page of this work; Simeon M.; Jeremiah C.; Henry F.; Margaret J.; Mary E.; and Sarah C., more familiarly known among her friends as "Sally." Mrs. Sally Hart died at an early age, leaving one son, Willie, who died in early manhood.

Mr. Hart married second, September 4, 1890, Mrs. Mattie (Harris) Keith, who was born in Terrell county, Georgia, a daughter of Edmond Jackson Harris and granddaughter of Edmond Harris, a pioneer settler of La Grange, Troup county. Edmond Jackson Harris was born in La Grange, and having received excellent educational advantages was admitted while young to the bar. Instead of entering upon a professional career, he chose the more peaceful pursuit of agriculture. Locating in Terrell county soon after its organization, he bought a tract of land lying twelve miles east of Dawson, and began its improvement. During the war between the states he served in the Confederate army, through exposure and privations while a soldier losing his health, and never fully recovering his former physical vigor. At the close of the war he sold his plantation and purchased land a mile and a half west of Dawson. For a while thereafter he was engaged in the warehouse business in Dawson, but he maintained his residence on the farm until his death, at the age of seventy-two years. The maiden name of the wife of Edmond Jackson Harris was Martha Ann Bryan, who was born in Thomas county, Georgia, of pioneer ancestry, her parents, Loverd and Edith (Wytch) Bryan, having been the first couple married in Thomas county, while her grandfather, Clement Bryan, was one of the first settlers of that county. She died at the age of seventy-five years, having outlived her husband. She reared eight children, as follows: Edmond S.; Mary Elizabeth, who became the first wife of John W. Peddy, and the mother of Mrs. Lee Clark Hoyl; Susan R.; Goodwin Hall; Mattie, now Mrs. Hart; Clare E.; Theo. Jackson; and Clementine Bryan.

Mattie Harris, now Mrs. Hart, married first Robert Anson Keith, who was born in Dalton, Georgia, a son of John W. Keith, who came to Terrell county many years ago, and having purchased land lying a mile west of Dawson resided there until his death. Robert Anson Keith was reared and educated in north Georgia. Coming to Georgia with his father, he became associated with him in the ownership of the land they bought, and in its management, living on the home farm until his death, which occurred three weeks after his marriage with Miss Harris. Mrs. Keith subsequently married, as previously stated, Mr. Hart. Of the union of Mr. and Mrs. Hart two children were born, namely: Thomas Jerome Hart and Edmund Harris Hart. Mr. Hart was reared an Episcopalian, but while a resident of Dawson attended the Methodist Episcopal church, of which Mrs. Hart is a member.

JEREMIAH CALVIN CARTER. A substantial and prosperous planter of Americus, and a successful manufacturer, Jeremiah Calvin Carter is numbered among the esteemed and useful citizens of Sumter county, where a large part of his life has been spent. A son of the late L. B. Walker Carter, he was born April 4, 1855, in that part of Warren county, Georgia, now included within the limits of Glascock county. His grandfather, Wiley Carter, was a son of James Carter, of whose history very little is known excepting the fact that he was a pioneer settler of Warren county, Georgia, and that he died at the home of one of his sons, in Quebec, Schley county, at a ripe old age.

Wiley Carter removed from Warren county to Schley county, where he purchased a large tract of land, which he operated with the help of slaves, and on the plantation which he improved spent the remainder of his life of three score and ten years.

L. B. Walker Carter was born on the home farm in Warren county, obtaining his education in the district schools. Coming to Sumter county in 1859, he located on land belonging to his father, situated near the present site of Bagley Station, and on which a few improvements had been previously made, a few acres of the tract having been cleared, and a log house having been erected. With the assistance of slaves, he continued the improvements already inaugurated and had placed a large part of the land under cultivation when his labors were interrupted by the breaking out of the Civil war. Enlisting then in Cutt's Battalion, he went with his command to Virginia, and subsequently was an active participant in many of the more important battles waged during the conflict, including those at Fredericksburg and Gettysburg, and the numerous engagements in and around Richmond and Petersburg, being at Appomattox at the final surrender. Returning home from there, he resumed farming, and continued in his free and independent ocenpation until his death, in 1873. The maiden name of his wife was Mary Ann Seals. She was born in Warren county, where her father, William Archibald Seals, was an early settler. Mr. Seals improved a water power on Rock Comfort creek, and in addition to managing a large plantation with slave labor owned and operated a large merchant flour mill, continuing a resident of that county until his death, in 1863. He married Eliza Ann Harris, who survived him several years. Mrs. Mary Ann (Seals) Carter outlived her husband but four days. Four children were born of their union, as follows: Jeremiah Calvin, of whom we write; Annie, now deceased, married N. A. Ray; William A., deceased; and N. I., wife of D. A. Jenkins.

As a small boy, Jeremiah Calvin Carter attended first the rural schools, afterwards being a pupil in the public schools of Americus. He received a practical training in agriculture while young, and at the age of eighteen years, being industrious and self-reliant, he began farming on his own account. He succeeded to the ownership of one-half of the parental homestead, the other half being in the possession of his brother-in-law, to whom he subsequently sold his share. As an agriculturist Mr. Carter has met with exceptional good success, owning upwards of sixteen hundred acres in Sumter county, Georgia, and having valuable tracts of lands in both Orange and Gadsden counties, Florida. Mr. Carter's sons manage his Sumter county farms, which are devoted to general farming, while his Florida lands are especially devoted to the culture of tobacco. In 1900 Mr. Carter established a cigar factory in Americus, and has since built up a good business in that line of industry.

On January 4, 1883, Mr. Carter was united in the holy bonds of matrimony with Mittie C. Wallace, who was born in Sumter county, a daughter of John B. and Eleanor W. Wallace. Mr. and Mrs. Carter are the parents of ten children, namely: John W.; Eleanor Brownie; William Edgar; Mamie; Walter G.; Calvin; Sallie Estelle; Otis; Oscar; and Nathaniel. Both Mr. and Mrs. Carter are members of the Methodist Episcopal church.

JAMES A. DAVENPORT. A man of pronounced ability, intelligence and much enterprise, James A. Davenport is numbered among the successful business men of Americus, and is a worthy representative of its native-born citizens, his birth having occurred in this city. He is a son of the late Col. Walter and Mary (Frederick) Davenport, and a brother of Daniel F. Davenport, in whose sketch, which appears elsewhere in this volume, further parental and ancestral history may be found.

Obtaining his preliminary education in the public schools of Americus, James A. Davenport was subsequently graduated from Bryant & Stratton's Business College, in Baltimore, 1874. Returning home he was afterwards for a time engaged in the drug trade with his father and brother, but for several years has carried on an extensive and highly remunerative business as an insurance agent, representing many large and well-known companies.

Mr. Davenport married October 23, 1895, Miss Chloe Belle White, who was born in Albany, Dougherty county, Georgia. Her father, John J. White, a Virginian by birth and breeding, entered the Confederate service while a boy in his teens, and served as a courier on the staff of Gen. Robert E. Lee. Subsequently coming to Sumter county, Georgia, he located at Albany, and purchasing a nearby plantation resided there a number of years. Going then to Chicago and St. Louis, he was there engaged in the brokerage business until his death. His wife, whose maiden name was Dora Hutchinson, was a native of Kentucky. Mr. and Mrs. Davenport are the parents of five children, namely: Catherine; James; Gertrude; Chloe Belle; and Virginia.

Public-spirited and actively interested in local affairs, Mr. Davenport has rendered excellent service as an alderman, and as a director of the Carnegie public library. Fraternally he is a member of Council Lodge, No. 95, Free and Accepted Masons; of Wells Chapter, Royal Arch Masons; and of DeMolay Commandery, Knights Templar.

LAURENCE JEFFERSON BLALOCK. Possessing a large measure of veritable talent, a distinctive intellectuality, and keen mental powers. Laurence Jefferson Blalock, of Americus, is a distinguished member of the Sumter county bar, and one of the leading criminal lawyers of Georgia, his success being due to a systematic application of his abilities to the profession of his choice. A son of Rev. David Blalock, he was born in Louisville, Jefferson county, Georgia, of pioneer stock, his paternal grandparents, natives of South Carolina, having been among the early settlers of Wilkes county, Georgia.

Rev. David Blalock was born, it is thought, in Wilkes county, and as a young man embarked in mercantile pursuits in Augusta, Georgia. Uniting with the Methodist Episcopal church in early manhood, he became a preacher in that denomination, and having, in 1850, joined the Georgia Methodist Episcopal conference held pastorates in different localities. In 1867 the state was divided, and he became a member of the South Georgia Conference, and remained active in the ministry until his death, which occurred in Americus, in 1881, at the age of seventy-two years. The maiden name of his wife was Mary Lalledstedcd. She was born in Augusta, of French Huguenot ancestry, and died at the age of fifty years, leaving four children, namely: Emma; Laura; Laurence J.; and Mary.

Acquiring his education in the different places in which his father was settled as a minister, Laurence J. Blalock began earning his living at the age of eighteen years, and for four years was in the employ of the Houston & Texas Central Railroad Company, being located in Texas. Returning then to Georgia, he was engaged in business at Americus as a general merchant for two years. His tastes and ambitions leading him to choose a professional career, Mr. Blalock then began the study of law, for which he was well adapted, and in October, 1875, was admitted to the bar. Locating in Americus, he met with encouraging success from the start, and now holds high rank among the foremost lawyers of the state, his specialty of criminal law having brought him into prominence in legal circles, and won for him an enviable reputation for professional skill and ability.

Mr. Blalock married in 1875, Mary A. Cobb, who was born in Americus, a daughter of Joseph A. Cobb, of whom further account is given elsewhere in this volume. Fraternally Mr. Blalock is a member of Americus Lodge, No. 13, Ancient Free and Accepted Order of Masons, of which he is past master; a member and 'past high priest of Wells Chapter, No. 42, Royal Arch Masons; and a member, and past noble grand of Sumter Lodge, Independent Order of Odd Fellows.

PRESTON B. WILLIFORD. A man of excellent business tact and judgment, Preston B. Williford, of Americus, is widely known throughout Sumter county as a dealer in city and farm property. A son of John Williford, he was born on a farm in Stewart county, Georgia, where his boyhood days were passed. His grandfather, William Williford, was, as far as known, a life-long resident of north Georgia. To him and his wife five children were born and reared, as follows: John; Henry; Samuel; Rachael; and another daughter.

A native of Madison county, Georgia, John Williford was there brought up on a farm, and while young was well drilled in the various branches of agriculture. Removing to Stewart county in early manhood, he purchased a tract of land, the greater part of which was covered with a heavy growth of pine, ash, and hickory timber. Putting up a small log cabin for himself and wife, he began the pioneer task of hewing a farm from the wilderness. Laboring with indomitable energy and perseverance, he met with very satisfactory success in his operations, being enabled in the course of a few years to erect a substantial set of frame buildings in place of the log structures that for a time answered the purpose of sheltering the family and the stock. He had cleared a goodly part of the land when his earthly labors were brought to an end, his death occuring in 1860, when he was but forty-four years of age.

The maiden name of the wife of John Williford was Elizabeth Allen Burke. She was born in Elbert county, Georgia, a daughter of William

P. Burke, and died at the age of seventy-six years, the latter part of her life having been spent with her children. Left a widow, in 1860, with twelve small children, the youngest but two years old, she assumed management of the home farm, carrying it on with great success, and keeping her family together until all were self-supporting. She reared five daughters and seven sons, as follows: Ann; Sarah; William; Mary; Henry; Louisa; John; Luther; Joseph; James; Preston B.; and Elizabeth.

The youngest son, and eleventh child, of the parental household, Preston B. Williford lived with his widowed mother until he was sixteen years old, when he went to Green Hill, in Stewart county, where he was for three years clerk in a general store. Returning then to the homestead, he assisted in its management for four years, after which he bought a farm five miles from his old home, and was there engaged in farming for a year. Going from there to Columbus, Muscogee county, Mr. Williford was clerk in a cotton warehouse for six years. On giving up that position, he was engaged in the retail shoe business in Americus until 1896, when he began selling real estate on commission, an industry in which he has since continued, being now an extensive dealer in city and farm property.

March 26, 1878, Mr. Williford was united in marriage with Sarah Matthews, who was born in Marion county, Georgia, a daughter of John L. and Frances J. (Herndon) Matthews. Of the union of Mr. and Mrs. Williford, four children have been born, namely: Amzie; Fannie Mae; Preston B., Jr.; and Lousie Mildred. Angie married Ralph Newton, and they have one child, Elizabeth Newton. Mr. and Mrs. Williford are members of the First Baptist church.

REV. WILLIAM WASHINGTON WEBB. The prosperity and advancement of a community depend upon the social character and public spirit of its members, and in every prosperous town or country center will be found citizens who take the leadership and give their energies not alone to their own well-being but to the things that mean better and fuller life for all. Such a citizen at Hahira in Lowndes county has Mr. W. W. Webb been recognized for a number of years.

William Washington Webb, who represents an old and prominent south Georgia family, was born on a plantation in Dooly county, the 6th of August, 1853. His father was John Webb, born in that portion of Washington county now Johnson county. The grandfather was Giles Webb, who it is thought was a native of North Carolina. According to a well authenticated family tradition, the father of Giles, known as General Webb, was an associate and traveling companion of John Wesley during his American tour. Grandfather Giles Webb came to Georgia and became a pioneer of Washington county, which at that time comprised a great scope of country in central Georgia. He bought a lot of land in what is now Johnson county, and with the aid of his slaves cleared and improved it into a fine plantation, where he was engaged in general farming until his death. He married a Miss Askue, and she survived him until 1861. The names of their five children were William, Thomas, Giles, John and Eli. Of these, Thomas and Giles died before the war, William died while a prisoner of war at Point Lookout, and Eli went through four years of service without wounds or capture.

John Webb, the father, after being reared to manhood in his native county, purchased land in Dooly county and was engaged in general farming there with slave labor up to the time of the war. As a Georgia soldier he participated in the defense of Atlanta and was so severely wounded that he lost a leg. As soon as he was able he returned home,, Having sold in 1868 his interests in Dooly county and also part of the where he was convalescing when the end of the great struggle came. old homestead in Johnson county, he settled in Lowndes county in 1869. He located here before the era of modern development had begun, and was able to buy seven hundred acres three miles southwest of the present site of Hahira for the sum of five hundred dollars. His first home was a log house, and he had to haul the lumber for floor and doors from the nearest sawmill, twenty-five miles away. By the continuous labor of years he improved a large part of this land, erected good buildings, and resided there until his death at the age of seventy-six in 1898.

John Webb married Elizabeth Lamb, who was a native of Houston county, this state, and a daughter of Luke and Mary (Burnham) Lamb. Luke Lamb was a son of Arthur Lamb, and both were born in North Carolina. Elijah Burnham, the father of Mary, was a native of North Carolina, and both the Lamb and Burnham families were pioneers of Houston county, Georgia, where they settled in 1826. Luke and Mary Lamb had the following children: Washington, Elizabeth, Mary Ann, Solomon and Laura. Mrs. John Webb, whose death occurred in 1900, was the mother of the following children: William W., of this sketch; Luke Lamb; Laura, who married J. B. Miley; John E.; Lula, who married Thomas Folsom; Eli D.; Harriet, who married John L. Redding; Thomas W., and Charles W.

William W. Webb was about eight years old when the war between the states was precipitated. That conflict swept away nearly all his father's wealth, and as a consequence all the boys had to work, and little opportunity was afforded for the education and advantages to which families of their position were accustomed. But he was able to get considerable knowledge in the neighboring schools, and the lack of earlier years his subsequent industry has largely supplied. While a youth he learned the trade of blacksmith, and that was his regular occupation for some years. In 1876 he established a business of his own at Thomasville, and conducted it four years. In the meantime he bought land three miles from the present town of Hahira, his four years at the forge giving him the money to pay for this property, and in 1881 he began his career as an independent farmer. For ten years he resided on his country place and did well in general farming, and in fact has been one of the enterprising agriculturists of this county ever since, directing his farm from his residence in town. In 1891 he moved to Hahira, where he has taken a very important part in the town life and activities.

Mr. Webb has been a member of the town council, and upwards of twenty years has served on the town board of education, and at the present time is also a member of the county board of education. Partly owing to his own early deprivations in schooling and also to his public-spirited interest in all that concerns the general welfare, he has devoted himself earnestly to the provisions for public education. To his efforts as much as to the efforts of any other citizen, the town is indebted for its present admirable school system. The Hahira schools are absolutely free to all, and in efficiency they are probably not surpassed in any town of the size in Georgia. His influence and efforts contributed in great measure to the erection of the present school building at a cost of twenty thousand dollars. Mr. Webb was also for some years a member of the Farmers Alliance, and was one of the promoters and still a useful member of the Farmers Union. He is president of the Georgia, Alabama & Western Railroad Company.

Mr. Webb was reared in the Methodist faith, and in 1895 was ordained a local preacher. He has been active in the ministry ever since. A fluent and forceful speaker, both in the pulpit and on social occasions he has used his talent for the advancement of righteousness and better ideals in his community. Mr. Webb has served eighteen years as worshipful master of Hahira Lodge, No. 346, F. & A. M., and is a member of Valdosta Chapter, R. A. M., and the Valdosta Commandery, K. T., having filled chairs in both these branches of Masonry. Another important public service by which he is perhaps best known to the citizens of Hahira is his management of the local postoffice, his duties as postmaster having been continuous since 1891.

In 1874 Mr. Webb was united in marriage with Miss Sarah Jane Vickers. Mrs. Webb was born in Lowndes county, a daughter of Henry and Malinda Vickers. They are the parents of seven children, named Solomon Wesley, Valeta, Henrietta, Ira E., Frankie Elizabeth, Minnie Lee and John A. Solomon W. married Lucy Lawson, and their four children are Willie Briggs, Louise, Roger and Dennis. Valeta is the wife of G. K. Johnson, and has two children, Emmett and Ira Edgar. Henrietta is the wife of M. M. Parish. Ira E. married Mattie Rowntree and has two children, Carrie Lou and Eugene. Frankie E. is the wife of Henry B. Lawson, and their children are Lillian, Hollis E. and Blanford. Minnie L. is the wife of Turner Folsom.

IVEY P. CRUTCHFIELD, as architect and builder, has made a name for himself in his locality in southeastern Georgia, and as he is yet a young man he has prospects for a broader, greater work.

Mr. Crutchfield was born at Irwinton, Georgia, in 1878, son of J. I. and Celia (Smith) Crutchfield, both natives of the Empire State of the South; and when he was a small boy the family moved to a farm near Cochran, where he lived until he was seventeen. Then he began life for himself. He learned the builder's trade in its every detail, beginning with hammer and saw, and while he contracted for and built houses of various descriptions he studied architecture; he was not content merely to erect according to the plans and specifications of others, he was ambitious to follow his own plans. For four years he made his home at Vidalia and previous to that time Cochran was the seat of his operations, at both of which places and others are to be found monuments of his skillful workmanship. As a contractor he erected seven of the principal mercantile buildings of Cochran, also the oil mills and a number of the most prominent residences of that town, among them being the $14,000 residence of P. L. Peacock. At Soperton he built a sale stable and cotton warehouse and fifteen mercantile buildings, and later on he planned a $20,000 bank building at Soperton, Georgia. His first work of note as an architect was the building occupied by the large store of Leader & Rosansky, Vidalia. Among his other architectural works are the First National Bank Building, the Thompson & Hamilton Building, the Crescent City Barber Shop Building, Vidalia Furniture Company Building, the Bank of Vidalia, the New Vidalia Cafe Building, the building occupied by the buggy business of S. B. & E. L. Medows, the annex of Vidalia College Institute, G. N. Mathews & Sons Store, and many residences in Vidalia. He drew the plans and erected the $16,000 residence of R. M. Garbett of Lyons, the county seat of Toombs county, and other buildings erected by him at that place are those of Moses Coleman and I. Q. Coleman respectively, and the school annex, also the home of F. M. Smith at Lyons. He was the architect of the Bank of Nashville, the Mount Vernon Bank of Mount Vernon, the Uvalda Bank of Uvalda, Georgia, the

Farmers-Merchants Bank of Nunez, and the Bank of Soperton. In January, 1913, he moved to Savannah and opened an office in the Germania, Building.

June 10, 1906, Mr. Crutchfield married Miss Annie Renfroe, daughter of Thomas Renfroe of Cochran, and they have two children: Lawrin and Ivy Thomas.

Mr. and Mrs. Crutchfield are members of the Methodist church, and, fraternally, he is identified with the Knights of Pythias.

WILLIAM H. GURR. An able and worthy representative of the legal fraternity of Terrell county, William H. Gurr, one of the leading attorneys of Dawson, is a fluent, earnest and convincing advocate, and through his industry and ability has built up a large and remunerative practice in his adopted city. A son of Edward M. Gurr, he was born in Bibb county, Georgia, February 9, 1871. His grandfather, Samuel Gurr, was born in South Carolina, a son of John Gurr, who is supposed to have been the founder of the American family of Gurr.

Samuel Gurr grew to man's estate in South Carolina, and was there reared to habits of industry and thrift. Early in life he migrated to Georgia, settling in Houston county in pioneer days, bravely daring all the privations and hardships of life in a new country, in order to pave the way for those who followed, and to establish a home for his children. Buying land that was in its original wildness, he was there engaged in agricultural pursuits during the remainder of his years. He married Elizabeth Bishop, a native of South Carolina, and she survived him, passing away at the age of four score years. They reared eight children, as follows: Elvira, Thomas Jefferson, Robert, Mattie, Edward M., James P., John W., and Samuel D.

Edward M. Gurr first opened his eyes to the light of the world on a farm in Houston county, Georgia, where he lived until sixteen years old. Then ambitious to become a wage-earner, he entered the employ of the Central Georgia Railroad, with which he was connected as an employe until thirty years old, in that capacity having been exempt from military service during the Civil war. After the death of his father, he purchased a part of the old homestead, and managed it for three years. He then traded that property for a farm in Crawford county, where he resided until his early death, at the age of forty-two years in 1887. His wife, whose maiden name was Nancy Balkcom, was a native of Quitman county. Her father, Ichabod Balkcom, who died in the Confederate army during the war between the states, moved with his family from Jones county to Quitman county, and on the farm which he purchased his wife, nee Caroline Moore, spent her remaining years. Both the Moore and Balkcom families were reared in Monroe county, and moved to Quitman county about the same time. Mrs. Edward M. Gurr survived her husband four years, dying in 1891. She was the mother of eight children as follows: James W., William H., Thomas Edward, Frank B., Mattie L., Fanny G., Ophelia, and Belle.

As a boy, William H. Gurr, in his efforts to obtain an education, used to walk three miles to the rural schools of his native county. The knowledge thus acquired was further advanced at higher institutions of learning, he having attended first the Cuthbert Military College, and later Emory College in Oxford, Georgia, from which he was graduated with the class of 1897. In June, 1898, Mr. Gurr enlisted in Ray's Regiment of Immunes, designated as Third Regiment United States Volunteer Infantry, and went with this command to Cuba, where he remained eight months, being stationed at Santiago, Baracoa, and Sagua de Tanamo. He was honorably discharged with his regiment, May 2, 1899, and on his return home turned his attention to the study of law, a profession for which he is well adapted. In January, 1900, Mr. Gurr was admitted to the bar, and immediately located at Dawson, where he has been in continuous practice ever since.

In September, 1900, Mr. Gurr married Helen H. Giles, who was born in Stewart county, Georgia, a daughter of William H. and Martha (Boyette) Giles. William H. Giles was born on a farm seven miles west of Lumpkin in Stewart county, February 5, 1851. His father was John Frank Giles, who it is thought, was a native of Baldwin county, this state. Anyhow he came from that portion of the state about 1835, and located in the wilderness of south Georgia. He was one of the men who bore the pioneer burden in a country sparsely settled without railroads, where wild game of all kinds was in abundance, and where the Indians roamed through the forest still claiming the privileges of hunting as they had for generations. Grandfather Giles was in south Georgia in time to participate in the final overthrow of the Indian tribes of Florida and Georgia, and fought in the battle of Roanoke in 1836. He was subsequently for a number of years an overseer on plantations in Stewart county, and his death occurred when about sixty-five years of age. He married Mary Armstrong, who was born in Baldwin county, a daughter of James H. and Mary (Davis) Armstrong. Her death occurred at the age of seventy-two. Their seven children were named Mary F., Sarah A., J. Alexander, William H., George P., John F., and Robert F. William H. Giles was reared on a farm, received his early education in some of the Stewart county schools, and a considerable part of his early youth was spent during the troublous times of the Civil war. He became one of the prosperous farmers of this county, and continued actively in those pursuits until 1893, at which time he removed to Richland, where he has since been proprietor of the principal hotel of that town. When twenty-two years of age he married Miss Maggie Boyett, who was born in Clay county, Georgia, a daughter of James and Sarah (Adams) Boyett. Mr. Giles and wife reared two children, the first being Helen Holmes, wife of Mr. Gurr, and the second being Willard James.

Mr. Gurr has served for five years as city attorney, and is now solicitor of the city court of Dawson. An active and influential party since casting his first presidential vote for William J. Bryan, Mr. Gurr has since served as a delegate to two state conventions, and was a delegate to the national Democratic convention held in Baltimore in 1912. Fraternally Mr. Gurr is a member of P. T. Schley lodge No. 229, Ancient Free and Accepted Order of Masons, and belongs to the Sigma Alpha Epsilon college fraternity.

ALEXANDER J. MCKINNON, the prominent farmer and stock grower of the Way district of Thomas county, can boast descent from two families who have been gentry in Scotland for many hundred years, the McIntosh and the McKinnon families. The grandfather of the subject of this sketch, John McKinnon, was the first representative of the family to make his home in Georgia. He was born in Robeson county, North Carolina, about two years after his parents had come to the United States from Scotland, about 1773. He spent his early youth in the locality of his birth, and was there married to Mary McIntosh, whose natal day occurred in Scotland in the year 1775, and who came to the United States with her parents when she was but six years old. Mary McIntosh McKinnon had two brothers, Daniel and Murdoch. Daniel had three children, John Anderson, Roderick, and Margaret McLoed. The offspring of Murdoch were John, Caroline, Benjamin,

Daniel, Mary and Charlotte. John McKinnon had two brothers, Hector and Kenneth, who passed their lives in Robeson county, North Carolina, and whose descendants still live in the turpentine and lumber district of that state.

After his marriage, John McKinnon left the community where he had been born, and migrated to Montgomery county, Georgia, in which locality he was a pioneer. He resided there as a farmer and stock raiser until about 1830, in which year he moved to Thomas county, settling about six miles east of Thomasville, on timbered land. He was quite a large slave holder, and used slave labor in clearing his new property, and engaging in farming and stock raising. He died five years after coming to Thomas county, in the spring of 1835, of measles. He had been raised in the faith of the Presbyterian church, but on coming to Thomas county, where there was no church of his denomination, he had united with the Methodist congregation, and in that church he died. A pious, God-fearing man all his life, it is said that almost with his dying breath he repeated snatches of the old hymn, commencing,

"Jesus, and shall it ever be, a mortal man ashamed of Thee."

And so passed to his eternal reward with his Master's name upon his lips.

After her husband had been laid away in the plot of ground which he had set aside for the family cemetery, the cares of a large family of children, and of the farm as well, devolved upon Mary McIntosh McKinnon. She did her duty well, managing the business of the farm so efficiently that when her children reached the age of maturity, she was able to start each one out in life with a plot of ground and two or three slaves. She fell asleep in the year 1857, after a life devoted to all that is loveliest and best in Christian womanhood.

John and Mary McIntosh McKinnon had twelve children, many of whose descendants are now honored and prosperous citizens of southern Georgia. They were Malcolm, who was born in the year 1799, and married Margaret McArthur; Roderick, whose natal day occurred in the year 1801, and who died unmarried; Neil, whose birth took place in 1803, and who married Sarah Rains Mitchell; Elizabeth, born in 1805, who became the wife of Thomas Pugh; John, born in 1807, whose wife was Mary Louise Jordan; Nancy, who married Murdoch McKinnon; Kenneth, husband of Ann McRae: Daniel, who died as a young man; Margaret, who became Mrs. Malcolm McKinnon; Murdoch, whose wife was Mary Ann McArthur; McIntosh, who married Margaret McArthur, sister to Mary Ann, and niece of the Margaret McArthur who married Malcolm McKinnon; Mary, who became the wife of Alexander McRae, the brother of Ann McRae.

The father of the subject of this history, Kenneth McKinnon, was born in Montgomery county, Georgia, July 14, 1814. He accompanied the family to Thomas county, and after his father's death continued to live with his mother on the old homestead until his marriage, when he settled on a tract of land in what is now the Way district of Thomas county. There he engaged in general farming and stock raising. In 1861, when the War of the Rebellion broke out, he joined the Georgia Reserves, and served until honorably discharged on account of physical disability. He was not the only one of John McKinnon's descendants to take part in the great struggle. At the very beginning of the conflict between the states, twenty grandsons of John McKinnon gave their lives in the aid of the Confederate cause, and later, two more grandsons died in the service of the stars and bars. Seven of these young men were unmarried, but the rest left wives to mourn them.

When the war was over, Kenneth McKinnon continued farming on his old farm, and remained there until his death, which occurred in the year 1882. His wife survived him by nearly twenty years, departing this life on the twenty-eighth of May, 1900. Mrs. Kenneth McKinnon, who was Ann McRae before her marriage, was born in Telfair county, Georgia, April 10, 1819. Her parents, Philip and Elizabeth McRae, were natives of Scotland, and pioneers of the county in which Mrs. McKinnon was born. Ann McRae McKinnon bore her husband seven children, by name, Mary, Isabelle, Philip, Margaret, William D., Alexander J., and Julia F.

Alexander J. McKinnon was born on the farm where he now makes his home on March 4, 1857. He attended the schools of the neighborhood, and resided with his parents until he gradually succeeded into the active management of the property, after which they made their home with him. He has continued to farm the home tract of eight hundred acres, but, as his prosperity has increased, he has added to it from time to time until he now possesses about twelve hundred acres.

Mr. McKinnon was married on May 8, 1882, to Mattie Dukes, the daughter of John W. and Wealthea (Peacock) Dukes. Six children are the issue of this marriage, namely, Frank L., Clara May, Wealthea Elizabeth, Lucy Alexander, George Remer, and Howell Edward.

Mr. McKinnon shares the dominant characteristics of the McKinnon family, and is a quiet, law-abiding citizen of his community. He and his wife are members of the Methodist Episcopal church, and are valued workers in the congregation.

WILLIAM RIDGELY LEAKEN. Distinguished not only for the high position which he has attained in legal circles and in public life, but for the honored ancestry from which he traces his descent, William Ridgely Leaken is widely known as collector of customs for the port of Savannah, and as special assistant attorney general of the United States. A son of Rev. George Armistead Leaken, he was born, February 13, 1859, in Baltimore, Maryland. Of Irish and English lineage, he comes of good old colonial stock, his great-grandfathers on both sides of the family having served in the colonial wars. One of them, Theodore Middleton, his mother's grandfather, having raised and equipped at his own expense two companies of soldiers, after which he served as lieutenant of Maryland troops in the Continental army, under Gen. Mountjoy Bailey.

Rev. George Armistead Leaken was named for Gen. George Armistead of Maryland, with whom his father, Gen. Sheppard Church Leaken, of Maryland, an officer in the War of 1812, was associated in the engagement at Fort McHenry, both having command of troops at the bombardment of that fort. He was born in Baltimore, Maryland, in 1818, and died July 10, 1912. Educated in Princeton College, he entered the priesthood of the Episcopal church in early manhood, and for half a century was rector of Trinity church in his native city. This long continuous period of useful activity, in the intimate relation naturally existing between pastor and parishioner, made him a greatly loved and revered character in Baltimore. Dr. Leaken is an author of several valuable books of a scientific and religious nature, one of which, "The Law of Periodicity," is known the world over. His wife, whose maiden name was Anna Maria Middleton, died several years ago.

Acquiring his rudimentary education in the schools of Baltimore, William Ridgely Leaken entered Trinity College, in Hartford, Connecticut, in 1876, and was there graduated in July, 1880, with the degree of

Bachelor of Arts, his alma mater subsequently conferring upon him the degree of Master of Arts. Removing soon after his graduation to Albany, Georgia, Mr. Leaken was there engaged in tutoring for two years, in the meantime taking up the study of law. Coming to Savannah in the autumn of 1882, he completed his legal studies in the office of Chisholm & Erwin, in 1883 being admitted to the bar. In 1885 he was admitted to practice in the United States courts of Georgia, and in 1897 to the supreme court of the United States. From 1883 until 1890 Mr. Leaken was associated with the firm of Chisholm & Erwin, but since that time has continued his practice alone.

Mr. Leaken's talents, skill and efficiency as a lawyer have received wide recognition, particularly in official circles. In 1897 he was appointed assistant district attorney for the southern district of Georgia, in which capacity he rendered satisfactory service for seven years. In 1904 he was made special assistant attorney general of the United States, a position that he is still filling most acceptably. On July 9, 1909, Mr. Leaken was appointed by President Taft collector of customs for the port of Savannah, and immediately entered upon the important and responsible duties of the position, which he still holds. His able administration of this post is greatly appreciated by the commercial and shipping interests of Savannah, which are constantly increasing in magnitude and value, while the city's status as the principal port of entry on the south Atlantic seaboard is each year being advanced with the continued development of the South.

In 1898, at the beginning of the Spanish-American war, Mr. Leaken enlisted as a private in the Second Georgia Regiment, United States Volunteers, and was subsequently promoted to second lieutenant of his company. He is now an honorary member, for service, of the Savannah Volunteer Guards, and formerly he was judge advocate of the First Battalion of Infantry, National Guard of Georgia.

Prominent in political life, Mr. Leaken was a delegate to the national Republican convention of 1900, and in 1897 was a Republican presidential elector from Georgia. He is identified with various patriotic, social and fraternal organizations, and does much to promote their good. He is a charter member, and former historian, of the Georgia Society of the Sons of the Revolution; governor of the Georgia Society of Colonial Wars; a member of the Oglethorpe Club; of the Savannah Board of Trade; of the Hibernian society; of the Ancient Free and Accepted Order of Masons, he is a Knights Templar, and a member of the Ancient Arabic Order Nobles of the Mystic Shrine. Religiously he is affiliated with Christ church, Episcopal, and is president of the choir guild.

Mr. Leaken has acquired note as an author, a series of romances from his facile pen having been published from time to time in the Savannah *Morning News*, the series including "The Romance of Oglethorpe and His Birth;" "The Romance of Salzburg and Ebenezer;" "The Romance of the Shamrock and the Lily," accounting for the presence of Irish regiments as assistants in the American cause at the siege of Savannah; and of other interesting stories.

At Savannah, in 1894, Mr. Leaken married Ruth, daughter of Maj. James T. Stewart, of Savannah. She was and is an accomplished leader of Savannah social set and engaged largely in charitable and literary work in the various organizations of her native city.

DAVID FLEMING CHAPMAN. A resident of Brooks county whose career of usefulness has extended through many years is David Fleming Chapman, now living in Barwick village. At the beginning of his career he was a soldier of the Confederacy, has served more than forty years as a justice of the peace and for shorter periods in other office of honor and trust, and has spent many profitable years in farming or in business.

Mr. Chapman was born in Liberty county, Georgia, April 5, 1840, and represents one of the oldest families of this state. Of the original stocks that settled in Georgia during the colonial period, the Scotch-Irish contributed many fine qualities of industry and civic ability, and it was to this racial stock that the Chapmans belonged. Mr. Chapman's great-grandfather was born in the north of Ireland, where the Scotch-Irish originated, and was one of seven sons. The oldest got the ancestral estate and all the other six emigrated to America, two settling in New York and the others in the Carolinas and Georgia. The great-grandfather located in McIntosh county, Georgia, and from there volunteered his service to the forces fighting for the cause of independence, and lost his life in a battle that occurred two miles from Savannah. He was twice married, having three sons by his first wife, and by his second had one, named Francis, who was an infant when his father was killed in battle.

Francis Chapman, the grandfather, was born in McIntosh county, and after reaching manhood's estate became one of the pioneer settlers of Liberty county, where he secured a large tract of land and was engaged in farming and stock raising until his death which occurred when he was seventy-two years of age. He kept a number of slaves and was one of the prosperous planters of his time. He married Mary Leigh, who was born in Tattnall county and who died in Liberty county aged eighty-six. She had ten children, all of whom grew up, and their names were Keziah, John, Mary, Jemima, Emily, Nancy, James, Nathaniel, Sheldon and Rosina. The descendants of Francis and Mary (Leigh) Chapman are now scattered through various localities of Georgia and elsewhere. They formerly held occasional reunions.

John Chapman, one of the children of Francis and Mary Chapman, was born in Liberty county, April 15, 1810, and was reared on the home farm in that county. He possessed a genius for mechanics, and with his own hands fabricated many of the tools used on his farm, and did all his own blacksmithing. He took up state land and also bought large quantities until at one time he was the owner of upward of six thousand acres. With the aid of his slaves he carried on general farming and stock raising on an extensive scale. He was eighty-six years old when he died. The maiden name of his wife was Elizabeth Delk, who was born in Liberty county and died at the age of seventy-five. Her father, David Delk, a native of Scotland, came to America and at the age of fourteen enlisted in the continental army as a drummer boy, serving seven years in the struggle for American independence. Among other campaigns he was present at the siege of Quebec. John Chapman and wife reared thirteen of their fifteen children, named as follows: Martha, Francis, John, Samuel N., Thomas J., Mary, Columbus, Elizabeth, Sheldon W., Ferdinand, Ann Eliza, Clifford, Talulah and David F.

Reared and educated in his native county, David F. Chapman began his career by teaching school for three terms. He had barely attained his majority when the war broke out, and on the 14th of August, 1861, he enlisted in Company I of the Twenty-fifth Georgia Infantry. He served in the coast defense of this state until honorably discharged on account of ill health. Returning home he was for some time station agent and express agent and also postmaster at Ludowici station in Liberty county. In 1866, having resigned from these positions, he moved to Brooks county and went into the merchandise business with his father-in-law and later by himself at Okapilco. He held the office of postmaster there for the long period of twenty-four years, and during that time was also engaged in farming. His residence at Okapilco continued until 1906, in which year he moved to Barwick, his present home. In 1868 Mr. Chapman was elected a justice of the peace. During a few months' residence in Quitman he had resigned this position, but with that brief exception has served continuously as a justice for the past forty-four years. In 1900 and 1910 he was census enumerator for his district, and has taken the census for three decades, having been substitute enumerator in 1890. He is a Democrat in politics and has long been one of the influential citizens of his community. He and his wife are members of the Primitive Baptist church, with which he has been identified for a period of thirty-seven years.

Mr. Chapman married in 1866 Martha Frances Wade. She was born in Dooly county, Georgia, and her parents, Judge Elijah and Elizabeth (Reddick) Wade, who were natives of Screven county, moved from Dooly county to what is now Brooks county in 1854, settling on a farm in Dry Lake district, where they spent the rest of their lives. After the death of Mrs. Chapman's mother, her father married for his second wife Mrs. Mary Peacock, widow of Dr. Peacock. Mrs. Chapman's brothers and sisters were named as follows: Mary, Lucy, Philip, Mitchel, Wesly Beaureguard, and her children named: Cornelia, John W., Mary J., David S., James E., William Francis, Samuel N., Henry V. and Anna C. All are married with the exception of two sons, and all are doing well.

HON. MERCER LAFAYETTE LEDFORD. One of the ablest attorneys and most prominent men in public affairs in Grady county, is the honorable Mercer Lafayette Ledford, who has been a resident of Cairo since the organization of Grady county, and who has for many years enjoyed success as a lawyer and numerous distinctions in political life.

Mercer Lafayette Ledford was born on a farm in Union county, Georgia, September 24, 1865. His father was Silas Ledford, born near Asheville, in Buncombe county, North Carolina, October 22, 1821. The grandfather was Benjamin Ledford, born in the same county of North Carolina, and a son of John Ledford, a native and life-long resident of North Carolina, and said to have been a soldier in the Revolutionary war. Grandfather Benjamin Ledford owned and occupied a farm upon which the town of Candler has since been built. In 1839 he immigrated to Georgia, coming overland with teams and wagons, and bringing his household goods, and his livestock. He located in Union county, buying land on Ivy Log creek, six miles northwest of Blairsville. There he built a log house in the woods, and at once began the heavy toil connected with creating a homestead of the wilderness. He resided on that estate until his death at the age of ninety-three years. He married a Miss Owensby, who was born in Buncome county, North Carolina, and her father, Porter Owensby, married a Miss Morgan. The grandmother died at the age of sixty-five, and Grandfather Ledford married again when he was sixty-eight years of age, Mrs. Salina (Chapman) Miller, becoming his second wife. She bore him three children, whose names were Solomon, Mary and Willie. By the first marriage the five children were Silas, Martha, Porter, Amy and Benjamin. The sons all gave service to the Confederacy during the war.

Silas Ledford, the father, was educated in the rural schools of Buncombe county, North Carolina, and on beginning his career his father gave him a tract of timbered land near his own home. On that he built a log house, and that was the home of his family for some years. Silas Ledford served the Confederate army for a time during the last year of the war. He finally sold his first homestead and bought a place a mile and a half east of Blairsville, which continued to be his home until his death in 1891. Silas Ledford married Eliza Arminda Bowling. She was born in Union county, Georgia, in February, 1837, and her father, Thomas Bowling, was born near Greenville in South Carolina. Thomas Bowling in 1833 settled in Union county, Georgia, buying land a mile and a half east of Blairsville, and clearing a farm which Mercer L. Ledford now owns. Thomas Bowling took a very active part in the early affairs of Union county, and assisted in clearing the land for the courthouse and in cutting and hewing the logs for the first building. He was also distinguished as one of the first sheriffs of Union county. After the death of his first wife he married the second time and moved to Fulton county, where he spent his last years. The maiden name of the first wife was Mary McDonald, and her children were Lewis, Gabriel, Elmira, Elliott, Jackson, Van Buren, Eliza, Arminda, Evlyn and Martha. The two older sons served in the Mexican war, and both died in service at Vera Cruz. Mrs. Silas Ledford died on January 2, 1897, and her eight children were Andrew J., Jane, John S., Alice, Mercer Lafayette, Ida, Virgil C., and Sarah Isabelle.

Mercer L. Ledford first attended school in Blairsville and subsequently was a student in the Ivy Log high school, whose principal was at that time Professor M. L. Mauney. When seventeen years of age he was licensed as a teacher, and his first school was at Ebenezer Church, the school house being situated on land where his father had first located. He subsequently taught in Gwinett county and there took up the study of law with Juhan & McDonald. Mr. Ledford was admitted to the bar in 1892 and practised for some time in Lawrenceville, moving from there to Blairsville. His first case in Union county was at Ebenezer Church, where he had taught school a number of years ago, and where his father first settled. He was engaged in practice at Blairsville until 1905, and then upon the organization of Grady county he located at Cairo and has enjoyed a large practice in this new county.

In 1897 Mr. Ledford married Florence Iowa Christopher. She was born in Union county, a daughter of John A. and Sarah (Martin) Christopher, her parents being natives of North Carolina and South Carolina respectively. Mrs. Ledford received her education at Blairsville and in the Baptist school in Hiawassee. She was a well educated woman and taught school for some time before her marriage. The four children of Mr. and Mrs. Ledford are Sarah, Ina, Curtis and Louisa.

Mr. Ledford's public services have been numerous. He served as a member of the board of education in Union county, and was also a county school commissioner. In 1902 he was elected to the office of state senator from Union county, and served during 1902-3-4. As senator he served on the committee on special and general judiciary, and the committee on finance, chairman on the committee of education, and also was a member of the committee on mines and mining and on public printing. He was influential in the passage of the franchise tax bill, a bill which imposed a tax upon the franchises of public utility corporations in this state. He was also author of the bill regulating the sale of domestic wines. For seven years Mr. Ledford served as county attorney of Grady county, and for two and one-half years as president of the county board of education, and was a prominent member of the Democratic party, has been on the congressional district executive committee and also the state executive committee. In 1904 he was a presidental elector from the ninth congressional district. Fraternally Mr. Ledford is past master of Allegheny lodge, A. F. & A. M., at Blairsville, and is now a member of Cairo lodge, No. 299, A. F. & A. M. He is also affiliated with the Cairo lodge of Odd Fellows, the Woodmen of the World and the Knights of Pythias. He and his wife are both members of the Missionary Baptist church and he has served as moderator of the Baptist Association.

PHILIP NEWBERN, now serving his second term as mayor of the city of Ocilla, Georgia, is a native of the state, his birth occurring in Broxton, Coffee county, on October 2, 1880. He is the son of Lawrence and Elizabeth (Douglas) Newbern, both natives of Coffee county. The mother was a daughter of Robert Douglas, and the town of Douglas, in Coffee county, was named for that gentleman. The early education of Philip Newbern was received in the public schools of Broxton, and when he had completed the curriculum of the high school of that place he entered the state normal at Athens in the autumn of 1899. Later he attended the Southern Normal Institute of Douglas and was graduated from that institution in 1902, after which he was engaged as a teacher in the school for a term of two years. In June, 1904, he resigned and became a candidate for election to the office of clerk of the superior court, but was defeated. He then taught school for one season in 1905 and in the autumn of that year entered Mercer Law School at Macon, Georgia, from which school he was graduated in June, 1906, and immediately thereafter admitted to the bar. He located in Broxton where he began the practice of his profession, remaining there until 1907, moving in that year to Ocilla, where he has since continued to live, and where he has conducted an ever growing practice, winning a prominence in his profession and as mayor of the city, holding the esteem of all who come within his influence.

On June 28, 1903, Mr. Newbern was united in marriage with Abbie Meeks, the daughter of Malcolm Meeks. One child was born of their union, a daughter named Ineva, born August 23, 1906. Mr. Newbern married a second time, Mrs. Margaret Brooker becoming his wife, a daughter of T. J. Tanner of McDonald, Coffee county, Georgia. They have one daughter, Varnelle, born on February 7, 1909.

Mr. Newbern is one of a family of ten, all living, as follows: Aleph, wife of H. V. Johnson of Broxton, a printer by trade, now engaged as a traveling salesman. J. Wesley, a minister, located in Washington, D. C. Laura, the wife of J. H. Long of Lake Charles, Louisiana. Bessie, the wife of Henry Parks, Inverness, Florida, where he is engaged as an engineer. J. L., a teacher in the schools of Brooklet, Georgia. D. F., living in Florida, where he is employed at the Phosphate mines. Maybel, Emma and Cloyce, at home with the mother.

In addition to his other interests, Mr. Newbern is occupied to some extent in farming, and is quite a successful man in that as well as in his legal work. He is a member of the Methodist Episcopal church. Both he and his wife are of Irish parentage.

W. L. PIERCE CLOWER. Prominent among the energetic, wide-awake young men who are so ably conducting the agricultural interests of Brooks county is W. L. Pierce Clower, who resides with his widowed mother in the Morven district. He was born at Rays Mill, in Berrien county, Georgia, on January 22, 1880, and is a descendant in the fourth generation from Daniel Clower, who was born in Germany, July 18, 1762, immigrated to America as a youth, and fought with the colonists in their struggle for independence.

Daniel P. Clower, the next in line of descent, was born on May 13, 1805, and died on his farm in Gwinnett county, Georgia, while yet in manhood's prime. He married Parthene Brandon, a daughter of William Brandon. She too died in early life, leaving four children as follows: John Thomas, father of the subject of this review; William P.; Mary Elizabeth; and Nancy J. Very young when their parents died, all of these children spent their early youth with an uncle, Joseph Brandon.

John Thomas Clower, M. D., the eldest child of the household, was born in Gwinnett county, in Georgia, May 13, 1830. He availed himself of every opportunity afforded him for the acquiring of an education while young, and subsequently went to Bartow county, Georgia, as an overseer on the plantation of his uncle, Thomas Brandon. Then, after working at the carpenter trade for a short time, he entered the Atlanta Medical College, from which he was graduated just as the war between the states was declared. Immediately enlisting as a soldier, he was made second lieutenant of his company, which was attached to Major Laden's Battalion, in the Ninth Georgia Regiment, and with his command joined the Western army. Later Dr. Clower was appointed surgeon, and was with the army in its many compaigns and battles until the last of the conflict.

Locating in Gwinnett county when he returned to Georgia, Dr. Clower was there engaged in the practice of medicine until 1870. The next seventeen years he practiced at Rays Mills, Berrien county, Georgia, from there coming to Brooks county in 1887. Buying a plantation in the Morven district, he carried on farming in connection with his professional work, becoming noted both as an agriculturist, and as a physician of skill and ability, and continuing thus until his death, March 12, 1893.

Dr. Clower married in January, 1869, Delusky Ann Brogdon, who was born in Gwinnett county, Georgia, on March 7, 1849, a daughter of Hope J. Brogdon. Her grandfather, George Brogdon, was born, it is supposed, in one of the Carolinas. Coming to Georgia at an early period of its settlement, he located first in Jackson county, from there going to Gwinnett county, where he took up land and from the virgin wilderness hewed a farm. Both he and his wife possessed the true pioneer grit and courage, and thrift indoors and out brought success to them. They started their wedded life without means, and by dint of persevering labor acquired sufficient property to be called rich in those times. Both he and his wife, whose maiden name was Sarah Jackson, lived long and happy lives. George Brogdon reared eight children as follows: Wiley, George, William, Noah, Charity, Faith, Hope J. and Sarah. He gave each of his children a tract of land.

Locating on the land presented to him by his father, Hope J. Brogdon erected a typical pioneer log cabin for his first home, and immediately began clearing a farm. There being no railways in those early days, he marketed his produce at Augusta, one hundred miles away, on the homeward trip bringing the needed supplies, including salt, molasses and iron for use in the making of farm implements. His wife, who for many years after her marriage cooked by the fireplace, became the proud possessor of one of the first stoves carried into Gwinnett county. Well versed in the domestic arts, she used to card, spin and weave cloth for the garments in which she clothed her family. He died on the farm he had improved, at the age of sixty-nine years, being survived by his wife, who reached the age of about seventy years. The maiden name of the wife of Hope Brogdon was Emily Bogan. Her father, Shadrach Bogan, removed from Augusta, Georgia, to Gwinnett county, becoming a pioneer of Lawrenceville, where he was wont to trade with the Indians. He built the first grist mill in that county, and also the first gin. Prominent in public affairs, he served for one or more terms as counsellor general of the state. Late in life he moved to Alabama, and his last days were spent at Cedar Bluff. Mr. Bogan married Ann Fee. Her father, Captain Fee, a native of England, sailed the seas as captain of a vessel. He brought his family to Georgia, locating in Augusta, and soon after started on an ocean voyage, but neither he nor his ship nor his crew were ever heard from again. Mrs. Hope J. Brogdon lived a few years after the death of her husband. She was the mother of thirteen children, as follows: Caroline, Frances, Mary, Elizabeth, George, Daniel, Noah, William, Wiley, Delusky Ann, Jackson, Emery and John.

Dr. Clower was an active member of the Methodist Episcopal church South, to which Mrs. Clower also belongs, and for a number of years served as a member of the county school board. Mrs. Clower has never forgotten the art of spinning and weaving which she learned as a girl, but occasionally gets out her wheel and spins the yarn which she later knits into stockings. The doctor and Mrs. Clower reared three sons, namely: John P., R. Jackson and W. L. Pierce Clower.

John P. Clower, of Moultrie, Georgia, is employed as a book-keeper by one of the leading firms of that place. He has been twice married. His first wife, whose maiden name was Fannie Lou Edmondson, died in early womanhood, leaving two children, Bamma and Warren Candler. He married for his second wife Mamie Pruitt, and to them two children have been born, Young and Lovic.

R. Jackson Clower, M. D., a practicing physician in Mowen, married Willie Brice and they are the parents of three children, named Mary Thomas, Emily Jackson and Tim Brice.

W. L. Pierce Clower, the immediate subject of this biographical sketch, resides with his mother on the old homestead, where he is carrying on general farming with excellent results.

CHARLES SCRIVEN JONES. Showing marked ability and enterprise in the management of his agricultural interests, Charles Scriven Jones occupies a noteworthy position among the leading farmers of Brooks county, his large estate, which is located in the Dixie district, being well improved, and furnished with an excellent group of farm buildings, and all of the latest approved kinds of machinery for carrying on his work successfully. A son of Andrew Jackson Jones, he was born, March 13, 1866, in Brooks county.

His great-grandfather, Abraham Jones, was born and reared in Wales. Crossing the Atlantic in his search for fortune, he lived for a few years in Virginia. Coming from there to Georgia, he purchased wild land in Putnam county, and on the farm which he cleared and improved both he and his wife spent the remainder of their lives.

James A. Jones, grandfather of Charles Scriven Jones, was a natural mechanic, and as a young man learned carpentering and cabinet making, becoming well skilled in each. For many years he followed these trades successfully, his home being in Putnam county, about seven miles north of Eatonton, where his death occurred while yet in the prime of life. His wife, whose maiden name was Nancy Banks, spent her entire eighty-three years of life in Putnam county, living with her children during her later days. In her girlhood she became well versed in the domestic arts and sciences, learning to card, spin and weave, and to cook by the open fireplace. After her marriage she did her full share of the pioneer labor devolving upon the mistress of a household, clothing her family in garments fashioned by her own hand from the homespun material which she had herself manufactured with the wheel and the loom. It is needless to say that she must have had very few leisure minutes while cooking and caring for her husband and eight children.

Born in Putnam county, Georgia, December 27, 1836, Andrew Jackson Jones was reared amid pioneer scenes, when people lived in a very primitive manner, with few modern conveniences. Travelling was mostly performed on horseback, by private conveyance, or by stage, railways being nowhere in evidence, while wild beasts and game of all kinds was abundant. But ten years old when his father died, he spent the next eight years at the home of a relative, where he was well drilled in the various branches of agriculture. Coming from there to Brooks county, he was plantation overseer until the breaking out of the Civil war, when he enlisted in the "Brooks Rifles," a company which was sent to Virginia to join the army of North Virginia. He continued with his command, taking part in its various marches, campaigns and battles, serving under Generals Joseph M. Johnston, Magruder and Longstreet. When the end came he was with other of his comrades on detached duty, striving to keep the cattle away from the Federals. Finding that he and his associates were nearly surrounded, with no chance of further saving the cattle, and not wanting to surrender, he started on foot for Georgia, and was fortunate to secure a ride a part of the way. At Macon, he and his companions met an officer of the Confederate army who told them that it was useless to continue their flight, and advised them to surrender, advice which they heeded. Returning to his old home, Andrew J. Jones resumed farming on rented land. A short time later he bought a tract of land in Dixie precinct, and was there successfully employed as a tiller of the soil for many years. He is now living retired from active pursuits, making his home with his son Charles. At the age of twenty-one years he married Catherine Norwood, who was born in Houston county, a daughter of Theodore and Hannah (Hicks) Norwood, who settled in that county in pioneer days, but later removed to Brooks county, where they spent their later years. She passed to the higher life in June, 1909, leaving five children, as follows: Mary Frances, James Jackson, Charles Scriven, Theodosia C., and Ada Virginia. Both parents united with the Missionary Baptist church when young, and were most faithful and valued members.

Gaining his early education in the district schools of Brooks county, Charles Scriven Jones worked on the home farm until becoming of age. Entering then the employ of the S., F. & W. Railroad Company, now the Atlantic Coast Line, he continued in its roadway department until 1892. Resigning his position in that year, Mr. Jones embarked in farming and in mercantile pursuits, and in his undertakings has met with signal success. He now owns four hundred and fifty acres of land, which includes the old homestead on which he was born and brought up. He has made improvements of value on his property, including the erection of a substantial set of buildings, his estate now ranking as one of the most desirable in the vicinity.

Mr. Jones married, in 1889, Lula E. Ward, who was born in Brooks county, a daughter of William H. and Lurana (Albritton) Ward. Eight children have been born to Mr. and Mrs. Jones, namely: Wesley Foy, Charles Hunter, Riva Annette, Lula Eunice, Bernice, Carl Leon, Nellie Ray, and Sam Scriven. Mr. and Mrs. Jones, true to the religious faith in which they were reared, are members of the Missionary Baptist church. Fraternally Mr. Jones belongs to Mount Horeb Lodge, Free and Accepted Masons.

JAMES FARIE, JR. One of the oldest and most prominent men in the naval stores industry at Savannah, Mr. Farie has for more than a quarter of a century been a resident of this city and engaged in the exportation of turpentine and rosin. During his early career he had experience in the same business in England, and on first coming to this country was representative of an English house dealing in naval stores. Both the business career and the family record of Mr. Farie have a proper place in the history of Savannah.

James Farie, Jr., was born on the twenty-seventh of July, 1857, at Bridge of Allan, county of Perth, Scotland, his birthplace being a well known resort in Scotland and quite famous for its curative waters. His parents, James and Agnes (Liddell) Farie, of Glasgow, Scotland, and later of London, England, are both deceased. James Farie, Sr., was originally engaged in the pottery business near Greenock, Scotland; later, he was interested in the manufacture of shale oil near Edinburgh. After the discovery of petroleum in America, he gave up this business and removed to London. In his tastes and inclinations he was more of a scientist than a business man, and he devoted considerable time to original research, particularly in geology. He was a prominent member of and honorary secretary for some time of the Geological Society of Glasgow, Scotland, which city was his home for many years. He was a juror on awards in Class C in the Glasgow Exposition of 1865-66. After his removal to London, England, he became a member of the Geological Society of that city, and took an active interest in various scientific subjects. The Farie family of Scotland is related to a number of well known families of that country, among them the Reids, Hamiltons, Adamses and Liddells.

James Farie, Jr., received his education in the schools of Glasgow, Edinburgh and London, and entered commercial life in the last named city. In 1881 he came to America and took up his residence at Wilmington, North Carolina, where he was a representative of English interests which were large distributors of turpentine in the United Kingdom and the continent of Europe. He remained at Wilmington two years, following which he was in Charleston, South Carolina, with the same business connections for nearly four years and in 1886 he came to Savannah. Since that date this city has been his home, and during this time he has devoted his attention to the turpentine and rosin business, thus having gained the distinction of being one of the oldest and most successful exporters of these products in Savannah.

On settling in Savannah he actively assisted in the reorganization of the Young Men's Christian Association in this city and for many years was chairman of the finance committee and treasurer and one of the board of directors and also for several years vice president of the association. He is also a member of the Savannah Baptist church, and served on the board of deacons of that church for many years and also for several years as honorary secretary of the board. Mr. Farie has been a member of the Savannah Board of Trade since 1886 and has given many continuous years of service as one of the board of directors of that corporation, having rendered valuable assistance throughout this period on several of its most important committees in connection with the naval stores trade interests. During the earlier years of the naval stores business in Savannah when the rosin and turpentine were exported in sail tonnage, he chartered a large number of sailing vessels each season to move these products to the various markets in the United Kingdom and the continent of Europe and in this way materially assisted in building up Savannah as the leading port for the exportation of naval stores.

Mr. Farie in 1892 was married to Miss Mary Harris Turner, daughter of Dr. John D. and Elmira C. (Weaver-Adams) Turner, of Atlanta, Georgia. Dr. Turner was one of the pioneers in the upbuilding of Atlanta, and at the time of his death he was president of the Exposition

Cotton Mills of that city. An interesting fact is that Mrs. Farie, through her father, is descended in direct line from Rev. William Turner, who was born in Scotland, not far from the home of Mr. Farie's ancestors, in Aberdeenshire in the year 1645. He married Mary McLemore, who was born in the same shire in 1650. On account of the persecution of the covenanters, he fled from Scotland with his young bride and settled in the north of Ireland. Persecution followed him, and he with his co-believers, who composed quite a colony, came to America in 1680, and settled in Worcester county, Maryland, not far from Snow Hill. His descendant, Zadoc Turner, who was the ancestor of Dr. Turner of Atlanta, immigrated with his family in 1793 to the state of Georgia. They left Chesapeake Bay on a sailing vessel, and after a rough and stormy voyage were driven by strong winds to the West Indian Islands, and finally landed in Savannah. One of Zadoc Turner's daughters died on the voyage, and would have been buried at sea but for the strong objections made by her brothers. Instead, her body was placed in a cedar chest and preserved until the vessel reached Savannah, where she was buried in the colonial cemetery. From Savannah the Turner family took boats on the Savannah river for Augusta, whence they crossed the country and settled in Hancock county east of the Oconee river soon after the Indians had been removed to the west. They settled at Mount Zion and took up land and cleared it and began planting. They were pioneers of that section of the state.

Zadoc Turner was a strong character. He was a soldier in the Continental army of the Revolutionary war, belonging to the Second Maryland Regiment, and took part in the battles of Brandywine and Trenton, and in the compaigns around New York and Philadelphia. He was also at Valley Forge, and with the Continental army until the surrender of the British at Yorktown. Zadoc Turner died in 1820.

Mr. and Mrs. Farie are the parents of two children: Cynthia Farie, born in 1895, and James Gilbert Farie, born in 1898.

HON. PATRICK HENRY HERRING. A former representative of Decatur county in the state legislature and a well-known citizen and business man of Cairo, Mr. Herring has had a long and honored career in this section of Georgia, and belongs to a family which did pioneer work in the development of this section of the state.

Patrick Henry Herring was born on a farm near Calvary, in Decatur county, June 5, 1845. His father was Hanson William Herring, born in Sampson county, North Carolina, in 1808, and the grandfather was Jackson Herring, also a native of North Carolina, and so far as known a life long resident of that state. Hanson William Herring was reared and married in his native state, and then in 1836, soon after his marriage, migrated to Georgia, making the journey across the country with teams and wagons and bringing his household goods, slaves and other possessions. He settled in the south part of Decatur county and bought a tract of land in the woods. He hewed out the timbers and constructed a double pen log house, a structure in which Patrick Henry Herring was born. The father directed his own labors and those of his slaves and dependents in clearing up the woods and brush from a large estate, and was engaged as a prosperous planter and farmer until his death in 1880, at the age of seventy-two years. The maiden name of his wife was Amy Caroline Anders, who was born in Bladen county, North Carolina, and who lived until 1891, being also seventy-two years of age at her death. The eleven children in the family were named Thomas W., Mary C., Julia, Anne E., Patrick Henry, Miles C., John A., Margaret, Counsel, Joe and Amelia.

Patrick Henry Herring grew up in Decatur county, attended the rural schools and the Calvary high school, and as a youth assisted in all the labors of the plantation. In 1863 when he was eighteen years of age he enlisted in the Confederate service and was stationed at St. Marks. He remained in the army until the close of the war and then returned home and assisted his parents until he was twenty-three years of age. At that time his father gave him a plantation situated two miles from the old homestead, and he turned his attention to its cultivation, and occupied his time until 1906. In that year he moved into Cairo, where he has since lived largely retired from strenuous activities, and enjoying the well earned competence of his early career.

Mr. Herring was married September 24, 1868, to Margaret Ann Maxwell. Mrs. Herring was born on a plantation in the southeastern part of Decatur county, a daughter of James G. Maxwell, who was born in Sampson county, North Carolina. He was reared and married in his native state and with his young bride came overland to Georgia. His location was in the southeastern part of Decatur county and in the wilderness which existed at that time he built a log house in which his daughter Mrs. Herring was born. He operated his large estate with slave labor, and enjoyed a generous prosperity and the esteem and respect of the community until his death in his ninety-fourth year. James G. Maxwell married Molcy Butter of Sampson county, North Carolina. Her death occurred at the age of seventy. The eight children in the Maxwell family were John R., Elizabeth, Thomas, William, James, Daniel, Margaret Ann and Mary. The sons were all soldiers in the Confederate army, and Thomas died while in service.

The eleven children including the large and happy family of Mr. and Mrs. Herring are named Thomas W., Ida Alice, Mary Ellen, Lillie May, Marvin, Ola, Pierce, Lochie, Maggie, Henry H., and Kedar. Thomas W. married Lucy Snider and has one son, George Ward. Ida Alice married A. E. Bell, and there are six children in this family, named Marion, Leta, Emery, Catherine, Elmer and Margaret. Mary Ellen is now deceased, and was the wife of Dr. George B. Carter, leaving one daughter named Margaret. Lillie May married Joseph Higdon and has five children named Grace, Lois, Sarah, Robert Henry and Thomas. Marvin married for his first wife Mattie Higdon, and for his second wife married Ida Waller, having one son named Ernest. Ola married Thomas Wight, and her five children are George, Henry, Carrie, Elizabeth and Mabel. Lochie married George L. Snider, and their three children are Leota, Lloyd and George J. Maggie married Ira Higdon, and they have three sons, John Buryl, Samuel Parrott and Patrick Henry. Henry H. married Annie May Maxwell.

Mr. Herring's official career began a number of years ago, when he was made overseer of roads in his district. He was at that time a boy in his teens, and has ever since taken an active part in local government and has been an influential man in his community. He served in the office of tax collector of Decatur county two years, and was subsequently elected county commissioner, an office in which he was continued by reelection for twenty years. He was in that office until Grady county was organized in January, 1906, and is prominent in the first government organization of this county in connection with the office of judge of ordinary, and he is still judge, having been reelected to the present term. In 1897 Mr. Herring was further honored by his district in election to the state legislature, and he served during the session of 1898-99. Mr. and Mrs. Herring are active members of the Methodist church at Cairo, and he is affiliated with Cairo Lodge No. 299, A. F. & A. M., with Cairo Lodge, I. O. O. F., and with Cairo Lodge, Knights of Pythias.

WILLIAM PHILIP SCHIRM. Savannah has known few citizens more worthy of the unqualified esteem and regard of the people as a whole than was the late William Philip Schirm, and it is a matter of great pleasure to record here that he never failed to receive his just meed of appreciation and esteem at the hands of the citizenship of the city and of the surrounding community. Foreign born, he came to these parts in early manhood, and at no time in his remaining years did he fail in his duty toward the country of his adoption. His life was from first to last one of the utmost usefulness and when he died on May 31, 1896, Savannah lost one of her most honored and loved citizens.

William Philip Schirm was born in the year 1836 in Schernern bei Nassau a/d Lahn (now known as Hessen-Nassau) Germany, where was also born his father. He came to America in 1857, and settled in Georgia in that year. He was a young man of excellent education and had served in the German army. After coming to Savannah his occupation was that of a teacher, and he was identified with a private institution in north Georgia of some repute, where he was known as an educator of exceptional ability. Some well known citizens of Savannah and other Georgian cities were his pupils in those early days. With the outbreak of the Civil war Mr. Schirm enlisted in the Confederate army and he served with distinction and valor throughout that conflict. Concerning his military career, it may be further said that he entered the service in February, 1862, with the rank of first lieutenant, Troop A, Georgia Cavalry, Clinch Light Battery, and was later detailed ordnance officer for the City of Savannah under General Anderson. Maj. G. W. Anderson, commander of Fort McAllister, says of him in his official report: "Lieut. William P. Schirm fought until the enemy entered the fort, and, notwithstanding a wound in the head, gallantly remained at his post, discharging his duties with a coolness and efficiency worthy of all commendation." He was taken prisoner on December 13, 1864, and was in prison at Hilton Head and Washington, and was released on June 6, 1865, at the close of the hostilities. He later became a member of Camp No. 756 Confederate Veterans, of which he was elected secretary, on March 6, 1894, and was re-elected on April 26, 1895.

Mr. Schirm was a director in the Chatham Real Estate & Improvement Company, and at the time of his death was a member of the Savannah Benevolent Association, a society the members of which are loved and respected by every true Savannahian. The following resolutions were adopted at the time of his passing by this well known society:

"The life he had led and the services he performed are all the legacies he could bequeath to us who remain, and when we examine these legacies and find that the life has been active, correct, exemplary and consistent, and the services well timed, practical and useful, we hold them in kindly remembrance and pay willing tribute to their worth.

"As a member of this association, Mr. Schirm was active and faithful, and as one of its directors he aided by his sound judgment and conservative business methods in advancing and establishing the prosperity and present financial strength of our Association. Quiet, modest and unobtrusive in all his ways, he never sought to attain higher positions than those allotted to him, and in every position acquitted himself honorably and well, always exhibiting those strong and commanding traits of character, which, through his long and eventful life, secured for him from time to time marked and substantial evidence of confidence.

"We mourn his loss and cherish his memory."

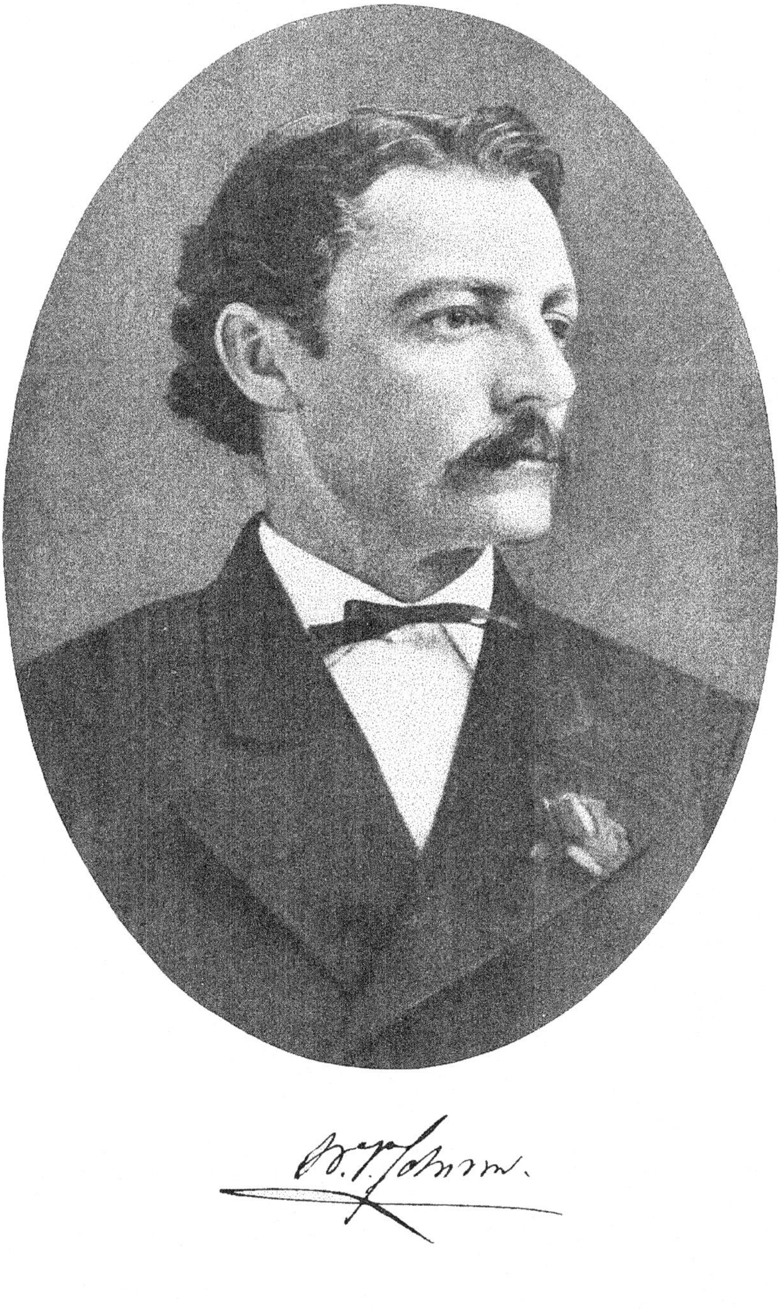

On January 20, 1876, Mr. Schirm married Ellen M. Lovell. Her parents were Edward and Mary (Bates) Lovell, both of whom passed away these many years gone. Mrs. Schirm is still living in Savannah.

After the close of the war, William P. Schirm returned to the quiet of civilian life and at the time of his death was connected with The Willcox and Gibbes Guano Company. He was a prominent member of the First Presbyterian church of this city, and a deacon of that body.

Among the sons of William P. Schirm may be mentioned in further detail, Edward L., the eldest son of his parents. He was born in Savannah in 1877; he was here reared and here he has passed all his life thus far. In 1900 Mr. Schirm entered The Citizens Bank of Savannah, beginning his labors there as junior clerk. In 1904 The Citizens Bank of Savannah established a branch office at Liberty and Montgomery streets and chose Mr. E. L. Schirm to be assistant cashier thereof, from which position he was in 1910 advanced to be cashier of the Liberty street branch of The Citizens and Southern Bank, which responsible office he now holds to the entire satisfaction of that institution.

On December 19, 1899, Mr. Schirm was married to Miss Elizabeth Brady. They have two children, Ellen L. and William Philip Schirm.

MOSES B. LINTON. Few families have been longer represented by residence in south Georgia, and none have contributed more industrious effort and worthier manhood and womanhood than the Lintons. One of the bearers of this name, Moses B. Linton, has for many years been successfully identified with the farming interests of the Everett district in Thomas county.

Mr. Linton was born in the southwest corner of Thomas county, October 18, 1850. His great-grandfather, a native of the north of Ireland and of Scotch ancestry, brought his young wife to America and settled in the Abbeville district of South Carolina, where they reared their family and spent the rest of their days in quiet industry and honor. Their four sons and two daughters were Moses W., Thomas, Sidney, Ben, Rebecca and Margaret.

Moses W., the grandfather, was born in Abbeville district. For some probably interesting reason that has escaped the knowledge of his descendants, when he was sixteen he became dissatisfied with home and ran away, finally reaching southwest Georgia. It was this boyhood adventure which brought the name of Linton so early into Georgia and accounts for the establishment of the family in this part of the state. Soon after his arrival the grandfather married Lucy Lanier, a native of Decatur county, her parents being pioneers there. She had some money, and with this capital the young people bought a tract of land in the southwest part of Thomas county. A small patch had been cleared by Indians, but all the rest was primeval forest. After getting this land into productive condition the grandfather had to haul his surplus crops to Tallahassee or Newport in Florida for market, the trip requiring several days, and many years passed before railroads were built to this region. By industry and good management he and his wife became very prosperous, and had a large amount of land and many slaves. At the close of the war he freed over a hundred of the blacks. Late in life he moved to Thomasville and lived retired until his death, which occurred at the age of seventy-eight, followed three days later by that of his wife. They reared four children, whose names were Benjamin F., James A., John L. and Margaret.

Benjamin F. Linton, the father, was born on the homestead in Thomas county, and at the time of his marriage bought land two miles from his birthplace. That was still a number of years before the war and before railroads brought modern conditions, so that he had the same difficulties of marketing as his father before him had encountered. In the household all the cooking was done by the fireplace, and the mother taught her slaves to card, spin and weave the wool and cotton, all members of the household being dressed in homespun. In 1865 the father sold his farm and for a time worked some of the lands of his father. Finally in 1880 he moved to Jefferson county, Florida, where he died at the age of fifty-two years. Benjamin F. Linton married Rebecca Rountree, who was born in Lowndes county of a pioneer family there, and she survived her husband by thirteen years. Their three sons and one daughter were Moses B., Frank J., Oscar R. and Lona E.

When Moses B. Linton was twenty-one his father gave him a pair of mules and a pair of oxen, a horse and buggy, a year's supply of material and the use of land for a crop. For an industrious worker this was a fair amount of capital, and he used his talent wisely, making a good crop the first year. Then after renting land for two years, he bought at the place where he still resides, in lot 153 in the locality known as Ancilla, in Everett district of Thomas county. For some years he was proprietor of a grist and saw mill and cotton gin, and for twelve years was engaged in merchandising, so that he has been identified with a varied enterprise and has won a commendable prosperity. His farm now consists of five hundred and eighty acres, devoted to general agriculture and stock raising.

Mr. Linton was married at the age of twenty to Miss Florence Virginia Kemp. She was born in Grooverville district of Brooks county, a daughter of Asa and Emily (Bryan) Kemp. Her mother was a native of Spring Hill, Florida. Her father was born in what is now Brooks county, where his father, Peter Kemp, was a pioneer settler. Mr. and Mrs. Linton reared two children, Lawrence E. and Maude. The son for a time conducted a store in Thomas county and later a saw mill in Brooks county. He came to his death by an accident in the mill when he was twenty-four years old, just when his promising career was fairly started. He married Marcia Austin, daughter of Robert Austin, and she with her two sons Russell and Lawrence survives her husband. The daughter Maude is the wife of Hecton L. Cook, and they have two sons, Emmett and Irvin. Mrs. Linton is a member of the Methodist church.

MATHEW JAMES HARRELL. Noteworthy among the native-born citizens of Brooks county who have spent their lives within its precincts, aiding in every possible way its growth and development, whether relating to its agricultural, manufacturing or financial interests, is Mathew James Harrell, an extensive land-owner, living on the Grooverville road, about four miles from Quitman. He was born in Brooks county, March 13, 1859, a son of Samuel J. Harrell.

His paternal grandfather, John Harrell, was born, reared, and married in North Carolina. Accompanied by his family, he subsequently migrated to Georgia, the private conveyance in which he made the journey, which was accomplished before the days of railways, was a cart made entirely of wood, their being no tires on the wheels. Bringing his provisions with him, he camped and cooked along the way, and on arriving in what is now Brooks county purchased land three miles west of the present site of Quitman. After settling on the land, he followed to some extent his trade of shoemaker, visiting the different plantations in this locality, and making shoes for the slaves. He spent a part of his time in farming, living in different places, but finally locating about three miles from Barwick, where he spent his remaining days, outliving the allotted three score and ten years of man's life. His wife, whose maiden name was Nancy Ausley, was born in North Carolina, and died before he did, leaving eight sons and one daughter.

Born in Brooks county, Georgia, Samuel J. Harrell at the age of nineteen years took upon himself the responsibilities of a married man, and began his independent career without other means than willing hands, a brave heart, and unlimited stock of energy and courage. At the breaking out of the war between the states, he enlisted and went through the war in the Confederate service. At the close of the conflict Mr. Harrell resumed his agricultural labors. Purchasing a small farm in Brooks county, he operated it for a time, but subsequently, desirous of enlarging his activities in that line, he rented a large plantation in the southern part of the county, and embarked in general farming on an extensive scale, in his undertaking being reasonably successful. A lifelong resident of Brooks county, he died at his home on the Grooverville road, at the age of sixty-four years. The maiden name of the wife of Samuel J. Harrell was Laura Jane Albritton. She was born in Brooks county, a daughter of Rev. George W. and Jane (Allen) Albritton. Mr. Albritton, who was a native of Georgia and a preacher in the Primitive Baptist church, enlisted during the Civil war for service in the Confederate army, and with his command took part in various campaigns and battles during the earlier part of the conflict, but in its last year was captured by the enemy and died from exposure while a prisoner of war. He carried with him as a soldier his bible and hymn book, saying he wanted to loan these to his comrades one and all. Capt. George W. Albritton was also a first lieutenant of the Florida Volunteers in the Indian wars of 1835, being commissioned by the governor before Florida was admitted as a state. His widow, who reared several children, survived him. Other members of the Albritton family were Mathew James and Isaac Abraham Albritton, both prominent lawyers of Brooks and Thomas counties and both reared near Quitman. Mrs. Samuel J. Harrell is still living on the homestead on the Grooverville road, and is the mother of eight children.

Having by diligent study acquired a practical education in the distriet schools, Mathew James Harrell remained with his parents until his marriage. Beginning then the struggle of life on his own account, he purchased seventy-five acres of land, fifteen acres only of which had been improved. His natural ability, early training and energetic spirit counted much in his favor, and through his own efforts he won success in his agricultural labors. Since that time, Mr. Harrell has bought and sold several tracts of land, and now has title to upwards of seven hundred and fifty acres, some of which is heavily timbered, while large fields are under a high state of cultivation, yielding abundant harvests each year. On his home place, situated four miles from Quitman, on the Grooverville road, Mr. Harrell has lived for the past fifteen years. Here he has a fine set of farm buildings, and in addition to carrying on mixed husbandry he has a well equipped saw mill, which he erected primarily for his own use. For a number of years he operated a threshing machine in various parts of the county.

Mr. Harrell first married, when but twenty years old, Annie Olive Winter, a daughter of Jeremiah and Lizzie (Boring) Winter, and granddaughter of Dr. Thomas and Martha (Le Noir) Boring. She passed to the higher life one short year after their marriage and her babe followed a few months later. Mr. Harrell married second Miss Addie Groover, who was born in Brooks county, Georgia, a daughter of Thomas and Susan (Joiner) Groover, and grand-daughter of James and Elizabeth (Denmark) Groover, pioneer settlers of Brooks county. Her mother died when she was but an infant, and her father subsequently married Sarah Joiner, a sister of his first wife, and an aunt of Mrs. Harrell. Eight children have blessed the union of Mr. and Mrs. Harrell, namely: Bennet, a well-known farmer; Walter, a clerk in the Quitman postoffice; Samuel T.; Annie Laurie, wife of W. D. Long; Ida Olivia, who was killed by a runaway horse at the age of fifteen on her way from school; Mathew J., Jr., Alma, and Wallace Eugene. Samuel T. Harrell, the third son, is a lawyer in Quitman, being in the firm of Bennett & Harrell. Mr. Harrell is a member of the Hickory Head Agricultural Society, and both he and his wife are faithful members of the Methodist Episcopal church.

JOHN HENRY EMANUEL. Since 1909 sheriff of Decatur county, Mr. Emanuel has been known to the citizens of this county since childhood, has been recognized as an industrious, independent man of action, and few men have entered office in this county with so thorough a confidence on the part of their supporters.

John Henry Emanuel was born on a farm five miles southwest of Faceville. His father Hilliard Marion Emanuel was born in the same locality, March 3, 1843. The father was reared on a farm and when a young man bought a tract of timbered land which is still included in his land holdings. There he built a log cabin, surrounded by the woods, and a primitive home it furnished to his family. He was one of the men who hewed out of the wilderness a fertile well developed farm, and thus added to the general prosperity of this section of the state. After a few years he built a more pretentious log house, and subsequently a good frame house which he still occupies as his residence. The maiden name of his wife was Martha J. Gray, who was born in Decatur county, a daughter of James and Jane (Cartledge) Gray. All the nine children of the parents were born in one of the log houses just mentioned. Their names are as follows: Martha F., James H., John Henry, Ella V., Hattie E., Amanda E., Letitia, William Lee and Daisey.

During his youth Mr. John Henry Emanuel was given the privileges of the neighborhood district schools, and at the same time assisted in the work of the home farm. When he was eighteen his father gave him his time and he started out for himself. He earned his first regular pay by cutting wood at fifty cents a cord, and later was for a time in the employ of the S. F. & W. Railroad Company, after which he returned to farming, which he followed for several years. He was clerk for a time and in carpenter work, and at various occupations until 1909, in which year he was elected to the office of sheriff, and his efficient record has caused his retention in that office to the present time.

In October 14, 1894, Mr. Emanuel married Miss Nancy Cora Campbell. She died June 8, 1902. In 1904 Mr. Emanuel married Emma L. Smith. The one daughter by the first marriage is named Dottie Lea, and the four children of the second union are Essie Pauline, John H., Jr., Frank W., and Woodrow.

ROBERT FRITZ ZEIGLER. Talented, enterprising, and progressive, Prof. Robert Fritz Zeigler is one of the more successful of the younger generation of educators in Ware county, as proprietor of Waycross Business College, at Waycross, helping many a young Georgian fit himself for a career of usefulness in industrial, business and professional fields. A native of South Carolina, he was born August 21, 1889, in Orangeburg county, where his father, Jesse Littleton Zeigler, was also born. His grandfather, George Josiah Zeigler, a life-long farmer in South Carolina, was a son of George John Zeigler, who was born in

Germany. He married Caroline Narcissus Averheart, who was the daughter of John Averheart, who came from Ireland during the Revolutionary war.

Brought up and educated in Orangeburg county, South Carolina, Jesse Littleton Zeigler was well drilled in agricultural pursuits as a boy, and as a young man, worked for several years in a mercantile establishment. Subsequently forming a partnership with Mr. F. J. Buyck, he became junior member of the firm of Buyck & Zeigler, farmers, merchants and millers, whose mills were located in and around Pine Grove township, at the same time being interested for awhile in a mercantile establishment at Fort Motte, owning that store with his oldest son, who had charge of it. The part of Orangeburg county in which he has lived for many years has been detached from that county, and now forms a part of Calhoun county, which he served as supervisor during the years 1909-12 inclusive.

Mr. Jesse Littleton Zeigler has been twice married. He married first Mary Fredonia Gaffney, who was born in Richland county, South Carolina, a daughter of William M. and Alice Euphenia Gaffney. She died in February 1904, leaving eight children, as follows: Jesse McLennan, Alice Euphenia, Ida Lee, Noland Theobald, Robert Fritz, Euna Fredonia, Jorene Buyck and George Josiah. Jorene Buyck and George Josiah are now attending Orangeburg College, Orangeburg, S. C. Jesse M. and Noland T.,who was a teacher for a few years, were engaged in the motor business for a short while at Orangeburg, after which Jesse M. accepted a position, which he now holds, with the International Harvester Company, as salesman and demonstrator. Noland T. is at present a traveling auditor, making Atlanta, Georgia, headquarters. Jesse M. married Maude Paulling Carroll, and they have three children, Sally Fredonia, Maude Carroll, and Myrtle May. Mr. J. L. Zeigler married for his second wife, in 1906, Lillian O. Jones, and they have three children, Capers Hayne, Jennie Lorene, and William Klauber.

Growing to manhood in Orangeburg county, South Carolina, Robert Fritz Zeigler was educated in the public and academical schools, later entering the Southern Business College, then at Orangeburg, for the study of book keeping and phonography. Under the instruction of Prof. A. H. White, a master penman and teacher of business science, he advanced rapidly, displaying unusual skill and ability. Recognizing in Mr. Zeigler those qualities that make a successful teacher, Prof. White organized the Orangeburg Business College, and offered him a position in the Shorthand Department, which he accepted and later became Principal of that department, which position he held for about two years. With the desire to better qualify himself, he took advantage of the home course offered to teachers of Pernin's Universal Phonography, by the Pernin Shorthand Institute, Detroit, Michigan.

Going then to Columbus, Georgia, he continued as a teacher there for a short time, when, having an opportunity to enter upon a broader sphere of action, he came to Waycross to assume charge of the Waycross Business College, which was then, in March 1908, owned by Benjamin J. Ferguson. Four months later, in July, 1908, Prof. Zeigler purchased the school from Mr. Ferguson, which he has since conducted with marked success. This institution is one of the leading ones of the kind in southeast Georgia, and under the efficient teaching of the professor and his assistants, the many pupils who come from various parts of Georgia and adjoining states, become familiar with typewriting, shorthand, bookkeeping, business mathematics, penmanship, English correspondence, office practice, and other branches of study used in the commercial world. As a penman, Mr. Zeigler has reached a high state of perfection, and his pupils find that he possesses not only the ability to write well himself, but that still rarer talent, which enables him to impart his knowledge to others.

True to the religious faith in which he was reared, Prof. Zeigler united with the Baptist church, and is now a deacon in the First Baptist church of Waycross, and the superintendent of its Sunday school.

NATHAN ATKINSON BROWN. A well-known and highly esteemed resident of Muscogee county, Nathan Atkinson Brown, of Columbus, Georgia, has served as deputy clerk of the United States circuit and district courts, and United States commissioner, for many years, and during the time has administered the affairs of his office so wisely and conscientiously, and with such thoroughness as to win the approval of all concerned.

He was born March 6, 1866, in Camden county, Georgia, on the same plantation that his father, the late Capt. Nathan Atkinson Brown, first drew the breath of life.

His grandfather David Brown was born in Pickens district, South Carolina. Coming to Georgia in pioneer days, he bought land in Camden county, and on this plantation, which he redeemed from its original wildness, spent the remainder of his life. He married Elizabeth Atkinson, and they reared a large family of children.

Capt. Nathan Atkinson Brown received his early education under the instruction of private tutors, later attending the Marietta Military Institute of Georgia. Although fitted for a professional career he chose the independent occupation of an agriculturalist, and with the assistance of slaves carried on farming successfully. During the war between the states, he entered the Confederate service on the fifth day of August, 1861, as a first lieutenant "Camden Rifles" in Company "I" of the 13th Georgia Regiment, Georgia Volunteers, C. S. A., commanded by Colonel Styles. He was honorably discharged from service by Col. Duncan L. Clinch on or about the 15th day of April, 1865, at which time he held the rank of captain of Company "C," 4th Georgia Cavalry. He was on duty the greater part of the war in south Georgia and Florida. The sword which he carried during the war was also used in the Revolutionary war by his grand-uncle John Atkinson, and in the War of 1812 by his uncle Nathan Atkinson, and is now one of the cherished possessions of his son Nathan A. Brown, of whom we write. He lived but a short time after the close of the war, his death occurring on February 23d, 1866.

Capt. Nathan Atkinson Brown married Louisa Tupper Nicholes, who was born in Beaufort district, South Carolina, a daughter of Dr. Henry J., and Eliza Witter (Turner) Nicholes, natives of the same state. Dr. Nicholes was a successful physician, and also an extensive planter. He operated his lands with his slaves' help, owning valuable rice plantations in Camden county, and cotton plantations in Glynn county, Georgia. During, or soon after the war, he removed from Camden to Cobb county, buying a home in Marietta and running a farm a few miles from that town. After spending a useful life, he departed this life for a more glorious one above. Left a widow when young, Mrs. Louisa Nicholes Brown, who had three small children, Eula, Lillie and Nathan Atkinson Brown, joined her father in Marietta. After his death she moved to Atlanta where she has resided up to the present time.

But an infant when his father died, Nathan A. Brown was partly brought up and educated in Marietta. After moving to Atlanta, he studied stenography, and secured a situation with the Richmond &

Danville Railroad Company, and was for several years stationed at Atlanta. Subsequently accepting a position with the Atlantic & Pacific Railroad Company he went to New Mexico, and was in the railway office at Albuquerque until 1890. During that period Mr. Brown spent his leisure time in reading law, and in that year returned to Georgia to still further pursue his legal studies. He entered the Atlanta Law School, and was among the first graduates receiving his degree of B. L., June 29, 1892. After completing his course he was admitted to the bar, and subsequently entered the office of Judge Henry B. Tompkins, formerly of the Savannah circuit. In 1897, Mr. Brown was appointed deputy clerk of the United States circuit and districts courts at Columbus, Georgia, and also United States commissioner, and he has continued in office ever since; his long record of service in those positions being ample proof of his ability and efficiency.

Mr. Brown first married in 1893, at Danville, New York, Miss Rose Hopkins, of Clay City, Illinois, a daughter of Wm. Hopkins and Miriam (Kelly) Hopkins. She bore him three sons, Donald Vincent, Nathan Atkinson, and William Hopkins Brown. The former was a beautiful child of four years when he died of scarlet fever. His devoted mother followed him to the beautiful mansion above in September, 1904. Mr. Brown's second marriage, which took place at Macon, Georgia, June 4, 1908, was to Miss Annie Daniel, of Macon, Georgia, a daughter of William Brantly and Urquhart (Evans) Daniel, and of this union two children have been born, namely: Mildred Daniel Brown and Louise Evans Brown. Religiously Mr. and Mrs. Brown are members of the Baptist church. Fraternally he belongs to Mount Hermon Lodge No. 304, Ancient Free and Accepted Order of Masons.

WILLIAM T. CHINA. A capable and intelligent business man of Lyons, Toombs county, William T. China, cashier of the Toombs County Bank, has long been identified with the best interests of the community, and has proved himself a valuable and worthy citizen. Born at Williamsburg, South Carolina, April 28, 1874, he was reared in the homes of relatives, his parents having died when he was a child.

Growing to manhood in his native state, Mr. China acquired a practical education in the public schools, and was early trained to habits of industry and thrift. Coming to Georgia in 1898, he first engaged in the turpentine business, and was afterwards bookkeeper for the Lyons Trading Company for a year. In 1906, Mr. China was elected cashier of the Toombs County Bank, a position which he has since filled ably and satisfactorily. This institution has a capital stock of $30,000, and is under the management of men of tried and true integrity and ability, Enoch J. Giles being its president; R. L. Page, vice-president; and Mr. China, cashier. Mr. China has never shirked the responsibilities of public office, but is now serving most acceptably as a member of the city council, and as city treasurer.

On December 28, 1899, Mr. China was united in marriage with Mamie J. Parker, a daughter of J. P. Parker, of Troy, Alabama. She is a most estimable woman, and a member of the Baptist church.

WILLIAM E. DAVIS. One of the oldest residents of the town of Meigs, and a representative of a family which has been identified with Georgia for several generations, Mr. Davis has had a long and interesting career. He is a native of Oglethorpe county, where he was born December 19, 1839.

His father, William J. Davis, who was born in Virginia, December 14, 1802, at an early age was left an orphan and then went to live with an uncle, Middleton Pope. Soon afterward the Pope family came to Georgia, and he was reared on a farm in Oglethorpe county, his uncle being one of the first settlers there. Middleton Pope acquired large tracts of land in that part of the state, operating them with slave labor. His wife survived him and spent her last days in Athens. Their only child married David C. Barrow, of which union was born Pope Barrow. Early in his career William J. Davis bought land in Oglethorpe county, having slaves to work it, and lived there until his death on September 8, 1858. He married Angelina Lumpkin on the 24th of December, 1827. She was born in Oglethorpe county, June 28, 1801, and belonged to one of the most prominent families in Georgia during the first half of the last century. Her father was Rev. George Lumpkin, a native and life-long resident of Oglethorpe county, where he conducted a farm and also performed the duties of a pioneer minister of the Missionary Baptist church. A brother of this minister was a governor of the state of Georgia, and another brother was Judge Joseph Lumpkin. Mrs. William J. Davis died on December 21, 1847. Both she and her husband were members of the Missionary Baptist church. They were the parents of eleven children, named as follows: George, Middleton, Sarah, Annie J., Matilda, Martha A., William E., Mary, Lucy Pope, Howell Cobb, and Josephine.

William E. Davis was sixteen years old when his father died, and his older brother Middleton then returned home and became head of the family until its members had found homes of their own. Not long after attaining manhood and taking up the serious duties of life, the war broke out and William E., then a young man of twenty-two, enlisted in May, 1861, in Company K of the Eighth Georgia Infantry under Colonel Barton. The command went to the front and was attached to Longstreet's corps in the army of North Virginia, participating in many of the campaigns and battles in the principal seat of the civil conflict. He was in the first battle at Manassas Junction, and a few days later was within a few miles and in plain sight of the city of Washington. The seven days' fighting around Richmond, the Wilderness, Williamsburg, Martinsburg, were other notable engagements in which he did a soldier's part. At Mechanicsburg, Company K and another company were sent out to meet the Yankees. All were lying on the ground when a shell burst above them. Mr. Davis was stunned by one of the fragments while the men on each side of him were killed outright, and he was covered with their blood. The companies retreated and he was left for dead among his slain comrades. After a time, when he recovered consciousness, he observed that the enemy had occupied the field all about him. Keeping still and watching his opportunity, he finally crawled into a swamp, and at night found his way back to camp, where he was passed by the pickets. He then lay down among his sleeping comrades, and the next morning afforded them a surprise as though returned from the dead, and they hailed him as the dead man. His captain had already dispatched a letter informing Mr. Davis' sister of his death on the field of battle, and it was some time before the truth came to end her bereavement. Mr. Davis performed a strenuous service as a southern soldier until the spring of 1864, when on account of disability he was honorably discharged and returned home. As soon as he had recovered, however, he was back in service, this time in the Twenty-ninth Battalion of Georgia Cavalry, and was in the coast defense until the close of the war.

In May, 1865, his duty to the southland had been discharged and he went to his sister's home in Decatur county. He arrived so destitute of clothing that she tore up one of her dresses to make him a shirt. Mr.

Davis is one of the honored citizens who, at the close of the war, set to work in the reconstruction of their own fortunes and the rebuilding of a new industrial society. His first employment was as overseer on a Decatur county farm, where he remained two years. He then paid six hundred dollars for sixty-two and a half acres of land in Mitchell county, rebuilt a log house that stood on the place, and there commenced his career as an independent farmer. From that time to the present, through much hard labor and careful management during the earlier years, he has been on the highroad to material prosperity. In a few years he sold his first place and bought two hundred and fifty acres fifteen miles southwest of Camilla, which continued to be his home for about ten years. He then sold and bought a farm of one hundred and twenty-five acres six miles southeast of Camilla, and lived there until 1884. In that year he transferred his residence to Thomas county and the vicinity of the present town of Meigs, buying one hundred and twenty-five acres close to the present townsite. A sawmill, a turpentine still and a commissary then comprised all the activities at the point, and he has witnessed every important addition to the town. He afterwards increased his land to three hundred acres, and continued to operate it and make it his home until 1911, in which year he moved into town and built a comfortable residence for his declining years. His home is surrounded by a considerable tract of land in the cultivation of which he keeps himself busy.

Mr. Davis was married in 1867 to Miss Martha Evans. She was born in Baker county, this state. Her father, Alfred Evans, a native of Alabama, who was left an orphan, came to Georgia, settling in Baker county, where he lived some years, then moved to Decatur and later to Mitchell county, and finally to Cairo, which was then in Thomas county but is now the county seat of Grady county. At Cairo he bought a farm now included in the town limits, and lived there till his death at the age of fifty-two. Alfred Evans married Grace Ann Smith, who died at Cairo aged seventy-two years, and she reared ten children.

Mr. and Mrs. Davis are the parents of eleven children, namely: William M., Alfred, Leonora, Russell, Mattie, Gordon, Lucy, Haggard, Clifford, Herbert and Rossa. William has been twice married, his first wife being Della Adams and his second Bessie Brandage. His eight children, all by the first wife, are Roscoe, Annie, Emma, Meda, Johnnie, Ernest, Ruby and George. Alfred, the second son, married Katie Wilkes, and their children include Lois, Wilkes, Edwin, Harrold and Kathleen. Leonora married J. J. Boswell, and they have one son, Julian. Russell married Nabbie Grant, and they have four children, Jewell, John, Evans and Nina. Mattie is the wife of J. D. Atkinson, and her two children are Grace and Clifford. Gordon married Mittie Lay. Lucy is the wife of J. A. Sasser, and their three children are Lucille, Ina and Mildred. Haggard married Hattie Redfern. Clifford is the wife of Hayward Singleton, and has two children, Huldah and Hagar. Herbert married Jimmie Golden, and they have one son, Frederick.

Mr. and Mrs. Davis have enjoyed long and prosperous lives, have provided well for themselves and children, and in the evening of life their greatest pleasure is in the large family of children and grandchildren who honor and venerate them. All the family are members of the Baptist church.

ROBERT E. BARFIELD. The present mayor of the town of Hahira has for a number of years been one of the progressive farmers of this vicinity and represents a pioneer family in Lowndes county. Mr. Barfield was born on the farm where he now resides on the 6th of March, 1878, his residence being within the corporate limits.

His grandfather was Frederick Jones Barfield, who was probably born in Jones county, this state, and in 1858 moved to Lowndes county, which was then much larger than at present, with the county seat at Troupville. No railroads had yet penetrated to this section, and he was one of the pioneers in development of the country. He bought a tract of timber land four miles south of the present site of Hahira, and with his slaves was engaged in general farming up to the time of his death, which occurred when he was fifty-five years old. The maiden name of his wife was Bethany Brewer, who was born either in Jones or an adjoining county, and she survived her husband several years.

The father of Robert E. Barfield was named Gen. Lafayette Barfield, and he was born in Jones county in 1857, but lived in Lowndes county from the time he was one year of age. On beginning life for himself he purchased a tract of land, part of which is now included in the town of Hahira. About thirty-five acres of it was cleared, and the log cabin in which Robert E. was born constituted the principal improvement on the place at the time. On the death of the grandfather he left this place and took charge of the old home estate in the interest of the other heirs, and later bought the other interests and became sole owner. There he lived until his death in 1896 at the age of thirty-nine. He married Feddie Wilson, a native of Lowndes county and daughter of Solomon and Sarah Wilson, pioneers of this county. She is now a resident of Arizona. She reared nine children, named as follows: Navie E., Robert E., Sally, Frederick, Maggie Gordon, General L., Jr., Maude, Pearl and Hester Eugene.

Robert E. Barfield, the oldest son of this family, was reared on the old homestead south of Hahira and attended school in Mineola. Being eighteen when his father died, the care of the estate devolved upon him, his father's will making him executor, and on coming of age he took full charge. The farm was his home until his marriage, and he then moved to Valdosta and served twenty-one months as deputy sheriff. After this official service he lived on the farm again for a year, and then managed the farm two years from his home in Valdosta. He was engaged in sawmilling for two years, at the end of which time he located in Hahira and the following year built his present residence in town, located on the same farm on which he was born. He has been chiefly occupied in general farming. As a resident of town he takes an active part in its affairs, and is now serving his second term in the office of mayor.

Mr. Barfield was married in 1898 to Miss Eula Belle Newton, who was born in Brooks county, a daughter of James and Sarah J. Newton. Mr. and Mrs. Barfield have one son, Robert E., Jr. Mrs. Barfield is a member of the Baptist church, which her husband also attends. Fraternally he affiliates with Valdosta Lodge No. 346, A. F. & A. M., and with Adele Chapter, R. A. M. In politics he is a Democrat.

JOHN ELIJAH WEBB. Now one of the most prosperous planters of Lowndes county and a citizen whose services have often contributed to the general advancement and public welfare of his community, John Elijah Webb began his career practically without any of the material equipment and capital which are supposed to be necessary to successful endeavor. He is one of the substantial men upon whom the solid prosperity and civic progress of south Georgia depend.

John Elijah Webb was born in Macon county, Georgia, July 16, 1861, a son of John and Elizabeth (Lamb) Webb. The Webb family with its connections has been identified with this state for nearly a century, and its members have been honorable and productive factors in the civic and material life of the state. A brief history of Mr. Webb's antecedents is published elsewhere in this work in the sketch of W. W. Webb, and hence need not be repeated here.

The war all but destroyed the fortunes of Mr. Webb's father, and as his childhood fell during the years of that struggle and the reconstruction period he was without many of the advantages which youths of the best families enjoyed before the war and in the modern era of prosperity. To the education supplied by the neighborhood schools he has since added by extensive reading. His assistance was early required on the farm, and when still a very young man the entire management of the home place devolved upon him through the retirement of his father from active labor on account of ill health. In meeting the responsibilities of this situation, his first act was to sell all the mules to pay off indebtedness, and this heroic measure left him without stock to run the place. Giving his personal note for $40.00 to a colored man in payment for a blind horse, he thus began his independent career at farming. He had his parents to support and a younger brother and sister to educate, but his industry and courage never failed to meet the responsibilities. Finally he sold his horse for $25.00 and bought a mule for $100.00. With $75.00 cash he gave his note for $40.00 for the balance. This brief sketch will not take up the details of the way in which he worked out success, and the above facts are mentioned merely to show some of the difficulties in his start. What he has accomplished from such a beginning is illustrated in his present possession of a plantation of eight hundred acres in one body, well stocked and with excellent building improvements, and he also owns an interest in a tract of four hundred acres. Mr. Webb is a director in the Hahira Bank, is a member of the Senith Mercantile Company, and a stockholder in the Tennessee Oil & Gas Company.

At the age of twenty-four Mr. Webb was married to Miss Anna P. Nichols, who was born in Lowndes county, a daughter of Thomas and Mary (Vickers) Nichols. Mr. and Mrs. Webb are parents of the following children: Mary, Elizabeth, Everett, Pearl, Vesta Van Buren, Minnie Eugenia. Mr. Webb and wife are members of the Methodist church.

In politics he is a Democrat, and has long taken an active part in public affairs. For four years he was member of the county board of education, and also did good service on the county board of road and revenue commissioners. He was a member of the latter when the court house was constructed, when the first definite steps were taken to straighten the county roads, and when the bridges at Troupville and over the Little river were built. These bridges can now be crossed at any stage of water, and are considered among the best improvements of the county.

C. C. CURRY. A man of distinctive energy and much force of character, C. C. Curry, of Vidalia, head of the law firm of Curry & Williams, possesses a natural aptitude for the work of his profession, being industrious, earnest and persistent in the advocacy of his client's cause, while his record gives evidence of his wide legal knowledge and his broad reasoning powers have won him success in his labors. A native of Washington county, Georgia, he was born May 7, 1871, near Curry's old mill site, in the vicinity of Warthen Station. His father, A. G. Curry, served in the Confederate army during the Civil war, enlisting in a company of Georgia Volunteer Infantry, and for awhile being a prisoner-of-war.

Leaving the old home farm at the age of twenty-one years, C. C. Curry began work for himself as a bridge constructor on a railroad in Florida, for three years standing guard over a gang of convict laborers in Dutton. During that period he attended school for the first time, and by night study progressed from the primer to the third reader. Going then to Hague, Florida, he found himself so far behind in his studies that he became somewhat discouraged, and returned to the convict camp, where he remained a year. Having while there made good use of his every leisure moment, Mr. Curry entered the Normal institute at Jasper, Florida. A year later the professors of that school established the Georgia Normal College and Business Institute, and Mr. Curry became one of its first pupils. For three years he paid his way through that institution by janitor service, and the succeeding two years by tutoring. Going then to Valparaiso, Indiana, he entered the Law department of the Northern Indiana Normal school, and by working as a waiter in a restaurant, and selling books, he maintained himself until his graduation, with the class of 1901, with a good record for scholarship.

Returning to Georgia, Mr. Curry began the practice of his profession at Abbeville, and as a lawyer has been eminently successful. He is now located at Vidalia, being senior member of the firm of Curry & Williams, attorneys, and has here built up a substantial and remunerative patronage. A man of pleasing address and personality, with a gift for oratory, Mr. Curry has won quite a reputation as a platform dialect entertainer, lecturer, elocutionist, humorist and musician, in the latter capacity being an expert banjo player. Fraternally he is a member of the Ancient Free and Accepted Order of Masons.

Mr. Curry married, at Abbeville, Georgia, Mattie Doster, a daughter of A. J. and Caroline Doster, and into their home four sons have made their advent, namely: Clifton, born in 1902; Olin Wimberly, born in 1904; A. J. (Jack), born in 1906; and Joe Brown, born in 1908.

WALTER EDWARD BRADLEY. Realizing the fact that the editor and proprietor of a newspaper occupies a vantage ground which may make or mar a reputation, or build up or break down a cause worthy of support, the citizens of Baxley have reason for congratulation that the Baxley *News-Banner* is in such safe, sagacious and thoroughly clean hands. It is considered one of the best general newspapers in the county, as well as an outspoken, fairplay exponent of all measures for the benefit of the community, and is in all respects well worthy of the care and sound judgment displayed in its columns, and reflects credit on its owner, Walter Edward Bradley. Mr. Bradley is a native of Appling county, and was born near the town of Graham, August 24, 1888, a son of Elijah and Annie (Downs) Bradley. His grandfather, Edward Bradley, was a native of Chatham county, where he was a large slave holder and planter, and his maternal grandfather, D. M. Downs, also came from that locality. Elijah Bradley was born and reared in Liberty county, served as second lieutenant in a Georgia regiment during the war between the states, under General Lee, and after the close of hostilities became a prominent merchant. He and his wife had the following children: J. R., who is thirty-four years of age; Walter Edward; Joseph, who is sixteen years old; Susie, the wife of T. M. Brown, a merchant of Tifton, Georgia; and Ruby, who married J. K. Kinzey, a locomotive engineer residing at Tallahassee, Florida.

Walter Edward Bradley was three years of age when his parents removed to Eastman, Dodge county, and there he resided twelve years, his early education being secured in the public schools of that place. He was graduated from the Eastman high school in 1900, and after attending Emory College for one term started to learn the printer's trade in the office of the Eastman *Times-Journal,* with which he was associated until coming to Baxley in the latter part of 1909. He then became the successor of D. M. Parker as editor and publisher of the *News-Banner,* which he has succeeded in making one of the most popular and reliable sheets in the county. This is a flourishing, bright, attractive and well-edited newspaper, and enjoys a large circulation in Baxley and the surrounding country. The office is fitted with all modern appliances found in first-class establishments, and the job printing department has a large and rapidly growing patronage. Mr. Bradley supports all movements which he believes will be of benefit to his community, and is recognized as wielding a great deal of influence in forming public opinion in public matters.

On April 23, 1910, Mr. Bradley was married to Miss Sallie Maie Melton, daughter of the late G. T. Melton, a planter and merchant of Baxley, and they have a bright, interesting son, Edward Melton, now aged two years. Mr. and Mrs. Bradley are popular in social circles, and are well known in religious work as members of the Methodist church South. He is fraternally connected with the Masons, the Odd Fellows, the Knights of Pythias and the Woodmen of the World.

GEORGE FLETCHER MCLEOD. The people who constitute the bone and sinew of this country are not those who are unstable and unsettled, who fly from this occupation to that, who do not know where they stand on political questions till they are told how to vote, and who take no active and intelligent interest in affairs affecting their schools, church and property. The backbone of this country is made up of families which have made their own homes, who are alive to the best interests of the community in which they reside, who are so honest that it is no trouble for their neighbors to know it, who attend to their own business and are too busy to attend to that of others, who work steadily on from day to day, taking the sunshine with the storm, and who rear a fine family to an honest name and comfortable home. Such people are always welcome in any community and any country. Among such people is the valiant ex-soldier and successful business man, who is the subject of this brief review—George Fletcher McLeod.

Mr. McLeod was born November 23, 1842, in Macon, Georgia, and when a child of four years removed with his parents John Fletcher and Harriet (Smith) McLeod, to near Abbeville, Wilcox county, Georgia. He resided upon his father's farm until about the age of seventeen years, giving over the roseate days of youth to obtaining a schooling, assisting his father in the work of the farm and in the usual pursuits and recreations dear to boyhood. He was the first young man to enlist in the Confederate army from Wilcox county, becoming a member of Company C, Eighth Georgia Infantry, of General Bartow's command. He participated in the first battle of Bull Run, was severely wounded in the head with a minnie ball and remained in the hospital at Charlottesville, Virginia, for about a year. As soon as he was able to leave the hospital he went back to service and served throughout the remainder of the great conflict as captain of the commissary department.

After the termination of the Civil war, Mr. McLeod accepted the new conditions with manly courage and fortitude and at once took his place in the business world, engaging in the saw-mill, lumber and timber business at Abbeville, Georgia, for a number of years and since then has been engaged in other pursuits. He has fine executive ability and fine business principles and has proved successful. He has also had important financial connections and was at one time president and is now director of the Bank of Abbeville, no small part of the high standing of this monetary institution being due to his discrimination. Mr. McLeod had five brothers and two sisters, but he is now the only surviving member of his family.

On December 20, 1881, the subject was united in marriage to Martha Wimberly, daughter of Lewis Dawson and Juliet (Powell) Wimberly, of Macon. Mrs. McLeod's family is a representative one of the South, her maternal grandfather, Hugh Powell, and his wife, Martha (Cottrell) Powell, having been well-known Virginians. The subject and his admirable wife have reared three fine sons and two charming and accomplished daughters to young manhood and womanhood. John Lewis is now located in Savannah; George Fletcher is in Abbeville; Wimberly is a student in the State University at Athens, Georgia; and Julia and Irene reside at home. Miss Julia is a rarely gifted elocutionist and teacher of the art and has given many dramatic readings for the benefit of churches, schools and societies. Irene is a gifted vocalist and is a much sought soloist and member of local choirs.

Mr. McLeod is a popular Mason and exemplifies in his own living the ideals of moral and social justice and brotherly love for which the order stands. He is also affiliated with the Independent Order of Odd Fellows and the S. D. Fullen Camp, United Confederate Veterans with whom he renews the old comradeship of other days. Mrs. McLeod, one of Abbeville's representative ladies, has been president of the Abbeville Chapter of the Daughters of the Confederacy since its organization some twelve years ago. The subject and his family are helpful members of the Methodist Episcopal church, South.

V. L. DARBY, M. D. A rising young physician of Denton, V. L. Darby, M. D., where he has a good practice, is fast winning for himself an honored name in the medical profession. He was born, February 29, 1884, on a farm near Monroe, Walton county, Georgia, and this year, 1912, had the pleasure of celebrating his natal day the seventh time. His parents, W. L. and Lulu (Hale) Darby, were both natives of Walton county, having been born on neighboring plantations.

Completing his early education in the Vidalia High school, V. L. Darby spent two years in the Medical department of the University of Georgia, in Augusta, and at the age of twenty-one years, in 1905, was graduated from the Maryland Medical College, in Baltimore, there receiving the degree of M. D. Then, after practicing medicine in Vidalia, Georgia, for a year, he took a post graduate course in New Orleans, while in that city spending some time at the Central America Yellow Fever Quarantine station for the state of Louisiana, gaining professional knowledge and experience impossible to acquire elsewhere. Returning to Georgia, Dr. Darby settled first in Hoschton, from there coming again to Vidalia, where he built up a good patronage, and about February 1, 1913, he moved to Denton; his success in dealing with difficult cases having won for him the confidence and good will of the people.

Dr. Darby has the distinction of being a charter member of the Chi Zeta Chi medical fraternity, which was organized at the University of Georgia in 1903, being the first Greek Letter society of that institution. He also belongs to several of Vidalia's fraternal lodges, including the Knights of Pythias, the Independent Order of Odd Fellows; and the Woodmen of the World. Both he and his wife are members of the Baptist church.

At Hoschton, Georgia, Dr. Darby was united in marriage with Ruth

Hosch, a daughter of Hon. John R. Hosch, her father having been a man of prominence and influence, and one of the leading lumber manufacturers and dealers of his community. The doctor and Mrs. Darby have one child, Virgil Hosch Darby, born in 1909.

REV. JOSEPH N. SMITH. An ardent believer and upholder of the truths of the Holy Scriptures, Rev. Joseph N. Smith, of Hazlehurst, Jeff Davis county, is known far and wide as a man of strong convictions, and deep consecration, and as one who is bound heart and soul to the work of the Christian ministry. A native of Georgia, he was born, March 31, 1852, in Emanuel county, on the farm of his father, John G. Smith.

Born in North Carolina, John G. Smith was but a small lad when brought by his parents to Georgia, where he grew to manhood, and subsequently made farming his chief occupation. During the Civil war he served bravely in a Georgia regiment, being commissioned as lieutenant of his company, and acting as captain in time of need. He took part in many engagements of note, and in a hard-fought battle just above Atlanta, was severely wounded. Two of his brothers, W. D. Smith and George W. Smith, also took part in the Civil war, serving in the Thirty-second Georgia Regiment, under Colonel Harrison. George W., the younger brother, died while in the army, at Mount Pleasant, South Carolina, while the elder brother, W. D., served as a private throughout the entire war, and at the engagement at Ocean Pond being severely injured by the falling of a tree.

Spending the first forty years of his life in Emanuel county, Joseph N. Smith acquired his early education in the district schools, and as a boy and youth became familiar with farm work. In early life he manifested strong religious tendencies, and almost as a matter of course entered the ministry, becoming associated with the Primitive Baptist church. In 1877 he was licensed to preach, and in November, 1878, Mr. Smith was ordained to full work in the denomination, and even now serves from one to four churches regularly. He also does contract work as a carpenter and builder, making good use of his natural mechanical ability and genius. Leaving his native county in 1894, Mr. Smith spent four years in Laurens county. Going then to Telfair county, he remained in Helena eight years, but for the past six years has maintained his home in Hazlehurst, and has here continued active work in the ministry, meeting with a due need of success in his labors.

Rev. Mr. Smith married, in 1873, Miss Georgia Gillis, a daughter of A. J. Gillis, who served as a member of the Georgia Cavalry in the Civil war, and of Elizabeth (Ricks) Gillis. Of the eleven children born of the union of Mr. and Mrs. Smith one child, Dora, has passed to the higher life, and ten are living, and all are married, namely: J. A., born in 1878; J. T., born in 1880; C. O., born in 1885; W. L., born in 1894; Hilrie, born in 1898; Lizzie, Mollie, Mamie, and Vernie. The family are all members of the Primitive Baptist church, and active workers therein.

ANDREW GILL, who is road-master for the Gulf Line Railroad at Sylvester, Georgia, was born on February 10, 1854, near Troupville, (Lowndes) now Brooks county, Georgia, on the farm of his father, John Gill. His mother was Nancy (McLeod) Gill, a native of Virginia, while his father was a native of South Carolina. Both were of Scotch ancestry. John Gill served in the Volunteer army of the Confederate states of America during the Civil war and saw much active service throughout its duration. He was wounded at Gettysburg and came home in January, 1865.

Until he was nineteen years of age, Andrew Gill assisted with the work of the farm, his actual school attendance in those years not aggregating nine months. After leaving the farm he went to work as a track hand, beginning October 3, 1873, in the employ of the Atlantic & Gulf Railroad, remaining thus employed for four months. At the end of that time he was promoted to the position of section foreman, a post which he held for sixteen years with that road and its successors, the Plant System and the Atlantic Coast Line. In 1890 he was promoted from the position of track foreman to that of conductor of a construction train, and he served three years in that capacity. In 1893 he was made supervisor of the Fifth Division of the Plant System, serving thus for nine years, after which he was promoted to the position of road-master, in which important position he continued for two years, making his entire service with this company, as measured by time, to cover a period of thirty years. In 1904, Mr. Gill quit the railroad service and engaged in business for himself as the operator of a naval store, and in this enterprise he continued through a period of seven years. In October, 1911, he took service as superintendent of construction with the Cotton State Construction Company in railroad building, the work being in connection with the Gulf Line Railroad where he is at present employed as road-master.

Mr. Gill has been twice married. On March 9, 1875, he was united in marriage with Sarah Martin, the daughter of A. V. Martin of Georgia. She died on October 20, 1877, leaving two children,—Mary, who died in her nineteenth year of life, and W. D., who died in infancy. On January 22, 1879, he was married to Mollie Foster, the daughter of Hampton C. Foster, a native of Tennessee, and Sarah (Smith) Foster, of Georgia. Of this latter union ten children were born, of which number nine are living. They are: Andrew W.; Fannie L.; Hampton C.; Lewis M.; Anna Vashti; M. W. Roy; Katie; Peter, and Robert L. Mr. Gill had two brothers,—Daniel and Angus, both of whom are deceased, and his sisters, Jane and Laura, are both married and make their homes in Georgia.

The Gill family is one held in high esteem in their community, where they have been well known for years. They have no definite church affiliations, but attend all churches impartially. Mr. Gill is a Mason of the Royal Arch degree.

R. LEE MOORE. The South perhaps more than any other region has been famous for the public-spirited men it has produced. Its lawyers have attained to the highest eminence in the jurisprudence of the nation; its publicists have determined wisely and well questions of public policy, and its military men have for their gallantry achieved undying fame in the hearts of the people. In this region and from such honored forebears resides R. Lee Moore, one of Statesboro's leading citizens and a former mayor of the community. In him there runs a strain of all these characteristics, which combined in splendid manhood have enabled him to attain to the position he occupies in the hearts of his fellow townsmen.

Mr. Moore has not yet attained to the meridian of life, despite the attainments which he bears and which usually mark the man of more advanced years. He was born at Scarboro, in Screven county, Georgia, on November 27, 1867, his parents being Zacariah and Mary (Jackson) Moore. The former was a native of Washington county, Georgia, October 2, 1825, being the date of his nativity. He died in 1887. His wife, who was born in Wilkinson county, Georgia, in 1840, is still living.

Reared on the home plantation in Screven county, R. Lee Moore was carefully educated for a profession. His early educational training was in Scarboro Academy, after which he continued his studies at the Middle Georgia Military Academy at Millidgeville, of which Gen. D. H. Hill was then president. Passing from college to active life he taught school for a time in Screven county, and later was employed as a salesman in a mercantile establishment at Millen.

His ambition beckoned him onward, however, and he went to the city of Savannah, whose larger field afforded the opportunity he so greatly desired. He found employment as a clerk and bookkeeper, and at once set about the study of law, the privilege of practicing at the bar being the goal toward which he set his course. He finally entered the law department of the University of Georgia, in which he graduated as a member of the class of 1890, receiving the degree of Bachelor of Laws. He was admitted to the bar of his native state at Athens, June 18, 1890 by Judge N. L. Hutchinson.

He located at Statesboro, the county seat of Bulloch county, and has resided there continuously ever since. His natural aptitude and comprehensive education were recognized and he met with pronounced success. He has been found equally at home in the various division of law practice and has achieved a high rank in the profession. Mr. Moore is known abroad as well as in his home community as one of the ablest lawyers in Middle Georgia. Besides his large practice he has a successful business in farm loans.

Always a stanch adherant of the principles of the democratic party, Mr. Moore has taken an active part in its affairs in his section of Georgia. His judgment is excellent as regards political situations and in the counsels of the party his advice is always sought. In 1912, Mr. Moore was promiently mentioned as a candidate for congress from the first congressional district, but he declined to enter the race. In December, 1905, his fellow townsmen gave significant evidence of their esteem by electing him to the office of Mayor, to which place he was re-elected for for the succeeding term. His administrations are spoken of in the highest terms by all.

On June 22, 1893, Mr. Moore was united in marriage with Miss Laura Alderman, daughter of Hiram and Emma (Jones) Alderman, of Melrose, Florida.

CHARLES WYNNE ATTWILL, attorney at law, and fast forging to the front in his profession, is a native born Georgian, his birth taking place at Savannah, on December 15, 1879. He is the son of Charles Wesley and Lupina Rebecka (Horn) Attwill. The father was a native of West Moreland county, Virginia, while the mother was born in Laurens county, near Dublin, and reared in Thomasville, Thomas county. Charles W. Attwill, the elder, was employed in Savannah by the Hogan Dry Goods Company until the time of his death, which occurred on March 20, 1881. They were the parents of two children: Charles W. of this brief personal review and Susie, who died at the age of four years.

The son, Charles W., attended school in Savannah until he was ten years of age, the old Chatham Academy being the scene of his studies, and he then came to Eastman accompanied by his mother and her stepfather, Dr. D. Cox, and in Eastman high school completed his studies and was graduated therefrom in 1896. In 1898 the young man took a business course at Ozark, Alabama, and later studied law at Mercer University in Macon, Georgia, from which institution he was graduated in 1904. On June 8th of that year he began the practice of his profession in Mount Vernon, in which he has since made continuous and consistent advance. In the years 1905, '06 and '07 Mr. Attwill was official stenographer for the city courts of Eastman, McRae and Baxley, a position which he filled most admirably, as a result of his efficient business training, and on January 1, 1910, he was appointed by Gov. Joseph Brown to fill out the unexpired term of 'W. M. Morrison as solicitor of the city court of Eastman, which he retained until the expiration of the term, on June 1, 1911. He has conducted a general law practice with most pleasing results, and is the legal representative of the Dodge Fertilizer Works, also the First National Bank of Eastman.

Mr. Attwill is unmarried, and makes his home with his mother, who still lives in Eastman.

SIDNEY DOUGLAS DELL. Broad-minded, talented, and progressive, Sidney Douglas Dell, a young and leading attorney of Hazlehurst, has acquired distinction in legal circles, both at the bar and the bench, his advancement along professional paths having been swift, while each step has been creditable to him both as a man and as a lawyer. A native of Georgia, he was born, August 18, 1885, in Sylvania, Screven county.

His father, John C. Dell, was for many years a prominent attorney of Screven county, and a citizen of influence. A stalwart supporter of the principles and policies of the Democratic party, he contributed largely towards the advancement of its cause, representing his district in the state legislature; serving as chairman of the Democratic executive committee of Screven county, and, in 1896, being delegate at large to the convention that first nominated William J. Bryan for the presidency. He married Fannie Sharpe, of Screven county, and to them seven children were born, as follows: Jesse, private secretary to the quarter master general at Washington, District of Columbia; E. P., who is reading law at Hazlehurst with his brother Sidney; Nellie P., wife of Dr. W. B. Mell, formerly of Effingham county, but now residing in Sylvania; Mary, who conducts a circulating library at Sylvania, Georgia; Sidney Douglas; and two that have passed to the higher life.

After a thorough preliminary course of study in his native town, Sidney D. Dell was sent to Washington, District of Columbia, and was there graduated from the academic department of the Georgetown University. While in that department, he spent his evenings in reading law, and subsequently entered the law department of that institution, from which he was graduated in 1908. The years previous to that date, Mr. Dell had, in addition to keeping up with his academic and legal studies, served as stenographer for the Southern Railway Company's treasurer, a position which he retained until November, 1908, when, on account of the illness and death of his mother, he was called home. Remaining to settle up the family estate, Mr. Dell concluded to locate permanently in Georgia. On January 24, 1909, he continued his studies at Mercer University, in Macon, where he was graduated on June 2, 1909, and on the same day was admitted to the Georgia bar, and likewise to practice in the United States circuit court before Hon. Emory Speer. On June 15, of the same year, Mr. Dell was admitted to practice in the appellate court of Georgia, and he has, in addition to all this, license to practice in the courts of the District of Columbia.

On June 7, 1909, Mr. Dell began to practice of his profession at Hazlehurst, and about a month later was appointed trustee in bankruptcy by the referee of bankruptcy of the eastern division of the southern district of Georgia in the celebrated Gilmore case, which, on account of the many intricate legal points involved, was one of great importance. In January, 1910, Mr. Dell became associated with Judge H. A. King, becoming junior member of the firm of King & Dell, which was recently dissolved. In November, 19—, Mr. Dell was made judge of the city court of Hazlehurst, and has the honor and distinction of being one of the youngest judges on the bench. Especially well informed in regard to the law of bankruptcy and insolvency, Mr. Dell is prepared to handle bankruptcy cases in both Baxley and McRae.

Mr. Dell married, June 30, 1909, Miss Sadie Norman, daughter of Rev. Robert R. and Mary Norman, of Wilkes county, Georgia. Both Mr. and Mrs. Dell are valued members of the Methodist church. Fraternally, Mr. Dell is a member and the secretary of his lodge of Ancient Free and Accepted Order of Masons; and belongs to the Knights of Pythias.

J. WADE JOHNSON, vice president and general manager of the Southern Loan and Investment Company, Vidalia, Georgia, was born November 29, 1882, fifteen miles from Vidalia, in what was then Montgomery, now Toombs county, son of J. C. and Anna (Sharp) Johnson, both natives of Georgia. His grandfather Sharp is said to be the oldest man now living in Montgomery county. J. C. Johnson is one of the representative farmers of Toombs county. He is a veteran of the Southern army, for two years, 1863 and 1864, having tented and marched and fought with the boys in gray, his command being Company F, Sixty-first Georgia Infantry.

His father a farmer, young Johnson was reared to farm life and received his education in the common schools of his native county. He remained with his father until he was twenty-two years of age. On leaving the homestead, he accepted a position as deputy clerk of the supreme court of Montgomery county, which place he filled acceptably for a period of five years. He was elected vice president of the First National Bank of Vidalia at the time it was organized, and occupied this position for some time. Meanwhile he became identified with other enterprises, and on account of the press of other business he resigned his place in the bank. The Southern Loan & Investment Company, of which he is vice president and general manager, and of which A. M. Moses is president, does a general real estate and loan business, lending large sums of eastern capital to the Georgia farmers. In 1911, this company placed loans to the amount of $262,000, and handled 20,000 acres of Georgia land.

Mr. Johnson has made his home in Vidalia the past five years. In 1906, he and Miss Mable Morrison, daughter of P. Morrison, were united in marriage, and to them have been given two children: J. Wade, Jr., and Margaret.

Mr. Johnson has fraternal relations with the Knights of Pythias, and he and Mrs. Johnson are members of the Baptist church.

CARLTON J. WELLBORN. A man of wide research and learning, possessing a comprehensive knowledge of law, Carlton J. Wellborn occupies among the leading attorneys of Jeff Davis county, having a large and remunerative practice, and is well known in public life. He was born, September 7, 1868, in Blairsville, Union county, Georgia, coming from a family of much prominence.

His father, Carlton J. Wellborn, Sr., was born, bred and educated in Union county, Georgia, and as a young man was admitted to the bar. He served during the Civil war as commissary general under Gen. Joseph Brown, and was afterwards engaged in the practice of law, for a number of years being judge of the superior court of the northeast circuit. He was very prominent in the affairs of state and nation, and during the second administration of President Cleveland served as assistant secretary of the interior under Hoke Smith. He was also state librarian under Gov. Allen D. Candler. His wife, whose maiden name was Sarah M. Candler, was born in Milledgeville, Georgia, a daughter of E. S. Candler, who was comptroller of the state of Georgia during the Civil war.

Being fitted for college at Dahlonega, Georgia, Carlton J. Wellborn turned his attention to the study of law, and was graduated from the law department of the University of Georgia, at Athens, with the class of 1889. Immediately locating at Blairsville, he remained there in active practice for upwards of a score of years, meeting with unmistakable prestige in his profession, and being influential in public affairs. In August, 1911, he removed to Hawkinsville, where he is continuing his legal work, having a lucrative patronage.

Mr. Wellborn has represented his district in the state legislature three terms, having been elected in 1898, 1899, and again in 1905, and was assistant clerk of the house of representatives under John T. Boifeuillet.

Mr. Wellborn married Lula, daughter of T. P. Griffies, of Greensboro, Georgia, and into their household six children have made their advent, namely: William J., born in 1891, is editor and proprietor of the Hazlehurst *News*; Charles G., born in 1894, is also a journalist, being connected with the McRae *Enterprise*, in Telfair county; John P., born in 1898; Sarah, born in 1900; Osman, born in 1903; and Minnie Lee, born in 1910. Mr. Wellborn and his family belong to the Methodist church.

CASON F. ADAMS. Industriously engaged in one of the most useful and independent callings to which a man may devote his energies, Cason F. Adams, of the Tallokas district, is carrying on general farming with much success, performing his full share in rendering this district one of the finest agricultural regions of Brooks county. A son of the late Lasa Adams, he was born September 12, 1853, in Madison county, Florida.

His paternal grandfather, Dennis Adams, migrated from one of the Carolinas to Florida at an early day, when that portion of our country was almost entirely a wilderness, the red skins being much more plentiful than white men. Purchasing a tract of land, he erected a set of buildings, and began to clear a homestead. One old Indian, "Sam," was a frequent caller at his house, and proved his friendship for the newcomer by telling him that the Indians were that night to make a raid on the white settlers. The family made preparations to receive the savages when they attempted to drive away the stock. One of the sons, Lasa Adams, started out with his gun, the other members of the family being likewise armed, and when the battle that ensued was over there were three dead Indians lying upon the ground. The following day, Dennis Adams, believing discretion to be the better part of valor, came with his wife and children to Georgia, which was much further from the Indians' headquarters, and where the protections against the dusky savages were much better, and here spent his remaining days. He was twice married, his second wife surviving him about twenty years. By his two marriages he was the father of ten children, as follows: Joshua, Lasa, Dennis, Caswell, Cason, Sally, Rachel, Irene Louisa, and Jane.

Born in one of the Carolinas, Lasa Adams was but a small boy when the family settled in Florida, where he experienced all the hardships and privations of pioneer life, and where he had his first scrimmage with the Indians. On coming to Georgia he joined the force organized for protection against the wily red man, and took an active part in the engagement at Brushy creek, in 1836, when the Indians took their last stand in Georgia against the advance of civilization. On attaining his majority, Lasa Adams bought a tract of timbered land in Madison county, Florida, and on the farm which he improved spent a few seasons. He subsequently lived for four years in Jefferson county, Florida, from there coming to Georgia, and settling first in Thomas county, and later in Brooks county. Here purchasing a grist mill, he operated it with water power a number of years, the mill then, and now, being known as Adams's Mill. He did much to develop the industrial resources of this part of the country, and was here a resident until his death, at the age of eighty-three years, one month, and fourteen days.

Lasa Adams married Orpha Lee Holloway, who was born in what is now Brooks county, Georgia, where her father, William Holloway, a native of Bulloch county, Georgia, settled in pioneer times, and was afterwards extensively engaged in agricultural pursuits, operating his plantation with slave labor. She died September 28, 1887, aged sixty-five years. She reared four children, namely: Rhoda; Jane; James C., of whom a brief sketch appears elsewhere in this volume; and Cason F.

Commencing as a boy to assist his father on the farm, Cason F. Adams remained beneath the parental roof-tree until twenty-seven years of age. In the meantime he had visited Brooks county in his search of a permanent place of location, and had purchased a part of the land now included in the farm he owns and occupies, it being situated in lot number three, Tallokas district. Here Mr. Adams has a fine farm of two hundred and fifty acres, which he is managing successfully, as a general farmer being quite prosperous. He has a comfortable set of farm buildings, which are amply shaded by fine forest trees, which add much to the attractiveness and picturesque value of the place.

Mr. Adams married, at the age of twenty-six years, Texas Smith. She was born in Lowndes county, Georgia, where her father, J. R. M. Smith, located on coming to Georgia from Arkansas. Her mother, whose maiden name was Martha Smith, was born in Lowndes county, a daughter of Owen Smith, a well-known pioneer of that county. Mr. and Mrs. Adams have lost one child, Claon, who died at the age of sixteen years, and have four children living, namely: Leila, wife of Harris J. McGraw, has two children, Alwilda and Eugene; Olivia; John B.; and William Lasa. Politically Mr. Adams is a straightforward Democrat, and religiously he and his family attend the Bethel Baptist church.

MARTIN V. MILLER, M. D. A skillful and successful physician of Barney, Brooks county, Martin V. Miller, M. D., has through his recognized ability and professional knowledge acquired a large and lucrative practice, and gained an honored name in the medical fraternity. He was born, September 8, 1870, in Decatur county, Georgia, a son of John Harrington Miller.

Buck Miller, the doctor's grandfather, was for many years a wealthy planter and slave holder of eastern Georgia. He subsequently removed to Florida, and spent his last years in Jackson county. He reared three sons, as follows: Elias, Henry, and John Harrington.

Born on his father's plantation, John Harrington Miller was reared and educated in the eastern part of Georgia. On attaining manhood he migrated to Decatur county, Georgia, where he was a pioneer settler. At that time nearly the whole of southwestern Georgia was in its virgin wildness, deer, bear, and wild game of all kinds being abundant. There were no railroads then in evidence in the state, the few settlers marketing their produce in the Gulf ports. He located thirteen miles northwest of Bainbridge, which was a small hamlet, its one store being kept in a log house. Buying a heavily timbered tract of land, Mr. J. H. Miller built a small log cabin, and began the clearing of a farm. As his means increased, he added to the improvements already inaugurated, and later erected a substantial double house of hewed logs, into which he moved with his family. During the war between the states he enlisted in a Georgia regiment, and for a time was stationed along the coast. He was later sent to the defense of Atlanta, and with his brave comrades fought Sherman's forces. Returning home at the close of the war, he resumed his agricultural labors, residing on his farm until his death, in 1885, at the age of sixty-five years.

The maiden name of the wife of John Harrington Miller was Margaret Rebecca Godby. She was born in Lee county, Georgia, in 1835, a daughter of William and Betsey (Williams) Godby, and died in 1911, aged seventy-six years. Eight children were born of their union, as follows: Henry Luther, engaged in the practice of medicine at Palatka, Florida; Caroline; Martin V., the subject of this brief sketch; Elias M., engaged in farming in Decatur county; Lura E.; Thomas M., a physician in Hampton, Florida; Evie J.; and Wesley Sherman, a well-known physician of Ocala, Florida.

Completing the course of study in the public schools, Martin V. Miller turned his attention to the study of medicine, which seemed to be a favorite one in the family, having for his tutor Dr. E. B. Bush, of Colquitt county. Subsequently entering the Atlanta Medical College, he was graduated from that institution with the class of 1893. Beginning the practice of his profession at Jakin, Early county, Dr. Miller remained there a year, and the following ten years was employed as a physician at Whigham, Georgia. A close student, ambitious to keep abreast of the times in his profession, Dr. Miller then spent a year in Atlanta, where in addition to his work as a physician he attended medical lectures. In 1909, he came to Barney, Brooks county, where he has since been actively and successfully engaged in the practice of his profession, having built up an extensive and remunerative patronage. He is a member of the Brooks County Medical Society.

Dr. Miller married, January 26, 1898, Maggie Grace Jones, who was born at Climax, Decatur county, Georgia, a daughter of Zoar Robert and Mary (Evans) Jones, natives of Georgia, her father having been born in Decatur county, and her mother in Mitchell county. Her grandparents, pioneer farmers of Decatur county, were Silas and Sally (Williams) Jones, and Albert and Grace (Smith) Evans. Mrs. Miller's father is now living retired from agricultural pursuits, his home being in Cairo, Grady county. Mrs. Miller is a woman of culture and refinement, and a member of the Methodist Episcopal church.

HENRY A. EMERSON, whose well-managed farm lies in Brooks county, about five miles from Quitman, is numbered among the enterprising and skillful agriculturists who are using excellent judgment and good business methods in their work, and are meeting with satisfactory results. He was born in Liberty, Florida, a son of Charles Warren Emerson.

He is of English ancestry, his grandfather, Joseph Emerson, having emigrated from England to Massachusetts, settling in the near vicinity of Boston, where he spent the remainder of his years.

Charles Warren Emerson was born and reared near Boston, Massachusetts, and there acquired his early education. While in his 'teens he spent two years on board a whaling vessel, and afterwards followed the sea for seven years. Feeling the lure of the South, he made his way to Florida, becoming a pioneer of Leon county. At that time there were no railroads in either Florida or Georgia, and the forests were inhabited by wild animals, game of all kinds, and the Indians were numerous and sometimes vicious, causing the newcomers much trouble.

He lived in various counties in Florida, but spent the closing days of his life in Lafayette county, dying in 1894. His wife, whose maiden name was Diana Byrd, was born, in 1824, in Liberty county, Georgia, a daughter of Aleck and Nancy (Sykes) Byrd, who removed from that county to Florida, locating as pioneers in Madison county, and there living until called to the life beyond. Charles Warren and Diana Emerson were the parents of seven children, as follows: Nancy, Susie, Joseph W., Henry A., Charles, Mary and John. Joseph W. and Henry A. are the only survivors of this family. Joseph W. Emerson, the oldest son, has been twice married. He married first Nancy Shaw, who died in early life, leaving five children: Katie, Susie, Lewis, Charles W., and Jeremiah. His second wife, whose maiden name was Sarah A. Starling, died in 1887, leaving two children, Lulu and Sophia.

Although his educational advantages were limited, Henry A. Emerson availed himself of every opportunity for advancing his knowledge, thus obtaining a good stock of general information. He was reared to habits of honesty, industry and thrift, and at the age of nineteen began earning wages as a farm laborer, finding employment in Brooks county, Georgia. In 1877, Mr. Emerson went to Jefferson county, Florida, where he remained as a plantation overseer until 1886. He then entered the roadway department of the Savannah, Florida & Western Railroad Company, now the Atlantic Coast Line, and remained with the company for twenty years, faithfully and capably performing all the duties connected with the position until handing in his resignation. In 1906, having previously bought land in lots four hundred and seventy-three and four hundred eighty-six, Dixie district, within five miles of Quitman, Mr. Emerson turned his attention to agriculture, assuming possession of the farm where he is now living. Successful in his new industry, he now owns four hundred and sixty acres of land, and now has a goodly portion of his farm in cultivation, and improvements of an excellent character, his buildings being substantial, commodious and convenient.

In 1879, Mr. Emerson was united in marriage with Mary Emma Johnson, who was born in Brooks county, Georgia, a daughter of Wilson Johnson. Her grandfather, Jared Johnson, who married Elizabeth Eckels, moved from Washington county, Georgia, to Brooks county in pioneer days, and built a grist mill at Water Lillie Pond, and operated for a time. He afterwards moved south, settling near Ancilla river, where he resided until his death. Born in Washington county, Georgia, Wilson Johnson came with his parents to Brooks county, and in this part of the state spent his active life as a tiller of the soil. He married Mary Dean, a daughter of John and Jane (Albritton) Dean, who came to Brooks county from Laurens county, her father having been a man of culture, and one of the pioneer school teachers of this part of the state. Mr. and Mrs. Emerson have seven children, namely: Azubah V., who married Bailey T. Waldron, and has two children, Nellie and Alma; Carrie V.; Susie R.; Lucy I.; Nancy W.; Henry B.; and Russell W.

In state and local affairs Mr. Emerson is a straightforward Democrat, but in national affairs he is independent, voting for the best men regardless of party restrictions. Fraternally he is a member of Dixie Lodge, No. 242, Free and Accepted Masons.

GEORGE WEBSTER QUINN. A prominent member of the agricultural community of Hickory Head district, George Webster Quinn holds an assured position among the successful and progressive farmers and stockraisers of Brooks county, where he was born, his birth having occurred March 10, 1877.

His father, Dr. Gideon Quinn, was reared in Georgia, in the vicinity of Augusta, and there received his elementary education. Leaving home at the age of eighteen years, he spent three years in Mississippi, and on returning to Georgia entered the Atlanta Medical College, from which he was graduated with the degree of M. D. He subsequently practised a short time in Warren county, Georgia, in Alabama, and in Louisiana. On his return to Georgia, Dr. Quinn located in Montezuma, Macon county, and during the Civil war gave up his local practice to serve as a surgeon in the Confederate army. Removing to Brooks county in 1867, the doctor purchased a plantation in the Hickory Head district, and was here a resident until his death, in 1888.

Dr. Quinn married Araville Concord Aminta Ivey, who was born about forty miles from the city of Augusta, a daughter of Thomas and Rebecca (Buckholten) Ivey. Her father was a native of Virginia, his mother of south Georgia, and both spent the closing year of their lives near Augusta. She survived the doctor nearly a quarter of a century, passing away March 16, 1911. Eight children were born of their union, namely: Charles, deceased; Ada; Eula; Terry, deceased; David, deceased; Cora; Samuel; and George Webster.

Acquiring a good education in his youthful days, George Webster Quinn began his active career at the age of eighteen years, for awhile being bookkeeper for a naval stores company in Tallahassee, Florida. Returning to Brooks county, he accepted a position in a mercantile establishment in Quitman. Tiring of clerical work, Mr. Quinn came back to the soil, beginning life as an independent farmer on rented land. Energetic and wide-awake, he paid close attention to his chosen work, and was well rewarded for his labors. He had in a comparatively brief time saved a sufficient sum to warrant him in buying one hundred and forty acres of land, and he has since continued buying at intervals, and now has title to two thousand acres of good land in the Hickory Head district. Fourteen hundred acres of his property are fenced, and well stocked with cattle, horses, sheep and hogs, while all of his farms are amply supplied with the machinery and implements required by an up-to-date agriculturist. Well educated, and an intelligent reader, Mr. Quinn keeps apace with the times in regard to current events, and takes much interest in local matters.

JOHN DOUGAL MCCALLUM, now one of the enterprising young merchants of Boston, Thomas county, began his business career here in a clerical capacity, and by industry and commercial ability has won a place among the independent business men of this community.

He was born at Alfordsville, Robeson county, North Carolina, April 22, 1878. His father, Joseph Brown McCallum, was a native of the same vicinity. The grandfather was John McCallum, who was born in Bladen county, North Carolina, of Scotch ancestors that were among the early settlers there. From Bladen county he removed to Robeson county, where he became an extensive planter and at the conclusion of the Civil war freed seventy-eight slaves. He resided in that county until his death. He married a Miss Brown and they reared a large family.

Joseph Brown McCallum, the father, who is still living in North Carolina, has had a varied career as educator, soldier and farmer. He was educated in common schools and at college, and then began teaching. The war broke into upon the pursuit of this profession, and he enlisted in the Twenty-fourth North Carolina Infantry, and fought in Virginia under General Beauregard in Jackson's corps. In one of its many battles the regiment was captured, and Mr. McCallum was the only member of it that escaped. He was then transferred to the Thirty-fourth Regiment, with which he served to the end of the war. His long and arduous services included many of the memorable battles and campaigns of the Army of North Virginia, including Manassas, Fredericksburg, the Wilderness, Gettysburg, and the engagements around Richmond and Petersburg. He was present at the surrender at Appomatox, after which he returned home. He has since refused a pension or any form of remuneration for his soldier's duty, and says that he served out of pure patriotism and not for pelf. After his military experience he spent two years more at teaching, and then engaged in farming on his land adjacent to Alfordsville, where he has since resided.

Joseph B. McCallum married Mary Elizabeth McIntyre, a native of Robeson county. Her father, Dougal C. McIntyre, who was born in Scotland and accompanied his parents to North Carolina, was a farmer throughout his active career and spent his last days in Robeson county. Joseph B. McCallum and wife reared the following named children: Gustavus A., John Dougal, Mary Edna, Rufus B., Lamar, Joseph B., Jr., William Duncan and Katie Blanche.

After his graduation from the Alfordsville high school, John D. McCallum prepared for a business career by attending Massey's Business College in Columbus, Georgia, where he graduated in 1901. In the same year he located at Boston, with which town he has been identified throughout his practical career. He was first a bookkeeper for the Comfort Trading Company a year, then in the same capacity with J. B. Way Company two years, and with J. B. and J. S. Norton until 1905. In that year he established a general store of his own, and has since built up a very prosperous business.

Mr. McCallum married, in 1905, Miss Jemmie Way. Mrs. McCallum is a native of Thomas county, and her grandfather, Moses Way, was one of the pioneer settlers of south Georgia. Mr. McCallum and wife are members of the Presbyterian church, in which he is elder, and he is affiliated with Boston Lodge No. 138, I. O. O. F. In politics he is a Democrat.

THOMAS ADAMS. A retired merchant of Boston, Georgia, and at present an extensive farmer of Thomas county, Thomas Adams has acquitted himself throughout his life in a manner worthy of his ancestors who were among the brave pioneers who cleared the way for civilization in southern Georgia. The grandfather of the subject of this history, also named Thomas Adams, was born in North Carolina, and came among the earliest settlers to that part of Irwin county, now called Thomas county. At the time of his coming, the Indians had newly ceded the territory included in southern Georgia to the state, but they did not always act in good faith, and Thomas Adams, and the other white men who had settled in the vicinity lived in constant fear of the depredations of the redskins. They united into a band to protect their homes from the savages, however, and erected a log stockade in each settlement, for the purpose of affording refuge to the women and children. Thomas Adams cleared a farm from the wilderness with the help of his slaves, and on this property he lived until his death. He and his wife, who was a Miss Swilley, reared a large number of children, one of whom was Thomas Adams, Junior, the father of the man whose name appears at the head of this sketch.

Thomas Adams, Junior, was born in the year 1818, on his father's plantation in Thomas county. Reared as he was amid the perilous scenes of frontier life, and growing up in constant fear of marauding savages, it is no wonder that he was ready and eager to enlist in the Indian war at the early age of eighteen years. He fought in three hard-won battles, including the one at Brushy creek, where the Indians made their last stand against their civilized masters. When he was ready to start out in life for himself, Mr. Adams bought some land in the southern part of the county, where he cultivated a large farm, using slave labor. He employed at this time more than one hundred slaves. After a few years, he sold this plantation, and bought land north of Thomasville. He only remained in that locality a few years,-however, before he disposed of the property and purchased a tract situated on the south side of the railroad, and now included in the town of Boston. He had surveys made of this land, and had it subdivided into town lots, which he sold, buying a plantation on the Sevilla river in Thomas county, where he remained for the rest of his life, passing away in the year 1906, after a long and useful career as public and private citizen. His services to his community in private capacities were rewarded with the office of county judge, in which capacity he acquitted himself with great credit.

The wife of Thomas Adams, Junior, was Georgia Everett, a native of Bulloch county, Georgia. Her father, Jesse Everett, was one of the pioneer settlers of Thomas county. Mrs. Adams died at the age of seventy-eight years, having reared a family of nine children to be honest and industrious citizens of their country.

One of these children was Thomas Adams, III. He first saw the light of day at his father's farm, four miles north of Thomasville, January 3, 1860. He attended school at Boston, and partook of the excellent tutelage of Professor Moody, an educator well-known in that district. Mr. Adams resided with his parents until he had reached the age of twenty-four years. At that time, he started out for himself, embarking in the mercantile business at Boston. He remained in that town for ten years, and is still remembered there as an enterprising merchant. At the end of a decade, however, having previously purchased the homestead upon which his wife was born, located in Lot No. 236, of Thomas county, he entered upon the pursuit of agriculture, and now has acquired the reputation of being one of the most substantial and progressive farmers of the locality.

In the year 1887, Mr. Adams was united in the bonds of holy matrimony with Alice Ida Mims, a native of Thomas county, and the daughter of Wilke Mims, also born in Thomas county. Mrs. Adams' grandfather, David Mims, came to Thomas county from Montgomery county, Georgia. He was one of the first settlers in southern Georgia, and bought a large tract of six hundred acres, which he cleared and cultivated. After residing on this property for several years, he sold out and moved to Colquitt county, where he remained until his death, at the age of eighty-four years. His wife, Sally Kemp Mims, had died some years before in Thomas county, having reared eight sons and eight daughters.

Wilke Mims was raised and educated in Thomas county. At the beginning of the struggle between the states, he enlisted, with six of his brothers, in the Confederate army. He was detailed for service in the quartermaster's department. He contracted some disease during the war, and died in June, 1865, only a month after his return home. Wilke Mims was married in 1851, to Belle Moore, who was a native of Leon county, Florida. Mrs. Mims' father, Howell Moore, was born in Washington county, Georgia, and was one of the pioneers of Leon county. He owned a farm about eighten miles from Tallahassee, cultivating it by means of slave labor. He was a carpenter by trade, and at length became a contractor, building many churches and dwellings in the district in which he spent his life. His wife, the grandmother of Mrs. Adams, was a Matilda Coleman, the daughter of Jacob and Betsy Coleman. She also died on the Florida farm, having spent a life in harmony with the precepts of the Methodist Episcopal church, in the congregation of which faith both she and her husband were members. Mr. and Mrs. Moore reared a family of eight children, including Mrs. Adams' mother.

Left a widow with a family of five children on her hands, Mrs. Mims, like so many of the brave and noble women whom the Civil war deprived of their natural protectors, managed to keep her family together until they had all found homes of their own. She still lives on the farm to which she came as a bride, and although she is very old, and has seventeen grandchildren, as well as eleven great-grandchildren, she is quite active, working in the garden, and doing many of the tasks that have been hers so long. She has an excellent memory, and it is with undimmed faculties and cheery spirit that she awaits the call of the Master.

JAMES WILLIAM DUREN. Representing some of the oldest and best known families of Thomas county, James William Duren is one of the progressive and successful young farmer citizens near Thomasville. His forefathers were pioneers of this region, clearing and developing homes out of the wilderness, and he in his turn has taken up the tasks of modern agriculture and has applied to it the energy and skill which make the twentieth century agriculturist the most independent citizen of America.

He was born on a farm in the Oak Hill district of Thomas county on the 23d of December, 1874. His father was Reno Duren, who was born in Gwinnett county April 6, 1853. The grandfather was William Duren and the great-grandfather George Duren, both identified with earlier generations of Georgians, and the history of the Duren family in greater detail will be found in a sketch of George L. Duren elsewhere in this work.

Reno Duren, the father, was a boy of twelve when he came with the family to Thomas county. At the age of twenty he was married to Miss Susan S. Hall, and they then resided at her father's farm a few years. Her father then gave her a tract of land in lot 128 Oak Hill district, and there Reno Duren located and was engaged in general farming until his death, which occurred in 1908. The mother, Susan S. Hall, was born in Leon county, Florida, in 1852. Her father, David J. Hall, a son of Juniper and Serena Hall, pioneer settlers of Florida, was himself a native of Florida, and afterwards settled at Thomasville when it was a village and all the surrounding country little improved from wilderness conditions. After a few years he bought a large tract of land in the Oak Hill district, and there engaged in farming and stockraising until his death in 1881. David J. Hall married Harriet Wilson, a native of Thomas county and daughter of Allen Wilson, who was also a pioneer settler here. Allen Wilson owned a large amount of land five miles northeast of Thomasville, cultivating with slave labor, and lived there till his death at a good old age. He was three times married and reared a large family of children. Susan (Hall) Duren, the mother, died in 1891, and her seven children are named as follows: Eva, James W., Clarence, Scellie, Maude, Lottie and Reno.

James W. Duren had the advantages of a good home and received a substantial education first in the common schools and later in the South Georgia College at Thomasville. He assisted in the labors of the home farm until his marriage, and then lived two years on his father-in-law's place, after which he bought the old Duren homestead, where he has since been prosperously engaged in general farming, horticulture and stock raising. He has built a comfortable residence and otherwise improved the farm since it came into his hands.

In 1900, he was united in marriage with Miss Bama Bulloch. Mrs. Duren is a native of Thomas county, and her parents were James N. and Susan (Singletary) Bulloch. Mr. and Mrs. Duren's six children are: Joseph D., James N., Susan, Evelyn, Ollie and Ray. Mr. and Mrs. Duren are members of the Missionary Baptist church.

WILLIAM ALBERT WALKER, M. D. For more than twenty years successfully engaged in practice and the proprietor of a large and well equipped sanitarium at Cairo, in Grady county, Dr. Walker has represented the highest ability and best personal qualities of the medical profession. He is the type of physician whose work has been quietly performed, and whose services, while without the conspicuous qualities of men in public life, have been none the less valuable to society and deserving of the mention which is bestowed on conscientious and efficient work. Dr. Walker is a physician who is always apace with the developments and discoveries of his profession, and has enjoyed a practice that has absorbed all his time and energy.

Representing an old family of southern Georgia, William Albert Walker was born on a plantation four miles from Thomasville. His father was Jonathan Walker, and his grandfather was Talton Walker. The latter, a native of North Carolina, where he was reared and married, came to Georgia and became an early settler in Banks county. At the time of his settlement the greater part of Georgia was a wilderness, with the forest untouched, game of all kinds in plentiful quantities, and the Indians still living here and claiming the region as their hunting ground. Talton Walker and his brother Jonathan both participated in the Cherokee Indian wars. He had a large plantation, cleared out of the wilderness, operated it with slave labor, and remained a resident there until his death at the age of seventy-six years. His wife also lived to a good old age, and they reared twelve children, nine sons and three daughters, namely: Jonathan, Thurman, Samuel, Benton, Lumpkin, Polk, Byron, Augustus, Obie, Mary, Ellen, and Margaret. All of these sons, except Obie, served in the Confederate army. When Governor Brown, toward the close of the war, called out all the boys and old men, the mother wrote the governor that she already had eight sons in the army and only one at home, who was just old enough for service under that call, and saying that she needed this son at home, and requested the governor to release him from military duty. She quickly received a letter from Governor Brown, granting her desire.

Jonathan Walker, the father, was reared in Banks county, and about 1850 moved to Thomas county, buying a farm four miles east of Thomasville. In 1862, he entered the Confederate army and went with his command into Virginia, where he was attached to Longstreet's corps, participating in many of the more important battles of the Virginia campaign. He escaped capture and was wounded but once and then not seriously. When the war was over he made his way back home as best he could, and resumed the quiet pursuits of agriculture. He resided on his farm until a few years before his death, when he came to Cairo, where he lived retired until death came to him in 1902, when he was seventy-six years of age. The maiden name of his wife was Nancy Jane Kitchen, who was born in Banks county, and who died in 1908 at seventy-nine years. She reared seven children whose names are Casper, Alice, Caledonia, Cornelia, Janie, Laura and William Albert. Both parents were members of the Methodist church.

Dr. Walker attended the rural schools of Thomas county until he was seventeen years old, and then became a student in the high school at Cairo. Two years later he entered the Louisville Medical College at Louisville, Kentucky, where he was graduated M. D. in February, 1889. In the same year he took a post graduate course at the New York Polyclinic. His ambition to keep his accomplishments abreast of the growing knowledge in medical science has caused him to take a post graduate course in the New York Polyclinic every two years since he began actual practice. He opened his first office in Cairo, and has been in the enjoyment of a large practice in this locality for nearly twenty-four years. In 1905 he established a sanitarium at Cairo. The building at first had only three rooms, but its popularity has grown and its equipment in proportion, so that in 1912, the doctor erected a commodious brick building with twelve rooms and in the best style of architecture and arrangement and furnishings to serve its purposes.

In 1893 Dr. Walker married Jessie Powell, who was born at Cairo, a daughter of Rev. William and Lucretia (Brockett) Powell. Dr. and Mrs. Walker have six children, whose names are Wyeth, Agnes, Ellen, William Wayne, Mae, and Martha. The doctor and wife worship in the Methodist church.

JOHN McKINSTRY HENDRY. A representative farmer of the Morven district, Brooks county, John McKinstry Hendry stands as a true type of the energetic, hardy and enterprising men who have actively assisted in the development and advancement of this fertile and productive agricultural region. A son of Rev. John McPhail Hendry, he was born, December 2, 1859, in Hamilton county, Florida.

William Hendry, his paternal grandfather, who was of Scotch-Irish ancestry, was one of the earlier settlers of Liberty county, Georgia. Migrating to the southwestern part of the state about 1825, he took up land not far from the present site of Barwick, in what is now Brooks county, improved the water power, and there erected the first mill in this part of Georgia. Clearing a part of his land, he was there engaged in farming and milling the remainder of his life, both he and his wife dying from typhoid fever. Her maiden name was McPhail. They were people of sterling character, and faithful members of the Methodist Episcopal church. To them ten children were born, as follows: Ely, James, William, Neal, John, David, Mary, Harriet, Betsey, and Nancy.

Rev. John McPhail Hendry was born in Liberty county, Georgia, July 5, 1822. Of a naturally religious temperament, he was converted in his youth, and at the age of eighteen years was licensed as a preacher in the Methodist Episcopal church. Subsequently going to Gadsden county, Florida, he bought land, and built a mill, which he operated for a time. Joining then the conference, he held pastorates in different parts of Florida. Afterwards, having joined the South Georgia conference, he preached in various parts of this state. Later he went back to Florida, once more became a member of the Florida conference, and for a number of years thereafter was active in the ministry. When ready to give up his ministerial work, he returned to Georgia, and spent his last days in Brooks county, passing away at the age of seventy-five years. Progressive and enterprising, ever interested in educational matters, he established, in 1850, an advanced schools for girls in Macanopy, Florida, the first institution of the kind in the state. The maiden name of the wife of Rev. Mr. Hendry was Caroline Matilda Bell. She was born, October 20, 1835, in Hamilton county, Florida, where her parents, James and Matilda (Johnson) Bell, natives of Georgia, were pioneer settlers. Five children were born of their union, as follows: John Mc-

Kinstry; James Edward; Caroline, who was called Minnie; George Pierce; and Marvin E.

Attending school, in both Florida and Georgia, John McKinstry Hendry obtained a practical education in the public schools. Choosing for himself the independent life of a farmer, he began work on his account on land belonging to his mother. In 1889 he purchased a tract of timber in the Morven district, Brooks county, Georgia, and in the midst of the fragrant woods built a small, two-room house, and immediately began the arduous task of redeeming a farm from the wilderness. Selling that property in 1899, Mr. Hendry bought his present farm, which is advantageously located on the Quitman and Adel road. It contains two hundred and forty acres of land, with a good set of buildings, and he is here profitably engaged in general farming and stock raising.

On March 17, 1889, Mr. Hendry was united in marriage with Susan Martha Wilkins. She was born in Florida, a daughter of John and Susan Ellen (Taylor) Wilkins, and a granddaughter of Rev. Richard Taylor, a pioneer preacher of the Methodist Episcopal church. Mr. and Mrs. Hendry have three children living, namely: John F., Olin McKinstry, and Clara Lee. In his political affiliations, Mr. Hendry is a Democrat, and fraternally he is a member of the Woodmen of the World. He also belongs to the Morven Farmers' union. Both Mr. and Mrs. Hendry are members of the Methodist Episcopal church, and contribute generously towards its support.

PROF. WILLIAM GREEN AVERA. The career of a man who for the greater part of a life time has been identified with the training and education of the youth is always one of the most valuable assets of a community. Probably no educator in south Georgia has been so long or so closely connected with educational progress and the practical work of the schools as the present superintendent of the Berrien county schools, Prof. William Green Avera. He belongs to a family of pioneer Georgians, and was born on a farm in Clinch county, the 1st of August, 1855.

His great-grandfather, Moore Avera, of Welsh ancestry, was born in Robeson county, North Carolina, and after arriving at mature years emigrated to Georgia, making the journey with his private conveyance and becoming a pioneer settler of Wilkinson county. There he bought land and was engaged in farming and stock raising until his death.

Daniel Avera, son of this pioneer and grandfather of Professor Avera, was a native of Wilkinson county, was reared on a farm, and in 1845 moved from that locality into south Georgia, establishing the name and family fortunes in Lowndes county. It may be remembered that all of south Georgia was then sparsely settled, much of the land still in state ownership and its value counted in cents rather than dollars per acre. The grandfather's purchase of land was near what was then the center of Lowndes county, the area of which has since been materially reduced by the organization of other counties. As railroads and market towns had not yet become features of this part of Georgia, the planters took their surplus products to the St. Mary's river or to the gulf ports. In 1858 the grandfather, having sold his possessions in Berrien county, (Berrien having been organized in 1856,) moved to the southern part of Clinch county, where he engaged in cattle grazing on the borders of the Okefenoke swamp, and lived in that neighborhood until his death at the age of eighty. The maiden name of his wife was Tabitha Cook, and she was a native of Wilkinson county, and she also reached the age of eighty years. Their ten children were named Cynthia, Nancy, William M., Stephen W., Elizabeth, Rebecca J., Mary Ann, Sally, John R. and Zanie.

Stephen Willis Avera, the father, was born in Wilkinson county, January 5, 1836, was reared on the farm and trained in its pursuits, and after his marriage settled in the western part of Clinch county, where he resided until 1856, and then came to Berrien county, which had just been organized that year. During the war he enlisted and became a soldier of Company E of the Fifty-fourth Georgia Infantry. His command joined the western army under Generals Joseph E. Johnston and Hood, and stubbornly resisted Sherman's advance all the way from Dalton to Atlanta. After the fall of the latter city he went to Hood's army, participating in the battles at Jonesboro, Franklin, Murfreesboro and Nashville, and after the last named engagement he was sent home on detached duty, the war closing before his recall to the front.

Laying aside the musket he again put his hand to the plow, and was engaged in farming in Berrien county until 1887, when he sold out and bought a farm in Colquitt county which he still occupies, having reached the good old age of seventy-six years. He married Martha Elizabeth Aikins, who was born in Clinch county, a daughter of William Green and Winnie Ann (Moore) Aikins. Stephen W. Avera and wife reared eleven children, whose names are William Green, Winnie Ann, Polly Ann, Sarah O'Neal, Daniel M., Lyman H., Phebe V., Lou, Junius H., Cordelia and Martha.

Reared in a good home and trained to habits of industry, William G. Avera early manifested special inclination for study and the pursuit of knowledge, and made the best of his early opportunities of schooling. He has been a lifelong student, and when he was eighteen he was entrusted with his first school, located three miles east of Nashville. For thirty-three years, an entire generation, he was in the active work of the schoolroom, and he taught children and children's children during that time. The aggregate length of his service out of those thirty-three years was twenty-five full years, a third of a long lifetime. In 1907 Professor Avera was elected superintendent of the Berrien county schools, and by re-elections has since served continuously in that office. His administration has been marked by many improvements in the county educational system.

In 1877 Professor Avera was united in marriage with Miss Eliza J. Sirmans. Mrs. Avera was born in Berrien county, daughter of Abner and Frances (Sutton) Sirmans. She died at Sparks in 1905. In 1911 Professor Avera married Margaret McMillan, a native of Berrien county and daughter of Randall McMillan. The following children were born to Professor Avera by his first marriage, namely: Sirman W., Marcus D., Bryant F., Aaron G., Alice J., Homer C., Abner J., Willis M., Lona, and Lula. Marcus D., Homer C., Abner J., and Lula are now deceased. Aaron G. married Fannie Key, now deceased, and has one son, William. Sirman W. married Annie Young and has a daughter named Georgia. Bryant F. married Mary Patton. Alice J. is the wife of William T. Parr, and has four children, J. W., Stella, Saren and Gladys. Lona married Austin Avera, son of I. C. Avera, sheriff of Berrien county.

In 1878 Professor Avera settled on a farm eight miles southeast of Nashville, and that was the home of his family until 1904, when it was temporarily removed to Sparks that the children might have the benefit of the superior educational advantages available in the Sparks Collegiate institute there. Prof. Avera's present home is at Nashville, the county seat of Berrien county. He still owns the old home where all of his children were born and reared, and where his beloved deceased wife and children are buried. Sacred is the memory of this home to the man who has given the best years of his life to the educational and moral upbuilding of this section of Georgia.

Professor Avera and wife are members of the Primitive Baptist church, and in politics he is a Democrat.

WILLIAM FOREST LOCKE. One of Terrell county's best known citizens and business men was the late W. F. Locke, who died at his home in Dawson, in 1910. He had been a merchant, farmer, warehouseman for a number of years, and with material success also won high personal esteem. Mrs. Locke, who survives him, belongs to one of the oldest and most prominent families of southwestern Georgia.

William Forest Locke was born in Eufaula, Alabama, June 13, 1865. His father was William H. Locke, who for many years was engaged in business at Eufaula where he kept a clothing store and had a large trade. He was also a large land owner and farmer, his lands being located near Eufaula. When the Civil war broke out, he entered the Confederate service as a member of the Eufaula Rifles. Being a man of unusual education and a fluent writer and frequent correspondent of newspaper, while in the army he often wrote his wife accounts of his experiences, and these letters were published by the press, and the little volume of them is now highly treasured by the descendants of this worthy man. His home remained in Eufaula until his death. His wife, before her marriage, was Ann Judson Sylvester, who was a native of Georgia, and a daughter of DeMarquis Sylvester. The latter removed from Georgia to Alabama and bought land five miles from Eufaula, which he operated with slave labor and continued a resident in that community until his death. Mr. Sylvester married a Miss Rembert, a native of South Carolina. Mrs. William H. Locke survived her husband for many years and died at the age of seventy-five. She was the mother of ten children, all of whom grew to maturity, namely: Ella Estelle, Lula, Clifford A., Nettie L., William F., Charles C., Pearl D., Judson S., Mattie B., and Leslie Roscoe.

The late Mr. Locke of Terrell county was reared and educated at Eufaula, and at an early age began his independent career as a clerk in a wholesale grocery store in that city. After a few years as clerk he moved to Montgomery, where he was clerk in a hotel for a few months, after which he returned to Eufaula and opened a fancy grocery store and conducted it for one year. At the end of that time he came to Dawson, where he established a men's furnishing store, and also became interested in farming on land which was his wife's inheritance, located two and a half miles from Dawson. As a merchant and farmer he prospered during all the remaining years of his life. As a farmer he raised large quantities of cotton and corn, and for several years was engaged in the warehouse business at Dawson, handling large quantities of cotton. The late Mr. Locke had unusual business talent, and succeeded in almost every venture to which he put his hand.

On October 10, 1888, he married Miss Lillie Belle Rogers. The Rogers family have long been prominent in this state. Her father, Harrison Rogers, was formerly a resident near Dalton before the war, and was a large planter and operated his plantation with slave labor. When the slaves were freed, as a result of the war, the bulk of his wealth was swept away, but he did not lose the courage and enterprise which were the essential features of his character, and moving to Dawson when it was but a village he bought land nearby and began once more as a farmer to build up his prosperity. He became one of the most successful men in this region, and as his means increased, he invested in land until he became a very large holder of Dawson property, where he resided until his death at the age of eighty-two. The maiden name of Harrison Rogers' wife was Lucy Hood, of Meriwether county, Georgia, daughter of Bynum Hood, of the same county and the cousin of Bynum Hood of Dalton, a sketch of whom appears elsewhere in this work. The five children in the Rogers family were named William, who died at the age of thirteen; John C.; Lee H.; Ella Elizabeth and Lillie Belle.

Mr. and Mrs. Locke were both members of the Baptist church. The five children in their family were William Harrison, Mamie Ailene, Ruth, Lillie and Rogers. William H. married Olive Thornton, and they have a son named William Forest.

WILLIAM MILLS LEWIS, attorney in Vidalia, is a native of the state of Georgia, born in Warren county on November 7, 1869. He is the son of Nathan Augustus and Sicily (Rogers) Lewis, the former of Green county and the latter of Warren county. Mr. Lewis lived in Green county until 1859, at which time his family moved to Alabama, and there he attended the Eastern Alabama Male College, from which institution he was gradated in June, 1861. Immediately thereafter he joined the Fifty-first Alabama regiment and was with Gen. Joseph E. Johnston until the close of the war. Returning then to Georgia he was engaged for some time in teaching school in Warren county. It was there he met the girl who later became his wife and the mother of William Mills Lewis of this personal review. He was one of the three children of his parents, the others being Marvin Lewis, a manufacturer of Coca Cola, in Dothan, Alabama, and Mariana, wife of Henry R. Hall of Warren county.

The son, William, attended school in Warrenton, and was duly graduated from the high school of that place. He thereafter engaged in farming until he was twenty-one, when he took a position as clerk and continued in that work for two years. Later he taught school in Jefferson county for a year and the same length of time in Warren county, following which he returned to his farming again and was thus occupied for another term of two years. He then decided to study law, with a view to entering the profession, and for nine months was a student under E. P. Davis of Warrenton, after which he successfully passed his examinations and was admitted to the bar. He initiated the active practice of his profession in Milledgeville, Baldwin county, and after two years in that place be located at Vidalia, and here he enjoys an ever increasing clientage, and is regarded as one of the important citizens of the city. He was judge of the city court of Mt. Vernon in 1901 and 1902 and solicitor of the city court in 1907 and 1908, and a member of the board of commissioners of roads and revenues of Montgomery county.

On January 16, 1898, Mr. Lewis was married to Miss Sallie Meadows, the daughter of S. B. Meadows, mayor of Vidalia, and the representative of Toombs county in the legislature in 1909-10. Two children have been born to Mr. and Mrs. Lewis,—Mattele, born October 17, 1899, and Urma, born April 1, 1902.

Mr. Lewis is a member of the Knights of Pythias, but is not further affiliated with any fraternal organization. Mrs. Lewis is a member of the Baptist church.

DOOLLY DEWITT GILMORE. Even in an age which recognizes young men and places responsibilities upon them which in the past have been laid only upon the shoulders of those of more mature years, and in a part of the country noted for its young men of ability and sound judgment, we seldom find one who in so short a time has attained the prominence in financial circles that has come to Doolly Dewitt Gilmore, cashier of the Citizens Banking Company of Baxley, Georgia, one of the soundest institutions of Appling county. That the trust placed in his hands is well merited has been proved by the universal confidence in which he is held by the citizens of the community in which he has discharged his duties. Born March 11, 1886, in McRae, Telfair county, Georgia, he is a son of James H. and Mary Elizabeth Gilmore, natives of Butts county, the latter of whom died when he was an infant.

James H. Gilmore, a prominent planter, merchant and lumberman, served the Confederacy in a regiment of Georgia volunteers during the War between the States. He had the following children: Jesse M., who is thirty-seven years of age; Henry Cephas, who died at the age of thirty-two years; James Ernest, who is twenty-nine years old; Doolly Dewitt; Annie, the wife of Dr. Dan Morrison of Waycross, Georgia; Sarah Etta, living at Baxley and caring for her dead brother's children; and Edna Belle, the wife of Robert L. White, a prominent merchant of Live Oak, Florida.

Doolly D. Gilmore was seven years of age when he was taken by his father to a farm near Lumber City, on the Ocmulgee river, where he resided for eight years, obtaining his education in the public schools. He then returned to McRae for one year, where he was employed as a clerk in a dry goods store, and spent a like period in the dry goods establishment of his brother in Baxley. Subsequently he became engaged in railroad clerical work at Macon for the Southern and Central Railroads, but after three years went to Live Oak, Florida, and for a short time acted as a bookkeeper in a furniture and jewelry store. During the year that followed he was bookkeeper for the International Harvester Company, at Atlanta, and then returned to Baxley and entered the Citizens Banking Company as assistant cashier, serving in that capacity from November, 1906, until January, 1907, when he was elected cashier, a position which he has held to the present time.

The Citizens Banking Company, an institution with an authorized capital of $50,000, is now installed in a new reinforced concrete and steel building, erected in 1912, where it has large, modern and elegant quarters, including brick vaults and safety deposit department. It has been in operation for five years, during which time it has paid yearly dividends, and has accumulated a surplus of $9,000. The deposits have grown rapidly and now amount to more than $100,000, and the bank is the state depository for Appling county. Mr. Gilmore is a young man of fine character and excellent abilities, and takes a great interest in everything that tends toward the welfare of his adopted community. He belongs to the blue lodge, chapter, commandery and Shriner degrees of Masonry and is also connected with the Knights of Pythias. He and Mrs. Gilmore are consistent members of the Methodist Episcopal church South, in which he is at present serving as steward.

In December, 1908, Mr. Gilmore was married to Miss Madena Griner, who was born at Attopulgas, Decatur county, Georgia, daughter of the Rev. J. B. Griner of the Methodist Episcopal church South. They have had one daughter, Dorothy, who was born December 4, 1910.

JERRY D. TILLMAN. Belonging to a Southern family of prominence and worth, and a representative of the agricultural community of Brooks county, Jerry D. Tillman is eminently deserving of mention in a work of this character. A Georgian by birth, he was born, December 28, 1828, at Berlin, Colquitt county, a place then known as the Robinson district, Irwin county, in the log cabin erected by his father, John Tillman.

His grandfather, Jeremiah Tillman, a native of South Carolina, was there a resident when the War of 1812 was declared. Enlisting as a soldier, he came with his regiment to Georgia, where he was stationed until receiving his honorable discharge at the close of the conflict in Savannah. Being then joined by his family, he lived for awhile in Ware county, Georgia, subsequently becoming one of the original householders of that part of Irwin county now included within the limits of Colquitt county. Buying a tract of wooded land, he cleared a portion of it, and was there industriously employed in tilling the soil until his death, at the age of seventy-five years. To him and his wife, whose maiden name was Dicey Brown, six children were born and reared.

Born in South Carolina, John Tillman was brought up and educated in Georgia, where his parents settled when he was a small child. Becoming a farmer from choice, he bought land in Colquitt county, and with slave help cleared and improved the homestead upon which he spent his remaining years, passing away at the venerable age of four score and six years. He married Sally Mercer, who was born in Robinson county, North Carolina. Her parents, John and Fereby (Musclewhite) Mercer, came from their native state, North Carolina, to Georgia in 1836, settling as pioneers in Ware county, where they both spent their last days. Mrs. Sally (Mercer) Tillman died at the age of seventy-five years. She reared a large family of children, eleven in number, as follows: Jerry D., the special subject of this brief sketch; Henry; Sarah; Sally; Elijah; John; Harrison; Elizabeth; Fereby; Roxie; and Rachel. The sons all served throughout the war between the states, Elijah, who was commissioned captain of his company, being the only one of them that was wounded.

Born in a rude log cabin, Jerry D. Tillman grew to manhood among pioneer scenes. The dusky savages still frequented the forests, oftentimes going on the war path, in 1836, when he was a lad of eight years, making their last fight on Georgia soil. The people in his boyhood days lived chiefly on the wild game so abundant in this section, and the productions of the land, and his mother, who was accomplished in the domestic art and sciences, did her cooking by the open fire, and from the cotton grown on the plantation, and the sheep raised, carded, spun and wove the homespun in which she dressed her family. Jerry D., the oldest son, was fourteen years old before he wore shoes, not because he was not allowed to, but because he preferred to go barefooted. There being no railways in those times, he, in common with his neighbors, used to team produce to Saint Marys, Georgia, or to Newport, Florida, being a week or more on the round trip, and invariably taking along a stock of provisions, and cooking and camping on the way.

As a youth Jerry D. Tillman acquired a very good education, and at the age of twenty-one started for himself as an overseer on a large plantation, a position which he filled acceptably for five years. He then bought land on Mule creek, in Lowndes county, and was there employed in tilling the soil five years. Selling out at the end of that time, he bought land in Madison county, Florida, and continued his former occupation. In 1861 he enlisted in the Second Florida Cavalry, under Captain Paramour. With his company, which was attached to General Finnegan's Brigade, he took an active part in numerous important campaigns and battles, remaining with his command until the close of the war. In November, 1869, Mr. Tillman disposed of his Florida land, returned to Georgia, and settled on lot number 196, Briggs district, Brooks county, where he has since resided. This plantation contains five hundred acres of land, pleasantly located on the Morven and Valdosta road, and is under a good state of cultivation, with attractive improvements, the residence sitting back from the road, and having a beautiful grove in front of it.

On September 1, 1852, Mr. Tillman married Elizabeth Allen, who was born in Thomas county, Georgia, a daughter of Isaac and Easter (Harrell) Allen, natives of North Carolina, and pioneers of Thomas county. Nine children have been born to Mr. and Mrs. Tillman, namely: Robert, Amelia, Sally, Jimmie, Ella, Ida and Idella, twins, Charlotte, and Gordon. Amelia, widow of A. D. Bass, resides in Quitman. Sally, wife of Charles Freer, of Florida, has five children, Mabel; Leon and Leonora, twins; Tillman; and Helen. Jimmie, wife of W. C. Dampier, of Brooks county, has seven children, Gertrude, Missiebob, Blanche, Glenn, Valora, Jim, and Duncan. Gordon married Elizabeth McPherson, and they have one child, Gordon Isaac. Ella lives in Morven. Robert superintends the management of the homestead farm, his sisters, Charlotte and Idella living with him on the old home farm, keeping house for their father and brother, their mother having passed to the life beyond at the age of seventy-two years. She was a woman of much force of character, and a valued member of the Methodist Episcopal church. Mr. Tillman was formerly a Whig in politics, but since the Civil war has been identified with the Democratic party.

OLIVER C. CLEVELAND, the prosperous and progressive farmer of Thomas county, has had a life rich in the adventures both of war and peace. When a mere youth of eighteen years, he saw service in the Mexican war. A few years later, he joined the great tide of men that surged toward the gold fields of California, and came safely home after a perilous journey thither and home again, only to find his country on the eve of a great Civil war. The South had need of such valiant young men and strong fighters as Oliver C. Cleveland was, and he knew no more of peaceful days until the war was over, and the cause for which he had given so much of his youth, was lost. It is fitting that after the hardships of his early days, Mr. Cleveland should spend the remainder of his life as an agriculturist in his native state, and it is doubly fitting that his biography be included in the annals of his community, not only because of the part he played in the historical events of the nineteenth century, but because of the place he has won for himself in the hearts of his fellow citizens, in the neighborhood of his home, by his kindly spirit and true manhood.

Mr. Cleveland first saw the light of day in Franklin county, Georgia, March 30, 1829. His father, Benjamin Cleveland, was born in the same county in the year of 1792, the son of John Cleveland, who was a native of the Greenville district of South Carolina, and was descended from English ancestors who settled in the colonies in early times. John Cleveland moved to Georgia from South Carolina as a young man, and he was among the first to settle in Franklin county. He resided in that locality for a great many years, and then moved to Mobile, Alabama, where he died at a good old age. His wife was a Miss Gilbert before her marriage, and she bore him one daughter, and six sons, of whom the father of the subject of this history was one.

Benjamin Cleveland was reared and educated in Franklin county. He was married in the district in which he had spent his boyhood, and a few years later moved to Troop county, where he purchased a tract of land, cultivating it by means of slave labor. He also engaged in the mercantile business in the same district for several years, but finally sold out and moved to Stewart county, where he remained until his death, at the age of eighty-seven years. His wife, Amelia Hooper Cleveland, died at the age of seventy-five years. She was a daughter of

Richard Hooper, and reared five sons and four daughters. All of these sons afterward served in the Confederate army. Their names were James M., Richard H., Benjamin F., John W., and Oliver C.

Reared and educated in the county to which his parents moved soon after his birth, that is Troop county, Oliver C. Cleveland received in its schools, as well as in its woods and meadows, the foundation of that education which he has since acquired, guiding a natural intelligence by wide reading and keen speculation. In the year 1847, he enlisted in Company B, Georgia Battalion of Mounted Infantry, of which Lieutenant-Colonel James S. Colhoun was commander. He was mustered in for service in the Mexican war at Mobile, and then set sail with his company over a difficult and circuitous route to Mexico City, which had surrendered before the arrival of the forces of which he was a part. After a few weeks in the City of Mexico, he was transferred to Cuernavaca, where he remained until peace was declared, and on his return home, he was honorably discharged from the army.

In 1850, the year after the famous gold-craze was inaugurated, Oliver Cleveland went to California. He chose to travel via the Isthmus, and was one hundred and twenty days en route. He landed at San Francisco, then a city of tents nestling among the sand hills, and from thence he went to the mines. He remained in California, engaged in mining and other occupations until the year 1860. At that time, he returned home, choosing the southern route, this time. He travelled the entire distance of 2,760 miles by stage, the trip consuming nineteen days and nights.

He had been home just a year when the war between the North and South broke out. On the nineteenth of April, 1861, he enlisted in Company A, Second Georgia Battalion, and was sent at once to Virginia to save the Gossport navy at Norfolk. From Norfolk, he went to Goldsboro, North Carolina, to drill new recruits to the Confederate ranks. His first term of enlistment expired in April, 1862, and he reenlisted in the same company. He was sent to Virginia, then, and served under Generals Welthers and Mahone in Longstreet's corps, and took part in many of the great battles of the war, including the battle of Gettysburg. A few days before Lee's surrender he was granted a furlough, and returned home, and was there when peace was declared.

After the war, Mr. Cleveland engaged in farming in Stewart county, until 1872, when he moved to Terrell county. He remained at the latter place until 1885, in which year he came to Thomas county, and settled in the Oak Hill district, on the farm where he has since resided. Mr. Cleveland has been twice married. His first wife was Martha L. Armour, and he was thirty-nine years of age when he was united in marriage with her. She was a native of Troop county, and a daughter of William and Sarah (Harper) Armour. She died in 1879, and later Mr. Cleveland married Mrs. Sarah Grace. Mrs. Sarah Cleveland was a native of Sampson county, North Carolina. Her father was John Shearman, of Scotch-Irish ancestry, and a life-long resident of North Carolina. Mrs. Cleveland was first married to John S. Herring, of Sampson county, North Carolina. Her second husband was Thomas Grace, who died in 1880. Mr. Cleveland had one son by his first wife. This is Monroe E. Cleveland, who is married and now resides in Oklahoma.

FRANK U. GARRARD. A lawyer of Columbus whose practice has brought him into relationship with many of the largest corporations and business concerns of the state, Mr. Frank U. Garrard represents an old family and his father before him was one of the ablest members of the Columbus bar.

Frank U. Garrard was born at Columbus, January 1, 1876, a son of the late Louis F. and Annie (Foster) Garrard. As a boy he attended private schools in Columbus, and when seventeen years old began the study in the law offices of his father. He continued in this way for several years, and on December 4, 1897, was admitted to the bar. He practiced law alone for several years and then was taken into partnership with his father under the firm name of Garrard & Garrard. This firm was counsel for many of the larger corporations of Columbus, and also had a large general practice, the ability of the firm being recognized both as trial and as counsel lawyers. On the death of the senior Garrard the son has continued the business formerly conducted by the joint firm, and now enjoys a large and successful business. Mr. Garrard is attorney for the Columbus Investment Company; The Columbus Railroad Company; The Muskogee Real Estate and Investment Company; The Columbus Power Company; The Gas Light Company of Columbus; The Stone & Webster Engineering Syndicate; and the Third National Bank and the Columbus Savings Bank. Mr. Garrard was married December 12, 1900, to Miss Sara Gardiner of Sparta. They are the parents of four children, namely: Louise Gardiner, born December 2, 1902; Margaret, born February 3, 1906; Frank, Jr., born January 5, 1910; and Gardiner, born May 14, 1912. Mr. Garrard is affiliated with Mt. Harmen lodge, No. 304, A. F. & A. M.; Darly Chapter No. 7, R. A. M.; and is a Knights Templar Mason and a member of the Alee Temple of the Mystic Shrine. He is also affiliated with Columbus lodge, No. 67, I. O. O. F., and with R. E. Lee lodge, of the Knights of Pythias, and belongs to the Improved Order of Red Men. He also has membership in the Georgia State Bar Association. Mr. and Mrs. Gardiner worship in the Presbyterian church of which he is an elder in the church at Columbus. His chief recreations are automobiling and hunting.

DWIGHT L. ROGERS, practicing attorney at Ocilla, Georgia, and one of the leading men of that place, is a native of Georgia, born at Shiloh, near Reidsville, Tattnall county, on August 17, 1886. He is the son of William and Isabella Augusta (Lang) Rogers. The father was a native of Tattnall county and the mother of Liberty county. William Rogers was a merchant and conducted a mercantile business for years in Reidsville. They were the parents of six children, named as follows: Sankey C., a merchant of Reidsville; Beulah C., the wife of Judge Collins, judge of the city court of Reidsville; J. M., engaged in the hotel business at Hazelhurst; Dwight L., of this review; Annabel, the wife of M. E. Flanders; and Henry Levy a student in the University of Georgia, who is now in his junior year and will graduate with the class of 1913 in law. The parents, who were both of Irish birth, are now deceased.

As a boy and youth, Mr. Rogers attended the schools of Reidsville finishing the high school at that place and then entering Locust Grove Institute. He finished his education with a course at the University of Georgia, graduating from the law department with the class of 1909, and receiving at that time his B. S. degree. He was one of the popular and prominent young men of his class, and was a member of the debating team representing the University of Georgia, versus the University of North Carolina, honors being carried off by the University of Georgia contingent. He was a member of the Sphinx fraternity, and also the captain of a company of militia while at the university. He finished his law studies at Mercer University at Macon, and was graduated in 1910, being admitted to the bar in June of the same year.

Mr. Rogers immediately located at Ocilla, where he formed a partnership with a Mr. Jordan, which partnership has endured up to the present time, and Mr. Rogers is fast forging to the front in the practice of his chosen profession.

ELIJAH MACK DANIEL LITTLEFIELD. One of the prosperous farmers and influential citizens of Decatur county, Elijah Mack Daniel Littlefield, began his career with limited opportunities, and has acquired one of the best country estates in Decatur county, and is a man of substantial position and influence.

He was born in Kershaw, district of South Carolina, October 15, 1848. His father was John Littlefield, who so far as known was born in South Carolina, and about 1850 went west, expecting to find a location and take his family out to the western country. He died of cholera in Mexico. His wife, thus left a widow, with two children, in 1860, removed to Florida, settling in Calhoun county where she married Samuel Etheridge, a planter of that county. Mr. and Mrs. Etheridge spent their last days in Florida. By her second marriage she reared one daughter, named Mary Drusilla, who now lives with Mr. Littlefield in Decatur county, and presides over his household. Mr. Littlefield has one brother, John Wesley Littlefield, who owns and occupies a farm only a short distance from Elijah's home. John Wesley married Jane Clinard, and has seven children whose names are Ida, Rosa, Cera, William C., John Daniel, Bertha and Eugene.

Elijah M. D. Littlefield as a boy made the best of limited opportunities to attain an education in the rural schools, which were much broken up by reason of the war, and his own time was largely required at home. During the latter part of the war he enlisted as a boy soldier in the State militia, but was never called out for active duty. When a young man he came to Decatur county, and began his career on rented land. He got a start, succeeded in practically every venture he undertook and after ten years bought four hundred acres comprising the fine farm which he now owns. This land he has improved and brought to a high state of cultivation. He has built a comfortable home, besides houses for his tenants, a large tobacco barn, and sheds for stock. Mr. Littlefield has recently planted an orange grove on his farm. He and his sisters are members of the Christian church and he affiliates with the Masonic lodge.

JOHN WEST MCMULLEN. A life-long resident of Brooks county, where his birth occurred on January 6, 1838, John West McMullen is a fine representative of those brave pioneers of old, who in their efforts to establish homes for themselves and their descendants endured hardships and trials difficult for the people of this generation to realize. How well they succeeded in their undertakings the broad expanse of cultivated fields to be seen in every direction, the commodious dwellings that have replaced the humble log cabins, and the long trains of palace cars used for transportation in place of the carts drawn by oxen or horses bear visible evidence. Mr. McMullen's paternal grandfather was one of the earlier settlers of Georgia, having located in Thomas county while that section of the country was in its pristine wildness. He was of thrifty Scotch ancestry, and a man of sterling integrity. His children, which included a son named James, who became the father of John West McMullen, were all born and reared in Georgia.

James McMullen was trained to habits of industry, and early showed natural ability as a mechanic. Although he never learned a trade, he became an expert with tools, and could do general blacksmithing, or make either a barrel or a wagon. After his marriage he lived for awhile in Thomas county, from there removing to that part of Lowndes county that is now a part of Brooks county. Purchasing land in the Hickory Head district, he was there a resident until his death, at the age of sixty years. He married Harriet Rountree, who was born in Lowndes county, where her father, a pioneer settler, was murdered by negroes while taking the produce of his farm to one of the marketing points in Florida, either Tallahassee or Newport. She, too, died at the age of three score years. To her and her husband eight children were born, as follows: Henrietta, William, Martha, John West, Josephine, Robert, George, and Margaret. In his political affiliations James McMullen was a Whig, and long before there were any railways in Georgia he served as a representative to the state legislature.

Brought up on the home farm, John West McMullen gleaned his knowledge of the three "R's" in the district schools, and as a boy became familiar with the various branches of agriculture. In June, 1861, he enlisted in Company H, Ninth Georgia Volunteer Infantry, which was assigned to Longstreet's Corps, Army of North Virginia. Continuing with his regiment in all of its engagements, he was at the front at the Battle of Antietam, where, on September 17, 1862, he was severely wounded, a minie ball lodging in his shoulder. Later the ball worked downward, and in 1864 his father extracted it, cutting it out. Having been incapacitated for active duty for nearly two years, Mr. McMullen then rejoined his regiment, and continued with his command, in Virginia, until the surrender of General Lee. Mr. McMullen and a few of his comrades refused to surrender, and having made their escape walked to their homes in Georgia. Resuming farming in Hickory Head precinct, Mr. McMullen resided there for many years, but is now living retired in Quitman.

In 1868 Mr. McMullen was united in marriage with Sarah J. Lee, who was born in that part of Thomas county now included within the boundaries of Brooks county, March 20, 1844, where her parents, John and Eliza (Groover) Lee, were pioneer settlers. His wife, who survived him, died in Thomasville. Mr. and Mrs. McMullen are the parents of four children, namely: Margaret, James, Florrie, and John Lee. Maggie, wife of Walter Avera, has three children, Mary Mec, Walter and James. James, son of John W. McMullen, married Hattie Arrington, and they have one child, James. Florrie, who married Charles Avera, died at the age of twenty-nine years, leaving two children, Daisy and Charles. J. Lee married Julia Arrington, and they have two children, John Lee and Thomas Briggs. Mr. and Mrs. McMullen are worthy members of the Hickory Head Missionary Baptist church.

JAMES FREDERICK SOUTER. For twenty years a member of the Georgia bar, and since 1902 located in practice at Preston, the county seat of Webster county, Mr. Souter easily stands in the very front rank of his profession in his home county, and has a large practice in all the courts and as large a general business as any other lawyer in that section.

James Frederick Souter who was born on a farm in Macon county, Georgia, June 8, 1865, on both his father's and mother's side represents old and respected families in this state. His father was John W. Souter, who was born near Columbia, South Carolina, in 1828, and his grandfather was Cullias Souter, who came from South Carolina to Georgia, and settled in Macon county about 1849. The grandfather bought a tract of land, ten miles west of Oglethorpe, and cleared away the wilderness and created an excellent farm and homestead. He died on that old estate, and was the father of several children.

John W. Souter, the father, was reared and educated in his native state, and after moving to Georgia, bought land in the same locality as his father had. He possessed a number of slaves, and employed their labor in operating his plantation until the breaking out of the Civil war. He was one of the loyal sons of Georgia, who responded to the call of the Confederacy, and he joined Rylander's Battalion, with which command he went to the front and was in many of the great battles of the war. He was wounded only once and that not severely, and escaped capture. Resuming his farm operations after the war, he continued in the quiet industry and substantial prosperity of his homestead until his death at the age of eighty-four years. The maiden name of his wife was Eliza Barfield. She was born in North Carolina, a daughter of Jesse Barfield, who was a native of the same state, and who came to Georgia, about 1835. This migration from North Carolina to Georgia was accomplished in real pioneer style. Several wagons and teams were required to haul the household goods, and many of the slaves either rode horseback or walked by the side of the wagons. The Barfields located in what is now Macon county and at that time nearly the entire western half of Georgia was in the condition it had been from the beginning of American history. No railroads were built for a number of years, and in all that vast district, devoted almost entirely to plantation, Macon was the one great market and depot for supplies. Mr. Barfield in this county became a farmer and remained there until his death. Mrs. Souter, the mother, died at the age of sixty-eight years. She reared four children, whose names are Nancy C., Mary, John M., and James Frederick.

Mr. James F. Souter when a boy attended the schools which were then found in the country district of Macon county, and was given a little better than ordinary educational equipment by attendance in the Tazewell high school. Reared on a farm he continued in that occupation until 1893. In the meantime he had taken up the study of law and pursued it industriously, and on being admitted to the bar he located at Oglethorp where he was engaged in practice until 1903. In that year he moved to Preston, where his office has since been, and where he has acquired a liberal share of professional business.

Mr. Souter in 1895 married Eliza Brooks, who was born in Macon county, a daughter of Benjamin C. and Sarah Brooks. Mr. and Mrs. Souter's four children are Laverne, Lester, Mary and Hoyle. As an able lawyer Mr. Souter has naturally been honored with public position and responsibility. He served as a member of the city council, and was mayor of Preston, and in 1911 was elected by the county board of education as county superintendent of schools, his choice and appointment being confirmed by election of the people during the same year. Fraternally he is a member of the Patriotic Order Sons of America.

JAMES BERRIEN FINCH. For many years intimately associated with the advancement of the mercantile interests of Quitman, the late James Berrien Finch, one of the most respected and highly esteemed citizens of his community, passed his later years retired from all business activities. His earliest association with this place was in the latter part of the Civil war, where he did service in the conscript department for some time, and when peace was finally restored, he opened a mercantile establishment in the city, and there continued to be actively engaged in that field of enterprise until his retirement in 1909. Mr. Finch was ever one of the most loyal and public-spirited of men, and one whose connection with Quitman was one of the fortunate circumstances of that place. He gave most praiseworthy service to the city as a public official in many and varied capacities, and to him may be traced directly the instigation of many an innovation in the communal life of the place. His death proved a loss indeed to the entire community, and one that will long be felt in the places where he was known, esteemed and honored.

James Berrien Finch was born in Madison county, Florida, on the plantation of his father, Charles Finch. Details concerning the parentage and ancestry of Mr. Finch are all too meager, but it is known that his father was of Scotch-Irish stock, and that his Grandfather Finch, was one of the early planters of Screven county, Georgia.

Reared and educated in Screven county, Charles Finch migrated as a young man to Madison county, Florida, where he bought land, and with the assistance of his slaves, tilled the soil there for a few years. Selling out his Florida interests in 1846, he returned to Georgia, and located some twelve miles south of the present site of Quitman, in what was then Lowndes county. Clearing a part of his purchase, here he continued a resident until his death, at the age of fifty-eight years. He married Rebecca Jones, who was born in Screven county, and who died in Brooks county a year or two after his death, at the age of sixty years, her death being resultant from an injury she sustained when thrown from a carriage. She was the mother of the following children: Andrew, Henry, Martha, James Berrien, and Hilliard J.

A boy of ten years when he came with his parents to Brooks county, James Berrien Finch became familiar with the different branches of agriculture on the home farm, but as a young man he embarked in mercantile pursuits at Nankin. At that time Tebeauville, now called Waycross, was the nearest railway station, and whenever his business called him to New York, where he replenished his stock, he had to travel by stage to that place, thence by rail to Savannah, where he took boat for New York City.

When the alarm of war rang throughout the land, Mr. Finch promptly enlisted in Company K, Fiftieth Georgia Volunteer Infantry, and as second lieutenant of his company went to the front, his regiment being assigned to the Army of the Potomac. He participated in many campaigns, marches and engagements, continuing in active service until after the battle of Sharpsburg, where he was hit on the head by the fragment of a shell, receiving a wound that resulted in his losing the sight of one eye. Thus disabled, Mr. Finch was not again eligible for active army service, but he was detailed for conscript work in Georgia, with headquarters at Quitman. After the close of the war he continued in Quitman, there opening up a mercantile establishment, and he continued to be actively and successfully engaged in that enterprise until 1909, when he retired from active business interests and took his ease as long as he lived.

Public-spirited and progressive, Mr. Finch was a man who ever manifested the most intelligent and wholesouled interest in the affairs of the public, and he was among the foremost in the inauguration of beneficial enterprises. For fifteen years he served as a member of the village and city council, a part of that time being president of the board. While he was thus active in the management of the affairs of the community, the first artesian well was opened, and the first opera house built, while other improvements of a similar value were made possible.

In 1865, Mr. Finch married Mary McCall, who was born in Screven county, Georgia, and who was a daughter of Francis S. and Ann (Dobson) McCall, of whom a more extended notice may be found elsewhere in this work. Six children were born to Mr. and Mrs. Finch, namely: J. L., Frank, George S., Nina A., Rebecca and Herbert. The first born, now the wife of Dan Boone, married for her first husband Dr. Will Wood, who at his death left her with one son, Will Wood, Jr. Frank

James L. Foster

attended Mercer College for two years and in his twentieth year was graduated from the University of Georgia. Entering then upon a professional career, he taught school but four months when he was thrown from a horse and killed, thus bringing to a sad end what promised to be a life of brilliant record and achievement. George S. Finch married Berta Griffin, and they have two children: Le Roy and Nina. Nina A., who married Thomas E. Hampton, has one child, Mary Lee. Rebecca married E. D. Lambright, and they have one daughter, Mary Wallace Lambright.

CAPT. JAMES LACHLISON FOSTER. A distinguished soldier and officer of the Confederate army during the Civil war, and for more than forty years prominent in the Georgia lumber industry, Captain Foster is one of the best loved citizens of Savannah.

Captain Foster was born in the city of Philadelphia, June 2, 1841, and was twelve years of age when brought to Savannah, Georgia, by his parents. After securing his education at Chatham Academy, Savannah, and Paris Hill Academy in Screven county, Georgia, he served an apprenticeship in the machine shop and foundry of his uncles R. and J. Lachlison. He was twenty years of age when the Civil war broke upon the country and, becoming a soldier, he attained distinction both as a member of the land and the naval forces of the Confederacy. In 1861, he answered his country's call for volunteers by enlisting in Company B, Oglethorpe Light Infantry, under Capt. Fred Simms.

He was captured in the fall of Fort Pulaski and was a prisoner at Governor's Island, Fort Columbus, and Fort Delaware, and after his exchange was commissioned in the Confederate navy in 1863. He was appointed to duty as third assistant engineer No. 84 on board the ironclad "Isondiga," Captain Kennard, in the fleet of Commodore Tatnall at Savannah, later becoming its chief engineer, and in December, 1864, when the Confederate forces evacuated that city he took a prominent part, his gunboat covering the retreat at the pontoon bridges on the Savannah river. He directed the burning of the bridges immediately following, thus preventing immediate pursuit by General Sherman's forces. He also burned the gunboat before leaving for Charleston. For this and other distinguished services he rose rapidly in the navy, being appointed chief engineer of the ironclad "Palmetto State" and afterwards the "Chicora," two of the most formidable gunboats in the Confederate navy. Early in 1865, he was placed in charge of the ram "Jackson" at Columbus. Escaping capture when the latter city fell, he reported for duty at Augusta a few days before the surrender at Appomattox. Mr. Foster attained the rank of first assistant engineer in the navy (assimilated rank of major in the army).

In 1869, Captain Foster joined his cousins, Thomas and Joseph Hilton, and formed the company of Hiltons and Foster to manufacture lumber at Union Island near Darien, Georgia. He has been associated with this company and its successors as superintendent, director and vice president in all its expansion and various changes since that time. During this time he resided first in McIntosh county, Georgia, and then on St. Simon's Island, Glynn county, Georgia. While living in Glynn county he was one of the commissioners for that county.

Captain Foster was for several years captain of the McIntosh Light Dragoons, and served with distinction as senator for the second senatorial district in the state legislature in 1904 and 1905. His geniality, sturdy Scotch determination, English courage and Yankee industry, to which was added the southern pride of the only home of his memory, were qualities which, when fused in the patriotic crucible of a most devastating and levelling war and in the face of depressing reconstruction demoralization, have redeemed the old South and brought this beloved section forward with strides to the forefront. Captain Foster has earned and honored his position as a prominent citizen of the rehabilitated south.

Captain Foster was first married in 1867 to Miss Lettice Austin of Savannah. She died in 1888, and he was subsequently married to Miss Elizabeth Lachlison. Captain Foster has by his first marriage one daughter, Lettice Elizabeth, who is married to Manley B. Tharin. Captain Foster also had a son, Robert Lachlison Foster, who married Miss Emma L. Mitchelson. The son died in 1899, leaving one daughter, Roberta Wymore Foster.

JOSHUA BARROW. An old resident and representative of one of the old families of Thomas county, Joshua Barrow died at his home in that vicinity, February 19, 1910. The record of the family has an appropriate place in this history, and is briefly as follows:

Joshua Barrow was born in Thomas county, Georgia, June 19, 1827. His father was John E. Barrow, who was born in North Carolina, March 14, 1798. The grandfather was Joseph Barrow, a native of North Carolina, who came to Georgia late in life and spent his declining years in Thomas county. John E. Barrow, the father, came to Georgia when a young man and located in Camden county, where for some years he was employed on the estate of General Coffee as overseer. After his marriage he came into southwest Georgia, accompanied by his bride, and made the journey with a horse and cart, bringing along all their earthly possessions. He traded the horse, saddle and bridle for a tract of land about three miles southwest of the present site of Boston, and began life in the unbroken wilderness. By his industrious efforts he cleared up a large tract of land and was a prosperous citizen of Thomas county until his death at the age of seventy-seven. The maiden name of his wife was Mary McCann, who was born in North Carolina, December 11, 1807. Her father was Joshua McCann, who came from North Carolina and lived on a farm in Camden county, Georgia, and then moved to Thomas county, locating southwest of the present city of Boston, where he remained until his death at a good old age. The maiden name of the wife of Joshua McCann was Sophie Passmore, who survived her husband several years. Mrs. John G. Barrow died at the age of ninety years.

Joshua Barrow, an only child of his parents, was reared and educated in Thomas county, and a few years after his marriage moved to Florida, where for a time he was engaged in the merchandising business. He then returned to Georgia, bought land in what is now Grady county, about two miles east of Cairo, and lived there until his death on February 19, 1910.

Mrs. Barrow, who survives her husband, was before her marriage Emeline E. Ramsey, and was born in Bladen county, North Carolina, January 20, 1830. Her parents were William S. and Flora McPherson Ramsey. Her grandfather was John W. Ramsey, one of the pioneers of southwest Georgia. Flora McPherson, her mother, was a daughter of John and Abigail Mulford McPherson. Mr. and Mrs. Barrow reared eight children named Joseph, John, Mary, Thomas, James, William C., McCullough and Foster.

THOMAS HUTSON HARDEN. Now city engineer of Dawson, Terrell county, Mr. Harden represents the Harden family in a younger generation and his forefathers were among the most prominent citizens of south Georgia from the time of the Revolution down. Thomas Hutson Harden was born in Terrell county, was a son of Daniel McWhir Harden, a native of Bryan county, and a grandson of Thomas Hutson Harden, and a great-grandson of William Harden, the founder of this branch of the family in Georgia.

William Harden was born in South Carolina. He served as captain of the Beauford Artillery from 1743 to 1785. In March, 1786, he was commander at Fort Lyttleton. He was promoted colonel of militia under Gen. Stephen Bull, and in 1779 attacked the British at Wiggins Hill. He served as colonel under Gen. Francis Marion during the campaign of 1780 and 1781, and was in a number of skirmishes with the British and captured Fort Balfour with one hundred prisoners.

Thomas Hutson Harden, grandfather of the city engineer of Dawson, was also prominent in military affairs, and was lieutenant colonel and division inspector with Gen. John McIntosh. Thomas H. Harden married Matilda Baker. She was a daughter of Col. John Baker of Liberty county, Georgia, and in whose honor Baker county, Georgia, was named. He was a colonel in Marion's command during the Revolution, and one of the most prominent of Georgia leaders during that war. He served as a member of the committee appointed by the convention at Savannah, on July 20, 1774, to prepare resolutions expressive of the sentiments and determinations of the people of the colony with regard to the Boston port bill. He was a member of the provincial congress from 1775 to 1777, and was on the Georgia council of safety in 1776. He subsequently was in active service and participated in the capture of Augusta during May and June of 1781.

Daniel McWhir Harden, the father, was ten months old when his father died, and he then was taken to live in the home of his grandmother, then the wife of Rev. Daniel McWhir in Liberty county, where he was reared and educated. He studied medicine, but owing to his deafness he never practiced. He inherited a large amount of land and slaves in Bryant county, and was engaged in farming there for a number of years until his removal to Lee county with his brother, Thomas H. They bought a large tract of land, seven miles southeast of Dawson, and were engaged in operating the plantation with the aid of their numerous slaves. A short time before the war they sold their land and returned to Bryant county, where they bought a plantation called Egypt. Daniel Harden's family remained in Terrell county, and he spent part of his time in each county looking after his interests. During the war his wife was one of a committee appointed to solicit clothing for the soldiers, in May, 1863, and she continued in that charitable undertaking until the fall of 1864. In 1867, Daniel Harden established a mercantile business, which he conducted for a year, and then sold out and moved to Bryant county. Four years later he returned to Terrell county, and made his home in Dawson until his death in 1886.

Daniel Harden was married in Columbus on July 18, 1854, to Mary Ann Foster. She also brings some important names into the family relationship. She was born on a farm five miles south of Dawson, which was then in Lee county, Georgia, on November 11, 1838. Her father was Newit Foster, who was born in South Hampton county, Virginia, a son of Christopher C. Foster. Christopher C. Foster, the maternal great-grandfather of Thomas H. Harden, of Dawson, was a Revolutionary soldier. A remarkable fact of his life was that he was one hundred and twelve years of age at his death, which occurred in Virginia. His wife, whose maiden name was Mary Ann Jordan, was almost equally remarkable for her longevity, since she attained the age of one hundred and eight years. One of the sons of this centenarian, named James, went to Ohio, while another son named Moses was a physician and came to Georgia, spending his career in Lee county. Newit Foster came to Georgia with his uncle Benjamin Jordan, being fourteen years old at the time. Benjamin Jordan was quite wealthy, and bought large tracts of land in what is now Dougherty county, and Newit Foster continued in his employ for about twenty years. He finally settled in that part of Lee county which is now Terrell, and bought large tracts of timbered land on which he built a one-room log house. It was an exceedingly crude shelter, having a chimney constructed of earth and sticks, and all its furniture and equipment were in accordance with the rude style then prevailing in many homes of south Georgia. Two of his children were born in that log cabin. He worked his land with slave labor, and cleared up a large area to the sunlight, and for many years raised crops and surrounded himself and his family with all the essentials of material prosperity. He later built good frame buildings, and continued to reside there until his death at the age of fifty-nine years.

Newit Foster married Catherine Woolbright. She was born in Wilkes county, a daughter of Daniel Woolbright, who had come to what is now Terrell county, in 1836, and settled seven miles southeast of the present site of Dawson, where he bought large amounts of land, and with his slaves improved a large plantation. That remained his home until his death in 1850. Daniel Woolbright married Mary McKnight, who died in 1837. The wife of Newit Foster died at the age of seventy-eight years. She was the mother of seven children, whose names are Mary A., Sarah J., Frances, M. William, James, John, and Emma. The son William Foster was a soldier in the Confederate army.

Mary Ann (Foster) Harden, the mother, is still living, making her home in Dawson. She reared six children, named Catherine, Rosa, Mamie, Neta, Thomas H., and William Edward. Catherine and William are now deceased.

Mr. Thomas H. Harden was educated in the South Georgia Male and Female College at Dawson, and remained at home on the farm until he was eighteen years of age. He is a civil engineer by profession and was trained for that work by practical experience. He began as a rodman, and has had a large and successful experience in different departments of the profession. In 1908, he was commissioned to make the surveys for the map of Terrell county, and in the same year was elected to the office of city engineer of Dawson, official responsibilities which he has since discharged most capably. William E. Harden, the youngest son of the family, was educated in the public schools of Dawson and, when seventeen years old, was given the responsible task of editing and publishing a newspaper at Newton, known as the *Baker County News*. William Harden, who was familiarly known as ''judge'' to his friends, was a humorist and an artist of rare genius. He had high aspirations in his chosen work, and in order to find a larger field moved to Atlanta, where he worked as an engraver and as cartoonist for the *Constitution* and the *Journal* of that city. Many of his cartoons and illustrations were as comical as those associated with the Uncle Remus pictures, and through his artistic work he represented many of the current events and political and social issues of the times. He possessed a genial nature, and ready wit, and had a host of friends in south Georgia. He was a man of fine Christian character, a member of Dr. Broughton's Tabernacle in Atlanta, and also acted as class reporter and as artist for the Baraca Class, of which he was a member. In the summer of 1904 his health failed, and he returned home, where he died, January 28, 1905, at the age of twenty-four years.

GEORGE W. ARD, whose death in 1904 removed one of the best known and most highly respected citizens of Stewart county, was a Confederate soldier and long identified with the official life of his home county in Georgia.

He was born in Dale county, Alabama, in 1833, was reared on an Alabama farm, and in young manhood came to Georgia, where he was employed for several years as a farm superintendent. At the outbreak of the war between the states he enlisted in Company K of the Second Regiment of Georgian Volunteers, this regiment being attached to Toombs' Brigade, and with that command went into Virginia. He fought in all the battles in which his regiment was engaged, and at the crucial conflict at Antietam, in 1863, he was severely wounded, one ball passing through his elbow and another through his thigh, which caused the loss of his left leg. After the battle he fell into the hands of the Federals, and a member of the Ninth New York Infantry cared for him until he was exchanged. This strange friendship between two soldiers of the opposite armies was continued by correspondence until the death of the Federal soldier. After his exchange Mr. Ard returned home and was soon afterwards elected tax collector of Stewart county. He was continued in that office by reelection until his death in 1904.

In 1867, Mr. Ard married Sarah Whitten, who was born in Heard county, Georgia, a daughter of Reverend Arphax and Matilda (Bennett) Whitten. The Reverend Whitten was born in the Spartansburg district of South Carolina, and was the son of Rev. James Whitten, a missionary Baptist preacher, who carried the gospel in the early days to the inhabitants of Harris and Muskogee counties, and who died in Columbus, Georgia, about the beginning of the Civil war. Mrs. Ard's father was also a Baptist preacher and held pastorates in both Georgia and Alabama, and his death occurred at Smith Station in Lee county, Alabama. Mrs. Ard's mother died in Heard county, Georgia. Mrs. Ard reared eight children, namely: Annie, Clifford, Charles R., Sarah, Mary, Georgia, Arphax, and John.

ROBERT HAMILTON HARRIS, A. M., D. D. With a long and distinguished career in the law, as an educator and in the ministry, Dr. Harris, who is now residing in Cairo, Georgia, but purposes to return about November 1, 1913, to Columbus, is one of the eminent Georgians whose lives extend over the greatest epochs of the last and present century, and his beneficent activities are a matter of pride to all residents of the state. Both his own career and the record of his family have unusual interest, and the following paragraphs will treat these subjects as fully as possible.

Robert Hamilton Harris was born on the Holly Springs Plantation, the country home of his father, Dr. Bennett Harris, an Augusta physician, in Jefferson county, Georgia, April 19, 1842.

Going back to the founder of the family in America, it is believed, from the best information obtainable, that the first ancestors were natives of either England or Wales, and during colonial times came and settled in Virginia. In Virginia, was born the head of the next generation, John Harris, who removed from his native state to Sampson county, North Carolina, where he spent the rest of his life. Benjamin Harris, grandfather of Dr. Harris and son of John, was born in Sampson county, was a soldier in the Revolutionary war, enlisting while a lad, and some time after the close of that conflict removed to South Carolina, and later to Georgia, becoming a pioneer settler in Walton county. He secured land there, which was virgin soil, cleared a plantation and made his home at Social Circle until his death. The maiden name of his wife was Bethany Odom, who had three brothers, named Elkanah, Halatia and Deldatha. She survived her husband and lived to be about ninety years of age.

Dr. Bennett Harris, father of the Rev. Dr. Harris, was born in Edgefield district, South Carolina, in 1805. Though his early life was spent in a period marked by a dearth of good schools and in a country just emerging from the wilderness state, he made the best use of his scant opportunities to secure a good education and became a student in the state university in Athens, Georgia, where he was contemporary of the Cobbs and Hillyers. He undertook to work his way through the latter institution, by manual service about the buildings and grounds; but his strength failed him, and he was prostrated by fever. He was beginning to despair of completing his education, when Major Walker, a prominent citizen of Athens, became interested in him and advanced him the necessary amount of money to carry him through school to graduation. He then became a teacher, and after paying off his indebtedness and accumulating some earnings, entered the Pennsylvania School of Medicine in Philadelphia. After receiving a full diploma in medicine and surgery from that institution he took a post graduate course in medicine at the Eclectic School, Cincinnati, Ohio. He subsequently went abroad, studied and acquired extensive experience in clinics at the noted medical institutions of Paris during two years, and later spent one year of like work in London. Returning to America, in 1839, he located in Augusta, Georgia, and was in that city when its first great epidemic of yellow fever occurred. He and Dr. Turpin, with the two Doctors Eve, were the only physicians with such a sense of devotion to duty as to remain in the plague-stricken city. Dr. Harris was, himself, ultimately stricken down with the fever, but recovered and continued in practice until his death in 1845. Dr. Harris was married, in 1840, to Rebekah Ann Baldy, who was born in Beaufort District, South Carolina, a daughter of Stephen and Elizabeth (Dixon) Baldy.

Many interesting things might be said about the family of Elizabeth Dixon. Her grandfather was James Smithson, one of the first landgraves of the province of South Carolina. It is related that an English sea captain was compelled to put his ship into Port Royal harbor for repairs and, while waiting, was entertained in the home of Governor Smithson. When the captain left he gave the governor a sack of seeds from India. Those seeds were grains of rice in the rough, which were planted by Governor Smithson; and the tradition is that from that little planting originated rice culture in America. The mother of Elizabeth Dixon was a lineal descendant of Gilbert Hamilton, of Scotland, a friend of William Wallace and Robert Bruce, whose cause for the liberation of Scotland he espoused, participating, as a soldier and prominent officer, in the great battle of Bannockburn, which resulted in seating Bruce upon the throne. For his distinguished services in that cause, Robert Bruce gave him a patent of nobility, by virtue of which he became progenitor of the noble line of Dukes of Hamilton. The present title-holder of that line is Duke Frederick Hamilton, residing on his Irish estate at Baroncourt.

Dr. Robert Harris has now in his home at Cairo, Georgia, among his family heirlooms, a beautiful collection of solid silver pieces, of inestimable value, upon all the large pieces of which is engraved the Hamilton "crest"—a saw cutting into an oak, with the word "through," in capitals above. This silver service has been handed down from generation to generation for many centuries, and is one of the rarest and most interesting collections to be found in America. Dr. Harris also possesses the original family coat-of-arms, beautifully hand-painted on parchment and containing no bar-sinister—a fact of which he is justly proud. He also has the little christening stole, with hood and mittens, worn by the Hamilton babies during that church ceremonial for ages in the past. Those heirlooms came down to him through his mother, who in her orphaned girlhood went with her aunt, Miss Elizabeth Hamilton, to reside with a great-aunt, Miss Margaret Hamilton, in Dublin, Ireland, by invitation and until the death of the latter, of whom she became the heir. At the death of Miss Margaret, Miss Baldy returned with her aunt, Miss Elizabeth, to America, and the two set up housekeeping in Augusta, Georgia, in 1839, where Miss Elizabeth died of yellow fever and where Miss Baldy met and was married to her first husband, Dr. Harris. In the death of Dr. Harris his wife was left a widow with two little children, Robert and Bennetta, the latter of whom died in 1861. Some years later Mrs. Harris was married the second time, to Rev. Robert Fleming, a distinguished teacher, a noted author and a prominent minister of the Baptist denomination. Her death occurred in Thomasville when she was sixty-one years of age, leaving as survivors her husband, Mr. Fleming, and three children; her son and two daughters, Alice and Adela Fleming. Alice and her father died a few years later. Adela, now Mrs. Smith, for the second time a widow, resides in Waco, Texas.

When the Civil war came on, Robert Hamilton Harris was in college at Mercer University, but he left school to join the Newman Guards, Company A, First Georgia Regiment. He was soon transferred, however, to the Thomasville Guards, Company F, Twenty-ninth Georgia, serving with that command twenty months, along the Atlantic coast, at Savannah, Charleston, Wilmington and Jacksonville. In March, 1863, he was promoted to a lieutenancy, in Company A, Fifty-seventh Georgia Regiment. The captain being absent and the first lieutenant *hors de combat*, he was placed in command of his company and so continued until the close of the war, the first lieutenant soon dying and the captain being promoted to major. Mr. Harris received in order two more promotions—to first lieutenant and brevet captain. In that command, he went through the entire Vicksburg campaign, ending with that dreadful siege; in Johnston's campaign from Dalton to Atlanta; in Hood's campaign, from Atlanta to Nashville, Tennessee, and back to Corinth, Mississippi. He was under fire on scores of occasions, many of them extremely bloody and sometimes when he lost nearly all of his men; but although bullets frequently pierced his clothing, he never received more than a scratch or two in the nature of wounds. Besides the service mentioned, he fought Stoneman at Macon, commanding a regiment part of that day, and starting that general's defeat by turning his right flank. He was not with his regiment when it surrendered, under Johnston, at Bentonville, North Carolina, being on detached service in command of a lunette in defense at Macon against Wilson. He declined to surrender there, and, breaking through the swarms of Federal cavalry, made his way home to Thomasville, with only two men who escaped with him.

While a paroled prisoner, after the siege of Vicksburg, Dr. Harris, then just twenty-one, was married to Mary Martha, daughter of Hon. Peter E. Love, of Thomasville. On reaching home he read law under his father-in-law, was admitted to the bar and soon secured a good practice. He was elected mayor of his city, then after serving two or three years became solicitor of the county court, and later was appointed counsel for the Atlantic and Gulf Railroad, which extended from Savannah to Bainbridge and Albany. His health having become greatly impaired in that service, he decided to abandon the practice of law and later, in 1876, entered upon the next important phase of his career, as an educator. He was elected principal of the chief school in Cairo, and spent six years as a teacher in the local academy. In the meantime he had entered the ministry of the Baptist denomination. In 1882, he was called to the charge of the school at Calvary, and, consolidating four rival schools at that point, established the Calvary High School.

In 1883, he was called to the pastorate of the Baptist church at La Grange, Georgia, where he continued for two years. From that city he was called to the great First Church in Columbus, and during his ministry of eight years there added six hundred members to his charge. His next location was at Troy, Alabama, where he remained for two years, whence he was called to Thomasville, where he served the Baptist church for five years. In the meantime and since, he has received calls and overtures from a number of prominent churches in large cities that he has not felt at a liberty to consider.

While pastor in La Grange, Dr. Harris was elected a member of the faculty of the Southern Female College, an institution which was later removed to College Park, near Atlanta, and became known as Cox College. Being reelected to a leading chair in Cox College, Dr. Harris resigned his pastorate at Thomasville and went to that institution, where he remained over three years. There his health broke down, and he went to Tampa, Florida. While in Tampa, in 1906, after he had somewhat recuperated, he was called to the Baptist church at Cairo, which town has since been his home.

Soon after taking charge in Cairo, Dr. Harris commenced a campaign, among his own members only, to raise funds for the erection of a new church building, and the result is the present beautiful edifice in that city. The church is built in the English abbey style of architecture, of the finest pressed brick, the interior being most unique and very beautiful, with exceedingly handsome furnishings, and it was finished and equipped without a dollar of debt.

Dr. Harris continued his pastorate in Cairo until March, 1912, at which time he resigned, in order to become apostolic messenger to the churches of the Mercer Association.

The degrees of A. M. and D. D. were conferred upon him years ago by Mercer University, and he has been for many years, as he still is, in great demand as a speaker on various important occasions in many sections of the country. In addition to other distinctions, he is also chaplain and major on the staff of the South Georgia Brigade, U. C. V.

Hon. Peter E. Love, the father of Dr. Harris' wife, was a lawyer by profession, occupied the superior court bench for many years, was a member of the United States congress at the time of secession and used his influence in vain effort to prevent Civil war. He was the Georgia member of the committee of thirty-three, one from each state of the Union, appointed some time prior to the outbreak of hostilities, to arrange some compromise which might avert the imminent war. He died, honored by all who knew him—and there were thousands—in November, 1866.

Mrs. Harris passed away in 1900, leaving, besides her husband, two sons and one daughter. Of the sons, James Hamilton Harris is an expert accountant, resident in Texas, and is unmarried. The other, Amos Love Harris, is in the real estate business in Tampa, Florida, and was married in 1902 to Mattie Ward Henderson, a daughter of W. B. Henderson, late deceased, and one of the wealthiest and most prominent citizens of that city. They have two children, named Robert Hamilton and Caroline Henderson. Mamie Anne, the third child and only daughter, was married in 1894 to Edgar Duncan Burts, a prominent young attorney of Columbus, of brilliant promise, who died in January, 1905, leaving three children, Mamie Love, Edgar Duncan, Jr., and Sarah Caroline. Besides the two sons and daughter named there have been born to Mr. and Mrs. Harris five other children, all boys, and all dead before 1888.

MALCOLM B. COUNCIL. Noteworthy among the energetic and enterprising men who have contributed largely towards the development and advancement of the agricultural and industrial prosperity of Sumter county is Malcolm B. Council, of Americus, a well-known capitalist, and one of the more extensive landholders of southwest Georgia. A son of Solomon B. Council, he was born June 26, 1838, near Fayetteville, Cumberland county, North Carolina.

His paternal grandfather, Michael Council, a native of Nansemond county, Virginia, migrated to North Carolina in early life, locating first in what is now Anson county, from there going to Robeson county, and finally settling permanently in Cumberland county, that state, where his death occurred at the venerable age of ninety years. He married a Miss Barlow, and they reared five sons, Solomon B., Thomas, Matthew, John and Jordan, and three daughters. Nothing definite is known of the Barlow family, to which his wife belonged, but history tells us that one of Sir Walter Raleigh's ships that sailed from England in April, 1584, was commanded by Capt. Arthur Barlow, who landed in North Carolina in that year.

Reared on his father's farm, Solomon B. Council remained a resident of Cumberland county, North Carolina, until 1842. Then, accompanied by his wife and children, he made an overland journey to Georgia, bringing with him all of his worldly possessions, camping and cooking by the wayside. Locating in Sumter county, he bought a tract of heavily timbered land lying three miles northeast of Americus, and immediately began the pioneer task of hewing a home from the forest. This part of the state was then in its primeval wildness, deer and other wild game native to this section being plentiful, and roaming at will. Americus was a small place, with but three or four stores, and there were no railways in the state. Hawkinsville and Macon, on the Ocmulgee river, and Columbus, on the Chattahoochee, were the principal trading points, although salt was obtained at the Gulf. For his first habitation in his new home, Solomon B. Council built a rude log-house, with a stick and earth chimney. In due course of time that was replaced by a more commodious structure, other substantial buildings were erected, and on the farm which he improved he spent the remainder of his life, passing away at the advanced age of eighty-four years.

Solomon B. Council married Elizabeth Blue, who was born in Cumberland county, North Carolina, and died on the home farm, in Sumter county, Georgia, when but seven days less than eighty-eight years old. Her father, Malcolm Blue, married Nancy Jacobs, a daughter of Henry and Sarah (Brown) Jacobs, grand-daughter of Neal and Barbara (McMillin) Brown, and great-granddaughter of Governor Brown, of Tennessee. Mr. and Mrs. Solomon B. Council reared six children, as follows: Mary, Margaret, Maria, Sarah, George, and Malcolm B.

A child of four years when he was brought by his parents to Sumter county, Malcolm B. Council was brought up in true pioneer style, attending a subscription school, which was kept in a small loghouse, furnished with home-made seats and benches, while he, in common with the members of all the families in the vicinity, wore garments made of homespun, and fashioned by the women of the households, each woman and girl doing her regular daily stint of carding, spinning and weaving. At the outbreak of the war between the states, he enlisted as a private in Cutt's artillery, and was subsequently made adjutant, with rank of lieutenant. He went to Virginia with his company, which was attached to Longstreet's corps, and took part in many of the hard-fought battles of the conflict, including the engagements at Centerville, Chancellorsville, the seven days' fight around Richmond, the battles at Antietam, Sharpsburg, the Wilderness, the second engagement at Manassas, the battle of Gettysburg, at Spottsylvania Court House, and in the many skirmishes in the vicinity of Richmond and Petersburg, later surrendering at Appomattox.

Returning to Americus at the close of the war, Mr. Council taught school for awhile, and was afterward employed as clerk in a cotton warehouse. Entering then the employ of Capt. John A. Cobb, who owned five large plantations, and worked more than one hundred and twenty-five negroes, he became overseer of the Cobb property, making his home on the plantation which had the nearest white neighbors, they being three miles distant, and retained the position eight years. Going then to De Soto, Mr. Council carried on general farming there for two years, and on returning to Americus at the expiration of that time, embarked in the warehouse business, with which he was prominently and successfully connected for thirty years. In the meantime he was also interested in agricultural pursuits, and now owns and operates several valuable plantations. Among his holdings are the old Council homestead, one of the finest plantations in Georgia; a plantation on the river, fourteen miles southeast of Americus; an estate lying sixteen miles northwest of the city; another situated fifteen miles to the south; one in Lee county; and another plantation in Dooly county. Mr. Council has always been a lover of the chase, keeping a well-trained pack of hounds, and owns a game preserve of five hundred acres, sixteen miles from Americus.

Mr. Council married, February 5, 1867, Martha Maria Harris, who was born in Houston county, Georgia, two miles east of Fort Valley, a daughter of Isaac C. Harris. Samuel Harris, her paternal grandfather, a life-long resident of Georgia, died in 1814, at a comparatively early age. He was a soldier in the Revolutionary war, and for his services therein was given a grant of land in Washington county, the grant bearing date of September 30, 1784. Isaac C. Harris was born in Warren county, Georgia, July 30, 1813, and was brought up on a farm. After attaining manhood he lived for a short time in Jones county, but from 1842 until 1863 was engaged in farming in Houston county, where he owned land. Coming to Sumter county in 1863, he bought a farm lying ten miles south of Americus, and occupied it for a time. Selling out, he purchased land in Lee county, and was there a tiller of the soil until 1877, when he returned to Warren county, where he remained a resident until his death, in 1879. He was a local preacher in the Methodist Episcopal church, and reared his family in that faith.

Isaac C. Harris was twice married. He married first Provvie Alsobrook, who was born November 19, 1811, in Jones county, Georgia, a daughter of Amos and Sarah (Jones) Alsobrook, the former of whom spent his entire life in Jones county, while his wife, who survived him, spent her last years at the home of a daughter, in Florida. Mrs. Provvie Alsobrook Harris died September 22, 1862. Mr. Harris subsequently married for his second wife Mary Pullen, who is now living on the old Harris homestead, in Warren county. By his first marriage Mr. Harris reared twelve children, as follows: Mary; Noffleet; Augustus; Samuel; John; Sarah; Martha Maria, wife of Mr. Council; Eugenia; Joseph;

Robert; Alonzo; and James. Of his second union, three children were, born, Anna, William, and George.

Mr. and Mrs. Council are the parents of six children, namely: Lena Harris; Emma Eugenia; John Malcolm; Elizabeth; Nell Lenoir and Harris Solomon. Lena Harris married John T. Argo, and has six children, Martha Helen, Herschel Council, Christine Elizabeth, Catherine, Malcolm Blue, and John Thomas. Emma Eugenia, wife of Elton C. Parker, has four children, Leonard Council, Mary Elizabeth, Martha Eugenia, and Elton Council. John M. Council married Luetta Cochran. Elizabeth is the wife of Dr. Stephen H. McKee. Nell L. married S. E. Statham. Fraternally, Mr. Council is a member of M. B. Council Lodge, No. 95, Free and Accepted Masons; of Wells Chapter, No. 42, Royal Arch Masons; and of De Molay Commandery, No. 5, Knights Templar.

CAPT. JOHN PEEL BEATY. For upwards of thirty years, Captain Beaty has served in the responsible office of treasurer of Webster county. Captain Beaty is one of the oldest citizens of Preston, being now in his eighty-eighth year, and with a long and varied career, stretching behind him in retrospect.

Capt. John Peel Beaty was born in Jefferson county, Georgia, August 18, 1825. His grandfather was Henry Beaty, a native of Ireland, who came to America, landing at Savannah, and thence made his way to Jefferson county, where he bought land, but some years later moved to Houston county, and then, in 1836, to what is now Webster county. In Webtser county he spent the rest of his days, and was about one hundred years old at the time of his death. Robert Beaty, the father of Captain Beaty, was born in Jefferson county, Georgia. He was reared and married in that county, and in 1828 moved to Houston county where he remained until 1836, and then came to that portion of Stewart county, which is now included within the limits of Webster county. He bought a large quantity of land near Preston, and cleared it and operated it with the aid of his large retinue of slaves. For a number of years no railroads penetrated this section of Georgia, and the father hauled all his cotton and other produce to Macon or to Columbus to market. In transporting the cotton or other goods, six mules were hitched to each wagon. Robert Beaty lived in that vicinity until his death when eighty-four years of age. The maiden name of his wife was Sarah Peel. Her father, John Peel, a native of Ireland, where he married Miss Gamble, came to America and located in Jefferson county, Georgia; Mrs. Robert Beaty died at the age of eighty-three, and the five children were named Margaret, Sarah, John P., Nancy and Elizabeth.

John Peel Beaty was reared in a far-off and pioneer epoch of Georgia, and became thoroughly familiar with all the old-time plantation life before the war. He attended rural schools and assisted in the work of the home farm. After he was twenty-one, he became associated in managing the estate with his father. In March, 1862, he enlisted in Company F of the Forty-sixth Regiment of Georgia Infantry, and spent the first year at Charleston, South Carolina, and then joined the western army. He was in many of the important engagements which took place in the Mississippi valley, beginning with the great battle of Chickamauga, and in the various engagements leading up to Atlanta, taking part in the defense of that city. After the fall of Atlanta, he was with Hood's regiments, and later was at Wainsborough, Buck county, Georgia, at the final surrender. He then made his way back home as best he could. On arriving home he again took up farm life, but after several years moved to Preston, which has been his home ever since. Captain Beaty has had one unique experience. Without any moving of residence, he has lived during his lifetime in three different counties of Georgia, first Stewart county, second Kinchafoonte, a county not now in existence under that name, and in Webster county. He has represented the county three different times in the Georgia legislature. For the past thirty years he has been honored with the office of county treasurer, and the people of Webster county feel a matter of pride in this venerable and faithful county official.

Captain Beaty has been twice married. In 1853, he married Eliza R. Prim, and his second marriage was with Mrs. Fannie C. (Snelling) Bell. The six children of the first marriage are named: Martha, Robert, John, Albert, Susie and Katie. Captain Beaty and wife are both members of the Baptist church.

ADAM JONES CUMBEST. As farmer and miller and a useful citizen of his community, Mr. Cumbest has been identified with south Georgia for many years. He was born in Wilkinson county, this state, August 14, 1846, the Cumbests being an old family of that vicinity. His grandfather was, so far as known, a lifelong resident of Wilkinson county, where he was a farmer.

Mr. Cumbest's father, James Cumbest, was a native of Wilkinson county, and spent all his active career in agricultural pursuits. From Wilkinson he moved to Lee county, thence to Irwin, and finally to Mitchell county, where he bought a farm and resided until his death at the advanced age of eighty-six years. He married Bethany Williams, who was born in Wilkinson county and died in Lee county. She reared six children, named Thomas, Adam J., Frances, Elizabeth, Ellafarr and Angeline.

Spending the early years of his life on the home farm first in Lee and then in Mitchell county, Adam Jones Cumbest was still a boy when the war between the states came on. He enlisted in Company E of the Seventeenth Georgia Infantry and went up into Virginia to join Lee's army. During many of the campaigns and battles he did his soldier's duty, and in 1864 was captured at Port Harrison and held a prisoner at Point Lookout, Maryland, until near the close of the war. Being released on parole, he was not exchanged before the surrender. The life of a soldier he exchanged for that of farmer, and after his marriage in the spring of 1865 he settled on a farm belonging to his wife in Mitchell county. Two years later he moved to Decatur county, buying a farm fifteen miles from Bainbridge; then bought a farm in Colquitt county, two years later bought one in Mitchell county, where he resided five years, and then came to Thomas county, where he owned and operated a farm three years. He was then made superintendent of the Thomas county infirmary, an institution which he capably managed for a period of twelve years. On retiring from that public responsibility, he bought his present farm and homestead in the Boston district. Located on this place, near his house, was a grist mill, which he has operated in addition to his general farm enterprises.

In April, 1865, Mr. Cumbest was married to Eliza (Grinner) Hudson, whose family is one of the oldest in southwest Georgia. She was born in Decatur county, a daughter of John Grinner and granddaughter of John Grinner, both of whom were natives of South Carolina. The grandfather moved from his native state to Georgia about 1822, being one of the pioneers of what is now Decatur county. He and his family made the migration with horses and wagons and brought all the household goods and implements for their settlement in the wilderness.

Grandfather Grinner bought timbered land about five miles from the present site of Whigham. That region was still the hunting ground for Indians, who soon viewed the arrival of the increasing number of whites with distrust and hostility. The Grinners and other settlers built a fort for the protection of their families, and at one time the mother of Mrs. Cumbest spent four weeks in that structure. After clearing quite a tract of land, the grandfather moved to Mitchell county, where he bought other timbered land five miles northeast of the present site of Camilla, and lived there until his death. He had served in the Indian wars and was in every sense one of the pioneers to whose enterprise and hardihood later generations were indebted for the advantages which they enjoyed. The maiden name of his wife was Susan Mills, also a native of South Carolina, and she died in Mitchell county. The father of Mrs. Cumbest, John Grinner, was about twelve years old when brought to Georgia, and was reared amid pioneer scenes. On beginning his own career he bought land in Decatur county, but after some years bought another farm five miles from Camilla in Mitchell county. His settlement there occurred a number of years before railroads had been built, and for a number of years he hauled his products to Albany or to Tallahassee to market. His wife, the mother of Mrs. Cumbest, plied all the domestic arts of that primitive period, including the spinning of cotton and wool, the making of all clothes from homespun, and cooking at the fireplace until the introduction of cookstoves. The father changed farms several times, and spent his last years in Colquitt county, where he died at the age of eighty-seven. He married Lottie Ford, a native of South Carolina, and her father, James Ford, came from that state and was also a pioneer of Decatur county. The mother of Mrs. Cumbest died at the age of about eighty, and she reared ten children.

Mrs. Cumbest was first married at the age of fourteen to Levi Butler, who was a native of Mitchell county and enlisted in the first company that went from that county to the war. He died in the service while at Yorktown, Virginia, in 1862. After his death Mrs. Butler married David Hudson, a native of middle Georgia. In 1864, he also enlisted and five months later sacrificed his life to the southern cause at Macon. Mrs. Cumbest was one of the martyrs to the tragedies of the great war. After losing two husbands she married a third who had recently returned from a northern prison, and she and Mr. Cumbest have had a happy wedded life of upwards of a half century.

By her first marriage Mrs. Cumbest had three children: William, John and Louisa Butler. She and Mr. Cumbest reared six children: Elias, Seaburn, Mary Anna, James, George and Mittie. Elias married Marzilla Shiver and has one son, Elias. Seaburn married Ophelia Holland and has four children: Lonnie, Eunice, John and Ellis. Mary Anna married Jeff Busby, and has eight children: Gordon, Henry, Ira, Annie, Frank, Ola, Charles and Ruby. James married Arrilla Holland and has one son, Lee. George married Annie Purvett and has two children: Mittie and Viver. Mittie, the youngest child of Mr. and Mrs. Cumbest, died at the age of two years. William Butler, the first of Mrs. Cumbest's children, married Ida Douglas and have the following children: Audrey, Mamie, Louis, and William. John Butler married Ida Smith, and their seven children are: Levi, Nonie, William, Calvin, Mamie, Lois and Jewell. Louisa Butler married George Williams and has six children: Lonie, Betey, George, Trudie, Eliza and Ola. Mrs. Cumbest has seven great-grandchildren.

FLETCHER W. GRIFFIN. Ranking high among the live, enterprising and successful business men of Sumter county is Fletcher W. Griffin, of Americus, a well-known cotton dealer, and an extensive land owner. He was born in 1857, on a farm lying eight miles east of Americus, a son of Thomas Griffin, and comes of substantial pioneer stock.

Mr. Griffin's grandfather, Dempsey Griffin, was born near Raleigh, North Carolina, of Welsh ancestry. Joining the little bands of immigrants that were steadily pushing their way westward, he left his native state in 1849, accompanied by his family. With wife and children he made his way through the almost pathless woods with teams, bringing his household goods, and driving his stock, to Georgia. After a tedious journey of several weeks, he arrived in Sumter county, and on Line creek, east of Americus, bought a tract of forest-covered land. Clearing an opening in the woods, he built a loghouse, which, with its stick and clay chimney, and large fireplace, was the first home of the Griffin family in Georgia. He lived in the typical pioneer style, his wife doing all of her cooking by the open fireplace, and dressing her family in homespun material, which she wove herself, having first carded and spun the wool. Clearing quite a patch of the land, he lived there with his family until after the close of the war between the states, when he sold out, and moved to the south part of the county, where he purchased land, and was a resident until his death, at the advanced age of eighty-seven years. His wife, whose maiden name was McCurkadle, died when but sixty-five years old, leaving seven children, as follows: Bryan, Caleb, Thomas, John, Nancy, Hannah, and Catherine.

Thomas Griffin, the third son in succession of birth of the parental household, was born near Raleigh, North Carolina, in 1837, and at the age of twelve years came with the family to Sumter county, where he assisted in the pioneer labor of reclaiming a farm from the wilderness. At the time of his marriage he began farming on his own account on a part of his father's homestead, continuing thus engaged until 1862. Early in that year he enlisted in the Confederate army, and went with his command to Virginia, where, in June of that same year, he died, his death occurring at Orange court house, in the twenty-fifth year of his age. His wife, whose maiden name was Eliza Gammage, was born in Macon county, Georgia, a daughter of Alsey Gammage, a native of South Carolina, and a pioneer of Macon county, where he resided several years, although he later bought land in Sumter county, three and one-half miles from Americus, where he spent the remainder of his life of sixty-eight years. Mrs. Thomas Griffin subsequently married for her second husband Jesse Chembliss, who died while yet in the prime of life, before she did, her death occurring when she was but forty-three years of age. By her first marriage she was the mother of two children, namely: Fletcher W. Griffin, the special subject of this sketch; and Thomas W. Griffin. By her second marriage she had one child, Jesse Lee Chembliss.

As a boy and youth, Fletcher W. Griffin attended the rural schools of his district, and assisted in the various labors incidental to life on a farm, remaining with his mother until attaining hs majority. He then began his career as an independent agriculturist, renting land on shares until he accumulated a sufficient sum to warrant him in buying. Mr. Griffin's first purchase of land consisted of a one hundred and forty acre tract ten miles east of Americus. Going to Plains, Sumter county, in 1887, he there carried on a successful business as a merchant until 1903, when he located in Americus, where he has since been profitably engaged in the cotton business. Mr. Griffin has always been extensively interested in agriculture, and having an abiding faith in the future of Sumter county, has invested largely in land, being now the owner of upwards of one thousand acres.

Mr. Griffin married, in 1885, Nancy Lelia Merritt, who was born in Marion county, Georgia, a daughter of Wade H. Merritt. Into their home four children have made their advent, namely: Leon C., Mazie M., Inman W., and Fletcher. Leon C. married Mamie Brooks, and they have one child, Edith. Mazie M., wife of James Walker, has two children, Griffin and William J. Mr. Griffin is a director of the Commercial City Bank. Religiously both Mr. and Mrs. Griffin are members of the Methodist Episcopal church South.

WILEY M. LEWIS. Industriously engaged in the prosecution of one of the most useful callings to which a man can devote his time and energies, Wiley M. Lewis holds a noteworthy position among the more active and progressive agriculturists of Brooks county. He was born June 18, 1847, in that part of Lowndes county now included within the boundaries of Brooks county, of pioneer ancestry.

His father, Irvin James Lewis, was born in Bulloch county, Georgia, and, when a small child, lost both of his parents. He subsequently made his home for many years with his uncle, Abner Groover, one of the very first settlers of what is now Brooks county. As a youth he became familiar with the various branches of agriculture, and on attaining manhood bought a tract of land lying seven miles northwest of Quitman, and was there engaged in general farming until his death, which was the result of a snake bite, his death occurring while he was yet in the prime of a vigorous manhood.

The maiden name of the wife of Irvin James Lewis was Susan Thigpin. She was born in Wilkes county, Georgia, where her father, Rev. Meles Thigpin, first settled on coming from one of the Carolinas to Georgia. He was a preacher in the primitive Baptist church, and an active worker in the Master's vineyard. From Wilkes county Rev. Mr. Thigpin removed to what is now Brooks county in pioneer days, the tedious journey through the woods being made with ox teams. All of south Georgia was then a howling wilderness, through which bear, deer, panthers, and wild game of many kinds roamed at will, while the Indians far outnumbered the whites, who were forced to build log forts in which the women and children would take refuge whenever the savages started out on the war path. Securing four hundred and ninety acres of land ten miles northwest of the present site of Quitman, Mr. Thigpin there spent his remaining years, as did his wife, whose maiden name was Sarah Whaley. Mrs. Susan (Thigpin) Lewis survived her husband many years. She was his helpmeet in every sense of the term, performing her full share of the pioneer labor, carding, spinning and weaving all of the homespun in which she clothed her family, in the early days of her marriage, doing all of her cooking by the open fireplace. She was the mother of six children, as follows: Mary, Sarah Blanche, Caroline, Janie, Valeria and Wiley M.

But two years old when his father died, Wiley M. Lewis was by his mother reared to habits of industry, honesty and thrift, and with her remained for several years after attaining his majority. He was afterwards engaged in tilling the soil on and near the old homestead until 1898. In that year Mr. Lewis formed a partnership with his nephew, I. E. Bozeman, and having purchased eleven hundred acres of timbered land on the Tallokas road, seven miles from Quitman, he erected a sawmill, and was there extensively engaged in the manufacture of lumber until the timber supply was exhausted. He and his partner have since put large tracts of the land which they cleared under cultivation, and he is there now engaged in general farming, in his operations being exceedingly prosperous.

Mr. Lewis married, in 1885, Ophelia Folsom, who was born in Jefferson county, Florida, where her parents, Isaac and Pamelia (Woods) Folsom, were pioneers. Eleven children have blessed the union of Mr. and Mrs. Lewis, namely: Wiley, James, Susie May, Pamelia Gertrude, Blanche S., Irvin Lee, Rosebud Folsom, Ernest W., Carlos, Clara Belle, and Wallace. Fraternally Mr. Lewis is a member of Shalto lodge, No. 237, Free and Accepted Masons, with which he united at the age of twenty-one years. He is also a member of the Farmer's Alliance, and of the Farmer's Union, No. 1406.

MAJOR WILLIAM BERRY STEPHENS. A record of well won success has been made by Major William Berry Stephens, a stalwart member of the Chatham county bar, who has proved his remarkable fitness for the profession he adorns in the heat of constant litigation. Among his many claims to distinction is his prominence in Georgian military affairs, for he holds the office of major of the Savannah Volunteer Guards and is a veteran of the Spanish-American war, in which he served as sergeant of Company B, of the Second Georgia Infantry, United States Volunteers. Major Stephens is the scion of one of the oldest and most distinguished American families, with the members of which through many generations patriotism has stood for far more than a mere rhetorical expression.

Major Stephens shares his natal day with the Father of the Country, his birth having occurred near Morven, Brooks county, Georgia, February 22, 1870. He is a son of John Hugh and Sarah C. (Hendry) Stephens, the former born at Society Hill, Darlington county, South Carolina, September 19, 1842, and the latter at Morven, Brooks county, August 19, 1846. It is a matter of well-confirmed tradition that Major Stephens' maternal great-great-grandfather, Robert Hendry, who came from Virginia to Georgia and lies buried at Taylor's Creek, Liberty county, served under "Lighthorse Harry" Lee in the Revolutionary war. The paternal grandfather of Major Stephens served with the South Carolina troops in Florida during the Seminole Indian war of 1835-42 and two maternal grand-uncles, William Hendry and Normal Campbell, are known to have served against the Indians in Georgia, participating in the battle of Brushy Creek. Major Stephens' maternal grandfather, Neal Hendry, was one whose conscientious conviction of the supreme right of the states to sever their union with the national government led him to give his influence and service to the Confederacy, at the time of the Civil war. He was major in command of a detachment in middle Florida, guarding salt works along the coast and supplying cattle to the southern armies. The subject's father, as a youth of twenty, entered the service of the South, enlisting on August 1, 1861, at Madison, Florida, as a private in Company C, Fourth Florida Volunteer Infantry and he served in turn in the brigades commanded by Preston, Palmer, Anderson, Finley, Stovall and Smith. He was in the thick of events; was wounded at the battle of Murfreesboro, Tennessee, and later participated in the battles of Jackson, Chickamauga and Missionary Ridge, as well as at Chapel Hill, North Carolina, April 9, 1865, thus serving until the close of the war. This highly respected gentleman now resides in Jacksonville, Florida, and finds pleasure in renewing associations with the comrades of other days as a member of Robert E. Lee Camp, No. 58, United Confederate Veterans. The Stephens family is a race of soldiers and three of the sons of the foregoing upheld its military prestige at the time of the war with Spain. John Hugh, Jr., and Robert D. were members of the First Florida Infantry, United States Volunteers, and the former lost his life by disease while in the service.

Major Stephens received his early education in the public schools of Thomas and Mitchell counties, Georgia, and his higher academic studies were prosecuted under the direction of private tutors. In early youth he became imbued with the desire to enter the law and in 1889 he became a clerical assistant in the law office of Chisholm & Erwin, of Savannah, under whose able preceptorship he prosecuted his legal studies. In 1896 he was admitted to the bar and his excellent preliminary training having given him a grasp upon essentials which he utilized to the last degree, he at once entered upon a career, which has given him both success and high renown. From 1898 to January 1, 1900, he was division counsel for the Plant system of railways and then, upon the dissolution of the firm of Erwin, DuBignon, Chisholm & Clay, he resigned the aforementioned office and entered into a professional partnership with Hon. Fleming G. DuBignon, under the firm name of DuBignon & Stephens, this association continuing until the latter part of the year 1902, when it was dissolved upon the removal of Mr. DuBignon to the city of Atlanta. Since that time Major Stephens has conducted an individual professional business in Savannah.

Major Stephens' connection with affairs military dates from May, 1890, when he became a private in Company B, Savannah Volunteer Guards, and was later promoted to corporal and sergeant. On May 2, 1898, he was enrolled as a private in Company B, Second Georgia Infantry, United States Volunteers, for service in the war with Spain. He was appointed sergeant as soon as mustered and proceeded with his command to the reserve camp at Tampa, Florida, where he remained in service until the close of the war. He was honorably discharged at Huntsville, Alabama, August 29, 1898, in compliance with his own request. Upon his return to Savannah he immediately re-enlisted, as a private in Company B, Savannah Volunteer Guards, serving as such until he was commissioned captain of his company, February 1, 1900. In March, 1904, he resigned the captaincy and re-enlisted as a private, serving as such until the following November, when he was commissioned major of battalion of the Savannah Volunteer Guards, the battalion having been converted into heavy artillery by act of the general assembly, December 18, 1900. He still holds the office of major of this battalion and is also a member of Francis S. Bartow Camp, No. 95, United Sons of Confederate Veterans in Savannah.

Major Stephens has always been loyal to the principles of the Democratic party. In 1906, he was urged by a strong representation of Savannah's best citizenship to become a candidate for the state senate in opposition to an already nominated candidate who, although personally a man of the highest character, represented a political element in the city that a great many people deemed dangerous and inimical to Savannah's best interests. Major Stephens, responding to this call in a spirit of patriotism, entered the race just seven days prior to the election, and after a spirited and exciting contest, was elected by a majority of about six hundred, as a member of the state senate, representing the first senatorial district, embracing the counties of Chatham, Bryan and Effingham. Major Stephens' most notable achievement in the senate was his success in bringing the senate and the lower house together in the passage of the law which terminated the convict lease system in Georgia, thus taking the hire of convicts out of the hands of corporations and putting them to work on the public roads. Public opinion upholds this as one of the most beneficent enactments of legislation that has taken place in Georgia in many years. Major Stephens accomplished this by skillful parliamentary tactics and a final speech in the senate, in the face of the strongest and most bitter opposition.

The following tribute to Major Stephens is contributed by Judge Walter G. Charlton, of Savannah, judge of the supreme court, and one of the ablest jurists in the state:

"In the pursuit of his profession, Major Stephens has not only attained to success, but his career has also been marked by a thorough devotion to the highest ideals of his calling. This has been the dominant purpose of his life, to which his active participation in public affairs has been the natural incident. Of a singularly open and candid nature, rapid in conclusions and entirely bold in expression, he has been an effective soldier because he has been a consistent and fearless lawyer."

Major Stephens was happily married on September 6, 1899, his chosen lady being Miss Clifford B. Dasher, daughter of Frank W. and Grace B. (Lovell) Dasher, of Savannah. Into their household, one of the favorite social gathering-places in the city, has been born one son, William Hugh, the date of whose birth was December 18, 1900.

Major Stephens is identified with the following organizations: Ancient Landmark Lodge, No. 231, Free and Accepted Masons; Georgia Chapter, No. 3, Royal Arch Masons; Georgia Council, No. 2, Royal and Select Masters; Palestine Commandery, No. 7, Knights Templar; Alee Temple, Ancient Arabic Order Nobles of the Mystic Shrine; Alpha Lodge, No. 1, Ancient Accepted Scottish Rite; the Savannah Bar Association; the Guards' Club; the Oglethorpe Club; the Savannah Yacht Club, and the Forest City Gun Club. He and his wife are members of the Methodist Episcopal church, South, and are active in church and philanthropic work.

CHARLES WOOD GUNNELL. A man of marked business capacity, intelligence and enterprise, the late Charles Wood Gunnell, of Bronwood, did much towards advancing the agricultural prosperity of Terrell county, through his wise experiments clearly demonstrating the advantage and profit to be derived from growing pecans for commercial purposes. A native of Terrell county, he was born on a farm near Bronwood, May 28, 1862, and his death, which occurred in Bronwood, November 13, 1908, was mourned as a loss not only to his immediate family and friends, but to the entire community.

William Henry Gunnell, his father, was engaged in agricultural pursuits in Terrell county when the war between the states broke out. Entering the Confederate army, he went with his command to Virginia, and was killed in the engagement at Maryland Heights. His wife, whose maiden name was Mary Powell, survived him a few years, passing away in 1875.

Industrious and studious, Charles Wood Gunnell acquired a practical education when young, and until his marriage was employed as a bookkeeper for Sheffield & Bell, at Albany, Georgia. Returning then to Terrell county, he located at Bronwood, and there maintained his residence during the remainder of his life. Mr. Gunnell was for many years engaged in the warehouse business in Bronwood, and while thus employed purchased land in and near his home, and embarked in agricultural and horticultural pursuits. In 1891 he planted pecan nuts, and the trees, which he patiently watched and nurtured, four hundred in number, on twelve acres of land, constitute one of the best and most highly productive pecan orchards in the entire Union. An expert from the United States Department of Agriculture inspected this large orchard, and five pounds of nuts from each of two trees were taken to Washington for exhibition. In competition with the best nuts elsewhere grown, the nuts from each of those two trees were awarded a silver loving cup. Those same two trees are now officially named, one being the "Gunnell," and the other being named "Bronwood. " Mr. Gunnell was one of the very first to experiment with the culture of pecan nuts in this section of the country, and he proved most satisfactorily that nuts of that variety are a profitable crop to raise. In 1912 the Gunnell orchard yielded three thousand, five hundred pounds of nuts, a large and valuable crop.

Mr. Gunnell married, October 18, 1888, Rushie Geise, who was born in Dawson, Georgia, a daughter of Reuben and Jerusha (Wood) Geise, of whom a brief sketch may be found on another page of this volume. Three children were born of the union of Mr. and Mrs. Gunnell, namely: Charles Will, who was graduated from Mercer College, and is now studying law in the University of Georgia, at Athens; Martha R., who possesses great artistic talent, is a student at Andrews College, in Cuthbert; and Ralph Leighton. Mrs. Gunnell is a member of the Methodist Episcopal church, to which Mr. Gunnell also belonged; she is likewise a member of Mary Brantley Chapter, United Daughters of the Confederacy; of Stone Castle Chapter, Daughters of the American Revolution; and of the Order of the Eastern Star.

REUBEN GEISE. A former highly respected resident of Dawson, the late Reuben Geise was for many years successfully engaged in the lumber business, and contributed his full share in advancing the industrial interests of this part of Terrell county. A son of George Adam Geise, Jr., he was born, September 8, 1821, in Newmanstown, Pennsylvania, of substantial German ancestry.

His paternal grandfather, George Adam Geise, Sr., was born, June 4, 1725, in Hanover, Germany, and was there bred and educated. At the age of twenty-nine years he came to America in the good ship "Peggy," and located in Bern township, Pennsylvania. He there bought land, and was engaged in farming until his death, June 29, 1784. He proved himself loyal to his adopted country, bravely assisting the colonists in their struggle for independence. He married Barbara Haag, who was born in Berks county, Pennsylvania, July 31, 1738, and there died in August, 1814, having survived him thirty years.

George Adam Geise, Jr., was born in Bernville, Berks county, Pennsylvania, June 17, 1772. He married April 15, 1797, Susanna Bright, who was born in Bern township, Berks county, a daughter of John and Anna Maria (Leis) Brecht, as the name was then spelled, though it was later changed to Bright, and a granddaughter of David Brecht. Her great-grandfather, Stephen Brecht, emigrated from Germany to America in colonial times, coming to this country a widower with three small children. Settling in Lancaster county, Pennsylvania, he bought a tract from three Pennbrothers, John, Thomas and Richard, the land having been a part of their original grant. David Brecht, whose birth occurred in the Fatherland, September 8, 1719, was one of the three children that came with his father to this country. He served in the Revolutionary army, after which he resumed farming at his old home in Berks county, residing there until his death, September 22, 1783. John Brecht, or Bright, as he spelled his name, and his wife were both life-long residents of Berks county, his death occurring February 9, 1834, and hers on May 24, 1842.

George Adam Geise, Jr., and wife were also life-long residents of their native county. He died March 29, 1858, while her death occurred October 9, 1856. Both were buried in the Lutheran cemetery, at Newmanstown, Pennsylvania. They were the parents of fourteen children, and when her death occurred they had sixty-three grandchildren, and twenty-nine great-grandchildren.

While a boy in his teens, Reuben Geise joined his brother George, in Tuscumbia, Alabama. Learning the trade of a miller, he subsequently built a flour mill at Big Spring, Tuscumbia, Franklin county, and operated it as a merchant mill. Being thus employed during the war between the states, he was exempted from military duty, but during the last year of the conflict he entered the Confederate service, and was assigned to duty in the transportation of leather. He went with the army from Dixon Station, Alabama, to Rome, Georgia, from there refugeeing to Dawson, Georgia. At the close of the war, Mr. Geise established a saw mill in Dawson, and embarked in the lumber business, subsequently furnishing the Central Georgia Railroad Company with lumber. Meeting with well merited success, he continued in the lumber business until his death, October 25, 1880.

Reuben Geise married Jerusha Halsey Wood, who was born in Huntsville, Alabama, November 16, 1831, a daughter of Lewis Wood. Her paternal grandfather, Joseph Wood, was born in Newark, New Jersey, October 14, 1760, of English lineage. He was well educated, and taught school in different places in his native state, and also served as a soldier in the Revolutionary war. He married April 2, 1780, Joanna Tuttle, whose birth occurred June 12, 1762. He was a personal friend of George Washington, with whom he served as a soldier. Lewis Wood was born in Newark, New Jersey, April 10, 1794, and as a young man migrated to Richmond, Virginia, from there going to Huntsville, Alabama, where he resided until his death, in 1836. Lewis Wood married, in Huntsville, Alabama, February 27, 1822, Mary Ann Woods, who, though of the same name, was not a relative. Her father, Leighton Wood, third, was a native of Richmond, Virginia, a son of Leighton Wood, second, who was born in England, in the city of Bristol, where his father, Leighton Wood, first, was, as far as known, a life-long resident. Leighton Wood, second, immigrated to America, and settled in Virginia, where he fought with the colonists in their struggle for independence. Elected auditor of Hanover county, Virginia, in 1780, he served from May until November, of that year, when the Virginia assembly elected him solicitor general, an office which he filled most efficiently until 1791. In 1801 he returned to England, and there died in 1805. He married a daughter of Rev. Benjamin Franklin Blagrove, an Episcopalian rector, and chaplain of the Virginia assembly in 1781.

Leighton Wood, third, served in the War of 1812. He married Mary Younghusband, whose father, William Younghusband, a resident of Richmond, Virginia, served as a soldier in the Revolutionary war, while her grandfather, Isaac Younghusband, was captain of a company of soldiers in the same war. After his marriage, Leighton Wood, third, went with his wife to Kentucky, where his death occurred. His widow subsequently moved to Huntsville, Alabama, where she spent her remaining days.

Mrs. Reuben Geise passed to the higher life September 3, 1885. To her and her husband five children were born and reared, namely: Owen Nelson, Mary Wood, Susie Bright, James Deshler, and Rushie Lee. Mary Wood is the wife of D. J. Ray, of Atlanta, Georgia. Susie Bright married Walter S. Dozier, of whom a brief sketch may be found elsewhere in this biographical work. Rushie Lee is the widow of Charles Wood Gunnell, of whom a brief sketch also appears in this volume. Mrs. Walter S. Dozier is a genealogist, and to her the Geise and Dozier families are greatly indebted for their family histories, she having devoted much time in searching records, and in corresponding with members of the different branches of both families.

BENJAMIN F. EVANS. A merchant at Fowlstown, formerly a substantial farmer, and a veteran of the Civil war, Mr. Evans has spent practically all his life in Decatur county, and is a resident well known to all the citizenship of this community.

Benjamin F. Evans was born in Decatur county, February 24, 1843. His father was William Evans, born in North Carolina, and came to Georgia accompanied by his wife and five children. The trip to this state was made with team and wagon, and William Evans located at Attapulgus Creek, buying timbered land there. All the country in this section was sparsely populated, and he had his share of pioneer labors and experiences. He participated in the battle of Roanoke, where the Indians made their last stand in contending for this country. He improved a part of his land, then sold and bought other land on the same creek, and remained a resident in that vicinity until his death at the age of eighty-five. The maiden name of his wife was Martha Pope of North Carolina. She died at the age of seventy-five. The nine children reared by them were Nathan, John, Nancy, William, Feth, Mary A., Martha, Benjamin F., and Margaret E.

Benjamin F. Evans attended the neighborhood schools and assisted on the farm while growing to manhood in this county. In April, 1862, when nineteen years of age he entered the Confederate service as a member of Company D in the Seventeenth Georgia Infantry. He was with the command in Virginia, and his record of battles includes many of the most important of the war, among them being the seven days' fight around the Richmond, the second Manassas, Sharpsburg, Fredericksburg, Gettysburg, Seven Pines, and others. At Chickamauga he was severely wounded and spent some time in a hospital at Macon. When able for duty he was placed on detached work in the enrolling service at home and so continued until the close of the war. After the war he rented a piece of land and engaged actively in farming until 1884. He then came to Fowlstown and opened a stock of goods and has been engaged in merchandising to the present time.

In 1867, Mr. Evans married Harriet Eliza Callahan, who was born in Gadsen county, Florida, a daughter of William and Eliza Cooper Callahan. She was left an orphan at the age of two years, and was reared in the home of her maternal grandparents, Samuel and Sarah Cooper. Mr. and Mrs. Evans have five children now living, whose names are Annie, Callie, Oliver, Ada and Lilla. Annie married W. M. Wells, and her six children are named Malory, Deloy, Thelma, Caroline, Ethal and Tula. Callie married F. C. Cooper and her two children are Agnes and Grace. Lilla is the wife of M. F. Laing, and has two children named May Lilla and Carleton.

ELIJAH A. J. RICH. The following sketch contains the important facts in the life and family record of a Georgian, whose name in Decatur county stands for all that is honest and of good report for successful thrift and business integrity, and for a position in the community which all must respect. The Rich family were among the pioneers of southwest Georgia, and made homes out of the wilderness, and later descendants fought for their homes and the Southland in the great war between the states. Mr. Rich himself spent his early life in the pioneer epoch of this region, and none would deny that the comforts and blessings of good children that now surround himself and wife were merited rewards to worthy and well spent lives.

Elijah A. J. Rich was born in Randolph county, Georgia, November 16, 1840, a son of Thomas J. Rich, who was born in North Carolina, and a grandson of Martin Rich, who was also born in North Carolina, and came from there to Georgia, as an early settler in the southern part of the latter state. The grandfather spent the remaining years of his life in Decatur county. The maiden name of his wife, the grandmother, was Sarah Overstreet, who survived her husband many years.

Thomas J. Rich, the father, was a youth when he came to Georgia, and for a time after his marriage he lived in Randolph county, and then in 1841 moved to Decatur county, buying a tract of timbered land ten miles northwest of Bainbridge on the Bainbridge & Blakely road. In the midst of the woods he built a log house, and after providing pioneer comforts for his family began making a farm out of the wilderness. In 1858 he sold out and bought a place in Miller county, but after a year's residence there, sold and returned to Decatur county, where he bought land five and a half miles northwest of Bainbridge. He was past military age at the time of the Civil war, but in 1864 enlisted in the Georgia Reserves, and went with that command to the defense of Atlanta. He was severely wounded in the battle of Grizzleville Station, and was taken to Macon, where he died a few weeks later at the age of fifty-five. His remains were brought back to Miller county and interred in the Fann cemetery. Thomas J. Rich married Lettie Fann, who was born in North Carolina, a daughter of Elijah Fann, of the same state. The Fann and Rich family came to Georgia at the same time, in company with other immigrating families. They made the removal overland, with teams and wagons and camped along the roadside every night. In their wagons they brought their household goods. This colony settled in the southern part of Decatur county, buying land six miles south of Colquit on Spring creek, where he resided until his death. After coming to Georgia, he had participated as a volunteer in the Indian wars. The mother of Mr. Elijah A. Rich died when forty years of age, and left ten children, namely: Martha J., Sarah, Elijah A. J., Susan L., Augustus M., Washington, John T., Charles F., Riley B., and Caroline. Of these Elijah A. J., Augustus M., Washington and John T., served all through the Civil war as soldiers, Charles going out as a boy in the last year of the struggle.

Elijah A. J. Rich was but one year old when his parents settled in Decatur county. At that time and for some years later, all southwest Georgia was sparsely settled, and all kinds of game abounded through this section. There were no railroads then nor for many years to come, and Bainbridge was the market for the settlers over a wide radius of country. Though the Rich family was probably as prosperous as any of their neighbors, they had all the privations and inconveniences of pioneer existence. The mother was a most diligent housekeeper and either by her own hands or with the aid of her house slave, spun and wove all the cloth and dressed all her children in homespun garments. As a boy, Elijah A. J. attended the pioneer schools, kept up in the neighborhood by subscriptions of the residents who were able to give their children such advantages. He had at an early age taken an active part in the farm, and soon after the breaking out of the Civil war he enlisted in Company A of the Fifty-ninth Georgia Infantry, with which he went into Virginia, and joined Lee's army. His regiment was assigned to General Longstreet's corps, and participated in many of the important battles of the Virginia campaign, including that at Seven Pines, Gettysburg, Fredericksburg, and the numerous struggles around Richmond and Petersburg. For his excellent service to the South he was elected first lieutenant in Company A. A short time before the surrender of General Lee, he was wounded, and was granted a furlough, and before its expiration, peace was declared, so that he never rejoined his command. He soon bought a piece of land about five miles from Bainbridge, and went in debt in order to secure this start in life. There he built a small log house, and it was to that rude shelter that he took his young bride on their marriage. All the furniture of the establishment was home-made, and Mr. Rich went to the mill and bought rough lumber, with which he made with his own hands all the furniture for his home, doing this of mornings before work, and at noon hour. In April, 1867, Mr. Elijah A. J. Rich, married Mrs. Hattie Pierce. She was born in Baker county, and at an early age was left an orphan, and was reared by her aunt, Harriet Bryant. Mrs. Rich, as a girl, received a very practical training and learned to card, spin and weave. She spun and wove and cut the cloth and made clothes for all her family, and sewed it all by hand. She also wove the sacks in which Mr. Rich was accustomed to carry corn to the local mill, and in which he brought the meal which furnished the great staple food of corn bread.

Mr. Elijah A. J. Rich was elected to the Georgia legislature in 1886 on the Democratic ticket from Decatur county, defeating his opponent with an overwhelming majority.

One among the many things Mr. Rich did for the good of his state and county, was to support the bill, leasing the Georgia railroad running from Atlanta to Chattanooga, Tennessee. He served two years with credit to himself and state, and was offered a second nomination but refused. Thrift indoors and without, brought its reward, and in a few years Mr. and Mrs. Rich were on the high road to prosperity. After paying for the first tract of land, he secured other tracts, and improved these and sold them out for a profit.

In 1875 Mr. and Mrs. Rich founded a school, known at this date, 1913, as the Bethel high school. This school is a living monument to Mr. and Mrs. Rich. When Mr. and Mrs. Rich first started up this school it was for the benefits of their own children, but later others joined them. This big-hearted man and woman not only desired a good education for their own children but that other children not so fortunate should have the same advantage. Mr. and Mrs. Rich maintained this school with their own funds, letting the poorer children go without any cost to their parents. One very poor boy, William H. Griffin, came to Mr. Rich and asked that he be admitted to this school, saying that he was a poor one-armed boy and wished to get an education so he would be able to make his own living. Mr. Rich seeing that the boy was very desirous of learning, allowed him to attend school. This man is now a professor of one of our southern colleges.

In 1895 Mr. Rich bought the land where he now resides in lot 391, in Bethel district. There he has built a most comfortable frame house, and various farm buildings for the shelter of his stock. Mrs. Rich is a very careful and tasteful housekeeper and their home is furnished nicely, and is a place showing the refinement and thrift and good cheer of the entire family. Mr. and Mrs. Rich have eight children, whose names are: Euzema, Minnie, Emory G., Arthur J., Dola, Hunnewell, Perry D., and Thomas E.

Euzema married Menla Powell, and their nine children are named, Leroy, Jewell, Lloyd, Ross, Jennings, Emory G., Gladys, Lois, and James Clay.

Minnie, now deceased, married Willie Powell, and has six children, named Lamar, Ellis, Dewey, Mable, Adonis and Willie G.

Emory G., married Cornelia Powell, both of whom are now deceased, leaving three children, named Kate, Lucile, and Clyde. Mr. and Mrs. Rich, in addition to raising their own large family, have raised these three grandchildren, taken when the youngest was four years old.

Kate married W. F. Wynn, and they have one child named Irene. Lucille has completed school and is now teaching. Clyde, the youngest, is now in college. Mr. and Mrs. Rich have been able to give these children more advantages than their own children received.

Arthur J. married Florence Powell, and their one son is named Charles.

Dola, married William J. Bush, and their two children are Myrtle and Hoke.

Hunnewell, married J. T. Powell, and their four children are Curtis, Jesse T., Louise, and Minnie.

Perry D., married for his first wife Julia Bush, and their four children are, Hattie Sue, Ruth, Forest, and Julia. By his second marriage to Huron Powell, he has one child, Mazie.

Thomas E., married Rosa Arline, and their three children are, Thomas E., Pauline, Alee Frank.

Mr. and Mrs. Rich are both members of the Missionary Baptist church, as are all their children. Mr. Rich and his sons are affiliated with the Masonic fraternity, he and three sons being Knight Templars.

That while we have done these things, we feel like it's not of ourselves but of the Holy Spirit has guided and directed us through this life.

GEORGE EMORY THORNTON. The thirty years' service of Mr. Thornton as clerk of Webster county is a record rarely equalled in the annals of county officials of Georgia, and his long continuance in one of the most important local positions is due to his faithful and intelligent service in behalf of the people and the relations of his office to the public welfare. Mr. Thornton is by profession a lawyer and practiced for ten years in Webster county before he became clerk. He represents one of the old families of this section of the state.

George Emory Thornton was born in Carroll county, Georgia, January 4, 1849. His parents were John J. and Emeline (Darnell) Thornton. The father was born either in Putnam or Monroe county, Georgia, in 1818. The founder of the family in this section of the state was the grandfather, William Thornton, who was born in Virginia. The father of William Thornton, and the great-grandfather of the Webster county clerk, was a soldier in the Revolutionary war, and a lifelong resident of Virginia. Grandfather William Thornton emigrated from Virginia into Georgia, as one of the pioneers of the central portion of this state. He was a very energetic business man, and when all the country was new he secured large tracts of government lands in different counties. One of his plantations bordered upon the Ocmulgee river in Monroe county. He was survived for many years by his widow, whose maiden name was Tempy Briggs, and who married a second time and died when one hundred and seven years old. She was the mother of six children whose names were Rakdum, Harrison, Robert F., Isham, Lucy and Millie.

Isham J. Thornton, the father, received his education in the country schools. He had a natural skill as a mechanic, and following the inclinations of this ability he became a machinist and a very skilled workman. In 1852 he removed to Roanoke, in Alabama, where he followed his trade and remained a resident until his death in 1896. His wife, Emeline Darnell Thornton, was born in Putnam county, Georgia, daughter of J. A. and Polly (Autry) Darnell, both of whom had been born in North Carolina, and had come to Georgia as early settlers of Putnam county, subsequently moving into Alabama and settling at Roanoke, where Mr. Darnell died. His widow subsequently moved to Lafayette in the same state, where she died at the remarkable age of one hundred and four years. Mrs. Thornton, the mother, died in 1907. The eight children in her family were Robert F., Louisa, Annie, Emma, George' Emory, Laura, Eugene and Lucile May.

George Emory Thornton spent his early life at Roanoke, Alabama, where he obtained his education. When he was sixteen years old, he left school and home, and has ever since been self-supporting and is a self-made man in the best sense of the term. He became a clerk at Montgomery, and also at Union Springs, but at the end of three years returned to Roanoke and soon turned his attention to the study of law. He was admitted to the bar in 1872 at the age of twenty-three years, and soon afterwards located at Preston, where he opened an office and had a large share of the practice during that decade in the local courts. Then in 1883 he was elected to the office of clerk of Webster county, and has been retained in office by successive elections almost too numerous to mention.

At Americus, Georgia, in 1871, Mr. Thornton married Ludie E. Birdsong, who was born in Talbot county, Georgia, a daughter of Charles and M. E. (Daniel) Birdsong. The children of Mr. Thornton and wife are named as follows: Mackie E., Jennie, Nannie, Sallie, Minnie, Claude and David B. Mackie E. married D. H. Smith, and they have six children of their own. Jennie is the wife of D. E. Hutchins, and she died leaving one son, George E., who lives with his grandparents. Nannie married S. T. Wilson, who died leaving three children, the youngest named Mamie, being but an infant at the time of her mother's death, and now being reared in the home of her grandparents Thornton. Minnie is the wife of R. L. Nickerson. David B. is now a resident of New York City, where he is office manager for the Giess Manufacturing Company. Mr. and Mrs. Thornton are members of the Methodist church and he is affiliated with Preston Lodge No. 188, A. F. & A. M., and with the Tri-County Chapter of the Royal Arch Masonry at Richland.

BENJAMIN R. HARRISON. A career of unusual accomplishment and success has been that of Benjamin R. Harrison of Grady county. When he was ready to take up the independent responsibilities of life, he had no capital and found his opportunities by working land on the crop-sharing plan. By thrift and industry he passed several successful seasons, and with the accumulations of his diligence he was able to make his first purchase of land. He bought a tract situated within the limits of his present splendid farm, and after that beginning his prosperity has been steady and undiminished until he ranks as one of the foremost farmers of Grady county.

Born in a log cabin about twelve miles south of Thomasville, Georgia on the twenty-eighth of October, 1849, Mr. Harrison belongs to a family which has been identified with Georgia for three generations. His father was Henry Jackson Harrison, born in Pulaski county, and the grandfather was Benjamin Harrison, who came from Pulaski county to Decatur county, becoming one of the early settlers in the latter vicinity. His settlement was at a time when all of south Georgia was a wilderness, and deer. wolves and wild turkeys were plentiful in the woods which covered nearly all the country. Another source of meat supply was fish. and in those days the Georgia streams were not "fished out" as they are now. As there was hardly a fence over the entire region, this portion of the state made an excellent range for cattle. The grandfather bought a tract of timbered land, and erected a log cabin about twelve miles southwest of the present site of Cairo. On that place he remained until his death.

Henry Jackson Harrison was a child when brought to Decatur

county, and was reared on a farm, and after reaching manhood bought a piece of woods land, south from the present site of Cairo. He lived there a few years and then moved into Thomas county, where he resided until his death in 1889 in his seventy-first year. He married Patsy Jones, who was born in Decatur county, a daughter of Robert Jones. Robert Jones came from Pulaski county at the same time with the Harrison family, and bought land five miles west of the present site of Cairo. The farm which he cleared out of the wilderness in that location is now owned by one of his grandsons, and it was his home until his death. Robert Jones married, as his second wife, Patsy Hawthorne, who was the grandmother of Benjamin R. Harrison. She survived her husband, and both are now buried in the family burial plot on the old farm. The ten children in the elder Harrison's family were Elizabeth, Martha Jane, William S., Benjamin R., Nancy, Temperance, Scely, John, Mary and James.

Many of the pioneer conditions still prevailed in this section of Georgia, during the youth of Benjamin R. Harrison. There were no railroads in this part of the state and Bainridge and Tallahassee were the principal markets and depots for supplies. As a boy he has hunted nearly all kinds of wild game, and knew the hardships and privations of early life in south Georgia. As already mentioned, he began life without capital.

His purchase of land was fifty acres, covered with woods and without anything that might be called a permanent improvement upon it. When he had cleared out a space in the midst of the timber and had built a log cabin, he brought his young bride to the humble home and there they started housekeeping and home making. During the succeeding years he cleared off the timber from the rest of the land, and with the aid of his thrifty wife he enjoyed a progressive prosperity from the start. As means increased he bought other land until Mr. Harrison is now known as the owner of more than eight hundred acres of fine farming land in Grady county, and one of the most suhtantial land owners and citizens in this vicinity. In recent years he has erected a comfortable frame residence, and on the outskirts of the family home has situated barns and sheds for the shelter of stock and machinery, and all the equipment and improvements are in keeping with modern standards of Georgia agriculture.

Mr. Harrison married Miss Elizabeth Clay. She was born in Terrell county, Georgia, daughter of Augustus and Isabelle (Sligall) Clay. Her father, a native of north Georgia, and her mother, a native of Terrell county, were married in Terrell county, and from there moved into Thomas county, where both spent their remaining years. Mrs. Harrison died November, 1912. Mr. and Mrs. Harrison reared the following children: Melinda, Leona, William Robert, Benjamin F., Evvie, and Eula. Another child, Jack, died at the age of fifteen. Melinda married Seab Sutten and has four children named Mattie, Belle, John Benjamin, Seba A. and Edna J Leona married Charles Connolly and their three children are named Ruth, Mary and Roberta. Evvie is the wife of Levi Harper.

WILLIS J. DUKE. Now in his early forties, Mr. Duke of Decatur county is one of the largest land owners and crop producers of this part of Georgia. His career has encouragement for young men who start without resources except those contained in themselves. He was a renter for several years, prospered in every undertaking, and thriftily turned his surplus into more land until he found himself independent and with better provision for the future of himself and family than most men have at the close of a long lifetime.

It is an old family of Georgia that is represented by Mr. Duke. He was himself born in Decatur county, December 8, 1870. His father was Maston Hendricks Duke, who was born in Butts county, Georgia, September 4, 1845. The grandfather was Weekly W. Duke, and it is thought that he also was a native of Butts county, where he was reared and married. From there the grandfather moved into Randolph county, buying land about eight miles north of Cuthbert. He built up a large plantation and had numerous slaves to do the work of the fields and the household. That remained his home until his death when he was about fifty years of age. The maiden name of his wife was Penelope McClenden, who was born in Butts county, and died in Randolph county. They were the parents of several children and both were members of the Baptist church, and the grandfather was a Mason.

Maston Hendricks Duke, the father, was a small boy when his family moved into Randolph county, where he was reared and married. When eighteen years old he enlisted in the Twenty-eighth Georgia Battalion, first accompanying the command to Florida, and subsequently to North Carolina. He participated in several of the campaigns and battles of the closing years of the war, the last engagement being that at Bentonville. He also fought at Ocean Pond in Florida, and was the great struggle at Chickamauga. He was never wounded or captured, and went with his command until the final surrender. On returning home he found that his father was dead, and he then took charge of the home farm. In the fall of 1866, he bought a farm of seven hundred acres in lots 382, 384, 264, 383, and 182 in the Faceville district. There he carried on general farming and made his home until his death on October 23, 1909.

By marriage, Maston H. Duke became connected with another old and prominent family of Georgia. He was married to Miss Frances Elizabeth Mounger, who was born in Stewart county, Georgia, January 11, 1847. Her father was Edwin Mounger, who was born in Jefferson county, Georgia, in 1806. Her grandfather, Edwin Mounger, was years ago treasurer of the state of Georgia, was also trustee of University of Georgia for years, and married Frances Clark, daughter of Gen. Elijah Clark. He was also cousin of Thomas Jefferson and was offered a position in his cabinet but refused on account of relationship. Edwin Mounger was left an orphan when a boy, and was reared by his uncle, Governor Clark, and for a time was a student in the State University. He then took up the printers' trade, becoming an expert compositor, and set type on the first newspaper published at Marianna, Florida. He subsequently taught school at Perry in Houston county, Georgia. After his marriage he bought a farm in Stewart county, where he lived three years, then sold out and moved into Randolph county, where he bought a plantation five miles north of Cuthbert, cultivating its broad acres with the aid of his slaves and remained there until his death. The maiden name of the wife of Edwin Mounger was Elizabeth Jane Ball, whose relationship has been traced back to Gen. George Washington. She was born in Milledgeville, a daughter of William Ball, who was a Virginian and said to have been a Revolutionary soldier. Coming to Georgia, he bought a home in Milledgeville and a plantation near by, and remained there the rest of his days. William Ball married Elizabeth Grey. Their daughter, Elizabeth Jane, first married a Mr. Allen, and was the mother of five children by her first marriage and seven by the second. The Allen children were named William H., Julia, John R., Thomas and Marcus. The children of Edwin Mounger and his wife, Elizabeth Jane, were Sarah A., Edwin O., Frances E., Mary Jane, Annie E., Selma, and Clara O.

Maston H. Duke and wife reared nine children, named as follows: Momelus W., Edwin Mounger, Willis J., Oscar Clark, Elizabeth P., Julia Frances, Clara P., Maston H., and Annie Pearl. The parents were both members of the Methodist church.

As a boy Willis J. Duke received such education as the rural schools could furnish, and remained at home and worked for his father until he was twenty-four years old. He then began an independent career on rented land. His industry and good management brought him success from the start, and for several years he continued as a renter. In the meantime, however, he had bought a tract of land in the south part of the county, and also bought a tract in lot No. 370 in the Bethel district, seven miles northwest of Bainbridge, and in 1901 took up his residence on that farm. Mr. Duke is a Progressive farmer, and has a homestead which in its improvement is equalled by few others in district. He has built a good frame house as a residence, has erected barns for the shelter of stock and shed to protect all his farm machinery, and from time to time has bought other tracts of land so that he now owns upwards of one thousand acres. He engages in farming, raising a variety of crops and feeding a large number of hogs and cattle each year.

In 1894, Mr. Duke married Martha Elizabeth Sunday, who was born on the south line of Decatur, Georgia. Her father was Joseph Larue Sunday, who was born in the same vicinity, but across the state line in Gadsden county, Florida, where his father, George Sunday, had been one of the early settlers. About 1873, George Sunday moved to Montgomery county, Texas, which was his home until his death. The maiden name of his wife was Martha Johnson. Both parents lived to a good old age. Joseph L. Sunday, the father of Mrs. Duke, lived in Decatur county for a few years after marriage and then returned to Gadsden county, Florida, where he now resides. Joseph L. Sunday married Nancy Ann Johnson, who was born in Decatur county, daughter of Noah and Nancy (Lewis) Johnson. The eight children in the Sunday family were named as follows: Jesse W., Martha E., Nannie J., Bera and Burrus, twins, Joseph Jarius, Jeptha L., and Mary Lou. Both Mr. and Mrs. Sunday were members of the Methodist church. Mr. and Mrs. Duke are the parents of five children, whose names are Vasta Elizabeth, Bernard Lamar, Wesley Allen, Fannie Mae, Annie Ruby. Mr. and Mrs. Duke are both members of the Methodist church.

DR. THOMAS FRANKLIN BIVINS has been in active practice in Vienna, Dooly county, Georgia, for more than twenty years. This statement is almost enough to call to the vision of people just what sort of a man Doctor Bivins is, for when a man occupying his position of family counselor and friend to people for a period of twenty years, remains in the same place during this time, he must be of a noble character, and of a sincere heart, else his clientele would have found him out long ago. We all admire and exclaim over the wonderful feats of the surgeons in our great hospitals, and of those medical investigators who are continually announcing remarkable discoveries from their laboratories; do we ever think that the practitioner in the small town or city runs just as great risks and has practically as great a number of calls upon his nerve force as has the city surgeon? In the first place what work could be more taxing than a general practice, where the physician does not have to know everything about something, but what is much more impossible, something about everything. Again when he has a critical case the patient is not simply a human being whose life must be saved but as a rule some one whom he has known for years so he has the same strain on his nerves that he would have if he were operating upon one of his own family. It is this type of hero that Doctor Bivins is, though he, himself, very likely, would never think of himself as doing anything but his duty.

Doctor Thomas Franklin Bivins was born on the 13th of September, 1862, at Haynesville, in Houston county, Georgia. He was the son of Franklin Ward Bivins, whose birthplace was in Jones county, Georgia. Franklin Bivins had the opportunity of giving his service to the cause he thought was right, and of becoming one of that splendid body of men, the veterans of the army of the Confederacy. He was a private soldier in a company of infantry, and after the war was over he returned to his plantation and set to work to build up again his shattered fortune. His wife was Betzy Blackshear Walker, a daughter of a Mr. Walker, a planter of Houston county, Georgia. The father of Franklin Ward Bivins was Stephen Bivins, who was a native of Maryland. He came with his family to Jones county, Georgia, when only a small lad, so the family has been closely identified with the state for a long time. Dr. Bivins has one brother, Stephen Fillmore Bivins, who is a planter in Houston county, Georgia. His sisters number four: Mrs. Ella Tiguin, who is the wife of Samuel Tiguin, of El Paso, Texas; Betzy Bivins, who lives in Macon, Georgia; Mrs. Georgia Baskin, who is the wife of J. D. Baskin, of Moultrie, Georgia, a farmer; Mary W., who married C. E. Mathis of Macon, Georgia, her husband being a locomotive engineer.

Dr. Thomas Franklin Bivins grew up on his father's farm, helping with the work of the place and attending the near-by school. He early determined upon his future profession, for even as a boy he saw the need of a good doctor in all the country communities through the South. There was a dearth of physicians, just as there was a dearth of everything else. When he was about sixteen he began to attend the country high school, and from that time he was so busy with his books that he had no time for anything else. After finishing his high school work, he attended the Louisville Medical College, in Louisville, Kentucky, and here he was graduated, with the degree of M. D. in 1886.

True to his determination the young doctor returned to the state of his birth, bent on goving his services to help the people among whom he had been reared. This was no small sacrifice for the young man, for he realized the opportunities to advance himself in his profession would be very few. While he had been in college he had been in constant contact with the leaders in his profession, and now he would have to struggle along by himself with neither the inspiration or the wise counsel that they could have given him, had he gone for example into hospital work in Louisville. However, if his career was not to be as brilliant as it might have been had he remained in the city, he was to receive a training and experience that would broaden his character and give him an insight into the real problems of this complex life such as no hospital practice could have done. He was to learn the souls of men, and to go through trials and tribulations with his people, as he would never have had the opportunity to do as a hospital physician. He first located in Eureka, in Dooly county, Georgia. After remaining here for five years he moved to Vienna, in the same county, and here he has been in practice ever since. His practice is general, and that means that he has to cover many miles a day, through every sort of weather, but he never falters, and his reward is in the devotion of the people whom he has served so well and so faithfully. Who shall not say that friends are better than fame.

Dr. Bivins married Mary E. Gammage, a daughter of James M. and

Winnifred (Lock) Gammage. She was also a native of Georgia, Lawrence county being her birthplace. Dr. Bivins is a member of the Masonic order, and the A. A. O. N. M. S., and he also belongs to the Knights of Pythias, and to the Odd Fellows. Both Dr. Bivins and his wife are members of the Baptist church in Vienna, Georgia.

WILLIAM ROBERT GIGNILLIAT. The subject of this sketch passed to his eternal reward on November 25, 1885, at Darien, McIntosh county, Georgia, at the comparatively early age of forty-five years, having entered upon this life at Baisden's Bluff, in the same county, on June 21, 1839. During this brief period came the great crisis in the history of the South, and with quiet modesty he faced the issue and rendered heroic services to his native state during the trying days of the four years' struggle, and even more notably during the fateful days of reconstruction which followed.

Delicately nurtured and accustomed to every luxury, the outbreak of the war found him in a state of health which his physicians assured him would terminate fatally, unless he turned his back on the impending struggle and sought the restorative influences of southern France. Casting to the winds such advice as unworthy the consideration of a man in the hour of his country's need, he enlisted promptly at Savannah in the Chatham Artillery, but soon afterward, in connection with his lifelong friend, Capt. John M. Guerard, organized the company known as Guerard's Battery. He was first lieutenant, but often was in active personal command, Capt. John M. Guerard being detailed to staff duty and other important service from time to time. At the battles of Olustee, Florida, and Honey Hill, South Carolina, under his command the battery rendered conspicuous service and took its full part throughout the campaign in the Carolinas and Virginia. A short time prior to the surrender, Lieutenant Gignilliat was promoted to the rank of captain and served on the staff of Gen. J. Lamb Buist.

Prior to the outbreak of hostilities, Mr. Gignilliat completed his collegiate and legal education at the University of Georgia and the University of Virginia, and entered upon the practice of his profession at Savannah, Georgia. Strikingly handsome and possessing great charm of manner, he formed many warm friendships at college and in business. His natural inclination at the close of the war was to return to Savannah or locate in Atlanta, so as to continue these attractive associations, but the country of his birth needed him most and, harkening to the call of duty, he located in Darien to take an active part in redeeming McIntosh county from carpet-bag rule and negro domination. The notorious negro leader, Tunis G. Campbell, there held an undisputed sway as any crowned monarch, being backed by a negro population outnumbering the whites at least five to one, and by the bayonets of the Federal troops encamped at Darien. The scenes enacted in Darien and its vicinity from this time until Campbell's deposition and imprisonment in the State Penitentiary. were as trying as in any place in the South. Bloodshed was not infrequent, and but for the unflinching determination and bravery of a few ex-Confederates, acting under Mr. Gignilliat's advice and leadership, the situation would have been even worse and the bringing order out of chaos long delayed.

Mr. Gignilliat was chairman of the Democratic Executive Committee, senior warden of the Episcopal church, and master of the Masonic lodge, and all these positions were used by him with rare tact and good judgment to allay race prejudice and restore good order. He was elected to the state senate and was a member of the Constitutional Convention of 1887. He was chairman of the famous Congressional Convention of the First district, held at Jesup in 1876, and was tendered the nomination by a conference committee appointed after hundreds of ineffectual ballots had been taken. His instant reply was that he was there as the friend and delegate of Hon. Julian Hartridge, and would stand by him to the last, and in a few more ballots Mr. Hartridge won. This incident, as well as Mr. Gignilliat's course at the outbreak of the war and at the termination of hostilities, serve to illustrate the high sense of duty and absolute loyalty to country and friends, which were his predominant traits of character. These qualities, inherited from ancestors who had been of the best citizenship of England, France and Scotland, and who had much to do with the establishment of this Republic on a firm foundation, were carried by him to full fruition in a life of devoted unselfishness around the sacred hearth of home as well as in the wider arena of public life. He has left to his children a heritage of high character, patriotism and zeal which they would do well to emulate and transmit to generations yet unborn.

His death was the occasion of universal sorrow and his funeral probably the most largely attended of any that ever took place in the county, the Masonic services being conducted by his devoted friend, Hon. Rufus E. Lester. Numerous obituaries and tributes of respect were penned at the time. From one we quote as follows:

"We shall miss him—we, the people of McIntosh county, for whose advancement and interest he was always ready to work and did work, when days were dark and friends were few."

From another: "The State and county have sustained a loss which will be felt by every good citizen, since by his death comes the want of wise counsel, always directed to the best interest and welfare of the public, an absence of one whose words were strong, forcible, magnetic, a parting from a man whose heart was always full of sympathy toward his fellow men." And from the resolutions of the Masonic Lodge: "An affectionate and beloved father, a zealous and proficient craftsman, a talented, eloquent and honest lawyer, an enterprising and public-spirited citizen, a courtly, educated and polished gentleman."

To such men is the South indebted for the halo of glory, which, notwithstanding the defeat in battle, was the outcome of the terrific struggle of the early sixties, and is still more indebted for her reconstruction. Much has been said and written regarding the New South, but the fact that its development is in large measure the work of the men who made the Old South a civilization beyond compare, and who fought and bled in defense of her constitutional rights, and that this work is being carried forward by their descendants, rather than any new element from other parts of our common country or from abroad, and that these younger sons of the South have also gone out and are potent factors elsewhere in the nation, has not yet been sufficiently recognized or presented with the clearness and force which it merits.

It is not within the scope of a brief biographical sketch like this to do justice to such a theme and the thought is only suggested here with the hope that some worthy writer of the Southland may take up the subject broadly and with an abler pen give it due place in history.

A brief notice of the descendants of the subject of this sketch may serve to give further point to the thought above presented, particularly when it is considered that every community in the south furnished to the cause just such men as William Robert Gignilliat—modest and faithful—letting their light shine serene, and differing from each other only as one star differeth from another in glory; and that their descendants, even more numerous, are today in every state from Canada to Mexico, and from the Atlantic to the Pacific, working out under the hand of

God, which guided their forefathers, not only the destiny of the south, but of the entire nation.

The subject of this sketch was survived by six sons and one daughter, and the tenor of their lives is only one of many instances in point.

The oldest son, William L. Gignilliat, born at Savannah, Georgia, April 21, 1861, following in the footsteps of his father, adopted the legal profession. On account of the war and its aftermath, his education was obtained with difficulty, and he was compelled to content himself with the facilities offered by the public schools at Savannah. He graduated on the seventh of June, 1881, and after a brief visit to the family home in McIntosh county, he returned to Savannah and entered the law offices of Tompkins & Denmark, afterwards becoming a member of the firm of Denmark & Adams. He was compelled to withdraw from this firm by ill health and sought the pine lands of Effingham county, in 1890, where he has ever since made his home. Upon recovering his health he resumed the practice of his profession in Savannah, becoming associated with Mr. W. B. Stubbs, under the firm name of Gignilliat & Stubbs. After this partnership was dissolved, he practiced alone for several years and then entered into partnership with Daniel G. Heidt, Jr., under the firm name of Gignilliat & Heidt, which firm is still in active practice. During this period of over twenty-five years, he has enjoyed a large practice in the surrounding counties, as well as in the city of Savannah, and is universally liked for his considerate and courteous treatment of all with whom he comes in contact.

Mr. Gignilliat manifested but little military spirit in times of peace, but promptly on the outbreak of the war with Spain, volunteered for service and joined the Effingham Hussars. He was spoken of as captain in case that command went to the front, but the United States Government, declining to enlist additional cavalry companies, he turned his attention in another direction, and at his own expense organized the Second Battalion, Georgia Naval Reserves, with the expectation of having a ship manned by Georgia men, and under the command of his brother, who was a graduate of the United States Naval Academy, take part in the struggle, but the battle of Santiago was fought before they were fully mustered in, and more than 200 men which he then had in various squads at Savannah, Brunswick, Waycross and Thomasville, were disbanded.

He has for many years been a member of the New church (Swedenborgian), actively identified with the society at Savannah, and often conducting the services at the chapel in this city in the absence of the regular minister. Shortly after his removal to Effingham county, Mr. Gignilliat became chairman of the Democratic Executive Committee, and he has been an active participant in various congressional and state conventions. He is recognized as one of the most effective workers and public-spirited citizens of this section of the state, and could obtain any position within the gift of the people, but he has avoided rather than sought public preferment, declining the judgeship of the county and the superior court and the collectorship of the port of Savannah, and avoiding nomination for the legislature and state senate and for congress, he has devoted his time with unflagging zeal to developing the natural resources of this section.

Mr. Gignilliat is thoroughly identified in the public mind with the town of Pineora, which was named and founded by him during the period of his retirement above mentioned, and which he has ever since carefully fostered. Besides the building up of the town, Mr. Gignilliat is interested in a large sawmill enterprise at this point, but his chief field of endeavor is the scientific development of the fine agricultural possibilities of that section, and the encouragement of the settling of the best type of farmers on a ten thousand acre tract of land in which he is largely interested and which adjoins the town.

Thomas Heyward Gignilliat, who was born at Aiken, South Carolina, February 10, 1863, and departed this life July 5, 1911, attained distinction in the arts of war and peace. He was a graduate of the United States Naval Academy, but retiring soon after his graduation, he spent years in the study of aeronautics and the actual construction of a flying machine at Hartford, Connecticut. He was a mathematician of unusual talent, the formulas of flight worked out by him during the two years, cruise following his graduation from the Naval Academy, and which he embodied in his machine, coming to the attention of the leading institutions of learning in the country and leading to the revision of the text of that portion of the mathematical works then used in dealing with that subject. In company with his brother, William L. Gignilliat, and Mr. William B. Stillwell, E. F. Bryan, T. F. Johnson and other prominent Savannah men, he organized the American Aeronautic Machine Company, which was the first corporation of its kind in the world, but for lack of funds, due to one of the financial panics, which swept over the country shortly after the incorporation of this company, he would have won the laurels in this field of endeavor which have since fallen to others, the correctness of the calculations and plans upon which he was working, having been since demonstrated by their achievements.

Following these experiments he spent some years in the United States Corps of Engineers and in the War Department at Washington, D. C. He was closely associated with Gen. John M. Wilson, then chief of engineers of the United States Army immediately prior to the outbreak of the Spanish-American War, and it is interesting to know that much of the designing of the Atlantic Coast fortifications and the proper equipment of the same with suitable ordnance and ammunition, involving the expenditure of large sums of money, devolved upon him. The energy displayed by him and his singular aptitude for the work, was highly appreciated by General Wilson and found expression in a letter written by him shortly afterwards.

After remaining in the War Department long enough to finish his work and complete the necessary details of the equipment of the fortifications, on the designing of which he had worked so well, Mr. Gignilliat resigned in order to take part in active hostilities, and was assigned to the fleet in the West Indies with the rank of lieutenant. From this service he received an honorable discharge, with the thanks of congress, and returned to his position in the War Department. His health had been impaired by a long attack of fever, contracted in the Spanish-American war, and at his request he was transferred to outdoor work and did good service at various points from New England to Florida, as a member of the United States Engineering Corps. He resigned from that organization to accept the position of principal of one of the public schools in Savannah. His career as principal of the Barnard school demonstrated his faculty for discipline and organization. During the earlier years of his stay in Savannah he assisted in reorganizing the naval reserves and became its commander.

His next effort combined both military and educational features, being the establishment of the Culver Summer Naval School at Culver, Indiana, in collaboration with his younger brother, Leigh R. Gignilliat, hereinafter mentioned. This service has been duly recognized by both national and state authorities, and though his stay in that state was only during the summer vacations of the Savannah school, the rank of commander of Naval Reserves was conferred upon him by the state of Indiana. Noting his demise, the Savannah *Press* of July 6, 1911, says of him:

"Passing from such matters as rest under the public gaze, to matters connected with the inner life, and which constitute the real man, it may be said that from earliest boyhood he was noted for a disposition singularly sweet but coupled with unflinching resolution. Not aggressive, but of unfailing physical and moral courage, he sought in a quiet way to impart to all with whom he came in contact his own love for all that was noble, true and beautiful in life, and his aversion to everything that tended to lower and degrade.

"Thus lived and thus has passed away, too soon, a son of the south, true to its best traditions—'*un. chevalier sans peur et sans reproche.*'"

Helen Mary Hart Gignilliat, the only daughter of the subject of this sketch, born at Aiken, South Carolina, June 23, 1865, possesses the notable traits of the southern gentlewoman, and is a devoted wife and mother. Her husband, Hon. Livingston Kenan, was for many years solicitor general of the Atlanta Judicial Circuit and a resident of Darien, but is now a resident of Milledgeville, Georgia, where he occupies the position of both city and county attorney.

Arthur Mathewson Gignilliat was born at Walthourville, Liberty county, Georgia, March 26, 1868, and died at Hampton county, South Carolina, December 11, 1890, from a gun-shot wound. He had spent several years in Texas in bridge building and other railroad work, but had returned to his native state and was a civil engineer on the construction of the bridge across the Savannah river, now a part of the Seaboard Air Line System, at the time of his death. He was noted for his great physical strength and for bravery amounting almost to recklessness, as well as for unusual energy and aptitude in his line of work. But for his untimely death he would, no doubt, have kept equal pace with his brothers in the endeavors of life.

Robert Deas Gignilliat, born in McIntosh county, Georgia, February 25, 1873, has shown ability of a high order as a civil engineer, and more particularly in the line of concrete construction. It fell to his lot to superintend the work on the fortifications at Fort Screven, Tybee Island, Georgia, which were in process of construction immediately preceding and during the war with Spain, and for months he worked night as well as day to put this important outpost in condition to make an effective defense of the city of Savannah, in case of attack by the Spanish fleet. The concrete construction at this fort has been pronounced unsurpassed by any work done during that period. Preceding and following this public service, he was actively engaged in river and harbor work and railroad construction, holding important positions which he filled with zeal and efficiency. About four years ago he removed to Milledgeville, Georgia, where he opened and still maintains an office as an engineer, surveyor and contractor in concrete construction.

Leigh Robinson Gignilliat, born at Savannah, Georgia, July 4, 1875, more nearly resembles his father than any of the sons, and has the same faculty for making friends and winning his way along paths calling for talent of a rare order. He graduated with distinction successively from the Emerson Institute at Washington, D. C., and from the Virginia Military Academy. At the latter institute he was private secretary to the superintendent, captain of one of the companies, president of the literary society, editor of the college publication and valedictorian of his class.

His first service in active life was with the corps of United States engineers engaged in road work and bridge building in Yellowstone

National park. Returning to the family home in Georgia, he spent a few months there before accepting the position of commandant of the Culver Military Academy, at Culver, Indiana, an institution then but newly founded. He spent considerable time in architectural study while in Washington, and on the house drainage system for the city of Savannah, and other practical work while in Georgia. This varied experience, as well as the positions held by him at the military academy in Virginia, stood him in good stead at Culver in directing the laying off of the grounds, the erection of larger and finer buildings as the school developed, as well as in the higher work of discipline and organization. It was his good fortune at the outset of his career at Culver to be thrown in close contact and intimate companionship with Col. A. E. Fleet, a Virginia gentleman of the old school and of the highest type of southern manhood, as well as one of the most prominent educators of his day. Their combined efforts placed the Culver Military Academy second only to the United States Military Academy at West Point. Mr. Gignilliat, upon Colonel Fleet's retirement, became superintendent of the institution, and has carried forward the work with great ardor and success, the annual enrollment numbering many hundreds of scholars and the equipment being now unsurpased. Not content with the regular work, almost herculean, of the Culver Military Academy, his energy and mental activity have found expression from time to time in writing for the leading magazines and periodicals, as well as in the establishment, in connection with his brother, Thomas Heyward Gignilliat, of the Culver Summer Naval school.

So much has been said and written in current publications of the Culver schools and of the active spirit that controls and directs them, that further elaboration in a sketch of this kind is unnecessary.

Ravenel Gignilliat, the youngest son, was born in McIntosh county, Georgia, January 9, 1879, and still has ample time to add a higher record to the good beginning which he has made. He was educated in the public schools of Savannah and at Emory College, after leaving which he engaged in civil engineering. Though still young in years, probably no one in his profession has seen more active or varied service. He has served with the United States engineering corps, also in the laying out and constructing of several railroad lines, in water and factory construction, besides miscellaneous surveying and engineering. He now has an office in Savannah, Georgia, where his proficiency and untiring energy are fully recognized, and he bids fair to win an enviable reputation in his chosen work.

To those who, noting family traits, are interested in tracing them back to their origin, a brief sketch of the family history will prove interesting.

The ancestry of the Gignilliat family can be traced in a direct line to Jean Francois Gignilliat, a French Hugenot, whose people fled from France to Switzerland, where Jean Francois was born. He came to America early in the eighteenth century, with the Ravenels, Porchers and other Hugenot families, and was granted a tract of 5,000 acres of land in South Carolina, at Purysburg, on the Savannah river, a short distance above Savannah, "he being the first of the Swiss nation to emigrate to these colonies," according to the records of the South Carolina Historical Society. It was not long afterwards that his descendants removed to the new colony of Georgia and the family became identified with the Scotch settlers in the early history of McIntosh county. Each succeeding generation has been represented by strong men who took a prominent part in the history of the state and left to their descendants the heritage of an honorable name, notable among them being James Gignilliat, a member of the first constitutional convention of Georgia in 1777.

The father of William Robert Gignilliat, for whom he was named, received his education at the state university in Athens. He was a typical ante-bellum rice planter, possessing culture and refinement, as well as wealth. His other sons, Thomas Hart Gignilliat and Gilbert West Gignilliat, were twins, who at the early age of nineteen years entered the service of the Confederacy and were with the Fifth Georgia cavalry, the former as lieutenant and the latter as private and non-commissioned officer, until the close of the war, both being noted for that daring and utter disregard of personal danger so generally manifested by young volunteers in those days.

The mother of William Robert Gignilliat was Helen Mary Hart, of an old English family, settling first in New Jersey and Pennsylvania, and afterwards spreading to the Carolinas and Georgia. This family was noted for men of vigor and eminence, furnishing to the nation one of the signers of the Declaration of Independence, besides several army officers and noted pulpit orators. She was a native of Liberty county, Georgia, but spent several years at Athens pursuing her studies in music, botany and astronomy. Possessing a nature absolutely spiritual, and retaining throughout her lifetime a deep interest in scientific study, the family residence at Greenwood plantation attracted kindred spirits, even from a distance—one of them, a native of Connecticut and graduate of Yale college, has of late years (recalling the visits of his early manhood to the old plantation) referred to the home life there as a "veritable paradise on earth."

The wife of William Robert Gignilliat was Hattie W. Heyward, also descended from an old English family, which settled in South Carolina and which, likewise, furnished a signer of the Declaration of Independence, as well as army officers, both in the Revolutionary war and the War between the states, a chief magistrate of the state of South Carolina and many minor public officials—being, in fact, one of the best known families in the south. She, like her mother, was endowed with noble traits of mind and soul and even amid hardship and adversity made her home a refuge and delight for her husband and a large circle of relatives and friends.

Other lines of ancestry are traced to the highlands of Scotland and particularly to the clans of Campbell and McDonald. To this triple twist of English, French and Scotch ancestry, many of the traits of character, as well as the indomitable energy of the various members of the family, may well be ascribed.

SAMPSON B. BARFIELD. Among the planters of south Georgia, few families have been for a longer time or more actively engaged as crop producers and contributors to the agricultural and civic wealth of this section than that of Barfield. Several generations of this family have been residents of the state, and one of its prosperous and worthy members is Sampson B. Barfield, whose home for many years has been in the Club House district of Lowndes county.

He was born in Twiggs county, this state, on the 28th of November, 1853. His great-grandfather was a native of England and on coming to America settled in South Carolina, but according to the best information at hand later settled in Georgia, being one of the pioneers of Twiggs county, where he spent the rest of his days. In the same county the grandfather, William Barfield, who was a native of South Carolina, owned and operated a farm and lived there until his death, which occurred before the war. His four sons and three daughters were named as follows: John, Richard, Sampson, Frederick,, Betsey, Polly and Patsy.

Frederick Barfield, the father, was born in Twiggs county, was reared on a farm and began his independent career on a tract of land about seventeen miles from Macon, where he lived until 1856. In that year he settled in Lowndes county, which was then a much larger civil division than at present and the county seat was located at the old town of Troupville. The Barfields came here after the manner of emigrants to a new land, bringing in wagons their household goods, farm implements, etc. During their first year's residence the trading center was Troupville, but all the surplus products had to be hauled on wagons to Tallahassee or Newport and Jacksonville, Florida. Frederick Barfield bought land about four miles south of the present site of Hahira. A clearing of twelve acres and a log house constituted the improvements, and he at once began the task of clearing more land for the plow and engaged in general farming. At the time of the war he was past the military age, but in 1864 joined the state militia and went to the defense of Atlanta, where he was soon discharged on account of disability. His death occurred in 1872. He married Bethany Brewer, a native of Twiggs county, and she died in 1889. They were the parents of thirteen children, named as follows: William, Mary, Sarah, John, Carrie, Frank, Emeline, Epsie, Columbus, Sampson, Lafayette, Tempy and Belle. Of these, Belle died in childhood and William at the age of twenty-four. John and Frank both served in the Confederate army.

Sampson B. Barfield spent his early youth in Lowndes county, being reared in habits of industry and thrift, and after the removal of the family to Lowndes county he bought two hundred and twenty-five acres of timbered land that is included in his present farm. There he built a substantial log house, which continued the dwelling of himself and family for twenty-seven years, when it was replaced by a commodious and attractive residence of frame. From the beginning of his independent career he succeeded and with increasing means bought lands until his present holdings aggregate about fourteen hundred acres, all located in the Club House district.

Mr. Barfield married Miss Lizzie Lawson, a native of Lowndes county and a member of one of the old families of this section. Her parents were William and Maley (Vickers) Lawson, and her grandfather was Ashley Lawson (see sketch of Lawson family elsewhere). Her father served in the army of northern Virginia and saw arduous service as a soldier of the south, and was captured and held prisoner at Point Lookout several months before the end of the war. For several years he owned and operated a farm, a part of which is now included in the village of Hahira. Mr. and Mrs. Barfield have reared ten children, namely: Willie, Carrie, Charlie, Eddie, Zeno, Hum Mason, Ruth, Rosa, Ethel and Christelle. Mr. Barfield has been a director of the Bank of Hahira since its founding, is a member of the Farmers' Union, and affiliates with Hahira Lodge No. 346, A. F. & A. M.

REV. WALTER C. JONES. Born in one of the early homes of south Georgia, Rev. Jones represents a family which had a pioneer part in the settlement and development of this section of the state, and during his own career has followed a life of service and benefit to the community as well as for his individual welfare. He has spent many years in the ministry of the Methodist church, and since retiring has become noted as a fruit grower and nurseryman at Cairo.

Walter C. Jones was born in the Hickory Head section of Brooks county, Georgia, June 26, 1855. His father was Malachi, who was born in the Black Creek section of Bulloch county, in 1809. The grandfather was Thomas Jones, born and reared in Warreu county, Georgia, going to Bullock county when a young man and rearing his family and spending his last days in the latter vicinity. Thomas Jones married a Miss Denmark. Malachi Jones was reared and married in Bulloch county, and from there came into southwestern Georgia, accompanied by his wife and three children. The journey was made across the country with team and wagon, and his first location was the present site of Dixie, which was then located in Thomas county. Buying a tract of timbered land, he cleared a space among the trees and there built a log cabin, which was the first shelter of himself and family in southwestern Georgia. Indians and wild game were still plentiful in the almost unbroken forest areas which surrounded his home on every side, and his labors contributed one more plantation to this section of Georgia.

About 1845 he sold his land and bought a place in the Hickory Head section of Lowndes county, now in Brooks county. There he again built a home and it was in that house that Rev. Walter C. Jones was born. For many years after the settlement of the family, no railroads were built through this country, and the father marketed his cotton either in Tallahassee or St. Marks. One year he sold his cotton at St. Marks for 3½ cents per pound, and then turned and invested part of the proceeds of the crop for a stock of salt for which he had to pay $2.00 per sack. Malachi Jones improved the fine farm and spent the remainder of his life in Brooks county, where he died at the age of seventy-one. The maiden name of his wife was Sarah Reissier Groover. Her father was Charles Groover, a native of Savannah, and her ancestors came to America with the Salzburgers. At that time the family name was spelled Gruber, and was subsequently changed to the present form. Charles Groover, clerk of court of Bulloch county, spelled his name Gruver until 1837, as shown by the records, and then changed it to Groover, and so far as known all other members of the family adopt this spelling. Charles Groover from Savannah moved to Bulloch county, where he bought a plantation, was soon afterwards elected clerk of the court, and served several years in that official capacity. He remained a resident of Bulloch county until his death. The maiden name of his wife was a Miss Reissier, who survived him and later married Nathan Jones, and spent her last days in Bulloch county. Her sons were Samuel of Statesboro; Charles E., a well known resident of Savannah, and Daniel who died a young man. Mrs. Malachi Jones died at the age of sixty-nine years, and of her fourteen children, eleven grew to maturity, named as follows: Sophronia, Nathan, Julia, Charles E., William M., M. Franklin, Andrew J., Thomas T., Clinton R., Walter, Colquit, and Sally A. The son, Nathan, enlisted at the breaking out of the war in the Confederate service and died while a soldier. Charles E., William M., and M. Franklin served all through the war, and Andrew entered the army when a boy in 1864, remaining until the final surrender.

Walter C. Jones attended the rural schools in Brooks county and the Hickory Head High School. The beginning of his career was as a merchant, engaging in that business at Quitman at the age of twenty-two and continuing in that line for nine years. In 1887 he joined the south Georgia conference of the Methodist church, and for nearly a quarter of a century was active in the ministry with pastorate in different sections of the state until failing health compelled him to retire, and he is now a superannuated minister. However, he still engages in the active work as preacher, when his health will permit, and is teacher of a fine Bible class of ninety members at Cairo.

On leaving the regular work of the ministry, Mr. Jones located at Cairo, and turned his attention to farm life. He established a nursery and has made a specialty of the culture of pecan trees and for several seasons has sold as high as 12,000 to 15,000 trees. He also has a large and profitable pecan grove of his own, and his farm located close to Cairo is considered one of the best in Grady county. In 1912 he erected an attractive and comfortable home, built in the colonial style, and located on Gordon Heights one mile from the court house in Cairo.

Rev. Walter C. Jones, on January 20, 1892, married Miss Martha Melvina Powell. Mrs. Jones is a native of Cairo, and a daughter of Rev. William Powell, who was born in that portion of Decatur county, which is now included within the limits of Grady county. The grandfather of Mrs. Jones was Kedar Powell, who was born in Decatur county, a son of parents who were natives of North Carolina, and among the first settlers of southwest Georgia. Kedar Powell established his home about six miles south of Cairo, where he improved a farm out of the wilderness and lived there until late in life, when he moved into Cairo, and spent his last days in this town. Rev. William Powell was one of the first merchants in Cairo, and after the railroad had been built through, he was appointed station agent, an office which he held until his death. He was also interested in farming, and his place was partly included with the incorporate limits of Cairo. William Powell married Lucretia Brocket, a daughter of Capt. Lemuel Brocket, a large planter of Florida. Mr. and Mrs. Jones have five children named Walter Colquit, Jr., Margaret, William Powell, Joseph Mabbett, and Lucretia.

HONORABLE GERMANICUS YOUNG TIGNER. A man of broad capabilities, resourceful, and quick to grasp a situation and utilize opportunities, Honorable Germanicus Young Tigner has for many years been an important factor in the public life of Muscogee county, serving his fellow-men in various capacities, at the present writing, in 1913, being judge of the Columbus city court of Columbus. A native of Georgia, he was born in Haralson, Coweta county, of excellent English ancestry, being a descendant in the fifth generation from the immigrant ancestor, George Tigner, his lineage being thus traced: George Tigner, Philip Tigner, Young Fletcher Tigner, William Archelaus Tigner, and Germanicus Young Tigner.

About 1750 George Tigner, accompanied by his brother Thomas, came from England, their native country, to America. They were seafaring men, engaged in the merchant marine service, and both located in Baltimore, Maryland. A year later Thomas Tigner returned to his old home in England, but George Tigner remained in Baltimore, and kept his ships in active service until the Revolution, when they were seized by the British government. After his marriage he lived for a time in Anne Arundel county, Maryland, from there moving to Accomac county, Virginia, and settling near Drummondtown, where he spent his remaining days, being engaged in farming. He was twice married, by his first wife having three children, namely: William, who reared a family, and has descendants living in Virginia, and in various other parts of the Union; Hannah married a Mr. Houghton, and settled in New York State; and Philip, the next in line of descent.

Philip Tigner was born in Accomac county, Virginia, December 25, 1760. Leaving home in the seventeenth year of his age, he went first to Norfolk, Virginia, from there going to Salisbury, North Carolina, where he married. With his bride, he came to Georgia, and after spending a short time in Greene county removed to that part of Franklin county that was later a part of Jackson county, and is now included within the boundaries of Clarke county. Purchasing a tract of land through which a creek flowed, he improved the water power, built a saw mill and a grist mill, and was there prosperously employed in farming and milling until his death, at the age of fifty-nine years. A devout Methodist in religion, he erected one of the first Methodist Episcopal churches in North Georgia, it having been known as Tigner's Chapel. He married first, March 7, 1780, in Salisbury, North Carolina, Nancy Forbish, who died in Green county, Georgia, May 28, 1792. He married second Nancy Hall, a daughter of John Hall, a native of Ireland, who came to America in colonial times, locating first in North Carolina, later coming to Georgia as pioneers. By his first marriage he reared five children, Sarah E., James, William, Elizabeth, and Hope H. His second wife, to whom he was married in 1793, bore him eight children, namely: Nancy; Innocence; Pamelia; Freeborn G.; John Wesley; Young Fletcher, through whom the line of descent was continued; Urban Cooper; and Philip Gillen.

Young Fletcher Tigner was born August 22, 1805, on a plantation located about three miles north of Salem, Clarke county, Georgia. Converted when young, he joined the Methodist Episcopal church, and became a preacher in that denomination, as a member of the Georgia conference, filling the pulpits of churches in various places. In Meriwether county he purchased a plantation near Durand, which was his home for many years. Late in life he removed to Columbus, and lived in that vicinity until his death.

Rev. Young Fletcher Tigner married Sarah Frances Tinsley, who was born in Clarke county, Georgia, a daughter of James Tinsley, and granddaughter of Thomas Tinsley, a native of Hanover county, Virginia. She was a lineal descendant, it is thought, of one Edward Tinsley, who came from Yorkshire, England, to America in the early part of the seventeenth century, locating in Virginia. Seven of his brothers, according to tradition, served, and were killed, in the Revolutionary war. James Tinsley was born near Richmond, Virginia, in 1764. During the progress of the Revolutionary war, he went to South Carolina, and settled on the Cooper river, ten miles from Chesterton, from there coming, in 1790, to Georgia, where he afterwards spent his remaining years, his home having been in Columbia county. He married first Elizabeth Zachery, of South Carolina. He married for his second wife Mrs. Lucy Ann (Crawford) Richards, a sister of Hon. William Harris Crawford, who served as secretary of war under President Madison, as secretary of the treasury under both President Madison and President Monroe, and minister to France, and who, in 1824, as candidate for president of the United States, shared the electoral vote with John Quincy Adams, Andrew Jackson, and Henry Clay. Of the union of Rev. Y. F. and Sarah F. (Tinsley) Tigner, nine children were born, namely: James Andrew, Eliza Boring, William Archelaus, Wesley Fletcher, Lucy A. E., Samuel Hodges, and Sarah, Julia, and Young Fletcher. Dr. Wesley Fletcher Tigner, uncle of G. Y. Tigner, is a well known Confederate veteran, having fought in all the leading battles of Lee's army from Bull Run to Appomattox; engaged in thirty pitched battles, and now a retired dentist, in comfortable circumstances, and loved by all who know him.

William Archelaus Tigner was born in Meriwether county, Georgia, July 13, 1832, and received his rudimentary education in the rural schools, afterwards studying under Prof. Thaddeus Oliver, of Buena Vista. He was graduated from Emory College, in Oxford, Georgia, with the class of 1854, and soon after began teaching in Haralson, Coweta county. Succeeding well as an educator, he was made president of a Male and Female College at Chunnenuggee Ridge, Alabama. He afterwards taught in a Lutheran settlement, both in Oglethorpe county, Georgia, and in Macon county. While thus occupied, he studied law in his leisure moments, and after his admission to the bar located as a lawyer in Vienna, Dooly county. After practicing awhile in both Dooly and Oglethorpe counties, he removed to Atlanta, where he formed a partnership with William H. Hulsey, under the firm name of Hulsey & Tigner. He was later associated with W. D. Ellis as senior member of the law firm of Tigner & Ellis. In 1884 he was elected as senator from the Thirty-fifth district, and took an active and intelligent part in the work of legislation. He was reared a Methodist, but when about thirty-five years old united with the Lutheran church, and became a preacher in that denomination, filling pulpits in Ebenezer and other places, and serving as president of the South Carolina, Georgia and Florida Synod. For several years prior to his death he lived in Jonesboro, his death occurring there February 19, 1894.

William Archelaus Tigner was twice married. He married first Eugenia R. Dozier, who was born in Marion county, Georgia, in 1834, a daughter of Thomas H. and Martha Thomas (Davie) Dozier. She died March 19, 1872, leaving three children, namely: Germanicus Young, the special subject of this sketch; Martha, wife of A. O. Osborne, now of Wilmington, North Carolina; and William A. Tigner, Jr., an attorney now in Jonesboro, Georgia. He married for his second wife Miriam Byington, who is now living in Jonesboro, Georgia.

Germanicus Young Tigner was carefully educated under his father's and mother's tutorship, attending private schools in Atlanta, and the Jonesboro Academy. A young man of excellent mental attainments, eminently capable and intelligent, he was appointed, in 1876, by Judge Martin J. Crawford, official stenographer of the superior court at Columbus, and met every requirement of that responsible position so efficiently and satisfactorily that he was continued in office for sixteen years. In 1888 Mr. Tigner was elected as a representative to the state legislature, and later was appointed stenographer of the supreme court. At the end of two years he resigned that position, and returned to Columbus. In 1902 he was again elected to represent his county in the state legislature, and served in the sessions of 1902, 1903, and 1904. In 1908 Mr. Tigner was appointed, by Gov. Hoke Smith, judge of the city court of Columbus, and served by appointment until 1912, when he was elected to the position by an overwhelming majority, receiving a flattering vote that proved his popularity with all classes of people.

Mr. Tigner married, June 27, 1889, Johnny Lindsay. She was brought up and educated in Columbus, and at the Moravian Institute at Bethlehem, Pennsylvania, being a daughter of John B. and Helen (Slade) Lindsay, and granddaughter of Rev. Thomas Slade, father of Hon. J. J. Slade, of whom a brief biographical sketch appears elsewhere in this volume. Two children have been born of the union of Mr. and Mrs. Tigner, namely: Helen; and John Lindsay, who died at the early age of seventeen years. Religiously Mr. Tigner belongs to to the Methodist Episcopal church, and Mrs. Tigner is a member of the Baptist church.

WESLEY FLETCHER TIGNER. After a career of forty years as a dental practitioner in Georgia, Dr. Tigner now lives retired at his home in Columbus, and is one of the most highly esteemed citizens of that locality.

Wesley Fletcher Tigner was born in Meriwether county, Georgia, August 13, 1834, and is thus one of the oldest native sons of the state. His parents were Rev. Young Fletcher and Sarah (Tinsley) Tigner, concerning whom and this interesting family, further details will be found in the sketch of G. Y. Tigner, in other pages of this work. Dr. Tigner was reared in a rural community and his earliest education was that afforded by one of the neighborhood schools which existed in Georgia before the war. He was very liberally educated for his time, and from the common schools attended Collingsworth institute and in 1856 graduated from Emory College. The following years were spent in teaching, up to the beginning of the Civil war. Then in May, 1861, he enlisted in a company first known as the Henry Grays, and subsequently designated as Company A and attached to the Sixth Regiment of Alabama infantry. Few Georgia soldiers saw a more active and strenuous career as soldier than Dr. Tigner. His regiment was sent into Virginia, and became part of the army of northern Virginia. Its campaigns were many, and the doctor's service can be briefly suggested by referring to the important battles which were Gettysburg, Fredericksburg, Seven Pines, Antietam, Chancellorsville, Yorktown, Williamsburg, Winchester, Kernstown, the Seven Days Fighting around Richmond, and the battles about Petersburg, concluding with the surrender of Lee's forces at Appomatox. He was paroled with the rest of the southern forces and made his way south riding on a pony. He passed through North Carolina and South Carolina in this way, and reached the banks of the Savannah river at Barksdale Ferry, and thence to his father's home in Chattahoochee. He soon afterwards began the study of dentistry at Baltimore college. After a term of two years he began active practice in Columbus, and subsequently returned to Baltimore, where he was graduated in dentistry. Dr. Tigner was for a great many years the family dentist for hundreds of the best people in Columbus and vicinity, and it is of interest to note that he occupied one office in this city for a period of forty years. He has since retired from his active profession and now lives quietly surrounded by family and friends in Columbus.

In 1869 he married Mary Eliza Cunningham, who was born at Talbotton, Georgia, a daughter of James D. and Caroline (Sallie) Cunningham. The two children of the doctor and wife are Mary Frances and Annie Louise, the latter being the wife of J. Ralston Cargill.

WALTER S. DOZIER. Clerk of the court of Terrell county at Dawson, Mr. Dozier is one of the most popular officials of the county, and has had a long and active career in business and public life in this section of the state. He represents one of the oldest and most prominent families of the south.

Walter S. Dozier was born in Warrenton county, Georgia, March 6, 1857. His American ancestry goes back for four or five generations. The family originated in France, among the Huguenots. Leonard Dozier was born in France, was a Huguenot in religious faith, and immigrated to America early in the eighteenth century, locating in Virginia. He was married in that colony in 1733 and died there in 1785. His son was James S. Dozier, who served as sergeant of artillery during the Revolutionary war, and later in life located in Georgia, dying in Warrenton county, January 18, 1808. He married Elizabeth Staples, who was also born in Virginia. Five of their sons were among the settlers and workers who did so much to develop the country in

Warren county. James S. Dozier, the founder of the family in Georgia, just mentioned, was born in Lunenburg county, Virginia, in 1769. Leonard Wesley Dozier, the head of the next generation, was a native of Virginia, and married Nancy Staples. He was one of the early settlers of Warren county, where he died. John Dozier, son of Leonard Wesley and grandfather of the Dawson clerk of courts, was born in Warren county, Georgia, about 1796, and married Antoinet Parham, a daughter of Richard Parham, who was a Virginian who served in the Civil war. John Dozier and wife, so far as known, were lifelong residents of Warren county.

Nathaniel Wesley Dozier, father of Walter S., was born in Warren county, August 12, 1826, was reared and educated in his native locality, and when a young man moved to Stewart county, where he taught school for some time. He entered the Confederate service in 1864, going with the other Georgia troops to the defense of Atlanta. After the fall of that city, he participated in the battle at Griswold's Station, where he was wounded. He was then granted a furlough and returned home and the war closed before he had recovered from his wound. After the war he located in Webster county, where he taught school at Weston for some time. In 1872 occurred his removal to Dawson, where he became identified with merchandising, and was later in the warehouse business and engaged in the sale of fertilizer, which continued until his death on May 4, 1910. Nathaniel W. Dozier, married Mary M. Fuller, who was born in Warren county, Georgia, January 26, 1832. She was a daughter of Spiney and Sarah (Harden) Fuller, and a granddaughter of Spiney Fuller, Sr. Sarah Harden, her mother, was a native of Warren county, and a daughter of Benjamin Harden, who was married in Warren county in 1796 to Mary Smith, whose mother was the widow of a revolutionary soldier, who had come to Georgia, and located in Warren county in 1789. Mrs. Nathaniel W. Dozier, the mother, is now a resident at Dawson. She reared four children whose names are Walter S., Mary C., George Wesley and Alice.

Mr. Walter S. Dozier and wife have six sons and one daughter, namely: James C., Raymond E., Walter C., Owen W., Oliver V., Wilson P., and Susie May. Mr. Dozier is affiliated with P. T. Schley lodge, A. F. & A. M. His wife belongs to the May Brantly Chapter of the United Daughters of the Confederacy, is a member of the Daughters of the American Revolution and an Eastern Star. Mr. and Mrs. Dozier both are members of the Methodist church.

BYRON ALONZO ALDERMAN. A retired business man and one of the leading citizens of Pine Park in Grady county, Mr. Alderman is a life-long resident of southwest Georgia, and beginning his own career in the woods and in a log cabin home he has used thrift and dilligence in acquiring a generous measure of prosperity and has provided well for his family, at the same time performing with fidelity his obligations to his community.

Byron Alonzo Alderman was born on a farm eight miles northwest of Thomasville, November 15, 1854. His father was Hon. Isaac Alderman, a man of unusual influence and ability. He was born December 5, 1826, in Sampson or Duplin county, North Carolina, where his parents were life-long residents. He was reared in his native state by his widowed mother, and acquired a better education than the ordinary. His great-grandfather, Daniel Alderman, married Abigail Harris and came to New Jersey from England about 1750; removed to North Carolina in the year 1755. Daniel Alderman had three sons: John, who married Mary Cashwell; Daniel, who married Sarah Newton, and

David, who married Jemima Hall. David Alderman, Jr., who was Isaac Alderman's grandfather, had three sons: David, who married Nancy Morgan; Isaac, who married Elizabeth Morgan, and Elisha, who married a cousin, Rebecca Alderman. Daniel Alderman also had five daughters: Jemima, who married James Bland; Rachel, who married Bryant Buxton; Sarah, who married James Newton; Mary, who married John Crumpler, and Elizabeth, who remained single. Elisha Alderman and Rebecca Alderman were the parents of Hon. Isaac Alderman, and they had ten children, whose names are: James, Jemima, Sarah, Amos, Joseph, David, Isaac, Daniel, Susan, William. Hon. Isaac Alderman when a young man, took the vocation of teaching and on coming to Georgia he followed that line of work for a number of years. His first residence was in Thomas county, where he taught school and bought a piece of land eight miles northwest of Thomasville, where he built a log house in which his son, Byron A., was born. He continued to teach while superintending the improvements of his land, and in time had acquired a substantial home and the means to provide well for his family. In the year 1863, he enlisted in the Confederate army and was in the struggle until the close. After the war he again took up teaching and farming, and remained on the old homestead until his death, September 24, 1900. The maiden name of his wife was Susan Alderman, daughter of Timothy and Sally (Williams) Alderman, and distantly related to the family of which Isaac Alderman was a member. She was born August 30, 1832, and died November 29, 1897. Timothy Alderman was a native of North Carolina and his wife, Sally, a native of Georgia. Isaac Alderman had a number of public honors during his career, serving as a member of the Thomas County Board of Education and also as a member of the board of county commissioners. He was also honored by election as a representative of Thomas county in the state legislature. Both he and his wife were members of the Baptist church. Their six children were: Byron Alonzo, Laura, Virginia, Marcas E., Fannie and Mattie.

Byron Alonzo Alderman, as a boy, attended the rural schools and was later given the privilege of attendance in the high schools at Warsaw, North Carolina. Though well-educated he did not adopt a learned profession, but chose the peaceful pursuits of agriculture. Early in his career he bought 250 acres of land covered with timber, and cornering upon his father's homestead. He went into the woods and at an eligible site cleared off some of the trees, erected a log cabin, and it was in that home that he and his young wife began married life. In time he effected the clearing of a large amount of land, and was a prosperous and successful farmer there until January, 1899, and in that year he moved into Pine Park and in September of the same year established himself in the mercantile business. In 1908 ill health compelled him to give up the close confinement of the store and he was then succeeded by his son, Early L.

Mr. Alderman was first married in 1878 to Janie Walker, who was born in Thomas county, a daughter of Jonathan and Mary (Kitchen) Walker. (See sketch of Dr. W. A. Walker.)

Mrs. Alderman died in the year 1881. In 1885 he married his present wife, Martha Harman Kemph. She was born near Camilla, in Mitchell county, Georgia. Her father was Jacob Henry Kemph, a native of Georgia, and a son of Faulton Kemph. Faulton Kemph was born in Germany and when a young man spent fourteen weeks on a sailing vessel, which brought him to Georgia. He lived for a time in Burke county, and thence moved to Lee county. He was a well educated man and was honored by official preferment in Lee county, where he spent his last years. He married a Miss Lewis, and reared two sons, of whom John enlisted in the Confederate service at the breaking out of the war and lost his life in battle. Jacob Henry Kemph, father of Mrs. Alderman, lived in Dougherty county for some years after his marriage and later moved to Mitchell county, buying a farm about three and one-half miles south of Camilla. That was his home and scene of labors when the war came on, and in 1863, the month not now being known, he entered the service of the Confederacy, and remained until the close. He returned home very ill, and died on the third day of May, 1865, three days after he reached home. The maiden name of his wife was Eveline Sapp, who was born in Mitchell county, daughter of DeLain and Mary (Chastain) Sapp, natives and life-long residents of Georgia. Mrs. Aldermans mother, who died at the age of seventy-two, reared five children, whose names are: Mary F., John Morgan, Julia L., Martha Harman and Henry DeLain. Mr. Alderman has just one son, by his first wife, named Early Lenwood. He is now engaged in the mercantile business as successor to his father at Pine Park.

Mr. Early·Alderman married Miss Maybelle Sanford, and has three children named: Lenwood, William S. and Elizabeth Jane.

Mr. and Mrs. Alderman worship in the Baptist church in which he is a deacon. In the year 1912, he was honored by appointment as a member of the board of county commissioners of Grady county to fill a vacancy, and in the fall of the same year, he was elected by the people to the same office.

JOHN R. CARTER. An industrious and well-to-do agriculturist of Brooks county, John R. Carter is the proprietor of a fine homestead, which in regard to its appointments compares favorably with any in the neighborhood. He is a native of Georgia, his birth having occurred in Appling county, June 24, 1857. His father, Richard Carter, came as a young man from Robinson county, North Carolina, his birthplace, to Georgia. He was accompanied by his brother, Philip Marion Carter. Both served in the Indian wars, and the brother, it is supposed, lost his life while fighting the dusky savages. Richard Carter purchased land in Appling county while it was yet on the extreme frontier line, and in the wilderness built the log cabin which the family occupied several years and in which his children were born. Although too old for military service in the war between the states, he joined, near the close of the conflict, the Georgia reserves, which was composed of boys and old men, and was called out for home protection. During that period he served as sheriff of Appling county, but soon after the close of the war resigned the position. Selling his Appling county land, he moved to Brooks county, and after living on rented land for a while, purchased a farm in the western part of Dixie district, and was there a resident until his death, at the age of seventy-six years. His wife, whose maiden name was Elizabeth Elliott, survived him but a few years. They reared ten children, as follows: George M., Jane, Philip Marion, Harriet E., Nancy A., Samuel W., Frank R., John R., C. H. and Martha L. The two oldest sons, George M. and Philip M., served throughout the Civil war. They enlisted at Holmesville, Appling county, Georgia, about sixty miles from Savannah, and were paroled at Thomasville, this state.

Growing to manhood beneath the parental roof-tree, John R. Carter assisted in the work of the home farm until he entered the employ of the S. F. & W. Railroad Company, now the Atlantic Coast Line, with which he was identified for twelve years, doing section work for eight years and being in the bridge building department four years. Resigning his position, Mr. Carter turned his attention to agriculture, having previously purchased five hundred acres of land, two hundred and five acres lying in Brooks county and the remainder just across the line in Thomas county, the tracts adjoining. He has now one hundred and fifty acres of his estate in a good state of cultivation, and has erected a substantial set of farm buildings, these being situated on high land, about four miles from the flourishing town of Boston.

Mr. Carter married April 26, 1896, Bertha Maddox, who was born in Thomas county, a daughter of Carey M. and Melissa (Singletary) Maddox. Mr. Maddox was born in Randolph county, Georgia, March 2, 1829. He removed to Thomas county, and was there married to Miss Melissa Singletary on the 11th of December, 1868. He served four years in the war between the states, and during his services therein received one wound. Mrs. Maddox was born and reared in Thomas county. Three children have been born to Mr. and Mrs. Carter, namely: Bama Louis, John Russell and Bertha Vivian. In his political relations Mr. Carter is a stanch supporter of the principles of the Democratic party, and has served three terms as a county commissioner, a position to which he was elected in 1903, re-elected in 1907 and again in 1911 to serve for four years, making a total of twelve years in the position. Fraternally he is a member of Mount Horeb lodge, Free and Accepted Masons. Religiously both Mr. and Mrs. Carter belong to the Missionary Baptist church.

MILTON H. EDWARDS. One of the wealthiest and most influential citizens of eastern Georgia was the late Milton H. Edwards, land owner and capitalist, whose death occurred at his home on the morning of October 8, 1912. Coming to this place as a small boy, he spent all of his active business life in building up productive enterprises that not only brought prosperity to himself, but materially aided the town and surrounding country. A man of energy and wide interests connected with many of the largest business concerns of the city, he was a prominent figure in social and commercial circles of Eastman.

Milton Henry Edwards, the son of William Henry and Eliza Ball Edwards, was born near Glenville, Tattnall county, Georgia on May 20, 1862. His father was a native of Tattnall county and his mother of South Carolina. Their son, Milton H., of this review, was one of the twelve children born to them, seven of whom, three sisters and four brothers, survive. James M. and T. H., of Eastman; Virgil of Lake Butler, Florida, and W. J., of Lake City, Florida; Ursula, the wife of the late Judge D. M. Roberts, of Eastman; Ophelia, the wife of C. H. Peacock of Macon; Melissa, the wife of E. P. Miller, deceased, of Walthourville and Virginia, deceased, the wife of S. A. Foster, deceased, who was for many years a resident of Eastman.

Mr. Edwards came to Eastman and attended the schools of that city and after completing the high school course, engaged in the mercantile business as a clerk in the store of C. H. Peacock. In 1884, he, with his brother, T. H. Edwards, formed a partnership under the name of M. H. Edwards & Bro., and throughout their long and active career were partners in every business undertaking, large or small. A large and lucrative business was established and for many years this firm was the leading mercantile house in this section of the state. In 1905 this business was dissolved only to become a real estate firm, of which he was president, and in which enterprise he was actively engaged at the time of his death. In connection with this he was vice-president of the Oconee River Cotton Mills at Dublin, vice-president of the Eastman Cotton Mill, secretary and treasurer of the Improved Fertilizer Works of Eastman, a director of the Citizens' Banking Company of Eastman and also of the Ocmulgee Fertilizer Works of Hawkinsville and the, Farmers' Fertilizer Works at Milan. Mr. Edwards was the leading figure in the establishing of most of these.

Milton Edwards joined the Baptist church in early manhood and ever remained a loyal and consistent member. He assisted in building the present edifice and was always one of the most liberal supporters. For a number of years he was superintendent of the Sunday school and faithfully served as one of the deacons until the time of his death. Although successful in every business undertaking, kindness and generosity were his dominant traits and rich and poor, black and white always found in him a true friend and wise counselor.

Twenty-eight years ago he was married to Orlena, daughter of John Council and Marcia McCulloch Czar of Elkton, Kentucky, who yet survive him. Eleven children were born to them, seven of whom are still living, viz: Carrie Belle, Nelle, Milton Carr, Christine, Edwin McCulloch, Willard Theodore, and Fannie Harris.

HON. MARK HARDIN BLANDFORD. A former justice of the supreme court of Georgia, a veteran of two wars, and a member of the Confederate congress, the late Mark Hardin Blandford, who died January 31, 1902, was one of the most eminent men of south Georgia.

He was born in Jones county, Georgia, July 13, 1826, being in his seventy-sixth year at the time of his death. His father was Clark Blandford, and his grandfather was also named Clark Blandford. The grandfather was a native of England and came to America in young manhood, during the colonial era, and was married in this country. At the breaking out of the Revolutionary war he returned to England, where he owned some property and was never heard of again by any of his family or friends. He left a wife and three children in America. These children were Clarke, Champion and Polly. Polly married a Mr. Hardison of Florida. Champion died unmarried.

Clarke Blandford, the father, moved from Trenton, New Jersey, to Georgia, and for a time lived in Warrenton, Jones county, and from there came to Harris county, where he served as one of the first clerks of the court. The maiden name of his wife was Nancy Hardin, who belonged to the Hardin family of Kentucky. The three children of the parents were named Francis, Mark Hardin and Carrie.

The late Judge Blandford attended school in Pennfield, known as Murphy University of Georgia. He was less than twenty years of age when the war with Mexico was declared, and without the knowledge of his parents he slipped away and enlisted in Captain Scott's Company, going into Mexico with that command and serving with the company in all its various marches and battles until the war was over. Returning home a veteran of this conflict, he took up the study of law in the office of Col. Hardeman of Macon, and was admitted to the bar by special act of the legislature.

He began practice at Tazewell, which was then the capital of Marion county. He rose to distinction in the law, and after a few years his practice was again interrupted by war. With the outbreak of the war between the states, he raised a company for the Confederate service, and this company took the name of the Buena Vista Guards, and was attached to the Twelfth Georgia Regiment. He went to the front in command of this company, and was severely wounded and lost his right arm at McDower in the Allegheny mountains. Thus being disabled for further active service as a soldier, he returned home and was soon afterwards elected to the Confederate congress, defeating Col. Hines

Holt. He continued in the Confederate congress until its dissolution at the close of the war, and then resumed the practice of law in Columbus, Georgia. In 1869 he formed a partnership with ·B. H. Thornton. This firm was dissolved later, and he was associated with Lewis Garrard, under the firm name of Blandford & Garrard.

In 1874 Mr. Blandford was elected associate justice of the supreme court of Georgia to fill an unexpired term, and at the next regular election was chosen for the full term. He served as associate justice for ten years, making an admirable record as judge of the highest court of the state, and on leaving the bench returned to Columbus, and formed a partnership for practice with Thomas W. Grimes. He continued in that association and in active practice until his death on January 31, 1902.

Judge Blandford married Sarah Daniels, daughter of John Daniels, of Talbot county, Georgia. They were the parents of eight children, three of whom survived their father, namely: Robert Hall, since deceased; John W. and Lucy Mary, who now occupy the old homestead near Columbus.

ASAHEL A. WILLETT. At this writing Asahel A. Willett of Americus has completed nearly a century of human life. He is one of the remarkable and venerable men of southwest Georgia.

Asahel A. Willett was born at Norwich, Connecticut, May 4, 1814. His father was Capt. Jedediah Willett, who was born at Norwich, and the grandfather was Jedediah Willett, who married Sarah Rogers. The family is lineally descended from the first governor of New York.

Grandfather Jedediah Willett was a shipbuilder and built some vessels for the government during the Revolutionary war. He later came into Georgia, locating at Macon, where he died. His son, Joseph E., was one of the first settlers of Macon, and it is said, cut the first tree ever felled on that site.

Capt. Jedediah Willett, the father, was reared in Norwich, Connecticut, and worked with his father in the ship yard. He early took up the life of a sailor, and in time reached the position of captain. His father then gave him a ship, and he was engaged in the coast-wise trade, making his home in Savannah, Georgia, during the winter and in Brooklyn in the summer. He died of yellow fever about 1827. The maiden name of his wife was Mary Adgate, who was born in Norwich, daughter of Asahel and Mary (Rogers) Adgate. She lived to a good old age and reared three children, whose names were Burnham, Asahel and Jared.

Asahel A. Willett, the almost centenarian, attended school at Penfield and Norwich, Connecticut and in his youth acquired the trade of carpenter. He worked at that trade in Connecticut a short time and then moved to Macon, Georgia, where his grandfather and uncle were living. At that time Macon was only a village, and all the surrounding country a wilderness. He lived in Macon until about 1840, and then came to what is now Sumter county, but then a part of Lee county. At that time there were four log cabins in Americus, and Indians lived in the woods near by. The first store was opened a few years after his location there, and a man named Montgomery was one of the first, if not the first, merchant. He worked at his trade in this little settlement, and subsequently entered the merchandise business himself in this north part of the county. There were no railroads and he had to bring in all his goods with teams and wagons. His store was located on the stage route from Macon to Tallahassee and from Macon to Lumpkin. After about three years he traded his store property for other property in Americus, and there built the first house which was erected for the purpose of renting. He engaged in business as a merchant and also in real estate, and conducted farming for many years.

When the Mexican war broke out he raised a company for service, and during the first year of the war between the states, manufactured salt in Florida for the Confederate government. In 1862 he enlisted as a private and was soon put on detach duty at headquarters, being on the staff of Generals Wright and Cummins. He remained until the close of the war, and then resumed mercantile business and farming. After several years in Americus, he moved to the plantation where he now resides, a mile and a half from the courthouse.

He married on October 1, 1844, Elizabeth White, who was born in Virginia, a daughter of Peter and Permelia (Andrews) White. Mrs. Willett died at the age of sixty-eight. Their eight children were: Adelaide, Hattie, Jedediah, James, Augustus, Mollie, Amanda and Joseph.

WALTER B. CHEATHAM, M. D. Of a Georgia family resident in this state since the beginning of the nineteenth century, Dr. Cheatham is one of the ablest representatives of the four generations which have lived and furnished their honorable activities to the civic and economic welfare of Georgia.

Walter B. Cheatham was born August 25, 1853, in Webster county, Georgia. His early life was surrounded by good home influences and he was trained in the public schools. For his career he prepared at the Louisville Medical College, from which he was graduated M. D. with the class of 1877. His first two years in practice were spent in Macon, Georgia, after which he returned to Dawson, and in the subsequent thirty-four years has built up an extensive patronage among the best families of Terrell county. He was in active practice as a physician until 1906. In that year he was elected judge of the Terrell county Court of Ordinary. To this office he brought not only the ability and experience which belonged to every capable physican, but also a competent knowledge and interest in public affairs and a common sense efficiency which have done much to promote the fiscal welfare of this county. For many years Dr. Cheatham was an influential member of both the Terrell County and the State Medical Association. He has taken a leading part in municipal affairs, having served as mayor of Dawson and as member of the Dawson board of education. He is now president of the Dawson Telephone Company.

Dr. Cheatham married in 1878 Miss Sallie G. Farrar. Mrs. Cheatham was born in Jackson county, Georgia, in June, 1856, a daughter of G. W. and Fanny (Day) Farrar. Their two children are Lillian G. Cheatham and Walter B. Cheatham, Jr. Dr. Cheatham takes much interest in social and fraternal work. He is affiliated with P. Schley Lodge No. 229 A. F. & A. M., with Lawrence Chapter No. 96 R. A. M., with Cuthbert Counsel R. & F. M., with the De Molay Commandery No. 5 Knights Templar, with Yaraab Temple of the Mystic Shrine, and also with the Dawson Lodge of the Independent Order of Odd Fellows.

If wholesome character and mental and moral endowment in ancestry count for anything in the lives of descendants, as science asserts, Dr. Cheatham owes much of what he is and what he has accomplished to forebears of whom any one might be proud. Virginia was the original family seat in America of the Cheathams. Dr. Cheatham's great-grandfather was Arthur Cheatham, who spent his earlier years in Charlotte county, Virginia, then moved to Pittsylvania county, and in 1800 came southward to Georgia, and in the pioneer days located with his family in Jefferson county.

The head of the next generation in descent was grandfather Obadiah P. Cheatham, who was born in Charlotte county, Virginia, in 1794. He was a child when his parents migrated to Georgia, and he grew to manhood in Jefferson county, where he learned the trade of a millwright. Public spirited and patriotic he served in the War of 1812 and in the Indian wars of 1836 and 1837. He participated in the battle of Echaway Nochaway. For some time his residence was in Butts county, Georgia, then in Stewart county, where he followed his trade, and also engaged in farming until his death in 1850. Obadiah C. Cheatham married Charity Bryan, who was born in Mecklenberg county, North Carolina. The Bryan family thus introduced to the Cheatham relationship was distinguished for soldierly qualities and solid civic worth. Clement Bryan, the father of Mrs. Cheatham, was a native of North Carolina, and her grandfather was Col. Needham Bryan, who was a Revolutionary soldier and while serving in the colonial army fought in the battle of Allemance. Col. Bryan subsequently settled in Smithfield, North Carolina, where he spent his last days. Clement Bryan from North Carolina became a pioneer of Randolph county, Georgia, and until his death was identified with the advancement of that county's agricultural and industrial interests. He married Edith Smith, a daughter of Col. David Smith, who was a soldier of the Revolution. Colonel Smith's wife was Charity Whitfield. The founder of the Smith family in America was John Smith, father of Colonel David, who was born in England in 1700, and came to America after reaching manhood, finally in 1742 locating in North Carolina at what is now the town of Smithfield, which was named in his honor. John Smith married Elizabeth Whitfield, also a native of England, and they both died in Smithfield, where their bodies were laid to rest in the churchyard.

The third generation of the Cheatham family in Georgia is represented by Clement A. Cheatham, father of Dr. Cheatham. Clement A. Cheatham was born in 1822 in Butts county, Georgia, acquired his elementary education in the public schools, finished preparation for his profession in the Charleston Medical College and immediately on leaving college located in Stewart county, Georgia. He next moved to Weston in Webster county, where he practiced and lived until the organization of Terrell county in 1856, in which year he took up his residence in Dawson, and was actively identified with the practice of medicine until his death at the age of sixty-six years. Dr. Clement A. Cheatham married Elizabeth Irwin, a daughter of Jared Irwin, the third, and the descendant of a pioneer family of Georgia. Concerning the Irwin family the following authentic information was written by Jared I. Irwin of Sandersville:—"The founder of the Irwin family in America was Hugh Irwin, a native of Ireland who came to this country in colonial days, and settled in Mecklenburg county, North Carolina, where he lived several years. He then removed to Burke county, Georgia, accompanied by his family, being an early settler of that locality. His three sons, John, William and Jared removed to Washington county, Georgia, and secured large tracts of land a few miles southwest of Sandersville. The son Jared, who became prominent in public affairs, was brigadier general of militia, and represented Washington county in the state legislature for several years, being president of the Senate. He was a member of the Constitutional Conventions of 1789 and 1798, serving as president of the latter body, and was governor of Georgia from 1796 to 1798, and from 1806 to 1809. He also had the honor of signing the act rescinding the Yazoo Law, and had the infamous Land Law, that was an imposition upon the people, burned in the public square at Louisville, which was then the capital of the state." Gov. Hugh Irwin died March 1, 1818, and his remains are buried at his old home in Union Hill, Washington county, where the state has erected a monument to his memory. Jared' Irwin, the third, father of Elizabeth Irwin, was born and reared in Washington county, where he lived until after his marriage with Ann Williams. When the country lying between the Oconee and Chattahoochee rivers was surrendered to the settlers he removed to Stewart county, and there met his untimely death during the battle of Shepards Plantation after the massacre at the Battle of Roanoke.

Mrs. Clement A Cheatham survived her husband several years, passing away at the age of seventy-six years. She reared eight children as follows: Loverd Bryan, Thomas A., Walter B., Annie I., Isabella, Katie, Fanny E., and Charlie V.

JOHN WRIGHT WHEATLEY. An early and honored resident of Sumter county, John Wright Wheatley, of Americus, has for many years been prominently identified with the leading business and public interests of that city, and influential in promoting its material growth and prosperity. He was born, June 30, 1833, in Northumberland county, Pennsylvania, which was likewise the birthplace of his father, John Wheatley, Jr.

His paternal grandfather, John Wheatley (1), was born and reared in the city of Nottingham, England, where as a young man he was engaged in mercantile pursuits. His sympathy with the French Revolutionists becoming the subject of warm discussions, he decided to seek a home on foreign shores, and in 1788 immigrated to America, locating in Northumberland county, Pennsylvania, carrying with him a stock of merchandise, which he afterwards traded for a farm. A man of much ability, he soon became prominent in public life, and served as justice of the peace and scrivener. He lived to a venerable age, passing away in 1840, at the age of eighty-eight years.

John Wheatley (2), who died in 1873, aged seventy-six years, married Harriett Withington, a daughter of Martin Withington, whose grandmother, Rachael Thornton, was the only female survivor of the Wyoming Massacre which occurred July 3, 1778.

Gleaning his early education in the village schools, John Wright Wheatley remained beneath the parental roof-tree until seventeen years old. A manly, self-reliant youth, full of pluck and determination, he bade good-bye to friends and relatives in 1850, and started forth in quest of fortune. On December 24th, of that year, he made his appearance in Americus, Georgia, which was then a small village, giving scant promise of its present prosperous condition, while the country roundabout was but thinly populated. There were few railways in the state, and he made his advent on foot, walking part of the way from Macon to Americus. Industrious and capable, he soon found employment with his cousin, Mr. R. T. McCoy, as a clerk in his general store, which was located on the corner of Lee and Lamar streets. When Mr. McCoy sold out, Mr. Wheatley, in partnership with Mr. McCoy's brother, H. Kent McCoy, embarked in the drug business in Americus. Subsequently Mr. H. Kent McCoy entered the legal profession, and was later made chief justice of the state of Georgia. In 1855 their store was burned, and Mr. Wheatley accepted a position as bookkeeper for P. H. Oliver, a general merchant, whose store stood at the corner of Colton avenue and Lamar street, near the site now occupied by the Commercial City Bank building. The firm failing in 1857, Mr. Wheatley took charge of the stock, which was later purchased by Nelson Tift, of Albany.

Being out of a situation, Mr. Wheatley returned to his old home in Pennsylvania, but his sympathies were so evidently with the South that he thought best to come back to Georgia, and on his return to Americus he entered the employ of Kendrick & Johnson, general merchants, as bookkeeper, and ere long bought out the entire business. Early in 1861 the building and stock were destroyed by fire, and during the same year he was elected clerk of the Court of Ordinary of Sumter county. During the latter part of the war Mr. Wheatley was appointed aide-de-camp, with the rank of major, on the staff of General McCoy, and with him went to the defence of Atlanta, and after the fall of that city was an active participant in the engagements at Jonesboro and Griswoldville. At the close of the war, his sole possessions consisted of about a hundred bales of cotton, for a part of which he received twenty-five cents a pound.

Forming a partnership with his brother-in-law, W. H. C. Dudley, in 1866, Mr. Wheatley, as senior member of the firm of J. W. Wheatley & Company, engaged in the banking business, being affiliated with William Bryce & Company, of New York. This firm continued successfully until 1887, when it was merged into the Bank of Southwest Georgia, of which bank Mr. Wheatley was elected vice president. In 1897 he was made president of that institution, and continued in that position until 1905, when he retired from active business. Upon the organization of the Commercial City Bank, he was made honorary president, an office which he has since filled most acceptably to all concerned. His beautiful home, "Harmony Hall," is pleasantly located on the Oglethorpe road, about two miles from the court house, and its hospitable doors are ever open to his many friends.

The record of Mr. Wheatley's public service has been as honorable and distinguished as his business achievements. For thirty years he rendered faithful service as secretary of the board of county commissioners. During that period the county buildings were erected, and much to the surprise of the majority of people in the county; all were paid for in full without any increase in the tax rate, payment being made from the sinking fund which Mr. Wheatley had created.

Mr. Wheatley married, May 10, 1855, Mary E. Dudley, who was born in Lexington, Georgia, November 20, 1835. Her father, George Edward Dudley, who settled in Americus in 1840, was one of the most prominent lawyers of the South, and the author of Dudley's Law Reports, which were the first records of the supreme court ever published, and which are standard authority today. Mr. Dudley married Caroline Crawford, whose father, Honorable William H. Crawford, a well-known statesman, served as secretary of the treasury in the cabinet of President Monroe, and was also minister to France, and was a presidential candidate in 1824 with Adams, Jackson and Clay. Four children have blessed the union of Mr. and Mrs. Wheatley, namely: Caroline Susan, wife of L. C. Smith, of New York City; John W. Wheatley, Jr., who married Emma Bird; George Dudley Wheatley, who married Maggie Calloway; and William H. Crawford Wheatley, of whom a brief personal account may be found on another page of this work.

HON. WILLIAM HARRIS CRAWFORD WHEATLEY. Enterprising, progressive, and possessing the attributes that would make him a leader in any sphere he might select, Hon. William H. C. Wheatley, of Americus, has long been an important factor in the development and promotion of the industrial, mercantile, manufacturing and agricultural prosperity of Sumter county, and a commanding figure in its financial circles. He was born December 6, 1866, in Americus, a son of John Wright and Mary (Dudley) Wheatley, of whom a brief sketch may be found elsewhere in this biographical volume.

. Obtaining his elementary education in the public schools of his native city, "Crawford Wheatley," as he is familiarly known, further advanced his studies at the Lehigh University, in South Bethlehem, Pennsylvania, and later entered Steven's Institute of Technology, at Hoboken, New Jersey, from which he graduated, in 1887, with the degree of Mechanical Engineer. Returning then to Americus, he was here city engineer for a year. In 1888, becoming superintendent of the Americus' Oil Company, he built a large oil mill in the city, it being one of the leading industrial plants of that time. Subsequently he entered the firm of C. M. Wheatley & Company, architects and builders, with which he was identified for three years. In 1891 Mr. Wheatley organized the Americus Construction Company, of which he was vice-president until 1893, at the same time serving as president of the Americus Refrigerating Company. During those two years both firms, aided by his untiring energy and activity, rapidly increased and extended their operations and their business. From 1893 until 1896 Mr. Wheatley was a member of the firm of T. A. Klatz & Company, architects, and carried on a substantial business. Giving up active labor in 1896, he spent four years in rest, recreation and observation, in the meantime visiting the West Indies, and traveling extensively throughout Europe.

Returning to Americus in 1900, Mr. Wheatley was elected treasurer of the Sheffield-Huntington Company, a position for which his executive and financial ability amply qualified him. Resigning from that firm in 1905, Mr. Wheatley accepted the position of vice president of the Americus National Bank and in 1908 organized the Commercial City Bank, of which he is vice president and the principal stockholder, and which is housed in one of the finest buildings in the city. He has also been officially connected with various other organizations of prominence, having served as president of the Americus Manufacturing and Improvement Company; as president of the Carnegie Library Association; and as president of the local Board of Trade, under whose auspices the automobile road extending from Andersonville to Thomasville was established.

Mr. Wheatley has likewise been a dominant power in public affairs, and has rendered his fellow-citizens valuable assistance in positions of trust and responsibility. He served on the staff of Governor Terrell, holding the rank of lieutenant colonel, and in 1905 and 1906 represented the thirteenth senatorial district in the state senate, in which he served as chairman of the joint committee on new counties, and was the author of the Lieutenant Governor Bill of that session.

He was a delegate to the Democratic national convention held in Denver, Colorado, in July, 1908, which put in nomination the name of William J. Bryan for presidential candidate, and in 1912 was delegate at large to Democratic national convention held in Baltimore, Maryland. In November, 1912, he was elected as a representative to the Georgia legislature without any solicitation on his part, his election being a proof of his great popularity as a man, and as a citizen. Mr. Wheatley is a member of the library commission of the state of Georgia, and is treasurer and fiscal agent of the third district agricultural and mechanical school, an organization of great value to the young men and boys of this section of the state. He is greatly interested in the advancement of the agricultural interests of the state and county, and is himself an extensive owner of real estate.

On October 12, 1897, Mr. Wheatley was united in marriage with Miss Helen Huntington, a daughter of Charles A. and Virginia (Wyatt) Huntington, and of their union one son has been born, Charles Huntington Wheatley. Socially Mr. Wheatley is a member of the New York Athletic Club, of the Capital City Club, and the Piedmont Driving Club, of Atlanta. Fraternally he is a member of the M. B. Council Lodge, Free and Accepted Masons; of Wells Chapter, No. 42, Royal Arch Masons; of De Molay Commandery, Knights Templar; and of Alee Temple, Ancient Arabic Order Nobles of the Mystic Shrine, and has served as potentate in the southwest district.

JOHN F. COCKE. A well-known and highly esteemed resident of Dawson, Terrell county, John F. Cocke is distinguished both for his own life and work and for the honored ancestry from which he traces his descent. The member of a Georgia family that dates back to colonial times, he was born June 16, 1857, on a plantation in Lee county, Georgia. He is a descendant in the fifth generation from Caleb Cocke, the immigrant ancestor, his lineage being thus traced: Caleb,[1] Zebulon,[2] John,[3] Isaac Perry,[4] and John F.[5]

Caleb[1] Cocke, said to have been a lineal descendant of Lord High Admiral Cocke, of France, immigrated to America from England about 1710, settling in North Carolina. It is said that he was a very large man, and was called the "Great Hunter." Zebulon[2] Cocke was born and bred in North Carolina. Coming from there to Georgia in 1764, he located in Burke county on a two-hundred-acre tract of land granted him by King George. During the Revolution he fought with the colonists in their struggle for independence. At the opening of that war he had upwards of five hundred head of cattle on his farm, and at its close he had but one ox left with which to do his farm work, all of the other cattle having been taken by the British. He was one of the very first Baptists in the state, and a charter member of the Back Camp Baptist church, which was organized in 1788, and to which he donated four acres of land. He was twice married, his second wife, great grandmother of Mr. Cocke, having been Mrs. Sarah Field, nee Perry.

John[3] Cocke was born on the parental homestead, in Burke county, Georgia, September 4, 1784. Inheriting the patriotic ardor of his father, he served as a soldier in the War of 1812. About 1828 he removed to Lee county, Georgia, where he bought land that was in its pristine wildness, and with the aid of his slaves cleared and improved a fine plantation, on which he spent the remainder of his life. The maiden name of his wife was Lydia Davis. She was a daughter of Benjamin and Elizabeth (Daniel) Davis, and a granddaughter on the paternal side of Rev. Elnathan Davis, a noted Baptist preacher of Virginia. On the maternal side, she was also of honored ancestry, her Grandfather Daniel having been governor of the Carolinas before they were divided, and afterwards governor of South Carolina. All of her grandparents spent the closing years of their lives in Lee county, Georgia.

Isaac Perry[4] Cocke was born in Burke county, Georgia, and subsequently went with the family to Lee county. There he began life for himself, working as a farm laborer at low wages. Industrious and economical, he accumulated quite a sum of money, which he invested in land, later buying slaves with which to work his property. During his earlier life in Lee county deer and other kinds of wild game were abundant, and often did much damage to the growing crops. There being no railways in the state, he used to team his cotton to Macon, one hundred miles distant, the trip being a long and tedious one. He did not depend entirely upon cotton as a crop, but raised various other things, including cattle, hogs and poultry. He was very successful in his operations, and as his means allowed invested in other tracts of land, at his death having title to five thousand acres of choice land. His home plantation, located eight miles west of Liberty, was furnished with substantial buildings, and well stocked. He maintained a summer home at Griffin, but otherwise lived on his home farm until his death, in 1863.

Isaac Perry[4] Cocke married Almeda Griffin, who was born in Henry county, Georgia, where her parents, William and Martha (Barnett) Griffin, were, as far as known, life-long residents. She survived her husband, and married a second time. By her first marriage she reared three children, namely: John Franklin, the special subject of this brief biographical review; Almira Florine; and Isaac Perry, Jr.

John F.[5] Cocke obtained his rudimentary education in the public schools of Carterville, later attending Bowdon College, in Bowdon, Georgia. Completing his studies, he settled in Lee county on land that had come to him by inheritance, and was there extensively and profitably engaged in agricultural pursuits until 1899. In order that his children might have better educational advantages, Mr. Cocke then rented his large plantation, and settled in Dawson, buying an estate of four acres, with good buildings thereon, in the village. He still lives on that place, but has since bought another plantation, consisting of two hundred and fifty acres of highly productive land, in Terrell county.

Mr. Cocke married, in 1877, Annie Eliza Moreland. She was born in Lee county, a daughter of John and Eliza (Sikes) Moreland, natives of Baker county, and life-long residents of Georgia. Mr. and Mrs. Cocke are the parents of five children, namely: Annie Elouise; Charles Dudley; Stephen Moreland; and John Edwin and Julian Franklin, twins. Annie E., wife of James Bascom Hoyle, has three children, Annie Elouise, Mary Elizabeth, and Myra. Mr. and Mrs. Cocke are both members of the Methodist Episcopal church. Fraternally Mr. Cocke belongs to P. T. Schley Lodge, No. 229, Ancient Free and Accepted Order of Masons.

COLONEL ROBERT LEE COLDING. Savannah has a legal fraternity of which she has every reason to be proud, some of the members of the profession having achieved nation-wide prominence. Among its eminent representatives is Col. Robert Lee Colding, whose excellent equipment has given him high standing and a practice of large proportions. As his Christian name indicates, Colonel Colding comes of staunch Southern origin and a glance at the history of his forbears reveals a number of soldiers and patriots. He himself is a public-spirited citizen of the best type, ever ready to give his support to any measure which in his judgment will be likely to advance the general welfare.

Colonel Colding, who has lived his entire life in the city of Savannah, is the son of Capt. Silas M. and Laura Frances (Sibley) Colding. The father, who died in 1886, when the subject was still a lad, was born in Screven county, Georgia, and came to Savannah a bare-footed boy. He served in the Confederate army throughout the war between the states, becoming a regimental staff captain in the Fiftieth Georgia Infantry, in the army of northern Virginia. For a long number of years he was a successful cotton merchant; in his latter career as such, however, suffering financial reverses. The mother of Colonel Colding was born in Bridgeton, New Jersey; when she was a year old her parents removed to Florida and later to Georgia. She was the daughter of Samuel Shute Sibley, a widely known newspaper man of the earlier days. Long before the war he was the proprietor of the *Savannah Georgian*, which was the predecessor of the present *Morning News*. The paternal grandfather, Henry Colding, was born in Screven county, Georgia, of parents who came from Barnwell District, South Carolina. Henry Colding's father, Blanchard Colding, of South Carolina, was a Continental soldier in the Revolutionary war. The family originated in Denmark, migrating thence to Scotland and in Colonial days coming to America. They located first in New York after their arrival in the land of the stars and stripes and subsequently came to South Carolina.

On account of the parental financial reverses above referred to, Colonel Colding was early in life thrown upon his own resources. But although in those early days the doors of the schools were locked in his face, the doors of education were not and he found in the school of life a training quite invaluable. After some attendance in the public schools of the city, he entered the Savannah Military Academy, paying for his tuition out of his own earnings. Meantime a long gathering desire to become a lawyer reached the point of crystallization and he began his legal studies here, being duly admitted to the bar on June 18, 1898. He has since been admitted to practice in the state, supreme and federal courts and in the United States supreme court. He has a fine legal mind and is a hard-working and successful lawyer, always having a large amount of legal business, and his conduct of his law business being notable for thoroughness and efficiency.

He is the sound and substantial type of citizen who wins the well-deserved confidence of the people and he has been called to serve in several public capacities. He was county attorney of Cheatham county for five years, from 1903 to 1908. He is an ex-member of the city council, of which body he was vice chairman and chairman of the fire committee. He was colonel on the staff of Governor Terrell and is now on the list of retired officers with the rank of lieutenant commander.

Colonel Colding is one of the most prominent Masons of the state. He is past master of Solomon's Lodge, No. 1; deputy grand master of the Grand Lodge of Georgia; past high priest of Georgia Chapter No. 3; past grand high priest of the Grand Royal Arch Chapter of Georgia; past thrice illustrious master, Georgia Council No. 2, Royal and Select Masters; past grand master, Grand Council of Georgia; past commander, Palestine Commandery, No. 7, Knights Templar. He is now preceptor of Richard Joseph Nunn Consistory, 32nd degree, A. and A. S. R. He is also a high priest and prophet and representative of Alee Temple, A. A. O. N. M. S. He is also past exalted ruler of the local lodge of Elks. Colonel Colding has been connected with the formation of many lodges and has been instrumental in spreading the fine principles of Masonry, especially in southeastern Georgia. During his progress through Masonry many honors have been conferred upon him, each succeeding honor bringing increased satisfaction to the brethren of Savannah. He enjoys a great degree of popularity and is well worthy of the success he has achieved and the honors that have been conferred upon him.

Colonel Colding married Miss Annie E. McIntyre, daughter of Edward McIntyre, of Savannah, who was for many years comptroller of the Central of Georgia Railroad. The demise of this lady occurred in 1898.

JOHN T. CHASTAIN. The Chastains, father and son, have taken part in the most important events of southern Georgia. The father was one of the early settlers of the district, and figured in the pioneer struggles with wild land and wilder men. The son, who is the subject of this brief history, not only fought with the hundreds of Georgia's brave sons for the cause of the Confederacy, but has given his later life in the interests of peace and good citizenship.

John T. Chastain was born on a plantation in Thomas county, Georgia, on the twenty-fourth of November, 1841. His father, John Chastain, came into the world in North Georgia, in 1798, the son of James Chastain, whose wife was a Miss Morgan before her marriage. James Chastain was of French Huguenot ancestry. His son, John, though he had but limited opportunities, managed to obtain a pretty fair education for those days, and migrated to southern Georgia as a very young man. Like him, his four brothers all left the home neighborhood to settle other parts of the country, James and Morgan going to Dougherty county, Georgia, Thomas locating in Thomas county, and the fourth making his way southwest to Texas.

When John Chastain, Senior, reached the southern part of Georgia, the country thereabouts presented a very different appearance from what it does now. The territory then comprised in Irwin and Early counties, but now subdivided into several additional counties, including Thomas county, was wild and uncultivated. The woods were full of game, and although the Indians had ceded the land in the district to the state, some few still lingered in the vicinity, though ostensibly making their home in Florida, across the line. No one felt much anxiety concerning the redskins, however, since they were supposed to be friendly, and under the complete control of the state. John Chastain, then single, settled with two other young men in a cabin which they built a few miles south of Thomasville. On Saturday they journeyed a short distance northward to a settlement to spend the Sabbath, and on their return, they found that their cabin had been looted, and everything of value stolen, including their guns, which they had very unwisely left behind them. Naturally, they were very angry, and started in pursuit of the marauders, and by nightfall came upon a camp of Indians.

For caution's sake, the young men waited until morning, and then entered the camp of the Indians. While the red men were at breakfast, they entered the camp, and John Chastain, who could talk Indian, asked them if they had seen a stray horse. The Indians of course had not seen any such animal, but the young men, looking about, saw their guns in the possession of some of the braves, and knew that they were on the track of the thieves. When the Indians invited them to partake of their fare, they accepted the offer, but complained that they had no knives to eat with. The Indians gave them knives, and they commenced to eat. They watched their chance, however, and finally made a rush, securing their guns, and putting the thieves at their mercy. The Indians confessed to the theft, but promised to return everything they took, if the young men would promise not to report the offense to the governor, who, they feared, would deprive them of their bounty. The youths assented to this, and the Indians packed the stolen goods on the back of a horse, and sent a warrior to accompany John Chastain and his companions on their homeward journey.

Unsuspecting, the little party set out, jubilant at having recovered their property so easily. They did not allow for the treacherous nature of the savages, however, and before they had gone far, they found themselves in the midst of an ambush. The two comrades of John Chastain were murdered, but he escaped with only the loss of an index finger. He made his way back through the woods to Thomasville, where a party of irate settlers at once started in pursuit of the savages, armed for vengeance, but unfortunately, the Indians made good their escape. The crime was reported to the governor, however, and he demanded the appearance of the tribe at Tallahassee, where John Chastain identified five of the band which had beset him and his two comrades. These Indians were sentenced to suffer the extreme penalty, and though one died in captivity, and one escaped, the other three were hanged as an example to all red men who contemplated molesting the white settlers. The trial and hanging took place at Thomasville, and the sentence of the Indians was the first death penalty ever executed in Thomas county.

After his adventure with the Indians, Mr. Chastain lived for some time at Thomasville. A natural mechanic, he was by trade a carpenter, and helped to build some of the first houses ever erected in Thomasville. After his marriage, which occurred in Thomasville, he lived on at that town for a while, and then bought land about nine miles north, where he engaged in farming until his death, which occurred in 1851. Even after he was settled on his own farm, he was frequently called upon to exercise his knowledge of carpentry in the repair and erection of houses, for in that newly settled country, artisans were much in demand.

Mary Carlton Chastain, the mother of the subject of this sketch, was a native of Sampson county, North Carolina. Her father, John Carlton, was also born in North Carolina, of early English ancestry. John Carlton moved from his native state to Georgia, first sojourning a short time in Bulloch county, and then going on to Thomas county, where a son and daughter had already taken up their abode. He bought land in lots Nos. 85 and 86, now adjoining the city of Thomasville He built a house on this property, and cleared a farm, upon which he resided for several years. There were many settlers from North Carolina in the community, and to them as to all comers, Mr. Carlton dispensed open-handed hospitality. He was noted in his community not only for his kindliness and generosity, but also for his true Christian character. Himself a faithful Methodist, he educated two of his sons to spread the Gospel as preachers of that denomination.

After spending several years as a resident of the Thomasville district, Mr. Carlton sold out, and moved across the river, where he resided a few years before going to the home in Taylor county, Florida, where he lived until his death at the ripe old age of ninety-four years. His wife also reached an advanced age, departing from this life at the age of ninety-three. Her name was Nancy Alderman Carlton, also a native of North Carolina. Mr. and Mrs. Carlton had a large family, one of the members of which was Mary, the mother of John T. Chastain. Mrs. Chastain survived her husband by a number of years, dying at the age of eighty-seven. She reared six children to take their places as useful and efficient members of the community. These are Hardy M., Sarah A., Elizabeth, Sophronia, John T., and Julia E.

After attending the Thomasville schools, and taking a course in Fletcher Institute, John T. Chastain learned to set type in the office of the *Southern Enterprise*, a paper published by L. C. Bryan and R. R. Renlah. Previously, while still a student at the Institute, in 1853, he had inked the type to print the first paper ever issued in Thomas county, the *Thomasville Watchman*, of which Freeman W. Johnson was editor and proprietor. In 1862, Mr. Chastain enlisted in Company E, of the Fiftieth Regiment, of Georgia Volunteer Infantry. He remained with this regiment for a time, as part of the Coast defense, and then was sent North, where he joined the Army of North Virginia. Late in the year 1862, he was detailed for hospital service and entered on detached duty until after the close of the war.

Upon his return home from his military duties in 1865, John Chastain secured a position in the office of the *Southern Enterprise*, remaining upon the staff of that paper until shortly before it was merged with the *Times*. Previous to leaving the employ of the newspaper, Mr. Chastain had purchased the old homestead which had belonged to his grandfarther Carlton; he has resided upon this property ever since. His dwelling is a commodious frame one, set well back from the street in a grove of fine live oaks, magnolias, holly and pecan trees, with palms and flowering shrubs lending to the attractiveness of the place.

In 1865, Mr. Chastain was married at Farmville, Virginia, to Tishia Davis, who was born at Farmville, the daughter of Sheldon and Mary (Meadows) Davis, both life-long residents of the Old Dominion state. The union of Mr. and Mrs. Chastain was blessed with six children, Olin S., Corinne, Elmo, Minnie, Mattie, and Arthur T. Of these, Olin married Maude Fallen; Corinne, now dead, became the wife of E. R. West of Albany, Georgia; Elmo married Annie Smith, and has five children, Catherine, Shelton, Margaret, Elmo, and Fred; Minnie, who was the wife of Judge T. H. Parker, of Moultrie, Georgia, died leaving three children, Aileen, Thaddeus Hall, and John Chastain; Mattie passed away at the untimely age of seventeen; Arthur T. is married to Aileen Wade, and has four children, Vivian, Josephine, Minnie and Madie.

Mr. and Mrs. John T. Chastain are passing their declining years happily at their beautiful home. Although a Democrat, and an ardent one, Mr. Chastain does not, nor has he ever, taken any active part in the political game, preferring to serve his country as a good citizen and a faithful voter. Both he and his wife are recognized as factors for good in the life of the community, and are valued workers in the Missionary Baptist church, of which they are members. Mr. Chastain has farming interest and the acres he has under cultivation yield him a substantial income.

VIVIAN L. STANLEY. Now that men are too busy to gather around the stove in the country store, or in the post office at meal time, for the discussion of politics, and weighty decisions as to how the government should be run, the newspaper has become of supreme importance, not only as a disseminator of news, but as a powerful influence on the minds of the people. The power of the written word! How little people realize its subtile influence, and how often one hears the words, "I believe nothing the newspapers say." But this very person though perhaps not believing the papers is yet unconsciously influenced by them, and herein lies the power of the editor. Therefore when people are as fortunate as the people of Dublin, Georgia, they should give thanks. Vivian Stanley, general manager and editor of the *Courier-Dispatch*, of this city, is a man who is fully conscious of the responsibility that rests upon his shoulders and in every crisis will be found standing on the side of the progressives, working for the cause that will benefit the greatest number of people, an eager champion of the right and quick to condemn the tricks and clever schemes of those who are working for self aggrandizement. Mr. Stanley has had a life-long experience as a newspaper man, and has won during this career the friendship of all classes of people.

The birth of Vivian L. Stanley occurred in Dublin, Georgia, his parents being Capt. Rollin A. Stanley and Martha (Lowthen) Stanley. His grandfather and father were both men of prominence in the state of Georgia, the former having been the first surveyor general in the state of Georgia, and the latter having been the first solicitor general in the Oconee circuit. Capt. Rollin Stanley won his military title through his service in the army, as a captain in one of the Georgia regiments. He was a lawyer by profession and both he and his wife were natives of Georgia. He was a successful lawyer, and his children were brought up amid the influences of a cultured home life. The family consisted of eight children, five of whom are alive. Of these Ira L. is interested in the newspaper work in Dallas, Texas; Frank L. lives in Midville, Georgia; Florrie is the wife of W. R. Haynes of Macon, Georgia, who is there engaged in business. Augusta married Judge J. S. Adams, and Rollin and Mattie died in infancy.

After the completion of the education of Vivian Stanley he went at once into the newspaper business, serving in various capacities and learning the profession of journalism from the bottom upward. He has been in this profession ever since save for the few years in which he gave up his work to serve the interests of the people. This was during the administration of President Cleveland, when he held the office of postmaster of Dublin, also serving two years at this post during the administration of President McKinley. After his resignation from this public office, he once more took up his newspaper work. At this time there were two others beside himself who were interested in the work, namely, his brother, H. M. Stanley, and Mr. Hilton, of the Commercial Bank. At the time of the organization of the committee of commerce and labor, H. M. Stanley retired from the newspaper business to take charge of this new office. The *Courier-Dispatch* is now owned by a stock company, and the increase in circulation during the years that Mr. Stanley has been in charge is sufficient proof of his able management. The circulation now amounts to five thousand, and Mr. Stanley has added greatly to the revenue of the paper by establishing an up-to-date job printing department, which has a reputation of doing unusually good work. The *Courier-Dispatch* is the result of the combination of three papers, the *Courier*, the *Dispatch* and the *Times*. The *Courier* and the *Dispatch* were consolidated about fifteen years ago, and about two years ago, in June, 1909, the *Times* was taken over, thus making a strong combination, but one that required a keen mind and a willing hand to manage successfully.

In addition to his newspaper work Mr. Stanley has been active in other fields. From constant study of the political outlook, both local and national, he became fitted to play an important part in such affairs, and though he never cared for political preferment, yet he was elected alderman and was also made clerk of the city council, serving one term in the first mentioned office and three years in the latter position. His honesty, and conscientious endeavor to obey the will of those who put him in office, as well as his knowledge of the economic and social evils of the times made him an invaluable servant to the people.

Mr. Stanley was married to Ella Martin, a daughter of William and Julia A. Martin, of Sandersville, Georgia. Four children have been born to Mr. and Mrs. Stanley, namely: Martha, Vivian, Elenore and Rollin. Both Mr. and Mrs. Stanley are members of the Baptist church, and Mr. Stanley is affiliated in a fraternal way with the Knights of Pythias.

DOCTOR ALGERINE T. SUMMERLIN holds an important position in Dublin, Georgia, not only in a professional way, but as an able business man, well known for his good management and his common sense. He is a dentist of high order of ability and is an honor to the profession that is now beginning to assume so much importance in the eyes of the public, and for which science has done so much in the last decade or so. As an extensive landed proprietor, Doctor Summerlin has the responsibility of the many people, men, women and children who live on his plantations, for the relationship between master and servant in this section of the country is still more or less a paternal one. It is in this relation that Doctor Summerlin has proved himself a man of more than average ability, and in thinking for others he has developed those traits of character that have so endeared him to the community.

Doctor Summerlin was born in Bulloch county, Georgia, near the town of Statesboro, in 1860. His father was James Summerlin and his mother was Eliza (Lanier) Summerlin, both of whom were natives of Bulloch county. The great-great-grandfather of Doctor Summerlin on the paternal side was a native of North Carolina, and came to Georgia when Bulloch county was more or less of a wilderness. The family has therefore been in this county since pioneer days and has become thoroughly identified with the interests of this section. James Bulloch was a farmer, but his peaceful life on the old plantation was interrupted by the call to arms and the outbreak of the Civil war. He enlisted in a Georgia regiment and served with a division of the army that caught deserters and punished renegades and carried on a kind of guerrilla warfare. His career was brought to a sudden termination by his death at the hands of bushwhackers in Coffer county and here he was buried.

The youth of Doctor Summerlin was spent on his father's plantation where he grew up, the eldest of a large family. Both his father and his mother were twice married. His father had four children by a previous marriage and three by his marriage with the doctor's mother, Eliza Lanier. After the death of James Summerlin, his widow married G. Green and became the mother of six children. Doctor Summerlin was the eldest of his mother's children. His sister Alice is now the wife of H. B. Kennedy, a successful farmer of Bulloch county, and his brother Willie A., is his partner in the dental practice in Dublin. Doctor Summerlin received his education in the schools near his home, and for his professional training entered the Baltimore Dental College, from which he was graduated in 1886. He at once began the practice of dentistry in Bulloch county, and the following year came to Dublin, where he has since resided, and where he has been so successful.

The confidence which his friends and neighbors and fellow townsmen repose in him has been shown by the fact that they have twice elected him mayor of Dublin. He proved an able executive, but with this exception, could never be induced to enter the political arena. Fraternally, he is a member of the Royal Arcanum. His wife is a member of the Christian church, but he believes in the creed of no especial denomination. His landed estates comprise about one thousand acres and of this large area five hundred acres are under cultivation.

Doctor Summerlin was married on the 10th of April, 1900, to Callie Prince, the daughter of Mrs. A. M. Prince, of Washington county. They have become the parents of three children, as follows: Carolyn was born in July, 1903, A. T., Junior, whose birth occurred in July, 1906, and George, who was born on the 8th of May, 1909.

REV. GEORGE T. HURST. Among the ministers of the gospel in south Georgia few have equaled the record of service and experience of Rev. George Thomas Hurst, now living retired at Cairo in Grady county.

George Thomas Hurst was born seven miles northeast of Thomasville, Georgia, December 1, 1833, so that he is now in his eightieth year. His father was John W. Hurst, born in Screven county and the grandfather was Thomas Hurst. The latter moved from Screven to Thomas county and became one of the early settlers in that vicinity. He bought land seven miles northeast of Thomasville, built a log cabin in the woods and cut and cleared a farm out of the wilderness. When he began raising cotton he had to find a market for it at Tallahassee. He spent all the rest of his life on that homestead, and his remains now rest in the family lot on the farm. His wife survived him several years. In their family were children named William, Thomas, Betsy, Susie, Serena, John W. and Harriet.

John W. Hurst, the father, was a boy when his parents moved to Thomas county, and after his marriage he settled on a tract of land one mile away from his father's home. A few years later, in 1842, he bought other land one mile east of Thomasville, and conducted his plantation with the aid of slave labor up to the time of the war. He continued to make his home there until his death at the age of thirty-nine. Soon after his marriage, he had engaged in one of the Indian campaigns, which marked the final struggle between the whites and the red man in Florida and Georgia. He participated in two battles with the Indians, and in the latter was severely wounded. John W. Hurst married Maria Hicks, a daughter of George Hicks, one of the first

Robert M Hitch

gia, the son of Stephen A. and Tabitha A. (Edwards) Wilson. The subject's great-grandfather, James Wilson, came from North Carolina to Georgia immediately after the Revolutionary war. He was the holder of land grants in Effingham and Wilkes counties. He was a Continental soldier in the Revolution and the records show quite clearly that he had the rank of captain.

Elihu Wilson, grandfather of Horace Emmet Wilson, was born in Effingham county, where he resided until his death. His son, Stephen A. Wilson, lived in the same county, and was ever loyal to the institutions of the South. He served in the army of the Confederacy throughout the war between the states, in which service he attained the rank of captain of Company I of the Forty-seventh Georgia Infantry. Captain Wilson was by occupation a merchant and farmer.

Mr. Wilson, the subject of this brief record, was reared in Effingham county where he received his preliminary education. He graduated from the North Georgia Agricultural College with the class of 1880, and in the fall of the same year located in Savannah. Later he matriculated at the University of Virginia and graduated from the law department in the class of 1885, in which year he returned to this city and began the practice of the law. In 1893 he formed a copartnership with James M. Rogers, his brother-in-law, under the firm name of Wilson & Wilson, and this copartnership has continued until the present time. Mr. Wilson is interested in public affairs, and has been an alderman, city attorney and captain in Savannah Volunteer Guards. He married Miss Tallulah (Lula) Rogers, a native of this city, and from this union a son, Rogers Murchison Wilson, has been born.

ROBERT MARK HITCH, of the Savannah bar, was born at Morven, Brooks county, Georgia, on February 14, 1872, the fourth son and sixth child of Dr. Robert Marcus Hitch and his wife Martha Serena (Fall) Hitch. He was educated at the Morven Academy and at Mercer University, graduating at the latter institution with the degrees of Bachelor of Arts in the class of 1892; studied law under private instructors at Quitman, Georgia, was admitted to practice in the Superior courts of this state by Judge A. H. Hansell, at Thomasville, Georgia, November 3, 1892, practiced law at Quitman for the next several months, and in June, 1893, moved to Savannah, where he has since resided and practiced his profession.

At the present time (1913) Morven is the junction point to two local lines of railroad. In 1872, however, and for a number of years thereafter, it was the country place of Dr. Hitch, at which was located the local postoffice, voting place and general store, a cotton gin, lumber plant and other establishments of minor importance. Near at hand was the public school and in the immediate neighborhood were Methodist, Baptist and Presbyterian churches and a Masonic lodge. From this point radiated several of the most important public roads of the county and the surrounding territory was inhabited by an unusually thrifty and intelligent class of farmers. Dr. Hitch was prominent in the community as a physician, merchant, farmer and business man, was active in church and educational matters and in all movements of public interest. He was born in Laurens county, South Carolina, on June 6th, 1832, graduated at the Augusta Medical College, was married to Martha Serena Fall, daughter of Dr. Calvin J. Fall, in Fayette county, Georgia, April 27th, 1859, at which time he was a practicing physician of that section. At the outbreak of the Civil war he was active in the organization of a military company in Henry, Fayette and adjoining counties; which afterwards became Company B of the Thirtieth Georgia Regiment. A history of that command has been recently written and published by one of its members, Mr. A. P. Adamson. Dr. Hitch served as captain of that company during a large part of the war and participated in numerous battles, including the battle of Chickamaugua and the battles around Atlanta. His services as a surgeon were necessarily required very frequently following engagements in which his command took part and during the latter part of the war he was detailed as regimental surgeon for a considerable part of the time and at the close of the war was mustered out with the rank of major. In commemoration of his services as a Confederate soldier, his son and namesake, the subject of this sketch, was awarded a Confederate Cross of Honor by the Savannah Daughters of the Confederacy on April 26th, 1912. He died at his home at Morven, Georgia, on April 15th, 1888, as the result of constitutional infirmities growing out of exposures to which he was subjected during the war.

The parents of Dr. Hitch were William Winder Hitch and his wife Nancy (Hunter) Hitch, both of Laurens county, South Carolina. William Winder Hitch was the son and oldest child of John Hitch, who was born February 4, 1773, in Somerset county, Maryland, lived there until he was of age, then moved to Laurens county, South Carolina, where he married Katharine Hanna, who became the mother of William Winder Hitch and a number of other children. John Hitch was county treasurer of Laurens county, South Carolina, for twenty years and over, and was well known in that section. He was a son of Louther Hitch, of Somerset county, Maryland, who moved to Laurens county, South Carolina, in his latter years and died there at the age of eighty-eight. The Revolutionary annals of Maryland disclose the names of nine members of the Hitch family on the muster rolls of that commonwealth, including Louther Hitch and Captain Robert Hitch. Several members of the Hanna family in South Carolina were likewise enrolled in the Revolutionary commands of that state. The Christian name of Robert has been handed down through many generations of the Hitch family and recurs with great regularity in the family records in England, particularly in the public records of Yorkshire, Gloucestershire, Berkshire, Worcestershire, Oxfordshire and Bedfordshire, where various branches of the family have resided for several centuries.

On the maternal side the grandparents of Robert M. Hitch were Dr. Calvin Jones Fall, born in Jasper county, Georgia, March 18, 1815, died at Senoia, Georgia, April 10, 1879, and his wife Sarah Battle (Stroud) Fall, born in Clarke county, Georgia, September 21, 1818, died at Senoia, Georgia, January 10, 1891. Dr. Fall and his wife were married in Clarke county, Georgia, November 21, 1839, by Dr. Alonzo Church, at that time president of the State University. Dr. Calvin J. Fall was a son of Dr. John Strader Fall, born in Guilford county, North Carolina, July 22, 1777, and his wife, Martha (Barnett) Fall, born in Mecklenburg, North Carolina, July 19, 1780. Their marriage took place on October 27, 1812. Dr. John Strader Fall lived for a great many years at Decatur, Georgia, died May 3, 1863, and is buried at Fayetteville, Georgia. Martha Barnett Fall died February 19, 1851, and is buried at Decatur, Georgia. Apparently the Fall family were of Scottish origin, Dunbar, Scotland, according to the best information, being the central point of the family in the old country. The Stroud line appears to be purely English, the family records indicating that the earliest settlers in America of that name came to this country shortly after the great civil conflict which grew out of the struggle between Charles I and the Parliament, and were either descended from or closely related to William Stroud, of the English House of Commons, who with Hampden, Pym, Holles and Heselrig constituted the celebrated "Five Members" who led the anti-royalist forces in resisting the encroachments of the Crown. Sarah Battle Stroud, who became the wife of Dr. Calvin J. Fall, was a daughter of William Stroud, who was born in North Carolina and reared in Hancock county, Georgia, and of his wife Serena Ragan Battle, who was a daughter of William Sumner Battle, of Hancock county, Georgia, but who was originally from North Carolina. William Stroud was a son of Mark Stroud and Martha (Strother) Stroud, of Orange county, North Carolina, and Mark Stroud was a son of John Stroud and Sarah (Connelly) Stroud. The Strouds, Strothers and Battles came to North Carolina from Virginia and were all of Revolutionary stock. William Sumner Battle was a member of the noted family of that name, which appears to have been originally of Norman-French origin, and which in both England and America claims among its numbers a numerous and distinguished array of scholars, ministers, lawyers and statesmen. At the present time the family is most numerous in Virginia, North Carolina and Georgia, but various branches of it have achieved distinction in numerous other states North, as well as South. Eight generations of that family are buried in Hancock county, Georgia.

During the year or two immediately prior to his matriculation at Mercer University, Robert M. Hitch was fortunate in having as his instructor Professor Howe, a graduate of Brown University, Rhode Island, and a pure and noble type of Christian gentleman. Being a man of genial, gentle and kindly manners, superior mental endowments, wide reading and profound scholarship, the impression which he made upon his pupils was naturally of a most lasting and elevating nature. Entering the freshman class at Mercer University in January, 1889, and being compelled to leave college in March, 1890, on account of illness, the record made by Mr. Hitch in the first two years of his college career was somewhat irregular. He secured a sophomore speaker's place, but was unable to take part in the speakers' contest at commencement because of illness. In his junior and senior years, however, he improved his record by making the highest average standing in his class. In his junior year he also won the medal for oratory and was one of the champion debaters of the Phi Delta Literary Society at commencement. In his senior year he was elected anniversary speaker for his society.

The first two years of his professional life in Savannah he spent in the offices of Garrard, Meldrim and Newman, where he received splendid instruction under capable lawyers who enjoyed a large and varied practice. In the fall of 1896 he opened law offices on his own account and practiced alone until January, 1898. At that time he formed a co-partnership with the late A. L. Alexander, under the firm name of Alexander & Hitch. That co-partnership was continued until March, 1904, and at that time he entered into his present co-partnership with Dr. Remer L. Denmark, under the firm name of Hitch & Denmark.

Mr. Hitch was admitted to the Supreme Court of Georgia on December 15, 1897; to the United States Circuit and District Courts on February 11, 1895; to the United States Circuit Court of Appeals on August 8, 1901; and to the Supreme Court of the United States on January 31, 1908. He is a member of the American Bar Association and of the Georgia Bar Association. Mr. Hitch is a hard worker, a constant student, and a wide reader. He is general counsel and a director of a number of railroad and banking institutions and commercial corporations, some of state and some of national importance, besides representing a large miscellaneous clientage.

For several years Mr. Hitch was prominent in local military organizations. He first enlisted as a private in June, 1892, in the Quitman

Grays, of Quitman, Georgia, remaining as such until his removal in the following year to Savannah. In January, 1894, he enlisted as a private in Company A of the Savannah Volunteer Guards and was promoted to the rank of corporal on November 7, 1894. Later he was appointed sergeant. Upon the outbreak of the Spanish-American war he promptly volunteered and was largely instrumental in persuading the majority of his company to enlist in a body. The Savannah Volunteer Guards became merged with the Second Georgia Regiment, and Mr. Hitch served in the same as a member of Company M, first as a private and later as sergeant. He was stationed with the Second Georgia Regiment at Tampa, Florida, and at Huntsville, Alabama, and was honorably discharged from service at the latter named station after the signing of the peace protocol by the two countries. On December 28, 1898, he was elected second lieutenant of Company A, Savannah Volunteer Guards, and served as such until June 8, 1900. During this term of service he was for several months recorder of the military examining board and from April 24, 1903, until October 24, 1904, he was captain of the Oglethorpe Light Infantry.

Mr. Hitch was a member of the state legislature from Chatham county in the years 1900 and 1901, and as such gave excellent representation to his constituents. He was a presidential elector from Georgia on the national Democratic ticket in 1908, and he is and has been a prominent and active figure in politics and public life.

Mr. Hitch is widely known as an orator and speaker, and is frequently sought for alumni addresses, club and social banquets and anniversaries, college and high school commencements, etc. Some of his addresses have been of a serious and thoughtful nature, discussing vital questions, and have been printed for general distribution by the several organizations before whom they were delivered. Among these may be mentioned his address on "The Power of Thought," the alumni address at Mercer University, in Macon, on June 1, 1909; the address on "Georgia Secession Convention of 1861 and its Causes," delivered before Francis S. Bartow Camp, United Sons of Confederate Veterans, Savannah, January 21, 1903; and the address delivered at Midway, Liberty county, Georgia, April 29th, 1904, upon the occasion of the marking of certain graves of Confederate soldiers by Liberty Chapter, Daughters of the Confederacy.

Mr. Hitch is a member of a number of clubs and societies. He is past chancellor commander and a charter member of Chivalry lodge, Knights of Pythias, and a member of Live Oak lodge, Independent Order of Odd Fellows. He is a past master of Ancient Landmark lodge, A. F. & A. M. He was twice master of this lodge and at the end of his second term was presented by the lodge with a beautiful past-master's jewel. He is a Royal Arch Mason, a Knight Templar, a thirty-second degree Scottish Rite Mason and a Shriner.

Mr. Hitch was married at Cedar Spring, Spartanburg county, South Carolina, November 20, 1900, to Miss Virginia Eppes Walker, the youngest child and only daughter of Dr. Newton F. Walker, L. L. D., and his wife Virginia (Eppes) Walker, of Cedar Spring. On both paternal and maternal sides Mrs. Hitch is related to a number of the leading families of South Carolina and Virginia. They have two children: Virginia Eppes and Robert M., Jr. In 1911 Mr. Hitch completed a handsome home on the southwest corner of Estill and Atlantic avenues, in Savannah, where he has since resided.

DANIEL FREDERICK DAVENPORT. Prominent among the successful business men of Sumter county is Daniel Frederick Davenport, for many years one of the leading druggists of Americus, where he is at the present time, in 1913, engaged in the insurance and real estate business. He was born in Americus, a son of Colonel Walter Davenport, a pioneer settler of this part of Georgia, and comes of Revolutionary stock, and of substantial Virginian ancestry. His grandfather, Hon. Thomas Davenport, and his great-grandfather Davenport were both life-long residents of Virginia. His great-grandfather, a soldier in the Revolutionary army, took part in several engagements of the war, and on one occasion, when pursued by the British made his escape by running into a swamp, and burying himself, all but his head, in the mud. For services rendered during the struggle for independence he received from the United States government a grant of land, and though he secured a tract of land in Georgia, he never assumed its possession.

Hon. Thomas Davenport, whose birth occurred in Halifax county, Virginia, became one of the largest landholders and tobacco raisers of that county, owning a large plantation, which he operated with slave labor. A man of strong personality, sound judgment and great influence, he was prominent in public life, and was five times honored with an election to Congress, in which he served acceptably for ten years. He married and reared three children, two sons, George and Walter, and a daughter.

Walter Davenport was born in 1817, at Halifax Court House, Virginia, and in his native state received a liberal education. Beginning his active career as an educator, he taught school for a few years, both in Virginia and in Tennessee. Coming to Georgia in 1842, he located in Sumter county, which was then in a state of comparative wildness, deer, wolves, bears, and other wild beasts of the forest being plentiful, often terrorizing the few inhabitants of that locality. There were at that time no railways, and all goods were transported by teams from either Macon or Savannah, the round trip to and from those places consuming several days, and being especially hard when the roads were in a bad condition. Settling in Americus, then a mere hamlet, he was first engaged in the dry goods trade, and later in the hardware business. At the outbreak of the war between the states, he recruited a regiment, of which he was commissioned colonel, but having been appointed tithing agent he did not go to the front. Soon after the close of the conflict, Colonel Davenport established an insurance business, now conducted by two of his sons, and continued a resident of Americus until his death, in 1910, at the venerable age of ninety-three years.

Colonel Davenport married Mary Frederick, a native of Orangeburg, South Carolina. Her father, Daniel Frederick, was born, reared, and married in South Carolina. Subsequently coming with his family to Georgia, he purchased a plantation in Houston county, and operated it successfully, with the help of slaves for a few years. Selling that property, he bought land in Macon county, and there lived until his death, when upward of eighty years of age. His wife, whose maiden name was Caroline Rumph, died at the age of four score years. They reared a family of six children, as follows: Elvira; Ann; Olivia; Mary, who married Colonel Davenport; Clara; and James D., who served as a major in the Confederate service. Colonel Davenport's wife died several years before he did, passing away in May, 1892. They were the parents of nine children, as follows: Florence, wife of Benjamin P. Hollis; Virginia, wife of A. W. Smith; Fanny, wife of Dupont Guerry; James A., of whom a brief personal sketch may be found on another page of this work; Addie, who married D. J. Baldwin; Anna, a twin sister of Addie, married Thomas Dickson; Daniel Frederick, the subject of this brief sketch; Thomas Edwin; and Leila, wife of Lawrence Stapleton.

After leaving the public schools of Americus, Daniel F. Davenport further advanced his education by an attendance in an academy, and at the Agricultural and Mechanical College in Auburn, Alabama. On returning home, he became associated with his father and brother in the drug business, with which he was connected for twenty-eight consecutive years, having built up a large and lucrative patronage in that line. In 1910 Mr. Davenport embarked in the real estate, and the life and accident insurance business, in company with his brother, James A. Davenport, and in his undertakings is meeting with good success.

On November 21, 1890, Mr. Davenport was united in marriage with Miss Leila Crisp, who was born in Ellaville, Georgia, a daughter of Honorable Charles F. and Clara (Burden) Crisp, of whom a brief account may be found elsewhere in this volume. Mr. and Mrs. Davenport have two children, namely: Clara Belle, and Mary Ella. Both Mr. and Mrs. Davenport are members of the Methodist Episcopal church. Mr. Davenport is a member of the college fraternity, Sigma Phi Epsilon; and also belongs to the Woodmen of the World; and to the Patriotic Order Sons of America.

EUGENIUS A. NISBIT, attorney and prominent citizen of Albany, Georgia, was born in Macon, on September 20, 1861. He is the son of James G. Nisbit, born in Madison county, on February 20, 1828, and his wife, Mary Winfield, born in Eatonton on August 18, 1837. The father enlisted in the Jacksonville Artillery and served three months. He was later appointed judge of inferior court of Macon. James G. Nisbit was the son of Eugenius A. Nisbit, the first, who was at one time judge of the superior court of Atlanta.

Eugenius A. Nisbit, of this brief review, was educated in Macon high school and Mercer College, graduating from the latter in 1880. He then engaged in railroad business and came to Americus with the old S. M. Railroad. He read law in the meantime, and in 1897 was admitted to the bar, since which time he has given his entire attention to the legal profession. In 1910 he was elected to the legislature by the Democratic party, to which he gives his political allegiance.

Mr. Nisbit is a Mason of the Royal Arch degree, and has twice been master of the blue lodge. He is a member of the Presbyterian church, and is not married.

JOHN BYRON WIGHT, proprietor of Pecan Grove farm, nursery and orchard at Cairo has been a man of much prominence, and among the pioneers in the agricultural development of this state. He was one of the very first, some twenty-five years ago, to undertake pecan culture on a commercial basis. His accomplishments as a successful grower of pecans are now known all over the southeastern states. He has had a career of varied and valuable service. Mr. Wight was born at Sofkee, in Decatur (now Grady) county, September 28, 1859.

His early life was spent during the decade of the Civil war and reconstruction. From the rural schools he entered Emory College, graduating with the degree of A. B. in 1881. For a brief while he taught in Sofkee; then in 1882 entered Vanderbilt University at Nashville, and spent two years preparing for the Methodist ministry, graduating from that institution in 1884. In the meantime he taught a year and a half at Cairo, and in December, 1886, joined the South Georgia Conference and served consecutively the Trinity circuit, Darien Station, and the Eden circuit. In 1888 he was chosen principal of the Macon District High School at Snow. He was there for one year, and then taught as principal of the Cairo high school for eight years.

The professions of teacher and minister were not to keep him permanently from his career as an agriculturist and pomologist. While at work in the school room he had become interested in farming and fruit growing. In 1887 he planted his first nuts for the cultivation of pecans on a commercial scale, and his first pecan grove was among the pioneer groves in Georgia. In a paper read by Mr. Wight before the American Pomological Society, February 11, 1911, he gave the productive records of a tree, a budded Frotscher, which had been set at his home in Cairo in January, 1892. Mr. Wight explained that it was an exceptional tree, by situation and care bestowed upon it, but its production is not less interesting as showing the possibilities of Georgia pecan culture. The first pound of nuts was gathered in 1897. In the ten year period from 1903 to 1912 inclusive, the average production of the single tree was one hundred and sixty-seven pounds, the largest seasonal yield, 352 pounds, being produced in 1909. The average value of the crop during the last five years has been one hundred dollars. The last three paragraphs of Mr. Wight's paper deserve quotation:—"The bugbear of overproduction has been haunting some who are afraid that more nuts will be produced than can be profitably marketed. With a product as nutritious and palatable as pecans, this generation nor the next will ever see a glut in the pecan market. As nuts become more plentiful, and consequently cheaper in price, there will not only be more consumed but those who are already eating them will use more. Furthermore, they will be introduced into the markets of the world, and hundreds of millions of people will be consuming them where there are now only millions. Our physicians and scientists are telling us that if more nuts and fruits were eaten and less meats, that we would be healthier, and if healthier, then happier. Pecans are getting to be more and more a staple product. Future generations may see over-production; but when that far distant time is reached, wheat will be a glut in the market, and porterhouse steak will go begging for a buyer.

"I cannot close this paper without urging that every person in the pecan belt, which is practically commensurate with the cotton growing region should grow at least a few pecan trees. The unfortunate dwellers in the most crowded parts of our cities may not have room. But there are few homes, even in our cities and large towns, where there is not enough space to accommodate one or more trees. One tree, when well established, will furnish nuts sufficient to last the average family for a year. And a farmer, though he may have only a few acres of land, is neglecting a most profitable money crop when he fails to set out a few pecan trees around his garden and yard. These trees will furnish a shade in summer, nuts in the winter, and will add beauty and stateliness and comfort all the time. There are few New England homes that have not their apple and other fruit trees; and the day should not be far distant when the same can be said of pecan trees growing about the homes in our Southland. As shade trees they are beautiful; and there are none that yield more in pleasure and profit than do pecans.

"Twenty-three years ago I read this advice from a veteran pecan grower, who still abides with us: 'Young man, set a pecan grove, and when you are old it will support you.' I believed then that the advice was sound; I now know it is so. And so I will pass the word along: Young man, plant a pecan grove. It will help to make your days happier and your pockets heavier. It will lighten your burdens while here; and when you are gone, your children and children's children will rise up and call you blessed."

Mr. Wight has prospered and built up a splendid enterprise as a farmer and nut grower. He is now owner of eight hundred acres of land, of which one hundred and fifty are planted in pecans. As a successful fruit and nut grower, he has a prominent place among Georgia horticulturists. He is a member of the Georgia Horticultural Society, and is now its treasurer. He is prominent in the National Nut Growers' Association, has served two years as president of the Association in 1908 and 1910, and is now its secretary.

On July 25, 1888, Mr. Wight married Miss Alice Slater. She was born in Bullock county, Georgia, June 20, 1864, daughter of John G. and Susan (Cone) Slater. Mr. and Mrs. Wight's seven children are George Ward, John Slater, Robert Pratt, Laleah Adams, Warren Candler, Edward Allen and John Byron, Jr. Mr. Wight has a beautiful home in Cairo, built in modern colonial style. Mr. Wight is a member of Cairo Lodge No. 299, A. F. & A. M., of which he is now worshipful master; and is also a Royal Arch Mason.

For more than eighty years the Wight family has been represented in southern Georgia. The first generation was among the earliest pioneers in the settlement and development of Decatur county. In the second generation were worthy men and women who bore with equal fidelity their responsibilities to the world, and several representatives of the name were soldiers in the Confederate army during the great struggle between the states.

The original American ancestor was Thomas Wight. He was born on the Isle of Wight, came to America as early as 1635,, remained for a short time at Watertown, in Massachusetts, and in 1637 became a resident and free holder in Dedham, Massachusetts. He moved to Medfield about 1650, spending the rest of his days on a farm in that town. One of his descendants, William Ward Wight, of Milwaukee, Wisconsin, has compiled a very interesting history of the Wight family. Its pages state that Thomas Wight and his four sons and a son-in-law contributed to the fund for the erection of the first brick college on the campus in Cambridge, which is now Harvard University. Thomas Wight's contribution was four bushels of Indian corn, which was good legal tender in those days.

The more immediate ancestry of the Georgia family begins with Rev. Henry Wight, D. D., who was a student in Harvard University, when the Revolutionary war broke out, and left his studies for a time to serve in the patriot army. He subsequently was graduated from Harvard, and became a minister of the Congregational church, and served as pastor of the church in Bristol, Rhode Island, for fifty years.

His son, Henry Wight, transferred the family history to Georgia. Born at Bristol, Rhode Island, November 5, 1791, in early life he followed the sea and was later commander of vessels in the coastwise trade. Leaving the sea, he engaged in the mercantile business, and in 1829 came South and located in Georgia. A boat brought him as far as Savannah. From there he used teams to convey his goods and family across the state to Decatur county. Decatur county at that time lay in the almost unbroken wilderness of Georgia. There were no regular roads except the trails cut out among the trees by the pioneers. The woods teemed with wild game of all kinds; and in the hills and valleys the Indians still lingered, loath to quit this country which had so long been their hunting ground. Mr. Wight bought a large tract of timberland; and in the first clearing built the log house which was the original home of the Wight family in Georgia. Henry Wight, in keeping with the traditions of New England where he was born and reared, was a man of superior education; and after coming to South Georgia, taught school. He later opened a store at Sofkee. His stock of goods was drawn overland in carts from St. Marks, Florida, wagons being then almost unknown as vehicles of transportation. Henry Wight was a resident of Sofkee, until his death in February, 1885, when in his ninety-fourth year. He had married in Bristol, Rhode Island, Miss Abby Wardwell. Her father, Capt. Samuel Wardwell, was a large ship owner, and eighteen of his vessels were destroyed by French privateers in 1798 and 1799, when there was a quasi state of war between France and the United States. In reparation for this loss payment was demanded from the French government, and the claim was still pending when the Louisiana purchase was made. At that time, in addition to the sum paid for the western territory, the United States assumed responsibility for the settlement of all claims against France. But in this case, an entire century passed before settlement was made, a remarkable illustration of government delay. In 1899 the heirs of Captain Wardwell were awarded payment for the loss of one ship destroyed a century before, and Mr. J. B. Wight, as one of such heirs, got a two hundred and fortieth part of the total sum, his share amounting to $8.33. Abby (Wardwell) Wight died in October, 1871, and her children were named: William Henry, Abby Wardwell, Samuel Bowen, John, Byron Diman, and George Alden.

George Alden Wight, father of John Byron, established a store at Sofkee, when nineteen years of age. In 1863 he enlisted in the Georgia Volunteers, and was in service with his company and regiment in Georgia and Florida until the close of the war. In 1871 he began business at Cairo, being one of the earliest merchants in the town. When he located there, business was conducted in two small stores kept in log cabins. Mr. Wight himself erected a good frame building and put in a stock of general merchandise. Wight & Powell was the first business title, and subsequently G. A. Wight & Sons. He continued as a merchant at Cairo until his death occurred on August 21, 1894. In the meantime having bought the property of White Springs, Florida, he erected a hotel which was operated by a lessee. George Alden Wight was married November 11, 1858, to Julia Florence Herring, who was born in Decatur county, Georgia, July 7, 1845, a daughter of Hanson and Amy C. (Anders) Herring. Her death occurred September 7, 1860. For his second wife he married Margaret Louisa Powell, a daughter of Kedar and Amanda Melvina Powell. John Byron Wight was the only child of the first marriage, and of the second union there were children named Henry, Kedar Powell, William Samuel, Carrie Bell, Thomas, Walter Lee, Alice Pearl, George Alden, and Margaret Augusta. All these ten children of George A. Wight have grown to maturity. Most of them are still living in Cairo where they are prominent factors in the social and business life of their section. The parents were both members of the Methodist church, and the father belonged to the Masonic fraternity.

JAMES WHITLEY, ordinary of Irwin county, and a resident of Ocilla, is a native born Georgian, born in this state in August, 1875. He is the son of John H. and Martha V. S. (Henderson) Whitley. The father was a native of Irwin county and the mother of Worth county.

John H. Whitley was a farmer, and his son, James, of this review, passed his early days upon the farm; in fact, he continued in his residence there until his election to the office of ordinary of the county, which he now fills. He received his education in the public schools of Irwin county, in common with other members of his family. He was the eldest of a family of six children, all of whom are living but one. They are Ella T., the wife of James Royal; Della, married to F. E. Ewing; Thomas T., Jr.; Lula, who makes her home with James, and Lillian, who is a student at Forsythe. All are residents of Irwin county.

On July 29, 1897, Mr. Whitley was married to Mattie Royal, a daughter of William and Mary (Schinholsten) Royal, of Irwin county. Four children have been born to them, named as follows: John William, born in 1899; LeRoy, born in 1903; Russell, born in 1905, and Troy E., born in 1909. Mrs. Whitley passed away on August 1, 1910, leaving her husband and little family of four to mourn her loss.

Mr. Whitley is a Mason of the blue lodge degree, and the family are members of the Primitive Baptist church.

DUNCAN D. PEACOCK. One of the most prosperous small towns of south Georgia is Pavo in Thomas county. It is on the Georgia Northern Railroad and is seventeen miles from the county sites of the three adjoining counties of Thomas, Brooks and Colquitt, viz., Thomasville, Quitman and Moultrie, and is surrounded by some of the most productive farm lands in south Georgia, with turpentine and sawmill timber enough to keep these enterprises alive for many years to come. Pavo has a naval stores factory, variety works, manufactory of yellow pine, guano factory, two live banking institutions, two drug stores, one dentist, four physicians, two hospitals, and one of the most skilled surgeons in the south. It also has a large cotton ginnery with capacity of turning out one hundred bales of cotton, ginning both the long and short staple, per day, and a large cotton warehouse that would do credit to a town twice its size. The originator of the commercial enterprise and one of the chief factors in its growth and development has been Duncan D. Peacock, who was the first merchant of the place.

When the town of Pavo was incorporated he was instrumental in having a prohibition clause inserted in the charter so that no intoxicants can ever be sold there, not even cider. He is one of the charter members of the Bank of Pavo and of the Planters Bank, and has served the town as councilman. He was postmaster for nineteen consecutive years until the spring of 1911, at which time the office was advanced to third class, becoming a presidential office, and although he secured the endorsement of ninety per cent of the entire patrons of the office, including the business, professional and banking interests of the town, the referee of the powers in control appointed his successor, against the wishes of the patrons, because he had incurred the displeasure of that official, in that he had failed to comply with his request to furnish him with the names of the patrons of the office, while to have done so would have been in direct violation of the postal laws and regulations. The first name of this place was McDonald, having been named in honor of Col. James McDonald, one of the pioneer settlers who represented his district as a member of Congress.

The present name, Pavo, is the Latinized form of Mr. Peacock's name. Duncan D. Peacock is a native of Thomas county, where he was born February 24, 1859, and represents an old family resident from colonial times in North Carolina and Georgia. His great-grandparents were Simon and Zilpha (Pittman) Peacock, who were, according to the best information at hand, lifelong residents of North Carolina, and their children were named as follows: Stephen, Seth, Patience, Polly, Noah, Demeris, Robert, Raiford, Zilpha and Simon.

Robert Peacock, the grandfather, was born on a farm near the present site of Goldsboro, in Wayne county, North Carolina, in 1791, lived in that vicinity until after his marriage and then became an early settler of Macon county, Georgia, where he bought land and made his home a few years. From there he migrated into south Georgia and settled in that part of Lowndes, now Brooks county. This was in the era of early settlement. He bought a tract of hammock land, heavily

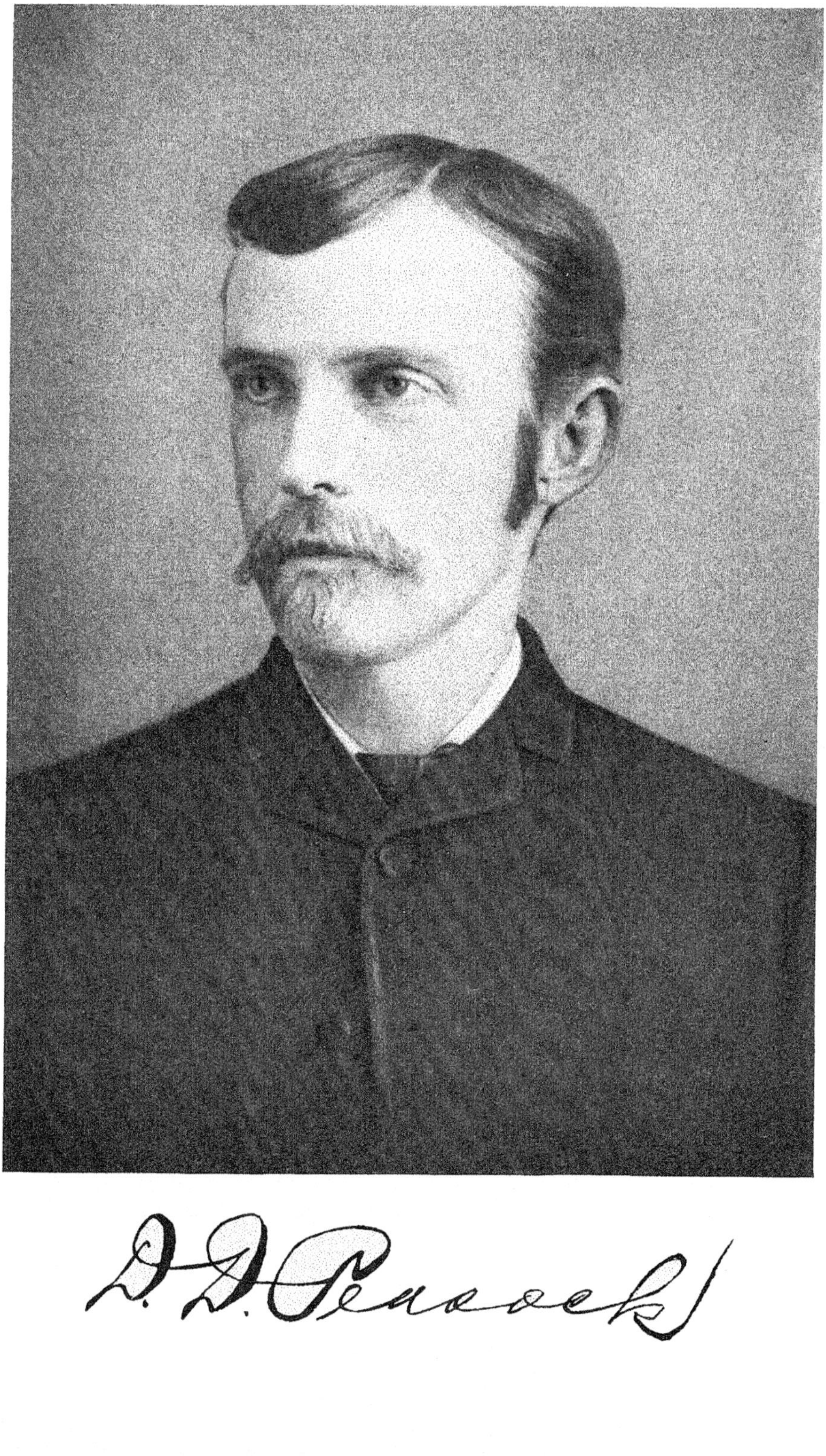

timbered with hard wood. His home was on the Coffee road, the main thoroughfare between Thomasville and Savannah, and at the place of his settlement has since grown up the little village of Okapilco. The grandfather resided there until his death in 1860. The maiden name of his first wife, the grandmother of Duncan D., was Wealthy Howell. She was born in Wayne county in North Carolina, and at her death in middle life left eight children, namely: Benajoh, Howell, Jane, Robert, Delamar, Edna, Byron and Morris. For his second wife the grandfather married America Howell and they reared ten children, named Sarah, Patience, John, Tyler, Virginia, Letitia, Laura, Margaret, Jasper and Eulalia.

Delamar C. Peacock, the father, who was born in Macon county, Georgia, in 1824, spent his active career in farming. He bought land east of Thomasville, where with the aid of slave labor he engaged in the tilling of the soil, and resided there until his death, at the age of forty-eight. He married Mary Ann McKinnon, a native Georgian and of a pioneer family of this section of the state. Her father was Malcom McKinnon, a native of Robeson county, North Carolina. Her grandfather, John McKinnon, was also probably a native of North Carolina and came to south Georgia and located in what is now Thomas county, along with the first pioneers who blazed the paths of civilization in this vicinity. He improved a farm five miles east of Thomasville, and his remains now rest on that original homestead. John McKinnon married Mary McIntosh, a native of Scotland, who came to America with her parents at the age of six years. She reared a large family of children. Mary (McKinnon) Peacock, the mother, died at the age of fifty-four, and her children were as follows: Malcom Robert, Rebecca, Josephene M., Moselle, Duncan D., Daniel Clayton, Wesley and Wealthy (twins) and John Howell. This family have gained particular distinction in the field of education.

Malcolm R. Peacock was for many years a teacher prominent in the public schools of Georgia, having spent the major part of his life in the schoolroom. Later he became one of the leading merchants of Thomasville, with a branch store in what was then McDonald (now Pavo), Georgia, and one in Boston, Georgia. In his old age he retired to his farm near Pavo, where he could enjoy a more quiet life aside from the heavy responsibilities and cares of the ever-hustling business mercantile life. He married Miss Lelia Culpepper, a daughter of William H. Culpepper, a native of Thomas county, who was a leading farmer in Georgia for many years, but who later moved to Florida where he purchased an orange grove. The children of Malcolm are: Emmitt, Wallace, Wesley and Howell (twins) and Mabelle.

Daniel Clayton is a graduate of the University of Georgia and also of Harvard, Massachusetts. He came from Harvard to Atlanta and established his school, "Peacock's School for Boys," in 1898. He now has a handsome three-story building in the finest residence part of the city, the school numbering one hundred and and twenty-five to one hundred and fifty boys from the age of twelve to eighteen, the annual receipts from which are eight or ten thousand dollars. Professor Clayton has a summer residence in Pavo, where he spends a part of the summer and winter, hunting during the winter and fishing during the summer and looking after his varied interests, including his large cotton ginnery and cotton warehouse, etc.

Wesley Peacock, next to the youngest of the family of nine, was born near Thomasville, Georgia, on December 24, 1865. At the age of fourteen he entered the South Georgia College in Thomasville, where after an attendance of four years, he was graduated in 1884 with first honor of his class and with a commission as first lieutenant in the military department. At the age of eighteen he taught school, the following year in Okapilco and in Stockton, Georgia, and was thus prepared to enter the University of Georgia in October, 1886, having received the appointment as a beneficiary of the Charles McDonald Brown scholarship fund by courtesy of ex-Governor Joseph E. Brown, of Georgia, which enabled him to graduate in the university in 1887 with second honor in his class. Mr. Peacock values a personal letter and a photograph from Governor Brown, received while teaching school in Texas two years after graduation, in recognition of his having been the first beneficiary of the Brown fund to repay the obligation.

While attending the University he became a member of the Sigma Alpha Epsilon fraternity and Phi Kappa Literary Society and in his junior year he enjoyed the unusual distinction of having won three speakers' places at commencement, one on oratory, another on original essay and a third on scholarship.

Immediately upon graduation Mr. Peacock went to Texas to join his older brother, D. C. Peacock, also a graduate of the University of Georgia, who had preceded him to Texas by two years, and in Jasper he was engaged for four years with his brother in conducting the South East Texas Male and Female College, after which he superintended the public schools of Uvalde, Texas, for three years.

On December 28, 1893, he married Miss Selina Egg, and in 1894 he established the Peacock School for Boys in San Antonio, Texas, which grew into the Peacock Military College, an institution enjoying the distinction of having been the first school in Texas or any gulf state to be classed A by the war department.

One son, Wesley Peacock, Jr., survived the death of his wife on November 28, 1898. On July 4, 1903, he married Miss Edith Wing in Chicago.

In 1911, after persuading congress to name Corpus Christi, Texas, as a site of a marine school under government patronage, Professor Peacock established and maintained in that city the Peacock Naval School in connection with the Peacock Military School of San Antonio, obtaining from the navy department navy cutters and other naval equipment.

Wealthy (Wessie), the twin sister of Professor Wesley, was educated at Young's Female College, Thomasville, Georgia, and died shortly afterwards with typhoid fever, at the age of eighteen, in the bloom of life. She was a devoted Christian and member of the Methodist church. She contracted the fever while in the performance of her Christian duties in attending the bedside of a sick neighbor, and was interred in Laurel Hill cemetery, Thomasville, Georgia. Thus her life was sacrificed in the service of her Master, but not in vain.

John Howell Peacock was also a graduate of the University of Georgia. He was head master for three years in Peacock's Military College at San Antonio, Texas, after holding chair of mathematics in San Antonio's Female College. He is now head master of Peacock's School for Boys, Atlanta, Georgia. Professor Howell married Miss Meda Perkins, of Alice, Texas, who was a graduate of San Antonio's Female College. The names of their two children are: John Howell, Jr., and Evelyn Louise.

Duncan D. Peacock also began his career as teacher when eighteen years old and continued four years. In 1879 he located at what was then McDonald, in Thomas county, where for two years he was in charge of the school. He was later appointed postmaster, and about the same time established the first general store in the village. There being several postoffices in the state similar to the name McDonald, viz., McDonald's Mill, Coffee county, McDonough, Henry county, McDaniel, Pickens county, resulting in much confusion of mail and freight, the patrons urged a change of name, and at the suggestion of the postoffice department several lists of names were sent to Washington, D. C., all the patrons who would do so having a part in the selection of the names listed, all of which were considered unavailable for the same reason that McDonald was unfit. In the last list Mr. Peacock added the name Pavo, which is the Latin for Peacock, and the postoffice authorities chose this as the designation for the postoffice, hence it was adopted for the entire village. After he had been in business for a few years Mr. Peacock was stricken with nervous prostration and rheumatism, which kept him in bed for one year and in a wheel chair for several years, then on crutches. Always a devout Christian, while suffering this affliction Mr. Peacock covenanted with God, that should he be restored to his former health he would thereafter direct his energies for the benefit of the Lord's work in the world. When fully restored and confronted with the problem how best to fulfill his promise, he resolved that he would consecrate his entire life as well as his business and honor Him in all of the same, in buying and selling, and all his transactions with his fellow-man, and that he would henceforth have a higher incentive in the prosecution of his business than the mere money relations accruing therefrom. God honored his consecration, his faith and trust in Him, making it an epoch in his Christian experience, which has ever since been predominant in his business. Having adopted as his motto, "Whether therefore ye eat or drink, or whatsoever ye do, do all to the glory of God," and all his "merchandise shall be holiness to the Lord," he therefore eliminated many articles formerly carried in stock which had been a source of profit, but which he could not now sell "to the glory of God," and which he thought the world would be better off without. His business cards and letter heads were made to read, "D. D. Peacock, Dealer in general merchandise of all kinds— EXCEPT tobacco, cigarettes, cigars, playing cards, pistols and cartridges." One morning after this, after he had made a fire in the heater in his store, he noticed his little son Clayton, who was only seven years old, with his arm full of books which he had taken from the shelving, cramming them in the stove. Asked what he was doing, the little fellow answered, "Papa, didn't you tell Mamma last night that these books are not good books, and that God did not want you to sell any more of them?" His father said: "Yes, son, and Papa will help you burn them all up; go and bring the others." So some seventy-five or one hundred novels which were being sold for the profit there was in them, without a thought of giving value received, were sacrificed, yes, "to the glory of God." A little later he purchased an entire stock of goods, a bankrupt stock, including quite a lot of playing cards, and a number of barrels of cider; he refused to take the cider, and reshipped it to the wholesale grocer, the merchant from whom he had bought the stock of goods protesting all the while that he had tried to get them to take the cider back and they had refused; but they were returned just the same and accepted, when they learned why it was refused by Mr. Peacock. The playing cards were destroyed.

Mr. Peacock is a Prohibitionist in the full sense of the word. He has never taken a drink of liquor nor a chew of tobacco, nor smoked a cigar or cigarette in his life. He has never visited any place that he could not consistently take his mother, sister, or wife, or daughter with him, and does not claim any credit for it, but gives the credit to his pious Christian mother and her training in his early life.

His unique trade device obtained a wide note through the country, and he was known far and wide as "The Except Merchant." This new name given to him by the commercial traveling salesmen, he later adopted, and had his return envelopes printed, "If not called for in five days, return to The Except Merchant." He frequently received letters addressed to "The Except Merchant," Pavo, Georgia. In April, 1912, he remitted his subscription to *The Ram's Horn*, Chicago, Illinois, an independent weekly, which has since become *The Home Herald*. This paper wrote an editorial, commenting and complimenting him for having the moral courage of his convictions in placing on the mast pole of his business cards and letter heads the line of eliminations included under the word "Except," which "indicated strength of Christian character worthy of note." This brought a number of letters from business men all over the country asking for copies of his letter heads; some desiring to emulate the example. One firm, a wholesale and retail house, as well as manufacturer, in the state of Maryland, wrote that they had never thought of printing their letter heads to show that they drew the line on tobacco, but that they would do so in future. Among other humorous comments he received a letter from a Savannah liquor house, stating they had not noticed wines as being "excepted" in his business and wanted to get him to handle their wines. Another house in New York sent him samples of playing cards. It was his custom in making remittances in liquidation of his indebtedness to write some scriptural references or quotations across the ends of the checks, such as John 3:16, Matthew 7:12, Heb. 10:14, 15. On one occasion the check was returned by the bank, with the inscription on the back, "Irregular," "Returned." Mr. Peacock wrote another check and mailed it to them with a new scriptural reference as follows: *"Mene, mene tekel, upharsin."* This time the bank kept the check, having concluded they "wanted the money" whether they were "weighed in the balance and found wanting" or not.

In his business career, Mr. Peacock has prospered, but he has also had his reverses. In 1905 having bought a large lot of cotton, the price dropped suddenly from eleven cents to seven cents per pound, and he was confronted with financial ruin. To make the situation worse, he was so ill he could not attend to business, and at that time his creditors offered him a settlement on a basis of thirty cents on the dollar. He refused a compromise, declaring his intentions of paying all his obligations in full. He paid part cash at the time, giving his notes for the remainder, and has since liquidated the entire amount with interest. It is this business integrity which has given him a high position among his associates, and he is today one of the most influential business men and citizens of Thomas county.

He has been an active member of the Methodist church, serving his church as trustee, steward, and has been superintendent of the Sunday School or teacher of the Bible class for a quarter of a century. He has a cottage at the Indian Springs camp ground, near Indian Springs, Georgia, where his family usually spends a part of the summer, he always joining them during the month of August during the annual Holiness Camp Meeting, which convenes during that month. He is an ardent supporter and believer in the doctrine for which that camp stands, and as taught by John Wesley, the founder of Methodism, a definite experience of holiness of heart in the believer instantaneously received by faith.

Duncan D. Peacock was married in June, 1888, to Mary J. Reddick, a native of Brooks county, and a member of an old Georgia family. Her grandfather, Nicholas Reddick, formerly a resident of

Screven county, became one of the early settlers of what is now Brooks county. He improved a large farm in what is now Brooks county, in the Tallokas district, employed a number of slaves to work the fields, and remained a resident of this vicinity until his death at a good old age. He was three times married, and his second wife, the grandmother of Mrs. Peacock, was a Miss Lewis. Mrs. Peacock's father was Rev. Moses Reddick, who was reared and educated in Brooks county. At the breaking out of the war he enlisted in Company C of the Seventh Georgia Battalion, was later transferred to the Sixty-first Georgia Infantry, and gave long and faithful service as a soldier in the army of North Virginia. He always carried his Bible in his breast pocket, and at one time it was penetrated by a bullet to the very last leaf, thus saving his life.

The Bible is now preserved by his descendants as a sacred relic. He escaped capture and was with his regiment until the close of the war, when he came home and took up farming. As a farmer and business man he prospered, and he also devoted much of his time and energies to his duties as a local preacher of the Methodist church. His death occurred at the age of sixty-three. He married Sarah Allen, who was born in the Dry Lake district of Brooks county, and they were the parents of eight children, named as follows: Elizabeth, Mary J., Sarah, James, Lucy, Virginia, Henry, and John Wesley. Sarah Allen's parents were from Wilmington, North Carolina, and were of Scotch-Irish descent.

Mr. and Mrs. D. D. Peacock have reared three children: Clayton Wesley, Moselle, and Lois Elizabeth. Clayton was educated at Meridian Male College, Meridian, Mississippi. He is a successful teacher, and is at present the principal of the Union Point High School at Union Point, Georgia. Clayton is quite a young man yet, and intends to further complete his education at the University of Georgia, or at Harvard, Massachusetts. Mosie Mae is a member of the graduating class of May, 1913, of Andrew Female College, at Cuthbert, Georgia. Having studied harmony, history, interpretation, sight reading, and having two years in practical pedagogy at Andrew College, she is well qualified. Besides receiving the B. L. diploma, she was awarded a certificate in piano music and received a diploma in Sunday School pedagogy. She was an active member and officer in the college Y. W. C. A. and president of the Kappa Gamma Literary Society. During her college course Miss Peacock was a leader in all the college activities and has at the same time taken a high rank in class work. She has good natural gifts, well developed by faithful study at college, and is an active religious worker. Lois Elizabeth is in school at Pavo. She is only seven years old now. Mr. Peacock and wife are both active members in the Pavo Methodist church.

Rebecca Peacock, the eldest daughter of Delamar Peacock, married Anthony Wayne Ivey, who was a son of Robert Ivey, one of the pioneer settlers of Thomas county. He was reared on a farm six miles east of Thomasville, Georgia. Wayne was a teacher in the public schools of Georgia for a number of years and was a member of the legislature for two years. He was also secretary and treasurer of the Farmers' State Alliance of Georgia, during which time he moved to Atlanta, where his wife died. After the death of his wife, he moved to Thomasville, where he died. His wife, Rebecca, was an invalid for several years and a patient sufferer, uncomplaining, and bore her sickness with Christian fortitude and grace. At the approach of death, she drew her loved ones around her, entreated them to meet her in heaven, and departed this life with shouts of victory, having called for a favorite hymn to be sung while she passed over. Their children were: Robert, Felton Bartow, Mamie, Elizabeth, Eula, Lee, and J. Duncan. Felton Bartow, after holding the responsible position as business manager for a large wholesale house in Savannah for a number of years, resigned this place in favor of his brother Duncan (who holds that position now) to go on the road as traveling salesman for the same company, viz., F. J. Cooledge & Bro., of Atlanta and Savannah. Mamie married Mr. Robert Varnedoe, of Thomasville; Lizzie married Henry Reddick, a merchant of Morven, Georgia. Miss Lee and Robert are living in Thomasville, where Felton B. makes his headquarters, his territory being south Georgia and Florida.

Josephene Peacock, the second daughter of Delamar Peacock, married Abraham Foreman, son of Glover and Malinda Foreman, of South Carolina. Her children are: Cora, James J., Delamar G., Mary (deceased), Blanch, Floy, Marion, and Dudly F.

Abraham Foreman was a farmer in Thomas county and moved to this place in the early days when it was called McDonald, with only two stores, and purchased the place which was known as the old McDonald dowery farm. In later years after the name was changed to Pavo and the place became an incorporated town, he opened up the most of the farm into resident lots and placed them on the market in one sale, thus offering the first big sale of land to those who were seeking homes in Pavo. He served the town in capacity of mayor and was always active at work in the development of Pavo. He is still one of the substantial residents of the town.

Cora, the oldest daughter of Josephene and Abraham Foreman, married P. A. Adams, a successful merchant of Pavo, who was one among the first of the town. James J., the oldest son, was educated in the public schools and graduated at the Stanley Business College of Thomasville, Georgia. He held important positions with business firms in Atlanta, Georgia, and was appointed a clerk in the pay department of the United States army. He did service in different departments of the United States and in the Philippine Islands and resigned in 1907 and came to Pavo, where he entered the cotton warehouse business. He has been an active citizen, having served as councilman, clerk, treasurer, as well as mayor of the town. He married Miss Ethell Mosely of Jakin, Georgia, in 1912. Blanch, the second daughter, married W. F. Harrison, of Slocum, Alabama. Floy, the third daughter of Abraham and Josephene Foreman, graduated at the Pavo high school, was a student of the state normal of Athens, Georgia, and is assistant teacher of the high school of Clayton, Georgia. Marion, the fourth daughter, also graduated at the Pavo high school and also at the state normal of Athens. She is now a teacher in the primary department in the Pavo high school.

Moselle Peacock, the third daughter of Delamar and Mary Peacock, married Hezekiah Roberts, a large landholder at Pavo. He is one of the chief factors in the growth and development of the town of Pavo and furnished many of the town resident lots on which are now erected the residences of many of her citizens. Mr. Roberts has served the town as mayor and councilman, and in many ways has been instrumental in building up the town and community, a more complete account of which is given in this volume in the history of Pavo.

To Moselle and Hezekiah Roberts were born: Mamie, Wessie, Frank, and Jack. Miss Wessie married Hugh C. Ford, the cashier of the Bank of Pavo. Mr. Ford is a graduate of Oxford and is of a prominent family of Cartersville, Georgia. Mrs. Ford attended Wesleyan

Female College and received a certificate in music. Jack is assistant cashier in the Bank of Pavo.

Mrs. Moselle Roberts died in August, 1895, and was buried in Lebanon cemetery at Pavo.

WILLIAM S. MANN, practicing attorney of McRae and senator from the Fifteenth Senatorial District, is readily conceded to be one of the most rapidly rising young professional men in Telfair county. Not yet four years in the professional world, he has in that brief time accomplished what it has taken other men many years of effort to attain, and those accomplishments give rich promise of the possibilities of his future career.

Born in Berrien county, in 1884, Mr. Mann is the son of Frank R. and Henrietta (Sykes) Mann. The father, a prominent turpentine operator and lumberman, who also conducted a naval store's supply house and did some farming, still lives in Berrien county, although his wife is deceased. She was a native of Montgomery county, and her husband of Tattnall county. When William S. Mann was an infant the family removed to Telfair county, and there he was reared and educated. He attended the common schools and later entered the University of Georgia at Athens, pursuing a literary course. He concluded his studies there with a course in law and in 1908 was graduated, receiving his degree. He immediately began the practice of his profession in McRae, and such progress did he make in his labors and so well did he impress the public with his ability and progressiveness that in 1910 he was nominated for the office of senator from the Fifteenth Senatorial District, comprising the counties of Telfair, Montgomery, Dodge, Ben Hill and Irwin, and his election duly followed. He is now discharging the duties of that position, and his labors thus far in behalf of his constituents have been all that could be desired.

On August 15, 1909, Mr. Mann was united in marriage with Miss Floris J. Perkins, daughter of J. W. Perkins, one time operator in turpentine in Georgia. Both parents are now deceased. They were former residents of St. Louis, Missouri, and there Mrs. Mann was born. One son, William S., Jr., was born to them on July 14, 1910.

The family affiliates with the Episcopalian church, of which Mrs. Mann is a member. Mr. Mann is a member of the Knights of Pythias. A sister of Mr. Mann, Aleph, is married to Oscar B. Burch and resides in Jackson, Georgia, while a brother, Frank R., Jr., is a physician and surgeon of Lumber City, Georgia

JOHN BURCH ROBERTS. A well-known and prosperous agriculturist of Terrell county, John Burch Roberts, living near Dawson, is distinguished both for his own life and works, and for the honored ancestry from which he is descended, the name of Roberts having been prominent in Georgia for upwards of a century.

His grandfather, Reverend Burch M. Roberts, was a Baptist preacher, holding pastorates in various places in Georgia, and meeting with a due meed of success in his ministerial labors. He married Harriet Hardwick, who also belonged to a well-known family of this state.

Honorable Joseph W. Roberts, father of John B. Roberts, was born, it is thought, in Hancock county, Georgia, where his father was then settled as a minister. Taking advantage of every offered opportunity for increasing his knowledge, he acquired a substantial education while young, but instead of entering upon a professional career chose the independent occupation of a farmer. He purchased land in Calhoun county when all of that section of Georgia was in its pristine wildness, being but sparsely populated, and far from any railroad. With the assistance of slaves he cleared and improved a good farm, upon which he lived until 1866. Locating then in Terrell county, he purchased a farm situated one and one-fourth miles west of the Court House, and was there engaged in agricultural pursuits a number of years. When ready to relinquish the management of his estate, he moved to Dawson, where he continued his residence until his death, at the good old age of seventy-eight years. He was long prominent and influential in public affairs, from 1861 to 1865, during the entire time that Georgia was one of the Confederate States, representing Calhoun county in the state legislature. He also served as judge of the inferior court, and at the time of his death was judge of the court of ordinary of Terrell county, a position which he had held for eighteen years. He married Mary J. Colley, daughter of John Colley, a Calhoun county farmer. She died at the age of sixty-four years, leaving six children, namely: John Burch, James W., Louisa, George M., Mary Ella and Charles.

Educated in the rural schools, and brought up on the home farm, John Burch Roberts acquired while young a valuable knowledge and expericuce in the art of agriculture, and naturally selected farming as his life occupation. At the time of his marriage he bought land lying ten miles east of Dawson, and managed it successfully for two years. The ensuing three yeares he was employed in mercantile pursuits, after which he returned to the soil, taking up farming near the old parental homestead, which has since come into his possession, and which he now occupies. It is a well improved estate, with substantial buildings, and under his wise management yields a good annual income.

Mr. Roberts married, November 17, 1870, Catherine Simpson, who was born in that part of Lee county now included within the boundaries of Terrell county. Her father, John James Simpson, was born in North Carolina, and when a small child was left fatherless. His widowed mother subsequently married Daniel Kennedy, and they came with their family to Georgia, locating in that section of Lee county that now forms a part of Terrell county. John James Simpson was a young man when he settled in Georgia, and he subsequently married Mary Elizabeth Blanchard, who was born in North Carolina, and came with her mother and her step-father, a Mr. Bradley, to Georgia. The Kennedy and Bradley families left North Carolina about the same time, the Bradleys being bound for Mississippi. While jorneying overland the two families met, and the Kennedys persuaded the Bradleys to locate in Lee county, Georgia, their point of destination. Four years later the two families became more closely united, John James Simpson, stepson of Daniel Kennedy, marrying Miss Blanchard, stepdaughter of Mr. Bradley. She died thirteen months after their marriage, leaving an infant daughter, Catherine, now the wife of Mr. Roberts. Mr. Simpson afterwards married for his second wife Florence Smith, daughter of Griffin Smith, a pioneer of South Georgia, and she is now living in South Georgia, and is the mother of four children, as follows: William, George, Edward and John. Mr. Simpson took an active interest in public affairs. and during the trying times of the Civil war served for four years as sheriff of Terrell county.

Ten children have blessed the marriage of Mr. and Mrs. Roberts, namely: Beulah, Blanchard, William, John James, Burch, Mary, George, Oscar, Alice and Cortez. All are still living, several being married, and having families of their own. Beulah, wife of Charles Wilkinson, has five children. Blanchard, wife of Sidney J. Cook, has three children, Ruth, Blanchard and Sidney. William married Sarah Brown, and has three children, Euzella, Catherine and Marion. John J., married Roxie Beckham, and they have three children, Pauline, Catherine and John. Burch married Willie Joiner, and they have one son, Burch. George married Bertha Haiston. Oscar married Nellie Kitchen. And Alice is the wife of Foy Haines. Mr. and Mrs. Roberts are members of the Methodist Episcopal church. Fraternally Mr. Roberts belongs to the Royal Arcanum.

JAMES D. WADE, JR. A prominent and prosperous member of the legal fraternity, James D. Wade, Jr., has been actively engaged in the practice of his profession in Quitman, Brooks county, for upwards of a quarter of a century, and during the time has gained for himself a fine reputation, not only as an able and skilful attorney, but as a man and a citizen. A son of Colonel James D. Wade, Sr., he was born, July 5, 1856, in Screven county, Georgia, of pioneer ancestry.

His paternal grandfather, Jesse Wade, who was of English lineage, was born in Green county, Georgia, where his parents, well-to-do farmers, were pioneer settlers. Brought up and educated in his native county, he began life for himself in Newton county, Georgia, but after living there ten years removed to Murray county, buying land in that part now included within the boundaries of Whitfield county, and on the farm which he cleared carrying on farming with the assistance of his slaves until they were freed. In 1863, being then well advanced in age, he refugeed to the home of his son Archibald, in Pierce county, and there resided until his death, in 1872, at the age of eighty-two years, his death having been the result of injuries received in an accident at a cotton gin. He married Bethany Middlebrooks, a daughter of Isaac Middlebrooks, a pioneer settler of Morgan county, Georgia. She died in 1882, aged eighty-eight years. To her and her husband nine children were born, as follows: Elizabeth, who married a Mr. White, and removed to Texas; Peyton L.; Isaac M.; James D.; Archibald P.; Edward C.; Seaborn H.; William P.; and Milton C.

James D. Wade, Sr., was born in Newton county, Georgia, February 13, 1826, and was brought up and educated in Whitfield county. Upon the breaking out of the Civil war he organized a company for the Confederate service, and was commissioned as its captain. He remained with his command until the close of the conflict, taking part in many engagements of note, and for bravery on the field of battle was promoted from rank to rank until receiving his commission as colonel of his regiment. Returning home at the close of the war, Col. James D. Wade remained in Screven county, where he had located prior to entering the army, until 1870. Selling his plantation in that year, the Colonel came to Brooks county, purchased land lying eight miles north of Quitman, and there continued his agricultural labors. Several years later he sold out, and subsequently lived retired in Quitman until his death, March 9, 1910, at the venerable age of four score and four years. Colonel Wade married Sarah Bowie, who was born in Screven county, Georgia, in 1830, and died in March, 1909. Her parents came from South Carolina, their native state, to Georgia, locating in Screven county at an early day, and there clearing and improving a farm, which they managed with slave labor, remaining on their homestead the rest of their days. To Colonel Wade and his wife five children were born, as follows: James D., Jr., the special subject of this biographical review; Jesse P.; Josephine F.; Seaborn H.; and William C.

Obtaining his early education in the common schools of Screven county, James D. Wade, Jr., subsequently attended the University of Georgia. His natural talents leading him to choose a profession, he then read law with Judge J. G. McCall, and being admitted to the bar in 1882 immediately began the practice of law in Quitman. In 1888 Mr.

Wade was elected clerk of court, and was continued in that office by continuous re-election for a period of twelve years. On retiring from the clerkship, Mr. Wade resumed his practice in Quitman, where he gained an extensive patronage.

Mr. Wade married, in 1888, Mary Jones, who was born in Thomas county, Georgia, a daughter of James Y. Jones. Mrs. Wade's grandfather, Thomas Jones, a native of Bulloch county, Georgia, was a pioneer settler of Thomas county, Georgia, and, it is said, was one of the three men whose Christian name was "Thomas," and for whom Thomas county and the city of Thomasville were named. Buying a tract of timber land, he erected a log cabin in the wilderness, and with slave labor cleared many acres of land, and carried on general farming with most satisfactory pecuniary results. He made improvements of great value, building a commodious brick house to replace the log structure in which he and his family first lived, and putting up substantial farm buildings. On the homestead which he wrested from the forest he spent the remainder of his long life. He married Lavina Young, who was born in Bulloch county, and died in Thomas county, at the venerable age of ninety years. James Y. Jones, Mrs. Wade's father, came to Brooks county many years ago, and in addition to buying a plantation bought a home in Quitman. He never lived upon his plantation, but made his home in Quitman until his death, at the comparatively early age of fifty-nine years. He married Margaret Holzendorf, who was born in Camden county, Georgia, of Holland ancestry. She died at the age of sixty-one years, leaving four children, as follows: Lavina; Mary, Now Mrs. Wade; Margaret; and James Y. Jones, Jr. Mr. and Mrs. Wade are the parents of nine children, all daughters, namely: Mary, wife of Wallace W. Hopper; Lillie; Maggie; Freddie; Sarah H.; Willie; Annie; Minnie; and Edna.

GEORGE ROBERT CHRISTIAN. Occupying a noteworthy position among the active and prosperous business men of Georgia and Florida, George R. Christian is distinguished not only for his own sterling traits of character but for the honored ancestry from whom he descended. He was born November 18, 1867, in Lowndes county, Georgia, nine miles south of Valdosta. The Christians were natives of the Isle of Man, where they had been prominent from time immemorial as the history of the Isle of Man shows (Peveril of the Peak). He is a son of Thomas Johnson Christian, whose father, Gabriel Christian, was the son of John Christian of Virginia, who came when a child with his father, Gilbert Christian, from the Isle of Man. They landed first at Philadelphia, and from there they came on down to the valley of Virginia, and were the second immigrants to settle there, John Lewis already being there, and having settled near where Staunton, Virginia, now stands.

John Christian, who married Elizabeth Crawford, a woman of vigorous intellect, was captain of horse in the Colonial army and fought the Indians along with Daniel Boone and Col. Wm. Christian, in whose honor Christian county, Kentucky, was named. (Life and Times of Caleb Wallace). John Christian was the only surviving member of a party of twelve attacked by the Indians while attempting to survey lands drawn by Col. Wm. Christian in western Kentucky as a bounty for services rendered in fighting the Indians.

Gabriel Christian, born in Virginia, received excellent educational advantages and was reared in the Presbyterian faith—he subsequently embraced the Protestant Methodist religion and became a preacher in that denomination. Coming to Georgia, he purchased a tract of wild land in Monroe county, and with his slaves began the improvement of the plantation. Continuing his work in the Master's vineyard as a circuit rider, he preached in numerous places in Georgia, remaining a resident of Monroe county until his death. The marriage of Gabriel Christian to Harrison Blair Gilmer also of Virginia was solemnized in Albermarle county in that state in the year of 1800. Her father, John Gilmer, married Mildred Merriwether, who was descended in the sixth generation from Nicholas Merriwether. Mildred Merriwether, who was the daughter of Thomas and Elizabeth (Thornton) Merriwether and who became the wife of John Gilmer was therefore a great-grandmother of George Robert Christian. Gabriel Christian and his wife reared seven children as follows: John Gilmer, Martha Taliaferro, Abner Hobbs, Julia Ann, Nicholas Thornton, Hope Hull and Thomas Johnson.

Thomas Johnson Christian was born in 1822 in Monroe county, at which place he remained until seventeen years of age. After the death of his father in 1839, he and his mother moved to Florida, carrying with them their slaves. He entered government land in Madison county and improved a plantation. Having sold this in 1856 to his brother-in-law, Dr. J. W. Hines, he moved to Georgia, and purchased lot No. 82, a timbered tract, eight miles south of Quitman, then in Lowndes, but now in Brooks county. He was on the first jury drawn in Brooks county. Having again sold in 1860, he moved to Hamilton county Florida, near Belleville, where he bought lands. There in company with Green McCall he built in the Withlacoochee river "a fall fish trap" from which he hauled fish by the two-horse wagon loads. The trap is still standing, having been in operation these many years. On account of failing health he sold his possessions in that locality and settled in 1862 in Berrien county, Georgia, four miles from Nashville, where he purchased Flat Creek mills, consisting of gins and grist with several adjoining lots of land.

During the war between the states he not being physically able to render active military service was detailed miller, and in that capacity did all that he could to help the Confederacy. He owned twenty-six slaves, for whom he was offered real estate in Savannah to their full value, but on account of the relation between master and slaves he refused to sell, saying that he always had treated them well, and he believed they would never leave him, and some of them did, after freedom, remain with him for several years. During the latter part of the war Captain Sharpe, an enrolling officer, was his guest while performing his duties for the Confederate army. The captain's whereabouts was discovered by the Confederate deserters, by whom he was brutally murdered. These deserters worked great damage to the property of Thomas J. Christian by killing his stock, burning his kitchen, setting on fire his dwellings, which would have burned had it not been for the prompt and active service of his slaves—especially the negro Summer, who carried the blankets into the well in order to wet them and smother the fire, the buckets having been taken off by those who set the house on fire. His life was constantly in danger. He was waylaid by the deserters who were jealous of his kind treatment to the soldiers and loyal persons connected with the Confederacy. His life was spared and he remained until 1867 in this trying community, in the center of the collection of the Confederate deserters, who congregated around this ten-mile bay and large swamp. From here he went to Lowndes county, nine miles south of Valdosta, at which place he remained for six months. He traded his Berrien county property for land in Madison county, Florida, just across the state line. Fifteen years later he exchanged that land for a farm located in Brooks county, Georgia, ten miles south of Quitman, and there he spent the remainder of his life, passing away January 6, 1885.

Thomas Johnson Christian married Mary Susannah McCall, who was born in Telfair county, Georgia, July 12, 1832, and died in Brooks county, Georgia, June 26, 1893. She was a daughter of Col. George Robert Francis McCall, a granddaughter of Rev. Wm. McCall, and great-granddaughter of Francis McCall, a native of Scotland who immigrated to America in Colonial days, settling in South Carolina. Rev. Wm. McCall served as a soldier in the Revolutionary war and was for many years a noted preacher in the Missionary Baptist church. Removing from Society Hill, South Carolina, to Screven county, Georgia, he was there a resident until his death. He was twice married. His first wife, Nancy Fletcher, the great-grandmother of George R. Christian, was the daughter of William Fletcher, who died in southeast Georgia at the advanced age of 132 years. The maiden name of his second wife was Mary Pierce.

Col. George R. McCall was born July 28, 1794, in Screven county, and was educated for a physician, having graduated at a medical college. Not caring for his professional life, he entered land in 1838 in what is now Brooks county, Georgia, and Madison county, Florida. The little Ancilla creek passed through his land and he improved the power, building first a grist mill and later putting up the first sawmill in South Georgia. He erected the first frame house in this section of the state, painted it white, and it was known for many miles around as the "White House." It was located about twelve miles south of Quitman in Lowndes county, now Brooks county, near the state line. Colonel McCall sold that estate to William Thomas, moved from there to the Land place, eight miles south of Quitman. Then he sold this and moved about one mile south of the state line into Madison county, Florida. On the same little Ancilla creek he built a larger grist and saw mill, and there resided until his death, November, 1884, in the ninety-first year of his age. The colonel was an important factor in the development of the resources of his community and during his career witnessed many wonderful transformations in the face of the country, villages and populous cities springing up. He saw Savannah grow from a small hamlet, when he first began trading there, to a large and enterprising city, one of the foremost in the state.

On January 15, 1817, Col. George R. McCall married Luvincia Fain, who was born in Telfair county, Georgia, January 15, 1801. She was a daughter of Thomas Fain and granddaughter of William Fain, a Revolutionary soldier who lies buried in Knoxville, Tennessee. William Fain was a native of Ireland, his trade was a linen weaver, and he left a land estate there when he came to America; when the Tories land was confiscated in this country he decided to give up his estate in Ireland. Luvincia (Fain) McCall died June 26, 1885. They lived a long and happy wedded life of sixty-eight years, and reared ten children.

Of the union of Thomas Johnson and Mary Susannah (McCall) Christian ten children were born, namely: Mary Blair, Thomas Addison, Rebecca Luvincia, Frank Gilmer, Moses Nathaniel, Hope Hull, Martha Virginia, Georgia Robert, Julia Ann and Cora Hull.

George R. Christian, the special subject of this sketch, attended common schools whenever opportunity offered, acquired a practical education when young, and assisted on the home farm until attaining his majority. He then went to a horological school at Oxford, North Carolina, and mastered the trade of watch maker, in which he engaged as watch maker and jeweler for eleven years in different parts of Georgia and Florida, during which time he permanently located at Quitman, Georgia. In November, 1899, he changed his business into an installment furniture business in which he was engaged seven years. Retiring from that business in 1906, he is at present a successful dealer in real estate, being one of the largest real estate owners in Quitman, Georgia. He is building a summer home on Pine mountain at Manchester, Georgia, and his winter home is on 15 Rhode avenue, St. Augustine, Florida, a place which is surrounded by palms, oranges, figs, mulberries and plums, trees and fruits which distinguish that section of the state. It is located near the famous Matanzas Bay, from which he gets his fish, oysters and deep-sea products. He has made a home for his unmarried sisters in Quitman, Georgia, since 1896, who still remain with him.

Captain Christian has never married. He takes special interest in his genealogy and has several relics handed from his ancestors.

AARON WILEY DOWDY. Left fatherless when still a babe in arms and forced at a tender age to begin to make his own way in the world to a great degree, life presented to Aaron Wiley Dowdy no primrose path of dalliance. With him it has been the order of the day to work and hustle from early youth and to attain success not through any adventitious chance, but by arduous effort and meritorious, self reliant service. That he has done this and has met with a large measure of success in his operations is made evident to all who visit his finely cultivated farm in Appling county, near Rockingham, where he has followed agricultural pursuits for the past thirteen years. Mr. Dowdy was born March 8, 1862, near Reidsville, Tattnall county, Georgia, and is a son of Aaron Wiley and America (Bacon) Dowdy.

Mr. Dowdy's paternal grandfather, Ben F. Dowdy, served as sheriff of Tattnall county during the war between the states, in which his son, the father of Aaron W., lost his life while serving in the Confederate ranks at Gettysburg. He married Emily Mattox. Mr. Dowdy's mother, a native of Bryant county, Georgia, who now resides in Appling county, is a daughter of Frederick and Emily (Stubbs) Bacon, farming people of Georgia.

The educational advantages of Aaron Wiley Dowdy were secured in the schools of the vicinity of the family home in Tattnall county, and he was reared to the life and pursuits of an agriculturist. Brought up under stern discipline, he early learned traits of self-reliance, industry, integrity and clean living, characteristics which have helped him in surmounting many obstacles and eventually achieving success. He continued to follow farming in his native county until he reached the age of thirty-seven years, at which time he came to Appling county, at that time locating on the farm which he now operates. Mr. Dowdy has been a hard-working, industrious man, living a frugal, correct and useful life. Whatever he has acquired is the result of his own thrift, energy and business capacity. He is one of the men who, in making money, do not so fall in love with it as to forget their duty to their fellow men. In all matters pertaining to the welfare of the people he takes a deep interest, and is one of the first to assist in promoting any good enterprise. In consequence of this disposition, together with his general worth and usefulness, he is well esteemed and has many friends in his community.

Mr. Dowdy was married to Miss Frances Weathers, daughter of the Rev. A. and Harriet (Smith) Weathers, the former a missionary Baptist minister who filled various charges throughout Tattnall and Liberty counties for a number of years. Mr. and Mrs. Dowdy have been the parents of seven children, as follows: Byron McFarland, thirty years of age, a farmer; Edward Cleveland, twenty-seven years old, who is also engaged in agricultural pursuits; Fannie, who is twenty-three years of age; Sidney, twenty, the wife of Frank Anderson, residing in Appling county, near Rockingham; Georgia, a sixteen-year-old student who has read the New Testament through three times; and Luther McLain, aged thirteen, and Henry, seven years old, both of whom are attending school. Mr. Dowdy is a master Mason, and he and his family attend the Methodist church, South.

WALTER BLAIR RODDENBERY. Born on the plantation in Decatur county, now in the new county of Grady, which he now occupies and cultivates, and which his father attained years ago when all the land was covered with forest, Walter Blair Roddenbery has unusual and prominent relations with the agricultural and civic affairs of his locality. He represents the third generation of a family which has resided in southern Georgia, and the family is one that has furnished men of ability not only to the agricultural and business affairs of the state, but also to the larger public life.

A special distinction belongs to Walter Blair Roddenbery as one of the prime movers in the formation and organization of Grady county. This movement, which was brought to a successful termination in 1906, met with a great deal of opposition from both Decatur and Thomas counties, neither of which wanted to lose some of their best territory. Mr. Roddenbery worked unceasingly, being convinced that the best interests of the locality would be subserved by a new county, and after the county had been created he became a member of the first board of county commissioners and chairman of the board. In this capacity he had much to do with the building of the present magnificent courthouse at Cairo, and continued as chairman of the board until that structure was built and paid for. It is believed that no county in Georgia has a finer courthouse building than Grady. Mr. Roddenbery is also president of the Roddenbery Hardware Company of Cairo, and of the Cairo Guano Company. He is a scientific farmer and a very successful one, raising diversified crops, but principally sugar cane, and every year from his own crop of cane he manufactures several thousand cases of syrup which he markets under the brand "Nigger in de Cane Patch." In the other important relations which he bears to his community, Mr. Roddenbery is chairman of deacons in the Baptist church, and for several years has served as superintendent of the Sunday School.

Walter Blair Roddenbery was born on his father's plantation near Cairo, on the twenty-eighth of April, 1862. His father was the late Dr. Seaborn Anderson Roddenbery, who was born on a farm in Thomas county, Georgia, in 1834. The paternal grandfather was Robert Roddenbery, a native of South Carolina, where for so far as known his parents spent all their lives. Two of the brothers of Robert Roddenbery also came south and located, one in Georgia, and one in Florida. Robert Roddenbery was a young man when he moved to Georgia, and began life in this state just even with the world. He had been reared to habits of industry, and after coming to Georgia, became a wage earner, saving his earnings and with the money buying land which in those days sold at very low prices, sometimes as low as $1.00 per acre. He bought a large quantity of land near the south line of Thomas county, where he built a log house in the woods, and with the labor of his own hand cleared land and cultivated it. He was one of the successful men of his time, and acquired a large estate. Before the war he owned many hundred acres of well improved land, and worked the plantation with the aid of slaves, freeing nearly a hundred of them at the close of the war. Late in life he moved into Thomasville, where he remained until his death, which resulted from his being thrown from a carriage. The maiden name of his wife was Vicey Anderson, who was born in Thomas county, where her father was a pioneer and she survived her husband several years, passing away in Cairo. They are both buried on the old home farm in Thomas county. The seven children in that generation were named Louisa, Mary Ann, Seaborn A., John K., Nancy, Margaret and Georgia.

Dr. Seaborn A. Roddenbery attained his early education in the rural schools of Thomas county. It was his desire to become a physician and there is a matter of curious interest in the disagreement between himself and father as to which school of practice he should adopt. The father wanted him to study homeopathy, and offered to pay his way through medical college, but the son was determined to follow the regular school of allopathy, and in consequence he cut himself loose from dependence upon his father, and secured a clerkship in a Thomasville store. After earning sufficient money he entered Oglethorpe Medical College at Savannah, where he was graduated M. D. in 1858. He then began practice in Decatur county, and engaged board and lodging in the home of Samuel Braswell, a planter living four miles northwest of the recent site of Cairo. He soon afterwards bought a tract of land at the "cross-roads," two miles from the present site of Cairo, and there built a log house. Into that humble shelter, he brought his bride and it was in that home that Walter Blair Roddenbery and other of the children were born. Dr. Roddenbery built up a very large and successful practice in his vicinity and like all the pioneer doctors he had to undergo the hardships of almost constant riding and driving across the country with few roads and with very inadequate accommodations for man or beast. This exposure and hard work undermined his health, so that in 1870 he moved into Cairo and engaged in the merchandise business. After that he practiced only when called upon by the families whom he had doctored for many years, and who refused to accept the services of any other physician. He continued as a farmer and merchant, until his death in 1896. During the last year of the war Dr. Roddenbery was called out with the Georgia militia.

Dr. Roddenbery married Miss Martha America Braswell. She was born on the south side of Thomas county in 1837, and now resides at the old homestead with her son Charles D. Her father was Samuel Braswell, who came from North Carolina to Georgia, being one of the early settlers in Thomas county. About 1845 he moved to Decatur county, and bought land four miles northwest of the present site of Cairo. In that locality he spent the rest of his day. Dr. Roddenbery and wife reared five sons and two daughters, named Walter Blair, Bertha, Robert S., Seaborn A., Jr., John W. and Charles D., and Kate. Bertha, now deceased, was first married to Dr. A. B. Coffman, and second to Charles W. Beale. Charles D. is a cigar manufacturer in Cairo. Robert S. is engaged in the real estate and insurance business at Moultrie, Georgia. Seaborn A. Roddenbery, Jr., an attorney at Thomasville, is one of the prominent men in public life of Georgia, and is now representing his district in congress for the third term.

Walter Blair Roddenbery as a boy attended school in Cairo, and was then sent to Prof. O. D. Scott's school in Thomasville, where he prepared for college. He entered the University of Virginia, and was a student there for two years. It was his intention to enter the law, but his father's ill health turned him aside from professional life, and he returned home to take charge of the store, a business to which he later succeeded. He has also become owner of the old homestead. Since his proprietorship he has supplanted the old residence with a comfortable and attractive rural home, and with many excellent farm buildings and improvements all of which are suitable evidence of the excellent manner in which he does his farming. He keeps a home dairy of jersey cows, and each season buys a number of stock cattle for fattening. He raises grain, cotton, vegetables and fruits but as already stated sugar cane is his chief crop.

Mr. Roddenbery was married June 1, 1887, to Miss Maude Bostwick. She was born in Homer, Louisiana, a daughter of Elijah and Rebecca (Scaife) Bostwick. Her maternal grandfather was Rev. Jimison Scaife, a pioneer of the Methodist ministry in Georgia. Mr. and Mrs. Roddenbery have four sons, named Albert C., Julien B., Walter Blair, Jr., and Frederick W. Mr. Roddenbery is a member of the Baptist church and his wife of the Methodist.

WILLIAM BERRIEN BURROUGHS, M. D. Bearing an old and distinguished name in Georgia, Dr. Burroughs has well performed the responsibilities and creditably lived up to the expectations of his family history. During the war between the states he earned distinction as a Georgia soldier. Fifteen years of his career were devoted to the exacting profession of medicine. Resigning a large practice on account of ill health he has since been in business in Brunswick. He has been honored with many of those offices in civic affairs, where the opportunities of service are great, and the duties vitally essential to the general welfare, but in which practically the only individual reward is the sense of public duty well done.

William Berrien Burroughs was born April 7, 1842, at Savannah, Georgia. The history of the family goes back to the Elizabethan days of England's glorious maritime exploits. An old record names Capt. Stephen Burroughs as captain of one of three vessels which attempted to reach China by way of Nova Zembla in 1553. Captain Burroughs published a book of his adventures, during which he reached "farthest north" at that time (seventy degrees and three minutes), and was "the first who observed the declination of the magnetic needle." In old books of heraldry is described the Burroughs' coat of arms, and many other records indicate the prominence of the name in England during the sixteenth and seventeenth centuries. Sir John Burroughs, who was knighted in 1624, was an attendant and court official to King Charles I. His descendants have been prominent in England from that time to this, one of them having been in recent years head of the largest drug house in the world at London.

The founder of the family in America was John Burroughs, who was born in Dorsetshire, England, in 1617, and came to America to Salem, Massachusetts, about 1642. As an adherent of Charles I, he had been one of those who fled from England at the time to escape the religious and political persecution after the dissolution of the long parliament of which he had been a member. Soon after arriving in this country, he located at Long Island, and was one of the original settlers of Middleburg in 1652, where he paid his share of the Indian rate. Being a leading man and skillful penman, he served as town clerk and clerk of court, and made the first map of Newtown. He was one of the seven patentees of Newtown in 1666, and continued in office as town clerk until his death, when his oldest son succeeded him to that office. His children, grandchildren and great-grandchildren moved to New York, New Jersey, Pennsylvania, and Connecticut.

Fourth in descent from this noted founder of the family in America was Benjamin Burroughs, grandfather of Dr. Burroughs. Benjamin Burroughs was born on Long Island at Newtown, March 31, 1779, and died at Savannah, Georgia, April 14, 1837. In 1795 he brought the name south to Augusta, Georgia, and in the following year moved to Savannah. On July 2, 1799, at the age of twenty he married in Savannah, Miss Catherine Eirick, daughter of Alexander Eirick, a member of the colonial parliament. Her youngest sister, Ruth, married Captain Francis H. Welman, an officer of the British navy, and their daughter, Mrs. John H. Reid, was long a prominent member of social circles in Savannah. Alexander Eirick married Ruth Erwin, a daughter of Christopher Erwin, who was born in county Antrim, Ireland, January 8, 1754. One sister of Ruth Erwin married a Captain Loyer, an officer of the French army, from whom is descended Capt. Richard J. Davant, the present mayor of Savannah. Another sister married Gov. Jared Irwin, her cousin, the letter being changed from e to i.

Grandfather Benjamin Burroughs was prominent as a cotton and commission merchant in Savannah. His partner, Mr. Oliver Sturges, and himself, owned a third interest in the steamship Savannah which in 1819 was the first vessel to cross the Atlantic ocean under her own steam. The partners shipped a large cargo of cotton to Liverpool on the first voyage of the Savannah. The vessel sailed from Savannah May 26, 1819, and reached Liverpool after a passage of twenty-five days, during which the engine was employed eighteen days. Benjamin Burroughs was an elder in the Independent Presbyterian church in Savannah, and gave five thousand dollars to assist in building the church in 1817. The names of the children of Benjamin Burroughs and wife were as follows: Joseph H.; William Howe, who married Ann McLeod; Benjamin, who married Rosa Williams; Dr. Henry Kollock Burroughs, a former mayor of Savannah, and who married Ella Dessaussure; Oliver S., who married Ann C. Maxwell; Elizabeth Reed, who married Dr. John S. Law; and Catherine, who married Charles Green.

Joseph Hallett Burroughs, father of Dr. Burroughs of Brunswick, was born in Savannah, Georgia, June 3, 1803. He was graduated from Yale College and then engaged in the cotton business with his father. On June 26, 1828, he married Miss Valeria Gibbons Berrien, who was born in Savannah, August 4, 1806. Her family was specially distinguished in the south and elsewhere. She was a daughter of John Macpherson Berrien and Eliza Anciaux. Mr. Berrien was quartermaster-treasurer of the French Royal Deux Ponts Regiment, and his commission, signed by Louis XVI, is now in the possession of Dr. Burroughs at Brunswick. Nicholas Anciaux was a son of Chevalier DeWiltteiseno, who was born in Frankfort-on-the-Main in Germany.

The Berrien family in America was founded by a Holland-French Huguenot, who settled on Long Island in 1669, and for several generations the family was prominent in the Dutch church and in the town and civil affairs of Long Island. Several generations later in the Berrien family was John Berrien, whose home was in Somerset county, New Jersey. He was a judge of the supreme court of the colony. General Washington made the Berrien home his headquarters for some time and from the doorstep of the Berrien house was delivered the farewell address of Washington to the army. One of the children of this Judge Berrien was John Berrien, the maternal great-grandfather of Dr. Burroughs. John Berrien emigrated to Georgia in 1775, and at the age of fifteen was lieutenant in the First Georgia Regiment, became captain at the age of seventeen, and at eighteen was appointed brigade-major in the Northern Army, by General Lachlan McIntosh. He served with distinction in the battle of Monmouth and at Valley Forge as well as in other engagements and continued to fight for independence until the close of the war. He married Miss Margaret Macpherson, a daughter of Capt. John Macpherson, an officer in the provincial navy, the Macpherson family having been especially prominent in military affairs during the Revolutionary war. One of the sons of Major John

Berrien was John Macpherson Berrien, the father of Valeria Gibbons Berrien. He was an attorney-general in Jackson's cabinet and declined the mission to England on account of domestic affliction.

Joseph Hallett Burroughs, the father of Dr. Burroughs, was a factor and commission merchant, was a member of the Presbyterian church, and an old-line Whig in politics. He served as paymaster of the First Regiment of Georgia militia. His death occurred in Savannah in 1854. He and his wife were the parents of ten children, and Dr. Burroughs has a brother, Richard B., who was also a physician, and Charles J., a physician at Jacksonville, Florida. His brother, John W., was a lawyer, in Savannah.

Dr. W. B. Burroughs received his primary education in Savannah, and completed it at Oglethorpe University, near Milledgeville, then the capital of Georgia. Oglethorpe University was destroyed during the war. At the breaking out of hostilities between the states, Dr. Burroughs left college and joined the Randolph Rangers as a private. This company and others subsequently became the Seventh Georgia Cavalry, and Dr. Burroughs was sergeant in Company G, of that regiment. The regiment was in Young's Brigade, Hampton's Division, Army of Northern Virginia. With this regiment Dr. Burroughs served all through the war, participating in the battle at Borden's Plank Road, Dinwiddie Courthouse, Stony Creek and other points, and received his parole at Appomattox.

At the close of the war he took up the study of medicine under a private preceptor in Savannah, and graduated in medicine at the Savannah Medical College in March, 1867. For fifteen years he was engaged in active practice in Camden county, and accumulated a considerable fortune by his professional activities. When his health failed, in 1881, he moved to Brunswick, and built one hundred houses, most of them small, consisting of about four rooms, and from that enterprise has ever since been engaged in the real estate and insurance business, and a recognized authority on all real estate matters.

Dr. Burroughs for fifteen years has been vice president of the Georgia State Agricultural Society, and for twelve years has been president of the Brunswick Agricultural Society. He has held a direetorship in the National Bank of Brunswick, in the Brunswick Savings & Trust Company, in the Kennon Cotton Factory, in the Board of Trade, and chairman of statistics in the latter body. He is grand vice chancellor of the Knights of Pythias of Georgia. Dr. Burroughs was appointed by Governor Northen to the national Nicaragua convention which assembled in New Orleans in 1893, and in St. Louis in 1892, and at each convention was elected an executive committeeman for his state by the Georgia delegation. For five years he has been lieutenant governor of the Society of Colonial Wars of Georgia. He was director and superintendent of the department of education at the Georgia State Fairs held in different towns in the state of Georgia, and was appointed by Gov. Joseph M. Terrell of Georgia, to the office of director of history, and made exhibits at Jamestown in 1907. Dr. Burroughs has made many historical contributions to current periodicals on cotton and on the early history of Georgia.

Dr. Burroughs was reared in the Presbyterian faith, and now attends all denominations. He has served eight years as a member of the Brunswick board of education. On January 17, 1872, Dr. Burroughs was married at Waynesville, in Wayne county, Georgia, to Miss Elizabeth Pettingill Wilson Hazlehurst, oldest daughter of Maj. Leighton Wilson Hazlehurst and Mary J. McNish, of Savannah. Her father was a wealthy rice planter of the Saltillo river, and during the war between the states was commissioned major of the Fourth Georgia Cavalry. Major Hazlehurst was a son of Robert Hazlehurst of Charleston, South Carolina. The children of Dr. Burroughs and wife are mentioned as follows: Mary McNish Burroughs, born in Camden county, Georgia, married Charles Walter Deming, who is in the oil and real estate business at Tulsa, Oklahoma; Lilla Hazlehurst Burroughs, born in Camden county, Georgia, and unmarried; Josephine Hallett Burroughs, born in Camden county, married Capt. Clyde A. Taylor, children, Clyde A. Taylor, Jr., and Lilla Hazlehurst Taylor; William Berrien, Jr., born in Camden county, married Ida D. Hartfelder of Elizabeth, New Jersey; Leighton Hazlehurst, born in Brunswick, unmarried; Mac Hazlehurst, born in Brunswick, married Miss Eliza F. McIntosh, of McIntosh county, Georgia.

JAMES R. BOURN. Noteworthy among the industrious and enterprising young agriculturists of Ware county, Georgia, is James R. Bourn, who has brought to his chosen calling excellent judgment and good business methods, and is meeting with signal success, his well-tilled farm lying near Waresboro, not far from the place of his birth, which occurred October 24, 1880. He is a son of John Bourn, of Ware county, and grandson of the late Col. Richard Bourn.

His great-grandfather, Bennett Bourn, the immigrant ancestor, was born in County Clare, Ireland, of Scotch ancestry. Coming when young to America, he located permanently in Georgia, buying land in Richmond county, and there being employed in tilling the soil until his death. He married a Miss Musie, who spent her entire life in Georgia, where her immediate ancestors were pioneer settlers.

Born in Richmond county, Georgia, Col. Richard Bourn grew to manhood on the home farm, as a boy and youth becoming well acquainted with the various branches of agriculture. Settling in Ware county when ready to begin life on his own account, he purchased a tract of unimproved land, and for a number of years was engaged in agricultural pursuits, employing slave labor in his farming operations, remaining there until 1859, when he migrated to Florida. At the outbreak of the Civil war, he offered his services to the Confederacy, and was commissioned colonel of a Florida regiment, which was assigned to the Army of the Potomac, in Virginia. With his regiment, he subsequently participated in numerous engagements, and was in Richmond when that city surrendered. Peace being declared, he returned to Ware county, Georgia, and was here a resident until his death, at the age of seventy-four years. Colonel Bourn married Mary Ann Taylor, who was born in Ware county. During the war between the states, she and two of her sons died of cholera, and another one of her four sons died in the army, the only survivor of her children being John Bourn, father of James R. Bourn.

Born in Ware county, John Bourn here grew to man's estate. Choosing for his life work the independent occupation to which he was reared, he purchased a tract of wild land lying about three miles from Waresboro, and soon after assuming its possession erected the substantial log house which he has since occupied. Having improved quite a large portion of the land, he is carrying on general farming to advantage. His wife, whose maiden name was Sarah Deen, was also born in Ware county. Eight children were born of their union, as follows: James R., the special subject of this brief sketch; Berry D.; John L.; Mary; Amy; Eva; Ruth; and Sarah. Berry D. Bourn and John L. Bourn both attended the Wareboro high school, John L. subsequently completing his studies at the university of Georgia, in

Athens. Both are now ministers, preaching in the Methodist Episcopal denomination, and being members of the South Georgia Conference.

Acquiring his rudimentary education in the rural schools of his district, James R. Bourn was graduated from the Waresboro high school, and for the next ten years taught school a part of each year. In the meantime he bought a farm lying one mile from the parental homestead, and in its management he is meeting with good success.

Mr. Bourn married, at the age of twenty-five years, Minnie North, of Clinch county, Georgia, a daughter of William B. and Harriet North. Mr. and Mrs. Bourn are the parents of three children, namely: Thelma, Elva, and Homer. Both are members of the Methodist Episcopal church and are rearing their family in the same faith. In his political relations Mr. Bourn is a Democrat and takes great interest in local affairs. In 1909 he was elected school commissioner of Ware county to fill out an unexpired term, and in 1910 had the honor of being re-elected to the same position for a term of four years.

CAPT. JOHN FLANNERY. The late Capt. John Flannery was born November 24, 1835, in Nenagh, County Tipperary, Ireland, and died May 9, 1910, in Savannah, Georgia, in which city he had been a prominent banker and cotton factor for many years. He was the eldest son of John and Hannah (Hogan) Flannery. His maternal grandmother was Catherine Fitzpatrick, descended from the prominent Fitzpatrick family who were Earls of Ossory. His education was received in private schools of his native town.

John Flannery, Sr., was a merchant in Nenagh and on account of general depression caused by famine and revolutions, his business became unsuccessful. The father and son determined to try their fortunes in America and together they landed in Charleston, South Carolina, on October 26, 1851, when the son was in his sixteenth year. The father soon decided to return to his home and died at sea on the passage to Ireland.

John Flannery, Jr., obtained his first business position as a clerk in Atlanta, but returned to Charleston as soon as he could find employment there. He removed to Savannah in December, 1854, where he filled various positions as clerk or bookkeeper until the opening of the war between the states.

On May 30, 1861, he enlisted as junior lieutenant in the Irish Jasper Greens, First Volunteer Regiment of Georgia, Confederate army, in which company he had served his state at Fort Pulaski earlier during the same year as a non-commissioned officer. Promoted January, 1862, to first lieutenant on October 20, 1862, he became captain of that historic company. He was in command of Lee Battery, Savannah River, for a year and until his regiment joined the army of Gen. Joseph E. Johnston. During the time he was stationed at Lee Battery the garrison, consisting nominally of nine officers and two hundred privates, was by illness reduced to nineteen privates and one officer, Lieut. John Flannery, who during the remainder of his life suffered from the effects of the malarial poison absorbed in the swamps around that post. He was with Hood's army in the disastrous Tennessee campaign, but, being at the time on detached service with his command, was not present at the battles of Franklin and Nashville. His activity in the war was brought to an end by serious illness at Corinth, Mississippi, in January, 1865. He was paroled in Augusta, Georgia, in May, 1865, and returned to Savannah the same month.

Prior to its consolidation with the Citizens Bank, under the name

Yours Truly
John Hanning

Citizens & Southern Bank, he was for twenty-five years president of the Southern Bank of the state of Georgia, which, during that period, was Savannah's largest bank, and of which institution he was one of the organizers and incorporators in November, 1870. After the consolidation he was made first vice president of the Citizens & Southern Bank, which position he held up to the time of his death.

For nearly half a century he was the leading member of one of Savannah's most prominent firms in the cotton trade. In July, 1865, he entered the cotton business as a partner in the firm J. L. Guilmartin & Co. In July, 1877, he bought out this business and changed the style to John Flannery & Co., admitting John L. Johnson as a partner. On June 1, 1901, he incorporated the business under the style, The John Flannery Company, and was elected president. In 1906 he sold his interest in this company, which still bears his name, and retired from active business in the cotton trade, but up to the time of his death remained one of Savannah's most public spirited citizens. Scarcely an enterprise of magnitude was launched in Savannah during the last fifty years of his life, which did not receive his aid or encouragement.

Captain Flannery was a director and vice president of the Chattahoochee & Gulf R. R. and director of the South Bound R. R. and of the Georgia & Alabama R. R. before they were merged into the Seaboard Air Line. He was a director of the United Hydraulic Cotton Compress Co., The Savannah Lighting Co., The Henderson-Hull Buggy Co., The Southern Pine Co. of Georgia, The Semmes Hardware Co., and the Savannah Hotel Co., owners of the magnificent Hotel DeSoto.

He was vice president, for Georgia, of the American-Irish Historical Society and was president of the Jasper Monument Association which erected the beautiful monument to the memory of Sergeant William Jasper, which has adorned Madison Square since its unveiling on February 22, 1888.

He was a member of the Savannah Cotton Exchange from 1875 and of the Hibernian Society from 1866 until his death. He was a member of The United Confederate Veterans, The Georgia Historical Society; The Savannah Yacht Club and of the Reform Club of New York City.

He was a staunch Democrat and took a lively interest in municipal affairs, but steadily refused to become a candidate for public office, though he served as chairman of the Savannah Sinking Fund Commission from 1878 to 1888, when he declined re-election.

He was a consistent member of the Roman Catholic church and contributed largely of his time and means to the handsome cathedral of St. John the Baptist erected in 1873 and burned in 1898. He was chairman of the building committee for the present magnificent cathedral of the same name which was erected in 1899 and 1900. In 1873 and 1874 he was largely instrumental in the conversion of the old cathedral into the present commodious home of the Catholic Library Association on Drayton street.

Through gifts made in 1903 and others arranged for not long before his death, he created a fund of one hundred thousand dollars known as the Flannery Trust Fund to be managed by a board of trustees, by whom the income shall be applied in shares to various Catholic institutions of Georgia.

His life was devoid of ostentation and filled with acts of charity. His purse was always open to those in distress and to young men laying the foundations for future success and to enterprises making for Savannah's improvement.

Captain Flannery was married in Savannah on April 30, 1867, to Miss Mary Ellen Norton, niece of Capt. John and Kate (Harty) Mc-

Mahon, with whom she lived, and daughter of Patrick and Honora (Harty) Norton of old Locust Grove (now Sharon), Taliaferro county, Georgia, who with their relatives came from Ireland and cast their lots with the Catholic colony in which were the families of Semmes, Brooke, Scott, Thompson and others, who came from Maryland during, or shortly before 1794, and established in that part of Warren county which later became part of Taliaferro county, the cradle of Catholicity in Georgia.

Mrs. Flannery died on June 11, 1899. Of the issue of six children, only two lived to maturity, John McMahon Flannery, who died December 29, 1900, and Kate Flannery, now the wife of Raphael T. Semmes of Savannah, Georgia.

HON. HENRY GRAY TURNER. In the death of Henry G. Turner in June, 1904, southwest Georgia lost one of its ablest public leaders and most influential citizens. For sixteen years he represented the second district in congress, was a successful lawyer, and had been identified by residence and professional activities for many years with the city of Quitman in Brooks county.

The late Mr. Turner was born in Granville, North Carolina, in 1839. His father, Archibald Turner, was born either in North Carolina or Dinwiddie county, Virginia, his parents having moved from Virginia to North Carolina and spent the rest of their days in the latter state. Archibald Turner was reared and spent his active life in North Carolina.

Henry Gray Turner was a child when his father died, and it was largely due to his self-reliant and purposeful efforts that he made advance to position and influence. He acquired a good education and when yet in his teens went to Alabama, where he taught school a year, and then taught for a time in Piscola Academy in the new town of Quitman, Georgia. In this way he first became known in the community where he was later so prominent. At the breaking out of the war between the states he returned home and offered his services to his native state. Commissioned captain of a company in the Twenty-third Regiment of North Carolina Infantry, he went to the front and soon joined the Army of the Potomac. He led his company in many of the hard-fought battles of the great war, and at Gettysburg was wounded and captured. He was held in federal prisons until near the close of the war, when he was paroled and returned south. The war ended before he was exchanged, and he spent some time in recuperating at Henderson, North Carolina, where his mother and sisters were living. From there he came again to Quitman, where he took up the study of law, and after being admitted at Nashville opened an office in Quitman.

In a short time success in his profession and distinction in public affairs came to him. He was elected and served several terms in the state legislature, and in 1878 was honored by election from the second district as its representative in congress. He served for eight consecutive terms until 1894. His adherence to the Democratic party was stanch and consistent, but he was unable to support the free-silver doctrine, and with the rise of that issue to dominance in the party he quietly withdrew from party leadership. During his residence at Quitman Mr. Turner had bought the land within the city limits which he improved into a beautiful park as a setting for his home, which has long been one of the most attractive places in this part of the state. Many trees adorn the grounds, and the native birds and squirrels have for years found a safe shelter among them. It was in this ideal envir-

JAMES O MORTON

onment that Mr. Turner spent his last years and where death found him.

The late Mr. Turner married Lavinia Calhoun Morton, who was born in Brooks county, a daughter of James Oliver and Sarah (Young) Morton. A sketch of her family follows. Mr. and Mrs. Turner were the parents of five children: James Morton, Henry, India, S. Morton and Archibald. The last named died in infancy, and James M. at the age of eleven. India is the wife of Samuel Stevens Bennett, an attorney in Albany, Georgia. S. Morton followed in his father's footsteps and is one of the rising young attorneys of Quitman. The late Mr. Turner was a member of the Methodist church, as is his wife.

JAMES OLIVER MORTON. One of the notable pioneers of south Georgia was the late James Oliver Morton, who died at his homestead in Brooks county in November, 1911, at the age of nearly ninety-one years. He assisted in the development of the natural resources of this region when almost the entire country was a wilderness. He was identified with the public as well as the industrial and business affairs of his community, and for many years as president directed the welfare of the Bank of Quitman. He served as one of the first four justices of the inferior court of Brooks county, and his name deserves a permanent record in the history of this portion of the state.

He was born in Screven county on the 20th of December, 1820, and by ancestry represented one of the oldest American families. He was a lineal descendant of George Morton, a native of England, who early in the seventeenth century, to avoid religious persecution, with others fled to Leyden, Holland, and from there in 1622 sailed on the ship Ann for America, joining the Pilgrim Fathers two years after their landing at Plymouth Rock. The Mortons and other Pilgrim families intermarried, and the Mortons of later generations have numerous relationship with the descendants of other Pilgrim sires. Oliver Morton, grandfather of the late Quitman banker, was born in Plymouth, Massachusetts, and afterwards came south and was one of the early settlers of central Georgia. The entire state was then sparsely settled, wild game abounded throughout the forests and all the Indians had not yet departed for their western homes and were sometimes troublesome to the settlements. Oliver Morton, like other pioneers, acquired a large amount of land and was engaged in farming in Jones county until his death.

Silas Morton, his son, was born in Jones county, and moved from there to Screven county, and bought a tract of land near Halcyondale which had been granted under patent from King George. There he managed a large estate with slave labor until his death. He married Sabina Archer, of Scotch-Irish ancestry, and so far as known she was a lifelong resident of Screven county.

James O. was a son of Silas and Sabina Morton, and was reared and educated in his native county. From there he moved to Bulloch county, which was his home until 1843, when he came to what is now Brooks county, then a part of Lowndes, the county seat being then at Troupville. Few white settlers had yet ventured into this region, railroads were not built for a number of years, and markets were many miles distant. The land which he first bought was located five miles from the present site of Quitman, but a year later he bought land a mile and a half from town. His settlement was in the midst of heavy timber, and his first home, occupied for several years, was a log house, in which his children were born. He owned a large number of slaves, and when these were freed by the war the greater part of his wealth was swept away. He was never a man to be discouraged by obstacles and reverses, and he continued steadily at producing the crops of the soil, employing many of his former slaves. After fifty years have gone, one of these old slaves, now blind and feeble, is being tenderly cared for on the old homestead. From a generous prosperity gained by the operations of his plantation Mr. Morton extended his interests into various other lines, especially banking, and was for a number of years president of the Bank of Quitman. It was his custom to drive into town every day and attend to the affairs of the bank, and he paid his last visit for this purpose just four days before his death. For more than seventy years he was constantly active, and his long and honorable career was associated with much disinterested service and kindness to those about him.

The late Mr. Morton was married on the 18th of August, 1843, to Sarah Young. It was their unusual fortune to spend sixty-eight years of wedded companionship, and she is still living on the old homestead, being physically frail but mentally strong. Sarah Young was born in Bulloch county, Georgia, December 7, 1825, and was a daughter of James and Lavinia (Jones) Young. Her paternal grandparents were William and Mary (Henderson) Young. William Young was a Georgian who took an active part in the movements for independence, was a member of the Council of Safety appointed at Savannah on June 22, 1775, and on the 4th of July following represented the town and district of Savannah at the assembling of the provincial congress. He was later a planter in Screven county, where he spent his last years, and the remains of himself and wife now repose on a hill overlooking the Ogeechee valley.

Mr. and Mrs. Morton were the parents of two children. The only son, Simeon L., in early life was a student of the Quitman Academy and when the war broke out enlisted with the Savannah Guards. He served throughout the war, participating in many of the most notable battles, and lost his life on one of the last battlefields of that four years' struggle between the states. The daughter, Lavinia Calhoun, is the widow of the late Henry G. Turner of Quitman.

WILLIAM HARDEN was born in Savannah, November 11, 1844, son of Edward J. and Sophia H. (Maxwell) Harden.

As the war came on and young Harden, when less than seventeen years of age, enlisted for service in the army, his education was not so complete as otherwise it would have been. Under the circumstances, he received the best educational training available at that day in private schools in Savannah. His first teacher was Miss Elizabeth Church; for about two years he was a student under Prof. Bernard Mallon, then principal of the Massie school, and later superintendent of the public schools of Atlanta. Also, for a time, Mr. Harden was a student under W. S. Bogart, principal of Chatham Academy. His student days, however, did not end with his academy days, for, indeed, he has been a student all his life—a student of human nature—a student of the motives and deeds of men and the histories of nations.

In April, 1861, Mr. Harden enlisted at Savannah in the Savannah Cadets, composed of very young men, which organization became a part of the state troops of Georgia, and of which, before it was mustered into the regular Confederate army, he was made sergeant. It was known as Savannah Cadets, and on account of the youthfulness of its members was not mustered into the Confederate army until May, 1862, at which time it was entirely reorganized, becoming Company F of the Fifty-fourth Regiment, Georgia Volunteers, in which William Harden was a

SAVANNAH AND SOUTH GEORGIA

private. This regiment was commanded by Col. Charlton H. Way. In January, 1863, Mr. Harden was detached from his company and detailed for service in the Signal Corps of the Confederate army, and was engaged in this capacity at Savannah till December 20, 1864, when he was ordered to Charleston and assigned to duty as military telegrapher at the headquarters of General Hardee. Leaving Charleston February 18, 1865, he was put in charge of the telegraph service at St. Stephens Depot for about ten days, after which he was sent to Florence, South Carolina. On further duty he made the trip from Florence to Timmonsville, that state, and while attempting to return to headquarters at Florence he was cut off by the enemy and turned back to Sumter. From there, accompanied by eleven men, he made his way to Augusta. Notwithstanding this detached service in Signal Corps, Mr. Harden's name was retained on the rolls of Company F, Fifty-fourth Regiment, till the close of the war.

Mr. Harden's duties as military telegrapher, involving the handling and transmission of secret messages of the greatest importance, were filled with many interesting incidents, sometimes tinged with romance, and occasionally fraught with danger. One incident that occurred while he was on duty at General Hardee's headquarters in Charleston in February, 1865, affords an illuminating glimpse of the life of the signal corps in time of war. On the afternoon of the 14th of that month, while Mr. Harden was at the telegraph key, there came a call from the Richmond office, and, the formal answer having been given, the Richmond operator began to send a message to General Hardee. The apparently unmeaning letters forming its beginning showed plainly at once that it was a cipher message. It was, as usual in such cases, received with much care, in order to be certain that no mistakes were made in so important a communication. Before sending it upstairs to General Hardee's staff officers, he and another young telegrapher who was on duty with him, John Mackay Elliott, decided that they would decipher it. They began in the usual way, using the key word that was in their possession as a basis of translation, but soon discovered that the message was entirely meaningless when written out according to their cipher. The key word on which the deciphering was based was "Complete Victory." The key word had been transmitted secretly to Mr. Harden before he left Savannah, from headquarters at Richmond, and had been used by him ever since in deciphering messages. On account of danger of discovery by the enemy, however, Mr. Harden concluded that the Richmond authorities had changed the key word, but that for some reason he had received no notice of what the new key word, if any, might be. With young Elliott, therefore, he accordingly set to work to figure out the new key so that the message might be deciphered, as neither General Hardee nor any of the members of his staff knew anything of a change in the key word, and they themselves could not have read it. After laborious and painstaking effort, by first deciphering the first word of the message and then each of the following words, Mr. Harden and his associate finally discovered that the new key was "Come Retribution," by using which they were overjoyed to find that they could make a full and intelligent translation of the message. Later this key was imparted to them in the official way, but if these two young telegraphers had not been able to discover it on this occasion, it would have been a serious matter to General Hardee. The message was from President Jefferson Davis at Richmond and was addressed to Gen. W. J. Hardee at Charleston, under date of February 14, 1865, the following being a copy of the same:

"Your dispatch of the 12th received to-day. The enemy may and probably does intend to attack Charleston, but it is by no means manifested by present operations. It is proper under the view presented, to remove whatever is not needful for defense of the place, and then to postpone evacuation as long as prudent. If General Beauregard can beat the enemy in the field, the course herein indicated may preserve the city and harbor for future use, and save us the pain of seeing it pass into the hands of the enemy. General Beauregard and yourself are so well informed of the condition of the armies and practicability of routes, that I must leave you to the free exercise of your judgment. It however seems to me that the bridge over the Santee can be defended against a boat expedition up that river, without materially interfering with other operations, and a movement of the enemy overland from Bull's Bay is hardly to be anticipated.''

After the close of the war, Mr. Harden engaged in telegraph service first at Jacksonville, Florida, and later at Savannah, until January, 1866, when he began the study of law under his father, Judge Edward J. Harden, in Savannah. However, as he then gave only a portion of his time to study, it was not until July 25, 1873, that he was admitted to the bar. From that date until the summer of 1883, he practiced law in Savannah. In the meantime he had been licensed to practice in the state supreme and United States courts in Georgia, and on November 15, 1877, he was appointed United States commissioner, U. S. district court, for the southern district of Georgia; which place he filled till he discontinued the practice of law.

July 5, 1882, Mr. Harden was appointed assistant county treasurer of Chatham county, which position he has filled ever since.

In 1902, upon the organization of the Savannah public library, Mr. Harden was elected librarian, his present position, he having been in charge of the library continuously since that time.

Mr. Harden was assistant librarian of the Georgia Historical Society from 1866 to 1869; in the latter year he was made librarian of the society and has filled this position ever since.

He is the custodian and treasurer of the Telfair Academy of Arts and Sciences. He organized on May 22, 1891, the Georgia Society of the Sons of the Revolution, and is secretary of the society. He is a Democrat in politics, as such having been elected to and served as a member of the Georgia house of representatives, his term being from 1900 to 1905.

He is a member of the American Antiquarian Society, American Historical Association, National Geographic Society, and American Library Association. Also he is a corresponding member of various local and state historical societies throughout the United States. He has contributed much valuable historical matter, particularly on Savannah and Georgia to various magazines and journals. His deep interest in the subject of history, together with the studious research he has made extending over a long number of years, the painstaking accuracy and devotion to truth in historical records which he has always maintained, his illuminating literary style and gifts as a writer; all these have combined to make Mr. Harden a historian of exceptional ability.

Mr. Harden's religious creed is that set forth by the Presbyterian church, and since 1877 he has been a ruling elder in the First Presbyterian church of Savannah.

December 11, 1879, in Savannah, Mr. Harden married Miss Mary E. Davenport of this city.

From this brief *resume* of Mr. Harden's own life, we turn back for a glimpse at the ancestry from which he sprang.

Judge Edward J. Harden, his father, distinguished both as lawyer and judge, was born at Republican Hall, Bryan county, Georgia, November 19, 1813, and died at Indian Springs, Georgia, April 19, 1873. He was reared in Bryan county and received much of his education under the noted educator, William McWhir, D. D., at Sunbury. He studied law in Savannah and in 1837 was licensed to practice in the superior court, and was judge of the court of oyer and terminer (now the city court) of Savannah, from November, 1845, to October, 1847, and his home remained in this city from that time till near his death. Judge Harden was widely known as one of the ablest lawyers of the Savannah bar. At the beginning of the war between the states he was appointed by President Davis to the position of judge of the Confederate state district court for Georgia, and served in that capacity till the fall of the Confederacy. He was city attorney of Savannah both before and after the war. At one time he was the junior partner in the law firm of Jackson & Harden, Col. Joseph W. Jackson being the senior member, and afterwards senior member of the firm of Harden & Lawton, of which Alexander R. Lawton, later quartermaster general of the Confederate states army and minister to Austria during the administration of President Grover Cleveland, was the junior. When the war between the states began he was senior partner of Harden & Gnerard, the younger member being John M. Gnerard. After the war he formed a law partnership with S. Y. Levy, with the firm name of Harden & Levy, which continued till his death. He was president of the Georgia Historical Society for two years, 1867 and 1868. He was the author of a notable work, "The Life of George M. Troup" (the "States Rights" governor of Georgia). This was a valuable contribution to the historical records of the South, but on account of its having been published at a period (1859) when the country was in such an unsettled state, the book did not receive as wide attention as otherwise it would have done. Too much could hardly be said in tribute to the exalted character and noble qualities of Judge Harden; he was the type of gentleman that represents all that was best of the old South. His passing away was a cause of universal regret, which was fittingly expressed in a memorial pamphlet compiled and issued by the Georgia Historical Society and containing tributes to his memory by the newspapers of the city, and various contributors thereto: the pastor of the First Presbyterian church, the Session of the Church, the Savannah Bar Association, and the Georgia Historical Society.

Mr. Harden's grandfather, Thomas Hutson Harden, was born July 22, 1786, in Prince William's parish, South Carolina. Left an orphan in his early childhood, he was brought to Georgia about 1792 or 1793 by a faithful old negro woman who had been one of his father's slaves. He had a cruel guardian, and it was to escape from him that the negro woman brought the young boy to Georgia and placed him in the care of his uncle, Edward Harden, in Savannah. Later the youth went to Bryan county, where he continued to live until his death on May 4, 1821. He was married there to Matilda Amanda Baker. When a young man he had studied law and was admitted to the bar, but never practiced his profession. He was a planter; was a colonel on General McIntosh's staff in the War of 1812. He died in the prime of life, at the age of thirty-four years.

Mr. Harden's great-grandfather was Col. William Harden, who was a colonel of a regiment under Gen. Francis Marion, South Carolina troops, in the War of the Revolution. He was born in Prince William's parish, South Carolina, November 8, 1742, and died there

November 28, 1785. He made a distinguished record as a soldier and officer in the Revolution.

Tracing back another generation, it is found that Mr. Harden's great-great-grandfather was William Harden of Prince William's parish, South Carolina. He was born November 22, 1720, and died in Prince William's parish September 12, 1760. His father, William Harden, was the first of the name that the family has any record of on the American continent. While it is not of authentic record, it is the supposition that this William Harden was born in Kent, England, and that he came to South Carolina from the Island of Barbadoes.

Mr. Harden's mother, Sophia H. (Maxwell) Harden, died December 12, 1812. She was born February 29, 1820, at Belfast, Bryan county, Georgia, daughter of Col. John Jackson Maxwell, who was born at Belfast, Bryan county, Georgia, June 10, 1784, and died at Belair, near Tallahassee, Florida, January 13, 1855. He was the youngest child of Capt. William and Constant (Butler) Maxwell. Col. J. J. Maxwell married Mary Ann Baker, the daughter of Col. John Baker of Revolutionary renown. Col. Maxwell was a promient figure and a man of large affairs in his day. He was a planter of large resources; he repeatedly represented Bryan county in the legislature, and was for many years one of the judges of the inferior (or county) court of Bryan county. He was also at one time one of the presidential electors from Georgia. He was one of the early members of the famous Midway Congregational church in Liberty county, Georgia. In 1835, he removed to Savannah and in this city became one of the ruling elders in the First Presbyterian church. He removed to Belair, a resort near Tallahassee, Florida, in January, 1847, and this place was his home until his death. Capt. William Maxwell, father of John J., was born in Amelia township, South Carolina, in 1739, and died in 1807 in Bryan county, Georgia, where he had come with his father in 1752. He was a member of the provincial congress of Georgia from 1775 to 1777; was appointed by the provincial congress one of the ''trustees for taking into their custody and management the (British) forfeited estates,'' May 4, 1778; privateersman commanding his own armed vessel, recovering property taken by British, and attacking parties of the enemy engaged in collecting forage and provisions for the Royal troops in Savannah, 1779; arrested, tried for ''treasonable practices'' and convicted by British authorities, January, 1780; fined 300 pounds and kept under parole until the evacuation of Savannah, July 11, 1782. Capt. William Maxwell was the son of James Maxwell, who came from South Carolina to Georgia in 1752 and settled on lands granted by the crown, on the Midway river, in what was then St. Philip parish (now Bryan county). He named his plantation ''Belfast'' and lived there all his life. He was married September 7, 1722, to Mary Simons of South Carolina, the daughter of Benjamin and Mary (DuPre) Simons. The Maxwell family is of Scotch origin, but came to America from the north of Ireland, where they had been established for two or three generations. The Maxwells have been a prominent family in the history of Georgia. Audly Maxwell, a brother of Mr. Harden's great-great-grandfather Maxwell, was a member of the first general assembly of Georgia, which met at Savannah, January 15, 1751.

Col. John Baker, the father of Mrs. John Jackson Maxwell, died in Savannah in 1792. He was a member of the committee appointed by convention at Savannah July 20, 1774, to prepare resolutions expressive of the sentiments and determination of the people of Georgia in regard to the Boston Port Bill; member of Provincial Congress of Georgia, 1775-1777; member of Georgia Council of Safety, 1776; colonel commanding a regiment of Liberty county (G.) militia, 1775-1783; wounded in skirmish at Bulltown Swamp, November 19, 1778;, defeated Captain Goldsmith at White House, Georgia, June 28, 1779; participated in battle of Augusta, Georgia, May-June, 1781.